NAVIGATOR SERIES

1500 + PROBLEMS

JEE Main & Advanced

Magnetism & Electromagnetic Induction

PRADEEP BENIWAL
IIT Kharagpur

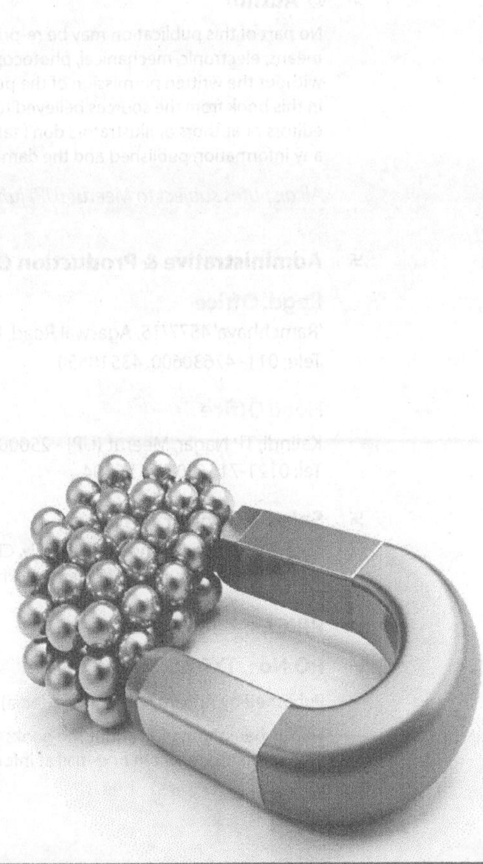

arihant
SUCCESS AND NOTHING LESS

NAVIGATOR SERIES

ARIHANT PRAKASHAN (Series), MEERUT

Administrative & Production Offices

Regd. Office
'Ramchhaya' 4577/15, Agarwal Road, Darya Ganj, New Delhi -110002
Tele: 011- 47630600, 43518550

Head Office
Kalindi, TP Nagar, Meerut (UP) - 250002
Tel: 0121-7156203, 7156204

Sales & Support Offices
Agra, Ahmedabad, Bengaluru, Bareilly, Chennai, Delhi, Guwahati, Hyderabad, Jaipur, Jhansi, Kolkata, Lucknow, Nagpur & Pune.

PRICE : ₹365.00

PO No : TXT-XX-XXXXXXX-X-XX

Published by Arihant Publications (India) Ltd.

For further information about the books published by Arihant, log on to www.arihantbooks.com or e-mail at info@arihantbooks.com

Follow us on

PREFACE

Physics is a subject that requires a lot of practice to master it and the best way to practice Physics is to solve more & more problems right from the beginner's level to the most complex ones. That's why the search for a good Physics Problems book has always been the top notch task of each good student.

During the last 15 Years while teaching & mentoring thousands of students preparing for JEE Main, JEE Advanced, KVPY, Olympiads etc. I always felt the need of such a book that can offer quality problems of Physics for all the topics of different chapters. There are many problems books available in the market but unfortunately none of them serve the purpose perfectly.

To fulfil the need of a good Physics Problems book, I have prepared the book **JEE Navigator, Magnetism & Electromagnetic Induction.** All the problems given in this book are arranged conceptually and systematically in order to test the conceptual understanding & analytical ability of the students.

All the problems given in each chapter of this book have been developed with the utmost care and arranged in a way to enhance the problem-solving skills of the students & to boost their confidence to tackle complex JEE Problems.

The Points given below will help you to learn the basic structure of the book;

- Each chapter is divided into three major heads; **Level 1 'Starter Level', Level 2 'JEE Main Level' & Level 3 'JEE Advanced Level'.**
- **Level 1 'Starter Level'** consists of preliminary questions that test basic concepts. After completing this level student will have a solid understanding of fundamentals of the chapter necessary to solve the problems.
- **Level 2 'JEE Main Level'** has single choice correct questions and numerical value questions aimed especially for JEE Main.
- **Level 3 'JEE Advanced Level'** consists of various types of questions; MCQ with one or more than one correct answer, Comprehension Based Questions, Match the Columns and Numerical Value problems as per JEE Advanced Pattern.
- The problems given in JEE Advanced Level are made to be conceptually challenging resulting in practical and relevant practice for JEE Advanced.
- Detailed solutions to all the problems have been provided at the end of every chapter just to help the students in case they stuck somewhere while solving some questions.

At the end, I can say confidently that if you rigorously practice the problems given in this book then surely you will get an edge in Physics and will increase your chance of getting good JEE Score.

However, I have taken the utmost care while writing this book but if any error or whatsoever has skipped my attention then please bring it to my notice so that it can be rectified. I would also like to appeal all my fellow Physics Teachers to have a look at the book and share their valuable suggestions for its further improvement.

Pradeep Beniwal
B.Tech, IIT Kharagpur
problemsinphysics@yahoo.com

CONTENTS

CHAPTER~01

MAGNETIC EFFECT OF CURRENT

LEVEL 01 Starter Level

1.1 Magnetic Field due to Straight Wire

1 A long wire carries a current of 90 A from east to west direction. Find the magnetic field due to current at a point which is 1.5 m just below the wire.

2 A long straight wire carrying current $i = 50$ A lies along X-axis. Find the magnetic field at point (2 cm, 3 cm, 4 cm).

3 A long, straight wire carrying a current of 1.0 A is placed horizontally in a uniform magnetic field $B = 1.0 \times 10^{-5}$ T pointing vertically upward as shown in figure. Find the magnitude of the resultant magnetic field at the points P and Q, both situated at a distance of 2.0 cm from the wire in the same horizontal plane.

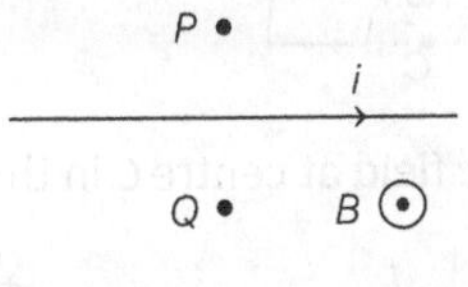

4 A long, vertical wire carrying a current of 10 A in the upward direction is placed in a region, where a horizontal magnetic field of magnitude 2.0×10^{-3} T exist from south to north. Find the point, where the resultant magnetic field is zero.

5 Find resultant magnetic field at point C in the figures shown.

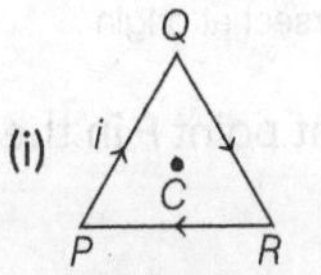

A loop in the shape of equilateral triangle of side a carrying current i

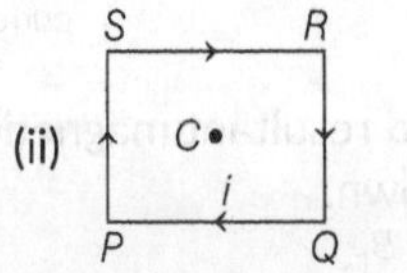

A loop in the shape of square of side a carrying current i

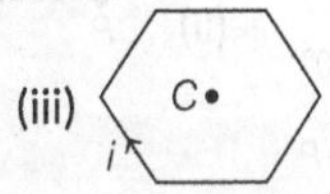

A loop in the shape of regular hexagon of side a carrying current i

6 Find resultant magnetic field at point C of the rectangular loop carrying current i as shown in figure.

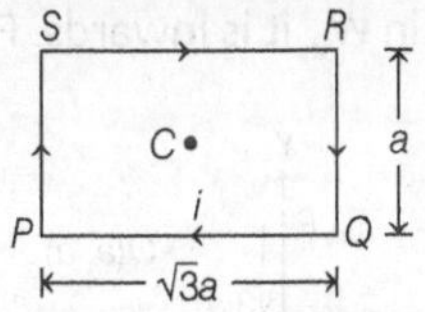

7 Figure shows a square loop $ABCD$ with edge length a. The resistance of the wire ABC is r and that of ADC is $2r$. Find the value of magnetic field at the centre of the loop assuming uniform wire.

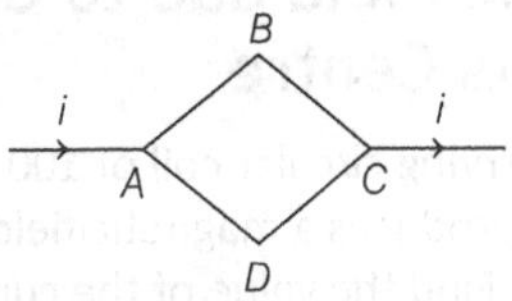

8 A current i flows along a thin wire shaped as a regular polygon with n sides which can be inscribed into a circle of radius R. Find the magnetic induction at the centre of the polygon. Analyse the obtained expression at $n \to \infty$.

9 Find resultant magnetic field at point P in the given figures.

(i)
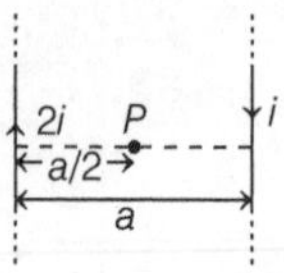

Two long parallel wires carrying current $2i$ and i in opposite directions

(ii)
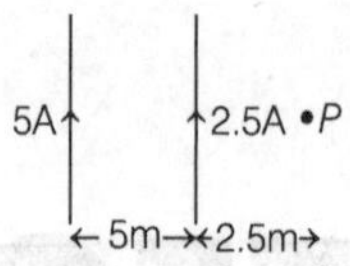

Two long parallel wires carrying current 5 A and 2.5 A in the same directions

(iii)
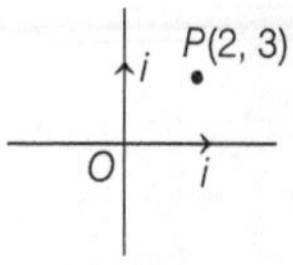

Two mutually perpendicular long wires carrying equal current i, intersect at origin

10 Find resultant magnetic field at point P in the figures shown.

(i)
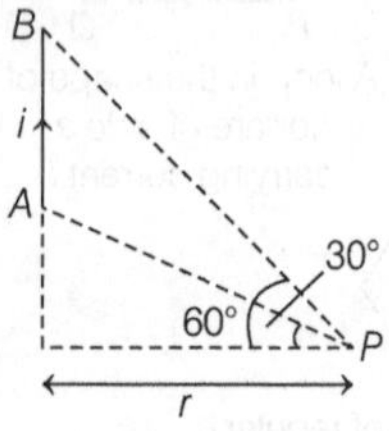

(ii)
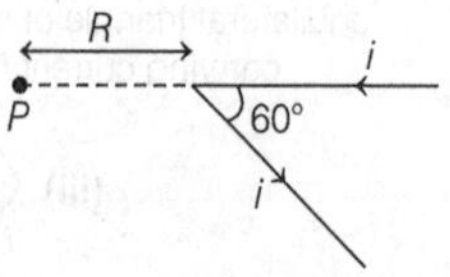

11 In the figure shown two long wires W_1 and W_2 each carrying current i are placed parallel to each other and parallel to Z-axis. The direction of current in W_1 is outward and in W_2 it is inwards. Find the **B** at points P and Q.

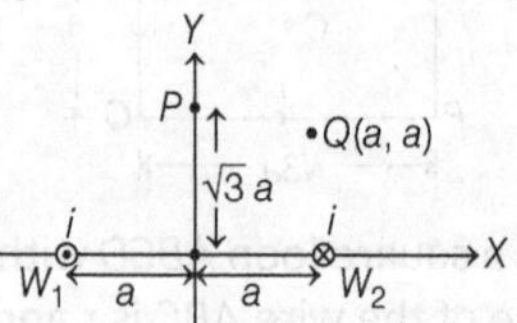

1.2 Magnetic Field due to Circular Arc at its Centre

1 A current carrying circular coil of 100 turns and radius 5 cm produces a magnetic field of 6×10^{-5} T at its centre. Find the value of the current.

2 A length of wire carries a steady current. It is first bent to form a circular coil of one turn. The magnetic field at the centre is B. The same length is now bent more sharply to give a double loop of a smaller radius. Find the new magnetic field at the centre caused by the same current.

3 An electron moving in a circular orbit of radius R makes n turns per second. Find the magnitude of magnetic field at the centre.

4 Find the magnetic field B due to a semi-circular wire of radius 10.0 cm carrying a current of 5.0 A at its centre of curvature.

5 A piece of wire carrying a current of 6.00 A is bent in the form of a circular arc of radius 10.0 cm, and it subtends an angle of 120° at the centre. Find the magnetic field B due to this piece of wire at the centre.

6 Find the magnetic field at centre C in the following cases.

(i)
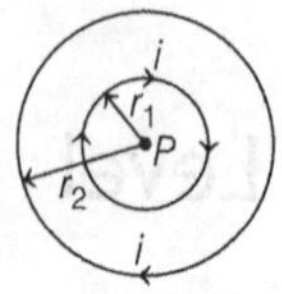

(ii)
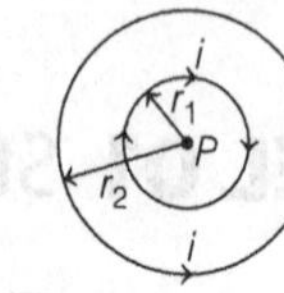

(iii)
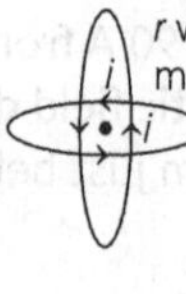

Two concentric loops each of radius r with their planes mutually perpendicular

7 Find the magnetic field at centre C in the following cases.

(i)
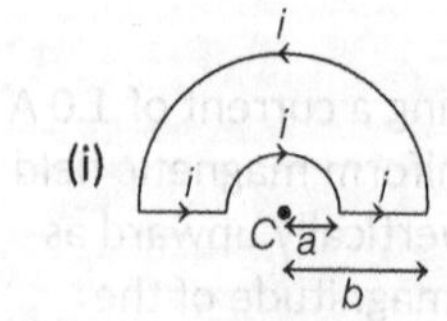

(ii)
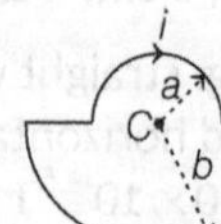

(iii)
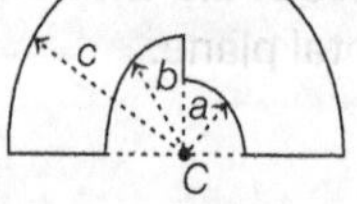

8 Find magnetic field at centre C in the following cases.

(i)
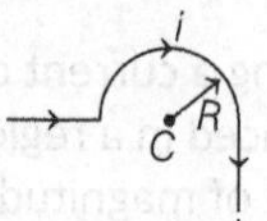

(ii)
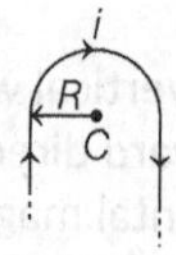

(iii)
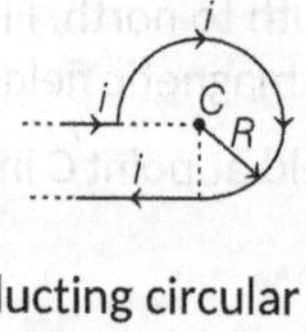

9 A conducting circular loop of radius a is connected to two long straight wires carrying current i as shown in figure. Find the magnetic field at the centre of the loop.

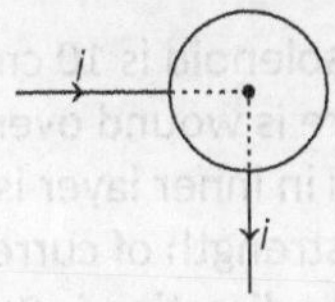

10 A current i flows along a thin wire shaped as shown in the figure. The radius of the circular part is R and the straight part subtends an angle 2ϕ at the centre of the circular part. Find the magnetic induction at the centre O.

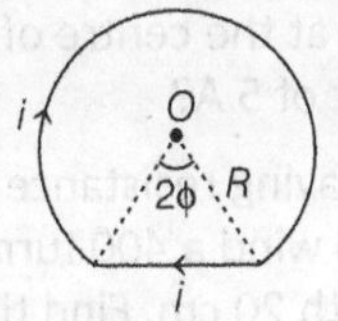

1.3 Magnetic Field due to Circular Coil on its Axis

1 A circular coil of 100 turns and radius 4.0 cm is placed in horizontal plane and carries an electric current of 5.0 A in the clockwise direction as seen from above. Find the magnetic field

(i) at a point 3.0 cm above the centre of the loop

(ii) at a point 3.0 cm below the centre of the loop.

2 An electric current i is flowing in a circular coil of radius a. At what distance from the centre of the axis of the coil will the magnetic field be (1/8)th of its value at the centre?

3 Two wires are wrapped over a wooden cylinder to form two coaxial loops carrying currents i_1 and i_2. If $i_2 = 8i_1$, find the value of x for which magnetic field at the origin O is zero.

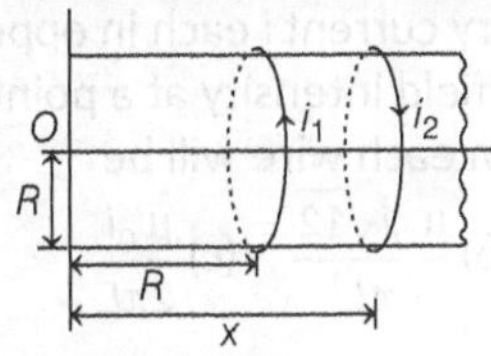

4 Two circular coils of wire each having a radius of 4 cm and 10 turns have a common axis and are 6 cm apart. If a current of 1 A passes through each coil in the opposite direction, find the magnetic induction

(i) at the centre of either coil and

(ii) at a point on the axis, midway between them.

1.4 Ampère's Law and its Applications

1 Find the values of $\oint \mathbf{B} \cdot d\mathbf{l}$ for the loops L_1, L_2 and L_3 in the given figure.

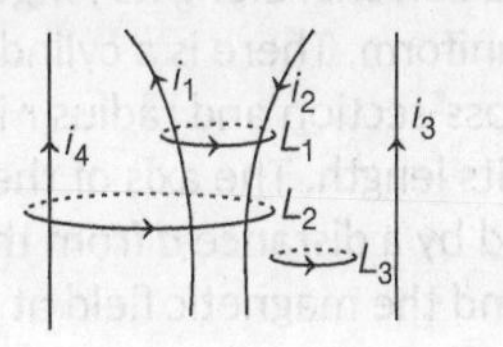

The sense of $d\mathbf{l}$ is mentioned in the figure.

2 What will be the value of $\int_A^B \mathbf{B} \cdot d\mathbf{l}$, where AB is line perpendicular to an infinite current carrying wire as shown in diagram ? (where $\mathbf{B}$ is magnetic field due to wire carrying current i)

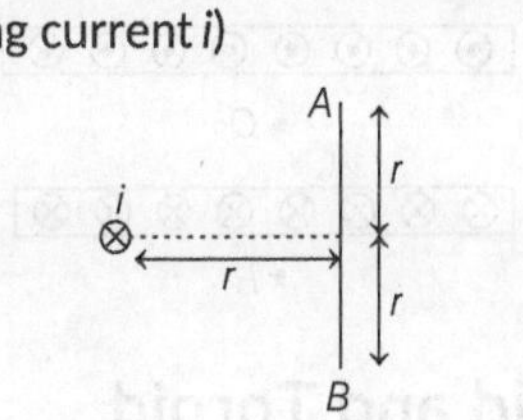

3 A thin but long, hollow, cylindrical tube of radius r carries a current i along its length. Find the magnitude of the magnetic field at a distance $r/2$ from the surface (i) inside the tube and (ii) outside the tube.

4 A solid wire of radius 10 cm carries a current of 5 A distributed uniformly over its cross-section. Find the magnetic field B at a point at a distance (i) 2 cm, (ii) 10 cm and (iii) 20 cm away from the axis. Draw a graph of B *versus* r, where r is the distance of the point from the axis.

5 A long, cylindrical tube of inner and outer radii a and b carries a current i distributed uniformly over its cross-section. Find the magnitude of the magnetic field at a point at a distance r from its axis for the following cases.

(i) $r < a$ (ii) $a \le r < b$ (iii) $r \ge b$

6 A cylindrical conductor of radius R carries a current along its length. The current density J over the cross-section of the conductor is a function of the radius according to $J = br$, where b is a constant. Find an expression for the magnetic field B at distance

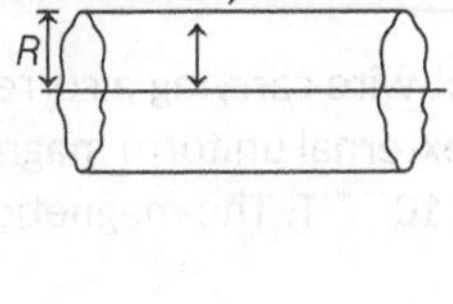

(i) $r_1 < R$ and

(ii) $r_2 > R$, measured from the axis

7 A long cylinder of uniform cross-section and radius R is carrying a current i along its length and the current density is uniform. There is a cylindrical cavity of uniform cross-section and radius r in the cylinder parallel to its length. The axis of the cylindrical cavity is separated by a distance d from the axis of the cylinder. Find the magnetic field at the axis of cylinder.

8 Two large metal sheets carry surface currents as shown in figure. The linear current density is λ A/m for each sheet. Find the magnetic field at the points P, Q and R.

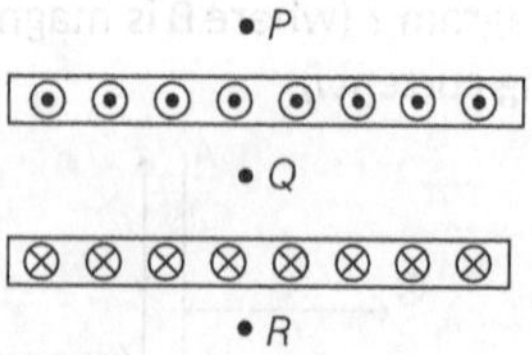

1.5 Solenoid and Toroid

1 A solenoid of length 0.4 m and diameter 0.6 m consists of a single layer of 1000 turns of fine wire carrying a current of 5.0×10^{-3} A. Find the magnetic field on the axis at the middle and at the ends of the solenoid.

2 The length of a solenoid is 10 cm and its diameter is very small. A wire is wound over it in two layers. The number of turns in inner layer is 50 and that of outer layer is 40. The strength of current flowing in two layers in opposite direction is 3 A. Find magnetic induction at the middle of the solenoid.

3 A long solenoid is fabricated by closely winding a wire of radius 0.5 mm over a cylindrical non-magnetic frame, so that the successive turns nearly touch each other. What would be the magnetic field B at the centre of the solenoid, if it carries a current of 5 A?

4 A copper wire having resistance 0.01 Ω in each metre is used to wind a 400 turns solenoid of radius 1.0 cm and length 20 cm. Find the emf of a battery which when connected across the solenoid will cause a magnetic field of 1.0×10^{-2} T near the centre of the solenoid.

5 The average radius of a toroid made on a ring of non-magnetic material is 0.1 m and it has 500 turns. If it carries 0.5 A current then what is the magnetic field produced along its circular axis inside the toroid?

LEVEL 02 JEE Main Level

Single Choice Correct Questions

1 The magnetic field at the origin due to a current element $i d\mathbf{l}$ placed at a position $\mathbf{r}$ is

(a) $\frac{\mu_0 i}{4\pi} \frac{d\mathbf{l} \times \mathbf{r}}{r^3}$ (b) $\frac{\mu_0 i}{2\pi} \frac{\mathbf{r} \times d\mathbf{l}}{r^3}$

(c) $\frac{\mu_0 i}{2\pi} \frac{\mathbf{r} \times d\mathbf{l}}{r^3}$ (d) $-\frac{\mu_0 i}{4\pi} \frac{d\mathbf{l} \times \mathbf{r}}{r^3}$

2 A long straight wire along the Z-axis carries a current i in the negative z-direction. The magnetic vector field $\mathbf{B}$ at a point having coordinates (x, y) in the $z = 0$ plane is

(a) $\frac{\mu_0 i}{2\pi} \frac{(y\mathbf{i} - x\mathbf{j})}{(x^2 + y^2)}$ (b) $\frac{\mu_0 i}{2\pi} \frac{(x\mathbf{i} + y\mathbf{j})}{(x^2 + y^2)}$

(c) $\frac{\mu_0 i}{2\pi} \frac{(x\hat{\mathbf{j}} - y\hat{\mathbf{i}})}{(x^2 + y^2)}$ (d) $\frac{\mu_0 i}{2\pi} \frac{(x\hat{\mathbf{i}} - y\hat{\mathbf{j}})}{(x^2 + y^2)}$

3 A long straight wire carrying a current of 30 A is placed in an external uniform magnetic field of induction 4×10^{-4} T. The magnetic field is acting parallel to the direction of current. The magnitude of the resultant magnetic induction (in T) at a point 2.0 cm away from the wire is

(a) 10^{-4} (b) 3×10^{-4}

(c) 5×10^{-4} (d) 6×10^{-4}

4 Two parallel straight long wires, separated by a distance L, carry current i each in opposite directions. The magnetic field intensity at a point located at a distance L from each wire will be

(a) $\frac{\mu_0 i\sqrt{3}}{2\pi L}$ (b) $\frac{\mu_0 i\sqrt{12}}{\pi L}$ (c) $\frac{\mu_0 i}{2\pi L}$ (d) $\frac{\mu_0 i\sqrt{3}}{\pi L}$

5 A rectangular loop of metallic wire is of length a and breadth b and carries a current i. The magnetic field at the centre of the loop is

(a) $\frac{\mu_0 i}{4\pi} \frac{8\sqrt{a^2 + b^2}}{ab}$ (b) $\frac{\mu_0 i}{4\pi} \frac{4\sqrt{a^2 + b^2}}{ab}$

(c) $\frac{\mu_0 i}{4\pi} \frac{2\sqrt{a^2 + b^2}}{ab}$ (d) $\frac{\mu_0 i}{4\pi} \frac{\sqrt{a^2 + b^2}}{ab}$

6 Equal currents $i = 1$ A are flowing through the wires parallel to Y-axis located at $x = +1$ m, $x = +2$ m, $x = +4$ m and so on..... , etc., but alternatively in opposite directions as shown. The magnetic field at origin (in T) would be

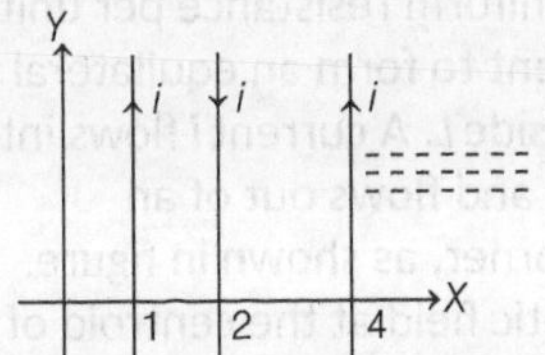

(a) $-1.33 \times 10^{-7}\hat{\mathbf{k}}$ (b) $1.33 \times 10^{-7}\hat{\mathbf{k}}$
(c) $2.67 \times 10^{-7}\hat{\mathbf{k}}$ (d) $-2.67 \times 10^{-7}\hat{\mathbf{k}}$

7 Equal current i is flowing in three infinitely long wires along positive x, y and z-directions. The magnetic field at a point $(0, 0, -a)$ would be

(a) $\frac{\mu_0 i}{2\pi a}(\hat{\mathbf{j}} - \hat{\mathbf{i}})$ (b) $\frac{\mu_0 i}{2\pi a}(\hat{\mathbf{i}} + \hat{\mathbf{j}})$
(c) $\frac{\mu_0 i}{2\pi a}(\hat{\mathbf{i}} - \hat{\mathbf{j}})$ (d) $\frac{\mu_0 i}{2\pi a}(\hat{\mathbf{i}} + \hat{\mathbf{j}} + \hat{\mathbf{k}})$

8 Two mutually perpendicular conductors carrying currents i_1 and i_2 lie in one plane. If i_1 is taken along X-axis and i_2 along Y-axis, the focus of points, where magnetic induction is zero, is

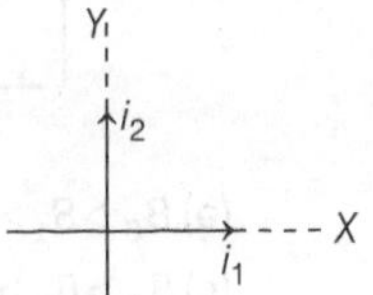

(a) a straight line passing through origin and having slope $\frac{i_1}{i_2}$
(b) a straight line passing through origin and having slope $\frac{i_2}{i_1}$
(c) a circle
(d) a hyperbola

9 Four long and parallel wires each carrying current i are kept at the corners of a square having side a. Magnetic field produced at centre C is

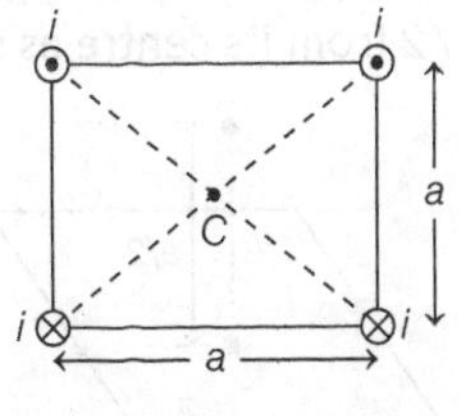

(a) $\frac{2\mu_0 i}{\pi a}$ (b) $\sqrt{2}\,\frac{\mu_0 i}{\pi a}$ (c) $\frac{\mu_0 i}{2\pi a}$ (d) $\frac{4\mu_0 i}{\pi a}$

10 Two long parallel wires are at a distance $2d$ apart. They carry steady equal currents flowing out of the plane of the paper as shown. The variation of the magnetic field B along the line XX' is given by

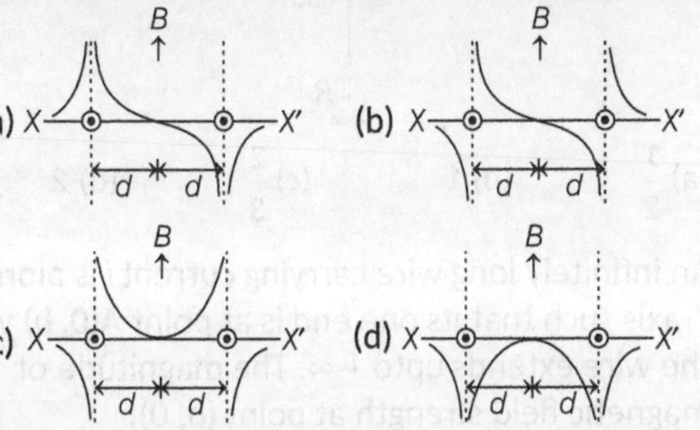

11 Two long straight parallel wires are kept at the ends of a diameter of a circular conductor of radius 1 m. The wire A carries a current of 1.6 A directed downwards perpendicular to the plane of the circle and B carries a current 1.2 A directed upwards perpendicular to the plane of the circle. The magnitude of magnetic induction at point S at a distance of 1.6 m from A on the circle is

(a) $2\sqrt{2} \times 10^{-7}$ T
(b) $\sqrt{2} \times 10^{-6}$ T
(c) $\sqrt{2} \times 10^{-7}$ T
(d) $2\sqrt{2} \times 10^{-6}$ T

12 Two long thin wires ABC and DEF are arranged as shown. They carry current i as shown in figure. The magnitude of the magnetic field at O is

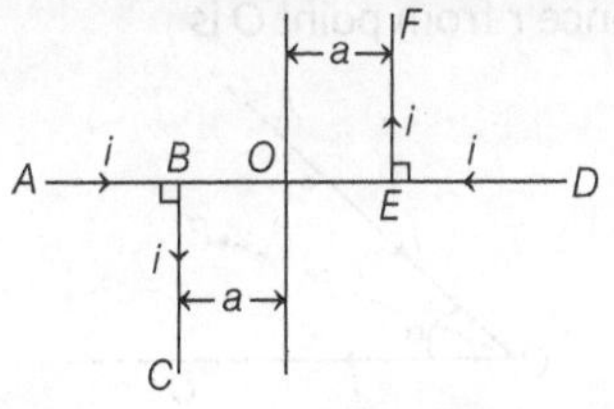

(a) zero (b) $\frac{\mu_0 i}{4\pi a}$
(c) $\frac{\mu_0 i}{2\pi a}$ (d) $\frac{\mu_0 i}{2\sqrt{2}\pi a}$

13 An infinitely long conductor PQR is bent to form a right angle as shown in figure. A current i flows through PQR. The magnetic field due to this current at the point M is B_1. Now, another infinitely long straight conductor QS is connected at Q, so that the current in PQ remaining unchanged. The magnetic field at M is now B_2. The ratio $\frac{B_1}{B_2}$ is given by

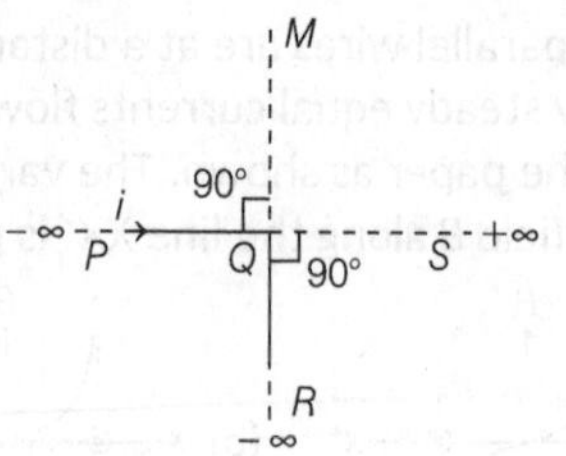

(a) $\frac{1}{2}$ (b) 1 (c) $\frac{2}{3}$ (d) 2

14 An infinitely long wire carrying current i is along Y-axis such that its one end is at point $A(0, b)$ while the wire extends upto $+\infty$. The magnitude of magnetic field strength at point $(a, 0)$.

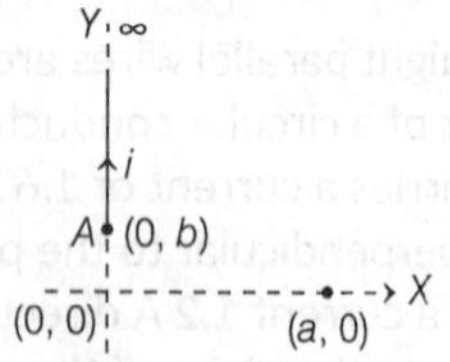

(a) $\frac{\mu_0 i}{4\pi a}\left(1+\frac{b}{\sqrt{a^2+b^2}}\right)$ (b) $\frac{\mu_0 i}{4\pi a}\left(1-\frac{b}{\sqrt{a^2+b^2}}\right)$

(c) $\frac{\mu_0 i}{4\pi a}\left(\frac{b}{\sqrt{a^2+b^2}}\right)$ (d) None of these

15 Two wires AO and OC carry equal currents i as shown in figure. One end of both the wires extends to infinity. Angle AOC is α. The magnitude of magnetic field at a point P on the bisector of these two wires at a distance r from point O is

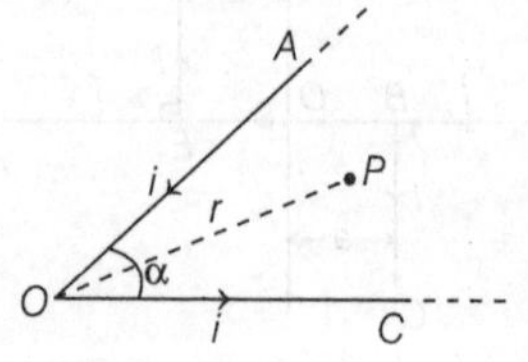

(a) $\frac{\mu_0}{2\pi}\frac{i}{r}\cot\left(\frac{\alpha}{2}\right)$ (b) $\frac{\mu_0}{4\pi}\frac{i}{r}\cot\left(\frac{\alpha}{2}\right)$

(c) $\frac{\mu_0}{2\pi}\frac{i}{r}\cot\left(\frac{\alpha}{4}\right)$ (d) None of these

16 A long straight wire, carrying current i, is bent at its mid-point to form an angle of 45°. Induction of magnetic field at point P, distant R from point of bending is equal to

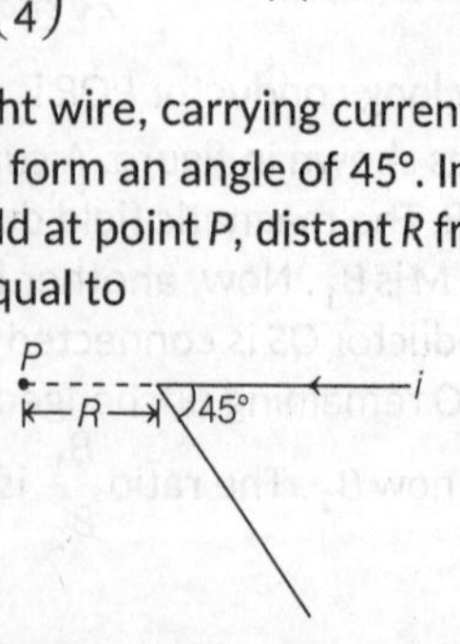

(a) $\frac{(\sqrt{2}-1)\mu_0 i}{4\pi R}$ (b) $\frac{(\sqrt{2}+1)\mu_0 i}{4\pi R}$

(c) $\frac{(\sqrt{2}-1)\mu_0 i}{4\sqrt{2}\pi R}$ (d) $\frac{(\sqrt{2}+1)\mu_0 i}{4\sqrt{2}\pi R}$

17 A wire of uniform resistance per unit length is bent to form an equilateral triangle of side L. A current i flows into one corner and flows out of an adjacent corner, as shown in figure. The magnetic field at the centroid of triangle due to the current in the triangular frame is

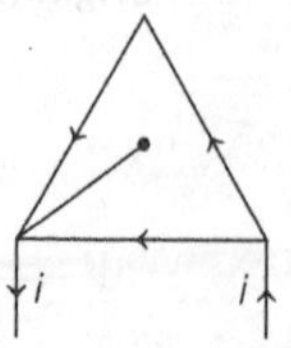

(a) $\frac{3\mu_0 i}{2\pi L}$ (b) $\frac{3\mu_0 i}{\pi L}$ (c) $\frac{3\sqrt{3}\mu_0 i}{2\pi L}$ (d) zero

18 The magnetic flux density in vacuum at the centre of any square coil (of one turn) of side a and carrying a current i is $\frac{ki}{a}$, where k is a constant. The magnitude of the induction at X, Y and Z are B_1, B_2 and B_3, respectively. Then,

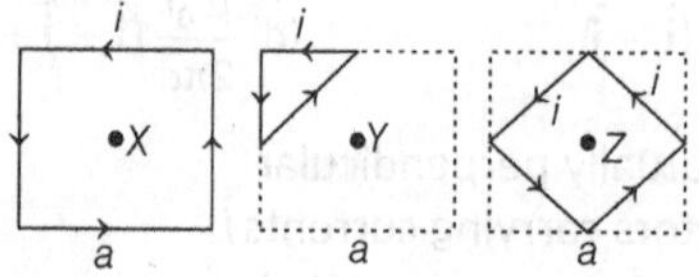

(a) $B_3 > B_1 > B_2$ (b) $B_2 > B_3 > B_1$

(c) $B_2 > B_1 > B_3$ (d) $B_1 > B_2 > B_3$

19 Two thick wires and two thin wires, all of the same materials and same length form a square in the three different ways P, Q and R with current connection as shown in figure. The magnetic field at the centre of the square is zero in cases

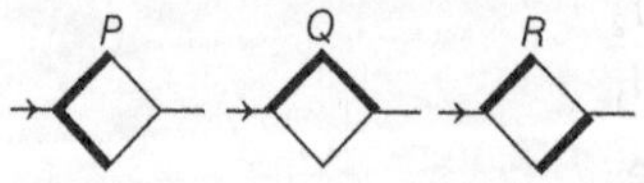

(a) P only (b) P and Q only

(c) Q and R only (d) P and R only

20 The magnetic field due to a current carrying square loop of side a at a point located symmetrically at a distance of $a/2$ from its centre as shown in figure is

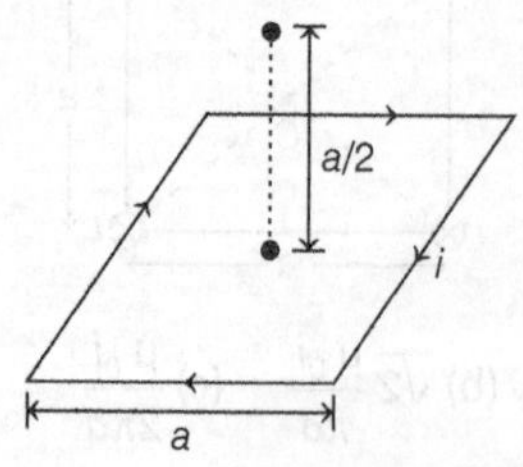

(a) $\frac{\sqrt{2}\,\mu_0 i}{\sqrt{3}\,\pi a}$ (b) $\frac{\mu_0 i}{\sqrt{6}\,\pi a}$

(c) $\frac{2\mu_0 i}{\sqrt{3}\,\pi a}$ (d) zero

21 A charge particle A of charge $q = 2\text{C}$ has velocity $v = 100$ m/s. When it passes through point A and has velocity in the direction as shown in figure, the strength of magnetic field at point B due to this moving charge is ($r = 2$ m)

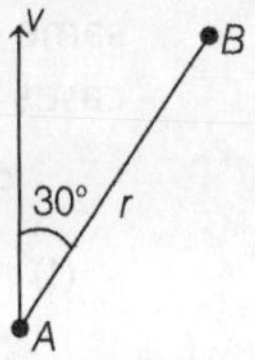

(a) $2.5\,\mu\text{T}$ (b) $5.0\,\mu\text{T}$

(c) $2.0\,\mu\text{T}$ (d) None of these

22 A charge $+2q$ moves vertically upwards with speed v, a second charge $-q$ moves horizontally to the right with the same speed v, and a third charge $+q$ moves horizontally to the right with the same speed v. The point P is located a perpendicular distance a away from each charge as shown in the figure. The magnetic field at point P is

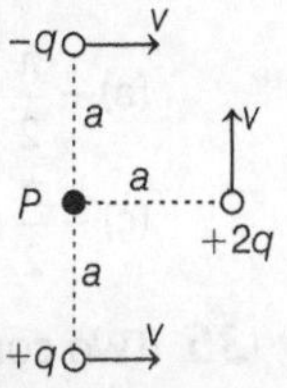

(a) $\frac{\mu_0}{4\pi}\frac{2qv}{a^2}\otimes$ (b) $\frac{\mu_0}{4\pi}\frac{4qv}{a^2}\otimes$

(c) $\frac{\mu_0}{4\pi}\frac{2qv}{a^2}\odot$ (d) $\frac{\mu_0}{4\pi}\frac{4qv}{a^2}\odot$

23 The ratio of magnetic field at centre of circular loop to the magnetic field at the centre of square loop, which are made by a constant length current carrying wire

(a) $\frac{\pi^2}{16}$ (b) $\frac{\pi^2}{8\sqrt{2}}$

(c) $\frac{\pi^2}{4\sqrt{2}}$ (d) $\frac{\pi^2}{2\sqrt{2}}$

24 An electron is revolving around a proton in a circular orbit of diameter 1 Å. If it produces a magnetic field of 14 Wb/m^2 at the proton, then its angular velocity will be about

(a) 4.375×10^{16} rad/s (b) 2.25×10^{14} rad/s

(c) 4×10^{15} rad/s (d) 8.75×10^{16} rad/s

25 A long wire carries a steady current. It is bent into circular loop of one turn and the magnetic field at the centre of the coil is B. It is then bent into circular loop of n turns. The magnetic field at the centre of the coil will be

(a) nB (b) n^2B

(c) $2nB$ (d) $2n^2B$

26 A conductor carrying current i is bent in the form of concentric semicircles as shown in the figure. The magnetic field at the centre O is

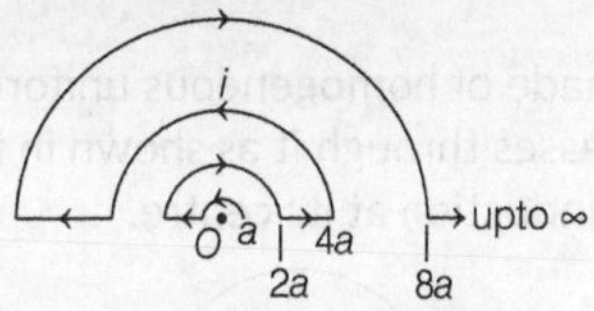

(a) zero (b) $\frac{\mu_0 i}{6a}$

(c) $\frac{\mu_0 i}{a}$ (d) $\frac{\mu_0 i \ln 2}{4a}$

27 The conductor $ABCDEF$ carries a current of 4 A. Find the net magnetic field at the centre O.

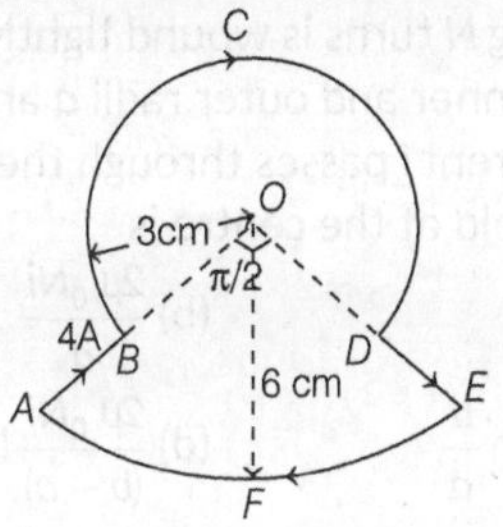

(a) $\frac{7}{3}\pi\times 10^{-3}$ T (b) $\frac{7}{3}\pi\times 10^{-5}$ T

(c) $\frac{7}{3}\pi\times 10^{-4}$ T (d) $\frac{7}{3}\pi\times 10^{-6}$ T

28 Net magnetic field at the centre of the circle O due to a current carrying loop as shown in figure is ($\theta < 180°$)

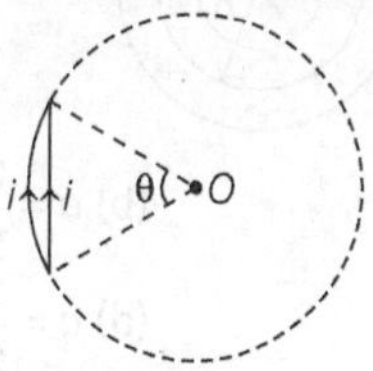

(a) zero

(b) perpendicular to paper inwards

(c) perpendicular to paper outwards

(d) is perpendicular to paper inwards if $\theta < 90°$ and perpendicular to paper outwards if $90° < \theta < 180°$

29 In the given figure, the magnitude of magnetic field at O is (all three wires are quarter circular arc)

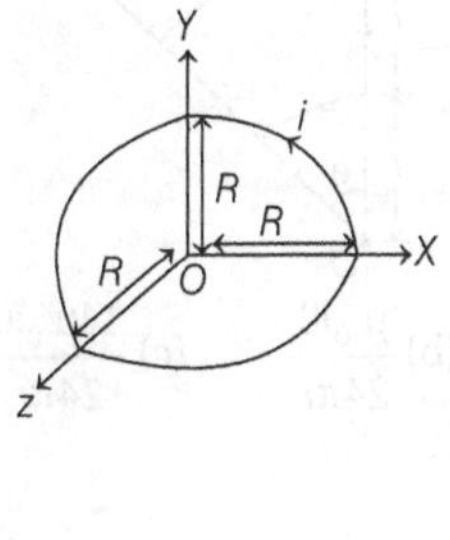

(a) $\frac{\mu_0 i}{4R}\sqrt{3}$ (b) $\frac{\mu_0 i}{2R}\sqrt{3}$

(c) $\frac{\mu_0 i}{8R}\sqrt{3}$ (d) None of these

30 A ring is made of homogeneous uniform wire. Current passes through it as shown in figure. Find magnetic induction at its centre.

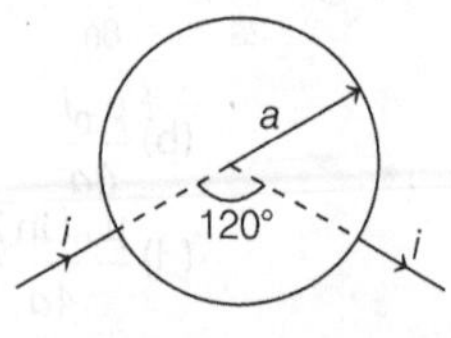

(a) $\frac{3\mu_0 i}{2a}$ (b) $\frac{3\mu_0 i}{4a}$ (c) $\frac{2\mu_0 i}{3a}$ (d) Zero

31 A coil having N turns is wound tightly in the form of a spiral with inner and outer radii a and b, respectively. When a current i passes through the coil, the magnetic field at the centre is

(a) $\frac{\mu_0 Ni}{b}$ (b) $\frac{2\mu_0 Ni}{a}$

(c) $\frac{\mu_0 Ni}{2(b-a)}\ln\frac{b}{a}$ (d) $\frac{2\mu_0 Ni}{(b-a)}\ln\frac{b}{a}$

32 For $c = 2a$ and $a < b < c$, the magnetic field at point P will be zero when

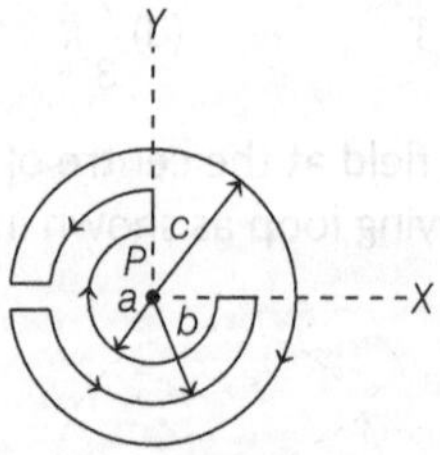

(a) $a = b$ (b) $a = \frac{3}{5}b$

(c) $a = \frac{5}{3}b$ (d) $a = \frac{1}{3}b$

33 Shown in the figure is a conductor carrying a current i. The magnetic field intensity at the point O (common centre of all the three arcs) is

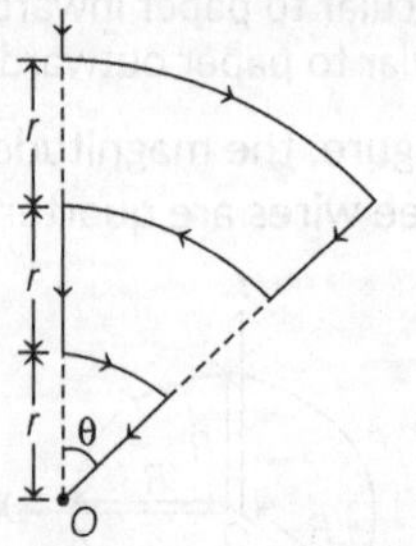

(a) $\frac{5\mu_0 i\theta}{24\pi r}$ (b) $\frac{\mu_0 i\theta}{24\pi r}$ (c) $\frac{11\mu_0 i\theta}{24\pi r}$ (d) zero

34 The magnetic field at the centre of a circular coil of radius r is π times that due to a long straight wire at a distance r from it, for equal currents. Figure here shows three cases, in all cases, the circular part has radius r and straight ones are infinitely long. For same current, the magnetic field at the centre P in cases 1, 2 and 3 have the ratio

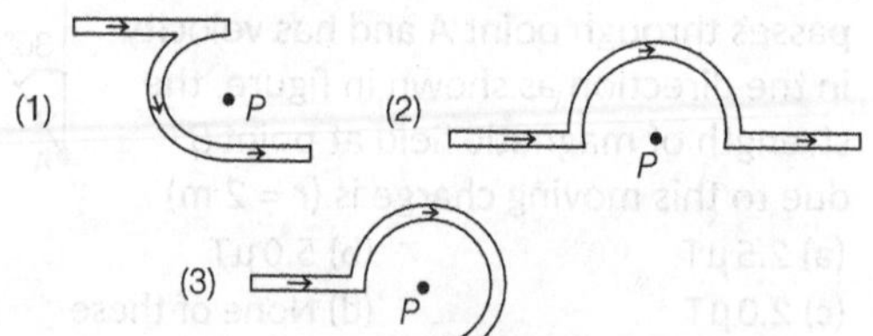

(a) $-\frac{\pi}{2}:\frac{\pi}{2}:\frac{3\pi}{4}-\frac{1}{2}$ (b) $-\frac{\pi}{2}+1:\frac{\pi}{2}+1:\frac{3\pi}{4}+\frac{1}{2}$

(c) $-\frac{\pi}{2}:\frac{\pi}{2}:3\frac{\pi}{4}$ (d) $-\frac{\pi}{2}-1:\frac{\pi}{2}-\frac{1}{4}:\frac{3\pi}{4}+\frac{1}{2}$

35 Two concentric coils X and Y of radii 16 cm and 10 cm lie in the same vertical plane containing north-south direction. X has 20 turns and carries 16 A. Y has 25 turns and carries 18 A. X has current in anti-clockwise direction and Y has current in clockwise direction for an observer, looking at the coils facing the west. The magnitude of net magnetic field at their common centre is

(a) $5\pi \times 10^{-4}$ T towards west

(b) $13\pi \times 10^{-4}$ T towards east

(c) $13\pi \times 10^{-4}$ T towards west

(d) $5\pi \times 10^{-4}$ T towards east

36 A long wire carrying current i is bent into the shape as shown in figure. The net magnetic field intensity at the centre O is

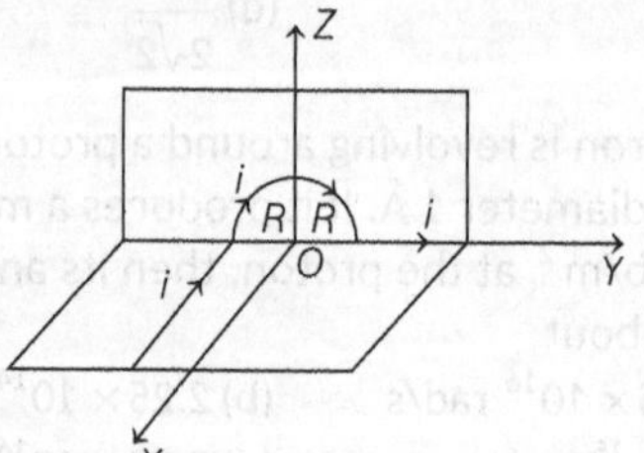

(a) $\frac{\mu_0 i}{4\pi R}\sqrt{1+\pi^2}$

(b) $\frac{\mu_0 i}{4\pi R}\sqrt{2+\pi^2}$

(c) $\frac{\mu_0 i}{4\pi R}\sqrt{4+\pi^2}$

(d) $\frac{\mu_0 i}{4\pi R}\sqrt{9+\pi^2}$

37 A conducting wire carrying a current i is bent into the shape as shown in figure. The net magnetic field at the centre O of the circular arc of radius R is

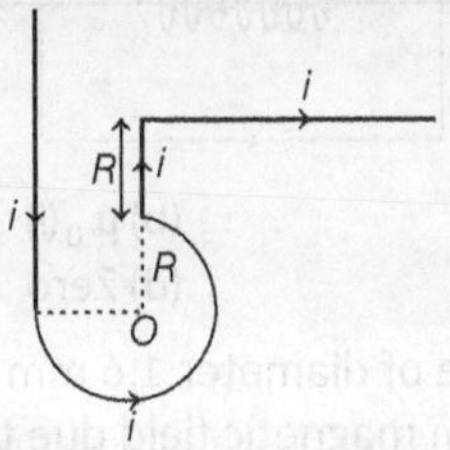

(a) $\frac{\mu_0 i}{2R}\left(\frac{1+3\pi}{\pi}\right)$ (b) $\frac{\mu_0 i}{4R}\left(\frac{1+3\pi}{\pi}\right)$

(c) $\frac{\mu_0 i}{8R}\left(\frac{1+3\pi}{\pi}\right)$ (d) $\frac{\mu_0 i}{8R}\left(\frac{2+3\pi}{\pi}\right)$

38 In the given figure, find the magnetic induction at O.

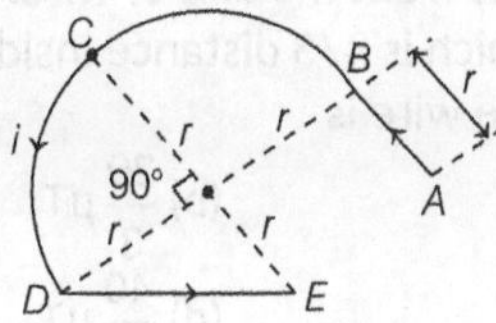

(a) $\frac{\mu_0 i}{4\pi r}(\pi+2+\sqrt{2})$ (b) $\frac{\mu_0 i}{4\pi r}\left(\pi+\sqrt{2}+\frac{1}{2}\right)$

(c) $\frac{\mu_0 i}{4\pi r}\left(\pi+\frac{1}{\sqrt{2}}+2\right)$ (d) $\frac{\mu_0 i}{4\pi r}(\pi+2+2\sqrt{2})$

39 Conductor $PQRSTU$ is carrying a current i as shown in figure and QR and ST are bent in the form of quarter circles. OX, OY and OZ are three orthogonal co-ordinate axes. $\hat{\mathbf{i}}$, $\hat{\mathbf{j}}$ and $\hat{\mathbf{k}}$ have usual meaning. The magnetic field at O is

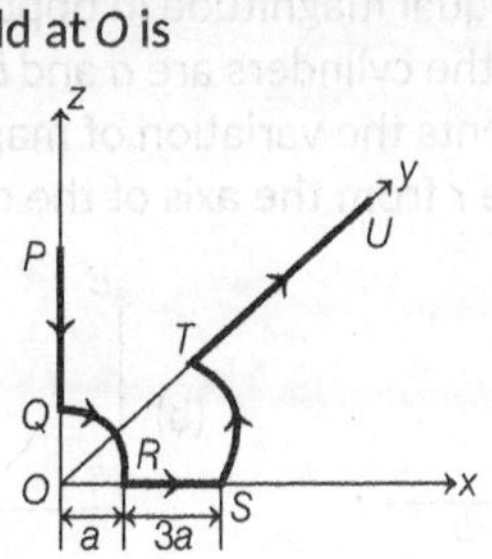

(a) $\frac{\mu_0 i}{8a}(\hat{\mathbf{j}}+\hat{\mathbf{k}})$ (b) $\frac{\mu_0 i}{8a}(\hat{\mathbf{j}}+0.25\hat{\mathbf{k}})$

(c) $\frac{\mu_0 i}{8a}(\hat{\mathbf{i}}+\hat{\mathbf{j}})$ (d) $\frac{\mu_0 i}{8a}(\hat{\mathbf{i}}+0.25\hat{\mathbf{j}})$

40 The diameter of a circular coil is 0.16 m and it has 100 turns. If a current of 5 A is passed through the coil, then the intensity of magnetic field at a point on the axis at a distance 0.06 m from its centre will be

(a) 2×10^{-3} Wb/m^2 (b) 2×10^{-2} Wb/m^2

(c) 2×10^{3} Wb/m^2 (d) 2×10^{2} Wb/m^2

41 An electric current is flowing through a circular coil of radius R. The ratio of the magnetic field at the centre of the coil and that at a distance $2\sqrt{2}R$ from the centre of the coil on its axis is

(a) $2\sqrt{2}$ (b) 27

(c) 36 (d) 8

42 Magnetic field at point P on the axis of two coplanar, concentric current carrying loop is zero if

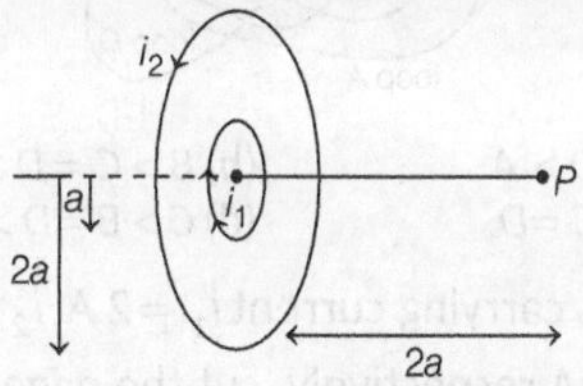

(a) $\frac{i_1}{i_2}=\frac{5}{2}\sqrt{\frac{5}{8}}$ (b) $\frac{i_2}{i_1}=\frac{5}{2}\sqrt{\frac{5}{8}}$

(c) $\frac{i_1}{i_2}=\frac{5}{2}\sqrt{\frac{8}{5}}$ (d) $\frac{i_2}{i_1}=\frac{5}{2}\sqrt{\frac{8}{5}}$

43 A point charge is moving in clockwise direction in a circle with constant speed. Consider the magnetic field produced by the charge at a point P (not centre of the circle) on the axis of the circle.

(a) It is constant in magnitude only

(b) It is constant in direction only

(c) It is constant in direction and magnitude both

(d) It is not constant in magnitude and direction both

44 The coils C_1 and C_2 have same number of turns and carry equal currents in the same sense. They subtend the same angle θ at P. If the magnetic field produced by C_1 at P is B, then that produced by C_2 will be

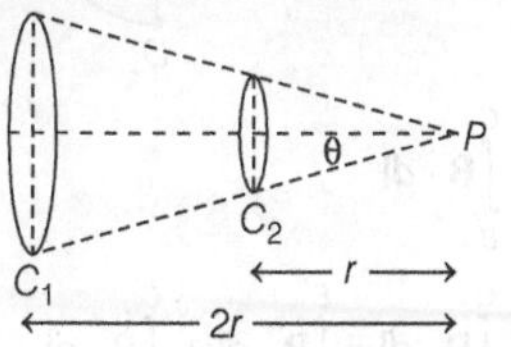

(a) B (b) $2B$

(c) $B/2$ (d) None of these

45 The field normal to the plane of coil of N turns, radius R carrying current i at a point lying a small distance h ($<<R$) from the centre of coil is B_1 and field at the centre of coil is B_2. Then, the value of $\frac{B_2-B_1}{B_2}$ is

(a) $\frac{2h^2}{3R^2}$ (b) $\frac{2h^2}{R^2}$ (c) $\frac{h^2}{3R^2}$ (d) $\frac{3h^2}{2R^2}$

46 Consider six wires coming into or out of the page, all with the same current. Rank the line integral of the magnetic field (from most positive to most negative) taken counterclockwise around each loop as shown in figure.

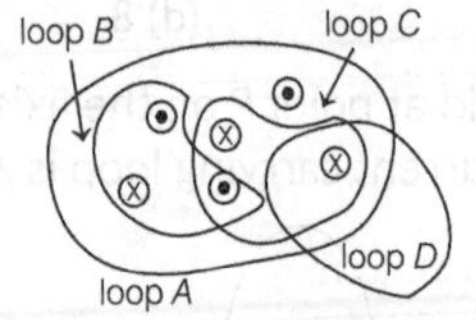

(a) $B > C > D > A$ (b) $B > C = D > A$
(c) $B > A > C = D$ (d) $C > B = D > A$

47 Four wires carrying current $i_1 = 2$ A, $i_2 = 4$ A, $i_3 = 6$ A and $i_4 = 8$ A respectively, cut the page perpendicularly as shown in figure. The value of $\int \mathbf{B} \cdot d\mathbf{l}$ for the loop shown would be

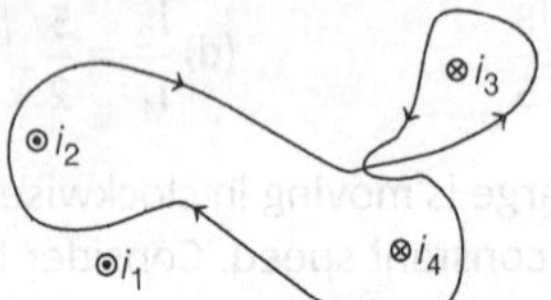

(a) $+2\mu_0$ Wb/m (b) $-2\mu_0$ Wb/m
(c) $+10\mu_0$ Wb/m (d) $-10\mu_0$ Wb/m

48 There is an infinitely long current carrying wire as shown in figure. Also shown an amperial path *ABCDE*. Mark the correct option.

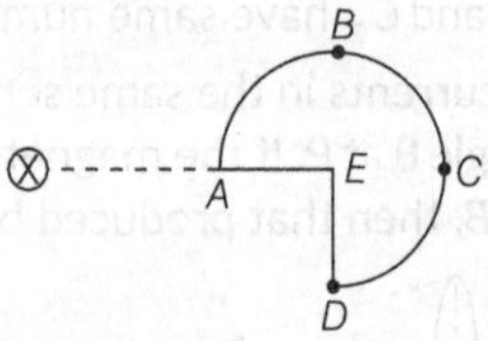

(a) $\int_A^B \mathbf{B} \cdot d\mathbf{l} = \int_B^C \mathbf{B} \cdot d\mathbf{l}$

(b) $\int_A^B \mathbf{B} \cdot d\mathbf{l} + \int_B^C \mathbf{B} \cdot d\mathbf{l} = \int_D^E \mathbf{B} \cdot d\mathbf{l} + \int_D^C \mathbf{B} \cdot d\mathbf{l}$

(c) $\int_A^B \mathbf{B} \cdot d\mathbf{l} + \int_B^C \mathbf{B} \cdot d\mathbf{l} = \int_E^D \mathbf{B} \cdot d\mathbf{l} + \int_D^C \mathbf{B} \cdot d\mathbf{l}$

(d) $\int_A^E \mathbf{B} \cdot d\mathbf{l} = \int_E^D \mathbf{B} \cdot d\mathbf{l}$

49 In the diagram shown, a wire carries current *I*. What is the value of the $\int \mathbf{B} \cdot d\mathbf{s}$ (as in Ampere's law) on the helical loop as shown in figure? The integration in done in the sense shown. The loop has *N* turns and part of helical loop on which arrows are drawn is outside the plane of paper.

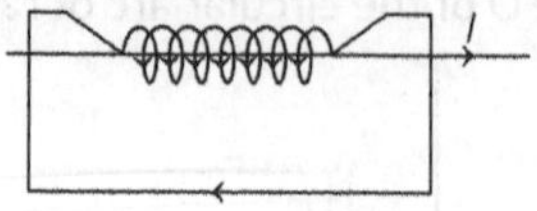

(a) $-\mu_0(NI)$ (b) $\mu_0(I)$
(c) $\mu_0(NI)$ (d) Zero

50 A copper wire of diameter 1.6 mm carries a current *i*. The maximum magnetic field due to this wire is 5×10^{-3} T. The value of *i* is

(a) 40 A (b) 5 A
(c) 20 A (d) 2 A

51 A solid cylindrical wire of radius *R* carries a current *i*. The magnetic field is 5μT at a point, which is $2R$ distance away from the axis of wire. Magnetic field at a point which is $R/3$ distance inside from the surface of the wire is

(a) $\frac{10}{3}$ μT (b) $\frac{20}{3}$ μT
(c) $\frac{5}{3}$ μT (d) $\frac{40}{3}$ μT

52 A hollow cylindrical wire carries a current *i*, having inner and outer radii *R* and 2*R* respectively. Magnetic field at a point which is $3R/2$ distance away from its axis is

(a) $\frac{5\mu_0 i}{18\pi R}$ (b) $\frac{\mu_0 i}{36\pi R}$ (c) $\frac{5\mu_0 i}{36\pi R}$ (d) $\frac{5\mu_0 i}{9\pi R}$

53 Two coaxial metallic long cylindrical shell carry current of equal magnitude in opposite direction. If the radii of the cylinders are *a* and *b* (>*a*), then which plot represents the variation of magnetic field with the distance *r* from the axis of the cylinder?

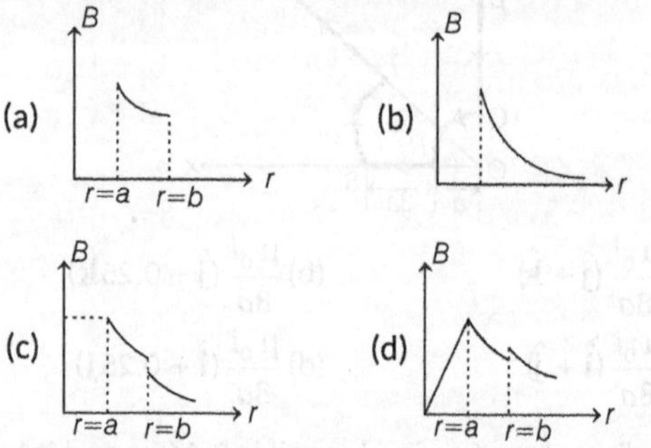

54 A long straight metal rod has a very long hole of radius *a* drilled parallel to the rod axis as shown in the figure. If the rod carries a current *i* find the value of magnetic induction on the axis of the hole, where OC = c

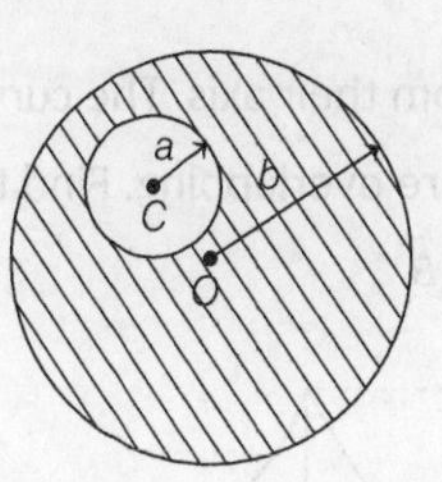

(a) $\frac{\mu_0 ic}{\pi(b^2-a^2)}$ (b) $\frac{\mu_0 ic}{2\pi(b^2-a^2)}$

(c) $\frac{\mu_0 i(b^2-a^2)}{2\pi c}$ (d) $\frac{\mu_0 ic}{2\pi a^2 b^2}$

55 A wire of length 100 m is tightly wounded on a hollow tube of radius 5 mm and length 1 m. A current of 1 A is flowing in the wire. Then magnetic field strength inside the tube will be

(a) 4 T (b) 4 mT

(c) 40 mT (d) 40 T

56 A long cylinder solenoid has tightly spaced turns wound in a single layer over its surface. The winding wire has a thickness of 0.1 mm. If a current of 1 A flows through the winding wire, what is the approximate value of magnetic field at the mid plane of the solenoid winding, on its axis?

(a) $2\pi\sqrt{2}\times10^{-3}$ T (b) $\pi\sqrt{2}\times10^{-3}$ T

(c) $2\pi\times10^{-3}$ T (d) $4\pi\times10^{-3}$ T

57 A current of $\frac{1}{4\pi}$ A is flowing through a toroid. It has 1000 number of turns per metre, then the value of magnetic field (in Wb/m^2) along its axis is

(a) 10^{-2} (b) 10^{-3}

(c) 10^{-4} (d) 10^{-7}

58 Constant current is flowing in toroid and top-view of toroid section in which loop *ABCD* is present as shown in figure. Then, choose the correct statement.

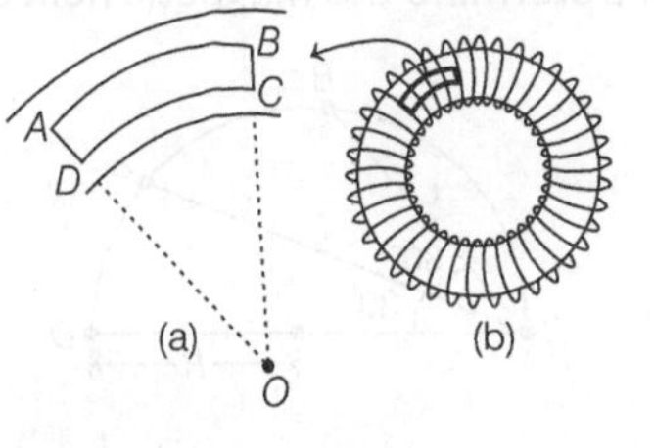

(a) $\int \mathbf{B}\cdot d\mathbf{l}$ is more for *AB* than *DC*.

(b) $\int \mathbf{B}\cdot d\mathbf{l}$ is less for *AB* than *DC*.

(c) $\int \mathbf{B}\cdot d\mathbf{l}$ is equal for both *AB* and *DC*.

(d) Can't say anything without knowing about cross-section shape of toroid.

Numerical Value Questions

1 A current element $i\delta l$ is located at origin. The current is in the direction of the $+Z$-axis, then the magnitude of *X* component of the magnetic field at a point *P* (3, 4, 12) is $\frac{n\frac{\mu_0}{4\pi}i\delta l}{2197}$. Find *n*.

2 A long straight wire lies on *Y*-axis and carries a current of 8 A in $-y$-direction. In addition to the magnetic field produced by the wire, a uniform magnetic field of $(1.4\times10^{-6}\hat{i})$T is also present. If the magnitude of net magnetic field at (1, 1, 1) is $\alpha\times10^{-7}$ T, then find α.

3 A current of $I=\sqrt{2}$ A flows in a circuit having the shape of an isosceles trapezium. The ratio of the bases of the trapezium is 2. Find the magnetic induction (in μT) at symmetric point *O* in the plane of the trapezium. The length of the smaller base of the trapezium is $l=10$ cm, the distance $h=5$ cm.

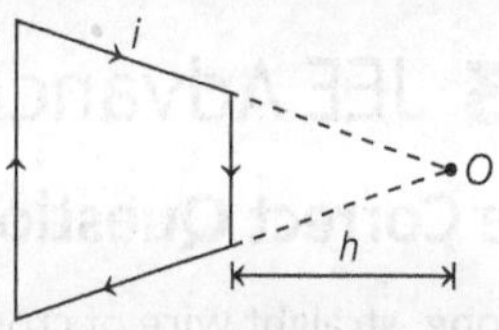

4 Infinite number of concentric squares each carrying equal current *i* and having side length *a*, 2*a*, 4*a*, 8*a*, ... respectively are placed co-planar. If alternate square coils carry currents along the same direction, magnetic field at their common centre is *K* times $\frac{\sqrt{2}\mu_0 i}{3\pi a}$. Find the value of *K*.

5 Two identical wires of same length carrying same current are bent into the shapes as shown in figure. If the ratio of magnitude of magnetic field at P_1 to magnetic field at P_2 is $\frac{\sqrt{n}}{\pi^2}$, then find *n*.

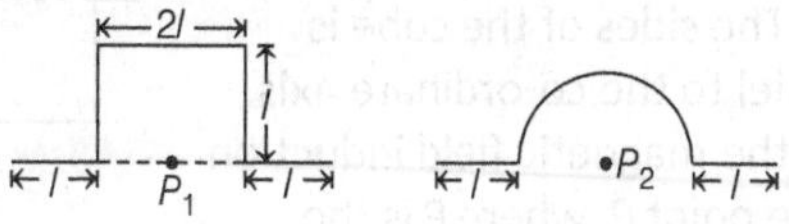

6 A thin rod is being rotated about point O in horizontal plane. The rod carries uniformly distributed charge over it having linear charge density $\frac{2}{\pi}$ C/m. The rod is rotating with a constant angular velocity 2π rad/s. If magnetic field strength at O is $\frac{\mu_0 n}{4\pi}\ln 2$ T, then find the value of n.

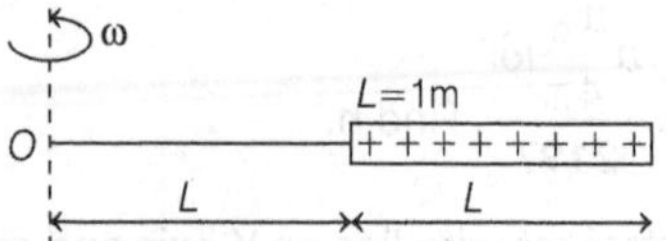

7 Current $i = 2.5$ A flows along the circular coil whose equation is given by $x^2 + y^2 = 9\text{ cm}^2$ (here x and y are in cm). If magnetic field at point (0, 0, 4 cm) is given by $n\pi \times 10^{-7}$ T, then state value of n.

8 We have two separate long cylindrical wires both having different but uniform current densities. The radius of one of the wires is twice of the other. The figure shows the graph of magnetic field B with radial distance r from their axis. The curved parts of the two graphs are overlapping. Find the ratio $\frac{B_1}{B_2}$.

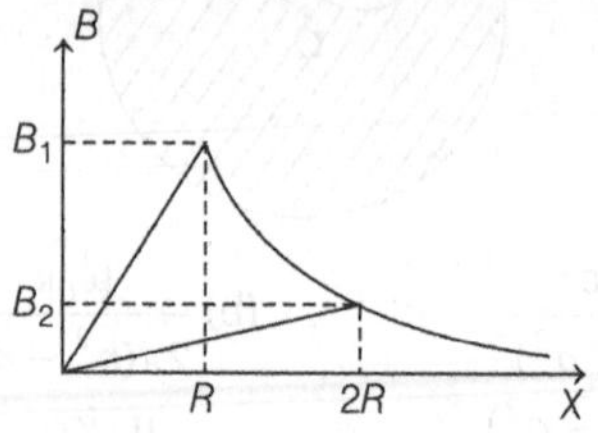

9 The current density $J(r)$ inside a long solid cylindrical wire of radius $R = 12$ mm is in the direction of the central axis and its magnitude varies linearly with radial distance r from the axis according to $J = \frac{J_0 r}{R}$, where $J_0 = 10^4\ \text{A/m}^2$. Find the magnitude of magnetic field (in μT) at $r = 6$ mm.

10 A solenoid is to be constructed with a magnetic field of 0.168 T at its centre. The radius of solenoid is to be 0.01 m and the wire carries a current of 2 A. If the solenoid is 1.4 m long, what is the length of wire needed (in m)?

LEVEL 03 JEE Advanced Level

Single Choice Correct Questions

1 Consider a long, straight wire of cross-section area A carrying a current i. Let there be n free electrons per unit volume. An observer sitting in the car moving in the same direction to the current with a speed $u = \left(\frac{i}{nAe}\right)$ and separated from the wire by a distance r. The magnetic field seen by the observer is

(a) $\frac{\mu_0 i}{2\pi r}$ (b) zero

(c) $\frac{\mu_0 i}{\pi r}$ (d) $\frac{2\mu_0 i}{\pi r}$

2 A current element (0.2 A-m) is placed along the X-axis at the centre of a cube of side length 2 m. The sides of the cube is parallel to the co-ordinate axis. Find the magnetic field induction at the point P, where P is the corner of the cube

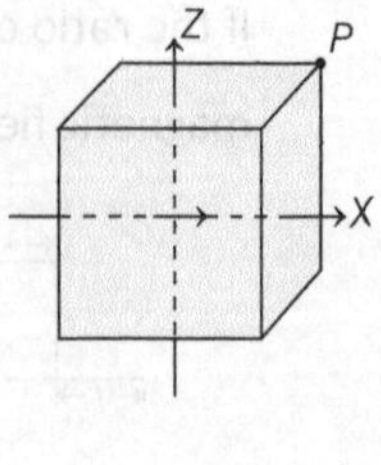

(a) $\frac{1}{\sqrt{2}} \times 10^{-7}$ T (b) $\sqrt{\frac{8}{27}} \times 10^{-8}$ T

(c) 1.77×10^{-9} T (d) $\frac{1}{8\sqrt{2}} \times 10^{-7}$ T

3 A current carrying wire is placed in the grooves of an insulating semi-circular disc of radius R, as shown in figure. The current enters at point A and leaves from point B. Determine the magnetic field at point D.

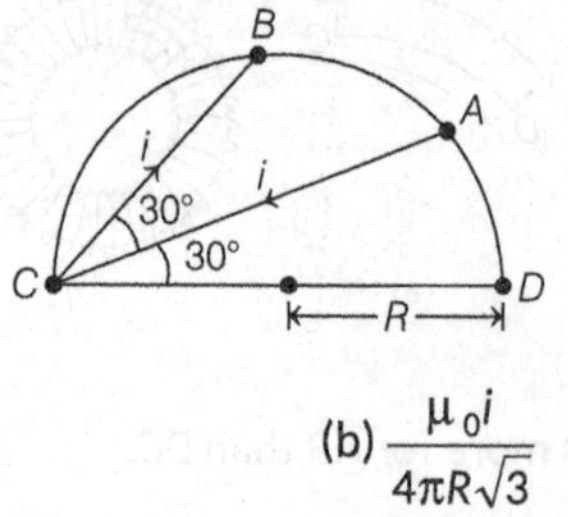

(a) $\frac{\mu_0 i}{8\pi R\sqrt{3}}$ (b) $\frac{\mu_0 i}{4\pi R\sqrt{3}}$

(c) $\frac{\mu_0 i}{2\pi R\sqrt{3}}$ (d) None of these

4 Determine the magnitude of magnetic field at the centre of the current carrying wire arrangement shown in the figure. The arrangement extends to infinity. (The wires joining the successive squares are along the line passing through the centre)

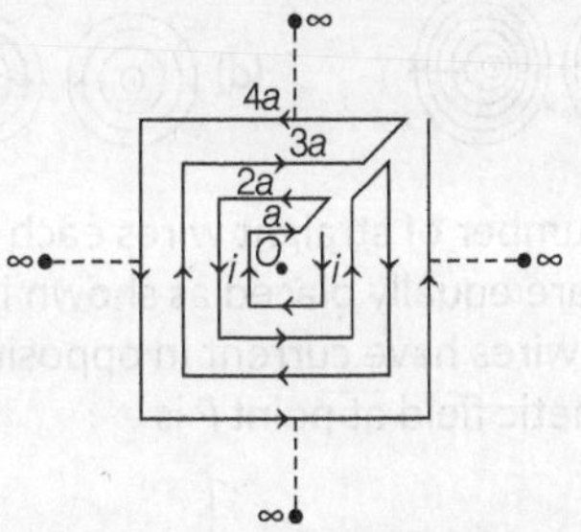

(a) $\frac{\mu_0 i}{\sqrt{2}\pi a}$ (b) 0

(c) $\frac{2\sqrt{2}\mu_0 i}{\pi a}\ln 2$ (d) None of these

5 In figure, AB is a non-conducting rod. Equal charges of magnitude q are fixed at various points on the rod as shown in figure. The rod is rotated uniformly about an axis passing through O and perpendicular to its length such that linear speed at the end A or B of the rod is 3 m/s. Magnetic field at O is

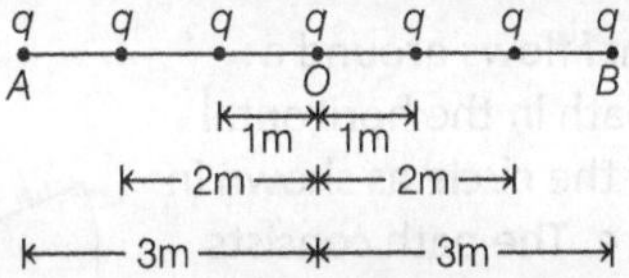

(a) $\frac{11\mu_0 q}{12\pi}$ (b) $\frac{3\mu_0 q}{7\pi}$

(c) $\frac{\mu_0 q}{2\pi}$ (d) $\frac{6\mu_0 q}{13\pi}$

6 A current carrying wire in the form of V alphabet is kept as shown in the figure. Magnetic field intensity at point P which lies on the angular bisector of V is

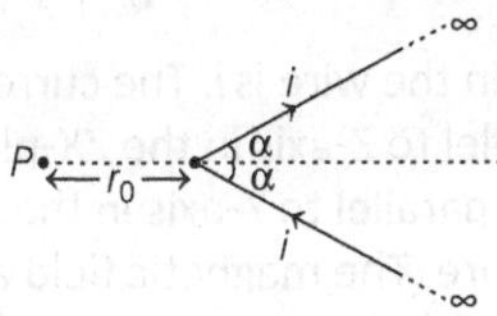

(a) $\frac{\mu_0 i}{4\pi r_0}\cot\left(\frac{\alpha}{2}\right)$ (b) $\frac{\mu_0 i}{2\pi r_0}\cot\left(\frac{\alpha}{2}\right)$

(c) $\frac{\mu_0 i}{4\pi r_0}\tan\left(\frac{\alpha}{2}\right)$ (d) $\frac{\mu_0 i}{2\pi r_0}\tan\left(\frac{\alpha}{2}\right)$

7 Equal current of 4 A is flowing in two parallel conductors kept at a distance of 2 m, in mutually opposite directions as shown in the figure. The magnetic induction (in μT) at a point P, equidistant from both the conductors at a distance 2 m will be

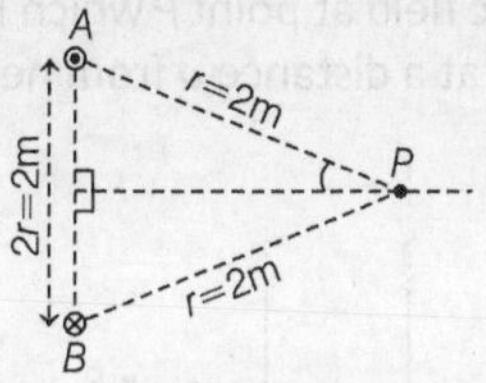

(a) 1.6 (b) 8

(c) 32 (d) 0.4

8 Six parallel infinite wires are placed at the vertices of a regular hexagon. These wires carry current as shown in figure. The resultant magnetic field at the centre O is

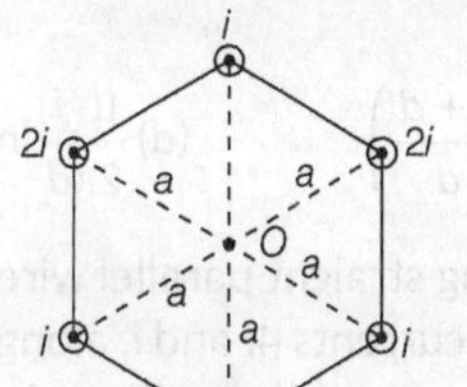

(a) zero (b) $\frac{\mu_0 i_0}{2\pi a}$ (c) $\frac{\mu_0 i_0}{\pi a}$ (d) infinite

9 A current i flows in the network shown in the figure. Resulting magnetic induction at point P is

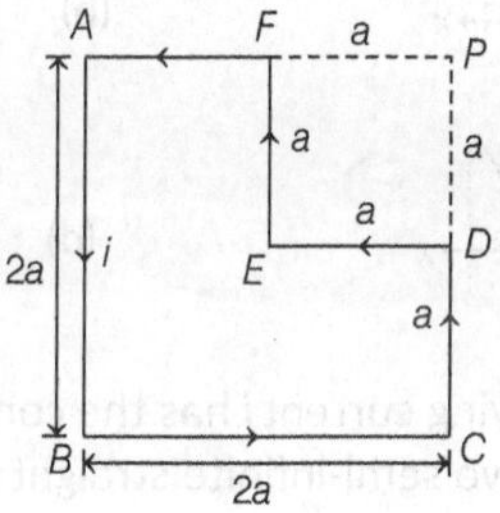

(a) $\frac{\mu_0 i}{4\pi a}$ (b) $\frac{\sqrt{2}\mu_0 i}{8\pi a}$ (c) $\frac{\mu_0 i}{8\sqrt{2}\pi a}$ (d) $\frac{\mu_0 i}{\sqrt{2}\pi a}$

10 Magnetic field at point P is

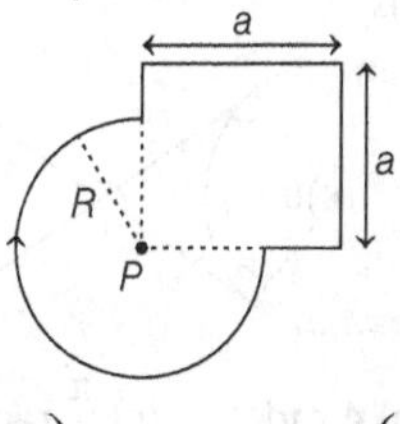

(a) $\mu_0 i\left(\frac{3}{8R}+\frac{1}{\sqrt{2}a}\right)$ (b) $\mu_0 i\left(\frac{3}{8R}+\frac{1}{4\sqrt{2}a}\right)$

(c) $\mu_0 i\left(\frac{3}{8R}+\frac{1}{2\sqrt{2}a}\right)$ (d) $\mu_0 i\left(\frac{3}{4R}+\frac{1}{4\sqrt{2}a}\right)$

11 An infinitely long thin metal sheet of width d carries a current i (uniformly distributed in its width d). Find the magnetic field at point P which lies in the plane of the sheet at a distance a from near end as shown in figure.

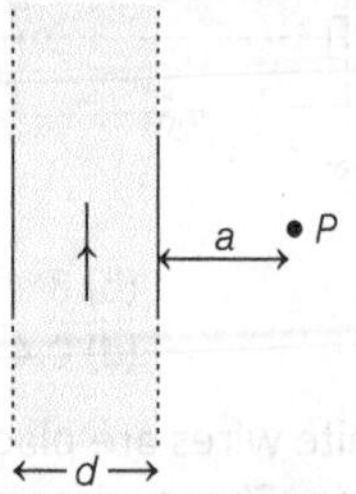

(a) $\frac{\mu_0 i}{2\pi a}\ln\left(\frac{a+d}{a}\right)$ (b) $\frac{\mu_0 i}{2\pi a}\ln\left(\frac{a+d}{d}\right)$

(c) $\frac{\mu_0 i}{2\pi d}\ln\left(\frac{a+d}{a}\right)$ (d) $\frac{\mu_0 i}{2\pi d}\ln\left(\frac{a+d}{d}\right)$

12 Two very long straight parallel wires, parallel to Y-axis, carry currents $4i$ and i, along $+y$-direction and $-y$-direction, respectively. The wires pass through the X-axis at the points $(d, 0, 0)$ and $(-d, 0, 0)$, respectively. The graph of magnetic field z-component as one moves along the X-axis from $x=-d$ to $x=+d$, is best given by

(a) 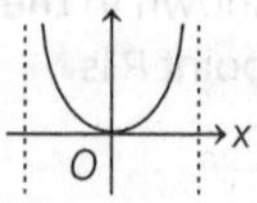

(b) 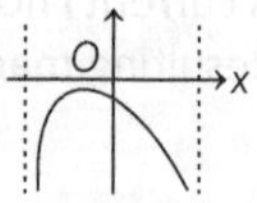

(c) 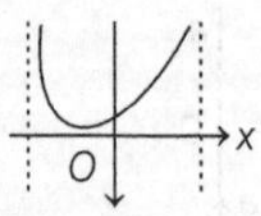

(d) 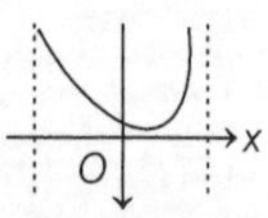

13 A wire carrying current i has the configuration shown in figure. Two semi-infinite straight sections, both tangent to the same circle, are connected by a circular arc, of central angle θ, along the circumference of the circle, with all sections lying in same plane. If magnetic field at centre O of the circle is zero, then θ is

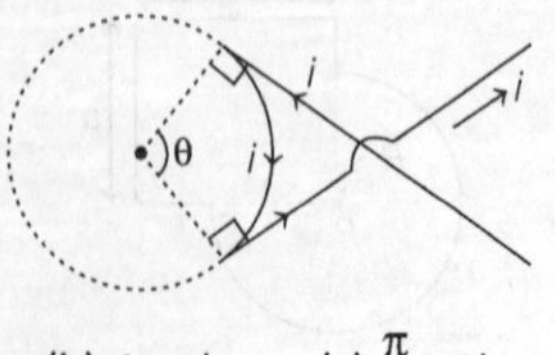

(a) 2 rad (b) 4 rad (c) $\frac{\pi}{2}$ rad (d) $\frac{\pi}{4}$ rad

14 Which of the following field patterns is correct for two long straight equal parallel current carrying wires as shown in figure?

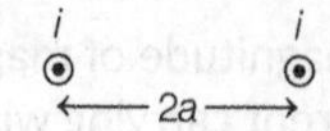

(a) 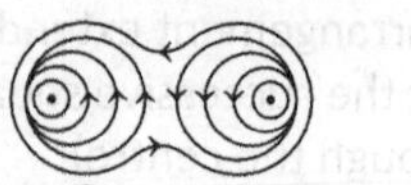
(b) 

(c) 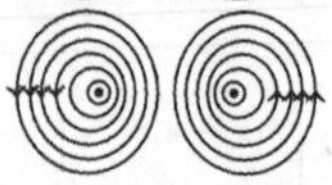
(d) 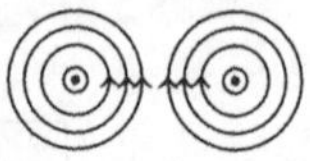

15 Infinite number of straight wires each carrying current i are equally placed as shown in the figure. Adjacent wires have current in opposite direction. Net magnetic field at point P is

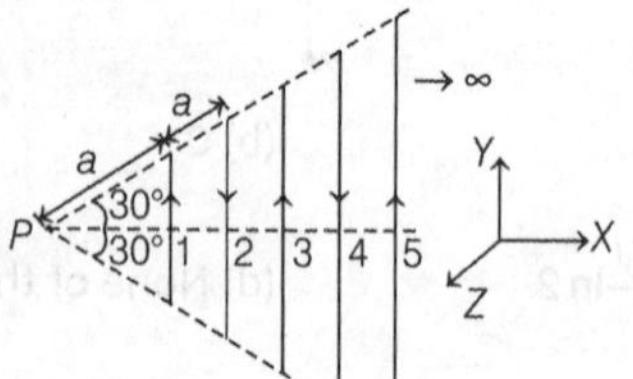

(a) $\frac{\mu_0 i}{4\pi}\frac{\ln 2}{\sqrt{3}a}\hat{\mathbf{k}}$ (b) $\frac{\mu_0 i}{4\pi}\frac{\ln 4}{\sqrt{3}a}\hat{\mathbf{k}}$

(c) $\frac{\mu_0 i}{4\pi}\frac{\ln 4}{\sqrt{3}a}(-\hat{\mathbf{k}})$ (d) zero

16 A current i flows around a closed path in the horizontal plane of the circle as shown in the figure. The path consists of eight arcs with alternating radii r and $2r$. Each segment of arc subtends equal angle at the common centre P. The magnetic field produced by current path at point P is

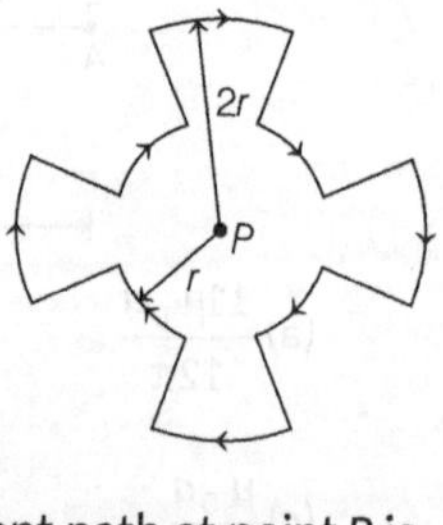

(a) $\frac{3}{8}\frac{\mu_0 i}{r}\otimes$ (b) $\frac{3}{8}\frac{\mu_0 i}{r}\odot$

(c) $\frac{1}{8}\frac{\mu_0 i}{r}\otimes$ (d) $\frac{1}{8}\frac{\mu_0 i}{r}\odot$

17 The current in the wire is i. The current comes from infinite parallel to Z-axis in the ZX-plane and finally goes infinite parallel to Y-axis in the XY-plane as shown in figure. The magnetic field at O is

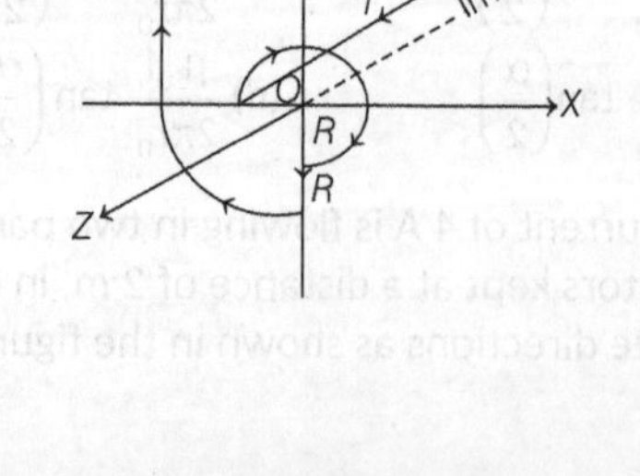

(a) $\frac{\mu_0 i}{2\pi R}\left[\hat{\mathbf{j}} + \frac{(2+7\pi)}{4}(-\hat{\mathbf{k}})\right]$

(b) $\frac{\mu_0 i}{4\pi R}\left[\hat{\mathbf{j}} + \frac{(2+7\pi)}{4}(\hat{\mathbf{k}})\right]$

(c) $\frac{\mu_0 i}{4\pi R}\left[\hat{\mathbf{j}} + \frac{(2+7\pi)}{4}(-\hat{\mathbf{k}})\right]$

(d) None of the above

18 A wire carrying a current i is bent into the shape of an exponential spiral, $r = e^{\theta}$, from $\theta = 0$ to $\theta = 2\pi$ as shown in figure. To complete a loop, the ends of the spiral are connected by a straight wire along the X-axis. Find the magnitude of B at the origin.

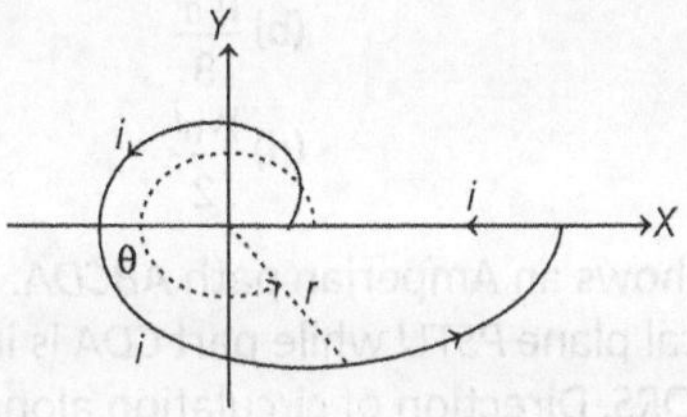

(a) $\frac{\mu_0 i}{2\pi\sqrt{2}}(1 - e^{-2\pi})$ (b) $\frac{\mu_0 i}{4\pi}\sqrt{2}\,(1 - e^{-2\pi})$

(c) $\frac{\mu_0 i}{2\pi}(1 - e^{-2\pi})$ (d) $\frac{\mu_0 i}{4\pi}(1 - e^{-2\pi})$

19 Current i is flowing along the path $ABCD$, along the four edges of the cube as shown in fig. (i), creates a magnetic field at the centre of the cube of B_0. Find the magnetic field B created at the centre of the cube by a current i flowing along the path of the six edges $ABCGHEA$ as shown in fig. (ii)

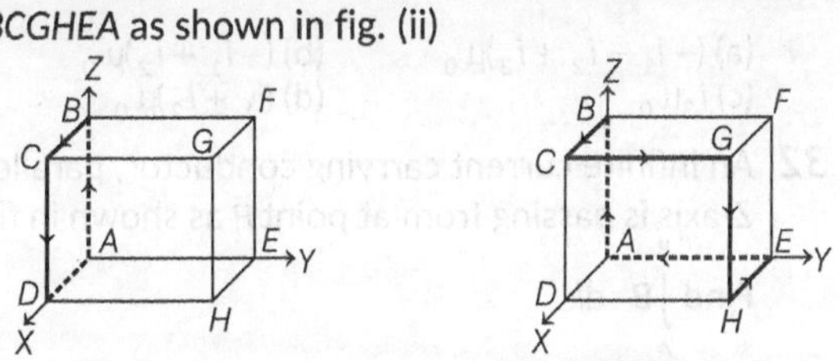

Fig.(i) Fig.(ii)

(a) $\sqrt{3}B_0$ towards corner F (b) $\sqrt{3}B_0$ towards corner E

(c) $\sqrt{\frac{3}{2}}B_0$ towards corner H (d) $\sqrt{\frac{3}{2}}B_0$ towards corner G

20 A non-planar loop of conducting wire carrying a current i is placed as shown in figure. Each of the straight sections of the loop is of length $2a$. The magnetic field due to this loop at the point P $(a, 0, a)$ points in the direction

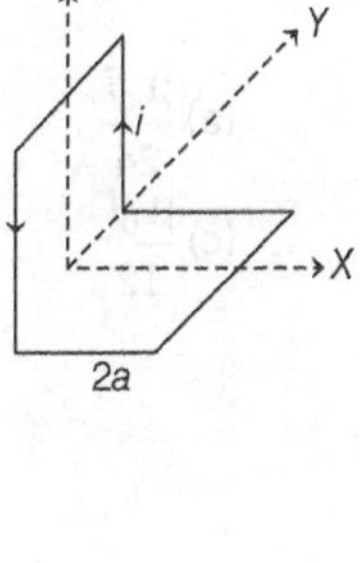

(a) $\frac{1}{\sqrt{2}}(-\hat{\mathbf{j}} + \hat{\mathbf{k}})$ (b) $\frac{1}{\sqrt{3}}(-\hat{\mathbf{j}} + \hat{\mathbf{k}} + \hat{\mathbf{i}})$

(c) $\frac{1}{\sqrt{3}}(\hat{\mathbf{i}} + \hat{\mathbf{j}} + \hat{\mathbf{k}})$ (d) $\frac{1}{\sqrt{2}}(\hat{\mathbf{i}} + \hat{\mathbf{k}})$

21 A square loop $ABCD$ of side a carrying current i is folded about an axis passing through its centre (Y-axis). The two halves are inclined at angle 30° with XY-plane as shown in figure. Find the magnetic field at origin. The origin coincides with the centre of loop.

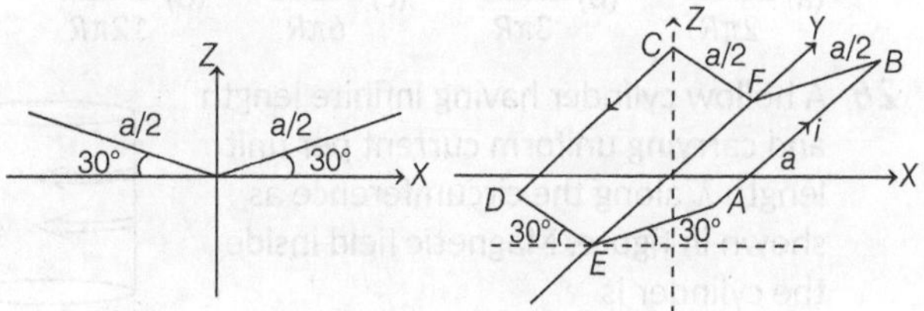

(a) $\frac{\sqrt{3}\mu_0 i}{\sqrt{2}\pi a}$ (b) $\frac{\sqrt{3}\mu_0 i}{2\sqrt{2}\pi a}$ (c) $\frac{3\mu_0 i}{2\sqrt{2}\pi a}$ (d) $\frac{\sqrt{6}\mu_0 i}{\pi a}$

22 A long thin walled pipe of radius R carries a current i along its length. The current density is uniform over the circumference of the pipe. The magnetic field at the centre of pipe due to quarter portion of the pipe as shown in figure, is

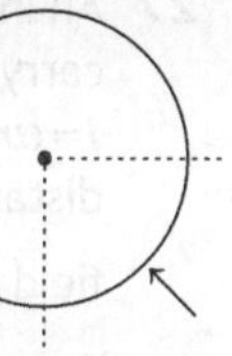

(a) $\frac{\mu_0 i\sqrt{2}}{4\pi^2 R}$ (b) $\frac{\mu_0 i}{\pi^2 R}$

(c) $\frac{2\mu_0 i\sqrt{2}}{\pi^2 R}$ (d) None of these

23 A positively charged disk is rotated clockwise as shown in figure. What is the direction of the magnetic field at point A in the plane of the disk?

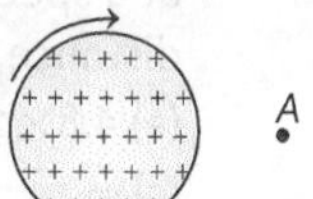

(a) ⊗ (into the plane)

(b) Rightwards

(c) Leftwards

(d) ⊙ (out of the plane)

24 Axis of a solid cylinder of infinite length and radius R lies along Y-axis. It carries a uniformly distributed current i along $+y$-direction. Magnetic field at a point $\left(\frac{R}{2}, y, \frac{R}{2}\right)$ is

(a) $\frac{\mu_0 i}{4\pi R}(\hat{\mathbf{i}} - \hat{\mathbf{k}})$ (b) $\frac{\mu_0 i}{2\pi R}(\hat{\mathbf{j}} - \hat{\mathbf{k}})$

(c) $\frac{\mu_0 i}{4\pi R}(\hat{\mathbf{j}})$ (d) $\frac{\mu_0 i}{4\pi R}(\hat{\mathbf{i}} + \hat{\mathbf{k}})$

25 A hollow non-conducting sphere of radius R has a positive charge q uniformly distributed on its surface. The sphere starts rotating with a constant angular velocity ω about an axis passing through center of sphere, as shown in figure. Then, the net magnetic field at centre of the sphere is

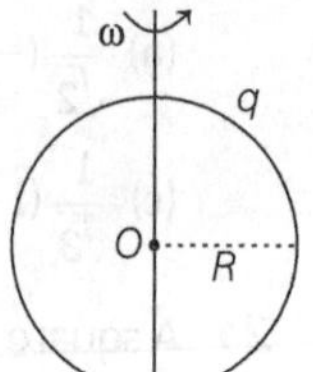

(a) $\frac{\mu_0 q\omega}{2\pi R}$ (b) $\frac{\mu_0 q\omega}{3\pi R}$ (c) $\frac{\mu_0 q\omega}{6\pi R}$ (d) $\frac{\mu_0 q\omega}{12\pi R}$

26 A hollow cylinder having infinite length and carrying uniform current per unit length λ along the circumference as shown in figure. Magnetic field inside the cylinder is

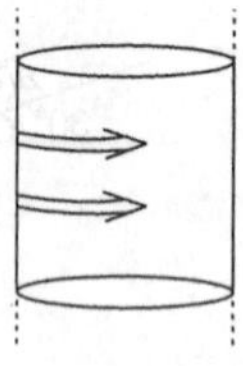

(a) $\frac{\mu_0\lambda}{2}$ (b) $\mu_0\lambda$
(c) $2\mu_0\lambda$ (d) None of these

27 An infinitely long cylindrical wire of radius R is carrying a current with current density $J = \alpha r^3$ (where, α is constant and r is the radial distance from the axis of the wire). If the magnetic field at $r = \frac{R}{2}$ is B_1 and at $r = 2R$ is B_2, then the ratio $\frac{B_2}{B_1}$ is

(a) 2 (b) 4 (c) 6 (d) 8

28 A long, straight, non-conducting string, painted with a charge density of 40 μC/m, is pulled along its length at a speed of 300 m/s. The magnetic field at a normal distance of 5 mm from the moving string is

(a) 4.8×10^{-7} T (b) zero
(c) ∞ (d) Cannot be found

29 A uniformly charged ring of radius R is rotated about its axis with constant linear speed v of each of its particles. The ratio of electric field to magnetic field at a point P on the axis of the ring distant $x = R$ from the centre of the ring is (c is speed of light).

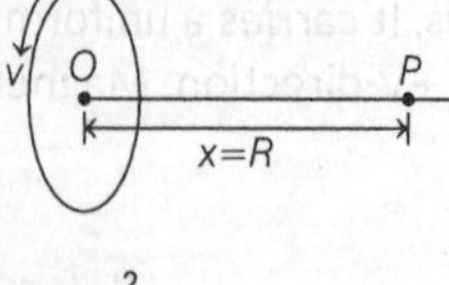

(a) $\frac{c^2}{v}$ (b) $\frac{v^2}{c}$ (c) $\frac{c}{v}$ (d) $\frac{v}{c}$

30 A current carrying wire (current = i) perpendicular to the plane of the paper produces a magnetic field, as shown in the figure. A square of side a is drawn with one of its vertices on the centre of the wire. The integral $\int \mathbf{B}\cdot d\mathbf{r}$ along $OPQRO$ has the value

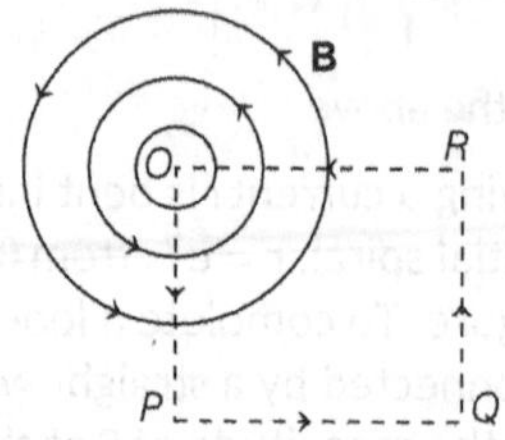

(a) $\mu_0 i$ (b) $\frac{\mu_0 i}{8}$
(c) $\frac{\mu_0 i}{4}$ (d) $\frac{\mu_0 i}{2}$

31 Figure shows an Amperian path $ABCDA$. Part ABC is in vertical plane $PSTU$ while part CDA is in horizontal plane $PQRS$. Direction of circulation along the path is shown by an arrow near point B and D. $\oint \mathbf{B}\cdot d\mathbf{l}$ for this path according to Ampere's law will be

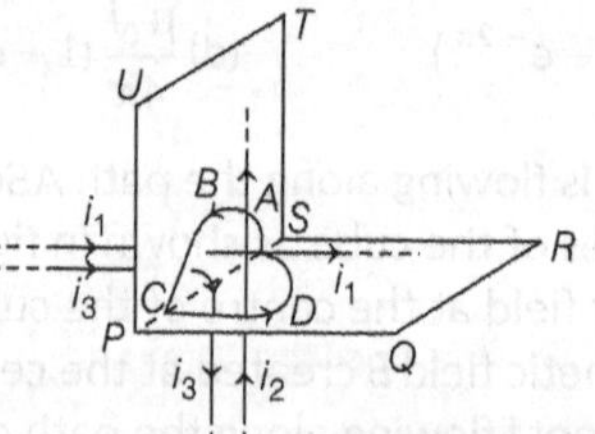

(a) $(-i_1 - i_2 + i_3)\mu_0$ (b) $(-i_1 + i_2)\mu_0$
(c) $i_3\mu_0$ (d) $(i_1 + i_2)\mu_0$

32 An infinite current carrying conductor, parallel to Z-axis is passing from at point P as shown in figure. Find $\int_A^B \mathbf{B}\cdot d\mathbf{l}$

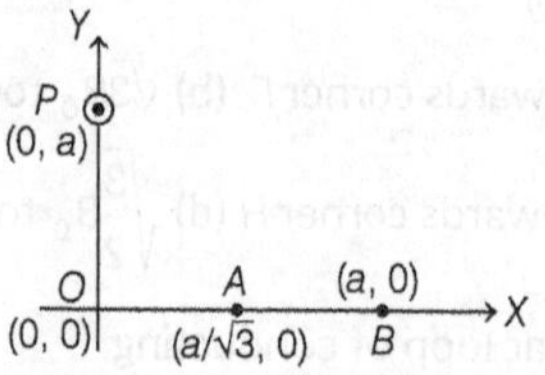

(a) $\frac{\mu_0 i}{24}$ (b) $\frac{\mu_0 i}{16}$
(c) $\frac{\mu_0 i}{12}$ (d) $\frac{\mu_0 i}{8}$

33 Let B_P, B_Q and B_R be the magnetic fields produced by the three infinite long wires P, Q and R, respectively. The three wires are placed symmetrically inside an equilateral triangular loop as shown in figure. The current in three wires are also shown in figure. If $\int_A^B \mathbf{B}_P \cdot d\mathbf{l} = 4\mu_0$ and $\int_C^A \mathbf{B}_Q \cdot d\mathbf{l} = -15\mu_0$, then considering SI units, the value of i is

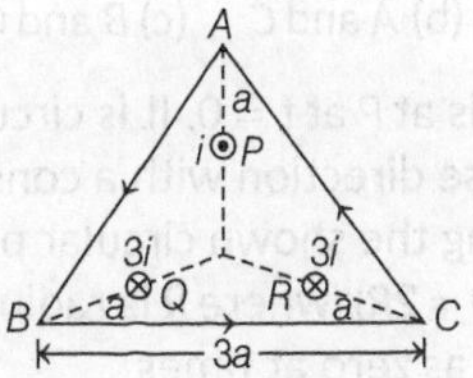

(a) 15 A
(b) 5 A
(c) 13 A
(d) Information insufficient

34 Current i_0 is flowing through a bent wire $a \to b \to c \to d$ in ZX-plane as shown in figure, then $\oint \mathbf{B} \cdot d\mathbf{l}$ over the loop $PQRS$ lying the the XY-plane as shown in figure, due to the bent wire $abcd$ is

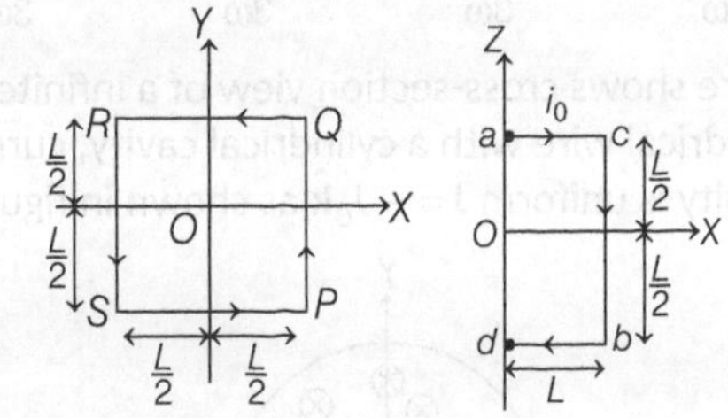

(a) $\frac{\mu_0 i_0}{8}$
(b) $\frac{\mu_0 i_0}{7}$
(c) $\frac{\mu_0 i_0}{5}$
(d) $\frac{\mu_0 i_0}{3}$

35 There is a long cylindrical pipe wire of internal radius r and external radius R carrying current i along its length. The variation of magnetic field with distance from the axis of the wire can be represented by the

(a) 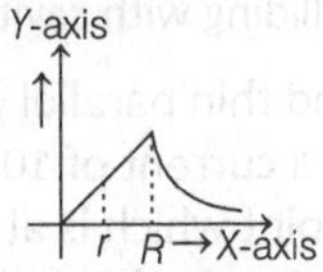

(b) 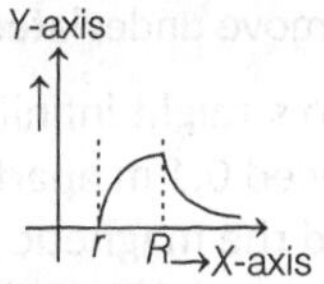

(c) 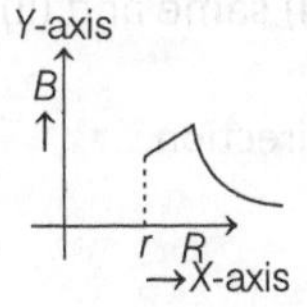

(d) 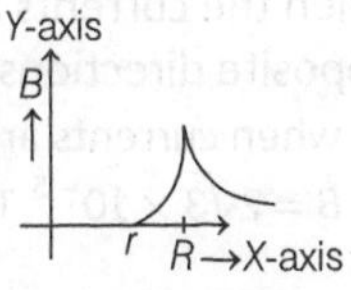

36 A small segment of length a is cut along Z-axis from a infinite sheet having a surface current density J (current per unit width). The magnetic field at P is

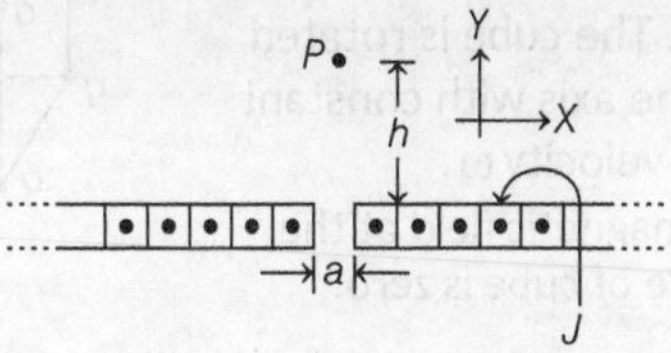

(a) $2\mu_0 J\left(1-\frac{h}{a\pi}\right)\hat{i}$
(b) $\frac{\mu_0 Jh}{2a\pi}\hat{i}$
(c) $\frac{\mu_0 J}{2}\left(\frac{a}{h\pi}-1\right)\hat{i}$
(d) $-\frac{\mu_0 J}{2}\left(\frac{h}{a\pi}-1\right)\hat{i}$

37 Two long conductors are arranged as shown above to form overlapping cylinders, each of radius r, whose centers are separated by a distance d. Current of density J flows into the plane of the page along the shaded part of one conductor and an equal current flows out of the plane of the page along the shaded portion of the other, as shown. What are the magnitude and direction of the magnetic field at point A?

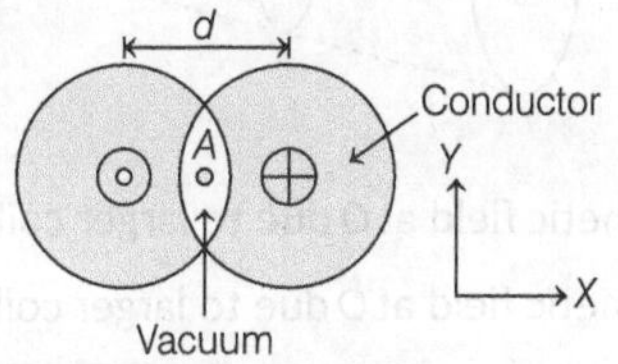

(a) $\left(\frac{\mu_0}{2\pi}\right)\pi dJ$, in the + y-direction
(b) $\left(\frac{\mu_0}{2\pi}\right)\frac{d^2}{r}$, in the + y-direction
(c) $\left(\frac{\mu_0}{2\pi}\right)\frac{4d^2 J}{r}$, in the − y-direction
(d) $\left(\frac{\mu_0}{2\pi}\right)\frac{Jr^2}{d}$, in the − y-direction

Multiple Choice(s) Correct Questions

1 A straight conductor carries a current i. Assume that all the free electrons in the conductor move with the same drift velocity v. A is a stationary observer while B is moving with same uniform velocity.

(a) A and B both observe the same magnetic field.
(b) A and B both observe zero electric field.
(c) A and B both observe the same current i.
(d) A observes zero electric field while the electric field observed by B is non-zero.

2 Consider a cube of side a as shown in figure. Eight point charges are placed at the corners. The cube is rotated about the axis with constant angular velocity ω.

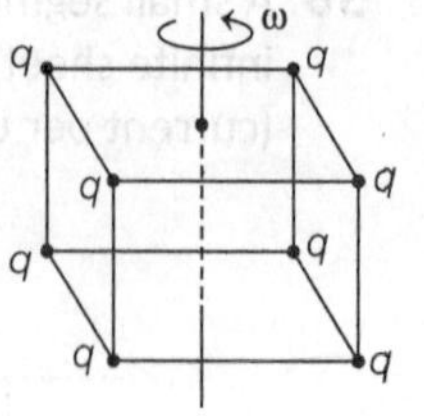

(a) Net magnetic field at the centre of cube is zero.

(b) Net magnetic field at the centre of cube is $\frac{\sqrt{2}\mu_0 q\omega}{\pi a}$.

(c) Net magnetic field at the centre of cube is $\frac{8\mu_0 q\omega}{3\sqrt{3}\pi a}$.

(d) If polarity of any four charges are reversed, then magnetic field at the centre of cube will be zero.

3 Two circular coils X and Y having equal number of turns and carrying equal current in same sense are placed co-axially, such that they subtend the same solid angle at O. Let B be the magnetic field at O due to smaller coil X, then

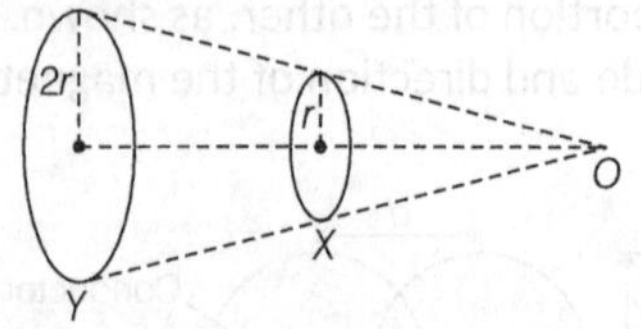

(a) Magnetic field at O due to larger coil $= 2B$

(b) Magnetic field at O due to larger coil $= \frac{B}{2}$

(c) Total magnetic field at O is $\frac{3B}{2}$.

(d) Total magnetic field at O is $\frac{\sqrt{5}B}{2}$.

4 Two identical long conducting wires AOB and COD are placed at right angle to each other, such that O is their common point for the two. The wires carry i_1 and i_2 currents, respectively. Point P is lying at distance d from O along a direction perpendicular to the plane containing the wires. The magnetic field at the point P will be

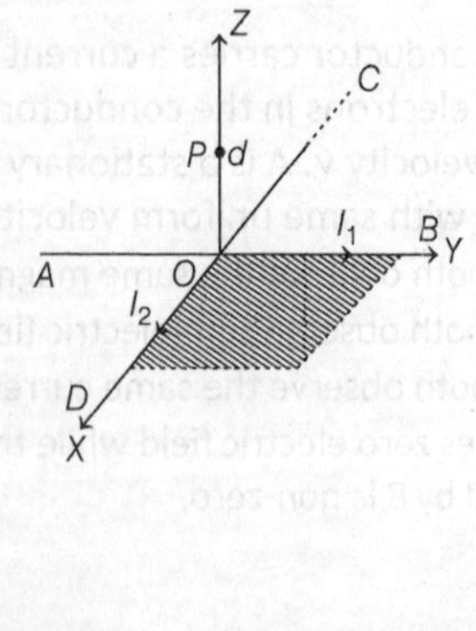

(a) in XY-plane (b) in XZ-plane

(c) $\frac{\mu_0}{2\pi d}(i_1^2 + i_2^2)$ (d) $\frac{\mu_0}{2\pi d}(i_1^2 + i_2^2)^{\frac{1}{2}}$

5 A long straight wire carries a current along the X-axis. Consider the points $A(0, 1, 0)$, $B(0, 1, 1)$, $C(1, 0, 1)$ and $D(1, 1, 1)$. Which of the following pairs of points will have magnetic fields of the same magnitude?

(a) A and B (b) A and C (c) B and C (d) B and D

6 An electron is at P at $t = 0$. It is circulating in anti-clockwise direction with a constant angular speed ω along the shown circular path. Magnetic field at $Q(CQ = 2R)$, where R is radius of the circle will be recorded as zero at times

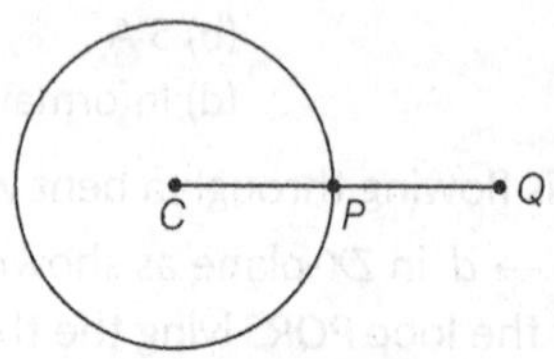

(a) $\frac{\pi}{3\omega}$ (b) $\frac{3\pi}{3\omega}$ (c) $\frac{5\pi}{3\omega}$ (d) $\frac{7\pi}{3\omega}$

7 Figure shows cross-section view of a infinite cylindrical wire with a cylindrical cavity, current density is uniform $\mathbf{J} = -J_0\hat{\mathbf{k}}$ as shown in figure.

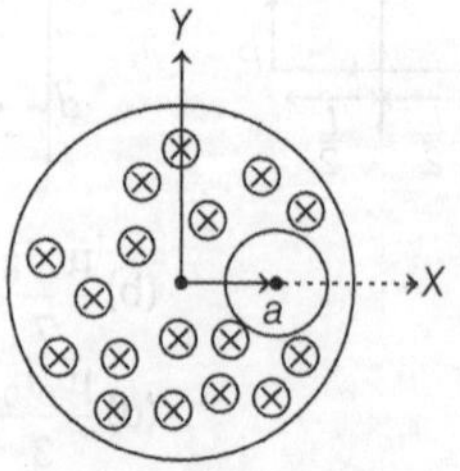

(a) Field inside cavity is uniform.

(b) Field inside cavity is along **a**.

(c) Field inside cavity is perpendicular to **a**.

(d) If an electron is projected with velocity $v_0\hat{\mathbf{j}}$ it will move undeviated before colliding with cavity wall.

8 Two straight infinitely long and thin parallel wires are spaced 0.1 m apart and carry a current of 10 A each. Find the magnetic field at a point which is at a distance of 0.1 m from both wires in the two cases when the currents are in the (i) same and (ii) opposite directions

(a) when currents are in same direction, $B = 2\sqrt{3} \times 10^{-5}$ T

(b) when current are in opposite direction
$B = 2 \times 10^{-5}$ T

(c) when currents are in same direction,
$B = 2 \times 10^{-5}$ T

(d) when currents are in opposite direction
$B = 2\sqrt{3} \times 10^{-5}$T

9 Two long thin, parallel conductors carrying equal current in the same direction are fixed parallel to the X-axis, one passing through $y = a$ and the other through $y = -a$. The resultant magnetic field due to the two conductors at any point is B. Which of the following are correct?

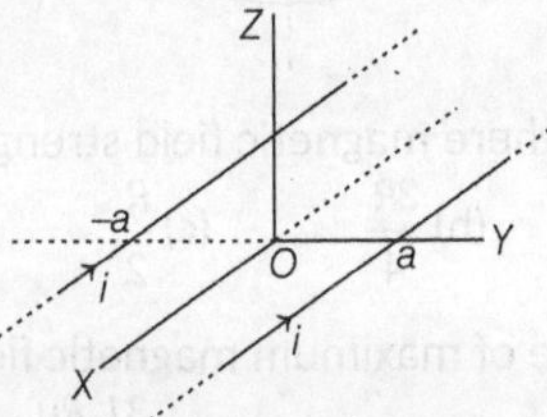

(a) $B = 0$ for all points on the X-axis
(b) At all points on the Y-axis, excluding the origin, B has only a z-component.
(c) At all points on the Z-axis, excluding the origin, B has only a y-component.
(d) B cannot have an x-component.

10 Consider a solid cylinder of radius R and very large length, with volume charge density ρ (charge/volume). Cylinder is rotated with constant angular velocity ω about its axis. Choose correct alternative(s).
(a) Magnetic field at the axis of cylinder is zero
(b) Magnetic field at the axis of cylinder is non zero
(c) Magnetic field at a point outside the cylinder is zero
(d) Magnetic field at a point outside the cylinder is non zero

11 Figure shows two perpendicular wires carrying the same current. In which of the following cases, there will not exist even one point at finite distance where magnetic field is zero.

(a) 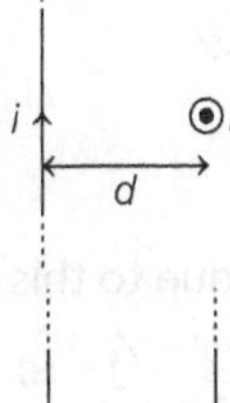

(b) 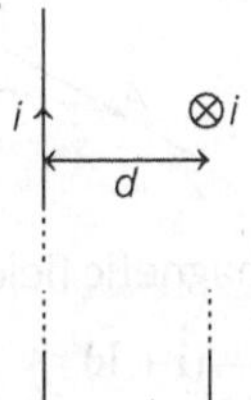

(c) 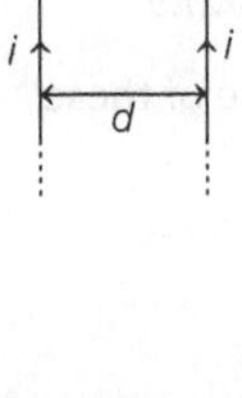

(d) 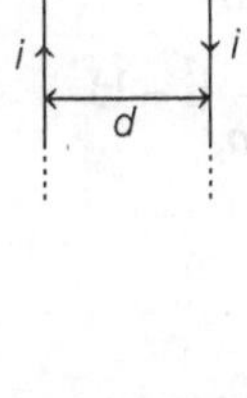

12 A large plate with uniform surface charge density σ is moving with constant speed v as shown in figure. The magnetic field at a small distance from plate is

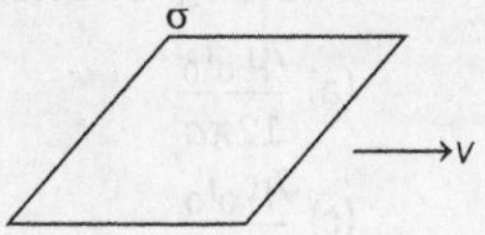

(a) $\mu_0 \sigma v$ in magnitude
(b) $\frac{\mu_0 \sigma v}{2}$ in magnitude
(c) perpendicular to plate
(d) parallel to plate

Comprehension Based Questions

Comprehension-1

Curves in the graph shown, give as function of radial distance r, the magnitude B of the magnetic field inside and outside four long wires a, b, c and d carrying currents that are uniformly distributed across the cross-sections of the wires. Overlapping portions of the plots are indicated by double labels.

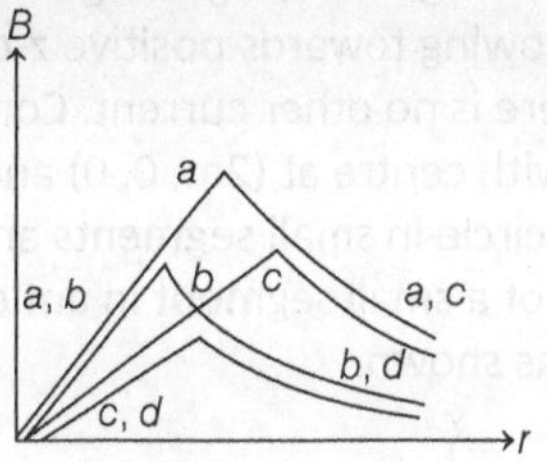

1 Which wire has the greatest radius ?
(a) a (b) b (c) c (d) d

2 Which wire has the greatest magnitude of the magnetic field on the surface ?
(a) a (b) b (c) c (d) d

3 The current density in wire a is
(a) greater than that in wire c
(b) less than that in wire c
(c) equal to that in wire c
(d) not comparable to that of in wire c due to lack of information.

Comprehension-2

In a coaxial cable, the inner conductor carries a current i_0 and the outer conductor provides the return path to the current

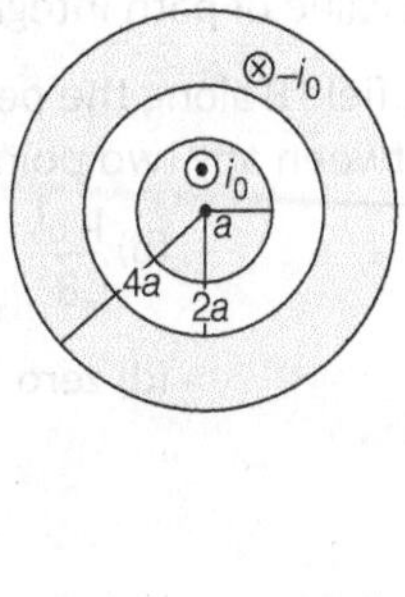

4 The magnetic field at a distance $r = 3a$ is

(a) $\frac{7\mu_0 i_0}{12\pi a}$ (b) $\frac{7\mu_0 i_0}{36\pi a}$

(c) $\frac{7\mu_0 i_0}{72\pi a}$ (d) None of these

5 The correct graph of $B = f(r)$ is

(a)
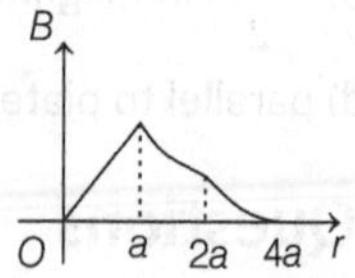

(b)
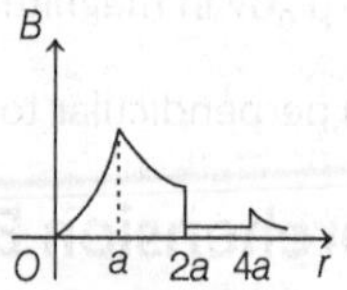

(c)
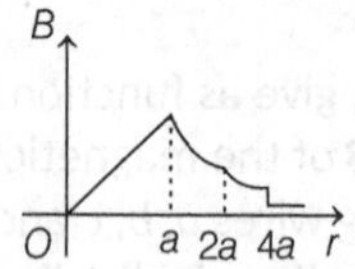

(d)
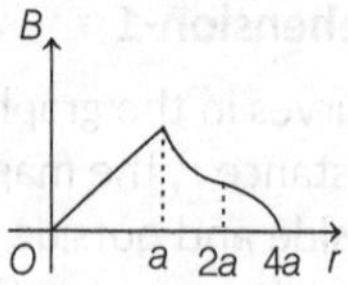

Comprehension-3

An infinitely long wire lying along Z-axis carries a current i, flowing towards positive z-direction (out of plane). There is no other current. Consider a circle in XY-plane with centre at (2m, 0, 0) and radius 1 m. Divide the circle in small segments and let $d\mathbf{l}$ denote the length of a small segment in anticlockwise direction, as shown.

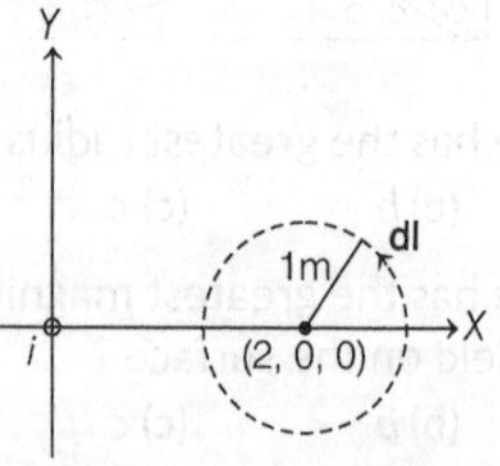

6 Consider two points A(3m, 0, 0) and B(2m, 1m, 0) on the given circle. The path integral $\int_A^B \mathbf{B} \cdot d\mathbf{l}$ of the total magnetic field **B** along the perimeter of the given circle from A to B is

(a) $\frac{\mu_0 i}{\pi} \tan^{-1}\frac{1}{2}$ (b) $\frac{\mu_0 i}{2\pi} \tan^{-1}\frac{1}{2}$

(c) $\frac{\mu_0 i}{2\pi} \sin^{-1}\frac{1}{2}$ (d) zero

7 The maximum value of path integral $\int \mathbf{B} \cdot d\mathbf{l}$ of the total magnetic field **B** along the perimeter of the given circle between any two points on the circle is

(a) $\frac{\mu_0 i}{12}$ (b) $\frac{\mu_0 i}{8}$

(c) $\frac{\mu_0 i}{6}$ (d) zero

Comprehension-4

An infinite cylindrical wire of radius R and having current density varying with its radius r as, $J = J_0\left(1 - \frac{r}{R}\right)$. Then answer the following questions.

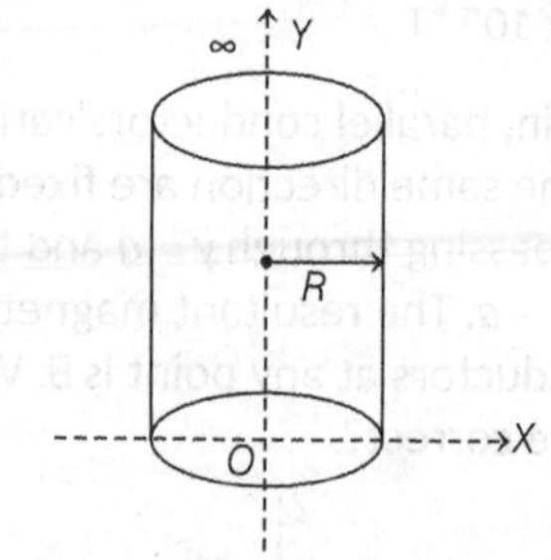

8 Position where magnetic field strength is maximum

(a) R (b) $\frac{3R}{4}$ (c) $\frac{R}{2}$ (d) $\frac{R}{4}$

9 Magnitude of maximum magnetic field is

(a) $\frac{J_0 R\mu_0}{6}$ (b) $\frac{3J_0 R\mu_0}{16}$

(c) $\frac{5J_0 R\mu_0}{16}$ (d) $\frac{5J_0 R\mu_0}{6}$

10 Graph between the magnetic field and radius is

(a)
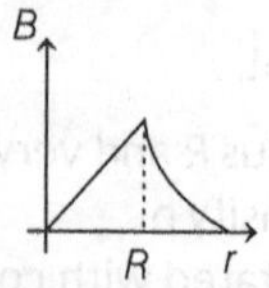

(b)
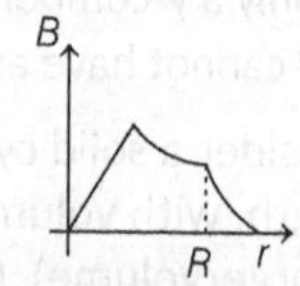

(c)
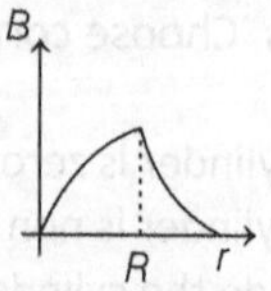

(d)
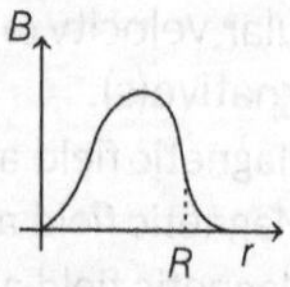

Comprehension-5

Figure shows a closed loop $AOCBA$ in which current i is flowing as shown in figure. Given $OA = OB = OC = a$.

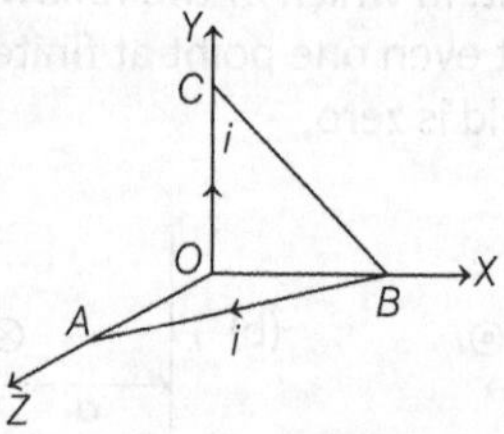

11 Find the magnetic field at point B due to this loop.

(a) $-\frac{\mu_0 i}{4\sqrt{2}\pi a}(\hat{\mathbf{i}} + \hat{\mathbf{k}})$ (b) $-\frac{\mu_0 i}{4\sqrt{2}\pi a}(\hat{\mathbf{j}} + \hat{\mathbf{k}})$

(c) $-\frac{\mu_0 i}{2\sqrt{2}\pi a}(\hat{\mathbf{i}} + \hat{\mathbf{k}})$ (d) None of these

12 Find the magnetic field at point O in figure.

(a) $-\dfrac{\mu_0 i}{4\pi a}(\hat{i}+\hat{k})$ (b) $-\dfrac{\mu_0 i}{4\pi a}(\hat{j}+\hat{k})$

(c) $-\dfrac{\mu_0 i}{2\pi a}(\hat{j}+\hat{k})$ (d) $-\dfrac{\mu_0 i}{2\sqrt{2}\pi a}(\hat{j}+\hat{k})$

Match The Columns Questions

1 Column I gives some current distributions and a point P lies in the space around these current distributions. Column II gives some expressions of magnetic field strength. Match column I to corresponding field strength at point P given in Column II

	Column I		Column II
A.	A conducting loop shaped as regular hexagon of side x, carrying current i. P is the centroid of hexagon	1.	$\dfrac{3\mu_0 i}{32\pi x}$
B.	A cylinder of inner radius x and outer radius $3x$, carrying current i. Point P is at a distance $2x$ from the axis of the cylinder	2.	$\dfrac{\sqrt{3}\mu_0 i}{\pi x}$
C.	Two coaxial hollow cylinders of radii x and $2x$, each carrying current i, but in opposite direction. P is a point at distance $1.5x$ from the axis of the cylinders	3.	$\dfrac{\mu_0 i}{2x}$
D.	Magnetic field at the centre of an n-sided regular polygon, of circum circle of radius x, carrying current i, $n \to \infty$, P is centroid of the polygon.	4.	$\dfrac{\mu_0 i}{3\pi x}$
		5.	Zero

2 Some current carrying wires are given in Column I and graphs of variation of magnetic field *versus* position of point P are given in Column II. Match the graph.

	Column I		Column II
A.	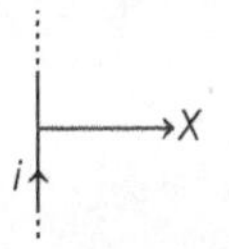 A long straight wire carrying current is placed along Y-axis. Its magnetic field is observed at $P(x, 0, 0)$.	1.	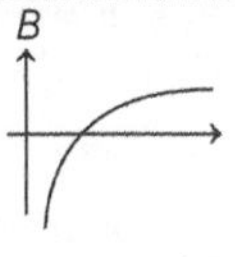
B.	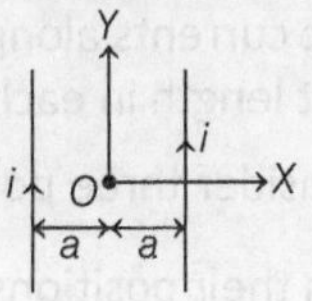 Two long parallel wire placed on XY-plane. O is origin. Its magnetic field is observed at $P(0, 0, z)$	2.	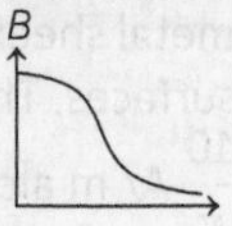
C.	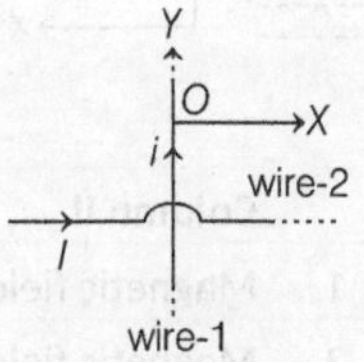 Two long wires placed along Y-axis and parallel to X-axis. Its magnetic field is observed at $P(x, 0, 0)$	3.	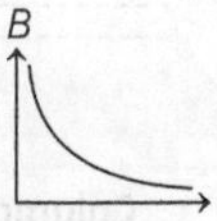
D.	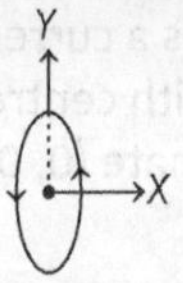 A current carrying ring is placed on YZ-plane. Origin is at the centre of ring. Its magnetic field is observed at point $P(x, 0, 0)$	4.	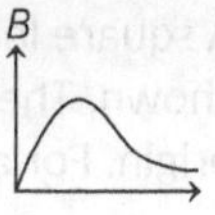

3 Consider a circular loop of radius R in ZX-plane with centre at origin. The magnitude of $\oint \mathbf{B} \cdot d\mathbf{l}$ is to be evalutated along the loop due to a semi-infinite current i carrying straight wire in XY-plane. Column I represents the position of wire and Column II represents the magnitude of $\oint \mathbf{B} \cdot d\mathbf{l}$

	Column I		Column II
A.	Wire extends from $(-R, R)$ to ∞ along the line $y = R$	1.	zero
B.	Wire extends from $(0, R)$ to ∞ along the line $y = R$	2.	equal to $\dfrac{\mu_0 i}{2}$
C.	Wire extends from $(0, R)$ to ∞ along the line $y = x + R$	3.	less than $\dfrac{\mu_0 i}{2}$
D.	Wire extends from $\left(\dfrac{R}{2}, 0\right)$ to ∞ along the line $y = x - \dfrac{R}{2}$	4.	greater than $\dfrac{\mu_0 i}{2}$

4 Figure shows cross-section of two large parallel metal sheets carrying electric currents along their surfaces. The current per unit length in each sheet is $\frac{10}{\pi}$ A/ m along the width. Consider three points *A*, *B* and *C* as shown in figure with their positions.

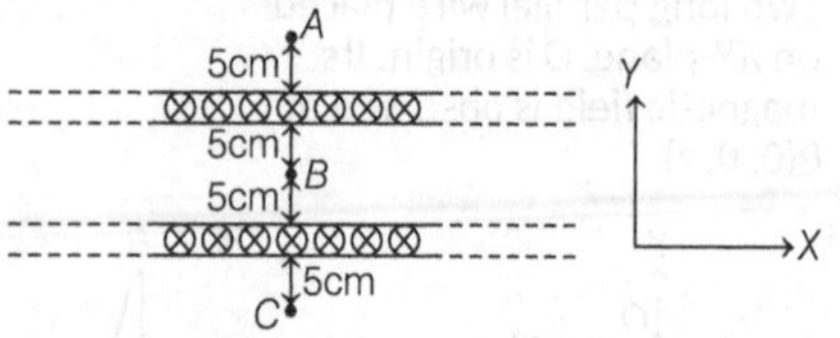

	Column I		Column II
A.	Towards right	1.	Magnetic field at *A*
B.	Towards left	2.	Magnetic field at *B*
C.	Zero	3.	Magnetic field at *C*
D.	Towards perpendicular to plane of paper	4.	Magnetic field at no point

5 A square loop *ABCD* of side *l*, carries a current *i* as shown. The loop lies in *XY*-plane with centre as origin. For a point *P* having co-ordinate (0, 0, *z*),

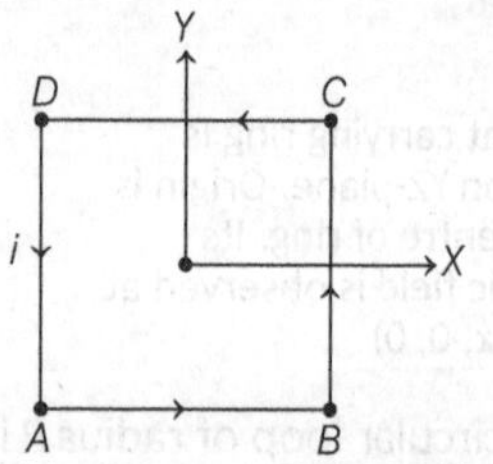

	Column I		Column II
A.	for $z > 0$, unit vector along magnetic field at *P* is	1.	$\dfrac{\mu_0 i l^2}{2\pi\left(z^2+\dfrac{l^2}{4}\right)^{\frac{3}{2}}}$
B.	for $z > 0$, unit vector along magnetic field at *P* only due to wire *AB* is	2.	$\dfrac{\dfrac{l}{2}\hat{\mathbf{k}}-z\hat{\mathbf{j}}}{\sqrt{\dfrac{l^2}{4}+z^2}}$
C.	for $z > 0$, unit vector along magnetic field at *P* only due to wire *BC* is	3.	$\dfrac{\mu_0 i l^2}{2\pi\left(z^2+\dfrac{l^2}{4}\right)\left(\sqrt{z^2+\dfrac{l^2}{2}}\right)}$
D.	for $z > 0$, the magnitude of magnitude field at *P* is	4.	$\dfrac{\dfrac{l}{2}\hat{\mathbf{k}}+z\hat{\mathbf{i}}}{\sqrt{\dfrac{l^2}{4}+z^2}}$
		5.	$\hat{\mathbf{k}}$

Numerical Value Questions

1 *ABCDEF* is a regular hexagon of side *a*. Resistance of *ABCD* is 2 times that of *AFED*. An electric current *i* enters at *A* and leaves at *D*. The magnetic field at the centre of the hexagon is $\left(\dfrac{\mu_0 i}{\sqrt{n}\pi a}\right)$ directed out of paper. Find the value of *n*.

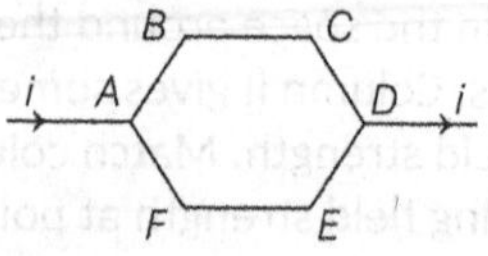

2 A thin conducting wire in the shape of a 'figure of eight' is situated with its circular loops in two planes making an angle of 120° with each other. The current in the loop is *i* and the radius is *a*. If the magnetic induction at a point of intersection of the two axes of the loops is $\dfrac{\sqrt{3}\mu_0 i}{na}$, then find *n*.

3 The circular and the straight parts of the wire are made of same material but have different diameters. If the ratio of their diameters for the magnetic field at the centre O to be zero is $\sqrt{n}:2$, then find *n*.

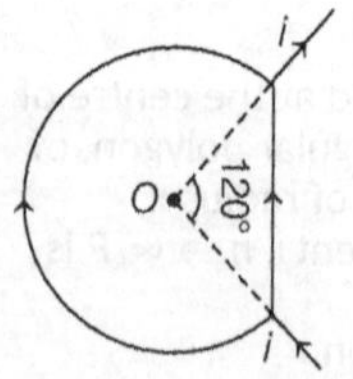

4 A thin wire is bent in the form of a semi circular ring of radius $R = 0.9$ m carries a current $i = 1$ A. The magnetic field at a point *P* as shown in figure is given by $n \times 10^{-7}$ T. Find the value of *n*. [$\ln(\sqrt{2}+1) = 0.9$]

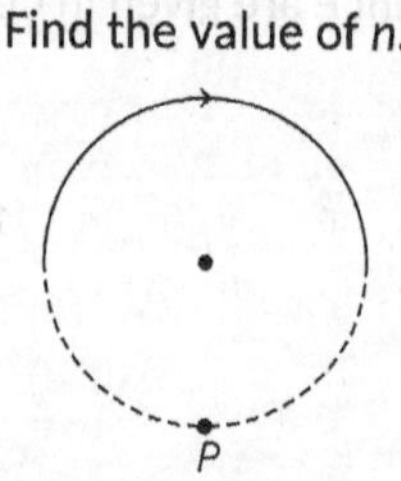

5 Let $\mathbf{B}_P$ and $\mathbf{B}_Q$ be the magnetic field produced by the wire *P* and *Q* which are placed symmetrically in a rectangular loop *ABCD* as shown in figure. Current in wire *P* is *i* directed inward and in *Q* is 2*i* directed

outwards. If $\int_A^B \mathbf{B}_Q \cdot d\mathbf{l} = 2\mu_0$, $\int_D^A \mathbf{B}_P \cdot d\mathbf{l} = -2\mu_0$ and

$\int_A^B \mathbf{B}_P \cdot d\mathbf{l} = -\mu_0$, then find the value of i (in A).

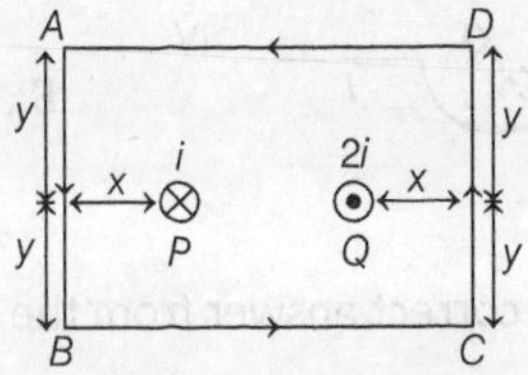

6 A circular disk of radius R with uniform charge density σ rotates with an angular speed ω. If the magnetic field at the center of the disk is $B = R\mu_0\sigma\omega/n$, then find n.

7 Consider a set of six infinite long straight parallel wires arranged perpendicular to the plane of paper in a hexagon as shown in figure. The length of the each side of the hexagon is 3 cm. What is the magnitude and direction of the magnetic field at point P? To express your answer, use the following method. Twelve direction at consecutive equal angles have been shown in figure. If the strength of magnetic field is 70 μT, directed along vector numbered 8, write your answer as 0870. Similarly If the strength of magnetic field is 70 μT, directed along vector numbered 12, write your answer as 1270.

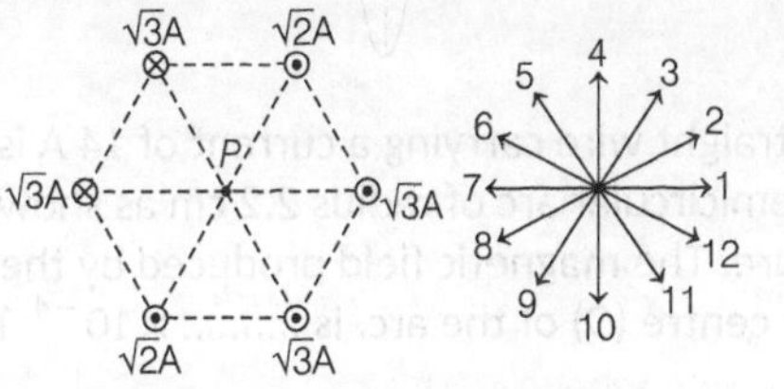

Previous Years Questions

JEE Main

1 Two long, straight wires carry equal currents in opposite directions as shown in figure. The separation between the wires is 5.0 cm. The magnitude of the magnetic field at a point P mid-way between the wires is .... μT.
(Given: $\mu_0 = 4\pi \times 10^{-7}$ TmA^{-1}) **[2024, 27 Jan Shift-I]**

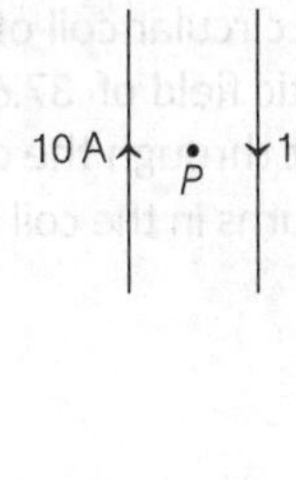

2 The magnetic field at the centre of a wire loop formed by two semicircular wires of radii $R_1 = 2\pi$ m and $R_2 = 4\pi$ m, carrying current $i = 4$A as per figure given below is $\alpha \times 10^{-7}$ T. The value of α is .... (Centre O is common for all segments) **[2024, 27 Jan Shift-II]**

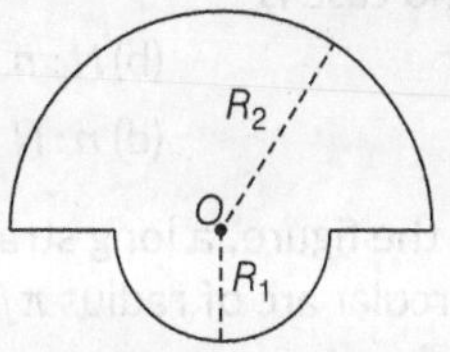

3 Two insulated circular loop A and B of radius a carrying a current of I in the anti-clockwise direction as shown in the figure. The magnitude of the magnetic induction at the centre will be **[2024, 30 Jan Shift-I]**

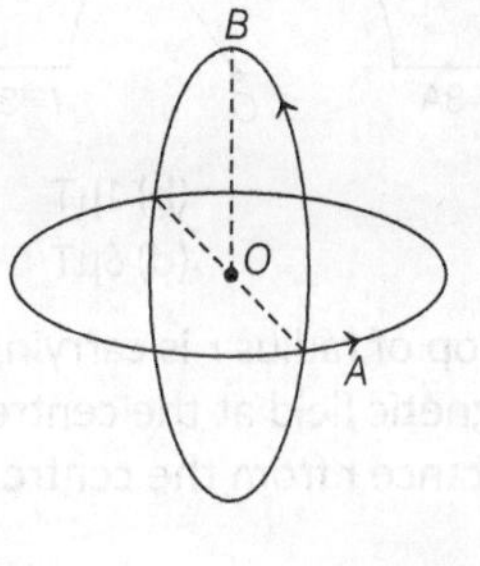

(a) $\dfrac{\sqrt{2}\,\mu_0 I}{a}$ (b) $\dfrac{2\,\mu_0 I}{a}$

(c) $\dfrac{\mu_0 I}{\sqrt{2}\,a}$ (d) $\dfrac{\mu_0 I}{2a}$

4 The current of 5 A flows in a square loop of sides 1 m is placed in air. The magnetic field at the centre of the loop is $x\sqrt{2} \times 10^{-7}$ T. The value of x is .... **[2024, 30 Jan Shift-II]**

5 As shown in the figure, a current of 2 A flowing in an equilateral triangle of side $4\sqrt{3}$ cm. The magnetic field at the centroid O of the triangle is **[2023, 30 Jan Shift-I]**

(Neglect the effect of earth's magnetic field)

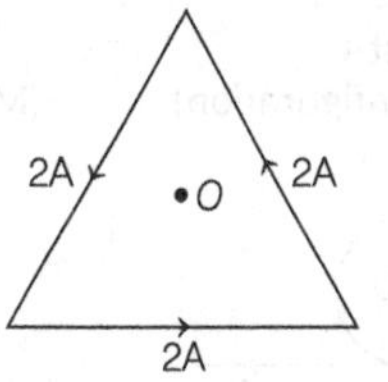

(a) $\sqrt{3} \times 10^{-4}$ T
(b) $4\sqrt{3} \times 10^{-4}$ T
(c) $3\sqrt{3} \times 10^{-5}$ T
(d) $4\sqrt{3} \times 10^{-5}$ T

6 A long conducting wire having a current I flowing through it, is bent into a circular coil of N turns. Then it is bent into a circular coil of n turns. The magnetic field is calculated at the centre of coils in both the cases. The ratio of the magnetic field in first case to that of second case is **[2023, 31 Jan Shift-II]**

(a) $N^2 : n^2$ (b) $N : n$

(c) $n^2 : N^2$ (d) $n : N$

7 As shown in the figure, a long straight conductor with semi-circular arc of radius $\pi/10$ m is carrying current $I = 3$ A.

The magnitude of the magnetic field at the centre O of the arc is (The permeability of the vacuum $= 4\pi \times 10^{-7}\ NA^{-2}$) **[2023, 1 Feb Shift-II]**

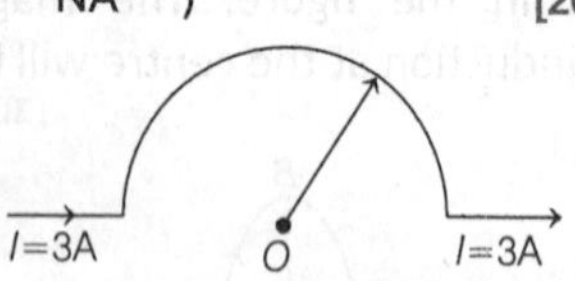

(a) $3\mu T$ (b) $1\mu T$

(c) $4\mu T$ (d) $6\mu T$

8 A circular loop of radius r is carrying current I A. The ratio of magnetic field at the centre of circular loop and at a distance r from the centre of the loop on its axis is **[2023, 24 Jan Shift-I]**

(a) $1 : \sqrt{2}$ (b) $1 : 3\sqrt{2}$

(c) $3\sqrt{2} : 2$ (d) $2\sqrt{2} : 1$

9 A solenoid of 1200 turns is wound uniformly in a single layer on a glass tube 2m long and 0.2m in diameter. The magnetic intensity at the centre of the solenoid when a current of 2A flows through it is **[2023, 25 Jan Shift-I]**

(a) $1 Am^{-1}$

(b) $1.2 \times 10^3\ A m^{-1}$

(c) $2.4 \times 10^3\ A m^{-1}$

(d) $2.4 \times 10^{-3}\ A m^{-1}$

10 Match List I with List II.

List-I (Current configuration)		List-II (Magnitude of Magnetic Field at point O)	
A.	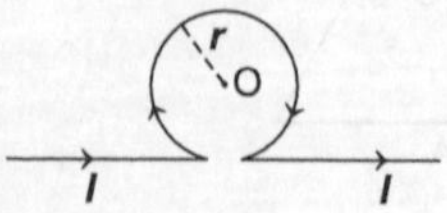	I.	$B_0 = \frac{\mu_0 I}{4\pi r}(\pi + 2)$
B.	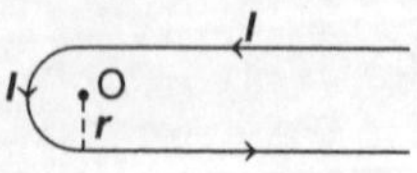	II.	$B_0 = \frac{\mu_0}{4}\frac{I}{r}$
C.	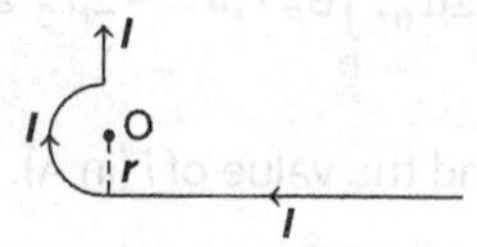	III.	$B_0 = \frac{\mu_0 I}{2\pi r}(\pi - 1)$
D.		IV.	$B_0 = \frac{\mu_0 I}{4\pi r}(\pi + 1)$

[2023, 25 Jan Shift-I]

Choose the correct answer from the options given below

(a) A-III, B-I, C-IV, D-II (b) A-III, B-IV, C-I, D-II

(c) A-I, B-III, C-IV, D-II (d) A-II, B-I, C-IV, D-III

11 The ratio of magnetic field at the centre of a current carrying coil of radius r from the magnetic field at distance r from the centre of coil on its axis is $\sqrt{x} : 1$. The value of x is .... **[2023, 8 April Shift-I]**

12 Two identical circular wires of radius 20 cm and carrying current $\sqrt{2}$ A are placed in perpendicular planes as shown in figure. The net magnetic field at the centre of the circular wires is ..... $\times 10^{-8}$ T. (Take, $\pi = 3.14$) **[2023, 6 April Shift-I]**

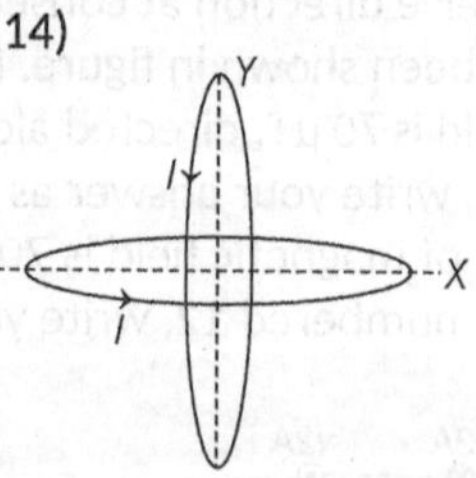

13 A straight wire carrying a current of 14 A is bent into a semicircular arc of radius 2.2 cm as shown in the figure. The magnetic field produced by the current at the centre (O) of the arc. is .... $\times 10^{-4}$ T **[2023, 10 April Shift-II]**

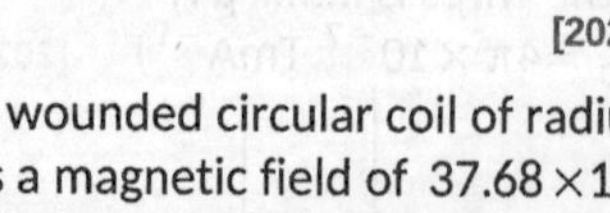

14 An electron in a hydrogen atom revolves around its nucleus with a speed of $6.76 \times 10^6\ ms^{-1}$ in an orbit of radius 0.52 Å. The magnetic field produced at the nucleus of the hydrogen atom is .... T. **[2023, 15 April Shift-I]**

15 A closely wounded circular coil of radius 5 cm produces a magnetic field of 37.68×10^{-4} T at its centre. The current through the coil is _______ A. (Given, number of turns in the coil is 100 and $\pi = 3.14$) **[2022, 29 July Shift-I]**

16 A triangular shaped wire carrying 10 A current is placed in a uniform magnetic field of 0.5 T, as shown in figure. The magnetic force on segment CD is (Given, $BC = CD = BD = 5$ cm). **[2022, 28 July Shift-II]**

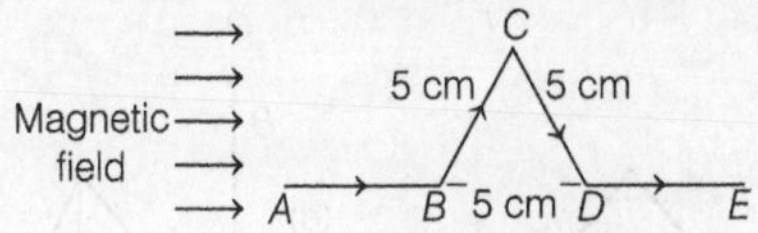

(a) 0.126 N (b) 0.312 N
(c) 0.216 N (d) 0.245 N

17 B_X and B_Y are the magnetic field at the centre of two coils X and Y, respectively each carrying equal current. If coil X has 200 turns and 20 cm radius and coil Y has 400 turns and 20 cm radius, the ratio of B_X and B_Y is **[2022, 26 July Shift-II]**

(a) 1 : 1 (b) 1 : 2
(c) 2 : 1 (d) 4 : 1

18 The electric current in a circular coil of 2 turns produces a magnetic induction B_1 at its centre. The coil is unwound and is rewound into a circular coil of 5 turns and the same current produces a magnetic induction B_2 at its centre. The ratio of B_2 / B_1 is **[2022, 25 July Shift-II]**

(a) $\frac{5}{2}$ (b) $\frac{25}{4}$
(c) $\frac{5}{4}$ (d) $\frac{25}{2}$

19 An infinitely long hollow conducting cylinder with radius R carries a uniform current along its surface. Choose the correct representation of magnetic field B as a function of radial distance (r) from the axis of cylinder. **[2022, 28 June Shift-I]**

(a)
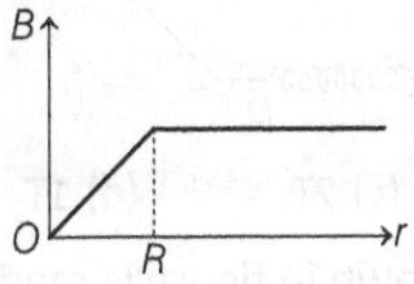

(b)
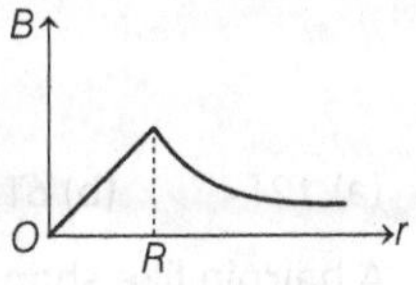

(c)
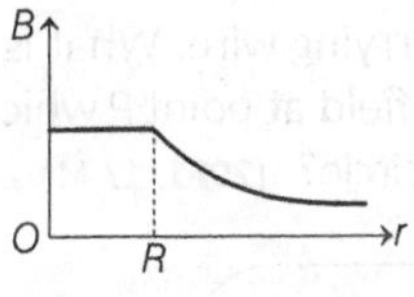

(d)
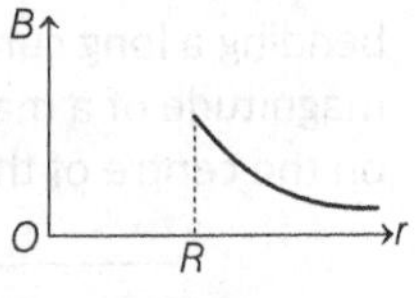

20 A long solenoid carrying a current produces a magnetic field B along its axis. If the current is doubled and the number of turns per cm is halved, the new value of magnetic field will be equal to **[2022, 25 June Shift-II]**

(a) B (b) $2B$
(c) $4B$ (d) $\frac{B}{2}$

21 A long straight wire with a circular cross-section having radius R, is carrying a steady current I. The current I is uniformly distributed across this cross-section. Then, the variation of magnetic field due to current I with distance r ($r < R$) from its centre will be **[2022, 25 June Shift-I]**

(a) $B \propto r^2$ (b) $B \propto r$
(c) $B \propto \frac{1}{r^2}$ (d) $B \propto \frac{1}{r}$

22 The magnetic field at the centre of a circular coil of radius r, due to current I flowing through it, is B. The magnetic field at a point along the axis at a distance $r/2$ from the centre is **[2022, 24 June Shift-I]**

(a) $B/2$ (b) $2B$
(c) $\left(\frac{2}{\sqrt{5}}\right)^3 B$ (d) $\left(\frac{2}{\sqrt{3}}\right)^3 B$

23 There are two infinitely long straight current carrying conductors and they are held at right angles to each other so that their common ends meet at the origin as shown in the figure given below. The ratio of current in both conductors is 1 : 1. The magnetic field at point P is **[2021, 1 Sep Shift-II]**

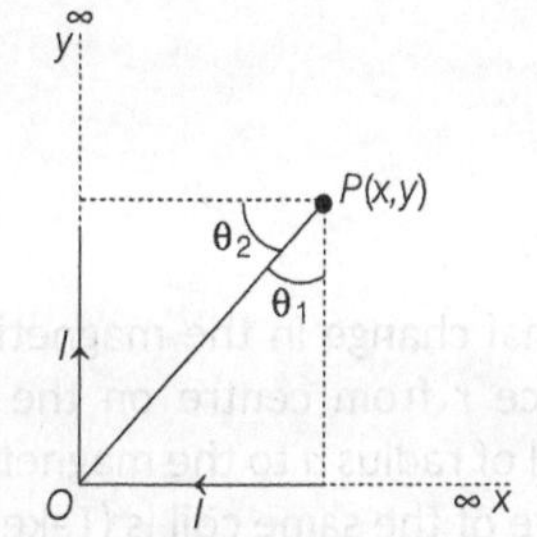

(a) $\frac{\mu_0 I}{4\pi xy}\left[\sqrt{x^2 + y^2} + (x + y)\right]$

(b) $\frac{\mu_0 I}{4\pi xy}\left[\sqrt{x^2 + y^2} - (x + y)\right]$

(c) $\frac{\mu_0 Ixy}{4\pi}\left[\sqrt{x^2 + y^2} - (x + y)\right]$

(d) $\frac{\mu_0 Ixy}{4\pi}\left[\sqrt{x^2 + y^2} + (x + y)\right]$

24 A coil having N turns is wound tightly in the form of a spiral with inner and outer radii a and b, respectively. Find the magnetic field at centre, when a current I passes through coil **[2021, 31 Aug Shift-I]**

(a) $\frac{\mu_0 IN}{2(b-a)} \ln\left(\frac{b}{a}\right)$ (b) $\frac{\mu_0 I}{8} \ln\left[\frac{a+b}{a-b}\right]$

(c) $\frac{\mu_0 I}{4(a-b)} \ln\left[\frac{1}{a} - \frac{1}{b}\right]$ (d) $\frac{\mu_0 I}{8} \ln\left(\frac{a-b}{a+b}\right)$

25 A current of 1.5 A is flowing through a triangle, of side 9 cm each. The magnetic field at the centroid of the triangle is
(Assume that, the current is flowing in the clockwise direction.) **[2021, 31 Aug Shift-II]**

(a) 3×10^{-7} T, outside the plane of triangle
(b) $2\sqrt{3} \times 10^{-7}$ T, outside the plane of triangle
(c) $2\sqrt{3} \times 10^{-5}$ T, inside the plane of triangle
(d) 3×10^{-5} T, inside the plane of triangle

26 A co-axial cable consists of an inner wire of radius a surrounded by an outer shell of inner and outer radii b and c, respectively. The inner wire carries an electric current i_0, which is distributed uniformly across cross-sectional area. The outer shell carries an equal current in opposite direction and distributed uniformly. What will be the ratio of the magnetic field at a distance x from the axis when (i) $x < a$ and (ii) $a < x < b$? **[2021, 27 Aug Shift-II]**

(a) $\frac{x^2}{a^2}$
(b) $\frac{a^2}{x^2}$
(c) $\frac{x^2}{b^2 - a^2}$
(d) $\frac{b^2 - a^2}{x^2}$

27 The fractional change in the magnetic field intensity at a distance r from centre on the axis of current carrying coil of radius a to the magnetic field intensity at the centre of the same coil is (Take, $r < a$) **[2021, 26 Aug Shift-II]**

(a) $\frac{3}{2}\frac{a^2}{r^2}$ (b) $\frac{2}{3}\frac{a^2}{r^2}$
(c) $\frac{2}{3}\frac{r^2}{a^2}$ (d) $\frac{3}{2}\frac{r^2}{a^2}$

28 Figures A and B shown two long straight wires of circular cross-section (a and b with $a < b$), carrying current I which is uniformly distributed across the cross-section. The magnitude of magnetic field B varies with radius r and can be represented as **[2021, 27 July Shift-II]**

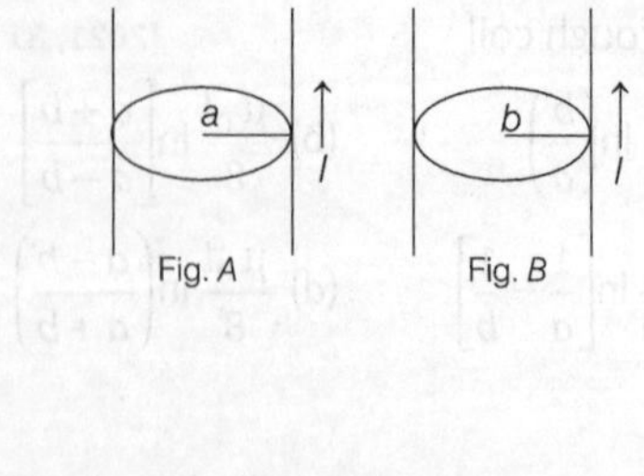

Fig. A Fig. B

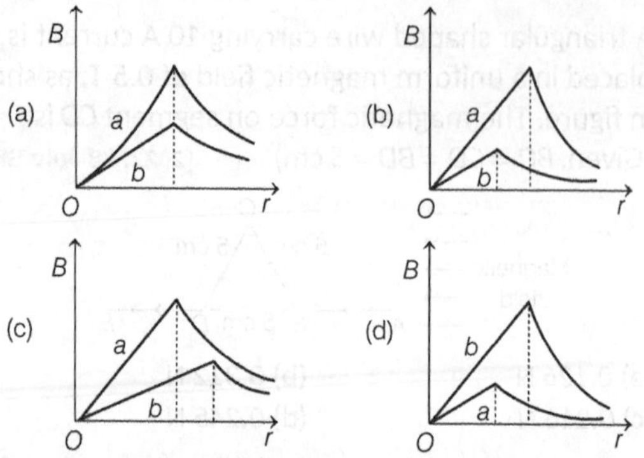

29 Match List I with List II.

List I	List II
A. Capacitance, C	I. $M^1 L^1 T^{-3} A^{-1}$
B. Permittivity of free space, ε_0	II. $M^{-1} L^{-3} T^4 A^2$
C. Permeability of free space, μ_0	III. $M^{-1} L^{-2} T^4 A^2$
D. Electric field, E	IV. $M^1 L^1 T^{-2} A^{-2}$

Choose the correct answer from the options given below. **[2021, 27 July Shift-II]**

	A	B	C	D		A	B	C	D
(a)	III	II	IV	I	(b)	III	IV	II	I
(c)	IV	II	III	I	(d)	IV	III	II	I

30 Four identical long solenoids A, B, C and D are connected to each other as shown in the figure. If the magnetic field at the centre of A is $3T$, the field at the centre of C would be (Assume that, the magnetic field is confined with in the volume of respective solenoid) **[2021, 18 March Shift-I]**

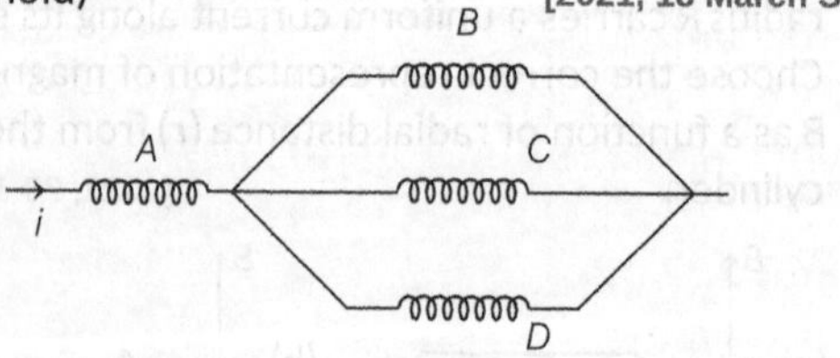

(a) 12T (b) 6T (c) 9T (d) 1T

31 A hairpin like shape as shown in figure is made by bending a long current carrying wire. What is the magnitude of a magnetic field at point P which lies on the centre of the semicircle? **[2021, 17 March Shift-II]**

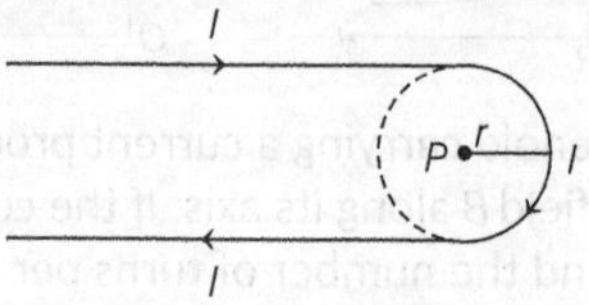

(a) $\frac{\mu_0 I}{4\pi r}(2 - \pi)$ (b) $\frac{\mu_0 I}{4\pi r}(2 + \pi)$
(c) $\frac{\mu_0 I}{2\pi r}(2 + \pi)$ (d) $\frac{\mu_0 I}{2\pi r}(2 - \pi)$

32 Magnetic fields at two points on the axis of a circular coil at a distance of 0.05 m and 0.2 m from the centre are in the ratio 8 : 1. The radius of coil is **[2021, 25 Feb Shift-I]**

(a) 0.2 m (b) 0.1 m (c) 0.15 m (d) 1.0 m

33 Magnitude of magnetic field (in SI unit) at the centre of a hexagonal shaped coil of side 10 cm, 50 turns and carrying current *I* ampere in units of $\frac{\mu_0 I}{\pi}$ is **[2020, 3 Sep Shift-I]**

(a) $250\sqrt{3}$ (b) $50\sqrt{3}$ (c) $500\sqrt{3}$ (d) $5\sqrt{3}$

34 A wire *A*, bent in the shape of an arc of a circle, carrying a current of 2 A and having radius 2 cm and another wire *B*, also bent in the shape of arc of a circle, carrying a current of 3 A and having radius of 4 cm, are placed as shown in the figure. The ratio of the magnetic fields due to the wires *A* and *B* at the common centre *O* is **[2020, 4 Sep Shift-I]**

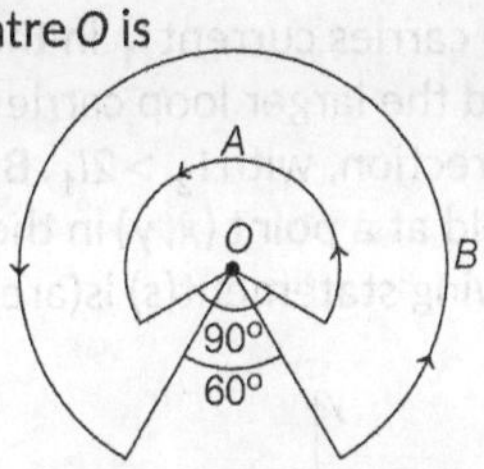

(a) 4 : 6 (b) 6 : 4 (c) 6 : 5 (d) 2 : 5

35 A very long wire *ABDMNDC* is shown in figure carrying current *I*. *AB* and *BC* parts are straight, long and at right angle. At *D* wire forms a circular turn *DMND* of radius *R*. *AB*, *BC* parts are tangential to circular turn at *N* and *D*. Magnetic field at the centre of circle is **[2020, 8 Jan Shift-II]**

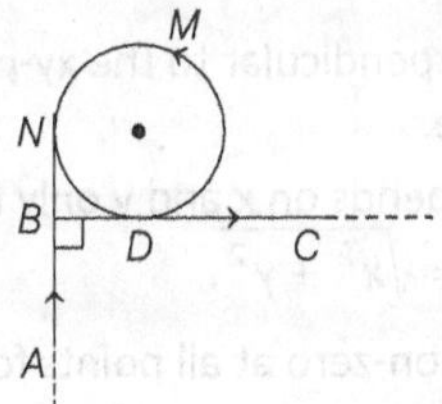

(a) $-\frac{\mu_0 I}{2\pi R}\left(\pi + \frac{1}{\sqrt{2}}\right)$ (b) $\frac{\mu_0 I}{2R}$

(c) $\frac{\mu_0 I}{2\pi R}(\pi + 1)$ (d) $\frac{\mu_0 I}{2\pi R}\left(\pi - \frac{1}{\sqrt{2}}\right)$

36 A long, straight wire of radius *a* carries a current distributed uniformly over its cross-section. The ratio of the magnetic fields due to the wire at distance $\frac{a}{3}$ and $2a$ respectively, from the axis of the wire is **[2020, 9 Jan Shift-I]**

(a) 3/2 (b) 2 (c) 2/3 (d) 1/2

37 The magnitude of the magnetic field at the centre of an equilateral triangular loop of side 1 m which is carrying a current of 10 A is [Take, $\mu_0 = 4\pi \times 10^{-7}\ \text{NA}^{-2}$] **[2019, 10 April Shift-II]**

(a) 9 μT (b) 1 μT
(c) 3 μT (d) 18 μT

38 A thin ring of 10 cm radius carries a uniformly distributed charge. The ring rotates at a constant angular speed of 40π rad s^{-1} about its axis, perpendicular to its plane. If the magnetic field at its centre is 3.8×10^{-9} T, then the charge carried by the ring is close to ($\mu_0 = 4\pi \times 10^{-7}$ N/A^2). **[2019, 12 April Shift-I]**

(a) 2×10^{-6} C
(b) 3×10^{-5} C
(c) 4×10^{-5} C
(d) 7×10^{-6} C

39 Find the magnetic field at point *P* due to a straight line segment *AB* of length 6 cm carrying a current of 5 A (See figure). (Take, $\mu_0 = 4\pi \times 10^{-7}$ N- A^{-2}) **[2019, 12 April Shift-II]**

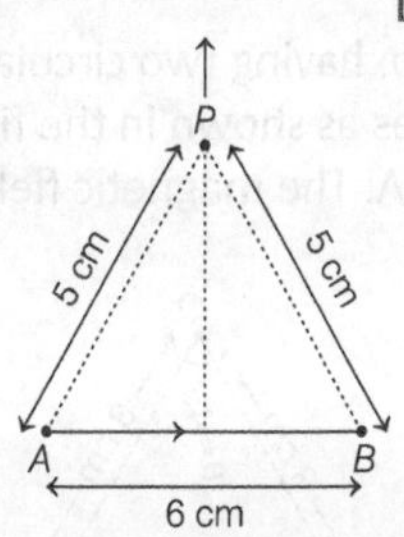

(a) 2.0×10^{-5} T (b) 1.5×10^{-5} T
(c) 3.0×10^{-5} T (d) 2.5×10^{-5} T

40 Two very long, straight and insulated wires are kept at 90° angle from each other in *xy*-plane as shown in the figure.

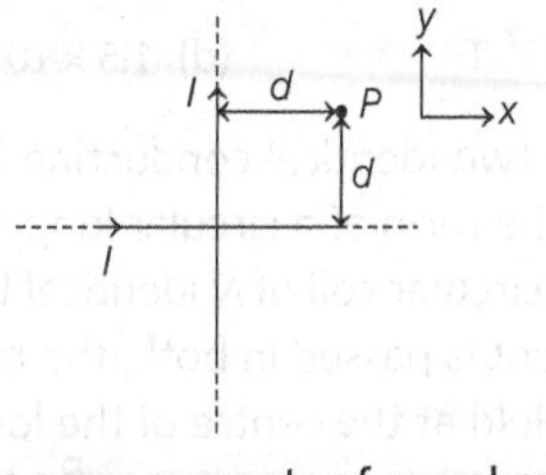

These wires carry currents of equal magnitude *I*, whose directions are shown in the figure. The net magnetic field at point *P* will be **[2019, 8 April Shift-II]**

(a) zero (b) $\frac{+\mu_0 I}{\pi d}(\hat{\mathbf{z}})$

(c) $-\frac{\mu_0 I}{2\pi d}(\hat{\mathbf{x}} + \hat{\mathbf{y}})$ (d) $\frac{\mu_0 I}{2\pi d}(\hat{\mathbf{x}} + \hat{\mathbf{y}})$

41 As shown in the figure, two infinitely long, identical wires are bent by 90° and placed in such a way that the segments LP and QM are along the X-axis, while segments PS and QN are parallel to the Y-axis. If $OP = OQ = 4$ cm and the magnitude of the magnetic field at O is 10^{-4} T and the two wires carry equal currents (see figure), the magnitude of the current in each wire and the direction of the magnetic field at O will be (Take, $\mu_0 = 4\pi \times 10^{-7}\ NA^{-2}$) **[2019, 12 Jan Shift-I]**

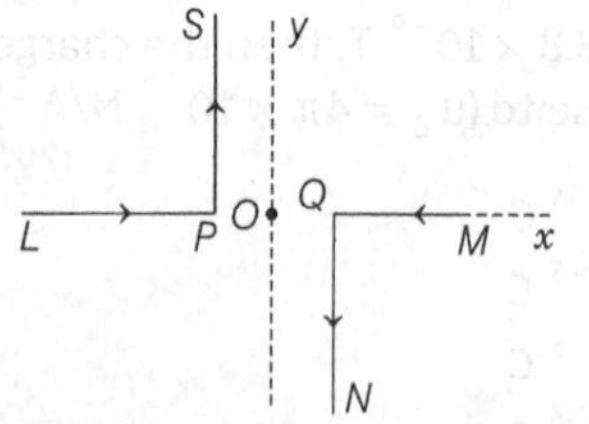

(a) 40 A, perpendicular out of the page
(b) 20 A, perpendicular into the page
(c) 20 A, perpendicular out of the page
(d) 40 A, perpendicular into the page

42 A current loop, having two circular arcs joined by two radial lines as shown in the figure. It carries a current of 10 A. The magnetic field at point O will be close to **[2019, 9 Jan Shift-I]**

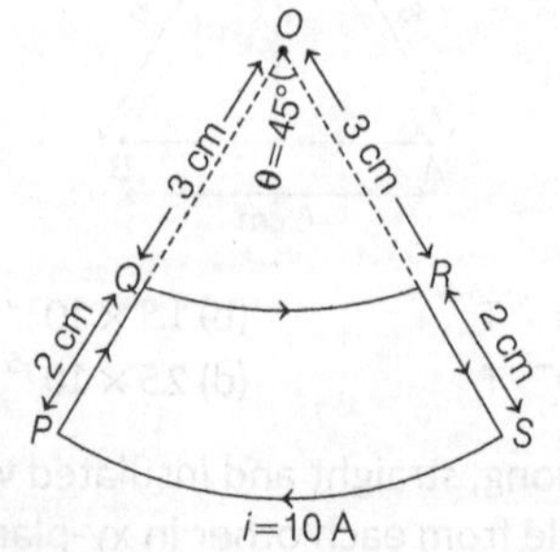

(a) 1.0×10^{-5} T
(b) 1.0×10^{-7} T
(c) 1.5×10^{-7} T
(d) 1.5×10^{-5} T

43 One of the two identical conducting wires of length L is bent in the form of a circular loop and the other one into a circular coil of N identical turns. If the same current is passed in both, the ratio of the magnetic field at the centre of the loop (B_L) to that at the centre of the coil (B_C), i.e. $\frac{B_L}{B_C}$ will be **[2019, 9 Jan Shift-I]**

(a) $\frac{1}{N}$
(b) N
(c) $\frac{1}{N^2}$
(d) N^2

44 Two identical wires A and B, each of length l, carry the same current I. Wire A is bent into a circle of radius R and wire B is bent to form a square of side a. If B_A and B_B are the values of magnetic field at the centres of the circle and square respectively, then the ratio $\frac{B_A}{B_B}$ is **[2016]**

(a) $\frac{\pi^2}{8}$
(b) $\frac{\pi^2}{16\sqrt{2}}$
(c) $\frac{\pi^2}{16}$
(d) $\frac{\pi^2}{8\sqrt{2}}$

JEE Advanced

1 Two concentric circular loops, one of radius R and the other of radius $2R$, lie in the xy-plane with the origin as their common centre, as shown in the figure. The smaller loop carries current I_1 in the anti-clockwise direction and the larger loop carries current I_2 in the clockwise direction, with $I_2 > 2I_1$. **B**(x, y) denotes the magnetic field at a point (x, y) in the xy-plane. Which of the following statement(s) is(are) correct? **(2021)**

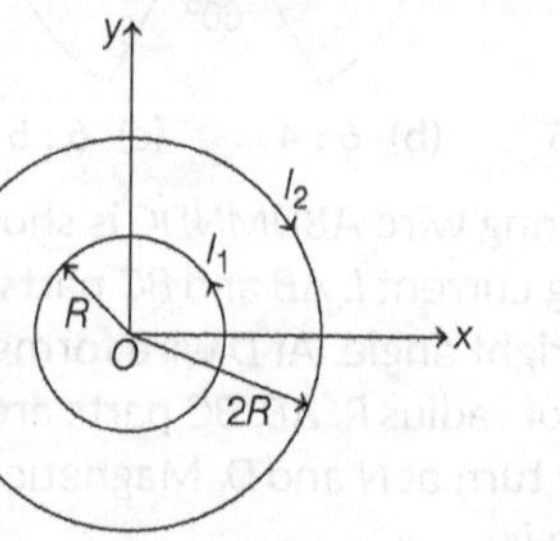

(a) **B**(x, y) is perpendicular to the xy-plane at any point in the plane.
(b) $|$**B**$(x, y)|$ depends on x and y only through the radial distance $r = \sqrt{x^2 + y^2}$.
(c) $|$**B**$(x, y)|$ is non-zero at all points for $r < R$.
(d) **B**(x, y) points normally outwards from the xy-plane for all the points between the two loops.

2 Two infinitely long straight wires lie in the xy-plane along the lines $x = \pm R$. The wire located at $x = +R$ carries a constant current I_1 and the wire located at $x = -R$ carries a constant current I_2. A circular loop of radius R is suspended with its centre at $(0, 0, \sqrt{3}R)$ and in a plane parallel to the xy-plane.
This loop carries a constant current I in the clockwise direction as seen from above the loop. The current in the wire is taken to be positive, if it is in the

$+\hat{\mathbf{j}}$-direction. Which of the following statements regarding the magnetic field $\mathbf{B}$ is (are) true? **(2018)**

(a) If $I_1 = I_2$, then $\mathbf{B}$ cannot be equal to zero at the origin (0,0,0)

(b) If $I_1 > 0$ and $I_2 < 0$, then $\mathbf{B}$ can be equal to zero at the origin (0,0,0)

(c) If $I_1 < 0$ and $I_2 > 0$, then $\mathbf{B}$ can be equal to zero at the origin (0,0,0)

(d) If $I_1 = I_2$, then the z-component of the magnetic field at the centre of the loop is $\left(-\dfrac{\mu_0 I}{2R}\right)$

3 A steady current I flows along an infinitely long hollow cylindrical conductor of radius R. This cylinder is placed coaxially inside an infinite solenoid of radius $2R$. The solenoid has n turns per unit length and carries a steady current I. Consider a point P at a distance r from the common axis. The correct statement(s) is (are) **(2013)**

(a) In the region $0 < r < R$, the magnetic field is non-zero

(b) In the region $R < r < 2R$, the magnetic field is along the common axis

(c) In the region $R < r < 2R$, the magnetic field is tangential to the circle of radius r, centered on the axis

(d) In the region $r > 2R$, the magnetic field is non-zero

4 An infinitely long hollow conducting cylinder with inner radius $R/2$ and outer radius R carries a uniform current density along its length. The magnitude of the magnetic field, $|\mathbf{B}|$ as a function of the radial distance r from the axis is best represented by **(2012)**

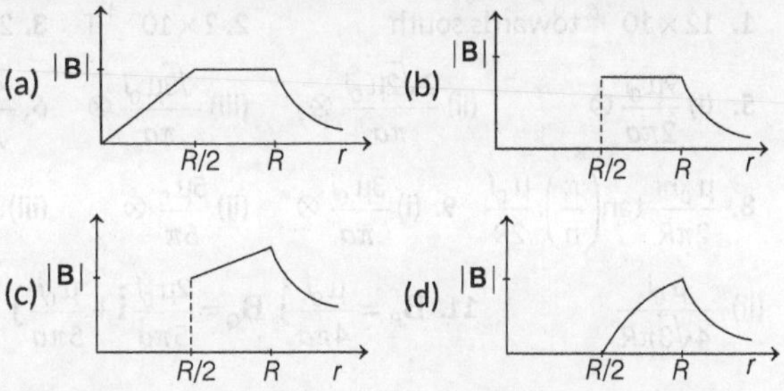

5 A cylindrical cavity of diameter a exists inside a cylinder of diameter $2a$ as shown in the figure. Both the cylinder and the cavity are infinitely long. A uniform current density J flows along the length. If the magnitude of the magnetic field at the point P is given by $\dfrac{N}{12}\mu_0 aJ$, then the value of N is **(2012)**

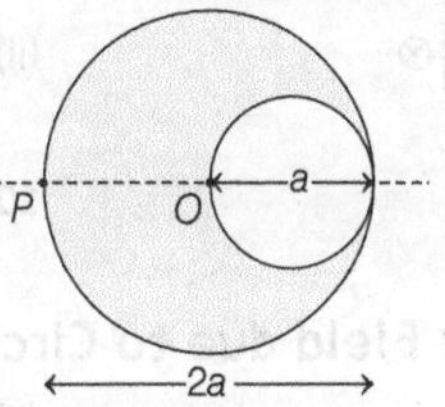

Answer Key

Level 1

1.1 Magnetic Field due to Straight Wire

1. 12×10^{-6} towards south 2. 2×10^{-4} T 3. 2.0×10^{-5} T, 0 4. 1.0 mm west to the wire

5. (i) $\frac{9\mu_0 i}{2\pi a} \otimes$ (ii) $\frac{2\sqrt{2}\mu_0 i}{\pi a} \otimes$ (iii) $\frac{\sqrt{3}\mu_0 i}{\pi a} \otimes$ 6. $\frac{4\mu_0 i}{\sqrt{3}\pi a}$ 7. $\frac{\sqrt{2}\mu_0 i}{3\pi a} \otimes$

8. $\frac{\mu_0 ni}{2\pi R} \tan\left(\frac{\pi}{n}\right), \frac{\mu_0 i}{2R}$ 9. (i) $\frac{3\mu_0 i}{\pi a} \otimes$ (ii) $\frac{5\mu_0}{6\pi} \otimes$ (iii) $\frac{\mu_0 i}{12\pi a} \otimes$ 10. (i) $\frac{\mu_0 i}{8\pi r}(\sqrt{3}-1)$

(ii) $\frac{\mu_0 i}{4\sqrt{3}\pi R}$ 11. $\mathbf{B}_P = \frac{\mu_0 i}{4\pi a}\hat{\mathbf{j}}, \mathbf{B}_Q = \frac{2\mu_0 i}{5\pi a}\hat{\mathbf{i}} + \frac{\mu_0 i}{5\pi a}\hat{\mathbf{j}}$

1.2 Magnetic Field due to Circular Arc at its Centre

1. 48 mA 2. $4B$ 3. $\frac{\mu_0 ne}{2R}$ 4. 1.6×10^{-5}T 5. 1.26×10^{-5} T

6. (i) $\frac{\mu_0 i}{2}\left(\frac{1}{r_1}+\frac{1}{r_2}\right)\otimes$ (ii) $\frac{\mu_0 i}{2}\left(\frac{1}{r_1}-\frac{1}{r_2}\right)\otimes$ (iii) $\frac{\mu_0 i}{\sqrt{2}r}$

7. (i) $\frac{\mu_0 i}{4}\left(\frac{1}{a}-\frac{1}{b}\right)\otimes$ (ii) $\frac{\mu_0 i}{4}\left(\frac{1}{a}+\frac{1}{b}\right)\otimes$ (iii) $\frac{\mu_0 i}{8}\left(\frac{1}{a}+\frac{1}{b}-\frac{2}{c}\right)\otimes$

8. (i) $\frac{\mu_0 i}{4R}\left(1+\frac{1}{\pi}\right)\otimes$ (ii) $\frac{\mu_0 i}{4R}\left(1+\frac{2}{\pi}\right)\otimes$ (iii) $\frac{\mu_0 i}{4R}\left(\frac{3}{2}+\frac{1}{\pi}\right)\otimes$

9. 0 10. $\frac{\mu_0 i}{2\pi R}(\pi - \phi + \tan\phi)$

1.3 Magnetic Field due to Circular Coil on its Axis

1. (i) 4×10^{-3} T, downwards (ii) 4×10^{-3} T, downwards 2. $\sqrt{3}a$

3. $\sqrt{7}R$ 4. (i) 1.3×10^{-4}T (ii) 0

1.4 Ampere's Law and its Applications

1. For L_1 $\oint \mathbf{B}\cdot d\mathbf{l} = \mu_0(i_1 - i_2)$; for $L_2 : \oint \mathbf{B}\cdot d\mathbf{l} = \mu_0(i_1 - i_2 + i_4)$; for $L_3 : \oint \mathbf{B}\cdot d\mathbf{l} = 0$

2. $\frac{\mu_0 i}{4}$ 3. (i) 0 (ii) $\frac{\mu_0 i}{3\pi r}$ 4. (i) 2×10^{-6} T (ii) 10^{-5} T (iii) 5×10^{-6} T

5. (i) 0 (ii) $\frac{\mu_0 i(r^2 - a^2)}{2\pi r(b^2 - a^2)}$ (iii) $\frac{\mu_0 i}{2\pi r}$ 6. (i) $B_1 = \frac{\mu_0 b r_1^2}{3}$ (ii) $B_2 = \frac{\mu_0 b R^3}{3r_2}$ 7. $\frac{\mu_0 i r^2}{2\pi d(R^2 - r^2)}$

8. $0, \mu_0\lambda$ towards right in the figure, 0

1.5 Solenoid and Toroid

1. (i) $\frac{\pi \times 10^{-5}}{\sqrt{13}}$ T (ii) $B = 2\pi \times 10^{-6}$ T 2. $12\pi \times 10^{-5}$ T 3. $2\pi \times 10^{-3}$ T

4. 1 V 5. 5×10^{-4} T

Level 2

Single Choice Correct Questions

1. (d)	2. (a)	3. (c)	4. (c)	5. (a)	6. (b)	7. (a)	8. (a)	9. (a)	10. (b)
11. (a)	12. (c)	13. (c)	14. (b)	15. (c)	16. (a)	17. (d)	18. (a)	19. (d)	20. (c)

21. (a)	22. (d)	23. (b)	24. (a)	25. (b)	26. (b)	27. (b)	28. (c)	29. (c)	30. (d)
31. (c)	32. (c)	33. (a)	34. (a)	35. (a)	36. (a)	37. (c)	38. (c)	39. (b)	40. (a)
41. (b)	42. (a)	43. (a)	44. (b)	45. (d)	46. (c)	47. (b)	48. (c)	49. (c)	50. (c)
51. (b)	52. (c)	53. (a)	54. (b)	55. (b)	56. (d)	57. (c)	58. (c)		

Numerical Value Questions

1. 4	2. 10	3. 2	4. 4	5. 32	6. 4	7. 36
8. 2	9. 12.56	10. 5880				

Level 3

Single Choice Correct Questions

1. (a)	2. (b)	3. (b)	4. (c)	5. (a)	6. (d)	7. (d)	8. (a)	9. (b)	10. (c)
11. (c)	12. (c)	13. (a)	14. (a)	15. (b)	16. (a)	17. (c)	18. (d)	19. (a)	20. (d)
21. (d)	22. (a)	23. (d)	24. (a)	25. (c)	26. (b)	27. (d)	28. (a)	29. (a)	30. (c)
31. (d)	32. (a)	33. (c)	34. (d)	35. (b)	36. (c)	37. (a)			

Multiple Choice(s) Correct Questions

1. (a, b, c)	2. (c, d)	3. (b, c)	4. (a, d)	5. (b, d)	6. (a, c, d)	7. (a, c, d)
8. (a, b)	9. (a, b, c, d)	10. (b, c)	11. (a, b, d)	12. (b, d)		

Comprehension Based Questions

1. (c)	2. (a)	3. (a)	4. (c)	5. (a)	6. (b)	7. (c)
8. (b)	9. (b)	10. (d)	11. (b)	12. (c)		

Match the Columns Questions

1. A→ 2; B→ 1; C→ 4; D→ 3
2. A→ 3; B→ 4; C→ 1; D→ 2
3. A→ 3; B→ 3; C→ 3; D→ 2
4. A→ 1; B→ 3; C→ 2; D→ 4
5. A→ 5; B→ 2; C→ 4; D→ 3

Numerical Value Questions

1. 12	2. 16	3. 8	4. 1	5. 6	6. 2	7. 0940

Previous Years Questions

JEE Main

1. (160)	2. (24)	3. (c)	4. (40)	5. (c)	6. (a)	7. (a)	8. (d)	9. (b)	10. (a)
11. (8)	12. (628)	13. (2)	14. (40)	15. (3)	16. (c)	17. (b)	18. (b)	19. (d)	20. (a)
21. (b)	22. (c)	23. (a)	24. (a)	25. (d)	26. (a)	27. (d)	28. (c)	29. (a)	30. (d)
31. (b)	32. (b)	33. (c)	34. (c)	35. (a)	36. (c)	37. (d)	38. (b)	39. (b)	40. (a)
41. (b)	42. (a)	43. (c)	44. (d)						

JEE Advanced

1. (a,b)	2. (a,b,d)	3. (a,d)	4. (d)	5. (5)

SOLUTIONS

Level 1

1.1 Magnetic Field due to Straight Wire

1. $B = \dfrac{\mu_0 i}{2\pi r} = \dfrac{4\pi \times 10^{-7} \times 90}{2\pi(1.5)} = 12 \times 10^{-6}\ \text{T}$

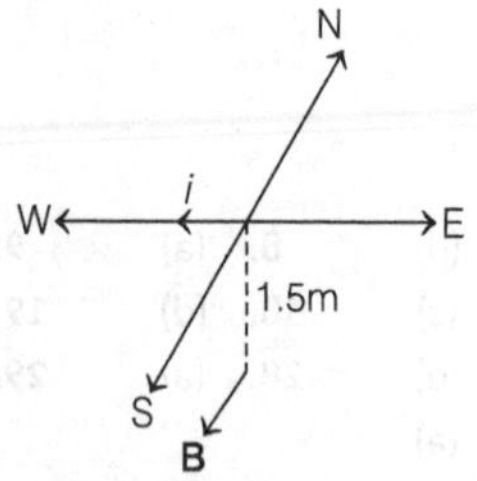

$B = 12 \times 10^{-6}$ T, towards south

2. $r = \sqrt{3^2 + 4^2} = 5$ cm

$B = \dfrac{\mu_0 i}{2\pi r} = \dfrac{4\pi \times 10^{-7} \times 50}{2\pi \times 5 \times 10^{-2}} = 2 \times 10^{-4}\ \text{T}$

3. $B_{\text{wire}} = \dfrac{\mu_0 i}{2\pi r} = \dfrac{4\pi \times 10^{-7} \times 1}{2\pi \times 2 \times 10^{-2}} = 1.0 \times 10^{-5}\ \text{T}$

$B_{\text{ext}} = 1.0 \times 10^{-5}\ \text{T}$

At point P, $B_{\text{net}} = B_{\text{wire}} + B_{\text{ext}} = 2.0 \times 10^{-5}\ \text{T}$

At point Q, $B_{\text{net}} = B_{\text{wire}} - B_{\text{ext}} = 0$

4. $B = \dfrac{\mu_0 i}{2\pi r} \Rightarrow 2.0 \times 10^{-3} = \dfrac{4\pi \times 10^{-7} \times 10}{2\pi \times r} \Rightarrow r = 1.0$ mm

So, point will be 1.0 mm west to the wire.

5. (i) $\mathbf{B} = 3\left[\dfrac{\mu_0 i}{4\pi r}(\sin\alpha + \sin\beta)\right] \otimes$

$= \dfrac{3\mu_0 i}{4\pi\left(\dfrac{a}{2\sqrt{3}}\right)}(\sin 60° + \sin 60°) \otimes = \dfrac{9\mu_0 i}{2\pi a} \otimes$

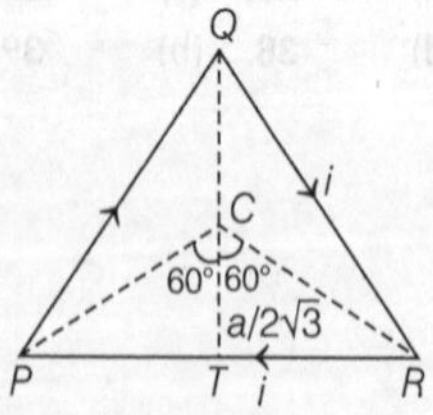

(ii) $\mathbf{B} = 4\left[\dfrac{\mu_0 i}{4\pi r}(\sin\alpha + \sin\beta)\right] \otimes$

$= 4\left[\dfrac{\mu_0 i}{4\pi\left(\dfrac{a}{2}\right)}(\sin 45° + \sin 45°)\right] \otimes$

$= \dfrac{2\sqrt{2}\mu_0 i}{\pi a} \otimes$

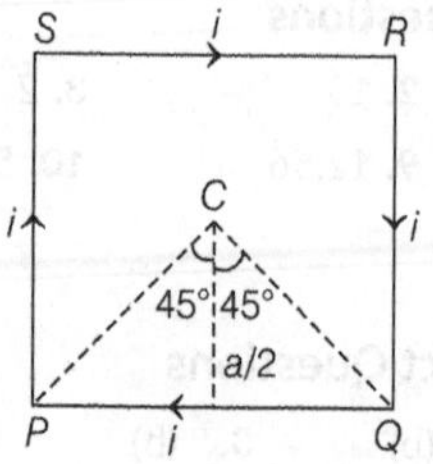

(iii) $\mathbf{B} = 6\left[\dfrac{\mu_0 i}{4\pi r}(\sin\alpha + \sin\beta)\right] \otimes$

$= 6\left[\dfrac{\mu_0 i}{4\pi\left(\dfrac{\sqrt{3}a}{2}\right)}(\sin 30° + \sin 30°)\right] \otimes = \dfrac{\sqrt{3}\mu_0 i}{\pi a} \otimes$

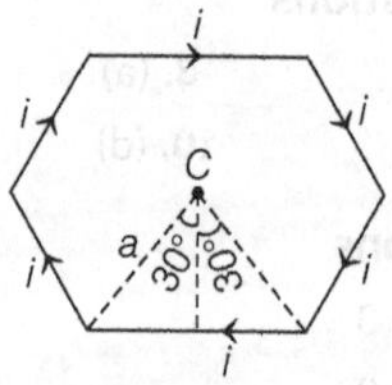

$r = a\cos 30° = \dfrac{\sqrt{3}a}{2}$

6. $B_{PQ} = B_{RS} = \dfrac{\mu_0 i}{4\pi\left(\dfrac{a}{2}\right)}(\sin 60° + \sin 60°) = \dfrac{\sqrt{3}\mu_0 i}{2\pi a}$

$B_{QR} = B_{SP} = \dfrac{\mu_0 i}{4\pi\left(\dfrac{\sqrt{3}a}{2}\right)}(\sin 30° + \sin 30°) = \dfrac{\mu_0 i}{2\sqrt{3}\pi a}$

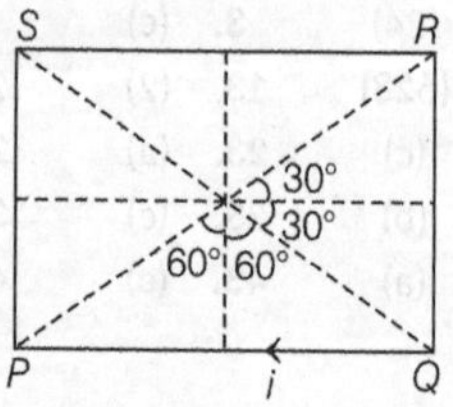

$B_{\text{net}} = 2(B_{PQ} + B_{QR}) = \dfrac{4\mu_0 i}{\sqrt{3}\pi a}$

7. $\dfrac{i_{ABC}}{i_{ADC}} = \dfrac{R_{ADC}}{R_{ABC}} = \dfrac{2r}{r} = 2$

$\mathbf{B}_{AB} = \mathbf{B}_{BC} = \left[\dfrac{\mu_0\left(\dfrac{2i}{3}\right)}{4\pi\left(\dfrac{a}{2}\right)}(\sin 45° + \sin 45°)\right] \otimes = \dfrac{\sqrt{2}\mu_0 i}{3\pi a} \otimes$

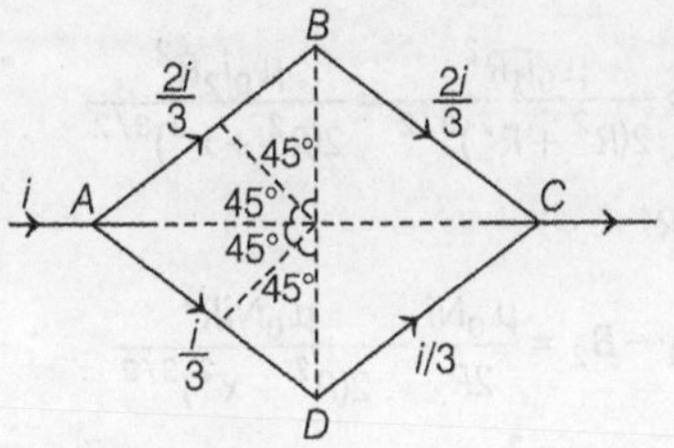

$$\mathbf{B}_{DA} = \mathbf{B}_{CD} = \left[\frac{\mu_0\left(\frac{i}{3}\right)}{4\pi\left(\frac{a}{2}\right)}(\sin 45° + \sin 45°)\right] \odot = \frac{\mu_0 i}{3\sqrt{2}\pi a} \odot$$

$$\mathbf{B}_{\text{net}} = 2\left(\frac{\sqrt{2}\mu_0 i}{3\pi a}\otimes\right) + 2\left(\frac{\mu_0 i}{3\sqrt{2}\pi a}\odot\right) = \frac{\sqrt{2}\mu_0 i}{3\pi a}\otimes$$

8. $B = n\left\{\frac{\mu_0 i}{4\pi\left[R\cos\left(\frac{\pi}{n}\right)\right]}\left[\sin\left(\frac{\pi}{n}\right) + \sin\left(\frac{\pi}{n}\right)\right]\right\}$

$$B = \frac{n\mu_0 i}{2\pi R}\tan\left(\frac{\pi}{n}\right)$$

If $n \to \infty$,

$$B = \frac{\mu_0 i}{2R}\lim_{n\to\infty}\left[\frac{\tan\left(\frac{\pi}{n}\right)}{\left(\frac{\pi}{n}\right)}\right] = \frac{\mu_0 i}{2R}$$

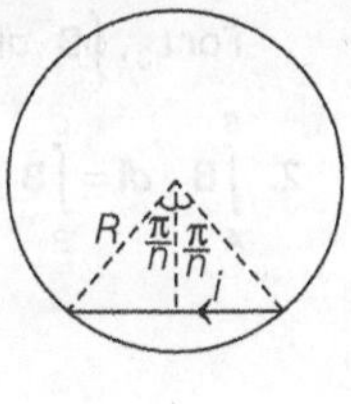

So, a polygon with infinite sides will be a circle.

9. (i) $\mathbf{B} = \frac{\mu_0(2i)}{2\pi\left(\frac{a}{2}\right)}\otimes + \frac{\mu_0 i}{2\pi\left(\frac{a}{2}\right)}\otimes = \frac{3\mu_0 i}{\pi a}\otimes$

(ii) $\mathbf{B} = \frac{\mu_0(5)}{2\pi(7.5)}\otimes + \frac{\mu_0(2.5)}{2\pi(2.5)}\otimes = \frac{5\mu_0}{6\pi}\otimes$

(iii) $\mathbf{B} = \frac{\mu_0 i}{2\pi(2)}\otimes + \frac{\mu_0 i}{2\pi(3)}\odot = \frac{\mu_0 i}{12\pi a}\otimes$

10. (i) $B = \frac{\mu_0 i}{4\pi r}(\sin\alpha + \sin\beta) = \frac{\mu_0 i}{4\pi r}[\sin 60° + \sin(-30°)]$

$= (\sqrt{3} - 1)\frac{\mu_0 i}{8\pi r}$

(ii) $B = \frac{\mu_0 i}{4\pi(R\cos 30°)}[\sin 90° + \sin(-30°)] + 0 = \frac{\mu_0 i}{4\sqrt{3}\pi R}$

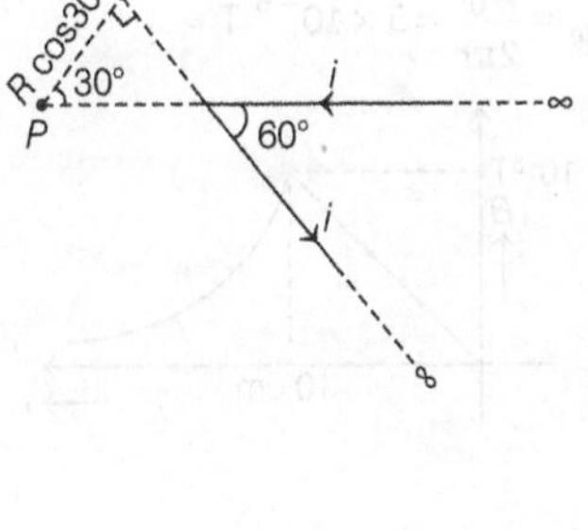

11. $B_1 = B_2 = \frac{\mu_0 i}{2\pi(2a)}$

$B_1' = \frac{\mu_0 i}{2\pi(\sqrt{5}a)}$

$B_2' = \frac{\mu_0 i}{2\pi a}$

$\tan\theta = \frac{a}{2a} = \frac{1}{2}$

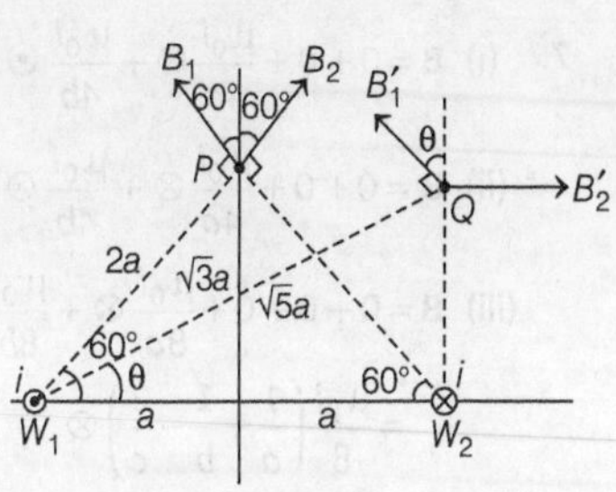

At point P,

$\mathbf{B}_P = (B_1\cos 60° + B_2\cos 60°)\hat{\mathbf{j}} = \frac{\mu_0 i}{4\pi a}\hat{\mathbf{j}}$

At point Q, $\mathbf{B}_Q = (B_2 - B_1'\sin\theta)\hat{\mathbf{i}} + B_1\cos\theta\hat{\mathbf{j}}$

$= \frac{2\mu_0 i}{5\pi a}\hat{\mathbf{i}} + \frac{\mu_0 i}{5\pi a}\hat{\mathbf{j}}$

1.2 Magnetic Field due to Circular Arc at its Centre

1. $B = \frac{\mu_0 Ni}{2R} \Rightarrow 6.0\times 10^{-5} = \frac{4\pi\times 10^{-7}\times 100\times i}{2\times 5\times 10^{-2}}$

$\Rightarrow \quad i = 48$ mA

2. $l = (2\pi r)N \Rightarrow r = \frac{l}{2\pi N}$

$$B = \frac{\mu_0 Ni}{2r} = \frac{\mu_0 Ni}{2\left(\frac{l}{2\pi N}\right)} = \frac{\mu_0 N^2 i\pi}{l} \Rightarrow \quad B \propto N^2$$

$$\Rightarrow \quad \frac{B_1}{B_2} = \frac{N_1^2}{N_2^2} \Rightarrow \frac{B}{B_2} = \frac{(1)^2}{(2)^2} \Rightarrow B_2 = 4B$$

3. $i = \frac{q}{T} = qf = en$

$B = \frac{\mu_0 i}{2R} = \frac{\mu_0 en}{2R}$

4. $B = \frac{\mu_0 Ni}{2R} = \frac{4\pi\times 10^{-7}\times\frac{1}{2}\times 5.0}{2\times 10.0\times 10^{-2}} = 1.6\times 10^{-5}$ T

5. $N = \frac{\theta}{2\pi} = \frac{120°}{360°} = \frac{1}{3}$

$B = \frac{\mu_0 Ni}{2R} = \frac{4\pi\times 10^{-7}\times\left(\frac{1}{3}\right)\times 6.00}{2\times 10.0\times 10^{-2}}$

$= 1.26\times 10^{-5}$ T

6. (i) $\mathbf{B} = \frac{\mu_0 i}{2r_1}\otimes + \frac{\mu_0 i}{2r_2}\otimes = \frac{\mu_0 i}{2}\left(\frac{1}{r_1} + \frac{1}{r_2}\right)\otimes$

(ii) $\mathbf{B} = \frac{\mu_0 i}{2r_1}\otimes + \frac{\mu_0 i}{2r_2}\odot = \frac{\mu_0 i}{2}\left(\frac{1}{r_1} - \frac{1}{r_2}\right)\otimes$

(iii) $B = \sqrt{\left(\frac{\mu_0 i}{2r}\right)^2 + \left(\frac{\mu_0 i}{2r}\right)^2} = \frac{\mu_0 i}{\sqrt{2}r}$

7. (i) $\mathbf{B} = 0 + 0 + \frac{\mu_0 i}{4a} \otimes + \frac{\mu_0 i}{4b} \odot = \frac{\mu_0 i}{4}\left(\frac{1}{a} - \frac{1}{b}\right) \otimes$

(ii) $\mathbf{B} = 0 + 0 + \frac{\mu_0 i}{4a} \otimes + \frac{\mu_0 i}{4b} \otimes = \frac{\mu_0 i}{4}\left(\frac{1}{a} + \frac{1}{b}\right) \otimes$

(iii) $\mathbf{B} = 0 + 0 + 0 + \frac{\mu_0 i}{8a} \otimes + \frac{\mu_0 i}{8b} \otimes + \frac{\mu_0 i}{4c} \odot$

$$= \frac{\mu_0 i}{8}\left(\frac{1}{a} + \frac{1}{b} - \frac{2}{c}\right) \otimes$$

8. (i) $\mathbf{B} = 0 + \frac{\mu_0 i}{4R} \otimes + \frac{\mu_0 i}{4\pi R} \otimes = \frac{\mu_0 i}{4R}\left(1 + \frac{1}{\pi}\right) \otimes$

(ii) $\mathbf{B} = \frac{\mu_0 i}{4\pi R} \otimes + \frac{\mu_0 i}{4R} \otimes + \frac{\mu_0 i}{4\pi R} \otimes = \frac{\mu_0 i}{4R}\left(1 + \frac{2}{\pi}\right) \otimes$

(iii) $\mathbf{B} = 0 + \frac{\mu_0 \left(\frac{3}{4}\right) i}{2R} \otimes + \frac{\mu_0 i}{4\pi R} \otimes = \frac{\mu_0 i}{4R}\left(\frac{3}{2} + \frac{1}{\pi}\right) \otimes$

9. $\mathbf{B} = 0 + 0 + \frac{\mu_0 \left(\frac{3}{4}\right)\left(\frac{i}{4}\right)}{2R} - \frac{\mu_0 \left(\frac{1}{4}\right)\left(\frac{3i}{4}\right)}{2R}$

$= 0$

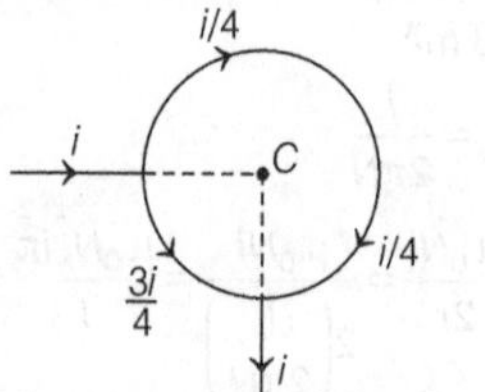

10. $\mathbf{B} = \frac{\mu_0 \left(\frac{2\pi - 2\phi}{2\pi}\right) i}{2R} + \frac{\mu_0 i}{4\pi (R\cos\phi)} (\sin\phi + \sin\phi)$

$$= \frac{\mu_0 i}{2\pi R} (\pi - \phi + \tan\phi)$$

1.3 *Magnetic Field due to Circular Coil on its Axis*

1. (i) $B = \frac{\mu_0 N i R^2}{2(R^2 + x^2)^{3/2}}$

$$= \frac{4\pi \times 10^{-7} \times 100 \times 5.0 \times (4.0 \times 10^{-2})^2}{2[(4.0 \times 10^{-2})^2 + (3.0 \times 10^{-2})^2]^{3/2}}$$

$= 4.0 \times 10^{-3}$ T, downwards

(ii) 4.0×10^{-3} T, downwards

2. $B_{\text{axis}} = \frac{1}{8} B_{\text{centre}}$

$$\Rightarrow \frac{\mu_0 N i a^2}{2(a^2 + x^2)^{3/2}} = \frac{1}{8}\left(\frac{\mu_0 N i}{2a}\right)$$

$\Rightarrow \quad x = \sqrt{3}a$

3. $B_1 = B_2 \Rightarrow \frac{\mu_0 i_1 R^2}{2(R^2 + R^2)^{3/2}} = \frac{\mu_0 i_2 R^2}{2(R^2 + x^2)^{3/2}}$

$\Rightarrow x = \sqrt{7}R$

4. (i) $B = B_1 - B_2 = \frac{\mu_0 N i}{2R} - \frac{\mu_0 N i R^2}{2(R^2 + x^2)^{3/2}}$

$$= \frac{4\pi \times 10^{-7} \times 10 \times 1}{2 \times 0.04} - \frac{4\pi \times 10^{-7} \times 10 \times 1 \times (0.04)^2}{2[(0.04)^2 + (0.06)^2]^{3/2}}$$

$= 1.3 \times 10^{-4}$ T

(ii) $B = B_1 - B_2$

$$= \frac{\mu_0 N i R^2}{2(R^2 + x^2)^{3/2}} - \frac{\mu_0 N i R^2}{2(R^2 + x^2)^{3/2}} = 0$$

1.4 *Ampere's Law and its Applications*

1. $\oint \mathbf{B} \cdot d\mathbf{l} = \mu_0 i_{\text{enclosed}}$

For L_1, $\oint \mathbf{B} \cdot d\mathbf{l} = \mu_0 (i_1 - i_2)$

For L_2, $\oint \mathbf{B} \cdot d\mathbf{l} = \mu_0 (i_1 - i_2 + i_4)$

For L_3, $\oint \mathbf{B} \cdot d\mathbf{l} = 0$ $\quad (\because i_{\text{enclosed}} = 0)$

2. $\int_A^B \mathbf{B} \cdot d\mathbf{l} = \int_B^C \mathbf{B} \cdot d\mathbf{l} = \int_C^D \mathbf{B} \cdot d\mathbf{l} = \int_D^A \mathbf{B} \cdot d\mathbf{l}$

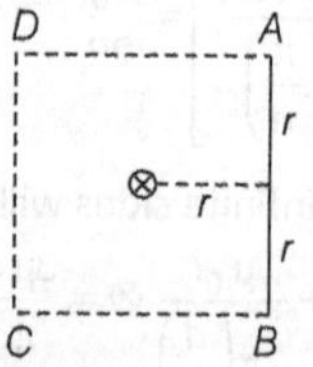

$$\int_A^B \mathbf{B} \cdot d\mathbf{l} = \frac{1}{4}\left(\oint \mathbf{B} \cdot d\mathbf{l}\right) = \frac{1}{4}(\mu_0 i)$$

3. (i) $B_{\text{inside}} = 0$

(ii) $B_{\text{outside}} = \frac{\mu_0 i}{2\pi\left(\frac{3r}{2}\right)} = \frac{\mu_0 i}{3\pi r}$

4. (i) $B_{\text{inside}} = \frac{\mu_0 i r}{2\pi R^2} = \frac{4\pi \times 10^{-7} \times 5.0 \times 2 \times 10^{-2}}{2\pi \times (10 \times 10^{-2})^2}$

$= 2 \times 10^{-6}$ T

(ii) $B_{\text{surface}} = \frac{\mu_0 i}{2\pi R} = 10^{-5}$ T

(iii) $B_{\text{outside}} = \frac{\mu_0 i}{2\pi r} = 5 \times 10^{-6}$ T

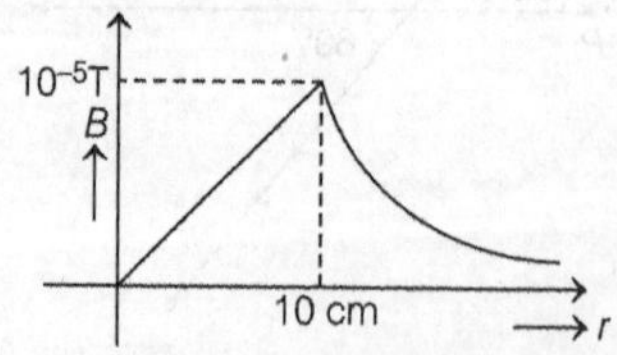

5. Current density, $J = \dfrac{i}{\pi(b^2 - a^2)}$

(i) $r < a$;

$$\oint \mathbf{B} \cdot d\mathbf{l} = \mu_0 i_{\text{enclosed}} \Rightarrow B(2\pi r) = 0 \Rightarrow B = 0$$

(ii) $a \le r < b$;

$$\oint \mathbf{B} \cdot d\mathbf{l} = \mu_0 i_{\text{enclosed}}$$

$$\Rightarrow B(2\pi r) = \mu_0 \left[\frac{i}{\pi(b^2 - a^2)} \pi(r^2 - a^2)\right]$$

$$\Rightarrow B = \frac{\mu_0 i(r^2 - a^2)}{2\pi r(b^2 - a^2)}$$

(iii) $r \ge b$;

$$\oint \mathbf{B} \cdot d\mathbf{l} = \mu_0 i_{\text{enclosed}}$$

$$\Rightarrow B(2\pi r) = \mu_0 i \Rightarrow B = \frac{\mu_0 i}{2\pi r}$$

6. (i) $r_1 < R$;

$$\oint \mathbf{B} \cdot d\mathbf{l} = \mu_0 i_{\text{enclosed}}$$

$$\Rightarrow B(2\pi r_1) = \mu_0 \int_0^r (br) 2\pi r dr$$

$$\Rightarrow B = \frac{\mu_0 b r_1^2}{3}$$

(ii) $r_2 > R$; $\oint \mathbf{B} \cdot d\mathbf{l} = \mu_0 i_{\text{enclosed}}$

$$\Rightarrow B(2\pi r_2) = \mu_0 \int_0^R (br) 2\pi r dr$$

$$\Rightarrow B = \frac{\mu_0 b R^3}{3 r_2}$$

7.

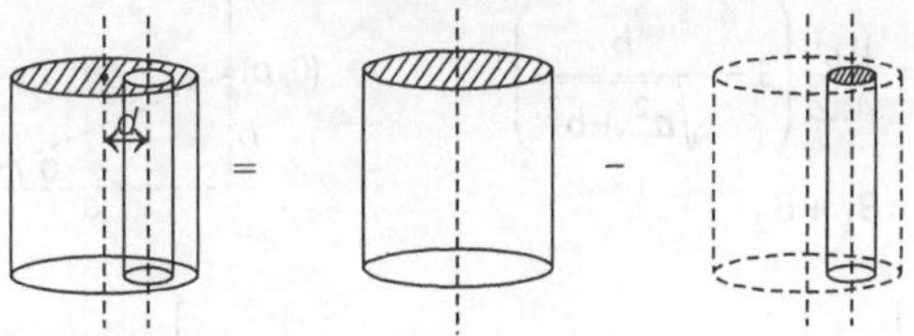

$$B = B_1 - B_2 = 0 - \left\{\frac{\mu_0 \left[\dfrac{i}{\pi(R^2 - r^2)} \times \pi r^2\right]}{2\pi d}\right\}$$

$$= -\frac{\mu_0 i r^2}{2\pi d(R^2 - r^2)}$$

8. Magnetic field due to large metal sheet $= \dfrac{\mu_0 \lambda}{2}$

$$B_P = \frac{\mu_0 \lambda}{2} - \frac{\mu_0 \lambda}{2} = 0$$

$$B_Q = \frac{\mu_0 \lambda}{2} + \frac{\mu_0 \lambda}{2} = \mu_0 \lambda$$

$$B_R = \frac{\mu_0 \lambda}{2} - \frac{\mu_0 \lambda}{2} = 0$$

1.5 *Solenoid and Toroid*

1. $n = \dfrac{N}{l} = \dfrac{1000}{0.4} = 2500$; $\cos\alpha = \cos\beta = \dfrac{0.2}{\sqrt{(0.2)^2 + (0.3)^2}}$

$$B_{\text{middle}} = \frac{\mu_0 n i}{2}(\cos\alpha + \cos\beta) = \frac{\pi \times 10^{-5}}{\sqrt{13}} \text{ T}$$

$$B_{\text{end}} = \frac{\mu_0 n i}{2}(\cos\alpha + \cos\beta)$$

$$= \frac{4\pi \times 10^{-7} \times 2500 \times 5 \times 10^{-3}}{2}\left[\frac{0.4}{\sqrt{(0.4)^2 + (0.3)^2}} + 0\right]$$

$$= 2\pi \times 10^{-6} \text{ T}$$

2. $B = \mu_0 n_1 i - \mu_0 n_2 i = \mu_0 (n_1 - n_2) i$

$$= 4\pi \times 10^{-7}\left(\frac{50}{0.1} - \frac{40}{0.1}\right) \times 3 = 12\pi \times 10^{-5} \text{ T}$$

3. $n = \dfrac{1}{2r} = \dfrac{1}{2 \times 0.5 \times 10^{-3}} = 1000$

$$B = \mu_0 n i = 4\pi \times 10^{-7} \times 1000 \times 5 = 2\pi \times 10^{-3} \text{ T}$$

4. $B = \mu_0 n i$

$$\Rightarrow 1 \times 10^{-2} = 4\pi \times 10^{-7}\left(\frac{400}{0.2}\right) \times i$$

$$\Rightarrow i = \frac{25}{2\pi} \text{ A}$$

$$R = (0.01)\,[400(2\pi r)] = 8\pi \times 10^{-2}\ \Omega$$

Using Ohm's law, $V = iR$

$$\varepsilon = \left(\frac{25}{2\pi}\right)(8\pi \times 10^{-2}) = 1 \text{ V}$$

5. $B = \dfrac{\mu_0 N i}{2\pi R} = \dfrac{4\pi \times 10^{-7} \times 500 \times 0.5}{2\pi(0.1)} = 5 \times 10^{-4}$ T

Level 2

Single Choice Correct Questions

1. $d\mathbf{B} = \left(\dfrac{\mu_0}{4\pi}\right) i \dfrac{d\mathbf{l} \times (0 - \mathbf{r})}{r^3} = -\dfrac{\mu_0 i}{4\pi}\left(\dfrac{d\mathbf{l} \times \mathbf{r}}{r^3}\right)$

2. $B = \dfrac{\mu_0 i}{2\pi r} = \dfrac{\mu_0 i}{2\pi\sqrt{x^2 + y^2}}$

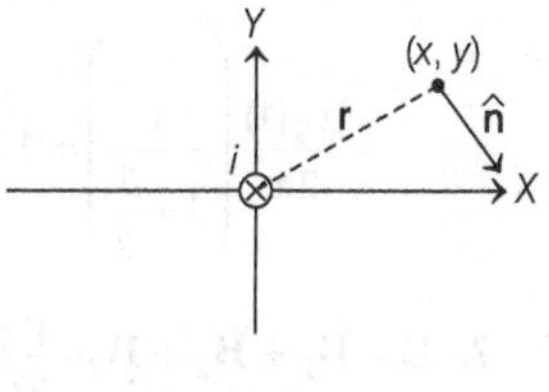

$$\mathbf{r} = x\hat{\mathbf{i}} + y\hat{\mathbf{j}}$$

$$\hat{\mathbf{n}} \perp \mathbf{r} \Rightarrow \hat{\mathbf{n}} = \frac{y\hat{\mathbf{i}} - x\hat{\mathbf{j}}}{\sqrt{x^2 + y^2}}$$

$$\mathbf{B} = B\hat{\mathbf{n}} = \frac{\mu_0 i}{2\pi\sqrt{x^2 + y^2}}\left(\frac{y\hat{\mathbf{i}} - x\hat{\mathbf{j}}}{\sqrt{x^2 + y^2}}\right) = \frac{\mu_0 i(y\hat{\mathbf{i}} - x\hat{\mathbf{j}})}{2\pi(x^2 + y^2)}$$

3. $B_{\text{wire}} = \dfrac{\mu_0 i}{2\pi r} = \dfrac{4\pi \times 10^{-7} \times 30}{2\pi \times 2 \times 10^{-2}} = 3 \times 10^{-4}$ T

$B_{ext} = 4 \times 10^{-4}$ T and $\mathbf{B}_{wire} \perp \mathbf{B}_{ext}$

$$\Rightarrow B_{net} = \sqrt{B_{wire}^2 + B_{ext}^2} = 5 \times 10^{-4}\ \text{T}$$

4. $B = \dfrac{\mu_0 i}{2\pi L}$

$$B_{net} = 2B\cos 60° = \frac{\mu_0 i}{2\pi L}$$

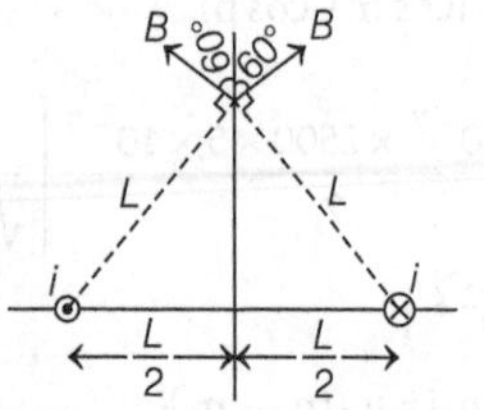

5. $B_{net} = 2(B_{AB} + B_{BC})$

$$= 2\left(\frac{\mu_0 i}{4\pi\left(\frac{b}{2}\right)}(\sin\theta + \sin\theta)\right) + 2\left(\frac{\mu_0 i}{4\pi\left(\frac{a}{2}\right)}(\sin\phi + \sin\phi)\right)$$

$$= \frac{2\mu_0 i}{\pi}\left[\frac{1}{b}\left(\frac{a/2}{\sqrt{(a/2)^2 + (b/2)^2}}\right) + \frac{1}{a}\left(\frac{b/2}{\sqrt{(a/2)^2 + (b/2)^2}}\right)\right]$$

$$= \left(\frac{\mu_0 i}{4\pi}\right)\left(\frac{8\sqrt{a^2 + b^2}}{ab}\right)$$

$$\sin\theta = \frac{a/2}{\sqrt{(a/2)^2 + (b/2)^2}}$$

$$\sin\phi = \frac{b/2}{\sqrt{(a/2)^2 + (b/2)^2}}$$

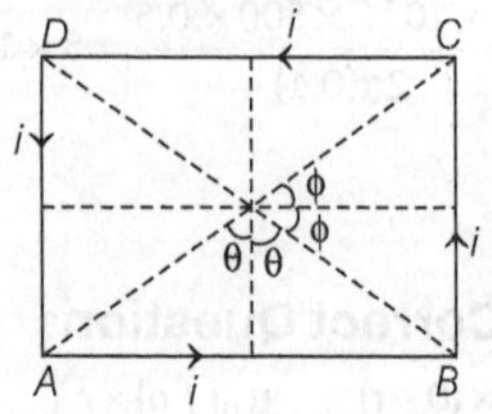

6. $$\mathbf{B} = \frac{\mu_0(1)}{2\pi}\left(1 - \frac{1}{2} + \frac{1}{4} - \frac{1}{8} + \ldots \infty\right)$$

$$= \frac{\mu_0(1)}{2\pi}\left(\frac{1}{1 + \frac{1}{2}}\right) = 1.33 \times 10^{-7}\,\hat{\mathbf{k}}\ \text{T}$$

7. $$\mathbf{B} = \mathbf{B}_1 + \mathbf{B}_2 + \mathbf{B}_3 = \frac{\mu_0 i}{2\pi a}\hat{\mathbf{j}} - \frac{\mu_0 i}{2\pi a}\hat{\mathbf{i}} + 0 = \frac{\mu_0 i}{2\pi a}(\hat{\mathbf{j}} - \hat{\mathbf{i}})$$

8. At point (X, Y), $$\mathbf{B} = \left(\frac{\mu_0 i_1}{2\pi Y} - \frac{\mu_0 i_2}{2\pi X}\right)\hat{\mathbf{k}} = 0$$

$$\Rightarrow \quad Y = \left(\frac{i_1}{i_2}\right)X$$

9. $$B = \frac{\mu_0 i}{2\pi\left(\frac{a}{\sqrt{2}}\right)}$$

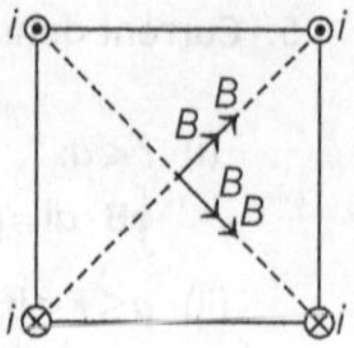

$$B_{net} = \sqrt{(2B)^2 + (2B)^2}$$

$$= 2\sqrt{2}B = \frac{2\mu_0 i}{\pi a}$$

11. $B_1 = \dfrac{\mu_0(1.6)}{2\pi(1.6)}$

and $B_2 = \dfrac{\mu_0(1.2)}{2\pi(1.2)}$

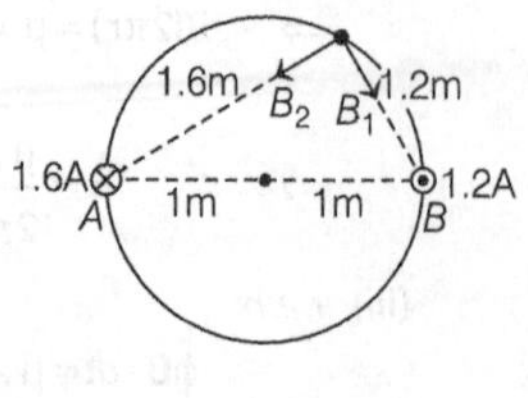

$$B_{net} = \sqrt{B_1^2 + B_2^2}$$

$$= 2\sqrt{2} \times 10^{-7}\ \text{T}$$

12. $B = B_{AB} + B_{BC} + B_{DE} + B_{EF}$

$$= 0 + \frac{\mu_0 i}{4\pi a} + 0 + \frac{\mu_0 i}{4\pi a} = \frac{\mu_0 i}{2\pi a}$$

13. $B_1 = \dfrac{\mu_0 i}{4\pi r} + 0 = \dfrac{\mu_0 i}{4\pi r}$

$$B_2 = \frac{\mu_0 i}{4\pi r} + 0 + \frac{\mu_0\left(\frac{i}{2}\right)}{4\pi r} = \frac{3}{2}\left(\frac{\mu_0 i}{4\pi r}\right)$$

$$\frac{B_1}{B_2} = \frac{2}{3}$$

14. $B = \dfrac{\mu_0 i}{4\pi r}(\sin\alpha + \sin\beta)$

$$= \frac{\mu_0 i}{4\pi a}(\sin 90° + \sin(-\theta))$$

$$= \frac{\mu_0 i}{4\pi a}\left(1 - \frac{b}{\sqrt{a^2 + b^2}}\right)$$

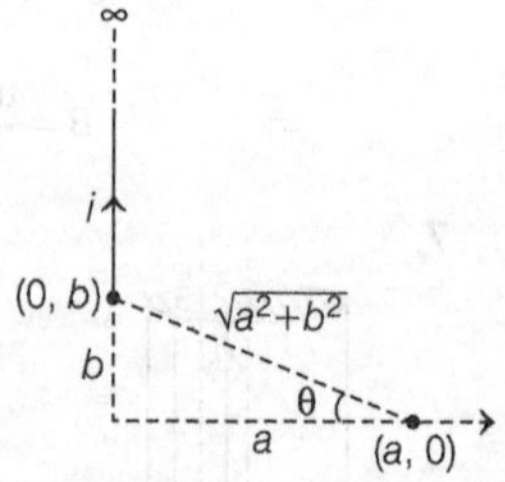

15. $B = B_1 + B_2$

$$= \left\{\frac{\mu_0 i}{4\pi\left[r\sin\left(\frac{\alpha}{2}\right)\right]}\left[\sin 90° + \sin\left(90° - \frac{\alpha}{2}\right)\right]\right\} \times 2$$

$$= \frac{\mu_0 i}{2\pi r}\left[\frac{1 + \cos\left(\frac{\alpha}{2}\right)}{\sin\left(\frac{\alpha}{2}\right)}\right] = \frac{\mu_0 i}{2\pi r}\cot\left(\frac{\alpha}{4}\right)$$

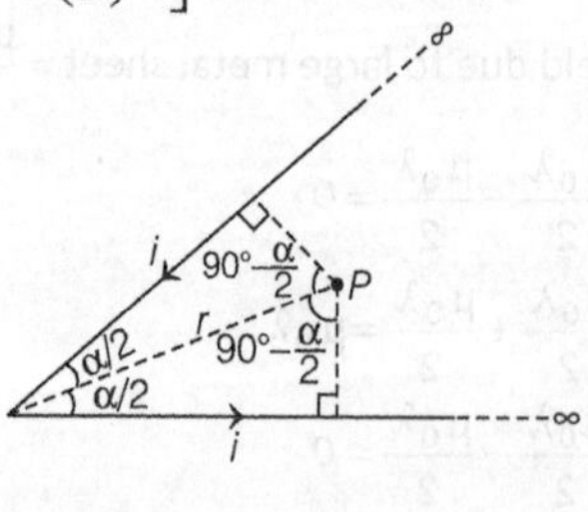

16. $B = 0 + \dfrac{\mu_0 i}{4\pi(R \sin 45°)}(\sin 90° - \sin 45°) = \dfrac{(\sqrt{2}-1)\mu_0 i}{4\pi R}$

17. $B = B_1 + B_2 + B_3$

$= \dfrac{\mu_0}{4\pi r}(\sin 60° + \sin 60°)\left(\dfrac{2i}{3} - \dfrac{i}{3} - \dfrac{i}{3}\right) = 0$

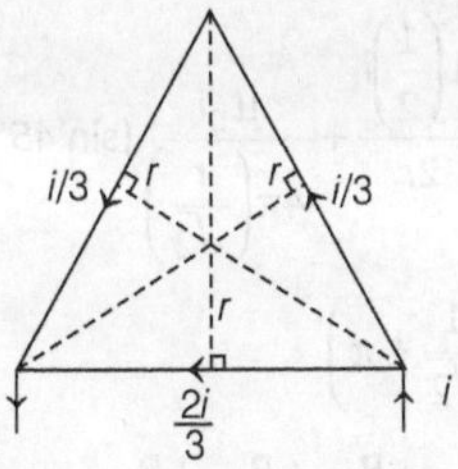

18. $B = \dfrac{ki}{a} \Rightarrow B \propto \dfrac{1}{a}$

$B_3 > B_1$ ($\because$ Third square is smaller than first square)

B_2 will be least. So, $B_3 > B_1 > B_2$

19. In P and R only, currents are divided in same proportion because the branches have equal resistance. Hence, magnetic field produced at centre due to each segment is of equal magnitude but of opposite direction, so net field is zero.

20. $RP = \sqrt{(QR)^2 + (PQ)^2} = \dfrac{a}{\sqrt{2}}$

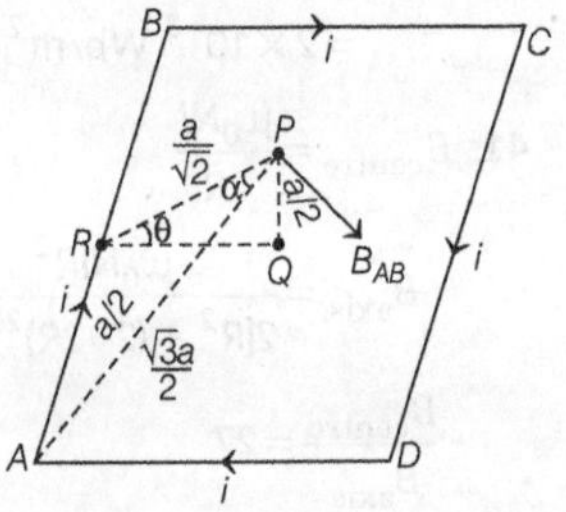

$AP = \sqrt{(RP)^2 + (RA)^2} = \dfrac{\sqrt{3}a}{2}$

$\sin\alpha = \dfrac{\frac{a}{2}}{\frac{\sqrt{3}a}{2}} = \dfrac{1}{\sqrt{3}}$

$B_{AB} = \dfrac{\mu_0 i}{4\pi\left(\frac{a}{\sqrt{2}}\right)}(\sin\alpha + \sin\alpha) = \dfrac{\mu_0 i}{\sqrt{6}\pi a}$

$B_{\text{net}} = 4B_{AB}\cos\theta = 4\left(\dfrac{\mu_0 i}{\sqrt{6}\pi a}\right)\cos 45° = \dfrac{2\mu_0 i}{\sqrt{3}\pi a}$

21. $B = \dfrac{\mu_0}{4\pi} q\left(\dfrac{vr \sin 30°}{r^3}\right) = 10^{-7} \times 2 \times \left(\dfrac{100 \times 2 \times \frac{1}{2}}{2^3}\right)$

$= 2.5\,\mu\text{T}$

22. $\mathbf{B} = \mathbf{B_1} + \mathbf{B_2} + \mathbf{B_3}$

$= \left(\dfrac{\mu_0}{4\pi}\right)\dfrac{1}{r^3}[q(\mathbf{v}\times\mathbf{r}) + 2q(\mathbf{v}\times\mathbf{r}) - q(-\mathbf{v})\times\mathbf{r})]$

$= \dfrac{\mu_0}{4\pi}\dfrac{4q(\mathbf{v}\times\mathbf{r})}{r^3}$

$= \left(\dfrac{\mu_0}{4\pi}\right)4q\left(\dfrac{va \sin 90°}{a^3}\right)\odot = \dfrac{\mu_0}{4\pi}\left(\dfrac{4qv}{a^2}\right)\odot$

23. $l = 4a \Rightarrow a = \dfrac{l}{4}$ and $l = 2\pi r \Rightarrow r = \dfrac{l}{2\pi}$

$\dfrac{B_{\text{circular loop}}}{B_{\text{square loop}}} = \dfrac{\dfrac{\mu_0 i}{2r}}{\left[\dfrac{\mu_0 i}{4\pi(a/2)}(\sin 45° + \sin 45°)\right] \times 4} = \dfrac{\pi^2}{8\sqrt{2}}$

24. $B = \dfrac{\mu_0 i}{2R} = \dfrac{\mu_0\left(\dfrac{q\omega}{2\pi}\right)}{2R}$

$= \dfrac{\mu_0}{4\pi}\left(\dfrac{q\omega}{R}\right) = 14$

$\Rightarrow \dfrac{10^{-7} \times 1.6 \times 10^{-19} \times \omega}{0.5 \times 10^{-10}} = 14$

$\Rightarrow \omega = 4.375 \times 10^{16}$ rad/s

25. $l = N(2\pi r) \Rightarrow r = \dfrac{l}{2\pi N}$

$B = \dfrac{\mu_0 Ni}{2r} = \dfrac{\mu_0 Ni}{2\left(\dfrac{l}{2\pi N}\right)} = \dfrac{\mu_0 N^2 \pi i}{l}$

$\Rightarrow B \propto N^2$

$\dfrac{B}{B_2} = \dfrac{(1)^2}{n^2} \Rightarrow \dfrac{B}{B_2} = \dfrac{1}{n^2} \Rightarrow B_2 = n^2 B$

26. $B = \dfrac{\mu_0 i}{4}\left(\dfrac{1}{a} - \dfrac{1}{2a} + \dfrac{1}{4a} - \dfrac{1}{8a} + \ldots\infty\right)$

$= \dfrac{\mu_0 i}{4a}\left(\dfrac{1}{1 - \left(-\dfrac{1}{2}\right)}\right) = \dfrac{\mu_0 i}{6a}$

27. $B = B_1 + B_2 = \dfrac{\mu_0\left(\dfrac{3}{4}\right)4}{2 \times 0.03} + \dfrac{\mu_0\left(\dfrac{1}{4}\right)4}{2 \times 0.06}$

$= \dfrac{7}{3}\pi \times 10^{-5}$ T

28. $\mathbf{B} = \mathbf{B_1} + \mathbf{B_2} = \dfrac{\mu_0 i\left[\sin\left(\dfrac{\theta}{2}\right) + \sin\left(\dfrac{\theta}{2}\right)\right]}{4\pi R\cos\left(\dfrac{\theta}{2}\right)}\odot + \dfrac{\mu_0\left(\dfrac{\theta}{2\pi}\right)\hat{\mathbf{i}}}{2R}\otimes$

$= \dfrac{\mu_0 i}{2\pi R}\left[\tan\left(\dfrac{\theta}{2}\right) - \dfrac{\theta}{2}\right]\odot$

For $0° < \theta < 180°$, $\tan\left(\dfrac{\theta}{2}\right) > \dfrac{\theta}{2}$

So, **B** will be perpendicular to paper outwards.

29. $\mathbf{B} = \dfrac{\mu_0\left(\dfrac{1}{4}\right)i}{2R}(\hat{\mathbf{k}} + \hat{\mathbf{i}} + \hat{\mathbf{j}}) = \dfrac{\mu_0 I}{8R}(\hat{\mathbf{i}} + \hat{\mathbf{j}} + \hat{\mathbf{k}})$

$$|\mathbf{B}| = \left(\frac{\mu_0 i}{8R}\right)\sqrt{3}$$

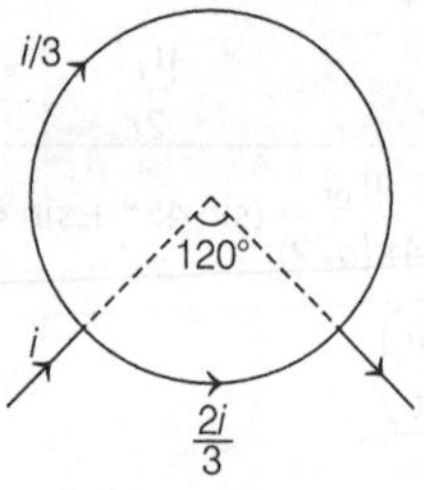

30. $B = \dfrac{\mu_0\left(\frac{2}{3}\right)\frac{i}{3}}{2a} - \dfrac{\mu_0\left(\frac{1}{3}\right)\left(\frac{2i}{3}\right)}{2a} = 0$

31. $\int dB = \int_a^b \dfrac{\mu_0\left(\frac{N}{b-a}dr\right)i}{2r}$

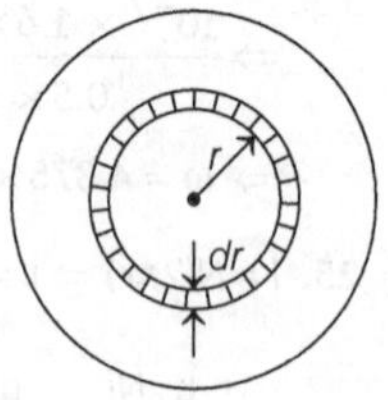

$$B = \frac{\mu_0 Ni}{2(b-a)}\ln\left(\frac{b}{a}\right)$$

32. $\mathbf{B} = \mathbf{B}_1 + \mathbf{B}_2 + \mathbf{B}_3 = \dfrac{\mu_0\left(\frac{3}{4}\right)i}{2a} - \dfrac{\mu_0\left(\frac{3}{4}\right)i}{2b} + \dfrac{\mu_0 i}{2c} = 0$

$$\Rightarrow \frac{\mu_0 i}{2}\left(\frac{3}{4a} - \frac{3}{4b} + \frac{1}{c}\right) = 0$$

$$\Rightarrow \frac{3}{4}\left(\frac{1}{a} - \frac{1}{b}\right) + \frac{1}{2a} = 0 \quad \Rightarrow a = \frac{5}{3}b$$

33. $B = \dfrac{\mu_2\left(\frac{\theta}{2\pi}\right)i}{2}\left(\dfrac{1}{r} - \dfrac{1}{2r} + \dfrac{1}{3r}\right) = \dfrac{5\mu_0 i\theta}{24r}$

34. $B_1 = -\dfrac{\mu_0 i}{4R} + \dfrac{\mu_0 i}{4\pi R} - \dfrac{\mu_0 i}{4\pi R} = -\dfrac{\mu_0 i}{4R}$

$$B_2 = \frac{\mu_0 i}{4R} + 0 + 0 = \frac{\mu_0 i}{4R}$$

$$B_3 = \frac{\mu_0\left(\frac{3}{4}\right)i}{2R} + 0 - \frac{\mu_0 i}{4\pi R} = \frac{\mu_0 i}{2\pi R}\left(\frac{3\pi}{4} - \frac{1}{2}\right)$$

$$B_1 : B_2 : B_3 = -\frac{\pi}{2} : \frac{\pi}{2} : \left(\frac{3\pi}{4} - \frac{1}{2}\right)$$

35. $\mathbf{B} = \mathbf{B}_1 + \mathbf{B}_2 = \dfrac{\mu_0 N_1 i_1}{2R_1}$, east $+ \dfrac{\mu_0 N_2 i_2}{2R_2}$, west

$$= \frac{4\pi\times 10^{-7}}{2}\left(\frac{20\times 16}{0.16}, \text{ east } \frac{25\times 18}{0.1}, \text{ west}\right)$$

$$= 5\pi\times 10^{-4}\text{ T towards west}$$

36. $\mathbf{B} = \dfrac{\mu_0 i}{4R}(-\hat{\mathbf{i}}) + \dfrac{\mu_0 i}{4\pi R}(-\hat{\mathbf{k}}) + 0$

$$\Rightarrow \mathbf{B} = -\frac{\mu_0 i}{4\pi R}(\pi\hat{\mathbf{i}} + \hat{\mathbf{k}})$$

$$\mathbf{B} = \frac{\mu_0 i}{4\pi R}\sqrt{1+\pi^2}$$

37. $B = \dfrac{\mu_0 i}{4\pi R} + \dfrac{\mu\left(\frac{3}{4}\right)i}{2R} + 0 - \dfrac{\mu_0 i}{4\pi(2R)} = \dfrac{\mu_0 i}{8R}\left(\dfrac{1}{\pi} + 3\right)$

38. $\mathbf{B} = \mathbf{B}_1 + \mathbf{B}_2 + \mathbf{B}_3$

$$B = \frac{\mu_0 i}{4\pi r}(\sin 90° + \sin 45°)$$

$$+ \frac{\mu\left(\frac{1}{2}\right)i}{2r} + \frac{\mu_0 i}{4\pi\left(\frac{r}{\sqrt{2}}\right)}(\sin 45° + \sin 45°)$$

$$= \frac{\mu_0 i}{4\pi r}\left(2 + \frac{1}{\sqrt{2}} + \pi\right)$$

39. $\mathbf{B} = \mathbf{B}_{PQ} + \mathbf{B}_{QR} + \mathbf{B}_{RS} + \mathbf{B}_{ST} + \mathbf{B}_{TU}$

$$= 0 + \frac{\mu_0 i}{8a}(+\hat{\mathbf{j}}) + 0 + \frac{\mu_0 i}{8(4a)}(+\hat{\mathbf{k}}) + 0$$

$$= \frac{\mu_0 i}{8a}(\hat{\mathbf{j}} + 0.25\hat{\mathbf{k}})$$

40. $B = \dfrac{\mu_0 NiR^2}{2(R^2+x^2)^{3/2}}$

$$= \frac{4\pi\times 10^{-7}\times 100\times 5\times (0.08)^2}{2[(0.08)^2 + (0.06)^2]^{3/2}}$$

$$= 2\times 10^{-3}\text{ Wb/m}^2$$

41. $B_{\text{centre}} = \dfrac{\mu_0 Ni}{2R}$

$$B_{\text{axis}} = \frac{\mu_0 NiR^2}{2[R^2 + (2\sqrt{2}R)^2]^{3/2}}$$

$$\frac{B_{\text{centre}}}{B_{\text{axis}}} = 27$$

42. $B = \dfrac{\mu_0 i_1 a^2}{2(a^2+(2a)^2)^{3/2}} - \dfrac{\mu_0 i_0 (2a)^2}{2((2a)^2+(2a)^2)^{3/2}} = 0$

$$\Rightarrow \frac{i_1}{5^{3/2}} = \frac{4i_2}{8^{3/2}}$$

$$\Rightarrow \frac{i_1}{i_2} = 4\left(\frac{5}{8}\right)^{3/2} = \frac{4(5\sqrt{5})}{8\sqrt{8}} \Rightarrow \frac{i_1}{i_2} = \frac{5}{2}\sqrt{\frac{5}{8}}$$

43. As point charge will move on the circle, $\mathbf{B}$ will rotate about the axis. So, $\mathbf{B}$ magnetic field is constant in magnitude only.

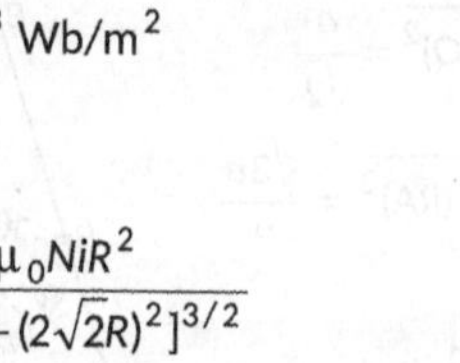

44. $B = \dfrac{\mu_0 NiR^2}{2(R^2+x^2)^{3/2}}$ and $R = x\tan\left(\dfrac{\theta}{2}\right)$

$$\Rightarrow B=\frac{\mu_0 Ni\left[x\tan\left(\frac{\theta}{2}\right)\right]^2}{2\left\{\left[x\tan\left(\frac{\theta}{2}\right)\right]^2+x^2\right\}^{3/2}}=\frac{\mu_0 Ni}{2x}\left[\frac{\tan^2\left(\frac{\theta}{2}\right)}{\sec^3\left(\frac{\theta}{2}\right)}\right]$$

$$\Rightarrow\ B\propto\frac{1}{x}\Rightarrow\frac{B_1}{B_2}=\frac{x_2}{x_1}\Rightarrow\frac{B}{B_2}=\frac{r}{2r}$$

$$\Rightarrow B_2=2B$$

45. $$B_1=\frac{\mu_0 NiR^2}{2(R^2+h^2)^{3/2}}=\left(\frac{\mu_0 Ni}{2R}\right)\frac{1}{\left(1+\frac{h^2}{R^2}\right)^{3/2}}$$

$$=\frac{\mu_0 Ni}{2R}\left(1-\frac{3h^2}{2R^2}\right)\Rightarrow\ B_2=\frac{\mu_0 Ni}{2R}$$

$$\therefore\quad\frac{B_2-B_1}{B_2}=\frac{3h^2}{2R^2}$$

46. $\oint \mathbf{B}\cdot d\mathbf{l}=\mu_0\, i_{\text{enclosed}}$

loop A; $\oint \mathbf{B}\cdot d\mathbf{l}=+i+i+i-i-i-i=0$

loop B; $\oint \mathbf{B}\cdot d\mathbf{l}=+i+i-i=i$

loop C; $\oint \mathbf{B}\cdot d\mathbf{l}=+i-i-i-i=-i$

loop D; $\oint \mathbf{B}\cdot d\mathbf{l}=-i$

$B>A>C=D$

47. $\oint \mathbf{B}\cdot d\mathbf{l}=\mu_0(-i_2-i_3+i_4)$

$=\mu_0(-4-6+8)=-2\mu_0$ Wb/m

48. $\oint \mathbf{B}\cdot d\mathbf{l}=0$

$$\Rightarrow\int_A^B \mathbf{B}\cdot d\mathbf{l}+\int_B^C \mathbf{B}\cdot d\mathbf{l}+\int_C^D \mathbf{B}\cdot d\mathbf{l}+\int_D^E \mathbf{B}\cdot d\mathbf{l}+\int_E^A \mathbf{B}\cdot d\mathbf{l}=0$$

$$\int_E^A \mathbf{B}\cdot d\mathbf{l}=0\Rightarrow \mathbf{B}\perp d\mathbf{l}$$

$$\Rightarrow\int_A^B \mathbf{B}\cdot d\mathbf{l}+\int_B^C \mathbf{B}\cdot d\mathbf{l}=-\int_C^D \mathbf{B}\cdot d\mathbf{l}-\int_D^E \mathbf{B}\cdot d\mathbf{l}$$

$$=\int_D^C \mathbf{B}\cdot d\mathbf{l}+\int_E^D \mathbf{B}\cdot d\mathbf{l}$$

49. $\oint \mathbf{B}\cdot d\mathbf{s}=\mu_0 i_{\text{enclosed}}=\mu_0(Ni)$

50. $$B_{\max}=\frac{\mu_0 i}{2\pi R}\Rightarrow 5\times10^{-3}=\frac{4\pi\times10^{-7}\times i}{2\pi(0.8\times10^{-3})}$$

$\Rightarrow\ i=20$ A

51. $$B_{\text{outside}}=\frac{\mu_0 i}{2\pi r}\Rightarrow 5=\frac{\mu_0 i}{2\pi(2R)}$$

$$B_{\text{inside}}=\frac{\mu_0 ir}{2\pi R^2}\Rightarrow B_{\text{inside}}=\frac{\mu_0 i\left(R-\frac{R}{3}\right)}{2\pi R^2}$$

$$\Rightarrow B_{\text{inside}}=\frac{20}{3}\mu\text{T}$$

52. $\int \mathbf{B}\cdot d\mathbf{l}=\mu_0 i_{\text{enclosed}}$

$$\Rightarrow B\cdot 2\pi\left(\frac{3R}{2}\right)=\mu_0\left\{\frac{i}{(\pi(2R)^2-R^2)}\pi\left[\left(\frac{3R}{2}\right)^2-R^2\right]\right\}$$

$$\Rightarrow\qquad B=\frac{5\mu_0 i}{36\pi R}$$

53. For $r<a, B=0$ $\quad(\because i_{\text{enclosed}}=0)$

For $a\le r<b, B=\frac{\mu_0 i}{2\pi r}$ $\quad(\because i_{\text{enclosed}}=i)$

For $r\ge b,\ B=0$ $\quad(\because i_{\text{enclosed}}=+i-i=0)$

54.

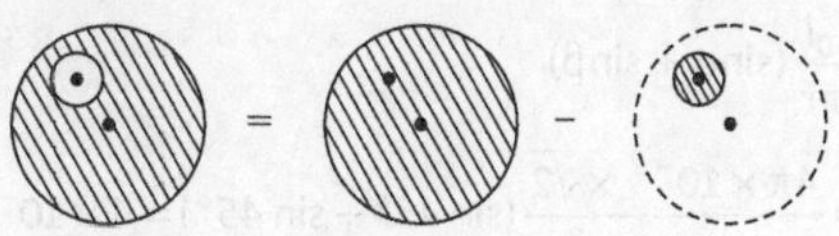

$B=B_1-B_2$

$$=\frac{\mu_0 ic}{2\pi(b^2-a^2)}-0=\frac{\mu_0 ic}{2\pi(b^2-a^2)}$$

55. $$N=\frac{100}{2\pi(5\times10^{-3})};\ n=\frac{N}{L}=\frac{100}{2\pi(5\times10^{-3})(1)}$$

$$B=\mu_0 ni=(4\pi\times10^{-7})\left[\frac{100}{2\pi(5\times10^{-3})(1)}\right]$$

$$=4\times10^{-3}\text{ T}=4\text{ mT}$$

56. $$n=\frac{1}{(0.1\times10^{-3})}=10^4\text{ turns/m}$$

$$B=\mu_0 ni=4\pi\times10^{-7}\times10^4\times1=4\pi\times10^{-3}\text{ T}$$

57. $$B=\frac{\mu_0 Ni}{2\pi R}=\mu_0 ni=4\pi\times10^{-7}\times1000\times\frac{1}{4\pi}=10^{-4}\text{ Wb/m}^2$$

58. $$\int_A^B \mathbf{B}\cdot d\mathbf{l}=\left(\frac{\mu_0 Ni}{2\pi r_1}\right)(r_1\theta)=\frac{\mu_0 Ni\theta}{2\pi}$$

$$\int_D^C \mathbf{B}\cdot d\mathbf{l}=\frac{\mu_0 Ni}{2\pi r_2}(r_2\theta)=\frac{\mu_0 Ni\theta}{2\pi}\quad\Rightarrow\quad\int_A^B \mathbf{B}\cdot d\mathbf{l}=\int_D^C \mathbf{B}\cdot d\mathbf{l}$$

Numerical Value Questions

1. $d\mathbf{l}=idl\,\hat{\mathbf{k}}$

$\mathbf{r}=3\hat{\mathbf{i}}+4\hat{\mathbf{j}}+12\hat{\mathbf{k}}$

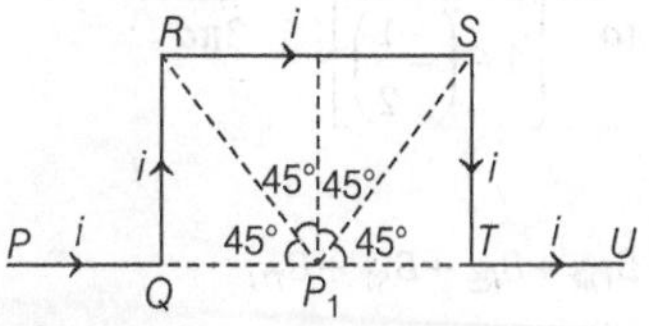

$$d\mathbf{B}=\left(\frac{\mu_0}{4\pi}\right)i\left(\frac{d\mathbf{l}\times\mathbf{r}}{r^3}\right)=\left(\frac{\mu_0}{4\pi}\right)idl\frac{(-4\hat{\mathbf{i}}+3\hat{\mathbf{j}})}{2197}$$

So, $n=4$

2. $\mathbf{n} = \mathbf{dl} \times \mathbf{r} = (-\hat{\mathbf{j}}) \times (\hat{\mathbf{i}} + \hat{\mathbf{j}} + \hat{\mathbf{k}}) = \hat{\mathbf{k}} - \hat{\mathbf{i}}$

$$\hat{\mathbf{n}} = \frac{\hat{\mathbf{k}} - \hat{\mathbf{i}}}{\sqrt{2}}$$

$$\mathbf{B}_{\text{wire}} = \frac{\mu_0 i}{2\pi r}\hat{\mathbf{n}} = \frac{4\pi \times 10^{-7} \times 8}{2\pi(\sqrt{2})}\left(\frac{\hat{\mathbf{k}} - \hat{\mathbf{i}}}{\sqrt{2}}\right)$$

$$= 0.8 \times 10^{-6}(\hat{\mathbf{k}} - \hat{\mathbf{i}})$$

$$\mathbf{B}_{\text{net}} = \mathbf{B}_{\text{wire}} + \mathbf{B}_{\text{ext}} = (0.6 \times 10^{-6})\hat{\mathbf{i}} + (0.8 \times 10^{-6})\hat{\mathbf{k}}$$

$$|\mathbf{B}_{\text{net}}| = 10 \times 10^{-7}\ \text{T}$$

So, $\alpha = 10$

3. $\mathrm{B} = \dfrac{\mu_0 i}{4\pi r}(\sin\alpha + \sin\beta)$

$$B_{AB} = \frac{4\pi \times 10^{-7} \times \sqrt{2}}{4\pi(5 \times 10^{-2})}(\sin 45° + \sin 45°) = 4 \times 10^{-6}\ \text{T}$$

$$B_{CD} = \frac{4\pi \times 10^{-7} \times \sqrt{2}}{4\pi(10 \times 10^{-2})}(\sin 45° + \sin 45°) = 2 \times 10^{-6}\ \text{T}$$

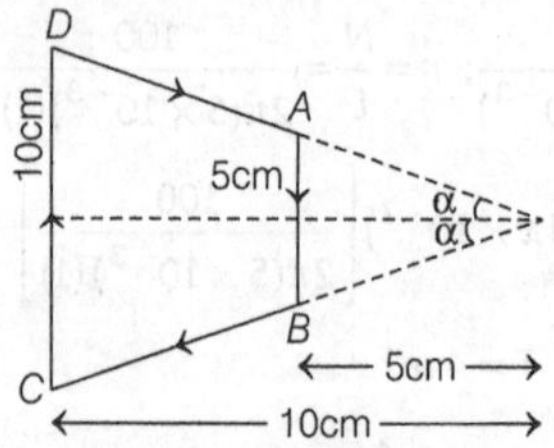

$$\mathbf{B}_{\text{net}} = \mathbf{B}_{AB} + \mathbf{B}_{BC} + \mathbf{B}_{CD} + \mathbf{B}_{DA}$$

$$\mathbf{B}_{\text{net}} = 4 \times 10^{-6} + 0 - 2 \times 10^{-6} + 0$$

$$= 2 \times 10^{-6}\ \text{T} = 2\mu\text{T}$$

4. Magnetic field due to a square coil

$$= 4\left[\frac{\mu_0 i}{4\pi\left(\frac{a}{2}\right)}(\sin 45° + \sin 45°)\right] = \frac{2\sqrt{2}\mu_0 i}{\pi a}$$

$$\mathbf{B} = \mathbf{B}_1 + \mathbf{B}_2 + \mathbf{B}_3 + \mathbf{B}_4 + \ldots$$

$$\Rightarrow B = \frac{2\sqrt{2}\mu_0 i}{\pi a}\left(1 - \frac{1}{2} + \frac{1}{4} - \frac{1}{8} + \ldots\infty\right)$$

$$= \frac{2\sqrt{2}\mu_0 i}{\pi a}\left[\frac{1}{1 - \left(-\frac{1}{2}\right)}\right] = \frac{4\sqrt{2}\mu_0 i}{3\pi a}$$

So, $K = 4$

5. $B_1 = B_{PQ} + B_{QR} + B_{RS} + B_{ST} + B_{TU}$

$$= 0 + \frac{\mu_0 i}{4\pi l}\sin 45° + \frac{\mu_0 i}{4\pi l}(2\sin 45°) + \frac{\mu_0 i}{4\pi l}\sin 45° + 0$$

$$= \frac{\mu_0 i}{\sqrt{2}\pi l}$$

$$2\pi R = 4l \Rightarrow R = \frac{2l}{\pi}$$

$$B_2 = \frac{\mu_0 i}{4\left(\frac{2l}{\pi}\right)} = \frac{\mu_0 i\pi}{8l}$$

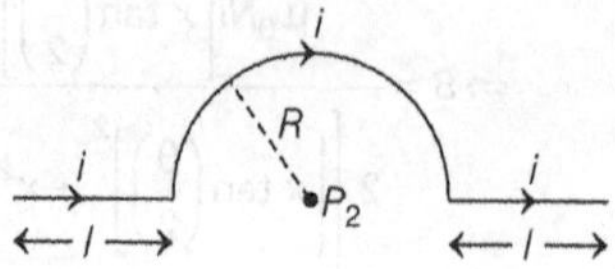

$$\frac{B_1}{B_2} = \frac{\sqrt{32}}{\pi^2}$$

So, $n = 32$

6. $$\int dB = \int_l^{2l} \frac{\mu_0\left[\lambda dx\left(\frac{\omega}{2\pi}\right)\right]}{2x}$$

$$\Rightarrow B = \frac{\mu_0\lambda\omega}{4\pi}\ln 2 = \frac{\mu_0\left(\frac{2}{\pi}\right)(2\pi)}{4\pi}\ln 2$$

So, $n = 4$

7. $$B_{\text{axis}} = \frac{\mu_0 N i R^2}{2(R^2 + x^2)^{3/2}}$$

$$= \frac{4\pi \times 10^{-7} \times 1 \times 2.5 \times (3 \times 10^{-2})^2}{2[(0.03)^2 + (0.04)^2]^{3/2}}$$

$$= 36\pi \times 10^{-7}\ \text{T}$$

So, $n = 36$

8. Curved parts are overlapping

$$\Rightarrow \quad \frac{\mu_0 i_1}{2\pi r} = \frac{\mu_0 i_2}{2\pi r} \Rightarrow i_1 = i_2$$

$$B_1 = \frac{\mu_0 i_1}{2\pi R_1} \text{ and } B_2 = \frac{\mu_0 i_2}{2\pi R_2}$$

$$\frac{B_1}{B_2} = \frac{R_2}{R_1} = \frac{2R}{R} = 2$$

9. $\oint \mathbf{B} \cdot \mathbf{dl} = \mu_0 i_{\text{enclosed}}$

$$\Rightarrow B(2\pi r) = \mu_0\left[\int_0^r \left(\frac{J_0 r}{R}\right) 2\pi r dr\right]$$

$$\Rightarrow B = \frac{\mu_0 J_0 r^2}{3R} = \frac{4 \times 3.14 \times 10^{-7} \times 10^4 \times (6 \times 10^{-3})^2}{3(12 \times 10^{-3})}$$

$$= 12.56\mu\text{T}$$

10. $B = \mu_0 n i \Rightarrow 0.168 = 4\pi \times 10^{-7} \times n \times 2$

$$n = \frac{21 \times 10^4}{\pi}$$

$$N = nl = \left(\frac{21 \times 10^4}{\pi}\right)(1.4)$$

Length of wire $= N(2\pi R)$

$$= \left(\frac{21 \times 10^4 \times 1.4}{\pi}\right)[(2\pi\ (0.01)]$$

$$= 5880\ \text{m}$$

Level 3

Single Choice Correct Questions

1. $B = \dfrac{\mu_0 i}{2\pi r}$ as magnetic field due to current carrying wire is independent of the reference frame.

2. $i d\mathbf{l} = 0.2\hat{\mathbf{i}}$, $\mathbf{r} = \hat{\mathbf{i}} + \hat{\mathbf{j}} + \hat{\mathbf{k}}$

$$d\mathbf{B} = \frac{\mu_0}{4\pi} i\left(\frac{d\mathbf{l} \times \mathbf{r}}{r^3}\right) = \frac{\mu_0}{4\pi}\frac{(0.2)(-\hat{\mathbf{j}} + \hat{\mathbf{k}})}{(\sqrt{3})^3}$$

$$d\mathbf{B} = \left(\frac{4\pi \times 10^{-7}}{4\pi}\right)(0.2)\frac{\sqrt{2}}{3\sqrt{3}} = \sqrt{\frac{8}{27}} \times 10^{-8}\ \text{T}$$

3. $$B_{\text{net}} = \frac{\mu_0 i(\sin 0° + \sin 60°)}{4\pi(2R\sin 30°)} - \frac{\mu_0 i(\sin 0° + \sin 30°)}{4\pi(2R\sin 60°)}$$

$$= \frac{\mu_0 i}{4\sqrt{3}\pi R}$$

$AD = 2R\sin 30°$
$BD = 2R\sin 60°$

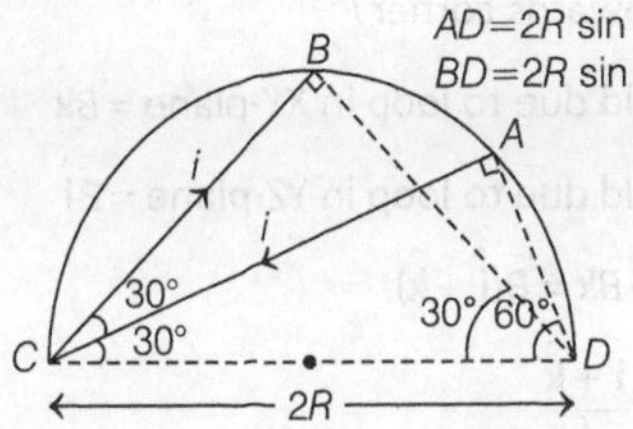

4. Magnetic field due to a square loop $= \dfrac{2\sqrt{2}\mu_0 i}{\pi a}$

$$B_{\text{net}} = \frac{2\sqrt{2}\mu_0 i}{\pi}\left(\frac{1}{a} - \frac{1}{2a} + \frac{1}{3a} - \frac{1}{4a} + \ldots\infty\right)$$

$$= \frac{2\sqrt{2}\,\mu_0 i}{\pi a}\ln 2$$

5. Magnetic field due to charge $q = \dfrac{\mu_0\left(\dfrac{q\omega}{2\pi}\right)}{2R}$

$$B_{\text{net}} = \frac{\mu_0 q\omega}{4\pi}\left(\frac{1}{1} + \frac{1}{2} + \frac{1}{3} + \frac{1}{1} + \frac{1}{2} + \frac{1}{3}\right)$$

$$= \frac{11\mu_0 q\omega}{12\pi} = \frac{11\mu_0 q\left(\dfrac{3}{3}\right)}{12\pi} = \frac{11\mu_0 q}{12\pi}$$

6.

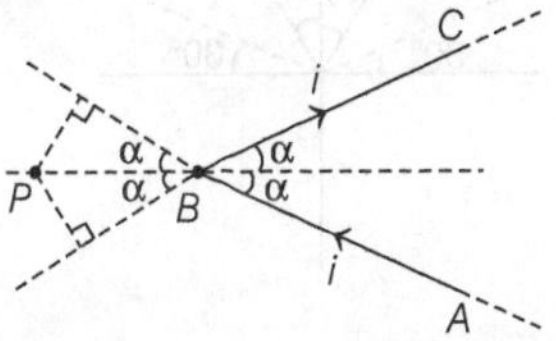

$$\mathbf{B} = \mathbf{B}_{AB} + \mathbf{B}_{BC}$$

$$\Rightarrow B = 2B_{AB} = \frac{2\mu_0 i[\sin 90° + \sin(-(90° - \alpha))]}{4\pi(r_0 \sin\alpha)}$$

$$= \frac{\mu_0 i}{2\pi r_0}\left(\frac{1 - \cos\alpha}{\sin\alpha}\right) = \frac{\mu_0 i}{2\pi r_0}\tan\left(\frac{\alpha}{2}\right)$$

7.

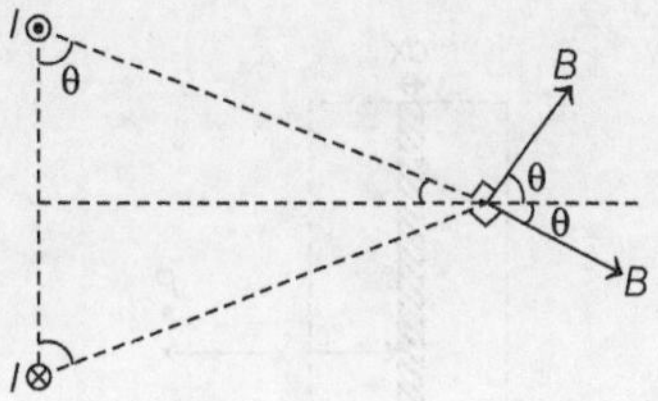

$$B_{\text{net}} = 2B\cos\theta = 2\left(\frac{\mu_0 I}{2\pi r}\right)\cos\theta$$

$$= 2\left(\frac{4\pi \times 10^{-7} \times 4}{2\pi(2)}\right)\cos 60°$$

$$= 0.4\,\mu\text{T}$$

8. Let $\dfrac{\mu_0 i}{2\pi a} = B$

$B_{\text{net}} = 0$

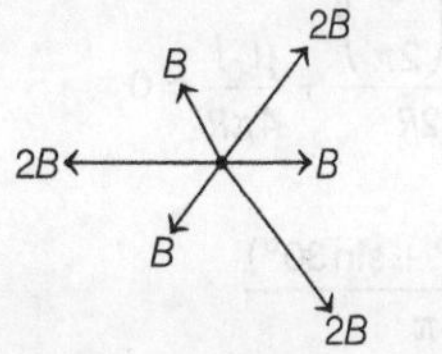

9. $$\mathbf{B}_{AB} = \mathbf{B}_{BC} = \frac{\mu_0 i}{4\pi(2a)}(\sin 0° + \sin 45°)\odot = \frac{\mu_0 i}{8\sqrt{2}\pi a}\odot$$

$$\mathbf{B}_{DE} = \mathbf{B}_{EF} = \frac{\mu_0 i}{4\pi a}(\sin 0° + \sin 45°)\otimes = \frac{\mu_0 i}{4\sqrt{2}\pi a}\otimes$$

$$\mathbf{B}_{CD} = \mathbf{B}_{FA} = 0$$

$$\mathbf{B}_{\text{net}} = 2\left(\frac{\mu_0 i}{4\sqrt{2}\pi a}\right) - 2\left(\frac{\mu_0 i}{8\sqrt{2}\pi a}\right) = \frac{\sqrt{2}\mu_0 i}{8\pi a}$$

10. $$\mathbf{B} = \mathbf{B}_{AB} + \mathbf{B}_{BC} + \mathbf{B}_{CD} + \mathbf{B}_{DE} + \mathbf{B}_{EA}$$

$$= \frac{\mu_0 i}{4\pi a}(\sin 0° + \sin 45°) + \frac{\mu_0 i}{4\pi a}(\sin 0° + \sin 45°) + 0 + \frac{\mu_0\left(\dfrac{3}{4}\right)i}{2R} + 0$$

$$= \mu_0 i\left(\frac{3}{8R} + \frac{1}{2\sqrt{2}a}\right)$$

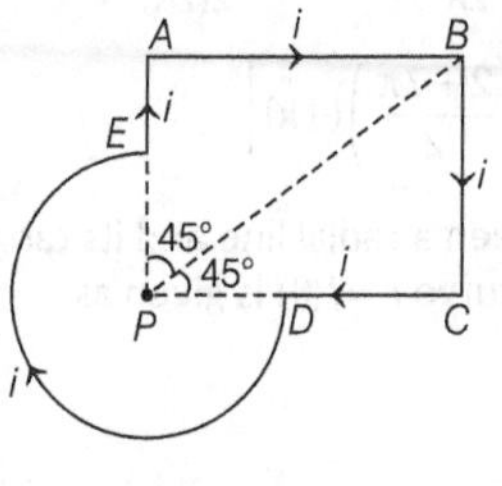

11. Current in dx width $= \left(\dfrac{i}{d}\right)dx$

$$B = \int dB = \int_a^{a+d}\frac{\mu_0\left(\dfrac{i}{d}dx\right)}{2\pi x} = \frac{\mu_0 i}{2\pi d}\ln\left(\frac{a+d}{a}\right)$$

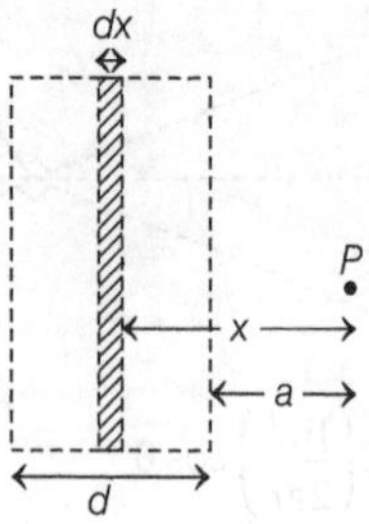

12. $\mathbf{B} = \mathbf{B}_1 + \mathbf{B}_2$

$$B = \frac{\mu_0 (4i)}{2\pi(d-x)} + \frac{\mu_0 i}{2\pi(d+x)}$$

$$= \frac{\mu_0 i}{2\pi}\left(\frac{5d+3x}{d^2-x^2}\right)$$

13. $$B = \frac{\mu_0 i}{4\pi R} - \frac{\mu_0\left(\frac{\theta}{2\pi}\right)i}{2R} + \frac{\mu_0 i}{4\pi R} = 0$$

$\Rightarrow \theta = 2$ rad

15. $$B = \frac{\mu_0 i(\sin 30^\circ + \sin 30^\circ)}{4\pi}\left(\frac{1}{a\cos 30^\circ} - \frac{1}{2a\cos 30^\circ} + \frac{1}{3a\cos 30^\circ} - \ldots\infty\right)$$

$$\mathbf{B} = \frac{\mu_0 i}{2\sqrt{3}\pi a}\left(1 - \frac{1}{2} + \frac{1}{3} - \frac{1}{4} + \ldots\infty\right)\hat{\mathbf{k}}$$

$$\mathbf{B} = \left(\frac{\mu_0 i}{2\sqrt{3}\pi a}\ln 2\right)\hat{\mathbf{k}}$$

16. $$\mathbf{B} = \left\{4\left[\frac{\mu_0\left(\frac{1}{8}\right)i}{2r}\right] + 4\left[\frac{\mu_0\left(\frac{1}{8}\right)i}{2(2r)}\right]\right\}\otimes$$

$$\mathbf{B} = \frac{3}{8}\frac{\mu_0 i}{r}\otimes$$

17. $$\mathbf{B} = \frac{\mu_0 i}{4\pi R}\hat{\mathbf{j}} + \frac{\mu_0\left(\frac{3}{4}\right)i}{2R}(-\hat{\mathbf{k}}) + \frac{\mu_0\left(\frac{1}{4}\right)i}{2(2R)}(-\hat{\mathbf{k}}) + \frac{\mu_0 i}{4\pi(2R)}(-\hat{\mathbf{k}})$$

$$\mathbf{B} = \frac{\mu_0 i}{4\pi R}\left[\hat{\mathbf{j}} + \left(\frac{2+7\pi}{4}\right)(-\hat{\mathbf{k}})\right]$$

18. Angle β between a radial line and its tangent line at any point on the curve $r = f(\theta)$ is given as

$$\tan\beta = \frac{r}{\frac{dr}{d\theta}}$$

For $r = e^{\theta}$; $\tan\beta = \frac{e^{\theta}}{e^{\theta}} = 1 \Rightarrow \beta = \frac{\pi}{4}$

So angle between **dl** and **r** $= \pi - \frac{\pi}{4} = \frac{3\pi}{4}$

Also, $dl = \frac{dr}{\sin\left(\frac{\pi}{4}\right)}$

$\Rightarrow dl = \sqrt{2}dr$

$$\int dB = \frac{\mu_0}{4\pi}i\int_{\theta=0}^{\theta=2\pi}\left(\frac{dl\, r\sin\theta}{r^3}\right)$$

$$\Rightarrow B = \frac{\mu_0 i}{4\pi}\int_{\theta=0}^{\theta=2\pi}\sqrt{2}\frac{dr}{r^2}\sin\left(\frac{3\pi}{4}\right)$$

$$= -\frac{\mu_0 i}{4\pi}[e^{-\theta}]_0^{2\pi} = \frac{\mu_0 i}{4\pi}(1 - e^{-2\pi})$$

19. $\mathbf{B}_{ABCGHEA} = \mathbf{B}_{ABCD} + B_{CGHD} + B_{ADHE}$

$= B_0\hat{\mathbf{j}} + B_0(-\hat{\mathbf{i}}) + B_0\hat{\mathbf{k}}$

$= B_0(-\hat{\mathbf{i}} + \hat{\mathbf{j}} + \hat{\mathbf{k}})$

$= \sqrt{3}B_0$ towards corner F

20. Magnetic field due to loop in XY-plane $= B\hat{\mathbf{k}}$

Magnetic field due to loop in YZ-plane $= B\hat{\mathbf{i}}$

$\mathbf{B} = B\hat{\mathbf{i}} + B\hat{\mathbf{k}} = B(\hat{\mathbf{i}} + \hat{\mathbf{k}})$

$$\hat{\mathbf{B}} = \frac{\mathbf{B}}{B} = \frac{\hat{\mathbf{i}} + \hat{\mathbf{k}}}{\sqrt{2}}$$

21. $$B_{CD} = B_{AB} = \frac{\mu_0 i}{4\pi\left(\frac{a}{2}\right)}(\sin 45^\circ + \sin 45^\circ) = \frac{\mu_0 i}{\sqrt{2}\pi a}$$

$$B_{BF} = B_{EA} = B_{FC} = B_{DE} = \frac{\mu_0 i}{4\pi\left(\frac{a}{2}\right)}(\sin 0^\circ + \sin 45^\circ)$$

$$= \frac{\mu_0 i}{2\sqrt{2}\pi a}$$

$B_1 = B_{AB} + B_{BF} + B_{EA}$

$$= \frac{\mu_0 i}{\sqrt{2}\pi a} + \frac{\mu_0 i}{2\sqrt{2}\pi a} + \frac{\mu_0 i}{2\sqrt{2}\pi a} = \frac{\sqrt{2}\mu_0 i}{\pi a}$$

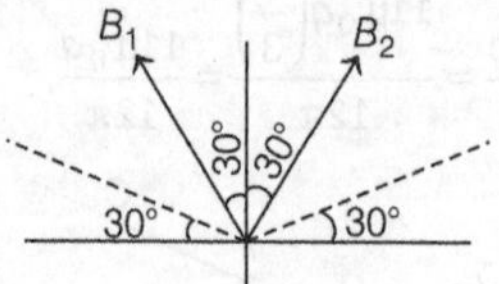

$$B_1 = B_2 = \frac{\sqrt{2}\mu_0 i}{\pi a}$$

$$B_{\text{net}} = B_1\cos 30^\circ + B_2\cos 30^\circ = \sqrt{6}\frac{\mu_0 i}{\pi a}$$

22. $$di = \frac{i}{2\pi R}(R\,d\theta) = \frac{i\,d\theta}{2\pi}$$

$$dB = \frac{\mu_0\left(\frac{i d\theta}{2\pi}\right)}{2\pi R} = \frac{\mu_0 i d\theta}{4\pi^2 R}$$

$$\int \mathbf{dB} = \int dB \sin\theta \hat{\mathbf{i}} + \int dB \cos\theta \hat{\mathbf{j}}$$

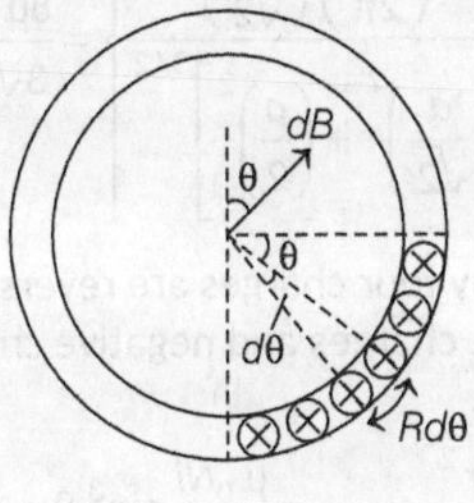

$$\mathbf{B} = \frac{\mu_0 i}{4\pi^2 R}\int_0^{\frac{\pi}{2}} \sin\theta d\theta \hat{\mathbf{i}} + \frac{\mu_0 i}{4\pi^2 R}\int_0^{\frac{\pi}{2}} \cos\theta d\theta \hat{\mathbf{j}}$$

$$\mathbf{B} = \frac{\mu_0 i}{4\pi^2 R}(\hat{\mathbf{i}} + \hat{\mathbf{j}}) \Rightarrow B = \frac{\mu_0 i\sqrt{2}}{4\pi^2 R}$$

23. Magnetic field at the centre of disc will be directed into the plane. As magnetic field lines form closed loops, magnetic field at *A* will be directed out of the plane.

24. $$B_{\text{in}} = \frac{\mu_0 i r}{2\pi R^2} = \frac{\mu_0 i\left(\frac{R}{2}\sqrt{2}\right)}{2\pi R^2} = \frac{\mu_0 i}{2\sqrt{2}\pi R}$$

$$\mathbf{n} = \mathbf{dl} \times \mathbf{r} = dl\hat{\mathbf{j}} \times \left(\frac{R}{2}\hat{\mathbf{i}} + y\hat{\mathbf{j}} + \frac{R}{2}\hat{\mathbf{k}}\right) = dl\frac{R}{2}(\hat{\mathbf{i}} - \hat{\mathbf{k}})$$

$$\hat{\mathbf{n}} = \frac{\hat{\mathbf{i}} - \hat{\mathbf{k}}}{\sqrt{2}}$$

$$\mathbf{B} = \left(\frac{\mu_0 i}{2\sqrt{2}\pi R}\right)\left(\frac{\hat{\mathbf{i}} - \hat{\mathbf{k}}}{\sqrt{2}}\right) = \frac{\mu_0 i}{4\pi R}(\hat{\mathbf{i}} - \hat{\mathbf{k}})$$

25. $$dq = \frac{q}{4\pi R^2}[(2\pi R\cos\theta)Rd\theta]$$

$$di = dq\frac{\omega}{2\pi} = \frac{q\omega}{4\pi}\cos\theta d\theta$$

$$\int dB = \int \frac{\mu_0\left(\frac{q\omega\cos\theta\, d\theta}{4\pi}\right)(R\cos\theta)^2}{2[(R\cos\theta)^2 + (R\sin\theta)^2]^{3/2}}$$

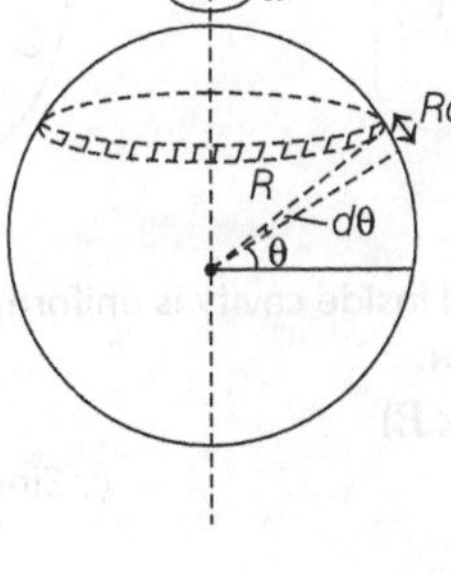

$$B = \frac{\mu_0 q\omega}{8\pi R}\int_{-\frac{\pi}{2}}^{\frac{\pi}{2}} \cos^3\theta\, d\theta = \frac{\mu_0 q\omega}{6\pi R}$$

26. Magnetic field inside a cylinder $= \mu_0 ni$

$$= \mu_0\frac{Ni}{l} = \mu_0\left(\frac{i}{l}\right) = \mu_0\lambda$$

27. $$\oint \mathbf{B}\cdot\mathbf{dl} = \mu_0 i_{\text{enclosed}}$$

$$\Rightarrow B_1\left[2\pi\left(\frac{R}{2}\right)\right] = \mu_0\left[\int_0^{\frac{R}{2}} \alpha r^3 2\pi r dr\right]$$

$$\Rightarrow B_1 = \frac{\mu_0\alpha}{5}\left(\frac{R^4}{16}\right) = \frac{\mu_0\alpha R^4}{80}$$

$$\oint \mathbf{B}\cdot\mathbf{dl} = \mu_0 i_{\text{enclosed}}$$

$$\Rightarrow B_2[2\pi(2R)] = \mu_0\left[\int_0^R \alpha r^3 2\pi r dr\right]$$

$$\Rightarrow \quad B_2 = \frac{\mu_0\alpha R^4}{10}$$

$$\therefore \quad \frac{B_2}{B_1} = 8$$

28. $$i = \frac{dq}{dt} = \lambda\frac{dl}{dt} = \lambda v$$

$$B = \frac{\mu_0 i}{2\pi r} = \frac{4\pi\times 10^{-7}\times 40\times 10^{-6}\times 300}{2\pi\times 5\times 10^{-3}}$$

$$= 4.8\times 10^{-7}\text{ T}$$

29. $$E = \frac{1}{4\pi\varepsilon_0}\frac{qx}{(R^2 + x^2)^{3/2}} \text{ and } B = \frac{\mu_0\left(\frac{q\omega}{2\pi}\right)R^2}{2(R^2 + x^2)^{3/2}}$$

$$\therefore \quad \frac{E}{B} = \left(\frac{1}{\mu_0\varepsilon_0}\right)\frac{1}{(\omega R)} = \frac{c^2}{v} \qquad \left(\because c = \frac{1}{\sqrt{\mu_0\varepsilon_0}}\right)$$

30. $$\int_P^Q \mathbf{B}\cdot\mathbf{dl} = \frac{1}{2}\int_U^Q \mathbf{B}\cdot\mathbf{dl}$$

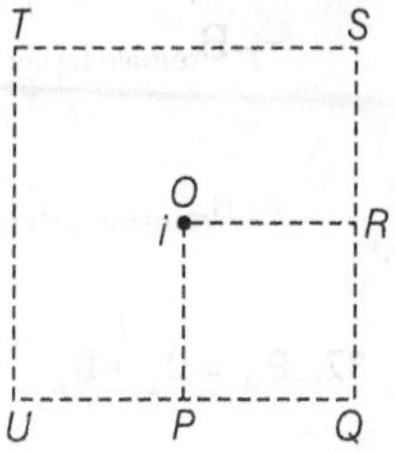

$$= \frac{1}{2}\left(\frac{\mu_0 i}{4}\right) = \frac{\mu_0 i}{8}$$

Similarly $\int_Q^R \mathbf{B}\cdot\mathbf{dl} = \frac{\mu_0 i}{8}$

$$\int_O^P \mathbf{B}\cdot\mathbf{dl} = \int_R^O \mathbf{B}\cdot\mathbf{dl} = 0 \qquad (\because \mathbf{B}\perp\mathbf{dl})$$

$$_{OPQRO}\oint \mathbf{B}\cdot\mathbf{dl} = \int_O^P \mathbf{B}\cdot\mathbf{dl} + \int_P^Q \mathbf{B}\cdot\mathbf{dl} + \int_Q^R \mathbf{B}\cdot\mathbf{dl} + \int_R^O \mathbf{B}\cdot\mathbf{dl}$$

$$= 0 + \frac{\mu_0 i}{8} + \frac{\mu_0 i}{8} + 0 = \frac{\mu_0 i}{4}$$

31. $\oint \mathbf{B}\cdot d\mathbf{l} = \mu_0(i_1 + i_3 - i_3 + i_2) = \mu_0(i_1 + i_2)$

32. $x = a\tan\theta$, $dx = a\sec^2 d\theta$

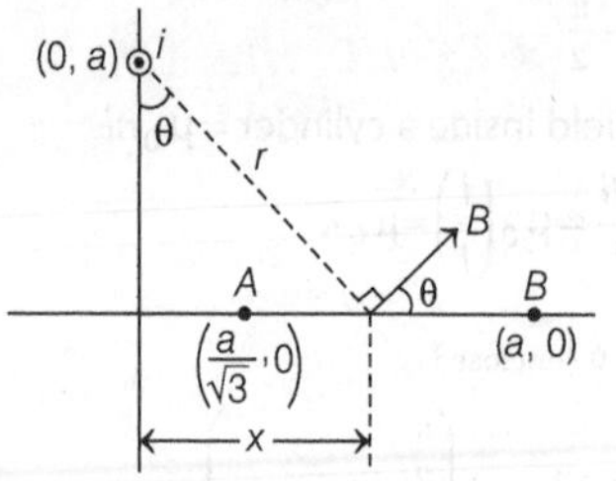

$$\mathbf{B}\cdot d\mathbf{l} = \left(\frac{\mu_0 i}{2\pi r}\right) dx\cos\theta = \frac{\mu_0 i}{2\pi\left(\frac{a}{\cos\theta}\right)} a\sec^2\theta d\theta\cos\theta \quad \Rightarrow$$

$$\int \mathbf{B}\cdot d\mathbf{l} = \frac{\mu_0 i}{2\pi}\int_{\pi/6}^{\pi/4} d\theta = \frac{\mu_0 i}{24}$$

33. $\mathbf{B} = \mathbf{B}_P + \mathbf{B}_Q + \mathbf{B}_R$ and $B \propto i$

$$\oint \mathbf{B}\cdot d\mathbf{l} = \int_A^B \mathbf{B}\cdot d\mathbf{l} + \int_B^C \mathbf{B}\cdot d\mathbf{l} + \int_C^A \mathbf{B}\cdot d\mathbf{l}$$

$$= (4\mu_0 - 12\mu_0 - 15\mu_0) + (5\mu_0 - 12\mu_0 - 12\mu_0) + (4\mu_0 - 15\mu_0 - 12\mu_0)$$

$$= -65\mu_0$$

Using Ampere's law, $\oint \mathbf{B}\cdot d\mathbf{l} = \mu_0 i_{\text{enclosed}}$

$\Rightarrow -65\mu_0 = \mu_0(-3I - 3I + I)$

$\Rightarrow \quad i = 13\text{A}$

35. $x < r; B = 0$

$r \le x < R; B = \dfrac{\mu_0 i(x^2 - r^2)}{2\pi x(R^2 - r^2)}$

$x \ge R; B = \dfrac{\mu_0 i}{2\pi x}$

36. $\mathbf{B}_{\text{remaining sheet}} + \mathbf{B}_{\text{small segment}} = \mathbf{B}_{\text{whole sheet}}$

$$\Rightarrow \mathbf{B}_{\text{remaining sheet}} + \left[\frac{\mu_0(Ja)}{2\pi h}\right](-\hat{\mathbf{i}}) = \left(\frac{\mu_0 J}{2}\right)(-\hat{\mathbf{i}})$$

$$\Rightarrow B_{\text{remaining sheet}} = \frac{\mu_0 J}{2}\left(\frac{a}{h\pi} - 1\right)\hat{\mathbf{i}}$$

37. $\mathbf{B}_A = \mathbf{B}_1 + \mathbf{B}_2 = \dfrac{\mu_0 J}{2}\left(\dfrac{d}{2}\right)\hat{\mathbf{j}} + \dfrac{\mu_0 J}{2}\left(\dfrac{d}{2}\right)\hat{\mathbf{j}}$

$$= \frac{\mu_0 Jd}{2}\hat{\mathbf{j}}$$

Multiple Choice (s) Correct Questions

1. Magnetic field produced by a current carrying wire is independent of reference frame. Conductor is electrically neutral. So, both observers will observe zero electric field.

2. Each rotating charge is equivalent to a current loop carrying current $= \dfrac{q\omega}{2\pi}$.

$$B_{\text{centre}} = 8\left\{\frac{\mu_0\left(\frac{q\omega}{2\pi}\right)\left(\frac{a}{\sqrt{2}}\right)^2}{2\left[\left(\frac{a}{\sqrt{2}}\right)^2 + \left(\frac{a}{2}\right)^2\right]^{3/2}}\right\} = \frac{8\mu_0 q\omega}{3\sqrt{3}\pi a}$$

If polarity of any four charges are reversed, then magnetic field of positive charges and negative charges will cancel out each other.

3. $B = \dfrac{\mu_0 Nir^2}{2[r^2 + (r\cot\theta)^2]^{3/2}} = \dfrac{\mu_0 Ni}{2r}\sin^3\theta$

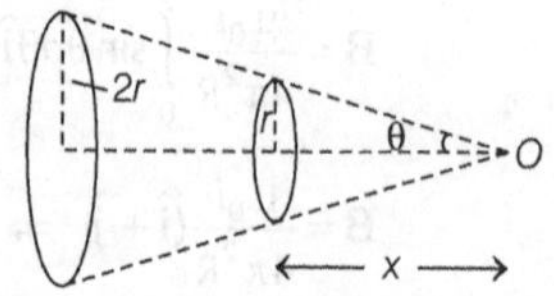

$B \propto \dfrac{1}{r} \quad \Rightarrow \quad \dfrac{B_1}{B_2} = \dfrac{r_2}{r_1}$

$\Rightarrow \quad \dfrac{B}{B_2} = \dfrac{2r}{r}$

$\Rightarrow \quad B_2 = \dfrac{B}{2}$

Total magnetic field at $O = B + \dfrac{B}{2} = \dfrac{3B}{2}$

4. $\mathbf{B} = \dfrac{\mu_0 i_1}{2\pi d}\hat{\mathbf{i}} - \dfrac{\mu_0 i_2}{2\pi d}\hat{\mathbf{j}}$

$B = \dfrac{\mu_0}{2\pi d}\sqrt{i_1^2 + i_2^2}$

5. *A* and *C* are equidistant from the wire. *B* and *D* are also equidistant from the wire.

6. Magnetic field at θ will be zero when velocity of electron will be directed towards *Q*.

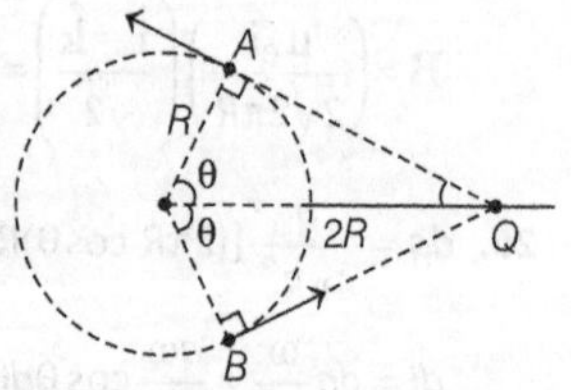

$\cos\theta = \dfrac{R}{2R} = \dfrac{1}{2} \Rightarrow \theta = \dfrac{\pi}{3}$

$\theta = \omega t = \left(\dfrac{\pi}{3}, 2\pi - \dfrac{\pi}{3}, 2\pi + \dfrac{\pi}{3}\right)$

$\Rightarrow \quad t = \left(\dfrac{\pi}{3\omega}, \dfrac{5\pi}{3\omega}, \dfrac{7\pi}{3\omega}\right)$

7. Magnetic field at point *P* in cavity,

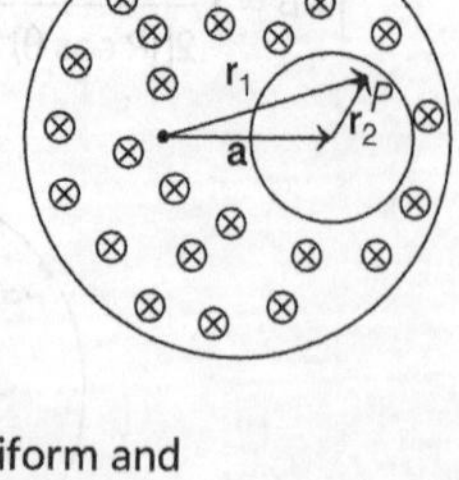

$\mathbf{B} = \mathbf{B}_1 - \mathbf{B}_2$

$$= \frac{\mu_0(\mathbf{J}\times\mathbf{r}_1)}{2} - \frac{\mu_0(\mathbf{J}\times\mathbf{r}_2)}{2}$$

$$= \mu_0\left[\frac{\mathbf{J}\times(\mathbf{r}_1 - \mathbf{r}_2)}{2}\right]$$

$$= \mu_0\left(\frac{\mathbf{J}\times\mathbf{a}}{2}\right)$$

So, magnetic field inside cavity is uniform and perpendicular to **a**.

$\mathbf{F} = q(\mathbf{v}\times\mathbf{B})$

$\mathbf{F} = 0 \qquad (\because \text{Since } \mathbf{v} \,||\, \mathbf{B})$

8. (a) When current are in same directions

$$B = \frac{\mu_0 i}{2\pi l}$$

$$B_{\text{net}} = 2B\sin\theta = \frac{\mu_0 i}{\pi l}\sin\theta$$

$$= \frac{4\pi\times10^{-7}\times10\times\sin60^\circ}{\pi(0.1)}$$

$$= 2\sqrt{3}\times10^{-5}\text{ T}$$

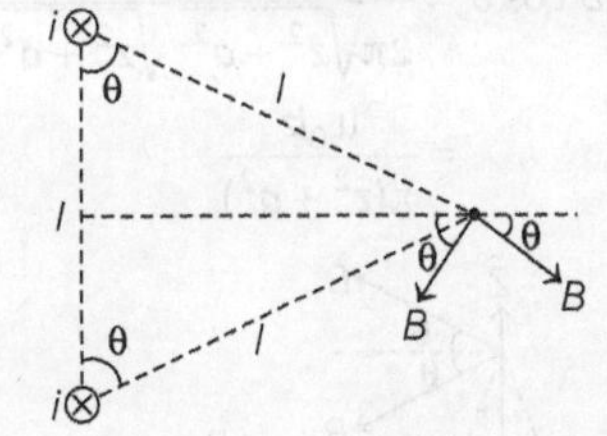

(b) When currents are in opposite directions.

$$B_{\text{net}} = 2B\cos60^\circ = 2\times10^{-5}\text{ T}$$

11. In options (a), (b) and (d) magnetic field is not zero at finite distance from the wires.

12. $q = \sigma(lb) \Rightarrow \frac{dq}{dt} = \sigma b\frac{dl}{dt} \Rightarrow \frac{i}{b} = \sigma v$

So, current per unit width, $J = \sigma v$

$$B = \frac{\mu_0 J}{2} = \frac{\mu_0 \sigma v}{2}, \text{ parallel to plate}$$

Comprehension Based Questions

1. Wire c has greatest radius.
2. Wire a has the greatest magnitude of the magnetic field on the surface.
3. $B = \frac{\mu_0 Jr}{2} \Rightarrow \frac{dB}{dr} = \frac{\mu_0 J}{2}$

   $\Rightarrow$ Slope $\propto J$

   Since, slope is greater for wire a than wire c, current density for wire a is greater than wire c.
4. $\oint \mathbf{B}\cdot d\mathbf{l} = \mu_0 i_{\text{enclosed}}$

   $$B[2\pi(3a)] = \mu_0\left[i_0 - \frac{i_0(\pi[(3a)^2-(2a)^2])}{\pi[(4a)^2-(2a)^2]}\right]$$

   $$B = \frac{7\mu_0 i_0}{72\pi a}$$
5. $\oint \mathbf{B}\cdot d\mathbf{l} = \mu_0 i_{\text{enclosed}}$

   For $r < a$, $B(2\pi r) = \mu_0\left(\frac{i_0}{\pi a^2}\pi r^2\right) \Rightarrow B = \frac{\mu_0 i_0 r}{2\pi a^2}$

   For $a < r < 2a$, $B(2\pi r) = \mu_0 i_0 \Rightarrow B = \frac{\mu_0 i_0}{2\pi r}$

   For $2a < r < 4a$, $B(2\pi r) = \mu_0\left(i_0 - \frac{i_0\pi[r^2-(2a)^2]}{\pi(4a)^2-(2a)^2}\right)$

   $$\Rightarrow \quad B = \frac{\mu_0 i_0(16a^2-r^2)}{24\pi a^2 r}$$

   For $r > 4a$, $B(2\pi r) = 0$

   $$\Rightarrow \quad B = 0$$
6. Lets draw an arc BC of radius OB with centre at origin.

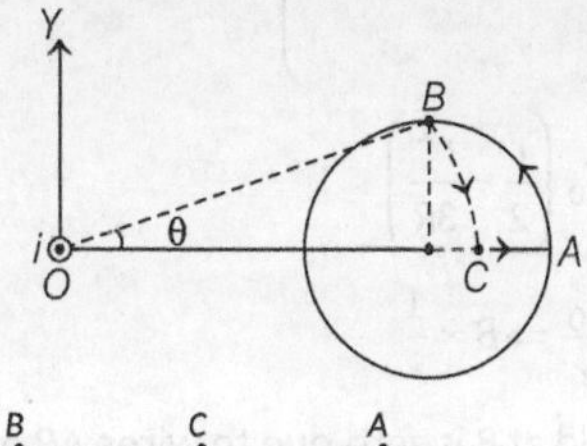

$$\oint_{ABCA}\mathbf{B}\cdot d\mathbf{l} = \int_A^B \mathbf{B}\cdot d\mathbf{l} + \int_B^C \mathbf{B}\cdot d\mathbf{l} + \int_C^A \mathbf{B}\cdot d\mathbf{l}$$

$$\Rightarrow \quad 0 = \int_A^B \mathbf{B}\cdot d\mathbf{l} + \left[-\left(\frac{\mu_0 i}{2\pi(OB)}\right)(OB\theta)\right] + 0$$

$$\Rightarrow \int_A^B \mathbf{B}\cdot d\mathbf{l} = \frac{\mu_0 i}{2\pi}\theta = \frac{\mu_0 i}{2\pi}\tan^{-1}\left(\frac{1}{2}\right)$$

7. Let take two points P and Q on the circle such that $OP = OQ$.

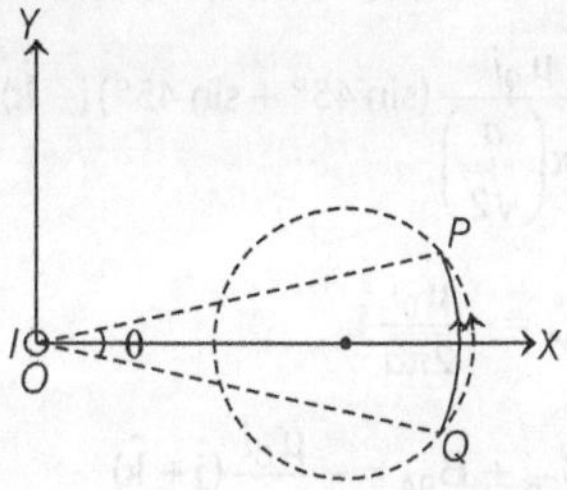

Value of $\int \mathbf{B}\cdot d\mathbf{l}$ along the dotted circle between points P and Q is also equal to value of $\int \mathbf{B}\cdot d\mathbf{l}$ along arc QP centered at origin.

Hence $\int \mathbf{B}\cdot d\mathbf{l} = \frac{\mu_0 i}{2\pi(OP)}[(OP)\theta] = \frac{\mu_0 i}{2\pi}\theta$

θ will be maximum when chords OQ and OP will be tangent to the dotted circle.

So, $\sin\left(\frac{\theta}{2}\right) = \frac{1}{2} \Rightarrow \theta = \frac{\pi}{3}$

$$\int \mathbf{B}\cdot d\mathbf{l} = \frac{\mu_0 i}{2\pi}\left(\frac{\pi}{3}\right) = \frac{\mu_0 i}{6}$$

8. $\oint \mathbf{B}\cdot d\mathbf{l} = \mu_0 i_{\text{enclosed}}$

$$\Rightarrow B(2\pi r) = \mu_0\int_0^r J_0\left(1-\frac{r}{R}\right)2\pi r\,dr$$

$$\Rightarrow \quad B = \mu_0 J_0\left(\frac{r}{2}-\frac{r^2}{3R}\right)$$

$$\frac{dB}{dr} = \mu_0 J_0\left(\frac{1}{2}-\frac{2r}{3R}\right) = 0$$

$$\Rightarrow \quad r = \frac{3R}{4}$$

9. $B_{max} = \mu_0 J_0 \left(\dfrac{\left(\frac{3R}{4}\right)}{2} - \dfrac{\left(\frac{3R}{4}\right)^2}{3R} \right) = \dfrac{3\mu_0 J_0 R}{16}$

10. $r < R, B = \mu_0 J_0 \left(\dfrac{r}{2} - \dfrac{r^2}{3R} \right)$

$r \geq R, B = \dfrac{\mu_0 i_0}{2\pi r} \Rightarrow B \propto \dfrac{1}{r}$

11. Magnetic field at B is zero due to wires AB and CB.

$$\mathbf{B}_{AO} = \frac{\mu_0 i}{4\pi a}(\sin 0° + \sin 45°)(-\hat{\mathbf{j}}) = -\frac{\mu_0 i}{4\pi\sqrt{2}a}\hat{\mathbf{j}}$$

$$\mathbf{B}_{OC} = \frac{\mu_0 i}{4\pi a}(\sin 0° + \sin 45°)(-\hat{\mathbf{k}}) = -\frac{\mu_0 i}{4\sqrt{2}\pi a}\hat{\mathbf{k}}$$

$$\mathbf{B}_{\text{net}} = \mathbf{B}_{AO} + \mathbf{B}_{OC} = -\frac{\mu_0 i}{4\sqrt{2}\pi a}(\hat{\mathbf{j}} + \hat{\mathbf{k}})$$

12. Magnetic field at O due to wires AO and OC will be zero.

$$\mathbf{B}_{CB} = \frac{\mu_0 i}{4\pi\left(\frac{a}{\sqrt{2}}\right)}(\sin 45° + \sin 45°)(-\hat{\mathbf{k}}) = -\frac{\mu_0 i}{2\pi a}\hat{\mathbf{k}}$$

Similarly, $\mathbf{B}_{BA} = -\dfrac{\mu_0 i}{2\pi a}\hat{\mathbf{j}}$

$$\mathbf{B}_{\text{net}} = \mathbf{B}_{CB} + \mathbf{B}_{BA} = -\frac{\mu_0 i}{2\pi a}(\hat{\mathbf{j}} + \hat{\mathbf{k}})$$

Match the Columns Questions

1. (A) $B = 6\left[\dfrac{\mu_0 i}{4\pi(x \cos 30°)}(\sin 30° + \sin 30°)\right] = \dfrac{\sqrt{3}\mu_0 i}{\pi x}$

(B) $\oint \mathbf{B} \cdot d\mathbf{l} = \mu_0 i_{\text{enclosed}}$

$$\Rightarrow B[(2\pi(2x)] = \mu_0 \left(\frac{i\pi[(2x)^2 - x^2]}{\pi[(3x)^2 - x^2]} \right)$$

$$\Rightarrow \qquad B = \frac{3\mu_0 i}{32\pi x}$$

(C) $\oint \mathbf{B} \cdot d\mathbf{l} = \mu_0 i_{\text{enclosed}}$

$$\Rightarrow B[2\pi(1.5x)] = \mu_0 i \quad \Rightarrow \quad B = \frac{\mu_0 i}{3\pi x}$$

(D) $B = n\left\{ \dfrac{\mu_0 i\left[\sin\left(\frac{\pi}{n}\right) + \sin\left(\frac{\pi}{n}\right)\right]}{4\pi x \cos\left(\frac{\pi}{n}\right)} \right\} = \dfrac{\mu_0 i}{2x} \dfrac{\tan\left(\frac{\pi}{n}\right)}{\left(\frac{\pi}{n}\right)}$

when $n \to \infty$, $\dfrac{\tan\left(\frac{\pi}{n}\right)}{\left(\frac{\pi}{n}\right)} = 1 \quad \Rightarrow \quad B = \dfrac{\mu_0 i}{2x}$

2. (A) $B = \dfrac{\mu_0 i}{2\pi x}$

$\Rightarrow B \propto \dfrac{1}{x}$

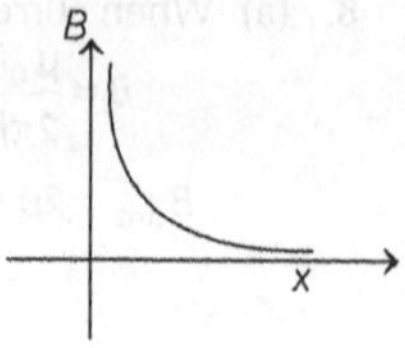

(B) $B = \dfrac{\mu_0 i}{2\pi\sqrt{z^2 + a^2}}$

$$B_{\text{net}} = 2B\cos\theta = \frac{2\mu_0 i}{2\pi\sqrt{z^2 + a^2}} \frac{z}{\sqrt{z^2 + a^2}}$$

$$= \frac{\mu_0 i z}{\pi(z^2 + a^2)}$$

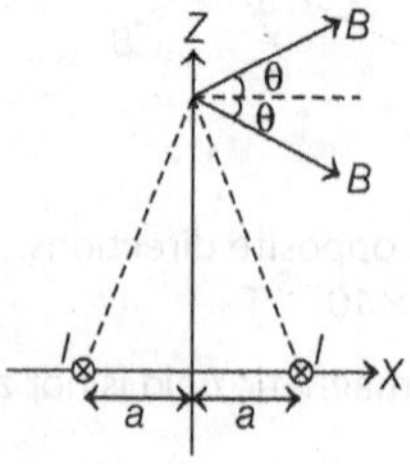

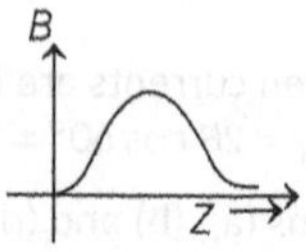

(C) $B = \left(\dfrac{\mu_0 i}{2\pi d} - \dfrac{\mu_0 i}{2\pi x} \right)$

$= \dfrac{\mu_0 I}{2\pi}\left(\dfrac{1}{d} - \dfrac{1}{x} \right)$

d = distance of wire-2 from X-axis.

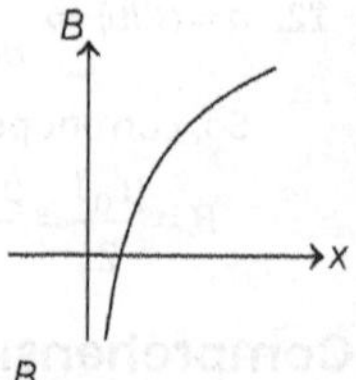

(D) $B = \dfrac{\mu_0 i R^2}{2(R^2 + x^2)^{3/2}}$

$\Rightarrow B \propto \dfrac{1}{(R^2 + x^2)^{3/2}}$

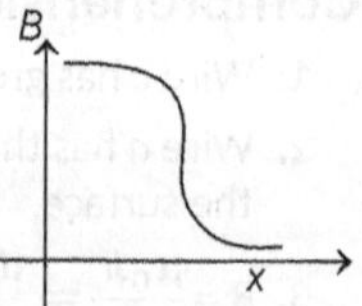

3. A → 3, B → 3, C → 3, D → 2

4. $\mathbf{B}_A = \left(\dfrac{\mu_0 J}{2} + \dfrac{\mu_0 J}{2} \right)$, towards right $= \mu_0 J$, towards right

$\mathbf{B}_B = \dfrac{\mu_0 J}{2} - \dfrac{\mu_0 J}{2} = 0$

$\mathbf{B}_C = \left(\dfrac{\mu_0 J}{2} + \dfrac{\mu_0 J}{2} \right)$, towards left $= \mu_0 J$, towards left

5. (A) Net magnetic field at P is along Z-axis. So, unit vector will be $\hat{\mathbf{k}}$.

(B) For wire AB,

$$\mathbf{n} = d\mathbf{l} \times \mathbf{r} = (dl\hat{\mathbf{i}}) \times \left[z\hat{\mathbf{k}} - \left(-\frac{l}{2}\hat{\mathbf{j}} \right) \right] = dl\left(\frac{l}{2}\hat{\mathbf{k}} - z\hat{\mathbf{j}} \right)$$

$$\hat{\mathbf{n}} = \frac{\mathbf{n}}{|\mathbf{n}|} = \frac{\frac{l}{2}\hat{\mathbf{k}} - z\hat{\mathbf{j}}}{\sqrt{\frac{l^2}{4} + z^2}}$$

(C) For wire BC,

$$\mathbf{n} = d\mathbf{l} \times \mathbf{r} = (dl\hat{\mathbf{j}}) + \left[z\hat{\mathbf{k}} - \left(\frac{l}{2}\hat{\mathbf{i}} \right) \right] = dl\left(z\hat{\mathbf{i}} + \frac{l}{2}\hat{\mathbf{k}} \right)$$

$$\hat{\mathbf{n}} = \frac{\mathbf{n}}{|\mathbf{n}|} = \frac{z\hat{\mathbf{i}} + \frac{l}{2}\hat{\mathbf{k}}}{\sqrt{z^2 + \frac{l^2}{4}}}$$

(D) $$B_{AB} = \frac{\mu_0 i}{4\pi\sqrt{z^2 + \frac{l^2}{4}}}\left(\frac{\frac{l}{2}}{\sqrt{z^2 + \frac{l^2}{2}}} + \frac{\frac{l}{2}}{\sqrt{z^2 + \frac{l^2}{2}}}\right)$$

$$= \frac{\mu_0 il}{4\pi\sqrt{z^2 + \frac{l^2}{4}}\sqrt{z^2 + \frac{l^2}{2}}}$$

$$B_{\text{net}} = 4B_{AB}\cos\theta$$

$$= 4\left(\frac{\mu_0 il}{4\pi\sqrt{z^2 + \frac{l^2}{4}}\sqrt{z^2 + \frac{l^2}{2}}}\right)\left(\frac{\frac{l}{2}}{\sqrt{z^2 + \frac{l^2}{4}}}\right)$$

$$= \frac{\mu_0 il^2}{2\pi\left(z^2 + \frac{l^2}{4}\right)\sqrt{z^2 + \frac{l^2}{2}}}$$

Numerical Value Questions

1. $\mathbf{B}_{AB} = \mathbf{B}_{BC} = \mathbf{B}_{CD}$

$$= \frac{\mu_0\left(\frac{i}{3}\right)(\sin 30° + \sin 30°)}{4\pi(a\cos 30°)} \otimes = \frac{\mu_0 i}{6\sqrt{3}\pi a} \otimes$$

$\mathbf{B}_{AF} = \mathbf{B}_{FE} = \mathbf{B}_{ED}$

$$= \frac{\mu_0\left(\frac{2i}{3}\right)(\sin 30° + \sin 30°)}{4\pi(a\cos 30°)} \odot = \frac{\mu_0 i}{3\sqrt{3}\pi a} \odot$$

$$\mathbf{B}_{\text{net}} = 3(\mathbf{B}_{AF} + \mathbf{B}_{AB}) = 3\left(\frac{\mu_0 i}{3\sqrt{3}\pi a} - \frac{\mu_0 i}{6\sqrt{3}\pi a}\right) = \frac{\mu_0 i}{\sqrt{12}\pi a}$$

$\therefore \quad n = 12$

2. B = Magnetic field at P due to one loop,

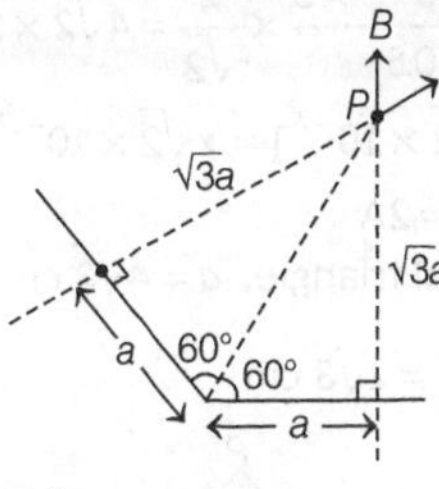

$$B = \frac{\mu_0 ia^2}{2[a^2 + (\sqrt{3}a)^2]^{3/2}} = \frac{\mu_0 i}{16a}$$

$$B_{\text{net}} = \sqrt{B^2 + B^2 + 2B(B)\cos 60°} = \sqrt{3}B$$

$$= \frac{\sqrt{3}\mu_0 i}{16a} = \frac{\sqrt{3}\mu_0 i}{na} \text{ (given)}$$

$\therefore n = 16$

3. Resistance of straight part $= R_1 = \dfrac{\rho(2R\sin 60°)}{\left(\dfrac{\pi d_1^2}{4}\right)}$

Resistance of circular part $= R_2 = \dfrac{\rho\left(\dfrac{4\pi R}{3}\right)}{\left(\dfrac{\pi d_2^2}{4}\right)}$

$$B_{\text{centre}} = \frac{\mu_0 i_1(\sin 60° + \sin 60°)}{4\pi(R\cos 60°)} - \frac{\mu_0 i_2}{2R}\left(\frac{\frac{4\pi}{3}}{2\pi}\right)$$

$$\Rightarrow \quad 0 = \frac{\sqrt{3}\mu_0 i_1}{2\pi R} - \frac{\mu_0 i_2}{3R} \quad \Rightarrow \quad \frac{i_1}{i_2} = \frac{2\pi}{3\sqrt{3}}$$

$$i \propto \frac{1}{R} \quad \Rightarrow \quad \frac{i_1}{i_2} = \frac{R_2}{R_1} \quad \Rightarrow \quad \frac{2\pi}{3\sqrt{3}} = \frac{4\pi d_1^2}{3\sqrt{3}d_2^2}$$

$$\Rightarrow \frac{d_2}{d_1} = \sqrt{2}$$

4. Lets take a current element of width $Rd\theta$ on the loop.

$$2\phi = \theta \quad \Rightarrow \quad \phi = \frac{\theta}{2}$$

$$r = 2R\cos\phi = 2R\cos\left(\frac{\theta}{2}\right)$$

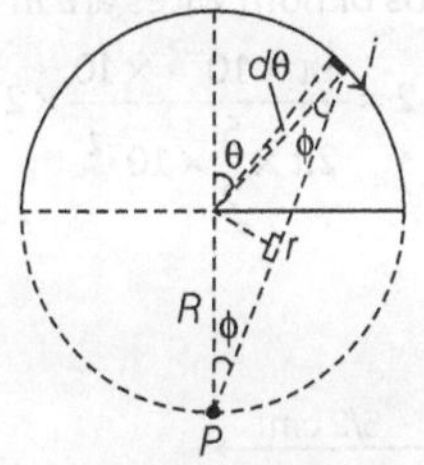

$$dB = \left(\frac{\mu_0}{4\pi}\right)i\frac{(Rd\theta)\left[2R\cos\left(\frac{\theta}{2}\right)\right]\sin(90 - \phi)}{\left[2R\cos\left(\frac{\theta}{2}\right)\right]^3}$$

$$\Rightarrow \int dB = 2\left(\frac{\mu_0 i}{4\pi R}\right)\int_0^{+\frac{\pi}{2}}\frac{d\theta}{4R\cos\left(\frac{\theta}{2}\right)} = \frac{\mu_0 i}{4\pi R}\ln(\sqrt{2} + 1)$$

5. $\mathbf{B} = \mathbf{B}_P + \mathbf{B}_Q$

$$\oint \mathbf{B}\cdot d\mathbf{l} = \int_A^B \mathbf{B}\cdot d\mathbf{l} + \int_B^C \mathbf{B}\cdot d\mathbf{l} + \int_C^D \mathbf{B}\cdot d\mathbf{l} + \int_D^A \mathbf{B}\cdot d\mathbf{l}$$

$$\Rightarrow \mu_0(2i - i) = (-\mu_0 + 2\mu_0) + (-2\mu_0 + 4\mu_0) + (-\mu_0 + 2\mu_0) + (-2\mu_0 + 4\mu_0)$$

$$\Rightarrow \quad \mu_0 i = 6\mu_0 \quad \Rightarrow \quad i = 6\text{ A}$$

6. $$\int dB = \int_0^R \frac{\mu_0\left((\sigma 2\pi r dr)\frac{\omega}{2\pi}\right)}{2r}$$

$$\Rightarrow B = \frac{\mu_0 \sigma \omega R}{2}$$

$$B = \frac{R\mu_0 \sigma\omega}{n} \quad \text{(given)}$$

So, $n = 2$

7. Let $B = \dfrac{\mu_0(1)}{2\pi(0.03)}$

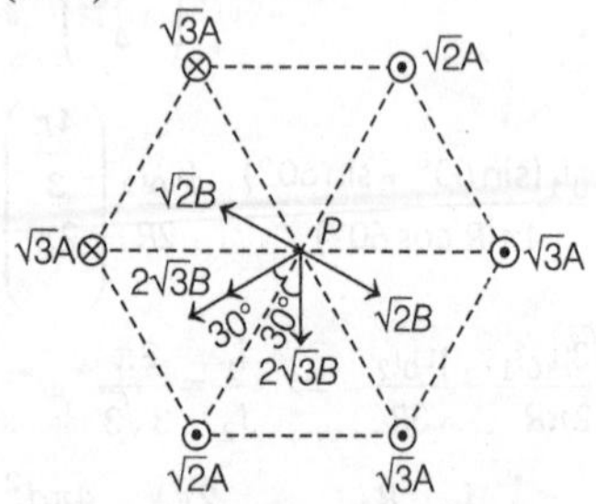

$$B_{\text{net}} = 2(2\sqrt{3}B\cos 30°) = 6B = 6\left(\frac{4\pi \times 10^{-7}}{2\pi(0.03)}\right) = 40\,\mu\text{T}$$

Net magnetic field is directed along vector numbered 09.

So, answer will be 0940.

Previous Years Questions

JEE Main

1. As magnetic fields of both wires are in same direction,

$$B = \frac{\mu_0 I}{2\pi D} \times 2 = \frac{4\pi \times 10^{-7} \times 10}{2\pi \times \frac{5}{2} \times 10^{-2}} \times 2$$

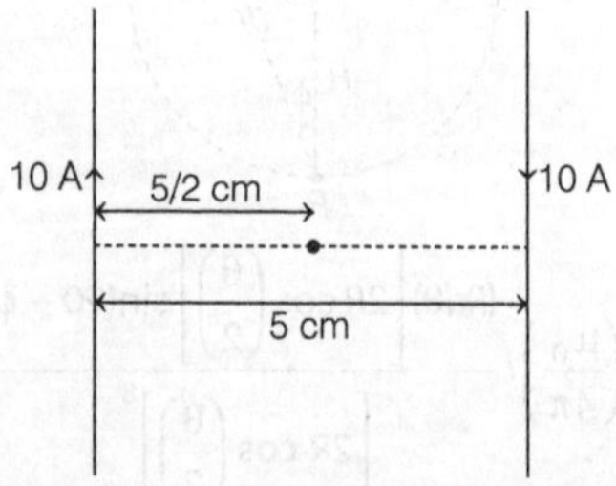

$$= 2 \times 2 \times 2 \times 2 \times 10^{-7} \times 10^2 = 16 \times 10^{-5} = 160 \times 10^{-6}$$

$$B = 160\,\mu\text{T}$$

2. Given, $R_1 = \dfrac{\pi}{2}$m

$$R_2 = \frac{\pi}{4}\text{m}$$

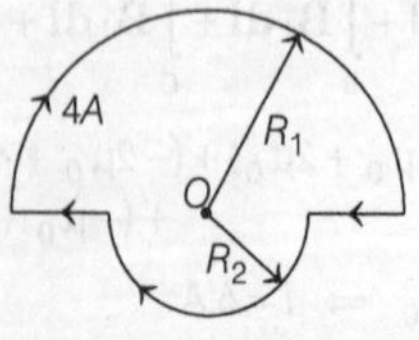

$$B_{\text{centre}} = \frac{\mu_0 I}{4R_1} + \frac{\mu_0 I}{4R_2} = \frac{\mu_0 \times 4}{4}\left[\frac{1}{R_1} + \frac{1}{R_2}\right]$$

$$= \frac{\mu_0 \times 4}{4}\left[\frac{2}{\pi} + \frac{4}{\pi}\right] = \frac{\mu_0 \times 4}{4}\left[\frac{6}{\pi}\right] = \frac{6\mu_0}{\pi}$$

$$\Rightarrow 4\pi \times 10^{-7} \times \left[\frac{6}{\pi}\right] = 24 \times 10^{-7}\,\text{T}$$

$\therefore \quad \alpha = 24$

3. Magnetic field at centre O due to current carrying loop is given by

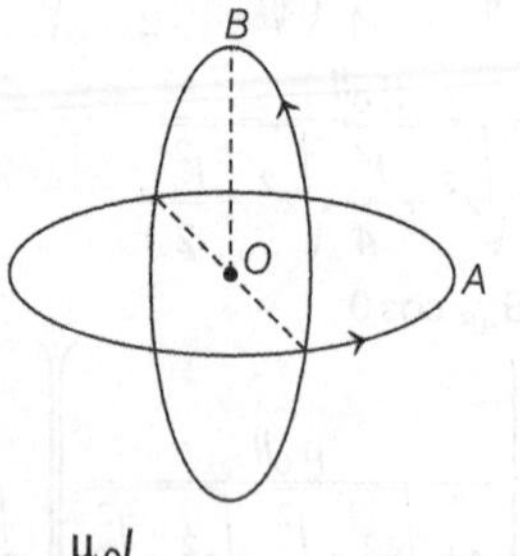

$$B = \frac{\mu_0 I}{2a} \quad \text{...(i)}$$

(I is current in loop, a is radius)

In our case, we have 2 perpendicular identical loops,

So, net magnetic field will be given by

$$B_{\text{net}} = \sqrt{B_1^2 + B_2^2}$$

$$B_{\text{net}} = \sqrt{2}\,B \quad [\because B_1 = B_2 = B]$$

$$B_{\text{net}} = \frac{\sqrt{2}\mu_0 I}{2a} \Rightarrow B_{\text{net}} = \frac{\mu_0 I}{\sqrt{2}a}$$

4. Magnetic field at centre is sum of magnetic fields produced by each side (obtained by Biot-Savart's law)

So, $B_{\text{centre}} = 4 \times \dfrac{\mu_0 I}{4\pi d}(\sin 45° + \sin 45°)$

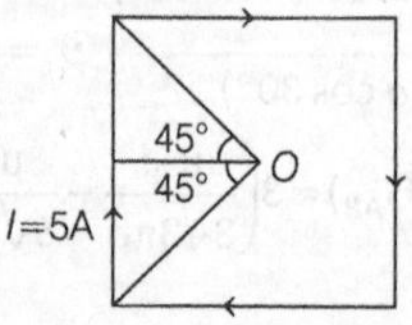

$$= \frac{4 \times 10^{-7} \times 5}{0.5} \times \frac{2}{\sqrt{2}} = 4\sqrt{2} \times 10^{-6}\,\text{T}$$

$$= 40\sqrt{2} \times 10^{-7}\,\text{T} = x\sqrt{2} \times 10^{-7}\,\text{T} \quad \text{(given)}$$

5. Given, current, $I = 2$A

Side of equilateral triangle, $a = 4\sqrt{3}$ cm

$$\therefore \quad QM = \frac{QR}{2} = \frac{a}{2} = 2\sqrt{3}\text{ cm}$$

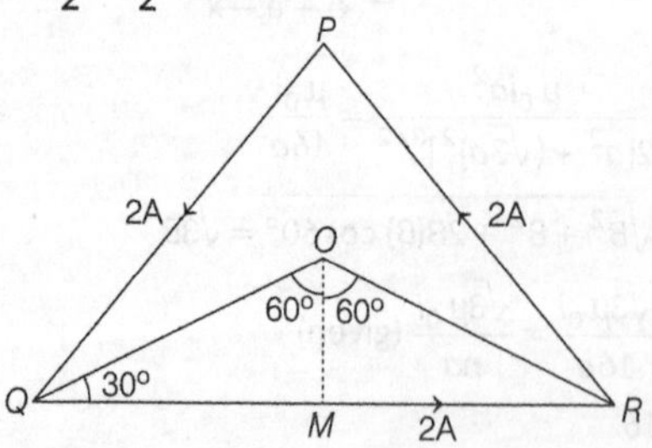

In ΔQOR

$$\tan 30° = \frac{OM}{QM}$$

$$\Rightarrow \quad \frac{1}{\sqrt{3}} = \frac{OM}{2\sqrt{3}} \Rightarrow OM = 2\text{ cm}$$

Magnetic field at 'O' due to current carrying wire QR,

$$B_{QR} = \frac{\mu_0}{4\pi}\cdot\frac{I}{OM}(\sin 60° + \sin 60°)$$

$$= \frac{\mu_0}{4\pi}\cdot\frac{2}{2\times10^{-2}}\left[\frac{\sqrt{3}}{2}+\frac{\sqrt{3}}{2}\right] = \sqrt{3}\times10^{-5}\text{ T}$$

Similarly, $B_{RP} = B_{PQ} = B_{QR} = \sqrt{3}\times10^{-5}$ T

Net magnetic field at 'O' due to all three wires,

$$B = B_{QR} + B_{PQ} + B_{RP} = 3B_{QR}$$

$$= 3\sqrt{3}\times10^{-5}\text{ T}$$

6. Magnetic field at the centre of current carrying coil of R having N number of turns is given as,

$$B = \frac{\mu_0 NI}{2R}$$

For two given situations

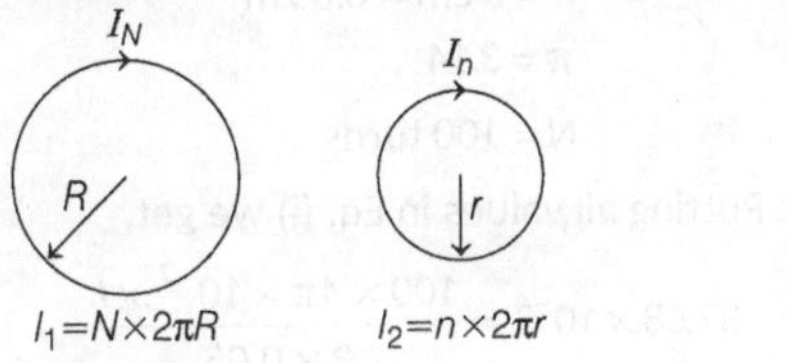

Length remains same, $l_1 = l_2$

$$N\times2\pi R = n\times2\pi r \text{ or } \frac{r}{R} = \frac{N}{n}$$

Since, $B_1 = \dfrac{\mu_0 NI}{2R}$ and $B_2 = \dfrac{\mu_0 nI}{2r}$

$$\therefore \quad \frac{B_1}{B_2} = \frac{\dfrac{\mu_0 NI}{2R}}{\dfrac{\mu_0 nI}{2r}} = \frac{N}{n}\left(\frac{r}{R}\right) = \left(\frac{N}{n}\right)\left(\frac{N}{n}\right) \Rightarrow \frac{B_1}{B_2} = \left(\frac{N}{n}\right)^2$$

7. Given that, $R = \dfrac{\pi}{10}$ m, $I = 3$A, $\mu_0 = 4\pi\times10^{-7}$N/A^2.

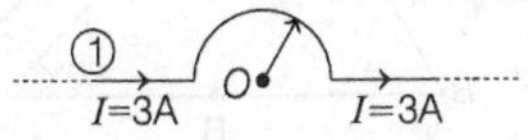

The point O lies on the line of wire-1 and wire-2. So, magnetic field is zero but due to semi-circular arc, it is non zero.

Magnetic field due to semi-circular arc,

$$B = \frac{\mu_0 I}{4R} = \frac{4\pi\times10^{-7}\times3}{4\times\dfrac{\pi}{10}} = 3\times10^{-6}\text{ T}$$

$$\Rightarrow \quad B = 3\ \mu\text{T}$$

8. Magnetic field at centre,

$$B_0 = \frac{\mu_0 I}{2r}$$

Magnetic field at axial point A,

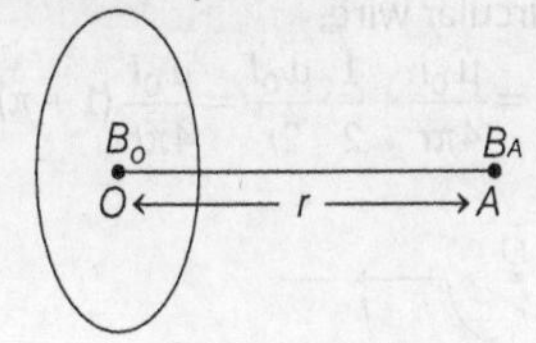

$$B_A = \frac{\mu_0 I r^2}{2(x^2+r^2)^{3/2}}$$

Here, $\quad x = r \quad$ [Given]

$$\Rightarrow \quad B_A = \frac{\mu_s I}{4\sqrt{2}r}$$

So, $\quad \dfrac{B_0}{B_A} = \dfrac{4\sqrt{2}}{2} = \dfrac{2\sqrt{2}}{1}$ or $2\sqrt{2}:1$

9. Given, Number of turns in solenoid

$$N = 1200$$

Length of glass tube,

$$l = 2\text{ m}$$

$\therefore$ Number of turns per unit length,

$$n = \frac{N}{l} = \frac{1200}{2} = 600\text{ turns/m}$$

$$I = 2\text{ A}$$

$\therefore$ Magnetic field intensity at the centre of the solenoid

$$H = \frac{B}{\mu_0} = \frac{\mu_0 ni}{\mu_0} = ni$$

$$H = ni = 600\times2 = 1200$$

$$H = 1.2\times10^3\text{ Am}^{-1}$$

10. A$\rightarrow$ III

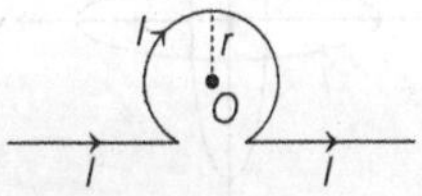

Magnetic field at centre O,

B_0 = Magnetic field due to circular wire − 2 × magnetic field due to straight wire

$$= \frac{\mu_0 I}{2r} - 2\times\frac{\mu_0 I}{4\pi r} = \frac{\mu_0 I}{2\pi r}(\pi - 1)$$

B$\rightarrow$ I

Magnetic field at point O

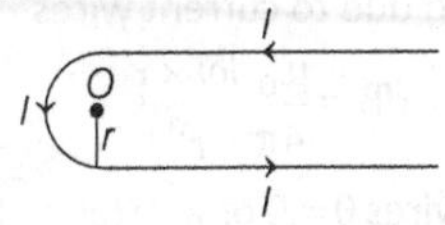

B_0 = 2 × Magnetic field due to straight wire + Magnetic field due to semi-circular wire.

$$= 2\times\frac{\mu_0 I}{4\pi r} + \frac{1}{2}\cdot\frac{\mu_0 I}{2r} = \frac{\mu_0 I}{4\pi r}(2+\pi)$$

C$\rightarrow$ IV

Magnetic field at O

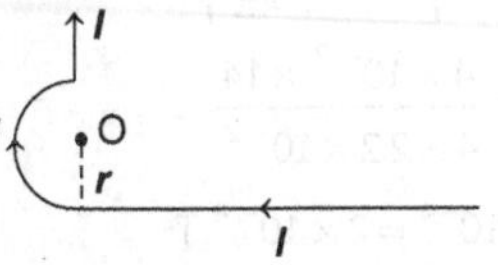

B_0 = Magnetic field due to straight wire + Magnetic field due to semi-circular wire,

$$= \frac{\mu_0 I}{4\pi r} + \frac{1}{2} \cdot \frac{\mu_0 I}{2r} = \frac{\mu_0 I}{4\pi r}(1+\pi)$$

D→ II,

Magnetic field due to straight wire will be zero.

$\therefore B_0$ = Magnetic field due to semi-circular wire.

$$= \frac{1}{2} \times \frac{\mu_0 I}{2r} = \frac{\mu_0 I}{4r}$$

11. Using $B_{\text{axis}} = \dfrac{\mu_0 I R^2}{2(R^2 + x^2)^{3/2}}$

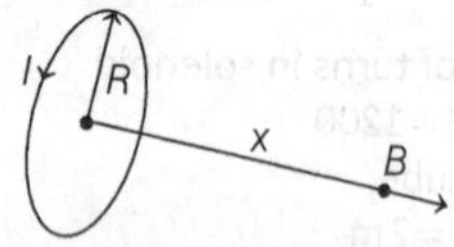

So, $\dfrac{B_{\text{axis}}(x=0)}{B_{\text{axis}}(x=r)} = \dfrac{\mu_0 I r^2}{2(r^2+0)^{3/2}} \times \dfrac{2(r^2+r^2)^{3/2}}{\mu_0 I r^2}$

$$= \frac{2^{3/2} r^3}{r^3} = \frac{\sqrt{8}}{1}$$

So, $x = 8$

12.

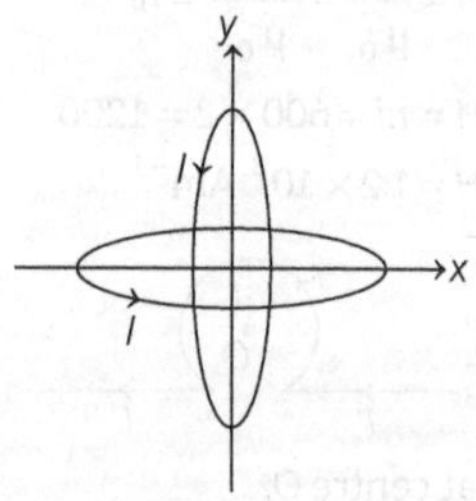

$$\mathbf{B}_{\text{net}} = \frac{\mu_0 i}{2r}\hat{i} + \frac{\mu_0 i}{2r}\hat{j} = \frac{\mu_0 i}{2r}\sqrt{2}$$

$$= 4\pi \times 10^{-7} \times \sqrt{2} \times \sqrt{2} \times \frac{1}{2 \times 0.2}$$

$$= 2 \times 3.14 \times 10^{-6} = 628 \times 10^{-8}\ \text{T}$$

13. Magnetic field due to current wires

$$d\mathbf{B} = \frac{\mu_0}{4\pi} \frac{I\delta l \times \mathbf{r}}{r^3}$$

For straight wires $\theta = 0$ or π

$\therefore \quad B = 0 \qquad (\because \delta l \times \mathbf{r} = \delta l r \sin\theta\, \hat{n})$

For semi circular arc $\sum dl = \pi r$ and

$$\theta = \frac{\pi}{2}$$

$$\therefore \quad \mathbf{B}_2 = \frac{\mu_0}{4\pi} \frac{\sum I\delta l \times \mathbf{r}}{r^3} = \frac{\mu_0}{4\pi} \frac{I}{r^2} \times \pi r$$

$$= \frac{\mu_0 I}{4r} = \frac{4 \times 10^{-7} \times 14}{4 \times 2.2 \times 10^{-2}}$$

$$= 1.9 \times 10^{-4} = 2 \times 10^{-4}\ \text{T}$$

14. Given, $v = 6.76 \times 10^6\ \text{ms}^{-1}$

$$r = 0.52\ \text{Å} = 0.52 \times 10^{-10}\ \text{m}$$

Current associated with revolving electron,

$$I = \frac{e}{T} = \frac{e}{\left(\frac{2\pi r}{v}\right)} = \frac{ev}{2\pi r}$$

$\therefore$ Magnetic field, $B = \dfrac{\mu_0 I}{2r} = \dfrac{\mu_0 ev}{4\pi r^2}$

$$= \left(\frac{\mu_0}{4\pi}\right) \cdot \frac{ev}{r^2}$$

$$= \frac{10^{-7} \times 1.6 \times 10^{-19} \times 6.76 \times 10^6}{(0.52 \times 10^{-10})^2} = 40\ \text{T}$$

15. We know that, formula for B_{centre} of a coil is

$$B_{\text{centre}} = \frac{\mu_0 NI}{2R} \qquad \text{... (i)}$$

where, N = total no. of turns in the coil

I = current in the coil

R = radius of coil

Given, $B_{\text{centre}} = 37.68 \times 10^{-4}$ T

$R = 5\ \text{cm} = 0.05\ \text{m}$

$\pi = 3.14$

$N = 100$ turns

$\therefore$ Putting all values in Eq. (i) we get,

$$37.68 \times 10^{-4} = \frac{100 \times 4\pi \times 10^{-7} \times I}{2 \times 0.05}$$

$$(\because \mu_0 = 4\pi \times 10^{-7}\ \text{TmA}^{-1})$$

$\Rightarrow \quad I = 3\text{A}$

16. Given, $i = 10$ A, $B = 0.5$ T

Since, $BC = CD = BD = l$ (say) $= 5$ cm, so ΔBCD is an equilateral triangle and angle between CD and BD is 60°. Also, as magnetic field is along BD, so angle between **B** and **l** is 60°

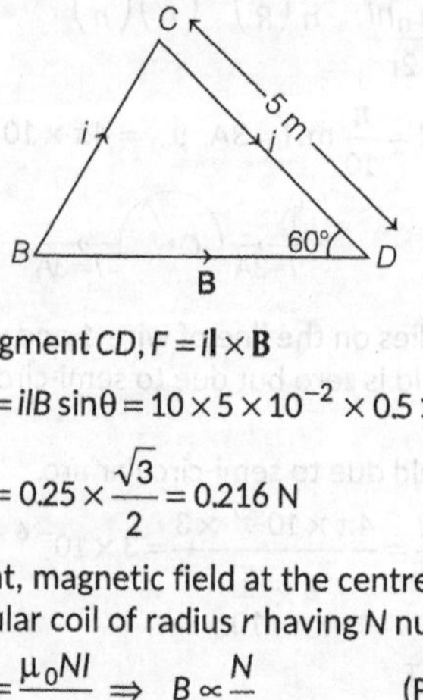

$\therefore$ Force of segment CD, $F = i\mathbf{l} \times \mathbf{B}$

$$= ilB\sin\theta = 10 \times 5 \times 10^{-2} \times 0.5 \times \sin 60°$$

$$= 0.25 \times \frac{\sqrt{3}}{2} = 0.216\ \text{N}$$

17. We know that, magnetic field at the centre of current I carrying circular coil of radius r having N number of turns is

$$B = \frac{\mu_0 NI}{2r} \Rightarrow B \propto \frac{N}{r} \qquad \text{(For same current)}$$

$$\Rightarrow \quad \frac{B_X}{B_Y} = \frac{N_X}{N_Y} \times \frac{r_Y}{r_X}$$

Here, $N_X = 200, N_Y = 400$

$$r_X = r_Y = 20 \text{ cm}$$

$\therefore \quad \frac{B_X}{B_Y} = \frac{200}{400} \times \frac{20}{20} = \frac{1}{2}$

$\Rightarrow \quad B_X : B_Y = 1 : 2$

18. **Case - I** Magnetic field at the centre of circular current carrying coil having $2(N_1 = 2)$ turns is given as

$$B_1 = \frac{\mu_0 N_1 I}{2r_1}$$

where, I = Current and r_1 = radius of circular coil.

$$B_1 = \frac{\mu_0 \times 2 \times I}{2r_1}$$

$\Rightarrow \quad B_1 = \frac{2\mu_0 I}{2r_1}$ ...(i)

Case -2 Magnetic field at the centre of circular current carrying coil having 5 turns ($N_2 = 5$) is given as

$$B_2 = \frac{\mu_0 N_2 I}{2r_2}$$

$\Rightarrow \quad B_2 = \frac{5\mu_0 I}{2r_2}$ ...(ii)

Dividing Eq. (ii) by Eq. (i), we get

$$\frac{B_2}{B_1} = \frac{5r_1}{2r_2} \quad \text{...(iii)}$$

According to given situation length of current carring wire in both cases is same.

i.e. $\quad l_1 = l_2$

$\Rightarrow \quad 2 \times 2\pi r_1 = 5 \times 2\pi r_2 \Rightarrow 2r_1 = 5r_2$

$\Rightarrow \quad \frac{r_1}{r_2} = \frac{5}{2}$

From Eq. (iii), $\frac{B_2}{B_1} = \frac{5}{2} \times \frac{5}{2} = \frac{25}{4}$

19.

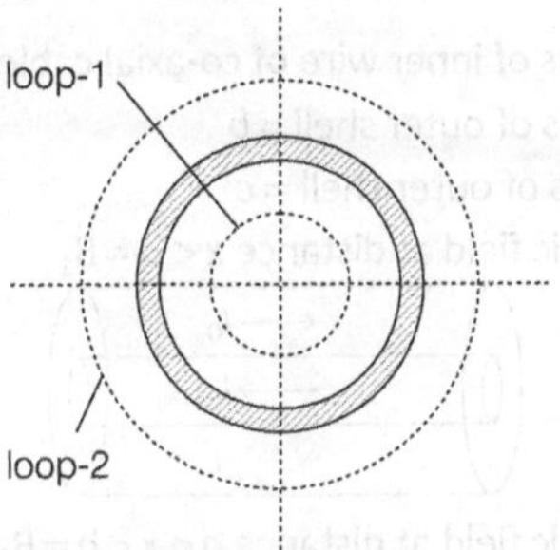

Consider two loops, loop-1 and loop-2.

For loop-1, there is no enclosed current so following Ampere's law,

$$\oint \mathbf{B} \cdot d\mathbf{l} = \mu_0 I_{\text{net}}$$

$\Rightarrow \quad B_{\text{in}} = 0$

Also, applying ampere circuital law for loop-2.

$$\oint \mathbf{B} \cdot d\mathbf{l} = B \times 2\pi r = \mu_0 I_{\text{net}}$$

$\Rightarrow \quad B_{\text{out}} = \frac{\mu_0 I}{2\pi r}$ or $B_{\text{out}} \propto \frac{1}{r}$

So, B varies with distance from centre as

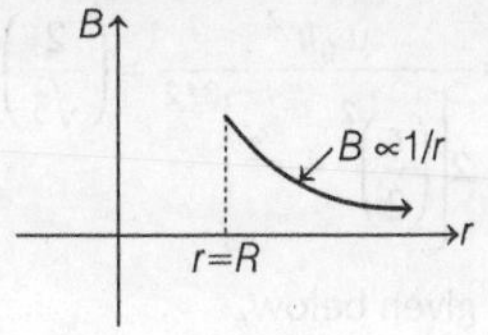

20. Magnetic field due to a long current carrying solenoid

$$B = \mu_0 nI \quad \text{...(i)}$$

where, μ_0 = permeability of free space,

n = number of turns per cm

and $\quad I$ = current flowing through the solenoid.

When $I' = 2I$ and $n' = \frac{n}{2}$, then

new value of magnetic field.

$$B' = \mu_0 n' I' = \mu_0 \left(\frac{n}{2}\right) \cdot 2I = \mu_0 nI = B \quad \text{[from Eq. (i)]}$$

21.

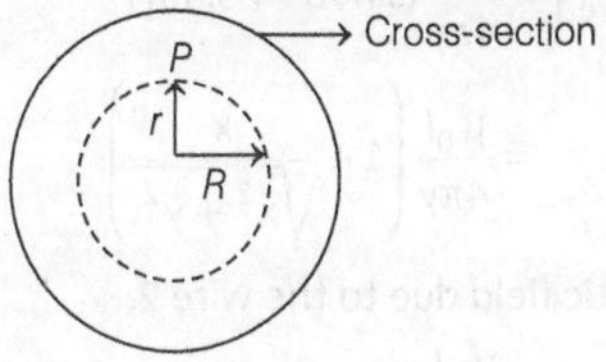

Current density, $J = \frac{I}{\pi R^2}$

$\therefore$ Current enclosed (i) in area

$$\pi r^2 = J\pi r^2 = \frac{I}{\pi R^2} \times \pi r^2 = \frac{I}{R}$$

Now, by using Ampere's circuital law, we get

$$\oint \mathbf{B} \cdot d\mathbf{l} = \mu_0 i$$

$\Rightarrow \quad \oint B \cdot dl \cos 0° = \mu_0 I \frac{r^2}{R^2}$

$\Rightarrow \quad B\oint dl = \mu_0 I \frac{r^2}{R^2}$

[$\because |\mathbf{B}|$ = constant on amperian loop]

$\Rightarrow \quad B \cdot 2\pi r = \mu_0 I \frac{r^2}{R^2}$

$\Rightarrow \quad B = \frac{\mu_0 I}{2\pi} \frac{r^2}{rR^2} = \left(\frac{\mu_0 I}{2\pi R^2}\right) r$

$\therefore \quad$ Clearly $B \propto r$ for $r < R$

22. According to given situation, magnetic field due to current carrying circular loop at the centre,

$$B_c = \frac{\mu_0 I}{2r} \quad \text{... (i)}$$

We know, magnetic field on the axis at a distance x from the centre of circular coil,

$$B = \frac{\mu_0 I r^2}{2(x^2 + r^2)^{3/2}}$$

Here, $x = \frac{r}{2}$,

Hence, $$B' = \frac{\mu_0 I r^2}{2\left[\left(\frac{r}{2}\right)^2 + r^2\right]^{3/2}} = \left(\frac{2}{\sqrt{5}}\right)^3 \frac{\mu_0 I}{2r} = \left(\frac{2}{\sqrt{5}}\right)^3 B$$

23. The diagram is given below,

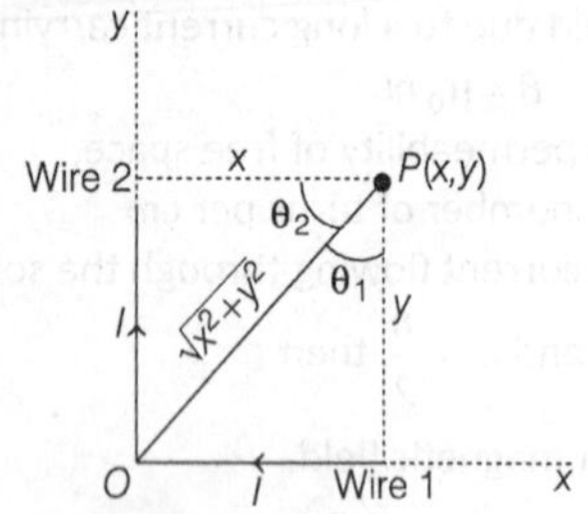

The magnetic field due to the wire 1,

$$B_{\text{wire 1}} = \frac{\mu_0 I}{4\pi y}(\sin 90° + \sin\theta_1)$$

$$= \frac{\mu_0 I}{4\pi y}\left(1 + \frac{x}{\sqrt{x^2 + y^2}}\right)$$

The magnetic field due to the wire 2,

$$B_{\text{wire 2}} = \frac{\mu_0 I}{4\pi x}(\sin 90° + \sin\theta_2)$$

$$= \frac{\mu_0 I}{4\pi x}\left(1 + \frac{y}{\sqrt{x^2 + y^2}}\right)$$

Thus, the total magnetic field,

$$B = B_1 + B_2$$

$$= \frac{\mu_0 I}{4\pi}\left(\frac{1}{y} + \frac{x}{y\sqrt{x^2 + y^2}} + \frac{1}{x} + \frac{y}{x\sqrt{x^2 + y^2}}\right)$$

$$= \frac{\mu_0 I}{4\pi xy}[\sqrt{x^2 + y^2} + (x + y)]$$

24. Given, number of turns $= N$

Inner radius $= a$, Outer radius $= b$

Current $= I$

Consider an element of thickness dr at a distance r from the centre.

Now, number of turns in dr element, $dN = \frac{N}{(b-a)} dr$

Magnetic field due to this element at the centre,

$$dB = \frac{\mu_0}{2} \frac{dN \cdot I}{r}$$

$$\therefore \quad dB = \frac{1}{2} \frac{\mu_0 I}{r} \frac{N}{(b-a)} dr$$

$\therefore$ Total magnetic field at the centre,

$$B = \int_a^b dB = \int_a^b \frac{\mu_0 IN}{2(b-a)} \frac{dr}{r}$$

$$= \frac{N}{2} \frac{\mu_0 I}{(b-a)} \ln r \Big|_a^b = \frac{N}{2} \frac{\mu_0 I}{(b-a)} \ln\left(\frac{b}{a}\right)$$

25. Given, electric current, $I = 1.5$ A

Side of triangle, $l = 9\text{ cm} = 9 \times 10^{-2}$ m

Let $OD = OE = OF = r \Rightarrow AD = \frac{l}{2}$

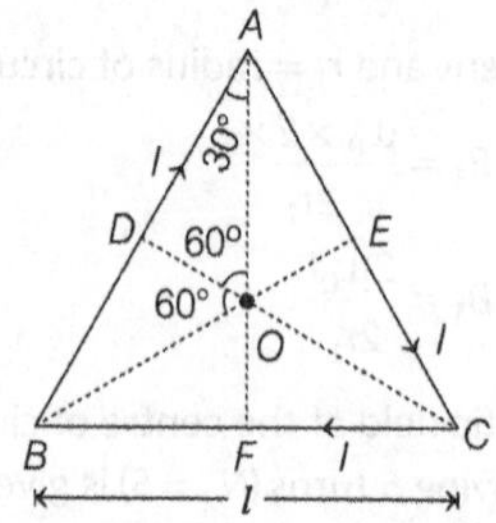

In ΔAOD, $\frac{OD}{AD} = \tan 30° \Rightarrow OD = AD \tan 30°$

$$\therefore \quad r = OD = \frac{l}{2} \times \frac{1}{\sqrt{3}} = \frac{l}{2\sqrt{3}}$$

Magnetic field due to AB at O,

$$B_1 = \frac{\mu_0 I}{4\pi r}[\sin 60° + \sin 60°] = \frac{\mu_0 I}{4\pi r} \times \frac{2\sqrt{3}}{2}$$

$$\Rightarrow \quad B_1 = \frac{\mu_0 I\sqrt{3}}{4\pi r} \quad \text{(perpendicular inward)}$$

Now, total magnetic field at O due to all sides,

$$B = 3B_1 = \frac{\mu_0 I}{4\pi r} 3\sqrt{3}$$

By substituting the values, we get

$$B = \frac{10^{-7} \times 1.5 \times 3\sqrt{3} \times 2\sqrt{3}}{9 \times 10^{-2}}$$

$$= 3 \times 10^{-5}\text{ T} \quad \text{(inside the plane of triangle)}$$

26. Given, radius of inner wire of co-axial cable $= a$

Innner radius of outer shell $= b$

Outer radius of outer shell $= c$

Let, magnetic field at distance $x < a = B_1$

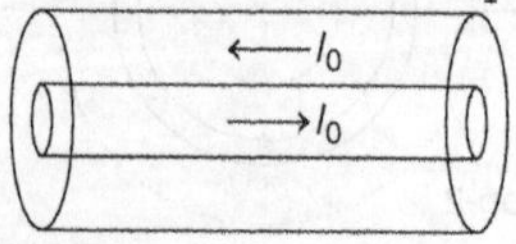

and magnetic field at distance $a < x < b = B_2$

By using Ampere circuital law,

$$\oint B \cdot dl = n\mu_0 I_{enc}$$

where, dl = perimeter of small circular element,

n = number of turns,

μ_0 = free space permeability

and I = current.

$$\therefore \quad B_1 \cdot 2\pi x = n\mu_0 I_{enc}$$

$$\Rightarrow \quad B_1 = \frac{\mu_0}{2\pi x}\frac{I_0}{\pi a^2}.\pi x^2 = \frac{\mu_0}{2\pi}\frac{I_0 x}{a^2} \quad \text{... (i)}$$

Now, for $B_2 (a < x < b)$

$$B_2 \cdot 2\pi x = \mu_0 I_0$$

$$B_2 = \frac{1}{2\pi}\frac{\mu_0 I_0}{x} \quad \text{...(ii)}$$

∴ From Eqs. (i) and (ii) we will get

$$\frac{B_1}{B_2} = \frac{\frac{\mu_0 I_0 x}{2\pi a^2}}{\frac{\mu_0 I_0}{2\pi x}} = \frac{x^2}{a^2}$$

27. According to question, the fractional change in the magnetic field intensity is given by

$$\frac{\Delta B}{B} = 1 - \frac{B_{axis}}{B_{centre}}$$

Substituting the values of B_{axis} and B_{centre}, we get

$$\frac{\Delta B}{B} = 1 - \frac{\frac{\mu_0}{4\pi}\frac{2\pi i a^2}{(a^2+r^2)^{3/2}}}{\frac{\mu_0}{4\pi}\frac{2\pi i}{a}} = 1 - \frac{a^3}{(a^2+r^2)^{3/2}}$$

$$= 1 - \frac{a^3}{a^3\left(1+\frac{r^2}{a^2}\right)^{3/2}} = 1 - \left(1+\frac{r^2}{a^2}\right)^{-3/2}$$

Given that, $r < a$, applying Binomial expansion,

$$(1-x)^{-n} = 1 - x + \frac{2x^2}{2!} - \frac{3\times 2x^3}{3!} \dots (-1)^n x^n, = (1+nx)$$

we get $\quad \dfrac{\Delta B}{B} = 1 - \left(1 - \dfrac{3}{2}\dfrac{r^2}{a^2}\right)$

$$\frac{\Delta B}{B} = 1 - 1 + \frac{3}{2}\frac{r^2}{a^2}$$

$\dfrac{\Delta B}{B} = \dfrac{3}{2}\dfrac{r^2}{a^2}$, which is the required expression.

28. We know that magnetic field inside circular cross-section carrying current I (which is uniformly distributed across the cross-section) is given as

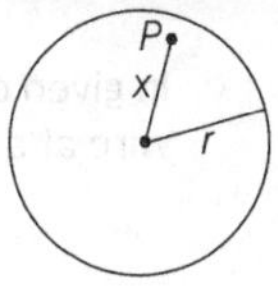

$$B = \frac{\mu_0 I x}{2\pi r^2}$$

$$\therefore \quad B \propto x$$

Magnetic field outside the circular cross-section is given as

$$B = \frac{\mu_0 I}{2\pi r} \Rightarrow B \propto \frac{1}{r}$$

Hence, graph between B and r showing in option (c) is correct.

29. **For capacitance (C),**

∵ Charge, $q = CV$

$$\Rightarrow \quad [C] = \left[\frac{q}{V}\right] = \frac{[AT]}{[ML^2T^{-3}A^{-1}]} = [M^{-1}L^{-2}T^4A^2]$$

For permittivity of free space (ε_0),

∵ According to Coulomb's law

$$F = \frac{kq_1q_2}{r^2} = \frac{1}{4\pi\varepsilon_0}\cdot\frac{q_1q_2}{r^2}$$

$$[\varepsilon_0] = \frac{[q_1][q_2]}{[F][r^2]} = \frac{[AT][AT]}{[MLT^{-2}][L^2]}$$

$$\Rightarrow \quad [\varepsilon_0] = [M^{-1}L^{-3}T^4A^2]$$

For permeability of free space (μ_0),

∵ Speed of light, $c = \dfrac{1}{\sqrt{\mu_0\varepsilon_0}} \Rightarrow \mu_0 = \dfrac{1}{\varepsilon_0 c^2}$

$$\Rightarrow \quad [\mu_0] = \frac{1}{[M^{-1}L^{-3}T^4A^2][LT^{-1}]^2}$$

$$\Rightarrow \quad [\mu_0] = [M^1L^1T^{-2}A^{-2}]$$

For electric field (E),

$$\because \quad [E] = \left[\frac{F}{q}\right] = \left[\frac{MLT^{-2}}{AT}\right]$$

$$\Rightarrow \quad [E] = [M^1L^1T^{-3}A^{-1}]$$

30. Given, magnetic field at the centre at A is 3T.

Since, the solenoid B, C and D are connected in parallel arrangement.

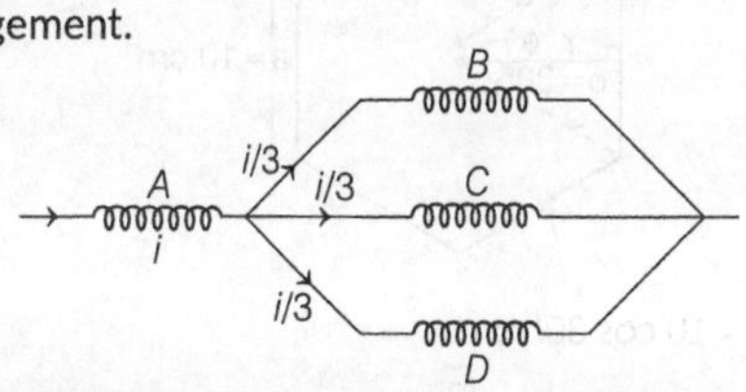

We know that,

The magnetic field in the circuit is directly proportional to the current in the circuit.

$$B \propto i$$

$$\Rightarrow \quad \frac{B_A}{B_C} = \frac{I_A}{I_C} \Rightarrow \frac{3T}{B_C} = \frac{i}{i/3}$$

$$\Rightarrow \quad B_C = 1\text{ T}$$

So, the field at the centre at $C = 1$ T.

31. For the straight wire, the expression of the magnetic field,

$$B_1 = B_3 = \frac{\mu_0 I}{4\pi r}$$

For the semicircular wire, the expression of the magnetic field, $\quad B_2 = \dfrac{\mu_0 I}{4r}$

Hence, the total magnetic field at the point P,

$B = B_1 + B_2 + B_3$

Substituting the values in the above equation, we get

$$B = \frac{\mu_0 I}{4\pi r} + \frac{\mu_0 I}{4r} + \frac{\mu_0 I}{4\pi r}$$

$$\Rightarrow \quad B = \frac{\mu_0 I}{4\pi r}(1+1+\pi) \Rightarrow B = \frac{\mu_0 I}{4\pi r}(2+\pi)$$

32. Given, $d_1 = 0.05$ m, $d_2 = 0.2$ m
and $B_1 : B_2 = 8:1$
Let radius of coil be r.
As we know that, magnetic field at a point on axis of a coil,

$$B = \frac{\mu_0}{2} \cdot \frac{Ir^2}{(d_1^2 + r^2)^{3/2}}$$

$$\therefore \quad \frac{B_1}{B_2} = \frac{r^2 \cdot (d_2^2 + r^2)^{3/2}}{(d_1^2 + r^2)^{3/2} \cdot r^2} = \frac{(d_2^2 + r^2)^{3/2}}{(d_1^2 + r^2)^{3/2}}$$

$$\Rightarrow \quad \frac{8}{1} = \left(\frac{d_2^2 + r^2}{d_1^2 + r^2}\right)^{3/2} \Rightarrow \frac{2^3}{1} = \left(\frac{d_2^2 + r^2}{d_1^2 + r^2}\right)^{3/2}$$

$$\Rightarrow \quad \frac{4}{1} = \frac{d_2^2 + r^2}{d_1^2 + r^2} \Rightarrow 4\,d_1^2 + 4r^2 = d_2^2 + r^2$$

$$\Rightarrow 4(0.05)^2 + 4r^2 = (0.2)^2 + r^2 \Rightarrow 3r^2 = 0.03$$

$$\Rightarrow \quad r = 0.1 \text{ m}$$

33. Magnitude of magnetic field due to one side of hexagonal loop at the centre is

$$B_1 = \frac{\mu_0 I}{4\pi r} \cdot 2\sin\phi$$

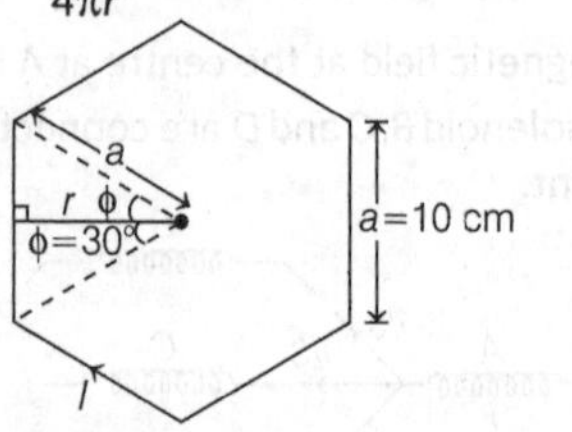

Here, $r = 10 \cos 30°$ cm

$$= 10 \times 10^{-2} \times \frac{\sqrt{3}}{2} \text{ m} = 5\sqrt{3} \times 10^{-2} \text{ m}$$

So, $B_1 = \dfrac{\mu_0 I \times 2\sin 30°}{4\pi(5\sqrt{3} \times 10^{-2})}$ $\quad (\because \phi = 30°)$

So, magnetic field due to complete 1 turn of loop of six sides is

$$B_2 = 6B_1 = \frac{6\,\mu_0 I \times 2\sin 30°}{4\pi(5\sqrt{3} \times 10^{-2})}$$

Magnetic field of 50 such turns at centre is

$$B_3 = 50B_2 = \frac{50 \times 6 \times \mu_0 I \times 2\sin 30°}{4\pi(5\sqrt{3} \times 10^{-2})}$$

$$= 500\sqrt{3}\left(\frac{\mu_0 I}{\pi}\right) \text{T} = 500\sqrt{3} \text{ in units of } \frac{\mu_0 I}{\pi}$$

Hence, option (c) is correct.

34. The ratio of magnetic fields due to wires A and B at the common centre O is

$$\frac{B_A}{B_B} = \frac{\dfrac{\mu_0 \theta_A I_A}{4\pi R_A}}{\dfrac{\mu_0 \theta_B I_B}{4\pi R_B}} = \frac{\theta_A I_A R_B}{\theta_B I_B R_A} = \frac{\dfrac{3\pi}{2} \times 2 \times 4 \times 10^{-2}}{\dfrac{5\pi}{3} \times 3 \times 2 \times 10^{-2}} = \frac{12}{10} = \frac{6}{5}$$

So, $B_A : B_B = 6:5$
Hence, correct option is (c).

35. Given arrangement consists of two current carrying wires and one current loop.
For wire ABN, magnetic field at O is given by

$$B_1 = \frac{\mu_0}{4\pi} \times \frac{I}{R}(\sin\phi_1 + \sin\phi_2)$$

$$\Rightarrow \quad B_1 = \frac{\mu_0}{4\pi} \times \frac{I}{R}[\sin 90° + \sin(-45°)]$$

$$= \frac{\mu_0}{4\pi R}\left(1 - \frac{1}{\sqrt{2}}\right) \otimes$$

Also, field of wire BDC at O,

$$B_2 = \frac{\mu_0 I}{4\pi R}(\sin\phi_1 + \sin\phi_2)$$

Here, $\phi_1 = 45°$ and $\phi_2 = 90°$.

$$\therefore \quad B_2 = \frac{\mu_0 I}{4\pi R}\left(\frac{1}{\sqrt{2}} + 1\right) \odot$$

Magnetic field of circular coil at O,

$$B_3 = \frac{\mu_0 I}{2R} \odot$$

Hence, net field at O,

$$B_{\text{net}} = B_1 \otimes + B_2 \odot + B_3 \odot$$

$$= \frac{\mu_0 I}{4\pi R}\left(1 - \frac{1}{\sqrt{2}}\right) - \frac{\mu_0 I}{4\pi R}\left(\frac{1}{\sqrt{2}} + 1\right) - \frac{\mu_0 I}{2R}$$

$$= \frac{-\mu_0 I}{2\pi R}\left(\pi + \frac{1}{\sqrt{2}}\right)$$

Negative sign is taken for outward field.

36. By Ampere's circuital rule, magnetic field inside and outside a wire carrying a uniformly distributed current is,

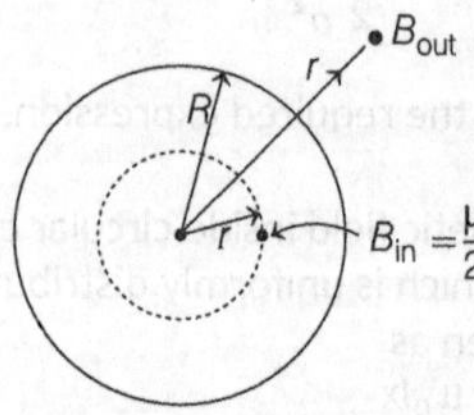

$$B_{\text{out}} = \frac{\mu_0 I}{2\pi r} \quad \text{...(i)}$$

$$B_{\text{in}} = \frac{\mu_0}{2\pi} \frac{ir}{R^2} \quad \text{...(ii)}$$

In given case, radius of wire is a. So, magnetic field due to wire at a distance $a/3$ from centre,

$$B_1 = \frac{\mu_0}{2\pi} \frac{i\left(\dfrac{a}{3}\right)}{a^2} = \frac{\mu_0 i}{6\pi a} \quad \text{[from Eq. (ii)]}$$

and magnetic field at a distance $2a$ from centre,

$$B_2 = \frac{\mu_0 i}{2\pi(2a)} = \frac{\mu_0 i}{4\pi a} \quad \text{[from Eq. (i)]}$$

Ratio of fields will be $\dfrac{B_1}{B_2} = \dfrac{\left(\dfrac{\mu_0 i}{6\pi a}\right)}{\left(\dfrac{\mu_0 i}{4\pi a}\right)} = \dfrac{2}{3}$

37.

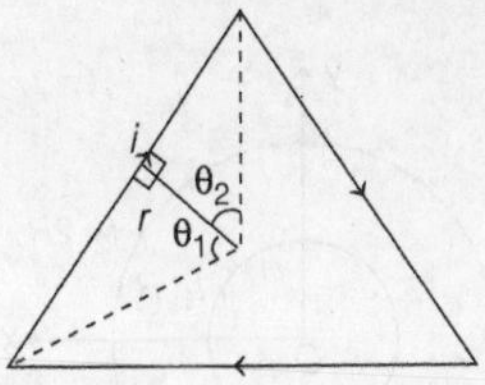

Due to symmetry of arrangement, net field at centre of triangle is

$$B_{net} = \text{Sum of fields of all wires (sides)}$$
$$= 3 \times \frac{\mu_0 i}{4\pi r}(\sin\theta_1 + \sin\theta_2)$$

So, $B_{net} = \dfrac{3 \times 10^{-7} \times 10 \times 2\left(\dfrac{\sqrt{3}}{2}\right)}{\left(\dfrac{1}{2\sqrt{3}}\right)} = 18 \times 10^{-6}$ T

$\Rightarrow \quad B_{net} = 18\,\mu$T

38. Magnetic field at the centre of a current carrying ring is given by

$$B = \frac{\mu_0 I}{2r} \text{ where } I = \frac{Q\omega}{2\pi}$$

$$\Rightarrow \quad B = \frac{\mu_0 Q\omega}{2r \times 2\pi} \text{ or } Q = \frac{2Br \times 2\pi}{\mu_0 \omega}$$

$$= \frac{2 \times 3.8 \times 10^{-9} \times 0.1 \times 2\pi}{4\pi \times 10^{-7} \times 40\pi} = 3 \times 10^{-5}\text{C}$$

39. The given figure can be drawn as shown below

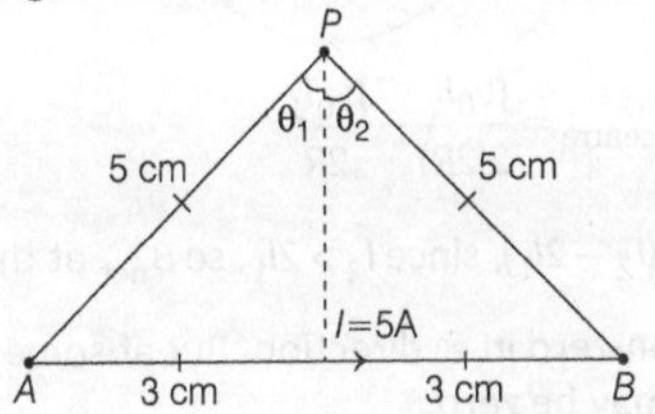

By Biot-Savart's law, magnetic field due to a wire segment at point P is

$$B = \frac{\mu_0 I}{4\pi d}(\sin\theta_1 + \sin\theta_2)$$

$$B = \frac{\mu_0 I}{4\pi d} \times 2\sin\theta = \frac{4\pi \times 10^{-7} \times 5}{4\pi \times 4 \times 10^{-2}} \times 2 \times \left(\frac{3}{5}\right)$$

$$= \frac{5 \times 2 \times 3}{4 \times 5} \times 10^{-5} = 1.5 \times 10^{-5}\text{ T}$$

40. Magnetic field due to wire 1 at point P is

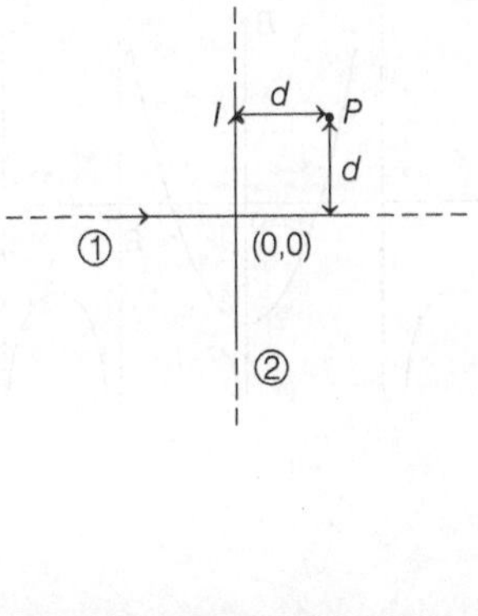

$$B_1 = \frac{\mu_0}{2\pi}\frac{I}{d}, \otimes$$

Similarly, magnetic field due to wire 2 at point P is

$$B_2 = \frac{\mu_0}{2\pi}\frac{I}{d}, \odot$$

Resultant field at point P is

$$B_{net} = B_1 + B_2$$

Since, $|B_1| = |B_2|$, but they are opposite in direction.

Thus, $B_{net} = 0$

∴ Net magnetic field at point P will be zero.

41. There is no magnetic field along axis of a current-carrying wire.

Also, magnetic field near one of end of an infinitely long wire is $\dfrac{\mu_0 I}{4\pi r}$ tesla.

Hence, magnetic field due to segments LP and MQ at O is zero. Using right hand rule, we can check that magnetic field due to segments PS and QN at 'O' is in same direction perpendicularly into the plane of paper.

Hence, $B_O = B_{PS} + B_{QN} = \dfrac{\mu_0 i}{4\pi r} + \dfrac{\mu_0 i}{4\pi r} = \dfrac{\mu_0 i}{2\pi r}$

So, $\quad i = \dfrac{2\pi r B_0}{\mu_0}$

Here, $r = OP = OQ = 4$ cm and $B_0 = 10^{-4}$ T.

Substituting values, we get

$$\Rightarrow \quad i = \frac{2\pi \times 4 \times 10^{-2} \times 10^{-4}}{4\pi \times 10^{-7}}$$

$\Rightarrow i = 20$ A, Also, magnetic field points perpendicular into the plane of paper.

42.

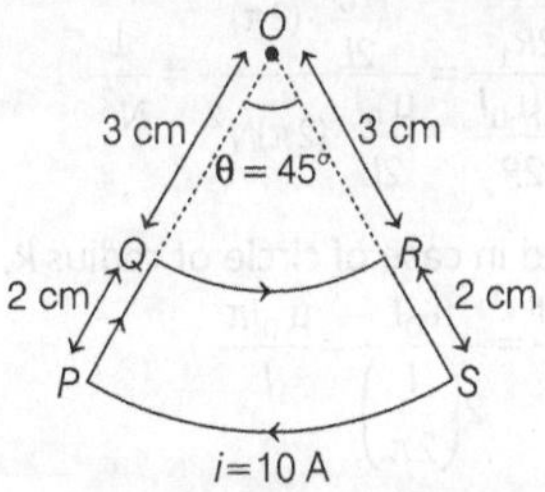

The magnetic field at point O due to wires PQ and RS will be zero.

Magnetic field due to arc QR at point 'O' will be

$$B_1 = \frac{\theta}{2\pi}\left(\frac{\mu_0 i}{2a}\right)$$

Here, $\theta = 45° = \dfrac{\pi}{4}$ rad, $i = 10$ A

and $\quad a = 3\text{ cm} = 3 \times 10^{-2}$ m

$$\Rightarrow \quad B_1 = \frac{\pi}{2\pi \times 4}\left(\frac{\mu_0 \times 10}{2 \times 3 \times 10^{-2}}\right) = \frac{5 \times \mu_0 \times 10^2}{24}$$

Direction of field B_1 will be coming out of the plane of figure.

Similarly, field at point 'O' due to arc SP will be

$$B_2 = \frac{\pi}{4}\left(\frac{1}{2\pi}\right)\left[\frac{\mu_0 \times 10}{2 \times (2+3) \times 10^{-2}}\right] = \frac{\mu_0 \times 10^2}{8}$$

Direction of B_2 is going into the plane of the figure.

$\therefore$ The resultant field at O is

$$B = B_1 - B_2 \cong 1 \times 10^{-5}\ \text{T}$$

43. Let consider the length of first wire is L, then according to question, if radius of loop formed is R_1, then,

For wire 1,

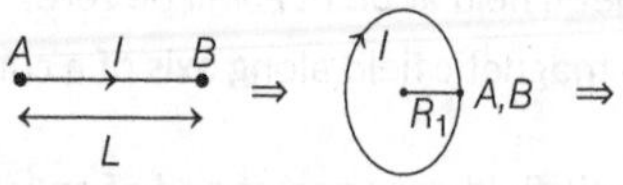

$$L = 2\pi R_1 \Rightarrow R_1 = \frac{L}{2\pi}$$

The magnetic field due to this loop at its centre is

$$B_L = \frac{\mu_0 I}{2R_1} = \frac{\mu_0 I}{2L} \times 2\pi \quad \text{...(i)}$$

Now, several wire is made into a coil of N- turns.

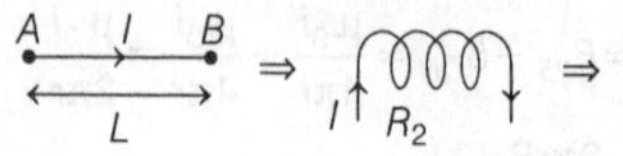

(R_2=radius of coil having N loops)

Thin, $L = N(2\pi R_2) \Rightarrow R_2 = L/2\pi N$

The magnetic field due to this circular coil of N-turns is

$$B_C = \left(\frac{\mu_0 I}{2R_2}\right) N = N \cdot \frac{\mu_0 I \cdot (2\pi N)}{2L} \quad \text{...(ii)}$$

Using Eqs. (i) and (ii), the ratio of $\frac{B_L}{B_C}$ is :

$$\Rightarrow \frac{B_L}{B_C} = \frac{\frac{\mu_0 I}{2R_1}}{N\frac{\mu_0 I}{2R_2}} = \frac{\frac{\mu_0 I}{2L}\cdot(2\pi)}{\frac{\mu_0 I}{2L}\cdot(2\pi)N^2} = \frac{1}{N^2}$$

44. Magnetic field in case of circle of radius R, we have

$$B_A = \frac{\mu_0 I}{2R} = \frac{\mu_0 I}{2\left(\frac{l}{2\pi}\right)} = \frac{\mu_0 I\pi}{l}$$

Magnetic field in case of square of side a, we get

$$B_B = 4 \times \frac{\mu_0}{4\pi} \times \frac{I}{\left(\frac{a}{2}\right)}\left(\frac{1}{\sqrt{2}} + \frac{1}{\sqrt{2}}\right) = \frac{\mu_0 2\sqrt{2} I}{a\pi}$$

As, $\quad 4a = l,\ a = l/4$

$$\Rightarrow \quad B_B = \frac{8\sqrt{2}\mu_0 I}{\pi l} \quad \text{... (ii)}$$

Dividing Eq. (i) by Eq. (ii), we get

$$\frac{B_A}{B_B} = \frac{\pi^2}{8\sqrt{2}}$$

JEE Advanced

1.

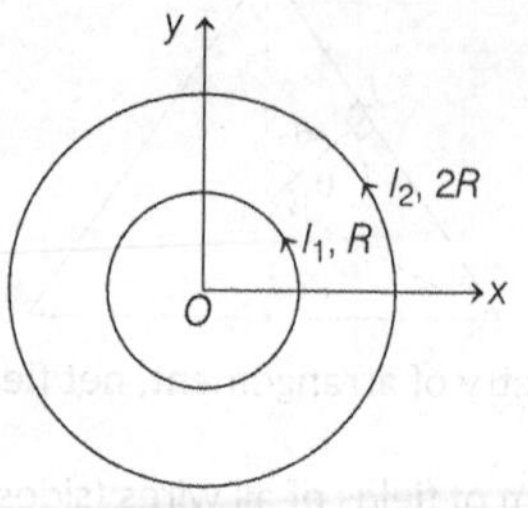

(a) Magnetic field at the plane of the ring is perpendicular to the plane. However, they bend as they move forward.

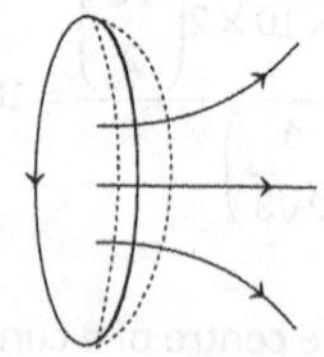

(b) By symmetry, we can say that $\mathbf{B}$ will be same at all the points having the same radial distance. So, $\mathbf{B}(x, y)$ will depend on the radial distance $r = \sqrt{x^2 + y^2}$.

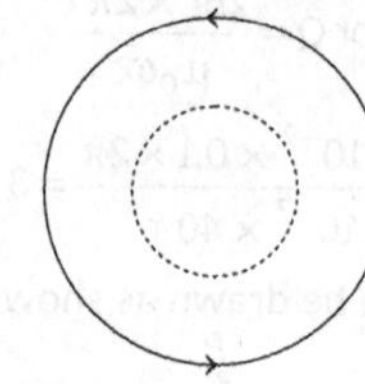

(c) $(B_{\text{net}})_{\text{centre}} = \frac{\mu_0 I_2}{2(2R)} - \frac{\mu_0 I_1}{2R}$

$= \frac{\mu_0}{4R}(I_2 - 2I_1)$, since $I_2 > 2I_1$, so B_{net} at the centre will be non-zero in ⊗ direction. But at some other point, B_{net} may be zero.

From the graph, it is clear that $B_{\text{net}} = 0$ for $r \in (O, R)$.

So, option (c) is incorrect.

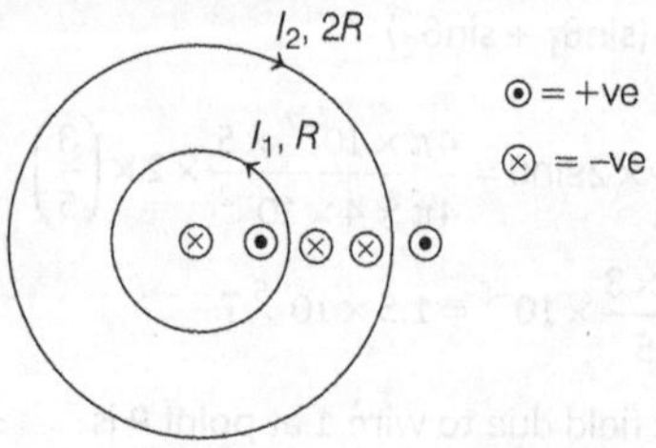

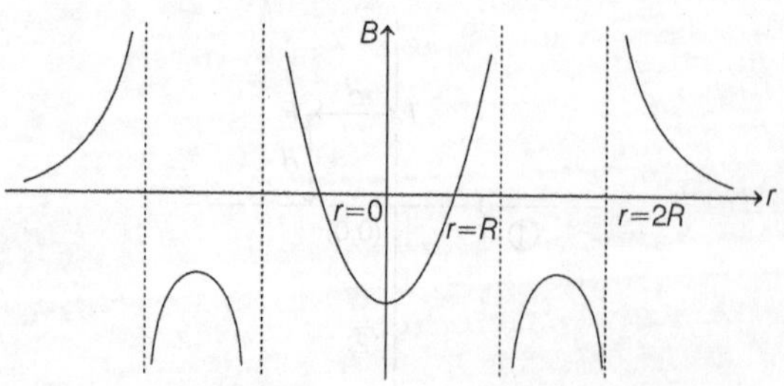

(d) For the graph, it is clear that $B = -$ ve
In, ⊗ direction for $r \in (R \text{ to } 2R)$, so option (d) is also incorrect.

2.

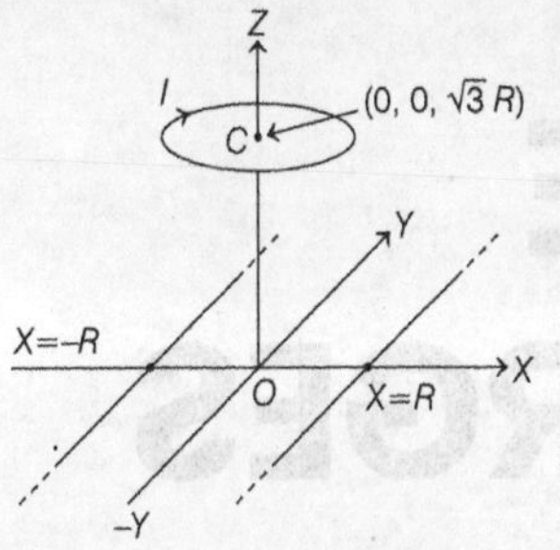

(a) At origin, $\mathbf{B} = 0$ due to two wires if $I_1 = I_2$, hence $(\mathbf{B}_{\text{net}})$ at origin is equal to $\mathbf{B}$ due to ring. which is non-zero.

(b) If $I_1 > 0$ and $I_2 < 0$, $\mathbf{B}$ at origin due to wires will be along $+\hat{\mathbf{k}}$. Direction of $\mathbf{B}$ due to ring is along $-\hat{\mathbf{k}}$ direction and hence $\mathbf{B}$ can be zero at origin.

(c) If $I_1 < 0$ and $I_2 > 0$, $\mathbf{B}$ at origin due to wires is along $-\hat{\mathbf{k}}$ and also along $-\hat{\mathbf{k}}$ due to ring, hence $\mathbf{B}$ cannot be zero.

(d)

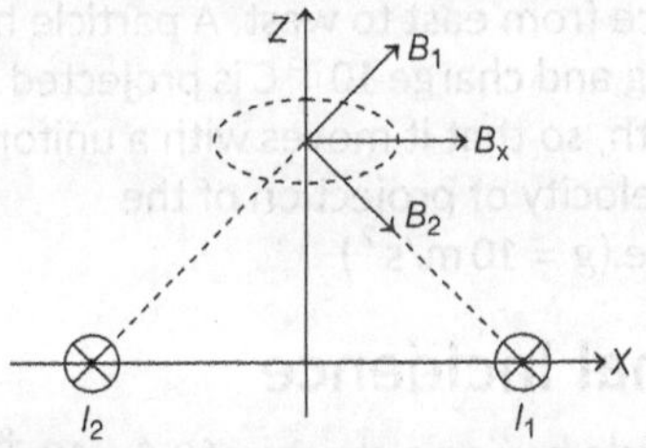

At centre of ring, $\mathbf{B}$ due to wires is along x-axis.
Hence, z-component is only because of ring which

$$\mathbf{B} = \frac{\mu_0 i}{2R}(-\hat{\mathbf{k}}).$$

3.

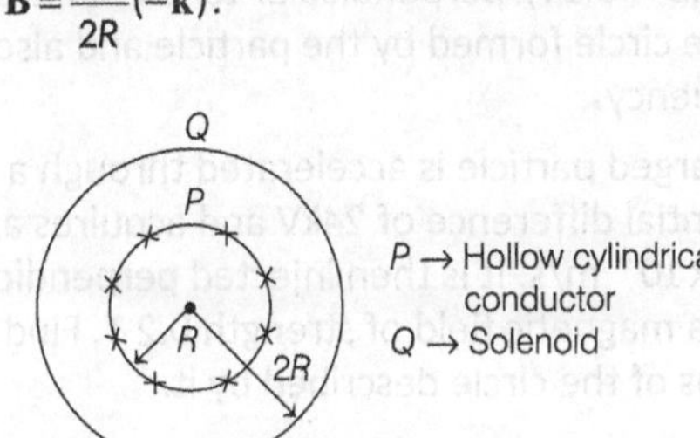

In the region, $0 < r < R$

$$B_P = 0,$$

$B_Q \neq 0$, along the axis

$$\therefore \quad B_{\text{net}} \neq 0$$

In the region, $\quad R < r < 2R$

$B_P \neq 0$, tangential to the circle of radius r, centred on the axis.

$B_Q \neq 0$, along the axis.

$\therefore B_{\text{net}} \neq 0$ not in the directions mentioned in options (b) or (c). In region, $r > 2R$

$$B_P \neq 0$$
$$B_Q \neq 0$$
$$\Rightarrow \quad B_{\text{net}} \neq 0$$

4.

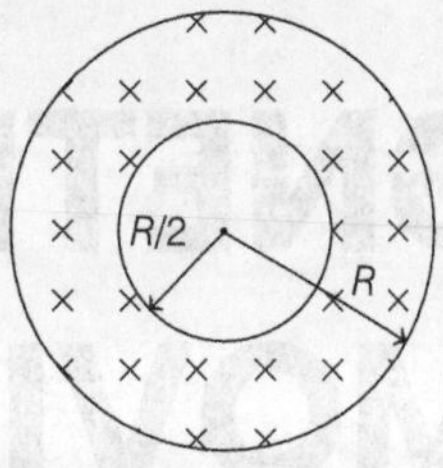

r = distance of a point from centre.

For $r \leq R/2$ Using Ampere's circuital law,

$$\oint \mathbf{B} \cdot d\mathbf{l} \quad \text{or} \quad Bl = \mu_0 (I_{\text{in}})$$

$$\text{or} \quad B(2\pi r) = \mu_0 (I_{\text{in}})$$

$$\text{or} \quad B = \frac{\mu_0}{2\pi} \frac{I_{\text{in}}}{r} \quad \text{...(i)}$$

Since, $\quad I_{\text{in}} = 0$

$$\therefore \quad B = 0$$

For $\frac{R}{2} \leq r \leq R$ $\quad I_{\text{in}} = \left[\pi r^2 - \pi\left(\frac{R}{2}\right)^2\right]\sigma$

Here, σ = current per unit area
Substituting in Eq. (i), we have

$$B = \frac{\mu_0}{2\pi} \frac{\left[\pi r^2 - \pi \frac{R^2}{4}\right]\sigma}{r} = \frac{\mu_0 \sigma}{2r}\left(r^2 - \frac{R^2}{4}\right) \text{ or } B = \alpha\left[\beta r - \frac{\gamma}{r}\right]$$

Here, α, β and γ are positive constant. So, we can see that B continuously increases as r increases.

At $\quad r = \frac{R}{2}, B = 0$

At $\quad r = R, B = \frac{3\mu_0 \sigma R}{8}$

For $r \geq R$ $\quad I_{\text{in}} = I_{\text{Total}} = I$ (say)
Therefore, substituting in Eq. (i), we have

$$B = \frac{\mu_0}{2\pi} \cdot \frac{I}{r} \quad \text{or} \quad B \propto \frac{1}{r}$$

5. $B_R = B_T - B_C$

R = Remaining portion
T = Total portion and
C = Cavity

$$B_R = \frac{\mu_0 I_T}{2a\pi} - \frac{\mu_0 I_C}{2(3a/2)\pi} \quad \text{...(i)}$$

$$I_T = J(\pi a^2) \Rightarrow I_C = J\left(\frac{\pi a^2}{4}\right)$$

Substituting the values in Eq. (i), we have

$$B_R = \frac{\mu_0}{a\pi}\left[\frac{I_T}{2} - \frac{I_C}{3}\right] = \frac{\mu_0}{a\pi}\left[\frac{\pi a^2 J}{2} - \frac{\pi a^2 J}{12}\right] = \frac{5\mu_0 a J}{12}$$

$$\therefore \quad N = 5$$

CHAPTER~02

MAGNETIC FORCE ON MOVING CHARGES

LEVEL 01 Starter Level

2.1 Magnetic Force on a Moving Charge

1 A charged particle of mass 5 mg and charge $q = +2\mu C$ has velocity $\mathbf{v} = 2\hat{i} - 3\hat{j} + 4\hat{k}$. Find out the magnetic force on the charged particle and its acceleration at this instant due to magnetic field $\mathbf{B} = 3\hat{j} - 2\hat{k}$. $\mathbf{v}$ and $\mathbf{B}$ are in m/s and Wb/m^2 respectively.

2 A charged particle is projected in a magnetic field of $(7.0\hat{i} - 3.0\hat{j}) \times 10^{-3}$ T. The acceleration of the particle is found to be $(x\hat{i} + 7.0\hat{j}) \times 10^{-6}$ m/s^2. Find the value of x.

3 A magnetic field of $8\hat{k}$ mT exerts a force of $(4.0\hat{i} + 3.0\hat{j}) \times 10^{-10}$ N on a particle having a charge of 5×10^{-10} C and going in the XY-plane. Find the velocity of the particle.

4 When a proton has a velocity $\mathbf{v} = (2\hat{i} + 3\hat{j}) \times 10^6$ m/s, it experiences a force $\mathbf{F} = -(1.28 \times 10^{-13}\hat{k})$ N. When its velocity is along the Z-axis, it experiences a force along the X-axis. What is the magnetic field?

5 The electrons in the beam of a television tube have a kinetic energy of 4.5×10^{-15} J. Initially, the electrons move horizontally from west and east. The vertical component of the earth's magnetic field points down, towards the surface of the earth, and has a magnitude of 2.25×10^{-5} T.

(i) In what direction, are the electrons deflected by this field component?

(ii) What is the acceleration of an electron in part (i)?

6 A uniform magnetic field of magnitude 0.20 T exists in space from east to west. A particle having mass 10^{-5} kg and charge 10^{-5} C is projected from south to north, so that it moves with a uniform velocity. Find velocity of projection of the particle.($g = 10$ m/s^2)

2.2 Normal Incidence

1 A particle having a charge of 2.0×10^{-8} C and a mass of 2.0×10^{-10} g is projected with a speed of 2.0×10^3 m/s in a region having a uniform magnetic field ($B = 0.1$T) perpendicular to it. Find the radius of the circle formed by the particle and also the frequency.

2 A charged particle is accelerated through a potential difference of 24kV and acquires a speed of 2×10^6 m/s. It is then injected perpendicularly into a magnetic field of strength 0.2 T. Find the radius of the circle described by it.

3 An electron having a kinetic energy of 400 eV circulates in a path of radius 20 cm in a magnetic field. Find the magnetic field and the number of revolutions per second made by the electron.

4 A proton describes a circle of radius 1 cm a magnetic field of strength 0.10 T. What would be the radius of the circle described by a deuteron moving with the same speed in the same magnetic field ?

5 A neutron, a proton, an electron and an α-particle enter a uniform magnetic field with equal velocities. The field is directed along the inward normal to the plane of the paper. Which of these tracks followed are by electron and α-particle?

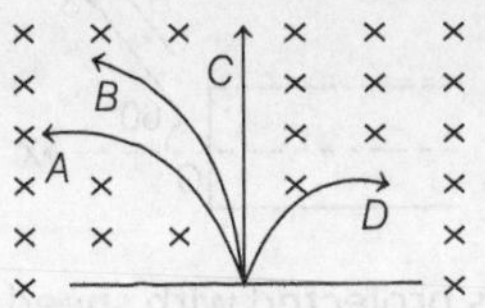

6 A proton (p), α-particle and deuteron (D) are moving in circular paths with same kinetic energies in the same magnetic field. Find the ratio of their radii and time periods. (Neglect interaction between particles)

7 A charge particle of mass m and charge q is projected with velocity v_0 along Y-axis at $t = 0$ in a uniform magnetic field $\mathbf{B} = B_0 \hat{\mathbf{i}}$. Find the velocity and position vector of the particle function of time.

8 An α-particle is accelerated by a potential difference of 10^4 V. Find the change in its direction of motion, if it enters normally in a region of thickness 0.1 m having transverse magnetic induction of 0.1 T. (Given, mass of α-particle is equal to 6.4×10^{-27} kg)

9 In the figure shown the magnetic field on the left of line PQ is zero and on the right of PQ it is uniform. A particle of mass m and charge q enters the magnetic field with speed u as shown in figure.

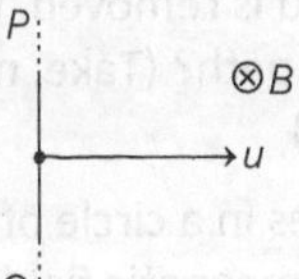

Find the

(i) time spent in the magnetic field.

(ii) distance travelled in the magnetic field.

(iii) impulse of magnetic force.

10 A charged particle having kinetic energy K enters into the region of a uniform magnetic field between two plates P and Q as shown in figure. The charged particle just misses hitting the plate Q. Find the magnetic field in the region between the two plates.

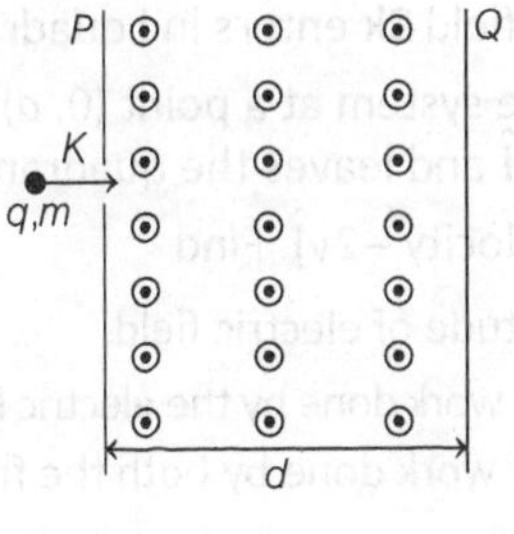

11 A particle of mass m and positive charge q, moving with a uniform velocity v, enters a magnetic field B as shown in figure.

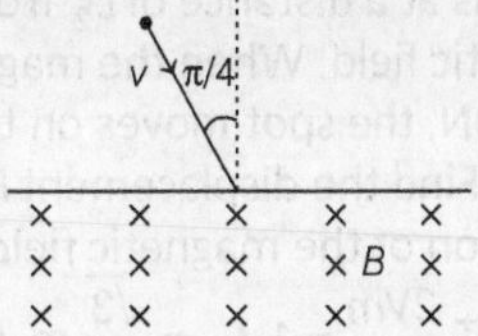

(i) Find the radius of the circular arc it describes in the magnetic field.

(ii) Find the angle subtended by the arc at the centre.

(iii) How long does the particle stay inside the magnetic field?

(iv) Solve the three parts of the above problem, if the charge q on the particle is negative.

12 A particle of mass m and charge q is projected into a region having a perpendicular magnetic field B. Find the angle of deviation (figure) of the particle as it comes out of the magnetic field if the width d of the region is very slightly smaller than

(i) $\dfrac{mv}{qB}$, (ii) $\dfrac{mv}{\sqrt{2}qB}$ and (iii) $\dfrac{3mv}{qB}$.

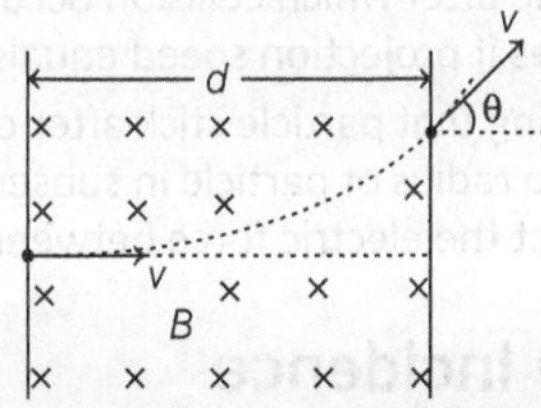

13 A tightly-wound, long solenoid has n turns per unit length, radius r and carries a current i. A particle having charge q and mass m is projected from a point on the axis of the solenoid in a direction perpendicular to the axis. What can be the minimum speed for which the particle should be projected to strike the solenoid ?

14 A beam of particles accelerated by a potential differences of V flies into a homogeneous magnetic field applied perpendicular to the plane of the paper and towards the observer.

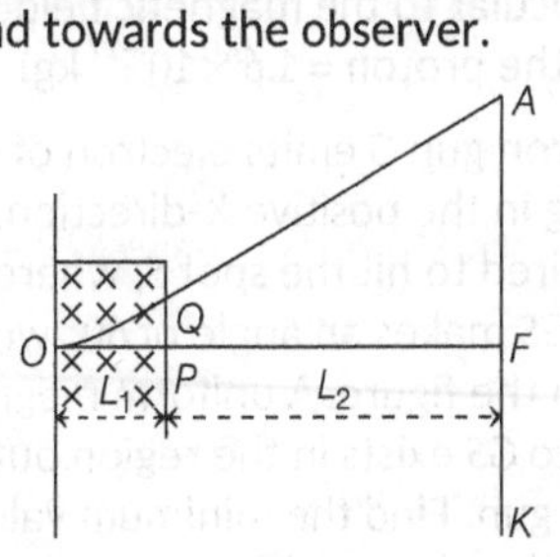

The width of the magnetic field is *OP*. In the absence of the magnetic field, the electron beam produces a spot at a point *F* in fluorescent screen *AK*, which is at a distance of L_2 from the edge of the magnetic field. When the magnetic field is switched ON, the spot moves on to *A* along the path *OQA*. Find the displacement *FA* of the spot, if the induction of the magnetic field is *B*.

(take, $B = 1\text{T}, \frac{2Vm}{q} = 1, L_1 = \frac{\sqrt{3}}{2}\text{ m}, L_2 = 3\frac{\sqrt{3}}{2}\text{ m}$)

15 A charged particle $+q$ of mass *m* is placed at a distance *d* from another charged particle $-2q$ of mass $2m$ in a uniform magnetic field *B* as shown in figure.

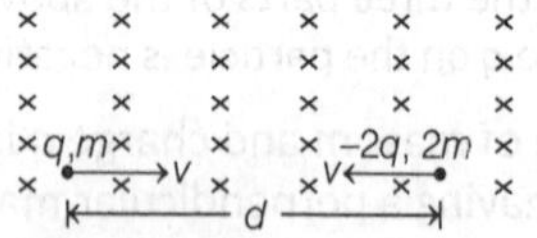

If the particles are projected towards each other with equal speeds *v*. Find

(i) the maximum value of projection speed v_m, so that the two particles do not collide.

(ii) the time after which collision occurs between the particles if projection speed equals $2v_m$.

(iii) Assuming that particle stick after collision, then find the radius of particle in subsequent motion. (Neglect the electric force between the charges)

2.3 Oblique Incidence

1 A particle having a charge of 5.0 mC and a mass of 5.0×10^{-12} kg is projected with a speed of 1.0 km/s in a magnetic field of magnitude 5.0 mT. The angle between the magnetic field vector and the velocity vector is $\sin^{-1}(0.90)$. Find the diameter of the helix and its pitch.

2 A proton projected in a magnetic field of 0.04 T travels along a helical path of radius 5.0 cm (of projected circle) and pitch 20 cm. Find, the components of the velocity of the proton along and perpendicular to the magnetic field. (Take, the mass of the proton $= 1.6 \times 10^{-27}$ kg)

3 An electron gun *G* emits electron of energy 2 keV travelling in the positive *X*-direction. The electrons are required to hit the spot *S*, where $GS = 0.1$m and the line *GS* makes an angle of 60° with the *X*-axis, as shown in the figure. A uniform magnetic field **B** parallel to *GS* exists in the region outside of electron gun. Find the minimum value of *B* needed to make the electron hit *S*.

(Take, mass of electron $= 9 \times 10^{-31}$ kg)

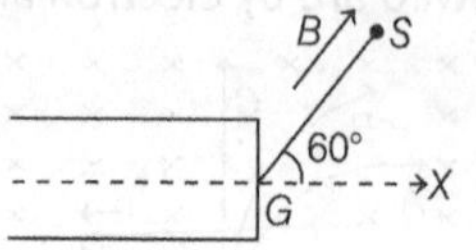

4 A particle is projected with speed v_0 at an angle θ with *X*-axis in *XY*-plane from origin at $t = 0$. Magnetic field in the region is $\mathbf{B} = B_0\hat{\mathbf{i}}$. Find the velocity and position vector of the particle function of time.

2.4 Electric and Magnetic Force on a Charge

1 When a proton is released from rest in a room, it starts with an initial acceleration a_0 towards west. When it is projected towards north with a speed u_0, it moves with an initial acceleration $3a_0$ towards west. Find the electric field and the minimum possible magnetic field in the room.

2 An electron beam passes through a magnetic field of 2×10^{-3} Wb/m^2 and an electric field of 3.2×10^4 V/m, both acting simultaneously ($\mathbf{E} \perp \mathbf{B} \perp \mathbf{v}$). If the path of electrons remains undeflected calculate the speed of the electron. If the electric field is removed, what will be the radius of the electron path? (Take, mass of electron $= 9.1 \times 10^{-31}$ kg)

3 A particle moves in a circle of radius 1.0 cm under the action of a magnetic field of 0.40 T. An electric field of 200 V/m makes the path straight. Find the charge/ mass ratio of the particle.

4 A particle having mass *m* and charge *q* is released from the origin in a region in which electric field and magnetic field are given by $\mathbf{B} = +B_0\hat{\mathbf{j}}$ and $\mathbf{E} = +E_0\hat{\mathbf{i}}$. Find the speed of the particle as a function of its *x*-coordinate.

5 A particle of charge $+q$ and mass *m* moving under the influence of a uniform electric field $E\hat{\mathbf{i}}$ and a magnetic field $B\hat{\mathbf{k}}$ enters in I quadrant of a coordinate system at a point $(0, a)$ with initial velocity $v\hat{\mathbf{i}}$ and leaves the quadrant at a point $(2a, 0)$ with velocity $-2v\hat{\mathbf{j}}$. Find

(i) magnitude of electric field.

(ii) rate of work done by the electric field at point $(0, a)$.

(iii) rate of work done by both the fields at $(2a, 0)$.

LEVEL 02 JEE Main Level

Single Choice Correct Questions

1 If the acceleration of a charge particle in magnetic field $\mathbf{B} = 2\hat{\mathbf{i}} + a\hat{\mathbf{j}} + \hat{\mathbf{k}}$ is $-5\hat{\mathbf{i}} + 3\hat{\mathbf{j}} + a^2\hat{\mathbf{k}}$, then the values of a are

(a) (– 2, 5) (b) (3, 7)
(c) (2, – 5) (d) (– 3, 7)

2 An electron experiences a force $(4.0\hat{\mathbf{i}} + 3.0\hat{\mathbf{j}}) \times 10^{-13}$ N in a uniform magnetic field when its velocity is $2.5\hat{\mathbf{k}} \times 10^7$ ms^{-1}. When the velocity is redirected and becomes $(1.5\hat{\mathbf{i}} - 2.0\hat{\mathbf{j}}) \times 10^7$ ms^{-1}, the magnetic force of the electron is zero. The magnetic field vector **B** is

(a) $-0.075\hat{\mathbf{i}} + 0.1\hat{\mathbf{j}}$ (b) $0.1\hat{\mathbf{i}} + 0.075\hat{\mathbf{j}}$
(c) $0.075\hat{\mathbf{i}} - 0.1\hat{\mathbf{j}} + \hat{\mathbf{k}}$ (d) $0.075\hat{\mathbf{i}} - 0.1\hat{\mathbf{j}}$

3 A long horizontal wire carries a current $i = 1$ A. A charged particle of mass $m = 1$ mg moves parallel to the wire with constant velocity $v = 10$ m/s. The distance of the charge from the wire is $r = 1$ cm. The magnitude of the charge is

(a) 50mC (b) 5mC
(c) 500mC (d) 5C

4 Two semi-circles carrying a current i are placed in a 3D coordinate system such that one of which lies in YZ-plane and the other is in XZ-plane with centre of both at origin of radius R. The magnetic force experienced by positive charge of value q moving with velocity v along x-direction when it is at the origin is

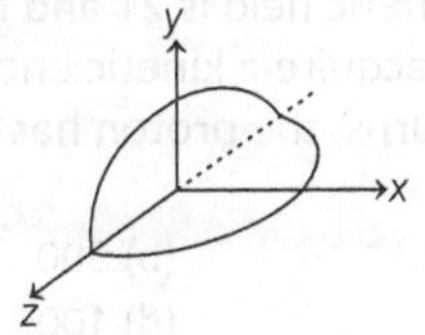

(a) $\dfrac{qv\mu_0 i}{4R}$ (b) $\dfrac{qv\mu_0 i}{2R}$
(c) $\dfrac{qv\mu_0 i}{2\sqrt{2}R}$ (d) 0

5 A beam of ions with velocity 2×10^5 m/s enters normally into a uniform magnetic field of 4×10^{-2} T. If the specific charge of the ion is 5×10^7 C/kg, then the radius of the circular path described will be

(a) 0.10 m (b) 0.16 m
(c) 0.20 m (d) 0.25 m

6 An electron, a proton and a deuteron move in a magnetic field with same momentum perpendicularly. The ratio of the radii of their circular paths will be

(a) 1 : 1 : 1 (b) 1 : 1 : 2 (c) 1 : 2 : 4 (d) 2 : 1 : 1

7 A proton and an α-particle enter a uniform magnetic field perpendicularly with the same speed. If proton takes 25 μs to make 5 revolutions, then the periodic time for the α-particle would be

(a) 50 μs (b) 25 μs (c) 10 μs (d) 5 μs

8 If an electron of velocity $(2\hat{\mathbf{i}} + 3\hat{\mathbf{j}})$ is subjected to magnetic field of $4\hat{\mathbf{k}}$, then its

(A) path will change
(B) speed does not change
(C) path must be circular
(D) momentum is constant

(a) A, B (b) All
(c) A, B, C (d) None of these

9 A car of mass 100 kg having charge of 0.1C is moving horizontally in a circular track of $R = 100$ m. If no friction acts on it in the presence of a vertical magnetic field of 10 T, then speed of the car is

(a) 1 m/s (b) 10 m/s
(c) 0.1 m/s (d) None of these

10 Which particles will have minimum frequency of revolution when projected with the same velocity perpendicular to a magnetic field?

(a) Li^+ (b) Electron
(c) Proton (d) He^+

11 A deutron of kinetic energy 50 keV is describing a circular orbit of radius 0.5 m in a plane perpendicular to magnetic field B. The kinetic energy of the proton that describes a circular orbit of radius 0.5 m in the same plane with the same B is

(a) 25 keV (b) 50 keV
(c) 200 keV (d) 100 keV

12 Two particles A and B of masses m_A and m_B respectively and having the same charge are moving in a plane. A uniform magnetic field exists perpendicular to this plane. The speeds of the particles are v_A and v_B respectively and the trajectories are as shown in the figure.

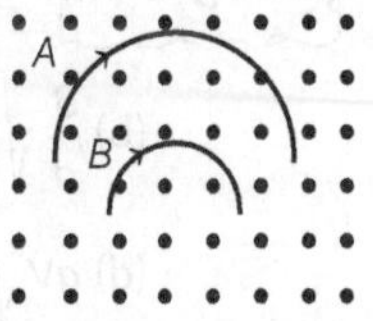

Then,

(a) $m_A v_A < m_B v_B$
(b) $m_A v_A > m_B v_B$
(c) $m_A < m_B$ and $v_A < v_B$
(d) $m_A = m_B$ and $v_A = v_B$

13 An electron and a proton each travel with equal speeds around circular orbits in the same uniform magnetic field as indicated (not to scale) in the diagram. The field is into the page on the diagram. The electron travels ________ around the ________ circle and the proton travels ________ around the ________ circle.

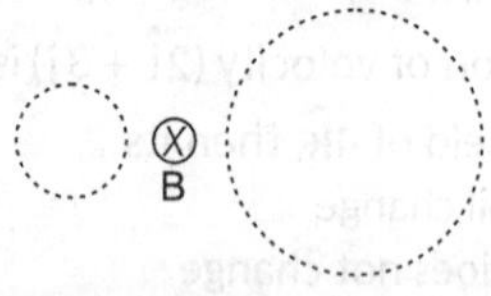

(a) clockwise, smaller, counter-clockwise, larger
(b) counter-clockwise, smaller, clockwise, larger
(c) clockwise, larger, counter-clockwise, smaller
(d) counter-clockwise, larger, clockwise, smaller

14 A charge particle having mass of 1.6×10^{-26} kg comes out of accelerator tube with kinetic energy 2×10^3 eV. Calculate the smallest magnitude of magnetic field that should be applied in vertically downwards direction to just prevent the charge particle from colliding the plate (Assume charge on particle = charge of proton)

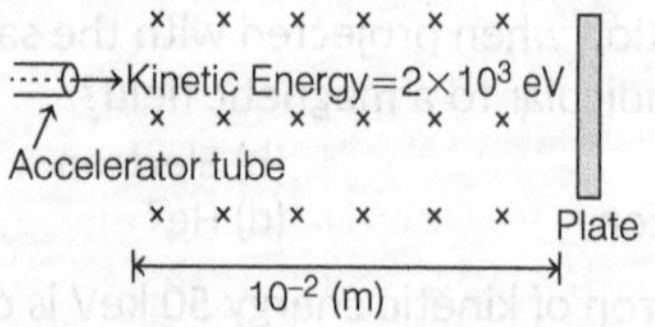

(a) 2 T (b) 4 T (c) 0.02 T (d) 0.04 T

15 A proton (mass m) accelerated by a potential difference V flies through a uniform transverse magnetic field B. The field occupies a region of space by width d. If α be the angle of deviation of proton from initial direction of motion (see figure), the value of $\sin \alpha$ will be

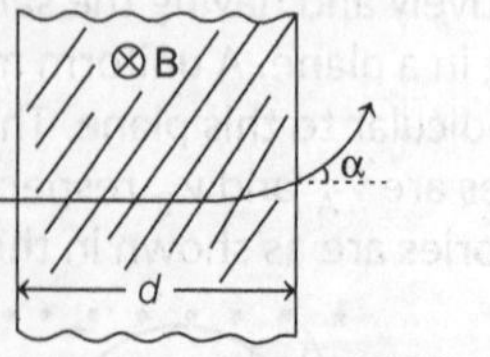

(a) $\frac{B}{2}\sqrt{\frac{qd}{mV}}$ (b) $\frac{B}{d}\sqrt{\frac{q}{2mV}}$

(c) $Bd\sqrt{\frac{q}{2mV}}$ (d) $qV\sqrt{\frac{Bd}{2m}}$

16 A particle having charge q enters a region of uniform magnetic field **B** (directed inwards) and is deflected a distance x after travelling a distance y. The magnitude of the momentum of the particle is

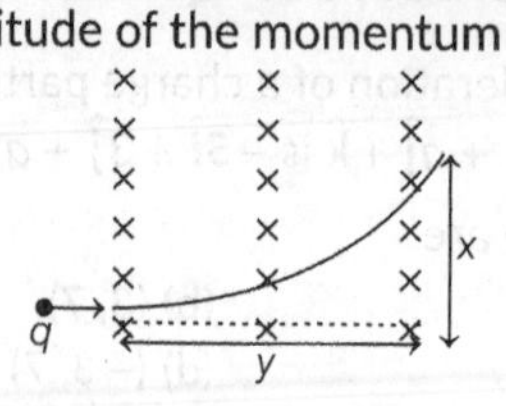

(a) $\frac{qBy}{2}$ (b) $\frac{qBy}{x}$

(c) $\frac{qB}{2}\left(\frac{y^2}{x} + x\right)$ (d) $\frac{qBy^2}{2x}$

17 A particle of mass m and charge q moves with a constant velocity v along the positive x- direction. It enters a region containing a uniform magnetic field B directed along the negative z-direction, extending from $x = a$ to $x = b$. The minimum value of v required, so that the particle can just enter the region $x > b$ is

(a) qbB/m (b) $q(b - a)B/m$
(c) qaB/m (d) $q(b + a)B/2m$

18 The frequency of a cyclotron oscillator is 10^7 Hz. The cyclotron is accelerating protons ($m_p = 1.67 \times 10^{-27}$ kg). If the radius of the dees of the cyclotron be 0.6 m, the kinetic energy of the proton beam produced by the accelerator will be nearly

(a) 1.2×10^{-13} J (b) 1.2×10^{-12} J
(c) 2.4×10^{-12} J (d) 4.8×10^{-12} J

19 A cyclotron is accelerating proton, where the applied magnetic field is 2T and the potential gap is 100 keV. To acquire a kinetic energy of 20 MeV, the number of turns, the proton has to move between the dees is

(a) 200 (b) 300
(c) 150 (d) 100

20 A tightly wound, long solenoid carries a current of 2.00 A. An electron is found to execute a uniform circular motion inside the solenoid with a frequency of 1.00×10^8 rev/s. The number of turns per metre in the solenoid will be

(a) 142 turns/m (b) 1420 turns/m
(c) 152 turns/m (d) 1520 turns/m

21 A mass spectrometer is a device that selects particles of a fixed mass. An ion with electric charge $q > 0$ and mass m starts at rest at a source S and is accelerated through a potential difference V. It passes through a hole into a region with a constant magnetic field **B** perpendicular to the plane as in the figure. The particle is deflected by the magnetic field and emerges through the hole in the bottom of the figure that is a distance d from the hole at the top. What is the mass of the particle?

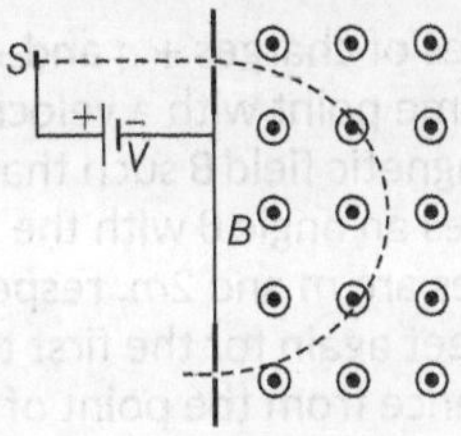

(a) $\frac{8qV}{B^2}$ (b) $\frac{qBd}{8V}$

(c) $\frac{q^2B}{3Vd^3}$ (d) $\frac{qB^2d^2}{8V}$

22 A charge particle having charge q_0 and mass m is entered into a magnetic field with velocity v_0 as shown. Uniform magnetic field B_0 is present only on right side of dotted line. Average force exerted on charge particle during time it is inside magnetic field is

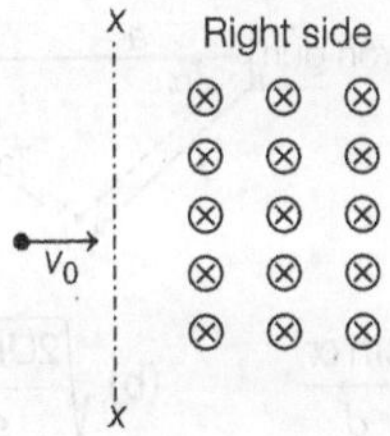

(a) $\frac{2qB_0v_0}{\pi}$ (b) qB_0v_0

(c) zero (d) $2qB_0v_0$

23 At $t = 0$, a charge q is at the origin and moving in the y-direction with velocity $\mathbf{v} = v\hat{\mathbf{j}}$. The charge moves in a magnetic field that is for $y > 0$ out of page and given by $B_1\hat{\mathbf{k}}$ and for $y < 0$ into the page and given by $-B_2\hat{\mathbf{k}}$. The charge's subsequent trajectory is shown in the sketch. From this information, we can deduce that

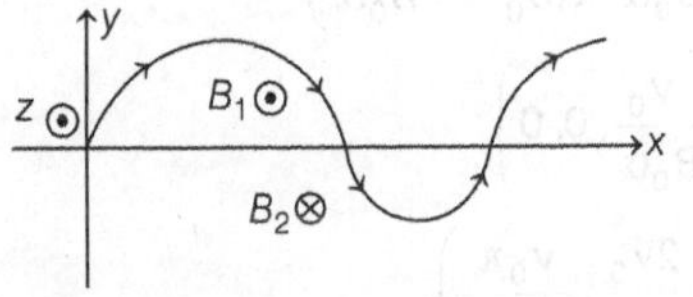

(a) $q > 0$ and $B_1 < B_2$

(b) $q < 0$ and $B_1 < B_2$

(c) $q > 0$ and $B_1 > B_2$

(d) $q < 0$ and $B_1 > B_2$

24 The magnetic field shown in the figure consists of two uniform regions. The width of the first part is 5 cm and the magnetic induction here is 0.001 T. The width of the other part is also 5 cm, with the direction of the induction being opposite in direction and 0.002 T in magnitude. What should be the minimum speed of the electron arriving from the direction indicated in the figure, so that it can pass through the magnetic field? Mass of electron $= 9 \times 10^{-31}$ kg

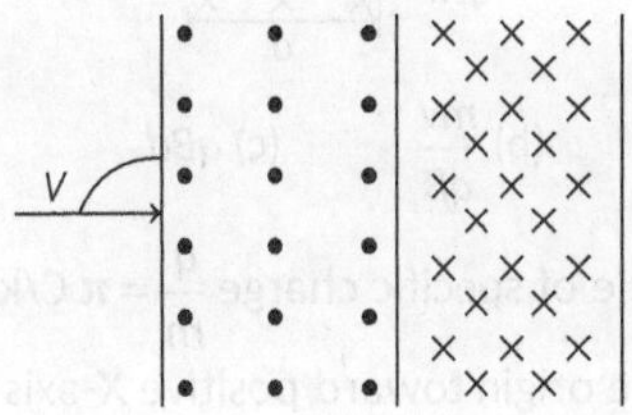

(a) $\frac{8}{9} \times 10^7$ m/s (b) $\frac{4}{9} \times 10^7$ m/s

(c) $\frac{16}{9} \times 10^7$ m/s (d) None of these

25 The region between $x = 0$ and $x = L$ is filled with uniform magnetic field $B_0\hat{\mathbf{k}}$. A particle of mass m positive charge q and velocity $v_0\hat{\mathbf{i}}$ travels along X-axis and enters the region of the magnetic field at origin (Neglect gravity). The particle emerges from the region of magnetic field with its velocity at an angle 30° to its initial. If the magnetic field is reduced to half of the initial value, then the angle of emergence will become

(a) $\sin^{-1}\left(\frac{1}{4}\right)$ (b) 60°

(c) 90° (d) $\sin^{-1}\left(\frac{1}{2}\right)$

26 A uniform magnetic field with a slit system as shown in figure is to be used as a momentum filter for high-energy charged particles. With a field B, it is found that the filter transmits α-particles each of energy 5.3 MeV. The magnetic field is increased to 2.3 B and deuterons are passed into the filter. The energy of each deuteron transmitted by the filter is

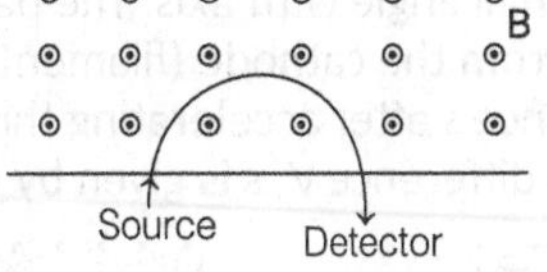

(a) 10.34 MeV (b) 8.34 MeV

(c) 14.02 MeV (d) None of these

27 A charged particle of mass m and charge q is projected into a uniform magnetic field of induction B with speed v which is perpendicular to B. The width of the magnetic field is d. The impulse imparted to the particle by the field is $\left(d << \frac{mv}{qB}\right)$

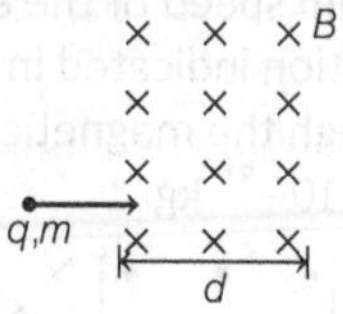

(a) qBv (b) $\frac{mv}{qB}$ (c) qBd (d) $\frac{2mv^2}{qB}$

28 A particle of specific charge $\frac{q}{m} = \pi$ C/kg is projected from the origin toward positive X-axis with a velocity of 10 m/s in a uniform magnetic field $\mathbf{B} = -2\hat{\mathbf{k}}$ T. The velocity $\mathbf{v}$ of particle after time $t = \frac{1}{12}$ s will be (in m/s)

(a) $5(\hat{i} + \sqrt{3}\hat{j})$ (b) $5(\sqrt{3}\hat{i} + \hat{j})$
(c) $5(\sqrt{3}\hat{i} - \hat{j})$ (d) $5(\hat{i} + \hat{j})$

29 A proton of mass 1.67×10^{-27} kg and charge 1.6×10^{-19} C is projected with a speed of 2×10^6 m/s at an angle of 60° to the X-axis. If a uniform magnetic field of 0.104 T is applied along Y-axis, the path of proton is a

(a) circle of radius 0.2 m, time period $\pi \times 10^{-7}$ s
(b) circle of radius 0.1 m, time period $2\pi \times 10^{-7}$ s
(c) helix of radius = 0.1 m and time period $2\pi \times 10^{-7}$ s
(d) helix of radius = 0.2 m and time period $4\pi \times 10^{-7}$ s

30 A charged particle is fired at an angle θ to a uniform magnetic field directed along the X-axis. During its motion along a helical path, if the pitch of the helical path is equal to the maximum distance of the particle from the X-axis

(a) $\cos\theta = \frac{1}{\pi}$ (b) $\sin\theta = \frac{1}{\pi}$
(c) $\tan\theta = \frac{1}{\pi}$ (d) $\tan\theta = \pi$

31 Figure shows an electron gun that emits electrons at very small angle with axis. The paraxial electrons emitted from the cathode (filament) are refocused at a distance s after accelerating through a potential difference V, s is given by (Take $\pi^2 = 10$)

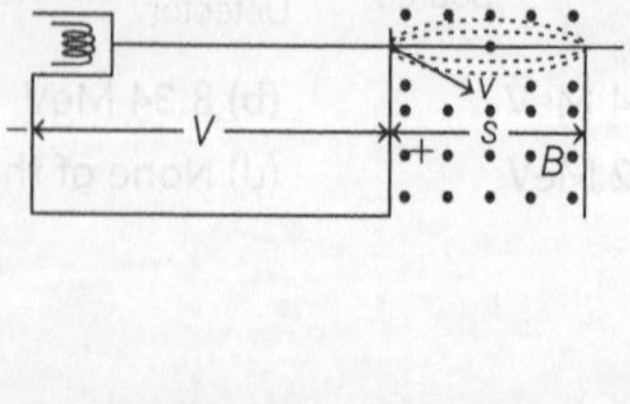

(a) $2\sqrt{\frac{20mV}{eB^2}}$ (b) $\sqrt{\frac{20mV}{eB^2}}$
(c) $\sqrt{\frac{10mV}{eB^2}}$ (d) None of these

32 Two particles of charges $+q$ and $-q$ are projected from the same point with a velocity v in a region of uniform magnetic field B such that the velocity vector makes an angle θ with the magnetic field. Their masses are m and $2m$, respectively. Then, they will meet again for the first time at a point whose distance from the point of projection is

(a) $\frac{2\pi mv\cos\theta}{qB}$ (b) $\frac{8\pi mv\cos\theta}{qB}$
(c) $\frac{\pi mv\cos\theta}{qB}$ (d) $\frac{4\pi mv\cos\theta}{qB}$

33 An electron gun T emits electron accelerated by a potential difference U in a vacuum in the direction of the line a as shown in figure. Target M is placed at a distance d as shown in figure. Find the magnetic field perpendicular to the plane determine by line a and the point M in order that electron hit the target M

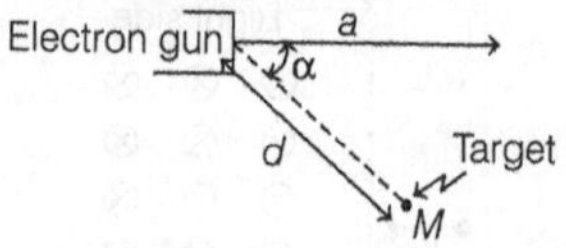

(a) $2\sqrt{\frac{2Um_e}{e}}\frac{\sin\alpha}{d}$ (b) $\sqrt{\frac{2Um_e}{e}}\frac{\sin\alpha}{2d}$
(c) $\sqrt{\frac{2Um_e}{e}}\frac{\sin\alpha}{d}$ (d) $8\sqrt{\frac{2Um_e}{e}}\frac{\sin\alpha}{d}$

34 A charged particle of specific charge α is released from origin at time $t = 0$ with velocity $\mathbf{v} = v_0\hat{\mathbf{i}} + v_0\hat{\mathbf{j}}$ in magnetic field $\mathbf{B} = B_0\hat{\mathbf{i}}$. The coordinates of the particle at time $t = \frac{\pi}{B_0\alpha}$ are (specific charge $\alpha = q/m$)

(a) $\left(\frac{v_0}{2B_0\alpha}, \frac{\sqrt{2}v_0}{\alpha B_0}, -\frac{v_0}{B_0\alpha}\right)$
(b) $\left(\frac{-v_0}{2B_0\alpha}, 0, 0\right)$
(c) $\left(0, \frac{2v_0}{B_0\alpha}, \frac{v_0\pi}{2B_0\alpha}\right)$
(d) $\left(\frac{v_0\pi}{B_0\alpha}, 0, -\frac{2v_0}{B_0\alpha}\right)$

35 An electrostatic field E and a magnetic field B act in the same region. Which one of the combinations shown in the figure can cause the electrons to pass undeflected?

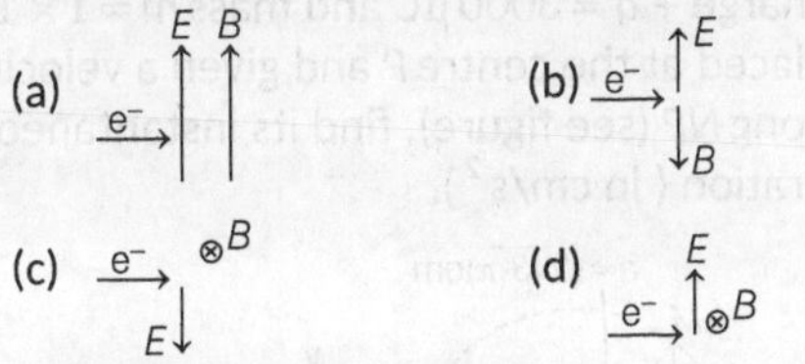

36 A particle having a charge 20 μC and mass 20 μg moves along a circle of radius 5 cm under the action of a magnetic field $B = 0.1$ T. When the particle is at P, a uniform electric field is switched ON and it is found that the particle continues on the tangent with a uniform velocity. Find the electric field.

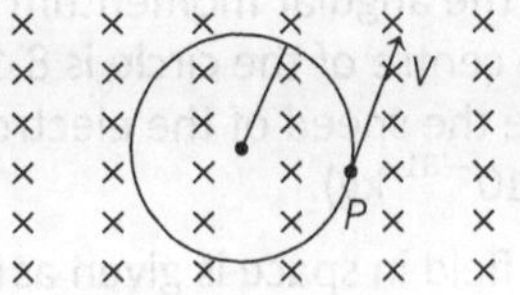

(a) 2 V/m (b) 1 V/m
(c) 0.5 V/m (d) 1.5 V/m

37 Electric and magnetic field are directed as $E_0\hat{i}$ and $B_0\hat{k}$ respectively. A particle of mass m and charge $+q$ is released from position (0, 2, 0) from rest. The velocity of that particle at (x, 5, 0) is $(5\hat{i} + 12\hat{j})$. The value of x will be

(a) $\dfrac{25m}{2qE_0}$ (b) $\dfrac{25m}{12qE_0}$

(c) $\dfrac{144m}{12qE_0}$ (d) $\dfrac{169m}{2qE_0}$

38 A particle of charge q and mass m starts moving from the origin under the action of an electric field $\mathbf{E} = E_0\hat{i}$ and $\mathbf{B} = B_0\hat{i}$ with velocity $\mathbf{v} = v_0\hat{j}$. The speed of the particle will become $2v_0$ after a time

(a) $t = \dfrac{2mv_0}{qE}$ (b) $t = \dfrac{2Bq}{mv_0}$

(c) $t = \dfrac{\sqrt{3}Bq}{mv_0}$ (d) $t = \dfrac{\sqrt{3}mv_0}{qE}$

39 An electron enters the space between the plates of a charged capacitor as shown. The charge density on the plate is σ. Electric field intensity in the space between the plates is E. A uniform magnetic field B also in that space perpendicular to the direction of E. The electron moves perpendicular to both $\mathbf{E}$ and $\mathbf{B}$ without any change in direction. The time taken by the electron to travel a distance l in that space is

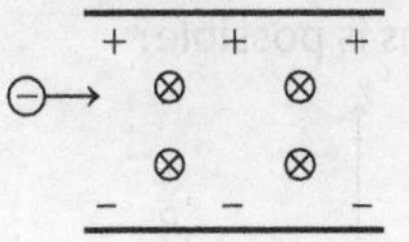

(a) $\dfrac{\varepsilon_0 lB}{\sigma}$ (b) $\dfrac{\varepsilon_0 l}{\sigma B}$

(c) $\dfrac{\sigma l}{\varepsilon_0 B}$ (d) $\dfrac{\sigma B}{\varepsilon_0 l}$

40 In a certain region uniform electric field E and magnetic field B are present in the opposite direction. At the instant $t = 0$, a particle of mass m carrying a charge q is given velocity v_0 at an angle θ, with the Y-axis, in the YZ-plane. The time after which the speed of the particle would be minimum is equal to

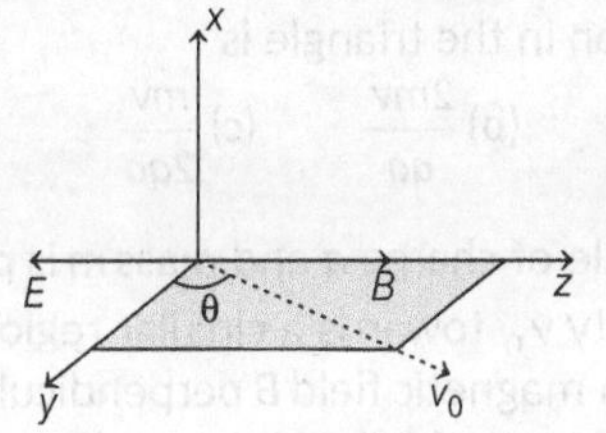

(a) $\dfrac{mv_0}{qE}$ (b) $\dfrac{mv_0 \sin\theta}{qE}$

(c) $\dfrac{mv_0 \cos\theta}{qE}$ (d) $\dfrac{2\pi m}{qB}$

41 Figure shows the path of an electron in a region of uniform magnetic field. The path consists of two straight sections, each between a pair of uniformly charged plates, and two half-circles. The plates are named 1, 2, 3 and 4. Then,

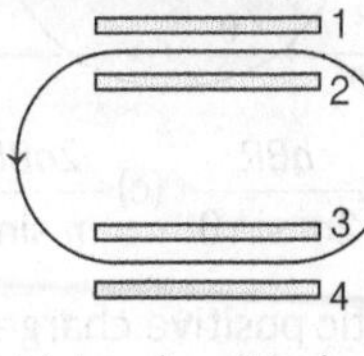

(a) 1 and 3 at higher (positive) potential and 2 and 4 at lower (negative) potential

(b) 1 and 3 at lower potential and 2 and 4 at higher potential

(c) 1 and 4 at higher potential and 2 and 3 at lower potential

(d) 1 and 4 at lower potential and 2 and 3 at higher potential

42 For a positively charged particle moving in a XY-plane initially along the X-axis, there is a sudden change in its path due to the presence of electric and / or magnetic fields beyond P. The curved path is shown in the XY-plane and is found to be non-circular. Which one of the following combinations is possible?

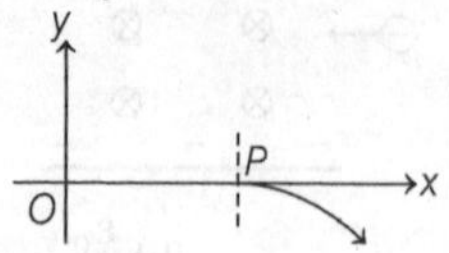

(a) $\mathbf{E} = 0$; $\mathbf{B} = b\hat{\mathbf{j}} + c\hat{\mathbf{k}}$ (b) $\mathbf{E} = a\hat{\mathbf{i}}$; $\mathbf{B} = c\hat{\mathbf{k}} + c\hat{\mathbf{i}}$

(c) $\mathbf{E} = 0$; $\mathbf{B} = c\hat{\mathbf{j}} + b\hat{\mathbf{k}}$ (d) $\mathbf{E} = a\hat{\mathbf{i}}$; $\mathbf{B} = c\hat{\mathbf{k}} + b\hat{\mathbf{j}}$

43 A uniform magnetic field exists in region which forms an equilateral triangle of side a. The magnetic field is perpendicular to the plane of the triangle. A charge q enters into this magnetic field perpendicular with speed v along perpendicular bisector of one side and comes out along perpendicular bisector of other side. The magnetic induction in the triangle is

(a) $\frac{mv}{qa}$ (b) $\frac{2mv}{qa}$ (c) $\frac{mv}{2qa}$ (d) $\frac{mv}{4qa}$

44 A particle of charge q and mass m is projected with a velocity v_0 towards a circular region having uniform magnetic field B perpendicular and into the plane of paper from point P as shown in figure. R is the radius and O is the centre of the circular region. If the line OP makes an angle θ with the initial line of motion then the value of v_0, so that particle passes through O is

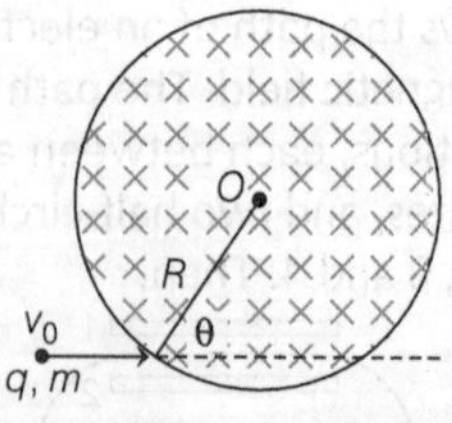

(a) $\frac{qBR}{m\sin\theta}$ (b) $\frac{qBR}{2m\sin\theta}$ (c) $\frac{2qBR}{m\sin\theta}$ (d) $\frac{3qBR}{2m\sin\theta}$

45 A non-relativistic positive charge particle of charge q and mass m is projected perpendicular to uniform magnetic field B as shown. Neglecting gravity calculate X-coordinate of point on screen at which the charge particle will hit. $d = \frac{r\sqrt{3}}{2}$, where $r = \frac{mv}{qB}$

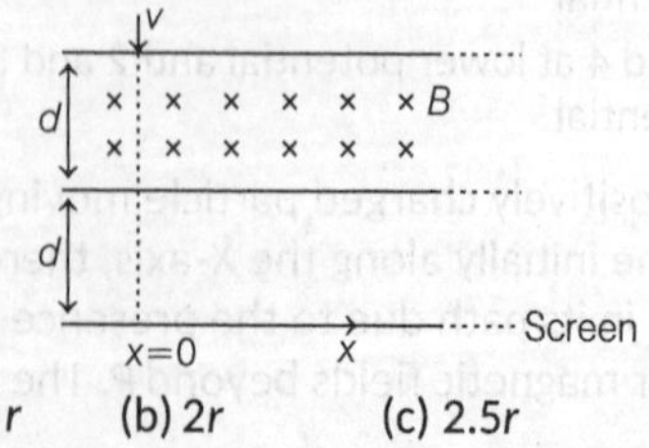

(a) $\sqrt{3}r$ (b) $2r$ (c) $2.5r$ (d) $0.5r$

Numerical Value Questions

1 A wire loop carrying a current $I = 10$ A is placed in the XY-plane as shown in the figure. If a particle with charge $+q = 3000\,\mu C$ and mass $m = 1 \times 10^{-5}$ kg is placed at the centre P and given a velocity 10 m/s along NP (see figure), find its instantaneous acceleration (in cm/s^2).

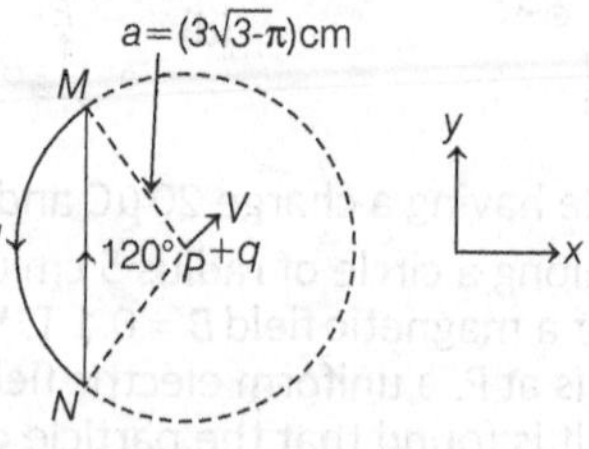

2 An electron moves in a circular path perpendicular to a constant magnetic field with a magnitude of 1.0 mT. If the angular momentum of the electron about the centre of the circle is 8.1×10^{-38} J-s, determine the speed of the electron (in m/s). (Take $m_e = 9 \times 10^{-31}$ kg).

3 Magnetic field in space is given as $\mathbf{B} = \sqrt{3}B_0\,\hat{\mathbf{i}} + B_0\,\hat{\mathbf{j}}$. A charged particle is projected along the line $y = \sqrt{3}x$ with velocity 2 m/s. Then find the distance (in m) travelled by particle in 3 s.

4 A particle of mass 1 mg and charge $1\,\mu C$ is projected with speed 50 m/s towards a region containing a uniform magnetic field 10 T. What should be the minimum thickness (d) of this region (in m), so that the particle returns back to left side?

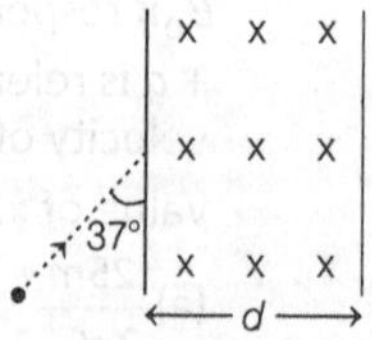

5 A beam of equally charged particles after being accelerated through a voltage V enters into a magnetic field B as shown in the figure. It is found that all the particles hit the plane between C and D. Find $\frac{m_{max}}{m_{min}}$, where m_{max} = the mass of the heaviest particle and m_{min} = the mass of lightest particles of the beam.

(Given $B = 4 \times 10^{-3}$ T, $V = 5$ volt, $l = 20$ cm and $d = 2$ cm)

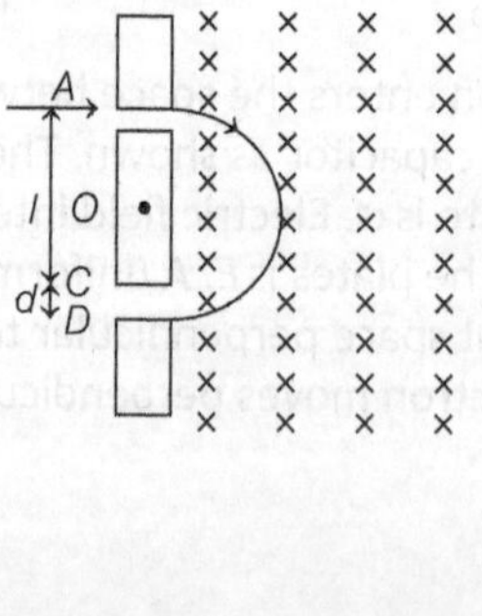

6 There is a constant homogeneous electric field of 200 V m^{-1} within the region $x = 0$ and $x = 0.167$ m pointing in the positive X-direction. There is a constant homogeneous magnetic field B within the region $x = 0.167$ m and $x = 0.334$ m pointing in the Z-direction. A proton at rest at the origin ($x = 0$, $y = 0$) is released. Find the strength of the magnetic field (in mT) B, so that the proton is deflected back to just reach $x = 0, y = -0.167$ m.
(mass of the proton $= 1.67 \times 10^{-27}$ kg)

7 A neutral particle of mass 28 g is at rest in a uniform magnetic field $B = 200/3$ T. At $t = 0$, particle decays into two particles of equal mass and one of them having charge 3 μC. Both of them move in separate paths lying in the plane perpendicular to magnetic field B. At later time t, the particles collide. Find the time (in s) of collision neglecting the interaction force.

8 A charge particle of mass m and charge $-q$ is released from rest from the given position. A uniform horizontal magnetic field B exists in space as shown. Find normal reaction (in N) acting on the charge at point P. ($m = 2$ kg, $q = 2$C, $R = 5$ m, $B = 0.5$ T, $g = 10$ m/s^2)

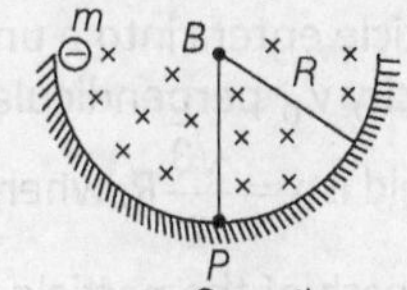

Smooth
Hemispherical Surface

9 A uniform magnetic field of intensity 1 T is applied in a circular region of radius 0.1 m, directed into the plane of paper. A charged particle of mass 5×10^{-5} kg and charge $q = 5 \times 10^{-4}$ C enters the field with velocity $\frac{1}{\sqrt{3}}$ m / s making an angle of $\frac{\pi}{n}$ with a radial line of circular region in such a way that it passes through the centre of the applied field. Find the value of n.

10 Electrons of kinetic energy 80 eV starting from a point source are allowed to spread out in the form of a cone of small vertex angle. If the axis of the cone is along the axis of a solenoid having 3000 turns/m, then calculate the minimum current (in mA) that must be circulated through the solenoid, so that the electrons are first focussed at a distance of 0.10 m from the source.
(Given : $m_e = 9 \times 10^{-31}$ kg, $e = 1.6 \times 10^{-19}$ C)

LEVEL 03 JEE Advanced Level

Single Choice Correct Questions

1 A small particle of mass $m = 1$ kg and charge of 1C enters perpendicularly in a triangular region of uniform magnetic field of strength 2T as shown in figure with velocity 48 m/s. The time that it spends in magnetic region is

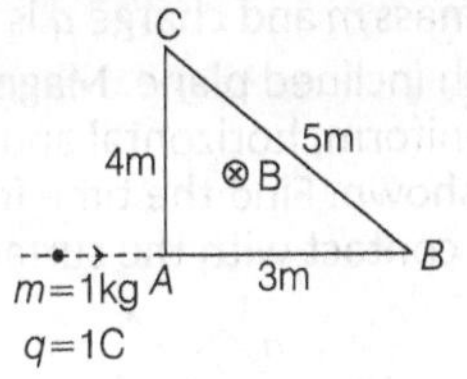

(a) $\frac{7\pi}{360}$ s (b) $\frac{\pi}{40}$ s
(c) $\frac{7\pi}{180}$ s (d) $\frac{11\pi}{180}$ s

2 Two protons move parallel to each other, keeping distance r between them, both moving with same velocity $\mathbf{v}$. Then, the ratio of the electric and magnetic force of interaction between them is

(a) $\frac{c^2}{v^2}$ (b) $\frac{2c^2}{v^2}$
(c) $\frac{c^2}{2v^2}$ (d) None of these

3 A neutral particle at rest in a magnetic field decays into two charged particles of different mass. The energy released goes into their kinetic energy. Then, what can be the path of the two particles? Neglect any interaction between the two charges.

(a) 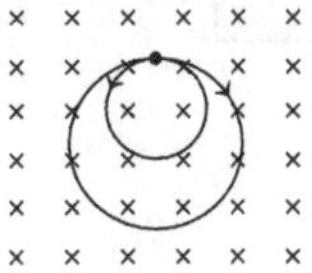

(b) 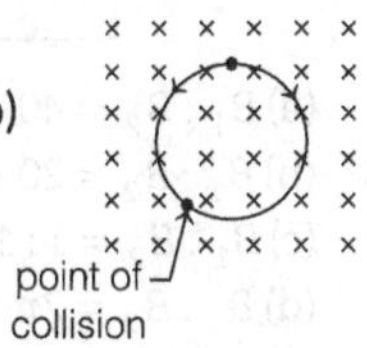

(c) 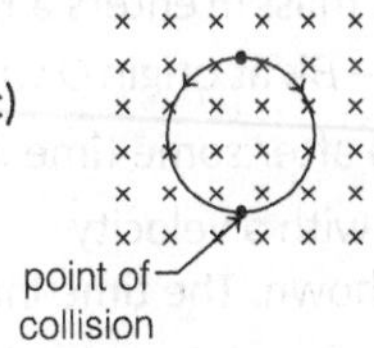

(d) 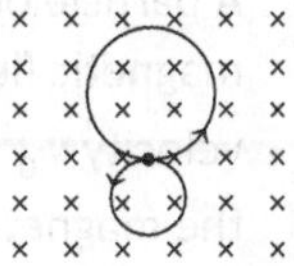

4 A charged particle enters into a uniform magnetic field with velocity v_0 perpendicular to it, the length of magnetic field is $x = \frac{\sqrt{3}}{2}R$, where R is the radius of the circular path of the particle in the field. The magnitude of change in velocity of the particle when it comes out of the field is

(a) $2v_0$ (b) $\frac{v_0}{2}$

(c) $\frac{\sqrt{3}v_0}{2}$ (d) v_0

5 Magnetic field is given by $(100\,\hat{k})$ T, in the region defined by $x^2 + y^2 = 16$ and $y > 0$. A charge particle of mass $m = 10^{-19}$ kg, $q = 1.6 \times 10^{-19}$ C enters at origin with a velocity $\mathbf{v}_0 = (640\,\hat{j})$ m/s. What is the angle of deviation (in degree) suffered by charge particle in the magnetic field?

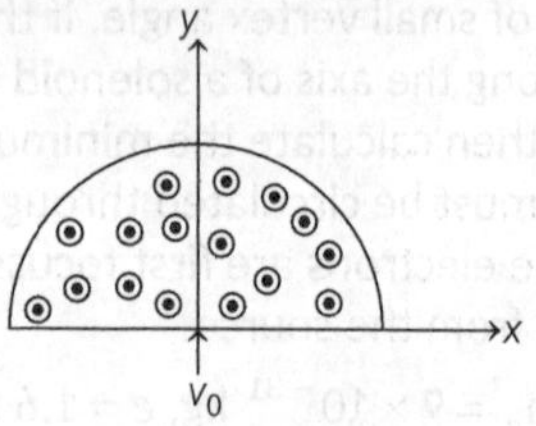

(a) 45° (b) 30°
(c) 60° (d) 37°

6 A charged particle is projected at a speed $v = 10^6$ m/s perpendicular to the boundary OX of two homogeneous magnetic fields. Magnetic induction vector fields are parallel to each other and perpendicular to the particle velocity. The average velocity of the particle till it completes a semi-circle in both magnetic fields is 10^5 m/s. Then,

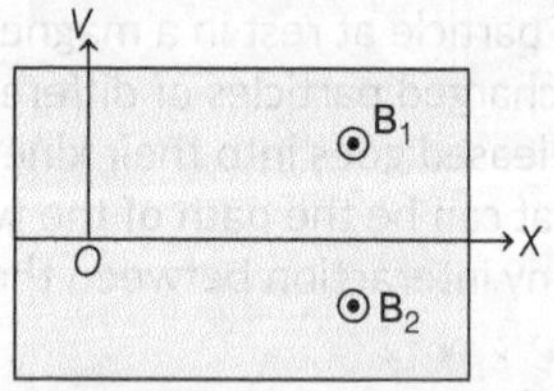

(a) $B_1 : B_2 = 40 - \pi : 40 + \pi$
(b) $B_1 : B_2 = 20 - \pi : 20 + \pi$
(c) $B_1 : B_2 = 1 : 1$
(d) $B_1 : B_2 = 2\pi : 2 + \pi$

7 A particle of charge q and mass m enters a uniform magnetic field region $\mathbf{B} = -B\hat{k}$ at origin O with a velocity $\mathbf{v}_0 = 6\hat{i}$ m/s and after some time it exits the magnetic field region with a velocity $\mathbf{v}_0 = (3\hat{i} + 3\sqrt{3}\hat{j})$ m/s as shown. The time interval for which the particle has moved in the magnetic field region is

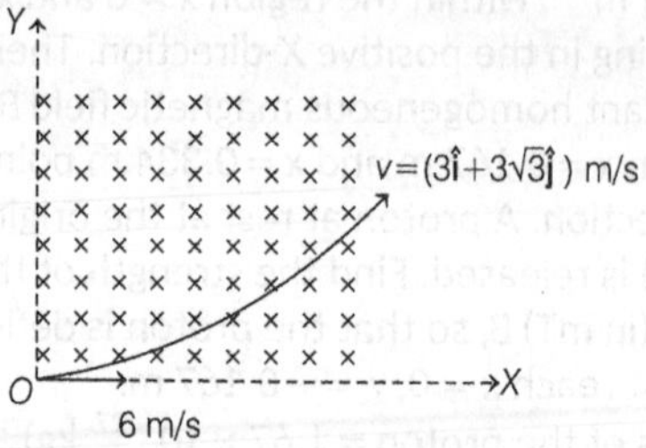

(a) $\frac{\pi m}{qB}$ (b) $\frac{\pi m}{2qB}$

(c) $\frac{\pi m}{3qB}$ (d) $\frac{\pi m}{4qB}$

8 Figure shows circular region of radius $R = \sqrt{3}$ m in which upper half has uniform magnetic field $\mathbf{B} = 0.2(-\hat{\mathbf{k}})$ T and lower half has uniform magnetic field $\mathbf{B} = 0.2\hat{\mathbf{k}}$ T. A very thin parallel beam of point charges each having mass $m = 2$ gm, speed $v = 0.3$ m/s and charge $q = +1$ mC are projected along the diameter as shown in figure. A screen is placed perpendicular to initial velocity of charges as shown. The distance between the points on screen where charges will strikes after being deflected by the magnetic field is

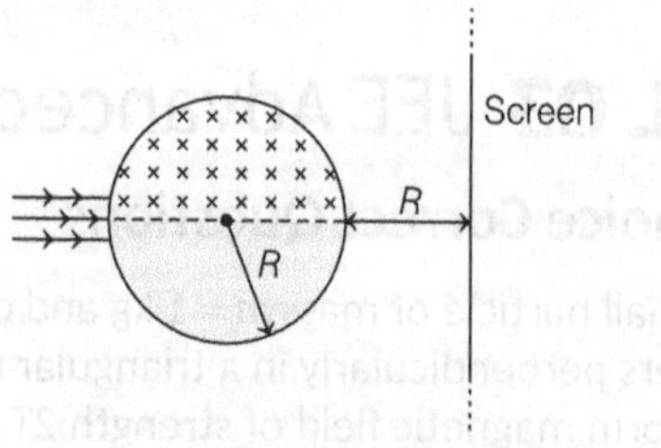

(a) 9 m (b) 10 m
(c) 12 m (d) 16 m

9 A block of mass m and charge q is released on a long smooth inclined plane. Magnetic field B is constant, uniform, horizontal and parallel to surface as shown. Find the time from start when block loses contact with the surface.

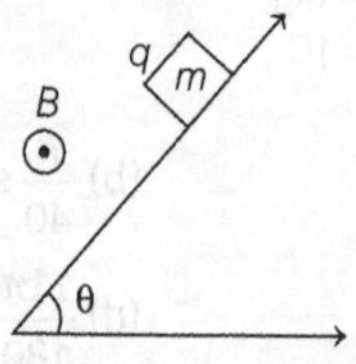

(a) $\frac{m\cos\theta}{qB}$ (b) $\frac{m\,\mathrm{cosec}\,\theta}{qB}$

(c) $\frac{m\cot\theta}{qB}$ (d) None of these

10 A particle of positive charge q and mass m enters with velocity $v\hat{j}$ at the origin in a magnetic field $B(-\hat{k})$ which is present in the whole space. The charge makes a perfectly inelastic collision with identical particle at rest but free to move at its maximum Y-coordinate. After collision the combined charge will move on trajectory (where $r = mv/qB$)

(a) $x^2 + y^2 = r^2$

(b) $(x+r)^2 + \left(y - \frac{r}{2}\right)^2 = \frac{r^2}{4}$

(c) $(x-r)^2 + (y-r)^2 = r^2$

(d) $(x-r)^2 + \left(y + \frac{r}{2}\right)^2 = \frac{r^2}{4}$

11 A charged particle moves inside a pipe which is bent as shown in figure. If $R < \frac{mv}{qB}$, then force exerted by the pipe on charged particle at P is (Neglect gravity)

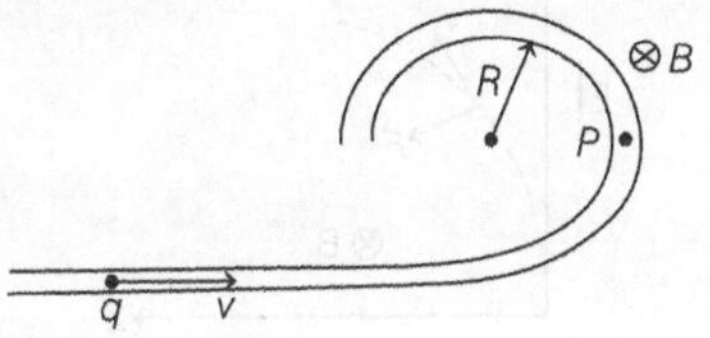

(a) towards centre
(b) away from centre
(c) zero
(d) None of the above

12 Suppose a hypothetical magnetic field exists in space $\mathbf{B} = B_0\hat{\mathbf{u}}_r$ above the earth surface where $\hat{\mathbf{u}}_r$ is a unit vector directed radially outward from origin. Origin is on surface of earth. A light charged particle has to perform uniform circular motion in the combined uniform (vertical) gravitational field of earth and magnetic field with speed v and radius r. Height of the plane of motion from earth surface will be

(a) $\frac{v^2}{g}$ (b) $\frac{v^2}{2g}$

(c) $\frac{2v^2}{g}$ (d) $\frac{\sqrt{2}v^2}{g}$

13 In the plane mirror, the coordinates of image of charged particle (initially at origin as shown) after two and half time periods are (initial velocity v_0 is in the XY-plane and the plane mirror is perpendicular to the X-axis. A uniform magnetic field $B\hat{i}$ exists in the whole space. P_0 is pitch of helix, R_0 is radius of helix).

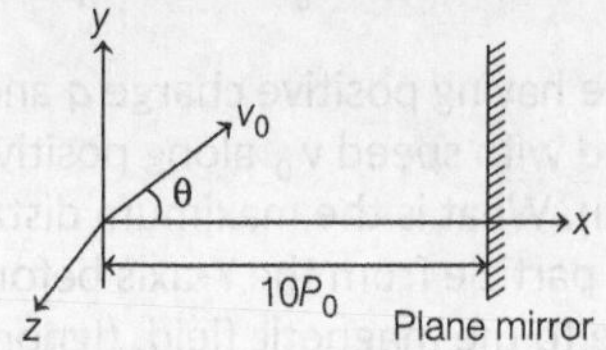

(a) $17P_0, 0, -2R_0$ (b) $3P_0, 0, -2R_0$

(c) $17.5P_0, 0, -2R_0$ (d) $3P_0, 0, 2R_0$

14 At time t_1, an electron is sent along the positive direction of X-axis, through both an electric field **E** and a magnetic field **B**, with **E** directed parallel to the Y-axis. Graph gives the y-component $F_{\text{net}, y}$ of the net force on the electron due to the two fields, as a function of the electron's speed v at time t_1. The magnitude of z-component of magnetic field is

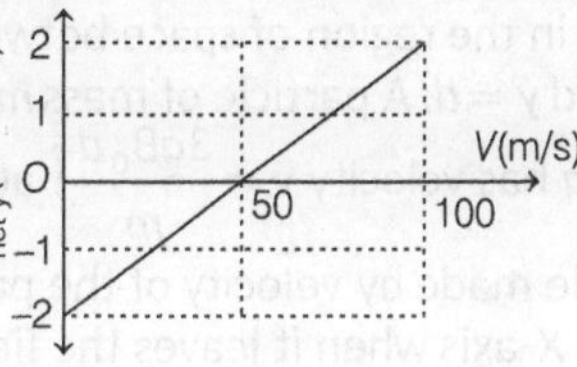

(a) 20×10^{-3} T (b) 25×10^{-3} T

(c) 50×10^{-3} T (d) 75×10^{-3} T

15 There exists a uniform magnetic and electric field of magnitude 1 T and 1 V/m respectively along positive Y-axis. A charged particle of mass 1 kg and of charge 1 C is having velocity 1 m/s along X-axis and is at origin at $t = 0$. Then the coordinates of particle at time π seconds will be

(a) (0, 1, 2) (b) $\left(0, -\frac{\pi^2}{2}, -2\right)$

(c) $\left(2, \frac{\pi^2}{2}, 2\right)$ (d) $\left(0, \frac{\pi^2}{2}, 2\right)$

16 In a certain region of space a uniform and constant electric field and a magnetic field parallel to each other are present. A proton is fired from a point A in the field with speed $v = 4 \times 10^4$ m/s at an angle of α with the field direction. The proton reaches a point B in the field where its velocity makes an angle β with the field direction. If $\frac{\sin\alpha}{\sin\beta} = \sqrt{3}$, find the electric potential difference between the points A and B. Take m_p (mass of proton) $= 1.6 \times 10^{-27}$ kg and e (magnitude of electronic charge) $= 1.6 \times 10^{-19}$ C

(a) 16 V (b) $\frac{16}{3}$ V (c) 90 V (d) 30 V

17 Magnetic field exists in the space and given as $\mathbf{B} = -\frac{B_0}{l^2} x^2 \hat{\mathbf{k}}$, where B_0 and l are positive constants. A particle having positive charge q and mass m is projected with speed v_0 along positive X-axis from the origin. What is the maximum distance of the charged particle from the Y-axis before it turns back due to the magnetic field. (Ignore any interaction other than magnetic field)

(a) $\left(\frac{ml^2 v_0}{3qB_0}\right)^{\frac{1}{3}}$ (b) $\left(\frac{3ml^2 v_0}{2qB_0}\right)^{\frac{1}{3}}$

(c) $\left(\frac{3ml^2 v_0}{qB_0}\right)^{\frac{1}{3}}$ (d) $\left(\frac{ml^2 v_0}{qB_0}\right)^{\frac{1}{3}}$

18 A non-uniform magnetic field $\mathbf{B} = B_0\left(1 + \frac{y}{d}\right)(-\hat{\mathbf{k}})$ is present in the region of space between $y = 0$ and $y = d$. A particle of mass m and positive charge q has velocity $\mathbf{v} = \frac{3qB_0 d}{m}\hat{\mathbf{i}}$ at origin O. Find the angle made by velocity of the particle with the positive X-axis when it leaves the field. (Ignore any interaction other than magnetic field)

(a) 90° (b) 30°
(c) 60° (d) 45°

19 A particle having mass m, charge q is projected with velocity v_0 along Y-axis in a region of uniform magnetic field B_0 which is outward and perpendicular to the plane of the paper as shown in the figure. The particle is continuously subjected to a frictional force which varies with velocity as $\mathbf{F}_r = -\alpha \mathbf{v}$, where α is a constant. Consequently the particle moves on a spiral path till it comes to rest at point P. The X-coordinate of point P is (Take, $\alpha = 10^{-3}$ kg/s, $q = 10^{-3}$ C, $B_0 = 1$ T, $v_0 = 1$ m/s, $m = 20$ gm)

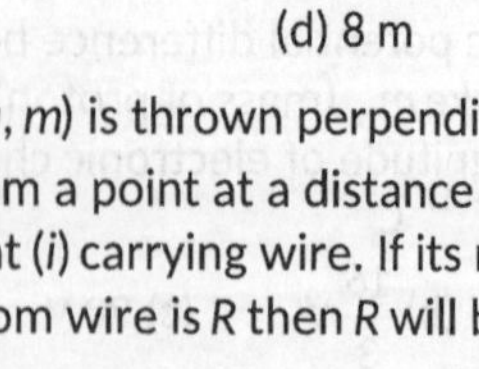

(a) 10 m (b) 4 m
(c) 6 m (d) 8 m

20 A charge (q, m) is thrown perpendicularly with speed v from a point at a distance r from an infinite long current (i) carrying wire. If its maximum distance from wire is R then R will be

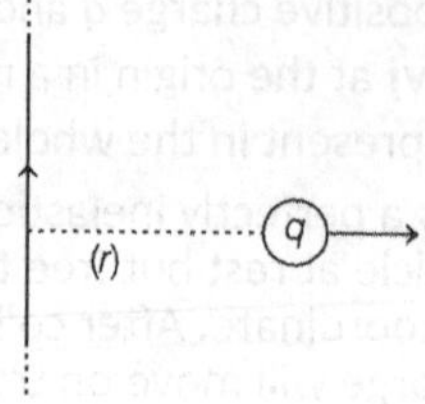

(a) infinite (b) $\left(re^{\frac{2\pi mv}{\mu_0 qi}}\right)$

(c) $\left(re^{\frac{4\pi mv}{\mu_0 qi}}\right)$ (d) $\left(re^{\frac{\pi mv}{\mu_0 qi}}\right)$

21 An electron is released from the origin at a place where a uniform electric field E and a uniform magnetic field B exist along the negative Y-axis and the negative Z-axis, respectively. Find the displacement of the electron along the Y-axis when its velocity becomes perpendicular to the electric field for the first time.

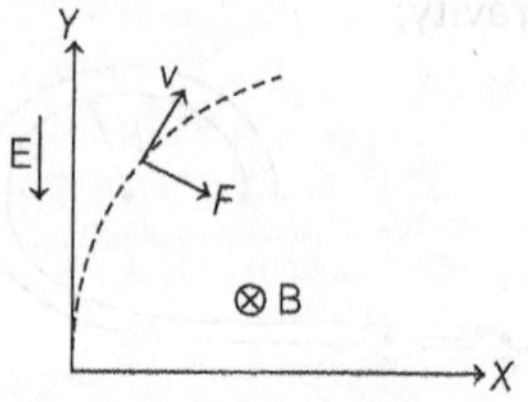

(a) $\frac{2Em}{eB^2}$ (b) $\frac{Em}{2eB^2}$ (c) $\frac{Em}{eB^2}$ (d) $\frac{Em}{3eB^2}$

22 A uniform electric field E is present horizontally along the paper throughout the region but uniform magnetic field B_0 is present horizontally (perpendicular to plane of paper in inward direction) right to the line AB. A charge particle having charge q and mass m is projected vertically upward and it crosses the line AB after time t_0. Find the speed of projection if particle moves with constant velocity after t_0. (Given $qE = mg$)

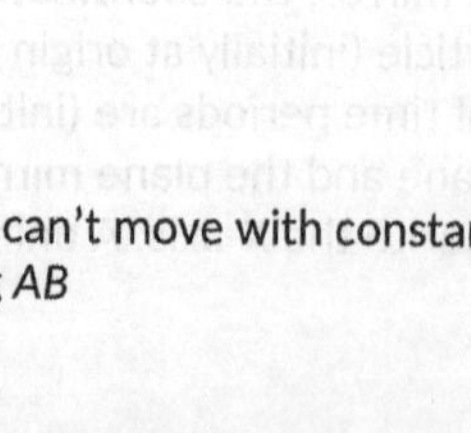

(a) gt_0
(b) $2gt_0$
(c) $\frac{gt_0}{2}$
(d) Particle can't move with constant velocity after crossing AB

23 A ring of mass m and radius r is made of an insulating material carries uniformly distributed charge. Initially it rests on a frictionless horizontal tabletop with its plane vertical. The charge on the ring, such that it starts rolling on entering completely into the region of the magnetic field, is

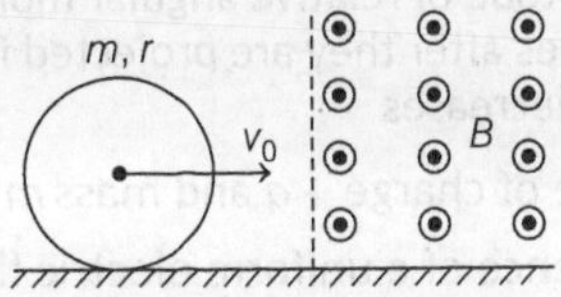

(a) $\frac{mv_0}{rB}$ (b) $\frac{\sqrt{2}mv_0}{rB}$

(c) $\frac{mv_0}{\sqrt{2}rB}$ (d) $\frac{2mv_0}{rB}$

Multiple Choice(s) Correct Questions

1 Velocity and acceleration vector of a charged particle moving in a magnetic field at some instant are $\mathbf{v} = 3\hat{\mathbf{i}} + 4\hat{\mathbf{j}}$ and $\mathbf{a} = 2\hat{\mathbf{i}} + x\hat{\mathbf{j}}$. Select the correct alternative (s)

(a) $x = -1.5$

(b) $x = 3$

(c) Magnetic field is along z-direction

(d) Kinetic energy of the particle is constant

2 A charged particle of unit mass and unit charge moves with velocity of $\mathbf{v} = (8\hat{\mathbf{i}} + 6\hat{\mathbf{j}})$ m/s in a magnetic field of $\mathbf{B} = (2\hat{\mathbf{k}})$ T. Choose the correct alternative(s).

(a) The path of the particle may be $x^2 + y^2 - 4x - 31 = 0$

(b) The path of the particle may be $x^2 + y^2 = 25$

(c) The path of the particle may be $y^2 + z^2 = 25$

(d) The time period of the particle will be π s

3 A charged particle is projected in magnetic field $\mathbf{B} = 10\hat{\mathbf{k}}$ from origin in XY-plane. The particle moves in a circle and just touches a line $y = 5$ m at $x = 5\sqrt{3}$ m. Then,

(Mass of particle $= 5 \times 10^{-5}$ kg, charge $= 1\,\mu$C)

(a) the particle is projected at an angle of 60° with X-axis

(b) the radius of circle is 10 m

(c) speed of particle is 2 m/s

(d) work done by magnetic force on the particle is zero

4 Two particles having the same specific charge (q/m) enter a uniform magnetic field with the same speed but at angles of 30° and 60° with the field. Let a, b and c be the ratios of their pitches, radii and periods of their helical paths respectively, then

(a) $abc = 1$ (b) $a + b = 2\sqrt{c}$

(c) $a^2 = c$ (d) $ab = c$

5 There are two points (X and Y) on the same B-line at a distance of 10 cm in a uniform magnetic field of magnetic induction $B = 0.02$ T. An electron, which was accelerated through a potential difference of 800 V, passes point X, such that its velocity encloses an angle of α with the induction line. What may the value of α be if the electron passes point Y as well ? (Take : $m_e = 9 \times 10^{-31}$ kg, $\pi^2 = 10$)

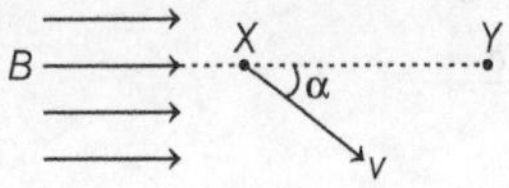

(a) $\cos^{-1}\left(\frac{5}{6}\right)$ (b) $\cos^{-1}\left(\frac{2}{3}\right)$

(c) 60° (d) Not possible for any α

6 A beam of charge particles is fired from a point on the X-axis, speed of each particle is v and its direction deviates by at most $\Delta\theta$ from the axis. Electric field E points in the X-direction along with the magnetic field B. The charge particles having mass m and charge q are observed to come back to the X-axis in the interval $(L, L - \Delta L)$.

(Distances are measured from the firing point)

(a) $\Delta L = \frac{\pi mv(\Delta\theta)^2}{qB}$

(b) $\Delta L = \frac{\pi mv(\Delta\theta)^2}{qB}$

(c) $L = \frac{2\pi mv}{qB} + \frac{2\pi^2 mE}{qB^2}$

(d) $L = \frac{\pi mv}{qB} + \frac{\pi^2 mE}{qB^2}$

7 In a region having an electric field and a magnetic field, a positive charge is released with the below given parameters, $\mathbf{E} = a\hat{\mathbf{i}}$, $\mathbf{B} = b\hat{\mathbf{i}} + c\hat{\mathbf{j}} + d\hat{\mathbf{k}}$, $\mathbf{v} = x\hat{\mathbf{i}} + y\hat{\mathbf{j}}$

(a) If $(yb + cx)\hat{\mathbf{k}} + xd\hat{\mathbf{j}} = 0$ charged particle moves along straight line

(b) For $c = 0$, $d = 0$, $y = 0$ charged particle moves along straight line with increasing speed

(c) For $c = 0$, $d = 0$, $y \neq 0$ charged particle moves along helix of varying pitch

(d) For $a = 0$, $\mathbf{v} \cdot \mathbf{B} = 0$ charged particle moves along circle

8 A particle of specific charge α is projected from origin at $t = 0$ with a velocity $\mathbf{v} = v_0(\hat{\mathbf{i}} + \hat{\mathbf{k}})$ in a magnetic field $\mathbf{B} = -B_0\hat{\mathbf{k}}$. Then,

(a) at $t = \dfrac{\pi}{\alpha B_0}$, velocity of the particle is $-v_0(\hat{\mathbf{i}} - \hat{\mathbf{k}})$.

(b) at $t = \dfrac{\pi}{4\alpha B_0}$, speed of the particle is v_0.

(c) at $t = \dfrac{2\pi}{\alpha B_0}$, magnitude of displacement of the particle is $\dfrac{2v_0}{\alpha B_0}$.

(d) at $t = \dfrac{2\pi}{\alpha B_0}$, distance travelled by the particle is $\dfrac{2\sqrt{2}\,\pi v_0}{\alpha B_0}$.

9 A charge particle of charge q, mass m is moving with initial velocity v as shown in figure in a uniform magnetic field $-B\hat{\mathbf{k}}$. Select the correct alternative/alternatives.

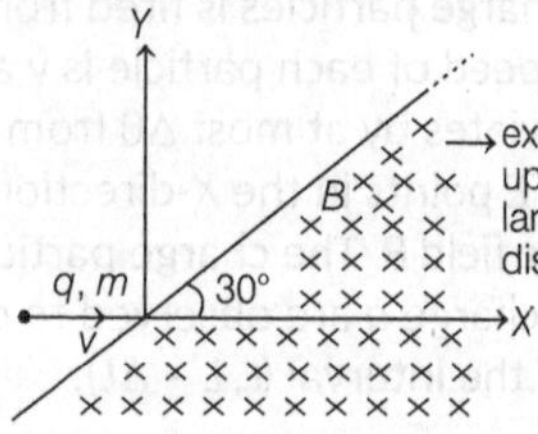

(a) Velocity of particle when it comes out from magnetic field is $\mathbf{v} = v\cos 60°\,\hat{\mathbf{i}} - v\sin 60°\,\hat{\mathbf{j}}$

(b) Time for which the particle was in magnetic field is $\dfrac{\pi m}{3qB}$

(c) Distance travelled in magnetic field is $\dfrac{\pi mv}{3qB}$

(d) The particle will never come out of magnetic field

10 Two identical charged particles (of mass m and having charge q) are simultaneously projected from origin (as shown) with equal speed v, in a region of transverse magnetic field.

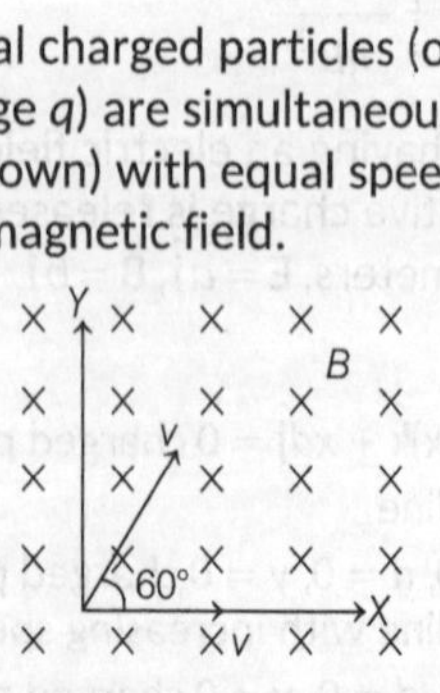

(a) If $\mathbf{r}_1$ and $\mathbf{r}_2$ are the position vectors of the particles at time $t = \dfrac{\pi m}{qB}$, then $\mathbf{r}_1 \cdot \mathbf{r}_2$ equals $2\left(\dfrac{mv}{qB}\right)^2$

(b) If $\mathbf{r}_1$ and $\mathbf{r}_2$ are the position vectors of the particles at time $t = \dfrac{\pi m}{qB}$, then $\mathbf{r}_1 \cdot \mathbf{r}_2$ equals $\dfrac{1}{2}\left(\dfrac{mv}{qB}\right)^2$

(c) Magnitude of relative speeds of the particles after they are projected remains constant

(d) Magnitude of relative angular momentum of the particles after they are projected first increases, then decreases

11 A particle of charge $+q$ and mass m moving under the influence of a uniform electric field $E\hat{\mathbf{i}}$ and uniform magnetic field $B\hat{\mathbf{k}}$ follows a trajectory from P to Q as shown in figure. The velocities at P and Q are $v\hat{\mathbf{i}}$ and $-2\hat{\mathbf{j}}$ respectively. Which of the following statement(s) is/are correct ?

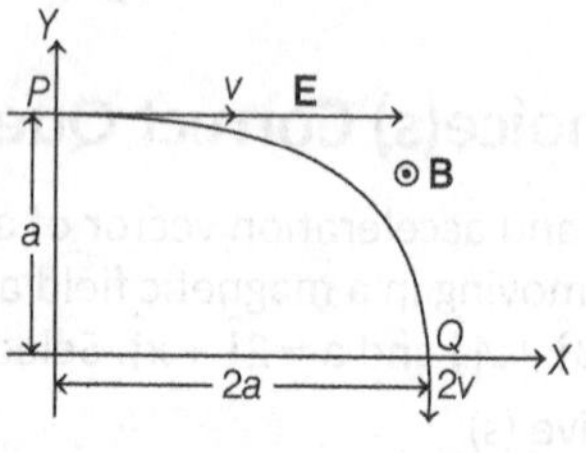

(a) $E = \dfrac{3}{4}\left[\dfrac{mv^2}{qa}\right]$

(b) Rate of work done by the electric field at P is $\dfrac{3}{4}\left[\dfrac{mv^3}{a}\right]$

(c) Rate of work done by the electric field at P is zero

(d) Rate of work done by both the fields at Q is zero

12 In a region magnetic field along X-axis changes with time according to the given graph. If time period, pitch and radius of helix path are T_0, P_0 and R_0 respectively, then which of the following is/are correct if the particle is projected at an angle θ with the positive X-axis in XY-plane?

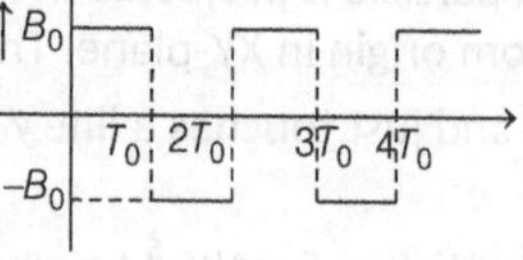

(a) At $t = \dfrac{T_0}{2}$, coordinates of charge are $\left(\dfrac{P_0}{2}, 0, -2R_0\right)$.

(b) At $t = \dfrac{3T_0}{2}$, coordinates of charge are $\left(\dfrac{3P_0}{2}, 0, 2R_0\right)$.

(c) Two extremes from X-axis are at a distance $2R_0$ from each other.

(d) Two extremes from X-axis are at a distance $4R_0$ from each other.

13 A ring of mass m and radius R is set into pure rolling on horizontal rough surface, in a uniform magnetic field of strength B as shown in the figure. A point charge q of negligible mass is attached to rolling ring. Friction is sufficient, so that it does not slip at any point of its motion.

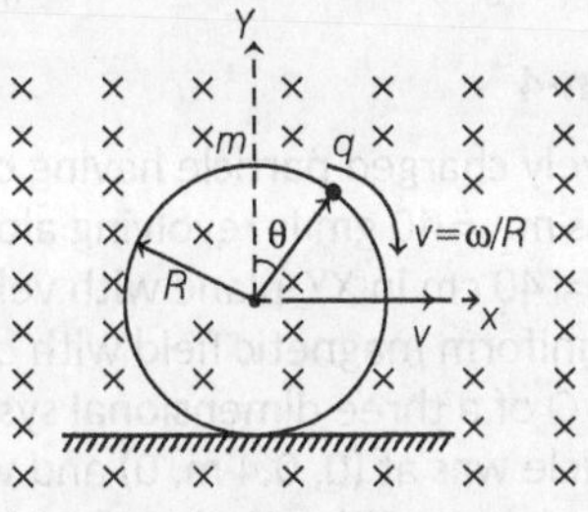

(q is measured in clockwise from positive Y-axis)

(a) Ring will continue to move with constant velocity
(b) The value of friction acting on ring is $Bqv\cos\theta$
(c) The value of friction acting on ring is $Bqv\sin\theta$
(d) Ring will lose contact with ground if v is greater than $\left(\frac{mg}{2qB}\right)$

14 A non-conducting cylindrical shell of radius R is placed in uniform magnetic field. The axis of the cylinder is parallel to the direction of magnetic field. A hole is drilled in cylinder and a particle having charge q and mass m is projected with velocity v perpendicular to magnetic field and directed towards the axis of cylinder as shown in diagram. The particle collides elastically with inner wall of the cylinder and rebounds.

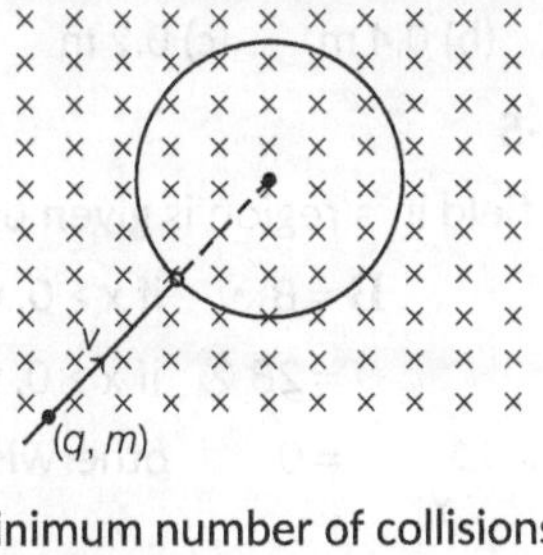

(a) The minimum number of collisions after which it will emerge is two
(b) The maximum speed v_0 for which it can come out is $v_0 = \left(\frac{qBR}{m}\right)\sqrt{3}$
(c) The minimum time in which it can come out will be $\left(\frac{\pi m}{qB}\right)$
(d) If the particle is projected with a velocity $\frac{v_0}{3}$ it will come out after five collisions.

15 A particle having charge 1C and mass 1 kg enters a region having uniform magnetic field of strength 2 T with a speed of 12 m/s, as shown in figure, then the CORRECT statement(s) is/are

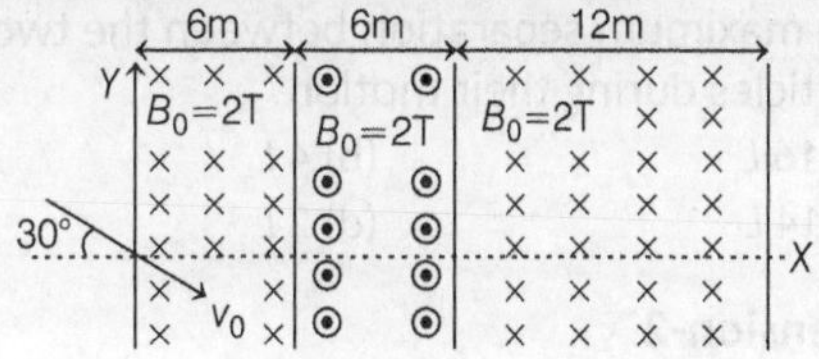

(a) The time for which the charge particle remains in magnetic field is $\frac{4\pi}{3}$ s.
(b) The velocity of charged particle becomes parallel to X-axis 6 times during its motion
(c) The distance between the point where the charge particle enters the uniform magnetic field and the point where it emerges out is 6 m
(d) The deviation of the charge particle when it emerges out of the magnetic field is $\frac{2\pi}{3}$ rad.

Comprehension Based Questions

Comprehension-1

Two charge particles each of mass m, carrying charge $+q$ and connected with each other by a massless inextensible string of length $2L$ are describing circular path in the plane of paper, each with speed $v = \frac{qB_0L}{m}$ (where B_0 is constant) about their centre of mass in the region in which an uniform magnetic field **B** exists into the plane of paper as shown in figure. Neglect any effect of electrical, gravitational and mutual interaction forces.

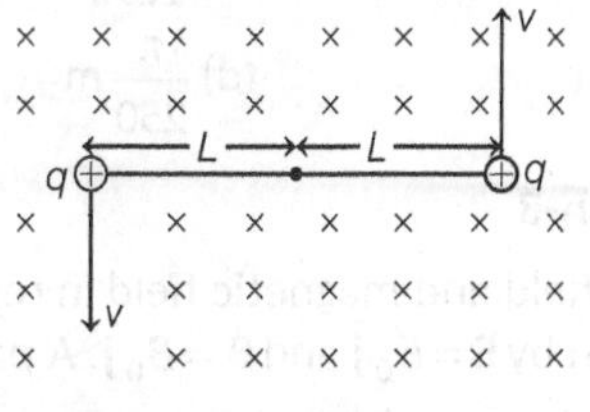

1 The magnitude of the magnetic field such that no tension is developed in the string will be

(a) $\frac{B_0}{2}$ (b) B_0 (c) $2B_0$ (d) 0

2 If the actual magnitude of magnetic field is half to that of calculated in part (i), then tension in the string will be

(a) $\frac{3}{4}\frac{q^2B_0^2L}{m}$ (b) zero (c) $\frac{q^2B_0^2L}{2m}$ (d) $\frac{2q^2B_0^2L}{m}$

3 Given that the string breaks when the tension is $T = \frac{3}{4}\frac{q^2B_0^2L}{m}$. Now, if the magnetic field is reduced to such a value that the string just breaks, then find the maximum separation between the two particles during their motion

(a) $16L$ (b) $4L$

(c) $14L$ (d) $2L$

Comprehension-2

A charged particle with charge to mass ratio $\left(\frac{q}{m}\right) = \frac{10^3}{19}$ C/kg enters a uniform magnetic field $\mathbf{B} = (20\hat{\mathbf{i}} - 30\hat{\mathbf{j}} + 50\hat{\mathbf{k}})$ T at time $t = 0$ with velocity $\mathbf{v} = (20\hat{\mathbf{i}} + 50\hat{\mathbf{j}} + 30\hat{\mathbf{k}})$ m/s. Assume that magnetic field exists in large space.

4 During the further motion of the particle in the magnetic field, the angle between the magnetic field **B** and velocity of the particle

(a) remains constant

(b) increases

(c) decreases

(d) may increase or decrease

5 The frequency of the revolution of the particle in cycles per second will be

(a) $\frac{10^3}{\pi\sqrt{19}}$ (b) $\frac{10^4}{\pi\sqrt{38}}$

(c) $\frac{10^4}{\pi\sqrt{19}}$ (d) $\frac{10^4}{2\pi\sqrt{19}}$

6 The pitch of the helical path of the motion of the particle will be

(a) $\frac{\pi}{100}$ m (b) $\frac{\pi}{125}$ m

(c) $\frac{\pi}{215}$ m (d) $\frac{\pi}{250}$ m

Comprehension-3

Electric field and magnetic field in region of space are given by $\mathbf{E} = E_0\hat{\mathbf{j}}$ and $\mathbf{B} = B_0\hat{\mathbf{j}}$. A particle of specific charge α (charge per unit mass) is released from origin with velocity $\mathbf{v} = v_0\hat{\mathbf{i}}$

7 Y-coordinate of particle when it crosses Y-axis for nth time is

(a) $\frac{2n^2\pi^2E_0}{B_0^2\alpha}$ (b) $\frac{n^2\pi E_0}{B_0^2\alpha}$

(c) $\frac{2\pi^2E_0}{n^2B_0^2\alpha}$ (d) 0

8 Angle between particle's velocity and Y-axis at that moment is

(a) $\tan^{-1}\left(\frac{v_0B_0}{2\pi E_0}\right)$ (b) $\tan^{-1}\left(\frac{v_0B_0}{2\pi nE_0}\right)$

(c) $\tan^{-1}\left(\frac{v_0B_0}{E_0}\right)$ (d) $\tan^{-1}\left(\frac{B_0}{E_0}\right)$

Comprehension-4

A positively charged particle having charge $q_1 = 1$C and mass $m_1 = 40$ gm is revolving along a circle of radius $R = 40$ cm in XY-plane with velocity $v_1 = 5$ ms^{-1} in a uniform magnetic field with centre of circle at origin O of a three dimensional system. At $t = 0$, the particle was at (0, 0.4 m, 0) and velocity was directed along positive X-direction. Another particle having charge $q_2 = 1$ C and mass $m_2 = 10$ g moving uniformly parallel to positive Z-direction with velocity $v_2 = \frac{40}{\pi}$ ms^{-1} collides with the revolving particle at $t = 0$ and gets stuck to it. Neglecting gravitational force and coulomb force.

9 After collision what is the path of combined particle?

(a) Circle (b) Helix

(c) Parabola (d) Hyperbola

10 Z-coordinate of combined particle at $t = \frac{\pi}{40}$ s

(a) 0.2 m (b) 0.4 m (c) 0.6 m (d) 0.8 m

11 Y-coordinate of combined particle at $t = \frac{\pi}{40}$ s

(a) 0.3 m (b) 0.4 m (c) 0.2 m (d) 0.6 m

Comprehension-5

Magnetic field in a region is given by

$$\mathbf{B} = B\odot \quad \text{if } x > 0, y > 0$$
$$= 2B\otimes \quad \text{if } x > 0, y < 0$$
$$= 0 \quad \text{otherwise}$$

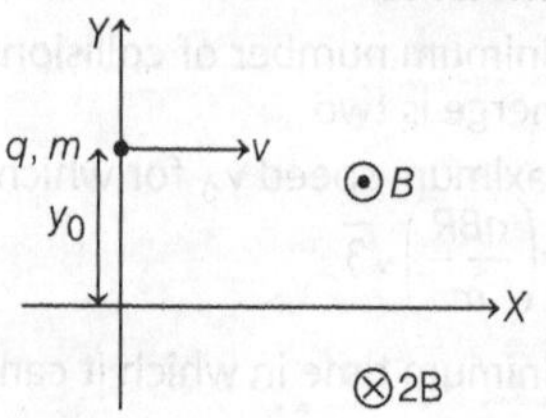

A particle of charge q mass m, speed v parallel to X-axis enters in the region at a distance $y_0 = \frac{R}{2}$, where $R = \frac{mv}{qB}$.

12 Time taken by the particle to hit the X-axis first time

(a) $\frac{\pi m}{qB}$ (b) $\frac{\pi m}{3qB}$

(c) $\frac{\pi m}{2qB}$ (d) $\frac{4\pi m}{3qB}$

13 Time taken by the particle when its velocity become parallel to X-axis first time after entering into magnetic field

(a) $\frac{\pi m}{qB}$ (b) $\frac{\pi m}{3qB}$

(c) $\frac{\pi m}{2qB}$ (d) $\frac{4\pi m}{3qB}$

Comprehension-6

A charge particle of mass m and charge q is projected on a rough horizontal XY-plane. Both electric and magnetic fields are given by $\mathbf{E} = -10\hat{\mathbf{k}}$ N/C and magnetic field $\mathbf{B} = -5\hat{\mathbf{k}}$ T are present in the region. The particle enters into the magnetic field at (4, 0, 0) m with a velocity $50\hat{\mathbf{j}}$ m/s. The particle starts into a curved path on the plane. If coefficient of friction $\mu = \frac{1}{3}$ between particle and plane, then ($qE = 2$ mg, $g = 10$ m/s^2)

14 Radius of curvature of the path followed by particle, initially, is

(a) 5 m (b) 2.5 m

(c) 1.25 m (d) 10 m

15 The time after which particle comes to rest, is

(a) 5 s (b) 4 s (c) 3 s (d) 1 s

16 Total work done by electric force on the particle is

(a) 250 J

(b) zero

(c) 125 J

(d) None of the above

Comprehension-7

A magnetic field B perpendicular to the XY-plane is restricted to a region of length l and width b as shown in the figure. An electron (mass of electron = m) enters into the region of $\mathbf{B}$ at origin O with a speed v_0 at an angle θ to the X-axis.

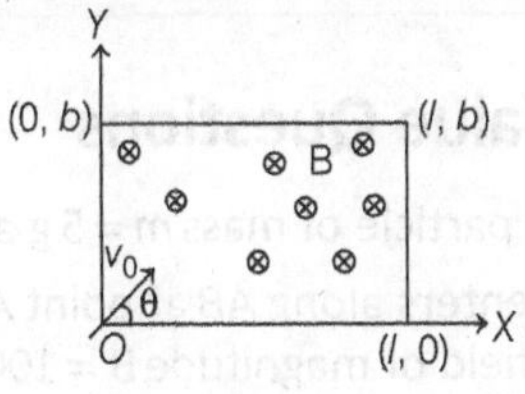

17 The range of θ for which the electron emerges out of the region of magnetic field on the side of the X-axis (i.e. at a point $(x, 0)$ such that $0 < x \le l$) is

$\left(\text{Given that } \frac{elB}{mv_0} = \sqrt{3}, \frac{ebB}{mv_0} = 1 - \frac{1}{\sqrt{2}}\right)$

(a) $45° \le \theta \le 60°$ (b) $0° \le \theta \le 60°$

(c) $30° \le \theta \le 60°$ (d) $0° \le \theta \le 45°$

18 Now, suppose that the electron was initially projected at an angle $\theta = \frac{\pi}{2}$ with a speed v. It emerges out of the region at a point (x, b) such that $0 < x < l$. Given that $\frac{beB}{mv} = 0.6$. Then, x is given by

(a) $\frac{4b}{3}$ (b) $\frac{2b}{3}$ (c) $\frac{b}{3}$ (d) $\frac{5b}{3}$

19 In the previous question, assume the instant at which electron emerges out of (x, b); $0 < x < l$, to be $t = 0$. At $t = 0$, an electric field $\mathbf{E} = E_0\hat{\mathbf{j}}$ is switched on in the entire region. Find the minimum value of E_0 for which the electron again re-enters the region of $\mathbf{B}$ on the same side on which it exited. Given that $\left(\frac{beB}{mv} = 0.6, \frac{leB}{mv} = 1\right)$

(a) Bv (b) $1.2\,Bv$ (c) $1.6\,Bv$ (d) $1.8\,Bv$

Comprehension-8

In the region between the plane $z = 0$ and $z = a (a > 0)$, the uniform electric and magnetic fields are given by $\mathbf{E} = E_0(\hat{\mathbf{k}} - \hat{\mathbf{j}})$, $\mathbf{B} = B_0\hat{\mathbf{i}}$. The region defined by $a \le z \le b$ contains only magnetic field $\mathbf{B} = -B_0\hat{\mathbf{i}}$. Beyond $z > b$ no field exits. A positive point charge q is projected from the origin with velocity $v_0\hat{\mathbf{k}}$. Assuming the mass of the particle to be $\frac{2}{3} \times \frac{qE_0 a}{v_0^2}$

20 The value of E_0 such that the particle moves undeviated upto the plane $z = a$ is

(a) $\frac{B_0 v_0}{\sqrt{2}}$ (b) $B_0 v_0$

(c) $B_0 v_0 \sqrt{2}$ (d) $\frac{B_0 v_0}{2}$

21 The minimum value of b, such that the particle reverses its direction completely is

(a) $\frac{4E_0 a}{3v_0 B_0}$ (b) $a\left\{1 + \frac{4E_0}{3v_0 B_0}\right\}$

(c) $\frac{2E_0 a}{3v_0 B_0}$ (d) $a\left\{1 + \frac{2E}{3v_0 B_0}\right\}$

22 When the particle just reverses its direction all the fields are switched OFF. Time taken by the particle to touch the plane $z=0$ from that instant

(a) $\frac{a}{v_0}$ (b) $\frac{a}{2v_0}$ (c) $\frac{a}{3v_0}$ (d) $\frac{a}{4v_0}$

Match the Columns Questions

1 A beam consisting of four types of ions A, B, C and D enters in a region that contains a uniform magnetic field as shown. The field is perpendicular to the plane of the paper. All ions in the beam travel with the same speed. The table below gives the masses and charges of the ions. The ions fall at different positions 1, 2, 3 and 4, as shown. Correctly match the ions with respective falling positions.

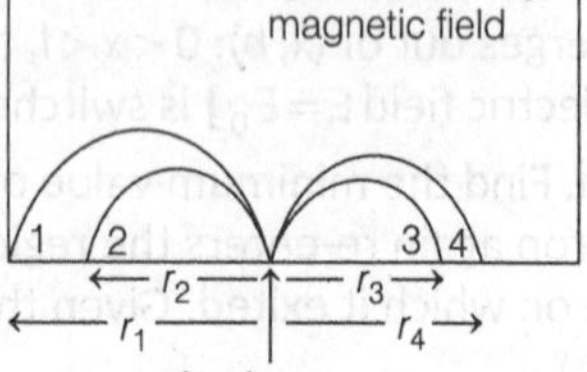

Ion beam $r_1 > r_2 = r_4 > r_3$

ION	MASS	CHARGE
A	$2m$	$+e$
B	$4m$	$-e$
C	$2m$	$-e$
D	m	$+e$

Column I	Column II
A. A	P. 1
B. B	Q. 2
C. C	R. 3
D. D	S. 4

2 A particle enters a space where exists uniform magnetic field $\mathbf{B}=B_x\hat{\mathbf{i}}+B_y\hat{\mathbf{j}}+B_z\hat{\mathbf{k}}$ and uniform electric field $\mathbf{E}=E_x\hat{\mathbf{i}}+E_y\hat{\mathbf{j}}+E_z\hat{\mathbf{k}}$ with initial velocity $\mathbf{u}=u_x\hat{\mathbf{i}}+u_y\hat{\mathbf{j}}+u_z\hat{\mathbf{k}}$. Depending on the values of various components the particle selects a path. Match the entries of Column I with the entries of Column II. The components other than specified in column I in each entry are non-zero. Neglect gravity.

Column I	Column II
A. $B_y=B_z=E_x=E_z=0$; $u=0$	P. Circle
B. $E=0, u_xB_x+u_yB_y \neq -u_zB_z$	Q. Helix with uniform pitch and constant radius
C. $\mathbf{u}\times\mathbf{B}=0, \mathbf{u}\times\mathbf{E}=0$	R. Cycloid
D. $\mathbf{u}\perp\mathbf{B}, \mathbf{B}\parallel\mathbf{E}$	S. Helix with variable pitch and constant radius
	T. Straight line

3 Assume that in space we have a charged particle moving with a certain kinetic energy entering a region as described in Column-I. Choose the correct alternative.

Column I	Column II
A. The region has a constant electric and magnetic field	P. Kinetic energy of the particle may/will remain constant during motion.
B. The region has constant electric field only	Q. Acceleration of the particle may/will be zero during motion.
C. The region has constant magnetic field only	R. Kinetic energy of particle changes during motion and it suffers deflection.
D. The region contains no field.	S. Kinetic energy of particle changes during motion but it suffers no deflection.
	T. Kinetic energy of particle does not change during motion but it suffers deflection

4 A charged particle having non-zero initial velocity is subjected to certain conditions given in Column I, Column II gives possible trajectories of the particle. Match the conditions in Column I with the results in Column II.

Column I	Column II
A. In only uniform electric field	P. The path of the charged particle may be a straight line
B. In only uniform magnetic field	Q. The path of the charged particle may be a parabola
C. In uniform magnetic and uniform electric field	R. The path of the charged particle may be circular
D. Subjected to a net force of constant magnitude	S. The path of the charged particle may be helical with uniform pitch
	T. The path of the charged particle may be helical with non-uniform pitch.

Numerical Value Questions

1 A charged particle of mass $m=5$ g and charge $q=12\,\mu\text{C}$ enters along AB at point A in a uniform magnetic field of magnitude $B=100$ T existing in a rectangular region of size ($8\,m \times 6\,m$) and into the plane of paper as shown in figure. The particle leaves the region at C. The speed of the charge particle (in m/s) as it leaves the region is

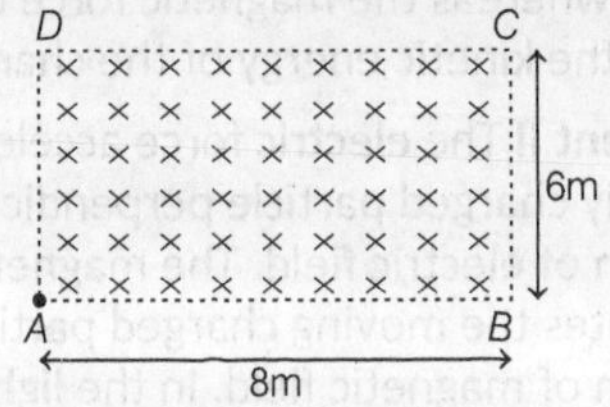

2 A particle having charge q and mass m is projected with velocity $(4\hat{i} - 6\hat{j} + 3\hat{k})$ m/s from the origin in a region occupied by electric field E and magnetic field B such that $\mathbf{E} = E_0\hat{j}$ and $\mathbf{B} = B_0\hat{j}$. Find the time (in s) when the magnitude of velocity of the charge particle becomes $5\sqrt{5}$ m/s. $\left(\text{Take, } \frac{qE_0}{m} = 2\right)$ and neglect the gravity.

3 A positively charged particle is given an initial velocity v_0 in XY-plane as shown in diagram. Initially the particle was at origin and the region contains uniform, mutually perpendicular electric and magnetic field. Let $\mathbf{E} = -E\hat{j}$ and $\mathbf{B} = B\hat{k}$. The minimum magnitude of the magnetic field, so that the charge particle crosses the origin again during its subsequent motion is $B_{min} = \frac{n\pi E}{B}$, find the integer value n.

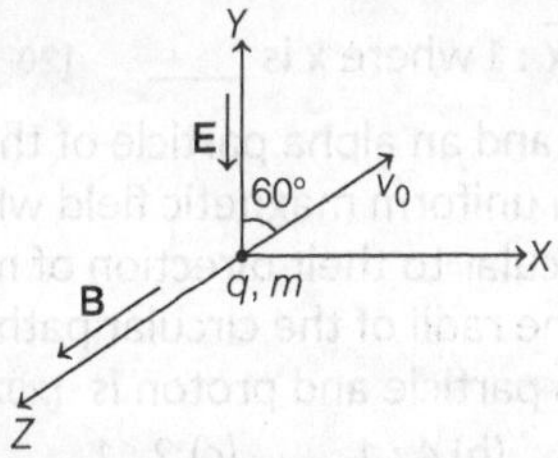

4 An electron is shot into one end of a solenoid. As it enters the uniform magnetic field within the solenoid, its speed is 800 m/s and its velocity vector makes an angle of 30° with the central axis of the solenoid. The solenoid carries 4.0 A current and has 8000 turns along its length. If the number of revolutions made by the electron within the solenoid by the time it emerges from the solenoid's opposite end is $N \times 10^5$ then find N. (Use, charge to mass ratio (e/m) for electron $\sqrt{3} \times 10^{11}$ C / kg).

5 A small ball of mass m carrying positive charge $+Q$ is dropped in uniform horizontal magnetic field B. The vertical depth of the deepest point of its path from initial position is $\frac{(3k-1)m^2 g}{Q^2 B^2}$. Find k.

6 XZ-plane is rough ground (friction coefficient $= \mu$). A charged particle is projected from point $(a, 0, 2a)$ with initial velocity $-v_0\hat{k}$ as shown. Charge on particle is $+q$, mass is m. Neglect gravity. An infinite wire carrying current i is on Y-axis. What should be minimum value of v_0, so that charge particle may cross X-axis? If $v_0 = \frac{\mu q \mu_0 i \ln x}{4\pi m}$ fill x in OMR Sheet

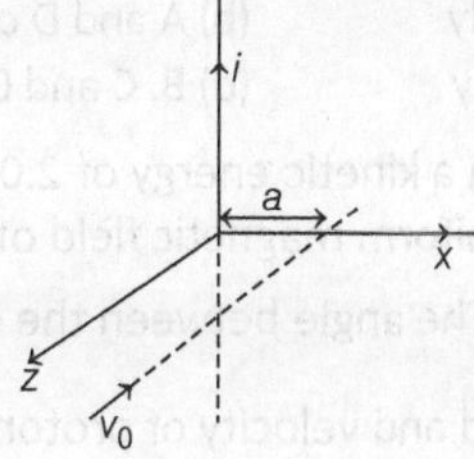

Previous Years Questions

JEE Main

1 Two particles X and Y having equal charges are being accelerated through the same potential difference. Thereafter they enter normally in a region of uniform magnetic field and describes circular paths of radii R_1 and R_2 respectively. The mass ratio of X and Y is **[2024, 29 Jan Shift-II]**

(a) $\left(\frac{R_2}{R_1}\right)$

(b) $\left(\frac{R_1}{R_2}\right)^2$

(c) $\left(\frac{R_2}{R_1}\right)^2$

(d) $\left(\frac{R_1}{R_2}\right)$

2 A charge of 4.0 μC is moving with a velocity of $4.0 \times 10^{-6}\ \text{ms}^{-1}$ along the positive Y-axis under a magnetic field $\mathbf{B}$ of strength $(2\hat{k})$ T. The force acting on the charge is $x\hat{i}$ N. The value of x is .... **[2024, 29 Jan Shift-II]**

3 An electron is allowed to move with constant velocity along the axis of current carrying straight solenoid. **[2023, 11 April Shift-II]**

A. The electron will experience magnetic force along the axis of the solenoid.
B. The electron will not experience magnetic force.
C. The electron will continue to move along the axis of the solenoid.
D. The electron will be accelerated along the axis of the solenoid.
E. The electron will follow parabolic path-inside the solenoid.

Choose the correct answer from the options given below.

(a) B and C only (b) A and D only
(c) B and E only (d) B, C and D only

4 A proton with a kinetic energy of 2.0 eV moves into a region of uniform magnetic field of magnitude $\frac{\pi}{2} \times 10^{-3}$ T. The angle between the direction of magnetic field and velocity of proton is 60°. The pitch of the helical path taken by the proton is ...... cm. (Take, mass of proton $= 1.6 \times 10^{-27}$ kg and charge on proton $= 1.6 \times 10^{-19}$ C). **[2023, 6 April Shift-II]**

5 A charge particle of 2 μC accelerated by a potential difference of 100 V enters a region of uniform magnetic field of magnitude 4 mT at right angle to the direction of field. The charge particle completes semicircle of radius 3 cm inside magnetic field. The mass of the charge particle is .... $\times 10^{-18}$ kg. **[2023, 1 Feb Shift-I]**

6 A velocity selector consists of electric field $\mathbf{E} = E\hat{\mathbf{k}}$ and magnetic field $\mathbf{B} = B\hat{\mathbf{j}}$ with $B = 12$ mT. The value of E required for an electron of energy 728 eV moving along the positive X-axis to pass undeflected is (Given, mass of electron $= 9.1 \times 10^{-31}$ kg) **[2022, 26 July Shift-II]**

(a) 192 kVm^{-1} (b) 192 mVm^{-1}
(c) 9600 kVm^{-1} (d) 16 kVm^{-1}

7 Two charged particles, having same kinetic energy, are allowed to pass through a uniform magnetic field perpendicular to the direction of motion. If the ratio of radii of their circular path is 6 : 5 and their respective masses ratio is 9 : 4. Then, the ratio of their charges will be **[2022, 25 July Shift-I]**

(a) 8 : 5 (b) 5 : 4
(c) 5 : 3 (d) 8 : 7

8 Given below are two statements

Statement I The electric force changes the speed of the charged particle and hence changes its kinetic energy, whereas the magnetic force does not change the kinetic energy of the charged particle.

Statement II The electric force accelerates the positively charged particle perpendicular to the direction of electric field. The magnetic force accelerates the moving charged particle along the direction of magnetic field. In the light of the above statements, choose the most appropriate answer from the options given below **[2022, 29 June Shift-II]**

(a) Both statement I and statement II are correct.
(b) Both statement I and statement II are incorrect.
(c) Statement I is correct but statement II is incorrect.
(d) Statement I is incorrect but statement II is correct.

9 A charged particle moves along circular path in a uniform magnetic field in a cyclotron. The kinetic energy of the charged particle increases to 4 times its initial value. What will be the ratio of new radius to the original radius of circular path of the charged particle **[2022, 29 June Shift-I]**

(a) 1 : 1 (b) 1 : 2
(c) 2 : 1 (d) 1 : 4

10 A deuteron and a proton moving with equal kinetic energy enter into to a uniform magnetic field at right angle to the field. If r_d and r_p are the radii of their circular paths respectively, then the ratio $\frac{r_d}{r_p}$ will be $\sqrt{x} : 1$ where x is ____. **[2022, 27 June Shift-II]**

11 A proton and an alpha particle of the same velocity enter in a uniform magnetic field which is acting perpendicular to their direction of motion. The ratio of the radii of the circular paths described by the alpha particle and proton is **[2022, 26 June Shift-I]**

(a) 1 : 4 (b) 4 : 1 (c) 2 : 1 (d) 1 : 2

12 A proton, a deuteron and an α-particle with same kinetic energy enter into a uniform magnetic field at right angle to magnetic field. The ratio of the radii of their respective circular paths is **[2022, 24 June Shift-II]**

(a) $1 : \sqrt{2} : \sqrt{2}$ (b) $1 : 1 : \sqrt{2}$
(c) $\sqrt{2} : 1 : 1$ (d) $1 : \sqrt{2} : 1$

13 Given below are two statements, one is labelled as Assertion (A) and the other is labelled as Reason (R).

Assertion (A) In a uniform magnetic field, speed and energy remains the same for a moving charged particle.

Reason (R) Moving charged particle experiences magnetic force perpendicular to its direction of motion. **[2022, 24 June Shift-I]**

(a) Both A and R are true and R is the correct explanation of A.

(b) Both A and R are true but R is not the correct explanation of A.

(c) A is true but R is false.

(d) A is false but R is true.

14 Two ions of masses 4 amu and 16 amu have charges +2e and +3e, respectively. These ions pass through the region of constant perpendicular magnetic field. The kinetic energy of both ions is same. Then, **[2021, 27 Aug Shift-I]**

(a) lighter ion will be deflected less than heavier ion

(b) lighter ion will be deflected more than heavier ion

(c) both ions will be deflected equally

(d) no ion will be deflected

15 If the maximum value of accelerating potential provided by a radio frequency oscillator is 12 kV. The number of revolution made by a proton in a cyclotron to achieve one sixth of the speed of light is .... [Given, $m_p = 1.67 \times 10^{-27}$ kg, $e = 1.6 \times 10^{-19}$ C, $c = 3 \times 10^8$ m/s] **[2021, 26 Aug Shift-II]**

16 Two ions having same mass have charges in the ratio 1 : 2. They are projected normally in a uniform magnetic field with their speeds in the ratio 2 : 3. The ratio of the radii of their circular trajectories is **[2021, 25 July Shift-II]**

(a) 1 : 4 (b) 4 : 3 (c) 3 : 1 (d) 2 : 3

17 A deuteron and an α-particle having equal kinetic energy enter perpendicular into a magnetic field. Let r_d and r_α be their respective radii of circular path. The value of $\frac{r_d}{r_\alpha}$ is equal to **[2021, 20 July Shift-I]**

(a) $\frac{1}{\sqrt{2}}$ (b) $\sqrt{2}$ (c) 1 (d) 2

18 A proton and an α-particle, having kinetic energies K_p and K_α, respectively, enter into a magnetic field at right angles. The ratio of the radii of trajectory of proton to that of α-particle is 2 : 1. The ratio of $K_p : K_\alpha$ is **[2021, 18 March Shift-II]**

(a) 1 : 8 (b) 8 : 1 (c) 1 : 4 (d) 4 : 1

19 A charge Q is moving *dl* distance in the magnetic field **B**. Find the value of work done by **B**. **[2021, 16 March Shift-II]**

(a) 1 (b) Infinite (c) Zero (d) −1

20 A proton, a deuteron and an α-particle are moving with same momentum in a uniform magnetic field. The ratio of magnetic forces acting on them is .... and their speed is .... in the ratio. **[2021, 25 Feb Shift-I]**

(a) 1 : 2 : 4 and 2 : 1 : 1 (b) 2 : 1 : 1 and 4 : 2 : 1

(c) 4 : 2 : 1 and 2 : 1 : 1 (d) 1 : 2 : 4 and 1 : 1 : 2

21 A particle of charge *q* and mass *m* is moving with a velocity $-v\hat{\mathbf{i}} (v \neq 0)$ towards a large screen placed in the *yz*-plane at a distance *d*. If there is a magnetic field $\mathbf{B} = B_0\hat{\mathbf{k}}$, the minimum value of *v* for which the particle will not hit the screen is **[2020, 6 Sep Shift-I]**

(a) $\frac{qdB_0}{3m}$ (b) $\frac{2qdB_0}{m}$ (c) $\frac{qdB_0}{m}$ (d) $\frac{qdB_0}{2m}$

22 A beam of protons with speed 4×10^5 ms^{-1} enters a uniform magnetic field of 0.3 T at an angle of 60° to the magnetic field. The pitch of the resulting helical path of protons is close to
(Take, mass of the proton = 1.67×10^{-27} kg and charge of the proton = 1.69×10^{-19} C) **[2020, 2 Sep Shift-I]**

(a) 2 cm (b) 4 cm (c) 5 cm (d) 12 cm

23 The figure shows a region of length *l* with a uniform magnetic field of 0.3 T in it and a proton entering the region with velocity 4×10^5 ms^{-1} making an angle 60° with the field. If the proton completes 10 revolutions by the time it cross the region shown, *l* is close to
(Take, mass of proton = 1.67×10^{-27} kg, charge of the proton = 1.6×10^{-19} C) **[2020, 2 Sep Shift-II]**

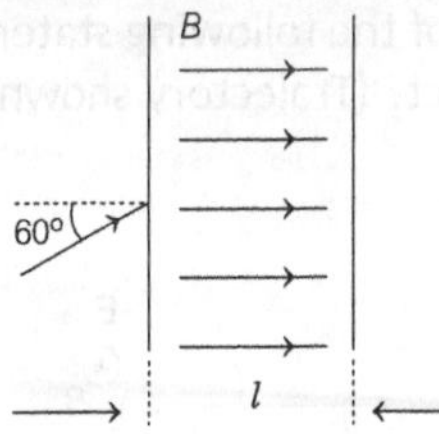

(a) 0.11 m (b) 0.88 m (c) 0.44 m (d) 0.22 m

24 A charged particle carrying charge 1 μC is moving with velocity $(2\hat{\mathbf{i}} + 3\hat{\mathbf{j}} + 4\hat{\mathbf{k}})$ ms^{-1}. If an external magnetic field of $(5\hat{\mathbf{i}} + 3\hat{\mathbf{j}} - 6\hat{\mathbf{k}}) \times 10^{-3}$ T exists in the region, where the particle is moving, then the force on the particle is $\mathbf{F} \times 10^{-9}$ N. The vector **F** is **[2020, 3 Sep Shift-I]**

(a) $-0.30\hat{\mathbf{i}} + 0.32\hat{\mathbf{j}} - 0.09\hat{\mathbf{k}}$

(b) $-30\hat{\mathbf{i}} + 32\hat{\mathbf{j}} - 9\hat{\mathbf{k}}$

(c) $-300\hat{\mathbf{i}} + 320\hat{\mathbf{j}} - 90\hat{\mathbf{k}}$

(d) $-3.0\hat{\mathbf{i}} + 3.2\hat{\mathbf{j}} - 0.9\hat{\mathbf{k}}$

25 An electron is moving along +x-direction with a velocity of 6×10^{6} ms^{-1}. It enters a region of uniform electric field of 300 V/cm pointing along +y-direction. The magnitude and direction of the magnetic field set up in this region such that the electron keeps moving along the x-direction will be **[2020, 6 Sep Shift-I]**

(a) 3×10^{-4} T, along $+z$-direction

(b) 5×10^{-3} T, along $-z$-direction

(c) 5×10^{-3} T, along $+z$-direction

(d) 3×10^{-4} T, along $-z$-direction

26 A particle of mass m and charge q has an initial velocity $\mathbf{v}=v_0\hat{\mathbf{j}}$. If an electric field $\mathbf{E}=E_0\hat{\mathbf{i}}$ and magnetic field $\mathbf{B}=B_0\hat{\mathbf{i}}$ act on the particle, its speed will double after a time **[2020, 7 Jan Shift-II]**

(a) $\dfrac{3mv_0}{qE_0}$ (b) $\dfrac{\sqrt{3}mv_0}{qE_0}$ (c) $\dfrac{2mv_0}{qE_0}$ (d) $\dfrac{\sqrt{2}mv_0}{qE_0}$

27 Proton with kinetic energy of 1 MeV moves from south to north. It gets an acceleration of 10^{12} m/s^2 by an applied magnetic field (west to east). The value of magnetic field (rest mass of proton is 1.6×10^{-27} kg) **[2020, 8 Jan Shift-I]**

(a) 71 mT (b) 0.071 mT

(c) 0.71 mT (d) 7.1 mT

28 A charged particle of mass m and charge q moving under the influence of uniform electric field $E\hat{\mathbf{i}}$ and a uniform magnetic field $B\hat{\mathbf{k}}$ follows a trajectory from point P to Q as shown in the figure. The velocities at P and Q are respectively, $v\hat{\mathbf{j}}$ and $-2v\hat{\mathbf{j}}$. Then, which of the following statements (A, B, C, D) are the correct? (Trajectory shown is schematic and not to scale)

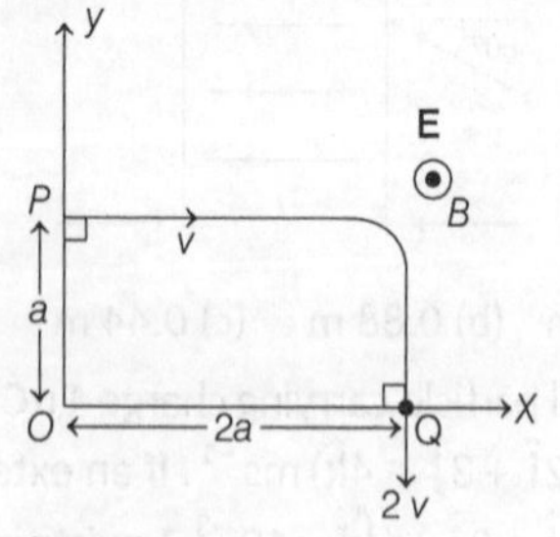

1. $E=\dfrac{3}{4}\left(\dfrac{mv^2}{qa}\right)$

2. Rate of work done by the electric field at P is $\dfrac{3}{4}\left(\dfrac{mv^3}{a}\right)$.

3. Rate of work done by both the fields at Q is zero.

4. The difference between the magnitude of angular momentum of the particle at P and Q is $2\,mav$. **[2020, 9 Jan Shift-I]**

(a) (1), (3), (4) (b) (1), (2), (3)

(c) (1), (2), (3), (4) (d) (2), (3), (4)

29 An electron gun is placed inside a long solenoid of radius R on its axis. The solenoid has n turns/length and carries a current I. The electron gun shoots an electron along the radius of the solenoid with speed v. If the electron does not hit the surface of the solenoid, maximum possible value of v is (all symbols have their standard meaning) **[2020, 9 Jan Shift-II]**

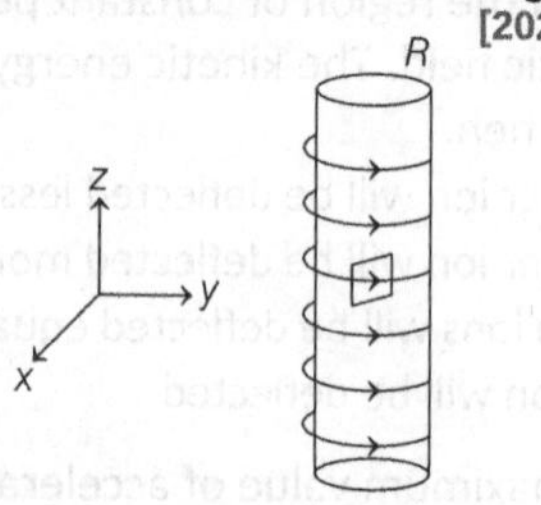

(a) $\dfrac{2e\mu_0 nIR}{m}$ (b) $\dfrac{e\mu_0 nIR}{4m}$

(c) $\dfrac{e\mu_0 nIR}{2m}$ (d) $\dfrac{e\mu_0 nIR}{m}$

30 A proton, an electron and a helium nucleus, have the same energy. They are in circular orbits in a plane due to magnetic field perpendicular to the plane. Let r_p, r_e and r_{He} be their respective radii, then **[2019, 10 April Shift-I]**

(a) $r_e < r_p = r_{He}$ (b) $r_e > r_p = r_{He}$

(c) $r_e < r_p < r_{He}$ (d) $r_e > r_p > r_{He}$

31 An electron moving along the X-axis with an initial energy of 100 eV, enters a region of magnetic field $\mathbf{B}=(1.5\times10^{-3}\ \text{T})\hat{\mathbf{k}}$ at S (see figure). The field extends between $x=0$ and $x=2$ cm. The electron is detected at the point Q on a screen placed 8 cm away from the point S. The distance d between P and Q (on the screen) is

(Take, electron's charge $=1.6\times10^{-19}$ C, mass of electron $=9.1\times10^{-31}$ kg) **[2019, 12 April Shift-II]**

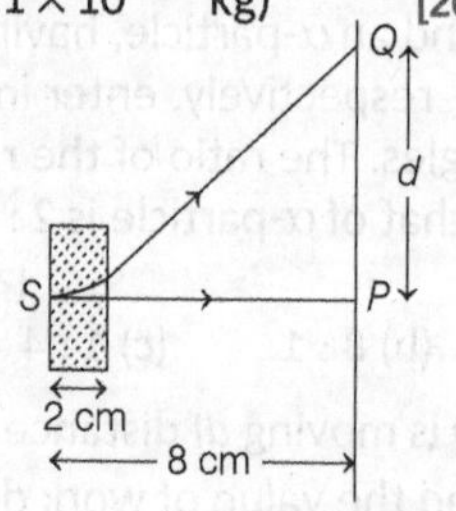

(a) 11.65 cm (b) 12.87 cm

(c) 1.22 cm (d) 2.25 cm

32 A particle having the same charge as of electron moves in a circular path of radius 0.5 cm under the influence of a magnetic field of 0.5 T. If an electric field of 100 V/m makes it to move in a straight path, then the mass of the particle is (Take, charge of electron $= 1.6 \times 10^{-19}$ C) **[2019, 9 Jan Shift-II]**

(a) 1.6×10^{-19} kg
(b) 1.6×10^{-27} kg
(c) 9.1×10^{-31} kg
(d) 2.0×10^{-24} kg

33 In an experiment, electrons are accelerated, from rest by applying a voltage of 500 V. Calculate the radius of the path, if a magnetic field 100 mT is then applied. (Take, charge of the electron $= 1.6 \times 10^{-19}$ C and mass of the electron $= 9.1 \times 10^{-31}$ kg) **[2019, 11 Jan Shift-I]**

(a) 7.5×10^{-2} m (b) 7.5×10^{-4} m
(c) 7.5×10^{-3} m (d) 7.5 m

34 A particle of mass m and charge q is in an electric and magnetic field is given by $\mathbf{E} = 2\hat{\mathbf{i}} + 3\hat{\mathbf{j}}$, $\mathbf{B} = 4\hat{\mathbf{j}} + 6\hat{\mathbf{k}}$. The charged particle is shifted from the origin to the point $P(x = 1; y = 1)$ along a straight path. The magnitude of the total work done is **[2019, 11 Jan Shift-II]**

(a) $(0.35)\,q$ (b) $(0.15)\,q$
(c) $(2.5)\,q$ (d) $5\,q$

35 The region between $y = 0$ and $y = d$ contains a magnetic field $\mathbf{B} = B\hat{\mathbf{k}}$. A particle of mass m and charge q enters the region with a velocity $\mathbf{v} = v\hat{\mathbf{i}}$. If $d = \frac{mv}{2qB}$ then the acceleration of the charged particle at the point of its emergence at the other side is **[2019, 11 Jan Shift-II]**

(a) $\frac{qvB}{m}\left(\frac{\sqrt{3}}{2}\hat{\mathbf{i}} + \frac{1}{2}\hat{\mathbf{j}}\right)$ (b) $\frac{qvB}{m}\left(\frac{1}{2}\hat{\mathbf{i}} - \frac{\sqrt{3}}{2}\hat{\mathbf{j}}\right)$

(c) $\frac{qvB}{m}\left(\frac{-\hat{\mathbf{j}} + \hat{\mathbf{i}}}{\sqrt{2}}\right)$ (d) $\frac{qvB}{m}\left(\frac{\hat{\mathbf{i}} + \hat{\mathbf{j}}}{\sqrt{2}}\right)$

36 A proton and an α-particle (with their masses in the ratio of 1 : 4 and charges in the ratio of 1 : 2) are accelerated from rest through a potential difference V. If a uniform magnetic field B is set up perpendicular to their velocities, the ratio of the radii $r_p : r_\alpha$ of the circular paths described by them will be **[2019, 12 Jan Shift-I]**

(a) $1 : \sqrt{2}$ (b) $1 : \sqrt{3}$
(c) $1 : 3$ (d) $1 : 2$

JEE Advanced

1. In the XY-plane, the region $y > 0$ has a uniform magnetic field $B_1\hat{\mathbf{k}}$ and the region $y < 0$ has another uniform magnetic field $B_2\hat{\mathbf{k}}$. A positively charged particle is projected from the origin along the positive Y-axis with speed $v_0 = \pi$ ms^{-1} at $t = 0$, as shown in figure. Neglect gravity in this problem. Let $t = T$ be the time when the particle crosses the X-axis from below for the first time. If $B_2 = 4B_1$, the average speed of the particle, in ms^{-1}, along the X-axis in the time interval T is .... **[2018]**

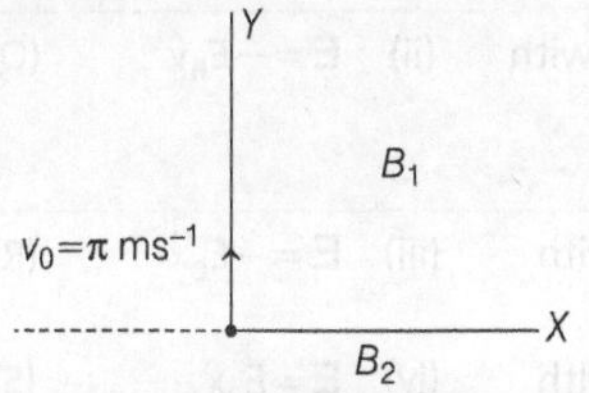

2. A uniform magnetic field B exists in the region between $x = 0$ and $x = \frac{3R}{2}$ (region 2 in the figure) pointing normally into the plane of the paper. A particle with charge $+Q$ and momentum p directed along X-axis enters region 2 from region 1 at point P_1 $(y = -R)$. **[2017]**

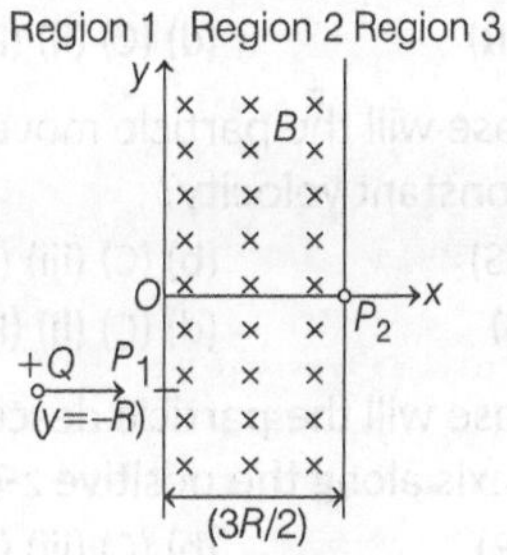

Which of the following option(s) is/are correct?

(a) When the particle re-enters region 1 through the longest possible path in region 2, the magnitude of the change in its linear momentum between point P_1 and the farthest point from Y-axis is $\frac{p}{\sqrt{2}}$.

(b) For $B = \frac{8}{13}\frac{p}{QR}$, the particle will enter region 3 through the point P_2 on X-axis.

(c) For $B > \frac{2}{3}\frac{p}{QR}$, the particle will re-enter region 1.

(d) For a fixed B, particles of same charge Q and same velocity v, the distance between the point P_1 and the point of re-entry into region 1 is inversely proportional to the mass of the particle.

Directions (Q.Nos. 3-5) Matching the information given in the three columns of the following table.

A charged particle (electron or proton) is introduced at the origin ($x = 0, y = 0, z = 0$) with a given initial velocity **v**. A uniform electric field **E** and a uniform magnetic field **B** exist everywhere. The velocity **v**, electric field **E** and magnetic field **B** are given in columns I, II and III, respectively. The quantities E_0, B_0 are positive in magnitude.

	Column I		Column II		Column III
A.	Electron with $\mathbf{v} = 2\frac{E_0}{B_0}\hat{x}$	(i)	$\mathbf{E} = E_0\hat{z}$	(P)	$\mathbf{B} = -B_0\hat{x}$
B.	Electron with $\mathbf{v} = \frac{E_0}{B_0}\hat{y}$	(ii)	$\mathbf{E} = -E_0\hat{y}$	(Q)	$\mathbf{B} = B_0\hat{x}$
C.	Proton with $\mathbf{v} = 0$	(iii)	$\mathbf{E} = -E_0\hat{x}$	(R)	$\mathbf{B} = B_0\hat{y}$
D.	Proton with $\mathbf{v} = 2\frac{E_0}{B_0}\hat{x}$	(iv)	$\mathbf{E} = E_0\hat{x}$	(S)	$\mathbf{B} = B_0\hat{z}$

[2017]

3. In which case would the particle move in a straight line along the negative direction of Y-axis (i.e. move along $-\hat{y}$)?

(a) (IV) (ii) (S) (b) (B) (iii) (Q)

(c) (C), (ii) (R) (d) (C) (ii) (P)

4. In which case will the particle move in a straight line with constant velocity?

(a) (B) (iii) (S) (b) (C) (iii) (P)

(c) (D) (i) (S) (d) (C) (ii) (R)

5. In which case will the particle describe a helical path with axis along the positive z-direction?

(a) (B) (ii) (R) (b) (C) (iii) (P)

(c) (D) (i) (S) (d) (D) (ii) (R)

Direction (Q. Nos. 6 and 7) In a thin rectangular metallic strip a constant current I flows along the positive x-direction, as shown in the figure. The length, width and thickness of the strip are l, w and d, respectively. A uniform magnetic field **B** is applied on the strip along the positive y-direction. Due to this, the charge carriers experience a net deflection along the z-direction. This results in accumulation of charge carriers on the surface $PQRS$ and appearance of equal and opposite charges on the face opposite to $PQRS$. A potential difference along the z-direction is thus developed. Charge accumulation continues until the magnetic force is balanced by the electric force. The current is assumed to be uniformly distributed on the cross section of the strip and carried by electrons.

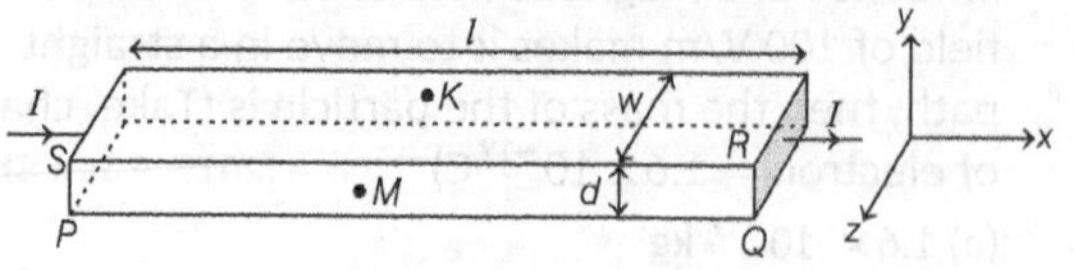

6. Consider two different metallic strips (1 and 2) of the same material. Their lengths are the same, widths are w_1 and w_2 and thicknesses are d_1 and d_2, respectively. Two points K and M are symmetrically located on the opposite faces parallel to the x-y plane (see figure). V_1 and V_2 are the potential differences between K and M in strips 1 and 2, respectively. Then, for a given current I flowing through them in a given magnetic field strength B, the correct statements is/are **[2015]**

(a) If $w_1 = w_2$ and $d_1 = 2d_2$, then $V_2 = 2V_1$

(b) If $w_1 = w_2$ and $d_1 = 2d_2$, then $V_2 = V_1$

(c) If $w_1 = 2w_2$ and $d_1 = d_2$, then $V_2 = 2V_1$

(d) If $w_1 = 2w_2$ and $d_1 = d_2$, then $V_2 = V_1$

7. Consider two different metallic strips (1 and 2) of same dimensions (length l, width w and thickness d) with carrier densities n_1 and n_2, respectively. Strip 1 is placed in magnetic field B_1 and strip 2 is placed in magnetic field B_2, both along positive y-directions. Then V_1 and V_2 are the potential differences developed between K and M in strips 1 and 2, respectively. Assuming that the current I is the same for both the strips, the correct options is/are **[2015]**

(a) If $B_1 = B_2$ and $n_1 = 2n_2$, then $V_2 = 2V_1$

(b) If $B_1 = B_2$ and $n_1 = 2n_2$, then $V_2 = V_1$

(c) If $B_1 = 2B_2$ and $n_1 = n_2$, then $V_2 = 0.5V_1$

(d) If $B_1 = 2B_2$ and $n_1 = n_2$, then $V_2 = V_1$

8 Two parallel wires in the plane of the paper are distance x_0 apart. A point charge is moving with speed u between the wires in the same plane at a distance x_1 from one of the wires. When the wires carry current of magnitude I in the same direction, the radius of curvature of the path of the point charge is R_1. In contrast, if the currents I in the two wires have directions opposite to each other, the radius of curvature of the path is R_2. If $\frac{x_0}{x_1} = 3$, and value of $\frac{R_1}{R_2}$ is **[2014]**

9. A particle of mass M and positive charge Q, moving with a constant velocity $\mathbf{u}_1 = 4\hat{\mathbf{i}}\ \text{ms}^{-1}$, enters a region of uniform static magnetic field normal to the x-y plane. The region of the magnetic field extends from $x = 0$ to $x = L$ for all values of y. After passing through this region, the particle emerges on the other side after 10 milliseconds with a velocity $\mathbf{u}_2 = 2(\sqrt{3}\hat{\mathbf{i}} + \hat{\mathbf{j}})\ \text{ms}^{-1}$. The correct statement(s) is (are) **[2013]**

(a) the direction of the magnetic field is $-z$ direction.

(b) the direction of the magnetic field is $+z$ direction

(c) the magnitude of the magnetic field is $\frac{50\pi M}{3Q}$ units.

(d) the magnitude of the magnetic field is $\frac{100\pi M}{3Q}$ units.

10. Consider the motion of a positive point charge in a region where there are simultaneous uniform electric and magnetic fields $\mathbf{E} = E_0\hat{\mathbf{j}}$ and $\mathbf{B} = B_0\hat{\mathbf{j}}$. At time $t = 0$, this charge has velocity $\mathbf{v}$ in the x-y plane, making an angle θ with the x-axis. Which of the following option(s) is(are) correct for time $t > 0$? **[2012]**

(a) If $\theta = 0°$, the charge moves in a circular path in the x-z plane.

(b) If $\theta = 0°$, the charge undergoes helical motion with constant pitch along the y-axis

(c) If $\theta = 10°$, the charge undergoes helical motion with its pitch increasing with time, along the y-axis.

(d) If $\theta = 90°$, the charge undergoes linear but accelerated motion along the y-axis.

Answer Key

Level 1

2.1 Magnetic Force on a Moving Charge

1. $2\times10^{-6}[-6\hat{i}+4\hat{j}+6\hat{k}]$ N; $0.8(-3\hat{i}+2\hat{j}+3\hat{k})$ m/s^2 **2.** 3.0 **3.** $(-75\hat{i}+100\hat{j})$ m/s

4. $-(0.4\hat{j})$ T **5.** (a) due south (b) 4.0×10^{14} m/s^2 **6.** 50 m/s

2.2 Normal Incidence

1. 20 cm, $\frac{5}{\pi}\times10^3\ \text{s}^{-1}$ **2.** 12 cm **3.** 3.4×10^{-4} T, 10^6 Hz **4.** 2 cm

5. D—electron, B—α-particle **6.** $R_p : R_\alpha : R_D = 1:1:\sqrt{2}$; $T_p : T_\alpha : T_D = 1:2:2$

7. $\mathbf{v} = v_0\cos\omega t\hat{\mathbf{j}} - v_0\sin\omega t\hat{\mathbf{k}}$; $\mathbf{r} = R\sin\omega t\hat{\mathbf{j}} - R(1-\cos\omega t)\hat{\mathbf{k}}$ **8.** 30°

9. (i) $\frac{\pi m}{qB}$ (ii) $\frac{\pi mu}{qB}$ (iii) $2mu$ **10.** $\frac{\sqrt{2mK}}{qd}$ **11.** (i) $\frac{mv}{qB}$ (ii) $\frac{\pi}{2}$ (iii) $\frac{\pi m}{2qB}$ (iv) $\frac{mv}{qB}, \frac{3\pi}{2}, \frac{3\pi m}{2qB}$

12 (i) $\frac{\pi}{2}$ (ii) $\frac{\pi}{4}$ (iii) π **13.** $\frac{\mu_0 qrni}{2m}$ **14.** 5 m **15.** (i) $\frac{Bqd}{2m}$ (ii) $\frac{m\pi}{6Bq}$ (iii) $\sqrt{3}d$

2.3 Oblique Incidence

1. 36 cm, $4\pi\sqrt{19}$ cm **2.** $\frac{4}{\pi}\times10^5$ m/s, 2×10^5 m/s **3.** $15\pi\times10^{-4}$ T

4. $\mathbf{v} = v_0\cos\theta\hat{\mathbf{i}} + v_0\sin\theta\cos\omega t\hat{\mathbf{j}} - v_0\sin\theta\sin\omega t\hat{\mathbf{k}}$;

$\mathbf{r} = (v_0\cos\theta)t\hat{\mathbf{i}} + R\sin\omega t\hat{\mathbf{j}} - R(1-\cos\omega t)\hat{\mathbf{k}}$, where $\omega = \frac{qB}{m}$ and $R = \frac{mv_0\sin\theta}{qB}$

2.4 Electric and Magnetic Force on a Charge

1. $\frac{ma_0}{e}$ towards west, $\frac{2ma_0}{ev_0}$ downward **2.** 1.6×10^7 m/s, 4.5 cm **3.** $\frac{5}{4}\times10^5$ C/kg

4. $\sqrt{\frac{2qE_0x}{m}}$ **5.** (i) $\frac{3mv^2}{4qa}$, (ii) $\frac{3mv^3}{4a}$, (iii) zero

Level 2

Single Choice Correct Questions

1. (c)	2. (a)	3. (a)	4. (a)	5. (a)	6. (a)	7. (c)	8. (c)	9. (a)	10. (a)
11. (d)	12. (b)	13. (a)	14. (a)	15. (c)	16. (c)	17. (b)	18. (b)	19. (d)	20. (b)
21. (d)	22. (a)	23. (a)	24. (a)	25. (a)	26. (c)	27. (c)	28. (b)	29. (c)	30. (d)
31. (a)	32. (d)	33. (a)	34. (d)	35. (c)	36. (c)	37. (d)	38. (d)	39. (a)	40. (b)
41. (c)	42. (b)	43. (b)	44. (b)	45. (b)					

Numerical Value Questions

1. (20)	2. (4)	3. (6)	4. (1)	5. (1.21)	6. (10)	7. (220)	8. (70)	9. (3)	10. (500)

Level 3

Single Choice Correct Questions

1. (a)	2. (a)	3. (b)	4. (d)	5. (c)	6. (b)	7. (c)	8. (c)	9. (c)	10. (b)
11. (a)	12. (a)	13. (c)	14. (b)	15. (d)	16. (a)	17. (c)	18. (c)	19. (a)	20. (b)
21. (a)	22. (b)	23. (b)							

Multiple Choice(s) Correct Questions

1. (acd)	2. (bd)	3. (abcd)	4. (ad)	5. (ab)	6. (ac)	7. (bcd)	8. (acd)	9. (bc)	10. (acd)
11. (abd)	12. (abd)	13. (acd)	14. (abcd)	15. (abd)					

Comprehension Based Questions

1. (b)	2. (c)	3. (c)	4. (a)	5. (b)	6. (d)	7. (a)	8. (b)	9. (b)	10. (a)
11. (c)	12. (b)	13. (c)	14. (a)	15. (a)	16. (b)	17. (d)	18. (c)	19. (b)	20. (b)
21. (b)	22. (b)								

Match the Columns Questions

1. A → S; B → P; C → Q; D → R
2. A → R; B → QT; C → T; D → S
3. A → PQRS; B → RS; C → PQT; D → PQ
4. A → PQ; B → PRS; C → PT; D → PQRST

Numerical Value Questions

1. (2)	2. (8)	3. (2)	4. (16)	5. (1)	6. (5)

Previous Years Questions

JEE Main

1. (b)	2. (32)	3. (a)	4. (40)	5. (144)	6. (a)	7. (b)	8. (c)	9. (c)	10. (2)
11. (c)	12. (d)	13. (a)	14. (b)	15. (543)	16. (b)	17. (b)	18. (d)	19. (c)	20. (b)
21. (c)	22. (b)	23. (c)	24. (b)	25. (c)	26. (b)	27. (c)	28. (b)	29. (c)	30. (c)
31. (*)	32. (d)	33. (b)	34. (d)	35. (*)	36. (a)				

JEE Advanced

1. (2)	2. (b,c)	3. (c)	4. (a)	5. (c)	6. (a,d)	7. (a,c)	8. (3)	9. (a,c)	10. (c,d)

SOLUTIONS

Level 1

2.1 Magnetic Force on a Moving Charge

1. $\mathbf{F} = q(\mathbf{v} \times \mathbf{B}) = (2 \times 10^{-6})[(2\hat{\mathbf{i}} - 3\hat{\mathbf{j}} + 4\hat{\mathbf{k}}) \times (3\hat{\mathbf{j}} - 2\hat{\mathbf{k}})]$

$\Rightarrow \mathbf{F} = 2 \times 10^{-6}(-6\hat{\mathbf{i}} + 4\hat{\mathbf{j}} + 6\hat{\mathbf{k}})$ N

$$\mathbf{a} = \frac{\mathbf{F}}{m} = 0.8(-3\hat{\mathbf{i}} + 2\hat{\mathbf{j}} + 3\hat{\mathbf{k}}) \text{ m/s}^2$$

2. $\mathbf{a} \perp \mathbf{B} \Rightarrow \mathbf{a} \cdot \mathbf{B} = 0$

$= (x\hat{\mathbf{i}} + 7\hat{\mathbf{j}}) \cdot (7\hat{\mathbf{i}} - 3\hat{\mathbf{j}}) = 0$

$= 7x - 21 = 0 \Rightarrow x = 3.0$

3. Let $\mathbf{v} = v_x\hat{\mathbf{i}} + v_y\hat{\mathbf{j}}$

$\mathbf{F} = q(\mathbf{v} \times \mathbf{B})$

$\Rightarrow (4\hat{\mathbf{i}} + 3\hat{\mathbf{j}}) \times 10^{-10} = (5 \times 10^{-10})[(v_x\hat{\mathbf{i}} + v_y\hat{\mathbf{j}}) \times (8 \times 10^{-3}\hat{\mathbf{k}})]$

$\Rightarrow \quad 4\hat{\mathbf{i}} + 3\hat{\mathbf{j}} = 0.04(v_y\hat{\mathbf{i}} - v_x\hat{\mathbf{j}})$

Comparing both sides,

$v_x = -75$ and $v_y = 100$

So, $\quad \mathbf{v} = (-75\hat{\mathbf{i}} + 100\hat{\mathbf{j}})$ m/s

4. Let $\mathbf{B} = B_1\hat{\mathbf{i}} + B_2\hat{\mathbf{j}} + B_3\hat{\mathbf{k}}$

$\mathbf{F} = q(\mathbf{v} \times \mathbf{B})$

$\Rightarrow \quad -1.28 \times 10^{-13}\hat{\mathbf{k}} = q(2\hat{\mathbf{i}} + 3\hat{\mathbf{j}}) \times 10^6 \times (B_1\hat{\mathbf{i}} + B_2\hat{\mathbf{j}} + B_3\hat{\mathbf{k}})$

$\Rightarrow \quad -1.28 \times 10^{-13}\hat{\mathbf{k}}$

$= q \times 10^6[3B_3\hat{\mathbf{i}} - 2B_3\hat{\mathbf{j}} + (2B_2 - 3B_1)\hat{\mathbf{k}}]$

Comparing, we get $B_3 = 0$ and $2B_2 - 3B_1 = \dfrac{-1.28 \times 10^{-19}}{q}$

$\mathbf{F} = q(\mathbf{v} \times \mathbf{B})$

$\Rightarrow \quad F\hat{\mathbf{i}} = q(v\hat{\mathbf{k}} \times (B_1\hat{\mathbf{i}} + B_2\hat{\mathbf{j}} + B_3\hat{\mathbf{k}})$

$\Rightarrow \quad F\hat{\mathbf{i}} = qv(+B_1\hat{\mathbf{j}} - B_2\hat{\mathbf{i}})$

Comparing, we get

$B_1 = 0$ and $B_2 = -0.4$

So, $\quad \mathbf{B} = -(0.4\hat{\mathbf{j}})$ T

5. (i) $\mathbf{F} = q(\mathbf{v} \times \mathbf{B})$

Force on electrons will be due south.

(ii) $\dfrac{1}{2}mv^2 = 4.5 \times 10^{-15}$

$\Rightarrow \dfrac{1}{2} \times 9.1 \times 10^{-31} v^2 = 4.5 \times 10^{-15}$

$\Rightarrow v \simeq 10^8$ m/s

$$a = \frac{qvB\sin\theta}{m} = \frac{1.6 \times 10^{-19} \times 10^8 \times 2.25 \times 10^{-5} \sin 90^\circ}{9.1 \times 10^{-31}}$$

$= 4.0 \times 10^4$ m/s^2

6. $F = mg \Rightarrow qvB\sin 90^\circ = mg$

$\Rightarrow \quad 10^{-5} v(0.2)(1) = 10^{-5}(10)$

$\Rightarrow \quad v = 50$ m/s

2.2 Normal Incidence

1. $R = \dfrac{mv}{qB} = \dfrac{(2.0 \times 10^{-13})(2.0 \times 10^3)}{(2.0 \times 10^{-8})(0.1)} = 20$ cm

$$f = \frac{qB}{2\pi m} = \frac{(2.0 \times 10^{-8})(0.1)}{2\pi \times 2.0 \times 10^{-13}} = \frac{5}{\pi} \times 10^3 \text{Hz}$$

2. $qV = \dfrac{1}{2}mv^2 \Rightarrow q(24 \times 10^3) = \dfrac{1}{2}m(2 \times 10^6)^2$

$\Rightarrow \dfrac{m}{q} = 12 \times 10^{-9}$

$$R = \frac{mv}{qB} = 12 \times 10^{-9} \times \frac{2 \times 10^6}{0.2} = 0.12 \text{ m} = 12 \text{ cm}$$

3. $R = \dfrac{\sqrt{2mK}}{qB}$

$\Rightarrow \quad B = \dfrac{\sqrt{2mK}}{qR}$

$\Rightarrow \quad B = \dfrac{\sqrt{2 \times 9.1 \times 10^{-31} \times 400 \times 1.6 \times 10^{-19}}}{1.6 \times 10^{-19} \times 0.2} = 3.4 \times 10^{-4}$T

$$f = \frac{qB}{2\pi m} = \frac{1.6 \times 10^{-19} \times 3.4 \times 10^{-4}}{2 \times 3.14 \times 9.1 \times 10^{-31}} = 10^6 \text{ Hz}$$

4. For proton, $\dfrac{mv}{qB} = 1$ cm

For deutron, $R = \dfrac{(2m)v}{qB} = 2$ cm

5. Since, electron is negatively charged, force $q(\mathbf{v} \times \mathbf{B})$ will be directed towards right initially. So, path D corresponds to electron.

$R = \dfrac{mv}{qB}$, $m_\alpha = 4m_p$ and $q_\alpha = 2q_p$

$\Rightarrow \quad R_\alpha > R_p$

So, path B will be of α-particle.

6. $m_p : m_\alpha : m_D = m_p : 4m_p : 2m_p$

$q_p : q_\alpha : q_D = q_p : 2q_p : q_p$

$R = \dfrac{\sqrt{2mK}}{qB} \Rightarrow R \propto \dfrac{\sqrt{m}}{q}$

$\Rightarrow R_p : R_\alpha : R_D = \dfrac{\sqrt{m_p}}{q_p} : \dfrac{\sqrt{4m_p}}{2q_p} : \dfrac{\sqrt{2m_p}}{q_p} = 1 : 1 : \sqrt{2}$

$T = \dfrac{2\pi m}{qB}$

$\Rightarrow \quad T \propto \dfrac{m}{q}$

$\Rightarrow T_p : T_\alpha : T_D = 1 : 2 : 2$

7. Since, $\mathbf{v} \perp \mathbf{B}$, the particle will move in a circle in *YZ*-plane. Centre of circle will lie on $-X$-axis.

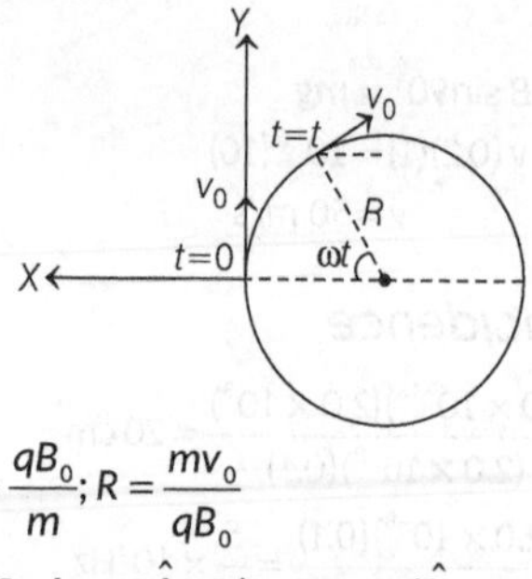

$$\omega = \frac{qB_0}{m};\ R = \frac{mv_0}{qB_0}$$

$$\mathbf{r} = R\sin\omega t\,\hat{\mathbf{j}} - R(1-\cos\omega t)\hat{\mathbf{k}}$$

$$\mathbf{v} = v_0\cos\omega t\,\hat{\mathbf{j}} - v_0\sin\omega t\,\hat{\mathbf{k}}$$

8. $R = \dfrac{\sqrt{2mqV}}{qB} = \dfrac{\sqrt{2\times4\times1.6\times10^{-27}\times3.2\times10^{-19}\times10^4}}{3.2\times10^{-19}\times0.1}$

$= 0.2$ m

$\sin\theta = \dfrac{d}{R} = \dfrac{0.1}{0.2} \Rightarrow \theta = 30°$

9. The particle will describe a semi-circular path in the magnetic field.

(i) $t = \dfrac{T}{2} = \dfrac{\pi m}{qB}$

(ii) Distance $= \pi R = \dfrac{\pi mv}{qB}$

(iii) Impulse $= mv - (-mv) = 2mv$

10. For just missing hitting the plate

$$d = R = \frac{\sqrt{2mK}}{qB} \Rightarrow B = \frac{\sqrt{2mk}}{qd}$$

11.

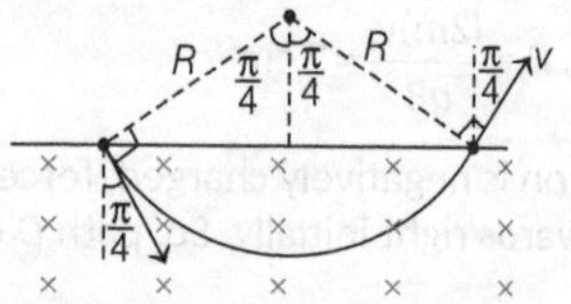

(i) $R = \dfrac{mv}{qB}$

(ii) $\dfrac{\pi}{4} + \dfrac{\pi}{4} = \dfrac{\pi}{2}$

(iii) $t = \dfrac{\theta}{\omega} = \dfrac{\pi m}{2qB}$

(iv) If *q* is negatively charged.

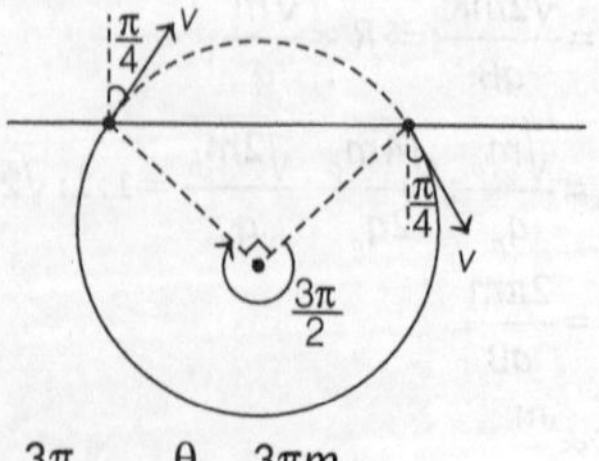

$$R = \frac{mv}{qB};\ \theta = \frac{3\pi}{2};\ t = \frac{\theta}{\omega} = \frac{3\pi m}{2qB}$$

12. (i) $\theta = \sin^{-1}\left(\dfrac{d}{R}\right) = \dfrac{\pi}{2}$

(ii) $\theta = \sin^{-1}\left(\dfrac{mv/\sqrt{2}qB}{mv/qB}\right) = \dfrac{\pi}{4}$

(iii) $d = 3R \Rightarrow$ particle will describe semi-circular path in the magnetic field.

So, $\theta = \pi$

13. For just striking the solenoid,

$$2R = r \Rightarrow \frac{2mv}{qB} = r$$

$$\Rightarrow \quad \frac{2mv_{\min}}{q(\mu_0 ni)} = r$$

$$\Rightarrow \quad v_{\min} = \frac{qr\mu_0 ni}{2m}$$

14.

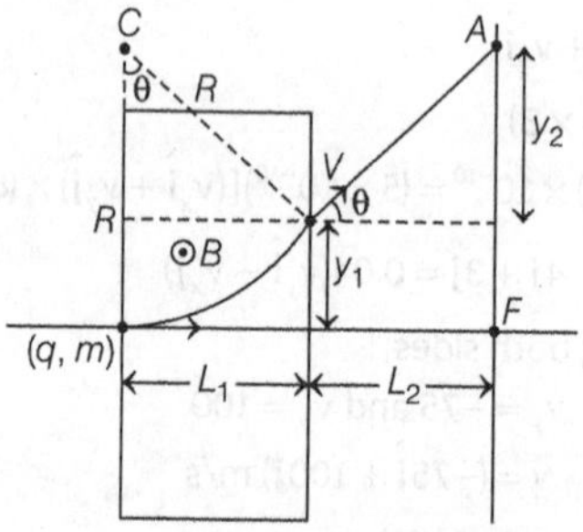

$$y_1 = R(1-\cos\theta),\quad y_2 = L_2\tan\theta$$

$$\sin\theta = \frac{L_1}{R} = \frac{L_1}{\dfrac{1}{B}\sqrt{\dfrac{2mv}{q}}} = \frac{\sqrt{3}/2}{1}$$

$$\Rightarrow \quad \theta = 60°$$

$$FA = y_1 + y_2 = \frac{L_1}{\sin\theta}(1-\cos\theta) + L_2\tan\theta$$

$$= \frac{\sqrt{3}/2}{\sqrt{3}/2}\left(1-\frac{1}{2}\right) + \frac{3\sqrt{3}}{2}(\sqrt{3}) = 5\text{ m}$$

15. (i) $R_1 = \dfrac{mv}{qB}$ and $R_2 = \dfrac{(2m)v}{(2q)B} = \dfrac{mv}{qB}$

So, both particles will go in circles of same radii.

For them not to collide, $d = 2R$

$$\Rightarrow \quad d = \frac{2mv_m}{qB} \Rightarrow v_m = \frac{qBd}{2m}$$

(ii) For $v = 2v_m$; $R = \dfrac{m(2v_m)}{qB} = 2d$

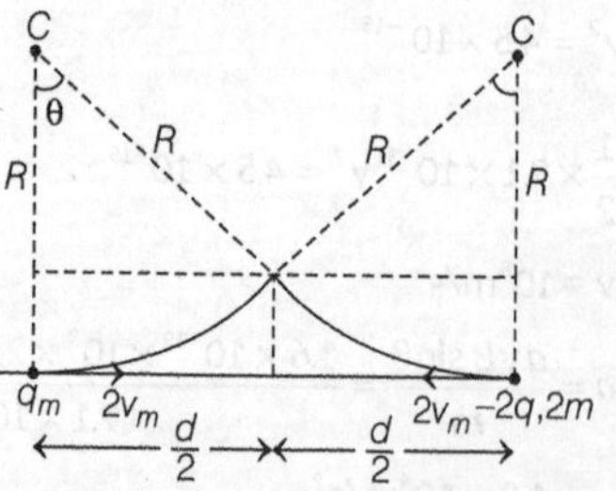

$$\sin\theta = \frac{d/2}{R} = \frac{d/2}{d} = \frac{1}{2} \Rightarrow \theta = \frac{\pi}{6}$$

$$\omega t = \theta \Rightarrow \left(\frac{qB}{m}\right)t = \frac{\pi}{6} \Rightarrow t = \frac{m\pi}{6qB}$$

(iii) Applying linear momentum conservation

$$m(2v_m\cos 30^\circ\,\hat{\mathbf{i}} + 2v_m\sin 30^\circ\,\hat{\mathbf{j}})$$

$$+2m(-2v_m\cos 30^\circ\,\hat{\mathbf{i}} + 2v_m\sin 30^\circ) = 3m\,\mathbf{v}$$

$$\Rightarrow \mathbf{v} = -\frac{v_m}{\sqrt{3}}\hat{\mathbf{i}} + v_m\hat{\mathbf{j}}$$

$$\Rightarrow |\mathbf{v}| = -\frac{2v_m}{\sqrt{3}}$$

$$\text{Radius of combined mass} = \frac{(3m)(2v_m/\sqrt{3})}{|-2q+q|B} = \sqrt{3}d$$

2.3 Oblique Incidence

1. $R = \dfrac{mv\sin\theta}{qB}$

$$= \frac{5\times10^{-12}\times1\times10^{3}\times0.9}{5\times10^{-6}\times5\times10^{-3}} = 0.18\,\text{m}$$

Diameter = 36 cm

$$\text{Pitch} = (v\cos\theta)\,T = (v\cos\theta)\frac{2\pi m}{qB}$$

$$= (1\times10^{3}\times\sqrt{1-0.81})\,\frac{(2\times3.14\times5\times10^{-12})}{5\times10^{-6}\times5\times10^{-3}} = 54\,\text{cm}$$

2. $R = \dfrac{mv_\perp}{qB}$

$$\Rightarrow v_\perp = \frac{qBR}{m} = \frac{1.6\times10^{-19}\times0.04\times5\times10^{-2}}{1.6\times10^{-27}} = 2\times10^{5}\,\text{m/s}$$

$$\text{Pitch} = v_{\parallel}T$$

$$\Rightarrow v_{\parallel} = \frac{(\text{Pitch})}{\left(\dfrac{2\pi m}{qB}\right)}$$

$$= \frac{20\times10^{-2}\times1.6\times10^{-19}\times0.04}{2\pi\times1.6\times10^{-27}}$$

$$= \frac{4}{\pi}\times10^{5}\,\text{m/s}$$

3. $K = \dfrac{1}{2}mv^2$

$$\Rightarrow 2\times10^{3}\times1.6\times10^{-19} = \frac{1}{2}\times9\times10^{-31}v^2$$

$$\Rightarrow \quad v = \frac{8}{3}\times10^{7}\,\text{m/s}$$

$$GS = (v\cos\theta)\,(nT)$$

$$\Rightarrow 0.1 = \left(\frac{8}{3}\times10^{7}\times\frac{1}{2}\right)n\left(\frac{2\times\pi\times9\times10^{-31}}{1.6\times10^{-19}B}\right)$$

$$\Rightarrow \quad B = n(15\pi\times10^{-4})$$

$$\Rightarrow B_{min} = 15\pi\times10^{-4}\,\text{T} \qquad [\because \text{for } B_{min}, n = 1]$$

4. In X-direction

$F_x = 0 \Rightarrow a_x = 0 \Rightarrow v_x = v_o\cos\theta = \text{constant}$

and $x = (v_o\cos\theta)t$

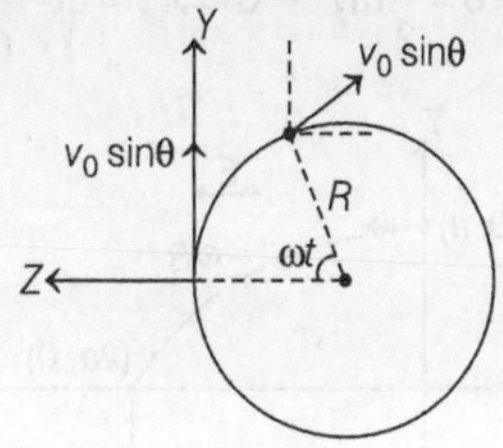

$$R = \frac{mv_0\sin\theta}{qB};\ \omega = \frac{qB}{m}$$

In YZ-plane ;

$$v_y = v_o\sin\theta\cos\omega t$$

$$v_z = -v_0\sin\theta\sin\omega t$$

$$y = R\sin\omega t$$

$$z = -R(1-\cos wt)$$

So, $\mathbf{v} = (v_o\cos\theta)\,\hat{\mathbf{i}} + v_o\sin\theta\cos\omega t\,\hat{\mathbf{j}} - v_o\sin\theta\sin\omega t\,\hat{\mathbf{k}}$

$$\mathbf{r} = (v_o\cos\theta)\,t\,\hat{\mathbf{i}} + R\sin\omega t\,\hat{\mathbf{j}} - R(1-\cos\omega t)\hat{\mathbf{k}}$$

2.4 Electric and Magnetic Force on a Charge

1. $\mathbf{F} = q\mathbf{E} + q(\mathbf{v}\times\mathbf{B})$

$$\Rightarrow \quad ma_0,\text{west} = e\mathbf{E} + 0$$

$$\Rightarrow \quad \mathbf{E} = \frac{ma_0}{e},\text{west}$$

$$\mathbf{F} = q\mathbf{E} + q(\mathbf{v}+\mathbf{B})$$

$$\Rightarrow m\,(3a_0),\text{west} = e\left(\frac{ma_0}{e},\text{west}\right) + e\,((u_0,\text{north})\times\mathbf{B})$$

$$\Rightarrow \quad 2ma_0,\text{ west} = eu_0B\sin\theta,\text{ west}$$

$$\Rightarrow \quad B = \frac{2ma_0}{eu_0\sin\theta}$$

$$\Rightarrow \quad B_{min} = \frac{2ma_0}{eu_0} \qquad [\because \text{for } B_{min}, \theta = 90^\circ]$$

$$\text{So, } \mathbf{B}_{min} = \frac{2ma_0}{eu_0},\text{downward}$$

2. For undeflected beam, $F_{net} = 0$

$$\Rightarrow \quad qE = qvB$$

$$\Rightarrow \quad v = \frac{E}{B} = \frac{3.2\times10^{4}}{2\times10^{-3}}$$

$$= 1.6\times10^{7}\,\text{m/s}$$

If electric field is removed,

$$r = \frac{mv}{qB} = \frac{9.1\times10^{-31}\times1.6\times10^{7}}{1.6\times10^{-19}\times2\times10^{-3}} = 4.5\,\text{cm}$$

3. $qE = qvB = E = vB$

$$\Rightarrow \quad 200 = v(0.4) = v = 500\text{ m/s}$$

$$R = \frac{mv}{qB} = \frac{q}{m} = \frac{v}{BR} = \frac{500}{0.4\times0.01} = 1.2\times10^{5}\,\text{C/kg}$$

4. Using work- energy theorem,

$$W_E + W_B = \Delta K$$

$$qE_0 x + 0 = \frac{1}{2}mv^2 - 0 \Rightarrow v = \sqrt{\frac{2qE_0 x}{m}}$$

5. (i)

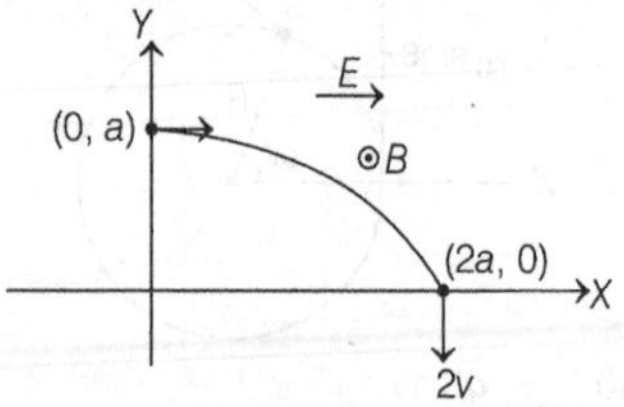

Using Work- energy theorem,

$$W_E + W_B = \Delta K$$

$$\Rightarrow \quad qE(2a) + 0 = \frac{1}{2}m(2v)^2 - \frac{1}{2}mv^2$$

$$\Rightarrow \quad E = \frac{3mv^2}{4qa}$$

(ii) At (0, a)

$$P_E = \mathbf{F}_E \cdot \mathbf{v} = (qE\hat{\mathbf{i}}) \cdot (v\hat{\mathbf{i}}) = qEv = \frac{3mv^2}{4a}$$

(iii) At (2a, 0)

$$P_E = (qE\hat{\mathbf{i}}) \cdot (-2v\hat{\mathbf{j}}) = 0$$

$$P_B = 0 \qquad (\because \mathbf{v} \perp \mathbf{F}_B)$$

Level 2

Single Choice Correct Questions

1. $\mathbf{a} \perp \mathbf{B}$

$$\Rightarrow \mathbf{a} \cdot \mathbf{B} = (-5\hat{\mathbf{i}} + 3\hat{\mathbf{j}} + a^2\hat{\mathbf{k}}).(2\hat{\mathbf{i}} + a\hat{\mathbf{j}} + \hat{\mathbf{k}}) = 0$$

$$\Rightarrow -10 + 3a + a^2 = 0$$

$$\Rightarrow a = 2 \text{ and } a = -5$$

2. Let $\mathbf{B} = B_x\hat{\mathbf{i}} + B_y\hat{\mathbf{j}} + B_z\hat{\mathbf{k}}$

$$\mathbf{F} = q(\mathbf{v} \times \mathbf{B})$$

$$\Rightarrow (4\hat{\mathbf{i}} + 3\hat{\mathbf{j}}) \times 10^{-13} = -1.6 \times 10^{-19}((2.5 \times 10^7\hat{\mathbf{k}}) \times (B_x\hat{\mathbf{i}} + B_y\hat{\mathbf{j}} + B_z\hat{\mathbf{k}}))$$

$$\Rightarrow \quad 0.1\hat{\mathbf{i}} + 0.075\hat{\mathbf{j}} = +B_y\hat{\mathbf{i}} - B_x\hat{\mathbf{j}}$$

Comparing both sides we get , $B_x = -0.075$ and $B_y = 0.1$

$$\mathbf{F} = q(\mathbf{v} \times \mathbf{B})$$

$$\Rightarrow \; 0 = -1.6 \times 10^{-19}[(1.5\hat{\mathbf{i}} - 2.0\hat{\mathbf{j}}) \times 10^7) \times (B_x\hat{\mathbf{i}} + B_y\hat{\mathbf{j}} + B_z\hat{\mathbf{k}})]$$

$$\Rightarrow B_z = 0$$

So, $\mathbf{B} = -0.075\hat{\mathbf{i}} + 0.1\hat{\mathbf{j}}$

3. $F_B = mg = qv\,B\sin 90^\circ = mg$

$$\Rightarrow \quad qv\left(\frac{\mu_0 j}{2\pi r}\right)\sin 90^\circ = mg$$

$$\Rightarrow \; q(10)\left(\frac{4\pi \times 10^{-7} \times 1}{2\pi(0.01)}\right)(1) = 1 \times 10^{-6} \times 10$$

$$\Rightarrow \quad q = 50 \times 10^{-3}\,\text{C} = 50\,\text{mC}$$

4.
$$\mathbf{B} = \frac{\mu_0 j}{4R}\hat{\mathbf{j}} + \frac{\mu_0 j}{4R}\hat{\mathbf{i}} = \frac{\mu_0 j}{4R}(\hat{\mathbf{i}} + \hat{\mathbf{j}})$$

$$\mathbf{F} = q(\mathbf{v} \times \mathbf{B}) = q\left(v\hat{\mathbf{i}} \times \left(\frac{\mu_0 j}{4R}\right)(\hat{\mathbf{i}} + \hat{\mathbf{j}})\right)$$

$$\Rightarrow \mathbf{F} = \frac{qv\mu_0 j\hat{\mathbf{k}}}{4R} \text{ and } F = \frac{qv\mu_0}{4R}$$

5. $R = \dfrac{mv}{qB} = \dfrac{2 \times 10^5}{5 \times 10^7 \times 4 \times 10^{-2}} = 0.10\text{ m}$

6. q is same for all of them.

$$R = \frac{P}{qB}$$

So, radius will be same for all of them.

7. $T_p = \dfrac{2\pi m_p}{q_p B}$ and $T_\alpha = \dfrac{2\pi(4m_p)}{(2q_p)B} = 2T_p$

$$\Rightarrow T_p = \frac{25\mu\text{s}}{5} = 5\mu\text{s} \Rightarrow T_\alpha = 2 \times 5 = 10\mu\text{s}$$

8. Since, $\mathbf{v} \perp \mathbf{B}$, electron will excute uniform circular motion. Magnitude of momentum is constant but direction will change.

So, momentum is not constant.

9. $qvB = \dfrac{mv^2}{R}$

$$\Rightarrow \quad v = \frac{qBR}{m} = \frac{0.1 \times 10 \times 100}{100} = 1\text{ m/s}$$

10. $f = \dfrac{qB}{2\pi m} \Rightarrow f \propto \dfrac{1}{m}$

11. $R = \dfrac{\sqrt{2mK}}{qB}$

$$\Rightarrow \quad K = \frac{q^2B^2R^2}{2m} \Rightarrow K \propto \frac{1}{m}$$

$$\Rightarrow \quad \frac{K_p}{K_d} = \frac{m_D}{m_p} \Rightarrow \frac{K_p}{50\text{keV}} = \frac{2m_p}{m_p}$$

$$\Rightarrow \quad K_p = 100\,\text{keV}$$

12. $R_A > R_B$

$$\Rightarrow \quad \frac{m_A v_B}{qB} > \frac{m_B v_B}{qB} \Rightarrow m_A v_A > m_B v_B$$

13. $R = \dfrac{mv}{qB} \Rightarrow R \propto m$

$$\Rightarrow \quad R_p > R_e \qquad [\because m_p > m_e \text{ and } q_p = q_e]$$

$$\mathbf{F} = q(\mathbf{v} \times \mathbf{B})$$

$\Rightarrow$ The electron travels clockwise around the smaller circle and the proton travels around the bigger circle.

14. For not hitting the plate,

$$R = 10^{-2}\text{m}$$

$$\Rightarrow \quad \frac{\sqrt{2mK}}{qB} = 10^{-2}$$

$$\Rightarrow \quad \frac{\sqrt{2 \times 1.6 \times 10^{-26} \times 2 \times 10^3 \times 1.6 \times 10^{-19}}}{1.6 \times 10^{-19} \times B} = 10^{-2}$$

$$\Rightarrow \quad B = 2\text{T}$$

15. $\sin\alpha = \dfrac{d}{R}$

$\Rightarrow \sin\alpha = \dfrac{d}{\left(\dfrac{\sqrt{2mqV}}{qB}\right)} = Bd\sqrt{\dfrac{q}{2mV}}$

16. Using Pythagoras theorem,

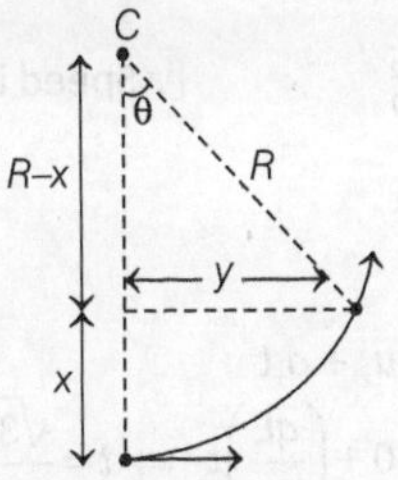

$R^2 = (R-x)^2 + y^2$

$\Rightarrow \quad R = \dfrac{x^2+y^2}{2x} \Rightarrow \dfrac{p}{qB} = \dfrac{x^2+y^2}{2x}$

$\Rightarrow \quad p = \dfrac{qB}{2}\left(\dfrac{y^2}{x} + x\right)$

17. $R = \dfrac{mv}{qB} \geq (b-a)$

$\Rightarrow \quad v \geq \dfrac{q(b-a)B}{m}$

$\Rightarrow v_{min} = \dfrac{q(b-a)B}{m}$

18. $K = \dfrac{q^2B^2R^2}{2m}$ and $f = \dfrac{qB}{2\pi m}$

$\Rightarrow K = \dfrac{(2\pi mf)^2R^2}{2m} = 2\pi^2 mf^2R^2$

$\Rightarrow K = 2\times(3.14)^2\times 1.67\times10^{-27}\times(10^7)^2(0.6)^2$

$\Rightarrow K = 1.2\times10^{-12}$ J

19. Number of turns $= \dfrac{K}{2qv} = \dfrac{20\times10^6 eV}{2\times100\times10^3 eV} = 100$

20. $f = \dfrac{qB}{2\pi m}$

$\Rightarrow f = \dfrac{q\mu_0 rni}{2\pi m}$

$\Rightarrow 10^8 = \dfrac{1.6\times10^{-19}\times4\pi\times10^{-7}\times n\times2}{2\pi(9.1\times10^{-31})}$

$\Rightarrow \quad n = 1420$ turns/m

21. $d = 2R = 2\left(\dfrac{\sqrt{2mqV}}{qB}\right)$

$\Rightarrow m = \dfrac{qB^2d^2}{8V}$

22. $F_{avg} = \dfrac{\Delta p}{\Delta t} = \dfrac{mv_0 - (-mv_0)}{\dfrac{\pi m}{qB}} = \dfrac{2qB_0v_0}{\pi}$

23. $\mathbf{F} = q(\mathbf{v}\times\mathbf{B})$

At $t = 0$, **F** is in X-direction **v** along Y-direction and **B** along Z-direction.

So, $q > 0$

$R = \dfrac{mv}{qB} \Rightarrow R \propto \dfrac{1}{B}$

$\Rightarrow \quad B_2 > B_1 \quad [\because R_2 < R_1]$

24. Let radius of circle described in the first and second region be r_1 and r_2 respectively.

Now, $r_1 > 5$ and $r_2 > 5$ and $r = \dfrac{mv}{qB}$

$\Rightarrow \quad v_{min} = \dfrac{rqB_{min}}{m}$

$\Rightarrow \quad v_{min} = \dfrac{5\times10^{-2}\times1.6\times10^{-19}\times0.001}{9\times10^{-31}} = \dfrac{8}{9}\times10^7$ m/s

25. $\sin\theta = \dfrac{d}{R} \Rightarrow \sin30^0 = \dfrac{L}{R} \Rightarrow R = 2L$

$R = \dfrac{mv}{qB} \Rightarrow R \propto \dfrac{1}{B}$

If magnetic field is halved, radius will get doubled.

Now, $\sin\theta = \dfrac{L}{4L}$

$\Rightarrow \quad \theta = \sin^{-1}\left(\dfrac{1}{4}\right)$

26. $R = \dfrac{mv}{qB} \Rightarrow R = \dfrac{\sqrt{2mK}}{qB}$

$\Rightarrow \quad K = \dfrac{q^2B^2R^2}{2m}$

$\dfrac{K_D}{K_\alpha} = \dfrac{\dfrac{q^2(2.3B)^2R^2}{2(2m)}}{\dfrac{(2q)^2B^2R^2}{2(4m)}}$

$\Rightarrow \quad \dfrac{K_D}{(5.3\text{MeV})} = \dfrac{(2.3)^2}{2}$

$\Rightarrow \quad K_D = 14.02$ MeV

27. $|\Delta\mathbf{v}| = 2v\sin\left(\dfrac{\theta}{2}\right) = 2v\left(\dfrac{\theta}{2}\right) = v\theta$

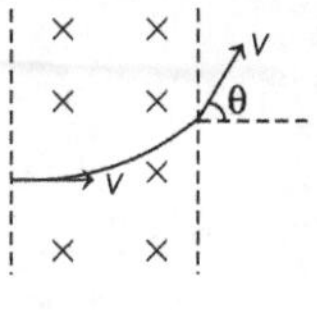

Impulse $= m|\Delta\mathbf{v}|$

$= mv\theta$

$= \dfrac{mvd}{R} = qBd$

28. $\theta = \omega t = \left(\dfrac{qB}{m}\right)t = \pi(2)\left(\dfrac{1}{12}\right) = \dfrac{\pi}{6}$

$\mathbf{v} = v\cos\theta\,\hat{\mathbf{i}} + v\sin\theta\,\hat{\mathbf{j}}$

$= 10\cos\left(\dfrac{\pi}{6}\right)\hat{\mathbf{i}} + 10\sin\left(\dfrac{\pi}{6}\right)\hat{\mathbf{j}} = 5\sqrt{3}\,\hat{\mathbf{i}} + 5\hat{\mathbf{j}}$

29. Path will be helical, radius $= \dfrac{mv\sin\theta}{qB}$

$$= \frac{1.67\times10^{-27}\times2\times10^{6}\times(0.5)}{1.6\times10^{-19}\times0.104} = 0.1\text{ m}$$

$$T = \frac{2\pi m}{qB} = \frac{2\pi\times1.67\times10^{-27}}{1.6\times10^{-19}\times0.104}$$

$$= 2\pi\times10^{-7}\text{ s}$$

30. Pitch $= 2R$

$$\Rightarrow (v\cos\theta)\left(\frac{2\pi m}{qB}\right) = 2\left(\frac{mv\sin\theta}{qB}\right)$$

$$\Rightarrow \quad \tan\theta = \pi$$

31. $eV = \frac{1}{2}mv^2 \Rightarrow v = \frac{\sqrt{2eV}}{m}$

$$\text{Pitch} = (v\cos\theta)\left(\frac{2\pi m}{qB}\right)$$

$$\Rightarrow S = \left(\frac{\sqrt{2eV}}{m}\right)(1)\left(\frac{2\pi m}{eB}\right) \qquad [\because \theta \approx 0^\circ]$$

$$\Rightarrow S = 2\sqrt{\frac{20\,mV}{eB^2}}$$

32. Distance of point $= (v\cos\theta)(n_1T_1) = (v\cos\theta)(n_2T_2)$

$$\Rightarrow \quad n_1\left(\frac{2\pi m}{qB}\right) = n_2\left(\frac{2\pi(2m)}{qB}\right)$$

$$\Rightarrow \quad n_1 = 2n_2$$

So, $n_2 = 1$ and $n_1 = 2$ for first meeting.

Distance $= (v\cos\theta)n_1T_1$

$$= (v\cos\theta)2\left(\frac{2\pi m}{qB}\right) = \frac{4\pi mv\cos\theta}{qB}$$

33. Since, $\mathbf{v} \perp \mathbf{B}$, electron will go in circular path.

For hitting the target,

$$d = 2R\sin\alpha$$

$$\Rightarrow \quad d = 2\left(\frac{\sqrt{2m_e eu}}{eB}\right)\sin\alpha$$

$$\Rightarrow \quad B = 2\sqrt{\frac{2Um_e}{e}}\frac{\sin\alpha}{d}$$

34. The particle will go in helical path,

$$x = v_0 t = v_0\left(\frac{\pi}{B_0\alpha}\right)$$

$$y = R\sin\omega t = \left(\frac{mv_0}{qB_0}\right)\sin\left(\frac{qB_0\pi m}{mB_0 q}\right) = 0$$

$$z = -R(1-\cos\omega t) = -2R = -\frac{2v_0}{B_0\alpha}$$

35. $q\mathbf{E} + q(\mathbf{v}\times\mathbf{B}) = 0$

36. $R = \frac{mv}{qB} \quad \Rightarrow \quad 0.05 = \frac{20\times10^{-9}\times v}{20\times10^{-6}\times0.1}$

$$\Rightarrow \quad v = 5\text{ m/s}$$

$$qE = qvB$$

$$\Rightarrow \quad E = vB = 5(0.1) = 0.5\text{ V/m}$$

37. Using Work-energy theorem, $W_E + W_B = \Delta K$

$$\Rightarrow \quad (qE_0)(x-0) + 0 = \frac{1}{2}m(\sqrt{5^2+12^2})^2 - 0$$

$$\Rightarrow \quad x = \frac{169m}{2qE_0}$$

38. $v = \sqrt{v_x^2+v_y^2+v_z^2}$

$$\Rightarrow 2v_0 = \sqrt{v_x^2+v_0^2} \qquad [\because \text{Speed in } YZ\text{-plane is constant } v_y^2+v_z^2 = v_0^2]$$

$$\Rightarrow \; v_x = \sqrt{3}v_0$$

In X-direction,

$$v_x = u_x + a_x t$$

$$\Rightarrow \quad \sqrt{3}v_0 = 0 + \left(\frac{qE}{m}\right)t \;\Rightarrow t = \frac{\sqrt{3}mv_0}{qE}$$

39. $qE = qvB$

$$\Rightarrow \; v = \frac{E}{B} = \frac{\sigma}{\varepsilon_0 B}; \quad t = \frac{l}{v} = \frac{\varepsilon_0 l}{\sigma}B$$

40. Speed will be minimum when $v_x = 0$

$$v_x = u_x + a_x t$$

$$\Rightarrow \quad 0 = v_0\sin\theta - \left(\frac{qE}{m}\right)t$$

$$\Rightarrow \quad t = \frac{mv_0\sin\theta}{qE}$$

41. Electron is going anti-clockwise. So, magnetic field will be directed out of the plane.

Between capacitor plates, magnetic force on electron should cancel out electric force on electron. So, electric field in the top capacitor should be directed down and in the lower capacitor vertically up.

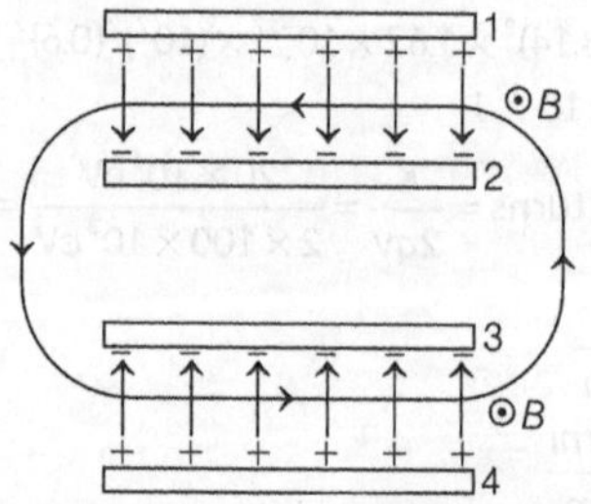

42. In options (A) and (C), path will be helical. Net force should be in XY-plane. So, option (D) is also ruled out.

43.

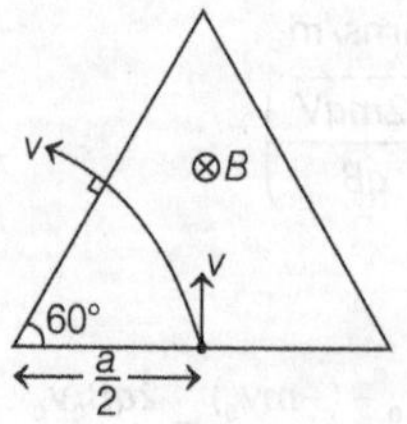

$$R = \frac{mv}{qB} \quad \Rightarrow \quad \frac{a}{2} = \frac{mv}{qB} \quad \Rightarrow B = \frac{2mv}{qa}$$

44.

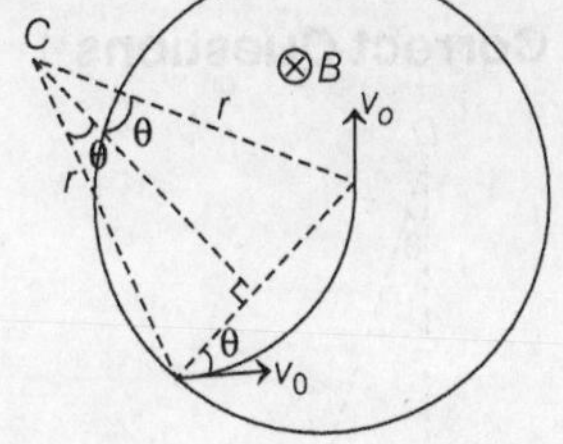

$$2r\sin\theta = R$$

$$\Rightarrow 2\left(\frac{mv_0}{qB}\right)\sin\theta = R \Rightarrow v_0 = \frac{qBR}{2m\sin\theta}$$

45.

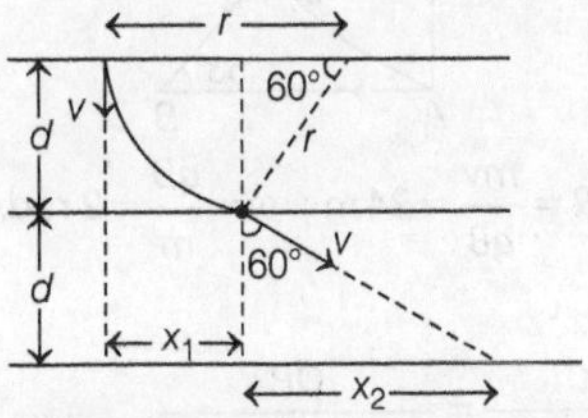

$$\sin\theta = \frac{d}{r} = \frac{\sqrt{3}r/2}{r}$$

$$\Rightarrow \quad \theta = 60^0$$

$$x_1 = r(1-\cos 60^0) = \frac{r}{2}$$

and $\quad x_2 = d\tan 60^0 = \frac{3r}{2}$

$$x = x_1 + x_2 = \frac{r}{2} + \frac{3r}{2} = 2r$$

Numerical Value Questions

1. $\mathbf{B} = \left[\frac{\mu_0 I(\sin 60^0 + \sin 60^0)}{4\pi(a\cos 60^0)} - \frac{\mu_0\left(\frac{1}{3}\right)I}{2a}\right](-\hat{\mathbf{k}})$

$$= \frac{\mu_0 I}{2\pi a}\left(\frac{3\sqrt{3}-\pi}{3}\right)(-\hat{\mathbf{k}})$$

$$= \frac{4\pi\times 10^{-7}\times 10(3\sqrt{3}-\pi)}{2\pi(3\sqrt{3}-\pi)\times 10^{-2}\times 3}(-\hat{\mathbf{k}}) = \frac{2}{3}\times 10^{-4}(-\hat{\mathbf{k}})$$

$$\mathbf{F} = q(\mathbf{v}\times\mathbf{B})$$

$$\Rightarrow F = qvB\sin\theta \Rightarrow a = \frac{qvB\sin\theta}{m}$$

$$= \frac{3000\times 10^{-6}\times 10\times\left(\frac{2}{3}\right)\times 10^{-4}\sin 90^0}{1\times 10^{-5}}$$

$$= 0.2\ \text{m/s}^2 = 20\ \text{cm/s}^2$$

2. $mvr = L$

$$\Rightarrow mv\left(\frac{mv}{qB}\right) = L$$

$$\Rightarrow \quad v = \sqrt{\frac{qBL}{m^2}}$$

$$\Rightarrow \quad v = \sqrt{\frac{1.6\times 10^{-19}\times 1\times 10^{-3}\times 8.1\times 10^{-38}}{81\times 10^{-62}}}$$

$$= 4\ \text{m/s}$$

3. Path of the particle will be helical.

Distance = Speed × time = 2 × 3 = 6 m

4.

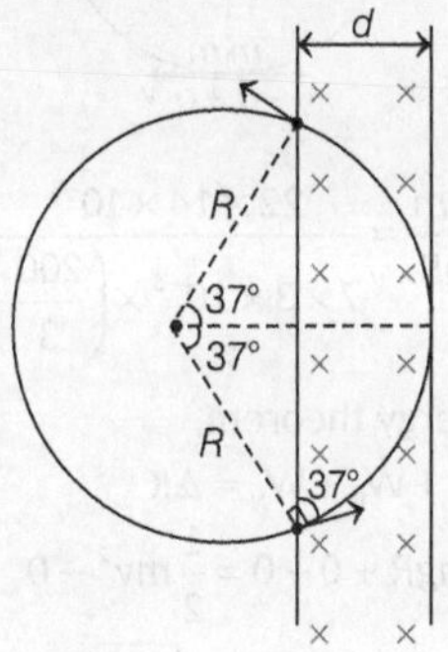

$$d = R - R\cos 37^0$$

$$d = \frac{R}{5} = \frac{1}{5}\left(\frac{10^{-6}\times 50}{10^{-6}\times 10}\right) = 1\ \text{m}$$

5. $R = \frac{\sqrt{2mqV}}{qB} \Rightarrow m = \frac{qB^2R^2}{2V} \Rightarrow m \propto R^2$

$$\Rightarrow \quad \frac{m_{max}}{m_{min}} = \left(\frac{R_{max}}{R_{min}}\right)^2 = \left(\frac{\frac{l+d}{2}}{\frac{l}{2}}\right)^2 = 1.21$$

6.

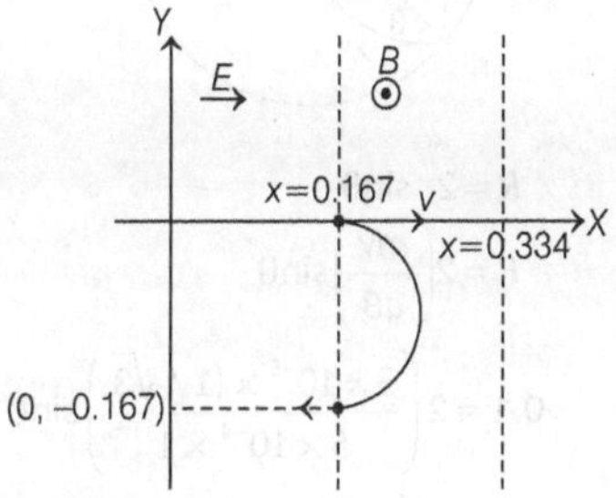

From $x = 0$ to $x = 0.167$ m,

$$v^2 = u^2 + 2as$$

$$\Rightarrow \quad v^2 = 0^2 + 2\left(\frac{qE}{m}\right)s$$

$$\Rightarrow \quad v^2 = 2\left(\frac{1.6\times 10^{-19}\times 200}{1.67\times 10^{-27}}\times 0.167\right)$$

$$\Rightarrow \quad v = 8\times 10^4\ \text{m/s}$$

For $x > 0.167$ m, $R = \frac{mv}{qB}$

$$\Rightarrow \quad \frac{0.167}{2} = \frac{1.67\times 10^{-27}\times 8\times 10^4}{1.6\times 10^{-19}\times B}$$

$$\Rightarrow \quad B = 10\ \text{mT}$$

7. They will collide after describing semi-circle.

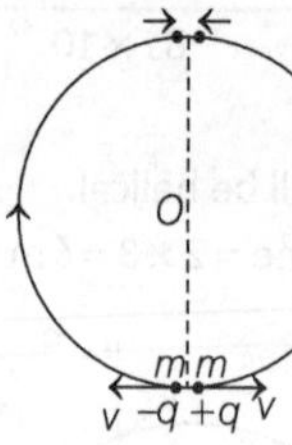

$$T = \frac{\pi m}{qB} = \frac{22 \times 14 \times 10^{-3}}{7 \times 3 \times 10^{-6} \times \left(\frac{200}{3}\right)} = 220 \text{ s}$$

8. Using Work-energy theorem,

$$W_{mg} + W_B + W_N = \Delta K$$

$$\Rightarrow \quad +mgR + 0 + 0 = \frac{1}{2}mv^2 - 0$$

$$\Rightarrow \quad v = \sqrt{2gR}$$

At P, $N_1 - mg - qvB\sin 90^\circ = \frac{mv^2}{R}$

$$\Rightarrow \quad N_1 = 3mg + qvB = 60 + 10 = 70\text{N}$$

9. Lets take radius of circle described by the particle in the magnetic field to be r.

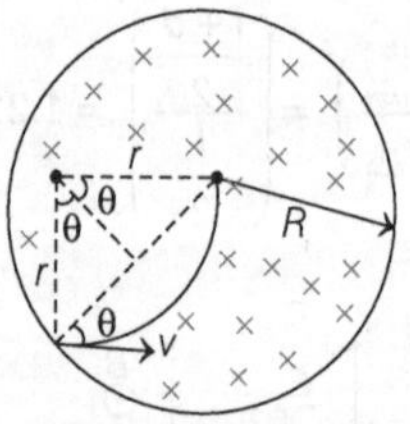

$$R = 2r\sin\theta$$

$$\Rightarrow \quad R = 2\left(\frac{mv}{qB}\right)\sin\theta$$

$$\Rightarrow \quad 0.1 = 2\left(\frac{5 \times 10^{-5} \times (1/\sqrt{3})}{5 \times 10^{-4} \times 1}\right)\sin\theta$$

$$\Rightarrow \quad \sin\theta = \frac{\sqrt{3}}{2} \Rightarrow \theta = \frac{\pi}{3}$$

10. Pitch $= (v\cos\theta)\frac{2\pi m}{qB} = \left(\frac{\sqrt{2qv}}{m}\right)\cos\theta\left(\frac{2\pi m}{qB}\right)$

$$\Rightarrow \text{Pitch} = \left(\sqrt{\frac{2mv}{q}}\right)\cos\theta\left(\frac{2\pi}{B}\right)$$

$$\Rightarrow \quad 0.1 = \left(\sqrt{\frac{2 \times 9 \times 10^{-31} \times 80}{1.6 \times 10^{-19}}}\right)\cos 0^\circ\left(\frac{2\pi}{B}\right)$$

$$\Rightarrow \quad B = 6\pi \times 10^{-4}\text{T}$$

For solenoid, $B = \mu_0 ni = 6\pi \times 10^{-4}$

$$\Rightarrow 4\pi \times 10^{-7} \times 3000 \times i = 6\pi \times 10^{-4}$$

$$\Rightarrow \quad i = 0.5\text{ A} = 500\text{ mA}$$

Level 3

Single Choice Correct Questions

1.

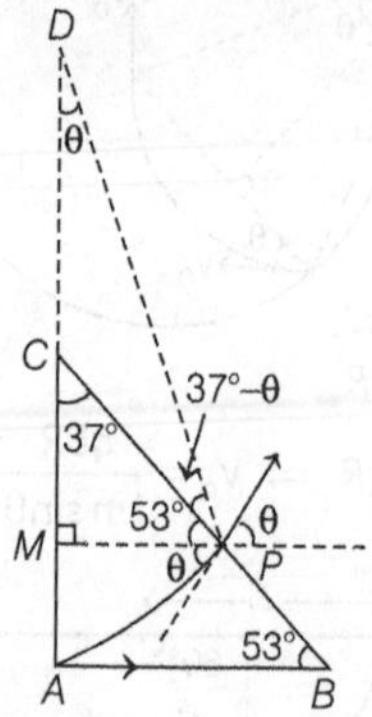

$$R = \frac{mv}{qB} = 24\text{ m}\ ;\ \omega = \frac{qB}{m} = 2\text{ rad/s}$$

In ΔCPO,

$$\frac{OC}{\sin(37^\circ - \theta)} = \frac{OP}{\sin(180^\circ - 37^\circ)}$$

$$\Rightarrow \quad \frac{20}{\sin(37^\circ - \theta)} = \frac{24}{\sin 37^\circ}$$

$$\Rightarrow \quad \sin(37^\circ - \theta) = \frac{1}{2} \Rightarrow \theta = 7^\circ$$

$$\Rightarrow \quad \theta = \omega t \Rightarrow \frac{7\pi}{180} = 2t$$

$$\Rightarrow \quad t = \frac{7\pi}{360}\text{ s}$$

2. $F_E = \frac{1}{4\pi\varepsilon_0}\frac{e^2}{r^2}$ and $F_B = \frac{\mu_0}{4\pi}\left(\frac{ev}{r^2}\right)(ev)$

$$\frac{F_E}{F_B} = \left(\frac{1}{\mu_0\varepsilon_0}\right)\frac{1}{v^2} = \frac{c^2}{v^2}$$

3. From linear momentum conservation

$$0 = m_1v_1 + m_2(-v_2)$$

$$\Rightarrow \quad m_1v_1 = m_2v_2$$

Charges will be $+q$ and $-q$.

So, they will rotate in opposite sense

$$R = \frac{mv}{qB} \Rightarrow R_1 = R_2$$

So, both particles will describe circles of same radius.

$T = \frac{2\pi m}{qB} \Rightarrow T \propto m$; Heavier particle will have more time period.

4. $\sin\theta = \frac{d}{R}$

$$\Rightarrow \quad \theta = \sin^{-1}\left(\frac{\sqrt{3}R}{2R}\right) \Rightarrow \theta = 60^\circ$$

$$|\Delta \mathbf{v}| = 2v_0\sin\left(\frac{\theta}{2}\right) = v_0$$

5.

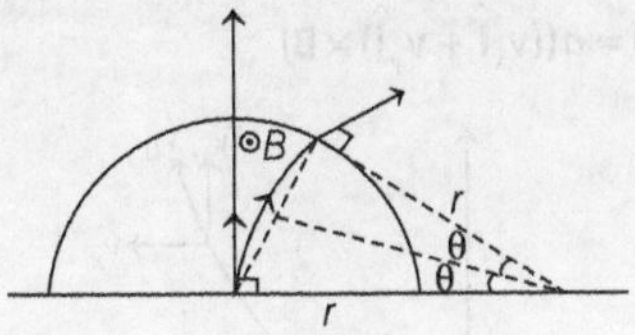

$$r=\frac{mv}{qB}=\frac{10^{-19}\times 640}{1.6\times 10^{-19}\times 100}=4\text{ m}$$

$$2r\sin\theta = R$$

$$\Rightarrow \quad 2(4)\sin\theta = 4 \Rightarrow \theta = 30^\circ$$

Deviation = $2\theta = 60^\circ$

6. $$v_{avg}=\frac{\text{displacement}}{\text{time}}=\frac{2(R_1-R_2)}{t_1+t_2}$$

$$\Rightarrow v_{avg}=\frac{2\left(\frac{mv}{qB_1}-\frac{mv}{qB_2}\right)}{\frac{\pi m}{qB_1}+\frac{\pi m}{qB_2}}$$

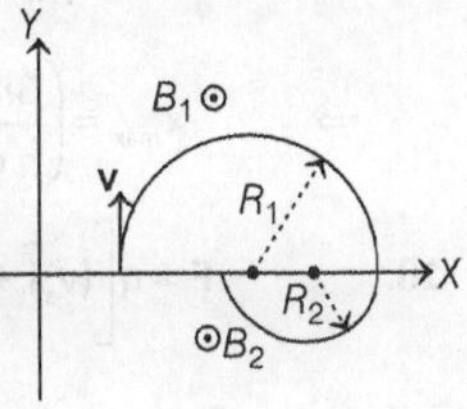

$$\Rightarrow 10^5=\frac{2(10^6)(B_2-B_1)}{\pi(B_1+B_2)}$$

$$\Rightarrow \frac{B_1}{B_2}=\frac{20-\pi}{20+\pi}$$

7. $\tan\theta=\frac{v_y}{v_x}=\frac{3\sqrt{3}}{3}=\sqrt{3} \Rightarrow \theta=\frac{\pi}{3}$

Deviation $=\frac{\pi}{3}=\omega t$

$$\Rightarrow \quad \frac{\pi}{3}=\left(\frac{qB}{m}\right)t \Rightarrow t=\frac{\pi m}{3qB}$$

8.

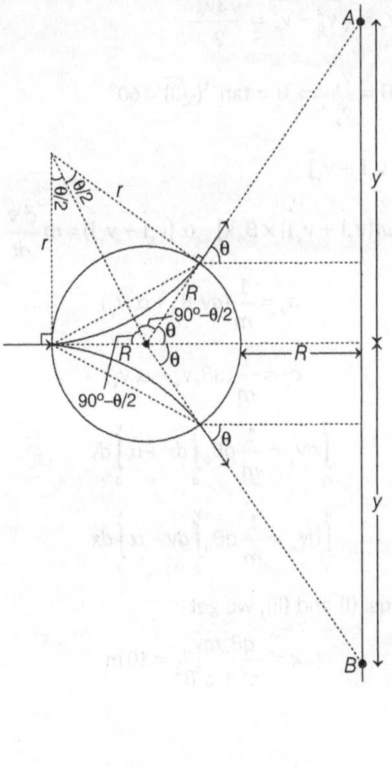

$$r=\frac{mv}{qB}=\frac{2\times 10^{-3}\times 0.3}{10^{-3}\times 0.2}=3\text{m}$$

$$2R\sin\left(90-\frac{\theta}{2}\right)=2r\sin\left(\frac{\theta}{2}\right)$$

$$\Rightarrow \quad \sqrt{3}\cot\left(\frac{\theta}{2}\right)=3 \Rightarrow \theta=60^\circ$$

$$\tan\theta=\frac{y}{2R}$$

$$\Rightarrow \quad y=2R\tan\theta=2\sqrt{3}(\sqrt{3})=6\text{m}$$

$$AB=2y=12\text{ m}$$

9. $N=mg\cos\theta-qvB$

$\Rightarrow 0=mg\cos\theta-q(g\sin\theta)t)B$

$\Rightarrow t=\frac{m\cot\theta}{qB}$

10. From momentum conservation,

$$-mv\hat{\mathbf{i}}=(2m)\mathbf{v}_1 \Rightarrow \mathbf{v}_1=-\frac{v}{2}\hat{\mathbf{i}}$$

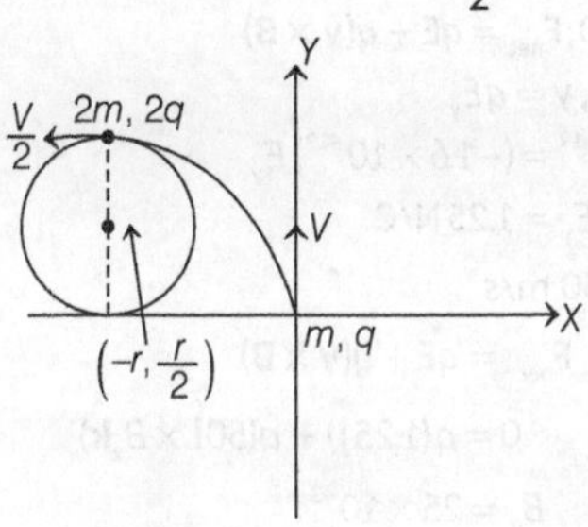

New radius $=\frac{(2m)\left(\frac{v}{2}\right)}{(2q)B}=\frac{r}{2}$

Equation of trajectory,

$$(x-(-r))^2+\left(y-\frac{r}{2}\right)^2=\left(\frac{r}{2}\right)^2$$

$$\Rightarrow \quad (x+r)^2+\left(y-\frac{r}{2}\right)^2=\frac{r^2}{4}$$

11. Since, $\frac{mv}{qB}>R$, the particle will be in contact with the outer wall of pipe. So, force on particle will be towards centre.

12. $qvB_o\cos\theta=mg$ ...(i)

$$qvB_0\sin\theta=\frac{mv^2}{r} \qquad \text{...(ii)}$$

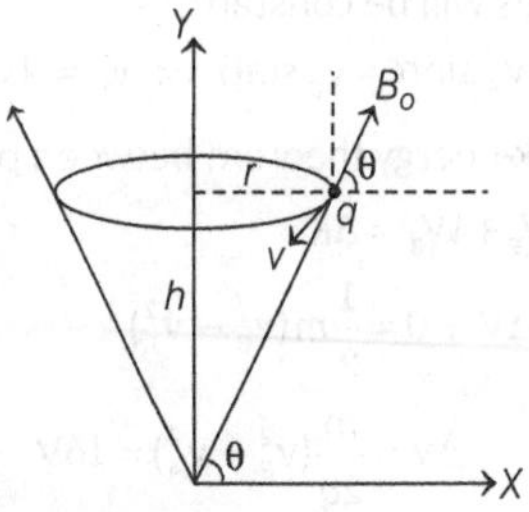

From Eqs. (i) and (ii), we get

$$\tan\theta = \frac{v^2}{gr}$$

Now, $$\tan\theta = \frac{h}{r} = \frac{v^2}{gr}$$

$$\Rightarrow \quad h = \frac{v^2}{g}$$

13. Coordinates of charged particle after two and half revolutions $= (2.5P_0, 0, -2R_0)$

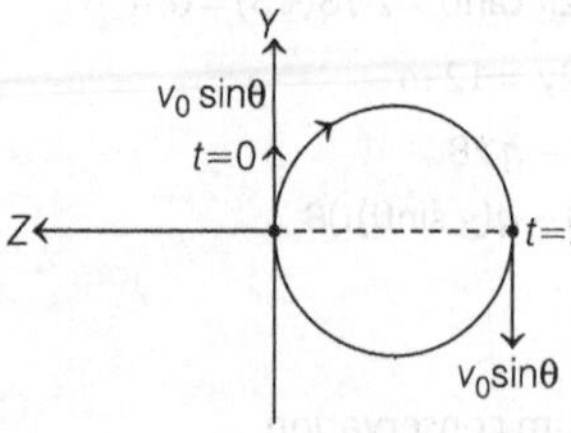

Coordinates of image $= (17.5P_0, 0, -2R_0)$

14. When $v = 0; \mathbf{F}_{net} = q\mathbf{E} + q(\mathbf{v}\times\mathbf{B})$

$\Rightarrow \quad F_{net}, y = qE_y$

$\Rightarrow -2\times10^{-19} = (-1.6\times10^{-19})E_y$

$\Rightarrow \quad E_y = 1.25$ N/C

When $v = 50$ m/s

$$\mathbf{F}_{net} = q\mathbf{E} + q(\mathbf{v}\times\mathbf{B})$$

$$\Rightarrow \quad 0 = q(1.25\hat{\mathbf{j}}) + q(50\hat{\mathbf{i}}\times B_z\hat{\mathbf{k}})$$

$$\Rightarrow \quad B_z = 25\times10^{-3}\text{T}$$

15. Particle will go along a helix of varying pitch. Projection of helix will be a circle in *ZX*-plane as shown.

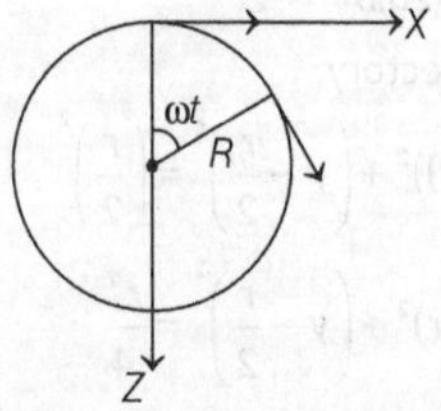

$$x = R\sin\omega t,\ y = \frac{1}{2}\left(\frac{qE}{m}\right)t^2;\ z = R(1-\cos\omega t)$$

$$\Rightarrow \quad x = 0, y = \frac{\pi^2}{2}; z = 2$$

16. Component of velocity perpendicular to electric and magnetic fields will be constant.

$$\Rightarrow \quad v_A\sin\alpha = V_B\sin\beta \Rightarrow V_B = 4\sqrt{3}\times10^4\text{m/s}$$

$\Rightarrow$ Using Work-energy theorem between points *A* and *B*,

$$W_E + W_B = \Delta K$$

$$\Rightarrow \quad q\Delta V + 0 = \frac{1}{2}m(v_B^2 - v_A^2)$$

$$\Rightarrow \quad \Delta v = \frac{m}{2q}(v_B^2 - v_A^2) = 16\text{V}$$

17. $\mathbf{F} = q(\mathbf{v}\times\mathbf{B}) = q((v_x\hat{\mathbf{i}} + v_y\hat{\mathbf{j}})\times\mathbf{B})$

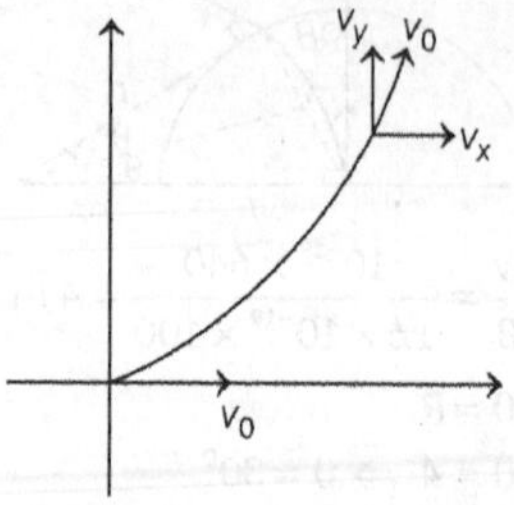

$$F_y = \frac{qB_0x^2}{l^2}v_x$$

$$\Rightarrow \quad \int_0^{v_0} dv_y = \frac{qB_0}{ml^2}\int_0^{x_{max}} x^2dx$$

$$\Rightarrow \quad x_{max} = \left(\frac{3ml^2v_0}{qB_0}\right)^{1/3}$$

18. $$\mathbf{F} = q\left[(v_x\hat{\mathbf{i}} + v_y\hat{\mathbf{j}})\times B_0\left(1+\frac{y}{d}\right)(-\hat{\mathbf{k}})\right]$$

$$\Rightarrow \quad F_x = -qB_0(1+\frac{y}{d})v_y$$

$$\Rightarrow \quad \frac{dv_x}{dt} = -\frac{qB_0}{m}(1+\frac{y}{d})\frac{dy}{dt}$$

$$\Rightarrow \int_{v_0}^{v_x} dv_x = \frac{-qB_0}{m}\int_0^d(1+\frac{y}{d})dy$$

$$\Rightarrow \quad v_x = v_0 - \frac{3qB_0d}{2m} = \frac{3qB_0d}{2m} = \frac{v_0}{2}$$

$$v_y = \sqrt{v_0^2 - v_x^2} = \frac{\sqrt{3}v_0}{2}$$

$$\tan\theta = \frac{v_y}{v_x} \Rightarrow \theta = \tan^{-1}(\sqrt{3}) = 60^\circ$$

19. Let $\mathbf{v} = v_x\hat{\mathbf{i}} + v_y\hat{\mathbf{j}}$

$$q[(v_x\hat{\mathbf{i}} + v_y\hat{\mathbf{j}})\times B_o\hat{\mathbf{k}}] - \alpha(v_x\hat{\mathbf{i}} + v_y\hat{\mathbf{j}}) = m\frac{d\mathbf{v}}{dt}$$

$$\Rightarrow \quad a_y = \frac{1}{m}(qv_xB_0 + \alpha v_y)$$

and $$a_x = \frac{1}{m}(qB_0v_y - \alpha v_x)$$

$$\int_{v_0}^{0} dv_y = \frac{1}{m}qB_0\int_0^x dx + \alpha\int_0^y dy \quad \text{...(i)}$$

$$\int_0^0 dv_x = \frac{1}{m}qB_0\int_0^y dy - \alpha\int_0^x dx \quad \text{...(ii)}$$

From Eqs. (i) and (ii), we get

$$x = \frac{qB_0mv_0}{\alpha^2 + q^2B^2} = 10\,\text{m}$$

20. Let $\mathbf{v} = v_x\hat{\mathbf{i}} + v_y\hat{\mathbf{j}}$

$$\mathbf{F} = q(v_x\hat{\mathbf{i}} + v_y\hat{\mathbf{j}}) \times \left(\frac{\mu_0 i}{2\pi x}(-\hat{\mathbf{k}})\right)$$

$$\Rightarrow \quad a_x = -\left(\frac{\mu_0 qi}{2\pi m}\right)\frac{v_y}{x} = -\frac{\lambda v_y}{x} \text{ where, } \lambda = \frac{\mu_0 qi}{2\pi m}$$

$$\Rightarrow \quad v_x\frac{dv_x}{dx} = -\frac{\lambda v_y}{x} \quad \text{...(i)}$$

$$v_x^2 + v_y^2 = v^2$$

$$\Rightarrow v_x\, dv_x + v_y dv_y = 0 \quad \text{...(ii)}$$

From Eqs. (i) and (ii), we get

$$\Rightarrow \quad -v_y\frac{dv_x}{dx} = -\frac{\lambda v_y}{x} \Rightarrow \int_r^R \frac{dx}{x} = \int_0^v \frac{dv_y}{\lambda}$$

$$\Rightarrow \quad R = re^{v/\lambda} = re^{\left(\frac{2\pi mv}{\mu_0 qi}\right)}$$

21. Let $\mathbf{v} = v_x\hat{\mathbf{i}} + v_y\hat{\mathbf{j}}$

$$\mathbf{F} = -e(-E\hat{\mathbf{j}}) + (-e)(v_x\hat{\mathbf{i}} + v_y\hat{\mathbf{j}}) \times (-B\hat{\mathbf{k}})$$

$$\Rightarrow \quad \mathbf{F} = eE\hat{\mathbf{j}} + eB(v_y\hat{\mathbf{i}} - v_x\hat{\mathbf{j}})$$

$$\Rightarrow \quad a_x = \frac{dv_x}{dt} = \frac{eB}{m}v_y \text{ and } a_y = \frac{dv_y}{dt} = \frac{e}{m}(E - v_xB)$$

$$\frac{d^2v_y}{dt^2} = -\frac{-eB}{m}\left(\frac{dv_x}{dt}\right) \Rightarrow \frac{d^2v_y}{dt^2} = \frac{-e^2B^2}{m^2}v_y$$

$$\Rightarrow \quad v_y = A\sin(\omega t + \phi), \text{ where, } \omega = \frac{eB}{m}$$

$$\Rightarrow \quad \frac{dv_y}{dt} = A\omega\cos(\omega t + \phi)$$

At $t = 0, v_y = 0, v_x = 0$ and $\frac{dv_y}{dt} = \frac{eE}{m}$

$$\Rightarrow \quad \phi = 0^\circ \text{ and } A = \frac{E}{B}$$

So, $v_y = \frac{E}{B}\sin\omega t$

$$\int_0^y dy = \frac{E}{B}\int_0^t \sin\omega t\,dt$$

$$\Rightarrow \quad y = \frac{E}{B\omega}(1 - \cos\omega t)$$

$$\mathbf{v} \perp \mathbf{E} \Rightarrow v_y = 0$$

$$\Rightarrow \quad \omega t = \pi \Rightarrow t = \frac{\pi}{\omega}$$

$$y = \frac{2E}{B\omega} = \frac{2Em}{eB^2}$$

22. At $t = t_0$

$$v_x = u_x + a_xt = 0 + \left(\frac{qE}{m}\right)t_0 = gt_0$$

$$v_y = u_y + a_yt = u - gt_0$$

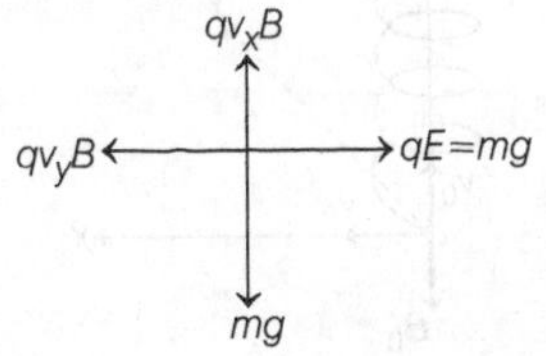

$$\Sigma F_y = 0 \Rightarrow qv_xB = mg$$

$$\Sigma F_x = 0 \Rightarrow qv_yB = qE = mg$$

$$\Rightarrow \quad v_x = v_y \Rightarrow gt_0 = u - gt_0$$

$$\Rightarrow \quad u = 2gt_0$$

23. Kinetic energy of ring will be constant.

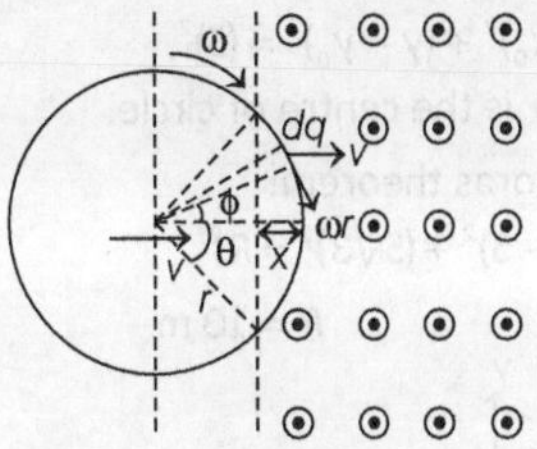

So, $\frac{1}{2}mv_0^2 = \frac{1}{2}mv^2 + \frac{1}{2}(mr^2)\omega^2$

$$\Rightarrow \quad \omega r = \sqrt{v_0^2 - v^2} \text{ and } v = v_0/\sqrt{2}$$

when pure rolling begins.

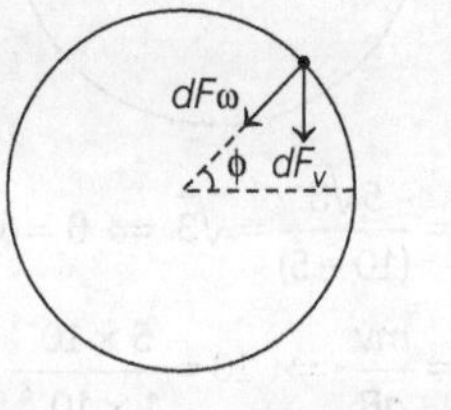

$$dF_\omega = (dq)(\omega r)B = \left(\frac{q}{2\pi R}Rd\phi\right)(\omega r)B$$

$$\Sigma F_x = \int dF_\omega \cos\phi = \int_{-\theta}^{\theta}\frac{q\omega rB}{2\pi}\cos\phi\, d\phi$$

$$\Rightarrow \quad -mv\frac{dv}{dx} = \frac{q\omega rB}{\pi}\sin\theta$$

$$\Rightarrow \quad -mv\frac{dv}{(r\sin\theta\, d\theta)} = \frac{q\omega rB}{\pi}\sin\theta$$

$$[\because x = r(1 - \cos\theta),\ dx = r\sin\theta\, d\theta]$$

$$\Rightarrow -\int_{v_0}^{v_0/\sqrt{2}}\frac{v\,dv}{\sqrt{v_0^2 - v^2}} = \frac{qBr}{\pi m}\int^{\pi}\sin^2\theta\, d\theta$$

$$\Rightarrow \quad \frac{v_0}{\sqrt{2}} = \frac{qBr}{\pi m}\left(\frac{\pi}{2}\right) \Rightarrow q = \sqrt{2}\frac{mv_0}{rB}$$

Multiple Choice(s) Correct Questions

1. $\mathbf{v} \perp \mathbf{a} \Rightarrow \mathbf{v}\cdot\mathbf{a} = 0$

$$\Rightarrow (3\hat{\mathbf{i}} + 4\hat{\mathbf{j}}).(2\hat{\mathbf{i}} + x\hat{\mathbf{j}}) = 0$$

$$\Rightarrow \quad 6 + 4x = 0 \Rightarrow x = -1.5$$

$$\mathbf{F} = q(\mathbf{v} \times \mathbf{B})$$

Magnetic field is along z-direction.

$$\mathbf{F} \perp \mathbf{v} \Rightarrow W = 0 \Rightarrow \Delta K = 0$$

$\Rightarrow K = \text{constant}$

2. Since, $\mathbf{v} \perp \mathbf{B}$; particle will go in uniform circular motion.

$$R = \frac{mv}{qB} = \frac{1 \times (\sqrt{8^2 + 6^2})}{1 \times 2} = 5\,\text{m}$$

$$T = \frac{2\pi m}{qB} = \frac{2\pi(1)}{(1)(2)} = \pi s$$

Path of particle,

$$(x - x_0)^2 + (y - y_0)^2 = (5)^2,$$

where (x_0, y_0) is the centre of circle.

3. Using pythagoras theorem,

$$(R - 5)^2 + (5\sqrt{3})^2 = R^2$$

$$\Rightarrow \quad R = 10\text{ m}$$

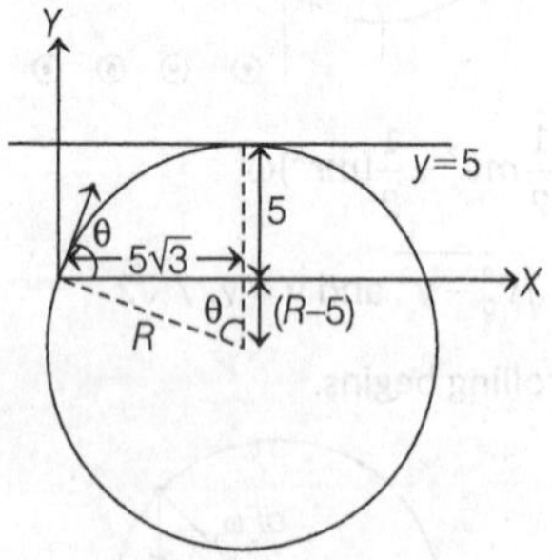

$$\tan\theta = \frac{5\sqrt{3}}{(10 - 5)} = \sqrt{3} \Rightarrow \theta = 60^\circ$$

$$R = \frac{mv}{qB} \Rightarrow 10 = \frac{5 \times 10^{-5} \times v}{1 \times 10^{-6} \times 10}$$

$$\Rightarrow \quad v = 2\text{ m/s}$$

$$W_B = 0 \quad \because \mathbf{v} \perp \mathbf{F_B}$$

4. $r = \dfrac{mv\sin\theta}{qB}$, $\quad T = \dfrac{2\pi m}{qB}$, $\quad P = (v\cos\theta)T$

$$a = \frac{P_1}{P_2} = \frac{\cos 30^\circ}{\cos 60^\circ} = \sqrt{3},$$

$$b = \frac{R_1}{R_2} = \frac{\sin 30^\circ}{\sin 60^\circ} = \frac{1}{\sqrt{3}},$$

$$c = \frac{T_1}{T_2} = 1$$

So, abc = 1 and ab = c

5. $XY = (v\cos\alpha)(nT)$, where, $n \varepsilon I$

$$\Rightarrow \quad XY = \left(\frac{\sqrt{2qV}}{m}\right)(\cos\alpha)(n)\left(\frac{2\pi m}{qB}\right)$$

$$\Rightarrow \quad XY = \left(\sqrt{\frac{8\pi^2 mV}{qB^2}}\right)(\cos\alpha)\,n$$

$$\Rightarrow \quad 0.1 = \left(\sqrt{\frac{8 \times 10 \times 9 \times 10^{-31} \times 800}{1.6 \times 10^{-19} \times 4 \times 10^{-4}}}\right) n\cos\alpha$$

$$\Rightarrow \cos\alpha = \frac{10}{3n}$$

$$\Rightarrow \quad \alpha = \cos^{-1}\left(\frac{10}{3n}\right)$$

For $n = 4, \alpha = \cos^{-1}\left(\dfrac{5}{6}\right)$

and $n = 5, \alpha = \cos^{-1}\left(\dfrac{2}{3}\right)$

6. $a_x = \dfrac{qE}{m}$ and $T = \dfrac{2\pi m}{qB}$

For $\theta = 0^\circ$;

$$s_x = u_x t + \frac{1}{2}a_x t^2$$

$$\Rightarrow \quad L = vT + \frac{1}{2}\left(\frac{qE}{m}\right)T^2 = \frac{2\pi mv}{qB} + \frac{2\pi^2 mE}{qB^2}$$

For $\theta = \Delta\theta$,

$$s_x = u_x t + \frac{1}{2}a_x t^2$$

$$L - \Delta L = v\cos\theta T + \frac{1}{2}\left(\frac{qE}{m}\right)T^2$$

So, $\quad \Delta L = vT(1 - \cos\Delta\theta);$

$$= 2vT\sin^2\left(\frac{\Delta\theta}{2}\right)$$

$$= \left(\frac{vT(\Delta\theta)^2}{2}\right) = \frac{\pi mv(\Delta\theta)^2}{qB}$$

7. (a) For particle to move along a straight line,

$$\mathbf{F} = q\mathbf{E} + q(\mathbf{v} \times \mathbf{B}) = 0$$

$$\Rightarrow qa\hat{\mathbf{i}} + q(x\hat{\mathbf{i}} + y\hat{\mathbf{j}}) \times (b\hat{\mathbf{i}} + c\hat{\mathbf{j}} + d\hat{\mathbf{k}}) = 0$$

$$\Rightarrow \quad (a + yd)\hat{\mathbf{i}} - xd\hat{\mathbf{j}} + (cx - by)\hat{\mathbf{k}} = 0$$

(b) $c = 0, d = 0, y = 0$

$\Rightarrow \mathbf{E} = a\hat{\mathbf{i}}, \mathbf{B} = b\hat{\mathbf{i}}, \mathbf{v} = x\hat{\mathbf{i}}$

$\mathbf{v} \| \mathbf{B}$, so magnetic force is zero. Charged particle will move along X-axis with increasing speed because of electric force.

(c) $c = 0;\ d = 0,\ y \neq 0$

$\Rightarrow \mathbf{E} = a\hat{\mathbf{i}},\ \mathbf{B} = b\hat{\mathbf{i}},\ \mathbf{v} = x\hat{\mathbf{i}} + y\hat{\mathbf{j}}$

Since, it is oblique incidence, particle will move along helix and because of electric force pitch will be varying.

(d) $a = 0 \Rightarrow \mathbf{E} = 0$

$\mathbf{v} \cdot \mathbf{B} = 0 \Rightarrow \mathbf{v} \perp \mathbf{B}$

Particle moves along circle.

8. Z-component of velocity is anti-parallel to magnetic field. So, Z-component of velocity will be constant. The particle will go into helical path as shown.

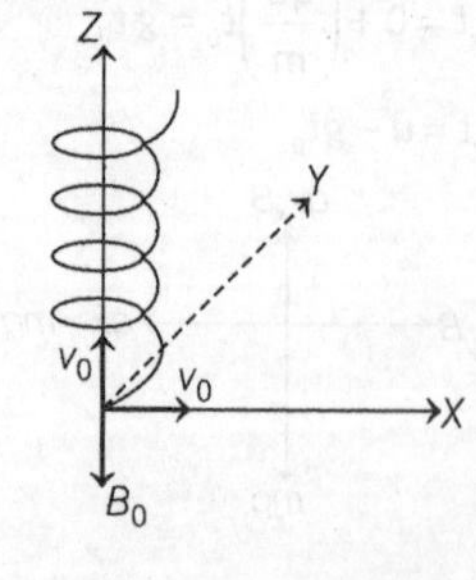

At $t = \frac{\pi}{\alpha B_0}$, particle will cover half revolution.

So, X-component of velocity will get reversed.

$$\mathbf{v} = -v_0\hat{\mathbf{i}} + v_0\hat{\mathbf{k}} = -v_0(\hat{\mathbf{i}} - \hat{\mathbf{k}})$$

Speed of the particle ($\sqrt{2}v_0$) is constant throughout.

At $t = \frac{2\pi}{\alpha B_0}$, particle will complete one revolution.

Displacement = pitch = $v_0 T = \frac{2\pi v_0}{\alpha B_0}$

Distance = Speed × Time

$$= (\sqrt{2}v_0)\left(\frac{2\pi}{\alpha B_0}\right) = \frac{2\sqrt{2}\pi v_0}{\alpha B_0}$$

9.

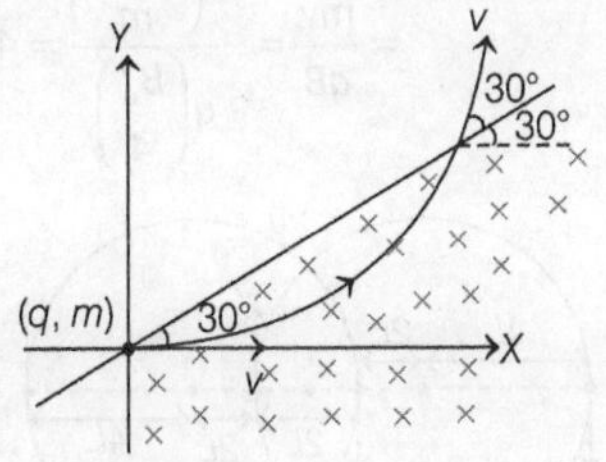

(a) The particle will describe an arc of circle as shown. Angle made by velocity with X-axis is $30^\circ + 30^\circ = 60^\circ$, while coming out of the magnetic field.

(b) Deviation of particle = $\frac{\pi}{3}$;

$$\omega t = \theta \Rightarrow \left(\frac{qB}{m}\right)t = \frac{\pi}{3} \Rightarrow t = \frac{\pi m}{3qB}$$

(c) Distance travelled = $vt = \frac{\pi m v}{3qB}$

10. At $t = \frac{\pi m}{qB}$, each particle will describe semi-circle.

So, magnitude of displacement = $2R$

$$\mathbf{r}_1 \cdot \mathbf{r}_2 = r_1 r_2 \cos\theta = (2R)(2R)\cos 60^\circ = 2R^2 = 2\left(\frac{mv}{qB}\right)^2$$

Speed of each particle is constant. So, the relative speed is zero throughout.

At $t = 0$ and $t = \frac{2\pi m}{qB}$, particles are at origin.

So, their relative angular momentum is zero.

So, magnitude of relative angular momentum first increases and then decreases as separation first increases and then decreases.

11. (a) Using work-energy theorem between P and Q.

$$W_B + W_E = \Delta K$$

$$\Rightarrow \quad 0 + qE(2a) = \frac{1}{2}m(2v)^2 - \frac{1}{2}mv^2$$

$$\Rightarrow \quad E = \frac{3}{4}\left(\frac{mv^2}{qa}\right)$$

(b) At point P,

$$P = \mathbf{F} \cdot \mathbf{v} = Fv\cos\theta$$

$$\Rightarrow \quad P_E = (qE)(v)\cos 0^\circ = \frac{3}{4}\frac{mv^3}{a}$$

(c) At point Q,

$$P_E = (qE)(2v)\cos 90^\circ = 0;\ P_B = 0 \quad \because (\mathbf{v} \perp \mathbf{F}_B)$$

12. At $t = \frac{T_0}{2}$, particle will complete half revolution.

So, coordinates $\left(\frac{P_0}{2}, 0, -2R_0\right)$

At $t = \frac{3T}{2}$, coordinates $\left(\frac{3P_0}{2}, 0, 2R_0\right)$

Distance between the two extremes from X-axis

$$= 2R_0 + 2R_0 = 4R_0$$

13.

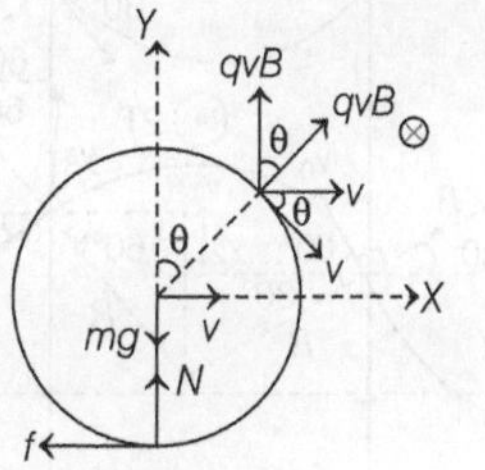

In X-direction, $f = qvB\sin\theta$

In Y-direction, $N + qvB + qvB\cos\theta = mg$

$$\Rightarrow \quad N = mg - qvB(1 + \cos\theta)$$

$$\Rightarrow \quad N_{min} = mg - qvB(1 + (-1)) \text{ when } \theta = \pi$$

$$\Rightarrow \quad N_{min} = mg - 2qvB$$

For losing contact, $N_{min} < 0$

$$\Rightarrow \quad mg - 2qvB < 0 \Rightarrow v > \frac{mg}{2qB}$$

14.

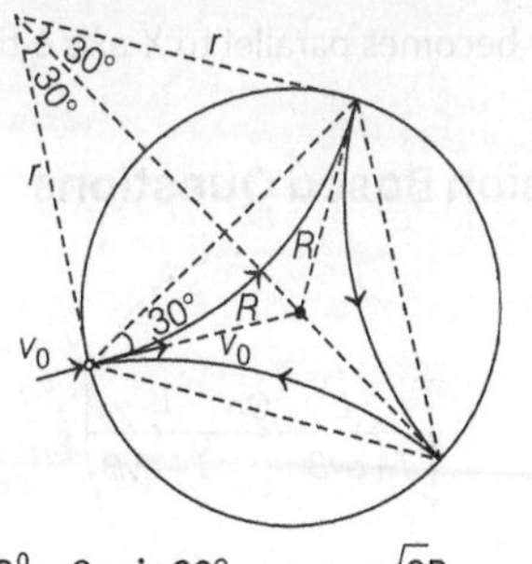

(b) $2R\cos 30^\circ = 2r\sin 30^\circ \Rightarrow r = \sqrt{3}R$

$$\Rightarrow \quad \frac{mv_0}{qB} = \sqrt{3}R$$

$$\Rightarrow \quad v_0 = \left(\frac{qBR}{m}\right)\sqrt{3}$$

(c) Each arc subtends $\frac{\pi}{3}$ of angle.

Total angle subtended = $\frac{\pi}{3} \times 3 = \pi$;

$$\theta = \omega t \Rightarrow \pi = \left(\frac{qB}{m}\right)t \Rightarrow t = \frac{\pi m}{qB}$$

(d) $2R\cos\theta = 2r\sin\theta$

$$\Rightarrow 2R\cos\theta = 2\left(\frac{m\left(\frac{qBR\sqrt{3}}{3m}\right)}{qB}\right)\sin\theta$$

$$\Rightarrow \quad \tan\theta = \sqrt{3} \Rightarrow \theta = 60°$$

So, particle will go along arcs inscribed in a regular hexagon, and number of collisions will be 5.

15. $R = \frac{mv}{qB} = 6$ m and $\theta = \sin^{-1}\left(\frac{d}{R}\right) = \frac{\pi}{2}$

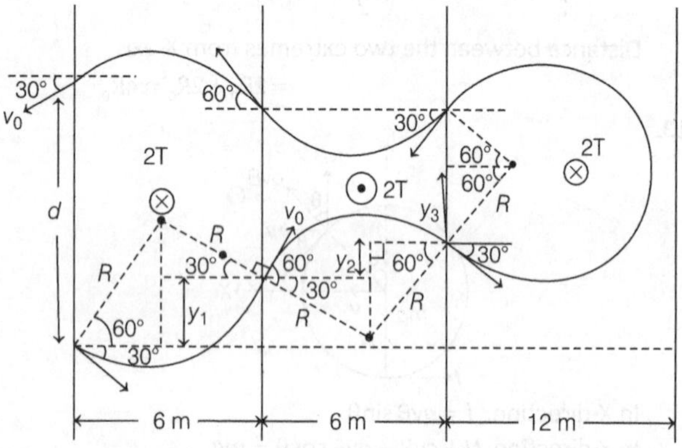

$$\text{Total deviation} = \frac{\pi}{2} - \frac{\pi}{2} + \frac{2\pi}{3} + \frac{\pi}{2} - \frac{\pi}{2} = \frac{2\pi}{3}$$

$$\theta = \omega t = \frac{8\pi}{3} = \left[\frac{(1)(2)}{(1)}\right]t$$

$$\Rightarrow \quad t = \frac{4\pi}{3}\text{ s}$$

The velocity becomes parallel to X-axis 6 times during the motion.

Comprehension Based Questions

1.

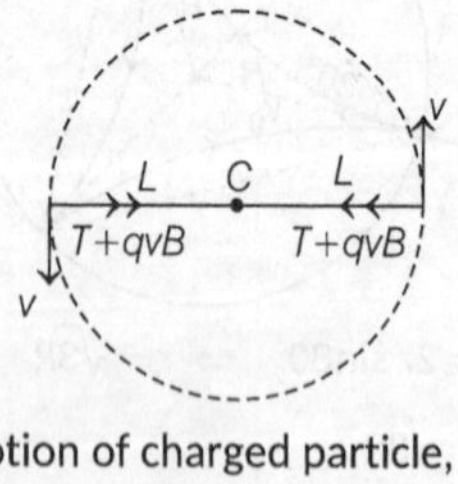

For circular motion of charged particle,

$$T + qvB = \frac{mv^2}{L}$$

$$\Rightarrow \quad 0 + qvB = \frac{mv^2}{L}$$

$$\Rightarrow \quad B = \frac{mv}{qL} = \frac{m}{qL}\left(\frac{qB_0L}{m}\right) = B_0$$

2. $T + qvB = \frac{mv^2}{L}$

$$\Rightarrow T + q\left(\frac{qB_0L}{m}\right)\frac{B_0}{2} = \frac{m}{L}\left(\frac{qB_0L}{m}\right)^2$$

$$\Rightarrow \quad T = \frac{q^2B_0^2L}{2m}$$

3. $T + qvB = \frac{mv^2}{L}$

$$\Rightarrow \frac{3}{4}\frac{q^2B_0^2L}{m} + q\left(\frac{qB_0L}{m}\right)B = \frac{m}{L}\left(\frac{qB_0L}{m}\right)^2$$

$$\Rightarrow \quad B = \frac{B_0}{4}$$

Radius of circle described by each particle

$$= \frac{mv}{qB} = \frac{m\left(\frac{qB_0L}{m}\right)}{q\left(\frac{B_0}{4}\right)} = 4L$$

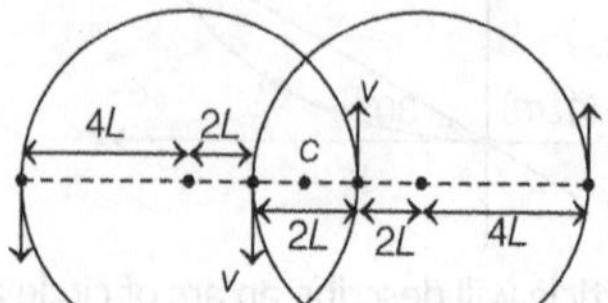

Maximum separation $= 4L + 2L + 2L + 2L + 4L$
$= 14L$

4. In helical motion, angle between **B** and **v** remains constant.

5. $f = \frac{qB}{2\pi m} = \left(\frac{1000}{19}\right)\left(\frac{\sqrt{20^2+30^2+50^2}}{(2\pi)}\right) = \frac{10^4}{\pi\sqrt{38}}$

6. Pitch $= (v\cos\theta)T$

$$= \left(\frac{\mathbf{v}.\mathbf{B}}{B}\right)\frac{2\pi m}{qB} = \frac{400}{\sqrt{3800}}\left(\frac{\pi\sqrt{38}}{10^4}\right) = \frac{\pi}{250}\text{ m}$$

7. The particle will follow helical path with increasing pitch. The axis of helix will be along Y-axis.

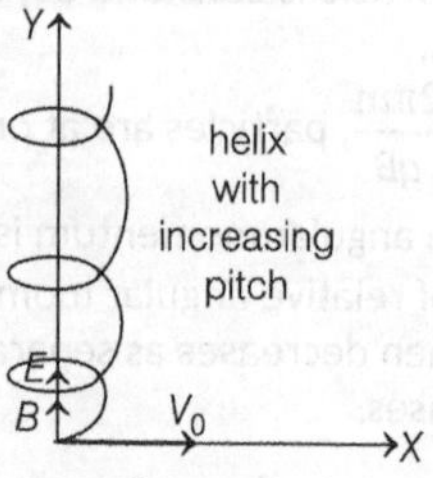

$$S_y = u_yt + \frac{1}{2}a_yt^2$$

$$\Rightarrow \quad y = 0 + \frac{1}{2}\left(\frac{qE_0}{m}\right)\left(\frac{n2\pi m}{qB_0}\right)^2 = \frac{2n^2\pi^2E_0}{B_0^2\alpha}$$

8. $v_y = u_y + a_yt = 0 + \left(\frac{qE_0}{m}\right)\left(\frac{n2\pi m}{qB_0}\right) = \frac{2\pi nE_0}{B_0}$

$$\tan\theta = \frac{v_x}{v_y} = \frac{v_0}{\dfrac{2\pi n E_0}{B_0}} \Rightarrow \theta = \tan^{-1}\left(\frac{v_0 B_0}{2\pi n E_0}\right)$$

9. $R = \dfrac{mv}{qB} \Rightarrow 0.4 = \dfrac{40 \times 10^{-3} \times 5}{1 \times B}$

$\Rightarrow \quad B = 0.5\,T$

So, $\mathbf{B} = (0.5T)\hat{\mathbf{k}}$

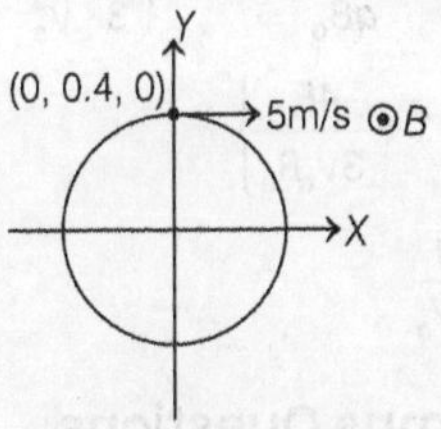

Using linear momentum conservation

$$(40 \times 10^{-3}) \times 5\hat{\mathbf{i}} + (10 \times 10^{-3}) \times \frac{40}{\pi}\hat{\mathbf{k}} = 50 \times 10^{-3} \times \mathbf{v}$$

$$\Rightarrow \qquad \hat{\mathbf{v}} = 4\hat{\mathbf{i}} + \frac{8}{\pi}\hat{\mathbf{k}}$$

Path of combined particle will be helix.

Z-component of velocity will be constant.

10. $s_z = u_z t + \dfrac{1}{2} a_z t^2$

$$\Rightarrow \quad z = \left(\frac{8}{\pi}\right)\left(\frac{\pi}{40}\right) = 0.2\text{ m}$$

11. $r = \text{Radius of helix} = \dfrac{(m_1 + m_2)v}{(q_1 + q_2)B}$

$$= \frac{50 \times 10^{-3} \times 4}{2 \times 0.5} = 0.2\text{ m}$$

$$\theta = \omega t = \left(\frac{2 \times 0.5}{50 \times 10^{-3}}\right)\left(\frac{\pi}{40}\right) = \frac{\pi}{2}$$

So, the combined particle will rotate an angle of $\dfrac{\pi}{2}$.

$Y\text{-coordinate} = R - r = 0.4 - 0.2 = 0.2\text{ m}$

12.

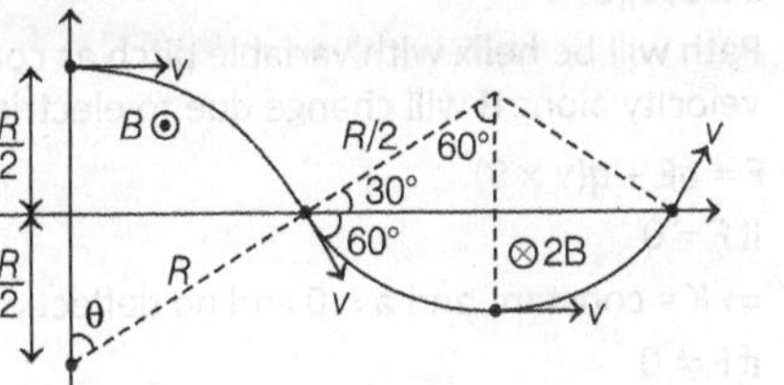

Time taken to hit the X-axis first time,

$$\cos\theta = \frac{R/2}{R}$$

$$\Rightarrow \qquad \theta = 60^0$$

$$\theta = \omega t_1$$

$$\Rightarrow \qquad \frac{\pi}{3} = \left(\frac{qB}{m}\right)t_1 \Rightarrow t_1 = \frac{\pi m}{3qB}$$

13. Velocity becomes parallel to X-axis when it further turns through an angle of 60^0.

$$\theta = \omega t$$

$$\Rightarrow \qquad \frac{\pi}{3} = \left(\frac{q(2B)}{m}\right)t_2 \Rightarrow t_2 = \frac{\pi m}{6qB}$$

$$\text{Total time taken} = t_1 + t_2 = \frac{\pi m}{2qB}$$

14. $R = \dfrac{mv}{qB} = \dfrac{m(50)}{\left(\dfrac{2mg}{E}\right)5} = 5\text{ m}$

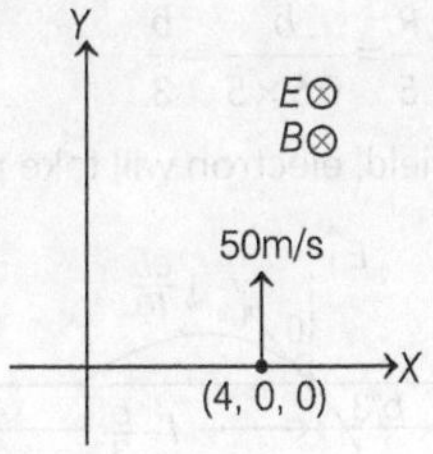

15. $N = mg + qE = 3mg$

$$f_K = \mu_k N = \frac{1}{3}(3mg) = mg$$

$$-mg = ma \Rightarrow -mg = m\frac{dv}{dt}$$

$$\Rightarrow \qquad \int_{50}^{0} dv = -g\int_{0}^{t} dt \Rightarrow t = 5\text{s}$$

16. $W_E = 0 \because \mathbf{F}_E \perp \mathbf{v}$

17.

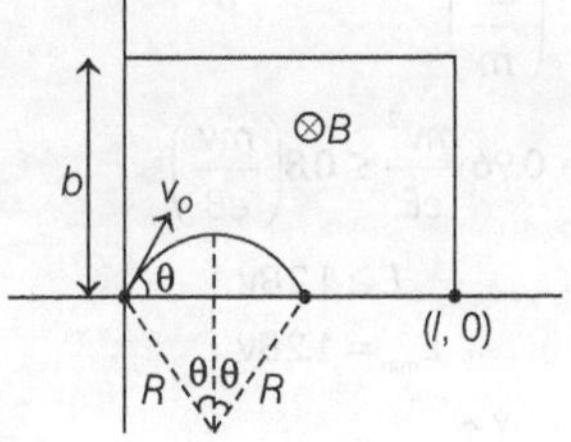

$$\frac{elB}{mv_0} = \sqrt{3} \Rightarrow l = \sqrt{3}R$$

$$\Rightarrow \qquad \frac{ebB}{mv_0} = 1 - \frac{1}{\sqrt{2}} \Rightarrow b = \left(1 - \frac{1}{\sqrt{2}}\right)R$$

$$2R\sin\theta \le l$$

$$\Rightarrow \qquad 2R\sin\theta \le \sqrt{3}R$$

$$\Rightarrow \qquad \sin\theta \le \frac{\sqrt{3}}{2} \Rightarrow \theta \le 60^0$$

$$R - R\cos\theta \le b$$

$$\Rightarrow R(1 - \cos\theta) \le \left(1 - \frac{1}{\sqrt{2}}\right)R$$

$$\Rightarrow \qquad \cos \ge \frac{1}{\sqrt{2}} \Rightarrow \theta \le 45^0$$

So, $0^0 \le \theta \le 45^0$

18.

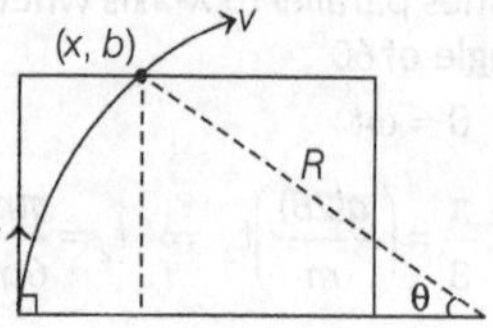

$$b = 0.6\frac{mv}{eB} = 0.6R$$

$$R\sin\theta = b$$

$$\Rightarrow \quad R\sin\theta = 0.6R \Rightarrow \theta = 37^0$$

$$x = R(1-\cos\theta) = R(1-\cos 37^0)$$

$$= \frac{R}{5} = \frac{b}{0.6\times 5} = \frac{b}{3}$$

19. Due to electric field, electron will take parabolic path.

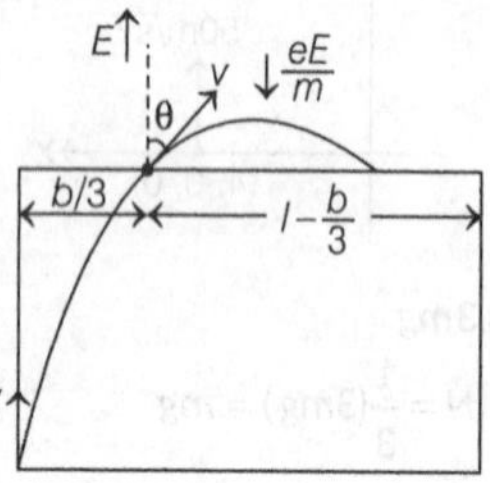

Horizontal range $\le l - \frac{b}{3}$

$$\Rightarrow \quad \frac{v^2(2\sin\theta\cos\theta)}{\left(\frac{eE}{m}\right)} \le l - \frac{b}{3}$$

$$\Rightarrow \quad \frac{v^2 2(0.6)(0.8)}{\left(\frac{eE}{m}\right)} \le R - \frac{0.6R}{3}$$

$$\Rightarrow \quad 0.96\frac{mv^2}{eE} \le 0.8\left(\frac{mv}{eB}\right)$$

$$\Rightarrow \quad E \ge 1.2Bv$$

$$\Rightarrow \quad E_{min} = 1.2Bv$$

20.

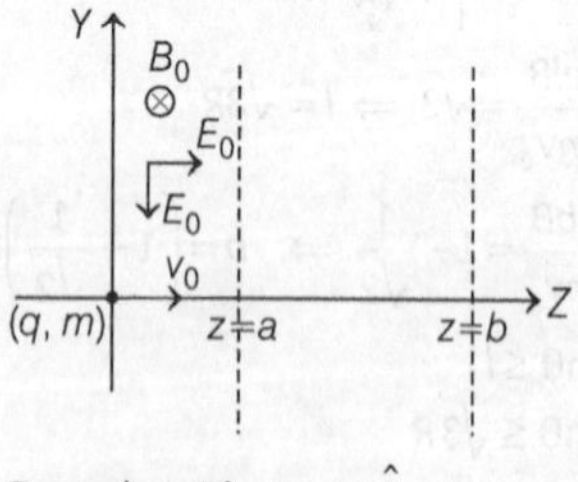

$$F_B = q(\mathbf{v}\times\mathbf{B}) = qv_0B_0\hat{\mathbf{j}}$$

$$F_E = qE_0(\hat{\mathbf{k}} - \hat{\mathbf{j}})$$

$$\Sigma F_y = 0$$

$$\Rightarrow qv_0B_0 - qE_0 = 0$$

$$\Rightarrow \quad E_0 = B_0v_0$$

21. From, $Z = 0$ to $Z = a$

$$W_E + W_B = \Delta K$$

$$\Rightarrow (qE_0)a + 0 = \frac{1}{2}mv^2 - \frac{1}{2}mv_0^2$$

$$v = \sqrt{\frac{v_0^2 + 2qE_0a}{m}} = 2v_0$$

Now, $b - a = R = \dfrac{m(2v_0)}{qB_0}$

$$\Rightarrow \quad b = a + \frac{2mv_0}{qB_0} = a + 2\left(\frac{2}{3}\frac{qE_0a}{v_0^2}\right)\frac{v_0}{qB_0}$$

$$\Rightarrow \quad b = a\left\{1 + \frac{4E_0}{3v_0B_0}\right\}$$

22. Time taken $= \dfrac{a}{2v_0}$

Match the Columns Questions

1. $R = \dfrac{mv}{qB} \Rightarrow R_B > R_A = R_C > R_D$

Least radius is for ion falling at portion 3.

So, $D \to 3$

Ions falling at 3 and 4 will have same sign of charge as both are rotating in the same sense. So $A \to 4$

Since, $R_B > R_C \Rightarrow B \to 1$ and $C \to 2$.

2. (A) $\mathbf{B} = B_x\hat{\mathbf{i}}$ and $\mathbf{E} = E_y\hat{\mathbf{j}}$ and $u = 0$

Path will be cycloid.

(B) $\mathbf{E} = 0$, $\mathbf{B} = B_x\hat{\mathbf{i}} + B_y\hat{\mathbf{j}} + B_z\hat{\mathbf{k}}$, $\mathbf{u} = u_x\hat{\mathbf{i}} + u_y\hat{\mathbf{j}} + u_z\hat{\mathbf{k}}$

$$\cos\theta = \frac{u_xB_x + u_yB_y + u_zB_z}{\sqrt{u_x^2+u_y^2+u_z^2}\sqrt{B_x^2+B_y^2+B_z^2}} \ne 0$$

$$\Rightarrow \theta \ne 90^0$$

So, path will be helix with uniform pitch, if $\theta \ne 0^0$ and straight line if $\theta = 0^0$.

(C) $\mathbf{u}\times\mathbf{B} = 0$; $\mathbf{u}\times\mathbf{E} = 0$

$\Rightarrow$ **u, B** and **E** all are parallel.

So, path will be straight line.

(D) $\mathbf{u}\perp\mathbf{B}$, $\mathbf{B}\|\mathbf{E}$

Path will be helix with variable pitch as component of velocity along **B** will change due to electric force.

3. (A) $\mathbf{F} = q\mathbf{E} + q(\mathbf{v}\times\mathbf{B})$

If $\mathbf{F} = 0$

$\Rightarrow K =$ constant and $\mathbf{a} = 0$ and no deflection

If $\mathbf{F} \ne 0$

$\Rightarrow$ Kinetic energy will change. Acceleration will be non-zero.

If $\mathbf{E}\|\mathbf{B}\|\mathbf{v}$ particle suffers no deflection otherwise particle will suffer deflection.

(B) If $\mathbf{u}\|\mathbf{E}$, kinetic energy changes but no deflection.

(C) Work done by magnetic field is zero. So, kinetic energy will be constant.

If $\mathbf{u}\|\mathbf{B}$; $\mathbf{a} = 0$ and no deflection.

(D) $\mathbf{F} = 0 \Rightarrow \mathbf{a} = 0$

$\Rightarrow K$ = constant and no deflection.

4. (A) It $\mathbf{u} \parallel \mathbf{E}$, path will be straight line and otherwise parabola.

(B) If $\mathbf{u} \parallel \mathbf{B}$, path will be straight line.

$\mathbf{u} \perp \mathbf{B}$; path will be circular.

$\theta \neq 0^\circ, 90^\circ, 180^\circ$; path will be helix with uniform pitch.

(C) $\mathbf{F} = q\mathbf{E} + q(\mathbf{v} \times \mathbf{B})$

If $\mathbf{F} = 0$, path will be straight line.

If $\theta \neq 0^\circ, 180^\circ$ $\mathbf{E} \parallel \mathbf{B}$, path will be helix with non- uniform pitch.

(D) All possibilities are there.

Numerical Value Questions

1.

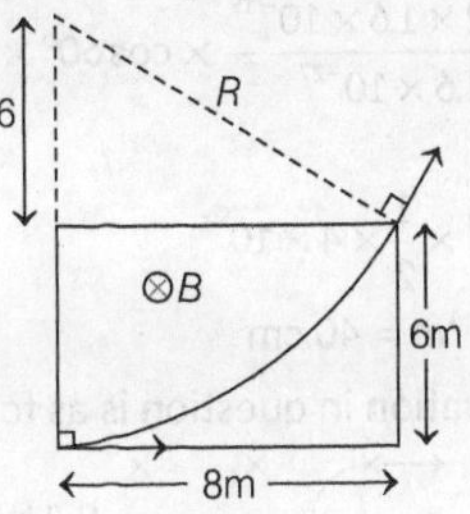

$$(R-6)^2 + 8^2 = R^2 \Rightarrow R = \frac{25}{3}\text{ m}$$

$$R = \frac{mv}{qB}$$

$$\Rightarrow \quad \frac{25}{3} = \frac{5\times10^{-3}\times v}{12\times10^{-6}\times100} \Rightarrow v = 2\text{ m/s}$$

2. Speed in ZX-plane will be constant.

$$v = \sqrt{v_x^2 + v_z^2} = \sqrt{4^2+3^2} = 5\text{ m/s}$$

Now, $\quad v = \sqrt{v_x^2 + v_y^2 + v_z^2}$

$$\Rightarrow \quad 5\sqrt{5} = \sqrt{v_y^2 + 5^2} \Rightarrow v_y = 10\text{ m/s}$$

$$v_y = u_y + a_y t$$

$$\Rightarrow \quad 10 = -6 + \left(\frac{qE_0}{m}\right)t \Rightarrow t = 8\text{ s}$$

3. $\mathbf{v} = \sqrt{3}\frac{v_0}{2}\hat{\mathbf{i}} + \frac{v_0}{2}\hat{\mathbf{j}}$

For crossing origin,

$$k\left(\frac{2\pi m}{qB}\right) = \frac{2\left(\frac{v_0}{2}\right)}{\frac{qE}{m}}, \text{ where } k \in I$$

$$\Rightarrow \quad B = \left(\frac{2\pi E}{v_0}\right)k$$

For B to be minimum $k = 1$,

$$\Rightarrow \quad B_{\min} = \frac{2\pi E}{v_0}$$

So, $n = 2$

4. $B = \mu_0 ni = 4\pi\times10^{-7}\times\left(\frac{8000}{L}\right)\times 4$

$$= \frac{128\pi\times10^{-4}}{L}\text{T}$$

$$\text{Pitch} = (v\cos\theta)T = (v\cos\theta)\frac{2\pi m}{qB}$$

$$\Rightarrow 800\left(\frac{\sqrt{3}}{2}\right)\frac{2\pi L}{\sqrt{3}\times10^{11}\times128\pi\times10^{-4}} = \frac{L}{16}\times10^{-5}\text{m}$$

$$\text{Number of revolutions} = \frac{L}{\frac{L}{16}\times10^{-5}} = 16\times10^5$$

So, $N = 16$

5.

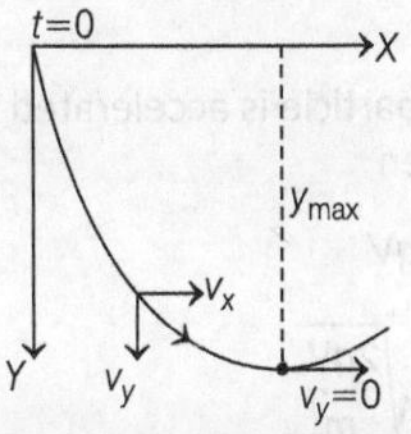

$$\mathbf{F} = mg\,\hat{\mathbf{j}} + q[(v_x\hat{\mathbf{i}} + v_y\hat{\mathbf{j}})\times(B\hat{\mathbf{k}})]$$

$$\Rightarrow \quad a_x = \frac{qv_yB}{m} \text{ and } a_y = g - \left(\frac{qB}{m}\right)v_x$$

$$\frac{d^2v_y}{dt^2} = -\left(\frac{qB}{m}\right)\frac{dv_x}{dt} = -\frac{q^2B^2}{m^2}v_y$$

$$\Rightarrow \quad v_y = A\sin\omega t \text{ where, } \omega = \frac{qB}{m}$$

At $t = 0$, $\frac{dv_y}{dt} = A\cos\omega t = g$

$$\Rightarrow \quad A = \frac{g}{\omega}$$

So, $\quad v_y = \frac{g}{\omega}\sin\omega t$

$$\Rightarrow \quad y = \frac{g}{\omega^2}(1-\cos\omega t)$$

$$y_{\max} = \frac{2g}{\omega^2} \text{ when } \cos\omega t = -1 = \frac{2gm^2}{q^2B^2}$$

So, $k = 1$

6.

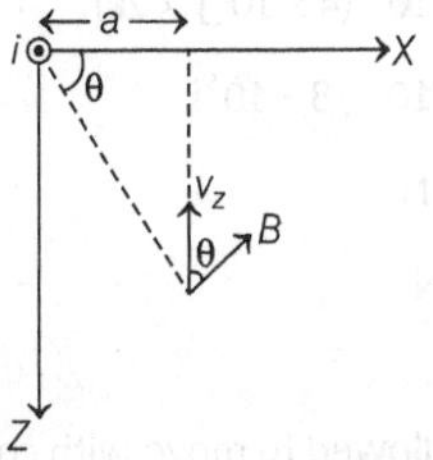

$$N = qv_zB\sin\theta = qv_z\frac{\mu_0 i}{2\pi\sqrt{z^2+a^2}}\left(\frac{z}{\sqrt{z^2+a^2}}\right)$$

$$\Rightarrow N = \frac{q\mu_0 i v_z z}{2\pi(z^2+a^2)}$$

$$f_k = \mu N = \frac{q\mu i v_z}{2\pi}\frac{z}{(z^2+a^2)}$$

$$\Rightarrow \frac{v_z dv_z}{dz} = \frac{\mu q \mu_0 j v_z}{2\pi m}\frac{z}{z^2+a^2}$$

$$\Rightarrow -\int_{v_0}^{0} dv_z = \frac{\mu q \mu_0 j}{2\pi m}\int_{2a}^{0}\frac{z\,dz}{z^2+a^2}$$

$$\Rightarrow \quad v_0 = \left(\frac{\mu q \mu_0 j}{4\pi m}\right)\ln 5$$

So, $x = 5$

Previous Years Questions

JEE Main

1. When a charge particle is accelerated with potential difference V, then

$$\frac{1}{2}mv^2 = qV$$

$$v = \sqrt{\frac{2qV}{m}}$$

$\therefore$ When charged particle enters into magnetic field B, then

$$R = \frac{mv}{Bq}$$

$$= \frac{m}{Bq}\times\sqrt{\frac{2qV}{m}}$$

$$= \frac{1}{B}\sqrt{\frac{2mV}{q}}$$

$\therefore R \propto \sqrt{m}$

Thus, $\frac{R_1}{R_2} = \sqrt{\frac{m_x}{m_y}}$

$$\Rightarrow \left(\frac{R_1}{R_2}\right)^2 = \frac{m_x}{m_y}$$

$$\Rightarrow \frac{m_x}{m_y} = \left(\frac{R_1}{R_2}\right)^2$$

2. $F = q(v \times B)$

$$= 4\times10^{-6}(4\times10^6\hat{j}\times 2\hat{k})$$

$$= 4\times10^{-6}\cdot 8\times10^6\hat{i}$$

$$= 32\hat{i}\text{ N}$$

$$= x\,\hat{i}\text{ N} \quad \text{(given)}$$

$\therefore \quad x = 32$

3. An electron is allowed to move with constant velocity along the axis of current carrying straight solenoid.

The electron will not experience magnetic force.

The electron will continue to move along the axis of the solenoid.

4. $B = \frac{\pi}{2}\times10^{-3}$ (given)

$KE = \frac{1}{2}mv^2$ and $v = \sqrt{\frac{2KE}{m}}$

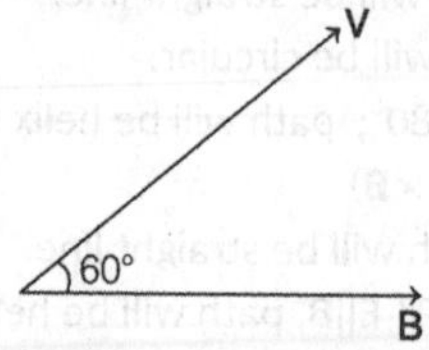

Pitch = $v\cos 60^\circ \times$ time period of one rotation

$$= v\cos 60^\circ \times \frac{2\pi m}{eB}$$

$$= \sqrt{\frac{2\times2\times1.6\times10^{-19}}{1.6\times10^{-27}}}\times\cos 60^\circ\times\frac{2\pi\times1.6\times10^{-27}}{1.6\times10^{-19}\times\frac{\pi}{2}\times10^{-3}}$$

$$= 2\times10^4\times\frac{1}{2}\times4\times10^{-5}$$

$$= 4\times10^{-1}\text{m} = 40\text{ cm}$$

5. The given situation in question is as follows.

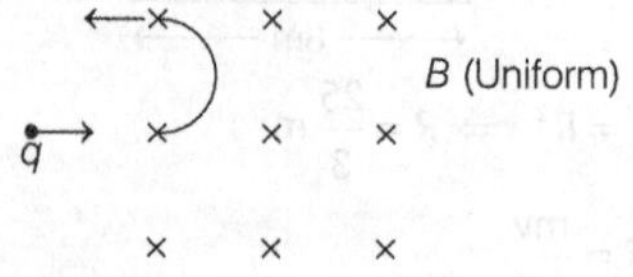

Kinetic energy of charged particle,

$$KE = qV$$

$$\Rightarrow \quad KE = 2\times10^{-6}\times100 = 2\times10^{-4}\text{ J}$$

Radius of circular path, $R = \frac{mv}{qB}$

$$R = \frac{p}{qB} = \frac{\sqrt{2(\text{KE})m}}{qB} \text{ or } m = \frac{q^2B^2R^2}{2(\text{KE})}$$

$$= \frac{(2\times10^{-6})^2\times(4\times10^{-3})^2\times(3\times10^{-2})^2}{2\times2\times10^{-4}}m = 144\times10^{-18}\text{ kg}$$

6. Given, $\mathbf{E} = E\hat{k}$

and magnetic field, $\mathbf{B} = B\hat{j} = 12\times10^{-3}\hat{j}\text{T} \quad (\because B = 12\text{ mT})$

Kinetic energy of electron,

$$K = 728\text{ eV} = 728\times1.6\times10^{-19}\text{ J}$$

$$= 1.16\times10^{-16}\text{ J}$$

We know that, electron will move along positive X-axis without deflection, thus,

$$v = E/B$$

Since, $K = \frac{1}{2}mv^2$

$$\Rightarrow \quad K = \frac{1}{2}m\left(\frac{E}{B}\right)^2 \Rightarrow K = \frac{1}{2}m\frac{E^2}{B^2}$$

$$\Rightarrow \quad E^2 = \frac{2KB^2}{m} \Rightarrow E = \sqrt{\frac{2KB^2}{m}}$$

$$= \sqrt{\frac{2 \times 1.16 \times 10^{-16} \times (12 \times 10^{-3})^2}{9.1 \times 10^{-31}}}$$
$$= 1.92 \times 10^5 \text{Vm}^{-1}$$
$$= 192 \times 10^3 \text{ Vm}^{-1}$$
$$= 192 \text{ kVm}^{-1}$$

7. Radius of circular path, $R = \frac{\sqrt{2mK}}{qB}$

$$\Rightarrow \quad q = \frac{\sqrt{2mK}}{RB}$$

$$\because \quad \frac{q_1}{q_2} = \sqrt{\frac{m_1}{m_2}} \times \frac{R_2}{R_1} = \sqrt{\frac{9}{4}} \times \frac{5}{6} = \frac{5}{4}$$

8. Statement I is correct.

As electric force and acceleration,

$$F = qE \text{ and } a = \frac{q}{m} \cdot E$$

Also magnetic force in a perpendicular magnetic field,

$$F = q(\mathbf{v} \times \mathbf{B}) \Rightarrow \mathbf{v} \perp \mathbf{F}$$

So, work done by force,

$$W = (\mathbf{F} \cdot \mathbf{v}) = \text{zero}$$

As work done is zero, so no change in kinetic energy occurs. Therefore, statement II is incorrect as electric force on a positive particle is along the direction of electric field.

9. Kinetic energy of a particle rotating in a magnetic field is

$$\text{KE} = \frac{1}{2}mv^2 = \frac{B^2q^2r^2}{2m} \quad \left[\because r = \frac{mv}{Bq} \Rightarrow v = \frac{rBq}{m}\right]$$

$$\Rightarrow \quad \text{KE} \propto r^2$$

$$\Rightarrow \quad \frac{K_f}{K_i} = \left(\frac{r_f}{r_i}\right)^2$$

Given, $K_f = 4K_i$

$$\Rightarrow \quad \left(\frac{r_f}{r_i}\right)^2 = 4 \Rightarrow r_f = 2r_i$$

or $\quad \frac{r_f}{r_i} = \frac{2}{1}$

10. Given, a deutron and a proton have equal KE enter into a uniform magnetic field.

$$\theta = 90° \qquad [\because \mathbf{v} \perp \mathbf{B}]$$

$$\frac{r_d}{r_p} = \frac{\sqrt{x}}{1}$$

To find x

Since, radius of circular path,

$$r = \frac{\sqrt{2mK}}{qB} \qquad (\because \text{KE and } B \text{ are same})$$

$$\Rightarrow \quad \frac{r_d}{r_p} = \frac{\sqrt{m_d}}{\sqrt{m_p}} \times \frac{q_d}{q_p} = \sqrt{2}$$

[Since, $m_d = 2m_p$ and $q_p = q_d$]

Comparing with given value, we get

$\therefore \quad x = 2$

11. Radius of a charged particle in uniform magnetic field is given by, $R = \frac{mv}{qB}$

For α particle, $R_\alpha = \frac{m_\alpha v}{q_\alpha B}$

For proton, $R_p = \frac{m_p v}{q_p \cdot B} \Rightarrow \frac{R_\alpha}{R_p} = \frac{\frac{m_\alpha}{q_\alpha}}{\frac{m_p}{q_p}} = \frac{2}{1}$

Therefore, the ratio of radii of the circular paths described by the alpha particle and proton is 2 : 1.

12. When a charged particle enters into magnetic field perpendicular to it, then it moves on circular path, and radius r of circular path is given as,

$$r = \frac{mv}{Bq} = \frac{p}{Bq} \qquad [\text{where, momentum } p = mv]$$

$$= \frac{\sqrt{2mK}}{Bq} \qquad \left[\begin{array}{l}\because p = \sqrt{2mK} \\ \text{where, } K = \text{kinetic energy}\end{array}\right]$$

$$\Rightarrow \quad r \propto \frac{\sqrt{m}}{q}$$

$$\therefore \; r_p : r_d : r_\alpha = \frac{\sqrt{m_p}}{q_p} : \frac{\sqrt{m_d}}{q_d} : \frac{\sqrt{m_\alpha}}{q_\alpha}$$

$$\left[\begin{array}{l}\text{Since, } m_d = 2m_p, m_\alpha = 4m_p, \\ q_p = q_d = e \text{ and } q_\alpha = 2e\end{array}\right]$$

$$\therefore \quad r_p : r_d : r_\alpha = \frac{\sqrt{m_p}}{e} : \frac{\sqrt{2m_p}}{e} : \frac{\sqrt{4m_p}}{2e} = 1 : \sqrt{2} : 1$$

13. In a uniform magnetic field, moving charged particle experiences magnetic force perpendicular to its direction of motion, which is called Lorentz force and is given as

$$F = q(\mathbf{v} \times \mathbf{B}) \text{ i.e. } \mathbf{F} \perp \mathbf{v}$$

where, v = velocity, q = charge and B = magnetic field

i.e. force on charged particle always remains perpendicular to its velocity i.e. its displacement.

Hence, work done $= \mathbf{F} \cdot \mathbf{s} = Fs\cos 90° = 0$

Hence, according to work-energy theorem,

$$\Delta E_K = W = 0$$

i.e. kinetic energy = constant.

Hence, in uniform magnetic field, speed and energy remains the same for moving charged particle. Therefore, both A and R are correct and R is the correct explanation of A.

14. $$r = \frac{\sqrt{2m\text{KE}}}{qB} \Rightarrow r \propto \frac{\sqrt{m}}{q}$$

$$\Rightarrow \quad \frac{r_1}{r_2} = \sqrt{\frac{m_1}{m_2}} \times \left(\frac{q_2}{q_1}\right)$$

$$\Rightarrow \quad \frac{r_1}{r_2} = \sqrt{\frac{4}{16}} \times \left(\frac{+3e}{2e}\right) = \frac{1}{2} \times \frac{3}{2} = \frac{3}{4}$$

$$\Rightarrow r_1 = \frac{3}{4} r_2 \Rightarrow r_1 < r_2$$

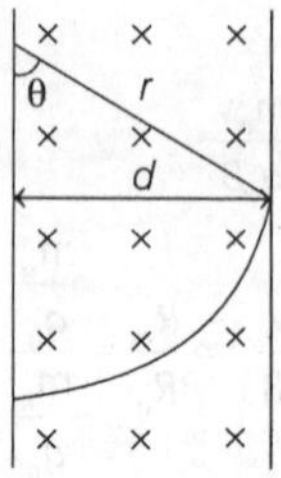

Now, the deflection of ion in region with constant magnetic field as shown in figure is denoted by θ.

From diagram,

$$\sin\theta = \frac{d}{r}$$

$$\theta \propto \frac{1}{r} \qquad [\because d = \text{constant}]$$

As, $r_1 < r_2$ from above expression $\theta_1 > \theta_2$.

Thus, deflection of lighter ion will be more than the deflection of heavier ion.

15. Given, maximum value of accelerating potential,

$$V = 12 \text{ kV} = 12000 \text{ V},$$

Speed achieved by a proton cyclotron, $v = c/6$

where, c is the speed of light $= 3\times 10^8 \text{ms}^{-1}$

Mass of proton, $m_p = 1.67\times 10^{-27}$ kg

Charge of proton, $q_p = 1.6\times 10^{-19}$ C

According to the question, assume a proton makes revolutions in the cyclotron to achieve the speed v.

The energy absorbed by proton due to the accelerating potential provided by the radio oscillator

$$= n \times 2 \times q_p \times V$$

This energy absorbed by proton will be equal to the kinetic energy gain by the proton i.e.,

$$2nq_pV = \frac{m_p v^2}{2}$$

Substituting the given values in above expression, we get

$$n \times 2 \times 1.6 \times 10^{-19} \times 12000 = \frac{1}{2} \times 1.67 \times 10^{-27} \times \left(\frac{3\times 10^8}{6}\right)^2$$

$$n \times 3.84 \times 10^{-15} = 2.0875 \times 10^{-12}$$

$$n = 543.62$$

As, n is number of revolutions, so it should be an integer.

$$\therefore \quad n = 543$$

16. Let masses of ions be m_1 and m_2 respectively, charges be q_1 and q_2 respectively and speed of charges be v_1 and v_2.

Given, $m_1 = m_2 = m$

$$q_1 : q_2 = 1:2$$

$$v_1 : v_2 = 2:3$$

As we know that,

$$r = \frac{mv}{qB}$$

$$\therefore \quad \frac{r_1}{r_2} = \frac{m_1 v_1}{q_1 B} \times \frac{q_2 B}{m_2 v_2} = \frac{m}{m} \times \frac{2}{1} \times \frac{2}{3} = \frac{4}{3}$$

17. $r = \dfrac{\sqrt{2Km}}{Bq}$

Since, m, K and B are same for both deuteron and α-particle.

$$r \propto \frac{\sqrt{m}}{q}$$

$$\therefore \quad \frac{r_d}{r_\alpha} = \sqrt{\frac{m_d}{m_\alpha}} \cdot \frac{q_\alpha}{q_d} = \sqrt{\frac{2}{4}}\left(\frac{2}{1}\right)$$

$$\left[\because m_d = 2m_p \text{ and } m_\alpha = 4m_p, \; q_\alpha = 2e \text{ and } q_d = e.\right]$$

$$\frac{r_d}{r_\alpha} = \sqrt{2}$$

18. Given, the charge on the proton, $q_p = +e$

The charge on the alpha particles, $q_\alpha = +2e$

The expression of the radius of the orbit,

$$r = \frac{mv}{qB} \Rightarrow r = \frac{p}{qB} \qquad (\because p = mv)$$

$$\therefore \quad \frac{r_p}{r_\alpha} = \frac{p_p}{q_p} \times \frac{q_\alpha}{p_\alpha}$$

$$\Rightarrow \quad \frac{2}{1} = \frac{+2e}{+e} \times \frac{p_p}{p_\alpha} \qquad \left[\because \frac{r_p}{r_\alpha} = \frac{2}{1}\right]$$

$$\Rightarrow \quad \frac{p_p}{p_\alpha} = 1$$

Since, kinetic energy and momentum are related as

$$K = \frac{p^2}{2m}$$

$$\therefore \quad \frac{K_p}{K_\alpha} = \frac{p_p^2 m_\alpha}{m_p p_\alpha^2}$$

$$\Rightarrow \quad \frac{K_p}{K_\alpha} = \frac{m_\alpha}{m_p} = \frac{4m_p}{m_p} \Rightarrow \frac{K_p}{K_\alpha} = \frac{4}{1}$$

19. According to question, a charge Q is moving $d\mathbf{l}$ distance in magnetic field B.

As we know that force acting on a point charge by magnetic field is always perpendicular to the velocity of particle **v**.

$$\therefore \quad \mathbf{F} = Q(\mathbf{v}\times\mathbf{B}) \qquad \text{... (i)}$$

The above, statement means that **F** is perpendicular to **v**.

$\because$ Work done, $W = F \cdot ds$

$$= Q(\mathbf{v}\times\mathbf{B})\cdot dl \qquad \text{[using Eq. (i)]}$$

$$= Q(\mathbf{v}\times\mathbf{B}) dl \cos\theta$$

$$= Q(\mathbf{v}\times\mathbf{B})\, dl \cos 90^\circ \qquad [\because \theta = 90^\circ\, F \perp \mathbf{v} \text{ or } d\mathbf{l}]$$

$$= 0$$

$\therefore$ The work done by the magnetic field will be zero.

20. Let F_p, F_d and F_α be the forces and v_p, v_d and v_α be the velocities of proton, deuteron and α-particle, respectively.

Since, $\quad F = Bqv$

On dividing and multiplying F by m, we get

$$F = Bqv\frac{m}{m}$$

$\Rightarrow \quad F = B\dfrac{q}{m}p \qquad (\because p = mv)$

$\Rightarrow \quad F \propto q/m \qquad (\because p \text{ and } B \text{ are same})$

$\therefore \quad F_p : F_d : F_\alpha = \dfrac{+q}{m} : \dfrac{+q}{2m} : \dfrac{+2q}{4m}$

$= 1 : 1/2 : 1/2$

$= 2 : 1 : 1$

and $\quad F = Bqv$

$\Rightarrow \quad v \propto F/q$

$\therefore \quad v_p : v_d : v_\alpha = \dfrac{F_p}{q_p} : \dfrac{F_d}{q_d} : \dfrac{F_\alpha}{q_\alpha}$

$= \dfrac{2x}{q} : \dfrac{x}{q} : \dfrac{x}{2q}$

$= 2 : 1 : 1/2$

$= 4 : 2 : 1$

21. As we know that, if a charge particle moves in a uniform magnetic field, then its path is always circular. Considering the charge positive, the direction of magnetic force acting on it, has been shown by dotted line.

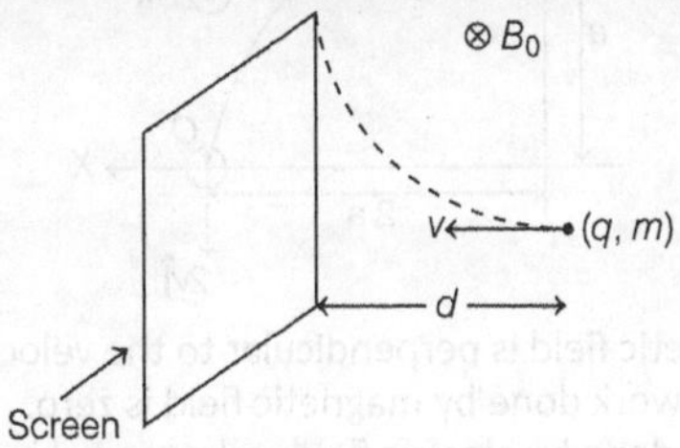

As, charge particle should not hit the screen this means radius of circular path must be less than screen distance d.

i.e. $\quad R \le d \Rightarrow \dfrac{mv}{qB_0} \le d \qquad \left[\because R = \dfrac{mv}{qB_0}\right]$

or $\quad v \le \dfrac{qB_0 d}{m}$

Maximum value of $v = \dfrac{qB_0 d}{m}$

Note In this problem, minimum value has been asked which is clearly an error, so read it maximum value.

22. Pitch of helical path shown below is given by

$$\text{Pitch} = T \cdot v\cos\theta = \frac{2\pi m}{Bq} \cdot v\cos\theta$$

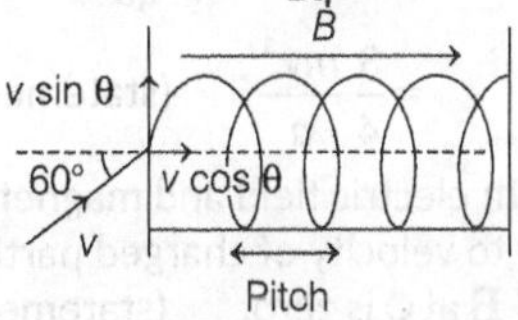

$\Rightarrow \quad \text{Pitch} = \dfrac{2 \times 3.14 \times 1.67 \times 10^{-27} \times 4 \times 10^5 \times \cos 60^\circ}{(1.69 \times 10^{-19})(0.3)}$

$= 0.04 \text{ m} = 4 \text{ cm}$

Hence, correct option is (b).

23. As $\mathbf{v}$ is not perpendicular to $\mathbf{B}$, so path of particle is helical in magnetic field as shown in figure,

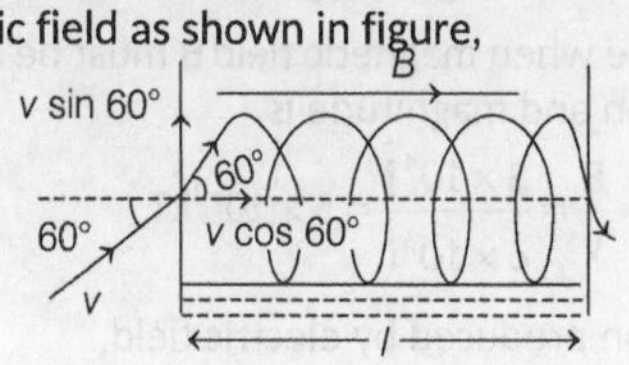

Let T be the time to complete 1 round, then

$$T = 2\pi m / Bq$$

So, total time to cross the length l of region of magnetic field is

$$t = 10T = 10 \times \frac{2\pi m}{Bq}$$

Hence, length of path l is

$l = \text{speed} \times \text{time} = v\cos\theta \times t$

$= v\cos 60^\circ \times 10 \times \dfrac{2\pi m}{Bq}$

$\Rightarrow \quad l = \dfrac{4 \times 10^5 \times \frac{1}{2} \times 10 \times 2\pi \times 1.67 \times 10^{-27}}{0.3 \times 1.6 \times 10^{-19}}$

$= 0.437 \approx 0.44 \text{ m}$

Hence, correct option is (c).

24. Force on a charged particle moving in region of a magnetic field is given by

$$\mathbf{F} = q(\mathbf{v} \times \mathbf{B})$$

Here, $q = 1\,\mu\text{C} = 1 \times 10^{-6}\,\text{C}$,

$\mathbf{v} = (2\hat{\mathbf{i}} + 3\hat{\mathbf{j}} + 4\hat{\mathbf{k}})\,\text{ms}^{-1}$

and $\quad \mathbf{B} = (5\mathbf{i} + 3\mathbf{j} - 6\mathbf{k}) \times 10^{-3}\,\text{T}$

So, force on the particle is

$$\mathbf{F} \times 10^{-9} = 1 \times 10^{-6} \begin{vmatrix} \hat{\mathbf{i}} & \hat{\mathbf{j}} & \hat{\mathbf{k}} \\ 2 & 3 & 4 \\ 5 \times 10^{-3} & 3 \times 10^{-3} & -6 \times 10^{-3} \end{vmatrix}$$

$$= 10^{-9} \begin{vmatrix} \hat{\mathbf{i}} & \hat{\mathbf{j}} & \hat{\mathbf{k}} \\ 2 & 3 & 4 \\ 5 & 3 & -6 \end{vmatrix}$$

$\Rightarrow \quad \mathbf{F} = -30\hat{\mathbf{i}} + 32\hat{\mathbf{j}} - 9\hat{\mathbf{k}}$

Hence, option (b) is correct.

25. Given that, $\mathbf{v} = 6 \times 10^6\,\hat{\mathbf{i}}$ m/s,

$\mathbf{E} = 300\hat{\mathbf{j}}$ V/cm $= 3 \times 10^4\,\hat{\mathbf{j}}$ V/m

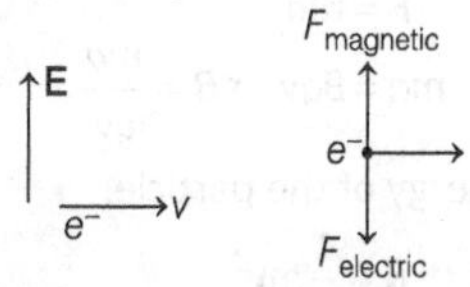

To keep the electron moving along x-direction,

$$\mathbf{F}_{\text{net}} = 0$$

or $\quad \mathbf{F}_{\text{electric}} + \mathbf{F}_{\text{magnetic}} = 0$

$$q\mathbf{E} + q(\mathbf{v} \times \mathbf{B}) = 0$$

or $\quad \mathbf{E} + \mathbf{v} \times \mathbf{B} = 0$

It is possible when magnetic field **B** must be along $+z$-direction and magnitude is

$$\mathbf{B} = \frac{\mathbf{E}}{\mathbf{v}} = \frac{3 \times 10^4 \hat{\mathbf{j}}}{6 \times 10^6 \hat{\mathbf{i}}} = 5 \times 10^{-3} \hat{\mathbf{k}} \text{T}$$

26. Acceleration produced by electric field,

$$\mathbf{a} = \frac{qE_0}{m} \hat{\mathbf{i}}$$

After time t, velocity of the particle,

$$\mathbf{v} = \mathbf{u} + \mathbf{a}t$$

$$\Rightarrow \quad \mathbf{v} = v_0 \hat{\mathbf{j}} + \left(\frac{qE_0 t}{m} \right) \hat{\mathbf{i}} \qquad [\because \mathbf{u} = \mathbf{v} = v_0 \hat{\mathbf{j}}]$$

So, speed of the particle,

$$|\mathbf{v}| = \sqrt{v_0^2 + \left(\frac{qE_0 t}{m} \right)^2}$$

Now, given $|\mathbf{v}| = 2v_0$ after time t, so

$$2v_0 = \sqrt{v_0^2 + \left(\frac{qE_0 t}{m} \right)^2}$$

$$\Rightarrow \quad 4v_0^2 = v_0^2 + \left(\frac{qE_0 t}{m} \right)^2 \Rightarrow 3v_0^2 = \left(\frac{qE_0 t}{m} \right)^2$$

So, time interval, $t = \dfrac{\sqrt{3}\, mv_0}{qE_0}$.

Here, we must note that no change in magnitude of velocity is caused by a perpendicular magnetic field. So, we are not taking effect of magnetic field while calculating change in speed.

27. Given, proton is moving from south to north and magnetic field is directed from west to east.

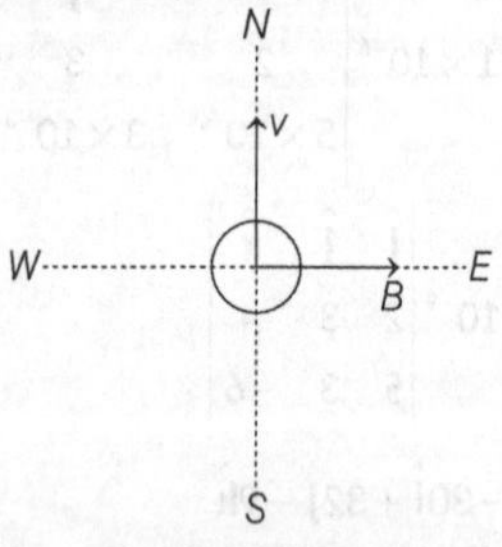

As $\mathbf{v} \perp \mathbf{B}$, force on the charged particle,

$$F = Bqv$$

If m = mass and a = acceleration of the particle, then

$$F = ma$$

So, $\quad ma = Bqv$ or $B = \dfrac{ma}{qv} \qquad$ ...(i)

If K = kinetic energy of the particle,

then $\quad K = \dfrac{1}{2} mv^2$

$$\Rightarrow \quad v = \sqrt{\frac{2K}{m}} \qquad \text{...(ii)}$$

From Eqs. (i) and (ii), we get

$$B = \frac{ma}{q\sqrt{\frac{2K}{m}}} = \frac{m^{3/2} \cdot a}{q \times \sqrt{2K}} \qquad \text{...(iii)}$$

Here, $m = 1.6 \times 10^{-27}$ kg, $a = 10^{12}$ ms^{-2},

$q = 1.6 \times 10^{-19}$ C,

$K = 1 \text{ MeV} = 1 \times 10^6 \times 1.6 \times 10^{-19}$ J

$= 1.6 \times 10^{-13}$ J

Substituting these given values in Eq. (iii), we get

$$B = \frac{(1.6 \times 10^{-27})^{3/2} \times 10^{12}}{1.6 \times 10^{-19} \times (2 \times 1.6 \times 10^{-13})^{1/2}}$$

$$= \frac{(1.6)^{3/2} \times 10^{-27 \times \frac{3}{2}} \times 10^{12}}{(1.6)^{3/2} \times 2^{1/2} \times 10^{-19} \times 10^{-13/2}}$$

$$= \frac{1}{\sqrt{2}} \times 10^{-3} = 0.71 \text{ mT}$$

28. Charged particle follows trajectory as shown in the figure.

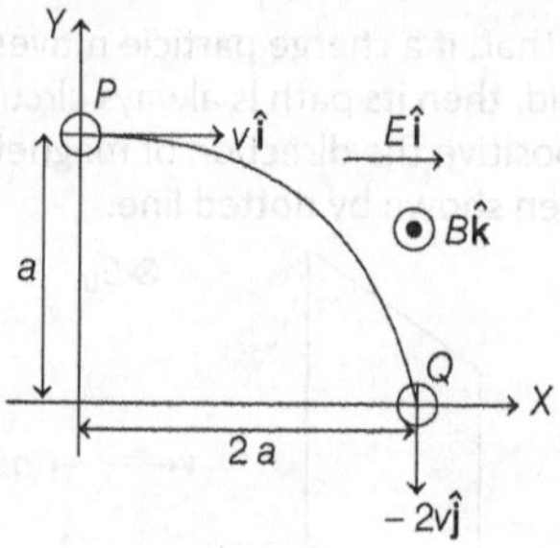

As magnetic field is perpendicular to the velocity of charged particle, work done by magnetic field is zero.

So, work done by electric field = change in kinetic energy of charged particle.

$$\Rightarrow \quad \int \mathbf{F} \cdot d\mathbf{s} = \frac{1}{2} m(-2v\hat{\mathbf{j}})^2 - \frac{1}{2} m(v\hat{\mathbf{i}})^2$$

$$\Rightarrow \quad (qE\hat{\mathbf{i}})(2a\hat{\mathbf{i}} - a\hat{\mathbf{j}}) = 2mv^2 - \frac{1}{2} mv^2$$

$$\Rightarrow \quad 2qaE = \frac{3}{2} mv^2$$

$$\Rightarrow \quad E = \frac{3}{4} \frac{mv^2}{qa} \qquad \text{(statement 1 is correct)}$$

Rate of work done = Power = $\mathbf{F} \cdot \mathbf{v} = qE\hat{\mathbf{i}} \cdot v\hat{\mathbf{i}}$

$$= qEv = q \cdot \frac{3}{4} \frac{mv^2}{qa} \cdot v$$

$$= \frac{3}{4} \frac{mv^3}{a} \qquad \text{(statement 2 is correct)}$$

At point Q, both electric field and magnetic field are perpendicular to velocity of charged particle, so work done by both **E** and **B** at Q is zero. (statement 3 is correct)

Angular momentum about origin at P = $mva\hat{\mathbf{k}}$.

Angular momentum about origin at Q = $-4mva\hat{\mathbf{k}}$.

Difference between magnitudes of angular momentum at

P and Q,

$$\Delta L = L_Q - L_P = 4mva - mva$$

$$= 3mva \quad \text{(statement 4 is incorrect)}$$

Thus, option (b) is correct.

29. In given arrangement, electron gun shoots electron perpendicularly to the direction of magnetic field.

Here, we are showing cross-section of solenoid.

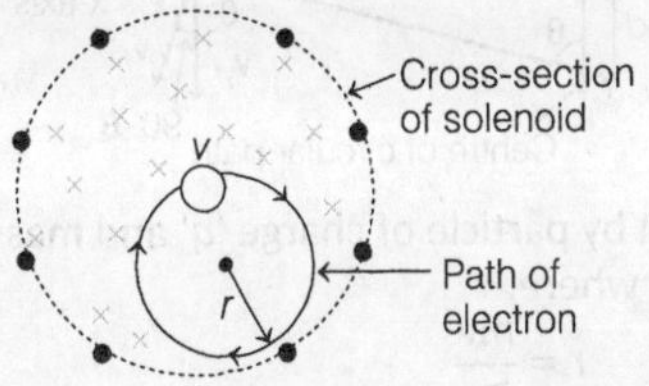

As electron is moving at 90° to magnetic field, its path is a circle. Maximum value of radius of path taken by electron, such that it does not collide with solenoid wall is $\frac{R}{2}$.

So, $$r_{\max} = \frac{R}{2} = \frac{mv_{\max}}{eB}$$

Here, $$B = \mu_0 nI$$

So, $$v_{\max} = \frac{ReB}{2m} = \frac{e\mu_0 nIR}{2m}$$

30. When a moving charged particle is placed in a magnetic field **B**.

Then, the net magnetic force acting on it is

$$\mathbf{F}_m = q(\mathbf{v} \times \mathbf{B})$$

$$\mathbf{F}_m = q\,vB\sin\theta$$

Here, $\theta = 90°$

$$\mathbf{F}_m = q\,vB$$

Also, due to this net force, the particle transverses a circular path, whose necessary centripetal force is being provided by F_m, i.e.

$$\frac{mv^2}{r} = q\,vB$$

$$\Rightarrow \quad r = \frac{mv^2}{qvB} = \frac{mv}{qB} \Rightarrow r \propto m$$

So, for electron,

$$r_e = \frac{m_e v}{eB} \text{ or } r_e \propto m_e$$

For proton,

$$r_p = \frac{m_p v}{eB} \text{ or } r_p \propto m_p$$

For He-particle,

$$r_{\text{He}} = \frac{4m_p v}{2eB} = \frac{2m_p v}{eB}$$

Clearly, $r_{\text{He}} > r_p$ $\quad (\because r_{\text{He}} = 2r_p)$

and we know that, $m_p > m_e$

$$\left[\begin{array}{l}\because m_p \approx 10^{-27}\text{kg},\\ m_e \approx 10^{-31}\text{ kg}\end{array}\right]$$

$$\therefore \quad r_p > r_e \Rightarrow r_{\text{He}} > r_p > r_e$$

31.

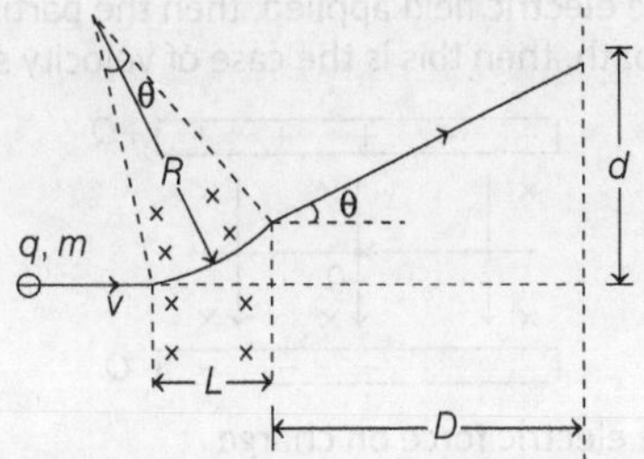

Radius of path of electron, $R = \frac{mv}{Bq}$

Now, from geometry of given arrangement, comparing values of $\tan\theta$, we have

$$\tan\theta = \frac{L}{R} = \frac{d}{D}$$

$$\Rightarrow \quad d = \frac{LD}{R} = \frac{Bq\,LD}{mv}$$

$$\Rightarrow \quad d = \frac{BqLD}{\sqrt{2mk}} \qquad [\because mv = \sqrt{2mk}]$$

where, k = kinetic energy of electron

Here, $B = 1.5 \times 10^{-3}$ T,

$q = 1.6 \times 10^{-19}$ C, $L = 2 \times 10^{-2}$ m,

$D = 6 \times 10^{-2}$ m,

$m = 9.1 \times 10^{-31}$ kg, $k = 100 \times 1.6 \times 10^{-19}$ J

So, $$d = \frac{(1.5 \times 10^{-3} \times 1.6 \times 10^{-19} \times 2 \times 10^{-2} \times 6 \times 10^{-2})}{\sqrt{(2 \times 9.1 \times 10^{-31} \times 100 \times 1.6 \times 10^{-19})}}$$

$$= \frac{28.8 \times 10^{-26}}{\sqrt{29.12 \times 10^{-48}}} = \frac{28.8 \times 10^{-26}}{5.39 \times 10^{-24}}$$

$$= 5.34 \times 10^{-2}\text{m}$$

$$= 5.34 \text{ cm}$$

No option is matching.

32. According to given condition, when a particle having charge same as electron move in a magnetic field on circular path, then the force always acts towards the centre and perpendicular to the velocity.

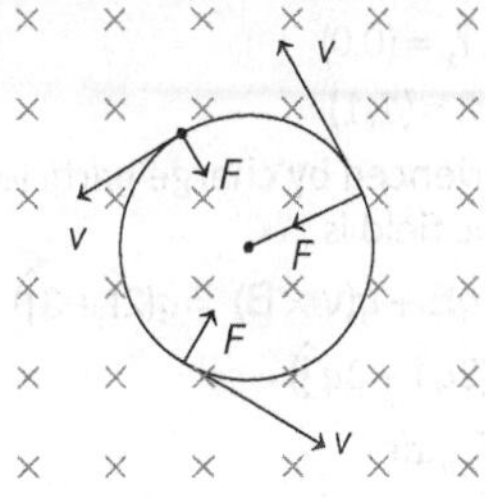

Here, $B = 0.5$ T

R = radius of circular path = 5 cm

Now, the magnetic force is

$$F_m = q(v \times B) = q\,vB\sin 90°$$

$$F_m = qvB \qquad \text{...(i)}$$

When the electric field applied, then the particle moves in a straight path, then this is the case of velocity selector.

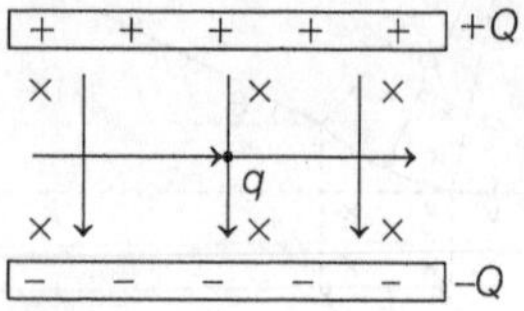

Here, the electric force on charge,

$$F_e = qE \quad \text{...(ii)}$$

In velocity selector,

$$F_m = F_e \Rightarrow qvB = qE \quad \text{...(iii)}$$

Initially particle moves under the magnetic field, So the radius of circular path taken by the particle is

$$R = \frac{mv}{qB} \quad \text{...(iv)}$$

From Eqs. (iii) and (iv), we get

$$m = \frac{qB^2R}{E}$$

$$m = \frac{1.6 \times 10^{-19} \times 0.25 \times 0.5 \times 10^{-2}}{10^2}$$

$$m = 2 \times 10^{-24} \text{ kg}$$

33. During the circular motion of accelerated electron in the presence of magnetic field, its radius is given by

$$r = \frac{mv}{Be} = \frac{\sqrt{2meV}}{eB}$$

where, v is velocity and V is voltage.

After substituting the given values, we get

$$= \frac{\sqrt{2 \times 9.1 \times 10^{-31} \times 1.6 \times 10^{-19} \times 500}}{1.6 \times 10^{-19} \times 100 \times 10^{-3}}$$

$$= 10\left[\frac{2 \times 9.1 \times 500}{1.6} \times 10^{-12}\right]^{1/2},$$

$$r = 7.5 \times 10^{-4} \text{ m}$$

34. Here, $\mathbf{E} = 2\hat{\mathbf{i}} + 3\hat{\mathbf{j}}$, $\mathbf{B} = 4\hat{\mathbf{j}} + 6\hat{\mathbf{k}}$,

q = charge on a particle.

Initial position, $r_1 = (0,0)$

Final position, $r_2 = (1,1)$

Net force experienced by charge particle inside electromagnetic field is

$$\mathbf{F}_{net} = q\mathbf{E} + q(\mathbf{v} \times \mathbf{B}) = q(2\hat{\mathbf{i}} + 3\hat{\mathbf{j}}) \quad [\text{here, } \mathbf{v} \times \mathbf{B} = 0]$$

$$= (2q\hat{\mathbf{i}} + 3q\hat{\mathbf{j}})$$

$$\therefore \quad dW = \mathbf{F}_{net} \cdot d\mathbf{r}$$

$$\Rightarrow \quad \int dW = \int_{r_1}^{r_2} (2q\hat{\mathbf{i}} + 3q\hat{\mathbf{j}}) \cdot (dx\,\hat{\mathbf{i}} + dy\,\hat{\mathbf{j}})$$

$$[\text{here } d\mathbf{r} = dx\,\hat{\mathbf{i}} + dy\,\hat{\mathbf{j}}]$$

$$\Rightarrow \quad W = 2q\int_0^1 dx + 3q\int_0^1 dy$$

or $\quad W = 2q + 3q$ or $W = 5q$

35. Situation given in question is shown below;

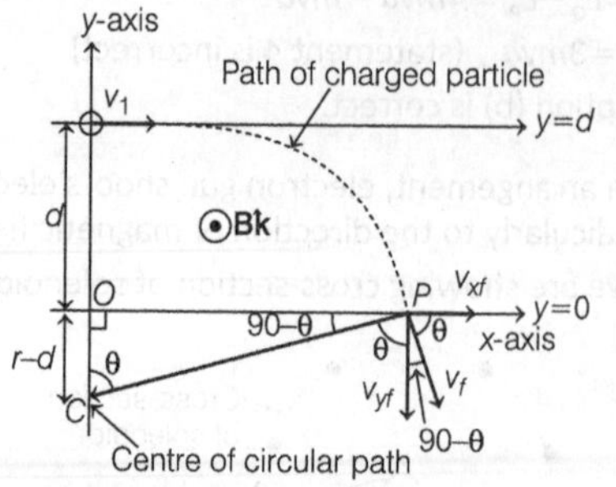

Path taken by particle of charge 'q' and mass 'm' is a circle of radius r where,

$$r = \frac{mv}{Bq}$$

Here final velocity

$$\mathbf{v}_f = \mathbf{v}_x\hat{\mathbf{i}} + \mathbf{v}_{yf}(-\hat{\mathbf{j}})$$

$$= v\cos 60\,\hat{\mathbf{i}} - v\sin 60°\,\hat{\mathbf{j}}$$

$$= v\left(\frac{1}{2}\hat{\mathbf{i}} - \frac{\sqrt{3}}{2}\hat{\mathbf{j}}\right)$$

So, change of velocity of charged particle is

$$\Delta\mathbf{v} = \mathbf{v}_f - \mathbf{v}_i$$

$$= v\left(\frac{1}{2}\hat{\mathbf{i}} - \frac{\sqrt{3}}{2}\hat{\mathbf{j}}\right) - v\hat{\mathbf{i}} = -v\left(\frac{1}{2}\hat{\mathbf{i}} + \frac{\sqrt{3}}{2}\hat{\mathbf{j}}\right)$$

It t = time taken by charged particle to cross region of magnetic field then,

$$t = \frac{\text{distance } OP}{\text{speed in direction } OP}$$

$$= \frac{r \times \frac{\sqrt{3}}{2}}{v} = \frac{\frac{mv}{Bq} \times \frac{\sqrt{3}}{2}}{v} = \frac{\sqrt{3}m}{2Bq}$$

So, acceleration of charged particle at the point its emergence is;

$$\text{Acceleration } \mathbf{a} = \frac{\Delta\mathbf{v}}{\Delta t} = \frac{-v\left(\frac{1}{2}\hat{\mathbf{i}} + \frac{\sqrt{3}}{2}\hat{\mathbf{j}}\right)}{\frac{\sqrt{3}\,m}{2\,Bq}}$$

$$= \frac{-Bqv}{m}\left(\frac{\hat{\mathbf{i}}}{\sqrt{3}} + \hat{\mathbf{j}}\right)\text{ms}^{-2}$$

None of the option given matches with answer.

36. Radius of path of charged particle q in a uniform magnetic field B of mass 'm' moving with velocity v is

$$r = \frac{mv}{Bq} = \frac{m\sqrt{(2qV/m)}}{Bq}$$

$$\Rightarrow \quad r \propto \frac{\sqrt{m}}{\sqrt{q}} \text{ so, required ratio is}$$

$$\Rightarrow \quad \frac{r_p}{r_\alpha} = \sqrt{\frac{m_p}{m_\alpha}} \times \sqrt{\frac{q_\alpha}{q_p}} = \sqrt{\frac{1}{4}} \times \sqrt{\frac{2}{1}} = \frac{\sqrt{2}}{2} = \frac{1}{\sqrt{2}}$$

JEE Advanced

1. If average speed is considered along X-axis,

$$R_1 = \frac{mv_0}{qB_1}, R_2 = \frac{mv_0}{qB_2} = \frac{mv_0}{4qB_1}$$

$$R_1 > R_2$$

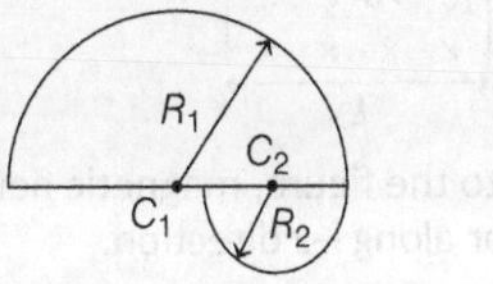

Distance travelled along x-axis, $\Delta x = 2(R_1 + R_2) = \dfrac{5mv_0}{2qB_1}$

$$\text{Total time} = \frac{T_1}{2} + \frac{T_2}{2} = \frac{\pi m}{qB_1} + \frac{\pi m}{qB_2} = \frac{\pi m}{qB_1} + \frac{\pi m}{4qB_1} = \frac{5\pi m}{4qB_1}$$

$$\text{Magnitude of average speed} = \frac{\dfrac{5mv_0}{2qB_1}}{\dfrac{5\pi m}{4qB_1}} = 2$$

2. (a)

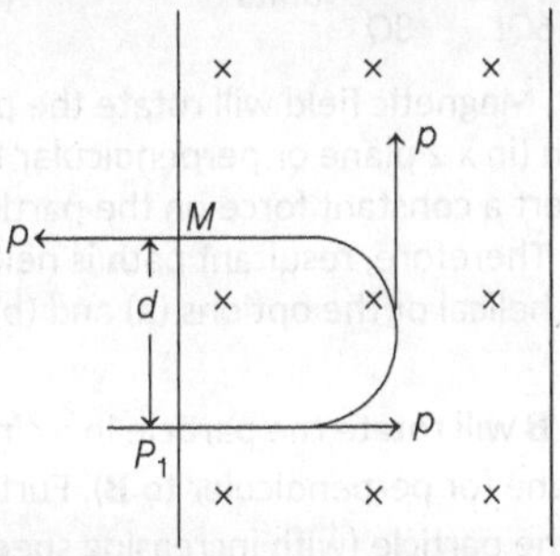

$|\Delta \mathbf{P}|$ = magnitude of change in momentum between points P_1 and $M = 2p$

(b) $r(1-\cos\theta) = R$

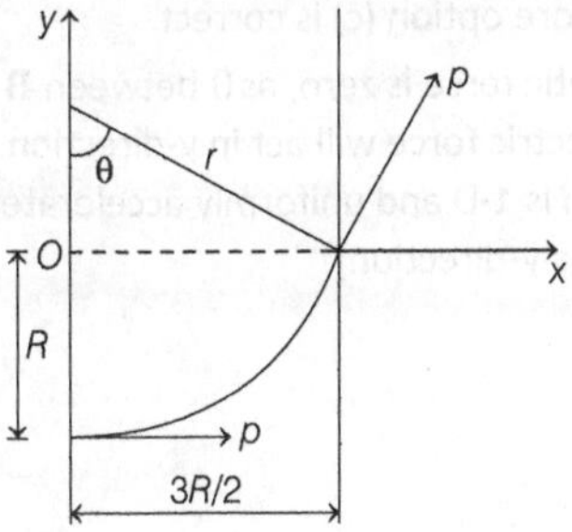

$$r\sin\theta = \frac{3R}{2}$$

$$\Rightarrow \quad \frac{\sin\theta}{1-\cos\theta} = \frac{3}{2}$$

$$\frac{2\sin\frac{\theta}{2}\cos\frac{\theta}{2}}{2\sin^2\frac{\theta}{2}} = \frac{3}{2}$$

$$\Rightarrow \quad \cot\frac{\theta}{2} = \frac{3}{2}$$

$$\Rightarrow \quad \tan\frac{\theta}{2} = \frac{2}{3} \Rightarrow \tan\theta = \frac{2\left(\frac{2}{3}\right)}{1-\frac{4}{9}} = \frac{\frac{4}{3}}{\frac{5}{9}} = \frac{12}{5}$$

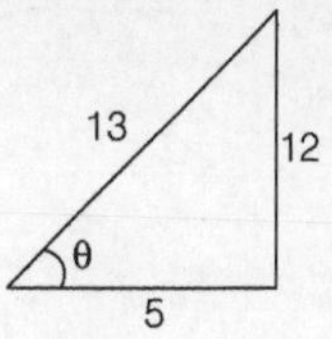

$$\sin\theta = 12/13$$

$$r\left(\frac{12}{13}\right) = \frac{3R}{2};\ r = \frac{13R}{8} = \frac{p}{QB};\ B = \frac{8p}{13QR}$$

(c) Particle will re-enter in region-1 if,

$$r < \frac{3R}{2}$$

or

$$\frac{P}{QB} < \frac{3R}{2}$$

$$\Rightarrow \quad B > \frac{2P}{3QR}$$

(d) $r = \dfrac{mv}{QB}$, $d = P_1M = 2r = \dfrac{2mv}{QB} \Rightarrow d \propto m$

3. For a particle to move in negative y-direction, either its velocity must be in negative y-direction (if initial velocity $\neq 0$) and force should be parallel to velocity or it must experience a net force in negative y-direction only (if initial velocity = 0)

4. $\mathbf{F}_{net} = \mathbf{F}_e + \mathbf{F}_B = q\mathbf{E} + q\mathbf{v} \times \mathbf{B}$

For particle to move in straight line with constant velocity,

$$\mathbf{F}_{net} = 0$$

$$\therefore \quad q\mathbf{E} + q\mathbf{v} \times \mathbf{B} = 0$$

or

$$\mathbf{E} = \mathbf{B} \times \mathbf{v}$$

5. For path to be helical with axis along positive z-direction, particle should experience a centripetal acceleration in xy-plane.

For the given set of options, only option (c) satisfy the condition. Path is helical with increasing pitch.

6. $F_B = Bev = Be\dfrac{I}{nAe} = \dfrac{BI}{nA}$ (v = drift velocity)

$$F_e = eE \Rightarrow F_e = F_B$$

$$eE = \frac{BI}{nA}$$

$$\Rightarrow \quad E = \frac{BI}{nAe}$$

$$V = Ew = \frac{BI}{nAe} \cdot w$$

$$= \frac{BIw}{n(wd)e} = \frac{BI}{ned}$$

or $$V \propto \frac{1}{d} \Rightarrow \frac{V_1}{V_2} = \frac{d_2}{d_1}$$

$\Rightarrow$ if $w_1 = 2w_2$ and $d_1 = d_2$

$$V_1 = V_2$$

7. $$V = \frac{BI}{ned}$$

$$\Rightarrow \quad \frac{V_1}{V_2} = \frac{B_1}{B_2} \times \frac{n_2}{n_1}$$

If $B_1 = B_2$ and $n_1 = 2n_2$, then $V_2 = 2\,V_1$

If $B_1 = 2B_2$ and $n_1 = n_2$, then $V_2 = 0.5\,V_1$

8. $$B_2 = \frac{\mu_0 I}{2\pi x_1} + \frac{\mu_0 I}{2\pi (x_0 - x_1)}$$

(when currents are in opposite directions)

$$B_1 = \frac{\mu_0 I}{2\pi x_1} - \frac{\mu_0 I}{2\pi (x_0 - x_1)}$$

(when currents are in same direction)

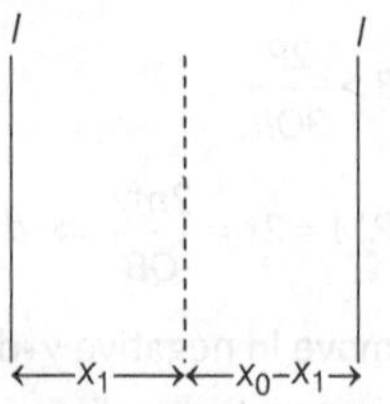

Substituting $x_1 = \frac{x_0}{3}$ (as $\frac{x_0}{x_1} = 3$)

$$B_1 = \frac{3\mu_0 I}{2\pi x_0} - \frac{3\mu_0 I}{4\pi x_0} = \frac{3\mu_0 I}{4\pi x_0}$$

$$R_1 = \frac{mv}{qB_1} \text{ and } B_2 = \frac{9\,\mu_0 I}{4\pi x_0}$$

$$R_2 = \frac{mv}{qB_2}$$

$$\Rightarrow \quad \frac{R_1}{R_2} = \frac{B_2}{B_1} = \frac{9}{3} = 3$$

9. $\mathbf{u}_1 = 4\hat{\mathbf{i}}$; $\mathbf{u}_2 = 2(\sqrt{3}\,\hat{\mathbf{i}} + \hat{\mathbf{j}})$

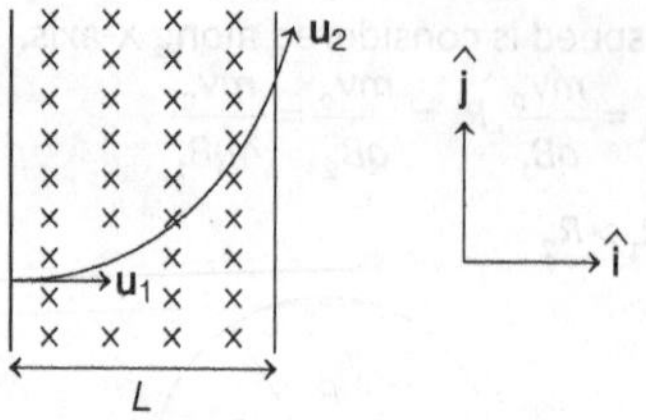

According to the figure, magnetic field should be in ⊗ direction, or along $-z$ direction.

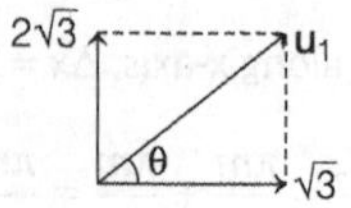

Further, $$\tan\theta = \frac{2}{2\sqrt{3}} = \frac{1}{\sqrt{3}}$$

$\therefore$ $$\theta = 30°$$

$\therefore$ $$\frac{\pi}{6} = \text{angle rotated by the particle} = \omega t = \left(\frac{BQ}{M}\right)t$$

$\therefore$ $$B = \frac{\pi M}{6Qt} = \frac{50\pi M}{3Q} \text{ units} \qquad (\text{as } t = 10^{-3}\text{ s})$$

10. (a) and (b) : Magnetic field will rotate the particle in a circular path (in x-z plane or perpendicular to B). Electric field will exert a constant force on the particle in positive y-direction. Therefore, resultant path is neither purely circular nor helical or the options (a) and (b) both are wrong.

(c) $v_\perp$ and **B** will rotate the particle in a circular path in x - z plane (or perpendicular to **B**). Further $v_{||}$ and **E** will move the particle (with increasing speed) along positive y-axis (or along the axis of above circular path). Therefore, the resultant path is helical with increasing pitch, along the y-axis (or along **B** and **E**). Therefore option (c) is correct.

(d) Magnetic force is zero, as θ between **B** and **v** is zero. But electric force will act in y-direction. Therefore, motion is 1-D and uniformly accelerated (towards positive y-direction).

CHAPTER~03

MAGNETIC FORCE ON CURRENT ELEMENTS

LEVEL 01 Starter Level

3.1 Magnetic Force on a Current Carrying Wire

1 Consider a 10 cm long portion of a straight wire carrying a current of 10 A placed in a magnetic field of 0.1 T making an angle of 37° with the wire. What magnetic force does the wire experience?

2 A thin straight horizontal wire of length 0.2 m whose mass is 10^{-4} kg floats in a magnetic induction field when a current of 10 A is passed through it. To make this possible, what should be the minimum magnetic strength? (Take, $g = 10\ \text{m/s}^2$)

3 A loop of wire has the shape of a right triangle as shown in figure and carries a current of $i = 5.0$ A. A uniform magnetic field is directed parallel to side AB and has a magnitude of 2.0 T.

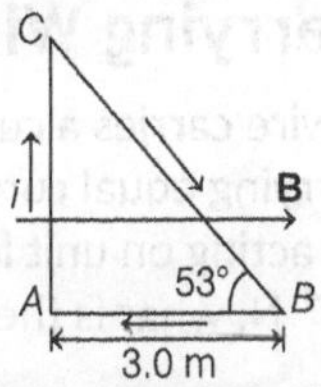

(i) Find the magnitude and direction of the magnetic force exerted on each side of the triangle.

(ii) Determine the magnitude of the net force exerted on the triangle.

4 A straight wire lies along a body diagonal of an imaginary cube of side $a = 20$ cm and carries a current of 5 A as shown in figure. Find the force on it due to a uniform magnetic field $\mathbf{B} = (2.0\ \text{T})\hat{\mathbf{k}}$.

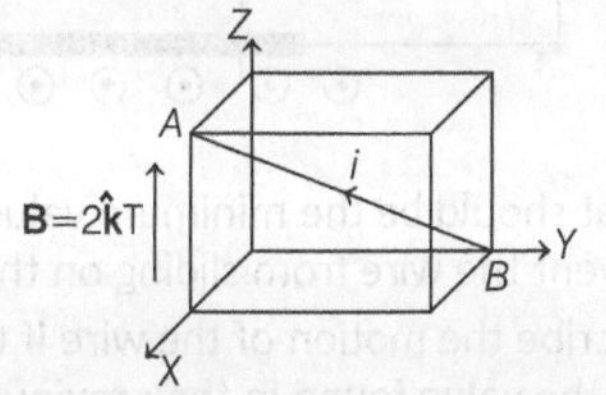

5 A wire of length l carries a current i along the Y-axis. A magnetic field exists which is given as $\mathbf{B} = B_0(\hat{\mathbf{i}} + \hat{\mathbf{j}} + \hat{\mathbf{k}})$ T. Find the magnitude of the magnetic force acting on the wire.

6 In the figure shown a semicircular wire is placed in a uniform $\mathbf{B}$ directed toward right. Find the resultant magnetic force and torque on it about point C.

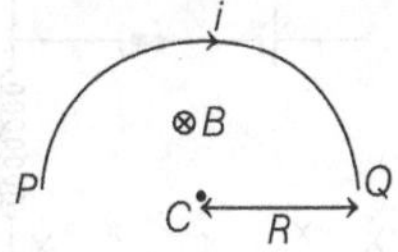

7 Calculate the force on a current carrying wire AB in a uniform magnetic field as shown in figure.

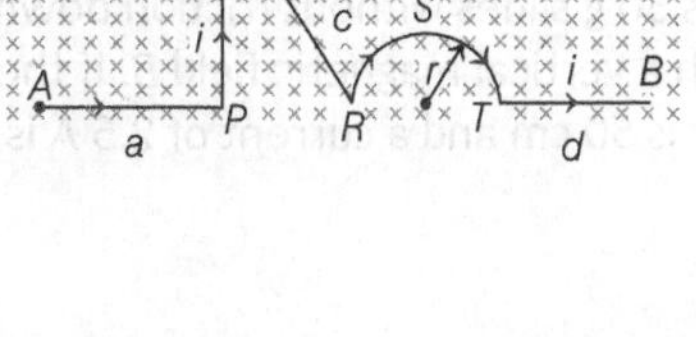

8 Find the magnetic force on the L-shaped wire AB carrying current i_2 due to the long wire carrying current i_1.

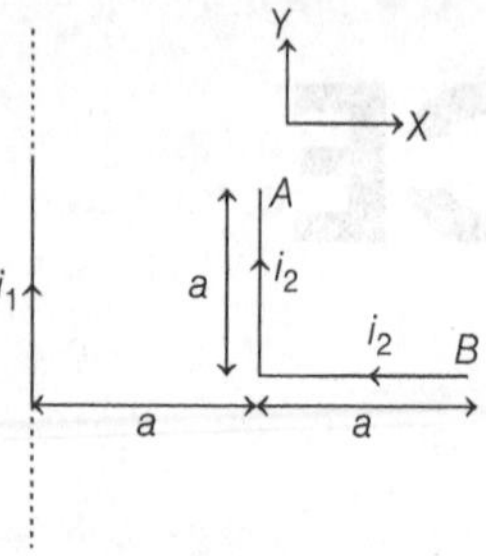

9 Figure shows two long metal rails placed horizontally and parallel to each other at a separation l. A uniform magnetic field B exists in the vertically upward direction.

A wire of mass m can slide on the rails. The rails are connected to a constant current source which drives a current i in the circuit. The friction coefficient between the rails and the wire is μ.

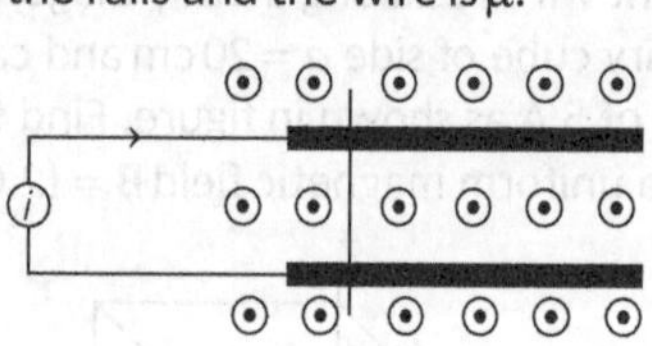

(i) What should be the minimum value of μ which can prevent the wire from sliding on the rails?

(ii) Describe the motion of the wire if the value of μ is half the value found in the previous part.

10 A metal rod of mass 10 g and length 25 cm is suspended on two springs as shown in figure. The springs are extended by 4 cm. When a 20 A current passes through the rod, it rises by 1 cm. Determine the magnetic field assuming acceleration due to gravity to be 10 m/s^2

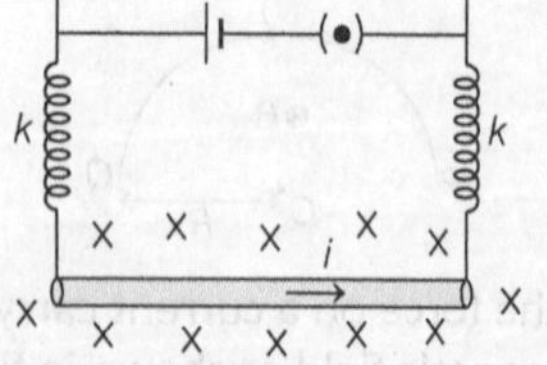

11 Two conducting rails are connected to a source of e.m.f. and form an incline as shown in figure. A bar of mass 50 g slides without friction down the incline through a vertical magnetic field B. If the length of the bar is 50 cm and a current of 2.5 A is provided by the battery, for what value of B will the bar slide at a constant velocity? (Take, $g = 10$ m/s^2)

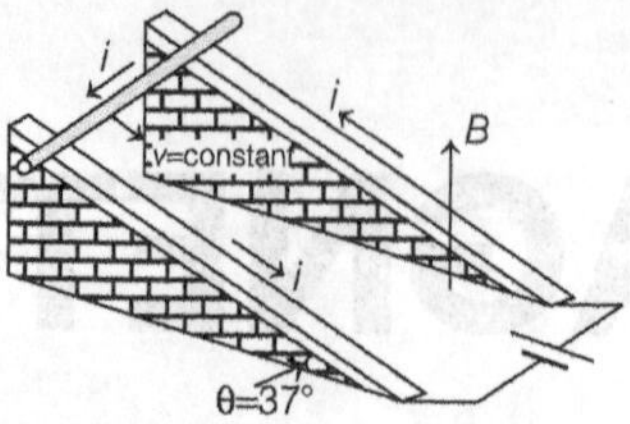

12 A circular loop of radius R, carrying a current i, is placed in a two-dimensional magnetic field. The centre of the loop coincides with the centre of the field as shown in figure. The strength of the magnetic field at the periphery of the loop is B. Find the magnetic force on the loop.

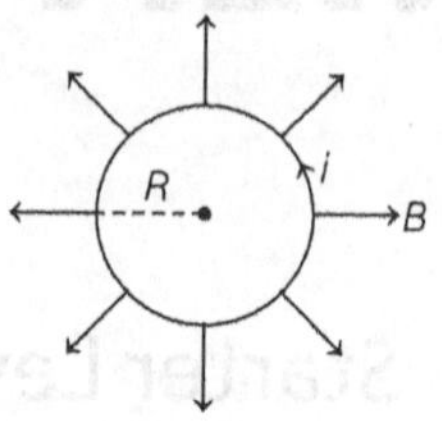

13 Figure shows a circular wire-loop of radius R, carrying a current i, placed in a perpendicular magnetic field B. (i) Consider a small part dl of the wire. Find the force on this part of wire exerted by the magnetic field in the radially outward direction. (ii) Find tension in the wire.

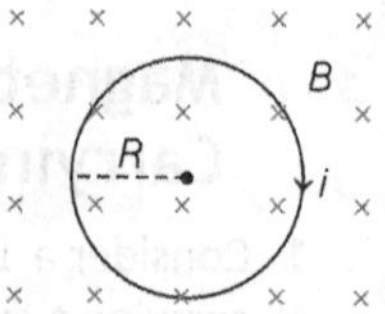

14 A hypothetical magnetic field existing in a region is given by $\mathbf{B} = B_0 \mathbf{e}_r$, where $\mathbf{e}_r$ denotes the unit vector along the radial direction of a point relative to the origin and B_0 = constant. A circular loop of radius a, carrying a current i, is placed with its plane parallel to the XY-plane and the centre at $(0, 0, a)$. Find the magnitude of the magnetic force acting on the loop.

3.2 Magnetic Force between Parallel Current Carrying Wires

1 A straight, long wire carries a current of 20 A. Another wire carrying equal current is placed parallel to it. If the force acting on unit length of the second wire is 2.0×10^{-4} N, what is the separation between them?

2 Two parallel wires separated by a distance of 10 cm carry currents of 20 A and 80 A along the same direction. Where should a third current carrying wire be placed so that it experiences no magnetic force?

3 Two long straight parallel conductors are separated by a distance of $r_1 = 5$ cm and carry constant currents $i_1 = 10$ A and $i_2 = 20$ A. What work per unit length of a conductor must be done to increase the separation between the conductors to $r_2 = 10$ cm, if currents flow in the same direction?

4 In the figure shown the wires *AB* and *PQ* carry constant currents i_1 and i_2 respectively. *PQ* is of uniform wire of mass *m* and length *l*. *AB* and *PQ* are both horizontal and kept in same vertical plane. The *PQ* is in equilibrium at height *h*. Find

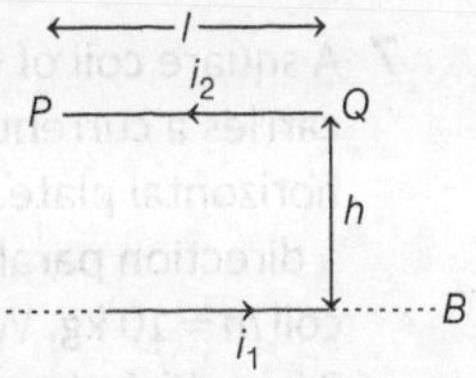

(i) *h* in terms of $i_1 i_2$, *l*, *m*, *g* and other standard constants.

(ii) If the wire *PQ* is displaced vertically by small distance, find time period of small oscillations.

3.3 Magnetic Dipole Moment

1 In a hydrogen atom the electron moves in an orbit of radius 0.5 Å making 10^{16} rev/s. What is the magnetic moment associated with the orbital motion of the electron ?

2 A charge *Q* is spread uniformly over an insulated disc of radius *R*. What is the magnetic moment of the disc if it is rotated with an angular velocity ω about its axis?

3 A circular loop of radius *R* is bent about its diameter along two mutually perpendicular planes as shown in figure. If the loop carries a current *i*, then determine its magnetic dipole moment.

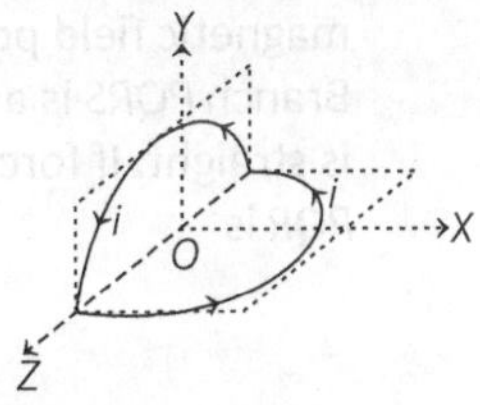

4 A conductor carries a constant current *i* along the closed path *abcdefgha* involving 8 of the 12 edges of length *l*. Find the magnetic dipole moment of the closed path.

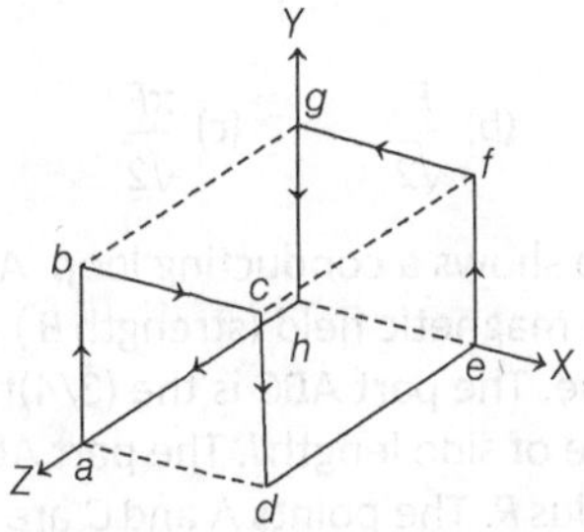

5 The wire loop *PQRSP* formed by joining two semicircular wires of radii R_1 and R_2 carries a current *i* as shown in figure. What is the magnetic moment of the loop in cases (i) and (ii)?

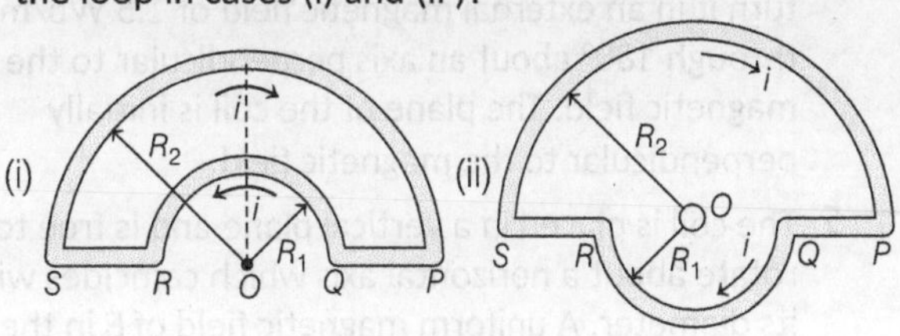

6 Find the magnetic moment of the current carrying coil *OABCO* of 100 turns as shown in figure. Given that, $i = 4.0$ A, $OA = 20$ cm and $AB = 10$ cm.

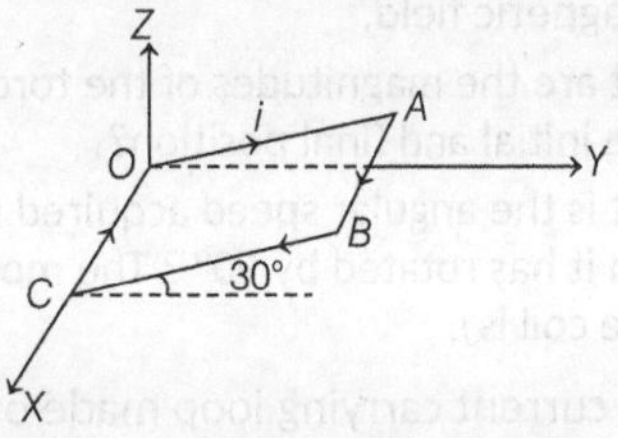

3.4 Magnetic Force and Torque on a Current Carrying Loop

1 A 50 turn circular coil of radius 4 cm carrying a current of 2.5 A is rotated in a magnetic field of strength 0.20 T.

(i) What is the maximum torque that acts on the coil?

(ii) In a particular position of the coil, the torque acting on it is half of this maximum. What is the angle between the magnetic field and the plane of the coil?

2 A closely wound solenoid of 2000 turns and area of cross-section 1.6×10^{-4} m^2, carrying a current of 4.0 A, is suspended through its centre allowing it to turn in a horizontal plane.

(i) What is the magnetic moment associated with the solenoid?

(ii) What is the force and torque on the solenoid if a uniform horizontal magnetic field of 7.5×10^{-2} T is set up at an angle of 30° with the axis of the solenoid?

3 Figure shows one quarter of a simple circular loop of wire that carries a current of 14 A. Its radius is $a = 5$ cm. A uniform magnetic field, $B = 300$ G, is directed in the + *X*-direction. Find the torque on the entire loop and the direction in which it will rotate.

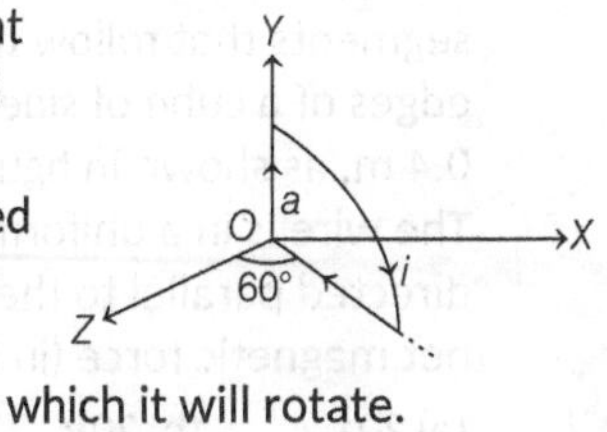

4 A circular coil of 100 turns has an effective radius 0.05 m and carries a current of 0.1 A (assume current remains constant). How much work is required to turn it in an external magnetic field of 1.5 Wb/m^2 through 180° about an axis perpendicular to the magnetic field. The plane of the coil is initially perpendicular to the magnetic field.

5 The coil is placed in a vertical plane and is free to rotate about a horizontal axis which coincides with its diameter. A uniform magnetic field of B in the horizontal direction exists such that initially the axis of the coil is in the direction of the field. The coil rotates through an angle of 90° under the influence of the magnetic field.

(i) What are the magnitudes of the torques on the coil in the initial and final position?

(ii) What is the angular speed acquired by the coil when it has rotated by 90° ? The moment of inertia of the coil is I.

6 A square current carrying loop made of thin wire and having a mass $m = 10$ g can rotate without friction with respect to the vertical axis OO_1, passing through the centre of the loop at right angles to two opposite sides of the loop. The loop is placed in a homogeneous magnetic field with an induction $B = 10^{-1}$ T directed at right angles to the plane of the drawing. A current $i = 2$ A is flowing in the loop. Find the period of small oscillations that the loop performs about its position of stable equilibrium.

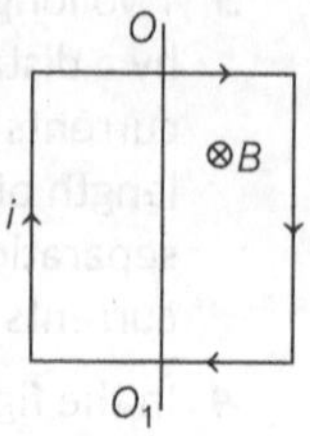

7 A square coil of edge $l = 1$ m having $n = 10$ turns carries a current $i = 1$ A. It is kept on a smooth horizontal plate. A uniform magnetic field B exists in a direction parallel to an edge. The total mass of the coil $m = 10$ kg. What should be the minimum value of B for which the coil will start tipping over?

8 A square cardboard of side l and mass m is suspended from a horizontal axis XY as shown in figure. A single wire is wound along the periphery of board and carrying a clockwise current i. At $t = 0$, a vertical downward magnetic field of induction B is switched ON. Find the minimum value of B so that the board will be able to rotate up to horizontal level.

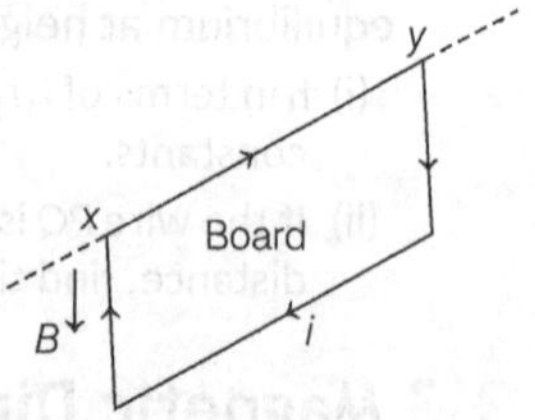

LEVEL 02 JEE Main Level

Single Choice Correct Questions

1 A conducting wire bent in the form of a parabola $y^2 = 2x$ carries a current $i = 2$ A as shown in figure. This wire is placed in a uniform magnetic field $\mathbf{B} = -4\hat{k}$ T. The magnetic force on the wire is (in N)

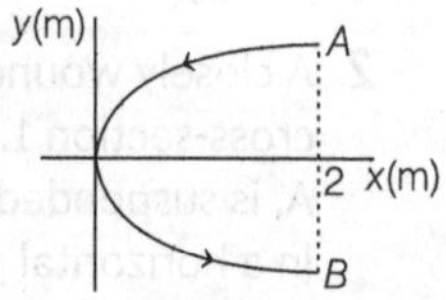

(a) $-16\hat{i}$ (b) $32\hat{i}$ (c) $-32\hat{i}$ (d) $16\hat{i}$

2 A long wire carries current of 25 A parallel to the positive X-axis, except for three of the four segments that follow the edges of a cube of side 0.4 m, as shown in figure. The wire is in a uniform magnetic field of 2.0 T directed parallel to the positive X-axis. What is the net magnetic force (in N) on the wire ?

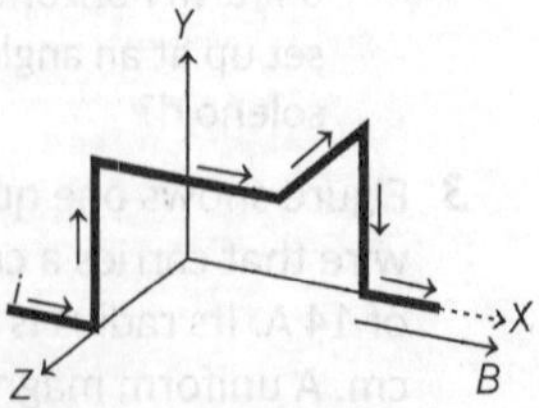

(a) $20\hat{j}$ (b) $20\hat{k}$ (c) $20(\hat{j} - \hat{k})$ (d) $-20\hat{j}$

3 A current carrying loop is placed in a uniform magnetic field pointing in negative z-direction. Branch $PQRS$ is a three quarter circle, while branch PS is straight. If force on branch PS is F, force on branch PQR is

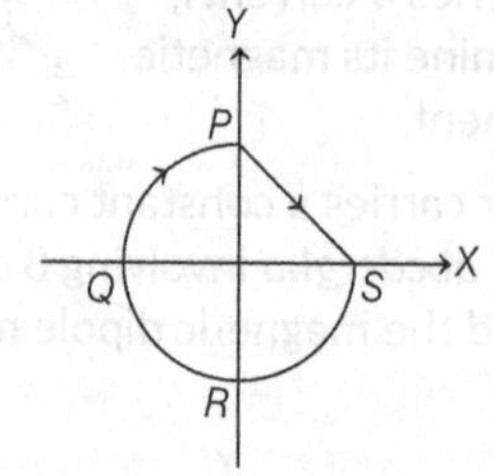

(a) $\sqrt{2}F$ (b) $\frac{F}{\sqrt{2}}$ (c) $\frac{\pi F}{\sqrt{2}}$ (d) $\sqrt{2}\pi F$

4 The figure shows a conducting loop $ABCDA$ placed in a uniform magnetic field (strength B) perpendicular to its plane. The part ABC is the (3/4)th portion of the square of side length l. The part ADC is a circular arc of radius R. The points A and C are connected to a battery which supply a current i to the circuit. The magnetic force on the loop due to the field B is

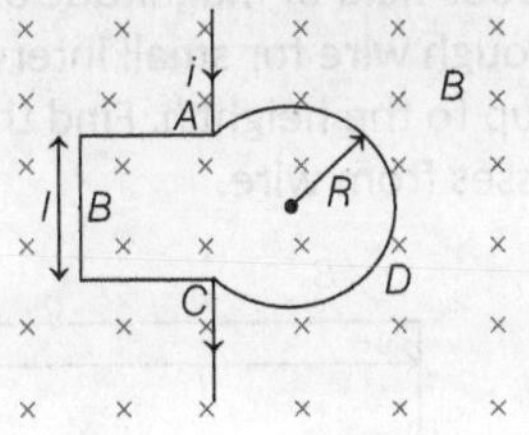

(a) zero (b) Bil (c) $2BiR$ (d) $\frac{BilR}{l+R}$

5 A square loop $ABCD$ carrying a current i_1 is placed near and coplanar with a long straight conductor XY carrying a current i_2, the net force on the loop will be

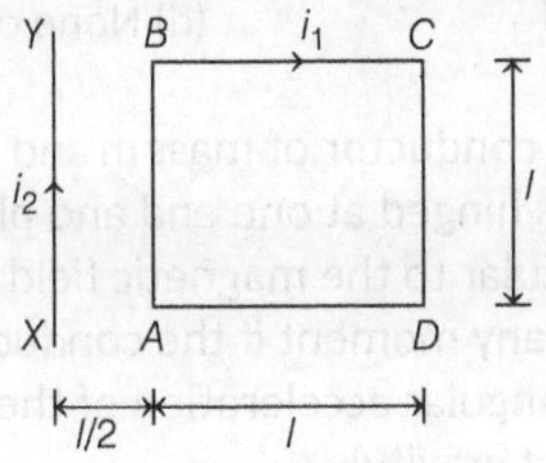

(a) $\frac{2\mu_0 i_1 i_2}{3\pi}$ (b) $\frac{\mu_0 i_1 i_2}{3\pi}$ (c) $\frac{2\mu_0 i_1 i_2 l}{3\pi}$ (d) $\frac{\mu_0 i_1 i_2 l}{2\pi}$

6 Loop $ABCD$ and long straight wire are in the same plane. Side $CD = 2AB$. Distance between long straight wire and AB is equal to distance BE. Net force on the loop is

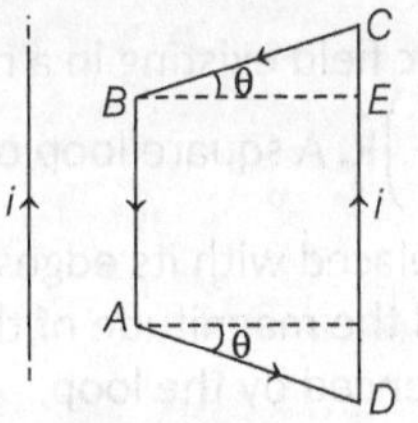

(a) towards the long straight wire
(b) away from the long straight wire
(c) parallel to the long straight wire
(d) net force on the loop will be zero

7 A uniform magnetic field $\mathbf{B} = (3\hat{\mathbf{i}} + 4\hat{\mathbf{j}} + \hat{\mathbf{k}})$ T exists in region of space. A semi-circular wire of radius 1 m carrying current 1 A having its centre at (2, 2, 0) is placed in XY-plane as shown in figure. The force on semicircular wire will be

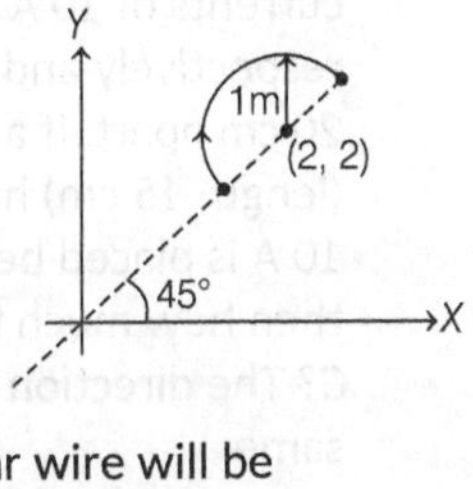

(a) $\sqrt{2}(\hat{\mathbf{i}} + \hat{\mathbf{j}} + \hat{\mathbf{k}})$ N (b) $\sqrt{2}(\hat{\mathbf{i}} - \hat{\mathbf{j}} + \hat{\mathbf{k}})$ N
(c) $\sqrt{2}(\hat{\mathbf{i}} + \hat{\mathbf{j}} - \hat{\mathbf{k}})$ N (d) $\sqrt{2}(-\hat{\mathbf{i}} + \hat{\mathbf{j}} + \hat{\mathbf{k}})$ N

8 The magnetic force between wires as shown in figure is

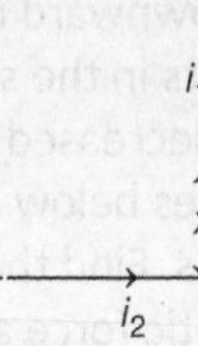

(a) $\frac{\mu_0 i_1 i_2}{2\pi}\ln\left(\frac{x+l}{2x}\right)$ (b) $\frac{\mu_0 i_1 i_2}{2\pi}\ln\left(\frac{2x+l}{2x}\right)$

(c) $\frac{\mu_0 i_1 i_2}{2\pi}\ln\left(\frac{x+l}{x}\right)$ (d) None of these

9 A uniform conducting wire ABC where angle between AB and BC is 37° has a mass of 10 g. The wire AB is parallel to Y-axis. A current of 2 A flows through it. The wire is kept in a uniform magnetic field $B = 2$ T (inwards). The acceleration of wire will be (assume no other force). Angle between AB and BC is 37° with AB along Y-axis.

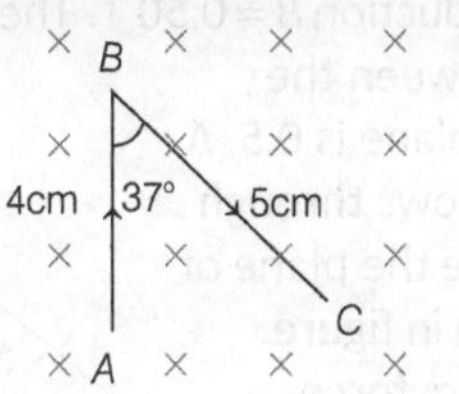

(a) zero
(b) 12 m/s^2 along y-direction
(c) 36 m/s^2 along x-direction
(d) 36 m/s^2 along y-direction

10 A straight rod of mass m and length l is suspended from the identical springs as shown in the figure. The springs are stretched by a distance of x_0 due to the weight of the wire. The circuit has total resistance R. When the magnetic field perpendicular to the plane of the paper is switched ON, springs are observed to extend further by the same distance. The magnetic field strength is

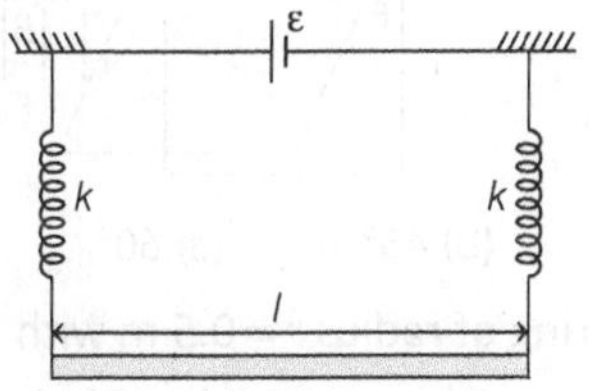

(a) $\frac{mgR}{\varepsilon l}$ ⊙ (b) $\frac{mgR}{2\varepsilon x_0}$ ⊙

(c) $\frac{mgR}{\varepsilon l}$ ⊗ (d) $\frac{mgR}{\varepsilon x_0}$ ⊗

11 A metal wire PQ of mass 10 g lies at rest on two horizontal metal rails separated by 4.90 cm as shown in figure. A vertically downward magnetic field of magnitude 0.800 T exists in the space. The resistance of the circuit is slowly decreased and it is found that when the resistance goes below 20.0 Ω, the wire PQ starts sliding on the rails. Find the coefficient of friction. Neglect magnetic force acting on wire PQ due to metal rails (Take, $g = 9.8 \text{ m/s}^2$)

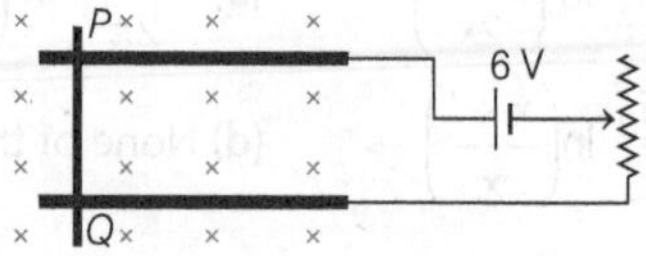

(a) 0.12 (b) 0.25
(c) 0.4 (d) 0.5

12 The figure shows a conductor of weight 5 N and length $l = 0.5$ m placed on a rough inclined plane making an angle 30° with the horizontal so that conductor is perpendicular to a uniform horizontal magnetic field of induction $B = 0.50$ T. The coefficient of static friction between the conductor and the plane is 0.5. A current of $i = 20$ A flows through the conductor inside the plane of this paper as shown in figure. What is the minimum force needed to be the applied parallel to the inclined plane to keep the conductor at rest?

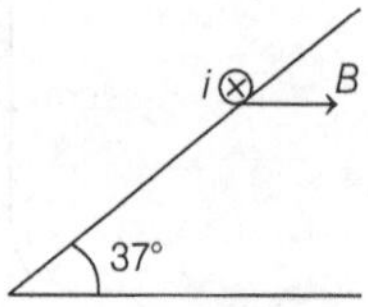

(a) 2 N (b) 3 N (c) 4 N (d) 5 N

13 As shown in figure, three sided frame is pivoted at P and Q and hangs vertically. Its sides are of same length and have a linear density of $\sqrt{3}$ kg/m. A current of $10\sqrt{3}$ A is sent through the frame, which is in a uniform magnetic field of 2 T directed upwards as shown in figure. Angle through which the frame will be deflected in equilibrium is

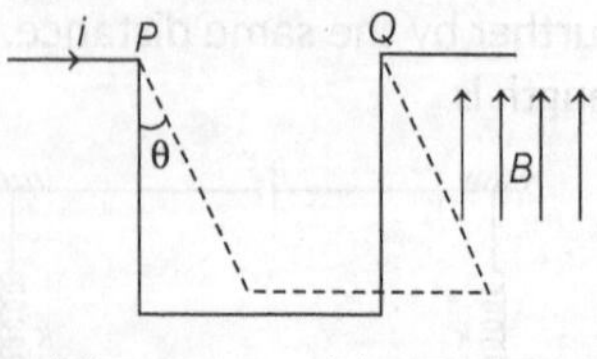

(a) 30° (b) 45° (c) 60° (d) 90°

14 A metal ring of radius $r = 0.5$ m with its plane normal to a uniform magnetic field B of induction 0.2 T carries a current $i = 100$ A. The tension developed in the ring is

(a) 100 N (b) 50 N (c) 25 N (d) 10 N

15 A U-shaped wire of mass m and length l is immersed with its two ends in mercury. The wire is in a homogeneous field of magnitude B. If a charge, passes through wire for small interval Δt, the wire will jump up to the height h. Find the amount of charge passes from wire.

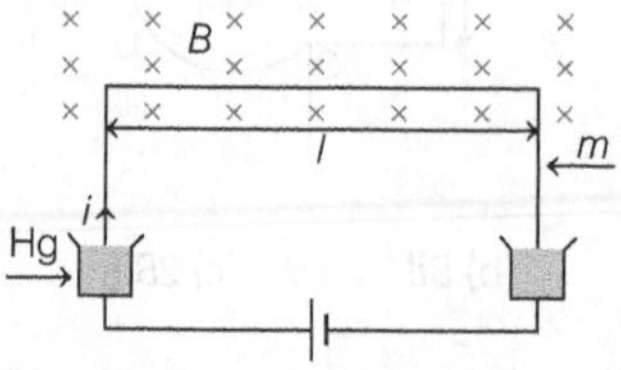

(a) $\dfrac{m\sqrt{2gh}}{Bl}$ (b) $\dfrac{m\sqrt{gh}}{Bl}$

(c) $\dfrac{2m\sqrt{2gh}}{Bl}$ (d) None of these

16 A straight conductor of mass m and carrying a current i is hinged at one end and placed in a plane perpendicular to the magnetic field B as shown in figure. At any moment if the conductor is let free, then the angular acceleration of the conductor will be (neglect gravity)

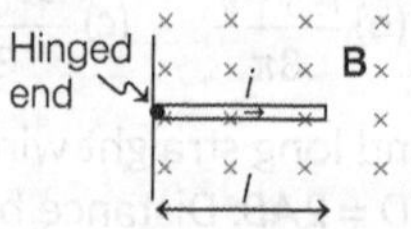

(a) $\dfrac{iB}{2m}$ (b) $\dfrac{2}{3}\dfrac{iB}{m}$ (c) $\dfrac{3iB}{2m}$ (d) $\dfrac{3i}{2mB}$

17 The magnetic field existing in a region is given by $\mathbf{B} = B_0\left(1 + \dfrac{x}{l}\right)\hat{\mathbf{k}}$. A square loop of edge l and carrying current i, is placed with its edges parallel to the XY-axis. Find the magnitude of the net magnetic force experienced by the loop.

(a) $2B_0il$ (b) $\dfrac{B_0il}{2}$ (c) B_0il (d) $4B_0il$

18 In the adjoining figure, two very long, parallel wires A and B carry currents of 10 A and 20 A, respectively and are at a distance 20 cm apart. If a third wire C (length 15 cm) having a current of 10 A is placed between them, then how much force will act on C? The direction of current in all the three wires is same

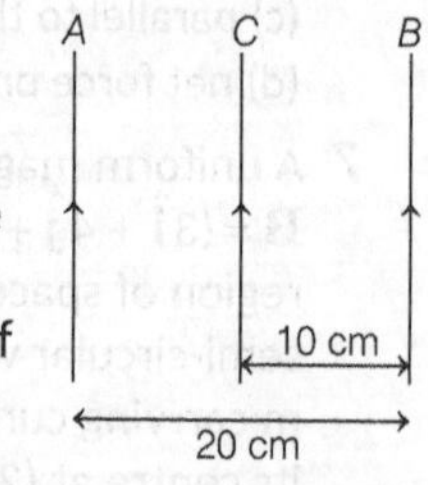

(a) 3×10^{-5} N (left) (b) 3×10^{-5} N (right)
(c) 6×10^{-5} N (left) (d) 6×10^{-5} N (right)

19 Two parallel conductors carrying current in the same direction attract each other, while two parallel beams of electrons moving in the same direction repel each other. Which of the following statements cannot be the reason for this?

(a) The conductors are electrically neutral .

(b) The conductors produce magnetic fields on each other.

(c) The electron beams do not produce magnetic fields on each other.

(d) The magnetic forces caused by the electron beams on each other are weaker than the electrostatic forces between them.

20 Electric charge q is uniformly distributed over a thin rod of length l. The rod is placed parallel to a long wire carrying a current i. The separation between the rod and the wire is a. The force needed to move the rod along its length with a uniform velocity v is

(a) $\frac{\mu_0 iqv}{2\pi a}$ (b) $\frac{\mu_0 iqv}{4\pi a}$ (c) $\frac{\mu_0 iqv}{2\pi l}$ (d) $\frac{\mu_0 iqv}{4\pi l}$

21 Two particles, each of mass m & charge q, are attached to the two ends of a light rigid rod of length $2R$. The rod is rotated at constant angular speed about a perpendicular axis passing through its centre. The ratio of the magnitudes of the magnetic moment of the system and its angular momentum about the centre of the rod is :

(a) $\frac{q}{2m}$ (b) $\frac{q}{m}$ (c) $\frac{2q}{m}$ (d) $\frac{q}{\pi m}$

22 A non-conducting rod AB of length l has a positive linear charge density λ. The rod is rotated about point A with an angular velocity ω in the plane of paper. The magnetic moment of the rod is

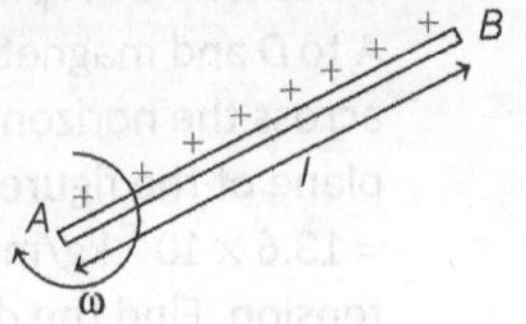

(a) $\frac{\lambda\omega l^3}{2}$ (b) $\frac{2\lambda\omega l^3}{3}$ (c) $\frac{3\lambda\omega l^3}{2}$ (d) $\frac{\lambda\omega l^3}{6}$

23 Find the magnetic dipole moment of the rectangular loop shown in figure. Sides, $a = 3$ m, $b = 2$ m and $c = 4$ m, current in the loop $i = 1$ A.

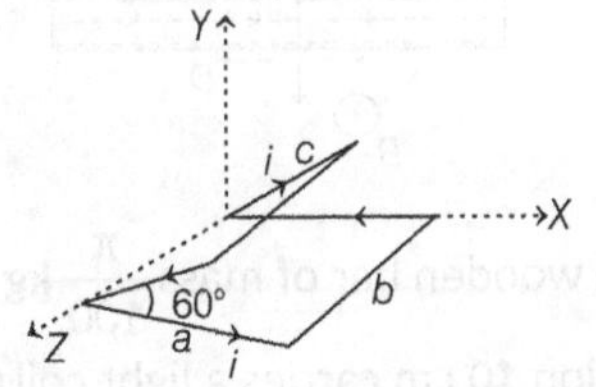

(a) 12.2 A-m^2 (b) 15.8 A-m^2

(c) 13.8 A-m^2 (d) 20.2 A-m^2

24 A rectangular coil PQ has $2n$ turns, an area $2a$ and carries a current $2i$ as shown in figure. The plane of the coil is at 60° to a horizontal uniform magnetic field of flux density B. The torque on the coil due to magnetic force is

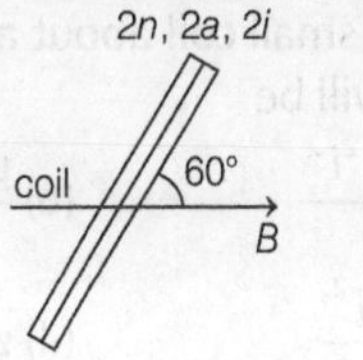

(a) $Bnai \sin 60°$ (b) $8Bnai \cos 60°$

(c) $4nai\, B \sin 60°$ (d) None of these

25 Four wires of equal length are bent in the form of four loops P, Q, R and S. These are suspended in a uniform magnetic field and same current is passed in them. The maximum couple will act on

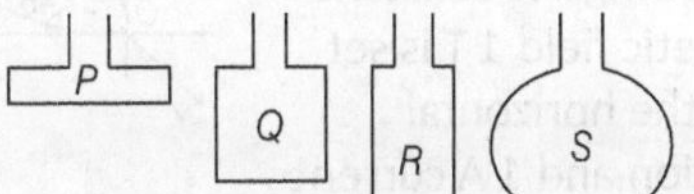

(a) P (b) Q (c) R (d) S

26 The given figure shows a coil bent with $AB = BC = CD = DE = EF = FG = GH = HA = 1$ m and carrying current 1 A. There exists in space a vertical uniform magnetic field of 2 T in the y-direction. Then, find out the torque (in vector form) on the loop.

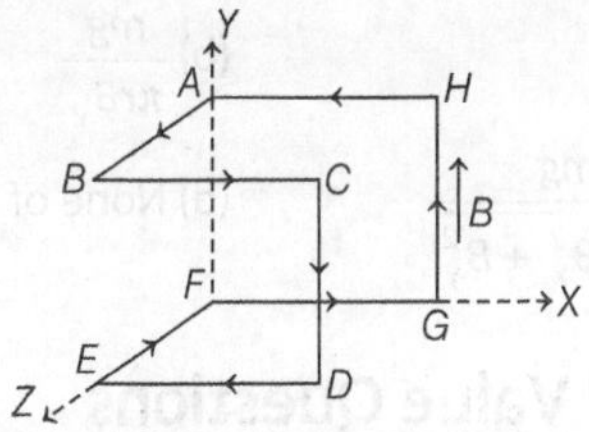

(a) $2\hat{k}$ (b) $-2\hat{k}$ (c) $2\hat{j}$ (d) $-2\hat{j}$

27 A conducting ring of mass 2 kg and radius 0.5 m is placed on a smooth horizontal plane. The ring carries a current $i = 4$ A. A horizontal magnetic field $B = 10$ T is switched ON at time $t = 0$ as shown in figure. The initial angular acceleration of the ring will be

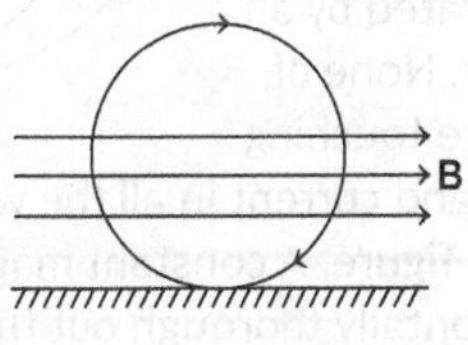

(a) 40π rad/s^2 (b) 20π rad/s^2

(c) 5π rad/s^2 (d) 15π rad/s^2

28 A small circular coil of radius r and number of turns n is placed at the centre of another big circular coil of radius R and number of turns N. Initially the two coils are coplanar and the same current i flows through both the coils. Then, the amount of work done in rotating the small coil about any of its diameter by an angle π will be

(a) $\frac{2\mu_0 \pi n N r^2 i^2}{R}$ (b) $\frac{\mu_0 \pi n N r^2 i^2}{2R}$

(c) $\frac{\mu_0 \pi n N r^2 i^2}{R}$ (d) zero

29 A current carrying circular coil of single turn of mass $\frac{\pi}{10}$ kg and radius 25 cm is hanging by two ideal strings. A constant magnetic field 1 T is set up in the horizontal direction and 1 A current flows through coil as shown in figure. Then, the ratio of tension (T_1/T_2) in the string will be

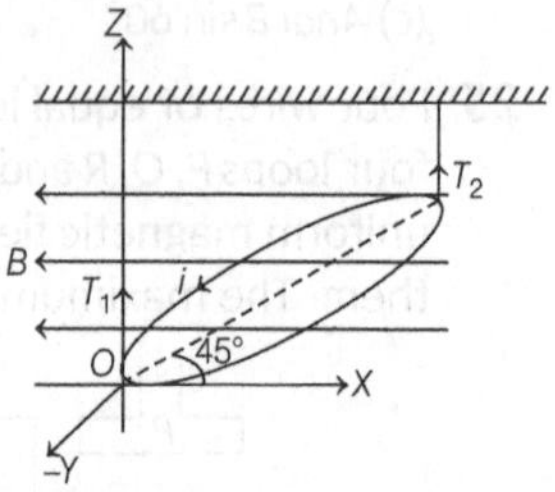

(a) 2 : 1 (b) 5 : 3 (c) 4 : 1 (d) 1 : 2

30 A rigid circular loop of radius r and mass m lies in the XY-plane on a flat table and has a current i flowing in it. At this particular place, the earth's magnetic field is $\mathbf{B} = B_x \hat{\mathbf{i}} + B_y \hat{\mathbf{j}}$. The minimum value of i for which one end of the loop will lift from the table is

(a) $\frac{mg}{\pi r B_x}$ (b) $\frac{mg}{\pi r B_y}$

(c) $\frac{mg}{2\pi r\sqrt{B_x^2 + B_y^2}}$ (d) None of these

Numerical Value Questions

1 Figure shows 12 current carrying wires wound around the sphere of radius 25 cm. Each wire carries the same current 0.5 A and is separated by an angle of 30°. None of the wires are touching each other and current in all the wires is moving up as shown in figure. A constant magnetic field 2 T exists horizontally thorough out the region of space. Find the net force (in N) on the wires.

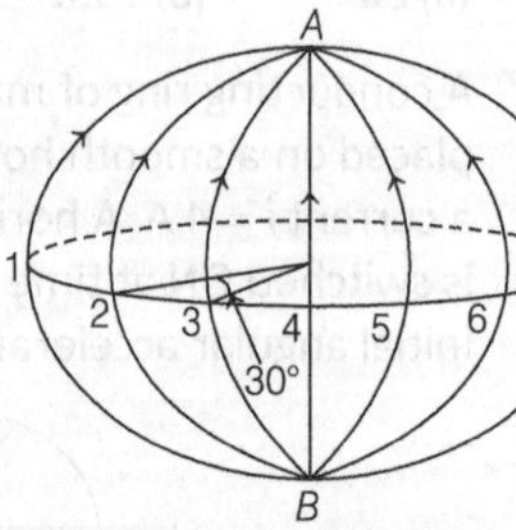

2 A long straight conductor carries current i_1. A wire PQ carrying current i_2 is placed as shown. The net force on PQ is $\frac{\mu_0 i_1 i_2}{2\pi}$ ln x, then write the value of x.

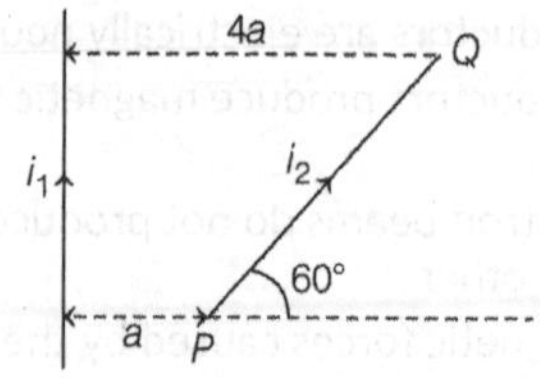

3 A superconducting current carrying ring of mass $m = 40$ g and $R = \frac{2}{\pi}$ cm floats in the magnetic field of a magnet. If the field lines make an angle $\theta = 30°$ with vertical and the ring is placed co-axially, assuming $i = 10$ A, find the magnetic field B (in T).

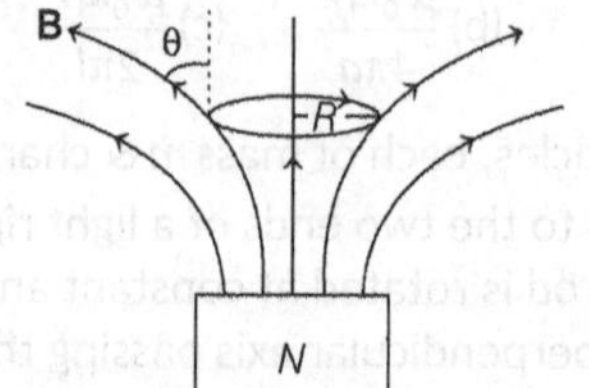

4 Mercury is contained in U-tube of uniform square cross-section of side $a = 4$ mm. Electrodes A and D are sealed inside as shown in figure. An electric current $I = 10$ A passes between the electrodes from A to D and magnetic field $B = 5.44$ Wb/m^2 is applied across the horizontal arm perpendicular into the plane of the figure. Here density of mercury $= 13.6 \times 10^3$ kg/m^3, $g = 10$ m/s^2, nelgect surface tension. Find the difference (in cm) in mercury level in limbs of U-tube.

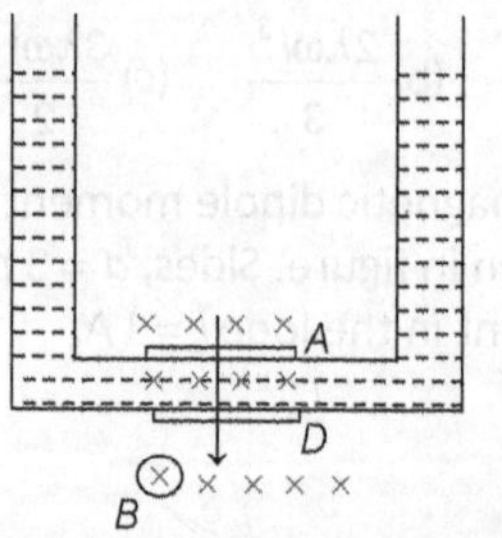

5 A uniform wooden bar of mass $\frac{\pi}{100}$ kg and radius of cross-section 10 cm carries a light coil C of 100 turns. The bar is smoothly pivoted at P. If the coil carries a current 2 A and subjected to an external magnetic

field 10^{-2} T, the bar remains in equilibrium. Find the distance x (in cm) of the centre of mass of the rod from the pivot.

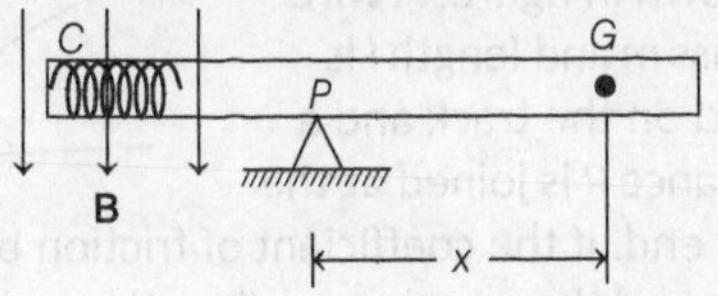

6 A wire carrying 3 A current is wrapped around a non-conducting cube of side 1 m as shown in figure. Find the magnitude of net magnetic moment (in A-m^2) due to the loop.

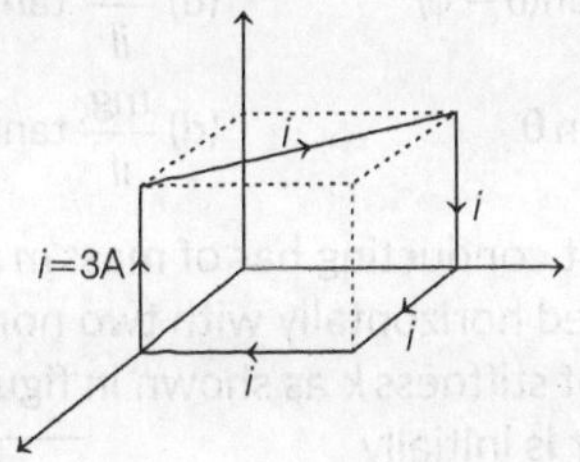

7 A closed loop carrying a current i is placed so that its plane is perpendicular to the long straight conductor which carries a current i_0 as shown in figure. The torque acting on the current loop is $n \times 10^{-7}$ N-m.

Then, find the value of n. (Given, $i = 2$ A, $i_0 = 1$ A, $r_0 = 2$ m, $\phi = 60°$)

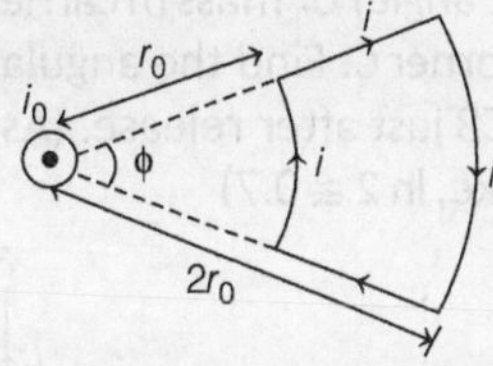

8 A current carrying uniform square frame is suspended from hinged supports as shown in figure such that it can freely rotate about its upper side. The length and mass of each side of the frame is 2 m and 4 kg, respectively. A uniform magnetic field $\mathbf{B} = (3\hat{\mathbf{i}} + 4\hat{\mathbf{j}})$ is applied. When the wire frame is rotated to 45° from vertical and released it remains in equilibrium. Find the magnitude of current (in A) in the wire frame.

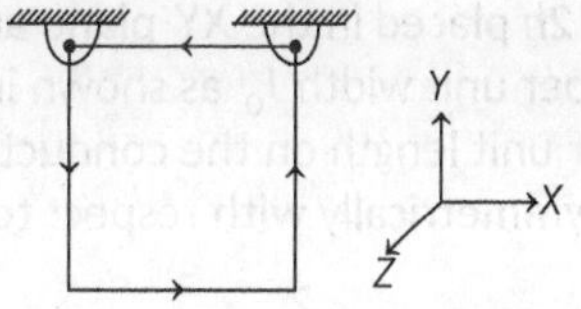

LEVEL 03 JEE Advanced Level

Single Choice Correct Questions

1 Shown in figure is a very long semicylindrical conducting shell of radius R and carrying a current i along its length. An infinitely long straight current carrying conductor is lying along the axis of the semicylinder. If the current flowing through the straight wire is i_0, then find the force per unit length on the semicylinder.

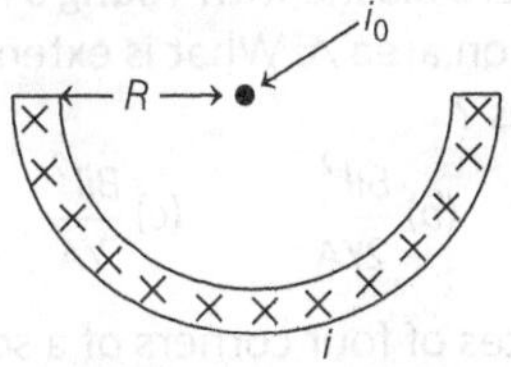

(a) $\dfrac{\mu_0 i_0 i}{\pi R}$ (b) $\dfrac{\mu_0 i_0 i}{2\pi r R}$ (c) $\dfrac{\mu_0 i_0 i}{\pi^2 R}$ (d) $\dfrac{\mu_0 i_0 i}{2\pi^2 R}$

2 A semicircular wire of radius R, carrying current i, is placed in a magnetic field as shown in figure. On left side of $X'X$, magnetic field strength is B and on right side $X'X$, magnetic field strength is $2B$. Both fields are directed inside the page. The magnetic force experienced by the wire would be

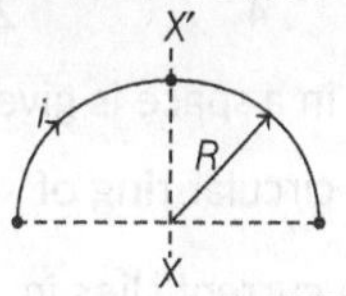

(a) $3BiR$ (b) $2BiR$ (c) $\sqrt{10}\,BiR$ (d) $\sqrt{5}\,BiR$

3 An infinitely long straight wire carries a current i_1, as shown in figure. Find the total force on another wire CD of length $2l$ which is placed so that C is at a distance l from the current carrying wire.

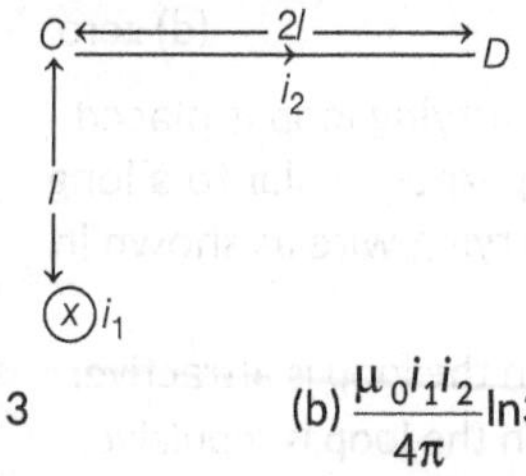

(a) $\dfrac{\mu_0 i_1 i_2}{2\pi} \ln 3$ (b) $\dfrac{\mu_0 i_1 i_2}{4\pi} \ln 3$

(c) $\dfrac{\mu_0 i_1 i_2}{2\pi} \ln 5$ (d) $\dfrac{\mu_0 i_1 i_2}{4\pi} \ln 5$

4 In the figure shown an infinitely long wire carries a current i_1 and another uniform rigid wire ACB (bent at C at right angle) of mass m carries a current i_2, it is hinged at corner C. Find the angular acceleration of this wire ACB just after release. (Assume gravity is absent) (Take, $\ln 2 \cong 0.7$)

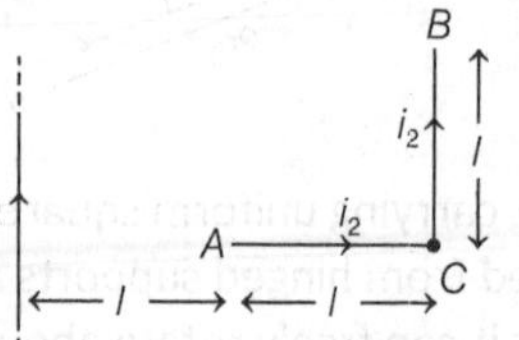

(a) $\dfrac{3\mu_0 i_1 i_2}{20\pi ml}$ (b) $\dfrac{3\mu_0 i_1 i_2}{40\pi ml}$

(c) $\dfrac{9\mu_0 i_1 i_2}{20\pi ml}$ (d) $\dfrac{9\mu_0 i_1 i_2}{40\pi ml}$

5 A conductor placed along the line $z = h$ carrying a current i is placed parallel to a very long current strip of width $2h$ placed in the XY-plane and carrying a current per unit width J_0 as shown in figure. Find the force per unit length on the conductor. The sheet is placed symmetrically with respect to Y-axis.

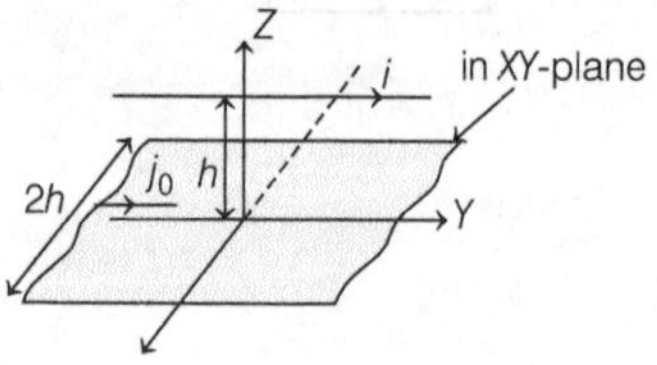

(a) $\dfrac{\mu_0 i J_0}{2}$ (b) $\dfrac{\mu_0 i J_0}{4}$ (c) $\dfrac{\mu_0 i J_0}{2\pi}$ (d) $\dfrac{\mu_0 i J_0}{4\pi}$

6 Magnetic field in a space is given as $\mathbf{B} = \dfrac{B_0 x}{R}\hat{\mathbf{k}}$. A circular ring of radius R having current i lies in the space with centre at origin as shown in the figure. Find the magnitude of net magnetic force acting on the circular ring due to the magnetic field.

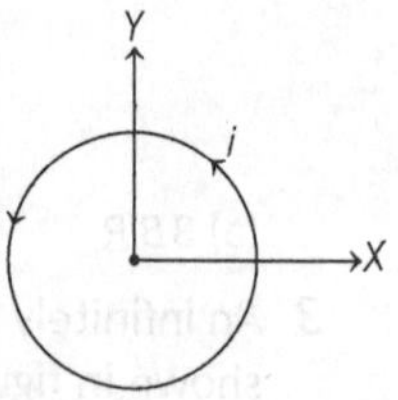

(a) $2iB_0R$ (b) πiB_0R

(c) $2\pi iB_0R$ (d) zero

7 A current carrying loop is placed in a plane perpendicular to a long current carrying wire as shown in figure.

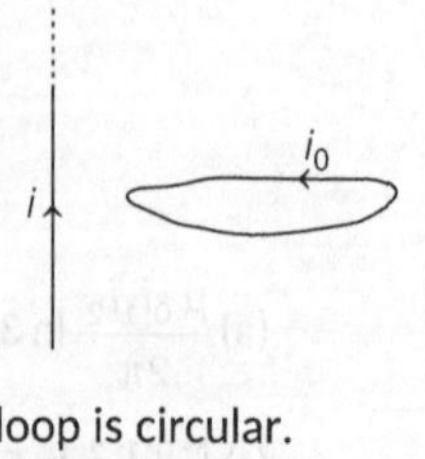

(a) Force on the loop is attractive.

(b) Force on the loop is repulsive.

(c) Force on the loop is zero, only if loop is circular.

(d) Force on the loop is zero, for any shape of loop.

8 Two conducting parallel rail tracks are inclined at an angle θ with the horizontal as shown in figure. A wire of mass m and length l is placed on the track and a resistance R is joined at the other end. If the coefficient of friction between the tracks and the wire is $\tan\phi$ (less than $\tan\theta$), then the minimum magnitude of magnetic field applied vertically so that the wire remains stationary is (the wire carries a current i)

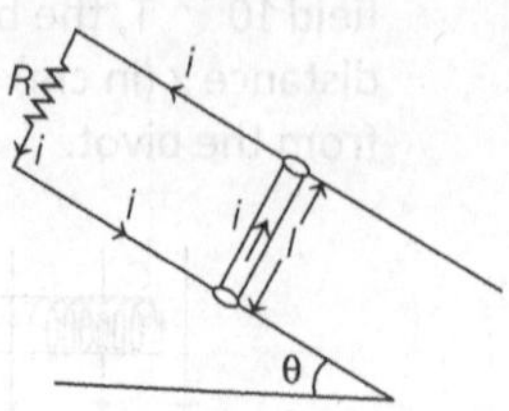

(a) $\dfrac{mg}{il}\tan(\theta - \phi)$ (b) $\dfrac{mg}{il}\tan(\theta + \phi)$

(c) $\dfrac{mg}{il}\sin\theta$ (d) $\dfrac{mg}{il}\tan\theta$

9 A straight conducting bar of mass m and length l is suspended horizontally with two non-conducting springs of stiffness k as shown in figure. The capacitor is initially charged to the potential difference U. At time $t = 0$, the switch S is closed and the capacitor discharges. The bar starts oscillating in vertical plane. Find the amplitude of these oscillations (assume the time of discharge of capacitor is much smaller than the period T of the mechanical oscillation of the bar)

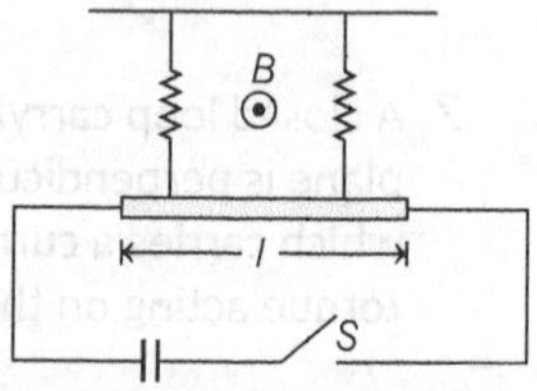

(a) $\dfrac{BlCU}{\sqrt{2km}}$ (b) $\dfrac{BlCU}{\sqrt{km}}$

(c) $\dfrac{BlCU}{\sqrt{8km}}$ (d) $\dfrac{BlCU}{4\sqrt{km}}$

10 A square wire frame of side l carries current i. It is kept inside a uniform magnetic field B perpendicular to its plane. Two of opposite sides are rigid and other two sides are elastic with Young's modulus Y, cross-section area A. What is extension in each of these wires ?

(a) $\dfrac{2Bil^2}{YA}$ (b) $\dfrac{Bil^2}{2YA}$ (c) $\dfrac{Bil^2}{YA}$ (d) $\dfrac{Bil^2}{4YA}$

11 Co-ordinates of four corners of a square loop are $A \equiv (0, 0, 0)$, $B \equiv (0, 0, a)$, $C \equiv \left(\dfrac{a}{\sqrt{2}}, \dfrac{a}{\sqrt{2}}, a\right)$ and $D \equiv \left(\dfrac{a}{\sqrt{2}}, \dfrac{a}{\sqrt{2}}, 0\right)$. A current i is flowing in the loop in $ABCDA$ direction. The magnetic moment of the loop will be

(a) $\left(\frac{a^2}{\sqrt{2}}\hat{\mathbf{j}}+\frac{a^2}{\sqrt{2}}\hat{\mathbf{k}}\right)i$ (b) $\left(-\frac{a^2}{\sqrt{2}}\hat{\mathbf{i}}+\frac{a^2}{\sqrt{2}}\hat{\mathbf{j}}\right)i$

(c) $\left(\frac{a^2}{\sqrt{2}}\hat{\mathbf{i}}+\frac{a^2}{\sqrt{2}}\hat{\mathbf{j}}\right)i$ (d) $\left(\frac{a^2}{\sqrt{2}}\hat{\mathbf{i}}-\frac{a^2}{\sqrt{2}}\hat{\mathbf{j}}\right)i$

12 Find the value of magnetic dipole moment (in A-m^2) of the following circuit. The current distribution is shown in figure.

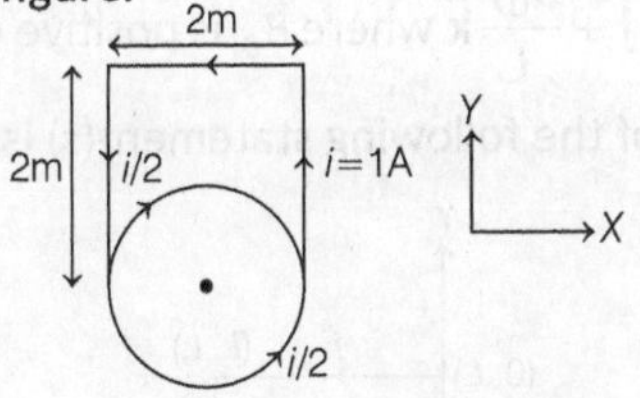

(a) $4\hat{\mathbf{k}}$ (b) $\left(4-\frac{\pi}{2}\right)\hat{\mathbf{k}}$

(c) $\left(4+\frac{\pi}{2}\right)\hat{\mathbf{k}}$ (d) $(4+\pi)\hat{\mathbf{k}}$

13 Q charge is uniformly distributed over the slant surface of a right circular cone of semi-vertical angle θ and height h. The cone is uniformly rotated about its axis at angular velocity ω. Calculate associated magnetic dipole moment.

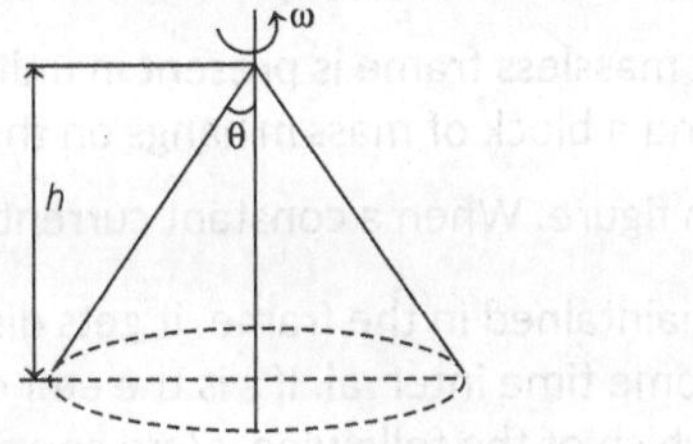

(a) $\frac{Q\omega}{2}h^2\cot^2\theta$ (b) $\frac{Q\omega h^2}{2}\tan^2\theta$

(c) $\frac{Q\omega}{4}h^2\tan^2\theta$ (d) $\frac{Q\omega h^2}{8}\tan^2\theta$

14 A wire carrying 10 A current is bent to pass through various side of a cube of side 10 cm as shown in figure. A magnetic field $\mathbf{B}=2\hat{\mathbf{i}}-3\hat{\mathbf{j}}+\hat{\mathbf{k}}$ is present in region then torque on the loop is

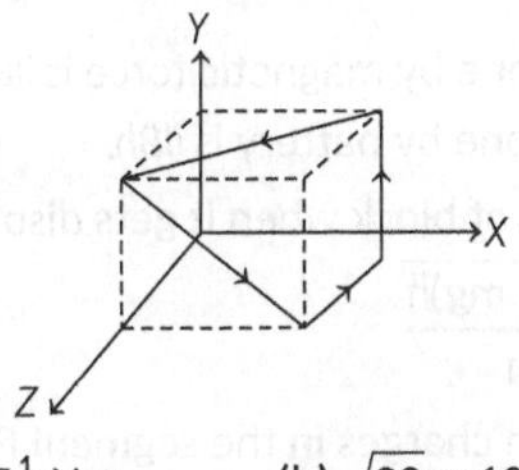

(a) $\sqrt{20}\times10^{-1}$ N-m (b) $\sqrt{20}\times10^{-2}$ N-m

(c) $\sqrt{150}\times10^{-1}$ N-m (d) $\sqrt{150}\times10^{-2}$ N-m

15 In the figure shown a coil of single turn is wound on a sphere of radius R and mass m. The plane of the coil is parallel to the plane and lies in the equatorial plane of the sphere. Current in the coil is i. The value of B if the sphere is in equilibrium is

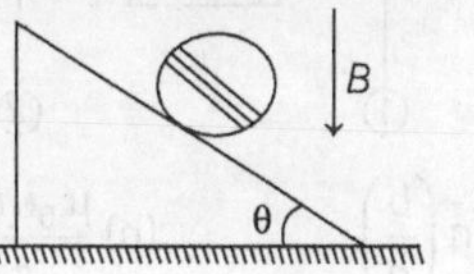

(a) $\frac{mg\cos\theta}{\pi iR}$ (b) $\frac{mg}{\pi iR}$

(c) $\frac{mg\tan\theta}{\pi iR}$ (d) $\frac{mg\sin\theta}{\pi iR}$

16 The circular current loop of radius b shown in figure is mounted rigidly on the axle, midway between the two supporting cords. In the absence of an external magnetic field the tensions in the cords are equal to T_0. Current is in anti-clockwise direction as seen from right side. What will be the tension in cord 1 when the vertical magnetic field B is present and the axle still in equilibrium?

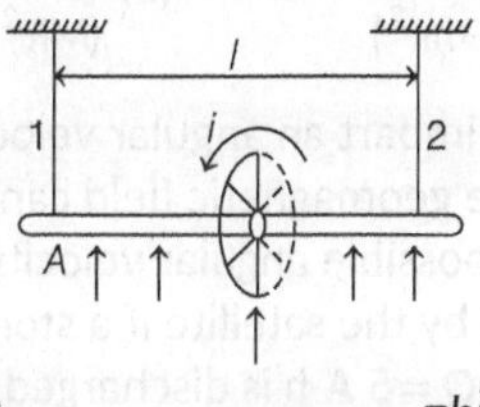

(a) $T_0+\frac{\pi b^2 iB}{2l}$ (b) $T_0+\frac{\pi b^2 iB}{l}$

(c) $T_0-\frac{\pi b^2 iB}{2l}$ (d) $T_0-\frac{\pi b^2 iB}{l}$

17 A uniform current carrying ring of mass m and radius R is connected by a massless string as shown in figure. A uniform magnetic field B_0 exist in the region to keep the ring in horizontal position, then the current in the ring is (l = length of string)

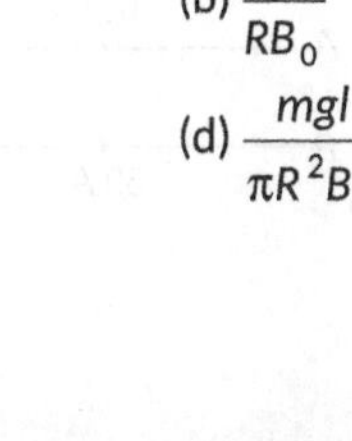

(a) $\frac{mg}{\pi RB_0}$ (b) $\frac{mg}{RB_0}$

(c) $\frac{mg}{3\pi RB_0}$ (d) $\frac{mgl}{\pi R^2B_0}$

18 What is the work done in transferring the wire from position (1) to position (2)?

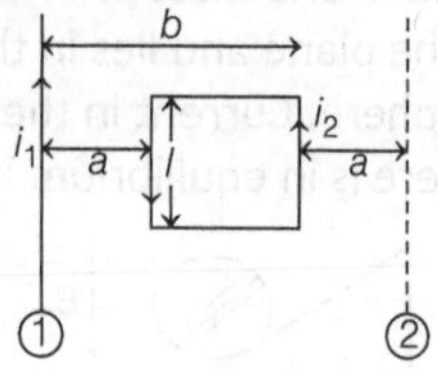

(a) $\frac{\mu_0 i_1 i_2 l}{2\pi} \ln\left(\frac{b}{a}\right)$ (b) $\frac{\mu_0 i_1 i_2 l}{\pi} \ln\left(\frac{b}{a}\right)$

(c) $\frac{\mu_0 i_1 i_2 l}{4\pi} \ln\left(\frac{b}{a}\right)$ (d) zero

19 A coil of radius R carries current i_1. Another concentric coil of radius ($r << R$) carries current i_2. Planes of two coils are mutually perpendicular and both the coils are free to rotate about common diameter. Find maximum kinetic energy of smaller coil when both the coils are released, masses of coils are M and m, respectively.

(a) $\frac{\mu_0 \pi i_1 i_2 M R r^2}{2(MR^2 + mr^2)}$ (b) $\frac{\mu_0 \pi i_1 i_2 M R r^2}{4(MR^2 + mr^2)}$

(c) $\frac{2\mu_0 \pi i_1 i_2 M R r^2}{(MR^2 + mr^2)}$ (d) $\frac{\mu_0 \pi i_1 i_2 M R r^2}{(MR^2 + mr^2)}$

20 In order to impart an angular velocity to an earth satellite the geomagnetic field can be used. Find the maximum possible angular velocity about its own axis gained by the satellite if a storage battery with a capacity of $Q = 5$ A-h is discharged suddenly through a coil of $N = 2000$ turns wound around the satellite's surface along the circumference of the largest circle. The satellite has a mass of $m = 10^3$ kg and is a thin walled uniform sphere. The geomagnetic field is parallel to the winding plane and its flux density is $B = 0.5$ G.

(a) 2π rad/s (b) 2.7π rad/s

(c) 3.6π rad/s (d) 4.5π rad/s

Multiple Choice(s) Correct Questions

1 Two long parallel conductors are carrying currents in the same direction as shown in the figure. The upper conductor A carries a current of 100 A and is held firmly in position. The lower conductor B carries a current of 50 A and is free to slide up and down. The linear mass density of the lower conductor is 0.01 kg m^{-1}.

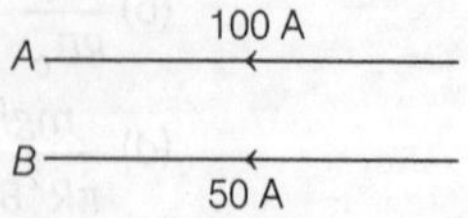

(a) Conductor B will be in equilibrium if the distance between the conductors is 0.01 m.

(b) Conductor B performs SHM with period $\frac{\pi}{50}$ s.

(c) Equilibrium of conductor B is stable.

(d) Equilibrium of conductor B is unstable.

2 Figure shows a square loop carrying current i is present in the magnetic field which is given by $\mathbf{B} = \frac{B_0 z}{L}\hat{\mathbf{j}} + \frac{B_0 y}{L}\hat{\mathbf{k}}$ where B_0 is positive constant.

Which of the following statement(s) is/are correct?

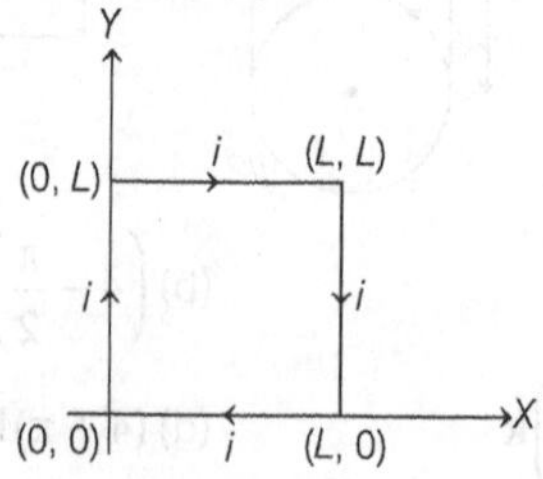

(a) Force on side (0, 0) to (0, L) is $\left(\frac{B_0 i L}{2}\right)\hat{\mathbf{i}}$.

(b) Force on side (0, L) to (L, L) is $-B_0 i L\,\hat{\mathbf{j}}$

(c) Net magnetic force on loop is zero.

(d) Force on side (L, 0) to (0, 0) is zero.

3 A massless frame is present in uniform magnetic field and a block of mass m hangs on the frame as shown in figure. When a constant current $i > \frac{mg}{lB}$ is maintained in the frame, it gets displaced by h in some time interval. If ε is the emf of battery then which of the following is/are correct?

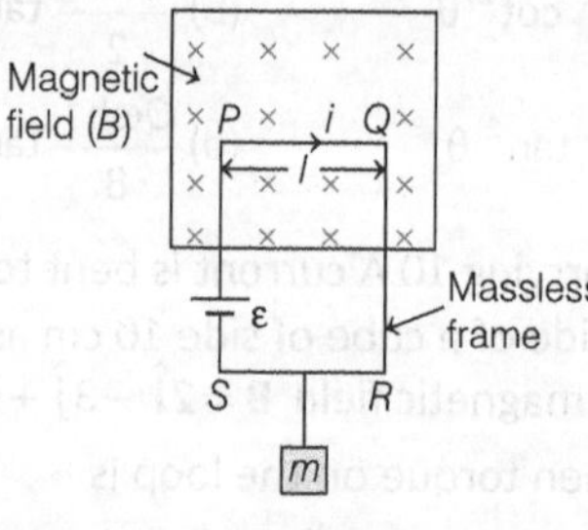

(a) Work done by magnetic force is $ilBh$.

(b) Work done by battery is $ilBh$.

(c) Velocity of block when it gets displacement by h is $\sqrt{\frac{2(ilB - mg)h}{m}}$.

(d) Force on charges in the segment PQ while the frame moves up is in the vertical direction.

4 In the figure, there is a uniform conducting structure in which each small square has side a. The structure is kept in uniform magnetic field B.

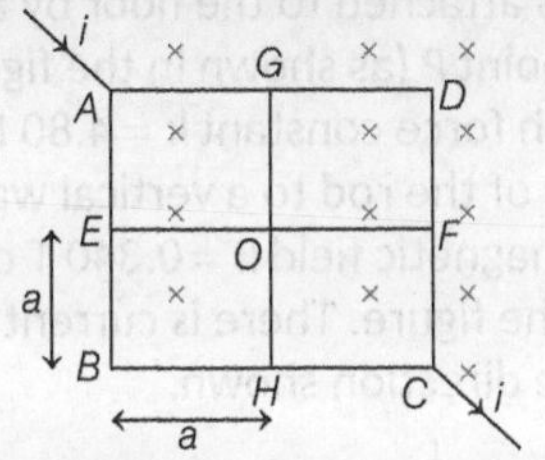

(a) The magnetic force on the structure is $2\sqrt{2}\,iBa$.

(b) Potential of point B = Potential of point D.

(c) Potential of point O = Potential of point B

(d) The magnetic force on the structure is $\sqrt{2}\,iBa$.

5. Rods AB, BC, CD and DA form a square loop having current i. Mass and length of each rod is m and l, respectively. The loop is situated in a uniform magnetic field B as shown in figure and it can rotate about axis P_1P_2, then

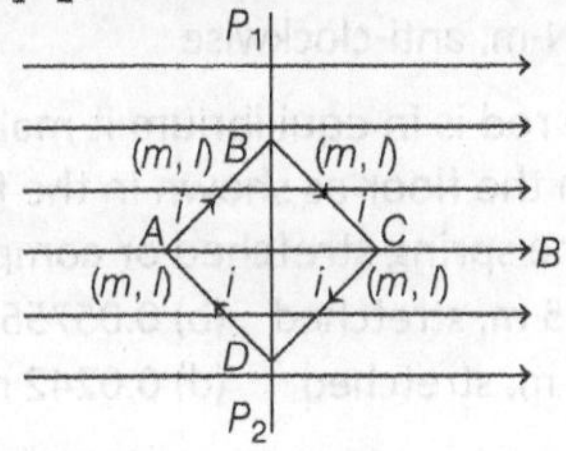

(a) angular acceleration of the square loop at $t = 0$, is $\frac{3}{2}\frac{Bi}{m}$

(b) angular velocity when square loop rotated by 30°, is $\sqrt{\frac{3iB}{2m}}$

(c) torque on the loop when it rotated by 60°, is $\frac{iBl^2}{2}$

(d) angular acceleration of the square loop when it is rotated from starting to 90°, decreases.

6. A uniform circular loop of mass m and radius R is lying in space where a uniform magnetic field $\mathbf{B} = B_0(\hat{\mathbf{i}} + \sqrt{3}\hat{\mathbf{j}})$. The loop carries constant current i in clockwise direction and lies in a gravity free region at rest in XY-plane with its centre at origin. Then choose the correct statement(s)

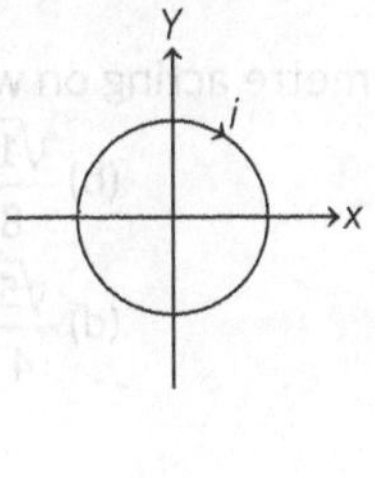

(a) The initial angular acceleration of the loop has magnitude $\frac{4\pi B_0}{m}$.

(b) The initial angular acceleration of the loop has magnitude $\frac{2\pi B_0}{m}$.

(c) The unit vector in the direction of initial angular acceleration is $\left(+\frac{\sqrt{3}}{2}\hat{\mathbf{i}} - \frac{1}{2}\hat{\mathbf{j}}\right)$.

(d) The initial acceleration of the point with coordinates $\left(\frac{\sqrt{3}}{2}R, \frac{-R}{2}\right)$ is zero.

7 A circular conducting loop of radius R and carrying current i_0 (direction not shown) is bent in two equal halves, one lying in XY-plane and other in ZX-plane. Centre is at the origin. Loop is immersed in uniform external magnetic field $\mathbf{B} = \frac{\mu_0 i_0}{2\pi R}(\hat{\mathbf{i}} + \hat{\mathbf{k}})$. If portion in XY-plane experiences a net force in positive Y-direction due to external field, then

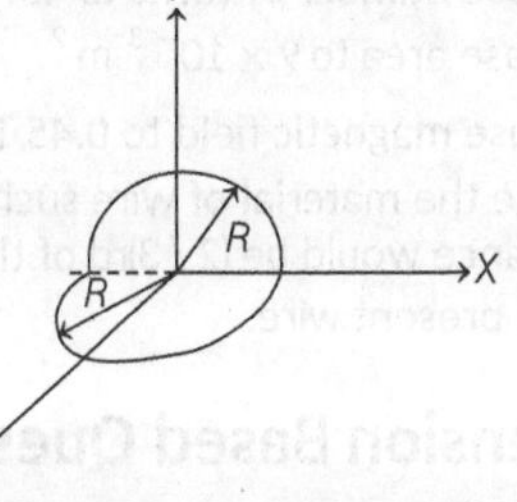

(a) magnetic dipole moment of the loop is $\frac{\pi R^2}{2} i_0(-\hat{\mathbf{k}} - \hat{\mathbf{j}})$.

(b) Net magnetic force due to external field on the portion lying in ZX-plane is $-\frac{\mu_0 i_0^2}{\pi}\hat{\mathbf{j}}$.

(c) Net torque experienced by the loop is $\frac{\mu_0 i_0^2 R}{4}(\hat{\mathbf{i}} + \hat{\mathbf{j}} - \hat{\mathbf{k}})$.

(d) Net magnetic field at the origin is $\frac{\mu_0 i_0}{4R}(\hat{\mathbf{j}} + \hat{\mathbf{k}})$.

8 A wooden cubical block $ABCDEFG$ of mass m and side a is wrapped by a square wire loop of perimeter $4a$, carrying current i. The whole system is placed at frictionless horizontal surface in a uniform magnetic field $\mathbf{B} = B_0\hat{\mathbf{j}}$ as shown in figure. In this situation, normal force between horizontal surface and block passes through a point at a distance x from center. Choose correct statement(s).

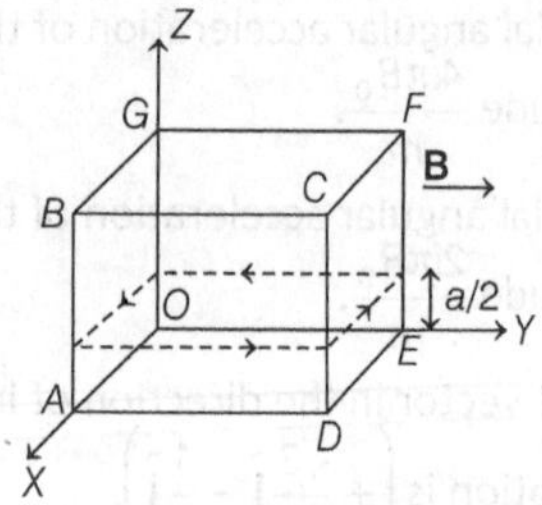

(a) The block must not topple if $i < \frac{mg}{aB_0}$.

(b) The block must not topple if $i < \frac{mg}{2aB_0}$.

(c) $x = \frac{a}{4}$ if $i = \frac{mg}{2aB_0}$.

(d) $x = \frac{a}{4}$ if $i = \frac{mg}{4aB_0}$.

9 In a moving coil galvanometer the number of turns $N = 30$, area of the coil $A = 4 \times 10^{-3}\ m^2$ and the magnetic field strength $B = 0.3$ T. To increase its voltage sensitivity by 50% we

(a) increase number of turns to 45.

(b) increase area to $9 \times 10^{-3}\ m^2$.

(c) increase magnetic field to 0.45 T.

(d) change the material of wire such that its specific resistance would be (2 / 3)rd of the specific resistance of the present wire.

Comprehension Based Questions

Comprehension-1

A thin, 50 cm long metal bar with mass 750 g rests on, but is not attached to, two metallic supports in a uniform 0.450 T magnetic field as shown in figure. A battery and a 25 Ω resistor in series are connected to the supports.

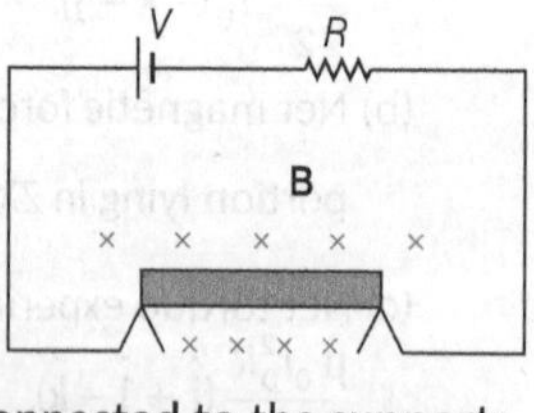

1 What is the largest voltage the battery can have without breaking the circuit at the supports?

(a) 817 V (b) 412 V

(c) 325 V (d) 160 V

2 The battery voltage has the maximum value calculated in above question. If the resistor suddenly gets partially short-circuited, decreasing its resistance to 2Ω, find the initial acceleration of the bar.

(a) 113 ms^{-2} (b) 55 ms^{-2}

(c) 180 ms^{-2} (d) 12.4 ms^{-2}

Comprehension-2

A thin, uniform rod with negligible mass and length 0.200 m is attached to the floor by a frictionless hinge at point *P* (as shown in the figure). A horizontal spring with force constant $k = 4.80$ N/m connects the other end of the rod to a vertical wall. The rod is in a uniform magnetic field $B = 0.340$ T directed into the plane of the figure. There is current $i = 6.50$ A in the rod, in the direction shown.

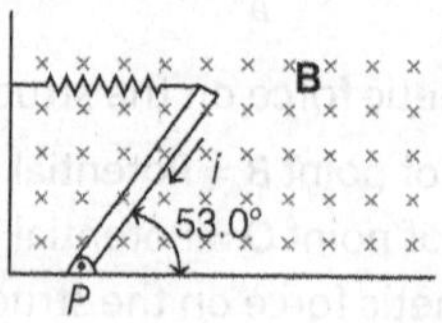

3 Calculate the torque due to the magnetic force on the rod, for an axis at *P*.

(a) 0.0442 N-m, clockwise

(b) 0.0442 N-m, anti-clockwise

(c) 0.022 N-m, clockwise

(d) 0.022 N-m, anti-clockwise

4 When the rod is in equilibrium it makes an angle of 53.0° with the floor as shown in the figure, how much is the spring stretched or compressed?

(a) 0.05755 m, stretched (b) 0.05755 m, compressed

(c) 0.0242 m, stretched (d) 0.0242 m, compressed

Comprehension-3

4 long wires each carrying current *i* as shown in figure are placed at the points *A*, *B*, *C* and *D*.

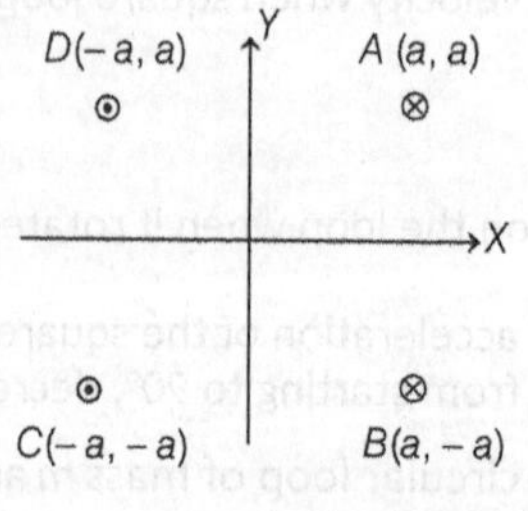

5 Magnetic field at the centre of the square is

(a) $\left(\frac{\mu_0 i}{4\pi a}\right)\hat{i}$ (b) $\left(\frac{\mu_0 i}{4\pi a}\right)\hat{j}$

(c) $\left(\frac{\mu_0 i}{\pi a}\right)\hat{i}$ (d) $\left(\frac{\mu_0 i}{\pi a}\right)\hat{j}$

6 The force per metre acting on wire at point *D* is

(a) $\frac{\sqrt{10}}{4}\frac{\mu_0 i^2}{\pi a}$ (b) $\frac{\sqrt{10}}{8}\frac{\mu_0 i^2}{\pi a}$

(c) $\frac{\sqrt{5}}{8}\frac{\mu_0 i^2}{\pi a}$ (d) $\frac{\sqrt{5}}{4}\frac{\mu_0 i^2}{\pi a}$

Comprehension-4

A hypothetical magnetic field $\mathbf{B} = B_0\hat{r}$ is present in a region, where B_0 is a positive constant and $\hat{r}$ is radially outward unit vector. A rough horizontal surface with coefficient of friction μ coincides with the XY-plane. A thin, non-conducting ring of mass m, radius R and charge $+q$ (uniformly distributed) is placed on the surface with its centre at origin and its plane parallel to XY-plane. If the ring is started with a certain angular velocity ω_0, it continues to move with the same angular velocity despite the surface being rough.

7 What is the value of ω_0?

(a) $\dfrac{mg}{qRB_0}$ (b) $\dfrac{mg}{2qRB_0}$

(c) $\dfrac{2mg}{3qRB_0}$ (d) $\dfrac{mg}{3qRB_0}$

8 If the ring is started with an angular velocity $\omega_0/2$, what is the time elapsed before its angular velocity reduces by half?

(a) $\dfrac{m \ln(1.5)}{2\mu qB_0}$ (b) $\dfrac{m \ln(3)}{2\mu qB_0}$

(c) $\dfrac{m \ln(1.5)}{\mu qB_0}$ (d) $\dfrac{m \ln(2)}{3\mu qB_0}$

Comprehension-5

A straight segment OC (of length $2a$) of a circuit carrying a current i is placed along the X-axis. Two infinitely long straight wire A and B, each extending $z = -\infty$ to $+\infty$ are fixed at $y = -a$ and $y = +a$ respectively, as shown in figure. The wires A and B each carry a current i into the plane of the paper.

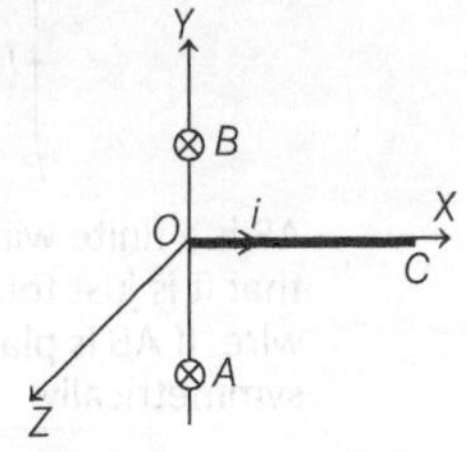

9 The force acting on segment OC is

(a) $\dfrac{\mu_0 i^2}{2\pi}\ln 3$ (b) $\dfrac{\mu_0 i^2}{4\pi}\ln 3$

(c) $\dfrac{\mu_0 i^2}{2\pi}\ln 5$ (d) $\dfrac{\mu_0 i^2}{4\pi}\ln 5$

10 What will be the force on OC if the current in the wire B is reversed?

(a) zero (b) $\dfrac{\mu_0 i^2}{4\pi}\ln 3$

(c) $\dfrac{\mu_0 i^2}{2\pi}\ln 5$ (d) $\dfrac{\mu_0 i^2}{4\pi}\ln 5$

Comprehension-6

A conducting ring of mass m and radius r has a weightless conducting rod PQ of length $2r$ and resistance $2R$ attached to it along its diameter. It is pivoted at its center C with its plane vertical and two blocks of mass m and $2m$ are suspended by means of a light in-extensible string passing over it as shown in figure. The ring is free to rotate about C and the system is placed in a magnetic field (into the plane of the ring). A circuit is now completed by connecting the ring at A and C to battery of emf. V. It is found that for certain value of V, the system remains static. (Neglect resistance of the ring)

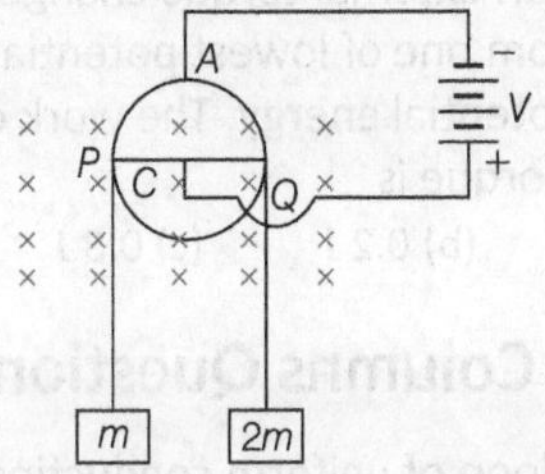

11 In static condition, find the current through rod PC

(a) $\dfrac{V}{R}$ (b) $\dfrac{V}{2R}$ (c) $\dfrac{4V}{R}$ (d) $\dfrac{2V}{R}$

12 Net torque applied by the tension in string on the ring can be related as

(a) $\dfrac{3BVr^2}{R}$ (b) $\dfrac{BVr^2}{R}$

(c) $\dfrac{BVr^2}{3R}$ (d) $\dfrac{BVr^2}{2R}$

13 The value of V can be related with m, B and r as

(a) $\dfrac{2mgR}{Br}$ (b) $\dfrac{mgR}{Br}$

(c) $\dfrac{mgR}{2Br}$ (d) $\dfrac{3mgR}{Br}$

Comprehension-7

A rigid circular loop has a radius of 0.20 m and is in the XY-plane. A clockwise current i is carried by the loop, as shown in figure. The magnitude of the magnetic moment of the loop is 0.75 A-m^2. A uniform external magnetic field, $B = 0.20$ T in the positive X-direction, is present

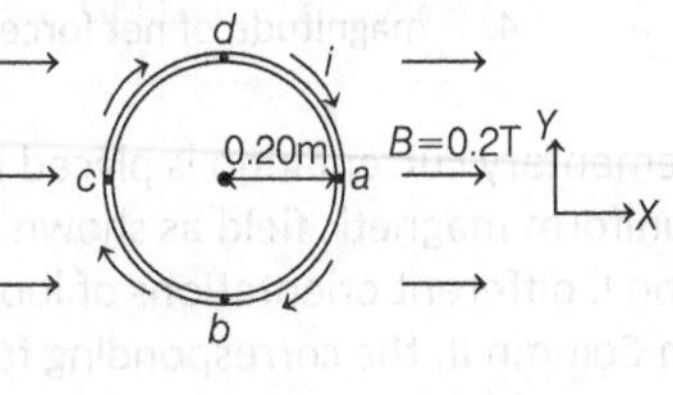

14 In figure, the magnitude of the magnetic torque exerted on the loop is

(a) 0.55 N-m (b) 0.15 N-m
(c) 0.45 N-m (d) 0.35 N-m

15 In figure the loop is released from rest. The initial motion of the loop is described by

(a) point *a* moves out of the plane, point *c* moves into the plane
(b) points *a*, *b*, *c* and *d* move counterclockwise
(c) points *a*, *b*, *c* and *d* move clockwise
(d) point *c* moves out of the plane, point *a* moves into the plane

16 In figure, an external torque changes the orientation of loop from one of lowest potential energy to one of highest potential energy. The work done by the external torque is

(a) 0.5 J (b) 0.2 J (c) 0.3 J (d) 0.4 J

Match The Columns Questions

1 A square loop of uniform conducting wire is as shown in figure. A current *i* enters the loop from one end and exits the loop from opposite end as shown in figure. The length of one side of square loop is *l*. The wire has uniform cross-section area and uniform linear mass density. In four situations of Column I, the loop is subjected to four different magnetic fields. Under the conditions of Column I, match the Column I with corresponding results of Column II (B_0 in Column I is a positive non-zero constant).

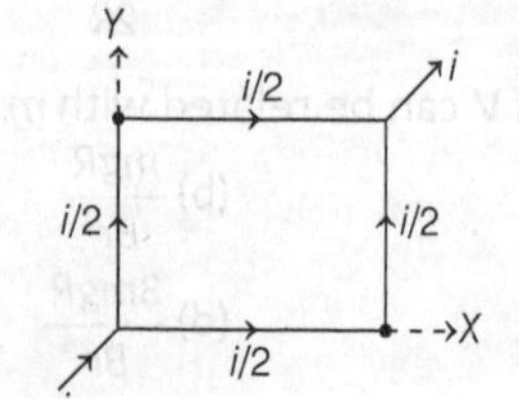

	Column I	Column II
A.	$\mathbf{B} = B_0\hat{\mathbf{i}}$	1. magnitude of net force on loop is $\sqrt{2}B_0il$.
B.	$\mathbf{B} = B_0\hat{\mathbf{j}}$	2. magnitude of net force on loop is zero
C.	$\mathbf{B} = B_0(\hat{\mathbf{i}} + \hat{\mathbf{j}})$	3. magnitude of net torque on loop is zero
D.	$\mathbf{B} = B_0\hat{\mathbf{k}}$	4. magnitude of net force on loop is B_0il.

2 An elementary current loop is placed in a non-uniform magnetic field as shown in figure. In Column I, different orientations of loop are described and in Column II, the corresponding forces experienced by the loop. P_m is magnetic moment of loop.

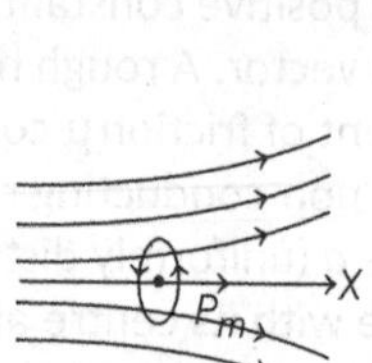

	Column I	Column II
A.	In the given situation,	1. resultant force is acting along $\mathbf{P}_m$
B.	If loop is rotated such that $\mathbf{P}_m$ is along + ve *z*-direction	2. resultant force is acting opposite to $\mathbf{P}_m$
C.	If loop is rotated such that $\mathbf{P}_m$ is along − ve *z*-direction	3. $F_x = 0, F_y = 0$
D.	If loop is rotated such that $\mathbf{P}_m$ is along + ve *y*-direction	4. $F_x = 0, F_z = 0$

3 In each of cases, assume that the wires are very thin.

	Column I	Column II
A.	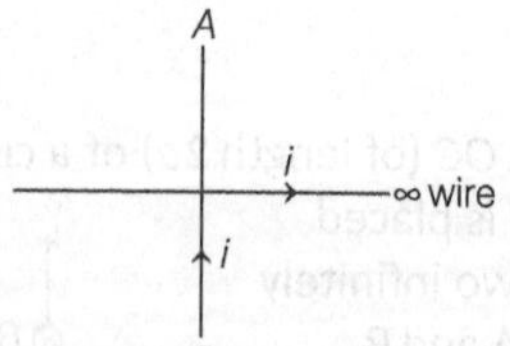 AB is a finite wire placed such that it is just touching the infinite wire. If AB is placed symmetrically	1. The force on AB is zero
B.	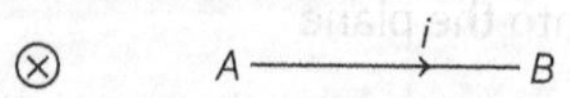 Infinite wire carrying current into the plane	2. The torque on AB about its centre is zero
C.	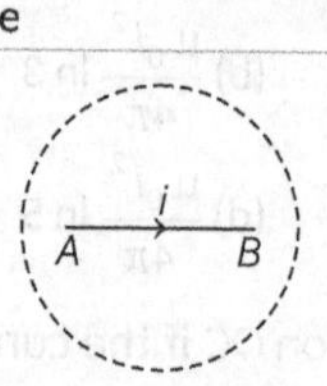 AB is kept inside an ideal solenoid along the diameter	3. The force on AB is non-zero
		4. The torque on AB about its centre is non-zero

Numerical Value Questions

1 A loop PQR formed by three identical uniform conducting rods each of length $a = 20$ cm is suspended from one of its vertices P, so that it can rotate about horizontal fixed smooth axis CD. Initially plane of loop is in vertical plane. A constant current $i = 10$ A is flowing in the loop. Total mass of the loop is $m = 600$ g. At $t = 0$, a uniform magnetic field of strength B directed vertically upwards is switched ON. Find the minimum value of B (in T), so that the plane of the loop becomes horizontal (even for an instant) during its subsequent motion.

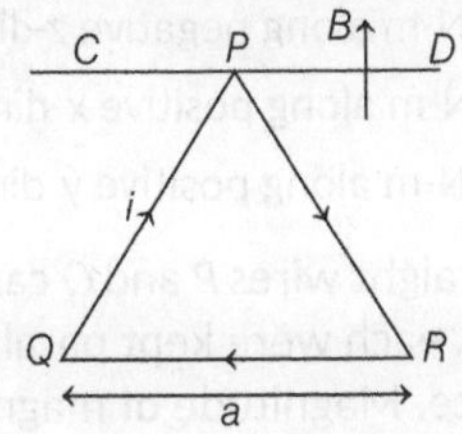

2 Figure shows a square loop 10 cm on each side in the XY-plane with its centre at the origin. An infinite wire is at $z = 12$ cm above Y-axis. What is torque on loop due to magnetic force? If torque is expressed as $x \times 10^{-7}$ N-m, find value of x.

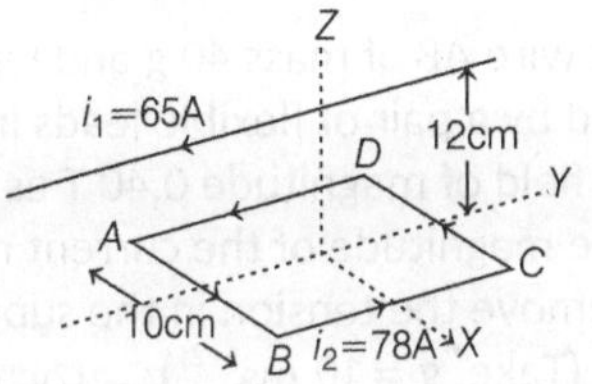

3 Metal rod with a mass $m = 10$ g and length $L = 0.2$ m is suspended by two light wires length $l = 1$ cm in a magnetic field induction $B = 1$ T which is directed vertically downwards as shown in figure. A capacitor of capacitance $C = 100\,\mu$F charged to a voltage of 100 V is connected as shown in figure. Determine the maximum deflection (in degree) of the rod from the initial position after the switch is closed. Resistance of wire and rod is not taken into account.

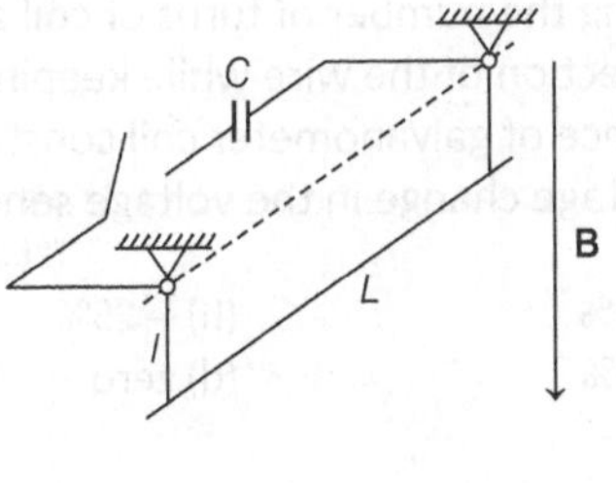

4 Calculate the magnetic moment (in A-m^2) of a thin wire with a current $i = 8.0$ A, wound tightly on a half a tore as shown in figure. The diameter of the cross-section of the tore is equal to $d = 5.0$ cm, and the number of turns in $N = 500$.

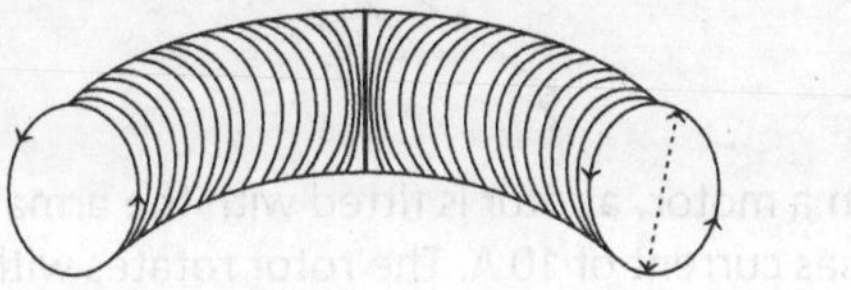

5 A non-conducting non-magnetic rod having square cross-section of side $\frac{l}{4}$ is suspended from a rigid support as shown in the figure. A light and small coil of 600 turns is wrapped tightly at the left end of the rod where uniform magnetic field B exists in vertically downward direction. Air of density ρ hits the half of the right part of the rod with velocity v as shown in figure.

What should be the current (in mA) in the coil so that rod remains horizontal? (Assume air particles come to rest after colliding with the rod)

(Take, $\rho = 1.05$ kg/m^3, $v = 10$ m/s, $B = 1$ T, $l = 2$m)

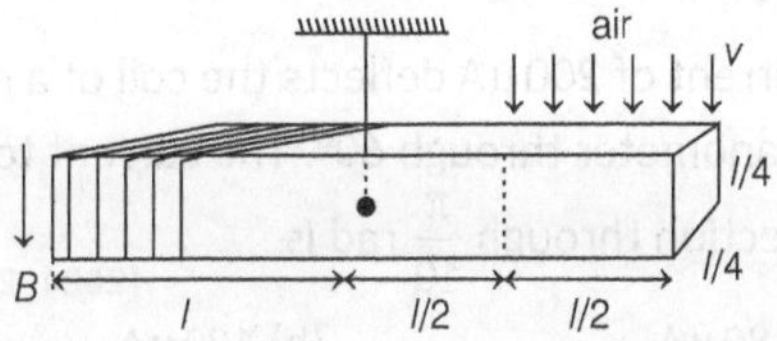

6 A coil carrying a current $i = 10$ A is placed in a uniform magnetic field so that its axis coincides with the field direction. The coil consists of only one turn and made up of copper. The diameter of the wire is 0.1 mm, the radius of the coil is $R = 3\pi$ cm. Find the value of external induction field (in T) at which the coil will rupture. Breaking stress of copper $= 3 \times 10^8$ Nm^{-2}.

7 On a smooth horizontal ground, we kept a square loop of mass 2 kg having sides 20 cm × 20 cm. Sides are parallel to X-axis and Z-axis. Beyond $x = +1$ m, uniform magnetic field of $\mathbf{B} = 2\hat{\mathbf{i}} + 4\hat{\mathbf{j}} + 6\hat{\mathbf{k}}$ (T) is present. The loop enters the magnetic field with negligible velocity. If the current in the loop is held constant at 1 A, what is the velocity(in m/s) of the loop when it has completely entered the region of the magnetic field?

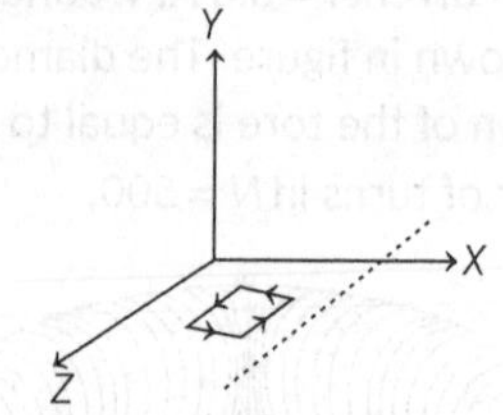

8 In a motor, a rotor is fitted with the armature that has current of 10 A. The rotor rotates with angular speed of 3 rad/s. Magnetic field of magnitude 2 T varies in direction in such a way that it is always perpendicular to the loop area. If the rotor coil has N number of turns and area of each loop is 0.45 m^2 then find the value N.

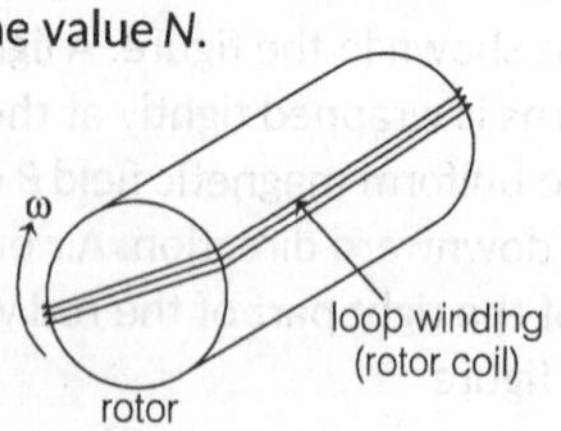

Given that motor consumes 2106 W power and there are no losses.

Previous Years Questions

JEE Main

1 A current of 200 μA deflects the coil of a moving coil galvanometer through 60°. The current to cause deflection through $\frac{\pi}{10}$ rad is **[2024, 27 Jan Shift-II]**

(a) 180 μA (b) 120 μA
(c) 30 μA (d) 60 μA

2 A rigid wire consists of a semicircular portion of radius R and two straight sections. The wire is partially immersed in a perpendicular magnetic field $B = B_0 \hat{j}$ as shown in figure. The magnetic force on the wire if it has a current i is **[2024, 31 Jan Shift-I]**

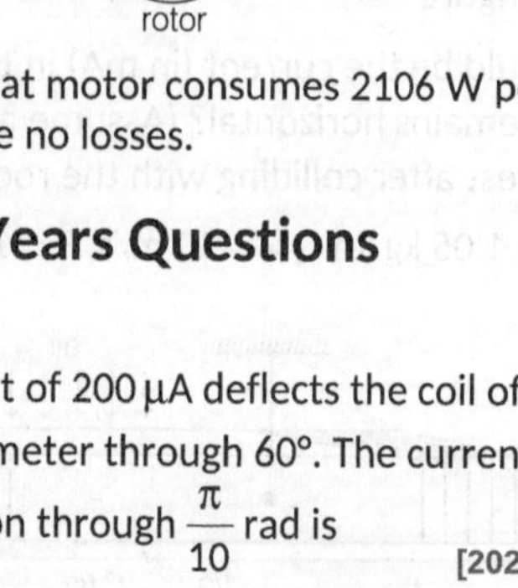

(a) $iBR\hat{j}$ (b) $-iBR\hat{j}$
(c) $2iBR\hat{j}$ (d) $-2iBR\hat{j}$

3 The horizontal component of earth's magnetic field at a place is 3.5×10^{-5} T. A very long straight conductor carrying current of $\sqrt{2}$ A in the direction from South East to North West is placed. The force per unit length experienced by the conductor is ...... $\times 10^{-6}$ N/m. **[2024, 30 Jan Shift-I]**

4 A uniform magnetic field of 2×10^{-3} T acts along positive Y-direction. A rectangular loop of sides 20 cm and 10 cm with current of 5A is in Y-Z plane. The current is in anti-clockwise sense with reference to negative X-axis. Magnitude and direction of the torque is **[2024, 31 Jan Shift-II]**

(a) 2×10^{-4} N-m along positive z-direction
(b) 2×10^{-4} N-m along negative z-direction
(c) 2×10^{-4} N-m along positive x-direction
(d) 2×10^{-4} N-m along positive y-direction

5 Two long straight wires P and Q carrying equal current 10 A each were kept parallel to each other at 4 cm distance. Magnitude of magnetic force experienced by 10 cm length of wire P is F_1. If distance between wires is halved and currents on them are doubled, force F_2 on 10 cm length of wire P will be **[2023, 1 Feb Shift-II]**

(a) $8F_1$ (b) $10F_1$ (c) $\frac{F_1}{10}$ (d) $\frac{F_1}{8}$

6 A straight wire AB of mass 40 g and length 50 cm is suspended by a pair of flexible leads in uniform magnetic field of magnitude 0.40 T as shown in the figure. The magnitude of the current required in the wire to remove the tension in the supporting leads is .... A. (Take, $g = 10 \text{ ms}^{-2}$) **[2023, 13 April Shift-II]**

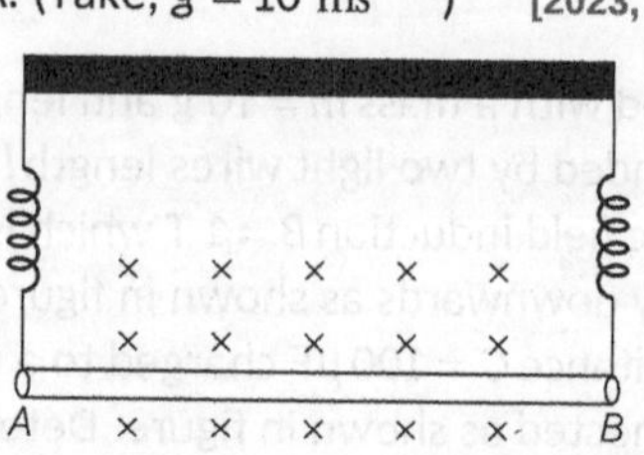

7 The current sensitivity of moving coil galvanometer is increased by 25%. This increase is achieved only by changing the number of turns of coil and area of cross-section of the wire while keeping the resistance of galvanometer coil constant. The percentage change in the voltage sensitivity will be **[2023, 11 April Shift-I]**

(a) + 25% (b) – 25%
(c) – 50% (d) zero

8 Given below are two statements

Statement I If the number of turns in the coil of a moving coil galvanometer is doubled then the current sensitivity becomes double.

Statement II Increasing current sensitivity of a moving coil galvanometer by only increasing the number of turns in the coil will also increase its voltage sensitivity in the same ratio.

In the light of the above statements, choose the correct answer from the options given below : **[2023, 10 April Shift-I]**

(a) Statement I is false but Statement II is true
(b) Statement I is true but Statement II is false
(c) Both Statement I and Statement II are false
(d) Both Statement I and Statement II are true

9 Certain galvanometers have a fixed core made of non magnetic metallic material. The function of this metallic material is **[2023, 8 April Shift-I]**

(a) to produce large deflecting torque on the coil
(b) to bring the coil to rest quickly
(c) to make the magnetic field radial
(d) to oscillate the coil in magnetic field for longer period of time

10 For a moving coil galvanometer, the deflection in the coil is 0.05 rad when a current of 10 mA is passed through it. If the torsional constant of suspension wire is 4.0×10^{-5} N-m rad^{-1} the magnetic field is 0.01 T and the number of turns in the coil is 200, the area of each turn (in cm^2) is **[2023, 25 Jan Shift-II]**

(a) 2.0 (b) 1.5 (c) 0.5 (d) 1.0

11 The magnetic moments associated with two closely wound circular coils A and B of radius $r_A = 10$ cm and $r_B = 20$ cm respectively are equal if: (where N_A, I_A and N_B, I_B are number of turn and current of A and B respectively) **[2023, 30 Jan Shift-I]**

(a) $2N_A I_A = N_B I_B$ (b) $4N_A I_A = N_B I_B$
(c) $N_A = 2N_B$ (d) $N_A I_A = 4N_B I_B$

12 A wire X of length 50 cm carrying a current of 2 A is placed parallel to a long wire Y of length 5 m. The wire Y carries a current of 3 A. The distance between two wires is 5 cm and currents flow in the same direction. The force acting on the wire Y is **[2022, 29 July Shift-II]**

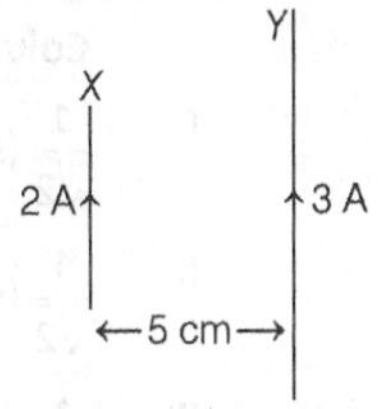

(a) 1.2×10^{-5} N directed towards wire X
(b) 1.2×10^{-4} N directed away from wire X
(c) 1.2×10^{-4} N directed towards wire X
(d) 2.4×10^{-5} N directed towards wire X

13 A coil in the shape of an equilateral triangle of side 10 cm lies in a vertical plane between the pole pieces of permanent magnet producing a horizontal magnetic field 20 mT. The torque acting on the coil when a current of 0.2 A is passed through it and its plane becomes parallel to the magnetic field will be $\sqrt{x} \times 10^{-5}$ Nm. The value of x is .... **[2021, 26 Aug Shift-II]**

14 A uniform conducting wire of length is 24 a, and resistance R is wound up as a current carrying coil in the shape of an equilateral triangle of side a and then in the form of a square of side a. The coil is connected to a voltage source V_0. The ratio of magnetic moment of the coils in case of equilateral triangle to that for square is $1 : \sqrt{y}$. The value of where y is .... **[2021, 27 Aug Shift-I]**

15 A loop of flexible wire of irregular shape carrying current is placed in an external magnetic field. Identify the effect of the field on the wire. **[2021, 18 March Shift-I]**

(a) Loop assumes circular shape with its plane normal to the field.
(b) Loop assumes circular shape with its plane parallel to the field.
(c) Wire gets stretched to become straight.
(d) Shape of the loop remains unchanged.

16 A wire carrying current I is bent in the shape $ABCDEFA$ as shown, where rectangle $ABCDA$ and $ADEFA$ are perpendicular to each other. If the sides of the rectangles are of lengths a and b, then the magnitude and direction of magnetic moment of the loop $ABCDEFA$ is **[2020, 2 Sep Shift-II]**

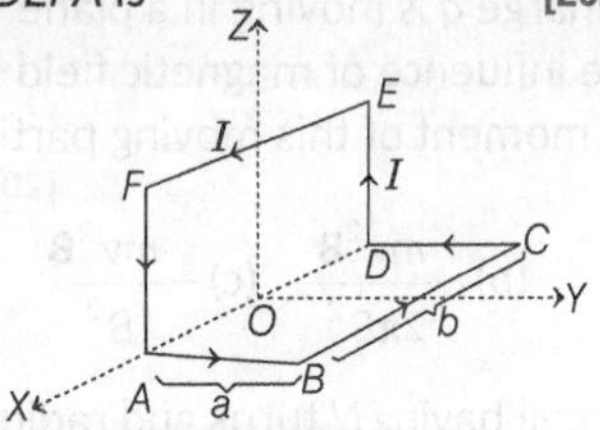

(a) abI, along $\left(\frac{\hat{j}}{\sqrt{2}} + \frac{\hat{k}}{\sqrt{2}}\right)$

(b) $\sqrt{2}\, abI$, along $\left(\frac{\hat{j}}{\sqrt{2}} + \frac{\hat{k}}{\sqrt{2}}\right)$

(c) $\sqrt{2}\, abI$, along $\left(\frac{\hat{j}}{\sqrt{5}} + \frac{2\hat{k}}{\sqrt{5}}\right)$

(d) abI, along $\left(\frac{\hat{j}}{\sqrt{5}} + \frac{2\hat{k}}{\sqrt{5}}\right)$

17 A galvanometer coil has 500 turns and each turn has an average area of 3×10^{-4} m^2. If a torque of 1.5 N-m is required to keep this coil parallel to a magnetic field when a current of 0.5 A is flowing through it, the strength of the field (in T) is .... **[2020, 3 Sep Shift-II]**

18 A circular coil has moment of inertia 0.8 kg m^2 around any diameter and is carrying current to produce a magnetic moment of 20 Am^2. The coil is kept initially in a vertical position and it can rotate freely around a horizontal diameter. When a uniform magnetic field of 4 T is applied along the vertical, it starts rotating around its horizontal diameter. The angular speed of the coil, acquired after rotating by 60°, will be **[2020, 4 Sep Shift-II]**

(a) 10 rad s^{-1} (b) 20π rad s^{-1}
(c) 10π rad s^{-1} (d) 20 rad s^{-1}

19 A square loop of side $2a$ and carrying current I is kept in xy-plane with its centre at origin. A long wire carrying the same current I is placed parallel to the Z-axis and passing through the point $(0, b, 0)$, ($b >> a$). The magnitude of the torque on the loop about Z-axis is given by **[2020, 5 Sep Shift-I]**

(a) $\frac{2\mu_0 I^2 a^3}{\pi b^2}$ (b) $\frac{2\mu_0 I^2 a^2}{\pi b}$
(c) $\frac{\mu_0 I^2 a^3}{2\pi b^2}$ (d) $\frac{\mu_0 I^2 a^2}{2\pi b}$

20 A charged particle going around in a circle can be considered to be a current loop. A particle of mass m carrying charge q is moving in a plane with speed v under the influence of magnetic field $\mathbf{B}$. The magnetic moment of this moving particle **[2020, 6 Sep Shift-II]**

(a) $\frac{mv^2\mathbf{B}}{2B^2}$ (b) $-\frac{mv^2\mathbf{B}}{2\pi B^2}$ (c) $-\frac{mv^2\mathbf{B}}{B^2}$ (d) $-\frac{mv^2\mathbf{B}}{2B^2}$

21 A circular coil having N turns and radius r carries a current I. It is held in the XZ-plane in a magnetic field $B\hat{\mathbf{i}}$. The torque on the coil due to the magnetic field (in N-m) is **[2019, 8 April Shift-I]**

(a) $\frac{Br^2 I}{\pi N}$ (b) $B\pi r^2 IN$
(c) $\frac{B\pi r^2 I}{N}$ (d) Zero

22 A rectangular coil (dimension 5 cm $\times$ 2.5 cm) with 100 turns, carrying a current of 3A in the clockwise direction, is kept centred at the origin and in the X-Z plane. A magnetic field of 1 T is applied along X-axis. If the coil is tilted through 45° about Z-axis, then the torque on the coil is **[2019, 9 April Shift-I]**

(a) 0.27 N-m (b) 0.38 N-m
(c) 0.42 N-m (d) 0.55 N-m

23 A rigid square loop of side a and carrying current I_2 is lying on a horizontal surface near a long current I_1 carrying wire in the same plane as shown in figure. The net force on the loop due to the wire will be **[2019, 9 April Shift-I]**

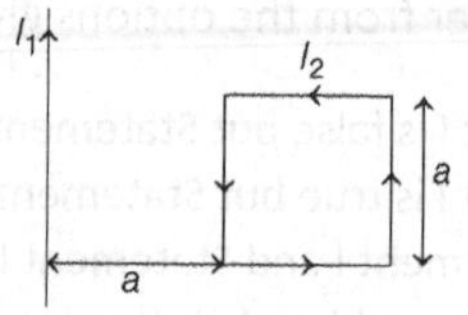

(a) repulsive and equal to $\frac{\mu_0 I_1 I_2}{2\pi}$
(b) attractive and equal to $\frac{\mu_0 I_1 I_2}{3\pi}$
(c) zero
(d) repulsive and equal to $\frac{\mu_0 I_1 I_2}{4\pi}$

JEE Advanced

1 A small circular loop of area A and resistance R is fixed on a horizontal XY-plane with the centre of the loop always on the axis $\hat{\mathbf{n}}$ of a long solenoid. The solenoid has n turns per unit length and carries current I counter clockwise as shown in the figure. The magnetic field due to the solenoid is in $\hat{\mathbf{n}}$ direction. Column-I gives time dependences of $\hat{\mathbf{n}}$ in terms of a constant angular frequency ω. Column-II gives the torques experienced by the circular loop at time $t = \pi/6\omega$. Let $\alpha = \frac{A^2\mu_0^2 n^2 I^2 \omega}{2R}$.

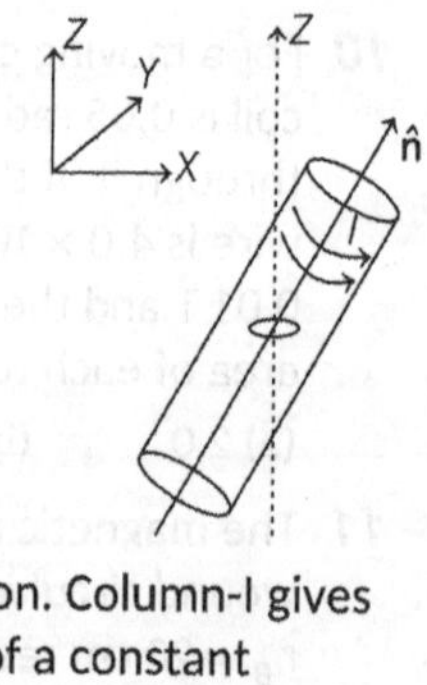

	Column-I		Column-II
I.	$\frac{1}{\sqrt{2}}(\sin\omega t\,\hat{\mathbf{j}} + \cos\omega t\,\hat{\mathbf{k}})$	P.	0
II.	$\frac{1}{\sqrt{2}}(\sin\omega t\,\hat{\mathbf{i}} + \cos\omega t\,\hat{\mathbf{j}})$	Q.	$-\frac{\alpha}{4}\hat{\mathbf{i}}$
III.	$\frac{1}{\sqrt{2}}(\sin\omega t\,\hat{\mathbf{i}} + \cos\omega t\,\hat{\mathbf{k}})$	R.	$\frac{3\alpha}{4}\hat{\mathbf{i}}$
IV.	$\frac{1}{\sqrt{2}}(\cos\omega t\,\hat{\mathbf{j}} + \sin\omega t\,\hat{\mathbf{k}})$	S.	$\frac{\alpha}{4}\hat{\mathbf{j}}$
		T.	$-\frac{3\alpha}{4}\hat{\mathbf{i}}$

Which one of the following option is correct? **(2022)**

	I	II	III	IV		I	II	III	IV
(a)	Q	P	S	T	(b)	S	T	Q	P
(c)	Q	P	S	R	(d)	T	Q	P	R

2 A circular coil of radius R and N turns has negligible resistance. As shown in the schematic figure, its two ends are connected to two wires and it is hanging by those wires with its plane being vertical. The wires are connected to a capacitor with charge Q through a switch. The coil is in a horizontal uniform magnetic field B_0 parallel to the plane of the coil. When the switch is closed, the capacitor gets discharged through the coil in a very short time. By the time the capacitor is discharged fully, magnitude of the angular momentum gained by the coil will be (assume that the discharge time is so short that the coil has hardly rotated during this time) **(2020)**

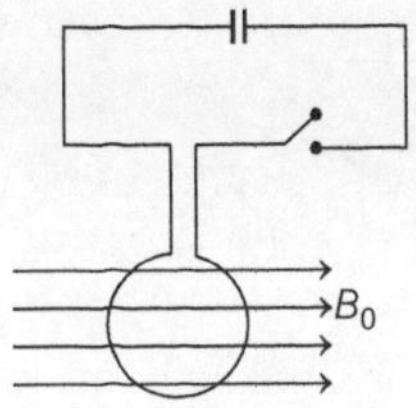

(a) $\frac{\pi}{2} NQB_0R^2$

(b) πNQB_0R^2

(c) $2\pi NQB_0R^2$

(d) $4\pi NQB_0R^2$

3 A conductor (shown in the figure) carrying constant current I is kept in the x-y plane in a uniform magnetic field $\mathbf{B}$. If F is the magnitude of the total magnetic force acting on the conductor, then the correct statements is/are **(2015)**

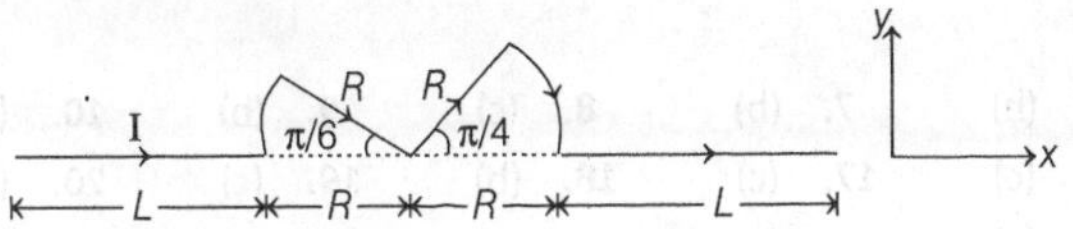

(a) if $\mathbf{B}$ is along $\hat{\mathbf{z}}$, $F \propto (L+R)$

(b) if $\mathbf{B}$ is along $\hat{\mathbf{x}}$, $F = 0$

(c) if $\mathbf{B}$ is along $\hat{\mathbf{y}}$, $F \propto (L+R)$

(d) if $\mathbf{B}$ is along $\hat{\mathbf{z}}$, $F = 0$

Direction (Q. Nos. 4 and 5) The figure shows a circular loop of radius a with two long parallel wires (numbered 1 and 2) all in the plane of the paper. The distance of each wire from the centre of the loop is d. The loop and the wires are carrying the same current I. The current in the loop is in the counter-clockwise direction if seen from above.

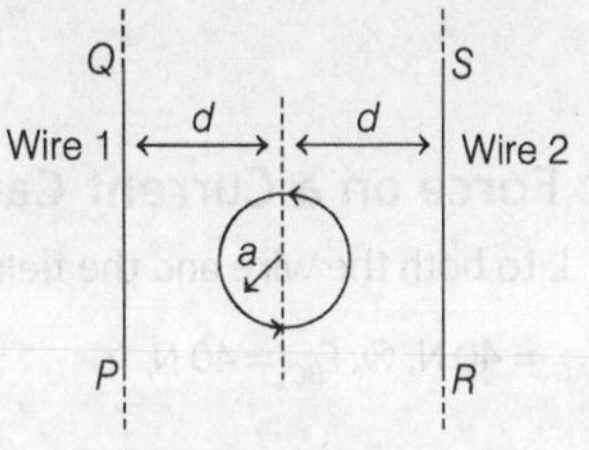

4 When $d \approx a$ but wires are not touching the loop, it is found that the net magnetic field on the axis of the loop is zero at a height h above the loop. In that case **(2014)**

(a) currents in wire 1 and wire 2 are in the directions PQ and RS, respectively and $h \approx a$

(b) currents in wire 1 and wire 2 are in the directions PQ and SR, respectively and $h \approx a$

(c) currents in wire 1 and wire 2 are in the directions PQ and SR, respectively and $h \approx 1.2a$

(d) currents in wire 1 and wire 2 are in the directions PQ and RS, respectively and $h \approx 1.2a$

5 Consider $d >> a$, and the loop is rotated about its diameter parallel to the wires by 30° from the position shown in the figure. If the currents in the wires are in the opposite directions, the torque on the loop at its new position will be (assume that the net field due to the wires is constant over the loop) **(2014)**

(a) $\frac{\mu_0 I^2 a^2}{d}$ (b) $\frac{\mu_0 I^2 a^2}{2d}$

(c) $\frac{\sqrt{3}\mu_0 I^2 a^2}{d}$ (d) $\frac{\sqrt{3}\mu_0 I^2 a^2}{2d}$

6 A loop carrying current I lies in the x-y plane as shown in the figure. The unit vector $\hat{\mathbf{k}}$ is coming out of the plane of the paper. The magnetic moment of the current loop is **(2012)**

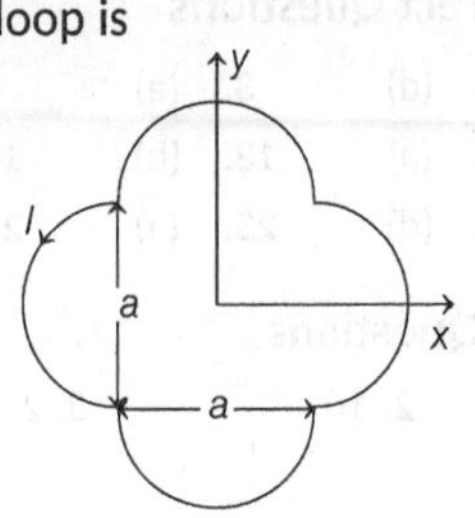

(a) $a^2 I\,\hat{\mathbf{k}}$ (b) $\left(\frac{\pi}{2}+1\right) a^2 I\,\hat{\mathbf{k}}$

(c) $-\left(\frac{\pi}{2}+1\right) a^2 I\,\hat{\mathbf{k}}$ (d) $(2\pi+1)\, a^2 I\,\hat{\mathbf{k}}$

Answer Key

Level 1

3.1 Magnetic Force on a Current Carrying Wire

1. 6×10^{-2} N, $\perp$ to both the wire and the field.
2. 5×10^{-4} T, horizontal and $\perp$ to the wire.
3. (i) $F_{AB}=0, F_{AC}=40$ N, $\otimes$, $F_{BC}=40$ N, $\odot$ (ii) 0
4. $-2(\hat{i}+\hat{j})$ N
5. $\sqrt{2}B_0 iL$
6. $F_{res}=2BIR$, $\tau=0$
7. $F_{net}=iB(a+\sqrt{c^2-b^2}+2r+d)$
8. $-\frac{\mu_0 i_1 i_2}{2\pi}[\hat{i}+(\ln 2)\hat{j}]$
9. (a) $\frac{Bil}{mg}$ (b) $\frac{Bil}{2m}$, towards right
10. 5×10^{-3} T
11. $B=0.3$ T
12. $2\pi BiR\otimes$
13. (a) $Bidl$ (b) BiR
14. $\sqrt{2}\pi aiB_0$

3.2 Magnetic Force between parallel Current Carrying Wires

1. 40 cm
2. 2 cm from 20 A current and 8 cm from the other
3. $40\ln 2\times10^{-6}$ J/m
4. (i) $\frac{\mu_0 i_1 i_2 l}{2\pi mg}$ (ii) $2\pi\sqrt{\frac{h}{g}}$

3.3 Magnetic Dipole Moment

1. $M=4\pi\times10^{-24}$ A-m^2
2. $\frac{Q\omega R^2}{4}$
3. $\frac{\pi R^2 I}{2}(\hat{i}+\hat{j})$
4. $(Il^2)\hat{j}$
5. (i) $\frac{1}{2}\pi i(R_2^2-R_1^2)$ (ii) $\frac{1}{2}\pi i(R_1^2+R_2^2)$
6. $4(\hat{j}-\sqrt{3}\hat{k})$ A-m^2

3.4 Magnetic Force and Torque on a Current Carrying Loop

1. (i) $4\pi\times10^{-2}$ N-m (ii) 60°
2. (i) 1.28 A-m^2 (ii) 0, 0.048 N-m
3. 7.1×10^{-4} N-m $-\hat{j}$ the loop will rotate about the Y-axis, so as to decrease the angle labelled 60°
4. $\pm75\pi\times10^{-3}$ J
5. (i) 0, MB (ii) $\left(\frac{2MB}{I}\right)^{\frac{1}{2}}$
6. 0.57 s
7. 4.9 T
8. $\frac{mg}{2il}$

Level 2

Single Choice Correct Questions

1. (b)	2. (d)	3. (a)	4. (b)	5. (a)	6. (b)	7. (b)	8. (c)	9. (b)	10. (a)
11. (a)	12. (a)	13. (b)	14. (d)	15. (a)	16. (c)	17. (c)	18. (b)	19. (c)	20. (a)
21. (a)	22. (d)	23. (a)	24. (b)	25. (d)	26. (a)	27. (a)	28. (c)	29. (b)	30. (c)

Numerical Value Questions

1. 6	2. 16	3. 2	4. 10	5. 20	6. 4.50	7. 8	8. 10

Level 3

Single Choice Correct Questions

1. (c)	2. (c)	3. (d)	4. (d)	5. (b)	6. (b)	7. (d)	8. (a)	9. (a)	10. (b)
11. (b)	12. (a)	13. (c)	14. (a)	15. (b)	16. (b)	17. (a)	18. (b)	19. (a)	20. (b)

Multiple Choice(s) Correct Questions

1. (a, d) 2. (a, b, d) 3. (b, c, d) 4. (a, b, c) 5. (a, b, c, d) 6. (a, c, d) 7. (b, c)
8. (b, d) 9. (b, c, d)

Comprehension Based Questions

1. (a) 2. (a) 3. (a) 4. (a) 5. (d) 6. (b) 7. (a)
8. (c) 9. (c) 10. (a) 11. (a) 12. (b) 13. (b) 14. (b)
15. (a) 16. (c)

Match the Columns Questions

1. A→ 3, 4 ; B→ 3, 4 ; C→ 2, 3 ; D→ 1, 3 2. A→ 2 ; B→ 1, 3 ; C→ 1, 3 ; D→ 1, 4
3. A→ 1, 4; B→ 3, 4; C→ 2, 3

Numerical Value Questions

1. 4 2. 720 3. 37 4. 5 5. 525 6. 2.5 7. 0.4 8. 78

Previous Years Questions

JEE Main

1. (d) 2. (c) 3. (35) 4. (a) 5. (a) 6. (2) 7. (a) 8. (b) 9. (b) 10. (d)
11. (d) 12. (a) 13. (3) 14. (3) 15. (a) 16. (b) 17. (20) 18. (*) 19. (b) 20. (d)
21. (b) 22. (a) 23. (d)

JEE Advanced

1. (*) 2. (b) 3. (a,b,c) 4. (c) 5. (b) 6. (b)

SOLUTIONS

Level 1

3.1 Magnetic Force on a Current Carrying Wire

1. $F = Bil\sin\theta = 0.1\times 10\times 0.1\times \sin 37° = 6\times 10^{-2}$ N,
perpendicular to both the wire and the field.

2. $Bil\sin\theta = mg$
$\Rightarrow B_{min}(10)\,(0.2)\sin 90° = 10^{-4}\times 10$
$(\because \theta = 90°$ for B to be minimum$)$
$\Rightarrow B_{min} = 5\times 10^{-4}$ T, horizontal and perpendicular to wire.

3. (i) $\mathbf{F}_{AC} = Bil\sin 90°\otimes = 2\times 5\times 4\sin 90°, \otimes = 40$ N, $\otimes$
$\mathbf{F}_{AB} = 0 \quad (\because \theta = 0°)$
$\mathbf{F}_{CB} = 2\times 5\times 5\sin 53°, \odot = 40$ N, $\odot$
(ii) $\mathbf{F}_{\text{net}} = \mathbf{F}_{AB} + \mathbf{F}_{AC} + \mathbf{F}_{CB} = 0$

4. Coordinates of point $A = (0.2, 0, 0.2)$
Coordinates of point $B = (0, 0.2, 0)$
$\mathbf{L} = \mathbf{r}_A - \mathbf{r}_B = 0.2\hat{i} - 0.2\hat{j} + 0.2\hat{k}$
$\mathbf{F} = i\,(\mathbf{L}\times\mathbf{B}) = 5[0.2(\hat{i} - \hat{j} + \hat{k})\times(2\hat{k})]$
$= -2(\hat{i} + \hat{j})$ N

5. $\mathbf{F} = i(\mathbf{L}\times\mathbf{B}) = i[L\hat{j}\times B_0(\hat{i}+\hat{j}+\hat{k})] = B_0 iL(\hat{i}-\hat{k})$
$F = \sqrt{2}\,B_0 iL$

6.

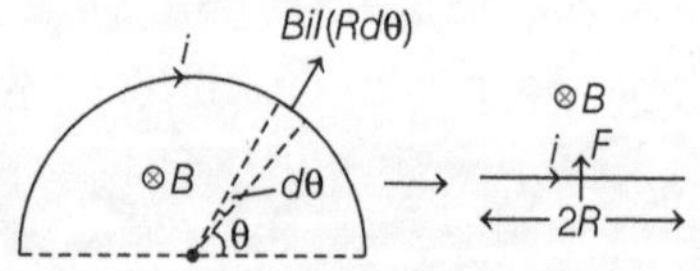

$F = Bil\sin\theta = Bi\,(2R)\sin 90° = 2BiR$

7. Effective length $= AB = a + \sqrt{c^2 - b^2} + 2r + d$
$F = Bil\sin\theta = Bi(a + \sqrt{c^2 - b^2} + 2r + d)\sin 90°$
$= Bi(a + \sqrt{c^2 - b^2} + 2r + d)$

8. $\mathbf{F}_{CA} = \left(\dfrac{\mu_0 i_1}{2\pi a}\right) i_2 a\sin 90°(-\hat{i}) = \dfrac{\mu_0 i_1 i_2}{2\pi}(-\hat{i})$

$\mathbf{F}_{BC} = \displaystyle\int_a^{2a}\left(\dfrac{\mu_0 i_1}{2\pi x}\right) i_2\,dx\sin 90°(-\hat{j})$

$= \dfrac{\mu_0 i_1 i_2}{2\pi}[\ln 2(-\hat{j})]$

$\mathbf{F}_{AB} = \mathbf{F}_{CA} + \mathbf{F}_{BC} = -\dfrac{\mu_0 i_1 i_2}{2\pi}[\hat{i} + (\ln 2)\hat{j}]$

9. (i) $f_L = \mu N = \mu\, mg$
To slide the wire,
$Bil = \mu\, mg \Rightarrow \mu = \dfrac{Bil}{mg}$

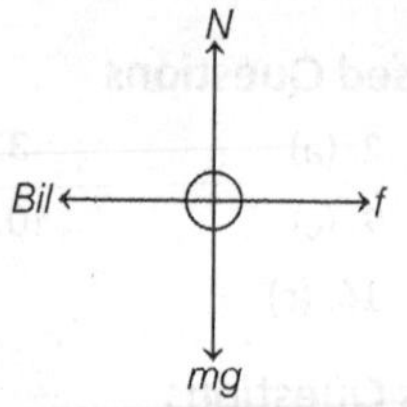

(ii) $\Sigma F = ma \Rightarrow Bil - \left(\dfrac{\mu}{2}\right) mg = ma$
$\Rightarrow a = \dfrac{Bil}{2m}$, towards right

10. Initially for equilibrium of rod, $2kx_0 = mg$
$\Rightarrow 2k(4\times 10^{-2}) = 10\times 10^{-3}\times 10$
$\Rightarrow \qquad k = 1.25$ N/m
When current is passed through rod, for new equilibrium,
$2k(x_0 - x) + Bil = mg$
$\Rightarrow 2\times 1.25\times 3\times 10^{-2} + B\,(20)\,(0.25) = 10\times 10^{-3}\times 10$
$\Rightarrow B = 5\times 10^{-3}$ T

11. Magnetic force on wire will be Bil, horizontal as shown in figure.

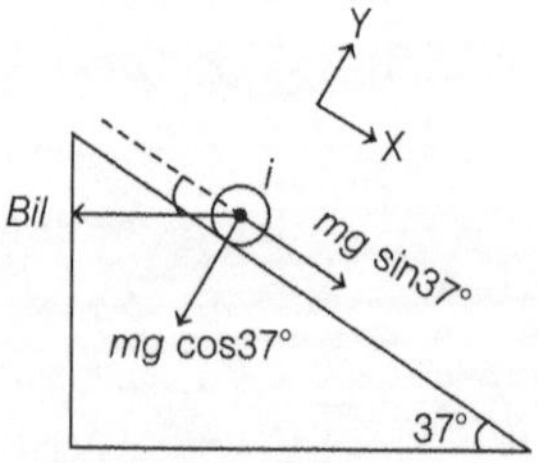

$\Sigma F_x = 0$
$\Rightarrow mg\sin 37° - Bil\cos 37° = 0$
$\Rightarrow \quad B = \dfrac{mg\tan 37°}{il} = \dfrac{50\times 10^{-3}\times 10\times 0.75}{2.5\times 0.5} = 0.3$ T

12. Force on small element,
$d\mathbf{F} = [Bi(Rd\theta)\sin 90°]\otimes$
$\int d\mathbf{F} = (BiR\int d\theta)\otimes$
$F = 2\pi BiR$, into the plane

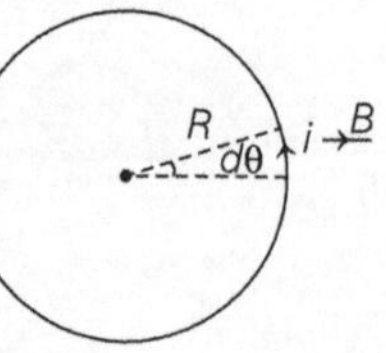

13. (i) Force on dl element $= Bidl$, radially out

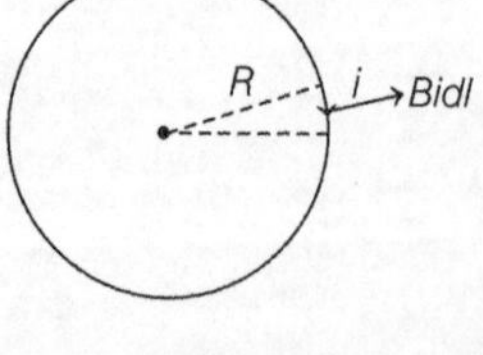

(ii) For equilibrium of dl element,

$$2T\sin\left(\frac{d\theta}{2}\right) = BiR\,d\theta$$

$$\Rightarrow \quad Td\theta = BiRd\theta$$

$$\Rightarrow \quad T = BiR$$

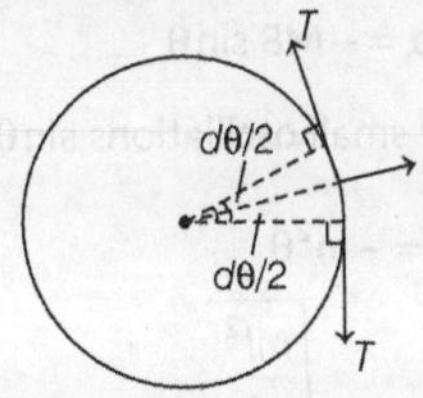

14. Force due to $B_0 \cos\theta$ on the loop is zero as forces on diametrically opposite elements will cancel out.

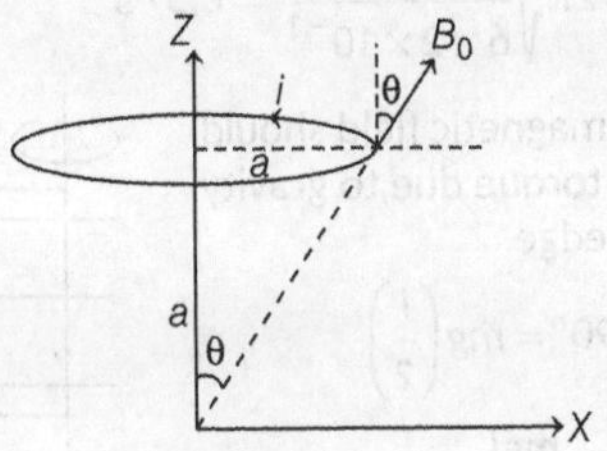

Force due to $B_0 \sin\theta = \int (B_0 \sin\theta)\, idl \sin 90°$

$$= B_0 i \sin 45°(2\pi a)$$

$$= \sqrt{2}\, B_0 i\pi a$$

3.2 Magnetic Force between Parallel Current Carrying Wires

1. $\dfrac{dF}{dl} = \dfrac{\mu_0 i_1 i_2}{2\pi r}$

$$\Rightarrow 2.0\times 10^{-4} = \frac{4\pi\times 10^{-7}\times 20\times 20}{2\pi r}$$

$$\Rightarrow \quad r = 40 \text{ cm}$$

2.

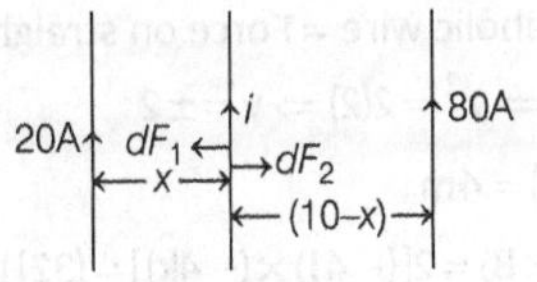

$$\frac{dF_1}{dl} = \frac{dF_2}{dl} \Rightarrow \frac{\mu_0(20)i}{2\pi x} = \frac{\mu_0 i(80)}{(10-x)}$$

$$\Rightarrow \quad x = 2 \text{ cm}$$

3. $W = \int F dr = \int_{r_1}^{r_2} \dfrac{\mu_0 i_1 i_2}{2\pi r}\, dr$

$$= \frac{\mu_0 i_1 i_2}{2\pi} \ln\left(\frac{r_2}{r_1}\right) = \frac{4\pi\times 10^{-7}\times 10\times 20}{2\pi} \ln\left(\frac{10}{5}\right)$$

$$= 40 \ln 2 \times 10^{-6} \text{ J/m}$$

4. (i) For equilibrium of wire PQ,

$$\left(\frac{\mu_0 i_1 i_2}{2\pi h}\right) l = mg$$

$$\Rightarrow \quad h = \frac{\mu_0 i_1 i_2 l}{2\pi mg}$$

(ii) Lets displace wire PQ by a distance x in vertically downward direction.

$$F = -\left[\frac{\mu_0 i_1 i_2 l}{2\pi h\left(1-\dfrac{x}{h}\right)} - mg\right]$$

$$\Rightarrow \quad F = -\left[\frac{\mu_0 i_1 i_2 l}{2\pi h}\left(1+\frac{x}{h}\right) - mg\right]$$

$$\Rightarrow \quad F = -\left(\frac{\mu_0 i_1 i_2 l}{2\pi h^2}\right)x = -\left(\frac{mg}{h}\right)x$$

Comparing it with $F = -kx \Rightarrow t = 2\pi\sqrt{\dfrac{h}{g}}$

3.3 Magnetic Dipole Moment

1. $M = i\pi R^2 = qf\pi R^2$

$$= 1.6\times 10^{-19} \times 10^{16} \times \pi \times (0.5\times 10^{-10})^2$$

$$= 4\pi \times 10^{-24} \text{ A-m}^2$$

2. $M = \displaystyle\int_O^R \left(\frac{Q}{\pi R^2} 2\pi r dr\right)\left(\frac{\omega}{2\pi}\right)\pi r^2 = \frac{Q\omega R^2}{4}$

3. We can keep two wires carrying currents in opposite directions along the diameter of the two halves. So, now we have two semicircular loops.

$$\mathbf{M} = i\left(\frac{\pi R^2}{2}\right)\hat{\mathbf{i}} + i\left(\frac{\pi R^2}{2}\right)\hat{\mathbf{j}} = \frac{i\pi R^2}{2}(\hat{\mathbf{i}} + \hat{\mathbf{j}})$$

4. Assume equal and opposite currents in wires ad and eh.

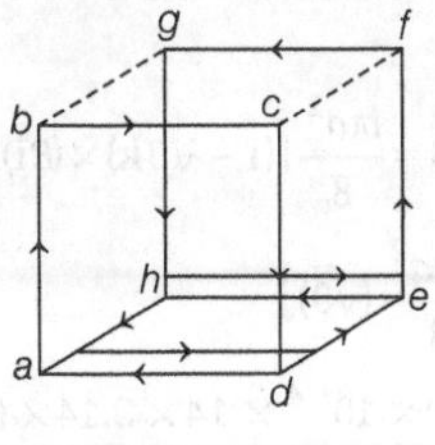

Now, we have 3 complete closed loops.

$$\mathbf{M}_{abcd} = il^2(-\hat{\mathbf{k}}),\ \mathbf{M}_{adeh} = Il^2(\hat{\mathbf{j}});\ \ \mathbf{M}_{efgh} = il^2(\hat{\mathbf{k}})$$

$$\mathbf{M} = \mathbf{M}_{abcd} + \mathbf{M}_{adeh} + \mathbf{M}_{efgh} = (il^2)\hat{\mathbf{j}}$$

5. (i) $\mathbf{M} = i\mathbf{A} \Rightarrow M = i\pi\left(\dfrac{R_2^2 - R_1^2}{2}\right)$

(ii) $M = i\pi\left(\dfrac{R_1^2 + R_2^2}{2}\right)$

6. $M = NiA = 100 \times 4.0 \times 20 \times 10^{-2} \times 10 \times 10^{-2} = 8 \text{ A-m}^2$

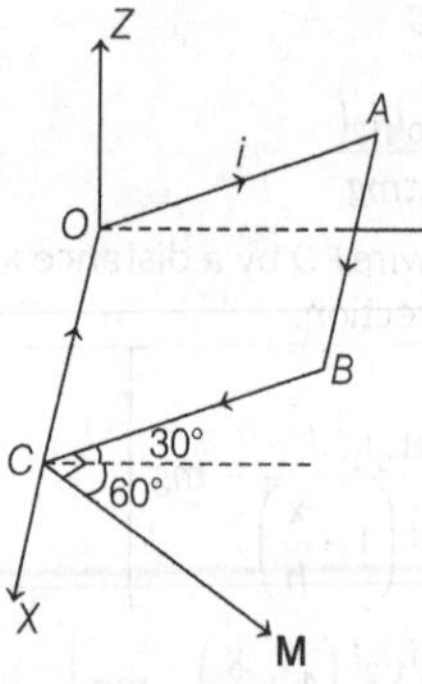

$\mathbf{M} = 8\cos 60°\,\hat{j} - 8\sin 60°\,\hat{k}$

$= 4(\hat{j} - \sqrt{3}\hat{k}) \text{ A-m}^2$

3.4 Magnetic Force and Torque on a Current Carrying Loop

1. (i) $\tau_{max} = NiAB = 50 \times 2.5 \times \pi(0.04)^2 \times 0.2$

$= 4\pi \times 10^{-2}$ N-m

(ii) $\tau = NiAB \sin\theta \Rightarrow \frac{NiAB}{2} = NiAB \sin\theta$

$\Rightarrow \sin\theta = \frac{1}{2} \Rightarrow \theta = 30°$

Angle between magnetic field and the plane of the coil $= 90° - 30° = 60°$

2. (i) $M = NiA = 2000 \times 4 \times 1.6 \times 10^{-4} = 1.28 \text{ A-m}^2$

(ii) $F = 0;\ \tau = MB\sin\theta = 1.28 \times 7.5 \times 10^{-2} \times \frac{1}{2}$

$= 4.8 \times 10^{-2}$ N-m

3. $\mathbf{M} = i\left(\frac{\pi a^2}{4}\right)(\cos 60°\,\hat{i} - \sin 60°\,\hat{k}) = \frac{i\pi a^2}{8}(\hat{i} - \sqrt{3}\hat{k})$

$\mathbf{B} = B\hat{i}$

$\tau = \mathbf{M} \times \mathbf{B} = \frac{i\pi a^2}{8}[(\hat{i} - \sqrt{3}\hat{k}) \times (B\hat{i})]$

$= -\frac{Bi\pi a^2}{8}(\sqrt{3})\hat{j}$

$= -\frac{300 \times 10^{-4} \times 14 \times 3.14 \times (0.05)^2 \times \sqrt{3}}{8}\hat{j}$

$= 7.1 \times 10^{-4}$ N-m $(-\hat{j})$

The loop will rotate about Y-axis, so as to decrease the angle labelled 60°.

4. $W_{ext} = \Delta U = \pm MB - (\mp MB) = \pm 2MB$

$= \pm 2 \times 100 \times 0.1 \times \pi(0.05)^2 \times 1.5$

$= \pm 75\pi \times 10^{-3}$ J

5. (i) Initially $\theta = 0°$, $\tau = MB\sin\theta = 0$

Finally $\theta = 90°$; $\tau = MB\sin\theta = MB$

(ii) $K_1 + U_1 = K_2 + U_2$

$\Rightarrow 0 - MB = \frac{1}{2}I\omega^2 + 0$

$\Rightarrow \omega = \sqrt{\frac{2MB}{I}}$

6. $\tau = -MB\sin\theta \Rightarrow I\alpha = -MB\sin\theta$

$\Rightarrow \alpha = -\frac{MB}{I}\theta$ (For small oscillations $\sin\theta \approx \theta$)

Comparing it with $\alpha = -\omega^2\theta$

$T = 2\pi\sqrt{\frac{I}{MB}} = 2\pi\sqrt{\frac{\frac{ml^2}{6}}{il^2B}}$

$= 2\pi\sqrt{\frac{10 \times 10^{-3}}{6 \times 2 \times 10^{-1}}} = 0.57$ s

7. Torque of magnetic field should overcome torque due to gravity about the edge.

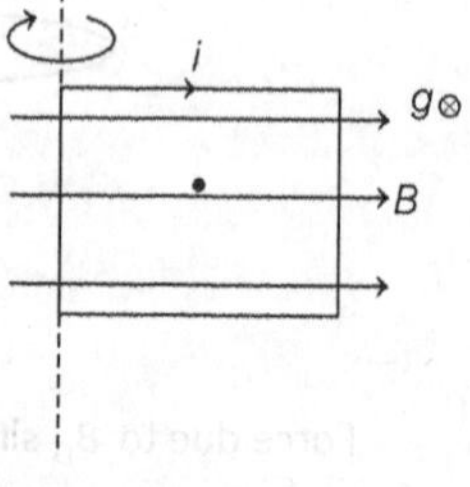

$MB_{min} \sin 90° = mg\left(\frac{l}{2}\right)$

$\Rightarrow nil^2B_{min} = \frac{mgl}{2}$

$\Rightarrow \quad B_{min} = \frac{mg}{2nil} = \frac{10 \times 9.8}{2 \times 10 \times 1 \times 1} = 4.9$ T

8. Loss in magnetic potential energy of loop = Gain in gravitational potential energy of cardboard

$\Rightarrow 0 - (-MB_{min}\cos 0°) = mg\left(\frac{l}{2}\right)$

$\Rightarrow \quad B_{min} = \frac{mg}{2il}$

LEVEL 2

Single Choice Correct Questions

1. Force on parabolic wire = Force on straight wire AB

$y^2 = 2x \Rightarrow y^2 = 2(2) \Rightarrow y = \pm 2$

$AB = 2(2) = 4$m

$F_{AB} = i(\mathbf{L} \times \mathbf{B}) = 2[(-4\hat{j}) \times (-4\hat{k})] = (32\hat{i})$ N

2. Force on the segment parallel to X-axis will be zero. Forces on the two segments parallel to Y-axis cancel out each other. Force on the segment parallel to Z-axis

$= i(\mathbf{L} \times \mathbf{B}) = 25(-0.4\hat{k} \times 2\hat{i}) = -20\hat{j}$

3. $F_{PS} = Bi(\sqrt{2}R) = F$

$F_{PQR} = Bi(2R) = 2\left(\frac{F}{\sqrt{2}}\right) = \sqrt{2}F$

4. $F = Bi_1l + Bi_2l = B(i_1 + i_2)l = Bil$

5. Forces on BC and DA cancel out each other.

$$F_{AB}=\left[\frac{\mu_0 i_2}{2\pi\left(\frac{l}{2}\right)}\right]i_1 l=\frac{\mu_0 i_1 i_2}{\pi}$$

$$F_{CD}=\left[\frac{\mu_0 i_2}{2\pi\left(\frac{3l}{2}\right)}\right]i_1 l=\frac{\mu_0 i_1 i_2}{3\pi}$$

$$F_{net}=F_{AB}-F_{CD}=\frac{2\mu_0 i_1 i_2}{3\pi}$$

6. Forces on AB and CD cancel out each other. Resultant of forces on DA and BC will be directed towards right. So, net force on the loop is away from the long wire.

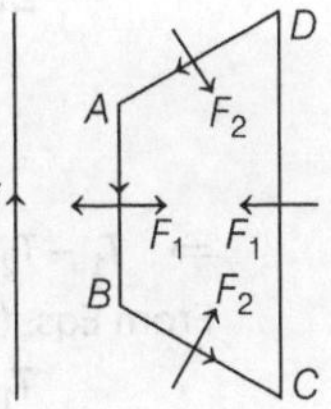

7. Semicircular wire can be replaced with a wire along its diameter.

$$\mathbf{L}=2\cos 45°\,\hat{\mathbf{i}}+2\sin 45\,\hat{\mathbf{j}}=\sqrt{2}(\hat{\mathbf{i}}+\hat{\mathbf{j}})$$

$$\mathbf{F}=i(\mathbf{L}\times\mathbf{B})=1[(\sqrt{2}(\hat{\mathbf{i}}+\hat{\mathbf{j}})\times(3\hat{\mathbf{i}}+4\hat{\mathbf{j}}+\hat{\mathbf{k}})]$$

$$=\sqrt{2}(\hat{\mathbf{i}}-\hat{\mathbf{j}}+\hat{\mathbf{k}})\text{ N}$$

8. $$\int dF=\int_x^{x+l}\left(\frac{\mu_0 i_2}{2\pi r}\right)i_1\,dr$$

$$F=\frac{\mu_0 i_1 i_2}{2\pi}\ln\left(\frac{x+l}{x}\right)$$

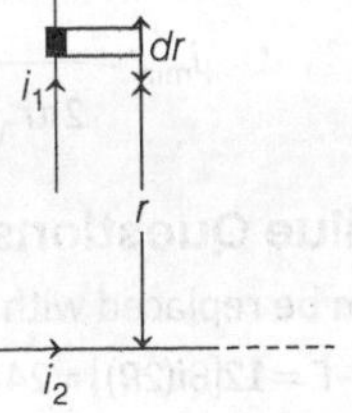

9. $$\mathbf{F}_{ABC}=\mathbf{F}_{AC}=I(\mathbf{L}_{AC}\times\mathbf{B})$$

$$=2[(3\times10^{-2})\hat{\mathbf{i}}\times(-2\hat{\mathbf{k}})]=(12\times10^{-2})\hat{\mathbf{j}}$$

$$\mathbf{a}=\frac{\mathbf{F}}{m}=\frac{(12\times10^{-2})\hat{\mathbf{j}}}{(10\times10^{-3})}=12\text{ m/s}^2(\hat{\mathbf{j}})$$

10. Initially, $2kx_0=mg$ ...(i)

After switching on magnetic field,

$2k(x_0+x_0)=mg+Bil$ ...(ii)

From Eqs. (i) and (ii), we get

$$B=\frac{mg}{il}=\frac{mgR}{\varepsilon l}$$

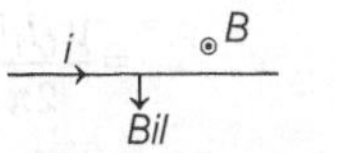

Direction of magnetic field will be out of the plane as current ⊙ through rod is flowing towards right and magnetic force is directed vertically down.

11. $Bil=\mu mg \Rightarrow B\left(\frac{\varepsilon}{R}\right)l=\mu mg$

$$\Rightarrow \mu=\frac{B\varepsilon l}{mgR}=\frac{0.8\times6\times4.9\times10^{-2}}{10\times10^{-3}\times9.8\times20}$$

$$=0.12$$

12. $N=(mg+Bil)\cos\alpha$

$f_L=\mu N=\mu(mg+Bil)\cos\alpha$

$F_{min}=(mg+Bil)\sin\alpha$

$-\mu(mg+Bil)\cos\alpha$

$=(mg+Bil)(\sin\alpha-\mu\cos\alpha)$

$=2\text{N}$

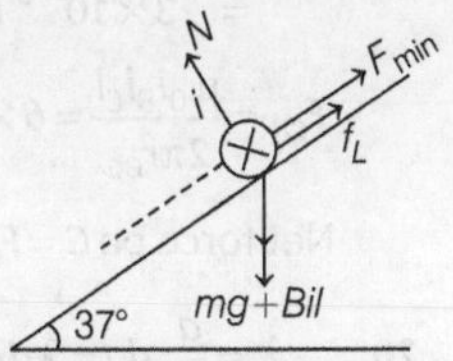

13. Net torque due to magnetic force on the two parallel sides is zero. So, for equilibrium

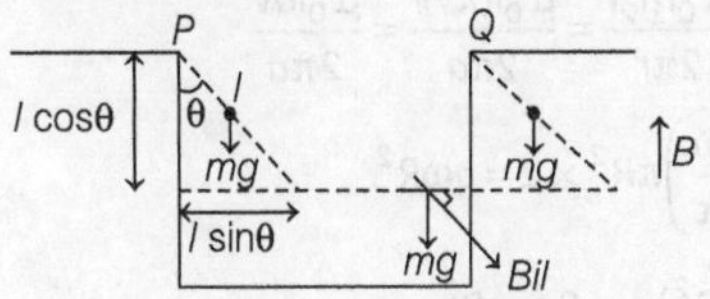

$$T_{\text{due to gravity}}=T_{\text{due to magnetic force on horizontal side}}$$

$$\Rightarrow(\lambda lg)l\sin\theta+(\lambda lg)\left(\frac{l}{2}\sin\theta\right)+(\lambda lg)\left(\frac{l}{2}\sin\theta\right)$$

$$=(Bil)(l\cos\theta)$$

$$\Rightarrow\tan\theta=\frac{Bi}{2\lambda g}=\frac{2\times10\sqrt{3}}{2\times\sqrt{3}\times10}=1$$

$$\Rightarrow\quad\theta=45°$$

14. $$2T\sin\left(\frac{d\theta}{2}\right)=Bi(Rd\theta)$$

$$\Rightarrow Td\theta=BiRd\theta$$

$$\Rightarrow\quad T=BiR$$

$$=0.2\times100\times0.5$$

$$=10\text{ N}$$

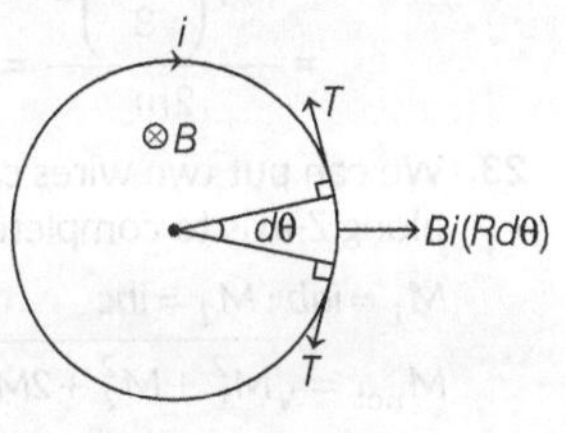

15. $Bil=ma\Rightarrow Bdql=md\theta$

$$\Rightarrow Bl\int dq=m\int d\theta$$

$$\Rightarrow\quad q=\frac{mv}{Bl}=\frac{m\sqrt{2gh}}{Bl}$$

16. $$\tau=i\alpha\Rightarrow(Bil)\frac{l}{2}=\left(\frac{ml^2}{3}\right)\alpha$$

$$\Rightarrow\alpha=\frac{3iB}{2m}$$

17. Forces on AB and CD will cancel out each other.

$$F_{DA}=\left[B_0\left(1+\frac{x}{l}\right)\right]il$$

$$F_{BC}=B_0\left(1+\frac{x+l}{l}\right)il$$

$$F_{\text{net}}=F_{BC}-F_{DA}=B_0 il$$

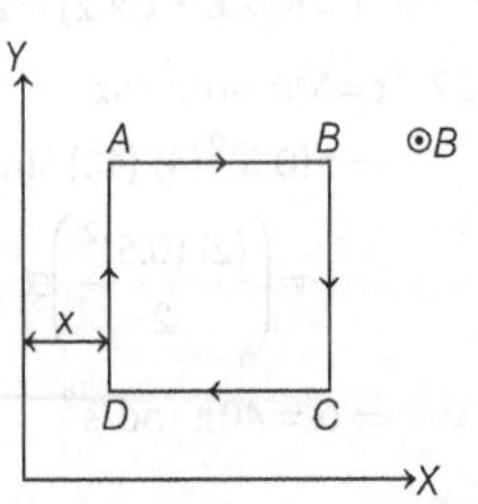

18. $F_{CA} = -\left(\dfrac{\mu_0 i_A i_C l}{2\pi r_{AC}}\right) = \dfrac{4\pi \times 10^{-7} \times 10 \times 10 \times 0.15}{2\pi(0.1)}$

$= -3 \times 10^{-5}$ N

$F_{CB} = \dfrac{\mu_0 i_B i_C l}{2\pi r_{BC}} = 6 \times 10^{-5}$ N

Net force on $C = F_{CA} + F_{CB} = 3 \times 10^{-5}$ N (right)

20. $\lambda = \dfrac{q}{l}$; $dq = \lambda dx \Rightarrow \dfrac{dq}{dt} = \lambda \dfrac{dx}{dt}$

$\Rightarrow i = \lambda v$

$F = \dfrac{\mu_0 i_1 i_2 l}{2\pi r} = \dfrac{\mu_0 i(\lambda v) l}{2\pi a} = \dfrac{\mu_0 i q v}{2\pi a}$

21. $M = \left(\dfrac{q\omega}{2\pi}\right)\pi R^2 \times 2 = q\omega R^2$

$L = (2mR^2)\omega = 2m\omega R^2$

$\Rightarrow \dfrac{M}{L} = \dfrac{q}{2m}$

22. $\dfrac{M}{L} = \dfrac{q}{2m}$

$\Rightarrow M = \dfrac{qL}{2m} = \dfrac{ql\omega}{2m}$

$= \dfrac{(\lambda l)\left(\dfrac{ml^2}{3}\right)\omega}{2m} = \dfrac{\lambda\omega l^3}{6}$

23. We can put two wires carrying equal and opposite currents along Z-axis to complete the two loops.

$M_1 = iab$; $M_2 = ibc$

$M_{net} = \sqrt{M_1^2 + M_2^2 + 2M_1M_2 \cos 60°} = 12.2$ A-m^2

24. $\tau = NiAB \sin\theta = (2n)(2i)(2a)B \sin 30° = 8Bnai \cos 60°$

25. $\tau = NiAB \sin\theta$

Couple (torque) will be maximum for circular loop as circle has the greatest area for a given perimeter.

26. We can put wires carrying equal and opposite currents along CH and DG to complete three loops.

$\mathbf{M} = \mathbf{M}_{ABCH} + \mathbf{M}_{CDGH} + \mathbf{M}_{DEFG}$

$= (1)^2(1)\hat{\mathbf{j}} + (1)^2(1)\hat{\mathbf{i}} + (1)^2(1)(-\hat{\mathbf{j}}) = (1)\hat{\mathbf{i}}$

$\tau = \mathbf{M} \times \mathbf{B} = \hat{\mathbf{i}} \times 2\hat{\mathbf{j}} = 2\hat{\mathbf{k}}$

27. $\tau = MB \sin\theta = I\alpha$

$\Rightarrow \pi(0.5)^2(4)(10) \sin 90°$

$= \left(\dfrac{(2)(0.5)^2}{2}\right)\alpha$

$\Rightarrow \alpha = 40\pi$ rad/s^2

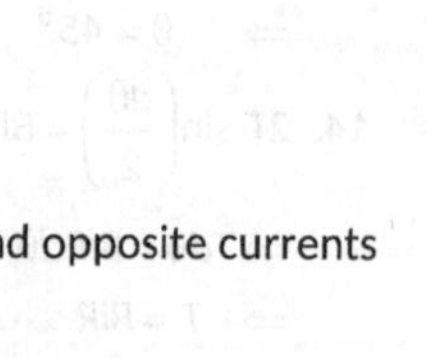

28. $U_1 = -MB\cos\theta = -(ni\pi r^2)\left(\dfrac{\mu_0 Ni}{2R}\right)\cos 0°$

$U_2 = -MB\cos\theta = -(ni\pi r^2)\left(\dfrac{\mu_0 Ni}{2R}\right)\cos\pi$

$W_{ext} = \Delta U = U_2 - U_1 = \dfrac{\mu_0 \pi n N r^2 i^2}{R}$

29. $\tau = \mathbf{M} \times \mathbf{B} = MB \sin\theta\, \hat{\mathbf{n}} = (i\pi R^2)B \sin 45°(-\hat{\mathbf{j}})$

$= \left(\dfrac{Bi\pi R^2}{\sqrt{2}}\right)(-\hat{\mathbf{j}})$

$\Sigma F = 0 \Rightarrow T_1 + T_2 = mg$ ...(i)

$\Sigma\tau = 0 \Rightarrow [T_1(R\cos 45°)]\hat{\mathbf{j}} + T_2(R\cos 45°)(-\hat{\mathbf{j}})$

$= \left(\dfrac{Bi\pi R^2}{\sqrt{2}}\right)(-\hat{\mathbf{j}})$

$\Rightarrow T_1 - T_2 = Bi\pi R$ ...(ii)

From Eqs. (i) and (ii), we get

$\dfrac{T_1}{T_2} = \dfrac{mg + Bi\pi R}{mg - Bi\pi R} = \dfrac{5}{3}$

30. $\tau = \mathbf{M} \times \mathbf{B} = (i\pi r^2)\hat{\mathbf{k}} \times (B_x\hat{\mathbf{i}} + B_y\hat{\mathbf{j}})$

$= i\pi r^2(-B_y\hat{\mathbf{i}} + B_x\hat{\mathbf{j}})$

To lift one end of loop from the table, $\tau_{magnetic} \geq \tau_{mg}$

$\Rightarrow \quad i\pi r^2\sqrt{B_x^2 + B_y^2} \geq mg\left(\dfrac{r}{2}\right)$

$\Rightarrow \quad i \geq \dfrac{mg}{2\pi r\sqrt{B_x^2 + B_y^2}}$

$\Rightarrow \quad i_{min} = \dfrac{mg}{2\pi r\sqrt{B_x^2 + B_y^2}}$

Numerical Value Questions

1. Each wire can be replaced with a straight wire along BA.

$F = 12[Bi(2R)] = 24BiR = 6$ N

2. $PQ = 3a \sec 60° = 6a$

Lets take an element dx on wire PQ.

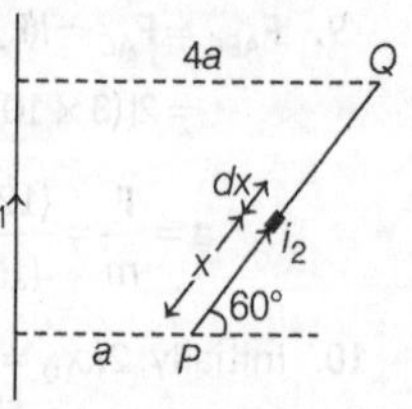

$\displaystyle\int dF = \int_0^{6a}\left(\frac{\mu_0 i_1}{2\pi(a + x\cos 60°)}\right) i_2\, dx$

$F = \dfrac{\mu_0 i_1 i_2}{2\pi}[2\ln(2a + x)]_0^{6a}$

$= \dfrac{\mu_0 i_1 i_2}{2\pi}\ln(16)$

$= \dfrac{\mu_0 i_1 i_2}{2\pi}\ln x$

So, $x = 16$

3. $F_B = mg \Rightarrow \int (B \sin 30°)\, i dl = mg$

$\Rightarrow (B \sin 30°)\, i(2\pi R) = mg$

$\Rightarrow \quad B = \dfrac{mg}{\pi i R} = \dfrac{40 \times 10^{-3} \times 10\pi}{\pi(10)(2 \times 10^{-2})} = 2$T

4. $F(\Delta p)A = Bil\sin\theta$

$$\Rightarrow eg(\Delta h)A = Bil\sin\theta \Rightarrow \Delta h = \frac{Bil\sin\theta}{egA}$$

$$= \frac{5.44\times 10\times 4\times 10^{-3}\ \sin 90°}{13.6\times 10^{3}\times 10\times (4\times 10^{-3})^2} = 10\text{ cm}$$

5. $mgx = MB\sin\theta$

$$\Rightarrow \left(\frac{\pi}{100}\right)(10)x = [100\times 2\times \pi(0.1)^2)(10^{-2})]\sin 90°$$

$$\Rightarrow \quad x = 20\times 10^{-2}\text{ m} = 20\text{ cm}$$

6. We can put wires along *BC*, *CD* and *CF* to complete 3 loops.

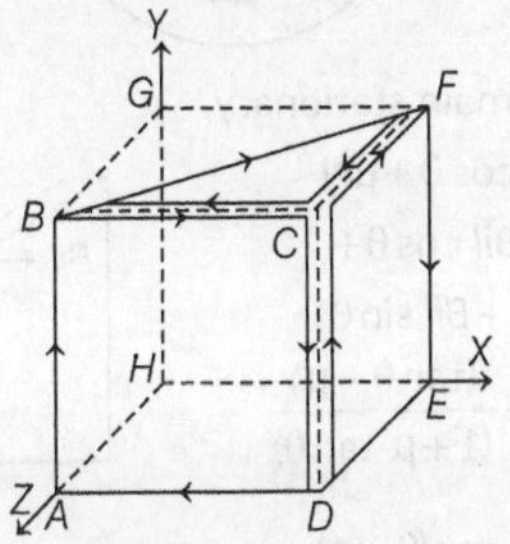

$$\mathbf{M} = \mathbf{M}_{CDEF} + \mathbf{M}_{BFC} + \mathbf{M}_{ABCD}$$

$$= (1)^2\,(3)(-\hat{i}) + \left(\frac{1}{2}\times 1\times 1\right)(3)(\hat{j}) + (1)^2(3)(-\hat{k})$$

$$= (-3\hat{i} + 1.5\hat{j} - 3\hat{k})\text{ A-m}^2$$

$$M = \sqrt{(3)^2 + (1.5)^2 + (3)^2} = 4.5\text{ A-m}^2$$

7. Torque on circular portions will be zero as magnetic field is tangential to circular portions.

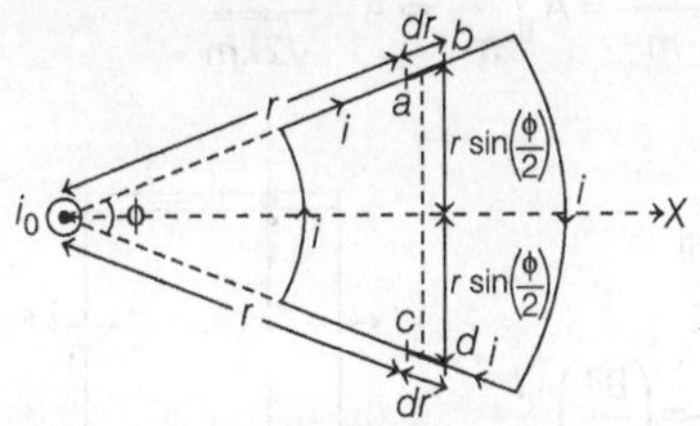

Force on *dr* element $= dF = \left(\frac{\mu_0 i_0}{2\pi r}\right) i\,dr\sin 90°$

Force on *ab* is out of the plane and force on *cd* is into the plane.

So, torque about *X*-axis,

$$\int d\tau = \int_{r_0}^{2r_0}\left[2r\sin\left(\frac{\phi}{2}\right)\right]\left(\frac{\mu_0 i_0 i}{2\pi r}\right)dr$$

$$\Rightarrow \quad \tau = \frac{\mu_0 i_0 i}{\pi}\sin\left(\frac{\phi}{2}\right)\int_{r_0}^{2r_0} dr$$

$$\Rightarrow \quad \tau = \frac{\mu_0 i_0 i r_0}{\pi}\sin\left(\frac{\phi}{2}\right) = 8\times 10^{-7}\text{ N-m}$$

8. **M** when it is lifted by $45° = il^2\cdot\left(\frac{\hat{j}+\hat{k}}{\sqrt{2}}\right)$

$$\tau_B = \mathbf{M}\times\mathbf{B} = \frac{il^2}{\sqrt{2}}[(\hat{j}+\hat{k})\times(3\hat{i}+4\hat{j})]$$

$$= \frac{il^2}{\sqrt{2}}(-4\hat{i} + 3\hat{j} - 3\hat{k})$$

$$\tau_{mg}\text{ (about top edge)} = \left(mg\frac{l}{2}\cos 45° + mg\frac{l}{2}\cos 45° + mgl\cos 45° + 0\right)\hat{i}$$

$$= 2mgl\cos 45°\,\hat{i}$$

For equilibrium net torque about *X*-axis = 0

$$2mgl\cos 45° = 4\left(\frac{il^2}{\sqrt{2}}\right)$$

$$\Rightarrow \quad i = \frac{mg}{2l} = 10\text{ A}$$

LEVEL 3

Single Choice Correct Questions

1.

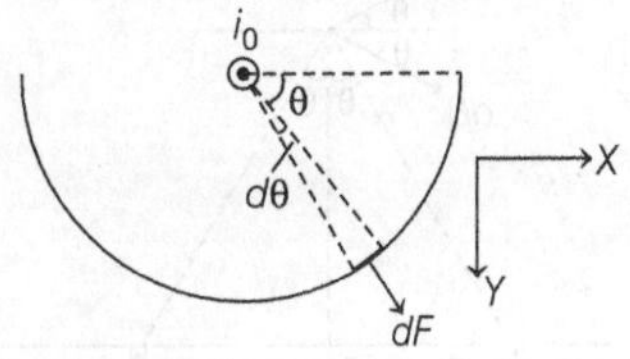

$$dF = \left(\frac{\mu_0 i_0}{2\pi R}\right)\left(\frac{i}{\pi R}R\,d\theta\right)$$

$$\int d\mathbf{F} = \int dF\cos\theta\,\hat{i} + \int dF\sin\theta\,\hat{j}$$

$$\mathbf{F} = \frac{\mu_0 i_0 i}{2\pi^2 R}\int_0^{\pi}\sin\theta\,d\theta(\hat{j}) \Rightarrow F = \frac{\mu_0 i_0 i}{\pi^2 R}$$

2.

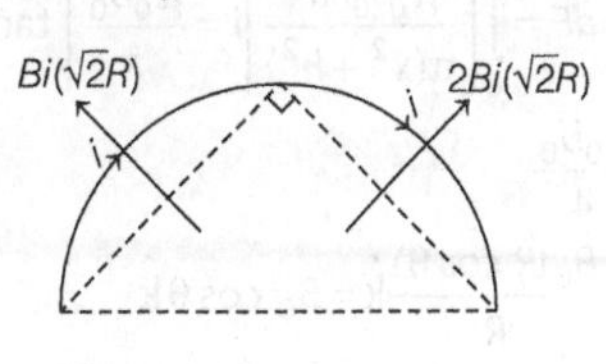

$$\text{Net force} = \sqrt{(\sqrt{2}\,BiR)^2 + (2\sqrt{2}\,BiR)^2} = \sqrt{10}\,BiR$$

3.

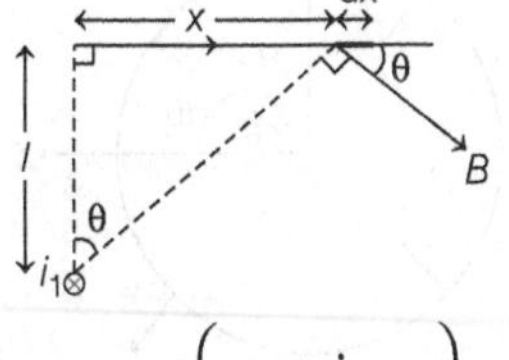

$$dF = Bi_2 dx\sin\theta = \left(\frac{\mu_0 i_1}{2\pi\sqrt{l^2+x^2}}\right) i_2 dx\left(\frac{x}{\sqrt{l^2+x^2}}\right)$$

$$\Rightarrow \quad \int dF = \frac{\mu_0 i_1 i_2}{4\pi}\int_0^{2l}\frac{2x\,dx}{l^2+x^2}$$

$$\Rightarrow \quad F = \frac{\mu_0 i_1 i_2}{4\pi}\ln 5$$

4.

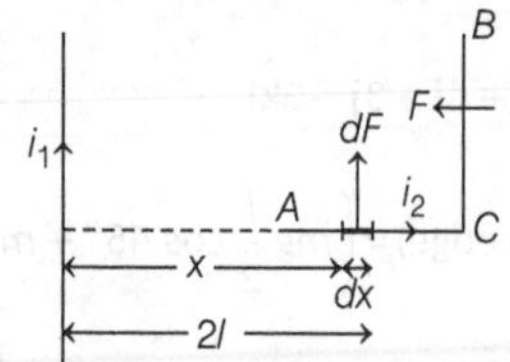

$$\tau_{AC} = \int_l^{2l}\left(\frac{\mu_0 i_1}{2\pi x}\right) i_2\,dx(2l-x) = \frac{\mu_0 i_1 i_2 l}{2\pi}(2\ln 2 - 1)$$

$$\tau_{CB} = \left(\frac{\mu_0 i_1 i_2 l}{2\pi(2l)}\right)\frac{l}{2} = \frac{\mu_0 i_1 i_2 l}{8\pi}$$

$$\tau_{net} = \tau_{AC} - \tau_{CB} = \frac{3\mu_0 i_1 i_2 l}{40} = \left(\frac{ml^2}{3}\right)\alpha$$

$$\Rightarrow \quad \alpha = \frac{9}{40}\frac{\mu_0 i_1 i_2}{\pi m l}$$

5.

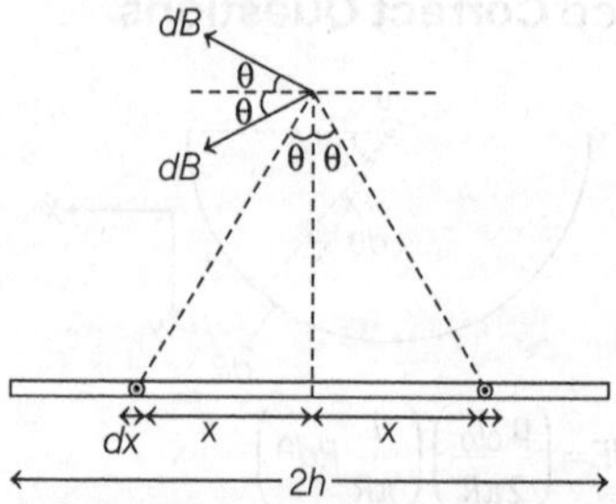

$$dB_{\text{net}} = 2\,dB\cos\theta = 2\left(\frac{\mu_0 J_0\,dx}{2\pi\sqrt{x^2+h^2}}\right)\frac{h}{\sqrt{x^2+h^2}}$$

$$F_{\text{net}} = \int dF = \int_0^h\left[\frac{\mu_0 J_0 h\,dx}{\pi(x^2+h^2)}\right] i = \frac{\mu_0 i J_0}{\pi}\left[\tan^{-1}\left(\frac{x}{h}\right)\right]_0^h$$

$$= \frac{\mu_0 i J_0}{4}$$

6. $\mathbf{B} = \frac{B_0 x}{R}\hat{\mathbf{k}} = \frac{B_0(R\cos\theta)}{R}\hat{\mathbf{k}} = B_0\cos\theta\,\hat{\mathbf{k}}$

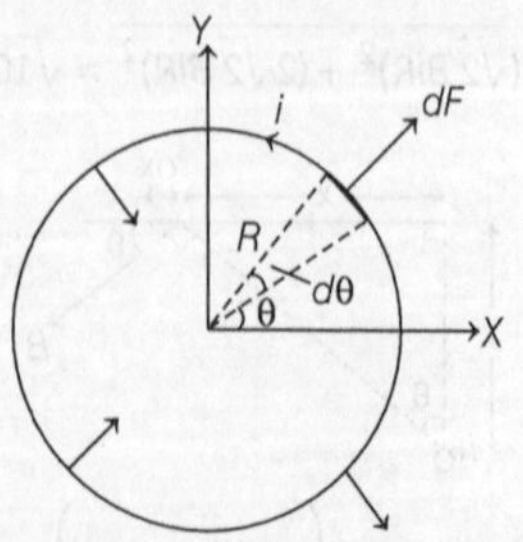

$$\int \mathbf{dF} = \int_0^{2\pi}(B_0\cos\theta)\;iRd\theta\cos\theta\,\hat{\mathbf{i}} + \int_0^{2\pi}(B_0\cos\theta)iRd\theta\sin\theta\,\hat{\mathbf{j}}$$

$$\Rightarrow \quad \mathbf{F} = B_0 iR\left(\int_0^{2\pi}\cos^2\theta\,d\theta\,\hat{\mathbf{i}} + \int_0^{2\pi}\frac{\sin 2\theta\,d\theta}{2}\hat{\mathbf{j}}\right)$$

$$\Rightarrow \quad \mathbf{F} = (B_0 iR\pi)\hat{\mathbf{i}}$$

7. Magnetic field lines of long wire are concentric circles. Force on loop of any shape will be zero.

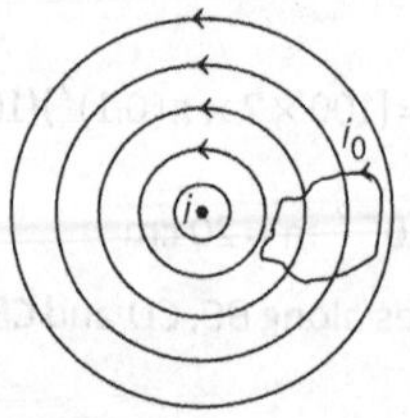

8. For wire to remain stationary,

$mg\sin\theta = Bil\cos\theta + \mu N$

$\Rightarrow mg\sin\theta = Bil\cos\theta + \mu(mg\cos\theta + Bil\sin\theta)$

$$B = \frac{mg}{il}\frac{(\tan\theta - \mu)}{(1+\mu\tan\theta)}$$

$$= \frac{mg}{il}\tan(\theta - \phi)$$

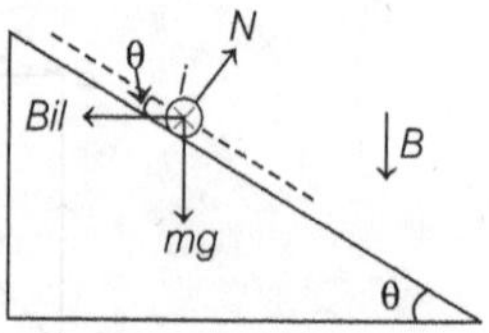

9. $F = ma \Rightarrow Bil = ma \Rightarrow B\frac{dq}{dt}l = m\frac{dv}{dt}$

$$\Rightarrow \quad Bl\int dq = m\int dv$$

$$\Rightarrow \quad v = \frac{Blq}{m} = \frac{BlCU}{m}$$

Now at mean position, $v = A\omega$

$$\Rightarrow \quad \frac{BlCU}{m} = A\sqrt{\frac{2k}{m}} \Rightarrow A = \frac{BlCU}{\sqrt{2km}}$$

10. $F = Bil$

$2T = F$

$\Rightarrow T = \frac{Bil}{2}$

$$\Delta l = \frac{FL}{AY} = \left(\frac{Bil}{2}\right)\frac{l}{AY}$$

$$= \frac{Bil^2}{2AY}$$

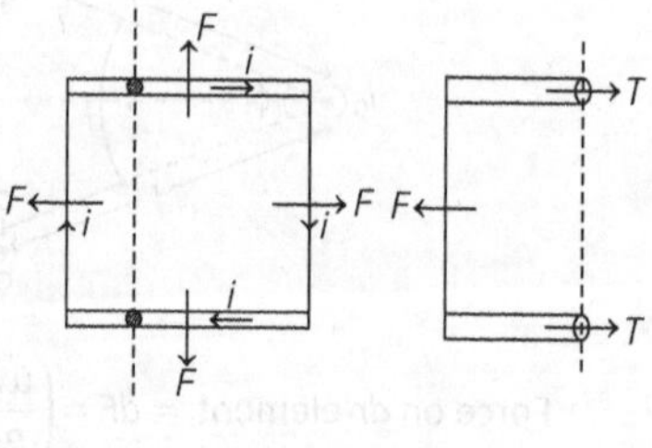

11. Vector perpendicular to the plane of square

$$= \mathbf{AB}\times\mathbf{BC} = (a\hat{\mathbf{k}})\times\left(\frac{a}{\sqrt{2}}\hat{\mathbf{i}} + \frac{a}{\sqrt{2}}\hat{\mathbf{j}}\right)$$

$$= \frac{a^2}{\sqrt{2}}(-\hat{\mathbf{i}}+\hat{\mathbf{j}})$$

$$\hat{\mathbf{n}} = \frac{-\hat{\mathbf{i}}+\hat{\mathbf{j}}}{\sqrt{2}}$$

$$\mathbf{M} = ia^2\hat{\mathbf{n}} = \frac{ia^2}{\sqrt{2}}(-\hat{\mathbf{i}}+\hat{\mathbf{j}})$$

12.

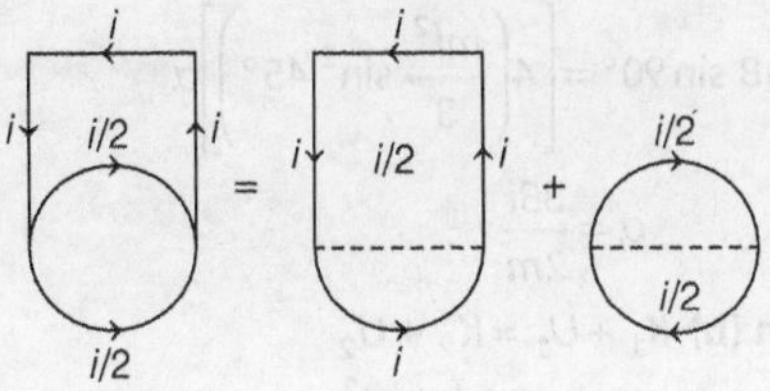

$$\mathbf{M}=\mathbf{M}_1+\mathbf{M}_2$$

$$=i\left(4+\frac{\pi r^2}{2}\right)\hat{\mathbf{k}}+\frac{i}{2}(\pi r^2)(-\hat{\mathbf{k}})=4\hat{\mathbf{k}}$$

13. $\frac{M}{L}=\frac{q}{2m}\Rightarrow M=\frac{ql\omega}{2m}=\frac{Q\left(\frac{mR^2}{2}\right)\omega}{2m}$

$$=\frac{Q\omega(h\tan\theta)^2}{4}=\frac{Q\omega h^2}{4}\tan^2\theta$$

14. $\mathbf{M}=\mathbf{M}_{ABCD}+\mathbf{M}_{ADF}+\mathbf{M}_{AFB}$

$$=(0.1)\,(0.1)\,(10)\hat{\mathbf{i}}+\frac{1}{2}\,(0.1)\,(0.1)\,(10)\hat{\mathbf{j}}$$

$$+\frac{1}{2}(0.1)\,(0.1)\,(10)\hat{\mathbf{k}}$$

$$=0.1\hat{\mathbf{i}}+0.05\hat{\mathbf{j}}+0.05\hat{\mathbf{k}}$$

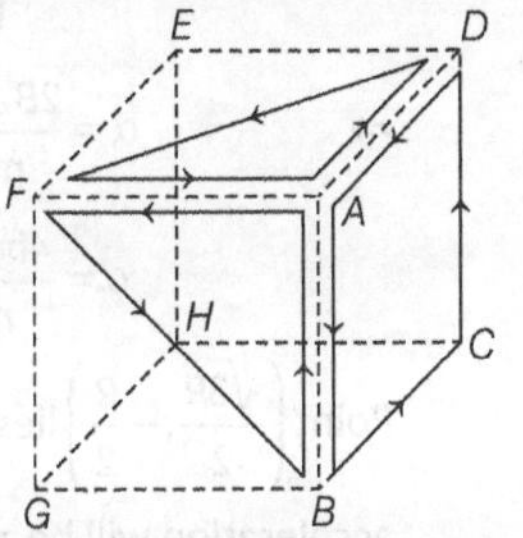

$$\boldsymbol{\tau}=\mathbf{M}\times\mathbf{B}$$

$$=0.05(2\hat{\mathbf{i}}+\hat{\mathbf{j}}+\hat{\mathbf{k}})$$

$$\times(2\hat{\mathbf{i}}-3\hat{\mathbf{j}}+\hat{\mathbf{k}})$$

$$=0.05(4\hat{\mathbf{i}}-8\hat{\mathbf{k}})\text{ N-m}$$

$$\tau=0.05\sqrt{4^2+8^2}$$

$$=\sqrt{20}\times10^{-1}\text{ N-m}$$

15. $\tau_B=MB\sin\theta=(i\pi R^2)B\sin\theta$

For rotational equilibrium about point P,

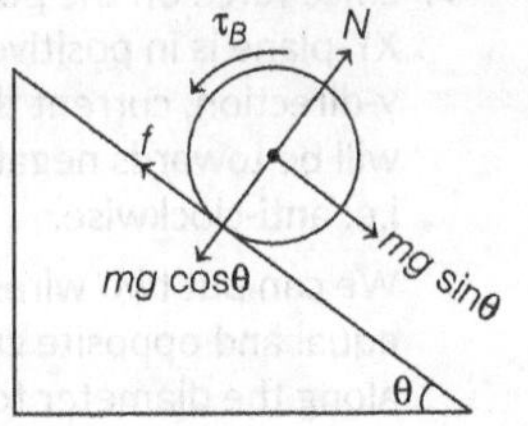

$$\tau_{mg}+\tau_N+\tau_f+\tau_B=0$$

$$\Rightarrow(mg\sin\theta)R+0+0$$

$$-i(\pi R^2)B\sin\theta=0$$

$$\Rightarrow B=\frac{mg}{\pi iR}$$

16.

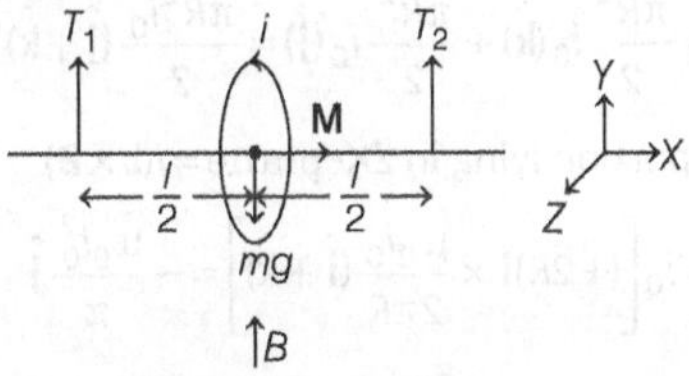

$$\tau_B=\mathbf{M}\times\mathbf{B}=(i\pi b^2)\hat{\mathbf{i}}\times B\hat{\mathbf{j}}=(\pi b^2 iB)\hat{\mathbf{k}}$$

For equilibrium, $\tau_{\text{net}}=0$

$$\Rightarrow\ T_1\left(\frac{l}{2}\right)\hat{\mathbf{k}}-T_2\left(\frac{l}{2}\right)\hat{\mathbf{k}}+(\pi b^2\,iB)\hat{\mathbf{k}}=0$$

$$\Rightarrow\quad T_1-T_2=\frac{2\pi b^2 iB}{l}\qquad\text{...(i)}$$

$$\Sigma F_y=0$$

$$\Rightarrow\quad T_1+T_2=mg=2T_0\qquad\text{...(ii)}$$

From Eqs. (i) and (ii), we get

$$T_1=T_0+\frac{\pi b^2 iB}{l}$$

17. $\tau_{mg}+\tau_B=0$

$$\Rightarrow mgR(-\hat{\mathbf{k}})+(i\pi R^2)B_0\sin90°\,(\hat{\mathbf{k}})=0$$

$$\Rightarrow i=\frac{mg}{\pi RB_0}$$

18. $U_1=-\int_a^b\left(\frac{\mu_0 i_1}{2\pi x}\right)(i_2 l dx)\cos\pi=\frac{\mu_0 i_1 i_2 l}{2\pi}\ln\left(\frac{b}{a}\right)$

By symmetry $U_2=-U_1$

$$W=-\Delta U=\frac{\mu_0 i_1 i_2 l}{\pi}\ln\left(\frac{b}{a}\right)$$

19. Kinetic energy will be maximum when they become coplanar.

Let ω_1 and ω_2 be the angular velocities of larger and smaller coils respectively when they become coplanar.

Conservation of angular momentum,

$$I_1\omega_1=I_2\omega_2\qquad\text{...(i)}$$

Conservation of energy,

$$K_1+U_1=K_2+U_2$$

$$\Rightarrow(0+0)-MB\cos90°=\left(\frac{1}{2}I_1\omega_1^2+\frac{1}{2}I_2\omega_2^2\right)+(-MB\cos0°)$$

$$\Rightarrow\ \frac{1}{2}I_1\omega_1^2+\frac{1}{2}I_2\omega_2^2=\left(\frac{\mu_0 i_1}{2R}\right)(i_2\pi r^2)\qquad\text{...(ii)}$$

Solving Eqs. (i) and (ii), we get

$$K_2=\frac{1}{2}I_2\omega_2^2=\frac{\mu_0\pi i_1 i_2 MRr^2}{2(MR^2+mr^2)}$$

20. $\tau=NiAB\sin\theta$

$$\Rightarrow\ \frac{2}{3}mR^2\frac{d\omega}{dt}=N\frac{dq}{dt}\pi R^2 B\sin90°$$

$$\Rightarrow\quad\int d\omega=\frac{3N\pi B}{2m}\int dq$$

$$\Rightarrow\quad\omega=\left(\frac{3N\pi B}{2m}\right)q=2.7\pi\text{ rad/s}$$

Multiple Choice(s) Correct Questions

1. For equilibrium of B, $F=mg$

$$\Rightarrow\quad\frac{\mu_0 i_1 i_2 l}{2\pi r}=(\lambda l)g$$

$$\Rightarrow\quad r=\frac{\mu_0 i_1 i_2}{2\pi\lambda g}=0.01\text{ m}$$

If we displace conductor B in upward direction, it will keep going up as magnetic force on B is greater than its weight. So, equilibrium of B is unstable.

2. Option (a), For side (0, 0) to (0, L), $z = 0$

$$\Rightarrow \quad \mathbf{B} = \left(\frac{B_0 y}{L}\right)\hat{\mathbf{k}}$$

$$\mathbf{F} = i\int (d\mathbf{l} \times \mathbf{B}) = I\int_0^L (dy\,\hat{\mathbf{j}}) \times \left(\frac{B_0 y}{L}\right)\hat{\mathbf{k}}$$

$$= \frac{B_0 i}{L}\left(\int_0^L y\,dy\right)\hat{\mathbf{i}} = \frac{B_0 i L}{2}\hat{\mathbf{i}}$$

Option (b), For side (0, L) to (L, L)

$$\mathbf{F} = i\left[L\hat{\mathbf{i}} \times \left(\frac{B_0 L}{L}\right)\hat{\mathbf{k}}\right] = -B_0 iL\hat{\mathbf{j}}$$

Option (d), For side (L, 0) to (0, 0), $\mathbf{B} = 0$

$$\Rightarrow \quad \mathbf{F} = 0$$

3. Work done by magnetic force on charges in wire PQ is zero as $\mathbf{F} \perp \mathbf{v}$. To maintain the current, work has to be done by battery.

$$W_{\text{battery}} = \int (nAl)\, euBV_d\, dt = ilB\int u\,dt = ilBh$$

Using work-energy theorem,

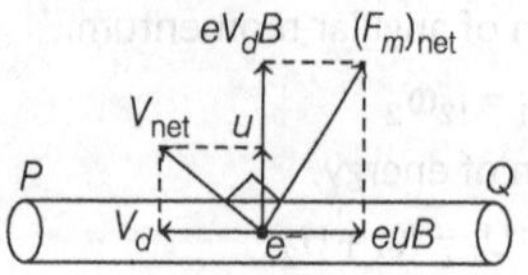

$$W_{\text{battery}} + W_{mg} = \Delta K$$

$$\Rightarrow \quad Bilh - mgh = \frac{1}{2}mv^2 - 0$$

$$\Rightarrow \quad v = \sqrt{\frac{2(Bil - mg)h}{m}}$$

4. Let $Bia = F$

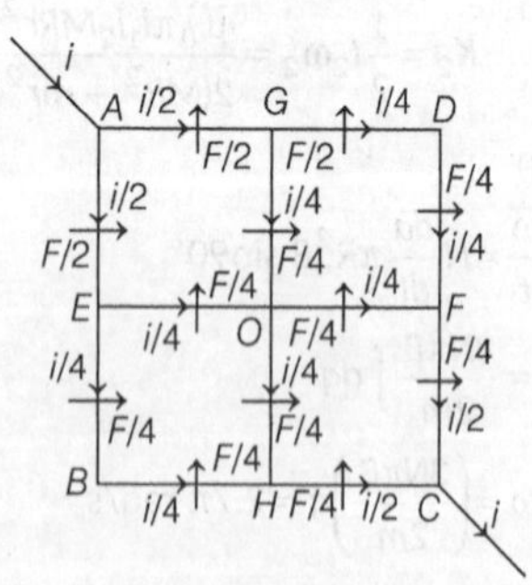

$$\mathbf{F}_{\text{net}} = 2F\hat{\mathbf{i}} + 2F\hat{\mathbf{j}}$$

$$F_{\text{net}} = 2\sqrt{2}F = 2\sqrt{2}iBa$$

Points B, O and D lie on perpendicular axis of symmetry. So, $V_B = V_O = V_D$

5. Option (a) $\tau = i\alpha$

$$\Rightarrow \quad MB\sin\theta = i\alpha$$

$$\Rightarrow (il^2)B\sin 90° = \left[4\left(\frac{ml^2}{3}\sin^2 45°\right)\right]\alpha$$

$$\Rightarrow \quad \alpha = \frac{3Bi}{2m}$$

Option (b) $K_1 + U_1 = K_2 + U_2$

$$\Rightarrow 0 - MB\cos 90° = \frac{1}{2}\left(\frac{4ml^2}{3}\sin^2 45°\right)\omega^2 - MB\cos 60°$$

$$\Rightarrow \quad \omega = \sqrt{\frac{3Bi}{2m}}$$

Option (c) $\tau = MB\sin\theta = (il^2)B\sin 30° = \dfrac{iBl^2}{2}$

Option (d) $i\alpha = \tau = MB\sin\theta$, As loop is rotated from starting to 90°, θ decreases from 90° to 0°. So, α decreases.

6.

$$\tau = \mathbf{M} \times \mathbf{B}$$

$$= (i\pi R^2)(-\hat{\mathbf{k}}) \times B_0(\hat{\mathbf{i}} + \sqrt{3}\hat{\mathbf{j}})$$

$$= B_0 i\pi R^2(\sqrt{3}\hat{\mathbf{i}} - \hat{\mathbf{j}})$$

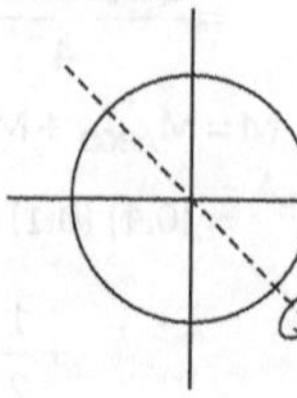

$$\tau = I\alpha$$

$$\Rightarrow B_0 i\pi R^2(\sqrt{3}\hat{\mathbf{i}} - \hat{\mathbf{j}}) = \left(\frac{mR^2}{2}\right)\alpha$$

$$\Rightarrow \quad \alpha = \frac{2B_0 i\pi}{m}(\sqrt{3}\hat{\mathbf{i}} - \hat{\mathbf{j}})$$

$$\alpha = \frac{4i\pi B_0}{m} \text{ and } \hat{\alpha} = \frac{\sqrt{3}\hat{\mathbf{i}} - \hat{\mathbf{j}}}{2}$$

Point $\left(\dfrac{\sqrt{3}R}{2}, -\dfrac{R}{2}\right)$ lies on the axis of rotation. So, its acceleration will be zero.

7. Since force on the portion in XY-plane is in positive y-direction, current through it will be towards negative X-axis i.e. anti-clockwise.

We can put two wires carrying equal and opposite currents along the diameter to complete two loops.

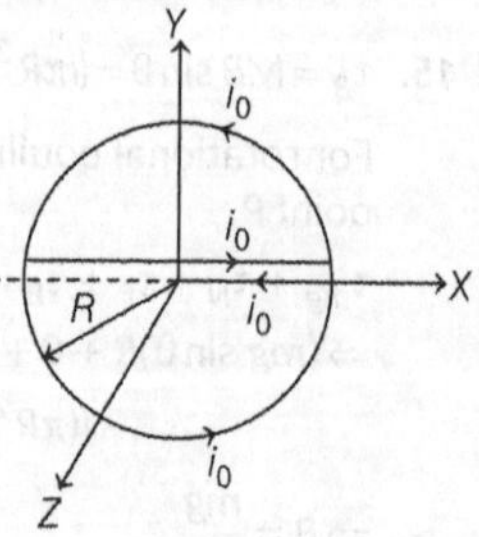

$$\mathbf{M} = \mathbf{M}_{XY\text{ loop}} + \mathbf{M}_{ZX\text{ loop}}$$

$$= \frac{\pi R^2}{2}i_0(\hat{\mathbf{k}}) + \frac{\pi R^2}{2}i_0(\hat{\mathbf{j}}) = \frac{\pi R^2 i_0}{2}(\hat{\mathbf{j}} + \hat{\mathbf{k}})$$

Force on portion lying in ZX-plane $= i(\mathbf{L} \times \mathbf{B})$

$$= i_0\left[(+2R)\hat{\mathbf{i}} \times \frac{\mu_0 i_0}{2\pi R}(\hat{\mathbf{i}} + \hat{\mathbf{k}})\right] = -\frac{\mu_0 i_0^2}{\pi}\hat{\mathbf{j}}$$

$$\tau = \mathbf{M} \times \mathbf{B} = \frac{\pi R^2 i_0}{2}(\hat{\mathbf{j}} + \hat{\mathbf{k}}) \times \frac{\mu_0 i_0}{2\pi R}(\hat{\mathbf{i}} + \hat{\mathbf{k}})$$

$$= \frac{\mu_0 i_0^2 R}{4}(\hat{\mathbf{i}} + \hat{\mathbf{j}} - \hat{\mathbf{k}})$$

8. Torque due to magnetic field

$$\tau = MB\sin 90° = ia^2B_0$$

For rotational equilibrium,

$$ia^2B_0 = mgx \Rightarrow x = \frac{ia^2B_0}{mg}$$

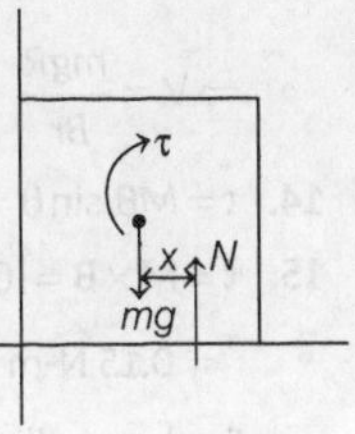

For the block not to topple,

$$x < \frac{a}{2}$$

$$\Rightarrow \frac{ia^2B_0}{mg} < \frac{a}{2} \Rightarrow i < \frac{mg}{2aB_0}$$

9. Voltage sensitivity $(VS) = \frac{\theta}{V} = \frac{NAB}{KR}$

(A) VS is independent of number of turns as we increase N, R also increases in the same ratio.

(B) $VS = \frac{NAB}{K\left(\frac{\rho l}{A'}\right)}$ and $l \propto \sqrt{A} \Rightarrow VS \propto \sqrt{A}$

(C) $VS \propto B$

(D) $VS \propto \frac{1}{\rho}$

Comprehension Based Questions

1. $Bil\sin\theta = mg \Rightarrow B\left(\frac{V}{R}\right)l\sin\theta = mg$

$$\Rightarrow 0.450\left(\frac{V}{25}\right)(0.5)\sin 90° = 0.750 \times 9.8$$

$$\Rightarrow V = 817\text{ V}$$

2. $i = \frac{817}{2} = 408.5\text{ A}$

$$Bil\sin\theta - mg = ma$$

$$\Rightarrow 0.450 \times 408.5 \times 0.5 - 0.750 \times 9.8 = 0.750a$$

$$\Rightarrow a = 113\text{ m/s}^2$$

3. $\tau = (Bil)\frac{l}{2} = (0.340)(6.50)\frac{(0.2)^2}{2}$

$= 0.0442$ N-m

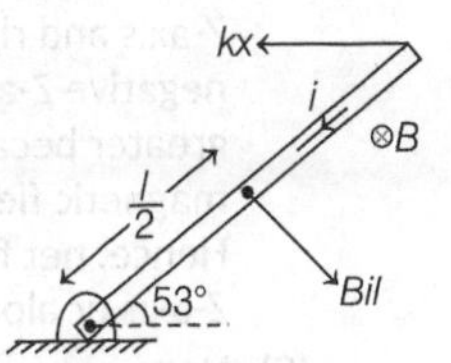

Bil force is acting on the rod as shown in figure.

Using $\tau = \mathbf{r} \times \mathbf{F}$ direction of torque due to force Bil about P will be clockwise.

4. Let elongation in the spring be x.

$$\tau_{net} = 0 = (Bil)\left(\frac{l}{2}\right) - (Kx)(l\sin 53°)$$

$$\Rightarrow \quad x = 0.05755\text{ m}$$

5. Magnetic field due to each wire,

$$B = \frac{\mu_0 i}{2\pi(\sqrt{2}a)}$$

$$\mathbf{B}_{net} = (4B\cos 45°)\hat{\mathbf{j}}$$

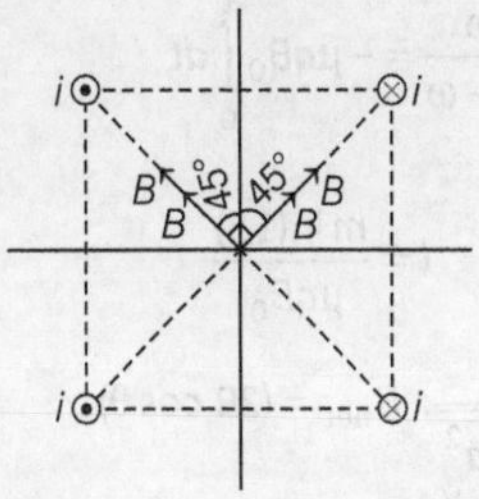

$$= \left(\frac{\mu_0 i}{\pi a}\right)\hat{\mathbf{j}}$$

6. $F_{DC} = F_{DA} = \frac{\mu_0(i)(i)}{2\pi(2a)}$

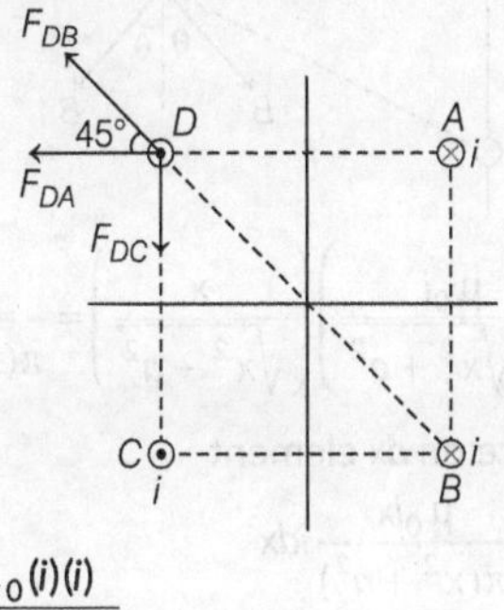

$$F_{DB} = \frac{\mu_0(i)(i)}{2\pi(2\sqrt{2}a)}$$

$$F_{net} = -(F_{DA} + F_{DB}\cos 45°)\hat{\mathbf{i}} + (F_{DB}\sin 45° - F_{DC})\hat{\mathbf{j}}$$

$$= -\frac{3}{8}\left(\frac{\mu_0 i^2}{\pi a}\right)\hat{\mathbf{i}} - \frac{1}{8}\left(\frac{\mu_0 i^2}{\pi a}\right)\hat{\mathbf{j}}$$

$$F_{net} = \frac{\mu_0 i^2}{8\pi a}\sqrt{(3)^2 + (1)^2}$$

$$= \frac{\sqrt{10}}{8}\frac{\mu_0 i^2}{\pi a}$$

7. Force due to magnetic field

$= B_0 i(2\pi R)$

$= B_0\left(\frac{q\omega_0}{2\pi}\right)(2\pi R)$

$= qRB_0\omega_0$

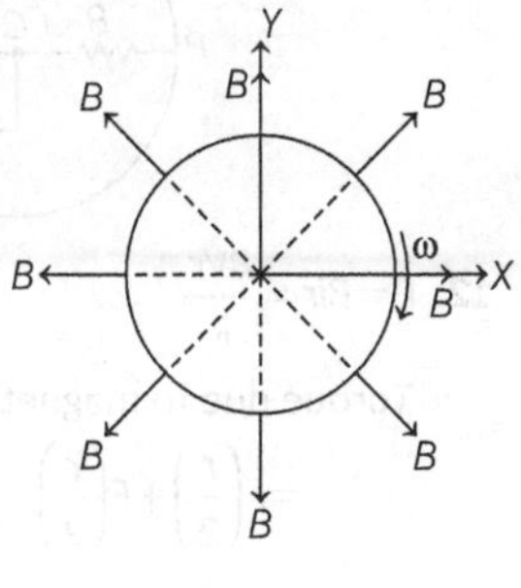

Friction force = 0

$\Rightarrow \quad N = 0$

$\Rightarrow \quad qRB_0\omega_0 = mg$

$\Rightarrow \quad \omega_0 = \frac{mg}{qRB_0}$

8. Let angular velocity be ω at any instant.

$$N = mg - (qRB_0)\omega$$

$$f_k = \mu N = \mu(mg - qRB_0\omega) = -\mu qRB_0(\omega_0 - \omega)$$

$$\tau = I\alpha \Rightarrow -\mu qRB_0(\omega_0 - \omega)R = (mR^2)\alpha$$

$$\Rightarrow m \int_{\frac{\omega_0}{2}}^{\frac{\omega_0}{4}} \frac{d\omega}{\omega_0 - \omega} = -\mu q B_0 \int_0^t dt$$

$$\Rightarrow \quad t = \frac{m \ln(1.5)}{\mu q B_0}$$

9. $B = \dfrac{\mu i}{2\pi\sqrt{x^2 + a^2}}$; $B_{net} = (2B\cos\theta)$

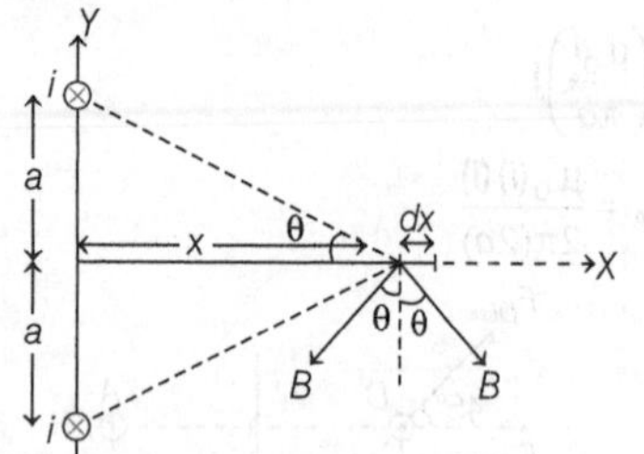

$$= 2\left(\frac{\mu_0 i}{2\pi\sqrt{x^2 + a^2}}\right)\left(\frac{x}{\sqrt{x^2 + a^2}}\right) = \frac{\mu_0 i x}{\pi(x^2 + a^2)}$$

Magnetic force on dx element

$$= dF = \frac{\mu_0 i x}{\pi(x^2 + a^2)} i dx$$

$$F = \frac{\mu_0 i^2}{\pi} \int_0^{2a} \left(\frac{x}{x^2 + a^2}\right) dx = \frac{\mu_0 i^2}{2\pi} \ln 5$$

10. If current in wire B is reversed, net magnetic field due to wires A and B will be along wire OC. So, net force on wire OC will be zero.

11. Current through PC and $CQ = i = \dfrac{V}{R}$

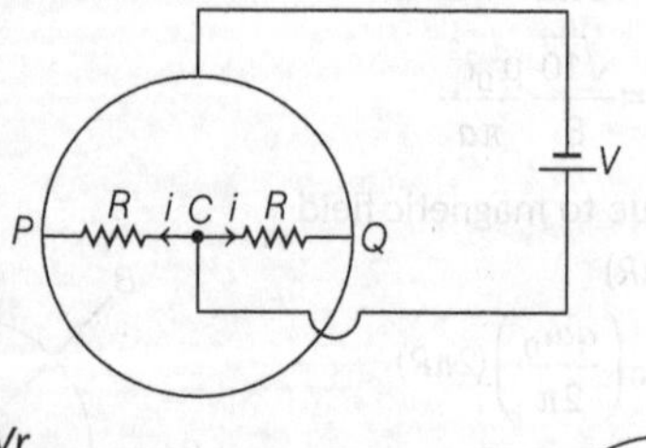

12. $F = Bir = \dfrac{BVr}{R}$

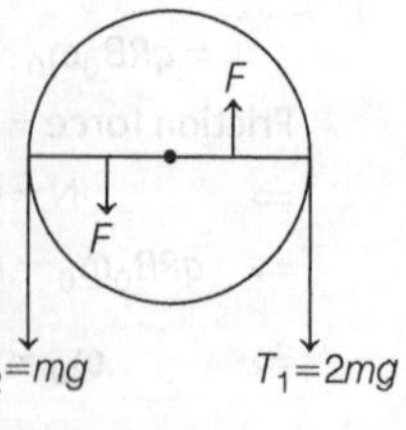

Torque due to magnetic forces

$$= F\left(\frac{r}{2}\right) + F\left(\frac{r}{2}\right)$$

$$= Fr = \frac{BVr^2}{R}$$

Net torque $= 0$

$\Rightarrow$ Torque on the ring due to tension $= \dfrac{BVr^2}{R}$

13. $\tau_{net} = 0 \Rightarrow (2\,mg)r - (mg)r = \dfrac{BVr^2}{R}$

$$\Rightarrow V = \frac{mgR}{Br}$$

14. $\tau = MB\sin\theta = 0.75 \times 0.2 \sin 90° = 0.15$ N-m

15. $\tau = \mathbf{M} \times \mathbf{B} = [0.75(-\hat{k})] \times [(0.2)\hat{i}]$

$= 0.15$ N-m $(-\hat{j})$

So, loop will rotate about Y-axis with point a moving out of the plane and point c moving into the plane.

16. $W_{ext} = \Delta U = -MB - (-MB) = 2MB$

$= 2 \times 0.75 \times 0.2 = 0.3$ J

Match the Columns Questions

1. (A) Because the magnetic field is parallel to X-axis, the forces on the wires parallel to X-axis is zero. The force on each wire parallel to Y-axis is $B_0\left(\dfrac{i}{2}\right)l$. Hence, net force is $B_0 il$.

(B) Similar to previous situation, net force on the loop is $B_0 il$.

(C) Since direction of current from the entry point to exist point is parallel to external magnetic field, net force is zero.

(D) $\mathbf{F} = i(\mathbf{L} \times \mathbf{B}) = i\left[\sqrt{2}l\left(\dfrac{\hat{i} + \hat{j}}{\sqrt{2}}\right) \times B_0\hat{k}\right]$

$\Rightarrow \quad \mathbf{F} = B_0 il(\hat{i} - \hat{j})$, $F = \sqrt{2}B_0 il$

Net torque in each case is zero.

2. (A) Resultant force is opposite to $\mathbf{P}_m$.

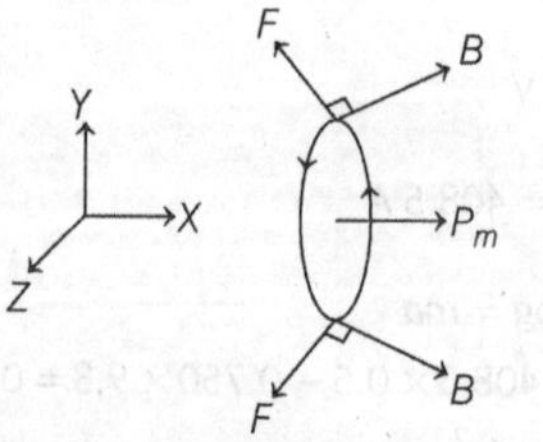

(B) Force on the left side is along Z-axis and right side is along negative Z-axis. But former is greater because of higher magnetic field on left side. Hence, net force is along Z-axis or along $\mathbf{P}_m$.

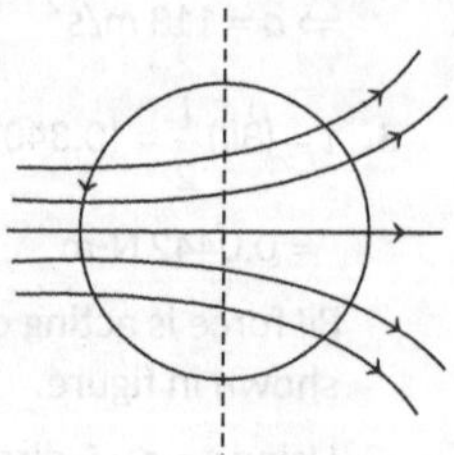

(C) Now, net force is reversed but $\mathbf{P}_m$ is also reversed.

(D) Force on left side is more than on right side. Net force will be along Y-axis or along $\mathbf{P}_m$.

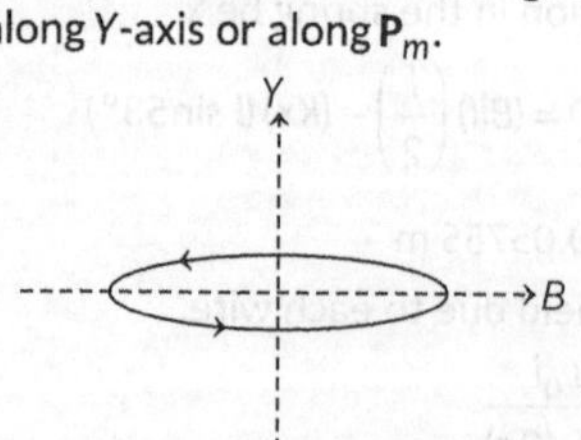

3. (A) Force will be zero. Net torque will be non-zero.

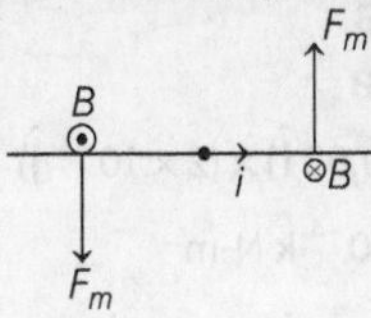

(B) Force and torque both are non-zero.

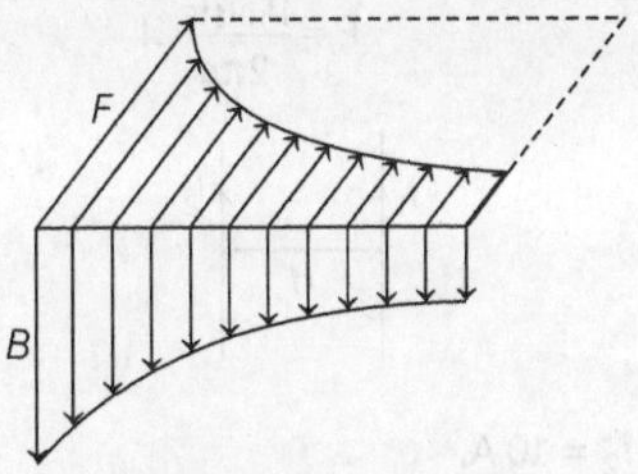

(C) Force is non-zero but torque about centre is zero.

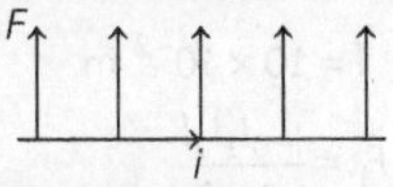

Numerical Value Questions

1. Loss in magnetic potential energy = Gain in gravitational potential energy

$$-MB\cos 90° - (-MB\cos 0°) = mgh$$

$$\Rightarrow \quad i\left(\frac{\sqrt{3}}{4}a^2\right)B = mg\left(\frac{a}{\sqrt{3}}\right) \Rightarrow B = \frac{4mg}{3Ia} = 4\text{T}$$

2. Forces on wires *AB* and *CD* will be zero.

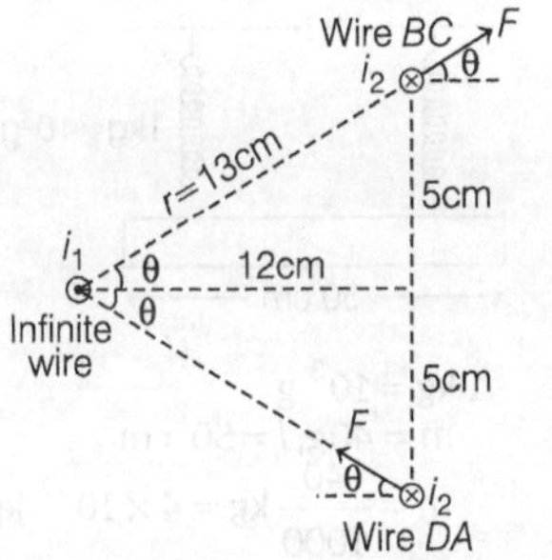

F = Force between long wire and wire *BC* or *DA*

$$= \left(\frac{\mu_0 i_i}{2\pi r}\right) i_2 l$$

$$\tau = (2F\cos\theta)\left(\frac{l}{2}\right) = \left(\frac{\mu_0 i_1 i_2 l}{2\pi r}\right) l\cos\theta$$

$$= 720 \times 10^{-7}\ \text{N-m} = x \times 10^{7}\ \text{N-m} \qquad \text{(given)}$$

So, $x = 720$

3. $ma = BiL \Rightarrow m\int dv = BL\int dq \Rightarrow v = \frac{BLCV}{m}$

Using energy conservation,

$$mgl(1-\cos\theta) = \frac{1}{2}mv^2$$

$$\Rightarrow \theta = \cos^{-1}\left(1 - \frac{B^2L^2C^2V^2}{2m^2gl}\right)$$

$$\Rightarrow \theta = \cos^{-1}(0.8) = 37°$$

4. $dM = i\left(\frac{\pi d^2}{4}\right)\left(\frac{N}{\pi r}rd\theta\right) = \frac{Nd^2 i}{4}d\theta$

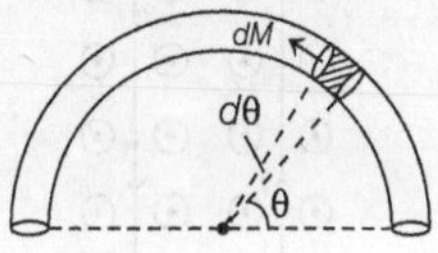

$$\mathbf{dM} = -dM\sin\theta\,\hat{\mathbf{i}} + dM\cos\theta\,\hat{\mathbf{j}}$$

$$\Rightarrow \mathbf{M} = -\int_0^{\pi}\frac{Nd^2 i}{4}\sin\theta\,d\theta\hat{\mathbf{i}} + \int_0^{\pi}\frac{Nd^2 i}{4}\cos\theta\,d\theta\hat{\mathbf{j}}$$

$$\Rightarrow \mathbf{M} = -\frac{Nd^2 i}{2}\hat{\mathbf{i}} \Rightarrow M = \frac{Nd^2 i}{2} = 5\ \text{A-m}^2$$

5. Force exerted by air on the rod $= \rho\left(\frac{l}{2}\right)\left(\frac{l}{4}\right)v^2 = F$

For rotational equilibrium of the rod, $\tau_{net} = 0$

$$\Rightarrow NiAB\sin\theta = F\left(\frac{3l}{4}\right)$$

$$\Rightarrow i = \frac{3\rho l v^2}{2NB} = 525 \times 10^{-3}\ \text{A} = 525\ \text{mA}$$

6. Tension in the loop $= BiR$

$$\text{Stress} = \frac{BiR}{\left(\frac{\pi d^2}{4}\right)} = \frac{4BiR}{\pi d^2}$$

$$\text{Breaking stress} = 3 \times 10^8 = \frac{4BiR}{\pi d^2} \Rightarrow B = 2.5\ \text{T}$$

7. $K_1 + U_1 = K_2 + U_2$

$$\Rightarrow 0 + 0 = \frac{1}{2}mv^2 - [1(0.2)^2\hat{\mathbf{j}}]\cdot(2\hat{\mathbf{i}} + 4\hat{\mathbf{j}} + 6\hat{\mathbf{k}})$$

$$\Rightarrow v = 0.4\ \text{m/s}$$

8. $P = \tau\omega = NiAB\sin\theta\omega$

$$\Rightarrow 2106 = N(10)(0.45)(2)\sin 90°(3) \quad \Rightarrow N = 78$$

Previous Years Questions

JEE Main

1. Given, $\theta_1 = 60° = \frac{\pi}{3}$ rad,

$$\theta_2 = \frac{\pi}{10}\ \text{rad}$$

In a galvanometer,

$\therefore \quad \theta \propto I$

$$\therefore \quad \frac{I_2}{I_1} = \frac{\theta_2}{\theta_1} = \frac{\frac{\pi}{10}}{\frac{\pi}{3}} = \frac{3}{10}$$

$\Rightarrow I_2 = \frac{3}{10} I_1 = \frac{3}{10} \times 200 = 60\,\mu A$

2. Force on wire $= i(l \times B)$

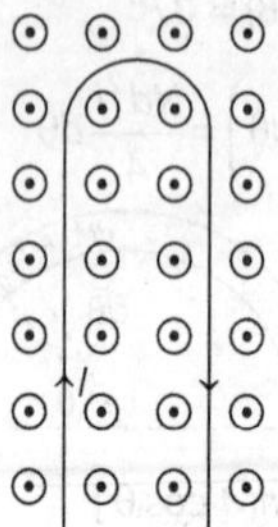

Here l is effective length vector,

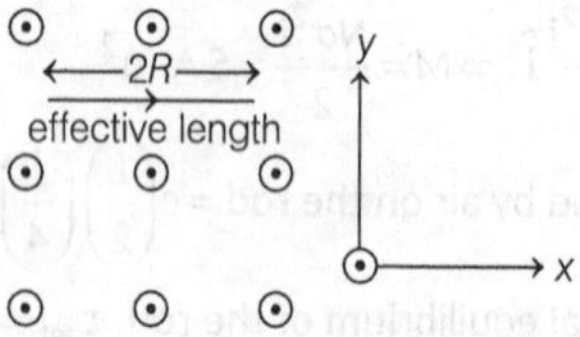

$l = (2R)\,\hat{i}$

So, force on wire is,

$\mathbf{F} = i(2R\hat{\mathbf{i}} \times B_0 \hat{\mathbf{k}})$

$= 2iRB_0(\hat{\mathbf{i}} \times \hat{\mathbf{k}})$

$= (2iRB_0)(-\hat{\mathbf{j}})$

Note In this question magnetic field in diagram is shown towards Z-axis but written $B = B_0\hat{\mathbf{j}}$.

3. Given,

$B_H = 3.5 \times 10^{-5}$ T

Current in wire, $i = \sqrt{2}$ A

$\theta = 45°$

Now,

Force per unit length is given by

$F = i\,lB\sin\theta$

$\frac{F}{l} = iB\sin\theta$

$= \sqrt{2} \times 3.5 \times 10^{-5} \times \frac{1}{\sqrt{2}}$ $(\because \theta = 45°)$

$= 3.5 \times 10^{-5}$ N/m

$= 35 \times 10^{-6}$ N/m

Hence, missing value is 35.

4.

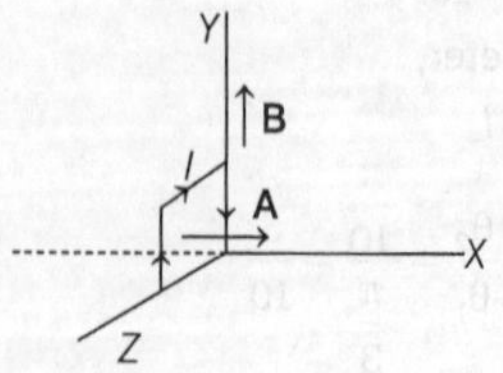

Torque on loop,

$= \mathbf{m} \times \mathbf{B}$

$= I\mathbf{A} \times \mathbf{B}$

$= (5 \times 0.02\,\hat{\mathbf{i}}) \times (2 \times 10^{-3}\,\hat{\mathbf{j}})$

$= 2 \times 10^{-4}\,\hat{\mathbf{k}}$ N-m

5. Force between two wires carrying current I_1 and I_2 is

$$F = \frac{\mu_0 I_1 I_2}{2\pi d}.l$$

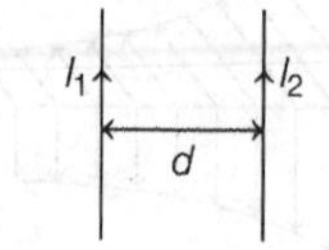

Here, $I_1 = I_2 = 10$ A,

$d = 5 \times 10^{-2}$ m,

$l = 10 \times 10^{-2}$ m

So, $F_1 = \frac{\mu_0 I_1 I_2 l}{2\pi d}$

If distance between wires is halved and currents are doubled.

Then, $F_2 = \frac{\mu_2 I_1' I_2' l}{2\pi d'} = \frac{\mu_0 4 I_1 I_2 l}{2\pi \frac{d}{2}}$

$= 8\left(\frac{\mu_0 I_1 I_2 l}{2\pi d}\right) = 8F_1$

6.

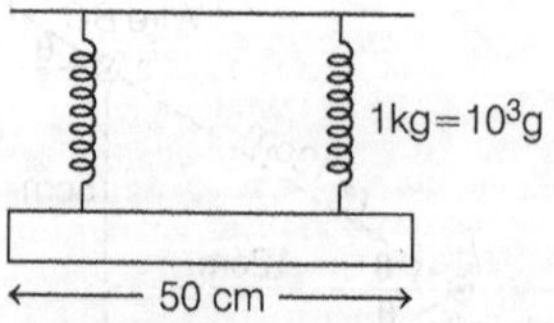

$1\text{ kg} = 10^3$ g

$m = 40\text{g}, l = 50$ cm

$m = \frac{40}{1000}\text{ kg} = 4 \times 10^{-2}$ kg

$l = 50$ cm

$1\text{ cm} = 10^{-2}$ m

$l = 50\text{ cm} = 50 \times 10^{-2}\text{ m} = 0.5$ m

$\because$ $iBl = mg$

$i = \frac{mg}{Bl}$

$i = \frac{4 \times 10^{-2} \times 10}{0.40 \times 0.5}$

$= \frac{10^{-1}}{0.5 \times 0.10}$

$= \frac{1}{5 \times 0.10}$

$= \frac{1}{0.50} = \frac{100}{50} = 2$ A

7. Given, $\tau = mB$

A = Area of coil

B = magnetic field

$$K\theta = IANB$$

$$\frac{\theta}{I} = \frac{ANB}{K}$$

$$\frac{\theta}{I} = \text{Current sensitivity.}$$

$$1.25\left(\frac{\theta}{I}\right)_1 = \left(\frac{\theta}{I}\right)_2 \quad \text{... (i)}$$

$$1.25\left[\frac{AN_1B}{K}\right] = \left[\frac{AN_2B}{K}\right]$$

$$1.25 = \frac{N_2}{N_1}$$

$$\frac{N_2}{N_1} = \frac{125}{100} = \frac{5}{4} \quad \text{...(ii)}$$

$$R = \rho\frac{l}{a} = \text{constants } l = a$$

Voltage sensitivity

$$= \frac{\theta}{V} = \frac{\theta}{IR} = \frac{\text{Current sensitivity}}{R}$$

R = Constant

Voltage sensitivity ∝ current sentivity + 25%

8. Current sensitivity of a galvanometer,

$$S_i = \frac{\theta}{I} = \frac{BNA}{K}$$

B = magnetic field of pole pieces;

N = number of turns of coil

A = area of coil

K = spring constant.

So, when number of turns is doubled,

'S_i' is also doubled.

Now voltage sensitivity of galvanometer is,

$$S_V = \frac{\theta}{IR} = \frac{BNA}{KR}$$

As $\frac{N}{R}$ remains constant, voltage sensitivity does not increases.

9. In a galvanometer to damp out the oscillations of the coil, core is either of a non-magnetic material or a magnetic core is covered with a sheet of a non-magnetic material. Eddy currents induced in the non-magnetic material converts oscillation energy into heat.

In this way oscillation of coil die out quickly.

10. Given, deflection in the coil,

$$\theta = 0.05 \text{ rad}$$

Current, $I = 10 \text{ mA} = 10^{-2}$ A

Magnetic field,

$$B = 0.01 \text{ T}$$

$$n = 200$$

Torsional constant,

$$C = 4\times10^{-5} \text{ N-m rad}^{-1}$$

We know that,

$$\frac{\theta}{I} = \frac{nBA}{C}$$

$$\Rightarrow \quad A = \frac{C\theta}{nBI} = \frac{4\times10^{-5}\times0.05}{200\times0.01\times10^{-2}}$$

$$= 1\times10^{-4} \text{ m}^2$$

$$= 1\times10^{-4}\times10^{4} \text{ cm}^2 = 1 \text{ cm}^2$$

11. Magnetic moment of a circular coil is, $M = NIA = NI(\pi r^2)$

When 2 coils A and B have same magnetic moments then,

$$M_A = M_B$$

$$\Rightarrow \quad N_AI_A(\pi r_A^2) = N_BI_B(\pi r_B^2)$$

$$\Rightarrow \quad N_AI_A(10)^2 = N_BI_B(20)^2$$

(Given, r_A = 10 cm and r_B = 20 cm)

$$\Rightarrow \quad N_AI_A = 4N_BI_B$$

12. Magnitude of force acting on both wires X and Y will be same and given as

$$F = \frac{\mu_0 I_X I_Y}{2\pi r}\times l_X$$

$$= 2\times10^{-7}\times\frac{2\times3\times0.5}{5\times10^{-2}}$$

$$= 1.2\times10^{-5} \text{ N}$$

∴ Force acting on the wire Y will be 1.2×10^{-5} N directed towards wire X because both wires having current in the same direction, hence they attract to each other.

13. Torque acting on coil can be calculated as

$$\tau = MB\sin\theta$$

$$\tau = i\left(\frac{\sqrt{3}}{4}a^2\right)B\sin\theta$$

$$\left[\because A = \frac{\sqrt{3}}{4}a^2 \text{ (for equilateral triangle)}\right]$$

$$= 0.2\times\frac{\sqrt{3}}{4}\times(0.1)^2\times20\times10^{-3}\times\sin90° \quad [\because \mathbf{A}\perp\mathbf{B}]$$

$$= \sqrt{3}\times10^{-5} \text{ N-m}$$

After comparing obtained value with the given value, x = 3.

14. Number of turns in equilateral triangle will be

$$n_T = \frac{24a}{3a} = 8 \quad [\because \text{Length of one turn is } 3a]$$

Number of turns in square will be

$$n_S = \frac{24a}{4a} = 6 \quad [\because \text{Length of one turn is } 4a]$$

The ratio of magnetic moment for triangular coil to square coil is given as

$$\frac{M_T}{M_S} = \frac{n_TIA_T}{n_SIA_S} \quad (\because I \text{ is same in both coils})$$

Substituting the values in above expression, we get

$$\frac{1}{\sqrt{y}} = \frac{\left(8 \times \frac{\sqrt{3}}{4} a^2\right)}{6 \times a^2}$$

$$= \frac{8\sqrt{3}}{24} = \frac{1}{\sqrt{3}}$$

$$\Rightarrow \quad \sqrt{y} = \sqrt{3} \Rightarrow y = 3$$

Hence, the value of y is 3.

15. A loop of wire will act like magnetic dipole. In equilibrium, direction of dipole will be parallel to direction of magnetic field and its plane remains normal to the field.

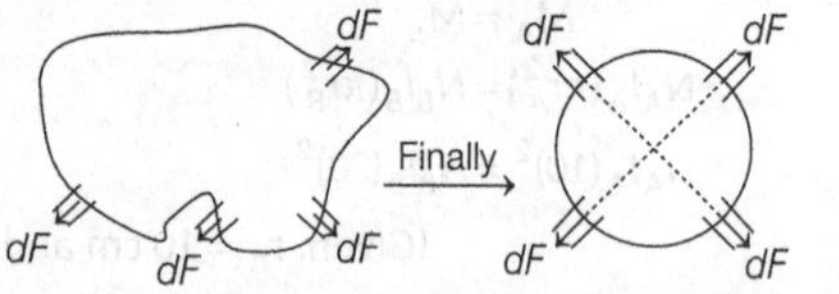

Now on each element of wire force due to magnetic field will be perpendicular to length of element and outward in direction. So, loop will become circular.

Hence, the correct option is (a).

16. Given rectangular loop can be viewed as a combination of two loops *ABCDA* and *ADEFA*.

So, $\mathbf{m}$ (loop) = $\mathbf{m}$ (*ABCDA*) + $\mathbf{m}$ (*ADEFA*)

The area vector of *ABCDA* is along *Z*-axis and that of *ADEFA* is along *Y*-axis as shown in figure,

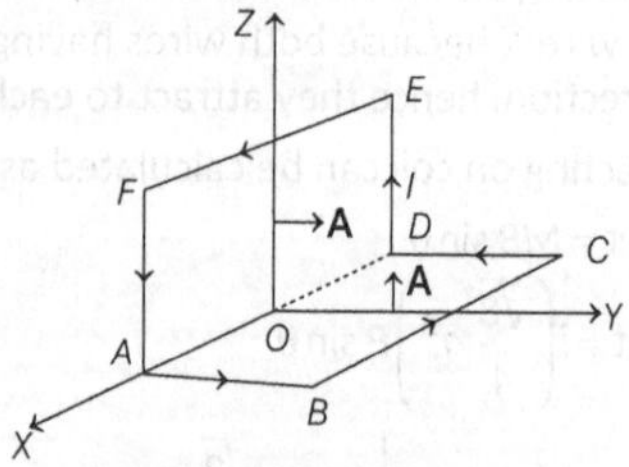

Now,

$$\mathbf{m}(ABCDA) = IA\hat{\mathbf{k}} = I(ab)\hat{\mathbf{k}}$$

and $\quad \mathbf{m}(ADEFA) = IA\hat{\mathbf{j}} = I(ab)\hat{\mathbf{j}}$

$\therefore \quad \mathbf{m}\text{ (loop)} = Iab\hat{\mathbf{k}} + Iab\hat{\mathbf{j}} = Iab(\hat{\mathbf{k}} + \hat{\mathbf{j}})$

$$= (Iab\sqrt{2})\left(\frac{\hat{\mathbf{k}}}{\sqrt{2}} + \frac{\hat{\mathbf{j}}}{\sqrt{2}}\right)$$

So, magnitude of $\mathbf{m} = \sqrt{2}Iab$

and direction of $\mathbf{m}$ is along $\frac{1}{\sqrt{2}}(\hat{\mathbf{j}} + \hat{\mathbf{k}})$.

Hence, correct option is (b).

17. Torque, $\tau = BINA \sin\theta$

Here, $\theta = 90° \Rightarrow \sin\theta = 1, \tau = 1.5$ N-m

$A = 3 \times 10^{-4}\,\text{m}^2, N = 500$ and $I = 0.5$ A

So, $\quad B = \frac{\tau}{INA} = \frac{1.5}{0.5 \times 500 \times 3 \times 10^{-4}} = 20$ T

18.

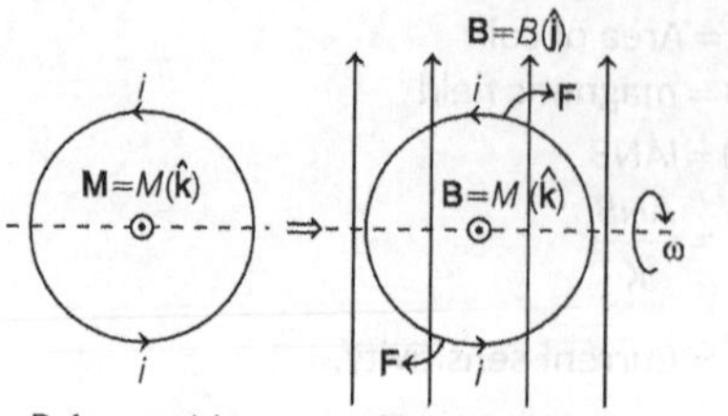

Before applying the magnetic field   After applying the magnetic field

Given that, $I_{\text{dia}} = 0.8$ kg-m^2,

$$M = 20\ \text{A-m}^2, B = 4\ \text{T}$$

$\theta =$ angle between M and B after rotation of 60° by coil $= 90° - 60° = 30°$ and $\omega = ?$

Applying the law of conservation of energy,

$(\text{TE})_{\text{initial}} = (\text{TE})_{\text{final}} \Rightarrow U_i + K_i = U_f + K_f$

$$0 + 0 = -MB\cos\theta + \frac{1}{2} I_{\text{dia}}\omega^2$$

$$0 = -20 \times 4 \cos 30° + \frac{1}{2} \times 0.8 \times \omega^2$$

$$\omega = \sqrt{173.2} = 13.16\ \text{rad/s}$$

Answer is unavailable in options. So, bonus marks should be provided.

19. The situation given in question is shown in the following figure

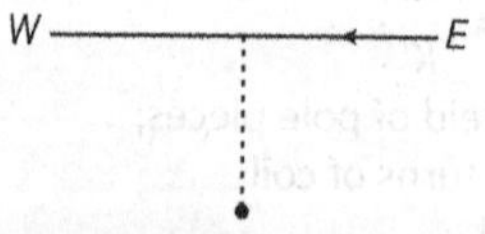

Force acting towards wire,

$$F_1 = \frac{\mu_0 I^2}{2\pi r} 2a$$

Force acting away from wire,

$$F_2 = \frac{\mu_0 I^2}{2\pi r} 2a$$

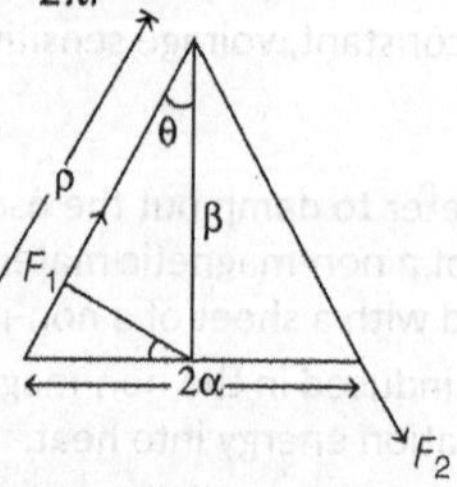

Torque acting on the loop about Z-axis,

$$\tau = F_1 a\cos\theta + F_2 a\cos\theta$$

$$= 2\left(\frac{\mu_0 I^2 2a}{2\pi r}\right) a \cdot \frac{b}{r} \qquad \left(\because \cos\theta = \frac{b}{r}\right)$$

$$= \frac{2\mu_0 I^2 a^2 b}{\pi(a^2 + b^2)} \qquad (\because r = \sqrt{a^2 + b^2})$$

$$= \frac{2\mu_0 I^2 a^2 b}{\pi b^2} \quad (\because b >>> a)$$

$$= \frac{2\mu_0 I^2 a^2}{\pi b}$$

Hence, correct option is (b).

20. Let us consider the direction of magnetic field be perpendicular to the plane in inward direction as shown below.

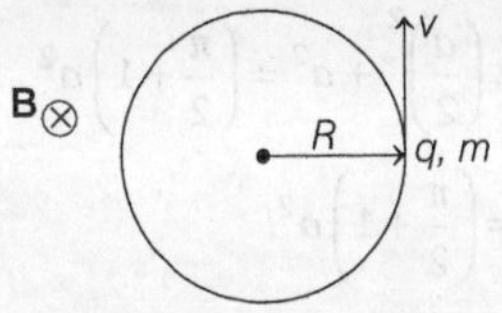

Current produced by the motion of charge particle, $i = \frac{q}{T}$

$$= \frac{qv}{2\pi R}$$

If motion of a charged particle is considered as a currnet loop, then magnetic moment of charged particle

$$M = iA = \frac{qv}{2\pi R} \times \pi R^2$$

$$\Rightarrow \quad M = \frac{1}{2} qvR \quad \text{...(i)}$$

As we know that, while moving in a circle, necessary centripetal force is provided by magnetic force.

i.e., $\frac{mv^2}{R} = qvB$ or $R = \frac{mv}{qB}$

Putting this value in Eq. (i), we get

$$M = \frac{1}{2} qv\left(\frac{mv}{qB}\right) \text{ or } M = \frac{mv^2}{2B}$$

Here the direction of **M** is determined by right hand thumb rule which is perpendicular to plane but in outward direction, i.e., opposite to that of **B**.

$$\therefore \quad \mathbf{M} = \frac{mv^2}{2B}(-\hat{\mathbf{B}})$$

$$\text{or} \quad \mathbf{M} = -\frac{mv^2 \mathbf{B}}{2B^2}$$

Hence, correct option is (d).

21. According to the question, the situation can be drawn as

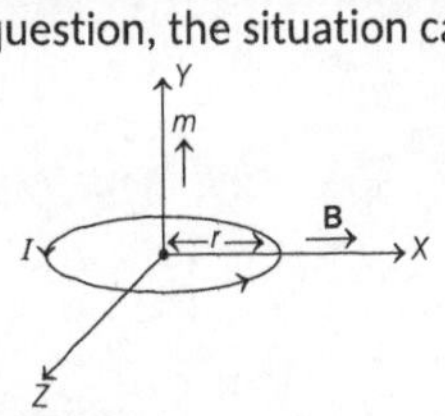

Torque on the current coil is

$$\tau = \mathbf{m} \times \mathbf{B} = mB \sin 90° = NIAB = NI\pi r^2 B \text{(N-m)}$$

22. $\tau = \mathbf{M} \times \mathbf{B} = NI(\mathbf{A} \times \mathbf{B}) = NIAB \sin\theta$

Substituting the given values, we get

$$\tau = 100 \times 3 \times 12.5 \times 10^{-4} \times 1 \times \sin 45° \approx 0.27 \text{ N-m}$$

23. Thus, the given square loop can be drawn as shown below

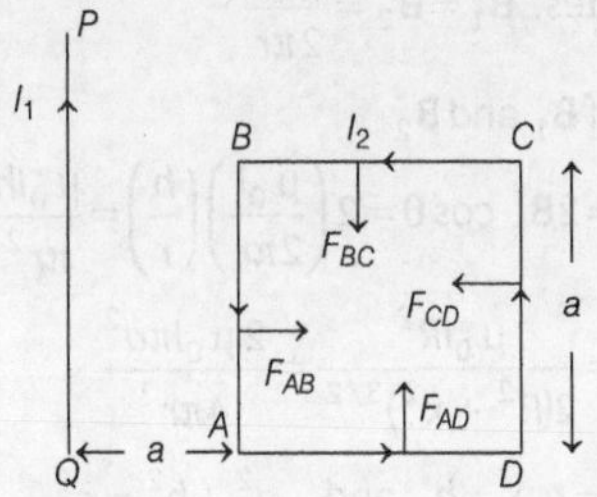

$$F_{AB} = \frac{\mu_0 I_1}{2\pi a} \cdot I_2 a \quad \text{(away from wire } PQ\text{)}$$

$$F_{BC} = F_{AD} = 0 \quad [\because \theta = 0°]$$

$$F_{CD} = \frac{\mu_0 I_1}{2\pi(2a)} \cdot I_2 a = \frac{\mu_0 I_1}{4\pi a} \cdot I_2 a \quad \text{(towards the wire } PQ\text{)}$$

$$\therefore \quad F_{\text{net}} = F_{AB} - F_{CD}$$

$$= \frac{\mu_0 I_1 I_2}{2\pi} - \frac{\mu_0 I_1 I_2}{4\pi} \quad \text{(away from wire)}$$

$$= \frac{\mu_0 I_1 I_2}{4\pi} \quad \text{(repulsive in nature)}$$

JEE Advanced

1. Question was dropped.
2. Torque experienced by circular loop = **M** × **B**
where, **M** is magnetic moment
and **B** is magnetic field.

$$\therefore \quad \tau = i\pi R^2 N B_0 \quad \text{(at the instant shown } \theta = \pi/2\text{)}$$

$$\therefore \tau dt = d\mathbf{L} = i\pi R^2 N B_0 dt$$

$$= Q\pi R^2 N B_0 \quad (\because \ idt = Q)$$

3.

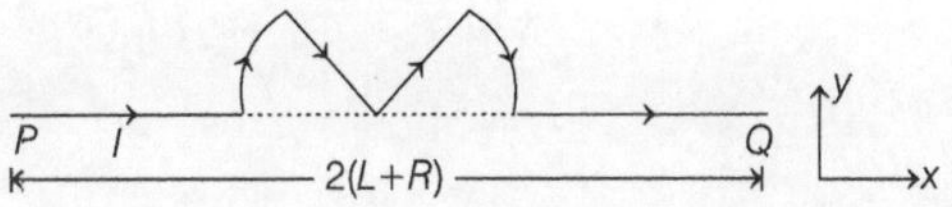

Force on the complete wire = force on straight wire PQ carrying a current I.

$$\mathbf{F} = I(\mathbf{PQ} \times \mathbf{B}) = I[\{2(L+R)\hat{\mathbf{i}}\} \times \mathbf{B}]$$

This force is zero if **B** is along $\hat{\mathbf{i}}$ direction or x-direction. If magnetic field is along $\hat{\mathbf{j}}$ direction or $\hat{\mathbf{k}}$ direction,

$$|\mathbf{F}| = F = (I)(2)(L+R)B \sin 90°$$

$$\text{or} \quad F = 2I(L+R)B \quad \text{or} \quad F \propto (L+R)$$

4. $\mathbf{B}_R = \mathbf{B}$ due to ring

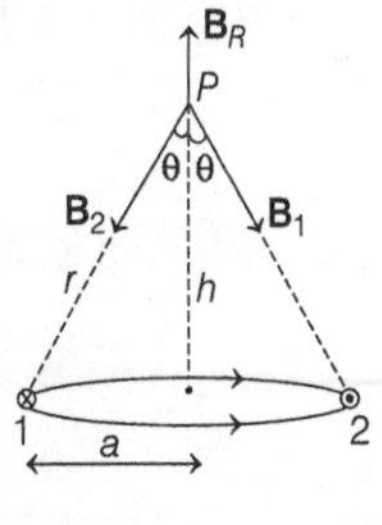

$\mathbf{B}_1 = \mathbf{B}$ due to wire-1 $\Rightarrow$ $\mathbf{B}_2 = \mathbf{B}$ due to wire-2

In magnitudes, $\mathbf{B}_1 = \mathbf{B}_2 = \frac{\mu_0 I}{2\pi r}$

Resultant of $\mathbf{B}_1$ and $\mathbf{B}_2$

$$= 2\mathbf{B}_1 \cos\theta = 2\left(\frac{\mu_0 I}{2\pi r}\right)\left(\frac{h}{r}\right) = \frac{\mu_0 I h}{\pi r^2}$$

$$B_R = \frac{\mu_0 I R^2}{2(R^2 + x^2)^{3/2}} = \frac{2\mu_0 I \pi a^2}{4\pi r^3}$$

As, $R = a, x = h$ and $a^2 + h^2 = r^2$

For zero magnetic field at P, $\frac{\mu_0 I h}{\pi r^2} = \frac{2\mu_0 I \pi a^2}{4\pi r^3}$

$\Rightarrow \quad \pi a^2 = 2rh \Rightarrow h \approx 1.2a$

5. Magnetic field at mid-point of two wires

$= 2$ (magnetic field due to one wire)

$$= 2\left[\frac{\mu_0}{2\pi}\frac{I}{d}\right] = \frac{\mu_0 I}{\pi d}$$

Magnetic moment of loop $M = IA = I\pi a^2$

Torque on loop $= MB \sin 150°$ or $MB \sin 30°$

$$= \frac{\mu_0 I^2 a^2}{2d}$$

6. Area of the given loop is

$A =$ (area of two circles of radius $a/2$ and area of a square of side a)

$$= 2\pi\left(\frac{a}{2}\right)^2 + a^2 = \left(\frac{\pi}{2} + 1\right)a^2$$

$$|\mathbf{M}| = IA = \left(\frac{\pi}{2} + 1\right)a^2 I$$

From screw law direction of $\mathbf{M}$ is outwards or in positive z-direction.

$\therefore \quad \mathbf{M} = \left(\frac{\pi}{2} + 1\right)a^2 I\hat{\mathbf{k}}$

CHAPTER~04

MAGNETIC PROPERTIES OF MATTER

LEVEL 01 Starter Level

4.1 Bar Magnet

1 Calculate the strength of the magnetic field at a distance of 20 cm from a pole of strength 40 A-m in air.

2 A north pole of strength 50 A-m and south pole of strength 100 A-m are separated by a distance of 10 cm in air. Find the force between them. Also find the force when the distance between them is doubled.

3 A bar magnet of magnetic moment 3.0 A-m^2 is placed in a uniform magnetic induction field of 2×10^{-5} T. If each pole of the magnet experiences a force of 6×10^{-4} N, what is the length of the magnet?

4 An iron rod of length L and magnetic moment M is bent in the form of a semicircle. Find its new magnetic moment.

5 Two thin bar magnets of pole strengths 25 A-m and 48 A-m respectively and lengths 20 cm and 25 cm respectively are placed at right angles to each other with the N-pole of first touching the S-pole of the second. Find the magnetic moment of the system.

6 A bar magnet has a pole strength of 3.6 A-m and magnetic length 8 cm. Find the magnetic field at a distance of 6 cm from its centre at a point on its

(i) axial line and

(ii) equitorial line

7 Find the magnetic field due to a dipole of magnetic moment 1.2 A-m^2 at a point 1 m away from it in a direction making an angle of 60° with the dipole-axis.

8. Figure shows two identical magnetic dipoles a and b of magnetic moments M each, placed at a separation d, with their axes perpendicular to each other. Find the magnetic field at the point P midway between the dipoles.

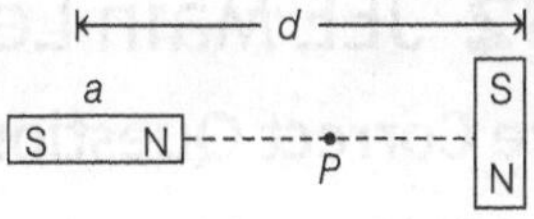

9 A bar magnet of length 0.2 m and pole strength 5 A-m is kept in a uniform magnetic induction field of strength 15 Wbm^{-2} making an angle of 30° with the field. Find the couple acting on it.

10 A bar magnet has a magnetic moment 2.5 J T^{-1} and is placed in a magnetic field of 0.2 T. Calculate the work done in turning the magnet from parallel to anti-parallel position relative to field direction.

11 Figure shows two small bar magnets having dipole moments M_1 and M_2 placed at separation r. Find the magnetic interaction energy of this system of dipoles for $r >> d$.

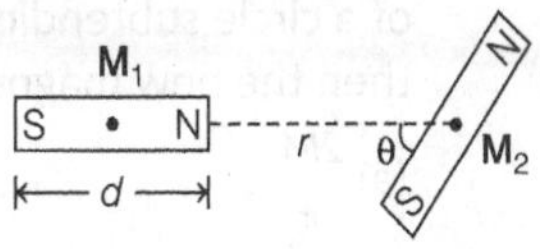

4.2 Magnetic Properties of Materials

1 The permeability of substance is 6.28×10^{-4} Wb/A-m. Find its relative permeability and susceptibility.

2 A magnetising field of 1600 Am^{-1} produces a magnetic flux of 2.4×10^{-5} Wb in a bar of iron of cross section 0.2 cm^2. Calculate permeability and susceptibility of the bar.

3 The magnetic moment of a magnet of mass 75 g is 9×10^{-7} A-m^2. If the density of the material of magnet is 7.5×10^3 kg m^{-3} then find intensity of magnetisation.

4 An iron bar of length 10 cm and diameter 2 cm is placed in a magnetic field of intensity 1000 Am^{-1} with its length parallel to the direction of the field. Determine the magnetic moment produced in the bar, if permeability of its material is 6.3×10^{-4} TmA^{-1}.

5 The susceptibility of magnesium at 300 K is 1.2×10^{-5}. At what temperature, will the susceptibility increase to 1.8×10^{-5}?

6 A domain in ferromagnetic iron is in the form of a cube of side length 1 μm. Estimate the number of iron atoms in the domain and the maximum possible dipole moment and magnetisation of the domain. The molecular mass of iron is 55 g/mol and its density is 7.9 g/cm^3. Assume that each iron atom has a dipole moment of 9.27×10^{-24} A-m^2.

7 A solenoid of 500 turns/m is carrying a current of 3 A. Its core is made of iron which has a relative permeability of 5000. Determine the magnitudes of the magnetic intensity, magnetisation and the magnetic field inside the core.

8 When a rod of magnetic material of size 10 cm $\times$ 0.5 cm $\times$ 0.2 cm is located in magnetising field of 0.5×10^4 A/m, then a magnetic moment of 5 A-m^2 is induced in it. Find out magnetic induction in rod.

9 The coercivity of a certain permanent is 4.0×10^4 Am^{-1}. This magnet is placed inside a solenoid 15 cm long and having 600 turns and a current is passed in the solenoid to demagnetise it completely. Find the current.

10 The hysteresis loss for a specimen of iron weighing 12 kg is equivalent to 300 Jm^{-3} $cycle^{-1}$. Find the loss of energy per hour at a frequency of 50 cycle s^{-1}. Density of iron is 7500 kg m^{-3}.

LEVEL 02 JEE Main Level

Single Choice Correct Questions

1 The magnetic field lines due to a bar magnet are correctly shown in

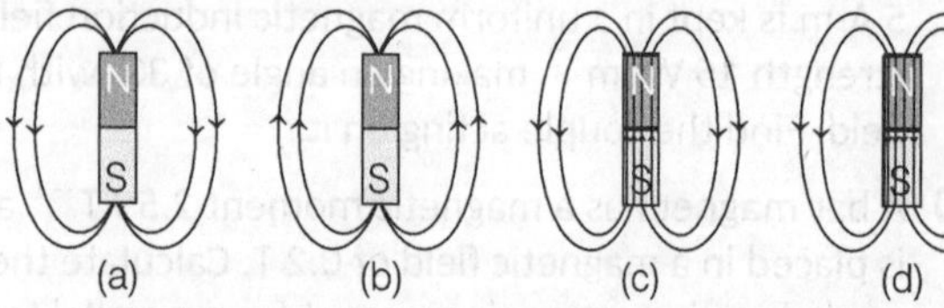

(a) (b) (c) (d)

2 A magnetised wire of moment *M* is bent into an arc of a circle subtending an angle 60° at the centre, then the new magnetic moment is

(a) $\frac{2M}{\pi}$ (b) $\frac{M}{\pi}$

(c) $\frac{3\sqrt{2}M}{\pi}$ (d) $\frac{3M}{\pi}$

3 If a magnet of pole strength *m* is divided into four parts such that the length and width of each part is half that of initial one, then the pole strength of each part will be

(a) $\frac{m}{4}$ (b) $\frac{m}{2}$ (c) $\frac{m}{8}$ (d) $4m$

4 The distance between the poles of a horse shoe magnet is 0.1 m and its pole strength is 0.01 A-m. The induction of magnetic field at a point midway between the poles will be

(a) 2×10^{-5} T (b) 4×10^{-6} T

(c) 8×10^{-7} T (d) Zero

5 Three indentical bar magnets each of magnetic moment *M*, are placed in the form of an equilateral triangle as shown in figure. The net magnetic moment of the system is

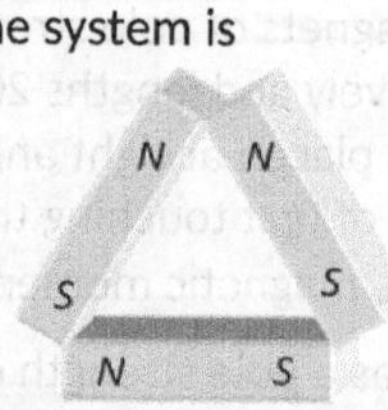

(a) zero (b) 2*M* (c) $\frac{3M}{2}$ (d) $M\sqrt{3}$

6 Two identical bar magnets with a length 10 cm and weight 50 gm-weight are arranged freely with their like poles facing in a arranged vertical glass tube. The upper magnet hangs in the air above the lower one so that the distance between the nearest pole of the magnet is 3mm. Pole strength of the poles of each magnet will be

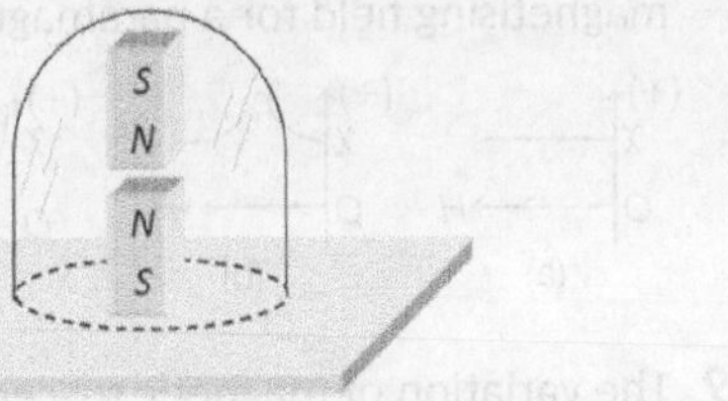

(a) 6.64 A-m (b) 2 A-m
(c) 10.25 A-m (d) None of these

7 The distance of two points on the axis of a magnet from its centre is 10 cm and 20 cm respectively. The ratio of magnetic intensity at these points is 12.5 : 1. The length of the magnet will be
(a) 5 cm (b) 25 cm (c) 10 cm (d) 20 cm

8 A bar magnet having centre *O* has a length of 4 cm. Point P_1 is in the broad side-on and P_2 is in the end side-on position with $OP_1 = OP_2 = 10$ m. The ratio of magnetic intensities *H* at P_1 and P_2 is
(a) $H_1 : H_2 = 16 : 100$ (b) $H_1 : H_2 = 1 : 2$
(c) $H_1 : H_2 = 2 : 1$ (d) $H_1 : H_2 = 100 : 16$

9 Two short magnets of equal dipole moments *M* are fastened perpendicularly at their centre (figure). The magnitude of the magnetic field at a distance *d* from the centre on the bisector of the right angle is

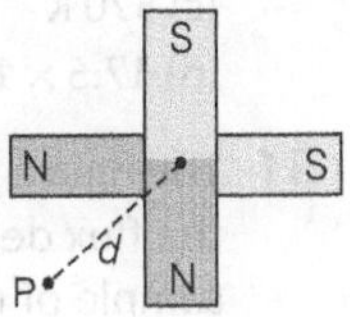

(a) $\frac{\mu_0}{4\pi} \frac{M}{d^3}$ (b) $\frac{\mu_0}{4\pi} \frac{M\sqrt{2}}{d^3}$
(c) $\frac{\mu_0}{4\pi} \frac{2\sqrt{2}M}{d^3}$ (d) $\frac{\mu_0}{4\pi} \frac{2M}{d^3}$

10 Two short magnets of magnetic moment 1000 A-m^2 are placed as shown at the corners of a square of side 10 cm. The net magnetic induction at *P* is

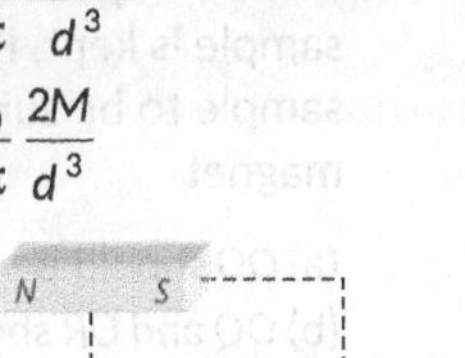

(a) 0.1 T (b) 0.2 T (c) 0.3 T (d) 0.4 T

11 Two identical short bar magnets, each having magnetic moment of 10 A-m^2, are arranged such that their axial lines are perpendicular to each other and their centres be along the same straight line in a horizontal plane. If the distance between their centres is 0.2 m, the resultant magnetic induction at a point midway between them is
(a) $\sqrt{2} \times 10^{-7}$ T (b) $\sqrt{5} \times 10^{-7}$ T
(c) $\sqrt{2} \times 10^{-3}$ T (d) $\sqrt{5} \times 10^{-3}$ T

12 Two magnets *A* and *B* are identical and these are arranged as shown in the figure. Their lengths are negligible in comparison to the separation between them. A magnetic needle is placed between the magnets at point *P* which gets deflected through an angle θ under the influence of magnets. The ratio of distance d_1 and d_2 will be

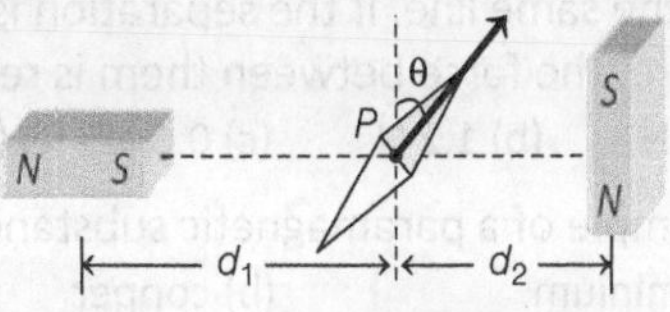

(a) $(2 \tan\theta)^{1/3}$ (b) $(2 \tan\theta)^{-1/3}$
(c) $(2 \cot\theta)^{1/3}$ (d) $(2 \cot\theta)^{-1/3}$

13 When a bar magnet is placed at 90° to a uniform magnetic field, it is acted upon by a couple which is maximum. For the couple to be half of the maximum value, at what angle should the magnet be inclined to the magnetic field (B)?
(a) 0° (b) 30° (c) 45° (d) 60°

14 A magnet of magnetic moment 50 Am is placed along the X-axis in a magnetic field $\mathbf{B} = (5.0\hat{i} + 3.0\hat{j})$ T. The torque acting on the magnet is
(a) $175\,\hat{k}$ N-m (b) $150\,\hat{k}$ N-m
(c) $75\,\hat{k}$ N-m (d) $25\sqrt{37}\,\hat{k}$ N-m

15 A bar magnet with its poles 25 cm apart and of pole strength 24.0 A-m rests with its centre on a frictionless pivot. A force *F* is applied on the magnet at a distance of 12 cm from the pivot so that it is held in equilibrium at an angle of 30° with respect to a magnetic field of induction 0.25 T. The value of force *F* is
(a) 5.62 N (b) 2.56 N (c) 6.52 N (d) 6.25 N

16 A magnetic needle lying parallel to a magnetic field requires *W* units of work to turn it through 60°. What is the torque needed to maintain the needle in this position?
(a) $\sqrt{3}W$ (b) W (c) $2W$ (d) $\frac{W}{\sqrt{3}}$

17 A magnetic dipole is under the influence of two magnetic fields. The angle between the two field directions is 75° and one of the fields has a magnitude of 2×10^{-3} T. If the dipole comes to stable equilibrium at an angle of 30° with this field, what is the magnitude of the other field?
(a) 1×10^{-3} T (b) $\sqrt{2} \times 10^{-3}$ T
(c) $2\sqrt{2} \times 10^{-3}$ T (d) $\sqrt{3} \times 10^{-3}$ T

18 The small magnets each of magnetic moment 10 A-m^2 are placed end-on position 0.1 m apart from their centres. The force acting between them is
(a) 0.03 N (b) 0.3 N (c) 0.6 N (d) 0.06 N

19 Force between two identical bar magnets whose centres are r metre apart is 4.8 N when their axes are in the same line. If the separation is increased to $2r$ metre, the force between them is reduced to
(a) 2.4 N (b) 1.2 N (c) 0.6 N (d) 0.3 N

20 An example of a paramagnetic substance is
(a) aluminium (b) copper
(c) iron (d) nickel

21 If a magnetic substance is kept in a magnetic field, then which of the following is thrown out?
(a) Paramagnetic (b) Ferromagnetic
(c) Diamagnetic (d) Anti-ferromagnetic

22 A superconductor exhibits perfect
(a) ferrimagnetism (b) ferromagnetism
(c) paramagnetism (d) diamagnetism

23 For an isotropic medium B, μ_0, H and M are related as (where B, μ_0, H and M have their usual meaning in the context of magnetic material
(a) $(B - M) = \mu_0 H$ (b) $M = \mu_0(H + M)$
(c) $H = \mu_0(H + M)$ (d) $B = \mu_0(H + M)$

24 When a piece of a ferromagnetic substance is put in a uniform magnetic field, the flux density inside it is four times the flux density away from the piece. The magnetic permeability of the material is
(a) 1 (b) 2 (c) 3 (d) 4

25 In the hysteresis cycle, the value of H needed to make the intensity of magnetisation zero is called
(a) retentivity (b) coercive force
(c) Lorentz force (d) None of the above

26 The materials suitable for making electromagnets should have
(a) high retentivity and low coercivity
(b) low retentivity and low coercivity
(c) high retentivity and high coercivity
(d) low retentivity and high coercivity

27 When a ferromagnetic material is heated to temperature above its Curie temperature, the material
(a) is permanently magnetized
(b) remains ferromagnetic
(c) behaves like a diamagnetic material
(d) behaves like a paramagnetic material

28 The variation of magnetic susceptibility (χ) with magnetising field for a paramagnetic substance is

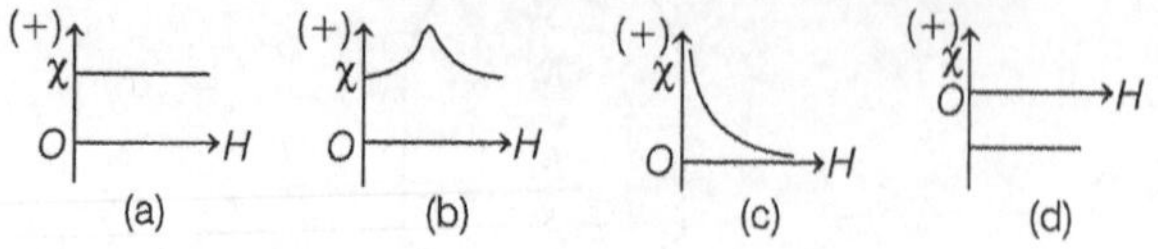

29 The variation of magnetic susceptibility (χ) with absolute temperature T for a ferromagnetic material is

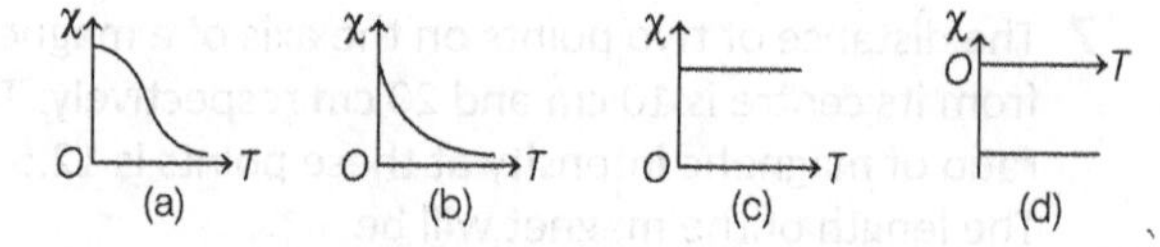

30 The $\chi - \frac{1}{T}$ graph for an alloy of paramagnetic nature is shown in figure, then the curie constant is

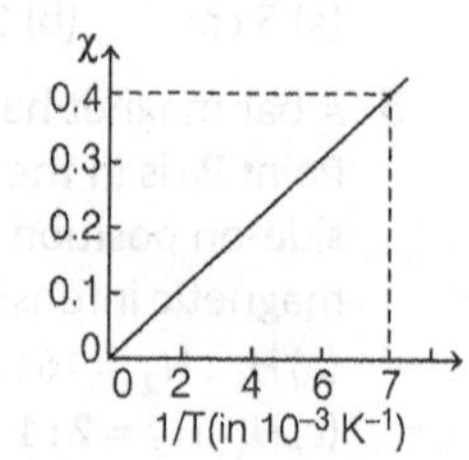

(a) 57 K
(b) 2.8×10^{-3} K
(c) 570 K
(d) 17.5×10^{-3} K

31 The figure illustrate how B, the flux density inside a sample of unmagnetised ferromagnetic material varies with B_0, the magnetic flux density in which the sample is kept. For the sample to be suitable for making a permanent magnet

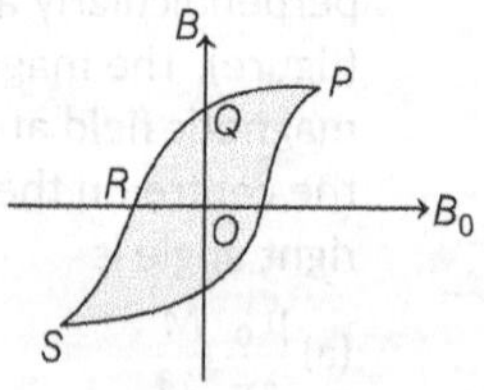

(a) OQ should be large, OR should be small
(b) OQ and OR should both be large
(c) OQ should be small and OR should be large
(d) OQ and OR should both be small

32 The variation of the intensity of magnetisation (I) with respect to the magnetising field (H) in a diamagnetic substance is described by the graph

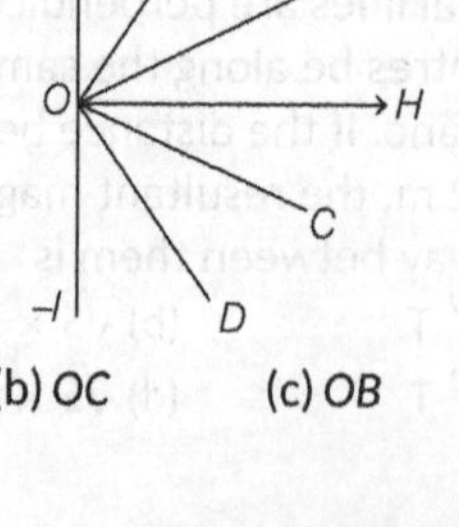

(a) OD (b) OC (c) OB (d) OA

33 For iron its density is 7.5 g/cc and mass 0.075 kg. If its magnetic moment is 8×10^{-7} A-m^2, its intensity of magnetisation is

(a) 8 A/m (b) 0.8 A/m
(c) 0.08 A/m (d) 0.008 A/m

34 On placing a piece of ferromagnetic material of cross-sectional area 1 cm^2 in magnetic field of 200 oersted, flux density of 3000 Gauss is produced in it. The values of relative permeability and magnetic susceptibility of the material will respectively be

(a) 11.9 and 150 (b) 150 and 11.9
(c) 50 and 11.9 (d) 15 and 14

35 The dipole moment of each molecule of a paramagnetic gas is 1.5×10^{23} A-m^2. The temperature of gas is 27°C and the number of molecules per unit volume in it is 2×10^{26} m^{-3}. The maximum possible intensity of magnetisation in the gas will be

(a) 3×10^3 Am^{-1} (b) 4×10^{-3} Am^{-1}
(c) 5×10^5 Am^{-1} (d) 6×10^{-4} Am^{-1}

36 A rod of ferromagnetic material with dimensions 10 cm × 0.5 cm × 0.2 cm is placed in a magnetic field of strength 0.5×10^4 Am^{-1} as a result of which a magnetic moment of 5 Am^2 is produced in the rod. The value of magnetic induction will be

(a) 0.54 T (b) 0.358 T
(c) 2.519 T (d) 6.28 T

37 The coercivity of a small bar magnet is 4×10^3 A/m. It is inserted inside a solenoid of 5000 turns and length 10 m to demagnetise it. The amount of current to be passed through the solenoid will be

(a) 2.5 A (b) 5 A
(c) 8 A (d) 10 A

38 A sample of paramagnetic salt contains 2.0×10^{24} atomic dipoles each of dipole moment 1.5×10^{-23} JT^{-1}. The sample is placed under a homogeneous magnetic field of 0.84 T, and cooled to a temperature of 4.2 K. The degree of magnetic saturation achieved is equal to 15%. What is the total dipole moment (approximate) of the sample for a magnetic field of 0.98 T and a temperature of 2.8K? (Assume Curie's law)

(a) 7.9 JT^{-1} (b) 52.5 JT^{-1}
(c) 30 JT^{-1} (d) 4.6 JT^{-1}

39 The mass of a specimen of a ferromagnetic material is 0.6 kg and its density is 7.8×10^3 kgm^{-3}. If the area of hysteresis loop of alternating magnetising field of frequency 50Hz is 0.722 MKS units, then the hysteresis loss per second will be

(a) 277.7×10^{-5} J (b) 277.7×10^{-6} J
(c) 277.7×10^{-3} J (d) 277.7×10^{-4} J

Previous Years Questions

JEE Main

1 The magnetic potential due to a magnetic dipole at a point on its axis situated at a distance of 20 cm from its centre is 1.5×10^{-5} Tm. The magnetic moment of the dipole is .... Am^2. (Given, $\frac{\mu_0}{4\pi} = 10^{-7}$ TmA^{-1})

[2024, 29 Jan Shift-I]

2 A bar magnet with a magnetic moment 5.0 A-m^2 is placed in parallel position relative to a magnetic field of 0.4 T. The amount of required work done in turning the magnet from parallel to antiparallel position relative to the field direction is

[2023, 31 Jan Shift-I]

(a) 2 J (b) zero (c) 4 J (d) 1 J

3 Given below are two statements: one is labelled as Assertion A and the other is labelled as Reason R

Assertion (A) Electromagnets are made of soft iron.

Reason (R) Soft iron has high permeability and low retentivity.

In the light of above, statements, choose the most appropriate answer from the options given below.

[2023, 8 April Shift-II]

(a) Both A and R are correct and R is the correct explanation of A
(b) Both A and R are correct but R is not the correct explanation of A
(c) A is not correct but R is correct
(d) A is correct but R is not correct

4 Given below are two statements:

Statement I For diamagnetic substance, $-1 \leq \chi < 0$, where χ is the magnetic susceptibility.

Statement II Diamagnetic substances when placed in an external magnetic field, tend to move from stronger to weaker part of the field.

In the light of the above statements, choose the correct answer from the options given below

[2023, 10 April Shift-II]

(a) Both Statement I and Statement II are true
(b) Statement I is incorrect but Statement II is true.
(c) Statement I is correct but Statement II is false
(d) Both Statement I and Statement II are False

5 Given below are two statements

Statement I The diamagnetic property depends on temperature.

Statement II The induced magnetic dipole moment in a diamagnetic sample is always opposite to the magnetising field.

In the light of above statements, choose the most appropriate answer from the options given below. **[2023, 12 April Shift-II]**

(a) Both Statement I and Statement II are False.
(b) Statement I is false but Statement II is true.
(c) Both Statement I and Statement II are true.
(d) Statement I is correct but Statement II is false.

6 The susceptibility of a paramagnetic material is 99. The permeability of the material in Wb/A-m is [Permeability of free space, $\mu_0 = 4\pi \times 10^{-7}$ Wb/A-m] **[2022, 27 June Shift-I]**

(a) $4\pi \times 10^{-7}$ (b) $4\pi \times 10^{-4}$
(c) $4\pi \times 10^{-5}$ (d) $4\pi \times 10^{-6}$

7 Which of the following statements are correct? **[2021, 18 March Shift-II]**

A. Electric monopoles do not exist, whereas magnetic monopoles exist.
B. Magnetic field lines due to a solenoid at its ends and outside cannot be completely straight and confined.
C. Magnetic field lines are completely confined within a toroid.
D. Magnetic field lines inside a bar magnet are not parallel.
E. $\chi = -1$ is the condition for a perfect diamagnetic material, where χ is its magnetic susceptibility.

Choose the correct answer from the options given below.

(a) C and E (b) B and D (c) A and B (d) B and C

8 A long solenoid with 1000 turns/m has a core material with relative permeability 500 and volume 10^3 cm^3. If the core material is replaced by another material having relative permeability of 750 with same volume maintaining same current of 0.75 A in the solenoid, the fractional change in the magnetic moment of the core would be approximately $(\chi / 499)$. Find the value of χ. **[2021, 31 Aug Shift-II]**

9 **Statement I** The ferromagnetic property depends on temperature. At high temperature, ferromagnet becomes paramagnet.

Statement II At high temperature, the domain wall area of a ferromagnetic substance increases.

In the light of the above statements, choose the most appropriate answer from the options given below. **[2021, 22 July Shift-II]**

(a) Statement I is true but Statement II is false
(b) Both Statement I and Statement II are true
(c) Both Statement I and Statement II are false
(d) Statement I is false but Statement II is true

10 The magnetic susceptibility of a material of a rod is 499. Permeability in vacuum is $4\pi \times 10^{-7}$ H/m. Absolute permeability of the material of the rod is **[2021, 20 July Shift-II]**

(a) $4\pi \times 10^{-4}$ H/m (b) $2\pi \times 10^{-4}$ H/m
(c) $3\pi \times 10^{-4}$ H/m (d) $\pi \times 10^{-4}$ H/m

11 A solenoid of 1000 turns per metre has a core with relative permeability 500. Insulated windings of the solenoid carry an electric current of 5 A. The magnetic flux density produced by the solenoid is (Permeability of free space $= 4\pi \times 10^{-7}$ H/m) **[2021, 17 March Shift-I]**

(a) π T (b) $2 \times 10^{-3} \pi$ T
(c) $\frac{\pi}{5}$ T (d) $10^{-4} \pi$ T

12 In a ferromagnetic material, below the Curie temperature, a domain is defined as **[2021, 25 Feb Shift-II]**

(a) a macroscopic region with zero magnetisation
(b) a macroscopic region with saturation magnetisation
(c) a macroscopic region with randomly oriented magnetic dipoles
(d) a macroscopic region with consecutive magnetic dipoles oriented in opposite direction

13 A small bar magnet placed with its axis at 30° with an external field of 0.06 T experiences a torque of 0.018 Nm. The minimum work required to rotate it from its stable to unstable equilibrium position is **[2020, 4 Sep Shift-I]**

(a) 9.2×10^{-3} J (b) 7.2×10^{-2} J
(c) 6.4×10^{-2} J (d) 11.7×10^{-3} J

14 A small circular loop of conducting wire has radius a and carries current i. It is placed in a uniform magnetic field B perpendicular to its plane such that when rotated slightly about its diameter and released, it starts performing simple harmonic motion of time period T. If the mass of the loop is m, then **[2020, 9 Jan Shift-II]**

(a) $T = \sqrt{\frac{\pi m}{iB}}$ (b) $T = \sqrt{\frac{2m}{iB}}$
(c) $T = \sqrt{\frac{2\pi m}{iB}}$ (d) $T = \sqrt{\frac{\pi m}{2iB}}$

15 An iron rod of volume 10^{-3} m^3 and relative permeability 1000 is placed as core in a solenoid with 10 turns/cm. If a current of 0.5 A is passed through the solenoid, then the magnetic moment of the rod will be **[2020, 5 Sep Shift-II]**

(a) 50×10^2 Am^2 (b) 5×10^2 Am^2

(c) 500×10^2 Am^2 (d) 0.5×10^2 Am^2

16 A paramagnetic sample shows a net magnetisation of 6 A/m, when it is placed in an external magnetic field of 0.4 T at a temperature of 4 K. When the sample is placed in an external magnetic field of 0.3 T at a temperature of 24 K, then the magnetisation will be **[2020, 4 Sep Shift-II]**

(a) 4 A/m (b) 0.75 A/m

(c) 1 A/m (d) 2.25 A/m

17 Magnetic materials used for making permanent magnets (*P*) and magnets in a transformer (*T*) have different properties, of the following, which property best matches for the type of magnet required? **[2020, 2 Sep Shift-I]**

(a) *T*: Large retentivity, small coercivity
(b) *P* : Large retentivity, large coercivity
(c) *P* : Small retentivity, large coercivity
(d) *T* : Large retentivity, large coercivity

18 A perfectly diamagnetic sphere has a small spherical cavity at its centre,which is filled with a paramagnetic substance. The whole system is placed in a uniform magnetic field **B**. Then, the field inside the paramagnetic substance is **[2020, 3 Sep Shift-II]**

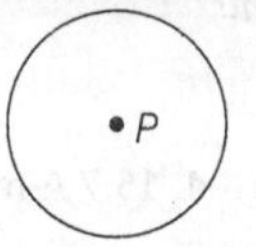

(a) much larger than |**B**| and parallel to **B**
(b) **B**
(c) zero
(d) much larger than | **B** | but opposite to **B**

19

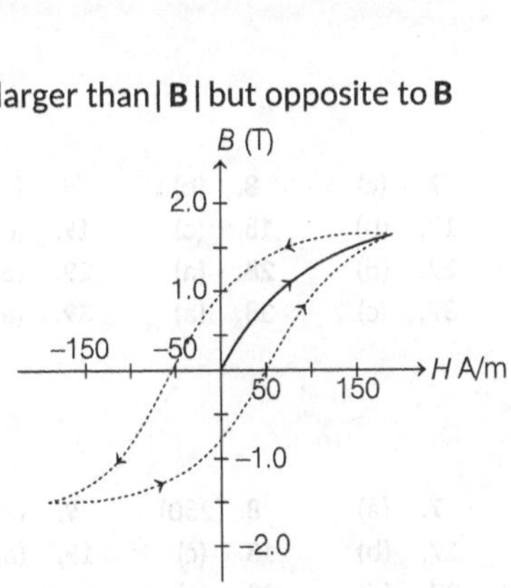

The figure gives experimentally measured *B versusH* variation in a ferromagnetic material. The retentivity, coercivity and saturation respectively of the material are **[2020, 7 Jan Shift-II]**

(a) 1.0 T, 50 A/m and 1.5 T
(b) 150 A/m, 1.0 T and 1.5 T
(c) 1.5 T, 50 A/m and 1.0 T
(d) 1.5 T, 50 A/m and 1.0 T

20 Two magnetic dipoles X and Y are placed at a separation *d*, with their axes perpendicular to each other. The dipole moment of Y is twice that of X. A particle of charge *q* is passing through their mid-point P, at angle $\theta = 45°$ with the horizontal line, as shown in figure. What would be the magnitude of force on the particle at that instant?
(*d* is much larger than the dimensions of the dipole) **[2019, 8 April Shift-II]**

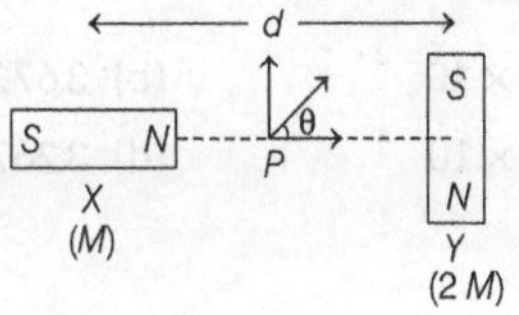

(a) $\left(\frac{\mu_0}{4\pi}\right)\frac{M}{(d/2)^3} \times qv$

(b) 0

(c) $\sqrt{2}\left(\frac{\mu_0}{4\pi}\right)\frac{M}{(d/2)^3} \times qv$

(d) $\left(\frac{\mu_0}{4\pi}\right)\frac{2M}{(d/2)^3} \times qv$

21 A magnet of total magnetic moment $10^{-2}\hat{i}$ A-m^2 is placed in a time varying magnetic field, $B\hat{i}(\cos\omega t)$, where $B = 1$ T and $\omega = 0.125$ rad/s. The work done for reversing the direction of the magnetic moment at $t = 1$ s is **[2019, 10 Jan Shift-I]**

(a) 0.01 J (b) 0.007 J (c) 0.014 J (d) 0.028 J

22 A hoop and a solid cylinder of same mass and radius are made of a permanent magnetic material with their magnetic moment parallel to their respective axes. But the magnetic moment of hoop is twice of solid cylinder. They are placed in a uniform magnetic field in such a manner that their magnetic moments make a small angle with the field. If the oscillation periods of hoop and cylinder are T_h and T_c respectively, then **[2019, 10 Jan Shift-II]**

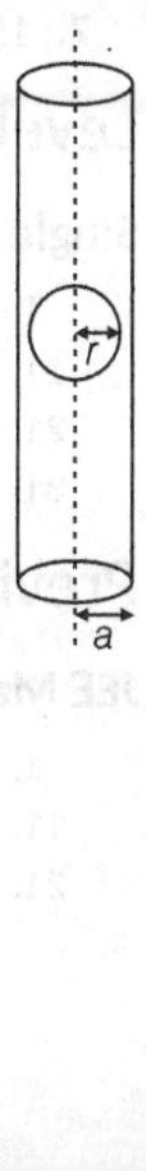

(a) $T_h = 0.5\,T_c$ (b) $T_h = T_c$

(c) $T_h = 2\,T_c$ (d) $T_h = 1.5\,T_c$

23 A bar magnet is demagnetised by inserting it inside a solenoid of length 0.2 m, 100 turns and carrying a current of 5.2 A. The coercivity of the bar magnet is **[2019, 9 Jan Shift-I]**

(a) 1200 A/m (b) 285 A/m
(c) 2600A/m (d) 520A/m

24 A paramagnetic substance in the form of a cube with sides 1 cm has a magnetic dipole moment of 20×10^{-6} J/T when a magnetic intensity of 60×10^{3} A/m is applied. Its magnetic susceptibility is **[2019, 11 Jan Shift-II]**

(a) 3.3×10^{-4} (b) 3.3×10^{-2}
(c) 4.3×10^{-2} (d) 2.3×10^{-2}

25 A paramagnetic material has 10^{28} atoms/m^3. Its magnetic susceptibility at temperature 350 K is 2.8×10^{-4}. Its susceptibility at 300 K is **[2019, 12 Jan Shift-II]**

(a) 3.726×10^{-4} (b) 3.672×10^{-4}
(c) 2.672×10^{-4} (d) 3.267×10^{-4}

26 A magnetic needle of magnetic moment 6.7×10^{-2} Am^2 and moment of inertia 7.5×10^{-6} kg m^2 is performing simple harmonic oscillations in a magnetic field of 0.01 T. Time taken for 10 complete oscillations is **[2017]**

(a) 8.89 s (b) 6.98 s (c) 8.76 s (d) 6.65 s

27 The magnetic lines of force inside a bar magnet **[AIEEE 2013]**

(a) are from North-pole to South-pole of the magnet
(b) do not exist
(c) depend upon the area of cross-section of the bar magnet
(d) are from South-pole to North-pole of the magnet

28 A magnetic needle is kept in a non-uniform magnetic field. It experiences **[AIEEE 2005]**

(a) a torque but not a force
(b) neither a force nor a torque
(c) a force and a torque
(d) a force but not a torque

Answer Key

Level 1

4.1 Bar Magnet

1. 10^{-4} Wb/m^2
2. 5×10^{-2} N, 12.5×10^{-3} N
3. 10 cm
4. $\frac{2M}{\pi}$
5. 13 A-m^2
6. (i) 8.6×10^{-4} T; (ii) 7.7×10^{-5} T
7. 1.6×10^{-7} T
8. $\frac{2\sqrt{5}\mu_0 M}{\pi d^3}$
9. 7.5 Nm
10. 1 J
11. $-\frac{\mu_0 M_1 M_2 \cos\theta}{2\pi r^3}$

4.2 Magnetic Properties of Materials

1. 500, 499
2. 7.5×10^{-4} Wb-m/A, 596.1
3. 0.09 A/m
4. 15.7 A-m^2
5. 200 K
6. 8.65×10^{10} atoms, 8.0×10^{-13} A-m^2, 8.0×10^{5} Am^{-1}
7. 1500 Am^{-1}, 7.5×10^{6} Am^{-1}, 9.4 T
8. 6.28 Wb/m^2
9. 10 A
10. 86400 J

Level 2

Single Choice Correct Questions

1. (d)	2. (d)	3. (b)	4. (c)	5. (b)	6. (a)	7. (c)	8. (b)	9. (c)	10. (a)
11. (d)	12. (c)	13. (b)	14. (b)	15. (d)	16. (a)	17. (b)	18. (c)	19. (d)	20. (a)
21. (c)	22. (d)	23. (d)	24. (d)	25. (b)	26. (c)	27. (d)	28. (a)	29. (a)	30. (a)
31. (b)	32. (b)	33. (c)	34. (d)	35. (a)	36. (d)	37. (c)	38. (a)	39. (a)	

Previous Years Questions

JEE Main

1. (6)	2. (c)	3. (a)	4. (a)	5. (b)	6. (c)	7. (a)	8. (250)	9. (a)	10. (b)
11. (a)	12. (b)	13. (b)	14. (c)	15. (b)	16. (b)	17. (b)	18. (c)	19. (a)	20. (b)
21. (c)	22. (b)	23. (c)	24. (a)	25. (d)	26. (d)	27. (d)	28. (c)		

SOLUTIONS

Level 1

4.1 Bar Magnet

1. $B = \left(\frac{\mu_0}{4\pi}\right)\frac{m}{r^2} = 10^{-7} \times \frac{40}{(0.2)^2} = 10^{-4}\ \text{Wb/m}^2$

2. $F = \left(\frac{\mu_0}{4\pi}\right)\frac{m_1 m_2}{r^2} = \frac{10^{-7} \times 50 \times 100}{(0.1)^2} = 5 \times 10^{-2}\ \text{N}$

$F \propto \frac{1}{r^2}$ force will become one-fourth if distance is doubled,

$F' = \frac{F}{4} = 12.5 \times 10^{-3}\ \text{N}$

3. $F = mB \Rightarrow 6 \times 10^{-4} = m\,(2 \times 10^{-5}) \Rightarrow m = 30$ A-m

$M = ml \Rightarrow 3 = 30 \times l \Rightarrow l = 10$ cm

4. $M = mL,\ M' = m(2R) = 2m\left(\frac{l}{\pi}\right) = \frac{2M}{\pi}$

5. $M_1 = 25 \times 0.2 = 5\ \text{A-m}^2$

$M_2 = 48 \times 0.25 = 12\ \text{A-m}^2$

$M = \sqrt{M_1^2 + M_2^2} = \sqrt{5^2 + 12^2} = 13\ \text{A-m}^2$

6. (i) $B = \left(\frac{\mu_0}{4\pi}\right)\frac{2Mr}{(r^2 - l^2)}$

$= \frac{10^{-7} \times 2 \times 3.6 \times 0.08 \times 0.06}{[(0.06)^2 - (0.04)^2]} = 8.6 \times 10^{-4}\ \text{T}$

(ii) $B = \frac{\mu_0}{4\pi}\frac{M}{(r^2 + l^2)^{\frac{3}{2}}} = \frac{10^{-7} \times 3.6 \times 0.08}{[(0.06)]^2 + (0.04)^2]^{\frac{3}{2}}}$

$= 7.7 \times 10^{-5}\ \text{T}$

7. $B = \frac{\mu_0 M}{4\pi r^3}\sqrt{1 + 3\cos^2\theta}$

$= \frac{10^{-7} \times 1.2}{(1)^3}\sqrt{1 + 3\left(\frac{1}{2}\right)^2} = 1.6 \times 10^{-7}\ \text{T}$

8.

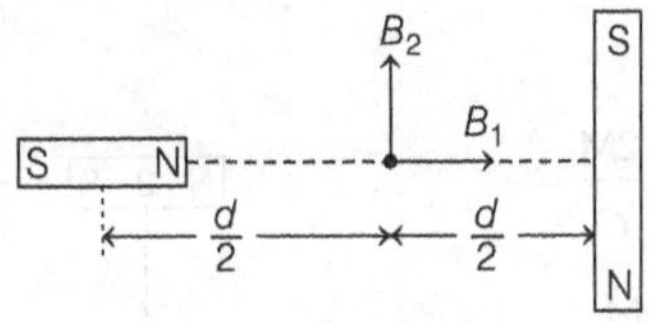

$B_1 = \left(\frac{\mu_0}{4\pi}\right)\frac{2M}{\left(\frac{d}{2}\right)^3}$ and $B_2 = \left(\frac{\mu_0}{4\pi}\right)\frac{M}{\left(\frac{d}{2}\right)^3}$

$B_{net} = \sqrt{B_1^2 + B_2^2} = \left(\frac{\mu_0}{4\pi}\right)\frac{M\sqrt{5}}{\left(\frac{d}{2}\right)^3} = \frac{2\sqrt{5}\mu_0 M}{\pi d^3}$

9. $\tau = MB\sin\theta \Rightarrow \tau = (5 \times 0.2)\ 15 \sin 30° = 7.5$ N-m

10. $U_1 = -MB\cos 0°$ and

$U_2 = -MB\cos 180°$

$W_{ext} = \Delta U = MB - (-MB) = 2MB$

$= 2 \times 2.5 \times 0.2 = 1$ J

11. Magnetic field at the location of M_2 due to M_1 is given as

$$B_1 = \frac{\mu_0 M_1}{2\pi r^3}$$

Interaction energy of M_2 in the field of M_1 is given as

$$U = -\mathbf{M}_2 \cdot \mathbf{B}_1 = -M_2 B_1 \cos\theta = -\frac{\mu_0 M_1 M_2}{2\pi r^3}\cos\theta$$

4.2 Magnetic Properties of Materials

1. $\mu_r = \frac{\mu}{\mu_0} = \frac{6.28 \times 10^{-4}}{4 \times 3.14 \times 10^{-7}} = 500$

$\chi_m = \mu_r - 1 = 499$

2. $\phi = BA \Rightarrow 2.4 \times 10^{-5} = B(0.2 \times 10^{-4})$

$\Rightarrow \quad B = 1.2\ \text{Wb/m}^2$

$\mu = \frac{B}{H} = \frac{1.2}{1600} = 7.5 \times 10^{-4}$ Wb/A-m

$\chi_m = \mu_r - 1 = \frac{\mu}{\mu_0} - 1 = 596.1$

3. $\text{Volume} = \frac{\text{Mass}}{\text{Density}} = \frac{75 \times 10^{-3}}{7.5 \times 10^3} = 10^{-5}\ \text{m}^3$

$I = \frac{M}{V} = \frac{9 \times 10^{-7}}{10^{-5}} = 0.09$ A/m

4. $\chi_m = \mu_r - 1 = \frac{6.3 \times 10^{-4}}{4\pi \times 10^{-7}} - 1 = 500.6$

$I = \chi_m H = (500.6)(1000) = 5 \times 10^5$ A/m

$M = IV = 5 \times 10^5 \times 3.14 \times (10^{-2})^2 \times (10^{-1}) = 15.7\ \text{Am}^2$

5. $\chi = \frac{1}{T}$

$\Rightarrow \quad \frac{\chi_1}{\chi_2} = \frac{T_2}{T_1}$

$\Rightarrow \quad \frac{1.2 \times 10^{-5}}{1.8 \times 10^{-5}} = \frac{T_2}{300}$

$\Rightarrow \quad T_2 = 200$ K

6. Number of iron atoms per unit volume

$= \left(\frac{7.9}{55} \times 6 \times 10^{23}\right)\ \text{cm}^{-3}$

$= 8.65 \times 10^{22}\ \text{cm}^{-3}$

Number of iron atoms in a domain

$$= (10^{-4})^3 \text{ cm}^3 \times (8.6 \times 10^{22} \text{ cm}^{-3})$$

$$= 8.65 \times 10^{10}$$

Maximum dipole moment of dipole

$$= 8.65 \times 10^{10} \times 9.27 \times 10^{-24}$$

$$= 8.0 \times 10^{-13} \text{ Am}^2$$

$$\text{Intensity of magnetisation} = \frac{M}{V} = \frac{8.0 \times 10^{-13}}{(10^{-6})^3} = 8.0 \times 10^5 \text{ A-m}^{-1}$$

7. $H = ni = 500 \times 3 = 1500 \text{ Am}^{-1}$

$\chi_m = \mu_r - 1 = 5000 - 1 = 4999$

$I = \chi_m H = 4999 \times 1500 = 7.5 \times 10^6 \text{ Am}^{-1}$

$B = \mu H = \mu_0 \mu_r H = 4\pi \times 10^{-7} \times 5000 \times 1500 = 9.4 \text{ T}$

8. $I = \frac{M}{V} = \frac{5}{(10 \times 0.5 \times 0.2) \times 10^{-6}} = 5 \times 10^6 \text{ Am}^{-1}$

$\chi_m = \frac{I}{H} = \frac{5 \times 10^{-6}}{0.5 \times 10^4} = 1000$

$\mu_r = 1 + \chi_m = 1001$

$\mu = \mu_0 \mu_r = 4\pi \times 10^{-7} \times 1001 = 12.56 \times 10^{-4}$

$B = \mu H = 12.56 \times 10^{-4} \times 0.5 \times 10^4 = 6.28 \text{ Wb/m}^2$

9. $n = \frac{600}{0.15} = 4000$

$H = ni \Rightarrow 4 \times 10^{-4} = 4000 i \Rightarrow i = 10 \text{ A}$

10. $\text{Volume} = \frac{\text{mass}}{\text{density}} = \frac{12}{7500} \text{ m}^3$

$\text{Energy loss} = 300 \times \frac{12}{7500} \times 50 \times 3600 = 86400 \text{ J}$

Level 2

Single Choice Correct Questions

1. Magnetic field lines inside a bar magnet are from South-pole to North-pole

2. $l = R\theta$

$\Rightarrow \quad l = \frac{\pi}{3} R$

$\Rightarrow \quad R = \frac{3l}{\pi}$

$M = ml; M' = ml' = m(2R \sin 30°)$

$= m\left(\frac{3l}{\pi}\right) = \frac{3M}{\pi}$

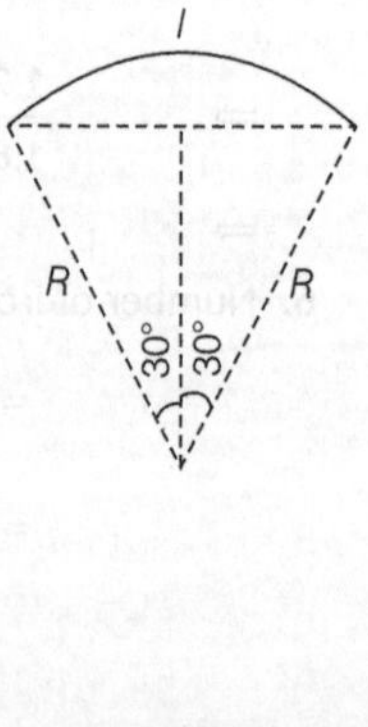

3. $m \propto A \Rightarrow \frac{m_1}{m_2} = \frac{A_1}{A_2} \Rightarrow \frac{m}{m_2} = \frac{A}{\left(\frac{A}{2}\right)}$

$\Rightarrow m_2 = \frac{m}{2}$

4. Magnetic field due to a monopole $= \left(\frac{\mu_0}{4\pi}\right) \frac{m}{r^2}$

$$B_{net} = 10^{-7} \left[\frac{0.01}{\left(\frac{0.1}{2}\right)^2} \right] + 10^{-7} \left[\frac{0.01}{\left(\frac{0.1}{2}\right)^2} \right] = 8 \times 10^{-7} \text{ T}$$

5.

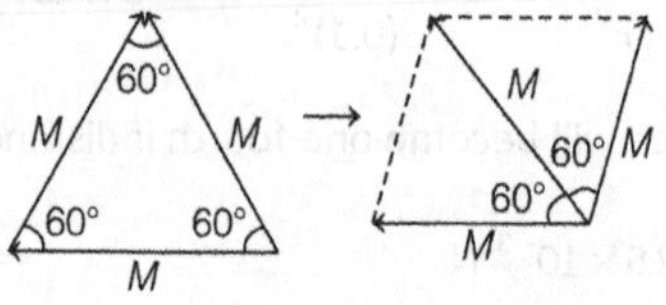

Resultant of three vectors $= M + M \cos 60° + M \cos 60° = 2M$

6. For equilibrium of upper magnet, $F = mg$

$\Rightarrow \quad \left(\frac{\mu_0}{4\pi}\right) \frac{m_1 m_2}{r^2} = mg$

$\Rightarrow \quad 10^{-7} \frac{m^2}{(3 \times 10^{-3})^2} = 50 \times 10^{-3} \times 9.8$

$\Rightarrow \quad m = 6.64 \text{ A-m}$

7. $B_{axis} = \left(\frac{\mu_0}{4\pi}\right) \frac{2Mr}{(r^2 - l^2)^2}$

$\Rightarrow \quad \frac{B_1}{B_2} = \frac{10[(20)^2 - l^2]^2}{[(10)^2 - l^2]^2 (20)} = 12.5$

$\Rightarrow \quad l = 5 \text{ cm}$

So length of the magnet $= 2l = 10$ cm

8. $H_1 = \left(\frac{\mu_0}{4\pi}\right) \frac{M}{r^3}; \quad H_2 = \left(\frac{\mu_0}{4\pi}\right) \frac{2M}{r^3}$

$H_1 : H_2 = 1 : 2$

9. $M_{net} = \sqrt{M^2 + M^2} = \sqrt{2} M$

$B_{axial} = \left(\frac{\mu_0}{4\pi}\right) \frac{2\sqrt{2} M}{d^3}$

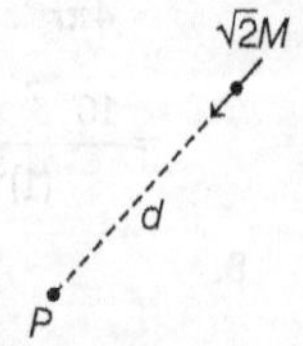

10. $B_1 = \left(\frac{\mu_0}{4\pi}\right) \frac{2M}{r^3}$

$B_2 = \left(\frac{\mu_0}{4\pi}\right) \frac{M}{r^3}$

$B_{net} = B_1 - B_2$

$= \frac{10^{-7} \times 1000}{(0.1)^3} = 0.1 \text{ T}$

11.

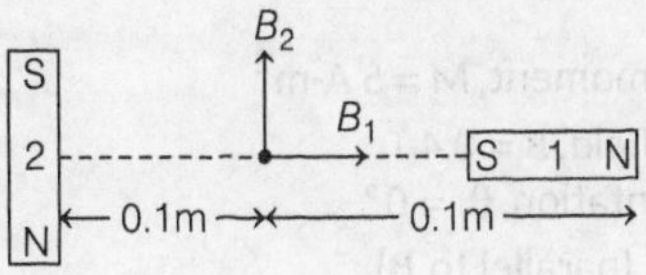

$$B_1 = \left(\frac{\mu_0}{4\pi}\right)\frac{2M}{r^3};\ B_2 = \left(\frac{\mu_0}{4\pi}\right)\frac{M}{r^3}$$

$$B_{net} = \sqrt{B_1^2 + B_2^2} = \frac{\sqrt{5} \times 10^{-7} \times 10}{(0.1)^3} = \sqrt{5} \times 10^{-3}\ \text{T}$$

12.

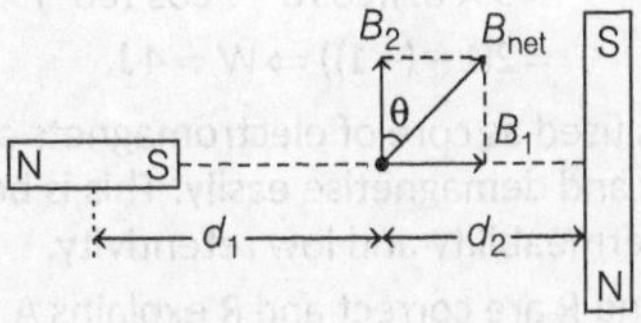

Magnetic needle will align itself in the direction of resultant magnetic field.

$$\tan\theta = \frac{B_1}{B_2} = \frac{\left(\frac{\mu_0}{4\pi}\right)\frac{2M}{d_1^3}}{\left(\frac{\mu_0}{4\pi}\right)\frac{M}{d_2^3}} = \frac{2d_2^3}{d_1^3}$$

$$\Rightarrow \quad \frac{d_1}{d_2} = (2\cot\theta)^{\frac{1}{3}}$$

13. $\tau_{max} = MB \sin 90°$

$\Rightarrow \tau = MB \sin\theta = \frac{1}{2}(MB \sin 90°) \quad \Rightarrow \theta = 30°$

14. $\tau = \mathbf{M} \times \mathbf{B} = 50\hat{\mathbf{i}} \times (5\hat{\mathbf{i}} + 3\hat{\mathbf{j}}) = (150\,\hat{\mathbf{k}})$ N-m

15. $\tau = MB \sin\theta = Fd$

$\Rightarrow (24 \times 25 \times 10^{-2})(0.25) \sin 30° = F(0.12)$

$\Rightarrow \quad F = 6.25$ N

16. $W = \Delta U = -MB \cos 60° - (-MB \cos 0°) = \frac{MB}{2}$

$$\tau = MB \sin 60° = (2W)\left(\frac{\sqrt{3}}{2}\right) = \sqrt{3}\ W$$

17.

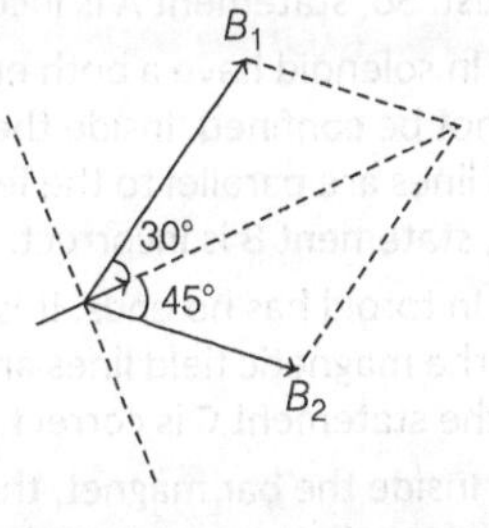

Components of the two fields perpendicular to resultant field should cancel out each other.

$$B_1 \sin 30° = B_2 \sin 45°$$

$$\Rightarrow \quad 2 \times 10^{-3} \times \frac{1}{2} = B_2\left(\frac{1}{\sqrt{2}}\right) \Rightarrow B_2 = \sqrt{2} \times 10^{-3}\ \text{T}$$

18. $F = \left(\frac{\mu_0}{4\pi}\right)\frac{6M_1M_2}{r^4} = 10^{-7} \times \frac{6 \times 10 \times 10}{(0.1)^4} = 0.6$ N

19. $F \propto \frac{1}{r^4} \Rightarrow \frac{F_1}{F_2} = \frac{r_2^4}{r_1^4} \Rightarrow \frac{4.8}{F} = \left(\frac{2r}{r}\right)^4 \Rightarrow F = 0.3$ N

20. Aluminium is paramagnetic, copper is diamagnetic and Iron and Nickel are ferromagnetic.

21. Diamagnetic materials are repelled by magnetism field. So, they will be thrown out.

22. A superconductor exhibits perfect diamagnetism as magnetic field lines don't enter a superconductor.

23. $B = B_{ext} + B_{induced} \Rightarrow B = \mu_0 H + \mu_0 M$

$\Rightarrow B = \mu_0(H + M)$

24. $\mu_r = \frac{B}{B_0} = \frac{4B_0}{B_0} = 4$

25. The value of H needed to make the intensity of magnetisation zero is called coercive force or coercivity.

26. The materials suitable for making electromagnetic should have high retentivity so that they retain strong magnetisation on removal of external magnetising is field and high coercivity so that they can't be easily demagnetised on applying reverse magneting field.

27. At temperatures above Curie temperature, a ferromagnetic material behaves like a paramagnetic material.

28. Magnetic susceptibility of paramagnetic substances is independent of the magnetising field.

29. Magnetic susceptibility of ferromagnetic materials decreases with rise in temperature and the substance becomes paramagnetic above Curie temperature.

30. $\chi_m = \frac{C}{T} \Rightarrow C =$ Slope of χ_m *versus* $\frac{1}{T}$ graph

$$= \frac{0.4}{7 \times 10^{-3}} = 57\ \text{K}$$

31. OQ = Retentivity; OR = Coercivity

For making a permanent magnet, both retentivity (OQ) and coercivity (OR) should be high.

32. $\chi_m = \frac{I}{H}$ = Slope of graph.

For diamagnetic material, magnetic susceptibility is small and negative.

33. Volume $= \frac{\text{Mass}}{\text{Density}} = \frac{0.075}{7.5 \times 10^3} = 10^{-5}\ \text{m}^3$

$$I = \frac{M}{V} = \frac{8 \times 10^{-7}}{10^{-5}} = 0.08\ \text{Am}^{-1}$$

34. $\mu_r = \frac{B}{B_0} = \frac{3000}{200} = 15$

$\chi_m = \mu_r - 1 = 15 - 1 = 14$

35. $I = (2 \times 10^{26}\ \text{m}^{-3}) \times (1.5 \times 10^{-23}\ \text{A-m}^2) = 3 \times 10^3\ \text{Am}^{-1}$

36. $V = 10 \times 0.5 \times 0.2 = 1\ cm^3$

$$I = \frac{M}{V} = \frac{5}{1 \times 10^{-6}} = 5 \times 10^6\ Am^2$$

$$B = \mu_0(H + I) = 4\pi \times 10^{-7}\ (0.5 \times 10^4 + 5 \times 10^6)$$
$$= 6.28\ T$$

37. $H = ni \Rightarrow 4 \times 10^3 = \left(\frac{5000}{10}\right) i \Rightarrow i = 8A$

38. Total dipole moment of sample

$= 2 \times 10^{24} \times 1.5 \times 10^{-23} = 30\ A\text{-}m^2$

Magnetic saturation is achieved at 15%.

$$\Rightarrow \quad M_1 = 30 \times \frac{15}{100} = 4.5\ JT^{-1}$$

When magnetic field is $B_2 = 0.98$ T, $T_2 = 2.8$ K, its total dipole moment is M_2.

According to Curie's Law,

$$\frac{\chi_1}{\chi_2} = \frac{T_2}{T_1}$$

$$\Rightarrow \quad \frac{M_1}{M_2} = \left(\frac{B_1}{B_2}\right)\left(\frac{T_2}{T_1}\right)$$

$$\Rightarrow \quad \frac{4.5}{M_2} = \left(\frac{0.84}{0.98}\right)\left(\frac{2.8}{4.2}\right)$$

$$\Rightarrow \quad M_2 = 7.9\ JT^{-1}$$

39. $\text{Volume} = \frac{\text{Mass}}{\text{Density}} = \frac{0.6}{7800}\ m^3$

Energy loss per second = (Area of loop) × (Volume) × (Frequency)

$$= 0.722 \times \frac{0.6}{7800} \times 50$$

$$= 277.7 \times 10^{-5}\ J$$

Previous Years Questions

JEE Main

1. $V = \frac{\mu_0}{4\pi}\frac{M}{r^2}$, $V = 1.5 \times 10^{-5}$ Tm

$$\frac{\mu_0}{4\pi} = 10^{-7}\ TmA^{-1}$$

$$1.5 \times 10^{-5} = 10^{-7}\frac{M}{r^2}$$

$$(1.5 \times 10^{-5}) = \frac{10^{-7} \times M}{(20 \times 10^{-2})^2}$$

$$M = \frac{(1.5 \times 10^{-5})(20 \times 10^{-2})^2}{10^{-7}}$$

$$M = 1.5 \times 4 = 6 \Rightarrow M = 6 \Rightarrow M = 6\ Am^2$$

2. Given,

Magnetic moment, $M = 5\ A\text{-}m^2$

Magnetic field, $B = 0.4$ T

Initial orientation, $\theta_i = 0°$ (parallel to B)

Final orientation, $\theta_f = 180°$ (anti-parallel to B)

work done in rotating a dipole from θ_i position to θ_f position,

$$W = MB(\cos\theta_i - \cos\theta_f)$$
$$= 5 \times 0.4(\cos 0° - \cos 180°)$$
$$= 2(1 - (-1)) \Rightarrow W = 4\ J$$

3. Soft iron is used as core of electromagnets as they gets magnetise and demagnetise easily. This is because soft iron has high permeability and low retentivity.

∴ Both A and R are correct and R explains A.

4. For a diamagnetic material,

$$\mu_r < 1 \quad \Rightarrow \quad -1 \le x < 0$$

Also diamagnetic material moves from stronger magnetic field to weaker magnetic fields.

Hence, statement I and II both are correct.

5. Diamagnetism is non-cooperative behaviour of orbitting electrons when exposed to an applied magnetic field.

Behaviour of the diamagnetic material is that the susceptibility is temperature independent.

Therefore, statement, I is false and statement II is true.

6. The relation between magnetic permeability and susceptibility of the material is given as,

$$\mu_R = 1 + \chi$$

$$\Rightarrow \quad \frac{\mu_m}{\mu_0} = 1 + 99$$

$$\Rightarrow \quad \mu_m = \mu_0 \times 100$$
$$= 4\pi \times 10^{-7} \times 100$$
$$= 4\pi \times 10^{-5}\ Wb/A\text{-}m$$

7. Statement (A) Magnetic monopoles do not exist, they always exist in pairs as South and North poles but electric monopoles exist. So, statement A is incorrect.

Statement (B) In solenoid have a both ends, so magnetic field lines cannot be confined. Inside the solenoids, the magnetic field lines are parallel to the length of the conductor. So, statement B is incorrect.

Statement (C) In toroid has no ends. It is closed loop conductor, so the magnetic field lines are completely confined. So, the statement C is correct.

Statement (D) Inside the bar magnet, the magnetic field lines are parallel. So, the statement D is incorrect.

Statement (E) Magnetic susceptibility of the diamagnetic material is −1. So, the statement E is correct.

Hence, the correct statements are C and E.

8. We know that $\mu_r = 1 + \chi$

$\Rightarrow \quad \chi = \mu_r - 1$

For 1st and 2nd material,

$$\chi_1 = \mu_1 - 1 = 500 - 1 = 499$$

and $\quad \chi_2 = \mu_2 - 1 = 750 - 1 = 749$

Now, magnetic intensity, $M = ni$

Let M_1 and M_2 be the magnetisation and m_1 and m_2 be the magnetic moments of material 1st and 2nd.

$$\frac{m_1}{m_2} = \frac{I_1}{I_2} = \frac{\chi_1}{\chi_2} \quad ...(iii)$$

Hence, fraction change in magnetic moment,

$$\frac{\Delta m}{m_1} = \frac{m_2 - m_1}{m_1} = \left(\frac{m_2}{m_1} - 1\right)$$

$$= \left(\frac{749}{499} - 1\right) = \frac{250}{499}$$

Thus, value of χ is 250.

9. Given, As we know that, ferromagnetism of any object decreases with increase in temperature and above Curie temperature, ferromagnetic material become paramagnetic material.

Hence, statement I is true.

But, in case of ferromagnetic material below Curie temperature, atoms are alligned and parallel. But above Curie temperature atoms losses their ordered magnetic moments.

Hence, statement II is false.

10. Given,

Magnetic susceptibility, $\chi_m = 499$

Permeability in vacuum, $\mu_0 = 4\pi \times 10^{-7}$ H/m

Absolute permeability of the material,

$$\mu = \mu_0(1 + \chi_m)$$

$$\Rightarrow \quad \mu = 4\pi \times 10^{-7}(1 + 499)$$

$$= 4\pi \times 10^{-7} \times 500$$

$$= 2\pi \times 10^{-4} \text{ H/m}$$

11. Given, number of turns per unit length,

$$n = 1000$$

Relative magnetic permeability,

$$\mu_r = 500$$

Current flowing through solenoid, $I = 5$ A

Magnetic permeability of free space,

$$\mu_0 = 4\pi \times 10^{-7} \text{ H/m}$$

We know that, magnetic field inside the solenoid can be given as

$$B = \mu n I \quad ...(i)$$

where, $\mu =$ permeability of medium.

As, $\quad \mu = \mu_r \mu_0 \quad ...(ii)$

From Eqs. (i) and (ii), we get

$$B = \mu_r \mu_0 n I = 500 \times 4\pi \times 10^{-7} \times 1000 \times 5$$

$$= 100\pi \times 10^{-7} \times 10^5 = \pi \text{ T}$$

12. Since, in ferromagnetic material, with increase in temperature susceptibility decreases,

∴ Ferromagnetic material below Curie temperature will show saturation magnetisation.

Hence, option (b) is the correct i.e. domain is defined as a macroscopic region with saturation magnetisation.

13. Torque on a bar magnet, $\tau = MB \sin\theta$

$$0.018 = M \times 0.06 \times \sin 30°$$

$$\Rightarrow \quad M = 0.6 \text{ A-m}^2$$

Now, work done to rotate bar magnet,

$$W = MB[\cos\theta_1 - \cos\theta_2]$$

Here, $\theta_1 = 0°$ (for stable equilibrium position)

and $\theta_2 = 180°$ (for unstable equilibrium position).

So, $\quad W = 0.6 \times 0.06[\cos(0°) - \cos(180°)]$

$$= 0.036[(1) - (-1)]$$

$$= 0.036(2) = 0.072 \text{ J}$$

$$= 7.2 \times 10^{-2} \text{ J}$$

Hence, correct option is (b).

14. Time period of oscillation of a magnetic dipole in a uniform magnetic field, $\quad T = 2\pi\sqrt{\frac{I}{\mu B}}$

where, $\mu =$ magnetic dipole.

Moment of dipole = Current × Area = $\pi a^2 i$

$I =$ moment of inertia of a coil $= ma^2/2$

So, $T = 2\pi\sqrt{\frac{ma^2/2}{\pi a^2 iB}} = 2\pi\sqrt{\frac{m}{2\pi iB}} = \sqrt{\frac{2\pi m}{iB}}$

15. Magnetic moment of an iron core solenoid, $M = \mu_r NiA$

where, $\mu_r =$ relative permeability = 1000,

$N =$ number of turns = 10 turns/cm,

$i =$ current = 0.5 A

and $\quad A =$ area of cross-section.

Now, $M = \mu_r Ni\frac{V}{l} \quad \left\{\because A = \frac{V}{l}\right\}$

Substituting all the given values in above equation, we get

$$M = 1000 \times \frac{10}{10^{-2}} \times 0.5 \times 10^{-3}$$

$$= 500 \text{ Am}^2 = 5 \times 10^2 \text{ Am}^2$$

Hence, correct option is (b).

16. Curie's law for paramagnetic materials,

$$\chi_m \propto \frac{1}{T} \Rightarrow \frac{I}{H} \propto \frac{1}{T}$$

$$\Rightarrow \quad \frac{I}{(B_0/\mu_0)} \propto \frac{1}{T} \Rightarrow \frac{\mu_0 I}{B_0} \propto \frac{1}{T}$$

$$\Rightarrow \quad I \propto \frac{B_0}{\mu_0 T} \Rightarrow I \propto \frac{B_0}{T} \quad (\because \mu_0 = \text{constant})$$

$$\Rightarrow \quad \frac{I_1}{I_2} = \frac{(B_0)_1}{(B_0)_2} \times \frac{T_2}{T_1}$$

On putting the given values in above equation, we get

$$\frac{6}{I_2} = \frac{0.4}{0.3} \times \frac{24}{4} \Rightarrow \frac{6}{I_2} = \frac{4}{3} \times \frac{6}{1}$$

$$\Rightarrow \quad I_2 = 0.75 \text{ A/m}$$

Hence, option (b) is correct.

17. Permanent magnets (*P*) must be able to hold large magnetism for a long time. So, they must have large coercivity and large retentivity.

Electromagnet and transformer cores (*T*) must be able to loose magnetisation quickly when current in their coils are zero. So, they must have small retentivity.

Hence, correct option is (b).

18. As, the sphere is perfectly diamagnetic, it completely expels field as shown below:

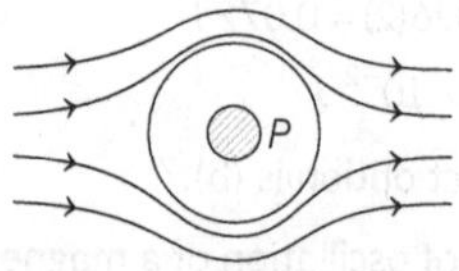

Therefore, there will be no magnetic field inside the cavity of sphere.

So, the paramagnetic sample at the spherical cavity at the centre of sphere remains uneffected by external field and field inside paramagnetic sample is zero.

Hence, correct option is (c).

19. We can obtain the values of retentivity (the remaining value of magnetic field *B* when $H = 0$), coercivity (value of *H* when $B = 0$) and saturation value of induced magnetic field (B_{max}) as shown in the figure.

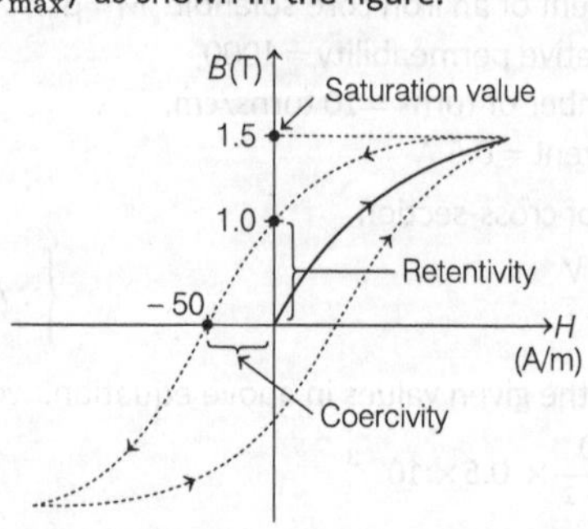

Clearly, retentivity = 1 T, coercivity = 50 Am^{-1} and saturation value = 1.5 T

20. For dipole *X*, point *P* lies on its axial line. So, magnetic field strength at *P* due to *X* is

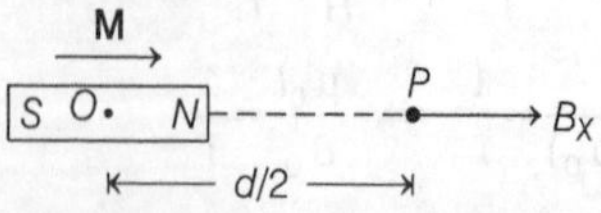

$$\Rightarrow \quad |\mathbf{B}_X| = \frac{\mu_0}{4\pi} \frac{2M}{(d/2)^3}$$

Similarly, for dipole *Y*, point *P* lies on its equatorial line. So, magnetic field strength at *P* due to *Y* is

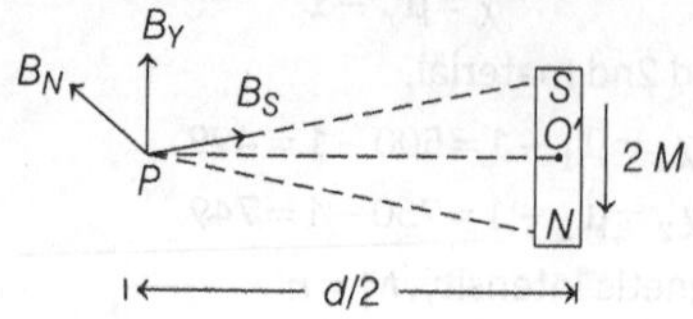

$$\Rightarrow \quad |\mathbf{B}_Y| = \frac{\mu_0}{4\pi} \frac{2M}{(d/2)^3}$$

Thus, the resultant magnetic field due to *X* and *Y* at *P* is

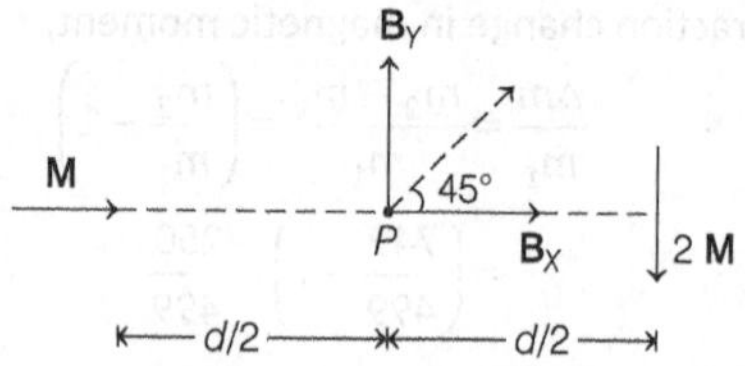

$$\mathbf{B}_{net} = \mathbf{B}_X + \mathbf{B}_Y$$

Since, $\quad |\mathbf{B}_Y| = |\mathbf{B}_X|$

Thus, the resultant magnetic field ($\mathbf{B}_{net}$) at *P* will be at 45° with the horizontal.

This means, direction of $\mathbf{B}_{net}$ and velocity of the charged particle is same.

$$\theta = 0 \quad \therefore \quad F = 0$$

Thus, magnitude of force on the particle at that instant is zero.

21. Work done in reversing dipole is

$$W = 2MB$$

where, $\quad M$ = magnetic dipole moment $= 10^{-2}$ A-m^2

and $\quad B$ = external field $= B \cos \omega t = 1 \times \cos(0.125 \times 1) = \cos(7°) = 0.992$

Substituting these values, we get

$$W = 2 \times 10^{-2} \times 0.992 = 0.0198 \text{ J}$$

which is nearest to 0.014 J.

22. The time-period of oscillations made by a magnet of magnetic moment *M*, moment of inertia *I*, placed in a magnetic field is given by

$$T = 2\pi \sqrt{\frac{I}{MB}} \qquad \text{... (i)}$$

For the hoop, let us assume its moment of inertia I_h and magnetic moment M_h, then its time period will be

$$T_h = 2\pi \sqrt{\frac{I_h}{M_h B}} \qquad \text{... (ii)}$$

Similarly, for solid cylinder, time period is,

$$T_c = 2\pi \sqrt{\frac{I_c}{M_c B}} \qquad \text{... (iii)}$$

Dividing Eq. (ii) by Eq. (iii), we get

$$\frac{T_h}{T_c} = \sqrt{\frac{I_h M_c}{M_h I_c}} \quad \text{... (iv)}$$

Now, it is given that, $M_h = 2M_c$

and we know that, moment of inertia of hoop $I_h = mR^2$ and moment of inertia of solid cylinder $I_c = \frac{1}{2} mR^2$

Substituting these values in Eq. (iv), we get

$$\frac{T_h}{T_c} = \sqrt{\frac{mR^2 \times M_c}{\frac{1}{2} mR^2 \times 2M_c}} = 1 \Rightarrow T_h = T_c$$

23. Coercivity of a bar magnet is the value of magnetic field intensity (H) that is needed to reduce magnetisation to zero.

Since, for a solenoid magnetic induction is given as,

$$B = \mu_0 nI \quad \text{...(i)}$$

where, n is the number of turns (N) per unit, length (l) and I is the current.

Also, $B = \mu_0 H$ ...(ii)

$\therefore$ From Eqs. (i) and (ii), we get

$$\mu_0 nI = \mu_0 H$$

or $H = nI = \frac{N}{l} I$

Substituting the given values, we get

$$H = \frac{100}{0.2} \times 5.2 = 2600 \text{ A/m}$$

Thus, the value of coercivity of the bar magnet is 2600 A/m.

24. Given, side of cube = 1 cm = 10^{-2} m

$\therefore$ Volume, $V = 10^{-6} \text{m}^3$

Dipole moment, $\mathbf{M} = 20 \times 10^{-6}$ J/T

Applied magnetic intensity,

$$\mathbf{H} = 60 \times 10^3 \text{ A/m}$$

Intensity of magnetisation

$$I = \frac{\mathbf{M}}{V} = \frac{20 \times 10^{-6}}{10^{-6}} = 20 \text{ A/m}$$

Now, magnetic susceptibility χ is

$$\chi = \frac{\text{Intensity of magnetisation}}{\text{Applied magnetic intensity}} = \frac{I}{H}$$

$$= \frac{20}{60 \times 10^3}$$

$$\Rightarrow \quad \chi = \frac{1}{3} \times 10^{-3} = 3.3 \times 10^{-4}$$

25. From Curie's law for paramagnetic substance, we have

Magnetic susceptiblity

$$\chi \propto \frac{1}{T}$$

$$\therefore \quad \frac{\chi_2}{\chi_1} = \frac{T_1}{T_2}$$

$$\Rightarrow \quad \chi_2 = \frac{\chi_1 \cdot T_1}{T_2}$$

$$\Rightarrow \quad \chi_2 = \frac{2.8 \times 10^{-4} \times 350}{300}$$

$$= 3.267 \times 10^{-4}$$

26. Time period of oscillation is

$$T = 2\pi \sqrt{\frac{I}{MB}}$$

$$\Rightarrow \quad T = 2\pi \sqrt{\frac{7.5 \times 10^{-6}}{6.7 \times 10^{-2} \times 0.01}} = 0.665 \text{ s}$$

Hence, time for 10 oscillations is $t = 6.65$ s.

27. Inside bar magnet, lines of force are from South to North.

28. Magnetic needle is placed in non-uniform magnetic field. It experiences force and torque both due to unequal forces acting on poles.

CHAPTER~05

ELECTROMAGNETIC INDUCTION

LEVEL 01 Starter Level

5.1 Induced EMF and Induced Current

1 The north pole of a magnet is brought down along the axis of a horizontal circular coil (figure). As a result, the flux through the coil changes from 0.4 Wb to 0.9 Wb in an interval of half of a second. Find the average emf induced during this period. Is the induced current clockwise or anti-clockwise as you look into the coil from the side of the magnet?

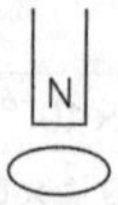

2 The flux of magnetic field through a closed conducting loop of resistance 0.4 Ω changes with time according to the equation $\phi = 0.20t^2 + 0.40t + 0.60$, where t is time in seconds. Find

(i) the induced emf at $t = 2$ s.

(ii) the average induced emf in $t = 0$ to $t = 5$ s.

(iii) average current in time interval $t = 0$ to $t = 5$ s.

(iv) heat produced in $t = 0$ to $t = 5$ s.

3 A conducting loop confined in a plane is rotated in its own plane with some angular velocity. A uniform and constant magnetic field exists in the region. Find the current induced in the loop.

4 A square-shaped copper coil has edges of length 50 cm and contains 50 turns. It is placed perpendicular to a 1.0 T magnetic field. It is removed from the magnetic field in 0.25 s and restored in its original place in the next 0.25 s. Find the magnitude of the average emf induced in the loop during

(i) its removal, (ii) its restoration and

(iii) its motion.

5 A closed circular loop of 200 turns of mean diameter 50 cm and having a total resistance of 10Ω is placed with its plane at right angle to a magnetic field of strength 10^{-2} T. Calculate the quantity of electric charge passed through it when the coil is turned through 180° about an axis in its plane.

6 A square loop of side 2 m and resistance 5Ω is placed in a magnetic field as shown in figure. Find magnitude and direction of current in the loop in each case.

(i) 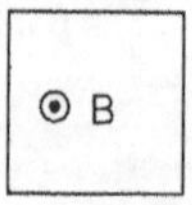

Uniform magnetic field of 10 T.

(ii) 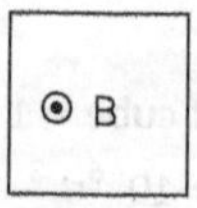

Magnetic field is increasing at a rate of 10T/s.

(iii) 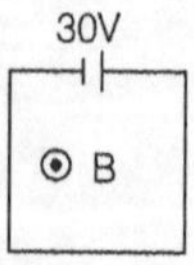

Magnetic field is decreasing at a rate of 5 T/s. Loop has a battery of emf 30V.

7 The radius of a coil decreases steadily at the rate of 10^{-2} m/s. A constant and uniform magnetic field of induction 10^{-3} Wb/m^2 acts perpendicular to the plane of the coil. Find the radius of the coil when the induced emf in the coil is 1μV.

8 Consider a long infinite wire carrying a time varying current $i = kt$ ($k > 0$). A circular loop of radius a and resistance R is placed with its centre at a distance d from the wire ($a << d$). Find out the induced current in the loop.

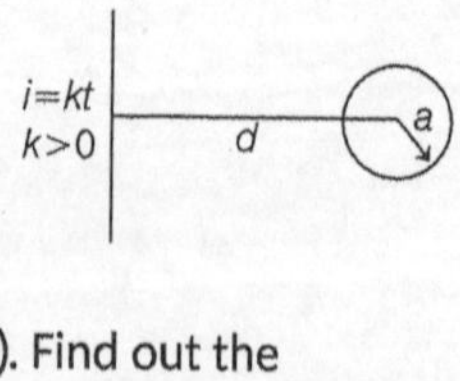

9 A heart pacing device consists of a coil of 50 turns and radius 1 mm just inside the body with a coil of 1000 turns and radius 2 cm placed concentrically and coaxially just outside the body. Calculate the average induced emf in the internal coil, if a current of 1A in the external coil collapses in 10 ms.

10 A solenoid has a cross_sectional area of $6.0 \times 10^{-4}\,m^2$, consists of 400 turns per metre and carries a current of 0.40 A. A 10 turn coil is wrapped tightly around the circumference of the solenoid. The ends of the coil are connected to a 1.5Ω resistor. Suddenly, a switch is opened, and the current in the solenoid dies to zero in a time 0.050s. Find the average current in the coil during this time.

11 A uniform magnetic field B exists in a cylindrical region of radius 1 cm as shown in figure. A uniform wire of length 16 cm and resistance 4.0Ω is bent into a square frame and is placed with one side along a diameters of the cylindrical region. If the magnetic field increases at a constant rate of 2 T/s, find the current induced in the frame.

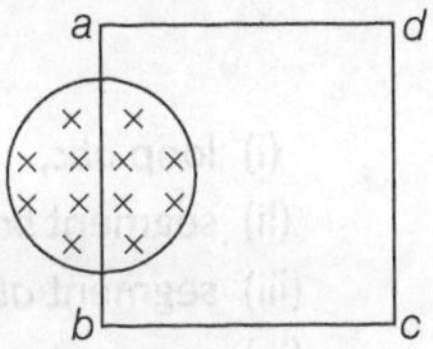

12 The magnetic field in the cylindrical region shown in figure increases at a constant rate of 20.0 mT/s. Each side of the square loop *abcd* and *defa* has a length of 1.00 cm and a resistance of 4.00Ω. Find the current (magnitude and sense) in the wire *ad* if (i) the switch S_1 is closed but S_2 is open (ii) S_1 is open but S_2 is closed, (iii) both S_1 and S_2 are open and (iv) both S_1 and S_2 are closed.

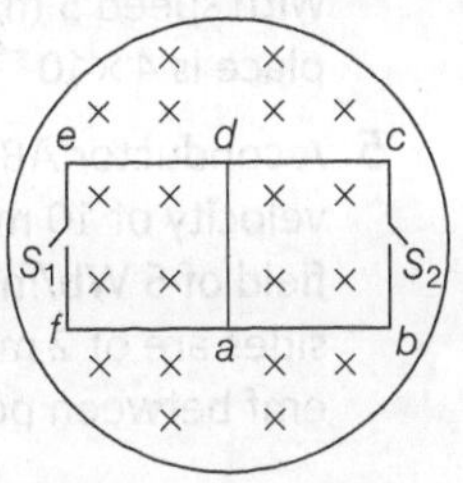

13 Figure shows a wire frame *PQSTXYZ* placed in a time varying magnetic field given as $B = \beta t$, where β is a positive constant. Resistance per unit length of the wire is λ. Find the magnitude and direction of current induced in the wire.

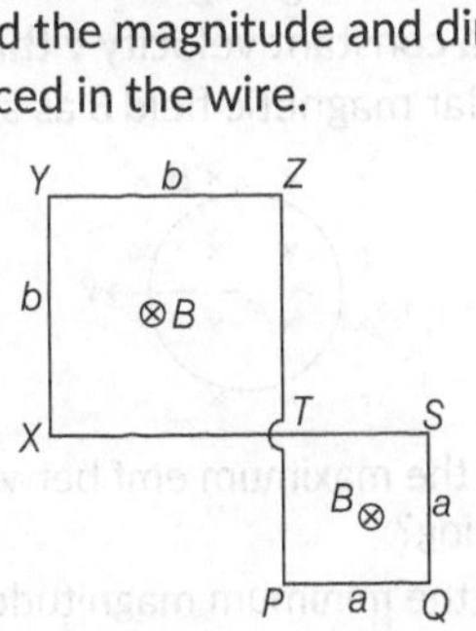

14 A coil of N turns and radius R carries a current of I and is placed on a horizontal table. A very small horizontal conducting ring of radius r is placed at a distance h_0 from the centre of the coil vertically above the coil . Find an expression for the emf established when the ring is allowed to fall freely. Express the emf in terms of instantaneous speed v and height h.

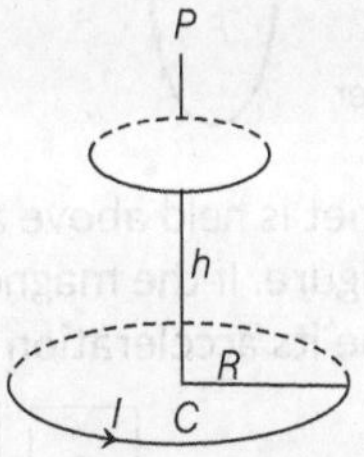

15 Figure shows a square loop of resistance 4Ω of side 1 m being moved towards right at a constant speed of 2 m/s. The front edge enters the 3 m wide magnetic field ($B = 2T$) at $t = 0$.

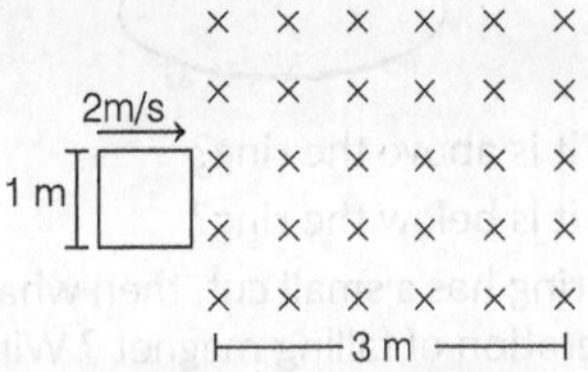

(i) Draw the graph of current induced in the loop as time passes. (Take anti-clockwise direction of current as positive)

(ii) Find the total heat produced in the loop during the interval 0 to 5 s.

5.2 Lenz's Law

1 Figure shows a long current carrying wire and two rectangular loops moving with velocity v. Find the direction of current in each loop.

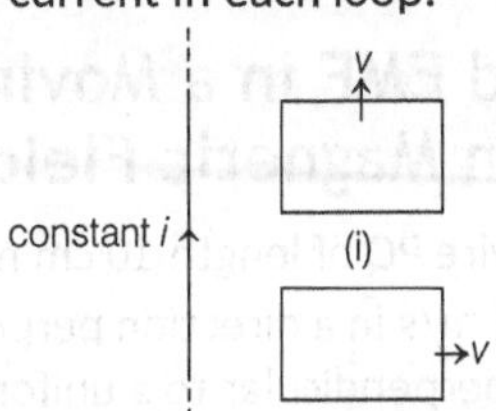

2 A magnet is moved in the direction indicated by an arrow between two coils as shown in the figure. Find the direction of induced current in straight wires *AB* and *CD*.

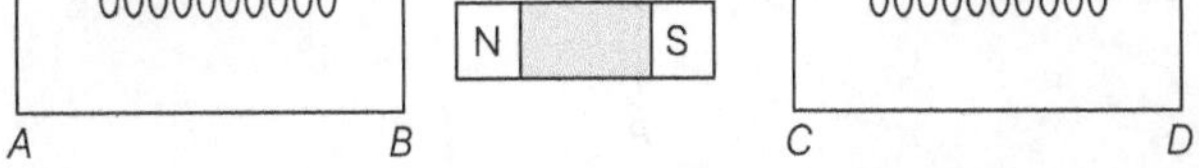

3 Two coils P and Q are lying a little distance apart coaxially. If an anti-clockwise current i is suddenly set-up in the coil P, then what will be the direction of current induced in coil Q? Will they attract or repel?

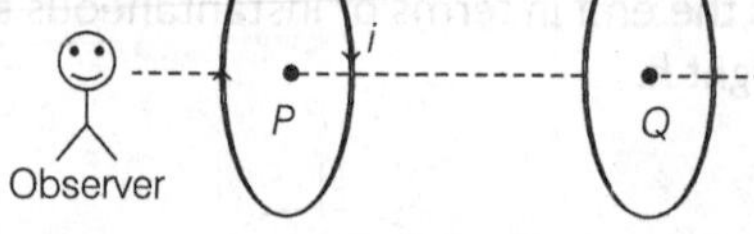

4 A bar magnet is held above a fixed metal ring as shown in figure. If the magnet is now dropped freely, what will be its acceleration compared to g

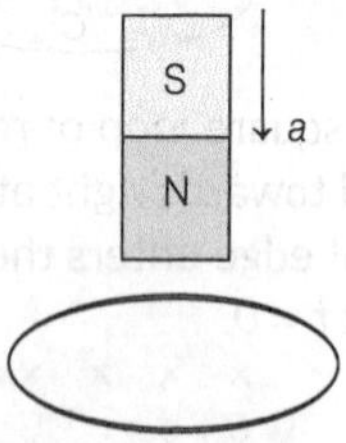

(i) when it is above the ring?

(ii) when it is below the ring?

(iii) If the ring has a small cut, then what will be acceleration of falling magnet ? Will there be induced emf in the ring ?

5 A small loop lies outside a circuit in the same plane. The key of the circuit is closed and opened alternately. What will be the direction of induced current in the closed loop?

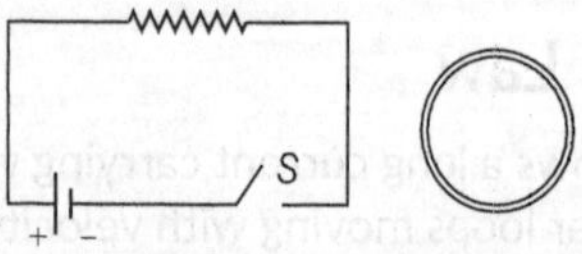

5.3 Induced EMF in a Moving Rod in Uniform Magnetic Field

1 A metallic wire PQ of length 10 cm moves with a velocity of 2 m/s in a direction perpendicular to its length and perpendicular to a uniform magnetic field of magnitude 2 T. Find the emf induced between the ends of the wire. Which end will be positively charged?

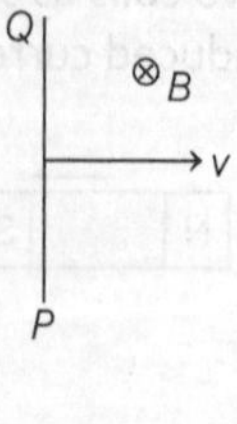

2 A metallic meter stick translates in a direction making an angle of 30° with its length. The plane of motion is perpendicular to a uniform magnetic field of 0.50 T that exists in the space. Find the emf induced between the ends of the rod, if the speed of translation is 20 cm/s.

3 A right angled triangle abc, made of a metallic wire, moves at a uniform speed v in its plane as shown in the figure. A uniform magnetic field B exists in the perpendicular direction of plane of triangle. Find the emf induced in the

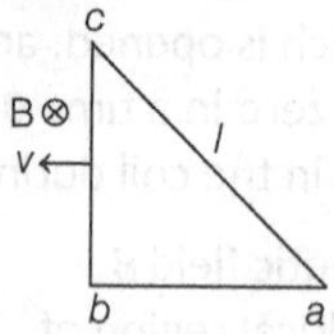

(i) loop abc,

(ii) segment bc,

(iii) segment ab and

(iv) segment ac.

4 The two rails, separated by 1m, of a railway track are connected to a voltmeter. What will be the reading of the voltmeter when a train travels on the rails with speed 5 m/s? The earth's magnetic field at the place is 4×10^{-4} T and the angle of dip is 30°.

5 A conductor $ABOCD$ moves along its bisector with a velocity of 10 m/s through a perpendicular magnetic field of 5 Wb/m^2, as shown in figure. If all the four sides are of 2 m length each, then find the induced emf between points A and D.

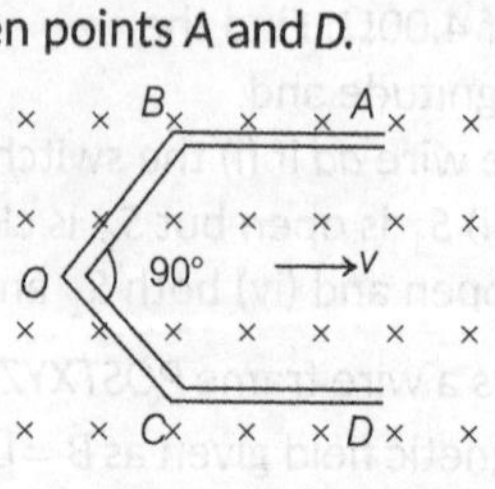

6 A circular conducting ring of radius r translates in its plane with a constant velocity v through a uniform perpendicular magnetic field B as shown in figure.

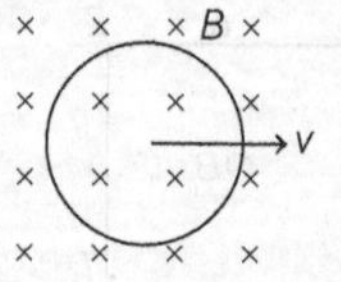

(i) What is the maximum emf between any two points on the ring?

(ii) What is the minimum magnitude of emf between any two points on the ring?

5.4 Circuit Problems

1 A rod PQ of mass m and resistance r is moving on two fixed smooth conducting rails (closed on both sides by resistances R_1 and R_2) kept in a uniform magnetic field B as shown in figure. Find the current in the rod at the instant its velocity is v.

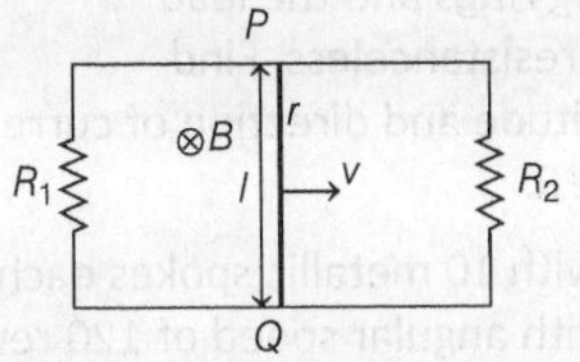

2 A rod of mass m and resistance r is placed on fixed smooth long conducting rails (closed by a resistance R) and it is projected with an initial velocity u as shown in figure. Find

(i) its velocity as a function of time.

(ii) distance travelled before coming to rest.

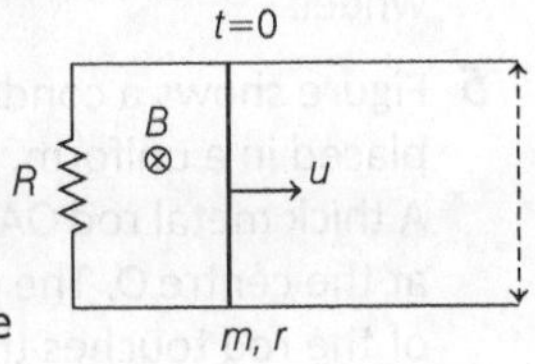

3 A long U-shaped wire of width l placed in a perpendicular uniform and constant magnetic field B (figure). A wire of length l is slid on the U-shaped wire with a constant velocity v towards right. The resistance of all the wires is r per unit length. At $t = 0$, the sliding wire is close to the left edge of the fixed U-shaped wire. Calculate

(i) the current in the circuit and

(ii) the force needed to keep the sliding wire moving with a constant velocity v at time t.

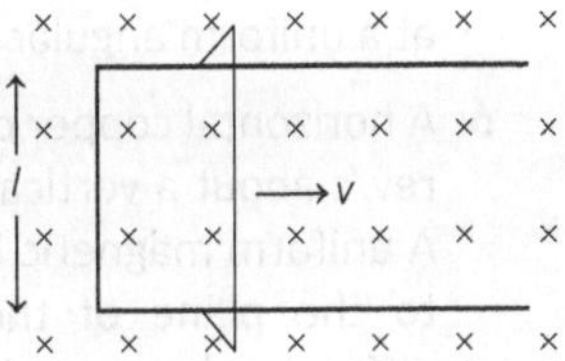

4 A square frame of wire $abcd$ of side 2 m has a resistance of 1Ω /m. It is pulled out of a magnetic field $B = 2$ T by applying a force of 10 N (figure). It is found that the frame moves with constant speed. Find (i) this constant speed, (ii) the emf induced in the loop, (iii) the potential difference between the points a and b and (iv) the potential difference between the points c and d.

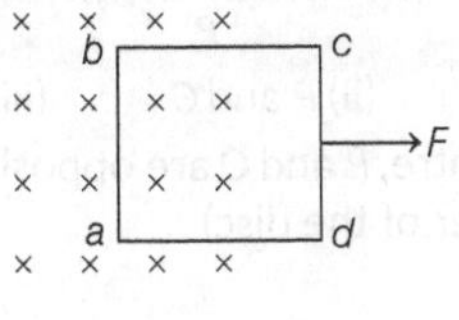

5 The wires P_1Q_1 and P_2Q_2 are made to slide on the conducting rails with the same speed 5 cm/s in a uniform magnetic field 1.0 T as shown in figure. Find the electric current in the 19Ω resistor, if

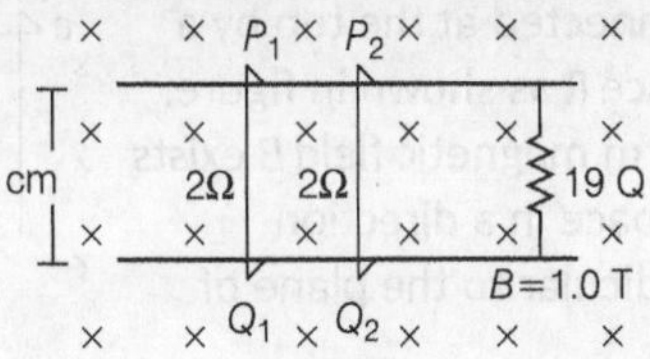

(i) both the wires move towards right and

(ii) P_1Q_1 moves towards left but P_2Q_2 moves towards right.

6 The current generator i_g, shown in figure sends a constant current i through the circuit. The wire cd is fixed and ab is made to slide on the smooth, thick rails with a constant velocity v towards right. Each of these wires has resistance r. Find the current through the wire cd.

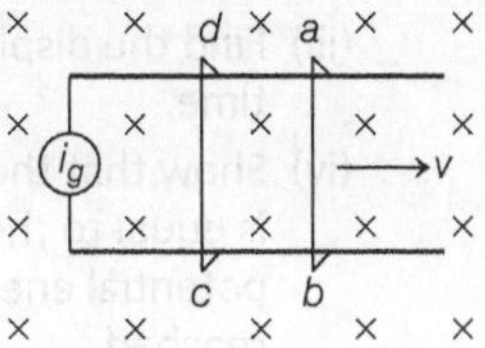

7 A wire ab of length l, mass m and resistance R slides on a smooth, thick pair of metallic rails joined at the bottom as shown in figure. The plane of the rails makes an angle θ with the horizontal. A vertical magnetic field B exists in the region. If the wire slides on the rails at a constant speed v, find value of B.

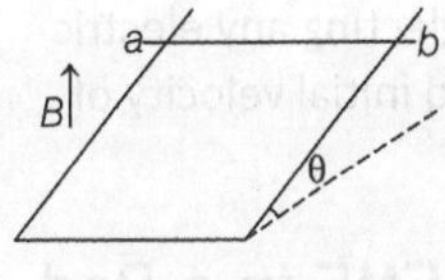

8 Figure shows a smooth pair of thick metallic rails connected across a battery of emf ε having a negligible internal resistance. A wire ab of length l and resistance r can slide smoothly on the rails. The entire system lies in a horizontal plane and is immersed in a uniform vertical magnetic field B. At an instant t, the wire is given a small velocity v towards right.

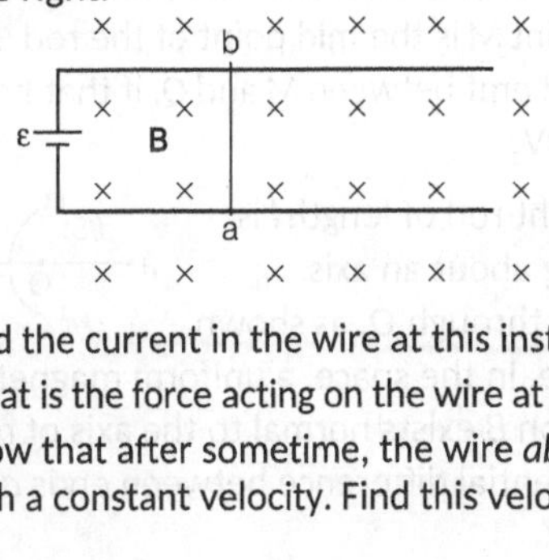

(i) Find the current in the wire at this instant.

(ii) What is the force acting on the wire at this instant ?

(iii) Show that after sometime, the wire ab will slide with a constant velocity. Find this velocity.

9 A copper wire *ab* of length *l*, resistance *r* and mass *m* starts sliding at $t = 0$ down a smooth, vertical, thick pair of conducting rails connected at the top by a resistance *R* as shown in figure. A uniform magnetic field *B* exists in the space in a direction perpendicular to the plane of the rails.

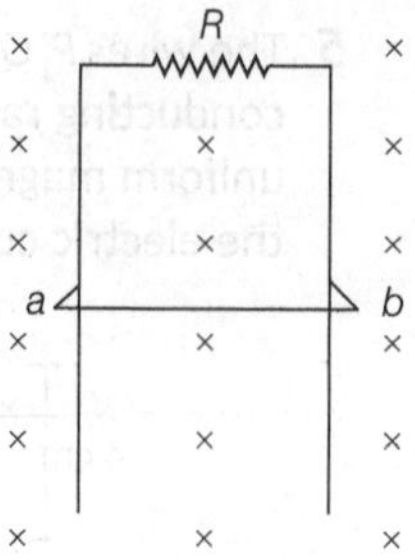

(i) Find the velocity of the wire as a function of time.

(ii) After sufficient time, the wire starts moving with a constant velocity v_m. Find v_m.

(iii) Find the displacement of the wire as a function of time.

(iv) Show that the rate of heat developed in the circuit is equal to the rate at which the gravitational potential energy is decreasing after steady state is reached.

10 A wire of mass *m* and length *l* can slide freely on a pair of fixed, smooth, vertical rails (figure). A magnetic field *B* exists in the region in the direction perpendicular to the plane of the rails. The rails are connected at the top end by an initially uncharged capacitor of capacitance *C*. Find the velocity of the wire at any time (*t*) after released. Neglecting any electric resistance and initial velocity of wire is zero.

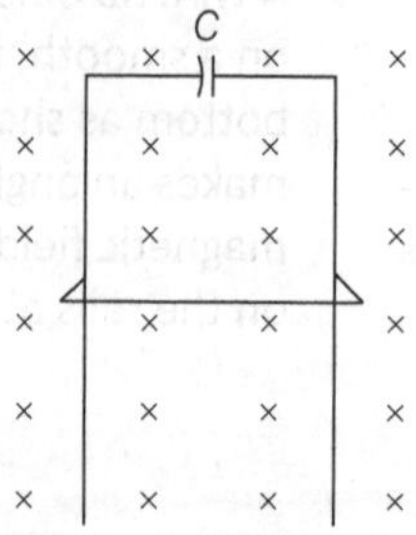

5.5 Induced EMF in a Rod, Ring and Disc Rotating in a Uniform Magnetic Field

1 A rod *PQ* of length 2 *l* is rotating about one end *P* in a uniform magnetic field *B* which is perpendicular to the plane of rotation of the rod. Point *M* is the mid point of the rod. Find the induced emf between *M* and *Q*, if that between *P* and *Q* = 100V.

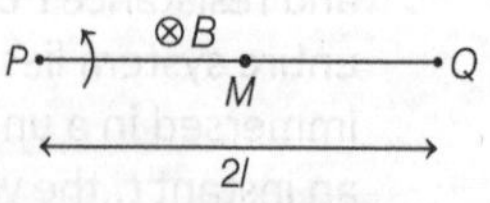

2 A straight rod of length *l* is rotating about an axis passing through *Q*, as shown in figure. In the space, a uniform magnetic field of induction *B* exists normal to the axis of rotation. Find the potential difference between ends *a* and *b*.

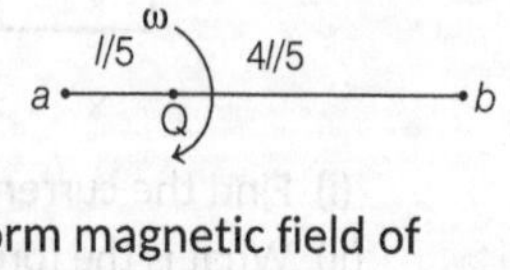

3 In the figure, there are two identical conducting rods each of length *a* rotating with angular speed ω in the directions shown. One end of each rod touches a conducting ring. Magnetic field *B* exists perpendicular to the plane of the rings. The rods, the conducting rings and the lead wires are resistanceless. Find the magnitude and direction of current in the resistance *R*.

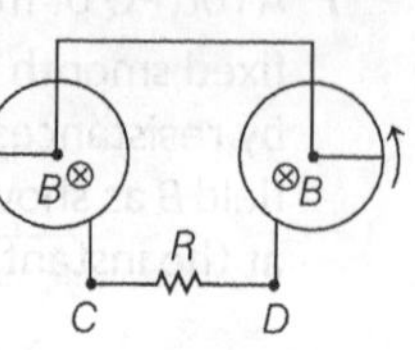

4 A wheel with 10 metallic spokes each 0.5 m long is rotated with angular speed of 120 rev/min in a plane normal to the earth's magnetic field. If the earth's magnetic field at the given place is 0.4 G, find the emf induced between the axle and the rim of the wheel.

5 Figure shows a conducting circular loop of radius *a* placed in a uniform, perpendicular magnetic field *B*. A thick metal rod *OA* is pivoted at the centre *O*. The other end of the rod touches the loop at *A*. The centre *O* and a fixed point *C* on the loop are connected by a wire of resistance *R*. A force *F* is applied at the middle point of the rod *OA* perpendicularly, so that the rod rotates clockwise at a uniform angular velocity ω. Find *F*.

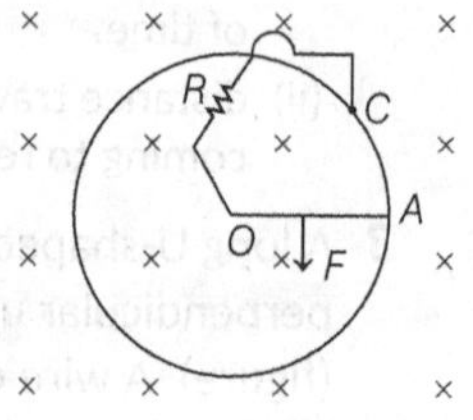

6 A horizontal copper disc of diameter 20 cm, makes 10 rev/s about a vertical axis passing through its centre. A uniform magnetic field of 100 G acts perpendicular to the plane of the disc. Calculate the potential difference between its centre and rim in volts.

7 A conducting disc of radius *R* is rolling without sliding on a horizontal surface with a constant velocity *v*. A uniform magnetic field of strength *B* is applied normal to the plane of the disc. Find the emf induced between (at this moment)

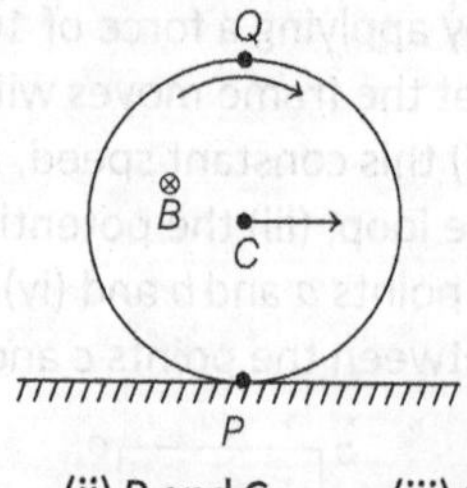

(i) *P* and *Q* (ii) *P* and *C* (iii) *Q* and *C*

(*C* is centre, *P* and *Q* are opposite points on vertical diameter of the disc)

8 A closed coil having 50 turns is rotated in a uniform magnetic field $B = 2 \times 10^{-4}$ T about a diameter which is perpendicular to the field. The angular velocity of rotation is 300 rev/min. The area of the coil is 100 cm^2 and its resistance is 4Ω. Find

(i) the maximum emf induced,

(ii) the emf induced as a function of time, if it is zero at $t = 0$ and is increasing in positive direction and

(iii) the average of the squares of emf over a long time.

5.6 EMF induced in a Rod or Loop in Non-uniform Magnetic Field

1 Figure shows a fixed square frame of wire having a total resistance R placed co-planarly with a long, straight wire. The wire carries a current i given by $i = i_0 \cos(2\pi t / T)$. Find

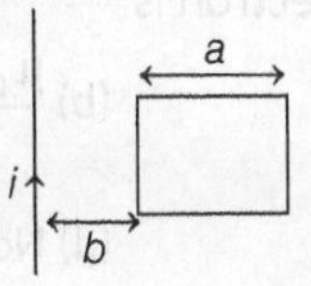

(i) the flux of the magnetic field through the square frame,

(ii) the emf induced in the frame and

(iii) the heat developed in the frame in the time interval 0 to $10T$.

2 The magnetic field in a region is given by $\mathbf{B} = (B_0 x / L)\hat{\mathbf{k}}$, where L is a fixed length. A conducting rod of length L lies along the X-axis between the origin and the point $(L, 0, 0)$. If the rod moves with a velocity $\mathbf{v} = v_0 \hat{\mathbf{j}}$, find the emf induced between the ends of the rod.

3 A long straight wire carries a current I_0. At distances a and b from it there are two other wires, parallel to the former one, which are interconnected by a resistance R (figure). A connector slides without friction along the wires with a constant velocity v. Assuming the resistances of the wires, the connector, the sliding contacts and the self-inductance of the frame to be negligible, then find

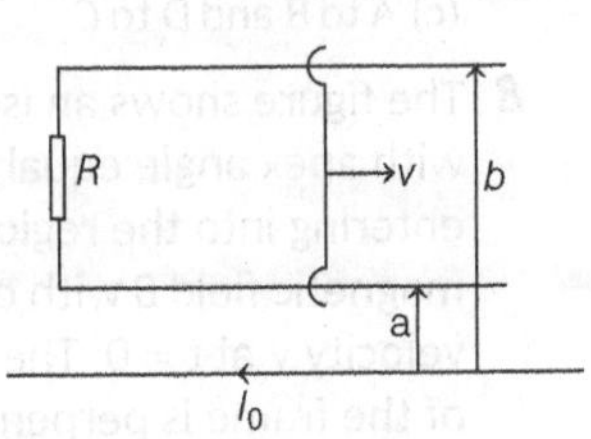

(i) the magnitude and the direction of the current induced in the connector

(ii) the force required to maintain the connector's velocity constant.

4 A triangular loop ABC is placed in the magnetic field of a long wire carrying a current i as shown in figure. The loop is placed in such a manner that the side BC is perpendicular to the wire and AC is parallel to the wire. The loop is kept in motion with a constant velocity directed parallel to the side BC and away from the wire. Find the emf induced in the loop at the instant when the distance of vertex B from the wire is a.

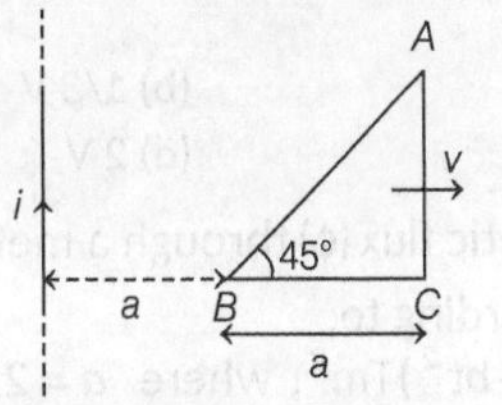

5.7 Induced Electric Field

1 What will be the electric field at a distance r from axis of changing cylindrical magnetic field B, which is parallel to the axis of cylinder?

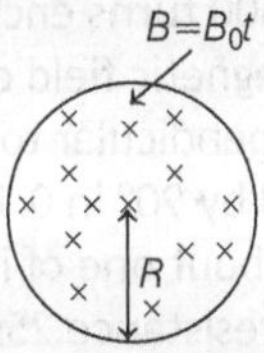

2 Find the emf induced in the rod AB as shown in the figure.

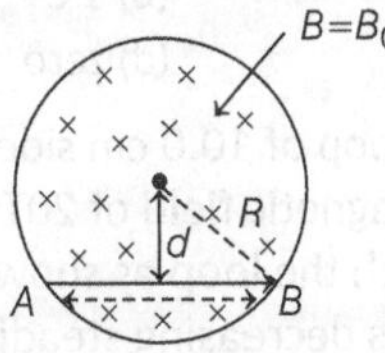

3 A thin, non-conducting ring of mass m, carrying a charge q, can rotate freely about its axis. At the instant $t = 0$, the ring was at rest and no magnetic field was present. Then, suddenly a magnetic field B was set perpendicular to the plane. Find the angular velocity acquired by the ring.

LEVEL 02 JEE Main Level

Single Choice Correct Questions

1 The magnetic flux (ϕ) *versus* time (t) graph for a coil is shown in the figure. The magnitude of average emf induced in the coil for a time interval of 0 s to 6 s is

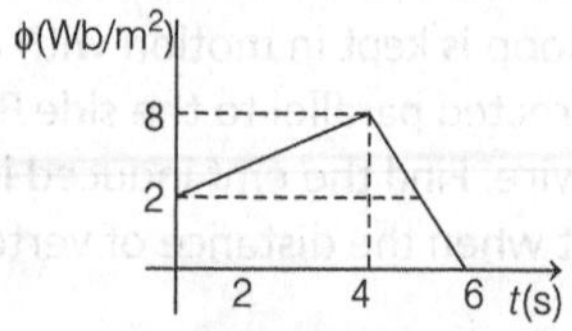

(a) 1 V (b) 1/3 V
(c) 2/3 V (d) 2 V

2 The magnetic flux (ϕ) through a metal ring varies with time t according to: $\phi = 3(at^3 - bt^2)\,\text{Tm}^2$, where $a = 2\,\text{s}^{-3}$ and $b = 6\,\text{s}^{-2}$. The resistance of the ring is 3Ω. The maximum current induced in the ring during the interval $t = 0$ to $t = 2\,\text{s}$, is

(a) 1 A (b) 2A
(c) 3A (d) 6 A

3 A circular coil of 500 turns encloses an area of 0.04 m^2. A uniform magnetic field of induction 0.25 Wb/m^2 is applied perpendicular to the plane of the coil. The coil is rotated by 90° in 0.1 second at a constant angular velocity about one of its diameters. A galvanometer of resistance 25Ω was connected in series with the coil. The total charge that will pass through the galvanometer is

(a) 0.4 C (b) 1 C
(c) 0.2 C (d) zero

4 A square wire loop of 10.0 cm side lies at right angles to a uniform magnetic field of 20T. A 10 V light bulb is in a series with the loop as shown in the fig. The magnetic field is decreasing steadily to zero over a time interval Δt. The bulb will shine with full brightness if Δt is equal to

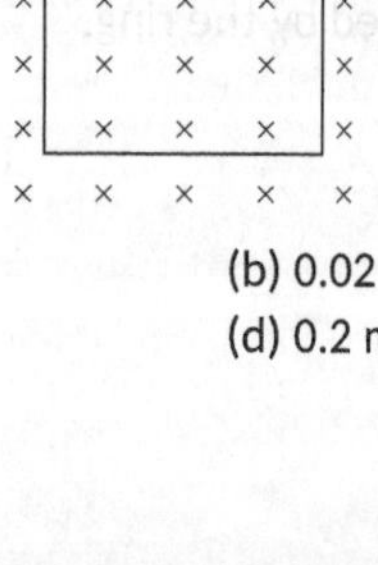

(a) 20 ms (b) 0.02 ms
(c) 2 ms (d) 0.2 ms

5 A conducting loop of radius R is present in a uniform magnetic field B perpendicular the plane of the ring. If radius R varies as a function of time t, as $R = R_0 + t$. The emf induced in the loop is

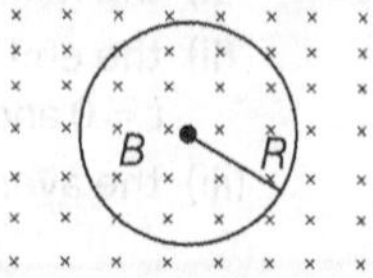

(a) $2\pi(R_0 + t)B$ clockwise
(b) $\pi(R_0 + t)B$ clockwise
(c) $2\pi(R_0 + t)B$ anti-clockwise
(d) zero

6 An electron is moving in a circular orbit of radius R with an angular acceleration α. At the centre of the orbit is kept a conducting loop of radius r, ($r << R$). The emf induced in the smaller loop due to the motion of the electron is

(a) zero (b) $\frac{\mu_0 er^2}{4R}\alpha$

(c) $\frac{\mu_0 er^2}{4\pi R}\alpha$ (d) None of these

7 A conducting wire frame is placed in a magnetic field which is directed into the paper. The magnetic field is increasing at a constant rate. The directions of induced currents in wires AB and CD are

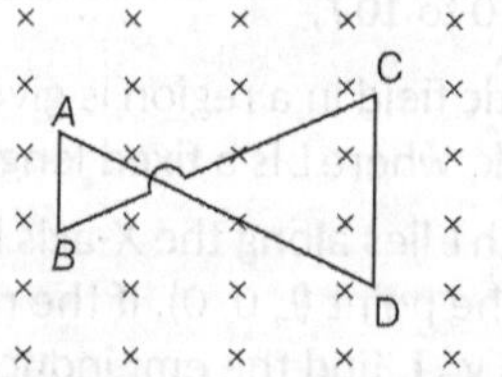

(a) B to A and D to C (b) A to B and C to D
(c) A to B and D to C (d) B to A and C to D

8 The figure shows an isosceles triangle wire frame with apex angle equal to $\pi/2$. The frame starts entering into the region of uniform magnetic field B with constant velocity v at $t = 0$. The longest side of the frame is perpendicular to the direction of velocity. If i is the instantaneous current through the frame then choose the alternative showing the correct variation of i with time.

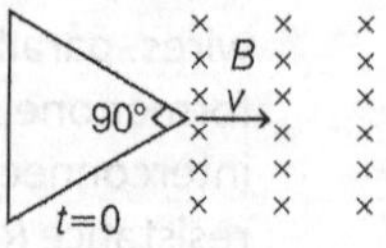

(a)
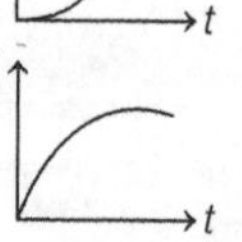

(b)
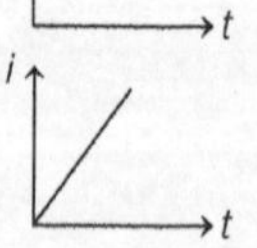

(c)

(d)

9 A square coil $ACDE$ with its plane vertical is released from rest in a horizontal uniform magnetic field B of length $2L$ (as shown in figure). The acceleration of the coil is

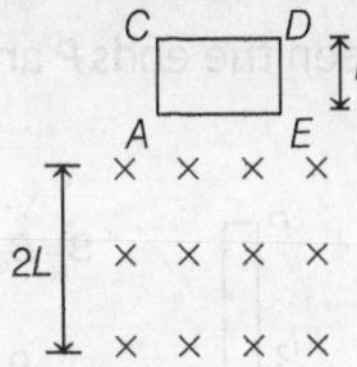

(a) less than g for all the time till the loop crosses the magnetic field completely
(b) less than g when it enters the field and greater than g when it comes out of the field
(c) g all the time
(d) less than g when it enters and comes out of the field but equal to g when it is within the field

10 The current i in the straight conductor varies sinusoidally with time as shown. (A positive value of i is in the direction indicated). At time t_1 the induced current in the rectangular loop is clockwise. What is the current in the rectangular loop at time t_2 and time t_3 respectively?

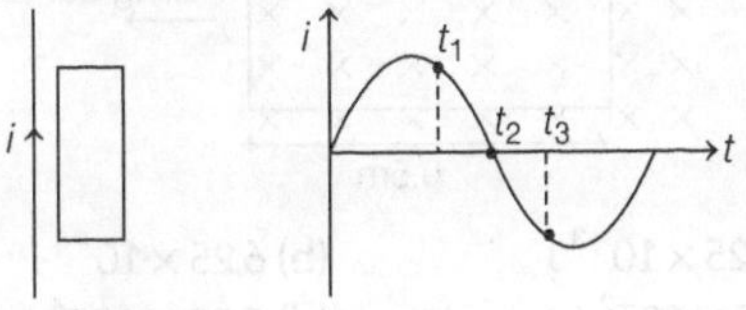

(a) zero; clockwise
(b) zero; counterclockwise
(c) clockwise; clockwise
(d) clockwise; counterclockwise

11 Three wire loops and an observer are positioned as shown in the figure. From the observer's point of view, a current i flows counterclockwise in the middle loop, which is moving towards the observer with a velocity v. Loops A and B are stationary. This same observer would notice that

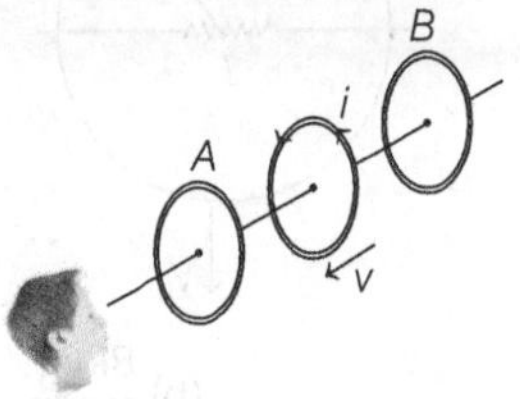

(a) clockwise current are induced in loops A and B
(b) counterclockwise current are induced in loops A and B
(c) a clockwise current is induced in loop A, but a counterclockwise current is induced in loop B
(d) a counterclockwise current is induced in loop A, but a clockwise current is induced in loop B

12 Two identical conductors P and Q are placed on two frictionless, flat, conducting rails R and S, in a uniform magnetic field directed into the plane. If conductor P is moved in the direction shown in the figure with a constant speed, then the conductor Q

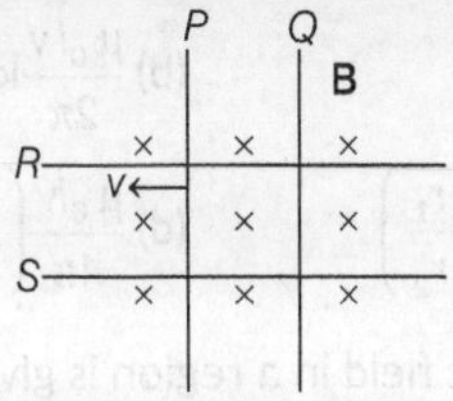

(a) will be attracted towards conductor P
(b) will be repelled away from conductor P
(c) will remain stationary
(d) first attracted and then repelled away from conductor P

13 A long metal bar of 30 cm length is aligned along a north-south line and moves eastward at a speed of $10\ ms^{-1}$. A uniform magnetic field of 4.0 T points vertically downwards. If the south end of the bar has a potential of 0 V, the induced potential at the north end of the bar is
(a) + 12 V
(b) − 12 V
(c) 0 V
(d) cannot be determined since there is not a closed circuit

14 A conducting rod PQ of length 5m oriented as shown is moving with $\mathbf{v} = (2ms^{-1})\hat{i}$ without any rotation in a uniform magnetic field) $(3\hat{j} + 4\hat{k})$ T. Emf induced in the rod is

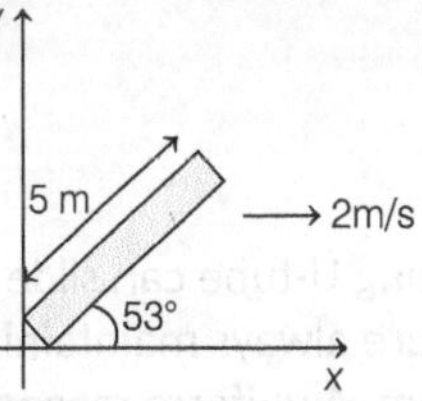

(a) 32 V (b) 40 V
(c) 50 V (d) None of these

15 A semi-circular loop of radius R is placed in a uniform magnetic field as shown. It is pulled with a constant velocity. The induced emf in the loop is

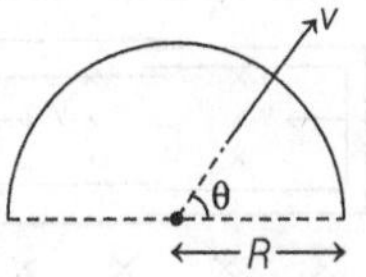

(a) $Bv(\pi R)\cos\theta$ (b) $Bv(\pi R)\sin\theta$
(c) $Bv(2R)\cos\theta$ (d) $Bv(2R)\sin\theta$

16 A uniform metal rod is moving with a uniform velocity v parallel to a long straight wire carrying a current i. The rod is perpendicular to the wire with its ends at distances r_1 and r_2 (with $r_2 > r_1$) from it. The emf induced in the rod is:

(a) 0 (b) $\frac{\mu_0 i v}{2\pi}\log_e\left(\frac{r_2}{r_1}\right)$

(c) $\frac{\mu_0 i v}{2\pi}\log_e\left(\frac{r_1}{r_2}\right)$ (d) $\frac{\mu_0 i v}{4\pi}\left(1-\frac{r_1}{r_2}\right)$

17 The magnetic field in a region is given by $\mathbf{B}=B_0\left(1+\frac{x}{a}\right)\hat{k}$. A square loop of resistance R and edge length d is placed with its edges along X and Y-axis. The loop is moved with constant velocity $\mathbf{v}=v_0\hat{i}$. The induced current in the loop is

(a) $\frac{v_0 B_0 d^2}{aR}$ (b) $\frac{v_0 B_0 d^2}{2aR}$

(c) $\frac{v_0 B_0 d^2}{4aR}$ (d) None of these

18 A wire bent as a parabola $y = kx^2$ is located in a uniform magnetic field of induction B, the vector B being perpendicular to the XY-plane. At the moment t = 0, a connector starts sliding translation wise from the parabola apex with a constant acceleration a (figure). The emf of electromagnetic induction in the loop thus formed as a function of y is

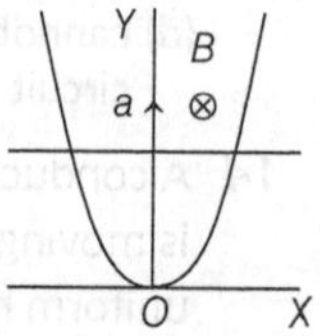

(a) $By\sqrt{2a/k}$

(b) $By\sqrt{a/2k}$

(c) $By\sqrt{8a/k}$

(d) $By\sqrt{4a/k}$

19 One conducting U-tube can slide inside another as shown in figure always maintaining electrical contact between them. A uniform magnetic field B is perpendicular to the plane of the figure. Each tube moves towards each other with a velocity v. If l is the width of each tube, then emf induced in circuit will be

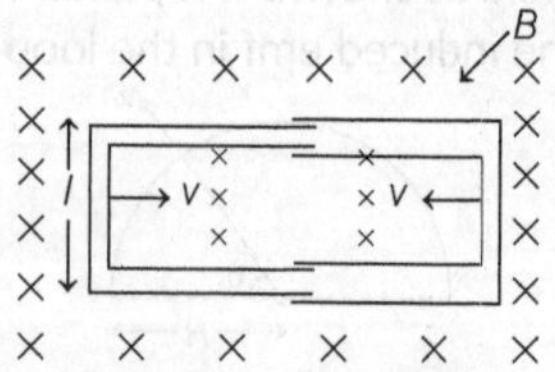

(a) Blv (b) $-Blv$

(c) zero (d) $2Blv$

20 A thin conductor PQR has length $PQ = l_2$ and $QR = l_1$ move with velocity $\mathbf{v}=(v_1\hat{i}+v_2\hat{j})$ m/s in XY-plane having uniform magnetic field $\mathbf{B}=B_0\hat{k}$. The potential difference between the ends P and R of the conductor is

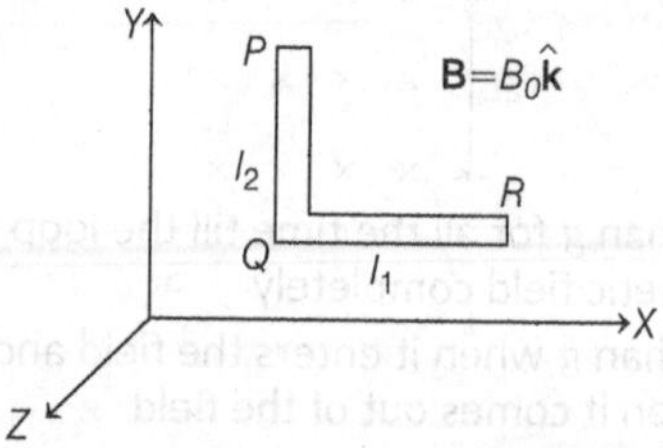

(a) $B_0(l_2v_1+l_1v_2)$ (b) $B_0(l_2v_2+l_1v_1)$

(c) $B_0(l_2v_1-l_1v_2)$ (d) $B_0(l_2v_2-l_1v_1)$

21 Figure shows a square loop of side 0.5m and resistance 10Ω. The magnetic field has a magnitude $B = 1.0$ T. The work done in pulling the loop out of the field uniformly in 2.0 s is

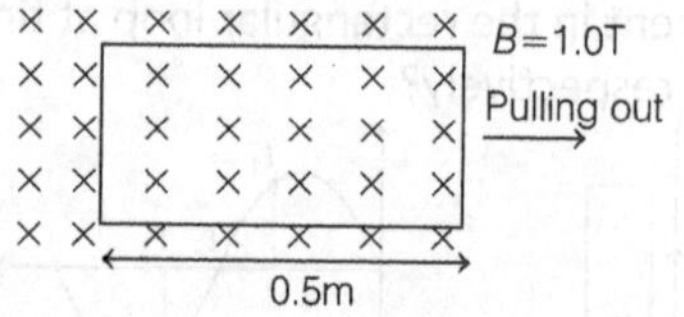

(a) 3.125×10^{-3} J (b) 6.25×10^{-4} J

(c) 1.25×10^{-2} J (d) 5.00×10^{-4} J

22 A metallic ring (radius R) of negligible resistance has a resistance r connected across its diameter as shown in the figure. It is moving with velocity v_0 in a constant magnetic field B acting perpendicular to the plane of paper in inward direction. The current in the resistance is

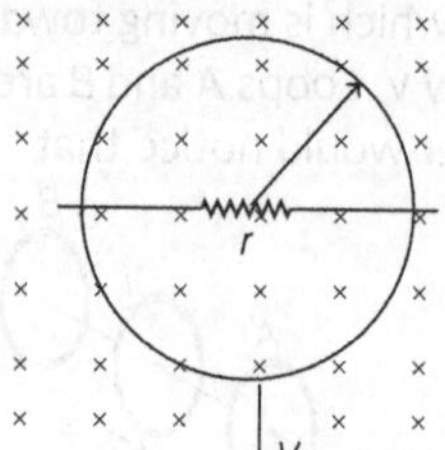

(a) $\frac{2BRv_0}{r}$ (b) $\frac{BRv_0}{r}$

(c) $\frac{BRv_0}{2r}$ (d) 0

23 A rectangular loop with a sliding connector of length 20 cm is situated in uniform magnetic field perpendicular to plane of loop. The magnetic induction is 10 T and resistance of connector is 1Ω.

The sides AB and CD have resistances 2Ω and 3Ω respectively. The external force required to keep the connector moving with a constant velocity $v = 4.4$ m/s is

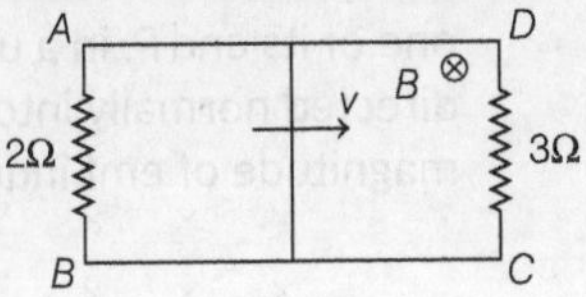

(a) 5 N
(b) 8 N
(c) 10 N
(d) 12 N

24 A long metal rod AB has resistance of unit length λ. It moves with constant speed $v (v \perp OC)$ in resistanceless triangular rails from O to C in a uniform magnetic field B as shown in the figure. The angle between the rails is α Find the current as a function of time.

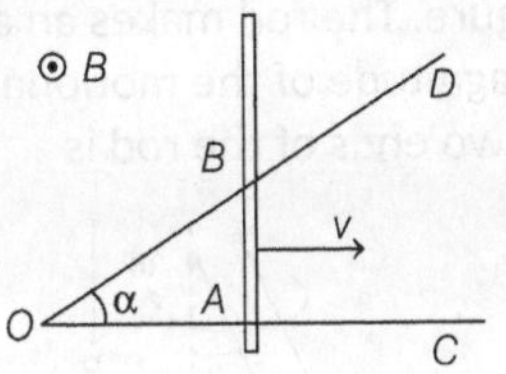

(a) $\frac{Bv}{\lambda}$ (b) $\frac{Bv}{2\lambda}$

(c) $\frac{2Bv\sin\alpha}{\lambda}$ (d) $\frac{Bv\sin\alpha}{2\lambda}$

25 A rectangular loop $PQRS$, is being pulled with constant speed into a uniform transverse magnetic field by a force F (as shown). Emf induced in side PS and potential difference between points P and S respectively are (Resistance of the loop $= r$)

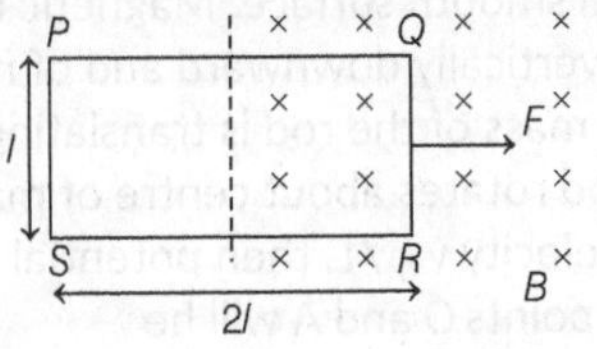

(a) zero, $\frac{Fr}{Bl}$ (b) zero, zero

(c) zero, $\frac{Fr}{6Bl}$ (d) $\frac{Fr}{6Bl}, \frac{Fr}{6Bl}$

26 A conducting rod of mass 50 g and length 10 cm can slide without friction on two long horizontal rails. A uniform magnetic field of magnitude 5 mT exists in the region, as shown. A source S is used to maintain a constant current 2A through the rod. If motion of the rod starts from the rest, its speed after 10 s from the start of the motion will be

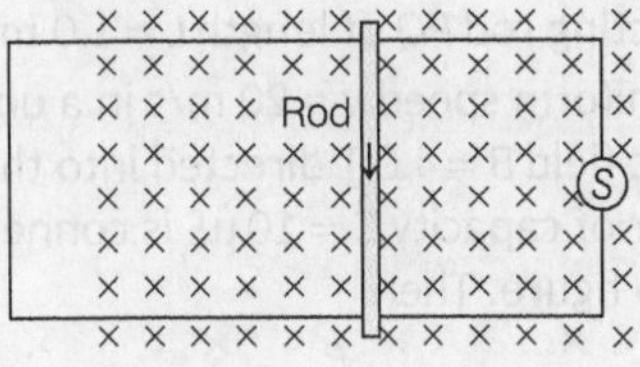

(a) 2 cm/s (b) 8 cm/s (c) 12 cm/s (d) 20 cm/s

27 A vertical ring of radius r and resistance R falls vertically. It is in contact with two vertical rails which are joined at the top with a conducting wire of zero resistance.

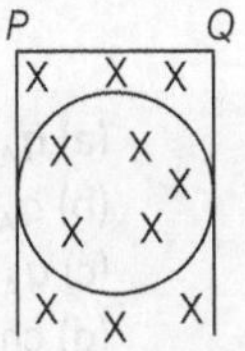

The rails are conducting, frictionless and have negligible resistance. Horizontal uniform magnetic field of magnitude B perpendicular to the plane of ring and rails exists. When the speed of ring is v, the current in the section PQ is

(a) zero (b) $\frac{2Brv}{R}$ (c) $\frac{4Brv}{R}$ (d) $\frac{8Brv}{R}$

28 A metal wire PQ slides on parallel metallic rails having separation 0.25 m, each having negligible resistance. There is a 2Ω resistor and 10V battery as shown in figure. There is a uniform magnetic field directed into the plane of the paper of magnitude 0.5 T. A force of 0.5N to the left is required to keep the wire PQ moving with constant speed to the right. With what speed is the wire PQ moving? (Neglect self-inductance of the loop)

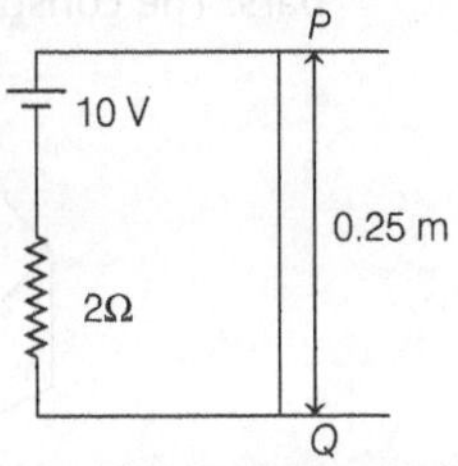

(a) 8 m/s (b) 16 m/s
(c) 24 m/s (d) 32 m/s

29 Two long parallel wires of zero resistance are connected to each other by a battery of 1.0 V as shown in figure. The separation between the wires is 0.5 m. A metallic bar, which is perpendicular to the wire and of resistance 10Ω moves on these wires when a magnetic field of 0.02 T is acting perpendicular to the plane containing the bar and the wires. The velocity of the bar as a function of time (if the mass of the bar is 0.002 kg and at $t = 0, v = 0$) is

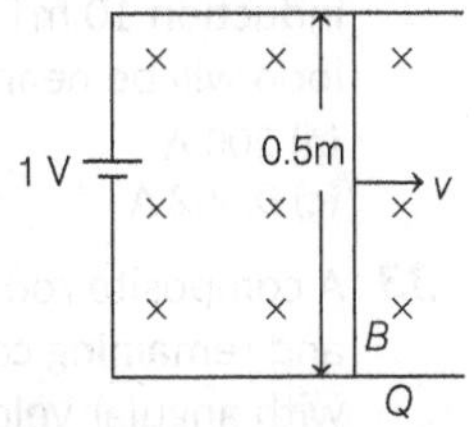

(a) $v = 100(1 - e^{-t/200})$ (b) $v = 100(1 - e^{-t/50})$
(c) $v = 200(1 - e^{-500t})$ (d) $v = 100(1 - e^{-200t})$

30 A conducting rod PQ of length $L = 1.0$ m is moving with a uniform speed $v = 20$ m/s in a uniform magnetic field $B = 4.0$ T directed into the paper. A capacitor of capacity $C = 10\,\mu F$ is connected as shown in figure. Then

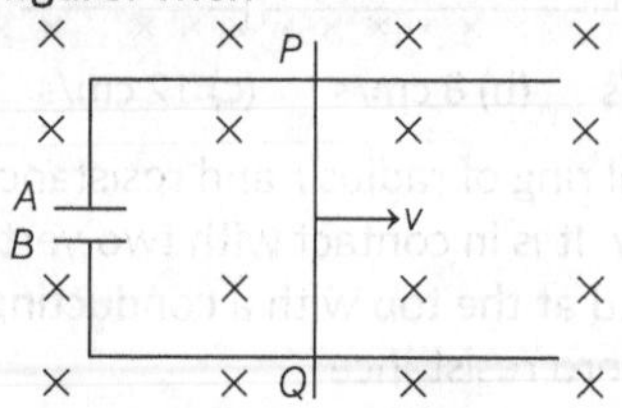

(a) $q_A = +800\,\mu C$ and $q_B = -800\,\mu C$
(b) $q_A = -800\,\mu C$ and $q_B = +800\,\mu C$
(c) $q_A = 0 = q_B$
(d) charged stored in the capacitor increases exponentially with time

31 A conducting wire of mass m slides down two smooth conducting bars, set at an angle θ to the horizontal as shown in figure. The separation between the bars is l. The system is located in the magnetic field B, perpendicular to the plane of the sliding wire and bars. The constant velocity of the wire is

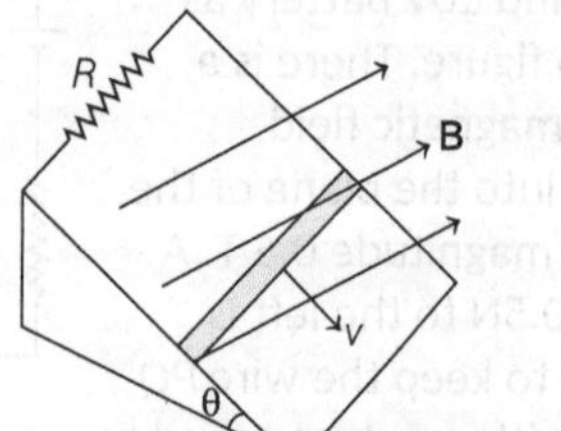

(a) $\dfrac{mgR\sin\theta}{B^2 l^2}$ (b) $\dfrac{mgR}{B^2 l^2}$
(c) $\dfrac{mgR\tan\theta}{B^2 l^2}$ (d) $\dfrac{mgR\sin\theta}{B^2 l^2 \cos^2\theta}$

32 A ring of resistance 10Ω, radius 10cm and 100 turns is rotated at a rate 100 rev/s about its diameter which is perpendicular to a uniform magnetic field of induction 10 mT. The amplitude of the current in the loop will be nearly (Take $\pi^2 = 10$)
(a) 200 A (b) 2 A
(c) 0.002 A (d) None of these

33 A composite rod of length l is one-fourth insulator and remaining conductor is made to rotate freely with angular velocity ω, in a uniform magnetic field B perpendicular to the plane of motion. Then potential difference across the rod will be (rotation is about insulating end).
(a) $\dfrac{1}{2}B\omega l^2$ (b) $\dfrac{7}{32}B\omega l^2$ (c) $\dfrac{15}{16}B\omega l^2$ (d) $\dfrac{15}{32}B\omega l^2$

34 When a J-shaped conducting rod is rotating in its own plane with constant angular velocity ω, about one of its end P, in a uniform magnetic field $\mathbf{B}$ directed normally into the plane of paper then magnitude of emf induced across it will be

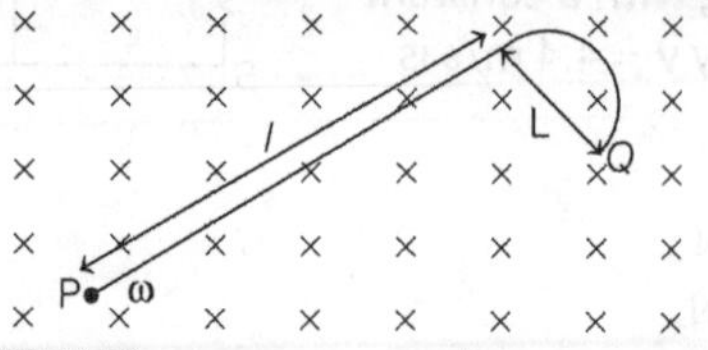

(a) $B\omega\sqrt{L^2 + l^2}$ (b) $\dfrac{1}{2}B\omega L^2$
(c) $\dfrac{1}{2}B\omega(L^2 + l^2)$ (d) $\dfrac{1}{2}B\omega l^2$

35 A rod of length L rotates in the form of a conical pendulum with an angular velocity ω about its axis as shown in figure. The rod makes an angle θ with the axis. The magnitude of the motional emf developed across the two ends of the rod is

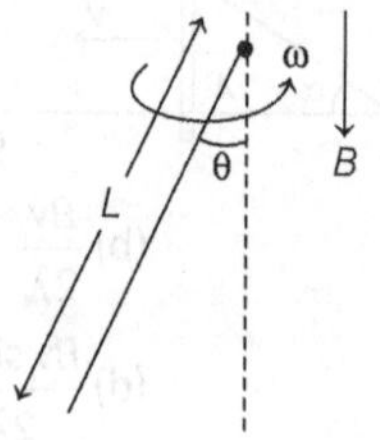

(a) $\dfrac{1}{2}B\omega L^2$ (b) $\dfrac{1}{2}B\omega L^2\tan^2\theta$
(c) $\dfrac{1}{2}B\omega L^2\cos^2\theta$ (d) $-\dfrac{1}{2}B\omega L^2\sin^2\theta$

36 A conducting rod of length L is moving on a horizontal smooth surface. Magnetic field in the region is vertically downward and of magnitude B_0. If centre of mass of the rod is translating with velocity v_0 and rod rotates about centre of mass with angular velocity v_0/L, then potential difference between points O and A will be

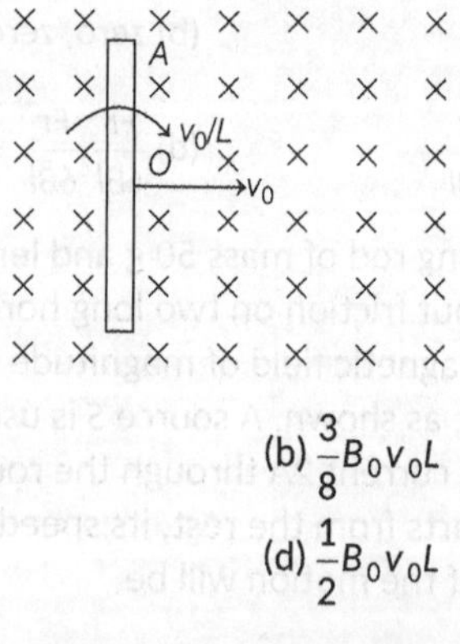

(a) $\dfrac{5}{8}B_0 v_0 L$ (b) $\dfrac{3}{8}B_0 v_0 L$
(c) $\dfrac{1}{8}B_0 v_0 L$ (d) $\dfrac{1}{2}B_0 v_0 L$

37 A conducting ring of radius R is rolling without slipping with a constant angular velocity ω as shown in figure. If the magnetic field strength is B and is directed into the page then the emf induced across PQ is

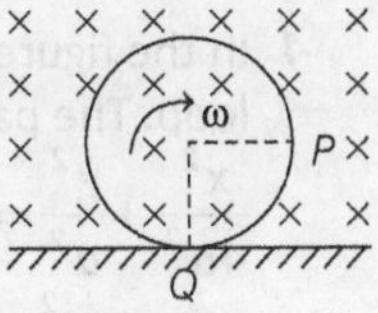

(a) $B\omega R^2$ (b) $\frac{1}{2}B\omega R^2$

(c) $4B\omega R^2$ (d) $\frac{1}{8}\pi^2 R^2 B\omega$

38 A metal rod of uniform resistance 20Ω is fixed at centre along a diameter of a conducting ring of radius 0.1 m and lies on XY-plane. There is a magnetic field $\mathbf{B} = (50\text{T})\hat{\mathbf{k}}$. The rod rotates with an angular velocity $\omega = 20$ rad/s about its axis passing through centre. An external resistance of 10Ω is connected across the centre of the ring and rim. The current through external resistance is

(a) 1/4 A (b) 1/2 A (c) 1/3 A (d) 0

39 A metallic ring of radius r with a uniform metallic spoke of negligible mass and length r is rotated about its axis with an angular velocity ω in a perpendicular uniform magnetic field B as shown in figure. The central end of the spoke is connected to the rim of the wheel through a resistor R as shown. The resistor does not rotate, its one end is always at the center of the ring and the other end is always in contact with the ring. A force F as shown is needed to maintain constant angular velocity of the wheel. F is equal to (the ring and the spoke has zero resistance)

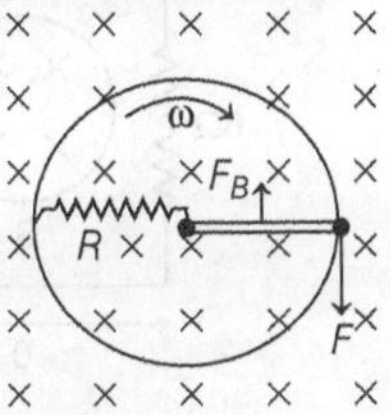

(a) $\frac{B^2\omega r^3}{8R}$ (b) $\frac{B^2\omega r^3}{2R}$ (c) $\frac{B^2\omega r^3}{4R}$ (d) $\frac{B^2\omega r^3}{16R}$

40 Figure shows three regions of magnetic field, each of area A and in each region magnitude of magnetic field decreases at a constant rate α. If $\mathbf{E}$ is induced electric field then value of line integral $\oint \mathbf{E} \cdot d\mathbf{r}$ along the given loop is equal to

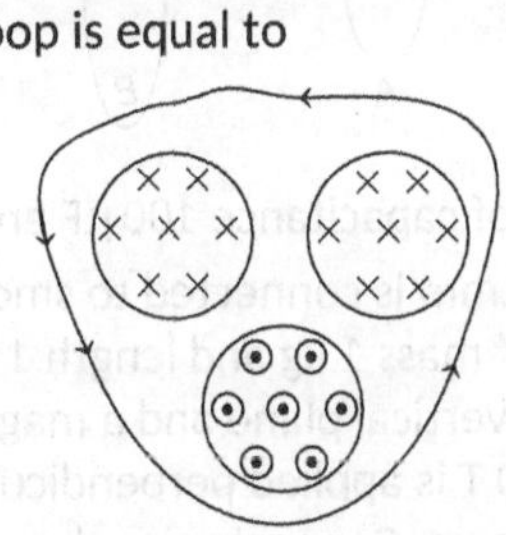

(a) αA (b) $-\alpha A$ (c) $3\alpha A$ (d) $-3\alpha A$

41 Figure shows a uniform magnetic field $B = kt$ confined to a cylindrical region of radius R. The instantaneous acceleration experienced by an electron placed at point P on the periphery of the field is

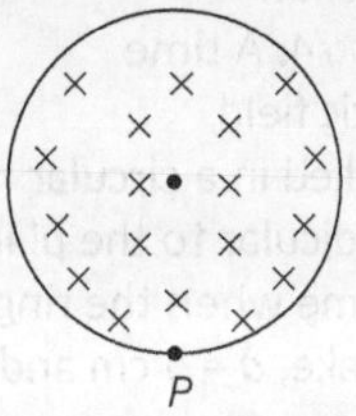

(a) zero (b) $\frac{keR}{2m}$ towards left

(c) $\frac{keR}{2m}$ towards right (d) $\frac{keR}{m}$ towards left

42 A time varying magnetic field $B = krt$ (where, k is a constant, r is the radial distance from centre O) is existing in a circular region of radius R as shown. If induced electric field at $r = \frac{R}{2}$ is E_1 and at $r = 2R$ is E_2 then the ratio $\frac{E_2}{E_1}$ is

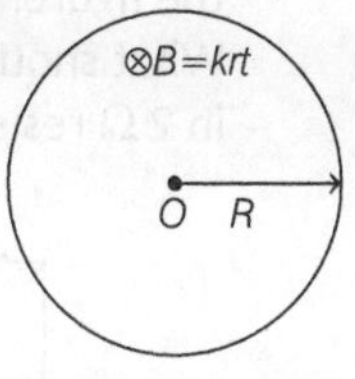

(a) 6 (b) 4

(c) 2 (d) 1

43 There exists a uniform but time varying magnetic field $B = a + bt$ normal to plane of paper in a cylindrical region as shown. A rectangular conducting loop is placed as shown. Induced emf in branches AB and BC are

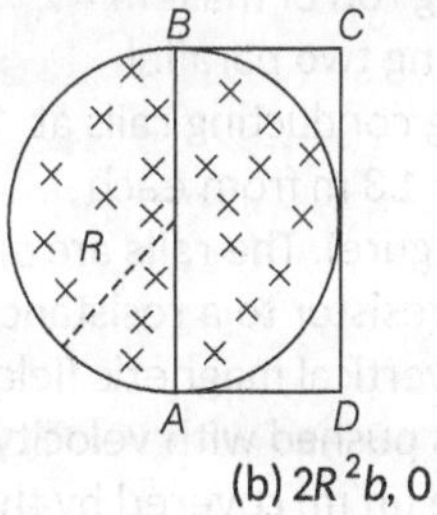

(a) $\pi R^2 b/2, 0$ (b) $2R^2 b, 0$

(c) $0, \pi R^2 b/8$ (d) $0, R^2 b/2$

44 In case of induced electric field due to a time dependent magnetic field in a cylindrical region, which of the statement is correct?

(a) It obeys the Gauss' law for electric flux.

(b) The work done by induced electric field while moving a charged particle in a closed loop is zero.

(c) The induced electric field and time varying magnetic field are parallel to each other at any instant of time.

(d) Electrostatic potential can be defined for the induced electric field.

45 A non conducting ring of mass 4 kg is uniformly charged with $\lambda = 4$ C/m and kept on rough horizontal surface with friction coefficient $\mu = \pi/4$. A time varying magnetic field $B = B_0 t^2$ is applied in a circular region of radius $a (a < r)$ perpendicular to the plane of ring as shown in figure. The time when the ring just starts to rotate on surface is (Take, $a = 5$ cm and $g = 10$ m/s^2 $B_0 = 125$ T/s^2)

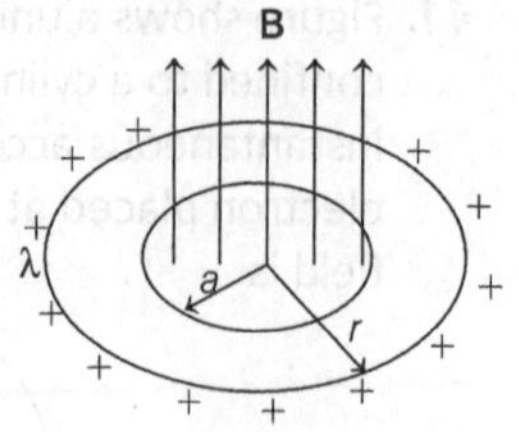

(a) 4 s (b) 5 s (c) 8 s (d) 10 s

Numerical Value Questions

1 A conducting rod PQ is sliding on two parallel conducting rod with constant velocity in a uniform magnetic field of induction $B = 2$ Wb/m^2 as shown in the figure. The rods are connected with a circuit. What should be velocity of rod PQ (in m/s) if current in 2 Ω resistor is 0.1 A?

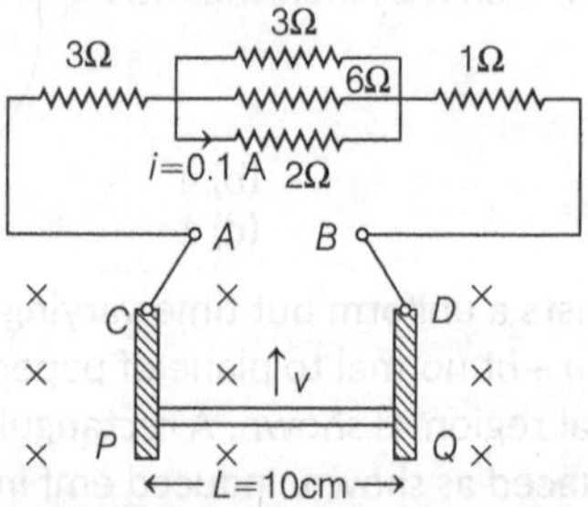

2 A conducting rod of mass $m = 2$ kg slides along two parallel smooth long conducting rails at distance $d = 1.3$ m from each other (see figure). The rails are joined by a resistor to a resistance $R = 0.32\Omega$ and placed in a vertical magnetic field of induction $B = 0.4$ T. The rod is pushed with velocity $v_0 = 3.38$ m/s. Find the distance (in m) covered by the rod until it stops.

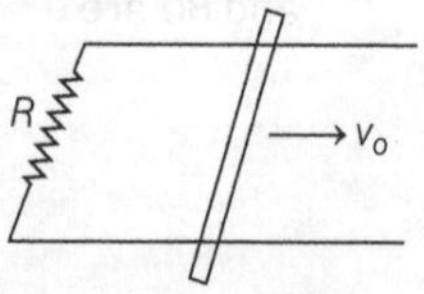

3 Two long parallel conducting horizontal rails are connected by a conducting wire at one end. A uniform magnetic field B exists in the region of space. A light uniform ring of diameter d which is practically equal to separation between the rails is placed over the rails as shown in the figure. If resistance of ring is λ per unit length, the force required to pull the ring with uniform velocity v is given by $NB^2 vd / \pi\lambda$ Find the value of N.

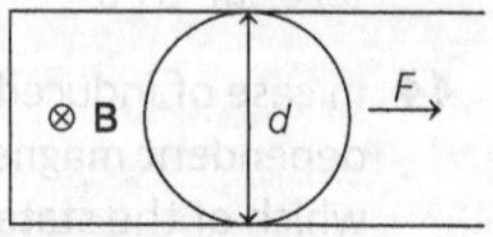

4 In the figure $ABCDEFA$ is a closed conducting wire loop. The part AFE is a portion of an ellipse, $\dfrac{x^2}{4a^2} + \dfrac{y^2}{a^2} = 1$ and BCD is a portion of the ellipse $\dfrac{x^2}{9a^2} + \dfrac{y^2}{4a^2} = 1$. A uniform magnetic field $\mathbf{B} = B_0 \hat{\mathbf{k}}$ exists in this region. If the frame is rotated about the Y-axis with a constant angular velocity ω. The maximum emf induced in the loop is $k\pi\omega B_0 a^2$. Find the value of k.

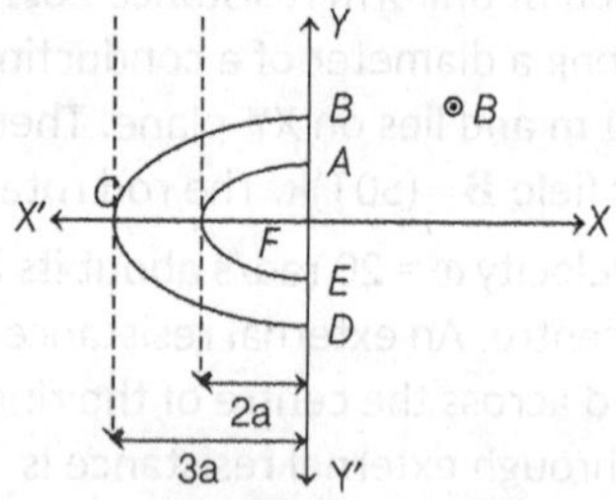

5 Two infinitely long solenoids (shown in cross-section) pass through a circuit as shown in the figure. The magnitude of **B** inside each is same and is increasing at the rate of 100 T/s. What is the current (in A) in 2Ω resistor?

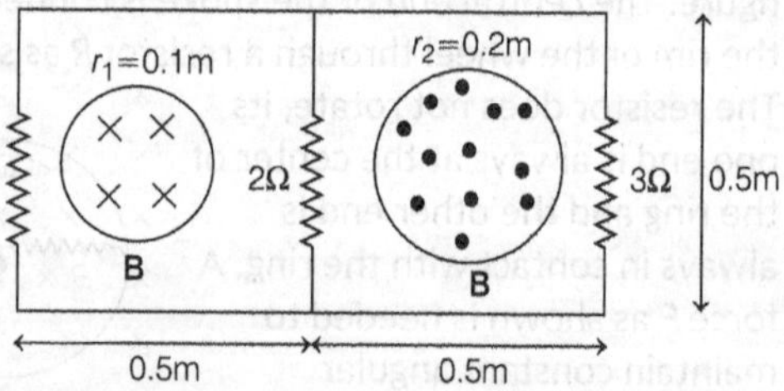

6 Loop A of radius $r (r << R)$ moves towards a stationary constant current carrying loop B with a constant velocity v in such a way that their planes are parallel and coaxial. Find the distance (in m) between the loops when the induced emf in loop A is maximum. (Take, $R = 6$ m)

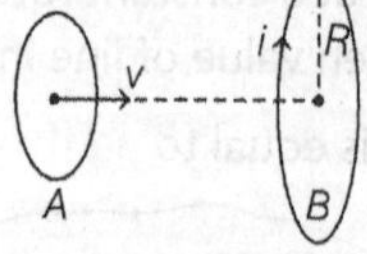

7 A capacitor of capacitance 100 μF and plates separation 1mm is connected to smooth rails and connector of mass 1 kg and length 1 m. The whole system is in vertical plane and a magnetic field of strength 100 T is applied perpendicular to plane of circuit as shown. Connector is released from rest. If the time after which dielectric of capacitor will burn out is $k \times 10^3$ s then find the value of k. Breaking strength of dielectric is 5×10^8 V/m.

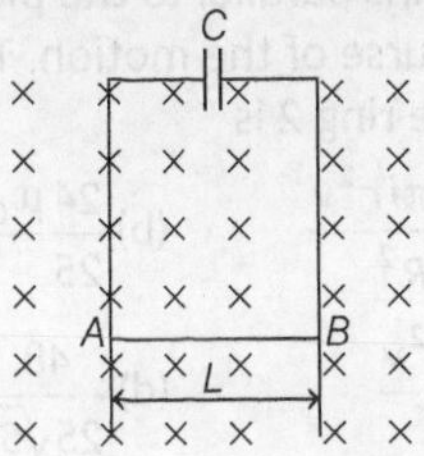

8 A conducting ring has 2 bulbs A and B rated at 2 V, 10 W and 2 V, 20W respectively. The ring encloses an ideal solenoid whose magnetic field is as shown. The radius of solenoid is 1m and the number of turns/length = 1000/m. The current changes at rate of 9 A/s. If the power dissipated in bulb B is $n \times 10^{-4}$ W, then find n.

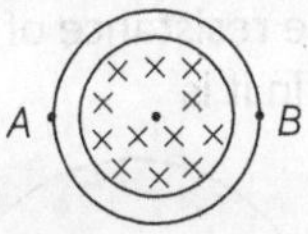

9 A conducting frame is placed in a horizontal plane as shown in the figure. The two sides are parallel and separated by a distance of 0.25 m. A massless conducting rod can slide without friction on the frame. The total resistance of the circuit is 40 Ω. The rod is connected to a 0.2 kg mass by a massless cord which passes over a massless and frictionless pulley. A uniform magnetic field of 2 T points vertically upward. The voltage of the battery is 100 V. Find the constant speed (in m/s) with which the rod and mass eventually move.

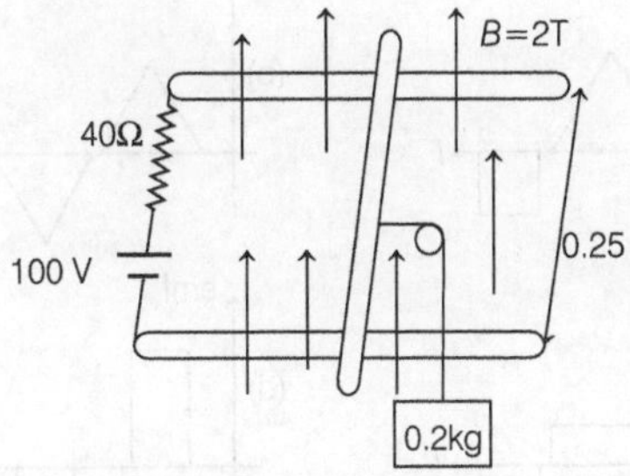

LEVEL 03 JEE Advanced Level

Single Choice Correct Questions

1 In the arrangement shown, a gas is filled inside a balloon, which is placed in a vertical magnetic field of intensity 1.5 T. The initial volume of balloon is 20π m^3 and the gas is filled inside it at the rate of 2 m^3/s. If there is no leakage, find the emf induced at t = 8π s, in a conducting ring, which is elastic and placed horizontally along the largest circumference of the balloon.

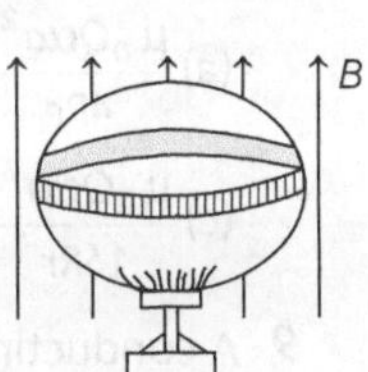

(a) 100 mV (b) 200 mV

(c) 500 mV (d) 800 mV

2 The given pattern of loop ($a > b$) is placed in a time varying magnetic field $dB/dt = k$, which is perpendicular to the planes of the loops. If the resistance per unit length of the wire is λ, then induced current is

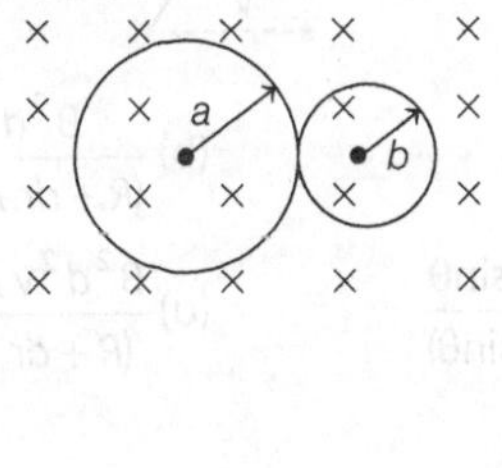

(a) $\dfrac{k(a^2+b^2)}{2\lambda(a+b)}$ (b) $\dfrac{k(a+b)}{2\lambda}$

(c) $\dfrac{k(a-b)}{2\lambda}$ (d) None of these

3 Two parallel long straight conductors lie on a smooth plane surface. Two other long parallel conductors rest on them at right angles, so as to form a square of side a. A uniform magnetic field exists at right angle to the plane containing the conductors. Now, conductors start moving outward with constant velocity v_0 at $t = 0$. Then, induced current in the loop at any time t is (λ is resistance per unit length of conductors)

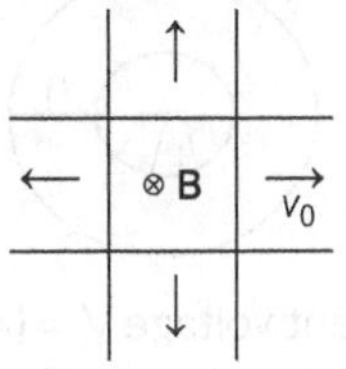

(a) $\dfrac{aBv_0}{\lambda(a+v_0t)}$ (b) $\dfrac{aBv_0}{2\lambda}$

(c) $\dfrac{Bv_0}{\lambda}$ (d) $\dfrac{Bv_0}{2\lambda}$

4 The magnetic field in a region $ABCD$ is as shown in the figure. A triangular loop is entered to this region at a constant speed (v) as shown. Then which graph represents the induced emf in loop w.r.t. time?

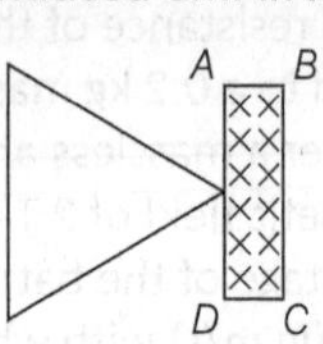

(a)
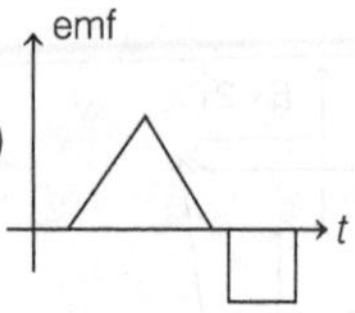

(b)
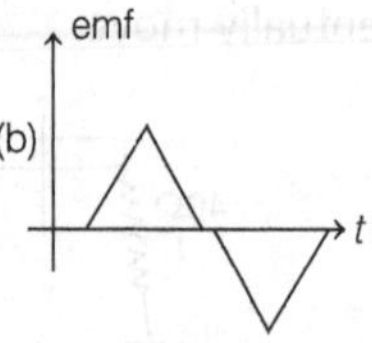

(c)
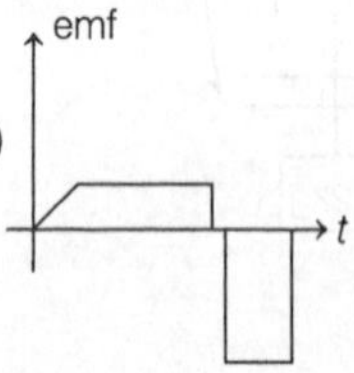

(d)
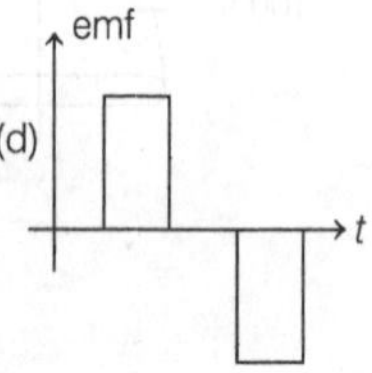

5 A uniform magnetic field of induction $B = 0.5$T exists in a circular region of radius $R = 5$m. A loop also of radius R encloses the magnetic field at $t = 0$ and then pulled at a uniform speed $v = 2$ m/s in the plane of the paper. The induced EMF in the loop at $t = 4$ s is

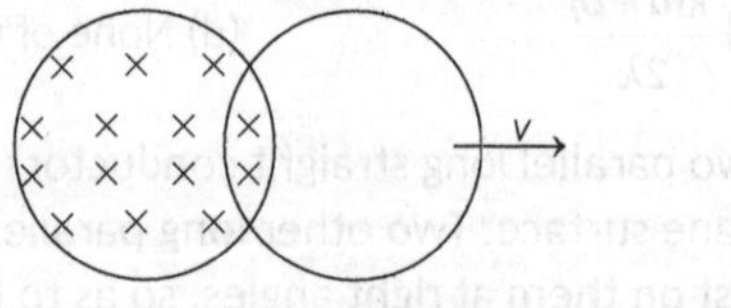

(a) 6 V (b) 8 V (c) 10 V (d) 12 V

6 Two concentric coplanar circular loops have diameters 20 cm and 2 m and resistance of unit length of the wire = 10^{-4} Ω/m.

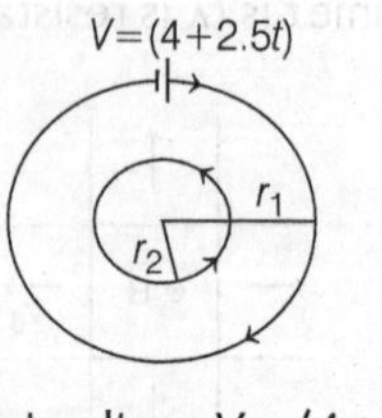

A time-dependent voltage $V = (4 + 2.5t)$ V is applied to the larger loop as shown. Find the current in the smaller loop.

(a) 1.25 A (b) 2.5 A (c) 4 A (d) 4.5 A

7 A current i is flowing in a circular ring 1 of radius R. A second ring 2 whose radius r is much smaller than that of the first, is moving with constant velocity v along the axis in such a manner that the plane of the ring remains parallel to the plane of the ring 1 during the course of the motion. The maximum emf induced in the ring 2 is

(a) $-\frac{24}{25\sqrt{5}}\frac{\mu_0 \pi i r^2 v}{R^2}$ (b) $\frac{24}{25}\frac{\mu_0 \pi i r^2 v}{R^2}$

(c) $\frac{2}{3\sqrt{3}}\frac{\mu_0 \pi i r^2 v}{R^2}$ (d) $\frac{48}{25\sqrt{5}}\frac{\mu_0 \pi i r^2 v}{R^2}$

8 A non-conducting ring of radius R having uniformly distributed charge Q starts rotating about XX' axis passing through diameter with an angular acceleration α as shown in the figure. Another small conducting ring having radius $a (a << R)$ is kept fixed at the centre of bigger ring in such a way that axis XX' is passing through its centre and perpendicular to its plane. If the resistance of small ring is r, the induced current in it is

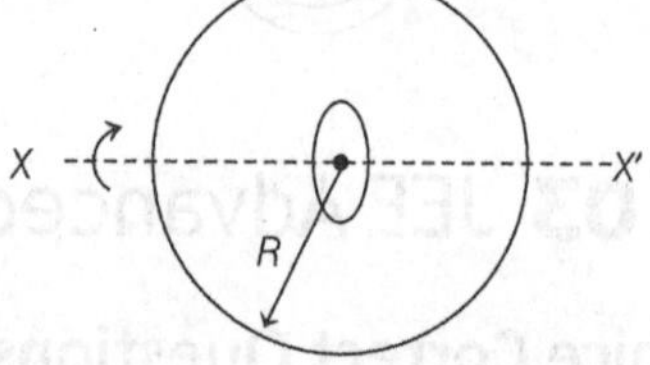

(a) $\frac{\mu_0 Q\alpha a^2}{4Rr}$ (b) $\frac{\mu_0 Q\alpha a^2}{8Rr}$

(c) $\frac{\mu_0 Q\alpha a^2}{16Rr}$ (d) $\frac{\mu_0 Q\alpha a^2}{32Rr}$

9 A conducting rod with resistance r per unit length is moving inside a vertical magnetic field B at constant speed v on two horizontal parallel ideal conductor rails. The ends of the rails are connected to a resistor R. The separation between the rails is d. The rod maintains a tilted angle θ to the rails. The external force required to keep the rod moving is

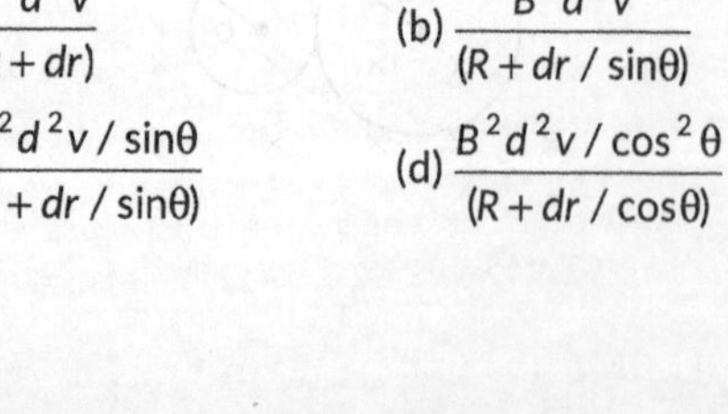

(a) $\frac{B^2 d^2 v}{(R + dr)}$ (b) $\frac{B^2 d^2 v}{(R + dr / \sin\theta)}$

(c) $\frac{B^2 d^2 v / \sin\theta}{(R + dr / \sin\theta)}$ (d) $\frac{B^2 d^2 v / \cos^2\theta}{(R + dr / \cos\theta)}$

10 In the arrangement shown in the figure, uniform magnetic field B is upward to the plane of paper. Connector AB is smooth and conducting, having mass m and length l. Initially spring has extension X_0. Spring is non-conducting (neglect induction in spring). Connector is released at $t = 0$. Maximum charge on the capacitor is

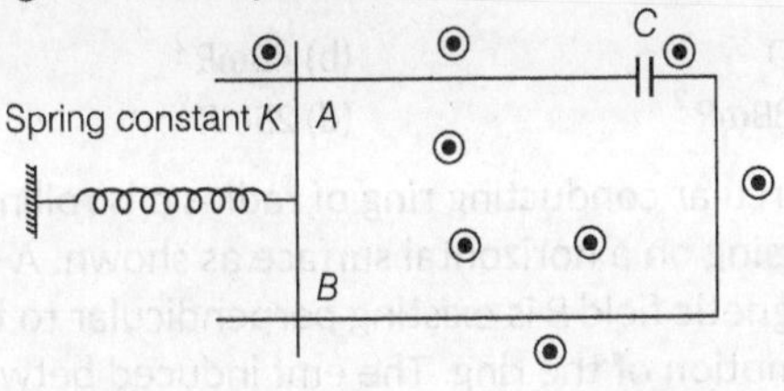

(a) $X_0\sqrt{\dfrac{KC}{1+\dfrac{B^2l^2C}{m}}}$ (b) $X_0\sqrt{\dfrac{KC}{1+\dfrac{m}{B^2l^2C}}}$

(c) $X_0\sqrt{\dfrac{KC}{2+\dfrac{B^2l^2C}{m}}}$ (d) $X_0\sqrt{\dfrac{4KC}{1+\dfrac{B^2l^2C}{2m}}}$

11 Two long parallel rails, a distance $d = 1$ m apart and each having a resistance per unit length $\lambda = 2\Omega$ /m are joined at one end by a resistance $R = 1\Omega$. A perfectly conducting rod MN of mass $m = 1$kg is free to slide along the rails without friction. There is a uniform magnetic field of induction $B = 1$ T normal to the plane of the paper and directed into the paper. A variable force F is applied to the rod MN such that, as the rod moves, a constant current $i = 1$ A flows through R. The applied force F at a distance $x = 1$m of the rod from R is

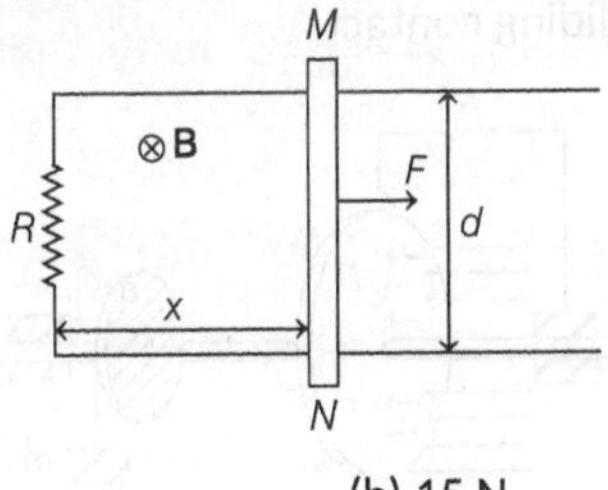

(a) 11 N (b) 15 N
(c) 21 N (d) 36 N

12 A long wire bent into the shape of a right angle is held stationary on a horizontal frictionless plane. A very long rod of mass 1 kg initially starts with velocity 4 m/s from the apex A of the bent wire. The resistance per unit length of the wire and the rod is $(\sqrt{2}-1)\times10^{-2}\ \Omega$ /m. The whole arrangement is put in a region of uniform magnetic field of 0.05 T directed normally into the horizontal plane. The distance travelled by the rod before it comes to rest is

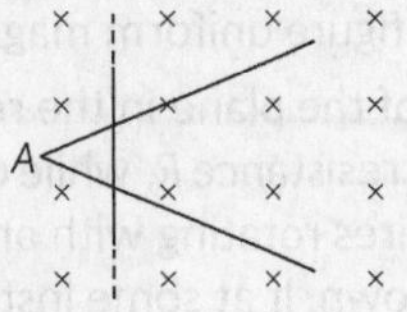

(a) 1 m (b) 2 m (c) 3 m (d) 4 m

13 In the circuit shown the speed of the rod is v, magnitude of magnetic field is B and rate of decrease of B with respect to time is K at the moment. At this moment, magnitude of the induced emf in the circuit is

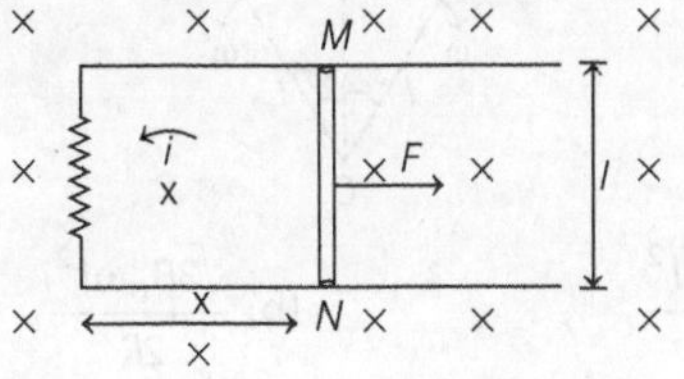

(a) $|lKx - Blv|$ (b) $|Blv|$
(c) $|lKx|$ (d) $|lKx + Blv|$

14 A conducting light string is wound on the rim of a metal ring of radius r and mass m. The free end of the string is fixed to the ceiling. A vertical infinite conducting smooth plane is always tangent to the ring. The ring is released and simultaneously a uniform magnetic field of strength B perpendicular to the plane of the ring is switched on. The string and the plane are connected by a resistance R. The ring is always immersed in the magnetic field. The terminal velocity of the ring will be

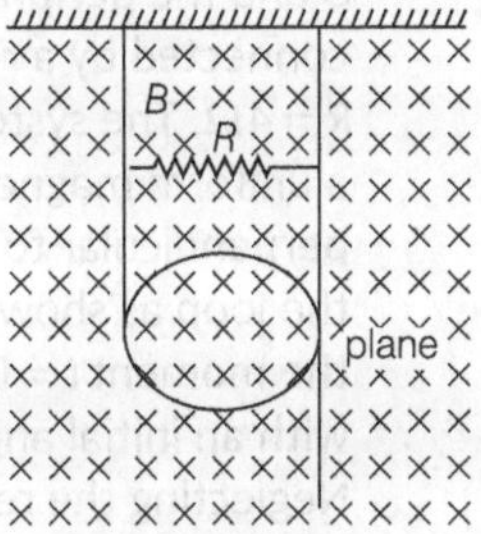

(a) $\dfrac{mgR}{B^2r^2}$ (b) $\dfrac{mgR}{2B^2r^2}$ (c) $\dfrac{2mgR}{B^2r^2}$ (d) $\dfrac{mgR}{4B^2r^2}$

15 Two parallel conducting rails, separated by a distance l, are placed horizontally in a region of uniform magnetic field B, perpendicular to the plane of the rails as shown in the figure. Two conducting wires, each of length l are placed, so as to slide on parallel conducting rails without friction. One of the wires is given a velocity v_0 parallel to the rails. Loss in kinetic energy of the system till the steady state is achieved will be

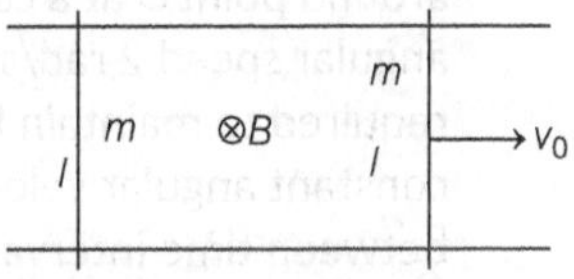

(a) 0 (b) $\dfrac{3}{4}mv_0^2$ (c) $\dfrac{3}{8}mv_0^2$ (d) $\dfrac{1}{4}mv_0^2$

16 In the shown figure uniform magnetic field B_0 is pointing out of the plane in the region. Wire CD is fixed and has resistance R, while OA and OB are conducting wires rotating with angular velocity ω about O as shown. If at some instant $OA = OB = l$ and each wire makes angle $\theta = 30°$ with Y-axis, then the current through resistance R is

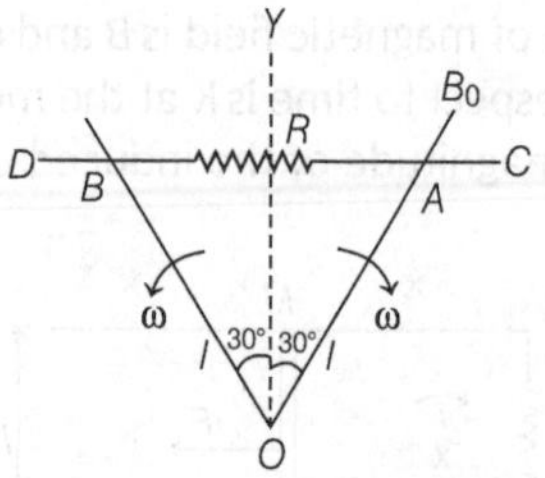

(a) $\dfrac{B_0\omega l^2}{R}$ (b) $\dfrac{\sqrt{3}B_0\omega l^2}{2R}$

(c) $\dfrac{\sqrt{3}B_0\omega l^2}{4R}$ (d) $\dfrac{B_0\omega l^2}{2R}$

17 A conducting rod PQ of mass $m = 1$ kg rotates without friction on a horizontal plane about O on circular rails of diameter $d = 2$ m. The center O and the periphery are connected by a resistance $R = 4\Omega$. The system is located in a uniform magnetic field $B = 2$ T perpendicular to the plane of the loop as shown in figure. At the moment $t = 0$, the rod starts rotating clockwise with an initial angular velocity $\omega_0 = 30\pi$ rad/s Neglecting the resistance of rails and rod, as well as self inductance, the number of revolutions made by the rod before it stops is

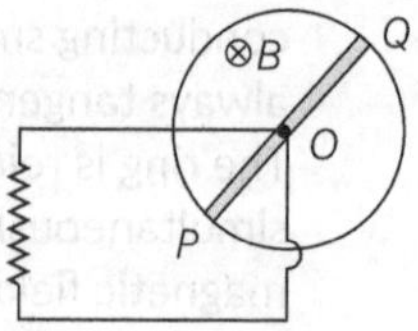

(a) 10 (b) 20 (c) 30 (d) 40

18 A uniform magnetic field 20 T exists on right side of the boundary in a gravity free space as shown in figure. The given circular arc of radius 2 cm made of conducting wire of total resistance 4Ω is rotated around point O at a constant angular speed 2 rad/s. Power required to maintain the constant angular velocity between time interval $t = \pi/6$ s to $t = \pi/3$ s is

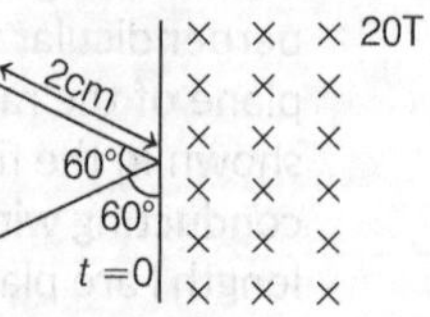

(a) 64 μW (b) 32 μW

(c) 128 μW (d) 16 μW

19 Two metallic rings of radius R are rolling on a metallic rod. A magnetic field of magnitude B is applied in the region. The magnitude of potential difference between point A and point C on the two rings (as shown), will be

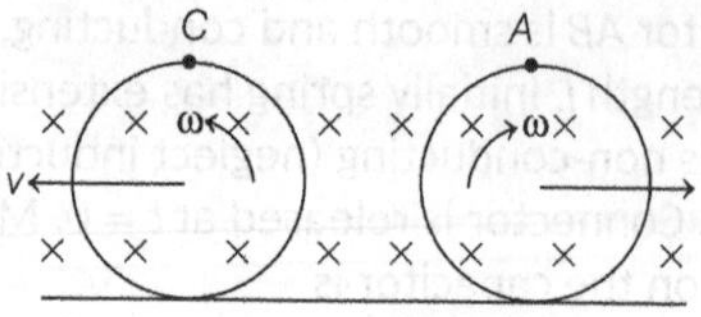

(a) 0 (b) $4B\omega R^2$

(c) $8B\omega R^2$ (d) $2B\omega R^2$

20 A circular conducting ring of radius a is rolling with slipping on a horizontal surface as shown. A uniform magnetic field B is existing perpendicular to the plane of motion of the ring. The emf induced between the points A and D of the ring is

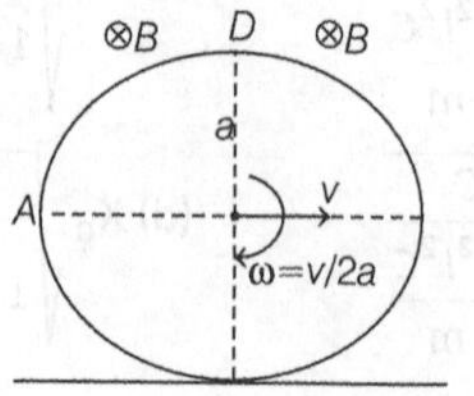

(a) $B\omega a^2$ (b) $2B\omega a^2$

(c) $4B\omega a^2$ (d) $6B\omega a^2$

21 A metallic disc of radius r is made of a material of negligible resistance and can rotate about a conducting horizontal shaft. A smaller non-conducting disc of radius a is fixed onto the same shaft and has a massless cord wrapped around it, which is attached to a small object of mass m as shown. Two ends of a resistor of resistance R are connected to the perimeter of the disc and to the shaft by sliding contacts.

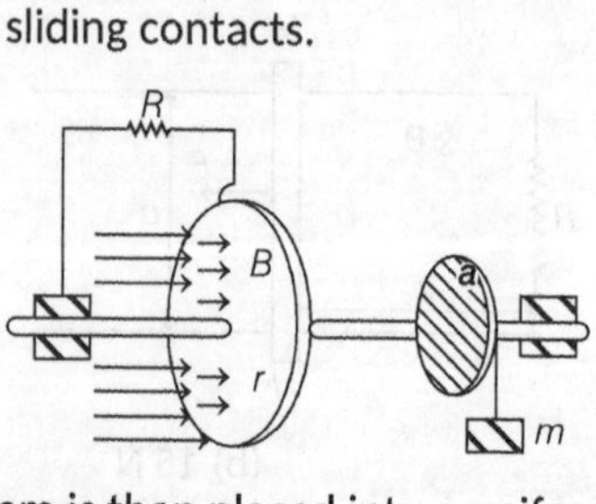

The system is then placed into a uniform horizontal magnetic field B and the mass m is released. Find the terminal angular velocity with which the disc will rotate finally.

(Take, $r = 10$ cm, $a = 2$ cm, $R = 0.01\Omega$, $B = 0.2$ T, $m =$ 50 g, $g = 10$ ms^{-2})

(a) 200 rad/s

(b) 300 rad/s

(c) 100 rad/s

(d) 10 rad/s

22 A thin strip 20 cm long is on a U-shaped wire of negligible resistance and it is connected to a spring of spring constant 0.5 N/m (see figure). The assembly is kept in a uniform magnetic field of 0.1T. If the strip is pulled from its equilibrium position and released, the number of oscillations it performs before its amplitude decreases by a factor of e is N. If the mass of strip is 50 g, its resistance 40Ω and air drag negligible, N will be close to

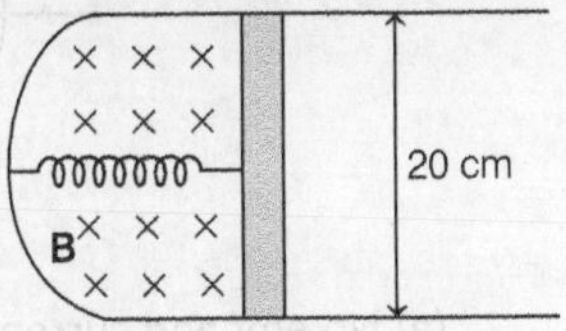

(a) 2000 (b) 5000 (c) 8000 (d) 10000

23 A closely and uniformly wound coil is in the form of a spiral of inner radius a and outer radius b as shown in the figure. The coil is having N turns and is placed in a time varying magnetic field $B = B_0 t$. The emf induced in the coil is

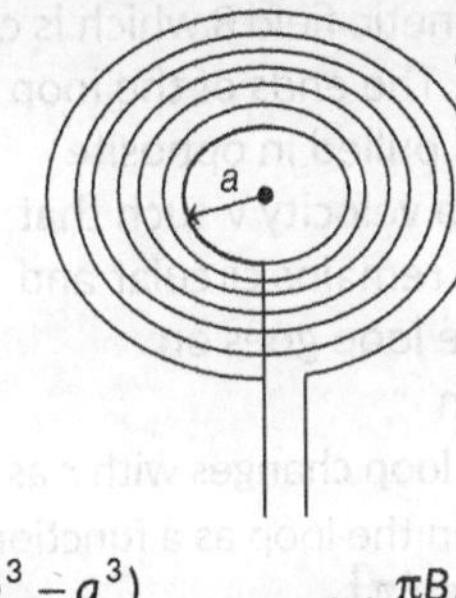

(a) $\dfrac{\pi B_0 N(b^3 - a^3)}{3(b-a)^2}$ (b) $\dfrac{\pi B_0 N(b^2 + a^2 + ab)}{3}$

(c) $\dfrac{\pi B_0 N}{3}$ (d) $\dfrac{\pi B_0 N(b^2 - a^2)}{2}$

24 A magnetic field, confined in a cylindrical region of radius R, is changing at the rate of 4 T/s. A conducting rod PQ of length $\sqrt{\dfrac{3}{2}}R$ is placed in the region as shown. The induced emf across the rod will be

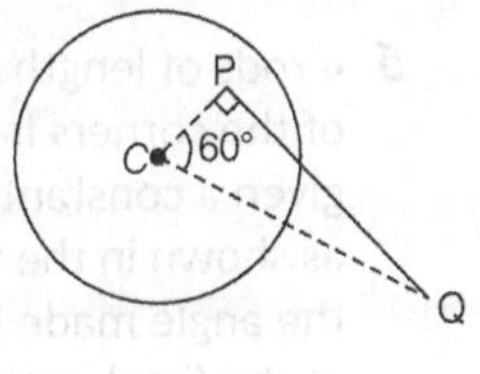

(a) $\dfrac{R^2}{24}(\pi + 6)$ V (b) $\dfrac{R^2\pi}{24}$ V

(c) $\dfrac{R^2\pi}{6}$ V (d) $\dfrac{R^2}{6}(\pi + 6)$ V

25 A triangular wire frame (each side = 2m) is placed in a region of time variant magnetic field having $\dfrac{dB}{dt} = \sqrt{3}$ T/s. The magnetic field is perpendicular to the plane of the triangle. The base of the triangle AB has a resistance 1Ω while the other two sides have resistance 2Ω each. The magnitude of potential difference between the points A and B will be

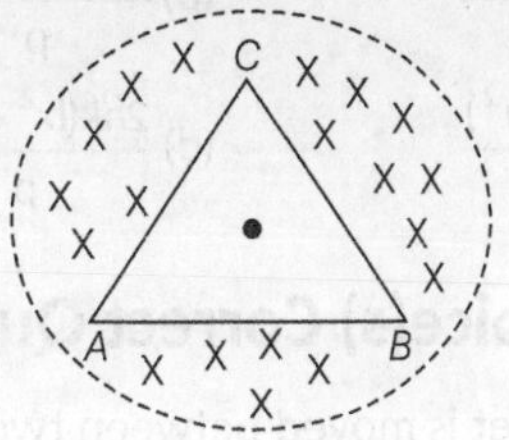

(a) 0.4 V (b) 0.6 V
(c) 1 V (d) 1.4 V

26 A uniform disc of radius r and mass m is charged uniformly with the charge q. This disc is placed flat on a rough horizontal surface having coefficient of friction μ. A uniform magnetic field is present in a circular region of radius $a(> r)$ but varying as kt^3 as shown in figure. Find the time after which the disc begins to rotate. (Given r = 1 m, m = 18 kg, q = 1C, μ = 0.1, k = 4, g = 10 ms^{-2})

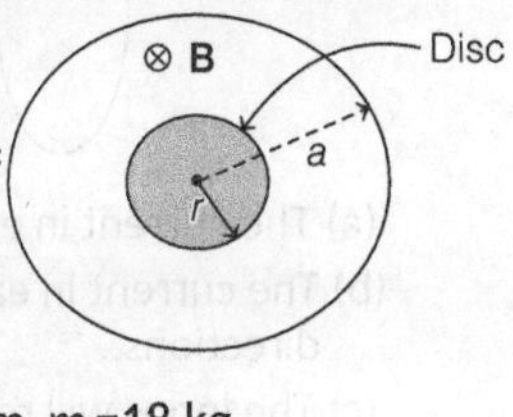

(a) 2 s (b) 4 s
(c) 8 s (d) None of these

27 A long solenoid of cross-sectional radius R has a thin insulated wire ring tightly put on its winding. One half of the ring has the resistance 10 times that of the other half. The magnetic induction produced by the solenoid varies with time as $B = bt$, where b is a constant. Find the magnitude of the electric field strength in the ring.

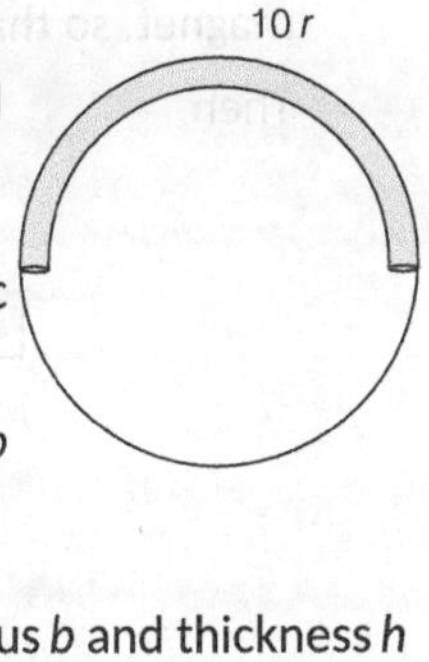

(a) $\dfrac{9}{11}Rb$ (b) $\dfrac{9}{22}Rb$
(c) 9 Rb (d) Rb

28 A ring of inner radius a outer radius b and thickness h is made of a material whose resistivity is ρ. The ring is placed in a uniform magnetic field (circular symmetry) varying in time. The magnetic field is directed along the axis of the ring and is given by $B = kt$, where k is a

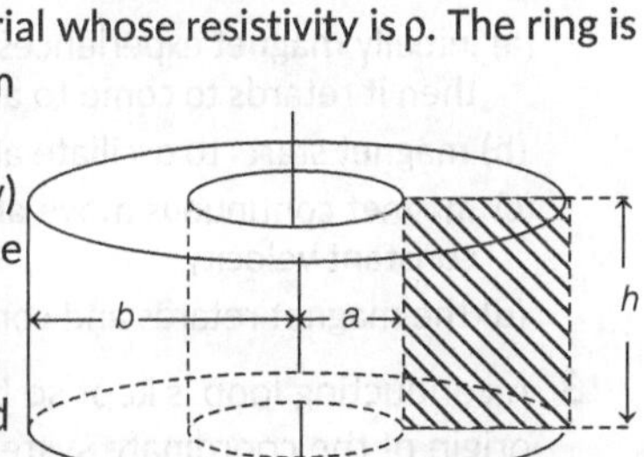

positive constant and t is time. What is the current induced in the ring?

(a) $\frac{hk(b^2-a^2)}{2\rho}$ (b) $\frac{hk(b^2-a^2)}{\rho}$

(c) $\frac{hk(b^2-a^2)}{4\rho}$ (d) $\frac{2hk(b^2-a^2)}{\rho}$

Multiple Choice(s) Correct Questions

1 A bar magnet is moved between two parallel circular loops A and B with a constant velocity v as shown in figure.

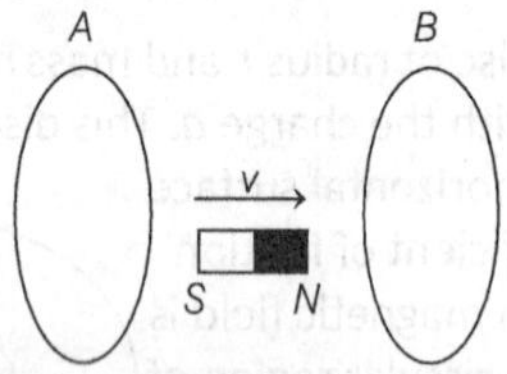

(a) The current in each loop flows in the same direction
(b) The current in each loop flows in the opposite directions.
(c) The loops will repel each other
(d) The loops attract each other

2 A conducting ring is fixed in a gravity free space and one point of the ring is earthed. Now a magnet is placed along axis of the ring at a distance from its centre such that the nearer pole is north pole as shown in figure. A sharp impulse is applied on the magnet, so that it starts to move towards the ring. Then

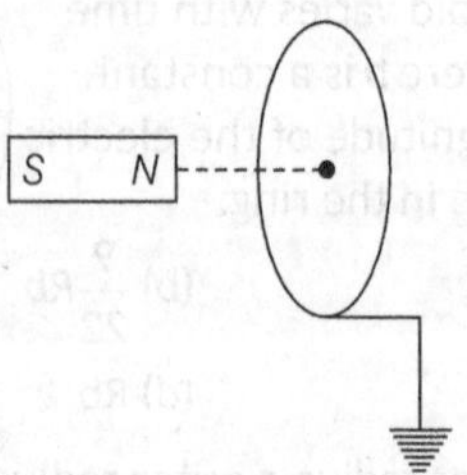

(a) initially magnet experiences an acceleration and then it retards to come to an instantaneous rest
(b) magnet starts to oscillate about centre of the ring
(c) magnet continuous move along the axis with constant velocity
(d) the magnet retards and comes to rest finally

3 A conducting loop is kept so that its center lies at the origin of the coordinate system. A magnetic field has the induction B pointing along Z-axis as shown in the figure.

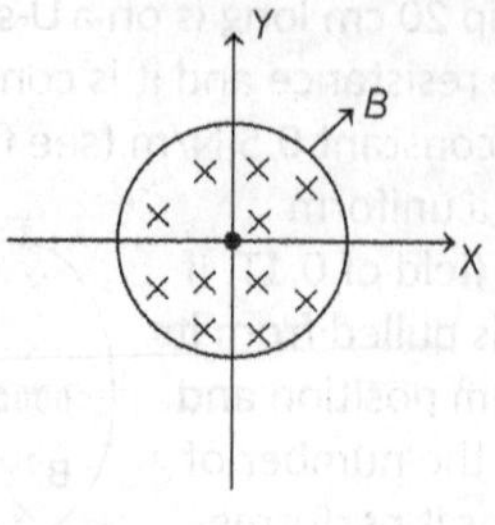

(a) No emf and current will be induced in the loop if it rotates about Z-axis.
(b) Emf is induced but no current flows if the loop is a fiber when it rotates about Y-axis.
(c) Emf is induced and induced current flows in the loop if the loop is made of copper and is rotated about Y-axis.
(d) If the loop moves along Z-axis with constant velocity, no current flows in it.

4 A circular conducting loop of radius r_0 and having resistance per unit length λ as shown in the figure is placed in a magnetic field B which is constant in space and time. The ends of the loop are crossed and pulled in opposite directions with a velocity v such that the loop always remains circular and the radius of the loop goes on decreasing, then

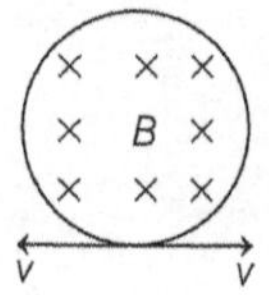

(a) radius of the loop changes with r as $r = r_0 - vt/\pi$
(b) emf induced in the loop as a function of time is $\varepsilon = 2Bv[r_0 - vt/\pi]$
(c) current induced in the loop is $i = \frac{Bv}{2\pi\lambda}$
(d) current induced in the loop is $i = \frac{Bv}{\pi\lambda}$

5 4 rods of length l are hinged to form a rhombus. One of the corners is held fixed and the opposite corner is given a constant velocity v as shown in the figure. 2θ is the angle made by the rods at the fixed corner. A magnetic field B_0 exists perpendicular to the plane of rhombus. Then

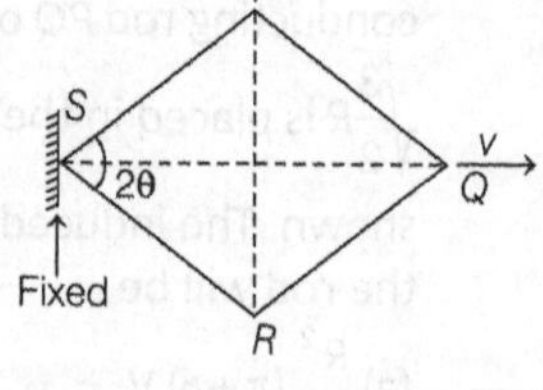

(a) angular velocity of rod PS is $\frac{v}{2l\sin\theta}$
(b) angular velocity of rod PS is $\frac{v}{2l\cos\theta}$
(c) total emf induced in the loop is $\frac{B_0 l v\cos 2\theta}{\cos\theta}$
(d) total emf induced in the loop is $\frac{B_0 l v\cos 2\theta}{\sin\theta}$

6 A plane rectangular loop is placed in a magnetic field. The emf induced in the loop due to this field is ε_i whose maximum value is ε_{im}. The loop was pulled out of the magnetic field at a variable velocity. Assume that $\mathbf{B}$ is uniform and constant. ε_i is plotted against t as shown in the graph.

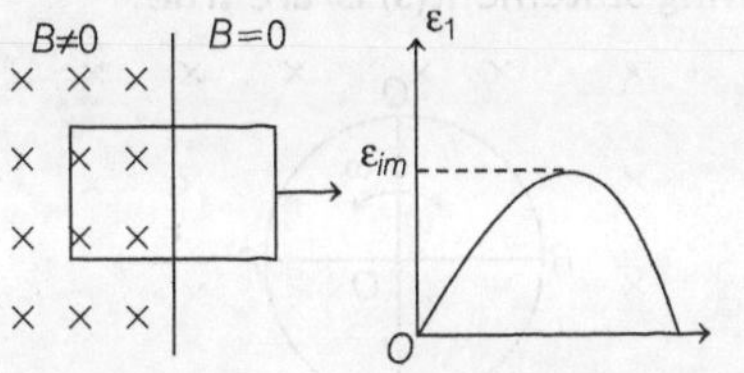

Which of the following are/is correct statement(s)?

(a) ε_{im} is independent of rate of removal of coil from the field.

(b) The total charge that passes through any point of the loop in the process of complete removal of the loop does not depend on velocity of removal.

(c) The total area under the curve (ε_i vs t) is independent of rate of removal of coil from the field.

(d) The area under the curve is dependent on the rate of removal of the coil.

7 The conductor $ABCD$ has the shape shown. It lies in the YZ-plane, with A and E on the Y-axis. When it moves with a velocity v in a magnetic field B, an emf ε is induced between A and E.

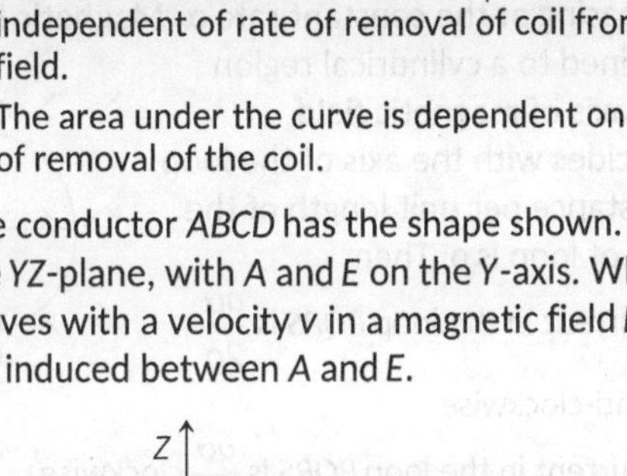

(a) $\varepsilon = 0$, if v is in the Y-direction and B is in the x-direction

(b) $\varepsilon = 2\,Bav$, if v is in the Y-direction and B is in the x-direction

(c) $\varepsilon = B\lambda v$, if v is in Z-direction and B is in the x-direction

(d) $\varepsilon = B\lambda v$, if v is in the X-direction and B is in the z-direction

8 In the figure shown, the wires P_1Q_1 and P_2Q_2 are made to slide on the rails with same speed of 5 cm/s. In this region a magnetic field of 1 T exists. The electric current in the 9Ω resistance is

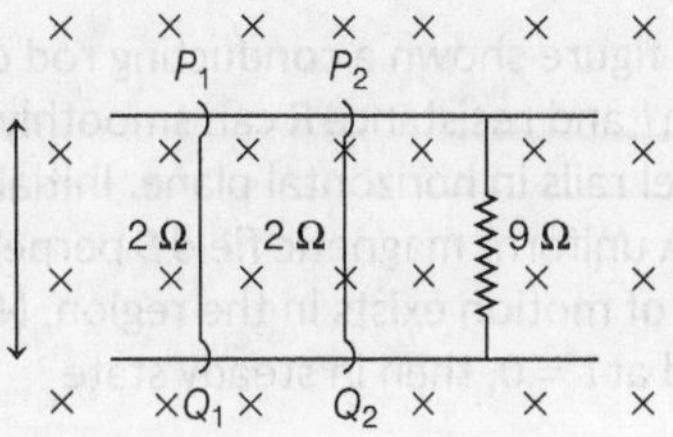

(a) zero if both wires slide towards left

(b) zero if both wires slide in opposite direction

(c) 0.2 mA if both wires move towards left

(d) 0.2 mA if both wires move in opposite direction

9 A conductor AB of mass 1 kg is sliding over two parallel conducting rails separated by a distance of 1m and is in a region of inward uniform magnetic field $\mathbf{B} = 0.1(-\hat{k})$. At time $t = 0$, AB is projected towards right with speed v_0.

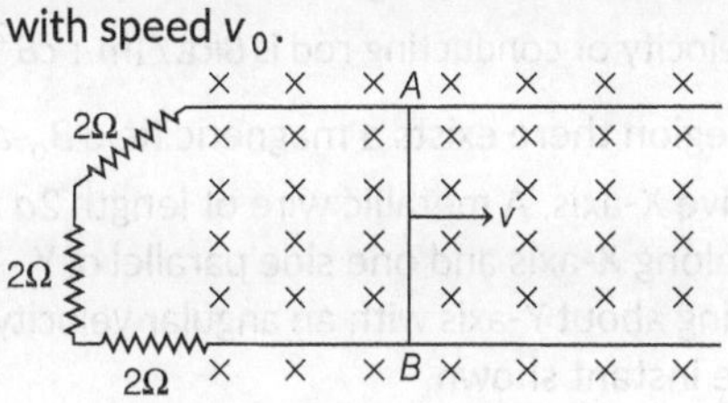

(a) The velocity of AB as a function of time is given as $v = v_0 e^{-\frac{t}{600}}$

(b) The velocity of rod becomes $v_0/2$ at $t = 600\ln 2$

(c) The induced current is $v_0/120$ at $t = 600\ln 2$

(d) The induced emf as a function of time is given as $\left(\dfrac{v_0}{10}\right)e^{-\frac{t}{600}}$

10 A square loop of finite resistance at time $t = 0$ starts moving parallel to X-axis with a constant acceleration $1\ m/s^2$ as shown in a space, where magnetic field is changing with position and time according to relations $\dfrac{dB}{dt} = 10^{-3}\ T/s$, $\dfrac{dB}{dx} = -10^{-3}\ T/m$.

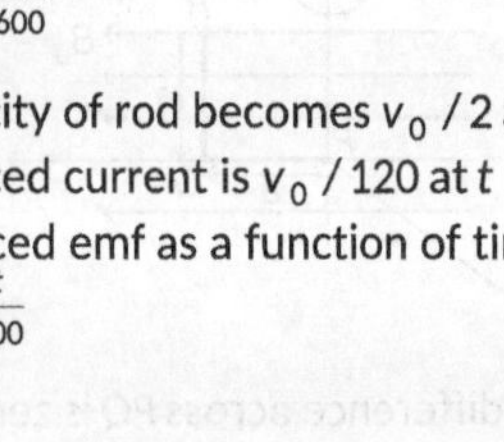

(a) Initially current in loop is anti-clockwise

(b) Initially current in loop is clockwise

(c) At t = 1s, current in loop is zero

(d) After $t > 1$s current is anti-clockwise

11 In the figure shown a conducting rod of mass m, length l and resistance R can smoothly move along parallel rails in horizontal plane. Initially, the rod is at rest. A uniform magnetic field B perpendicular to the plane of motion exists in the region. Now switch S is closed at $t = 0$, then in steady state

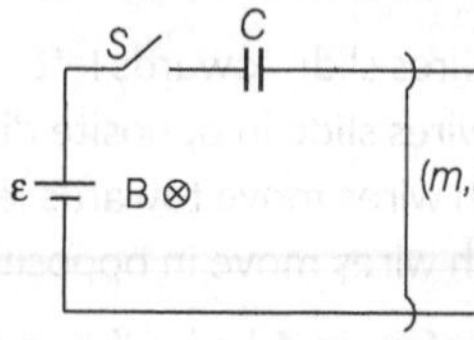

(a) the charge on the capacitor is $mc\varepsilon/(m + cB^2l^2)$
(b) the charge on the capacitor is $2mc\varepsilon/(m + cB^2l^2)$
(c) velocity of conducting rod is $2Blc\varepsilon/(m + cB^2l^2)$
(d) velocity of conducting rod is $Blc\varepsilon/(m + cB^2l^2)$

12 In a region there exists a magnetic field B_0 along positive X-axis. A metallic wire of length $2a$ and one side along X-axis and one side parallel of Y–axis is rotating about Y-axis with an angular velocity ω. Then at the instant shown,

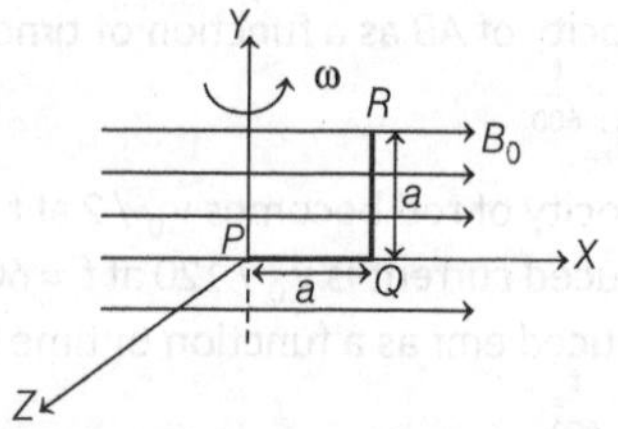

(a) potential difference across PQ is zero.
(b) potential difference across PQ is $B_0\omega a^2/2$.
(c) potential difference across QR is $B_0\omega a^2/2$.
(d) potential difference across QR is $B_0\omega a^2$.

13 In figure, there is a conducting ring having resistance R placed in the plane of paper in a uniform magnetic field B_0. If the ring is rotating in the plane of paper about an axis passing through point O and perpendicular to the plane of paper with constant angular speed ω in clockwise direction.

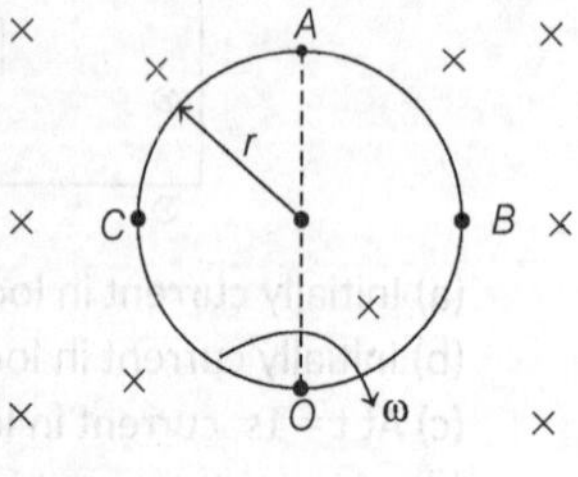

(a) Point A will be at higher potential than O.
(b) The potential of point B and C will be same.
(c) The current in ring will be zero.
(d) The current in the ring will be $2B_0\omega r^2/R$.

14 A disc of radius R is rolling without sliding on a horizontal surface with a velocity of center of mass v and angular velocity ω in a uniform magnetic field B which is perpendicular to the plane of the disc as shown in figure. O is the center of the disc and P, Q, R and S are the four points on the disc. Which of the following statement(s) is/are true?

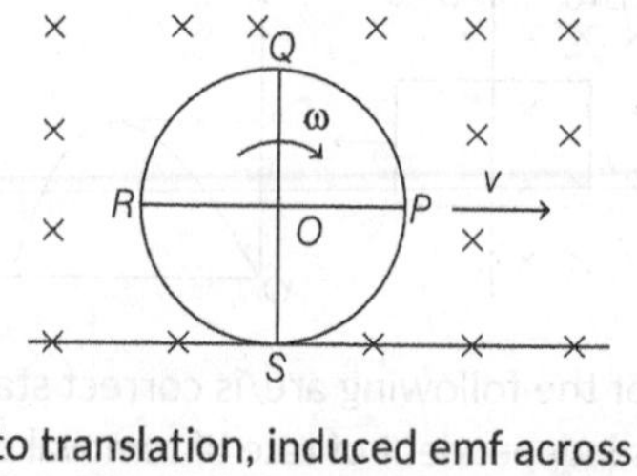

(a) Due to translation, induced emf across $PS = Bvr$
(b) Due to rotation, induced emf across $QS = 0$
(c) Due to translation, induced emf across $RO = 0$
(d) Due to rotation, induced emf across $OQ = Bvr$

15 The radius of the circular loop is a. Magnetic field is increasing at the constant rate α. Magnetic field is confined to a cylindrical region and axis of magnetic field coincides with the axis of the loop. Resistance per unit length of the wire of loop is ρ. Then

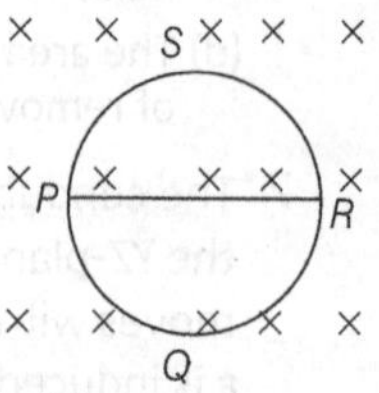

(a) current in the loop $PQRS$ is $\dfrac{a\alpha}{2\rho}$ anti-clockwise
(b) current in the loop $PQRS$ is $\dfrac{a\alpha}{\rho}$ clockwise
(c) current in the wire PR is zero
(d) current in the wire PR is $\dfrac{\pi a\alpha}{2\rho}$

16 Four identical charged particles each of mass 0.1 kg and charge 2 C connected to each other via massless non-conducting rods of equal length. The whole arrangement is placed in a cylindrical region carrying a uniform magnetic field as shown in the figure ($B_0 = 4\,\text{T}, a = 1\text{m}$) Suddenly the magnetic field is switched off. Then choose the correct statement(s)

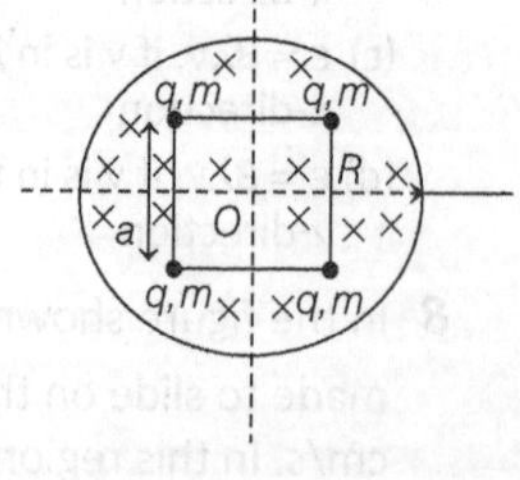

(a) the angular momentum of the system is 8 Nm/s
(b) the angular momentum of the system is $8\sqrt{2}$ Nm/s
(c) Angular velocity of the system is 40 rad/s
(d) the magnetic field at point O immediately after the magnetic field is switched off is non-zero.

17 A uniform conducting ring of mass $m = 2$ kg, radius $r = 2$ m and resistance 8Ω is kept on smooth, horizontal surface. A time varying magnetic field $\mathbf{B} = (\hat{i} + t^2\hat{j})$ T is present in the region, where t is time in second and take vertical as Y-axis. (Take $\pi^2 = 10$). Then
(a) time when ring starts toppling is 1 s.
(b) time when ring starts toppling is 3/4 s.
(c) heat generated through the ring till the instant when the ring start toppling is 40/3 J.
(d) heat generated through the ring till the instant when the ring start toppling is 80/3 J.

Comprehension Based Questions

Comprehension-1

Figure below shows a circular wire loop of radius $r = 0.1$ m with $N = 100$ turns and resistance $R = 2\,\Omega$.

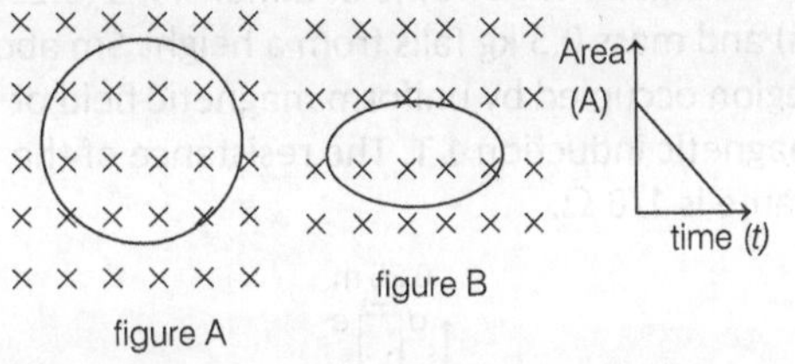

The plane of the loop coincides with the plane of paper. There is a uniform magnetic field $B = 4$ T perpendicular to the plane of the paper and directed into page. Since, the loop is flexible copper wire, you can grab it on opposite sides and pull it flat. Figure B shows the loop when you are in the middle of pulling it flat. You can assume that with no magnetic field, it would take almost no work to pull the loop flat. Figure C shows now the area enclosed by the loop changes with time. It starts at its initial area and drops linearly to zero in Δt = 3s.

1 While you are flattening the loop, there is an induced current in the loop. The induced current
(a) is anti-clockwise
(b) will increase during flattening the loop
(c) will decrease during flattening the loop
(D) will remain same during flattening the loop

2 At t = 2 s the magnitude of current is
(a) 2.09 A (b) 6.08 A
(c) 1.09 A (d) 0.09 A

3 Average force required to flatten it is
(a) 111N (b) 231 N
(c) 350 N (d) 160 N

Comprehension-2

The mobile side of the triangular conducting frame shown in the figure is sliding at uniform speed of v = 0.1 m/s along the other two sides. This horizontal frame is in a vertical homogeneous magnetic field with an induction of $B = 0.4$ T. Resistance per unit length is 1Ω/m. Initially at $t = 0$ sliding rod was at O.

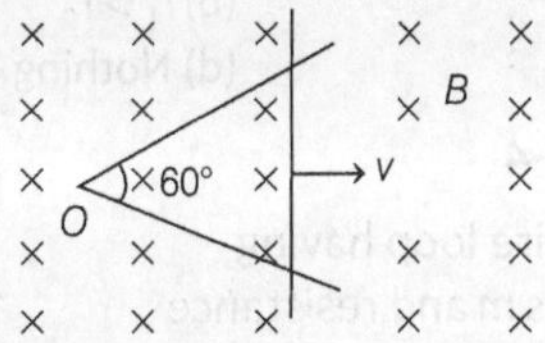

4 How does induced emf vary with time?
(a) Increases with time
(b) Decreases with time
(c) Remains constant
(d) Initially increases then decreases

5 Induced current in frame
(a) increases with time
(b) decreases with time
(c) remains constant
(d) initially increases then decreases

6 Work required for sliding during 10 s
(a) 3.1×10^{-3} J (b) 9.1×10^{-3} J
(c) 12.1×10^{-3} J (d) 14.1×10^{-3} J

Comprehension-3

The adjoining figure shows two different arrangements in which two square wire frames of same resistance are placed in a uniform constantly decreasing magnetic field B.

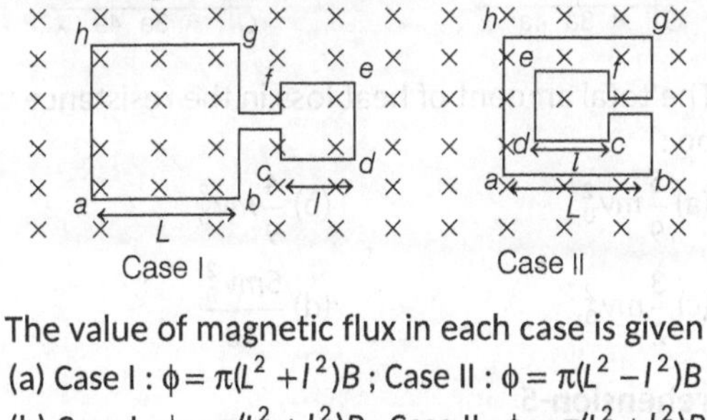

7 The value of magnetic flux in each case is given by
(a) Case I : $\phi = \pi(L^2 + l^2)B$; Case II : $\phi = \pi(L^2 - l^2)B$;
(b) Case I : $\phi = \pi(L^2 + l^2)B$; Case II : $\phi = \pi(L^2 + l^2)B$;
(c) Case I : $\phi = (L^2 + l^2)B$; Case II : $\phi = (L^2 - l^2)B$;
(d) Case I : $\phi = (L + l)^2 B$; Case II : $\phi = (L - l)^2 B$;

8 The direction of induced current in the case I is
(a) from a to b and from c to d
(b) from a to b and from f to e
(c) from b to a and from d to c
(d) from b to a and from e to f

9 The direction of induced current in the case II is
(a) from a to b and from c to d
(b) from b to a and from f to e
(c) from b to a and from c to d
(d) from a to b and from d to c

10 If i_1 and i_2 are the magnitudes of induced current in the cases I and II, respectively, then
(a) $i_1 = i_2$ (b) $i_1 > i_2$
(c) $i_1 < i_2$ (d) Nothing can be said

Comprehension-4

A square wire loop having side a, mass m and resistance R is moving along positive X-axis with speed v_0 enters uniform steady magnetic field $\mathbf{B} = B_0(-\hat{\mathbf{k}})$ at $t = 0$ s as shown in the figure. The magnitude of v_0 is sufficient so that the loop comes out from region of magnetic field with v_1. Neglect any type of energy loss other than heat loss in resistances of wires of square (given : $v_0 = 3B^2a^3/mR$)

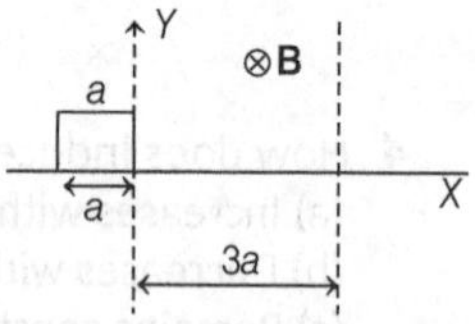

11 The plot of speed of square loop *versus* position x will be represented by

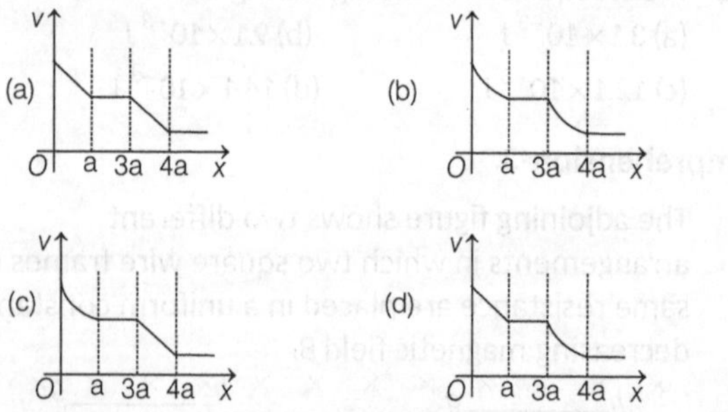

12 The total amount of heat loss in the resistance will be :
(a) $\frac{5}{9}mv_0^2$ (b) $\frac{4}{9}mv_0^2$
(c) $\frac{3}{2}mv_0^2$ (d) $\frac{5mv_0^2}{18}$

Comprehension-5

A train of mass 100 tons (1 ton = 1000 kg) runs on a meter gauge track (distance between the two rails is 1 m.) The coefficient of friction between the rails and the train is 0.045. The train is powered by an electric engine of 90% efficiency. The train is moving with uniform speed of 72 km/h at its highest speed limit. Horizontal and vertical component of earth's magnetic field are $B_H = 10^{-5}$ T and $B_v = 2\times10^{-5}$ T. Assume the body of the train and rails to be perfectly conducting.

13 The electrical power consumed by the train is
(a) 1.11 MW (b) 1 MW
(c) 0.50 MW (d) 0.90 MW

14 The potential difference between the two rails is
(a) 0.1 mV (b) 0.2 mV
(c) 0.4 mV (d) 0.8 mV

15 If now a resistor of 10^{-3} Ω is attached between the two rails, the extra units of energy (electricity) consumed during a 360 km run of the train is (1 unit of power = 1 kWh) (assume the speed of train to remain unchanged)
(a) 8×10^{-4} k Wh (b) 8×10^{-5} kWh
(c) 8×10^{-6} kWh (d) 8×10^{-7} kWh

Comprehension-6

A rectangular wire frame of dimensions (0.25m × 2.0 m) and mass 0.5 kg falls from a height 5m above a region occupied by uniform magnetic field of magnetic induction 1 T. The resistance of the wire frame is 1/8 Ω.

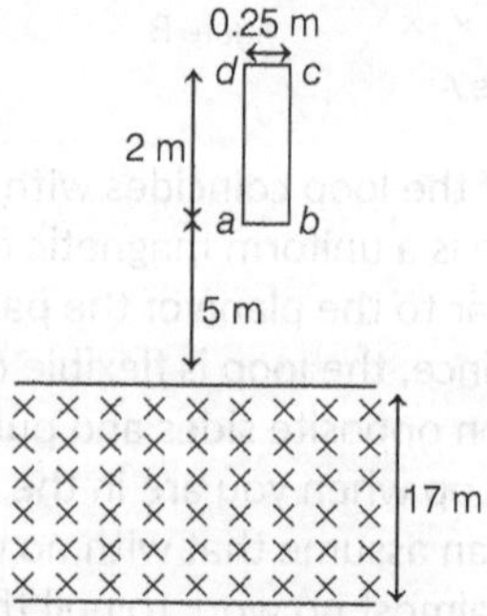

16 Time taken to completely enter into the field is
(a) 0.2 s (b) 1 s (c) 2.2 s (d) $\sqrt{0.2}$ s

17 Time taken by the wire frame when it just starts coming out of the magnetic field is
(a) 0.2 s (b) 1 s (c) 2.2 s (d) $\sqrt{0.2}$ s

Comprehension-7

Consider a square loop of wire with dimension a. One side of which is parallel to a long straight wire carrying current i_0, at a distance a. The resistance of the loop is R. Neglect the self-inductance of the loop.

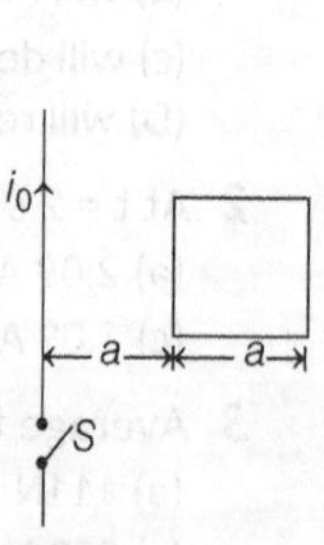

Initially switch S was closed and at $t = 0$, it is opened.

18 What is the net amount of charge that will flow after t = 0 through a fixed cross-section of the wire of the loop?

(a) $\dfrac{\mu_0 i_0 \ln(2) a}{\pi R}$ (b) $\dfrac{2\mu_0 i_0 \ln(2) a}{\pi R}$

(c) $\dfrac{\mu_0 i_0 \ln(2) a}{2\pi R}$ (d) $\dfrac{4\mu_0 i_0 \ln(2) a}{\pi R}$

19 What is the net momentum p given to the loop during the switching-off of the current?

(a) $\dfrac{\mu_0^2 i_0^2 \times \ln(2) a}{2\pi^2 R}$ (b) $\dfrac{\mu_0^2 i_0^2 \times \ln(2) a}{4\pi^2 R}$

(c) $\dfrac{\mu_0^2 i_0^2 \times \ln(2) a}{\pi^2 R}$ (d) $\dfrac{\mu_0^2 i_0^2 \times \ln(2) a}{8\pi^2 R}$

Comprehension-8

A circular loop of wire of radius a is bent about its diameter such that the angle between the two halves becomes 60°. The resistance per unit length of the wire is r_0. A uniform magnetic field directed along (+) Z-axis, is varying as $B = B_0 t$. (Neglect self-inductance of the loops)

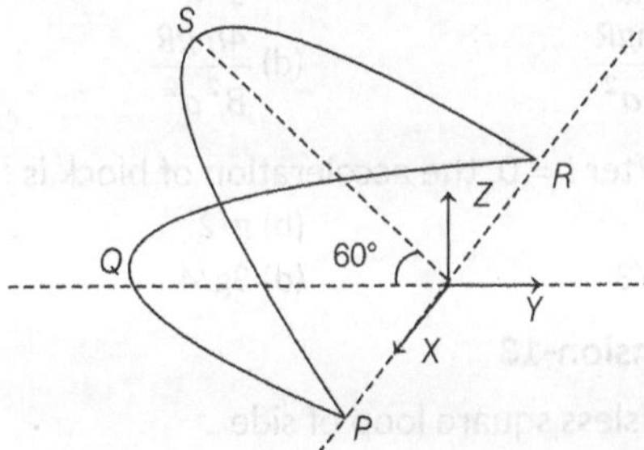

20 Magnitude of induced emf in the loop is

(a) $\dfrac{B_0 \pi a^2}{8}$ (b) $\dfrac{B_0 \pi a^2}{4}$

(c) $\dfrac{B_0 \pi a^2}{2}$ (d) $2B_0 \pi a^2$

21 If the system is maintained in the position shown at all the time the external torque needed to keep the loop in the position shown at any time t is

(a) $\dfrac{\sqrt{3} B_0^2 \pi a^3 t}{32 r_0}$ (b) $\dfrac{\sqrt{3} B_0^2 \pi^2 a^4 t}{16 r_0}$

(c) $\dfrac{B_0^2 \pi^2 a^4 t}{16 r_0}$ (d) $\dfrac{B_0^2 \pi a^3 t}{32 r_0}$

Comprehension-9

Figure shows a conducting rod of negligible resistance that can slide on smooth U-shaped rails made of wire of resistance $1\Omega / \text{m}$. Position of the conducting rod at $t = 0$ is shown. A time t dependent magnetic field $B = 2t$ T is switched on at $t = 0$.

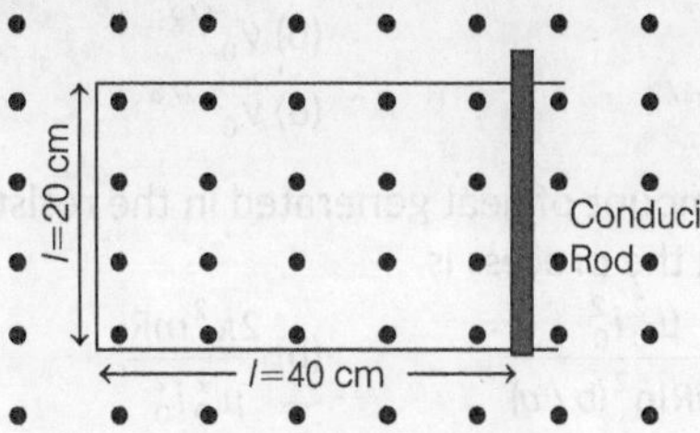

22 The current in the loop at $t = 0$ due to induced emf is

(a) 0.16 A, clockwise

(b) 0.08 A, clockwise

(c) 0.08 A, anti-clockwise

(d) zero

23 At $t = 0$, when the magnetic field is switched on, the conducting rod is moved to the left at constant speed 5 cm/s by some external means. The rod moves perpendicular to the rails.
At $t = 2$ s, induced emf has magnitude :

(a) 0.12 V (b) 0.08 V

(c) 0.04 V (d) 0.24 V

24 Following situation of the previous question, the magnitude of the force required to move the conducting rod at constant speed 5 cm/s at $t = 5$ s, is equal to

(a) 0.48 N (b) 0.12 N

(c) 0.08 N (d) 0.16 N

Comprehension-10

A long straight wire carries a current i_0. At distances a and b from it, there are two other wires, parallel to the former one, which are interconnected by a resistance R. A connector of mass m slides without friction along the wires with a initial velocity v_0 at time $t = 0$. Assuming the resistances of the wires, the connector, the sliding contacts and the self-inductances of the frame to be negligible

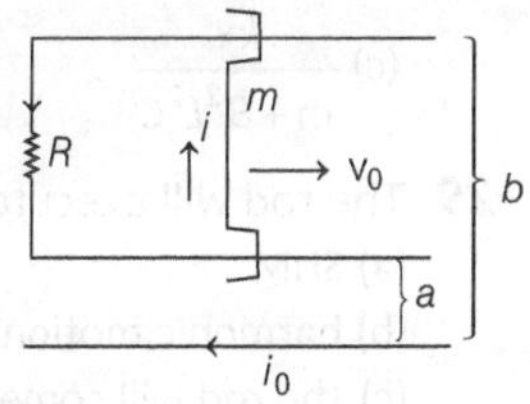

25 The time after which velocity becomes half is

(a) $\dfrac{4\pi^2 mR \ln 2}{\mu_0^2 i_0^2 \ln^2(b/a)}$

(b) infinity

(c) $\dfrac{2\pi^2 mR}{\mu_0^2 i_0^2 \ln(b/a)}$

(d) the motion will be periodic

26 The distance covered by the rod until it comes to rest is proportional to

(a) v_0 (b) $v_0^{1/2}$

(c) $v_0^{-1/2}$ (d) $v_0^{-2/3}$

27 The amount of heat generated in the resistance R during the process is

(a) $\frac{\mu_0^2 i_0^2}{4mR\ln^2(b/a)}$ (b) $\frac{2\pi^2 mR}{\mu_0^2 i_0^2}$

(c) $\frac{mv_0^2}{4}$ (d) None of these

Comprehension-11

The conducting connector *ab* mass *m* and length *L* can freely slide on a horizontal long conducting parallel rails connected by capacitor *C* at one end (as shown in figure). A non-conducting light spring (spring constant *k*) connected to the connector *ab* and it is in a relaxed state. The whole system is placed in uniform magnetic field of strength *B* directed into the plane of rails (as shown in figure). Now at time $t = 0$, connector is suddenly given a velocity v_0 in rightward direction. If resistance of circuit is negligible then

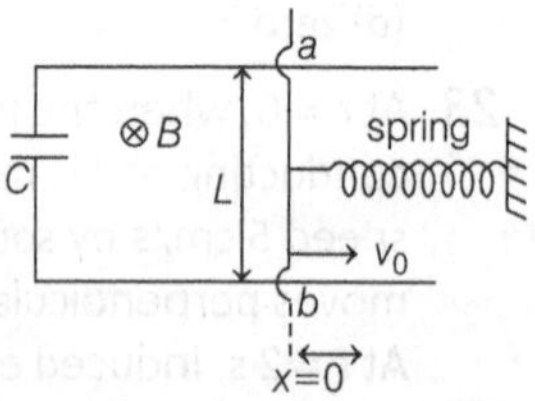

28 The acceleration of connector as a function of x is

(a) $\frac{kx}{m}$ (b) $\frac{kx}{m - B^2L^2C}$

(c) $\frac{kx}{m + B^2L^2C}$ (d) None of these

29 The rod will execute (after projecting it at $t = 0$)

(a) SHM

(b) harmonic motion but not SHM

(c) the rod will come at rest at certain position, then afterward it will not move

(d) None of the above

30 The maximum compression in the spring is

(a) $v_0\sqrt{\frac{m - B^2L^2C}{K}}$ (b) $v_0\sqrt{\frac{m + B^2L^2C}{K}}$

(c) $v_0\sqrt{\frac{m}{K}}$ (d) None of these

Comprehension-12

Consider a perfectly conducting uniform disc of mass *m* and radius *a* hinged in a vertical plane from its centre and free to rotate with respect to hinge. A resistance *R* is connected between centre of the disc and periphery by using two sliding contacts C_1 and C_2. A long non-conducting massless string is wrapped around the disk, whose another end is attached with a block of mass *m*. There exists a uniform horizontal magnetic field *B*, whose arrangement is shown in figure. Given system is released from rest at $t = 0$. Assume friction between string and disc is sufficient, so that there is no slipping between them. Let at any instant *t*, velocity of block is *v*, angular velocity of the disc is ω and current in resistance is *i*.

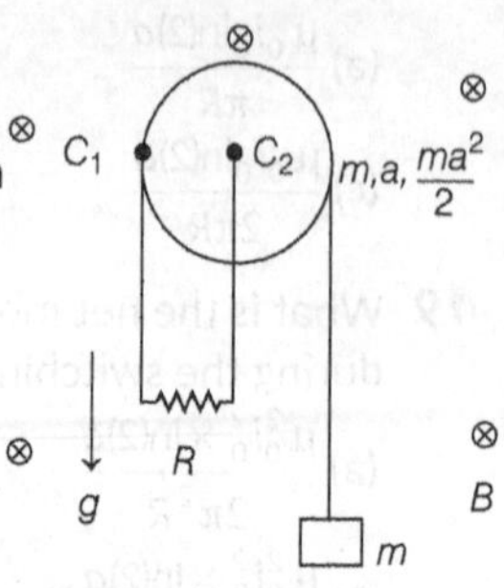

31 The terminal speed of the block of mass *m* is (Terminal speed = constant speed attained by the block after very long time)

(a) $\frac{mgR}{B^2a^2}$ (b) $\frac{2mgR}{B^2a^2}$

(c) $\frac{3mgR}{B^2a^2}$ (d) $\frac{4mgR}{B^2a^2}$

32 Just after $t = 0$, the acceleration of block is

(a) g (b) g/2

(c) 2g/3 (d) 3g/4

Comprehension-13

A massless square loop of side *a* is kept in *XZ*-plane as shown. Magnetic field in space is non-uniform given by $B = \frac{B_0 y}{a}\hat{k}$. The loop is rotated about *X*-axis with constant angular velocity ω.

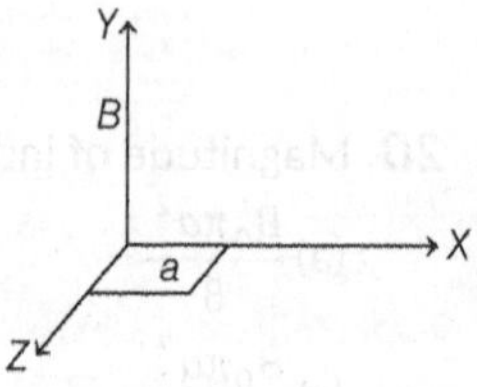

33 Emf induced in the loop as function of time is equal to

(a) $\frac{B_0 a^2}{2}\omega\sin 2\omega t$ (b) $\frac{B_0 a^2 \omega}{2}(1 + \sin 2\omega t)$

(c) $2B_0 a^2 \omega\cos\omega t$ (d) $B_0 a^2 \omega\cos\omega t$

34 Torque required to rotate the loop with constant angular velocity as a function of time is (Take resistance of loop = *R*)

(a) $\frac{B_0^2 a^4 \omega}{4R}(1 + \sin 2\omega t)^2$ (b) $\frac{B_0^2 a^4 \omega}{4R}\sin^2 2\omega t$

(c) $\frac{4B_0^2 a^4 \omega}{R}\cos^2\omega t$ (d) $\frac{B_0^2 a^4 \omega}{R}\cos^4\omega t$

Comprehension-14

A conducting rod PQ of mass M rotates without friction on a horizontal plane about O on circular rails of diameter l. The centre O and the periphery are connected by resistance R. The system is located in a uniform magnetic field perpendicular to the plane of the loop. At $t = 0$, PQ starts rotating clockwise with angular velocity ω_0. Neglect the resistance of the rails and rod, as well as self-inductance. $\left(\alpha = \dfrac{3B^2l^2}{8RM}\right)$

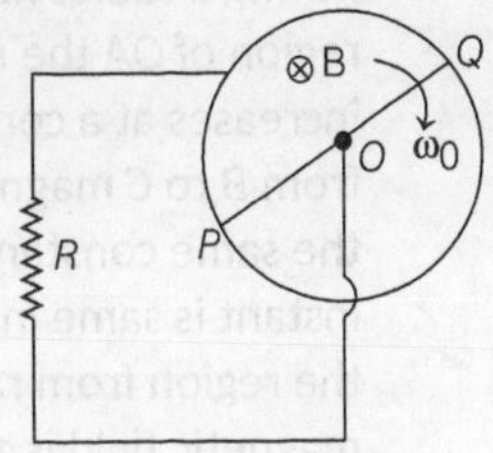

35 Magnitude of current as a function of time is

(a) $\dfrac{B\omega_0 l^2}{2R}e^{-\alpha t}$ (b) $\dfrac{B\omega_0 l^2}{16R}e^{-2\alpha t}$

(c) $\dfrac{B\omega_0 l^2}{8R}e^{-\alpha t}$ (d) $\dfrac{B\omega_0 l^2}{8R}e^{-2\alpha t}$

36 Total charge flown through resistance till rod PQ stop rotating is

(a) $\dfrac{\omega_0 M}{8B}$ (b) $\dfrac{\omega_0 M}{3B}$ (c) $\dfrac{\omega_0 M}{6B}$ (d) $\dfrac{\omega_0 M}{9B}$

37 Heat generated in the circuit by $t = \infty$ is

(a) $\dfrac{Ml^2\omega_0^2}{24}$ (b) $\dfrac{Ml^2\omega_0^2}{8}$ (c) $\dfrac{Ml^2\omega_0^2}{3}$ (d) $\dfrac{Ml^2\omega_0^2}{32}$

Match the Columns Questions

1 Magnetic flux in a circular coil of resistance 100Ω changes with time as shown in figure. Then match the following columns

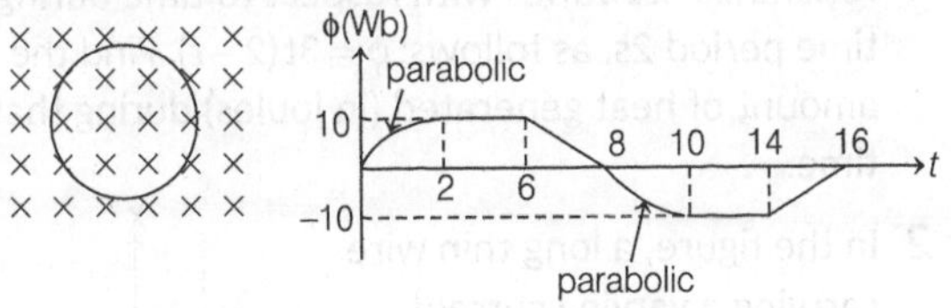

Column I	Column II
(a) At 1s induced current is	(P) Clockwise
(b) At 5s induced current is	(Q) Anti-clockwise
(c) At 9s induced current is	(R) Zero
(d) At 15s induced current is	(S) Magnitude is linearly Increasing
	(T) Magnitude is linearly decreasing

2 A circular conducting coil of radius 1m and resistance 1Ω is placed such that half of its area is in a region of uniform magnetic field $B_1\,(\hat{k})$ and the remaining half is in another region of uniform magnetic field $B_2\,(-\hat{k})$ as shown in figure. Column I shows values of B_1 and B_2 as a function of time t, (for $t \geq 0$), while Column II predicts possible directions of current and magnitude of force.

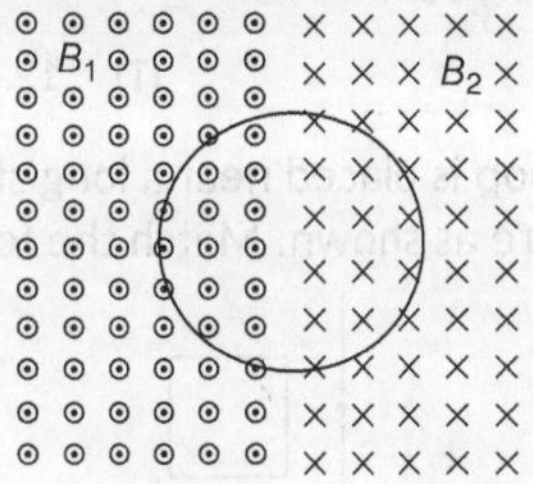

Column I	Column II
(a) $B_1 = 0; B_2 = 10$	(P) Current either always clockwise or always zero or always anti-clockwise.
(b) $B_1 = 10;$ $B_2 = 10t + 14$	(Q) Current sometimes clockwise, some times anti-clockwise, and at some time zero
(c) $B_1 = t^2;$ $B_2 = t^2 + 4$	(R) Force may be non-zero
(d) $B_1 = t^2;$ $B_2 = 4t + 4$	(S) Force must be non-zero

3 A uniform wire of length l can be bent into several configurations as shown in Column I to form a closed loop. The loop is kept in the time varying magnetic field $B = B_0 t^2$. Due to some phenomenon, the length of the wire is also changing with time as $l = l_0 t$. Column II gives the induced emf for the various situation. (given $B_0 = 0.1$ SI unit, $l_0 = 5$ SI unit, $\pi^2 = 10$)

Column I	Column II
(a) 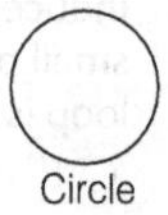 Circle at $t = \pi$ s	(P) 2.5 SI unit
(b) 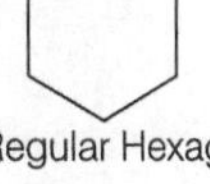 Regular Hexagon at $t = \sqrt{3}$ s	(Q) 25 SI unit

(c)	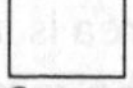 Square at $t = 2$ s	(R)	3.75 SI unit
(d)	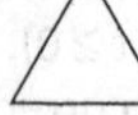 Equilateral triangle at $t = \sqrt{3}$ s	(S)	5 SI unit
		(T)	12.5 SI unit

4 A square loop is placed near a long straight current carrying wire as shown. Match the following

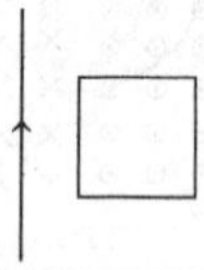

	Column I		Column II
(a)	If current is increased	(P)	Induced current in loop is clockwise
(b)	If current is decreased	(Q)	Induced current in loop is anti-clockwise
(c)	If loop is moved away from the wire	(R)	Wire will attract the loop
(d)	If loop is moved toward the wire	(S)	Wire will repel the loop
		(T)	None of these

5

	Column I		Column II
(a)	A circular conducting loop rotating about its axis in a uniform constant magnetic field perpendicular to its plane.	(P)	Net induced emf in the loop is non zero
(b)	A circular conducting loop moving along its plane in pure translation in a uniform constant magnetic field perpendicular to its plane.	(Q)	Net induced emf is zero but a small part of the loop may have some emf induced across it
(c)	A circular conducting loop placed in a magnetic field perpendicular to its plane which is decreasing with time	(R)	Induced emf in any small part of the loop is zero.
(d)	A square conducting loop rotating about its side in a uniform constant magnetic field perpendicular to its axis. Consider a time when the plane of the loop is parallel to the magnetic field.	(S)	Induced electric field outside the conductor is zero.
		(T)	Current flows in the loop

6 In the diagram shown the inner cylindrical region is having a radius R. $OB = 2R$, $OC = 3R$. In the circular region of OA the magnetic field points down and increases at a constant rate α. In the annular space from B to C magnetic field points up and increases at the same constant rate α. Magnetic field at any instant is same in magnitude in both the regions. In the region from radius R to $2R$ and radius > $3R$ the magnetic field is zero. As one travels from O to D along a straight line,

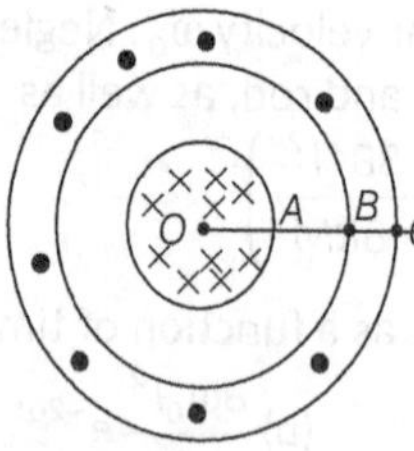

	Column I		Column II
(a)	magnitude of induced electric field increases continuously	(P)	O to A
(b)	magnitude of induced electric field decreases continuously	(Q)	A to B
(c)	magnitude of induced electric field first decreases and then increases	(R)	B to C
(d)	direction of induced electric field changes direction	(S)	C to D

Numerical Value Questions

1 Magnetic flux linked with a stationary loop of resistance 4Ω varies with respect to time during the time period 2s, as follows: $\phi = 3t(2-t)$. Find the amount of heat generated (in joules) during that time.

2 In the figure, a long thin wire carrying a varying current $i = 2\sin 5t$ lies at a distance y above one edge of a rectangular wire loop of length L and width W lying in the XZ-plane.

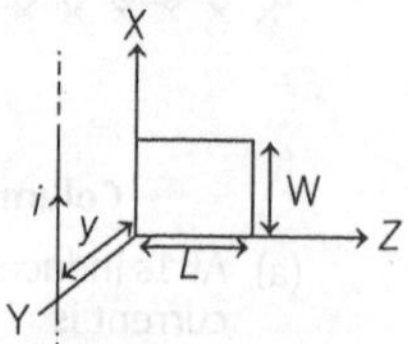

Magnitude of emf (in V) induced in the loop at $t = \frac{\pi}{15}$ s is $\alpha \times 10^{-7} \ln \frac{\beta}{4}$. Then the value of $\left(\frac{\alpha+\beta}{2}\right)$ is

($y = 2$m, $L = 3$m, $W = 1$m).

3 A square loop of side 2 cm with a capacitor of capacity 1 μF is located centrally between two current carrying wires separated by a distance of 6 cm as shown in the figure. When current in wires is $i = 5\sin(50\,\pi t)$ A, then maximum value of the current in square loop is $10^{-k}\,\pi^{2}\log 2$ A. Find the value of k.

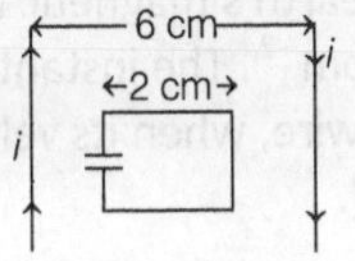

4 The L-shaped conductor as shown in figure moves at a speed of 10 m/s across a stationary L-shaped conductor in a 0.10 T magnetic field. The two vertices overlap, so that the enclosed area is zero at t = 0. The conductor has resistance of 0.010 Ω / m. If the current at $t = 0.10$s is $n\sqrt{2}$ A then find n.

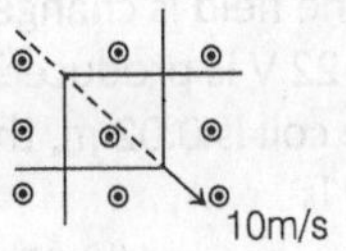

5 A conducting square loop of resistance $R = 50\Omega$ of side $a = 1$ m, with sides parallel to X and Y axis is moved with velocity $v = 1$ m/s in the positive x–direction in a magnetic field along the negative z–direction. The value of magnetic field varies with time as well as along x–direction given by B $(x,t) = 100\,xt$ T where x in meter and t in second. The left edge of the loop is at origin at $t = 0$. Find the value of current induced in the loop at $t = 1$s in ampere.

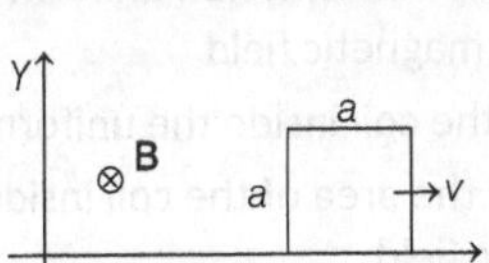

6 An inverted L shaped conductor PRQ is made by joining two perpendicular conducting rods, each of length 1.5 L, at end R. This structure is moving in XY-plane containing variable magnetic field, $\mathbf{B} = -3x\,\hat{\mathbf{k}}$ with a velocity $v\hat{i} + v\hat{j}$. If potential of P is V_P and that of Q is V_Q, then, value of $|V_P - V_Q|$ at the instant when P is at origin as shown in figure is $\alpha\left(\frac{9vL^2}{8}\right)L$.

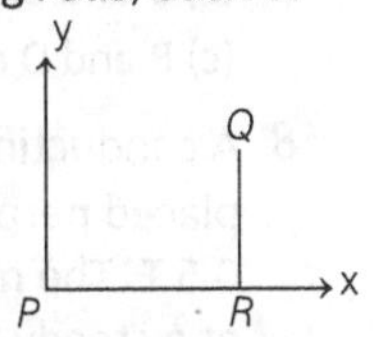

Find α.

7 Two parallel conducting rails are connected to a source of emf E and internal resistance r. Another conducting rod of length l having negligible resistance lies at rest and can slide without friction over the rails. A uniform magnetic field B is applied perpendicular to the plane of the rails. At $t = 0$, the rod is pulled along the rails by applying a force F. The velocity of the rod is observed to be $v = v_0\cos(\omega t)$ then find the power (in watt) spent by the force over 1 cycle. (Given, $B = 2$ T, $r = 2\times10^{-4}\,\Omega$, $v_0 = 2\,ms^{-1}$, l = 1 cm)

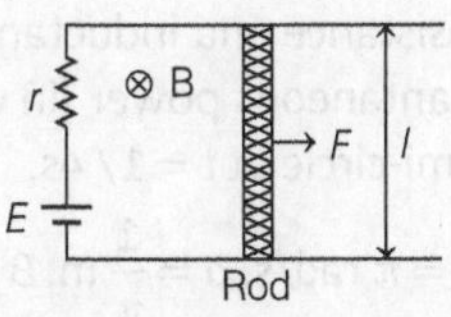

8 A pair of parallel horizontal conducting rails of negligible resistance shorted at one end is fixed on a table. The distance between the rail is L. A conducting massless rod of resistance R can slide on the rails frictionlessly. The rod is tied to massless string which passes over a pulley fixed to the edge of the table. A mass m, tied to the other end of the string hangs vertically. A constant magnetic field B exists perpendicular to the table. If the system is released from rest, calculate the acceleration (in ms^{-2}) of the mass at the instant when the velocity of the rod is half the terminal velocity.

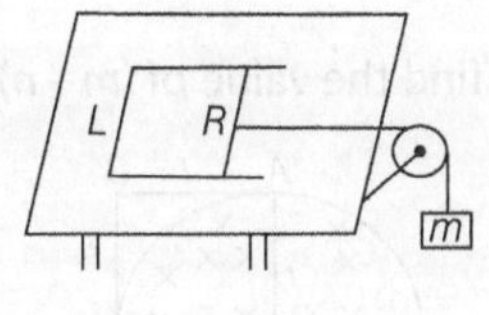

9 A resistance $R = 1\text{k}\Omega$ connected to a conducting rod PQ that can slide on a conducting circular ring of radius 2m with center at P. A constant uniform magnetic field 10 T exist as shown in figure. At t = 0, switch S is closed and simultaneously an external torque is applied on the rod so that it rotates with constant angular velocity 20 rad/s. Find the magnitude of power(in W) delivered by external agent . (Neglect the gravity, friction and self inductance of circular loop)

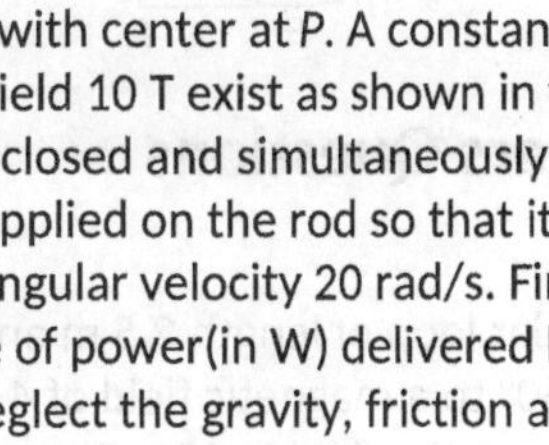

10 A copper rod is bent into a semi-circle of radius a and at ends straight parts are bent along diameter of the semi-circle and are passed through fixed, smooth and conducting rings O and O′ as shown in figure. A capacitor having capacitance C is connected to the rings. The system is located in a uniform magnetic field of induction B such that axis of rotation OO' is perpendicular to the field direction. At initial moment of time ($t = 0$), plane of semi-circle was normal to the field direction and the semi-circle is set in rotation with constant angular velocity ω. Neglecting resistance and inductance of the circuit, calculate instantaneous power (in watt) required to rotate the semi-circle at $t = 1/4$ s.

$$[\text{Take } \omega = \pi \text{ rad/s}, a = \frac{1}{\pi} \text{ m}, B = 4 \text{ T}, C = \frac{1}{\pi} \text{F}]$$

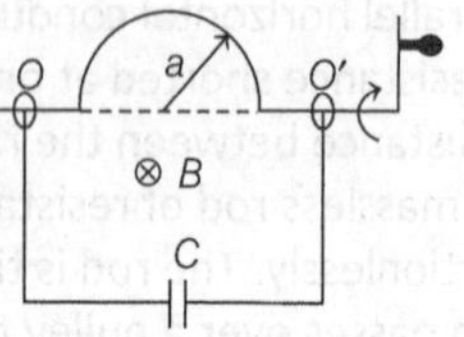

11 There is a cylindrical region of variable magnetic field $\frac{dB}{dt} = \alpha$ having a wire frame inside as shown. Each part of the wire frame has resistance r. If $i_{DE} = \left\{\frac{-me}{nr}\right\}$, where e is the emf developed in the rod AC then find the value of $(m + n)$.

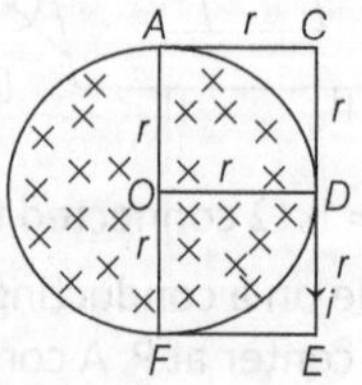

Previous Years Questions

JEE Main

1 A rectangular loop of length 2.5 m and width 2 m is placed at 60° to a magnetic field of 4 T. The loop is removed from the field in 10 s. The average emf induced in the loop during this time is **[2024, 27 Jan Shift-I]**

(a) – 2 V (b) – 1 V
(c) + 2 V (d) + 1 V

2 A square loop of side 10 cm and resistance 0.7 Ω is placed vertically in east-west plane. A uniform magnetic field of 0.20 T is set up across the plane in north-east direction. The magnetic field is decreased to zero in 1 s at a steady rate. Then, magnitude of induced emf is $\sqrt{x} \times 10^{-3}$ V. The value of x is .... **[2024, 29 Jan Shift-I]**

3 A horizontal straight wire 5 m long extending from east to west falling freely at right angle to horizontal component of earth's magnetic field 0.60×10^{-4} Wbm^{-2}. The instantaneous value of emf induced in the wire, when its velocity is 10 ms^{-1} is .... $\times 10^{-3}$ V. **[2024, 29 Jan Shift-II]**

4 A ceiling fan having 3 blades of length 80 cm each is rotating with an angular velocity of 1200 rpm. The magnetic field of earth in that region is 0.5 G and angle of dip is 30°. The emf induced across the blades is $N\pi \times 10^{-5}$ V. The value of N is .... **[2024, 30 Jan Shift-I]**

5 A coil is places perpendicular to a magnetic field of 5000 T. When the field is changed to 3000 T in 2s, an induced emf of 22 V is produced in the coil. If the diameter of the coil is 0.02 m, then the number of turns in the coil is **[2024, 31 Jan Shift-I]**

(a) 140 (b) 35
(c) 7 (d) 70

6 The magnetic flux ϕ (in weber) linked with a closed circuit of resistance 8 Ω varies with time (in seconds) as $\phi = 5t^2 - 36t + 1$. The induced current in the circuit at $t = 2$ s is .... A. **[2024, 31 Jan Shift-II]**

7 The induced emf can be produced in a coil by

A. moving the coil with uniform speed inside uniform magnetic field
B. moving the coil with non uniform speed inside uniform magnetic field
C. rotating the coil inside the uniform magnetic field
D. changing the area of the coil inside the uniform magnetic field

Choose the correct answer from the options given below : **[2023, 6 April Shift-I]**

(a) B and C only (b) A and C only
(c) B and D only (d) C and D only

8 A conducting circular loop of radius $10/\sqrt{\pi}$ cm is placed perpendicular to a uniform magnetic field of 0.5 T. The magnetic field is decreased to zero in 0.5 s at a steady rate. The induced emf in the circular loop at 0.25 s is **[2023, 24 Jan, Shift-I]**

(a) emf = 5 mV
(b) emf = 100 mV
(c) emf = 1 mV
(d) emf = 10 mV

9 A square loop of area 25 cm^2 has a resistance of 10 Ω. The loop is placed in uniform magnetic field of magnitude 40.0 T. The plane of loop is perpendicular to the magnetic field. The work done in pulling the loop out of the magnetic field slowly and uniformly in 1.0 sec. will be **[2023, 29 Jan, Shift-II]**

(a) 2.5×10^{-3} J

(b) 1.0×10^{-3} J

(c) 5×10^{-3} J

(d) 1.0×10^{-4} J

10 The magnetic field B crossing normally a square metallic plate of area 4m^2 is changing with time as shown in figure. The magnitude of induced emf in the plate during $t = 2\,s$ to $t = 4\,s$, is .... V. **[2023, 11 April shift-I]**

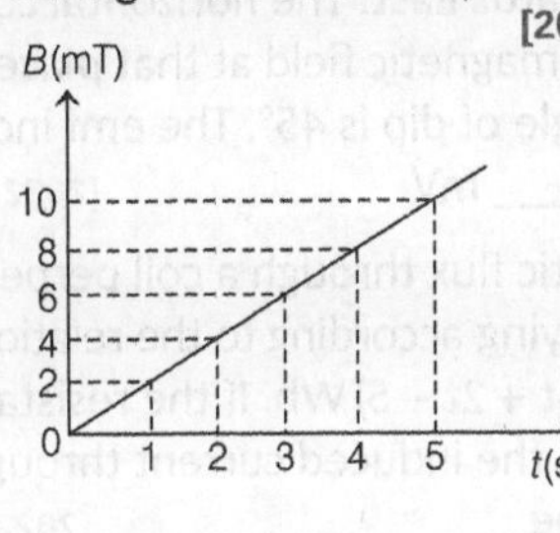

11 An insulated copper wire of 100 turns is wrapped around a wooden cylindrical core of the cross-sectional area 24 cm^2. The two ends of the wire are connected to a resistor. The total resistance in the circuit is 12 Ω. If an externally applied uniform magnetic field in the core along its axis changes from 1.5 T in one direction to 1.5 T in the opposite direction, the charge flowing through a point in the circuit during the change of magnetic field will be .... mC. **[2023, 13 April shift-II]**

12 An emf of 0.08 V is induced in a metal rod of length 10 cm held normal to a uniform magnetic field of 0.4 T, when moves with a velocity of **[2023, 8 April Shift-II]**

(a) 0.5 ms^{-1} (b) 2 ms^{-1}

(c) 20 ms^{-1} (d) 3.2 ms^{-1}

13 Given below are two statements, One is labelled as **Assertion (A)** and the other is labelled as **Reason (R)**.

Assertion (A) A bar magnet dropped through a metallic cylindrical pipe takes more time to come down compared to a non-magnetic bar with same geometry and mass.

Reason (R) For the magnetic bar, Eddy currents are produced in the metallic pipe which oppose the motion of the magnetic bar.

In the light of the above statements, choose the most appropriate answer from the options given below. **[2023, 11 April Shift-II]**

(a) Both A and R are true but R is not the correct explanation of A

(b) A is false but R is true

(c) A is true but R is false

(d) Both A and R are true and R is the correct explanation of A

14 A metallic rod of length L is rotated with an angular speed of ω normal to a uniform magnetic field B about an axis passing through one end of rod as shown in figure. The induced emf will be **[2023, 24 Jan, Shift-II]**

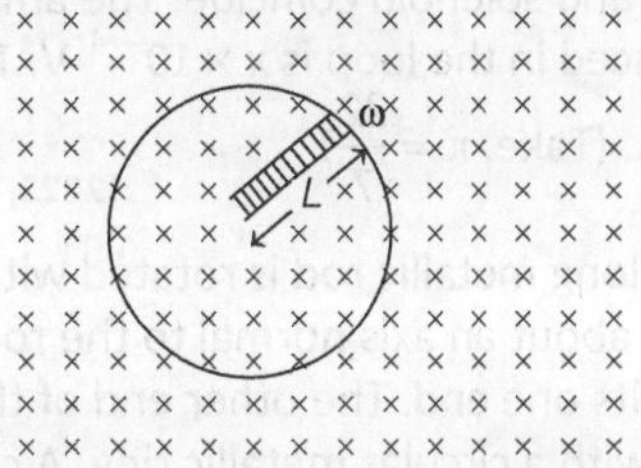

(a) $\frac{1}{2}BL^2\omega$ (b) $\frac{1}{4}BL^2\omega$

(c) $\frac{1}{2}B^2L^2\omega$ (d) $\frac{1}{4}B^2L\omega$

15 A wire of length 1 m moving with velocity 8 m/s at right angles to a magnetic field of 2T. The magnitude of induced emf between the ends of wire will be **[2023, 25 Jan, Shift-II]**

(a) 8 V (b) 12 V

(c) 16 V (d) 20 V

16 A metallic cube of side 15 cm moving along Y-axis at a uniform velocity of 2 ms^{-1}. In a region of uniform magnetic field of magnitude 0.5T directed along Z-axis. In equilibrium the potential difference between the face of higher and lower potential developed because of the motion through the field will be .... mV. **[2023, 11 April Shift-II]**

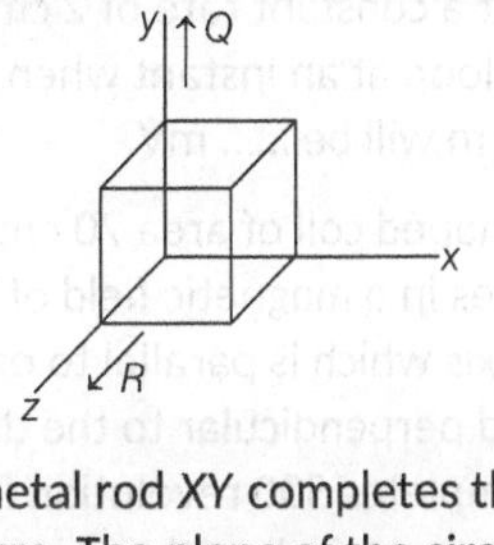

17 A 1 m long metal rod XY completes the circuit as shown in figure. The plane of the circuit is perpendicular to the magnetic field of flux density 0.15 T. If the resistance of the circuit is 5Ω, the force needed to move the rod in direction, as indicated, with a constant speed of 4 m/s will be .... 10^{-3} N. **[2023, 10 April Shift-I]**

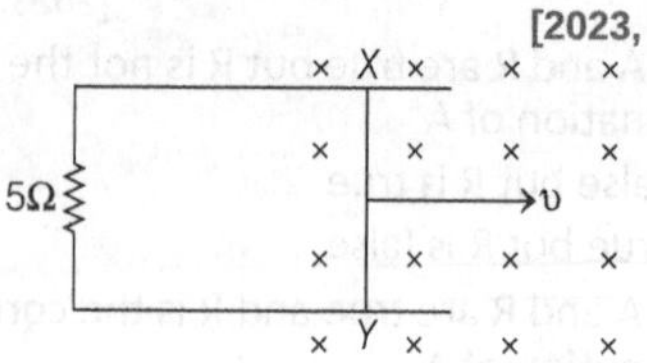

18 A square loop of side 2.0 cm is placed inside a long solenoid that has 50 turns per centimetre and carries a sinusoidally varying current of amplitude 2.5 A and angular frequency 700 rad s^{-1}. The central axes of the loop and solenoid coincide. The amplitude of the emf induced in the loop is $x \times 10^{-4}$ V. The value of x is .... (Take, $\pi = \frac{22}{7}$) **[2023, 10 April Shift-II]**

19 A 20 cm long metallic rod is rotated with 210 rpm about an axis normal to the rod passing through its one end. The other end of the rod is in contact with a circular metallic ring. A constant and uniform magnetic field 0.2 T parallel to the axis exists everywhere. The emf developed between the centre and the ring is .... mV.
$\left(\text{take, } \pi = \frac{22}{7}\right)$ **[2023, 15 April Shift-I]**

20 A conducting circular loop is placed in a uniform magnetic field of 0.4 T with its plane perpendicular to the field. Somehow, the radius of the loop starts expanding at a constant rate of 1 mm/s. The magnitude of induced emf in the loop at an instant when the radius of the loop is 2 cm will be .... μV. **[2023, 12 April Shift-I]**

21 A certain elastic conducting material is stretched into a circular loop. It is placed with its plane perpendicular to a uniform magnetic field $B = 0.8$ T. When released, the radius of the loop starts shrinking at a constant rate of 2 cms^{-1}. The induced emf in the loop at an instant when the radius of the loop is 10 cm will be ...... mV. **[2023, 29 Jan, Shift-I]**

22 A square shaped coil of area 70 cm^2 having 600 turns rotates in a magnetic field of 0.4 Wbm^{-2}, about an axis which is parallel to one of the side of the coil and perpendicular to the direction of field. If the coil completes 500 revolution in a minute. The instantaneous emf when the plane of the coil is inclined at 60° with the field, will be .... V.
$\left(\text{Take, } \pi = \frac{22}{7}\right)$ **[2023, 1 Feb Shift-II]**

23 A conducting circular loop is placed in XY-plane in presence of magnetic field $\mathbf{B} = (3t^3 \hat{j} + 3t^2 \hat{k})$ in SI unit. If the radius of the loop is 1 m, the induced emf in the loop, at time $t = 2$ s is $n\pi$ V. The value of n is .... **[2022, 27 July shift-II]**

24 In a coil of resistance 8 Ω, the magnetic flux due to an external magnetic field varies with time as $\phi = \frac{2}{3}(9 - t^2)$. The value of total heat produced in the coil, till the flux becomes zero, will be .... J. **[2022, 26 July Shift-II]**

25 A metallic rod of length 20 cm is placed in North-South direction and is moved at a constant speed of 20 m/s towards East. The horizontal component of the Earth's magnetic field at that place is 4×10^{-3} T and the angle of dip is 45°. The emf induced in the rod is ________ mV. **[2022, 27 June Shift-II]**

26 The magnetic flux through a coil perpendicular to its plane is varying according to the relation, $\phi = (5t^3 + 4t + 2t - 5)$ Wb. If the resistance of the coil is 5 Ω, then the induced current through the coil at $t = 2$ s will be **[2022, 26 June Shift-I]**
(a) 15.6 A (b) 16.6 A
(c) 17.6 A (d) 18.6 A

27 A metallic conductor of length 1m rotates in a vertical plane parallel to East-West direction about one of its end with angular velocity 5 rad/s. If the horizontal component of earth's magnetic field is 0.2×10^{-4} T, then emf induced between the two ends of the conductor is **[2022, 26 June Shift-II]**
(a) 5 μV (b) 50 μV (c) 5 mV (d) 50 mV

28 A circular coil of 1000 turns each with area 1 m^2 is rotated about its vertical diameter at the rate of one revolution per second in a uniform horizontal magnetic field of 0.07T. The maximum voltage generation will be ...... V. **[2022, 24 June Shift-II]**

29 A coil is placed in a magnetic field **B** as shown below.

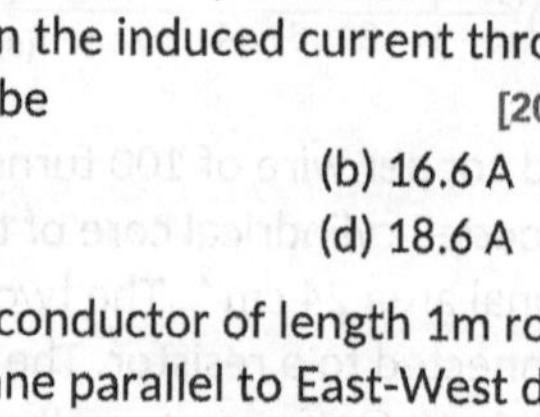

A current is induced in the coil because **B** is **[2021, 31 Aug Shift-II]**
(a) outward and decreasing with time
(b) parallel to the plane of coil and decreasing with time
(c) outward and increasing with time
(d) parallel to the plane of coil and increasing with time

30 In the given figure, the magnetic flux through the loop increases according to the relation $\phi_B(t) = 10t^2 + 20t$, where ϕ_B is in milliwebers and t is in seconds.

The magnitude of current through $R = 2\,\Omega$ resistor at $t = 5$ s is ...... mA. **[2021, 20 July Shift-II]**

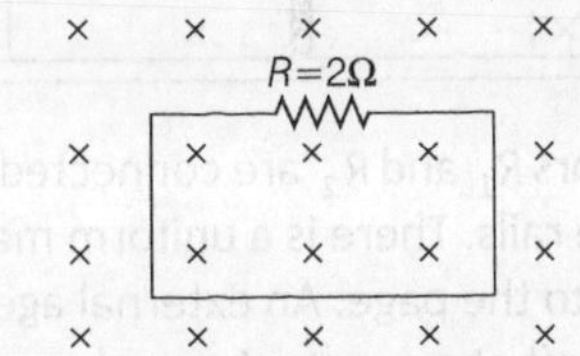

31 A square loop of side 20 cm and resistance 1Ω is moved towards right with a constant speed v_0. The right arm of the loop is in a uniform magnetic field of 5 T. The field is perpendicular to the plane of the loop and is going into it. The loop is connected to a network of resistors each of value 4 Ω. What should be the value of $\mathbf{v}_0$, so that a steady current of 2 mA flows in the loop ? **[2021, 1 Sep Shift-II]**

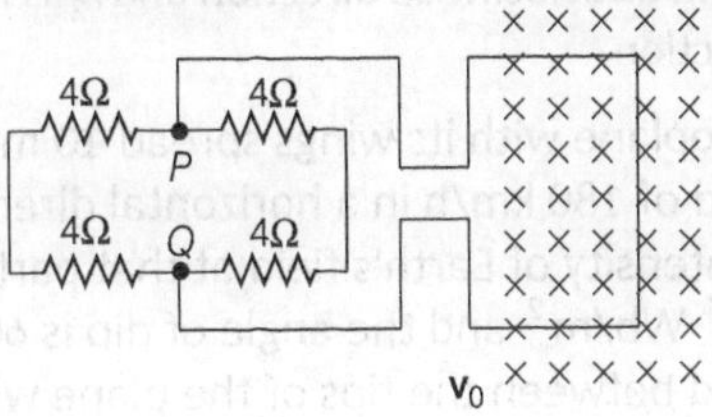

(a) 1 m/s
(b) 1 cm/s
(c) 10^2 m/s
(d) 10^{-2} cm/s

32 A constant magnetic field of 1 T is applied in the $x > 0$ region. A metallic circular ring of radius 1 m is moving with a constant velocity of 1 m/s along the X-axis. At $t = 0$ s, the centre of O of the ring is at $x = -1$ m. What will be the value of the induced emf in the ring at $t = 1$ s? (Assume the velocity of the ring does not change.) **[2021, 27 Aug Shift-II]**

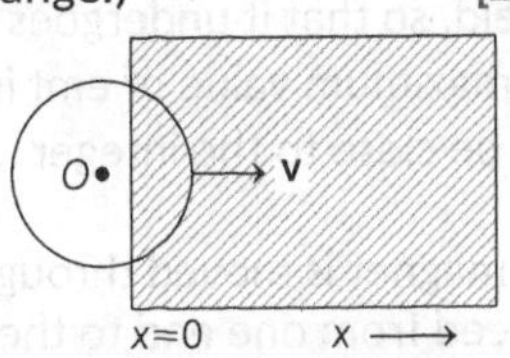

(a) 1 V (b) 2π V
(c) 2 V (d) 0

33 A bar magnet is passing through a conducting loop of radius R with velocity v. The radius of the bar magnet is such that it just passes through the loop. The induced emf in the loop can be represented by the approximate curve **[2021, 26 Aug Shift-I]**

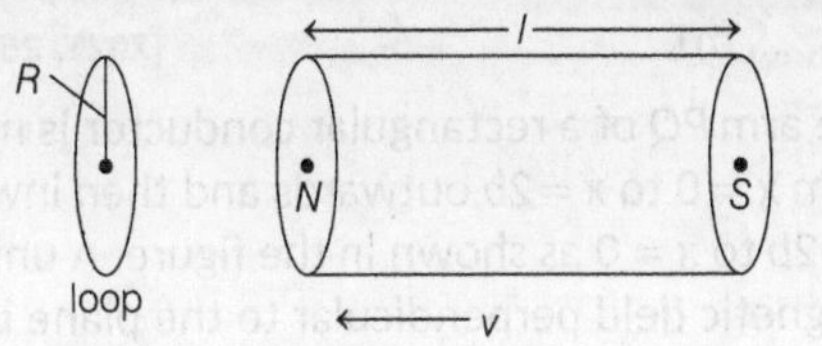

(a)
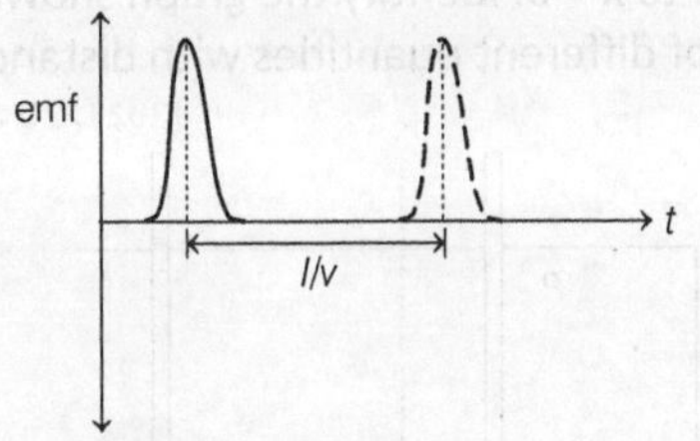

(b)
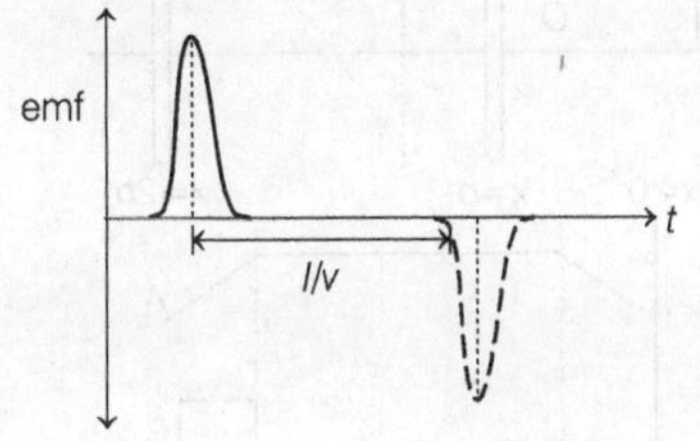

(c)
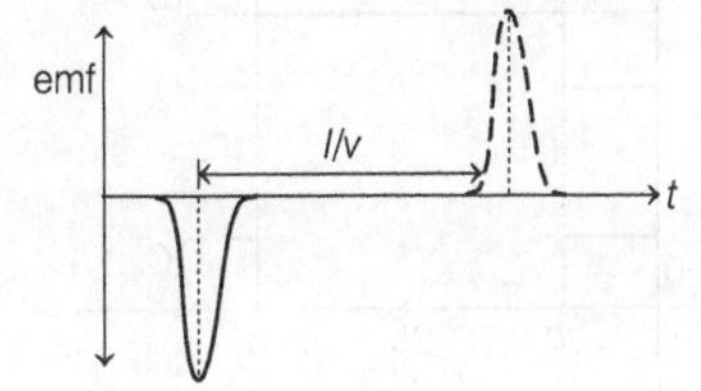

(d)
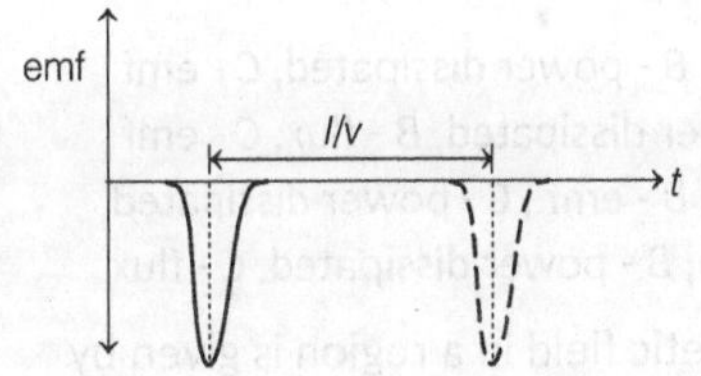

34 A circular coil of radius 8.0 cm and 20 turns is rotated about its vertical diameter with an angular speed of 50 rad s^{-1} in a uniform horizontal magnetic field of 3.0×10^{-2} T. The maximum emf induced in the coil will be ...... $\times 10^{-2}$ V.
(rounded off to the nearest integer.)
[2021, 26 Aug Shift-I]

35 A circular conducting coil of radius 1 m is being heated by the change of magnetic field **B** passing perpendicular to the plane in which the coil is laid. The resistance of the coil is 2 μΩ. The magnetic field is slowly switched off such that its magnitude changes in time as

$$B = \frac{4}{\pi} \times 10^{-3}\left(1 - \frac{t}{100}\right)\text{T}$$

The energy dissipated by the coil before the magnetic field is switched off completely is $E = \ldots\ldots$ mJ. **[2021, 25 July Shift-I]**

36 The arm PQ of a rectangular conductor is moving from $x = 0$ to $x = 2b$ outwards and then inwards from $x = 2b$ to $x = 0$ as shown in the figure. A uniform magnetic field perpendicular to the plane is acting from $x = 0$ to $x = b$. Identify the graph showing the variation of different quantities with distance. **[2021, 20 July Shift-I]**

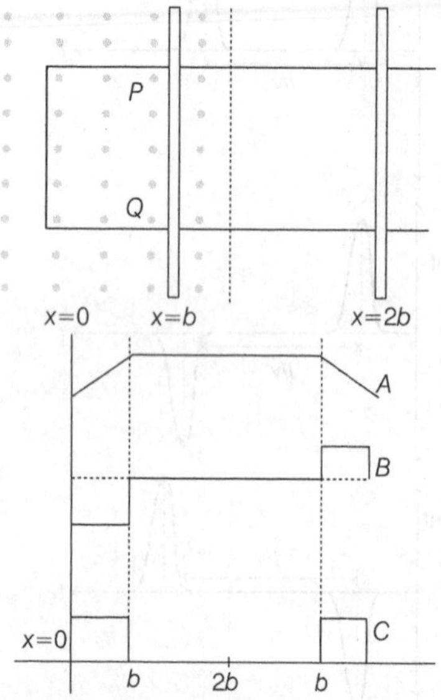

(a) A - flux, B - power dissipated, C - emf
(b) A - power dissipated, B - flux, C - emf
(c) A - flux, B - emf, C - power dissipated
(d) A - emf, B - power dissipated. C - flux

37 The magnetic field in a region is given by $\mathbf{B} = B_0\left(\frac{x}{a}\right)\hat{\mathbf{k}}$. A square loop of side d is placed with its edges along the X and Y-axes. The loop is moved with a constant velocity $\mathbf{v} = v_0\hat{\mathbf{i}}$. The emf induced in the loop is **[2021, 16 March Shift-II]**

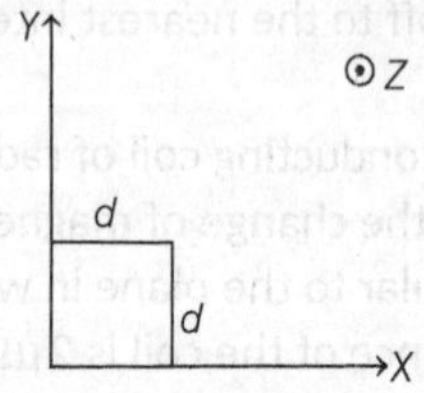

(a) $\frac{B_0 v_0^2 d}{2a}$ (b) $\frac{B_0 v_0 d}{2a}$
(c) $\frac{B_0 v_0 d^2}{a}$ (d) $\frac{B_0 v_0 d^2}{2a}$

38 A conducting bar of length L is free to slide on two parallel conducting rails as shown in the figure

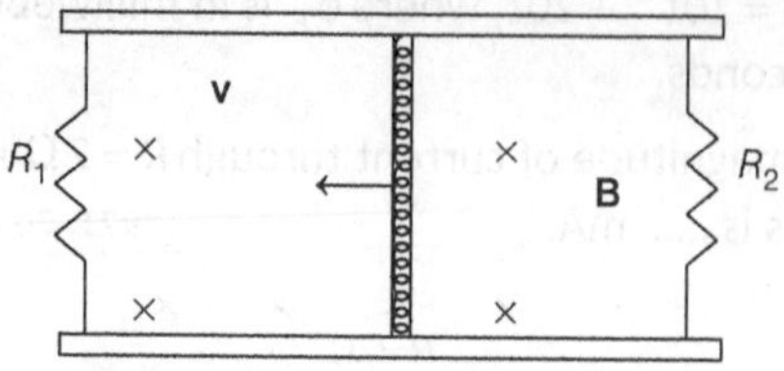

Two resistors R_1 and R_2 are connected across the ends of the rails. There is a uniform magnetic field **B** pointing into the page. An external agent pulls the bar to the left at a constant speed v.

The correct statement about the directions of induced currents I_1 and I_2 flowing through R_1 and R_2 respectively is **[2021, 16 March Shift-I]**

(a) both I_1 and I_2 are in anti-clockwise direction.
(b) both I_1 and I_2 are in clockwise direction.
(c) I_1 is in clockwise direction and I_2 is in anti-clockwise direction.
(d) I_1 is in anticlockwise direction and I_2 is in clockwise direction.

39 An aeroplane with its wings spread 10 m, is flying at a speed of 180 km/h in a horizontal direction. The total intensity of Earth's field at that part is 2.5×10^{-4} Wb/m^2 and the angle of dip is 60°. The emf induced between the tips of the plane wings will be **[2021, 26 Feb Shift-II]**

(a) 108.25 mV
(b) 54.125 mV
(c) 88.37 mV
(d) 62.50 mV

40 A circular coil of radius 10 cm is placed in a uniform magnetic field of 3.0×10^{-5} T with its plane perpendicular to the field initially.
It is rotated at constant angular speed about an axis along the diameter of coil and perpendicular to magnetic field, so that it undergoes half of rotation in 0.2s. The maximum value of emf induced (in μV) in the coil will be close to the integer .... **[2020, 2 Sep Shift-I]**

41 A small bar magnet is moved through a coil at constant speed from one end to the other. Which of the following series of observations will be seen on the galvanometer G attached across the coil?

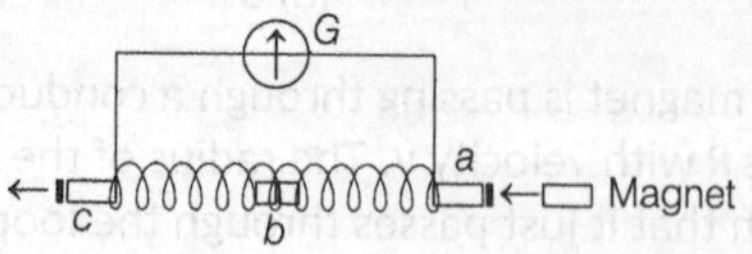

Three positions shown describe: (i) the magnet's entery (ii) magnet is completely inside and (iii) magnet's exit. **[2020, 4 Sep Shift-I]**

(a) 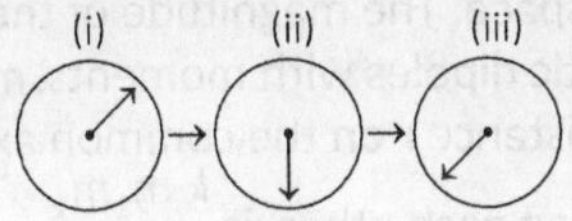

(b) 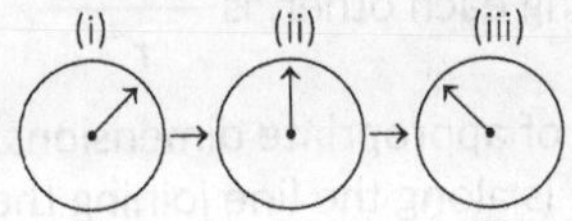

(c) 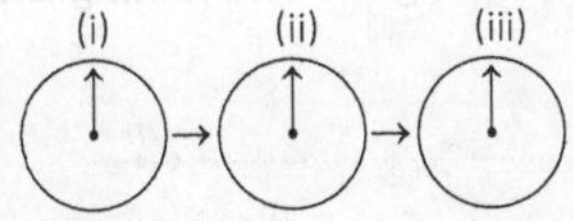

(d) 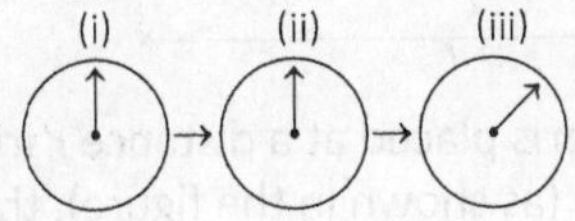

42 A uniform magnetic field B exists in a direction perpendicular to the plane of a square loop made of a metal wire. The wire has a diameter of 4 mm and a total length of 30 cm. The magnetic field changes with time at a steady rate $dB/dt = 0.032\ \text{Ts}^{-1}$. The induced current in the loop is close to
(Take, resistivity of the metal wire $= 1.23 \times 10^{-8}\ \Omega\text{m}$) **[2020, 3 Sep Shift-II]**

(a) 0.61 A (b) 0.43 A
(c) 0.53 A (d) 0.34 A

43 Two concentric circular coils C_1 and C_2 are placed in the xy-plane. C_1 has 500 turns and radius of 1 cm. C_2 has 200 turns and radius of 20 cm. C_2 carries a time dependent current $I(t) = (5t^2 - 2t + 3)$A, where t is in secon(d) The emf induced in C_1 (in mV), at the instant $t = 1$ s is $4/x$. The value of x is .... **[2020, 5 Sep Shift-I]**

44 A loop $ABCDEFA$ of straight edges has six corner points $A(0, 0, 0)$, $B(5, 0, 0)$, $C(5, 5, 0)$, $D(0, 5, 0)$, $E(0, 5, 5)$ and $F(0, 0, 5)$. The magnetic field in this region is $\mathbf{B} = (3\hat{\mathbf{i}} + 4\hat{\mathbf{k}})$T. The quantity of flux through the loop $ABCDEFA$ (in Wb) is .... **[2020, 7 Jan Shift-I]**

45 Consider a circular coil of wire carrying constant current I, forming a magnetic dipole. The magnetic flux through an infinite plane that contains the circular coil and excluding the circular coil area is given by ϕ_i. The magnetic flux through the area of the circular coil area is given by ϕ_o. Which of the following option is correct ? **[2020, 7 Jan Shift-I]**

(a) $\phi_i > \phi_o$ (b) $\phi_i < \phi_o$
(c) $\phi_i = \phi_o$ (d) $\phi_i = -\phi_o$

46 A very long solenoid of radius R is carrying current $I(t) = kte^{-\alpha t}$ $(k > 0)$, as a function of time $(t \geq 0)$.

Counter clockwise current is taken to be positive. A circular conducting coil of radius $2R$ is placed in the equatorial plane of the solenoid and concentric with the solenoi(d) The current induced in the outer coil is correctly depicted, as a function of time, by **[2019, 9 April Shift-II]**

(a) 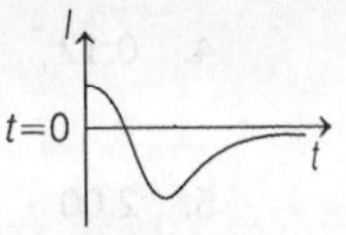

(b) 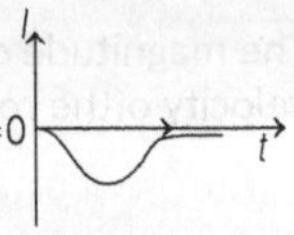

(c) 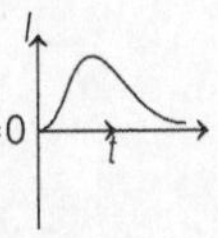

(d) 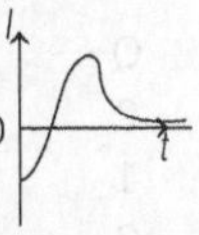

47 A conducting circular loop is made of a thin wire has area $3.5 \times 10^{-3}\ \text{m}^2$ and resistance $10\ \Omega$. It is placed perpendicular to a time dependent magnetic field $B(t) = (0.4\text{T})\sin(0.5\pi t)$. The field is uniform in space. Then the net charge flowing through the loop during $t = 0$ s and $t = 10$ ms is close to **[2019, 9 Jan Shift-I]**

(a) 6 mC
(b) 21 mC
(c) 7 mC
(d) 14 mC

JEE Advanced

1 A thin conducting rod MN of mass 20 g, length 25 cm and resistance $10\ \Omega$ is held on frictionless, long, perfectly conducting vertical rails as shown in the figure. There is a uniform magnetic field $B_0 = 4\text{T}$.directed perpendicular to the plane of the rod-rail arrangement. The rod is released from rest at time $t = 0$ and it moves down along the rails. Assume air drag is negligible. Match each quantity in List-I with an appropriate value from List-II and choose the correct option.
[Given, The acceleration due to gravity, $g = 10\ \text{ms}^{-2}$ and $e^{-1} = 0.4$] **(2023)**

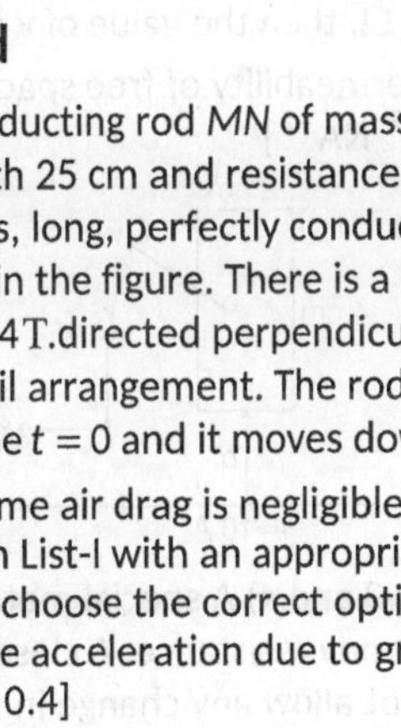

List-I	List-II
P. At $t = 0.2$ s, the magnitude of the induced emf in Volt	1. 0.07
Q. At $t = 0.2$ s, the magnitude of the magnetic force in Newton	2. 0.14
R. At $t = 0.2$ s, the power dissipated as heat in Watt	3. 1.20
S. The magnitude of terminal velocity ofthe rod in ms^{-1}	4. 0.12
	5. 2.00

	P	Q	R	S
(a)	5	2	3	1
(b)	3	1	4	5
(c)	4	3	1	2
(d)	3	4	2	5

2. A rectangular conducting loop of length 4 cm and width 2 cm is in the *XY*-plane as shown in the figure. It is being moved away from a thin and long conducting wire along the direction $\frac{\sqrt{3}}{2}\hat{\mathbf{x}} + \frac{1}{2}\hat{\mathbf{y}}$ with a constant speed *v*. The wire is carrying a steady current $I = 10$ A in the positive *x*-direction. A current of 10 μA flows through the loop when it is at a distance $d = 4$ cm from the wire. If the resistance of the loop is 0.1 Ω, then the value of v is .... ms^{-1}.
[Given : The permeability of free space $\mu_0 = 4\pi \times 10^{-7}$ NA^{-2}] **(2023)**

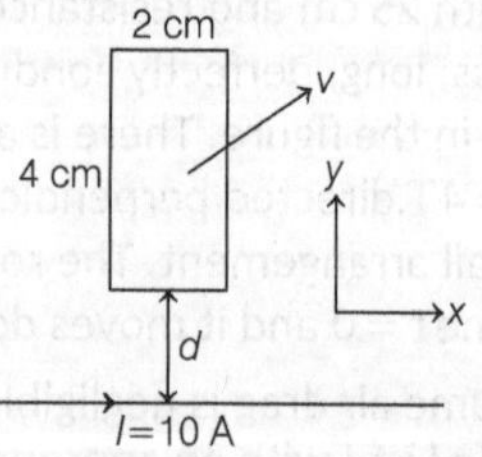

Direction (Q. Nos. 3 and 4) A special metal *S* conducts electricity without any resistance. A closed wire loop, made of *S*, does not allow any change in flux through itself by inducing a suitable current to generate a compensating flux. The induced current in the loop cannot decay due to its zero resistance. This current gives rise to a magnetic moment which in turn repels the source of magnetic field or flux. Consider such a loop, of radius *a*, with its center at the origin. A magnetic dipole of moment *m* is brought along the axis of this loop from infinity to a point at distance $r (>> a)$ from the center of the loop with its North pole always facing the loop, as shown in the figure below.

The magnitude of magnetic field of a dipole *m*, at a point on its axis at distance *r*, is $\frac{\mu_0 m}{2\pi r^3}$, where μ_0 is the permeability of free space. The magnitude of the force between two magnetic dipoles with moments, m_1 and m_2, separated by a distance *r* on the common axis, with their North poles facing each other, is $\frac{k\, m_1 m_2}{r^4}$, where *k* is a constant of appropriate dimensions. The direction of this force is along the line joining the two dipoles. **(2021)**

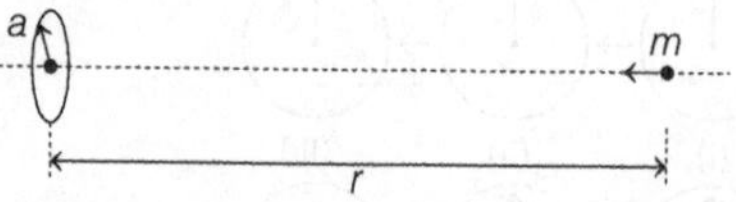

3 When the dipole *m* is placed at a distance *r* from the center of the loop (as shown in the figure), the current induced in the loop will be proportional to
(a) m/r^3 (b) m^2/r^2 (c) m/r^2 (d) m^2/r

4 The work done in bringing the dipole from infinity to a distance *r* from the centre of the loop by the given process is proportional to
(a) m/r^5 (b) m^2/r^5 (c) m^2/r^6 (d) m^2/r^7

5 A long straight wire carries a current, $I = 2$ A. A semi-circular conducting rod is placed beside it on two conducting parallel rails of negligible resistance. Both the rails are parallel to the wire. The wire, the rod and the rails lie in the same horizontal plane, as shown in the figure. Two ends of the semi-circular rod are at distances 1 cm and 4 cm from the wire. At time $t = 0$, the rod starts moving on the rails with a speed $v = 3.0$ m/s (see the figure).

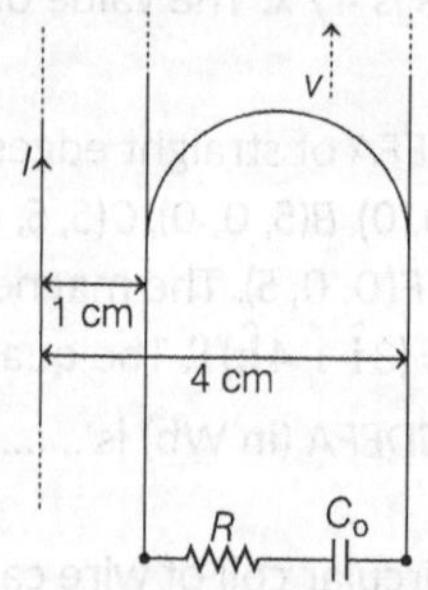

A resistor $R = 1.4$ Ω and a capacitor $C_o = 5.0$ μF are connected in series between the rails. At time $t = 0$, C_o is uncharged. Which of the following statement(s) is(are) correct?
[$\mu_0 = 4\pi \times 10^{-7}$ SI units. Take, ln2 = 0.7] **(2021)**
(a) Maximum current through *R* is 1.2×10^{-6} A.
(b) Maximum current through *R* is 3.8×10^{-6} A.

(c) Maximum charge on capacitor C_0 is 8.4×10^{-12} C.

(d) Maximum charge on capacitor C_0 is 2.4×10^{-12} C.

6 A light disc made of aluminium (a nonmagnetic material) is kept horizontally and is free to rotate about its axis as shown in the figure. A strong magnet is held vertically at a point above the disc away from its axis. On revolving the magnet about the axis of the disc, the disc will (figure is schematic and not drawn to scale) **(2020)**

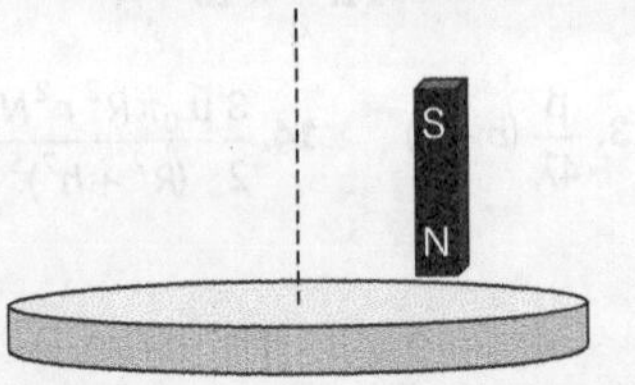

(a) rotate in the direction opposite to the direction of magnet's motion

(b) rotate in the same direction as the direction of magnet's motion

(c) not rotate and its temperature will remain unchanged

(d) not rotate but its temperature will slowly rise.

7 A circular insulated copper wire loop is twisted to form two loops of area A and $2A$ as shown in the figure. At the point of crossing, the wires remain electrically insulated from each other. The entire loop lies in the plane (of the paper). A uniform magnetic field **B** points into the plane of the paper. At $t = 0$, the loop starts rotating about the common diameter as axis with a constant angular velocity ω in the magnetic field. Which of the following options is/are correct? **(2017)**

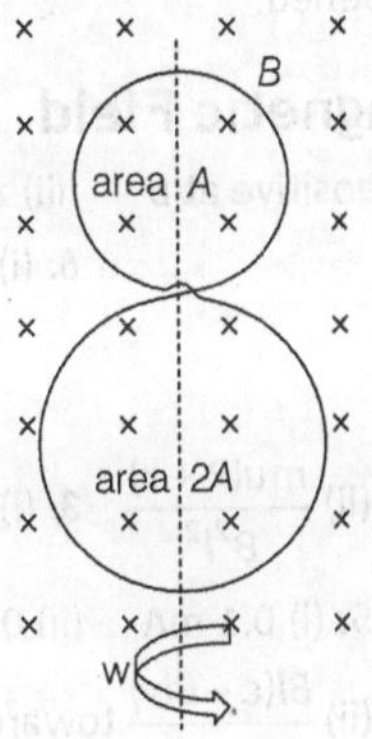

(a) The emf induced in the loop is proportional to the sum of the areas of the two loops.

(b) The rate of change of the flux is maximum when the plane of the loops is perpendicular to plane of the paper.

(c) The net emf induced due to both the loops is proportional to $\cos \omega t$.

(d) The amplitude of the maximum net emf induced due to both the loops is equal to the amplitude of maximum emf induced in the smaller loop alone.

8 A conducting loop in the shape of a right angled isosceles triangle of height 10 cm is kept such that the 90° vertex is very close to an infinitely long conducting wire (see the figure). The wire is electrically insulated from the loop. The hypotenuse of the triangle is parallel to the wire. The current in the triangular loop is in counterclockwise direction and increased at a constant rate of $10\ \text{As}^{-1}$. Which of the following statement(s) is (are) true? **(2016)**

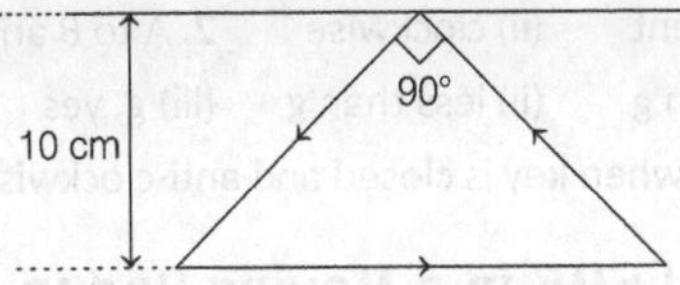

(a) There is a repulsive force between the wire and the loop.

(b) If the loop is rotated at a constant angular speed about the wire, an additional emf of $\left(\frac{\mu_0}{\pi}\right)$ volt is induced in the wire.

(c) The magnitude of induced emf in the wire is $\left(\frac{\mu_0}{\pi}\right)$ volt.

(d) The induced current in the wire is in opposite direction to the current along the hypotenuse.

Answer Key

Level 1

5.1 Induced EMF and Induced

1. 1.0 V, anti-clockwise
2. (i) 1.2 V (ii) 1.4 V (iii) 3.5 A (iv) 86/3 J
3. zero
4. (a) 50 V, (b) 50 V, (c) zero
5. 0.078 C
6. (i) 0 (ii) 8 A, anti-clockwise (iii) 2A clockwise
7. $5/\pi$ cm
8. $\frac{\mu_0 a^2 k}{2dR}$, anti-clockwise
9. 4.93 μV
10. 1.6×10^{-5}A
11. $\frac{\pi}{4}\times10^{-4}$ A
12. (i) 1.25×10^{-7}A, *a* to *d* (ii) 1.25×10^{-7}A, *d* to *a*, (iii) zero, (iv) zero
13. $\frac{\beta}{4\lambda}(b-a)$
14. $\frac{3}{2}\frac{\mu_0\pi R^2 r^2 Nihv}{(R^2+h^2)^{5/2}}$
15. (i)

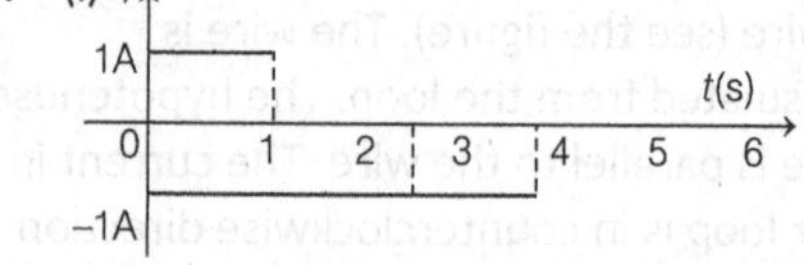

(ii) 8 J

5.2 Lenz's Law

1. (i) no current (ii) clockwise
2. *A* to *B* and *D* to *C*
3. Clockwise, repel
4. (i) less than g (ii) less than g (iii) g, yes
5. Clockwise when key is closed and anti-clockwise when key is opened.

5.3 Induced EMF in a Moving Rod in Uniform Magnetic Field

1. 0.4 V, Q
2. 0.05 V
3. (i) zero (ii) *Blv* sinθ , positive at *b* (iii) zero (iv) Blv sin θ, positive at a
4. 1 mV
5. 141.4 V
6. (i) 2*rvB* (ii) zero

5.4 Circuit Problems

1. $\frac{Blv(R_1+R_2)}{r(R_1+R_2)+R_1R_2}$
2. (i) $v=ue^{-\frac{B^2l^2t}{(R+r)m}}$ (ii) $\frac{mu(R+r)}{B^2l^2}$
3. (i) $\frac{Bvl}{2(l+vt)r}$ (ii) $\frac{B^2l^2v}{2r(l+vt)}$
4. (i) 5 m/s (ii) 20 V (iii) 15 V (iv) 5 V
5. (i) 0.1 mA (ii) 0
6. $\frac{ir-Blv}{2r}$
7. $\sqrt{\frac{mgR\sin\theta}{vl^2\cos^2\theta}}$
8. (i) $\frac{\varepsilon-blv}{r}$, from *b* to *a* (ii) $\frac{Bl(\varepsilon-Blv)}{r}$ towards right (iii) $\frac{\varepsilon}{Bl}$
9. (i) $v_m(l-e^{-gt/v_m})$ (ii) $v_m=\frac{mgr}{B^2l^2}$ (iii) $v_mt-\frac{v_m^2}{g}(l-e^{-gt/v_m})$ (iv) mgv_m
10. $\frac{mgt}{m+CB^2l^2}$

5.5 Induced EMF in a Rod, Ring and Disc Rotating in a Uniform Magnetic Field

1. 75 V
2. $3B\omega l^2/10$
3. $B\omega a^2/R$ from *C* to *D*
4. 6.28×10^{-5}V
5. $\frac{\omega a^3B^2}{2R}$
6. 3.14 mV.
7. (i) 2BR v (ii) BRv/2 (iii) 1.5 BRv
8. (i) 3.14 mV (ii) (3.14 mV) sin (10πt) (iii) $4.93\times10^{-6}V^2$

5.6 EMF induced in a Rod or Loop in Non-uniform Magnetic Field

1. (i) $\frac{\mu_0 ia}{2\pi}\ln\left(\frac{a+b}{b}\right)$ (ii) $\frac{\mu_0 i_0 a}{T}\ln\left(\frac{a+b}{b}\right)\sin\left(\frac{2\pi t}{T}\right)$ (iii) $\left(\frac{5\mu_0^2 i_0^2 a^2}{TR}\right)\left[\ln\left(\frac{a+b}{b}\right)\right]^2$
2. $\frac{B_0v_0L}{2}$
3. (i) $I=\frac{\mu_0 i_0 v}{2\pi R}\ln\frac{b}{a}$ (ii) $F=\frac{v}{R}\left[\frac{\mu_0 i_0}{2\pi}\ln\frac{b}{a}\right]^2$
4. $\frac{\mu_0 iv}{2\pi}\left(\ln 2-\frac{1}{2}\right)$

5.7 Induced Electric Field

1. For $r < R; E = \dfrac{B_0 r}{2}$ and for $r > R; E = \dfrac{B_0 R^2}{2r}$ 2. $E = \dfrac{B_0 l d}{2}$ 3. $qB/2m$

Level 2

Single Choice Correct Questions

1. (b)	2. (d)	3. (c)	4. (a)	5. (c)	6. (b)	7. (a)	8. (d)	9. (d)	10. (c)
11. (c)	12. (a)	13. (a)	14. (a)	15. (d)	16. (b)	17. (a)	18. (c)	19. (d)	20. (a)
21. (a)	22. (d)	23. (b)	24. (a)	25. (c)	26. (d)	27. (d)	28. (b)	29. (a)	30. (a)
31. (a)	32. (b)	33. (d)	34. (c)	35. (d)	36. (a)	37. (a)	38. (c)	39. (c)	40. (b)
41. (b)	42. (c)	43. (c)	44. (a)	45. (a)					

Numerical Value Questions

1. 5.00 2. 8 3. 4 4. 2 5. 2.36 6. 3 7. 1 8. 7.2 9. 120

Level 3

Single Choice Correct Questions

1. (c)	2. (c)	3. (c)	4. (c)	5. (a)	6. (a)	7. (a)	8. (b)	9. (c)	10. (b)
11. (c)	12. (d)	13. (a)	14. (d)	15. (d)	16. (a)	17. (b)	18. (d)	19. (b)	20. (b)
21. (c)	22. (b)	23. (b)	24. (d)	25. (a)	26. (a)	27. (b)	28. (c)		

Multiple Choice(s) Correct Questions

1. (b, c) 2. (d) 3. (a, c, d) 4. (a, b, d) 5. (a, d) 6. (b, c) 7. (a, c, d)
8. (b, c) 9. (a, b, c, d) 10. (a, c) 11. (a, d) 12. (a, d) 13. (a, b, c) 14. (a, b, c)
15. (a, c) 16. (a, c, d) 17. (a, d)

Comprehension Based Questions

1. (d)	2. (a)	3. (b)	4. (a)	5. (c)	6. (a)	7. (c)	8. (c)	9. (b)	10. (b)
11. (a)	12. (b)	13. (b)	14. (c)	15. (d)	16. (a)	17. (c)	18. (c)	19. (d)	20. (b)
21. (a)	22. (a)	23. (b)	24. (d)	25. (a)	26. (a)	27. (d)	28. (c)	29. (a)	30. (b)
31. (d)	32. (c)	33. (a)	34. (b)	35. (c)	36. (b)	37. (a)			

Match the Columns Questions

1. (a) → (QT); (b) → (R); (c) → (PT); (d) → (Q)
2. (a) - (P); (b) - (PS); (c) - (P); (d) - (QR)
3. (a) → (Q); (b) → (R); (c) → (S); (d) → (P);
4. (a) → (QS); (b) → (PR); (c) → (PR); (d) → (QS)
5. (a) → (RS); (b) → (QS); (c) → (PT); (d) → (PST)
6. (a) → (P); (b) → (QS); (c) → (R); (d) → R

Numerical Value Questions

1. 6 2. 9 3. 10 4. 25 5. 2 6. 3 7. 4 8. 5 9. 160 10. 2 11. 5

Previous Years Questions

JEE Main

1. (d)	2. (2)	3. (3)	4. (32)	5. (d)	6. (2)	7. (d)	8. (d)	9. (b)	10. (8)
11. (60)	12. (b)	13. (d)	14. (a)	15. (c)	16. (150)	17. (18)	18. (44)	19. (88)	20. (50)
21. (10)	22. (44)	23. (12)	24. (2)	25. (16)	26. (a)	27. (b)	28. (440)	29. (a)	30. (60)
31. (b)	32. (c)	33. (c)	34. (60)	35. (c)	36. (c)	37. (c)	38. (c)	39. (a)	40. (15)
41. (b)	42. (a)	43. (5)	44. (175)	45. (d)	46. (d)	47. (d)			

JEE Advanced

1. (d) 2. (4) 3. (a) 4. (c) 5. (a, c) 6. (b) 7. (b, d) 8. (a, c)

SOLUTIONS

Level I

5.1 Induced EMF and Induced Current

1. $\varepsilon_{avg} = \left|\frac{\Delta\phi}{\Delta t}\right| = \frac{0.9-0.4}{0.5-0} = 1.0\,\text{V}$

Induced current will be anti-clockwise as seen from top, so that upper face becomes north-pole.

2. (i) $\varepsilon = \left|\frac{d\phi}{dt}\right| = 0.4t + 0.4$

At $t = 2$; $\varepsilon = 0.4(2) + 0.4 = 1.2\,\text{V}$

(ii) $\varepsilon_{avg.} = \left|\frac{\Delta\phi}{\Delta t}\right| = \left|\frac{\phi_2 - \phi_1}{t_2 - t_1}\right| = \frac{7.6 - 0.6}{5 - 0} = 1.4\,\text{V}$

(iii) $i_{avg} = \frac{\varepsilon_{avg}}{R} = \frac{1.4}{0.4} = 3.5\,\text{A}$

(iv) $i = \frac{\varepsilon}{R} = \frac{0.4t + 0.4}{0.4} = t + 1$

Heat produced $= \int_0^5 i^2 R dt = \frac{86}{3}\,\text{J}$

3. $i = \frac{\varepsilon}{R} = \frac{1}{R}\left|\frac{d\phi}{dt}\right| = 0;\quad \because \{\phi \text{ is constant}\}$

4. $\phi = NBA\cos\theta = 50 \times 1.0 \times (0.5)^2 \cos 0° = 12.5\,\text{Wb}$

(i) $\varepsilon_{avg} = \left|\frac{\Delta\phi}{\Delta t}\right| = \left|\frac{0 - 12.5}{0.25}\right| = 50\,\text{V}$

(ii) $\varepsilon_{avg} = \left|\frac{\Delta\phi}{\Delta t}\right| = \left|\frac{12.5 - 0}{0.25}\right| = 50\,\text{V}$

(iii) $\varepsilon_{avg} = 0 \qquad [\because \Delta\phi = 0]$

5. $q = \frac{\Delta\phi}{R} = \frac{NBA - (-NBA)}{R} = \frac{2NBA}{R} = 0.078\,\text{C}$

6. (i) $i = \frac{1}{R}\frac{d\phi}{dt} = 0$

$\because \quad \phi = BA = \text{constant}$

(ii) $\varepsilon = \frac{d\phi}{dt} = A\frac{dB}{dt} = (2)^2(10) = 40\,\text{V}$

$i = \frac{\varepsilon}{R} = \frac{40}{5} = 8\text{A}$

Flux is increasing into the plane. According to Faraday's law to oppose this, induced current in the loop will be anti-clockwise.

(iii) $\varepsilon = \frac{d\phi}{dt} = A\frac{dB}{dt}$

$= (2)^2(5) = 20\,\text{V}$

$i = \frac{30 - 20}{5} = 2\text{A}$

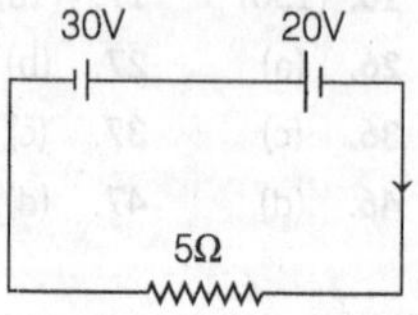

7. $\phi = B(\pi r^2)\cos 0°$

$\varepsilon = \left|\frac{d\phi}{dt}\right| = \pi B 2r\frac{dr}{dt}$

$\Rightarrow \quad 1\times10^{-6} = \pi(10^{-3})2r(10^{-2})$

$\Rightarrow \quad r = \frac{5}{\pi}\,\text{cm}$

8. $\phi = \left(\frac{\mu_0 i}{2\pi d}\right)(\pi a^2)\cos 0° = \frac{\mu_0 i a^2}{2d}$

$\varepsilon = \left|\frac{d\phi}{dt}\right| = \left(\frac{\mu_0 a^2}{2d}\right)\frac{di}{dt} = \frac{k\mu_0 a^2}{2d}$

Induced current $= \frac{\varepsilon}{R} = \frac{k\mu_0 a^2}{2dR}$, anti-clockwise.

9. $\phi = \left(\frac{\mu_0 N_1 i_1}{2R}\right)(N_2\pi r^2)\cos 0° = 4.93\times10^{-6}\,\text{Wb}$

$\phi_2 = 0 \qquad \because (i_1 = 0)$

$\varepsilon_{avg} = \left|\frac{\Delta\phi}{\Delta t}\right| = \left|\frac{0 - 4.93\times10^{-6}}{10\times10^{-3} - 0}\right| = 4.93\,\mu\text{V}$

10. $\phi = N(\mu_0 n i_1)A\cos 0°$

$= 10\times(4\pi\times10^{-7}\times400\times0.4)(6.0\times10^{-4})$

$= 1.2\times10^{-6}\,\text{Wb}$

$\phi_2 = 0$

$i_{avg} = \frac{1}{R}\left|\frac{\Delta\phi}{\Delta t}\right| = 1.6\times10^{-5}\,\text{A}$

11. $\varepsilon = \left|\frac{d\phi}{dt}\right| = A\frac{dB}{dt} = \left[\frac{\pi(0.01)^2}{2}\right]\times2 = \pi\times10^{-4}\,\text{V}$

$i = \frac{\varepsilon}{R} = \frac{\pi}{4}\times10^{-4}\,\text{A}$

12. (i) In loop *defa*,

$\varepsilon = \left|\frac{d\phi}{dt}\right| = A\frac{dB}{dt}$

$= (1\times10^{-2})\times20\times10^{-3} = 2\times10^{-6}\,\text{V}$

$i_{ad} = \frac{\varepsilon}{R_{defa}} = \frac{2\times10^{-6}}{4\times4}$

$= 1.25\times10^{-7}\,\text{A along } ad$

(ii) In loop *abcd*,

$\varepsilon = 2\times10^{-6}\,\text{V}$

$R_{abcd} = 4\times4 = 16\Omega$

$i = \frac{2\times10^{-6}}{16} = 1.25\times10^{-7}\,\text{A along } da$

(iii) Since both S_1 and S_2 are open, no current in the circuit.

(iv) Since the both S_1 and S_2 are closed, the circuit forms a balanced wheatstone bridge and no current flows along *ad*.

13. $\varepsilon = \left|\frac{d\phi}{dt}\right| = A\frac{dB}{dt}$

ε_1 = Induced emf in loop $XYZT = b^2\beta$

ε_2 = Induced emt in loop $PQST = a^2\beta$

Applying KVL, $+\varepsilon - iR_1 - \varepsilon_2 - iR_2 = 0$

$$\Rightarrow \quad i = \frac{\varepsilon_1 - \varepsilon_2}{R_1 + R_2}$$

$$i = \frac{b^2\beta - a^2\beta}{\lambda(4b) + \lambda(4a)}$$

$$= \frac{(b-a)\beta}{4\lambda}$$

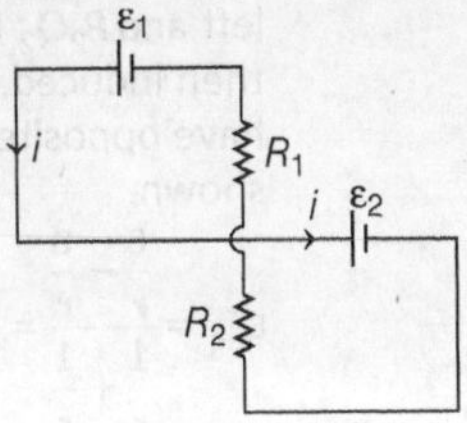

14. $\phi = BA\cos\theta$

$$= \left(\frac{\mu_0 NiR^2}{2(R^2+h^2)^{3/2}}\right)(\pi r^2)\cos 0°$$

$$\varepsilon = \left|\frac{d\phi}{dt}\right| = \left(\frac{\mu_0 Ni\pi R^2 r^2}{2}\right)\left(-\frac{3}{2}(R^2+h^2)^{-5/2} 2h\frac{dh}{dt}\right)$$

$$= \frac{3\mu_0 \pi R^2 r^2 Nihv}{2\ (R^2+h^2)^{5/2}}$$

15. (i) When loop enters ($t = 0$ to $t = 1$)

$\phi = Bx(1) = Bx$

$$\varepsilon = \left|\frac{d\phi}{dt}\right| = B\frac{dx}{dt} = (2)(2) = 4\text{ V}$$

$$i = \frac{\varepsilon}{R} = \frac{4}{4} = 1\text{ A, anti-clockwise}$$

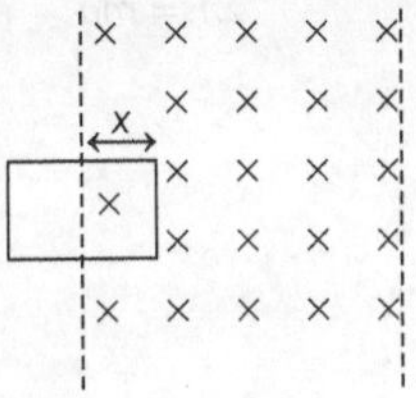

When loop comes out of magnetic field ($t = 3$ to $t = 4$)

$$i = \frac{\varepsilon}{R} = 1\text{ A, clockwise}$$

For $t = 1$ to $t = 3; i = 0$ {$\because$ Flux is constant}

$t = 4$ to $t = 5; i = 0$ {$\because \phi = 0$}

(ii) Heat produced $= \int i^2 R\,dt = (1)^2(4)(2) = 8\text{ J}$

5.2 Lenz's Law

1. In loop 1, flux is constant. So, induced current will be zero. In loop 2, flux into the plane is decreasing. So, to oppose decrease in flux current in the loop will be clockwise.

2.

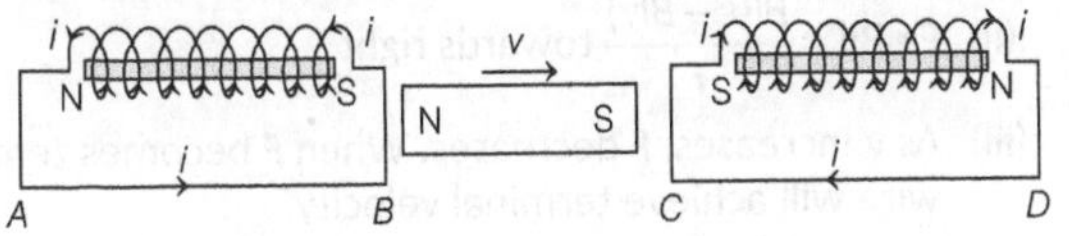

3.

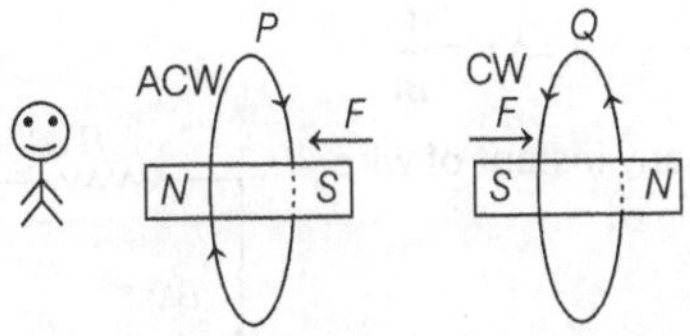

To oppose sudden flux, coil Q will repel and hence clockwise current in coil Q.

4.

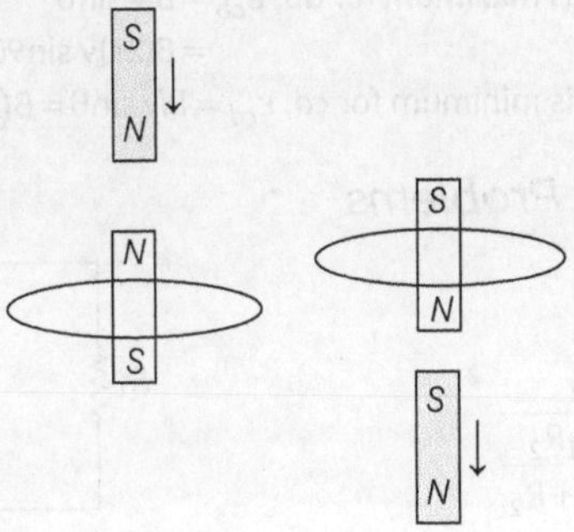

(i) When bar magnet is above the ring, it will be repelled. So, $a < g$.

(ii) When bar magnet is below the ring, it will be attracted. So, again $a < g$.

(iii) If the ring has a small cut, there will be induced emf in the ring but induced current will be zero. So, it will not exert any force on magnet and $a = g$

5. When the key is closed, current in the circuit will be clockwise and hence magnetic field inside circuit will be directed into the plane. So, magnetic flux through the loop is out of the plane and increasing. To oppose this, induced current in the loop will be clockwise. Similarly, when key is open, flux through the loop is out of the plane and decreasing. So, current will be anti-clockwise.

5.3 Induced EMF in a moving rod in Uniform Magnetic Field

1. $\varepsilon = Blv\sin\theta = 2(0.1)2\sin 90° = 0.4\text{V}$

Due to magnetic force ($\mathbf{F} = q(\mathbf{v}\times\mathbf{B})$), electrons will accumulate at end P. So, end Q will be positively charged.

2. $\varepsilon = Blv\sin\theta = (0.5)(1)(0.2)\sin 30° = 0.05\text{V}$

3. (i) $\phi = BA$ = constant, so $\varepsilon = \left|\frac{d\phi}{dt}\right| = 0$

(ii) $\varepsilon_{bc} = Blv\sin\theta$

$= B(l\sin\theta)v\sin 90° = Blv\sin\theta$

(iii) $\varepsilon_{ab} = Blv\sin\theta$

$= B(l\cos\theta)v\sin 0° = 0$

(iv) $\varepsilon_{ac} = Bl(v\sin\theta)\sin 90° = Blv\sin\theta$

4. Emf will be induced due to the vetical component of earth's magnetic field.

$$\varepsilon = B_v l v\sin\theta = (B\sin 30°)lv\sin 90°$$

$$= (4\times 10^{-4}\times 0.5)(1)(5) = 1\text{ mV}$$

5. $\varepsilon_{ABOCD} = \varepsilon_{AD} = Blv\sin\theta$

$= 5(2\sqrt{2})(10)\sin 90° = 100\sqrt{2}\text{V} = 141.4\text{ V}$

6.

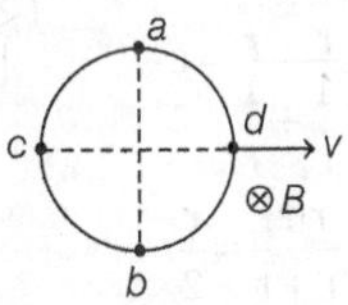

(i) Emf is maximum for ab, $\varepsilon_{ab} = Blv\sin\theta$
$= B(2r)v\sin 90° = 2Bvr$

(ii) Emf is minimum for cd, $\varepsilon_{cd} = Blv\sin\theta = B(2r)v\sin 0° = 0$

5.4 Circuit Problems

1. $i = \dfrac{Blv}{R_{eq}}$

$= \dfrac{Blv}{r + \dfrac{R_1R_2}{R_1 + R_2}}$

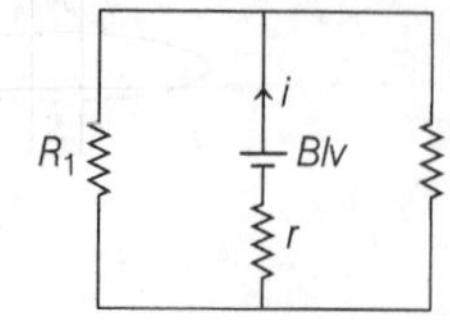

2. (i) Let at any instant velocity be v

$i = \dfrac{Blv}{R+r}$

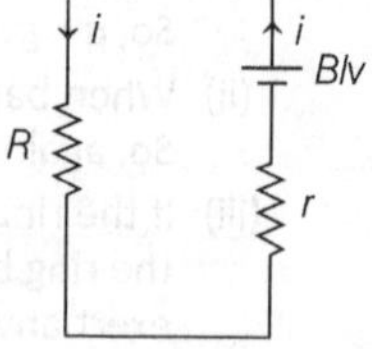

For rod,

$\Sigma F = ma$

$\Rightarrow -Bil = ma \Rightarrow -B\left(\dfrac{Blv}{R+r}\right)l = m\dfrac{dv}{dt}$

$\Rightarrow \displaystyle\int_u^v \frac{dv}{v} = -\frac{B^2l^2}{m(R+r)}\int_0^t dt$

$\Rightarrow \quad v = ue^{-B^2l^2t/(m(R+r))}$

(ii) $\dfrac{-B^2l^2v}{R+r} = mv\dfrac{dv}{dx}$

$\Rightarrow \displaystyle\int_u^0 dv = -\frac{B^2l^2}{m(R+r)}\int_0^x dx \Rightarrow x = \frac{mu(R+r)}{B^2l^2}$

3. (i) $i = \dfrac{Blv}{2rl + 2rvt} = \dfrac{Blv}{2r(l+vt)}$

(ii) $F = Bil = \dfrac{B^2l^2v}{2r(l+vt)}$

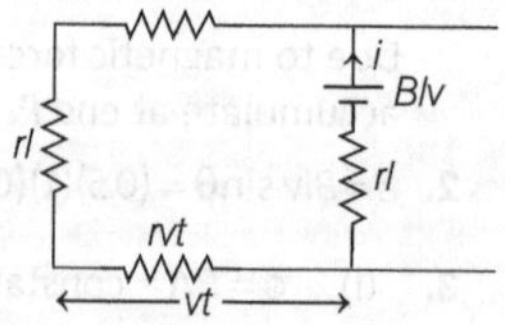

4. (i) $i = \dfrac{Blv}{8}$;

$F = Bil \Rightarrow F = \dfrac{B^2l^2v}{8}$

$\Rightarrow v = 5$ m/s

(ii) $\varepsilon = Blv = 2(2)(5) = 20$V

(iii) $V_b - V_a = \varepsilon - ir$

$= 20 - (2.5)(2) = 15$V

(iv) $V_c - V_d = ir$

$= (2.5)(2) = 5$V

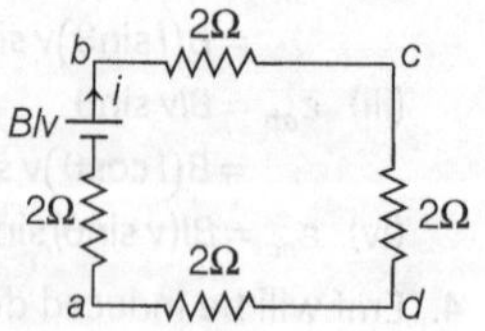

5. (i) $\varepsilon = Blv = 1 \times 0.04 \times 0.05 = 2$ mV

When both wires move towards right, induced emfs in them will have same polarities as shown.

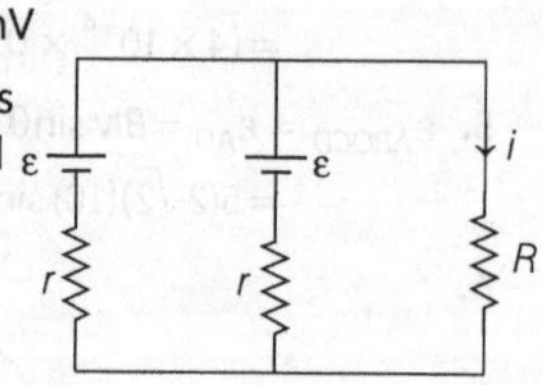

$\varepsilon_{eq} = \dfrac{\dfrac{\varepsilon}{r} + \dfrac{\varepsilon}{r}}{\dfrac{1}{r} + \dfrac{1}{r}} = \varepsilon$

and $\quad r_{eq} = \dfrac{r(r)}{r+r} = \dfrac{r}{2}$

So, $\quad i = \dfrac{\varepsilon_{eq}}{R + r_{eq}} = \dfrac{\varepsilon}{R + \dfrac{r}{2}} = 0.1$ mA

(ii) When P_1Q_1 moves towards left and P_2Q_2 towards right then induced emfs will have opposite polarities as shown.

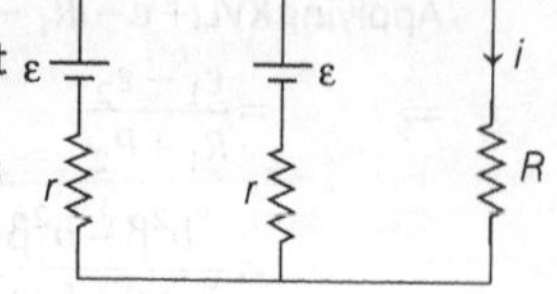

$\varepsilon_{eq} = \dfrac{\dfrac{\varepsilon}{r} - \dfrac{\varepsilon}{r}}{\dfrac{1}{r} + \dfrac{1}{r}} = 0$

So, $i = \dfrac{\varepsilon_{eq}}{R + r_{eq}} = 0$

6. Applying KVL in the loop,

$+Blv + xr - (i - x)r = 0$

$\Rightarrow \quad x = \dfrac{ir - Blv}{2r}$

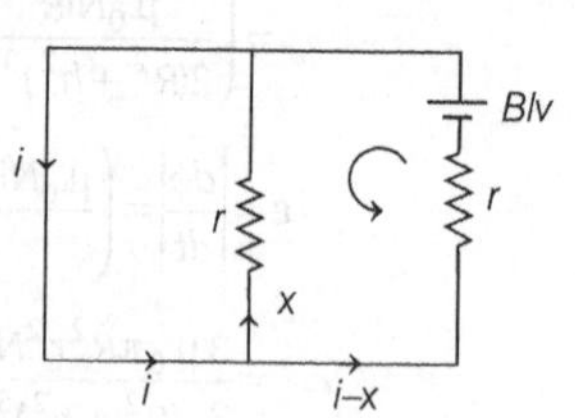

7. Along the inclined plane,

$\Sigma F = ma$

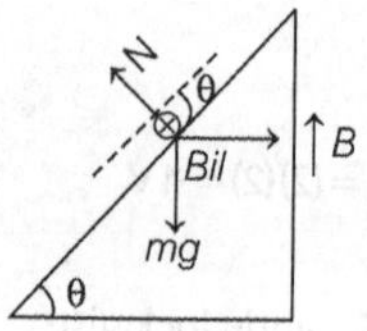

$\Rightarrow mg\sin\theta - Bil\cos\theta = 0$

$\Rightarrow mg\sin\theta - B\left(\dfrac{(B\cos\theta)lv}{R}\right)l\cos\theta = 0$

$\Rightarrow \quad B = \sqrt{\dfrac{mgR\sin\theta}{vl^2\cos^2\theta}}$

8. (i) $\varepsilon > Blv \;\because$ {v is small}

$\Rightarrow$ Current in the loop will be clockwise.

Applying KVL,

$+\varepsilon - Blv - ir = 0$

$\Rightarrow i = \dfrac{\varepsilon - Blv}{r}$

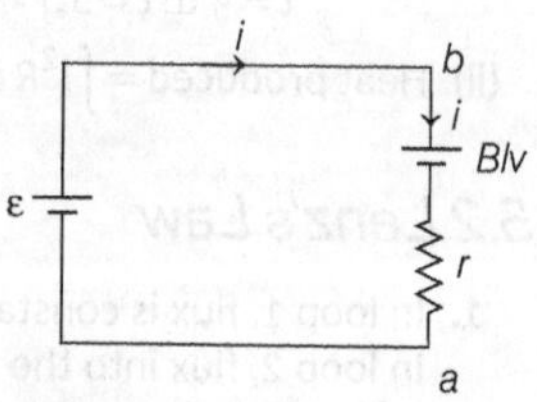

(ii) $F = Bil = \dfrac{Bl(\varepsilon - Blv)}{r}$ towards right

(iii) As v increases, F decreases. When F becomes zero, wire will achieve terminal velocity.

$F = \dfrac{Bl(\varepsilon - Blv)}{r} = 0 \Rightarrow v = \dfrac{\varepsilon}{Bl}$

9. (i) Let velocity at any instant of wire be v.

$i = \dfrac{Blv}{R+r}$

$\Sigma F = ma \Rightarrow mg - Bil = ma$

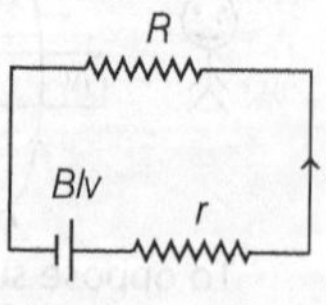

$$\Rightarrow mg - B\left(\frac{Blv}{R+r}\right)l = m\frac{dv}{dt}$$

$$\Rightarrow \int_0^v \frac{dv}{g - \frac{B^2l^2v}{m(R+r)}} = \int_o^t dt \Rightarrow v = v_m(1-e^{-gt/v_m})$$

where, $v_m = \dfrac{mg(R+r)}{B^2l^2}$

(ii) At $t=\infty$; $v = v_m = \dfrac{mg(R+r)}{B^2l^2}$

(iii) $v = \dfrac{dx}{dt} = v_m(1-e^{-gt/v_m})$

$$\Rightarrow \int_0^x dx = v_m\int_0^t (1-e^{-gt/v_m})dt$$

$$\Rightarrow x = v_m t - \frac{v_m^2}{g}(1-e^{-gt/v_m})$$

(iv) In steady state,

Rate of heat developed $= \dfrac{(Blv_m)^2}{R+r}$

Rate of loss of gravitational potential energy

$$= \frac{dU}{dt} = mg\frac{dh}{dt} = mg\,v_m$$

10. Let velocity be v at any instant of time and charge on capacitor be q.

$$+\frac{q}{c} - Blv = 0$$

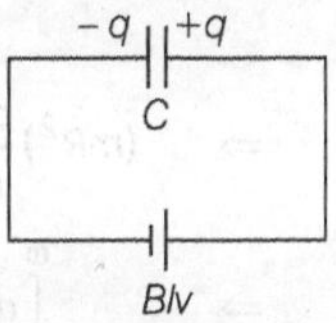

$\Rightarrow \quad q = BlCv$

$\Rightarrow \quad \dfrac{dq}{dt} = BlC\dfrac{dv}{dt}$

$\Rightarrow \quad i = Blca$

$\Sigma F = ma \Rightarrow mg - Bil = ma$

$\Rightarrow mg - B(Blca)l = ma$

$\Rightarrow \quad a = \dfrac{mg}{m + B^2l^2C}$

$v = u + at$

$\Rightarrow \quad v = 0 + \left(\dfrac{mg}{m+B^2l^2C}\right)t$

$\Rightarrow \quad v = \dfrac{mgt}{m+B^2l^2C}$

5.5 Induced EMF in a Rod, Ring and Disc Rotating in a Uniform Magnetic Field

1. $V_P - V_Q = \dfrac{1}{2}B\omega(2l)^2 = 100$

$\Rightarrow \quad \dfrac{1}{2}B\omega l^2 = 25\text{V}$

$V_p - V_m = \dfrac{1}{2}B\omega l^2 = 25\text{V}$

$V_M - V_Q = (V_P - V_Q) - (V_P - V_M) = 100 - 25 = 75\text{V}$

2. $V_a - V_b = \displaystyle\int_{-l/5}^{4l/5} \frac{1}{2}B(\omega x)dx = \frac{3}{10}B\omega l^2$

3. $\varepsilon = \dfrac{1}{2}B\omega a^2 + \varepsilon + \varepsilon - iR = 0$

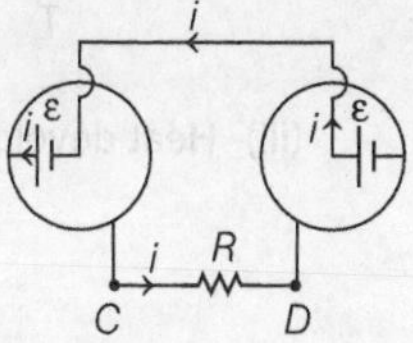

$\Rightarrow \quad i = \dfrac{2\varepsilon}{R} = \dfrac{B\omega a^2}{R}$, C to D

4. Emf induced in each spoke $= \dfrac{1}{2}B\omega l^2$

$$= \frac{1}{2}\times 0.4\times 10^{-4}\times\left(\frac{120}{60}\times 2\pi\right)(0.5)^2 = 6.28\times 10^{-5}\text{V}$$

5. $i = \left(\dfrac{1}{2}B\omega a^2\right)/R$

$\Sigma\tau = 0$

$$\Rightarrow F\left(\frac{a}{2}\right) - \int_0^a (Bidx)x = 0 \Rightarrow F = Bia = \frac{B^2\omega a^3}{2R}$$

6. $\varepsilon = \dfrac{1}{2}B\omega R^2 = \dfrac{1}{2}\times 100\times 10^{-4}\times(10\times 2\pi)\times(0.1)^2 = 3.14\text{mV}$

7. (i) $\varepsilon_{PQ} = \dfrac{1}{2}B\omega(2R)^2 = \dfrac{1}{2}B\left(\dfrac{v}{R}\right)(2R)^2 = 2BvR$

(ii) $\varepsilon_{PC} = \dfrac{1}{2}B\omega R^2 = \dfrac{1}{2}B\left(\dfrac{v}{R}\right)(R)^2 = \dfrac{BvR}{2}$

(iii) $\varepsilon_{QC} = \varepsilon_{PQ} - \varepsilon_{PC} = 2BvR - \dfrac{BVR}{2} = \dfrac{3BVR}{2}$

8. (i) $\phi = NBA\cos\omega t$

$$\varepsilon = \left|\frac{d\phi}{dt}\right| = NBA\omega\sin\omega t$$

$$\varepsilon_{max} = NBA\omega = 50\times 2\times 10^{-4}\times 100\times 10^{-4}\times\left(\frac{300}{60}\times 2\pi\right)$$

$= 3.14$ mV

(ii) $\varepsilon = NBA\omega\sin\omega t = (3.14\text{mV})\sin(10\pi t)$

(iii) $\varepsilon^2 = (NBA\omega)^2\sin^2\omega t$

$$<\varepsilon^2> = (NBA\omega)^2 < \sin^2\omega t> = \frac{1}{2}(NB\,A\omega)^2$$

$$= \frac{1}{2}(3.14\times 10^{-3})^2 = 4.93\times 10^{-6}$$

5.6 EMF Induced in a Rod or Loop in Non-uniform Magnetic Field

1. (i) $\displaystyle\int d\phi = \int_b^{b+a}\left(\frac{\mu_0 i}{2\pi x}\right)(adx)\cos 0°$

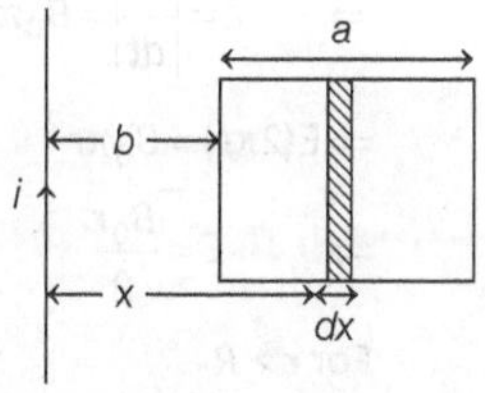

$$\Rightarrow \phi = \frac{\mu_0 ia}{2\pi}\ln\left(1+\frac{a}{b}\right)$$

(ii) $\varepsilon = \left|\dfrac{d\phi}{dt}\right|$

$$= \frac{\mu_0 a}{2\pi} \ln\left(\frac{a+b}{b}\right) \left|\frac{di}{dt}\right|$$

$$= \frac{\mu_0 a i_0}{T} \left(\ln\left(\frac{a+b}{b}\right)\right) \sin\left(\frac{2\pi t}{T}\right)$$

(iii) Heat developed $= \int_0^{10T} \frac{\varepsilon^2}{R} dt$

$$= \left(\frac{5\mu_0^2 i_0^2 a^2}{TR}\right)\left[\ln\left(\frac{a+b}{b}\right)\right]^2$$

2. $\varepsilon = \int_0^L \left(\frac{B_0 x}{L}\right) dx v_0 = \frac{B_0 v_0 L}{2}$

3. (i) $\varepsilon = \int_a^b \left(\frac{\mu_0 i_0}{2\pi x}\right) dx\, v$

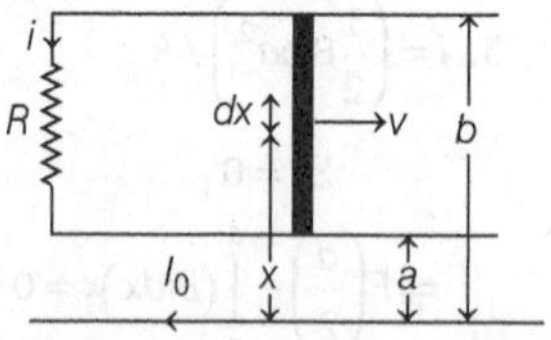

$$= \frac{\mu_0 i_0 v}{2\pi} \ln\left(\frac{b}{a}\right)$$

$$i = \frac{\varepsilon}{R} = \frac{\mu_0 i_0 v}{2\pi R} \ln\left(\frac{b}{a}\right)$$

(ii) $F = \int_a^b \left(\frac{\mu_0 i_0}{2\pi x}\right) i dx$

$$= \left(\frac{\mu_0 i_0}{2\pi}\right) i \ln\left(\frac{b}{a}\right) = \frac{v}{R}\left[\frac{\mu_0 i_0}{2\pi} \ln\left(\frac{b}{a}\right)\right]^2$$

4. $\tan 45° = \frac{h}{y - x}$

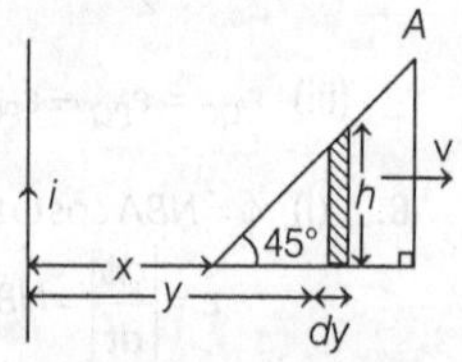

$\Rightarrow \quad h = y - x$

$$\phi = \int d\phi = \int_x^{x+a} \frac{\mu_0 i}{2\pi y}(y - x)\, dy \cos 0°$$

$$= \frac{\mu_0 i}{2\pi}\left[a - x \ln\left(\frac{x+a}{x}\right)\right]$$

$$\varepsilon = \left|\frac{d\phi}{dt}\right| = \frac{\mu_0 i}{2\pi}\left[x\left(\frac{x}{x+a}\right)\left(\frac{-a}{x^2}\right)\frac{dx}{dt} + \ln\left(\left(\frac{x+a}{x}\right)\frac{dx}{dt}\right)\right]$$

$$= \frac{\mu_0 i v}{2\pi}\left[\ln 2 - \frac{1}{2}\right]$$

5.7 Induced Electric Field

1. For $r < R$,

$$\phi = BA\cos\theta$$

$\Rightarrow \quad \phi = (B_0 t)\pi r^2 \cos 0°$

$\Rightarrow \quad \varepsilon = \left|\frac{d\phi}{dt}\right| = B_0 \pi r^2$

$\Rightarrow E(2\pi r) = B_0 \pi r^2$

$\Rightarrow \quad E = \frac{B_0 r}{2}$

For $r > R$

$$\phi = B(\pi R^2)\cos 0° = (B_0 t)\pi R^2$$

$\Rightarrow \quad \varepsilon = \left|\frac{d\phi}{dt}\right| = B_0 \pi R^2$

$\Rightarrow E(2\pi r) = B_0 \pi R^2$

$\Rightarrow \quad E = \frac{B_0 R^2}{2r}$

2. For closed loop ABC,

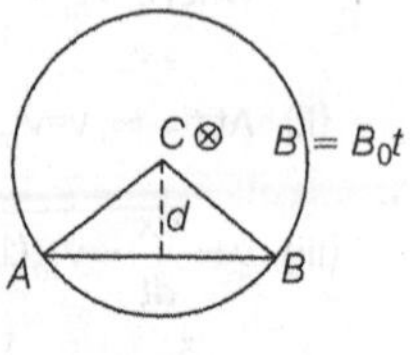

$$\phi = (B_0 t)\left(\frac{1}{2} l\, d\right)$$

$\Rightarrow \quad \varepsilon = \left|\frac{d\phi}{dt}\right| = \frac{B_0 l d}{2}$

$\Rightarrow \varepsilon_{AB} + \varepsilon_{BC} + \varepsilon_{CA} = \frac{B_0 l d}{2}$

$\Rightarrow \quad \varepsilon_{AB} + 0 + 0 = \frac{B_0 l d}{2}$

$\Rightarrow \quad \varepsilon_{AB} = \frac{B_0 l d}{2}$

3. $\phi = B(\pi R^2)\cos 0°$

$\Rightarrow \quad \varepsilon = \left|\frac{d\phi}{dt}\right| = \pi R^2 \frac{dB}{dt}$

$\Rightarrow \quad E(2\pi R) = \pi R^2 \frac{dB}{dt}$

$\Rightarrow \quad E = \frac{R}{2}\frac{dB}{dt}$

$$\tau = (qE)R$$

$\Rightarrow \quad (mR^2)\frac{d\omega}{dt} = q\left(\frac{R}{2}\frac{dB}{dt}\right)R$

$\Rightarrow \quad \int_0^{\omega} d\omega = \frac{q}{2m}\int_0^{B} dB$

$\Rightarrow \quad \omega = \frac{qB}{2m}$

Level 2

Single Choice Correct Questions

1. $|\varepsilon_{avg}| = \left|\frac{\Delta\phi}{\Delta t}\right| = \left|\frac{0-2}{6}\right| = \frac{1}{3}$ V

2. $\varepsilon = -\frac{d\phi}{dt} = -3(3at^2 - 2bt)$

$$i = \frac{\varepsilon}{R} = -(3at^2 - 2bt)$$

$$\frac{di}{dt} = -(6at - 2b) = 0$$

$\Rightarrow \quad t = \frac{b}{3a}$

At $\quad t = \frac{b}{3a}$;

$$i_{max} = -\left[3a\left(\frac{b}{3a}\right)^2 - 2b\left(\frac{b}{3a}\right)\right] = \frac{b^2}{3a} = 6\text{ A}$$

3. $\phi_1 = NBA\cos 0°$;

$\phi_2 = NBA\cos 90° = 0$

$$q = \frac{|\Delta\phi|}{R} = \frac{|0 - NBA|}{R}$$

$$= \frac{NBA}{R} = 0.2\,C$$

4. $$\varepsilon_{avg} = \left|\frac{\Delta\phi}{\Delta t}\right|$$

$$\Rightarrow \quad 10 = \frac{\left|0 - 20\times(0.1)^2\right|}{\Delta t}$$

$$\Rightarrow \quad \Delta t = 20\text{ ms}$$

5. $$|\varepsilon| = \left|\frac{d\phi}{dt}\right| = \frac{d(B\pi R^2)}{dt} = B\pi 2R\frac{dR}{dt} = 2\pi(R_0 + t)B$$

As radius increases, magnetic flux through the loop increases. To oppose that induced current will be anti-clockwise.

6. Let angular speed of electron be ω at any time

$$i = \frac{e\omega}{2\pi}; B = \frac{\mu_0 i}{2R}$$

$$\phi = \left(\frac{\mu_0}{2R}\left(\frac{e\omega}{2\pi}\right)\right)\pi r^2;$$

$$\varepsilon = \frac{d\phi}{dt} = \frac{\mu_0 e r^2}{4R}\frac{d\omega}{dt} = \frac{\mu_0 e r^2}{4R}\alpha$$

7. The emf will be induced in each loop in such a way that induced current will be anti-clockwise in each loop to oppose the flux increasing in ⊗ direction :

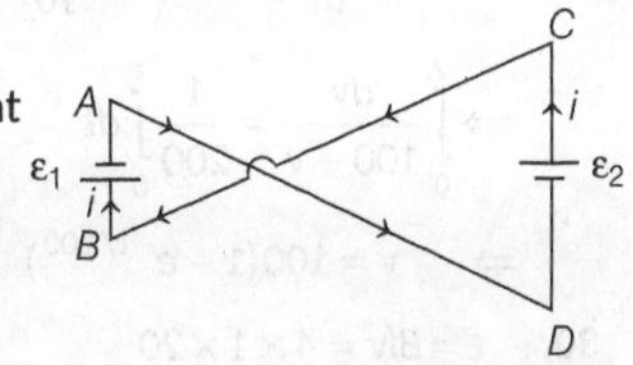

$\varepsilon_2 > \varepsilon_1$ ∵ {Induced emt will be greater in the bigger loop}

So, current in bigger loop will be anti-clockwise and in the smaller loop clockwise.

8. $$\phi = BA = B\left(\frac{1}{2}(2x)(x)\right) = Bx^2$$

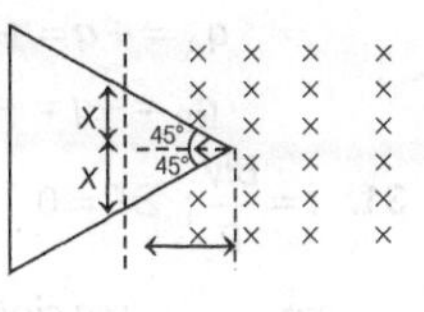

$$\varepsilon = \frac{d\phi}{dt} = 2Bx\frac{dx}{dt}$$

$$= 2Bxv$$

$$i = \frac{\varepsilon}{R} = \frac{2Bv(vt)}{R} = \left(\frac{2Bv^2}{R}\right)t$$

$$\Rightarrow \quad i \propto t$$

9. When loop enter or comes out of magnetic field, according to Lenz's law induced current will oppose motion. So, $a < g$. When loop is completely inside magnetic field, induced current will be zero as flux is constant, So $a = g$.

10. Current at t_1, t_2, t_3, will be in same direction as $\frac{di}{dt}$ is of same sign (negative) at t_1, t_2 and t_3.

11.

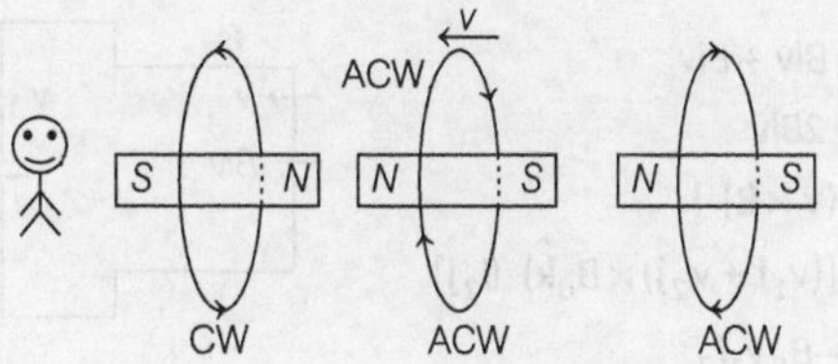

12. According to Lenz's law, conductor Q will be attracted to conductor P to oppose change of flux.

13. $$\varepsilon = Blv\sin 90°$$

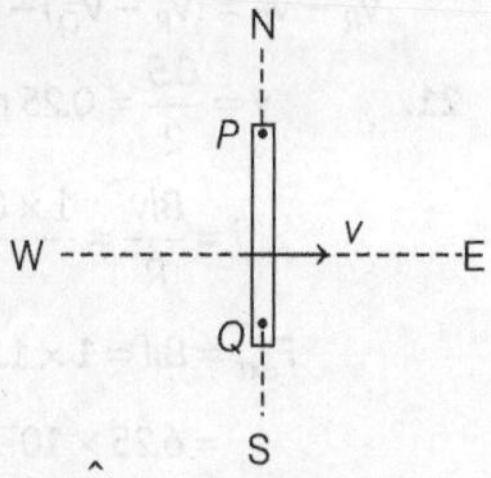

$$\Rightarrow V_P - V_Q = 4(0.3)(10)$$

$$\Rightarrow \quad V_p - 0 = 12$$

$$\Rightarrow \quad V_P = 12\text{V}$$

14. $$\varepsilon = (\mathbf{v}\times\mathbf{B})\cdot\mathbf{l}$$

$$= (2\hat{i}\times(3\hat{j} + 4\hat{k}))\cdot(5\cos 53°\,\hat{i} + 5\sin 53°\,\hat{j})$$

$$= (-8\hat{j} + 6\hat{k})\cdot(3\hat{i} + 4\hat{j})$$

$$= -32\text{ V}$$

15. $$\varepsilon = Bv(2R)\sin\theta$$

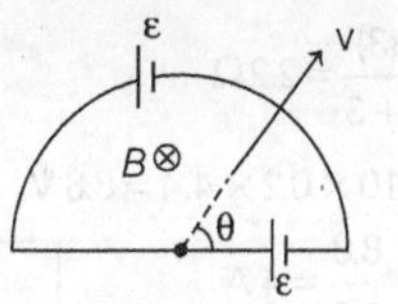

16. $$\int d\varepsilon = \int_{r_1}^{r_2}\left(\frac{\mu_0 i}{2\pi x}\right)v\,dx$$

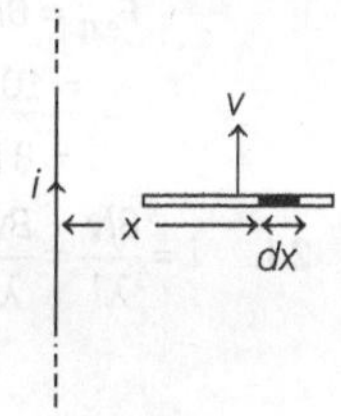

$$\Rightarrow \quad \varepsilon = \frac{\mu_0 iv}{2\pi}\ln\left(\frac{r_2}{r_1}\right)$$

17. $$\varepsilon_{BC} = \left[B_0\left(1 + \frac{x+d}{a}\right)\right]v_0 d$$

$$\varepsilon_{DA} = B_0\left(1 + \frac{x}{a}\right)v_0 d$$

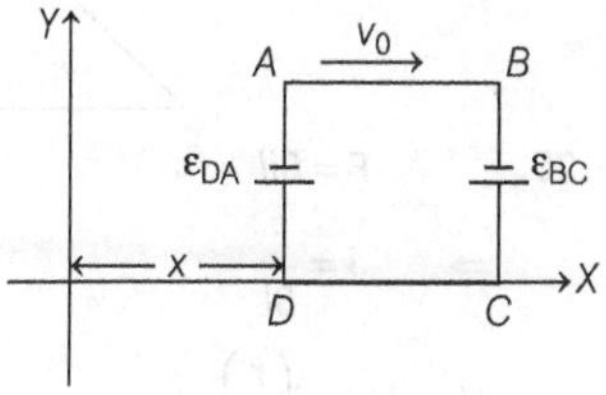

ε_{AB} and ε_{CD} will be zero as **v**|| **dl**

$$\varepsilon_{net} = \varepsilon_{BC} - \varepsilon_{DA}$$

$$= \frac{B_0 v_0 d^2}{a}$$

$$i = \frac{\varepsilon_{net}}{R} = \frac{B_0 v_0 d^2}{aR}$$

18. $$v^2 = u^2 + 2as$$

$$\Rightarrow \quad v = \sqrt{2ay}$$

$$\varepsilon = Blv = B(2x)\sqrt{2ay}$$

$$= 2B\sqrt{\frac{y}{k}}\sqrt{2ay} = By\sqrt{\frac{8a}{k}}$$

19. $\varepsilon_{net} = Blv + Blv$

$= 2Blv$

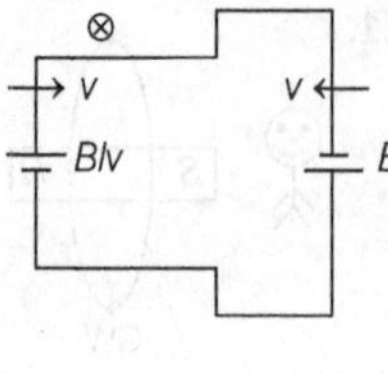

20. $\varepsilon = (\mathbf{v} \times \mathbf{B}) \cdot \mathbf{l}$

$V_P - V_Q = [(v_1\hat{\mathbf{i}} + v_2\hat{\mathbf{j}}) \times B_0\hat{\mathbf{k}}) \cdot (l_2\hat{\mathbf{j}}]$

$= -B_0 v_1 l_2$

$V_R - V_Q = [v_1\hat{\mathbf{i}} + v_2\hat{\mathbf{j}}) \times B_0\hat{\mathbf{k}}] \cdot (l_1\hat{\mathbf{i}}) = B_0 v_2 l_1$

$V_R - V_P = (V_R - V_Q) - (V_P - V_Q) = B_0(l_2 v_1 + l_2 v_2)$

21. $v = \frac{0.5}{2} = 0.25$ m/s

$i = \frac{Blv}{R} = \frac{1 \times 0.5 \times 0.25}{10} = 1.25 \times 10^{-2}$ A

$F_{ext} = Bil = 1 \times 1.25 \times 10^{-2} \times 0.5$

$= 6.25 \times 10^{-3}$ N

$W = F_{ext} l = 6.25 \times 10^{-3} \times 0.5 = 3.125 \times 10^{-3}$ J

22. $\varepsilon = Bv_0(2R)$

P.d. across $r = 0$

So $i = 0$

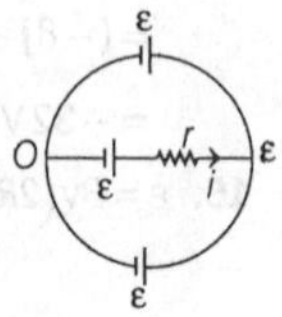

23. $R_{eq} = 1 + \frac{2(3)}{2+3} = 2.2\Omega$

$\varepsilon = Blv = 10 \times 0.2 \times 4.4 = 8.8$ V

$i = \frac{\varepsilon}{R_{eq}} = \frac{8.8}{2.2} = 4$ A

$F_{ext} = Bil$

$= 10 \times 4 \times (0.2)$

$= 8$ N

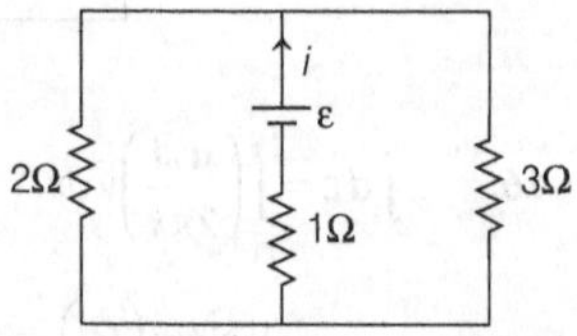

24. $i = \frac{Blv}{\lambda l} = \frac{Bv}{\lambda}$

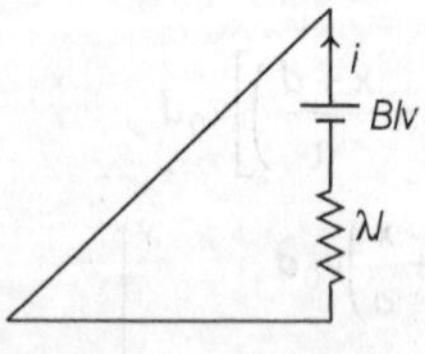

25. $F = Bil$

$\Rightarrow \quad i = \frac{F}{Bl}$

$V_P - V_S = i\left(\frac{r}{6}\right)$

$= \frac{Fr}{6Bl}$

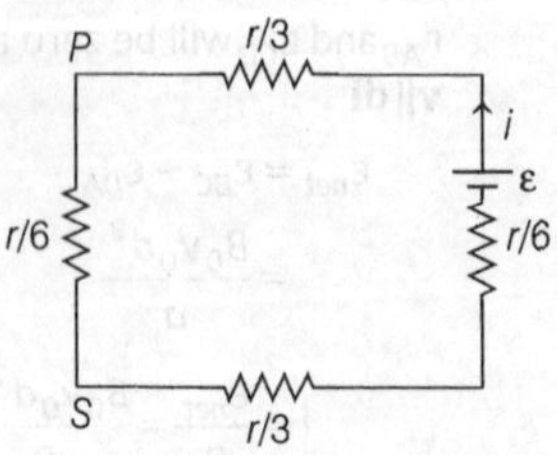

Induced emf in $PS = 0$

26. $F = Bil = 5 \times 10^{-3} \times 2 \times 0.1 = 10^{-3}$ N

$a = \frac{F}{m} = \frac{1 \times 10^{-3}}{50 \times 10^{-3}} = 0.02 \text{ m/s}^2$

$v = u + at = 0 + (0.02)(10)$

$= 0.2$ m/s $= 20$ cm/s

27. $\varepsilon = B(2r)v = 2Bvr$

$i = \frac{\varepsilon}{R/2} = \frac{2\varepsilon}{R}$

Current through

$PQ = 2i = \frac{4\varepsilon}{R}$

$= \frac{8Bvr}{R}$

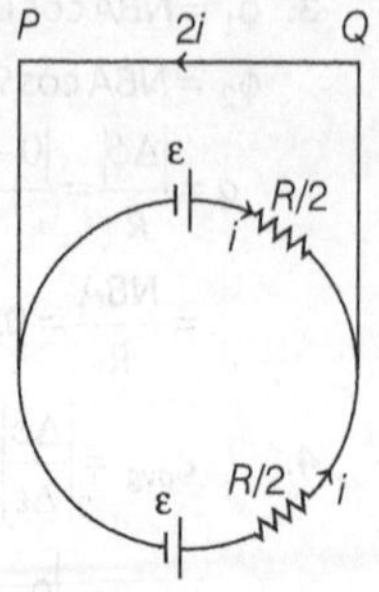

28. $F_{ext} = Bil$

$\Rightarrow \quad 0.5 = 0.5 \times i \times 0.25$

$\Rightarrow \quad i = 4$ A

$i = \frac{10 - \varepsilon}{2} \Rightarrow 4 = \frac{10 - Blv}{2}$

$\Rightarrow \quad v = 16$ m/s

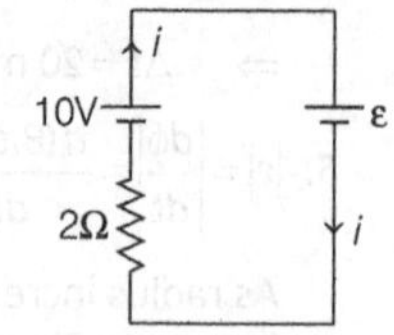

29. Let velocity be v at any time.

$\varepsilon = Blv = 0.02 \times 0.5 \times v$

$\Rightarrow \quad \varepsilon = 0.01v$

$i = \frac{1 - \varepsilon}{10} = \frac{1 - 0.01v}{10}$

$F = Bil$

$\Rightarrow m\frac{dv}{dt} = Bil$

$\Rightarrow 0.002\frac{dv}{dt} = 0.02\left(\frac{1 - 0.01v}{10}\right)(0.5)$

$\Rightarrow \int_0^v \frac{dv}{100 - v} = \frac{1}{200}\int_0^t dt$

$\Rightarrow \quad v = 100(1 - e^{-t/200})$

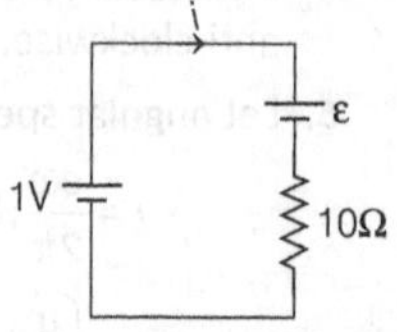

30. $\varepsilon = Blv = 4 \times 1 \times 20$

$= 80$ V

$q = C\varepsilon = (10\mu\text{F})(80\text{V})$

$= 800\mu$C

$q_A = +q = +800\mu$C;

$q_B = -q = -800\mu$C

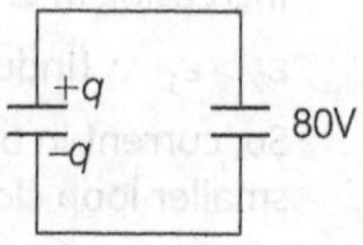

31. $i = \frac{Blv}{R}$; $\Sigma F = 0$

$\Rightarrow \quad mg \sin\theta - Bil = 0$

$\Rightarrow \quad mg \sin\theta - B\left(\frac{Blv}{R}\right)l = 0$

$\Rightarrow \quad v = \frac{mgR \sin\theta}{B^2 l^2}$

32. $\phi = NBA \cos\omega t,$

$\varepsilon = \left|\frac{d\phi}{dt}\right| = NBA\omega \sin\omega t$

$i = \frac{\varepsilon}{R} = \frac{NBA\omega}{R} \sin\omega t$

$$i_m = \frac{NBA\omega}{R}$$

$$= \frac{100\times 10\times 10^{-3}\times \pi(0.1)^2\times(100\times 2\pi)}{10} = 2A$$

33. $\varepsilon = \int_{l/4}^{l} B(\omega x)dx = B\omega\left[\frac{x^2}{2}\right]_{l/4}^{l} = \frac{15B\omega l^2}{32}$

34. $\varepsilon_{rod} = \varepsilon_{PQ} = \frac{1}{2}B\omega\left(\sqrt{L^2+l^2}\right)^2$

$$= \frac{1}{2}B\omega(L^2+l^2)$$

35. $\varepsilon = \int(\mathbf{v}\times\mathbf{B})\cdot dl$

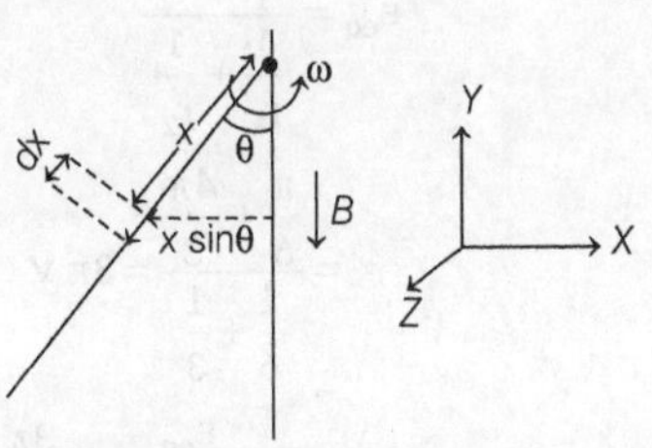

$\mathbf{v} = \omega(x\sin\theta)\hat{\mathbf{k}}$

$\mathbf{B} = -B\hat{\mathbf{j}}$

$\mathbf{dl} = -dx\sin\theta\hat{\mathbf{i}}$

$-dx\cos\theta\,\hat{\mathbf{j}}$

$$\varepsilon = \int[\omega(x\sin\theta\hat{\mathbf{k}})\times(-B\hat{\mathbf{j}})]\cdot(dx\sin\theta\hat{\mathbf{i}} - dx\cos\theta\hat{\mathbf{j}})$$

$$= \int[(B\omega x\sin\theta\hat{\mathbf{i}})\cdot(-dx\sin\theta\hat{\mathbf{i}} - dx\cos\theta\hat{\mathbf{j}})]$$

$$= -B\omega\sin^2\theta\int_0^L x\,dx = \frac{-1}{2}B\omega L^2\sin^2\theta$$

36. $\varepsilon = \int Bv\,dx = \int_0^{L/2} B_0\left(v_0 + \frac{v_0}{L}x\right)dx = \frac{5}{8}B_0v_0L$

37. About instantaneous axis of rotation through Q, ring is in pure rotation. So,

$$\varepsilon = \frac{1}{2}B\omega l^2 = \frac{1}{2}B\omega(\sqrt{2}R)^2 = B\omega R^2$$

38. $\varepsilon = \frac{1}{2}B\omega R^2 = \frac{1}{2}\times 50\times 20\times(0.1)^2$

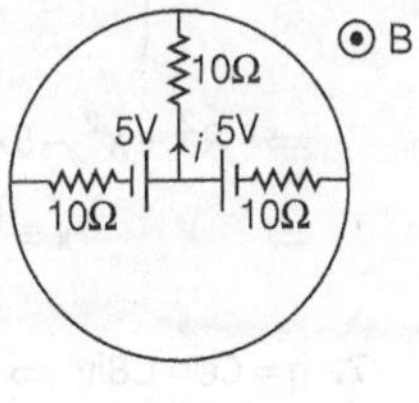

$= 5\text{ V}$

$$\varepsilon_{eq} = \frac{\frac{5}{10}+\frac{5}{10}}{\frac{1}{10}+\frac{1}{10}} = 5\text{ V};$$

$$r_{eq} = \frac{10(10)}{10+10} = 5\Omega$$

$$i = \frac{\varepsilon_{eq}}{R + r_{eq}} = \frac{5}{10+5} = \frac{1}{3}\text{A}$$

39. $\varepsilon = \frac{1}{2}B\omega r^2,\ i = \frac{\varepsilon}{R} = \frac{1}{2}\frac{B\omega r^2}{R}$

$$F_b = Bir$$

$$\Sigma\tau = 0$$

$$\Rightarrow \quad Fr - (Bir)\frac{r}{2} = 0$$

$$\Rightarrow \quad F = \frac{B^2\omega r^3}{4R}$$

40. $\phi = -B_1A - B_2A + B_3A$

$$= (B_3 - B_1 - B_2)A$$

$$\frac{d\phi}{dt} = \left(\frac{dB_3}{dt} - \frac{dB_1}{dt} - \frac{dB_2}{dt}\right)A$$

$$= (-\alpha - (-\alpha) - (-\alpha))A = \alpha A$$

$$\varepsilon = -\frac{d\phi}{dt}$$

$$\Rightarrow \oint \mathbf{E}\cdot d\mathbf{r} = -\alpha A$$

41. $\varepsilon = \frac{d\phi}{dt} \Rightarrow E(2\pi r) = \pi r^2\frac{dB}{dt}$

$$\Rightarrow \quad E = \frac{r}{2}\frac{dB}{dt}$$

At point P, $\mathbf{E} = \frac{R}{2}\frac{dB}{dt}$ towards right,

$\mathbf{a} = \frac{q\mathbf{E}}{m} = \frac{keR}{2m}$ towards left.

42. For $r \le R$,

$$E(2\pi r) = \frac{d}{dt}\left(\int_0^r B(2\pi r)dr\right)$$

$$\Rightarrow \quad Er = \frac{d}{dt}\left(\frac{ktr^3}{3}\right)$$

$$\Rightarrow \quad E = \frac{kr^2}{3}$$

For $r > R$,

$$E(2\pi r) = \frac{d}{dt}\left(\int_0^R B2\pi r dr\right) \Rightarrow E = \frac{kR^3}{3r}$$

At $r = \frac{R}{2}, E_1 = \frac{kR^2}{12}$ and $r = 2R, E_2 = \frac{kR^2}{6}$

$$\therefore \quad \frac{E_2}{E_1} = 2$$

43. For loop EBC,

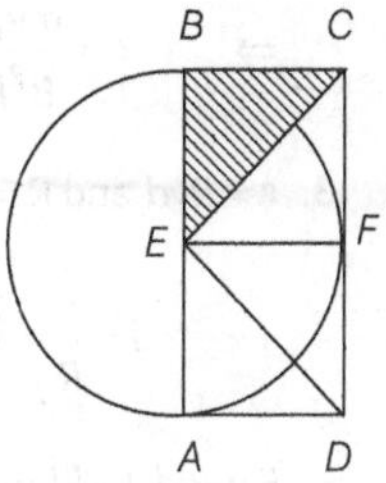

$$\phi = BA = B\left(\frac{R^2}{2}\left(\frac{\pi}{4}\right)\right)$$

$$|\varepsilon| = \left|\frac{d\phi}{dt}\right|$$

$$\Rightarrow \oint \mathbf{E}\cdot\mathbf{dl} = \left(\frac{\pi R^2}{8}\right)\frac{dB}{dt}$$

$$\Rightarrow \int_E^B \mathbf{E}\cdot\mathbf{dl} + \int_B^C \mathbf{E}\cdot\mathbf{dl} + \int_C^E \mathbf{E}\cdot\mathbf{dl} = \left(\frac{\pi R^2}{8}\right)\frac{dB}{dt}$$

$$\Rightarrow 0 + \int_B^C \mathbf{E}\cdot\mathbf{dl} + 0 = \left(\frac{\pi R^2}{8}\right)b = \varepsilon_{BC} = \frac{\pi R^2 b}{8}$$

$$\Rightarrow \quad \varepsilon_{AB} = \int_A^B \mathbf{E}\cdot\mathbf{dl} = 0 \ \therefore\ \mathbf{E}\perp\mathbf{dl}$$

45. $\varepsilon = \left|\frac{d\phi}{dt}\right| \Rightarrow E(2\pi r) = \pi a^2 \frac{dB}{dt} \Rightarrow E = \frac{a^2}{2r}\frac{dB}{dt} = \frac{a^2 B_0 t}{r}$

When the ring just starts to rotate,

$\tau_E = \tau_{friction}$

$\Rightarrow (qE)r = (\mu mg)r$

$\Rightarrow (\lambda 2\pi r)\left(\frac{a^2}{r}B_0 t\right)r = \mu mgr$

$\Rightarrow \quad t = \frac{\mu mg}{2\pi\lambda B_0 a^2} = 4\text{ s}$

Numerical Value Questions

1.

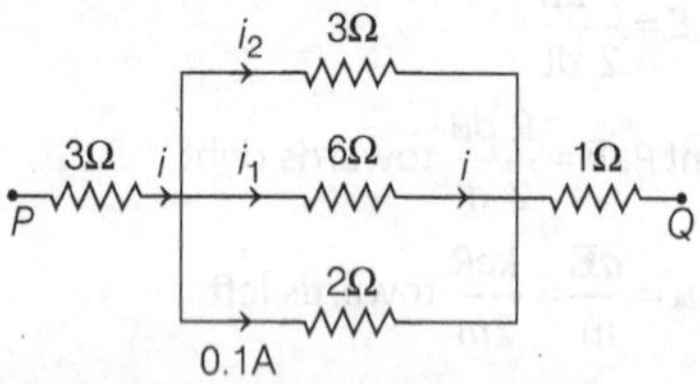

$i = i_1 + i_2 + 0.1$

$= \frac{0.1}{3} + \frac{(0.1)2}{3} + 0.1 = 0.2\text{ A}$

$V_P - V_Q = i\left(3 + 1 + \left(\frac{1}{3} + \frac{1}{6} + \frac{1}{2}\right)^{-1}\right) = 1\text{ V}$

$V_P - V_Q = Blv = 1$

$\Rightarrow \quad 2 \times 0.1 \times v = 1$

$\Rightarrow \quad v = 5\text{ m/s}$

2. $i = \frac{Blv}{R}, \quad F = Bil = ma$

$\Rightarrow \frac{B^2 l^2 v}{R} = -mv\frac{dv}{dx}$

$\Rightarrow \int_0^x dx = -\frac{mR}{B^2 l^2}\int_{v_0}^0 dv$

$\Rightarrow \quad x = \frac{mv_0 R}{B^2 l^2} = 8\text{ m}$

3. $\varepsilon = Bvd$ and $R = \lambda\left(\frac{\pi d}{2}\right)$

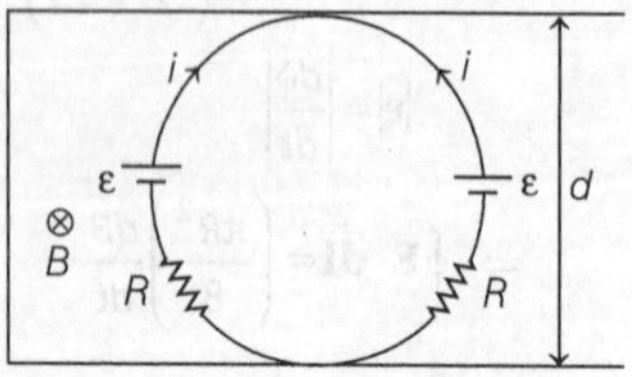

$i = \frac{\varepsilon}{R} = \frac{2Bv}{\pi\lambda}$

$F = Bid + Bid = \frac{4B^2 vd}{\pi\lambda}$

So, N=4

4. Area of loop $= A_{BCD} - A_{AFE}$

$= \frac{\pi(3a)(2a)}{2} - \frac{\pi(2a)(a)}{2} = 2\pi a^2$

$\phi = BA\cos\omega t = B_0(2\pi a^2)\cos\omega t$

$\varepsilon = \frac{d\phi}{dt} = -B_0(2\pi a^2)\omega\sin\omega t$

$\Rightarrow \varepsilon_{max} = 2\pi\omega B_0 a^2$ So, $K = 2$

5. $\varepsilon_1 = A_1\frac{dB}{dt} = \pi(0.1)^2(100) = \pi\text{ V}$

$\varepsilon_2 = A_2\frac{dB}{dt} = \pi(0.2)^2(100) = 4\pi\text{V}$

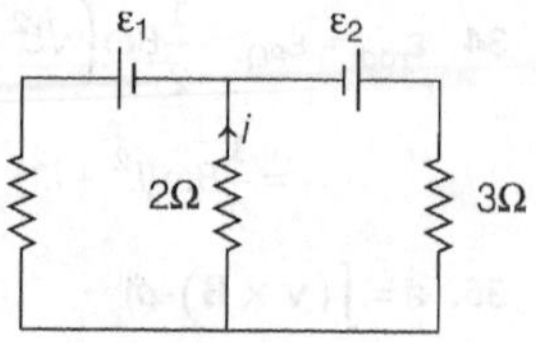

$r_{eq} = \frac{6(3)}{6+3} = 2\Omega$

$\varepsilon_{eq} = \frac{\frac{\varepsilon_1}{r_1} + \frac{\varepsilon_2}{r_2}}{\frac{1}{r_1} + \frac{1}{r_2}}$

$= \frac{\frac{\pi}{6} + \frac{4\pi}{3}}{\frac{1}{6} + \frac{1}{3}} = 3\pi\text{ V}$

$= i = \frac{\varepsilon_{eq}}{R + r_{eq}} = \frac{3\pi}{2+2} = \frac{3\pi}{4}\text{A} = 2.36\text{ A}$

6. $\phi = BA\cos\theta = \left(\frac{\mu_0 NIR^2}{2(R^2 + x^2)^{3/2}}\right)\pi r^2\cos 0°$

$\varepsilon = \left|\frac{d\phi}{dt}\right| = \left(\frac{\mu_0 NIR^2\pi r^2}{2}\right)\left(-\frac{3}{2}\frac{2x}{(R^2 + x^2)^{5/2}}\frac{dx}{dt}\right)$

To maximize ε, $\frac{d\varepsilon}{dt} = 0$

$\Rightarrow \quad -\frac{3}{2}\mu_0 NIR^2\pi r^2 v$

$\left(\frac{(R^2 + x^2)^{5/2}v - \frac{5}{2}(R^2 + x^2)^{3/2}(2x^2)v}{(R^2 + x^2)^5}\right) = 0$

$\Rightarrow R^2 + x^2 - 5x^2 = 0$

$\Rightarrow \quad x = \frac{R}{2} = 3\text{ m}$

7. $q = C\varepsilon = CBlv \Rightarrow i = \frac{dq}{dt} = Blca$

$mg - Bil = ma$

$\Rightarrow \quad mg - B^2 l^2 Ca = ma$

$\Rightarrow \quad a = \frac{mg}{m + B^2 l^2 C} = 5\text{m/s}^2$

$E = \frac{V}{d} = \frac{Blv}{d} = 5 \times 10^8$

$\Rightarrow \quad v = 5000\text{ m/s}$

$v = u + at$

$\Rightarrow 5000 = 0 + 5t$

$\Rightarrow \quad t = 1000\text{ s} = 1 \times 10^3\text{ s}$

8. $\varepsilon=\dfrac{d\phi}{dt}=\dfrac{d}{dt}(\mu_0 ni\pi R^2)$

$$=\mu_0 n\pi R^2\frac{di}{dt}=36\times10^{-3}\,\text{V}$$

$$i=\frac{\varepsilon}{R_1+R_2}=\frac{36\times10^{-3}}{\dfrac{(2)^2}{10}+\dfrac{(2)^2}{20}}=6\times10^{-2}\text{ A}$$

$$P_2=i^2R_2$$

$$=(6\times10^{-2})^2\left(\frac{(2)^2}{20}\right)=7.2\times10^{-4}\,\text{W}$$

So, $n=7.2$

9. $i=\dfrac{100+Blv}{R}=\dfrac{100+0.5v}{40}$

$$\Sigma F=0$$

$\Rightarrow$ $Bil=mg$

$\Rightarrow$ $2\left(\dfrac{100+0.5v}{40}\right)(0.25)=0.2\times10$

$\Rightarrow$ $v=120$ m/s

Level 3

Single Choice Correct Questions

1. New volume $=20\pi+8\pi(2)=\dfrac{4}{3}\pi r^3$

$\Rightarrow$ $r=3$ cm

$$V=\frac{4}{3}\pi r^3$$

$\Rightarrow$ $\dfrac{dV}{dt}=\dfrac{4}{3}\pi3r^2\dfrac{dr}{dt}$

$\Rightarrow$ $\dfrac{dr}{dt}=\dfrac{1}{4\pi r^2}\dfrac{dV}{dt}$

$\Rightarrow$ $\varepsilon=\dfrac{d\phi}{dt}=\dfrac{d}{dt}(B\pi r^2)$

$$=B2\pi r\frac{dr}{dt}=\frac{B(2\pi r)}{4\pi r^2}\frac{dV}{dt}=\frac{B}{2r}\frac{dV}{dt}=500\text{ mV}$$

2. $\varepsilon=\dfrac{d\phi}{dt}=A\dfrac{dB}{dt}$

$\Rightarrow$ $\varepsilon_1=\pi a^2k$

and $\varepsilon_1=\pi b^2k$

$$i=\frac{\varepsilon_1-\varepsilon_2}{R_1+R_2}=\frac{\pi(a^2-b^2)k}{\lambda2\pi(a+b)}=\frac{k(a-b)}{2\lambda}$$

3. l = Side of square at any time t

ε = Motional emf across each side = Blv_0

$$i=\frac{4\varepsilon}{4\lambda l}=\frac{Blv_0}{\lambda l}=\frac{Bv_0}{\lambda}$$

5. $C_1C_2=vt$

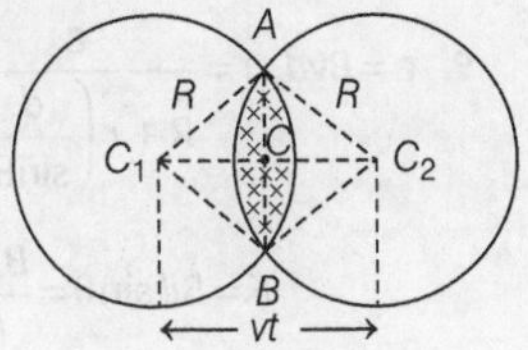

$$C_1C=\frac{vt}{2}$$

$$AC=\sqrt{R^2-\left(\frac{vt}{2}\right)^2}$$

Motional emf across $AB=Blv$

$$=B\left(2\sqrt{R^2-\left(\frac{vt}{2}\right)^2}\right)v=Bv\sqrt{4R^2-v^2t^2}=6\text{ V}$$

6. $i_1=\dfrac{V}{R}=\dfrac{4+2.5t}{\lambda(2\pi r_1)}$

$$\phi_2=\left(\frac{\mu_0 i_1}{2r_1}\right)\pi r_2^2;\quad \varepsilon_2=\frac{d\phi_2}{dt}=\frac{\mu_0\pi r_2^2}{2r_1}\frac{di_1}{dt}$$

$$i_2=\frac{\varepsilon_2}{R_2}=\frac{\mu_0\pi r_2^2}{2r_1(\lambda2\pi r_2)}\left(\frac{2.5}{\lambda(2\pi r_1)}\right)=1.25\text{ A}$$

7.

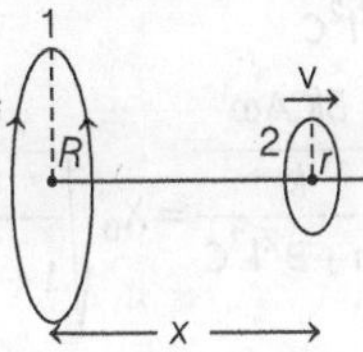

$$\phi_2=\left(\frac{\mu_0 iR^2}{2(R^2+x^2)^{3/2}}\right)(\pi r^2)\cos0^\circ$$

$$\varepsilon_2=-\frac{d\phi_2}{dt}=-\left(\frac{\mu_0 i\pi R^2r^2}{2}\right)\left[-\frac{3}{2}(R^2+x^2)^{-5/2}2x\frac{dx}{dt}\right]$$

$$\Rightarrow\ \varepsilon_2=\frac{3\mu_0 i\pi R^2r^2vx}{2(R^2+x^2)^{5/2}}=\frac{24}{25\sqrt5}\left(\frac{\mu_0 i\pi r^2v}{R^2}\right)$$

For ε_2 to be maximum, $\dfrac{d\varepsilon_2}{dt}=0\Rightarrow x=\dfrac{R}{2}$

$$(\varepsilon_2)_{max}=\frac{24}{25\sqrt5}\left(\frac{\mu_0\pi ir^2v}{R^2}\right)$$

8. $i=\left(\dfrac{Q}{2\pi R}R d\theta\right)\dfrac{\omega}{2\pi}=\dfrac{Q\omega d\theta}{4\pi^2}$

$$\int d\phi=\int\left(\frac{\mu_0 i(R\sin\theta)^2}{2((R\sin\theta)^2+(R\cos\theta)^2)^{3/2}}\right)\pi a^2\cos0^\circ$$

$\Rightarrow$ $\phi=\dfrac{\mu_0Q\omega a^2}{8\pi R}\displaystyle\int_0^{2\pi}\sin^2\theta d\theta$

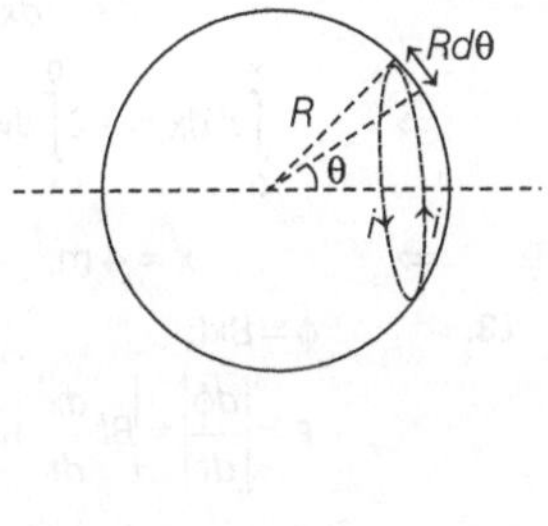

$$=\frac{\mu_0Q\omega a^2}{8R}$$

$$i=\frac{\varepsilon}{r}=\frac{1}{r}\frac{d\phi}{dt}$$

$$=\frac{\mu_0Qa^2}{8Rr}\frac{d\omega}{dt}=\frac{\mu Qa^2\alpha}{8Rr}$$

9. $\varepsilon = Bvd,\ i = \dfrac{\varepsilon}{R + r\left(\dfrac{d}{\sin\theta}\right)}$

$$F = Bil\sin\theta = \frac{B^2d^2v/\sin\theta}{\left(R + \dfrac{dr}{\sin\theta}\right)}$$

10. $q = C\varepsilon = C(Blv) \quad \Rightarrow \quad i = \dfrac{dq}{dt} = Blca$

q is maximum when v is maximum which will occur at mean position.

$$\Sigma F = ma$$

$$\Rightarrow \quad -kx - Bil = ma$$

$$\Rightarrow \quad a = -\frac{kx}{m + B^2l^2C}$$

So, the rod will execute SHM with

$$\omega = \sqrt{\frac{k}{m + B^2l^2C}}$$

$$q_{max} = BlCv_{max} = BlCA\omega$$

$$= BlCX_0\sqrt{\frac{k}{m + B^2l^2C}} = X_0\sqrt{\frac{kC}{1 + \dfrac{m}{B^2l^2C}}}$$

11. $i = \dfrac{Bdv}{R + 2\lambda x} \Rightarrow v = \dfrac{i(R + 2\lambda x)}{Bd}$

$$a = \frac{dv}{dt} = \frac{2i\lambda}{Bd}v$$

$$= \frac{2i\lambda}{Bd}\left(\frac{i(R + 2\lambda x)}{Bd}\right) = \frac{2i^2\lambda(R + 2\lambda x)}{B^2d^2}$$

$$\Sigma F = ma$$

$$\Rightarrow F - Bil = ma$$

$$\Rightarrow \quad F = \frac{2mi^2\lambda(R + 2\lambda x)}{B^2d^2} + Bid = 21\text{ N}$$

12. $\varepsilon = Bv(2x)$

$$i = \frac{\varepsilon}{R} = \frac{Bv(2x)}{\lambda(2x + 2\sqrt{2}x)} = \frac{Bv}{\lambda(\sqrt{2} + 1)} = 5v$$

$$\Sigma F = ma$$

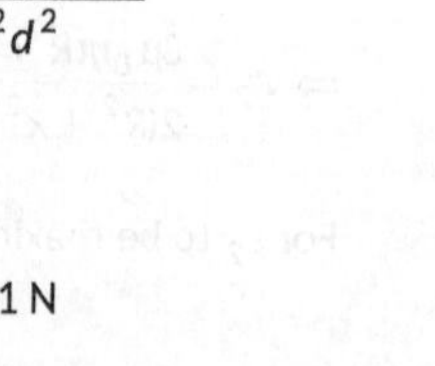

$$\Rightarrow \quad -Bil = ma$$

$$\Rightarrow \quad -B(5v)(2x) = mv\frac{dv}{dx}$$

$$\Rightarrow \quad \int_0^x x\,dx = -2\int_4^0 dv$$

$$\Rightarrow \quad x = 4\text{ m}$$

13. $\phi = Bxl;$

$$\varepsilon = \left|\frac{d\phi}{dt}\right| = \left|Bl\frac{dx}{dt} + xl\frac{dB}{dt}\right|$$

$$= |Blv - lKx|$$

14. $2i = \dfrac{\varepsilon}{R} \Rightarrow i = \dfrac{\varepsilon}{2R}$

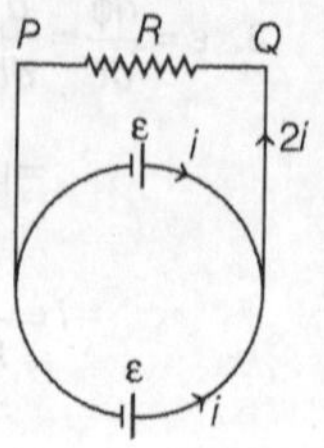

$$= \frac{Bv(2r)}{2R} = \frac{Bvr}{R}$$

$$\Sigma F = ma \Rightarrow mg - 2(Bi2r) = 0$$

$$\Rightarrow \quad v_T = \frac{mgR}{4B^2r^2}$$

15. In steady state both conductors move with same velocity v

$$mv_0 + 0 = mv + mv$$

$$\Rightarrow \quad v = \frac{v_0}{2}$$

$$\text{Loss in } K.E. = \left(\frac{1}{2}mv_0^2 + 0\right) - \left(\frac{1}{2}m\left(\frac{v_0}{2}\right)^2 + \frac{1}{2}m\left(\frac{v_0}{2}\right)^2\right)$$

$$= \frac{1}{4}mv_0^2$$

16. $\varepsilon = \dfrac{1}{2}B\omega l^2$

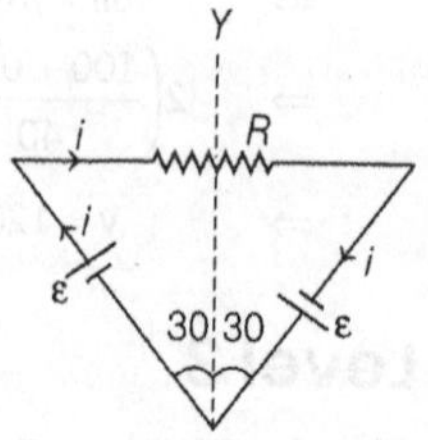

$$i = \frac{2\varepsilon}{R}$$

$$= \frac{B\omega l^2}{R}$$

17. $\varepsilon = \dfrac{1}{2}B\omega r^2$ and $i = \dfrac{\varepsilon}{R} = \dfrac{B\omega r^2}{2R}$

$$\text{Retarding torque on rod} = \left(B\left(\frac{i}{2}\right)r \times \frac{r}{2}\right) \times 2$$

$$\Rightarrow \quad \tau = -\frac{Bir^2}{2} = -\frac{B^2\omega r^4}{4R}$$

$$\tau = I\alpha$$

$$\Rightarrow \quad \frac{-B^2\omega r^4}{4R} = \frac{m(2r)^2}{12}\omega\frac{d\omega}{d\theta}$$

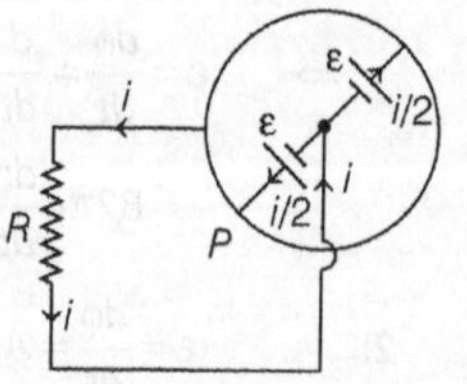

$$\Rightarrow \quad \int_0^\theta d\theta = -\frac{4mR}{3B^2r^2}\int_{\omega_0}^0 d\omega$$

$$\Rightarrow \quad \theta = \frac{4mR\omega_0}{3B^2r^2}$$

Number of revolutions

$$= \frac{\theta}{2\pi} = \frac{2mR\omega_0}{3B^2\pi r^2} = 20$$

18. $\phi = B\left(\dfrac{1}{2}r^2\theta\right)$

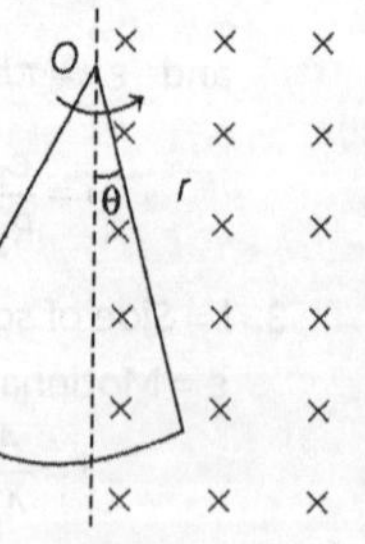

$$\varepsilon = \frac{d\phi}{dt} = \frac{Br^2}{2}\frac{d\theta}{dt} = \frac{B\omega r^2}{2}$$

To maintain ω to be constant,

P_{ext} = Power dissipated in the loop

$$= \frac{\varepsilon^2}{R} = \frac{B^2\omega^2r^4}{4R} = 16\mu\text{W}$$

19. Potential difference between bottom and topmost point of one ring

$$= \varepsilon = \frac{1}{2}B\omega(2R)^2 = 2B\omega R^2$$

$$V_A - V_C = \varepsilon - (-\varepsilon) = 2\varepsilon = 4B\omega R^2$$

20. $V_D - V_C = \varepsilon_{\text{Translational}} + \varepsilon_{\text{Rotational}}$

$$= B(2\omega a)a + \frac{1}{2}B\omega a^2 = \frac{5}{2}B\omega a^2$$

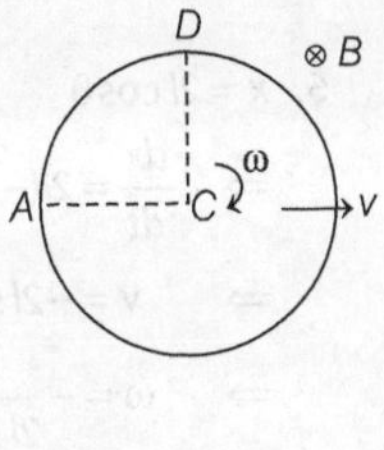

$V_A - V_C = \varepsilon_{\text{Translational}} + \varepsilon_{\text{Rotational}}$

$$= 0 + \frac{1}{2}B\omega a^2$$

$$V_D - V_A = \frac{5}{2}B\omega a^2 - \frac{1}{2}B\omega a^2 = 2B\omega a^2$$

21. $\varepsilon = \frac{1}{2}B\omega r^2;\ i = \frac{\varepsilon}{R} = \frac{1}{2}\frac{B\omega r^2}{R}$

$$\tau = \int_0^r (Bidr)r = \frac{Bir^2}{2} = \frac{B^2\omega r^4}{4R}$$

For terminal velocity, $\Sigma\tau = 0$

$$\Rightarrow \frac{-B^2\omega r^4}{4R} + mga = 0$$

$$\Rightarrow \quad \omega = \frac{4mgaR}{B^2r^4} = 100 \text{ rad/s}$$

22. $T = 2\pi\sqrt{\frac{m}{k}} = \frac{2\pi}{\sqrt{10}}$

$$F_m = Bil = B\left(\frac{Blv}{R}\right)l = \frac{B^2l^2v}{R}$$

$$F = -kx - \frac{B^2l^2v}{R}$$

For damped oscillations

$$A = A_0e^{-bt/2m} \quad \Rightarrow \frac{A_0}{e} = A_0e^{-bt/2m}$$

$$\Rightarrow \quad t = \frac{2m}{b} = \frac{2m}{\left(\frac{B^2l^2}{R}\right)} = 10^4\text{s}$$

$$\text{Number of oscillations} = \frac{t}{T} = \frac{10^4}{2\pi/\sqrt{10}} = 5000$$

23. $dN = \left(\frac{N}{b-a}\right)dr$

$$d\phi = dN(B_0t)\pi r^2$$

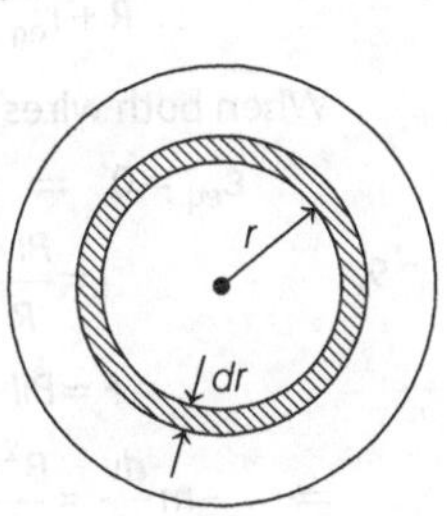

$$\Rightarrow \int d\phi = \int_a^b \left(\frac{N}{b-a}\right)dr(B_0t)\pi r^2$$

$$\Rightarrow \quad \phi = \frac{N\pi B_0t}{3(b-a)}(b^3 - a^3)$$

$$\varepsilon = \frac{d\phi}{dt} = \frac{N\pi B_0}{3}(b^2 + a^2 + ab)$$

24. $\tan 60° = \frac{PQ}{CP}$

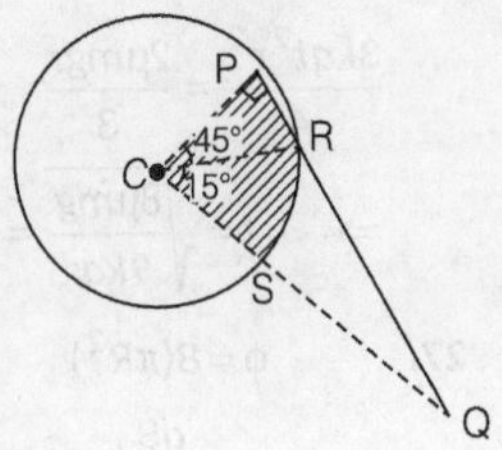

$$\Rightarrow \quad \sqrt{3} = \frac{1}{CP}\sqrt{\frac{3}{2}}R$$

$$\Rightarrow \quad CP = \frac{R}{\sqrt{2}}$$

$$(PR)^2 = (RC)^2 - (CP)^2 \Rightarrow PR = \frac{R}{\sqrt{2}}$$

Area (PQRS) = Area (CPR)+Area (RCS)

$$= \frac{1}{2}\left(\frac{R}{\sqrt{2}}\right)\left(\frac{R}{\sqrt{2}}\right) + \frac{1}{2}R^2\left(\frac{15\pi}{180}\right) = \frac{R^2}{4} + \frac{\pi R^2}{24}$$

$$\phi = B\left(\frac{\pi R^2}{24} + \frac{R^2}{4}\right)$$

$$\Rightarrow \quad \varepsilon = \frac{d\phi}{dt} = \frac{dB}{dt}\left(\frac{\pi R^2}{24} + \frac{R^2}{4}\right) = \frac{R^2}{6}(\pi + 6)$$

$$\varepsilon_{CP} + \varepsilon_{PQ} + \varepsilon_{QC} = \varepsilon = \frac{R^2}{6}(\pi + 6)$$

$$\Rightarrow \quad 0 + \varepsilon_{PQ} + 0 = \frac{R^2}{6}(\pi + 6)$$

$$\Rightarrow \quad \varepsilon_{PQ} = \frac{R^2}{6}(\pi + 6)\text{ V}$$

25. $\varepsilon = \frac{d\phi}{dt} = A\frac{dB}{dt}$

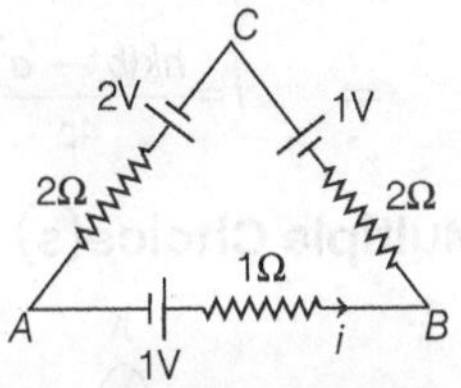

$$= \frac{\sqrt{3}}{4}(2)^2 \times \sqrt{3} = 3\text{ V}$$

$$i = \frac{\varepsilon}{R_{eq}}$$

$$= \frac{3}{(2+2+1)} = 0.6\text{ A}$$

$$\varepsilon_{AB} = \varepsilon_{BC} = \varepsilon_{CA} = \frac{1}{3}(3) = 1\text{ V}$$

$$V_B - V_A = \varepsilon_{AB} - ir = 1 - (0.6)(1) = 0.4\text{ A}$$

26. $\phi = B(\pi r^2) = kt^3\pi r^2$

$$\Rightarrow \quad \varepsilon = \frac{d\phi}{dt} = 3kt^2\pi r^2$$

$$\Rightarrow E(2\pi r) = 3kt^2\pi r^2$$

$$\Rightarrow \quad E = \frac{3kt^2r}{2}$$

$$\tau_E = \int_0^r \left(\frac{q}{\pi r^2}2\pi x dx\right)\left(\frac{3kt^2x}{2}\right)x = \frac{3kqt^2r^2}{4}$$

$$\tau_{fr} = \int_0^r \mu\left(\frac{m}{\pi r^2}2\pi x dx\right)gx = \frac{2\mu mgr}{3}$$

When the disc begins to rotate

$$\tau_E = \tau_{fr}$$

$$\frac{3kqt^2r^2}{4}=\frac{2\mu mgr}{3}$$

$$\Rightarrow \quad t=\sqrt{\frac{8\mu mg}{9kqr}}=2\text{ s}$$

27. $\phi=B(\pi R^2)$

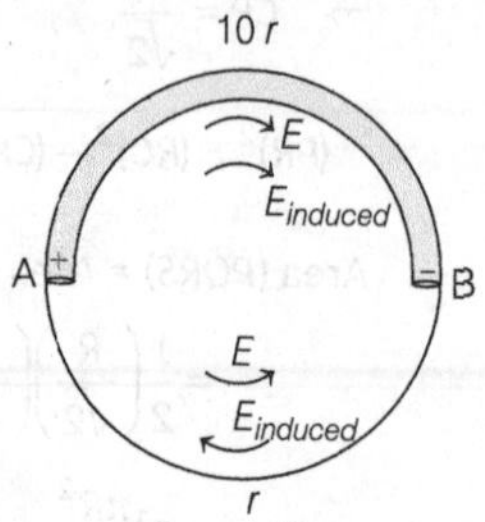

$$\Rightarrow \quad \varepsilon=\frac{dB}{dt}(\pi R^2)=b\pi R^2$$

$$i=\frac{\varepsilon}{(10r+r)}=\frac{b\pi R^2}{11r}$$

$$\varepsilon_{\text{induced}}=\frac{R}{2}\frac{dB}{dt}=\frac{bR}{2}$$

$$V_A-V_B=i(10r)$$

$$\Rightarrow \varepsilon(\pi R)+\varepsilon_{\text{induced}}(\pi R)=\left(\frac{b\pi R^2}{11r}\right)(10r)$$

$$\Rightarrow \quad \varepsilon=\frac{9}{22}Rb$$

28. $E=\frac{r}{2}\frac{dB}{dt}=\frac{kr}{2}$

$$J=\sigma E$$

$$\Rightarrow \frac{di}{(hdr)}=\frac{1}{\rho}\left(\frac{kr}{2}\right)\Rightarrow \int di=\frac{hk}{2\rho}\int_0^b r\,dr$$

$$\Rightarrow \quad i=\frac{hk(b^2-a^2)}{4\rho}$$

Multiple Choice(s) Correct Questions

1.

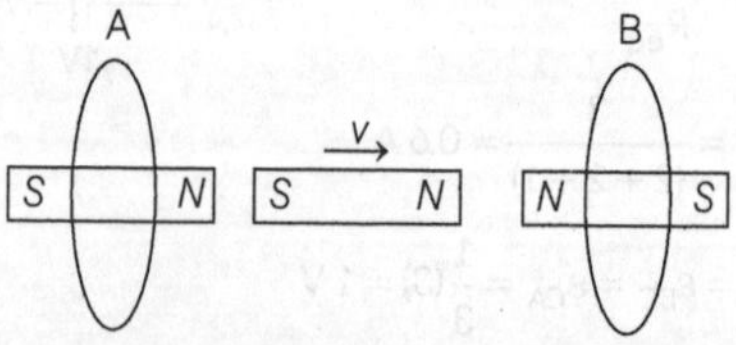

The current in the loops flows in opposite directions and the loops will repel each other.

2. Current will be induced in the ring such that it will oppose the motion of the magnet. The magnet will retard and eventually come to rest.

3. (a) $\phi=\text{constant}$

$$\Rightarrow \quad \varepsilon=\frac{d\phi}{dt}=0$$

(b) No motional emf in insultors

(c) $\varepsilon=-\frac{d\phi}{dt}$ and $i=\frac{\varepsilon}{R}$

(d) $\phi=\text{constant}\Rightarrow\varepsilon=0\Rightarrow i=0$

4. $2\pi r=2\pi r_0-2vt$

$$\Rightarrow \quad r=r_0-\frac{vt}{\pi}$$

$$\varepsilon=-\frac{d\phi}{dt}=-B\frac{d}{dt}(\pi r^2)=-2\pi Br\frac{dr}{dt}$$

$$=-2\pi B\left(r_0-\frac{vt}{\pi}\right)\left(-\frac{v}{\pi}\right)=2Bv\left(r_0-\frac{vt}{\pi}\right)$$

$$i=\frac{\varepsilon}{R}=\frac{2Bv\left(r_0-\frac{vt}{\pi}\right)}{\lambda 2\pi\left(r_0-\frac{vt}{\pi}\right)}=\frac{Bv}{\pi\lambda}$$

5. $x=2l\cos\theta$

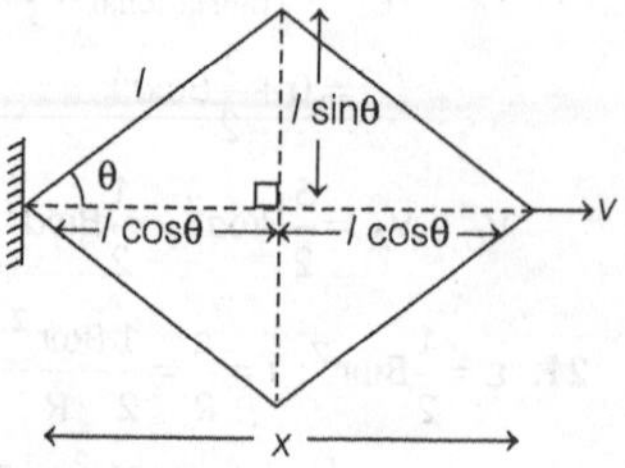

$$\Rightarrow \quad \frac{dx}{dt}=2l(-\sin\theta)\frac{d\theta}{dt}$$

$$\Rightarrow \quad v=-2l\sin\theta\times\omega$$

$$\Rightarrow \quad \omega=-\frac{v}{2l\sin\theta}$$

$$\phi=BA\cos 0^\circ$$

$$=B_0\left[\frac{1}{2}(2l\cos\theta)(2l\sin\theta)\right]$$

$$\varepsilon=\frac{d\phi}{dt}=B_0l^2\cos 2\theta\times 2\times\frac{d\theta}{dt}$$

$$=2B_0l^2\cos 2\theta\left(\frac{v}{2l\sin\theta}\right)=\frac{B_0lv\cos 2\theta}{\sin\theta}$$

6. $\varepsilon_i=-\frac{d\phi}{dt}\Rightarrow\int d\phi=-\int\varepsilon_i\,dt$

$\Rightarrow \quad \Delta\phi=-$ Area under ε_i vs t curve

$$q=\frac{\Delta\phi}{R}$$

7. $\varepsilon=(\mathbf{v}\times\mathbf{B})\cdot\mathbf{l}$

8. Induced emf across each wire $(\varepsilon)=Blv$

$$=1\times 4\times 10^{-2}\times 5\times 10^{-2}=2\text{ mV}$$

When both wires move left,

$$\varepsilon_{eq}=\frac{\frac{\varepsilon_1}{r_1}+\frac{\varepsilon_2}{r_2}}{\frac{1}{r_1}+\frac{1}{r_2}}=2\text{ mV}$$

$$i=\frac{\varepsilon_{eq}}{R+r_{eq}}=\frac{2\times 10^{-3}}{9+1}=0.2\text{ mA}$$

When both wires move in opposite direction,

$$\varepsilon_{eq}=0\Rightarrow i=0$$

9. $i=\frac{Blv}{R}$;

$$F=Bil$$

$$\Rightarrow \quad -m\frac{dv}{dt}=\frac{B^2l^2v}{R}$$

$$\Rightarrow \quad \int_{v_0}^{v}\frac{dv}{v}=-\frac{B^2l^2}{mR}\int_0^t dt$$

$\Rightarrow \quad v = v_0 e^{-t/600}$

At $\quad t = 600\ln 2,$

$v = v_0 e^{-600\ln 2/600} = \dfrac{v_0}{2}$

$i = \dfrac{Blv}{R} = \dfrac{(0.1)1(v_0/2)}{6} = \dfrac{v_0}{120}$

$\varepsilon = Blv = Blv_0 e^{-t/600} = \dfrac{v_0}{10} e^{-t/600}$

10. Induced emf due to variation of B with time $= A\dfrac{dB}{dt}$

Induced emf due to variation of B with x

$= A\dfrac{dB}{dt} = A\left(\dfrac{dB}{dx} \times \dfrac{dx}{dt}\right) = Av\dfrac{dB}{dx}$

Net induced emf $= A\dfrac{dB}{dt} + Av\dfrac{dB}{dx}$

$\varepsilon = A\left[\dfrac{dB}{dt} + at\dfrac{dB}{dx}\right] = A \times 10^{-3}(1-t)$

$i = \dfrac{\varepsilon}{R} = \dfrac{A \times 10^{-3}(1-t)}{R}$

At $\quad t = 1; i = 0$

At $\quad t = 0;$

Flux is increasing into the plane. So, induced current will be anti-clockwise.

11. $\quad F = Bil = ma$

$\Rightarrow B\dfrac{dq}{dt}l = m\dfrac{dv}{dt}$

$\Rightarrow Bl\int_0^q dq = m\int_0^v dv \Rightarrow q = \dfrac{mv}{Bl}$

In steady state, $q =$ constant, v =constant and $i = 0$

$q = CV = C(\varepsilon - Blv)$

$\Rightarrow \dfrac{mv}{Bl} = C(\varepsilon - Blv) \Rightarrow v = \dfrac{BlC\varepsilon}{m + CB^2l^2}$

and $\quad q = \dfrac{mv}{Bl} = \dfrac{mC\varepsilon}{m + CB^2l^2}$

15. $\varepsilon = \dfrac{d\phi}{dt} = \dfrac{d}{dt}(B\pi a^2) = \pi a^2\dfrac{dB}{dt} = \pi a^2\alpha$

$i_{PQRS} = \dfrac{\varepsilon}{R} = \dfrac{\pi a^2\alpha}{\rho(2\pi a)} = \dfrac{a\alpha}{2\rho}$

Induced current will be anti-clockwise to oppose the flux increasing into the plane.

$i_{PR} = 0$

$\because \quad \mathbf{E} \perp \mathbf{dl}$

16. $E = \dfrac{r}{2}\dfrac{dB}{dt};$

$\tau = 4(qEr) = 2qr^2\dfrac{dB}{dt}$

$\Rightarrow \quad \dfrac{dL}{dt} = 2qr^2\dfrac{dB}{dt} \Rightarrow \int_0^L dL = 2qr^2\int_{B_0}^0 dB$

$\Rightarrow \quad L = 2qB_0r^2 = 8$ Nm/s

$L = I\omega \Rightarrow 8 = (mr^2 \times 4)\omega$

$\Rightarrow \quad \omega = 40$ rad/s

Magnetic field at O immediately after switching magnetic field will be due to rotating charges.

17. $\phi = \mathbf{B}\cdot\mathbf{A} = (t^2)\pi r^2;$

$\varepsilon = \dfrac{d\phi}{dt} = 2\pi r^2 t; \quad i = \dfrac{\varepsilon}{R} = \dfrac{2\pi r^2 t}{R}$

For toppling, $\tau = |\mathbf{M} \times \mathbf{B}| \geq mgr$

$\Rightarrow (i\pi r^2)(1) \geq mgr$

$\Rightarrow \quad t \geq \dfrac{mgR}{2\pi^2 r^3} = 1$ s

Heat $= \int i^2R\,dt = \int_0^1 \left(\dfrac{2\pi r^2 t}{R}\right)^2 R\,dt = \dfrac{80}{3}$ J

Comprehension Based Questions

1. Flux is decreasing into the plane. So to oppose it, induced current will be clockwise.

$i = \dfrac{\varepsilon}{R} = \dfrac{1}{R}\dfrac{d\phi}{dt} = \dfrac{1}{R}\dfrac{d(NBA)}{dt} = \dfrac{NB}{R}\dfrac{dA}{dt}$

since, $\dfrac{dA}{dt}$ = constant $\Rightarrow i$ = constant

2. $i = \dfrac{NB}{R}\dfrac{dA}{dt} = \dfrac{100 \times 4}{2}\dfrac{\pi(0.1)^2}{3} = 2.09$ A

3. Heat produced $= i^2R\,\Delta t = (2.09)^2(2)(3) = 26$ J

Loop was initially $2r$ wide and it became πr long after it is flattened.

W_{ext} = Heat produced

$\Rightarrow F(\pi r - 2r) = 26$

$\Rightarrow \quad F = 231$ N

4. $\quad \varepsilon = Blv\sin\theta$

$= B\left(\dfrac{2vt}{\sqrt{3}}\right)v\sin 90°$

$= \dfrac{2Bv^2t}{\sqrt{3}}$

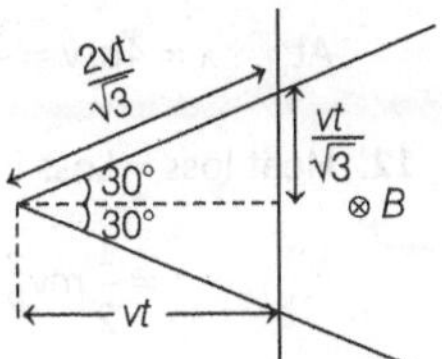

$\varepsilon \propto t$

5. $R = \lambda\left(\dfrac{2vt}{\sqrt{3}} + \dfrac{2vt}{\sqrt{3}} + \dfrac{2vt}{\sqrt{3}}\right) = \dfrac{6\lambda\,vt}{\sqrt{3}}$

$i = \dfrac{\varepsilon}{R} = \dfrac{Bv}{3\lambda}$ = constant

6. Work required $= \int_0^{10} i^2R\,dt$

$$= \int_0^{10} \left(\frac{Bv}{3\lambda}\right)^2 \left(\frac{6\lambda\, vt}{\sqrt{3}}\right) dt$$

$$= \frac{6B^2v^3}{9\sqrt{3}\lambda} \times \frac{10^2}{2} = 3.1 \times 10^{-3}\,\text{J}$$

7. Case- I, $\phi = BA\cos\theta = B(L^2 + l^2)$

Case- II, $\phi = BA\cos\theta = B(L^2 - l^2)$

8. To oppose the decreasing flux, induced current in each loop will be clockwise.

9. To oppose the decreasing flux, emf will be induced in each loop such that current is clockwise. But induced emf in bigger loop is greater. So current in bigger loop will be clockwise and in smaller loop anti-clockwise.

10. $i_1 = \dfrac{\varepsilon_1 + \varepsilon_2}{R}$ and $i_2 = \dfrac{\varepsilon_1 - \varepsilon_2}{R}$

where ε_1 and ε_2 are induced emf in bigger and smaller loops respectively.

So, $i_1 > i_2$

11. When loop enters the field,

$$i = \frac{Blv}{R} = \frac{Bav}{R};\ F = Bil = \frac{B^2a^2v}{R}$$

$$\Rightarrow\ -mv\frac{dv}{dx} = \frac{B^2a^2v}{R}$$

$$\Rightarrow\ \int_{v_0}^{v} dv = -\frac{B^2a^2}{mR}\int_0^x dx$$

$$\Rightarrow\ v = v_0 - \frac{B^2a^2x}{mR}$$

At $x = a,\ v = v_0 - \dfrac{B^2a^3}{mR} = \dfrac{2v_0}{3}$

For $x = a$ to $x = 3a$, $v = \dfrac{2v_0}{3}$ = constant

For $x = 3a$ to $x = 4a$,

$$v = \frac{2v_0}{3} - \frac{B^2a^2}{mR}(x - 3a)$$

At $x = 4a,\ v = \dfrac{v_0}{3}$

12. Heat loss = Loss in KE

$$= \frac{1}{2}mv_0^2 - \frac{1}{2}m\left(\frac{v_0}{3}\right)^2 = \frac{4}{9}mv_0^2$$

13. Electrical power consumed $= \dfrac{\mu mgv}{\eta}$

$$= \frac{0.045 \times 10^5 \times 10 \times 20}{\left(\frac{90}{100}\right)} = 1\,\text{MW}$$

14. $\varepsilon = B_v l v = 2 \times 10^{-5} \times 1 \times 20 = 0.4\,\text{mV}$

15. $i = \dfrac{Blv}{R} = \dfrac{0.4 \times 10^{-3}}{10^{-3}} = 0.4\,\text{A}$

Extra Energy consumed $= i^2Rt$

$$= (0.4)^2(10^{-3})\left(\frac{360}{72}\text{hr}\right)$$

$$= 8 \times 10^{-7}\,\text{kWh}$$

16. Velocity of frame when it starts entering the magnetic field, $v = \sqrt{2gh} = 10\,\text{m/s}$

time taken $= \sqrt{\dfrac{2h}{g}} = 1\,\text{s}.$

When the frame has partially entered the magnetic field.

$$i = \frac{\varepsilon}{R} = \frac{Blv}{R};$$

$$F = Bil = \frac{B^2l^2v}{R} = 5\,\text{N, upward}$$

$$\Sigma F = ma \Rightarrow mg - Bil = ma$$

$$\Rightarrow (0.5)(10) - 5 = ma\ \Rightarrow\ a = 0$$

So, velocity of frame will be constant.

Time taken to completely enter the magnetic field

$$= \frac{2}{10} = 0.2\,\text{s}.$$

17. When the frame is completely inside magnetic field, induced current is zero.

So, $mg - Bil = ma$

$$\Rightarrow\quad a = g = 10\,\text{m}/\text{s}^2$$

$$s = ut + \frac{1}{2}at^2$$

$$\Rightarrow 17 - 2 = 10t + \frac{1}{2}(10)t^2$$

$$\Rightarrow\quad t = 1\,\text{s}$$

Total time $= 1 + 0.2 + 1 = 2.2\,\text{s}$

18. $\displaystyle\int d\phi = \int_a^{2a} \frac{\mu_0 i_0}{2\pi x} a\,dx \cos 0°$

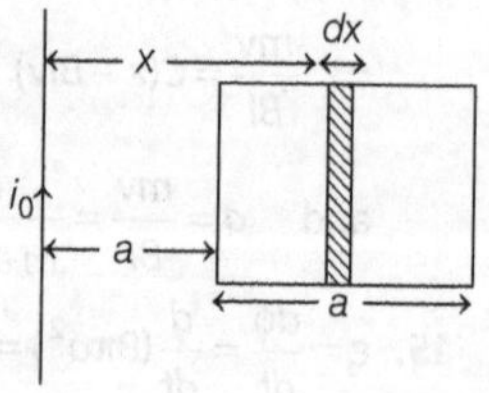

$$\phi_1 = \frac{\mu_0 i_0 a}{2\pi}\ln 2$$

$$\phi_2 = 0$$

$$q = \frac{\Delta\phi}{R} = \frac{\mu_0 i_0 a \ln 2}{2\pi R}$$

19. $F_1 = \left(\dfrac{\mu_0 i_0}{2\pi a}\right) ia$

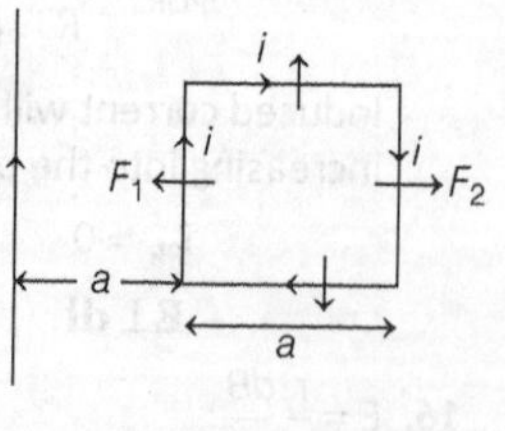

$$F_2 = \left(\frac{\mu_0 i_0}{2\pi(2a)}\right) ia$$

$$F_{net} = F_1 - F_2 = \frac{\mu_0 i_0 i}{4\pi}$$

$$\Rightarrow\quad \frac{dp}{dt} = \frac{\mu_0 i_0}{4\pi}\frac{dq}{dt}$$

$$\Rightarrow \int dp = \frac{\mu_0 i_0}{4\pi}\int dq$$

$$\Rightarrow \quad P = \frac{\mu_0 i_0}{4\pi}q = \frac{\mu_0 i_0^2 a\ln 2}{8\pi^2 R}$$

20. For loop *PQR*,

$$\phi_1 = (B_0 t)\left(\frac{\pi a^2}{2}\right)\cos 0°; \quad \varepsilon_1 = \frac{d\phi_1}{dt} = \frac{B_0\pi a^2}{2}$$

For loop *PSR*,

$$\phi_2 = (B_0 t)\left(\frac{\pi a^2}{2}\right)\cos 60°; \quad \varepsilon_2 = \frac{d\phi_2}{dt} = \frac{B_0\pi a^2}{4}$$

$$\varepsilon = \varepsilon_1 - \varepsilon_2 = \frac{B_0\pi a^2}{4}$$

21. $i = \frac{\varepsilon}{R} = \frac{B_0\pi a^2}{4(2\pi a r_0)} = \frac{B_0 a}{8r_0}$

For loop *PQR*, $\tau = 0$

For loop *PSR*, $\tau = MB\sin 60°$

$$= \left(\frac{i\pi a^2}{2}\right)B_0 t\left(\frac{\sqrt{3}}{2}\right) = \frac{\sqrt{3}B_0^2\pi a^3 t}{32r_0}$$

22. To oppose magnetic flux increasing out of the plane, induced current will be clockwise.

$$\varepsilon = \frac{d\phi}{dt} = A\frac{dB}{dt} + B\frac{dA}{dt}$$

At $\quad t = 0,\ \varepsilon = 0.16$ V

$$i = \frac{\varepsilon}{R} = \frac{0.16}{1} = 0.16 \text{ A}$$

23. $\varepsilon = \frac{d\phi}{dt} = A\frac{dB}{dt} + B\frac{dA}{dt}$

At $\quad t = 2$ s,

$$\varepsilon = (0.3 \times 0.2)(2) + 4 \times (-0.05 \times 0.2) = 0.08 \text{ V}$$

24. At $t = 5$ s,

$$\varepsilon = (0.15 \times 0.2)(2) + 10 \times (-0.05 \times 0.2) = -0.04 \text{ V}$$

$$i = \frac{\varepsilon}{R} = \frac{0.04}{0.5 \times 1} = 0.08 \text{ A}$$

$$F = Bil = 10 \times 0.08 \times 0.2 = 0.16 \text{ N}$$

25. & 26. $\varepsilon = \int Bv\,dx = \int_a^b \frac{\mu_0 i_0}{2\pi x}v\,dx = \frac{\mu_0 i_0 v}{2\pi}\ln\left(\frac{b}{a}\right)$

$$i = \frac{\varepsilon}{R} = \frac{\mu_0 i_0 v}{2\pi R}\ln\left(\frac{b}{a}\right)$$

$$F = \int Bi\,dx = \int_a^b \frac{\mu_0 i_0}{2\pi R}i\,dx = \frac{\mu_0 i_0 i}{2\pi}\ln\left(\frac{b}{a}\right)$$

$$\Sigma F = ma$$

$$\Rightarrow \quad -\frac{\mu_0 i_0}{2\pi}\left(\frac{\mu_0 i_0 v}{2\pi R}\ln\left(\frac{b}{a}\right)\right)\ln\left(\frac{b}{a}\right) = m\frac{dv}{dt}$$

$$\Rightarrow \int_{v_0}^{v_0/2}\frac{dv}{v} = -\frac{\mu_0 i_0^2\ln^2\left(\frac{b}{a}\right)}{4\pi^2 mR}\int_0^T dt$$

$$\Rightarrow \quad T = \frac{4\pi^2 mR\ln 2}{\mu_0^2 i_0^2\ln^2\left(\frac{b}{a}\right)}$$

$$F = \frac{\mu_0^2 i_0^2 v}{4\pi^2 R}\ln^2\left(\frac{b}{a}\right) = -mv\frac{dv}{dx}$$

$$\Rightarrow \quad \frac{\mu_0^2 i_0^2\ln^2\left(\frac{b}{a}\right)}{4\pi^2 Rm}\int_0^x dx = -\int_{v_0}^0 dv \Rightarrow x \propto v_0$$

27. Heat generated = Loss in kinetic energy $= \frac{1}{2}mv_0^2$

28. Let velocity at any instant be *v*.

$$q = CV = C(BLV)$$

$$\Rightarrow \quad i = \frac{dq}{dt} = BLCa$$

$$\Sigma F = ma$$

$$\Rightarrow \quad -Bil - kx = ma$$

$$\Rightarrow -B^2L^2Ca - kx = ma$$

$$\Rightarrow \quad a = \frac{-kx}{m + B^2L^2C} = -\omega^2 x$$

$$\Rightarrow \quad \omega = \sqrt{\frac{k}{m + B^2L^2C}}$$

29. $a \propto -x \Rightarrow$ Rod will excute SHM.

30. $v_{max} = A_{max}\omega \Rightarrow A_{max} = \frac{v_{max}}{\omega}$

$\Rightarrow$ Maximum compression $= v_0\sqrt{\frac{m + B^2L^2C}{k}}$

31. $mgv = \left(\frac{dK}{dt}\right)_{\text{Translational}} + \left(\frac{dK}{dt}\right)_{\text{Rotational}} + i^2R$

$$\Rightarrow mgv = \frac{d}{dt}\left(\frac{1}{2}mv^2\right) + \frac{d}{dt}\left(\frac{1}{2}I\omega^2\right) + \left(\frac{B\omega a^2}{2R}\right)^2 R$$

$$\Rightarrow mgv = mv\frac{dv}{dt} + \left(\frac{ma^2}{2}\right)\left(\frac{v}{a}\right)\left(\frac{1}{a}\frac{dv}{dt}\right) + \frac{B^2\left(\frac{v}{a}\right)^2 a^4}{4R^2} \times R$$

$$\Rightarrow \quad mg = m\frac{dv}{dt} + \frac{m}{2}\frac{dv}{dt} + \frac{B^2va^2}{4R}$$

$$\Rightarrow \quad mg = \frac{3m}{2}\frac{dv}{dt} + \frac{B^2va^2}{4R}$$

$$\Rightarrow \quad mg = 0 + \frac{B^2v_T a^2}{4R}$$

$$\Rightarrow \quad v_T = \frac{4mgR}{B^2a^2}$$

32. At $t=0$, $v=0$

$$\Rightarrow \quad mg=\frac{3m}{2}\frac{dv}{dt}$$

$$\Rightarrow \quad a=\frac{2g}{3}$$

33. $\int d\phi=\int_0^a\left(\frac{B_0 l\sin\omega t}{a}\right)a\,dl\sin\omega t$

$$\phi=\frac{B_0a^2}{2}\sin^2\omega t$$

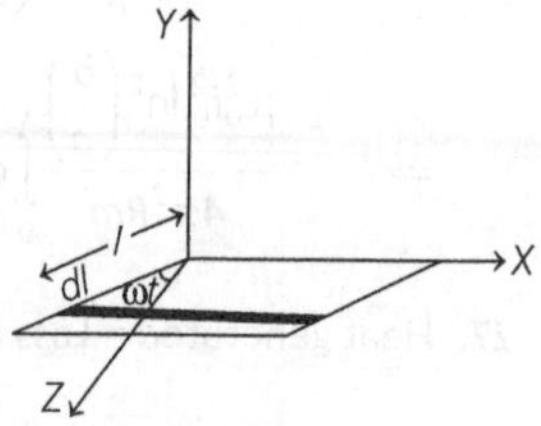

$$\varepsilon=\frac{d\phi}{dt}=\frac{B_0a^2}{2}2(\sin\omega t\cos\omega t)\omega$$

$$=\frac{B_0a^2}{2}\omega\sin 2\omega t$$

34. $i=\frac{\varepsilon}{R}=\frac{B_0a^2\omega}{2R}\sin\omega t$

$$\tau=\int(\mathbf{dM}\times\mathbf{B})=\int(iad\,l)\left(\frac{B_0 l\sin\omega t}{a}\right)\cos\omega t$$

$$=\int_0^a\left(\frac{B_0a^2\omega}{2R}\sin 2\omega t\,ad\,l\right)\left(\frac{B_0 l\sin\omega t}{a}\right)\cos\omega t$$

$$=\frac{B_0^2a^4\omega}{4R}\sin^2 2\omega t$$

35. Induced emf across OP

$$=\frac{1}{2}B\omega\left(\frac{l}{2}\right)^2=\frac{B\omega l^2}{8}$$

$$i=\frac{\varepsilon}{R}=\frac{B\omega l^2}{8R}$$

Torque on the rod $=2\int_0^{l/2}Bix\,dx=\frac{Bil^2}{4}$

$$\tau=I\alpha$$

$$\Rightarrow \quad -\frac{B}{4}\left(\frac{B\omega l^2}{8R}\right)l^2=\left(\frac{ml^2}{12}\right)\frac{d\omega}{dt}$$

$$\Rightarrow \quad \int_{\omega_0}^{\omega}\frac{d\omega}{\omega}=-\frac{3B^2l^2}{8mR}\int_0^t dt$$

$$\Rightarrow \quad \omega=\omega_0e^{-\alpha t}$$

$$i=\frac{B\omega l^2}{8R}=\frac{B\omega_0 l^2}{8R}e^{-\alpha t}$$

36. $q=\int_0^\infty i\,dt=\frac{B\omega_0 l^2}{8R}\int_0^\infty e^{-\alpha t}dt=\frac{\omega_0 M}{3B}$

37. Heat generated = Initial K.E. of rod

$$=\frac{1}{2}I\omega^2=\frac{1}{2}\left(\frac{Ml^2}{12}\right)\omega_0^2=\frac{Ml^2\omega_0^2}{24}$$

Match The Columns Questions

1. (a) At $t=1$, to oppose the increasing flux into the plane, induced current will be anti-clockwise.

$\phi=at^2+bt+c$ (equation of parabola with $a<0$)

$$i=\frac{\varepsilon}{R}=\frac{1}{R}\left|\frac{d\phi}{dt}\right|=\frac{2at+b}{R}$$

So, i will decrease linearly with time.

(b) At $t=5$,

$$i=\frac{\varepsilon}{R}=\frac{1}{R}\frac{d\phi}{dt}=0 \qquad \because \{\phi=\text{constant}\}$$

(c) At $t=9$, $i=\frac{2at+b}{R}$ but $a>0$.

So, i will increase linearly with time. To oppose the flux increasing out of plane, induced current will be clockwise.

(d) At $t=15$, to oppose the decreasing flux out of the plane, induced current will be anti-clockwise.

2. $\phi_1=\frac{B_1\pi R^2}{2}$, $\quad \phi_2=\frac{B_2\pi R^2}{2}$

(a) $\frac{d\phi_1}{dt}=0$ and $\frac{d\phi_2}{dt}=0$,

induced current is zero and force is also zero.

(b) $\frac{d\phi_1}{dt}=0$ and $\frac{d\phi_2}{dt}=\frac{10\pi R^2}{2}$, and inward field is increasing. So, the current will be always anti-clockwise and force on the ring will be towards left.

(c) $\frac{d\phi_1}{dt}=(2t)\frac{\pi R^2}{2}=t\pi R^2$ and $\frac{d\phi_2}{dt}=t\pi R^2$

As both the induced emf are equal in magnitude therefore, net current in the coil is zero. so force will also be zero.

(d) $\frac{d\phi_1}{dt}=t(\pi R^2)$, $\frac{d\phi_2}{dt}=2\pi R^2$

For $t<2$, $\frac{d\phi_2}{dt}>\frac{d\phi_1}{dt}$, current will be anticlockwise.

At $t=2$, $\frac{d\phi_1}{dt}=\frac{d\phi_2}{dt}$, current will be zero.

$\therefore$ force will be zero at $t=2$

For $t>2$; $\frac{d\phi_1}{dt}>\frac{d\phi_2}{dt}$, current will be clockwise.

3. (a) $l=2\pi r=l_0t \quad \Rightarrow \quad r=\frac{l_0t}{2\pi}$

$$\phi=BA=(B_0t^2)\pi\left(\frac{l_0t}{2\pi}\right)^2=\frac{B_0l_0^2t^4}{4\pi}$$

$$\varepsilon=\frac{d\phi}{dt}=\frac{B_0l_0^2}{4\pi}(4t^3)=25 \text{ SI unit}$$

(b) $6a=l_0t \quad \Rightarrow \quad a=\frac{l_0t}{6}$

$$\phi = BA = (B_0t^2)\left[6\frac{\sqrt{3}}{4}\left(\frac{l_0t}{6}\right)^2\right] = \frac{\sqrt{3}B_0l_0^2t^4}{24}$$

$$\varepsilon = \frac{d\phi}{dt} = \frac{\sqrt{3}B_0l_0^2}{24}(4t^3) = 3.75 \text{ SI unit}$$

(c) $4a = l_0t \Rightarrow a = \frac{l_0t}{4}$

$$\phi = BA = (B_0t^2)\left(\frac{l_0t}{4}\right)^2 = \frac{B_0l_0^2t^4}{16}$$

$$\varepsilon = \frac{d\phi}{dt} = \frac{B_0l_0^2}{16}(4t^3) = 5 \text{ SI unit}$$

(d) $3a = l_0t \Rightarrow a = \frac{l_0t}{3}$

$$\phi = BA = (B_0t)\left[\frac{\sqrt{3}}{4}\left(\frac{l_0t}{3}\right)^2\right] = \frac{\sqrt{3}}{36}B_0l_0^2t^4$$

$$\varepsilon = \frac{d\phi}{dt} = \frac{\sqrt{3}}{36}B_0l_0^2(4t^3) = 2.5 \text{ SI unit}$$

4. (a) When current is increased, inward flux through loop increases. To oppose this induced current will be anti-clockwise and wire will repel the loop.
(b) When current is decreased, inward flux through loop decreases. To oppose this induced current will be clockwise and wire will attract the loop.
(c) If loop is moved away, inward flux decreases. So, induced current is clockwise and wire will attract the loop.
(d) It loop is moved towards the wire, inward flux increases. To oppose this induced current will be anti-clockwise and the wire will repel the loop.

5. (a) $\frac{d\phi}{dt} = 0$

(b) $\left.\frac{d\phi}{dt}\right|_{\text{loop}} = 0;\ \left.\frac{d\phi}{dt}\right|_{\text{any small part}} \neq 0;$

(c) $\left.\frac{d\phi}{dt}\right|_{\text{loop}} \neq 0;\ \left.\frac{d\phi}{dt}\right|_{\text{any small part}} \neq 0;$

(d) $\left.\frac{d\phi}{dt}\right|_{\text{loop}} \neq 0;$

6. O to A ; $\phi = B(\pi r^2) \Rightarrow \varepsilon = \frac{d\phi}{dt} = \frac{dB}{dt}\pi r^2$

$$\Rightarrow E(2\pi r) = \alpha\pi r^2 \Rightarrow \quad E = \frac{r}{2}\alpha$$

A to B ; $\phi = B(\pi R^2) \Rightarrow \varepsilon = \frac{d\phi}{dt} = \frac{dB}{dt}\pi R^2$

$$\Rightarrow E(2\pi r) = \alpha\pi R^2 \Rightarrow \quad E = \frac{\alpha R^2}{2r}$$

B to C; $\phi = B(\pi R^2) - B\pi[r^2 - (2R)^2] = B\pi(5R^2 - r^2)$

$$\Rightarrow \quad \varepsilon = \frac{d\phi}{dt} = \alpha\pi(5R^2 - r^2)$$

$$\Rightarrow E(2\pi r) = \alpha\pi(5R^2 - r^2)$$

$$\Rightarrow \quad E = \frac{\alpha}{2}\left(\frac{5R^2}{r} - r\right)$$

C to D,

$$\phi = B\pi R^2 - B\pi(3R)^2 - (2R)^2 = -B(4\pi R^2)$$

$$\Rightarrow \quad \varepsilon = \frac{d\phi}{dt} = -\alpha(4\pi R^2)$$

$$\Rightarrow E(2\pi r) = -\alpha(4\pi R^2) \Rightarrow \ E = -\frac{2\alpha R^2}{r}$$

Numerical Value Questions

1. $\phi = 3t(2-t), |\varepsilon| = \left|\frac{d\phi}{dt}\right| = 6|t-1|$

$$\text{Heat produced} = \int \frac{\varepsilon^2}{R}dt = 9\int_0^2 (t-1)^2\,dt = 6 \text{ J}$$

2. $d\phi = BdA\cos\theta$

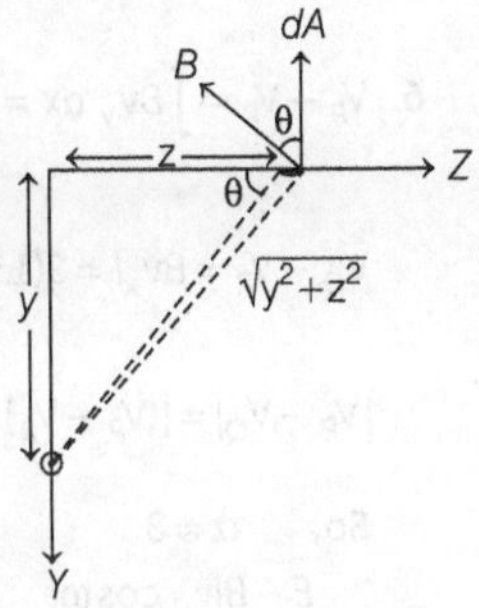

$$\Rightarrow \quad \phi = \int \frac{\mu_0 i}{2\pi\sqrt{y^2+z^2}}(wdz)\frac{z}{\sqrt{y^2+z^2}}$$

$$\Rightarrow \quad \phi = \frac{\mu_0 iw}{2\pi}\int_0^L \frac{zdz}{y^2+z^2}$$

$$\Rightarrow \quad \phi = \frac{\mu_0 iw}{4\pi}\ln\left(\frac{y^2+L^2}{y^2}\right)$$

$$\varepsilon = \frac{d\phi}{dt}$$

$$= \frac{\mu_0 w}{4\pi}\left(\frac{di}{dt}\right)\ln\left(\frac{y^2+L^2}{y^2}\right)$$

$$\Rightarrow \quad \varepsilon = \frac{\mu_0 w}{4\pi}\left(\ln\left(\frac{y^2+L^2}{y^2}\right)\right)(10\cos 5t)$$

At $\quad t = \frac{\pi}{15}$; $\varepsilon = 5\times10^{-7}\ln\left(\frac{13}{4}\right)$

so, $\quad \alpha = 5$ and $\beta = 13$

$$\Rightarrow \frac{\alpha+\beta}{2} = 9$$

3. $\int d\phi = \int_2^4 \left[\frac{\mu_0 i}{2\pi x(10^{-2})} + \frac{\mu_0 i}{2\pi(6-x)(10^{-2})}\right](2\times10^{-2})(dx\times10^{-2})$

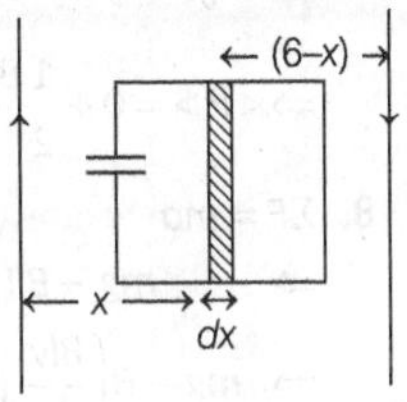

$$\Rightarrow \phi = \frac{\mu_0 i}{100\pi}\int_2^4\left(\frac{1}{x} + \frac{1}{6-x}\right)dx = \frac{\mu_0 i\ln 2}{50\pi}$$

$$\varepsilon = \frac{d\phi}{dt} = \frac{\mu_0\ln 2}{50\pi}\frac{di}{dt}$$

$$= 5\mu_0\ln 2\cos(50\pi t)$$

$$q = C\varepsilon$$

$$= (5\times10^{-6})\mu_0\ln 2\cos(50\pi t)$$

$$i = \frac{dq}{dt} = [(5\times10^{-6})\mu_0\ln 2]50\pi\sin(50\pi t)$$

$$i_{max} = 250\pi\times10^{-6}\times4\pi\times10^{-7}\ln 2$$

$$= 10^{-10}\pi^2\log_e 2$$

4. Length of diagonal at time $t = 10t$

$$\phi = BA = B\left(\frac{10t}{\sqrt{2}}\right)^2 = 50Bt^2$$

$$\varepsilon = \frac{d\phi}{dt} = 100Bt = 10t$$

$$R = (0.01)4\left(\frac{10t}{\sqrt{2}}\right) = \frac{0.4t}{\sqrt{2}}$$

$$i = \frac{\varepsilon}{R} = 25\sqrt{2}\text{A}$$

5. ε_1 = Emf induced in the left edge $= Blv$

$= [100(1)(1)](1)(1) = 100$ V

ε_2 = Emf induced in the right edge $= Blv$

$= [100(2)(1)](1)(1) = 200$ V

Emf induced in the other two edges will be zero as $\mathbf{v} \| \mathbf{dl}$

$$i = \frac{\varepsilon_1 - \varepsilon_2}{R} = \frac{200 - 100}{50} = 2\text{ A}$$

6. $$V_P - V_R = \int Bv_y\, dx = \int_0^{1.5L} 3xv dx = \frac{27vL^2}{8}$$

$$V_Q - V_R = Bv_x l = 3(1.5L)v(1.5L) = \frac{27vL^2}{4}$$

$$|V_P - V_Q| = |(V_P - V_R) - (V_Q - V_R)| = \frac{27vL^2}{8}$$

So, $\alpha = 3$

7. $i = \dfrac{E - Blv_0 \cos\omega t}{r}$; $F_m = Bil$

$$\Sigma F = ma$$

$$\Rightarrow F + F_m = ma$$

$$F + B\left(\frac{E - Blv_0 \cos\omega t}{r}\right)l = m(-v_0\omega \sin\omega t)$$

$$\Rightarrow \quad F = -\frac{BE}{r} + \frac{B^2l^2v_0 \cos\omega t}{r} - mv_0\omega \sin\omega t$$

$$P = Fv = -\frac{BE}{r}v_0 \cos\omega t + \frac{B^2l^2v_0^2 \cos^2 \omega t}{r}$$

$$- mv_0^2\omega \sin\omega t \cos\omega t$$

$$\Rightarrow \langle P \rangle = 0 + \frac{1}{2}\frac{B^2l^2v_0^2}{r} + 0 = 4\text{ W}$$

8. $\Sigma F = ma$

$$\Rightarrow \quad mg - BiL = ma$$

$$\Rightarrow mg - B\left(\frac{Blv}{R}\right) = ma \Rightarrow a = g - \frac{B^2L^2v}{mR}$$

For terminal velocity $a = 0$

$$\Rightarrow \quad 0 = g - \frac{B^2L^2}{mR}v_T \Rightarrow v_T = \frac{mgR}{B^2L^2}$$

When $v = \dfrac{v_T}{2}$, $a = g - \dfrac{B^2L^2}{mR}\left(\dfrac{mgR}{2B^2L^2}\right) = \dfrac{g}{2}$

9. $$i = \frac{\varepsilon}{R} = \frac{1}{2}\frac{B\omega r^2}{R}$$

$$\tau = \int_0^r (Bidx)x = \frac{Bir^2}{2} = \frac{B^2\omega r^4}{4R}$$

$$P = \tau\omega = \frac{B^2\omega^2 r^4}{4R} = 160\text{ W}$$

10. $$\phi = B\left(A + \frac{\pi a^2}{2}\cos\omega t\right)$$

$$\Rightarrow \quad \varepsilon = \left|\frac{d\phi}{dt}\right| = \frac{B\omega\pi a^2}{2}\sin\omega t$$

$$q = C\varepsilon \Rightarrow i = \frac{dq}{dt} = \frac{B\omega^2\pi a^2 C}{2}\cos\omega t$$

$$\tau = MB\sin\theta = \left(\frac{B\omega^2\pi a^2 C}{2}\cos\omega t\right)\frac{\pi a^2}{2}B\sin\omega t$$

$$\Rightarrow \quad \tau = \frac{1}{8}(B^2\omega^2\pi^2 a^4 C \sin 2\omega t)$$

$$P = \tau\omega = \frac{B^2\omega^2\pi^2 a^4 C \sin 2\omega t}{8}$$

At $t = \dfrac{1}{4}$ s; $P = 2$ W

11. $\varepsilon_{AC} = \varepsilon_{CD} = \varepsilon_{DE} = \varepsilon_{EF} = e$

$\varepsilon_{OA} = \varepsilon_{OD} = \varepsilon_{OF} = 0$

$i_{OD} = 0$

for loop $ACEF$, $i = \dfrac{\varepsilon}{R} = \dfrac{4e}{6r} = \dfrac{2e}{3r}$

So, $m = 2$ and $n = 3$

$\Rightarrow m + n = 2 + 3 = 5$

Previous Years Questions

JEE Main

1. $$E_{avg} = \frac{\Delta\phi}{\Delta t} = \frac{BA\cos\theta}{10}$$

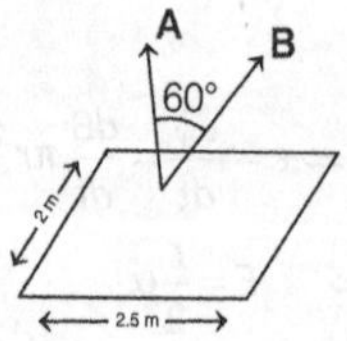

$$= 4 \times 2 \times \frac{5}{2} \times \frac{\cos 60°}{10} = 4 \times 5 \times \frac{1}{10 \times 2} = 1\text{ V} = 1\text{ V}$$

2.

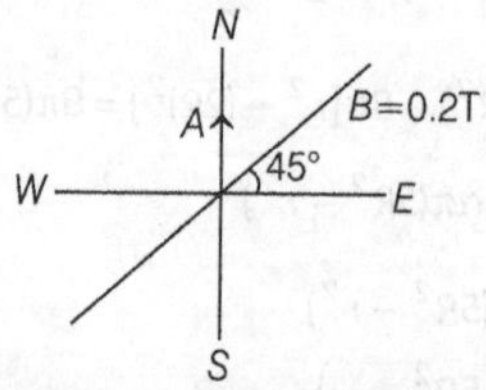

$$\mathbf{A} = (0.1)^2\hat{\mathbf{j}}; \quad \mathbf{B} = \frac{0.2}{\sqrt{2}}\hat{\mathbf{i}} + \frac{0.2}{\sqrt{2}}\hat{\mathbf{j}}$$

Magnitude of induced emf,

$$e = \frac{\Delta\phi}{\Delta t} = \frac{BA - 0}{1}$$

$$= \sqrt{2} \times 10^{-3}\ V$$

$$x = 2$$

3. Given, $l = 5$ m

$$B_H = 0.6 \times 10^{-4}\ Wbm^{-2}$$

$$v = 10\ m/s$$

∴ Instantaneous value of induced emf

$$e = Bvl$$

$$= 0.6 \times 10^{-4} \times 10 \times 5$$

$$= 3 \times 10^{-3}\ V$$

4. Given,

Length of blade (l) = 80 cm

Rotational speed = 1200 rpm

Angular speed, $\omega = 2\pi \times f$

$$= \frac{2\pi}{60} \times 1200\ rad/s$$

$$\omega = 40\pi\ rad/s$$

Induced emf, $\varepsilon = \frac{1}{2} B_V \omega l^2$ ...(i)

$$B_V = B_H \sin\theta$$

$$B_H = 0.5G = 0.5 \times 10^{-4}\ T$$

$$\theta = 30°, \sin 30 = \frac{1}{2}$$

$$B_V = \frac{1}{4} \times 10^{-4}$$

$$\varepsilon = \frac{1}{2} \times \frac{1}{4} \times 10^{-4} \times 40\pi \times (80)^2 \times 10^{-4}$$

$$\varepsilon = 3.2\pi \times 10^{-4}\ V = 32\,\pi \times 10^{-5}\ V$$

5. EMF produced in the coil is given by,

$$\varepsilon = \frac{d}{dt}\phi_B = NA \cdot \frac{dB}{dt}$$

$$= NA \cdot \frac{\Delta B}{\Delta t}$$

$$= N \times \frac{\pi D^2}{4}\left(\frac{\Delta B}{\Delta t}\right)$$

Here, change in magnetic field

$$\Delta B = B_2 - B_1$$

$$= 5000 - 3000 = 2000\ T$$

Time interval, $\Delta t = 2$ s

Diameter, $D = 0.02$ m

Emf induced $= 22$ V

So, we have,

$$22 = \frac{N\pi(0.02)^2 \times 2000}{4 \times 2}$$

$$\Rightarrow \quad N = 70 \text{ turns}$$

6. Induced current,

$$I = -\frac{e}{R} = -\left(\frac{\frac{d}{dt}\phi_B}{R}\right) = -\left(\frac{10t - 36}{8}\right)$$

Induced current at $t = 2s$ is,

$$I = -\left(\frac{10 \times 2 - 36}{8}\right) = 2\ A$$

7. Induced emf can be induced in coil by changing magnetic flux as

$$\phi = \mathbf{B} \cdot \mathbf{A} = BA\cos\theta$$

By rotating coil, angle θ changes and hence flux changes. By changing area, magnetic flux also changes.

8. It is given,

In 0.5 s, magnetic field of 0.5 T becomes zero.

So, rate of decay of magnetic field,

$$\frac{\Delta B}{\Delta t} = \frac{0 - 0.5}{0.5} = -1\ T/s$$

(Negative sign shows field is reducing)

Hence, magnetic field at 0.25 s will be

$$\frac{\Delta B}{0.25} = -1\ T/s$$

$$\Rightarrow \quad \frac{B_2 - B_1}{0.25} = -1$$

or $\quad B_2 = 0.5 - 0.25 = 0.25$ T

So, magnitude of induced emf in coil at $t = 0.25$ s will be

$$\varepsilon = \frac{d}{dt}\phi = \left(\frac{dB}{dt}\right) \cdot A$$

$$= \frac{\Delta B}{\Delta t} \cdot \pi r^2 = \frac{0.25}{0.25} \times \pi \times \left(\frac{10}{\sqrt{\pi}} \times 10^{-2}\right)^2$$

$$= 10^{-2}\ V = 10 \times 10^{-3}\ V = 10\ mV$$

9. Work done in pulling the loop out of region of magnetic field,

$$W = V \cdot q = VIt$$

$$\Rightarrow \quad W = \frac{V^2}{R} t$$

$$\Rightarrow \quad V = IR = \left(\frac{d}{dt}\phi\right)^2 \cdot \frac{t}{R} = \left(\frac{d}{dt}BA\right)^2 \cdot \frac{t}{R}$$

$$\Rightarrow \quad W = B^2 \cdot \frac{A^2}{t^2} \cdot \frac{t}{R} = \frac{B^2 A^2}{tR}$$

Here, $B = 40$ T, $A = 25 \times 10^{-4}\ m^2$, $t = 1$ s, $R = 10\ \Omega$

$$\therefore \text{Work done} = W = \frac{(40)^2 \times (25 \times 10^{-4})^2}{1 \times 10}$$

$$= 1.0 \times 10^{-3}\ J$$

10. We know that induced emf,

$$e = \frac{d\phi}{dt}$$

$$e=\frac{dBA}{dt}=\frac{AdB}{dt}$$

$e=A\times$ slope of B-t curve

$$=A\left[\frac{8-4}{4-2}\right]=4\times\frac{4}{2}$$

$$e=8\text{ V}$$

11. $\Delta Q=\frac{\Delta\phi}{R}=\frac{2NBA}{R}$

$$=\frac{2\times100\times1.5\times24\times10^{-4}}{12}$$

$$=6\times10^{-2}\text{ C}=60\text{ mC}$$

12. When a rod is moving perpendicular to an uniform magnetic field, magnitude of induced emf is;

$E=Bl\,V$

Here $E=0.08$ V

$l=10$ cm $=10\times10^{-2}$ m

$v=?, B=0.4$ T

So, velocity v is

$$v=\frac{E}{Bl}=\frac{0.08}{0.4\times10\times10^{-2}}=2\text{ m/s}$$

13. Moving magnet in conducting pipe causes change in flux and hence emf is induced. This emf causes eddy current in conducting pipe in such a way that it tries to oppose the change in flux, therefore magnet slows down.

So, both A and R are true and R is the correct explanation of A.

14. Induced emf in a rotating rod

$$=\frac{d\phi}{dt}=B\left(\frac{dA}{dt}\right)=\frac{B\cdot A}{T}$$

$$=B\cdot\frac{\pi L^2}{2\pi/\omega}=\frac{1}{2}BL^2\omega$$

15. Given, length of wire, $l=1$ m, Velocity, $v=8$ m/s

$\theta=90°$

Magnetic field, $B=2$ T

$\therefore$ Induced emf, $e=Bvl\sin\theta=2\times8\times1\times\sin90°=16$ V

16. Given,

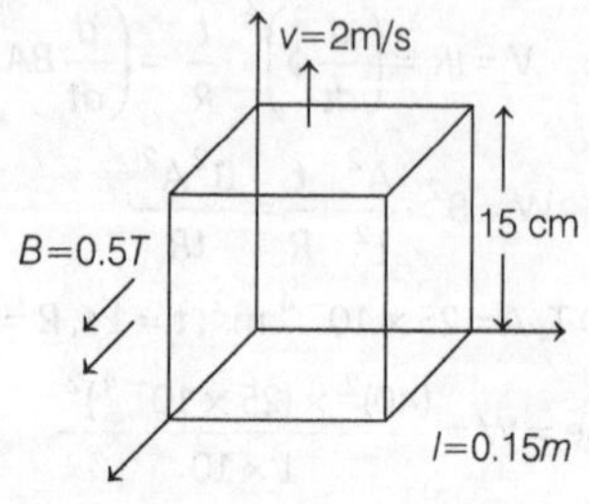

$l=0.15$ m

$$\text{Emf}=Bvl=0.5\times2\times0.15$$

$$=0.15\text{V}$$

$$=150\text{ mV}$$

17. Force on rod is given by

$$F=\frac{B^2l^2v}{R}$$

Substituting valuer we get

$$F=\frac{(0.15)^2\,(1^2)\times4}{5}=18\times10^{-3}\text{ N}$$

18. Given, side of square loop,

$a=2.0$ cm $=2\times10^{-2}$ m

Area of loop $=(2\times10^{-2})^2=4\times10^{-4}$ m^2

Amplitude of current $=2.5$ A

Angular frequency $=700$ rad/s

No. of turns in solenoid $=50$ turns per cm

$=\frac{50}{10^{-2}}$ turns per m

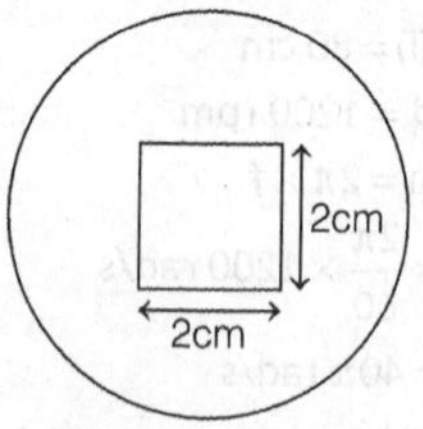

B due to selenoid $=\mu_0nI$

$\phi_{\text{through square}}=\mu_0nI\times A$

Emf induced, $\varepsilon=\mu_0nA\times\frac{dI}{dt}$

$=\mu_0nAI_0\omega\cos\omega t$ $\quad[\because I=I_0\sin\omega t]$

$|\varepsilon|=\mu_0nAI_0\omega$

$$=4\pi\times10^{-7}\times\frac{50}{10^{-2}}\times4\times10^{-4}\times2.5\times700$$

$$=44\times10^{-4}\text{ V}$$

19. Given, Angular speed of metallic rod.

$$\omega=2\pi\times\frac{210}{60}\text{ rad/s}=7\pi\text{ rad/s}$$

Length of rod, $l=20$ cm $=0.2$ m

Magnetic field, $B=0.2$ T

The emf induced between the centre and the ring,

$$e=\frac{1}{2}B\omega l^2$$

$$=\frac{1}{2}\times0.2\times7\pi\times(0.2)^2$$

$$=0.088\text{ V}=88\text{ mV}$$

20. Magnetic field $(B)=0.4$ T

Expansion in the radius of loop

$$\left(\frac{dr}{dt}\right)=1\text{ mm/s}=10^{-3}\text{m/s}$$

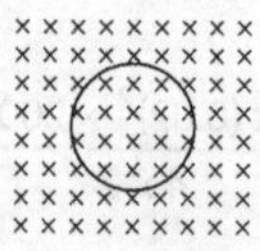

Thus, $\dfrac{dA}{dt} = 2\pi r \dfrac{dr}{dt}$

emf induced, $\varepsilon = \left(-\dfrac{d\phi}{dt}\right) = \dfrac{BdA}{dt} = 0.4\, 2\pi r \dfrac{dr}{dt}$

$$|\varepsilon|_{r\,=\,2\,\text{cm}} = 0.4 \times 2 \times \pi \times 2 \times 10^{-2} \times 10^{-3}\ \text{V}$$

$$= 16\pi\,\mu\text{V} = 50.24\,\mu\text{V} \simeq 50\,\mu\text{V}$$

21.

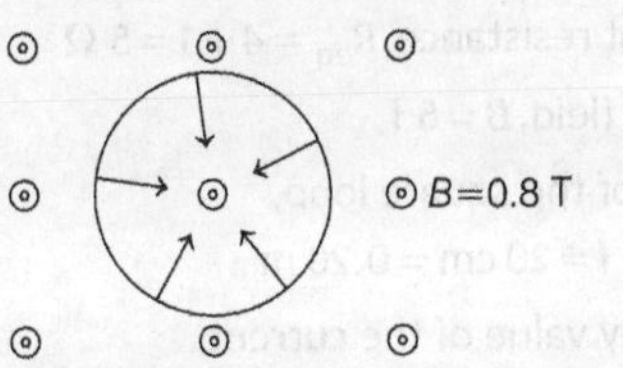

For loop given that, $\dfrac{dr}{dt} = 2\ \text{cm/s}$

Magnitude of induced emf in loop,

$$E = \frac{d\phi}{dt} = \frac{d}{dt}BA = B \cdot \frac{d}{dt}\pi r^2 = 2\pi Br \cdot \frac{dr}{dt}$$

Here, $B = 0.8\,\text{T}$, $r = 10$ cm, $\dfrac{dr}{dt} = 2$ cm/s

So, $E = 2 \times \pi \times 0.8 \times 10 \times 10^{-2} \times 2 \times 10^{-2}$

$$= 100 \times 10^{-4}\ \text{V} = 10\ \text{mV}$$

22. Given that, area,

$$A = 70\ \text{cm}^2 = 70 \times 10^{-4}\ \text{m}^2$$

No. of turns,

$$N = 600$$

Magnetic field,

$$B = 0.4\ \text{Wbm}^{-2}$$

Angular velocity,

$$\omega = 500\ \text{rpm} = 500 \times \frac{\pi}{30}\ \text{rad/s}$$

$$\Rightarrow \quad \omega = \frac{50\pi}{3}\ \text{rad/s}$$

The angle between the normal to coil and the direction of magnetic field,

$$\theta = 90° - 60° = 30°$$

Induced emf in rotating coil is given as

$$e = N\omega BA \sin\theta$$

$$= 600 \times \frac{50\pi}{3} \times 0.4 \times 70 \times 10^{-4} \times \sin 30°$$

$$\Rightarrow \quad e = 44\ \text{V}$$

23.

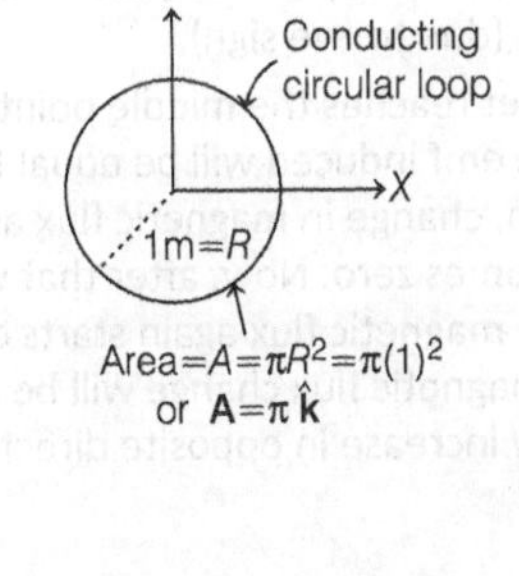

Given, $\mathbf{B} = (3t^3\hat{\mathbf{j}} + 3t^2\hat{\mathbf{k}})\text{T}$

∴ Flux through loop, $\phi_B = \mathbf{B} \cdot \mathbf{A} = (3t^3\hat{\mathbf{j}} + 3t^2\hat{\mathbf{k}}) \cdot (\pi\hat{\mathbf{k}}) = 3\pi t^2$ Wb

We know,

Induced emf, $\varepsilon = -\dfrac{Nd\phi_B}{dt}$

(where, N = no. of turns)

$$\Rightarrow \quad \varepsilon = -1\frac{d\,3\pi t^2}{dt} = -3\pi\frac{dt^2}{dt} \qquad (\because N = 1)$$

$$\Rightarrow \quad \varepsilon = -3\pi \times 2t = -6\pi t\ \text{V}$$

Now, at $t = 2$ s

$$\varepsilon = -6 \times \pi \times 2 = -12\pi\ \text{V}$$

$$\therefore \quad n\pi = -12\pi$$

$$\Rightarrow \quad n = -12 \Rightarrow |n| = 12$$

24. Given, resistance of coil, $R = 8\,\Omega$

Magnetic flux, $\phi = \dfrac{2}{3}(9 - t^2)$

According to Faraday's law of electromagnetic induction induced emf in the coil

i.e $= -\dfrac{d\phi}{dt} = \dfrac{-d}{dt}\dfrac{2}{3}(9 - t^2) = -\dfrac{2}{3} \times (-2t) = \dfrac{4}{3}t$

Heat produced during, $t = 0$ to $t = 3$ s

$$H = \int_0^3 \frac{e^2}{R}dt = \int_0^3 \frac{1}{8}\left(\frac{4}{3}t\right)^2 dt$$

$$= \int_0^3 \frac{2}{9}t^2 dt = \frac{2}{9}\left[\frac{t^3}{3}\right]_0^3$$

$$= \frac{2}{9}\left[\frac{3^3}{3} - \frac{0^3}{3}\right] = \frac{2}{9} \times 9 = 2\ \text{J}$$

25. Given a metallic rod, $L = 20$ cm

It is placed in *N-S* direction

$v = 20$ m/s (towards East)

$$B_H = 4 \times 10^{-3}\ \text{T}$$

$$\theta = 45°$$

To find emf induced in rod,

$$E = Blv \sin\theta$$

$$= 4 \times 10^{-3} \times \frac{20}{100} \times 20 \qquad (\because \theta = 90° \Rightarrow \sin 90° = 1)$$

$$= 16 \times 10^{-3}\ \text{V} = 16\ \text{mV}$$

26. Given, flux, $\phi = (5t^3 + 4t^2 + 2t - 5)$ Wb

$$t = 2\ \text{s}, R = 5\,\Omega$$

Induced emf, $\quad e = \dfrac{d\phi}{dt} = 15t^2 + 8t + 2$

At, $t = 2$ s,

$$e = (15 \times 2^2) + (8 \times 2) + 2 = 78\ \text{V}$$

We have, $e = IR$

$\therefore$ Induced current, $I = \frac{e}{R} = \frac{78}{5} = 15.6\,A$

27. Given, $l = 1\,m$

$$\omega = 5\,rad/s$$
$$B_H = 0.2 \times 10^{-4}\,T$$

Induced emf between the two ends of conductor due to its rotation in B_H,

$$e = \frac{B_H \omega l^2}{2} = \frac{0.2 \times 10^{-4} \times 5 \times 1^2}{2}$$
$$= 5 \times 10^{-5}\,V = 50 \times 10^{-6}\,V = 50\,\mu V$$

28. Given, number of turns in coil

$$N = 1000$$

Area, $A = 1\,m^2$

Angular velocity, $\omega = 2\pi \times$ number of revolutions per second

$$= 2\pi \times 1$$
$$\Rightarrow \quad \omega = 2\pi = 2 \times 3.14 = 6.28\ rad/s$$
$$B = 0.07\,T$$

$\therefore$ Maximum voltage produced due to revolution of coil,

$$V_{max} = NBA\omega$$
$$= 1000 \times 0.07 \times 1 \times 6.28$$
$$= 439.6 \simeq 440\,V$$

29. In the given figure, the magnetic field is outward, means N-pole is formed on outward face and S-pole is formed on inward (back) face.

As the induced current is anti-clockwise which is also making N-pole on outward face.

According to the Lenz's law, the induced current always opposes the nature by which it is produced.

Hence, induced current is in the direction, so the strength of N-pole is maintained as it is decreasing.

30. As per question, flux through the loop increases according to

$$\phi_0(t) = 10t^2 + 20t \qquad \text{...(i)}$$

where, ϕ_0 is in milliwebers and t in seconds.

Differentiate Eq. (i) with respect to t, we get

Induced emf $|E| = \frac{d\phi}{dt} = (20t + 20)\,mV$

Current, $i = \frac{|E|}{R} \Rightarrow i = \frac{20t + 20}{2}$

$$\Rightarrow \quad i = (10t + 10)\,mA$$

$\therefore$ Current, $= (10 \times 5 + 10)\,mA \qquad [\because i(t = 5\,s)]$

$$= (50 + 10)\,mA$$
$$i = 60\,mA$$

31. According to given circuit diagram, equivalent resistance between point P and Q.

$$R_{PQ} = (4 + 4)\,||\,(4 + 4) = \frac{8 \times 8}{8 + 8} = 4\,\Omega$$

The equivalent circuit can be drawn as

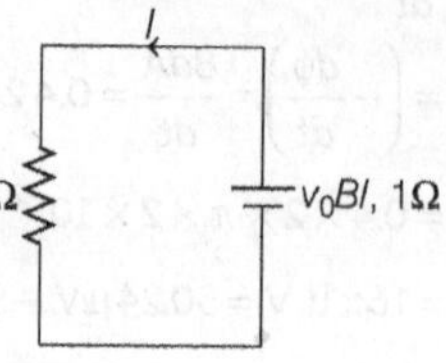

Equivalent resistance, $R_{eq} = 4 + 1 = 5\,\Omega$

Magnetic field, $B = 5\,T$

The side of the square loop,

$$l = 20\,cm = 0.20\,m$$

The steady value of the current,

$$I = 2\,mA = 2 \times 10^{-3}\,A$$

Induced emf, $e = Bv_0 l$

Induced current, $I = \frac{e}{R_{eq}}$

Substituting the values in the above equation, we get

$$2 \times 10^{-3} = \frac{5 \times v_0 \times 0.2}{5}$$
$$\Rightarrow \quad v_0 = 10^{-2}\,m/s = 1\,cm/s$$

$\therefore$ The value of $v_0 = 1\,cm/s$, so that a steady current of 2 mA flows in the loop.

32. Given, magnetic field, $B = 1\,T$

Radius of ring, $R = 1\,m$

Velocity of ring, $v = 1\,m/s$

Time taken, $t = 1\,s$

Let emf be ε.

Since, $\varepsilon = Blv \sin\theta$

$$\therefore \quad = 1 \times 2R \times 1 \times \sin 90^\circ$$
$$= 2R = 2\,V$$

33. Given, radius of loop is R and velocity of the bar magnet is v.

According to Faraday's law of electromagnetic induction, the emf induced in loop is given by

$$e = -\frac{Nd\phi}{dt} \qquad \text{...(i)}$$

As initially the bar magnet is moving towards the coil, so the rate of change of magnetic flux linked with the coil will increase. Thus, initially the emf induced in coil will decrease as per Eq. (i) (due to –ve sign).

When magnet reaches the middle point in the coil, for that moment the emf induced will be equal to zero because in this situation, change in magnetic flux associated with bar magnet becomes zero. Now, after that when magnet moves forward, the magnetic flux again starts changing but the polarity of magnetic flux change will be reversed. So, the emf will now increase in opposite direction.

The graph for change in emf of coil is shown below.

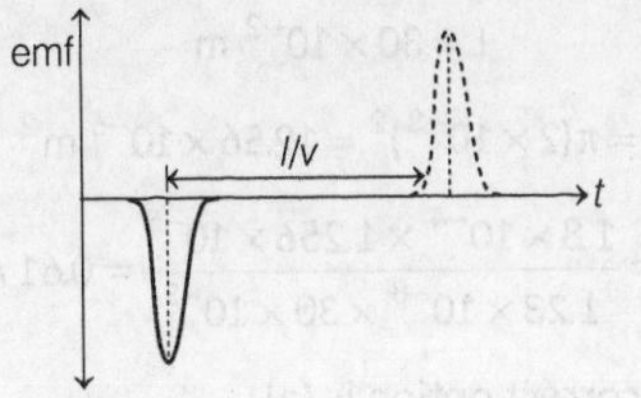

34. Given, radius of circular coil, $r = 8.0\text{ cm} = 0.08\text{ m}$

Number of turns, $N = 20$

Angular speed of coil, $\omega = 50\text{ rad s}^{-1}$

Magnetic field, $B = 3.0 \times 10^{-2}\text{ T}$

The maximum emf induced in a coil can be expressed as $\varepsilon = \omega NBA$

Here, A is the area of coil.

$$\varepsilon = NB\omega(\pi r^2)$$

Substituting the given values, we get

$$\varepsilon = 20 \times 3.0 \times 10^{-2} \times 50 \times \pi \times (0.08)^2$$

$$= 60.3 \times 10^{-2}\text{ V} \approx 60 \times 10^{-2}\text{ V}$$

35. Given,

Radius of coil, $r = 1\text{ m}$

Resistance of coil, $R = 2\mu\Omega = 2 \times 10^{-6}\,\Omega$

Magnetic field, $B = \frac{4}{\pi} \times 10^{-3}\left(1 - \frac{t}{100}\right)\text{T}$

As we know that,

Induced emf $(\varepsilon) = -\frac{d\phi}{dt} = -A\frac{dB}{dt}$ $\quad (\because \phi = \mathbf{B} \cdot \mathbf{A})$

where, $\frac{d\phi}{dt}$ = rate of charge of flux

A = area of coil

$\frac{dB}{dt}$ = rate of change of magnetic field strength

$$\Rightarrow \quad \varepsilon = -(\pi r^2)\frac{d}{dt}\left[\frac{4}{\pi} \times 10^{-3}\left(1 - \frac{t}{100}\right)\right]$$

$$= -\pi r^2 \times \frac{4}{\pi} \times 10^{-3} \times \frac{-1}{100}$$

$$= r^2 \times 4 \times 10^{-5} = 1^2 \times 4 \times 10^{-5}$$

$$= 4 \times 10^{-5}\text{ V}$$

If $B = 0$,

Then, $\frac{4}{\pi} \times 10^{-3}\left(1 - \frac{t}{100}\right) = 0 \Rightarrow t = 100\text{ s}$

Since, Energy (E) = Power (P) × Time (t)

Also, $P = \frac{\varepsilon^2}{R}$

$$\Rightarrow \quad E = \frac{\varepsilon^2}{R} \times t = \frac{(4 \times 10^{-5})^2}{2 \times 10^{-6}} \times 100$$

$$= \frac{16 \times 10^2}{2} = 8 \times 10^{-2} = 0.08 = 80\text{ mJ}$$

36. As the rectangular conductor moves in field area, so flux is increasing up to $x = b$, then flux is generated on return journey from $x = b$ to $x = 0$. The flux is shown by plot A of the graph.

As, emf, $e = -\frac{d\phi}{dt}$, which is shown by curve B.

and power dissipated, $P = VI$ which is shown by curve C.

37. The given situation can be shown as

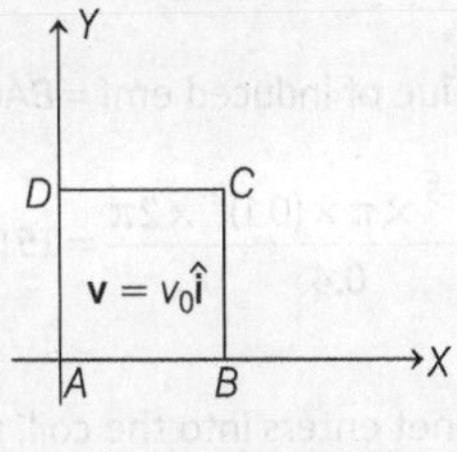

From the above figure, it can be seen that emf induced in side DC and AB will be zero. It is because **v** is parallel to length of conductor along X-axis.

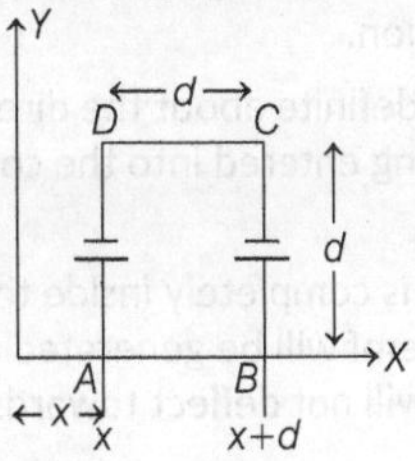

$\therefore$ Net emf induced $= E_{BC} - E_{AD}$

$$= \frac{B_0(x+d)v_0 d}{a} - \frac{B_0 x v_0 d}{a} = \frac{B_0 v_0 d^2}{a}$$

38. According to Lenz's law, "An induced current flows in a direction in such a way that it always opposes the cause that induced it".

Considering this, it can be concluded that I_1 is in the clockwise direction and I_2 is in the anti-clockwise direction and the effective circuit with the directions of I_1 and I_2 can be shown as follows

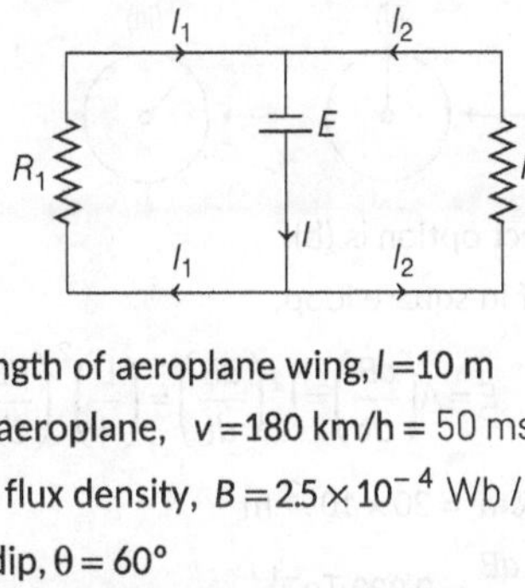

39. Given, length of aeroplane wing, $l = 10\text{ m}$

Speed of aeroplane, $v = 180\text{ km/h} = 50\text{ ms}^{-1}$

Magnetic flux density, $B = 2.5 \times 10^{-4}\text{ Wb/m}^2$

Angle of dip, $\theta = 60°$

The emf induced between the tips of plane wings,

$$\varepsilon = Blv\sin\theta$$

$$= 2.5 \times 10^{-4} \times 10 \times 50 \sin 60°$$

$$= 2.5 \times 5 \times 10^{-2} \times \sqrt{3}/2$$

$= 6.25 \times 1.732 \times 10^{-2}$

$= 108.25 \times 10^{-3} = 108.25$ mV

40. Flux linked with the coil is

$$\phi = B \cdot A = BA\cos\omega t$$

Magnitude of emf induced in coil

$$= \left|\frac{d}{dt}\phi\right| = |BA\omega \sin\omega t|$$

Maximum value of induced emf $= BA\omega = \dfrac{BA2\pi}{T}$

$$= \frac{3\times 10^{-5} \times \pi \times (0.1)^2 \times 2\pi}{0.4} = 15\,\mu V$$

41. At point (i)

The bar magnet enters into the coil, so the magnetic flux passing through the loops will change. In order to oppose that, an emf gets generated and an induced current starts to flow. So, the pointer of galvanometer will deflect in a particular direction.

(We can not be definite about the direction, as which pole of magnet is being entered into the coil is not given.)

At point (ii)

The bar magnet is completely inside the coil, so the flux will not change. No emf will be generated and no current flows. So, the pointer will not deflect towards any side. It will show zero.

At point (iii)

The bar magnet exits from the coil, so again the flux will change in opposite manner to what happened at point (i), so again an opposing emf gets generated and an induced current starts to flow in a direction opposite to that when the magnet was entering.

So in this case, the pointer will deflect in the direction opposite to the case when magnet was entering.

Looking at the options, following cases seems to be possible.

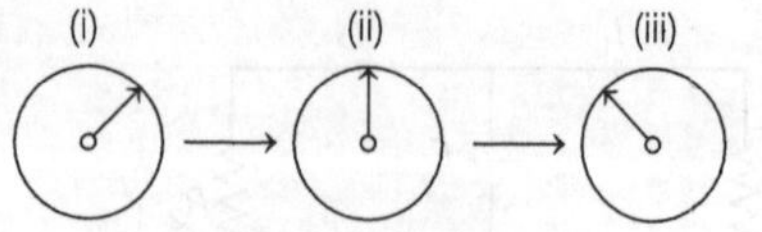

Hence, correct option is (b).

42. Induced emf in square loop,

$$E = A\left(\frac{dB}{dt}\right) = l^2\left(\frac{dB}{dt}\right) = \left(\frac{L}{4}\right)^2\left(\frac{dB}{dt}\right)$$

Here, $L = 30$ cm $= 30 \times 10^{-2}$ m

$$\frac{dB}{dt} = 0.032\ \text{Ts}^{-1}$$

$\therefore \quad E = 1.8 \times 10^{-4}$ V

Induced current $= \dfrac{E}{R} = \dfrac{E}{\rho\dfrac{L}{A}} = \dfrac{EA}{\rho L}$

Here, $\rho = 1.23 \times 10^{-8}\ \Omega$-m

$L = 30 \times 10^{-2}$ m

$A = \pi r^2 = \pi(2\times 10^{-3})^2 = 12.56 \times 10^{-6}\ \text{m}^2$

So, $\quad I = \dfrac{1.8\times 10^{-4} \times 1.256 \times 10^{-5}}{1.23 \times 10^{-8} \times 30 \times 10^{-2}} = 0.61$ A

Hence, correct option is (a).

43. Given, $I(t) = 5t^2 - 2t + 3$

$$\frac{dI}{dt} = 10t - 2$$

At $t = 1$ s, $\dfrac{dI}{dt} = 8$ A/s

Magnetic flux, $\phi = \left(\dfrac{\mu_0 I n_2}{2R}\right)(\pi r^2 n_1)$

Induced emf, $e = \left|\dfrac{d\phi}{dt}\right| = \left(\dfrac{\mu_0 n_2}{2R}\right)\pi r^2 n_1 \dfrac{dI}{dt}$

Given, $n_1 = 200$,

$r = 1$ cm $= 10^{-2}$ m,

$n_2 = 500$,

$R = 20$ cm $= 20 \times 10^{-2}$ m

and $\quad \mu_0 = 4\pi \times 10^{-7}$

$$\therefore \quad e = \frac{4\pi \times 10^{-7} \times 200 \times \pi \times 10^{-4} \times 500}{2 \times 20 \times 10^{-2}} \times 8$$

$= 8 \times 10^{-4}$ V $= 0.8$ mV

According to question,

$$0.8\text{mV} = \frac{4}{x} \Rightarrow x = \frac{4}{0.8} = 5$$

44. If given situation, loop and magnetic field are given as shown in the figure.

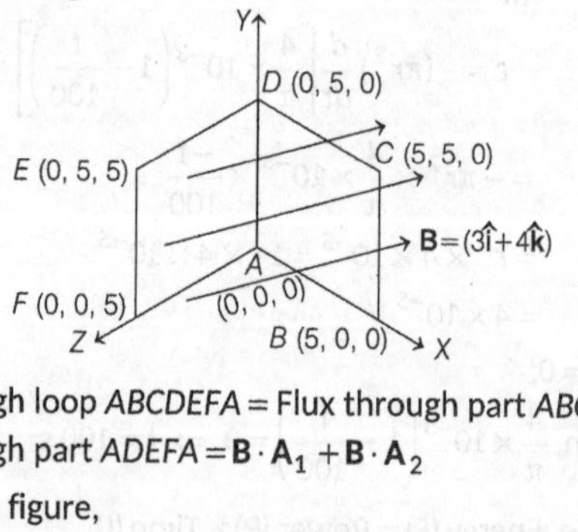

Flux through loop $ABCDEFA$ = Flux through part $ABCDA$ + Flux through part $ADEFA = \mathbf{B}\cdot\mathbf{A}_1 + \mathbf{B}\cdot\mathbf{A}_2$

Here, from figure,

$$\mathbf{A}_1 = 25\hat{k} \text{ and } \mathbf{A}_2 = 25\hat{i}$$

So, flux associated with complete loop

$= (3\hat{i} + 4\hat{k})\cdot 25\hat{k} + (3\hat{i} + 4\hat{k})\cdot 25\hat{i}$

$= 100 + 75$

$= 175$ Wb

45. We are given with following situation,

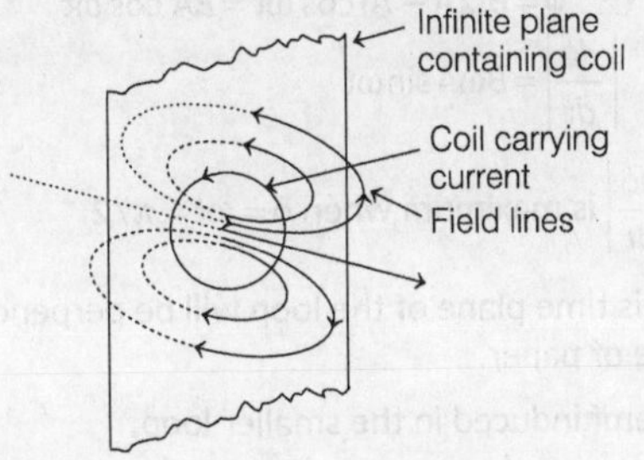

From the diagram of field lines, we can observe that whatever be the number of field lines emitted from coil, all of them goes back into the infinite plane only.

So, magnetic flux emanating from coil is equal and opposite to the flux linked with infinite plane.

So, $\phi_i = -\phi_o$

46. Magnetic flux associated with the outer coil is

$$\phi_{\text{outer}} = \mu_0 \pi NR \cdot I$$
$$= \mu_0 N\pi R(kte^{-\alpha t})$$
$$= Cte^{-\alpha t}$$

where,

$$C = \mu_0 N\pi Rk = \text{constant}$$

Induced emf,

$$e = \frac{-d\phi_{\text{outer}}}{dt} = Ce^{-\alpha t} + (-\alpha C t e^{-\alpha t})$$
$$= Ce^{-\alpha t}(1-\alpha t)$$

$\therefore$ Induced current, $I = \dfrac{e}{\text{Resistance}}$

$\Rightarrow$ At $t = 0, I = -$ ve

$\therefore$ The correct graph representing this condition is given in option (d).

47. Since, the magnetic field is dependent on time, so the net charge flowing through the loop will be given as

$$Q = \frac{\text{change in magnetic flux, } \Delta\phi_B}{\text{resistance, } R}$$

As, $\Delta\phi_B = B A = BA\cos\theta$

where, A is the surface area of the loop and 'θ' is an angle between B and A.

Here, $\theta = 0 \Rightarrow \Delta\phi_B = BA$

$\therefore$ For the time interval, $t = 0$ ms to $t = 10$ ms,

$$Q = \frac{\Delta\phi_B}{R} = \frac{A}{R}(B_{f \text{ at } 0.01 \text{ s}} - B_{i \text{ at } 0 \text{ s}})$$

Substituting the given values, we get

$$= \frac{3.5\times 10^{-3}}{10}[0.4\sin(0.5\pi) - 0.4\sin 0]$$
$$= 3.5\times 10^{-4}(0.4\sin \pi/2)$$
$$= 1.4\times 10^{-4}\text{ C}$$
$$= 14\text{ mC}$$

JEE Advanced

1.

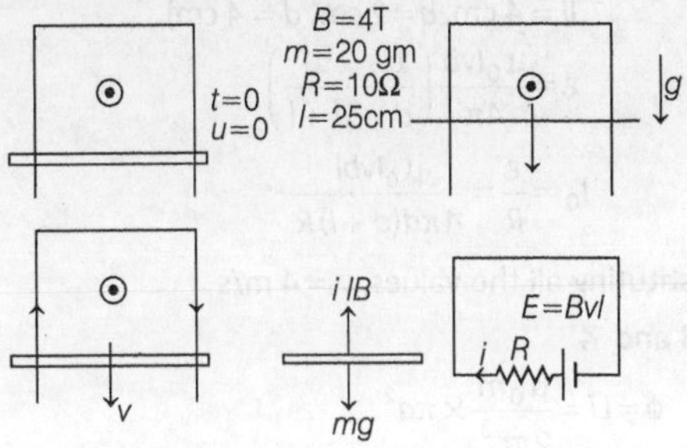

$$mg - IlB = m\frac{dv}{dt}$$
$$Bvl = IR$$
$$mg - \left(\frac{Bvl}{R}\right)Bl = m\frac{dv}{dt}$$
$$\frac{B^2l^2}{mR} = \frac{1}{20\times 10^{-3}\times 10} = 5$$
$$\frac{mgR}{B^2l^2} = \frac{20\times 10^{-3}\times 10\times 10}{4\times 4\times \frac{1}{4}\times\frac{1}{4}} = 2$$

Since, $\dfrac{mgR}{B^2l^2} - v\dfrac{mR}{B^2l^2}\dfrac{dv}{dt} = 0$

$$\frac{B^2l^2}{mR}\int_0^1 dt = \int_0^v \frac{dv}{\frac{mgR}{B^2l^2} - v}$$
$$5t = -\ln\left[\frac{2-v}{2}\right]$$
$$v = 2[1-e^{-5t}]$$

for $t = 0.2$ s

$$v = 2(1-e^{-1}) \Rightarrow v = 2(1-04)$$
$$v = 1.2\text{ ms}^{-1}$$
$$E = Bvl = 4\times 1.2\times\frac{1}{4} = 1.2\text{ V}$$
$$I = \frac{Bvl}{R} = \frac{1.2}{10} = 0.12\text{ A}$$
$$F = mg \quad ilB = 20\times 10^{-3}\times 10 - 0.12 = 0.08\text{ N}$$
$$P = I^2R = 0.12\times 0.12\times 10 = 0.144\text{ W}$$

Terminal velocity $v = 2$ for $t = \infty$

2. $v_y = \dfrac{v}{2}$

Emf induced in the loop is

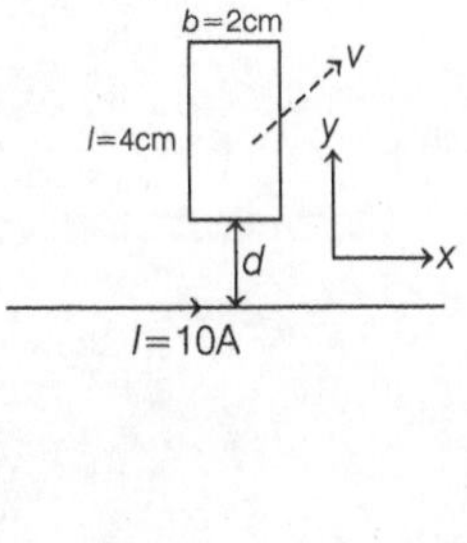

$$\varepsilon = \frac{\mu_0 I}{2\pi d}\cdot\frac{v}{2}b - \frac{\mu_0 I}{2\pi(d+l)}\cdot\frac{v}{2}b$$

$(l = 4\text{ cm}, b = 2\text{ cm}, d = 4\text{ cm})$

$$\Rightarrow \quad \varepsilon = \frac{\mu_0 I v b}{4\pi}\left(\frac{1}{d} - \frac{1}{d+l}\right)$$

$$\Rightarrow \quad I_0 = \frac{\varepsilon}{R} = \frac{\mu_0 I v b l}{4\pi d(d+l)R}$$

Substituting all the values, $v = 4$ m/s

Solution 3 and 4

$$\phi = Li = \frac{\mu_0 m}{2\pi r^3}\times \pi a^2$$

$$\Rightarrow \quad i = \frac{\mu_0 m\pi a^2}{2\pi r^3 L} \quad \Rightarrow \quad i \propto \frac{m}{r^3}$$

$$m' = \pi a^2 i = \frac{\mu_0 m\pi^2 a^4}{2\pi r^3 L}$$

$$\Rightarrow \quad F = \frac{km^2\pi^2 a^4}{2\pi r^7 L}$$

$$W = \int F dr \propto \int \frac{m^2 dr}{r^7} \quad \Rightarrow \quad W \propto \frac{m^2}{r^6}$$

5. Emf induced across the semi-circular conducting rod.

$$\varepsilon = \int_1^4 \frac{\mu_0 I v dx}{2\pi x} = \frac{\mu_0 I v}{2\pi}\ln(4) = \frac{\mu_0 I v}{\pi}\ln(2)$$

Since, the semi-circular conducting rod is moving with a constant speed $v = 3$ m/s, then

$$\varepsilon = \frac{\mu_0 I v}{\pi}\ln(2) = \text{constant}$$

Maximum current through the resistor R is

$$i_{max} = \frac{\varepsilon}{R} = \frac{\mu_0 I v}{\pi R}\ln(2) = \frac{4\times 10^{-7}\times 2\times 3\times 0.7}{1.4} = 1.2\times 10^{-6}\text{ A}$$

Maximum charge on the capacitor C_0 is

$$q_{max} = C_0\varepsilon = C_0\left(\frac{\mu_0 I v}{\pi}\ln(2)\right)$$

$$= 5\times 10^{-6}\times 4\times 10^{-7}\times 2\times 3\times 0.7$$

$$= 8.4\times 10^{-12}\text{ C}$$

6. When the magnet is moved, it creates a state, where the plate moves through the magnetic flux, due to which an electromotive force is generated in the plate and eddy currents are induced. These currents are such that it opposes the relative motion $\Rightarrow$ disc will rotate in the direction of rotation of magnet.

7. The net magnetic flux through the loops at time t is

$$\phi = B(2A - A)\cos\omega t = BA\cos\omega t$$

So, $$\left|\frac{d\phi}{dt}\right| = B\omega A\sin\omega t$$

$\therefore$ $\left|\frac{d\phi}{dt}\right|$ is maximum when $\phi = \omega t = \pi/2$

At this time plane of the loop will be perpendicular to the plane of paper.

The emf induced in the smaller loop,

$$\varepsilon_{smaller} = -\frac{d}{dt}(BA\cos\omega t) = B\omega A\sin\omega t$$

$\therefore$ Amplitude of maximum net emf induced in both the loops

= Amplitude of maximum emf induced in the smaller loop alone.

8. By reciprocity theorem of mutual induction, it can be assumed that current in infinite wire is varying at 10A/s and EMF is induced in triangular loop.

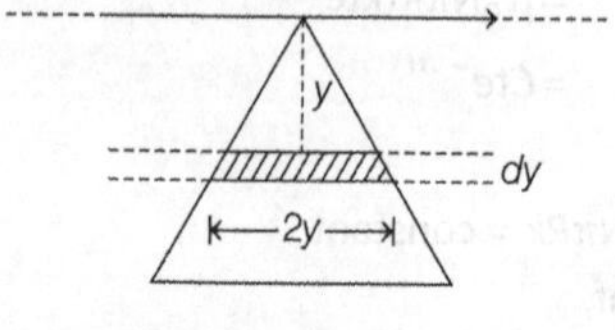

Flux of magnetic field through triangle loop, if current in infinite wire is ϕ, can be calculated as follows

$$d\phi = \frac{\mu_0 i}{2\pi y}\cdot 2y\, dy$$

$$d\phi = \frac{\mu_0 i}{\pi}dy \Rightarrow \phi = \frac{\mu_0 i}{\pi}\left(\frac{l}{\sqrt{2}}\right)$$

$$\Rightarrow \text{EMF} = \left|\frac{d\phi}{dt}\right| = \frac{\mu_0}{\pi}\left(\frac{l}{\sqrt{2}}\right)\frac{di}{dt}$$

$$= \frac{\mu_0}{\pi}(0.1\text{ m})\left(10\frac{\text{A}}{\text{s}}\right) = \frac{\mu_0}{\pi}\text{ volt}$$

If we assume the current in the wire towards right then as the flux in the loop increases we know that the induced current in the wire is counter clockwise. Hence, the current in the wire is towards right

Field due to triangular loop at the location of infinite wire is into the paper. Hence, force on infinite wire is away from the loop. By cylindrical symmetry about infinite wire, rotation of triangular loop will not cause any additional emf.

CHAPTER~06

INDUCTANCE

LEVEL 01 Starter Level

6.1 Self-Inductance

1 A coil of 100 turns carries a current of 5 mA and creates a magnetic flux of 10^{-5} Wb. Find self-inductance of coil.

2 In a coil, an average emf of 16 V is induced when the value of current changes from 2 A to 4 A in 0.05 s. What would be the value of coefficient of self-induction of the coil?

3 The current in a coil varies w.r.t. to time t as $i = 3t^2 + 2t$. If the inductance of coil be 10 mH, find the value of induced emf at $t = 2$ s.

4 Calculate the coefficient of self-induction of a solenoid of 2000 turns, length 0.5 m and radius 5 cm with
(i) air core and (ii) soft iron core
The magnetic permeability constant for soft iron = 1000

5 A superconducting loop of radius R has self-inductance L. A uniform and constant magnetic field B is applied perpendicular to the plane of the loop. Initially current in this loop is zero. The loop is rotated about its diameter by 180°. Find the current in the loop after rotation.

6 Find the self inductance of a system of two co-axial pipes of radii a and b ($b > a$), of length l (>> b), if current enters at one end of inner pipe, and comes back through the outer pipe because of a wire connecting the two pipes at the other end.

6.2 Mutual Inductance

1 How does the mutual inductance of a pair of coils change when
(i) the distance between the coils is increased ?
(ii) the number of turns in each coil is decreased ?
(iii) a thin iron rod is placed between the two coils, other factors remaining the same ?

2 Find the mutual inductance of two concentric loops of radii a_1 and a_2 ($a_1 << a_2$) if
(i) the planes of loops are same
(ii) the planes of loops are perpendicular
(iii) the planes of loops make θ angle with each other.

3 A small square loop of wire of side l is placed inside a large square loop of wire of side L(L>>l).
The loops are co-planar and their centres coincide. A current $i = 2t$ flows in the smaller loop. Neglect self-inductance of larger loop.
(i) Find the mutual inductance of the two coils.
(ii) Find the emf induced in the larger coil.
(iii) If the resistance of the larger loop is R, find the current in it as a function of time.

4 A solenoid of length 20 cm, area of cross-section 4.0 cm^2 and 4000 turns is placed inside another solenoid of 2000 turns having a cross-sectional area 8.0 cm^2 and length 10 cm. Find the mutual inductance between the solenoids.

5 Find the mutual inductance of a straight long wire and a rectangular loop, as shown in the adjacent figure.

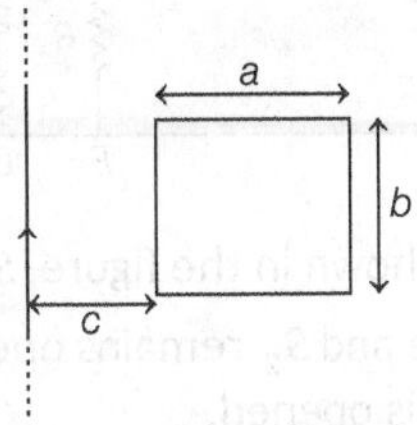

6 Two identical coils 1 and 2 lie close to each other such that 50% of the magnetic flux generated by one links with the other. A current of 1 A in coil (1) generates in it flux of 10^{-5} Wb. If this current is reversed in 0.1 s, determine the average induced emf in coil 2. Also calculate self inductances of coils and mutual inductance between them.

6.3 Inductor in a Circuit

1 *AB* is a part of circuit. Find the potential difference $V_A - V_B$ if current $i = 2$A and is

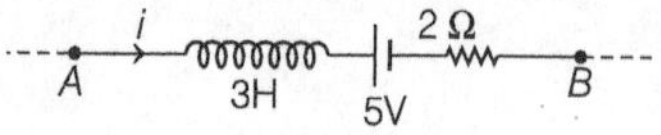

(i) constant

(ii) increasing at the rate of 4 A/s.

(iii) decreasing at the rate 4 A/s.

2 A circuit contains an ideal cell and an inductor with a switch. Initially the switch is open and it is closed at $t = 0$. Find

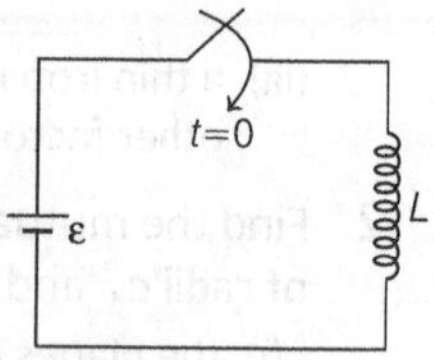

(i) the current as a function of time

(ii) energy stored in the inductor as a function of time

3 Suppose the EMF of the battery, the circuit shown varies with time *t* so the current is given by $i(t) = 3 + 5t$, where *i* is in amperes and *t* is in seconds. Take $R = 4\ \Omega$, $L = 6$H and find an expression for the battery EMF as a function of time.

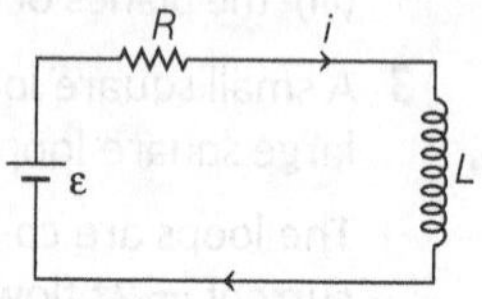

6.4 *LR* Circuit at $t = 0$ and $t = \infty$

1 In the following circuit, the switch is closed at $t = 0$. Initially all currents are zero. Find the currents i_1, i_2, i_3 and $\frac{di_3}{dt}$ at

(i) $t = 0$ (ii) $t = \infty$.

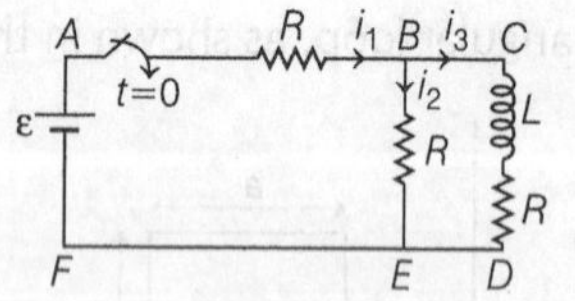

2 In the circuit shown in the figure, S_1 remains closed for a long time and S_2 remains open. Now, S_2 is closed and S_1 is opened.

Find out the $\frac{di}{dt}$ just after that moment.

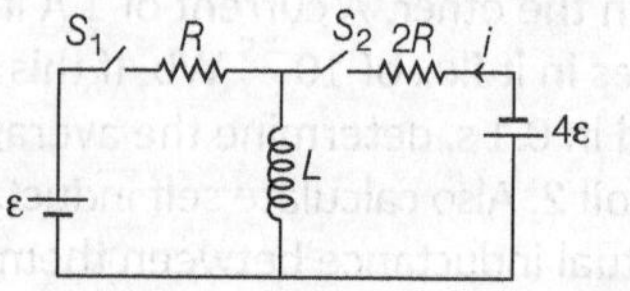

3 The circuit shown in figure is at steady state with the switch *S* closed. Find the currents through the resistors immediately after the switch *S* is opened. ($R_1 = R_2 = R_3 = R$)

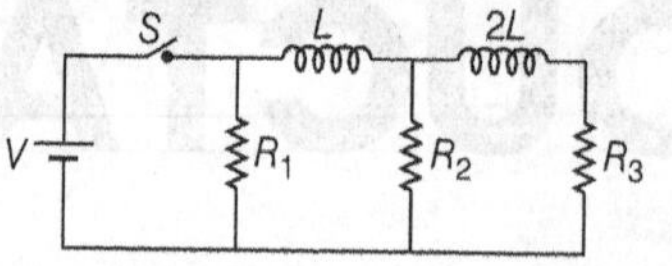

4 Two identical bulbs B_1 and B_2 are connected in parallel with a battery of emf ε. The bulb B_2 is connected in series with an ideal inductor *L*. How the brightness of the bulbs will change after closing the key *K*? What will happen when we open the key *K* after a long time?

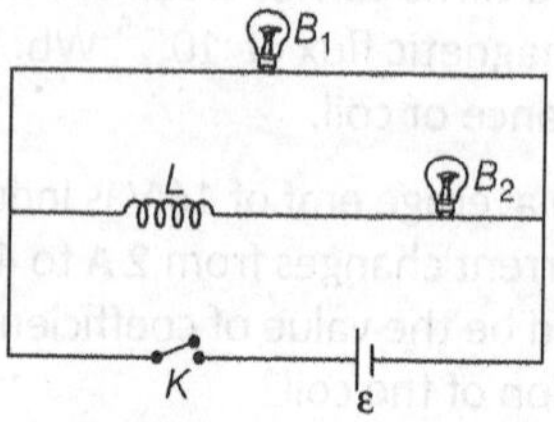

6.5 Growth of Current in Series *LR* Circuit

1 A coil having resistance 20 Ω and inductance 2 H is connected to a battery of emf 4.0 V. Find

(i) the current at 0.20 s after the connection is made and

(ii) the magnetic field energy in the coil at this instant.

2 A coil of resistance 4Ω is connected across a 0.4 V battery. The current in the coil is 63 mA, 1 s after the battery is connected. Find the inductance of the coil. $[e^{-1} \approx 0.37]$

3 A coil of negligible resistance and inductance 5H, is connected in series with a 100 Ω resistor and a battery of emf 2.0 V. Find the potential difference across the resistor 20 ms after the circuit is switched ON. $(e^{-0.4} = 0.67)$

4 An *LR* circuit has $L = 1.0$ H and $R = 20\ \Omega$. It is connected across an emf of 2.0 V at $t = 0$. Find $\frac{di}{dt}$ and $\frac{Ldi}{dt}$ at $t = 50$ ms.

5 An inductor-coil of inductance 20 mH having resistance 10 Ω is joined to an ideal battery of emf 5.0 V. Find the rate of change of the magnitude of induced emf at (i) $t = 0$, (ii) $t = 10$ ms.

6 An inductor of inductance 2H is joined in series with a resistor of resistance 200 Ω and a battery of emf 2 V. At $t = 10$ ms, find :

(i) the power delivered by the battery

(ii) the power dissipated in heating the resistor and

(iii) the rate at which energy is being stored in magnetic field.

7 An *LR* circuit having a time constant of 50 ms is connected with an ideal battery of emf ε. Find the time elapsed before

(i) the current reaches half its maximum value,

(ii) the power dissipated in heat reaches half its maximum value and

(iii) the magnetic field energy stored in the circuit reaches half its maximum value.

8 Figure shows a circuit consisting of a ideal cell, an inductor L and a resistor R connected in series. Let the switch S be closed at $t = 0$. Suppose at $t = 0$ current in the inductor is i_0 then find out equation of current as a function of time.

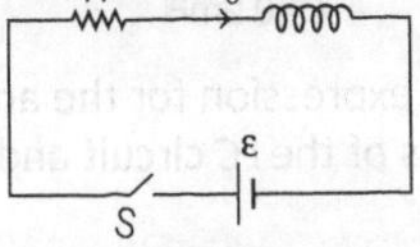

9 In the following circuit the switch is closed at $t = 0$. Initially there is no current in inductor. Find out current in the inductor coil as a function of time.

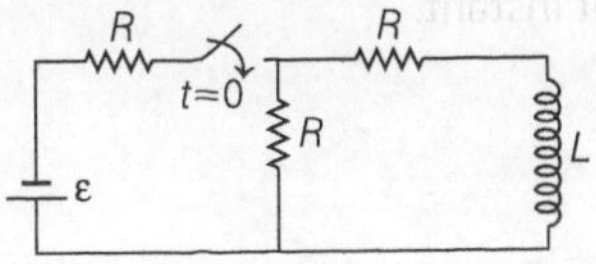

6.6 Decay of Current in *LR* Circuit (Without Battery)

1 The current in a discharging *LR* circuit without the battery drops from 2.0 A to 1.0 A in 0.10 s.

(i) Find the time constant of the circuit.

(ii) If the inductance of the circuit is 4.0 H, what is its resistance?

2 Consider the circuit shown in figure.

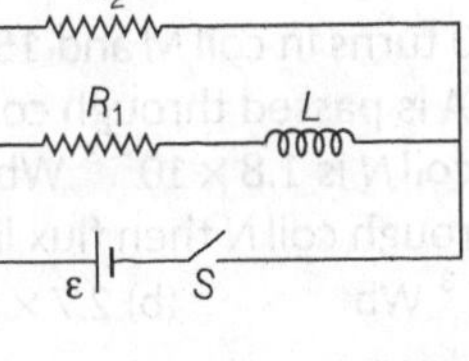

(i) Find the current through the battery a long time after the switch S is closed.

(ii) Suppose the switch is opened at $t = 0$. What is the time constant of the decay circuit?

(iii) Find the current through the inductor after one time constant.

3 In the circuit shown, initially the switch is in position 1 for a long time. Then the switch is shifted to position 2 for a long time. Find the total heat produced in R_2.

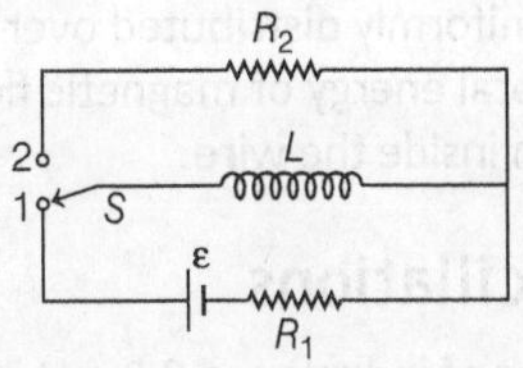

4 In a *L-R* decay circuit, the initial current at $t = 0$ is I. Find the total charge that has flown through the resistor till the energy in the inductor has reduced to one-fourth of its initial value.

6.7 Combination of Inductors

1 The equivalent inductance of two inductors is 2.4 H when connected in parallel and 10 H when connected in series. What is the value of inductance of the individual inductors?

2 In the circuit shown in figure an emf E, a resistance R, and coils inductance L_1 and L_2 are known. The internal resistance of the source and the coil resistances are negligible. Find the steady-state currents in the coils after the switch S was shorted.

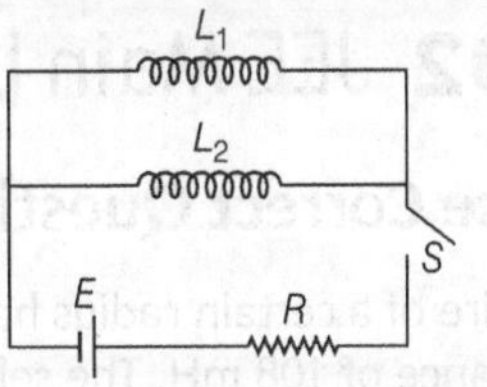

3 Find equivalent inductance between A and B.

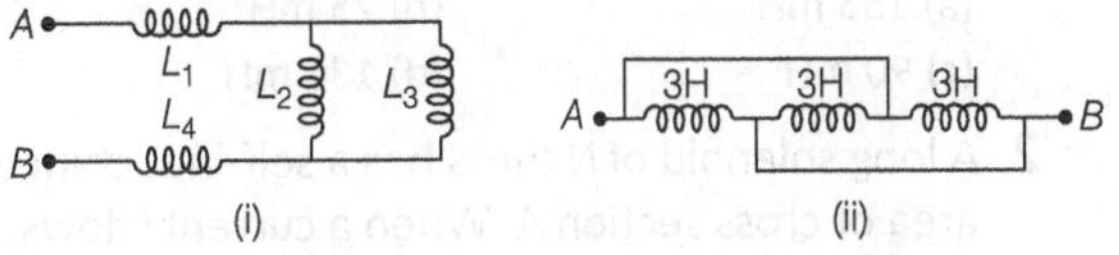

(i) (ii)

4 Two identical solenoid coils, each of self inductance L are connected in series. Their turns are in the same sense, and the distance between them is such that the coefficient of coupling is half. Find the equivalent inductance of the combination.

5 On a cylindrical rod two coils are wound one above the other. What is the coefficient of mutual induction if the inductance of each coil is 0.1 H ?

6.8 Magnetic Energy Density

1 Find the energy stored in the magnetic field inside a volume of 1.00 mm^3 at a distance of 10.0 cm from a long wire carrying a current of 4 A.

2 A long cylindrical wire of radius *R* is carrying a current *i* uniformly distributed over its cross-section. Find the total energy of magnetic field stored per unit length inside the wire.

6.9 *L-C* Oscillations

1 An inductor of inductance 2.0 mH is connected across a charged capacitor of capacitance 5.0 μF, and the resulting *LC* circuit is set oscillating at its natural frequency. Let *Q* denote the instantaneous charge on the capacitor, and *i* the current in the circuit. It is found that the maximum value of *Q* is 200 μC.

(i) When Q = 100 μC, what is the value of $\left|\frac{di}{dt}\right|$?

(ii) When Q = 200 μC, what is the value of *i* ?

(iii) Find the maximum value of *i*.

(iv) When *i* is equal to one half its maximum value, what is the value of $|Q|$?

2 At time $t = 0$, the *LC* circuit shown in the figure has equal amount of energy stored in the capacitor C = 20 μF and in the inductor, each equal to 200 μJ. The current amplitude in the circuit is $1/\sqrt{10}$ A. Find

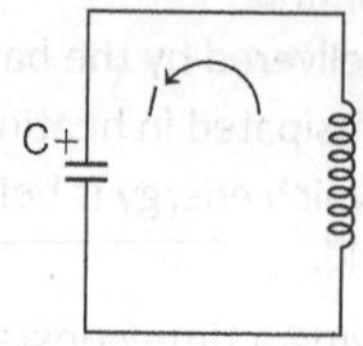

(i) the value of the inductance *L*.

(ii) the natural frequency of oscillation

(iii) the equation for charge and current in terms of *t*.

3 A circuit containing capacitors C_1 and C_2, shown in the figure is in the steady state with key K_1 closed. At the instant $t = 0$, K_1 is opened and K_2 is closed.

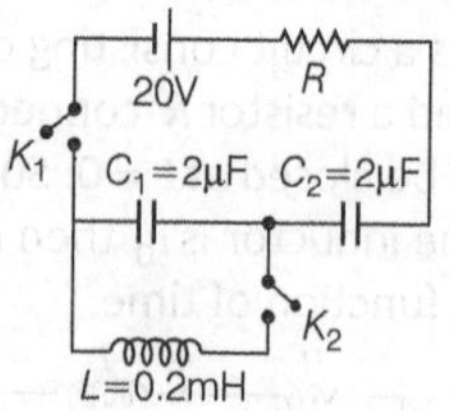

(i) Obtain an expression for the angular frequency of oscillations of the *LC* circuit and determine its value.

(ii) Determine the first instant *t*, when energy in the inductor becomes one third of that in the capacitor.

(iii) Calculate the charge on the plates of the capacitor at that instant.

LEVEL 02 JEE Main Level

Single Choice Correct Questions

1 A coil of wire of a certain radius has 600 turns and a self inductance of 108 mH. The self-inductance of a second similar coil of 500 turns will be

(a) 155 mH (b) 75 mH

(c) 90 mH (d) 130 mH

2 A long solenoid of *N* turns has a self-inductance *L* and area of cross section *A*. When a current *i* flows through the solenoid, the magnetic field inside it has magnitude *B*. The current *i* is equal to

(a) $\frac{BAN}{L}$ (b) $BANL$

(c) $\frac{BN}{AL}$ (d) $\frac{B}{ANL}$

3 A thin copper wire of length 100 m is wound as a solenoid of length *l* and radius *r*. Its self-inductance is found to be *L*. Now if the same length of wire is wound as a solenoid of length *l* but of radius $\frac{r}{2}$, then its self inductance will be

(a) 4*L* (b) 2*L*

(c) *L* (d) $\frac{L}{2}$

4 There are 10 turns in coil *M* and 15 turns in coil *N*. If a current of 2A is passed through coil *M*, then the flux linked with coil *N* is 1.8×10^{-3} Wb. If a current of 3A is passed through coil *N* then flux linked with coil *M* is

(a) 1.7×10^{-3} Wb (b) 2.7×10^{-3} Wb

(c) 1.7×10^{-5} Wb (d) 2.7×10^{-5} Wb

5 Two coils are at fixed locations. When coil 1 has no current and the current in coil 2 increases at the rate 15.0 A/s the emf in coil 1 in 25.0 mV, when coil 2 has no current and coil 1 has a current of 3.6 A, the flux linkage in coil 2 is

(a) 16.00 mWb (b) 10.00 mWb
(c) 4.00 mWb (d) 6.00 mWb

6 A current $i = 10 \sin(100\pi t)$ A is passed in first coil, which induces a maximum emf of 5π V in second coil. The mutual inductance between the coils is

(a) 10 mH (b) 15 mH (c) 25 mH (d) 5 mH

7 Two coaxial solenoids are made by winding thin insulated wire over a pipe of cross-sectional area $A = 10\ cm^2$ and length = 20 cm. If one of the solenoids has 300 turns and the other 400 turns, their mutual inductance is ($\mu_0 = 4\pi \times 10^{-7}\ T\ mA^{-1}$)

(a) $2.4\pi \times 10^{-5}$ H (b) $4.8\pi \times 10^{-4}$ H
(c) $4.8\pi \times 10^{-5}$ H (d) $2.4\pi \times 10^{-4}$ H

8 A circular loop of radius r is placed on the axis of a current carrying circular ring of radius $R (R >> r)$, at a distance $R\sqrt{3}$ from the centre of the ring. The plane of the loop is making an angle of 53° with the plane of the ring. The coefficient of mutual induction between them is

(a) $\frac{\mu_0 \pi r^2}{20R}$ (b) $\frac{3\mu_0 \pi r^2}{80R}$ (c) $\frac{3\mu_0 \pi R^2}{80r}$ (d) None

9 Two circular coils can be arranged in any of the three situations shown in the figure. Their mutual inductance will be

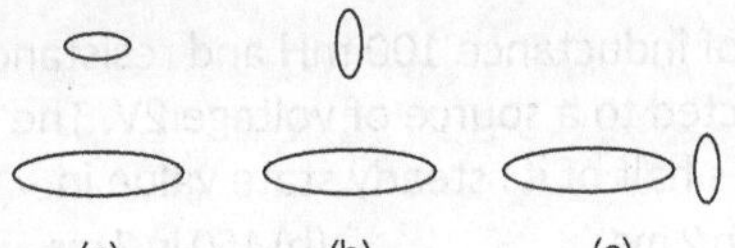

(a) maximum in situation (a)
(b) maximum in situation (b)
(c) maximum in situation (c)
(d) the same in all situations

10 A very long straight conductor and isosceles triangular conductor lie in a plane and are separated from each other as shown in the figure. If $a = 10$cm, $b = 20$ cm and $h = 10$ cm, the coefficient of mutual induction is

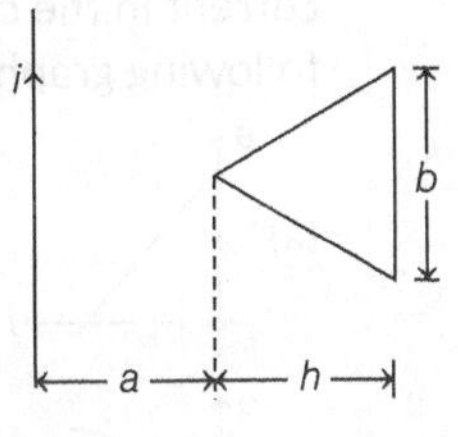

(a) 4.8×10^{-6} H (b) 3.6×10^{-8} H
(c) 2.4×10^{-8} H (d) 1.2×10^{-8} H

11 The figure shows a part of a complete circuit. The potential difference $V_B - V_A$ when the current i is 5A and is decreasing at a rate of $10^3\ A\ s^{-1}$ is given by

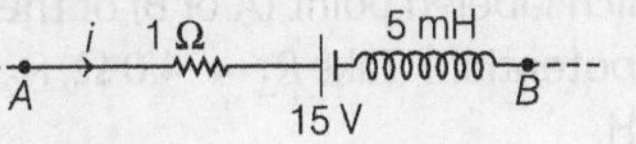

(a) 15 V (b) 10 V (c) – 15 V (d) 20 V

12 When the current in a certain inductor coil is 5.0 A and is increasing at the rate of 10.0 A/s, the potential difference across the coil is 140 V. When the current is 5.0 A and decreasing at the rate of 10.0 A/s, the potential difference is 60 V. The self inductance of the coil is

(a) 2 H (b) 4 H (c) 8 H (d) 12 H

13 A current is increasing at a rate of 4 A/s through a coil of inductance 2 H. Find rate of change of stored energy in the inductor at the moment when current is 2 A.

(a) 2 J/s (b) 1 J/s (c) 16 J/s (d) 4 J/s

14 Self inductance of a coil is 8 H. The power (in watt) consumed by coil (purely inductive) is given by $P = 8i^2$, where i is current in ampere. The time for the current to change from i_0 to $2i_0$ will be

(a) ln 2 (b) $5i_0$
(c) $\frac{i_0^2}{\ln 2}$ (d) None of these

15 A time varying voltage $V = 2t$ volt is applied across an ideal inductor of inductance $L = 2$H as shown in figure. Then select incorrect statement

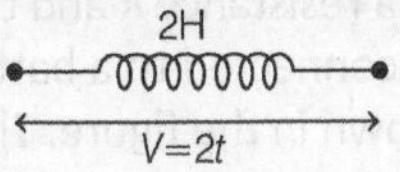

(a) current *versus* time graph is a parabola
(b) energy stored in magnetic field at $t = 2$ s is 4J
(c) potential energy at time $t = 1$s in magnetic field is increasing at a rate of 1 J/s
(d) energy stored in magnetic field is zero all the time

16 Two resistors of 10 Ω and 20 Ω and an ideal inductor of 10 H are connected to a 2 V battery as shown. The key K is inserted at time $t = 0$. The initial ($t = 0$) and final ($t \to \infty$) currents through battery are

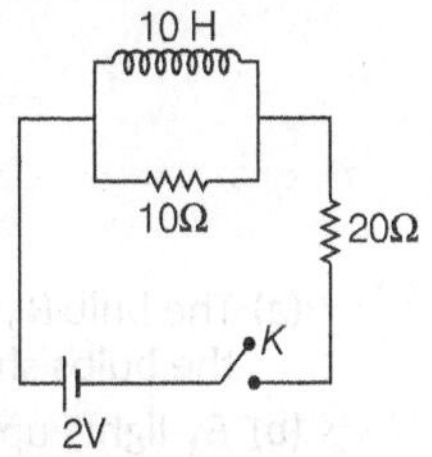

(a) $\frac{1}{15}$ A, $\frac{1}{10}$ A (b) $\frac{1}{10}$ A, $\frac{1}{15}$ A
(c) $\frac{2}{15}$ A, $\frac{1}{10}$ A (d) $\frac{1}{15}$ A, $\frac{2}{25}$ A

17 The circuit shown has been operating for a long time. The instant after the switch in the circuit labeled S is opened, what is the voltage across the inductor V_L and which labeled point (A or B) of the inductor is at a higher potential ? Take $R_1 = 4.0\,\Omega$, $R_2 = 8.0\,\Omega$, and $L = 2.5$ H.

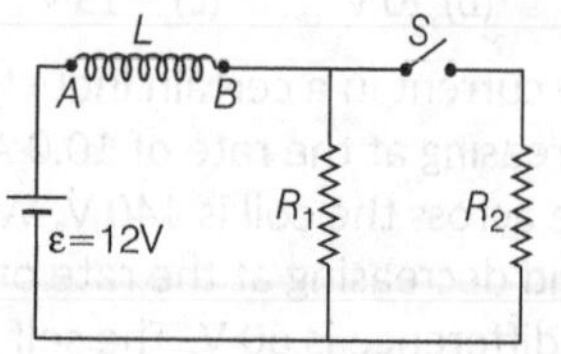

(a) $V_L = 12$ V; Point A is at the higher potential
(b) $V_L = 12$ V; Point B is at the higher potential
(c) $V_L = 6$V; Point A is at the higher potential
(d) $V_L = 6$V; Point B is at the higher potential

18 In the circuit shown, switch is closed at $t = 0$. Then the ratio $\frac{U_1}{U_2}$ of potential energy stored in the inductors L_1 and L_2 in steady state is

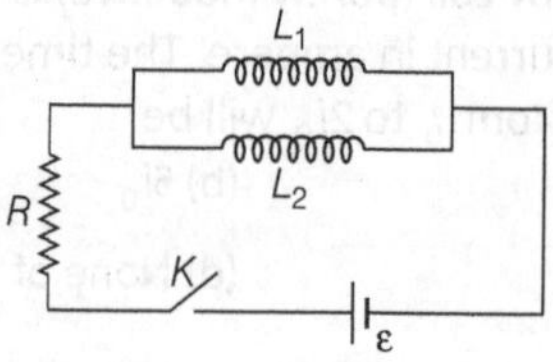

(a) $\frac{L_1}{L_2}$ (b) $\frac{L_2}{L_1}$ (c) $\left(\frac{L_1}{L_2}\right)^2$ (d) $\left(\frac{L_2}{L_1}\right)^2$

19 An inductor L, a resistance R and two identical bulbs B_1 and B_2 are connected to a battery through a switch S as shown in the figure. The resistance of coil having inductance L is also R. Which of the following statement gives the correct description of the happenings when the switch S is closed?

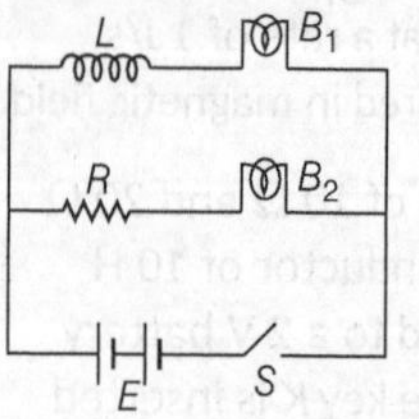

(a) The bulb B_2 lights up earlier than B_1 and finally both the bulbs shine equally bright.
(b) B_1 lights up earlier and finally both the bulbs acquire equal brightness.
(c) B_2 lights up earlier and finally B_1 shines brighter than B_2.
(d) B_1 and B_2 light up together with equal brightness all the time.

20 The circuit shown in the diagram is in steady state. If the switch S is suddenly opened which of the following statement is correct just after opening the switch?

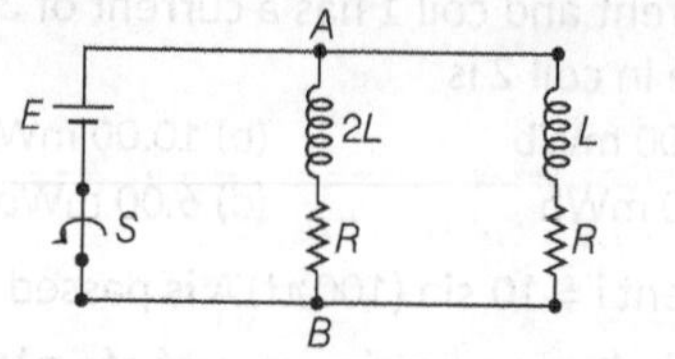

(a) The current in the inductor L will be 0
(b) The current in the inductor L will remain constant.
(c) The current in the inductor L will be flow from A to B
(d) The current in the inductor L will flow from B to A.

21 An LR circuit with a battery is connected at $t = 0$. Which of the following quantities is not zero just after closing the circuit?
(a) current in the circuit
(b) magnetic field energy in the inductor
(c) power delivered by the battery
(d) emf induced in the inductor

22 An emf of 15 V is applied in a circuit containing 5 H inductance and 10 Ω resistance. The ratio of the currents at time $t = \infty$ and $t = 1$s is
(a) $\frac{e^2+1}{e^2}$ (b) $\frac{e^2}{e^2-1}$ (c) $\frac{e^2+1}{e^2-1}$ (d) $\frac{e^2-1}{e^2}$

23 A coil of inductance 5 H is joined to a cell of emf 6 V through a resistance 10 Ω at time $t = 0$. The emf across the coil at time $t = \ln\sqrt{2}$ s is
(a) 3 V (b) 1.5 V (c) 0.75 V (d) 4.5 V

24 A coil of inductance 100 mH and resistance 2Ω is connected to a source of voltage 2V. The current reaches half of its steady state value in
(a) 50 ln 2 ms (b) 150 ln 2 ms
(c) 50 ms (d) 150 ms

25 In an L-R circuit connected to a battery of constant emf E switch S is closed at time $t = 0$. If e denotes the magnitude of induced emf across inductor and i the current in the circuit at any time t, then which of the following graphs shows the variation of e with i ?

(a)
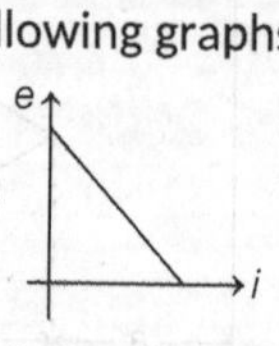

(b)
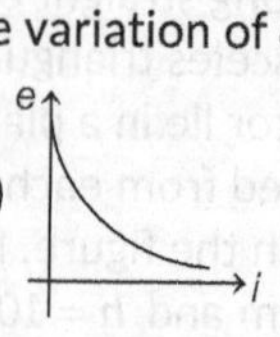

(c)
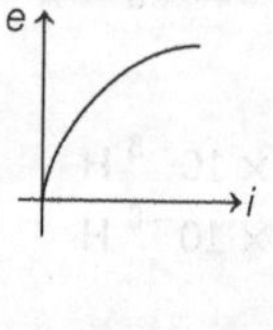

(d)
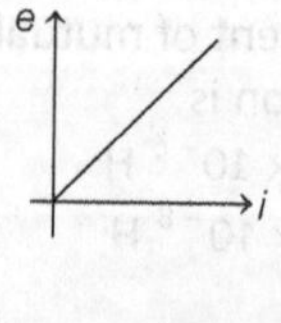

26 A resistor and an inductor in series are connected to a battery through a switch S. After the switch has been closed, what is the magnitude of the current flowing when the rate of increase of magnetic energy stored in the coil is maximum?

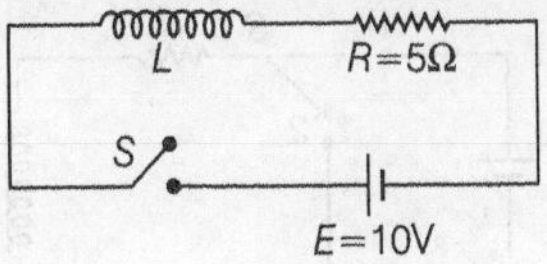

(a) 1A (b) 2A

(c) 2.5A (d) 1.5A

27 An inductor coil stores U energy, when i current is passed through it and dissipates energy at the rate of P. The time constant of the circuit, when this coil is connected across a battery of zero internal resistance is

(a) $\frac{4U}{P}$ (b) $\frac{U}{P}$

(c) $\frac{2U}{P}$ (d) $\frac{2P}{U}$

28 In the circuit shown, the cell is ideal. The coil has an inductance of 4H and zero resistance. F is a fuse of zero resistance and will blow when the current through it reaches 5A. The switch is closed at $t = 0$. The fuse will blow

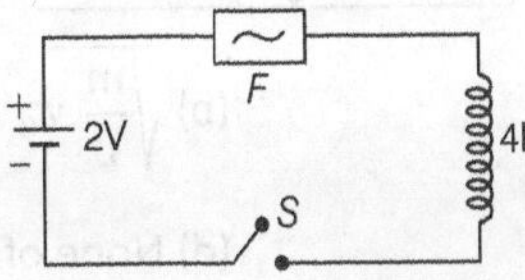

(a) almost at once (b) after 2 s

(c) after 5 s (d) after 10 s

29 In the circuit shown in figure, A is a sliding contact which can move over a smooth rod PQ. Resistance per unit length of the rod PQ is 1 Ω/m. Initially slider is just left to the point P and circuit is in the steady state. At $t = 0$ slider starts moving with constant velocity $v = 5$ m/s towards right. Current in the circuit at $t = 2$ s is

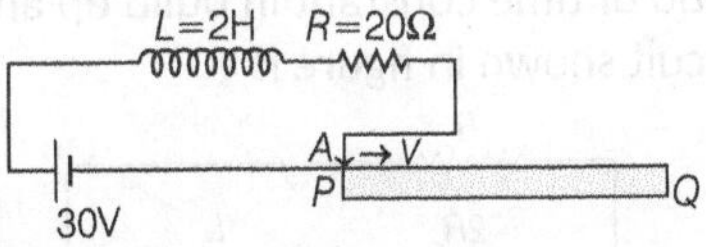

(a) 1 A

(b) less than 0.5 A

(c) more than 1 A

(d) in between 0.5 to 1.0 A

30 In the steady state of the circuit shown in the figure, the ratio of energy stored in the inductor to the energy stored in the capacitor is

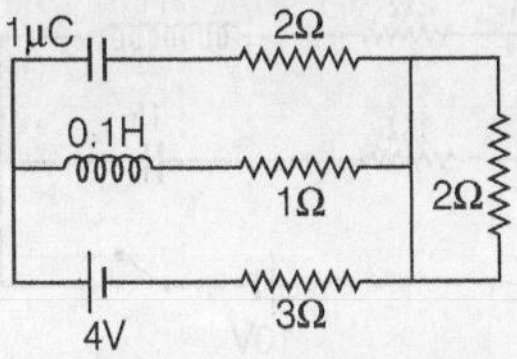

(a) 0.00001 (b) 100000

(c) 1000 (d) None of these

31 A resistor of resistance R, an inductor of inductance L and a capacitor of capacitance C are connected in series and the combination is connected to a battery of emf ε as shown. At $t = 0$, the switch S is closed. Let, after a very long time, the thermal energy developed in circuit be Q, energy stored in circuit be U and energy supplied by battery be E. Then

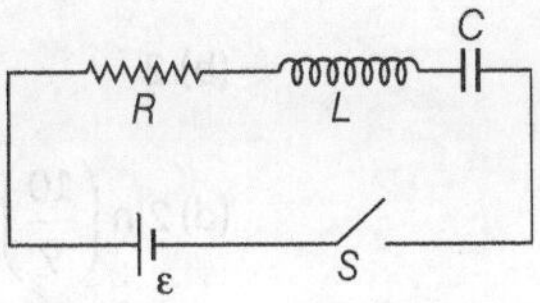

(a) $Q : U : E = 1 : 1 : 2$ (b) $Q : U : E = 1 : 3 : 4$

(c) $Q : U : E = 3 : 1 : 4$ (d) $Q : U : E = 1 : 2 : 3$

32 The current in the given circuit is increasing with a rate 4 A/s. The charge on the capacitor at an instant when the current in the circuit is 2 A will be :

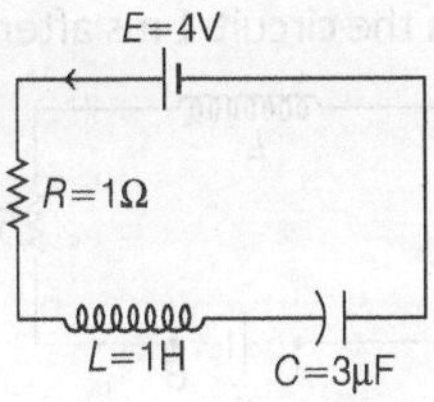

(a) 4 μC (b) 5 μC

(c) 6 μC (d) none of these

33 In the given circuit diagram, the key K is switched on at $t = 0$.
The ratio of the current i through the cell at $t = 0$ and at $t = \infty$ will be

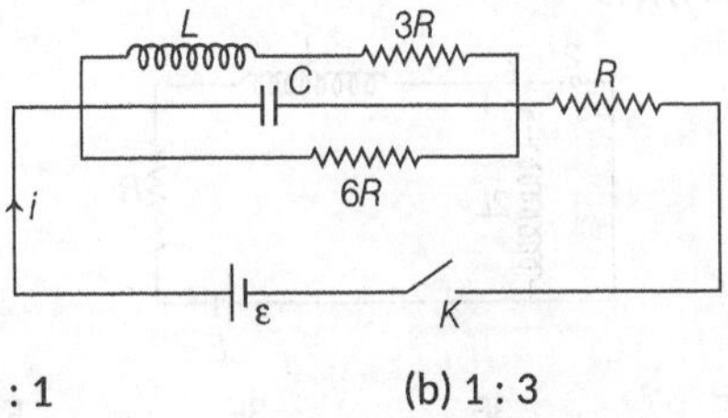

(a) 3 : 1 (b) 1 : 3

(c) 1 : 2 (d) 2 : 1

34 In the given circuit shown, the switch is closed at $t = 0$. The battery is ideal.

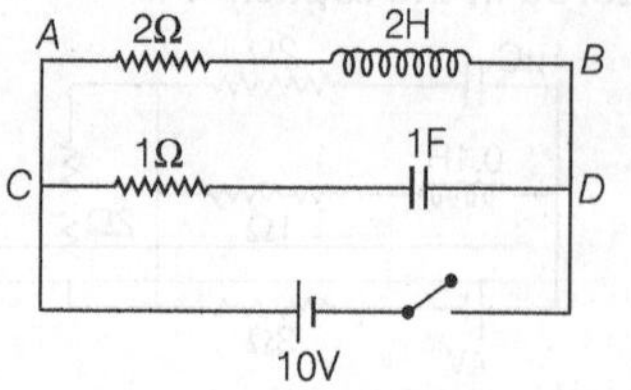

(a) Initial current through battery is 5A.
(b) Current through battery after a long time is 10 A.
(c) The time when current in both branches (*AB* and *CD*) are equal is ln 2 s.
(d) The time when current in both branches (*AB* and *CD*) are equal is ln 3 s.

35 In an *LR* circuit current at $t = 0$ is 20 A. After 2s, it reduces to 18 A. The time constant of the circuit is (in s)

(a) $\ln\left(\frac{10}{9}\right)$ (b) 2

(c) $\frac{2}{\ln\left(\frac{10}{9}\right)}$ (d) $2\ln\left(\frac{10}{9}\right)$

36 An inductor ($L = 100$ mH), a resistor ($R = 100\Omega$) and a battery ($E = 10$ V) are initially connected in series as shown in the figure. After a long time the battery is disconnected by short circuiting the points *A* and *B*. The current in the circuit 1 ms after the short circuit is

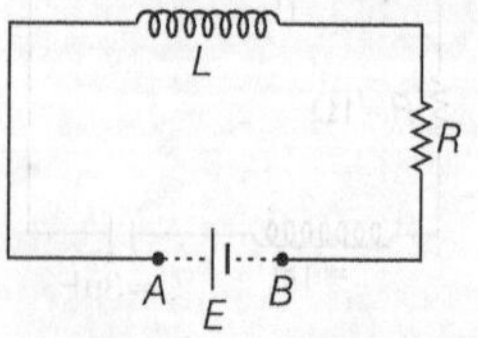

(a) $\frac{1}{10e}$ A (b) $\frac{e}{10}$ A (c) $\frac{10}{e}$ A (d) 1 A

37 In the circuit shown switch is connected to 1 for a very long time. At a particular instant $t = 0$, switch is shifted to 2, the current in the circuit after a time gap of *L/R* is

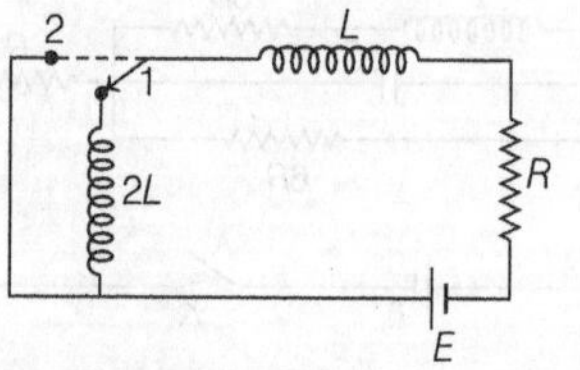

(a) $\frac{E}{2Re}$ (b) $\frac{3E}{R}$ (c) $\frac{3E}{Re}$ (d) $\frac{E}{R}$

38 In the circuit shown in the figure, the switch is kept in position 1 for long time and then it shifted to 2 at $t = 0$. The energy dissipated as thermal energy through resistor *R* in time $t = 0$ to $t = \frac{2L}{R}$ is

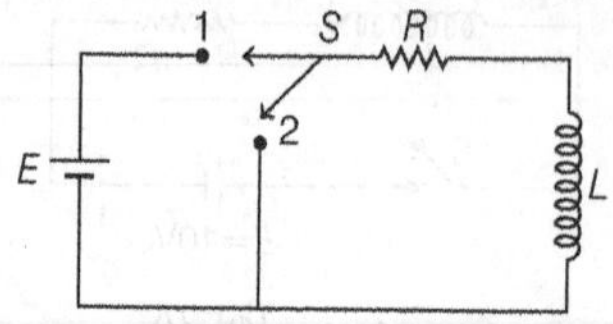

(a) $\frac{LE^2}{2R^2}$ (b) $\frac{LE^2}{2R^2}\left(\frac{-1+e^2}{e^2}\right)$

(c) $\frac{LE^2}{2R^2}(1-e^4)$ (d) $\frac{LE^2}{2R^2}\left(\frac{e^4-1}{e^4}\right)$

39 Two ends of an inductor of inductance *L* is connected to two parallel conducting wires. A rod of length *l* and mass *m* is given velocity v_0 as shown. The whole system is placed in perpendicular magnetic field B. Find the maximum current in the inductor. (Neglect gravity and friction)

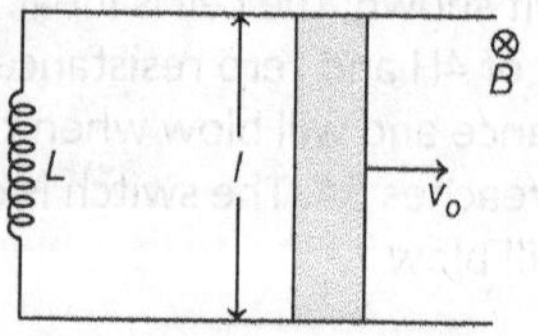

(a) $\sqrt{\frac{2m}{L}}\, v_0$ (b) $\sqrt{\frac{m}{L}}\, v_0$

(c) $\sqrt{\frac{2m}{3L}}\, v_0$ (d) None of these

40 A long solenoid is made of a superconducting wire carrying a current i_0. The solenoid is slowly stretched so that its cross section does not change but its length changes from L_0 to L_1. What is the new current in the solenoid assuming the solenoid is still tightly wound?

(a) $\frac{L_0 i_0}{L_1}$ (b) $\frac{L_1 i_0}{L_0}$ (c) $\frac{L_0^2 i_0}{L_1^2}$ (d) $\frac{L_1^2 i_0}{L_0^2}$

41 The ratio of time constant in build up and decay in the circuit shown in figure is

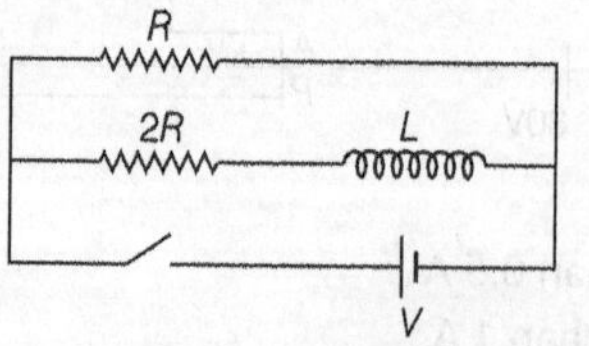

(a) 1 : 1 (b) 3 : 2
(c) 2 : 3 (d) 1 : 3

42 The frequency of oscillation of current in the inductor is

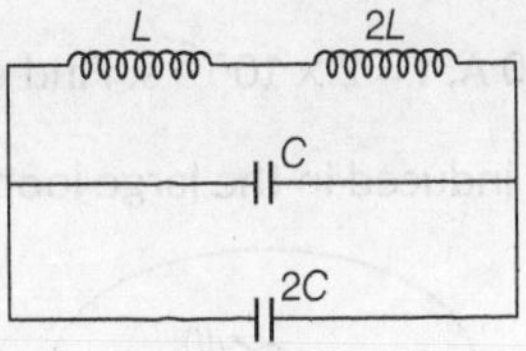

(a) $\frac{1}{3\sqrt{LC}}$ (b) $\frac{1}{6\pi\sqrt{LC}}$ (c) $\frac{1}{\sqrt{LC}}$ (d) $\frac{1}{2\pi\sqrt{LC}}$

43 A condenser of capacity 6 μF is fully charged using a 6 V battery. The battery is removed and a resistanceless 0.2 mH inductor is connected across the condenser. The current which is flowing through the inductor, when one-third of the total energy is in the magnetic field of the inductor is

(a) 0.1 A (b) 0.2 A (c) 0.4 A (d) 0.6 A

44 For the circuit shown, the switch was closed at switch S_1 for a long time till steady state condition reached. At time $t = 0$, the switch S_1 is opened and S_2 is closed. The current through inductor as a function of time will be

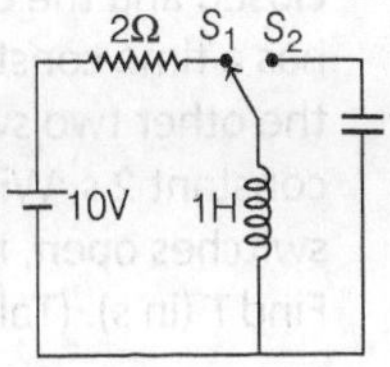

(a) 5 cos 100t (b) 10cos 100t
(c) 5 cos 1000t (d) 10 cos 1000t

45 In an LC circuit shown in the figure, $C = 1$ F, $L = 4$ H. At time $t = 0$, charge in the capacitor is 4C and it is decreasing at a rate of $\sqrt{5}$ C/s. Choose the correct statement.

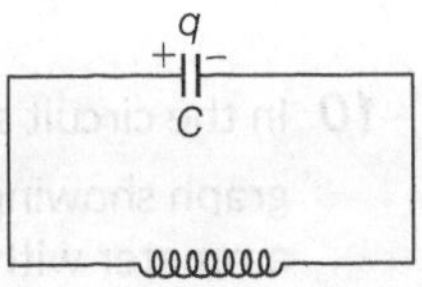

(a) Maximum charge in the capacitor can be 6C
(b) Maximum charge in the capacitor can be 8C
(c) Maximum current in the circuit can be 9 A
(d) Maximum current in the circuit can be 2/3 A

46 In an LC circuit the capacitor has maximum charge q_0. The value of $\left(\frac{dI}{dt}\right)_{max}$ is

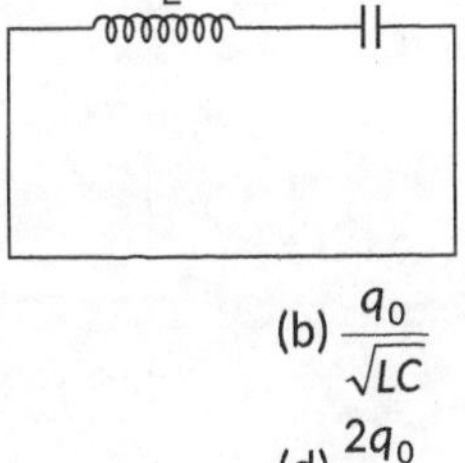

(a) $\frac{q_0}{LC}$ (b) $\frac{q_0}{\sqrt{LC}}$
(c) $\frac{q_0}{2LC}$ (d) $\frac{2q_0}{LC}$

47 The switch in the circuit pictured is in position a for a long time. At $t = 0$ the switch is moved from a to b. The current through the inductor will reach its first maximum after moving the switch in a time

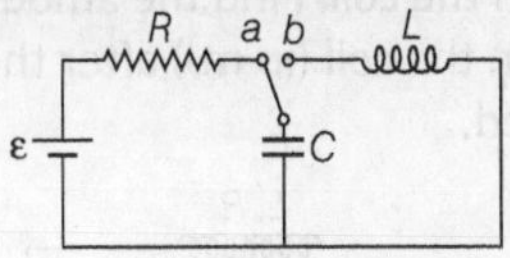

(a) $2\pi\sqrt{LC}$ (b) $\frac{1}{4}\sqrt{LC}$
(c) $\frac{\pi}{2}\sqrt{LC}$ (d) $\pi\sqrt{LC}$

48 Initially capacitor A is charged to a potential drop ε and capacitor B is uncharged. At $t = 0$, switch S is closed, then the maximum current through the inductor is

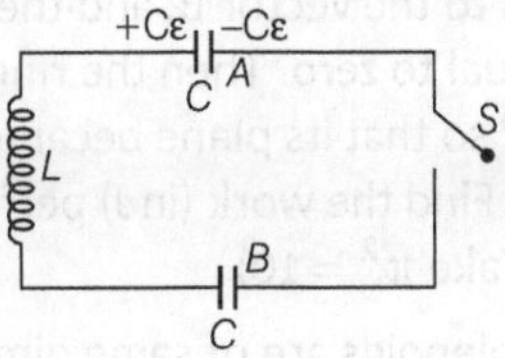

(a) $\varepsilon\sqrt{\frac{C}{2L}}$ (b) $\varepsilon\sqrt{\frac{C}{L}}$ (c) $2\varepsilon\sqrt{\frac{C}{L}}$ (d) $\frac{\varepsilon}{2}\sqrt{\frac{C}{L}}$

Numerical Value Questions

1 Find the value of instantaneous power (in W) supplied by battery at the moment after the switch is closed.

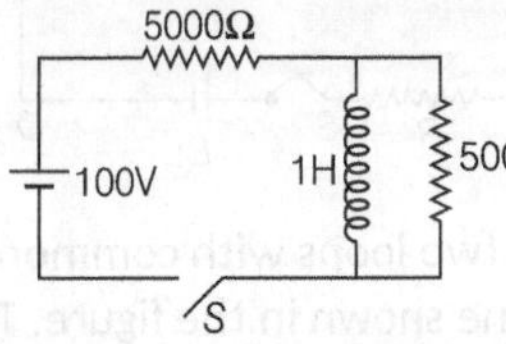

2. How many metres of a thin wire are required to design a solenoid of length 1m and $L = 1$ mH? Assume cross-sectional diameter is very small.

3. A resistor and an inductor in series are connected to a battery through a switch. After the switch has been closed, at what time (in s) will the Joule heat dissipated in the resistor change at the fastest rate?

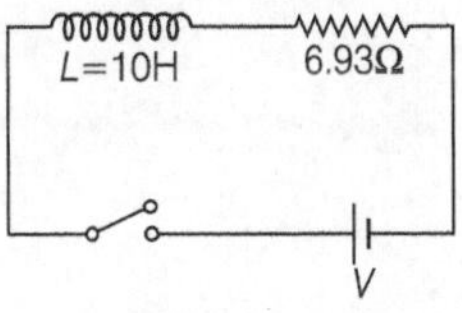

4 A coil of inductance $L = 2$ mH and resistance $R = 1\Omega$ is connected to a source of constant emf 3V as shown in the figure. A resistance $R_0 = 2\Omega$ is connected in parallel with the coil. Find the amount of heat generated in the coil (in mJ) after the switch S is disconnected.

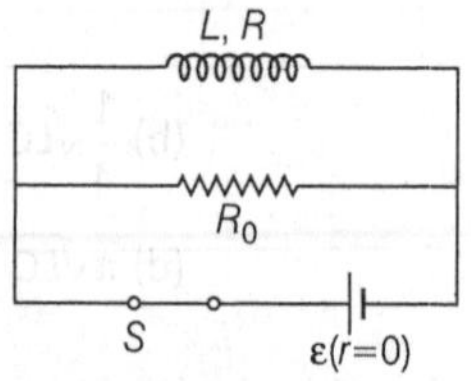

5 A superconducting round ring of radius $a = 20$cm and inductance $L = 0.1$H was located in a uniform magnetic field of induction $B = 10$ T. The plane of ring was parallel to the vector B, and the current in the ring was equal to zero. Then the ring was turned through 90° so that its plane became perpendicular to the field. Find the work (in J) performed during the turn. (Take $\pi^2 = 10$)

6 Two ideal solenoids are of same dimensions. One is air cored with 600 turns while other is Aluminium cored with 200 turns (relative permeability of Aluminium is 3), are connected in a circuit as shown in the figure. The switch S is closed at $t = 0$. Find the ratio of potential difference across air-cored solenoid to that of Aluminium cored solenoid at any time t.

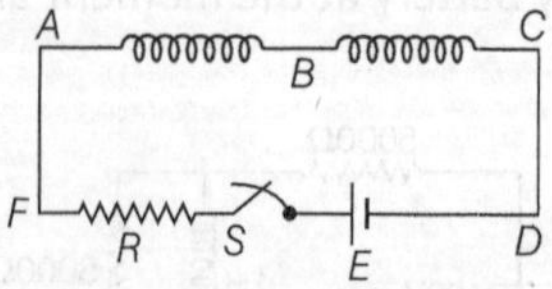

7 Consider the two loops with common centre and on the same plane shown in the figure. The large circular loop has radius R= 10 cm, and the small square loop has side $a = 1$ cm. There is a current circulating in the small loop given by $i(t) = \frac{i_0 t}{\tau}$, with $i_0 = \frac{2}{\pi} \times 100$ A, $\tau = 2 \times 10^{-2}$ s. Find emf (in microvolts) induced in the large loop.

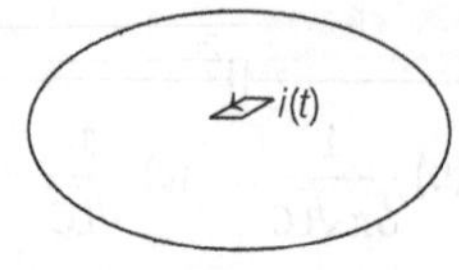

8 If two small current carrying loops each of radius r are kept in same plane such that separation between their centres is a ($a >>> r$), then their mutual inductance will be $\frac{\mu_0 \pi r^4}{ka^3}$. Find out the value of k.

9 Consider the circuit shown in figure. With switch S_1 closed and the other two switches open, the circuit has a time constant 0.05 s. With switch S_2 closed and the other two switches open, the circuit has a time constant 2 s. With switch S_3 closed and the other two switches open, the circuit oscillates with a period T. Find T (in s). (Take $\pi^2 = 10$)

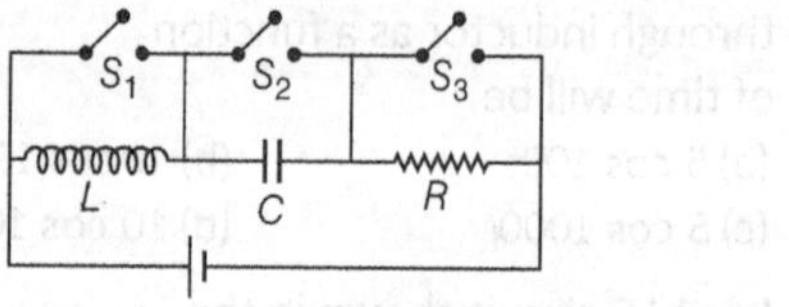

10 In the circuit shown, switch is closed at $t = 0$. The graph showing variation of current passing through ammeter with time is given below. If $C = 4\mu$F and $L = 0.1$ mH then find the value of R (in Ω).

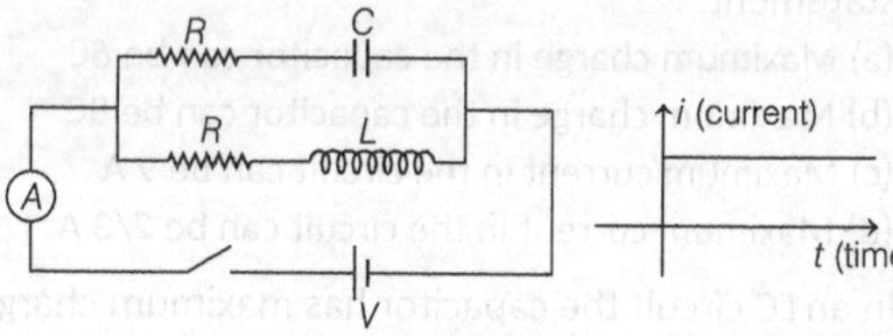

LEVEL 03 JEE Advanced Level

Single Choice Correct Questions

1 In the circuit shown, charge q varies with time t as $q = t^3 - t^2 + 4t$, where q is in coulombs and time t is in second. Find $V_A - V_B$ at $t = 1$ s.

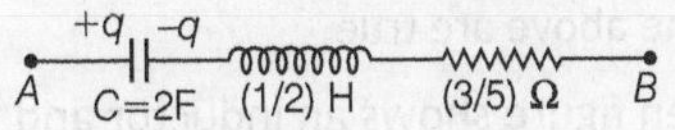

(a) 4 V (b) 5 V (c) 6 V (d) 7 V

2 The ratio of power dissipated by the bulb at $t = 1$ s and $t = 2$ s after closing the switch is

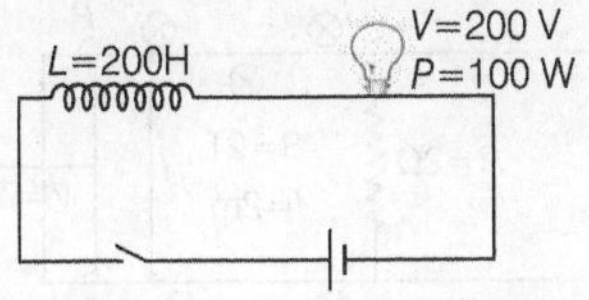

(a) $\frac{e^2}{e^4 - 1}$ (b) $\frac{e^4}{(e^2 + 1)^2}$

(c) $\frac{e^2 - 1}{e^4 + 1}$ (d) None of these

3 Rate of increment of energy in an inductor with time in series *LR* circuit getting charge with battery of emf *E* is best represented by : [inductor has initially zero current]

(a) 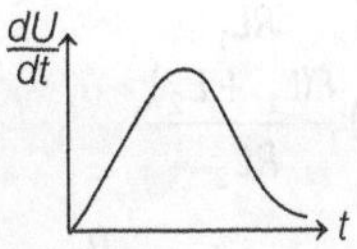

(b) 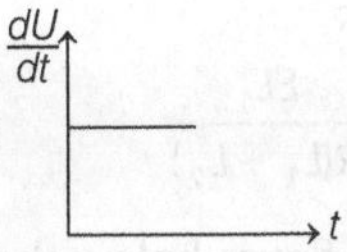

(c) 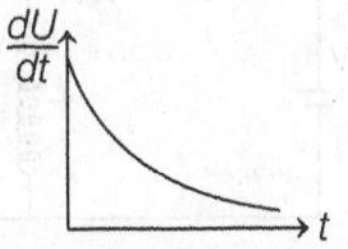

(d) 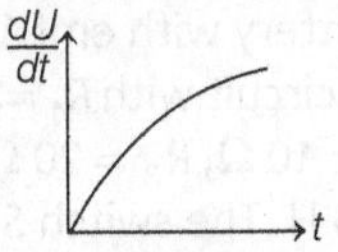

(c)

4 In the circuit shown in figure switch S is closed at time $t = 0$. Find the charge which passes through the battery in one time constant.

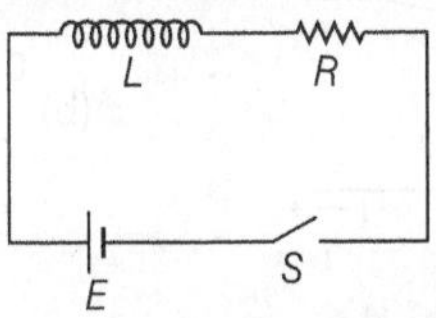

(a) $\frac{EL}{(e-1)R^2}$ (b) $\frac{EL(e+1)}{eR^2}$

(c) $\frac{EL}{eR^2}$ (d) $\frac{ELe}{(e-1)R^2}$

5 An inductor L and a resistor R are connected in series with a direct current source of emf E. The maximum rate at which energy is stored in the magnetic field is

(a) $\frac{E^2}{4R}$ (b) $\frac{E^2}{R}$ (c) $\frac{4E^2}{R}$ (d) $\frac{2E^2}{R}$

6 When induced emf in inductor coil is 50% of its maximum value then stored energy in inductor coil in the given circuit will be

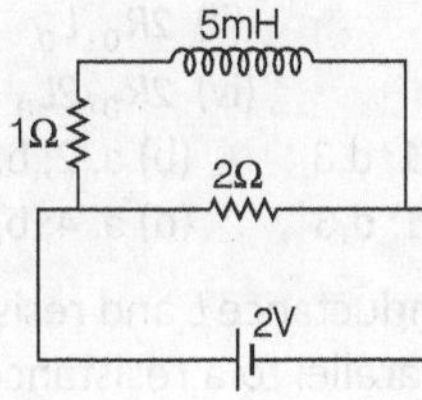

(a) 2.5 mJ (b) 5 mJ (c) 15 mJ (d) 20 mJ

7 The decay of current in a certain *L-R* circuit is shown in Figure. The fraction of the magnetic potential energy lost by the inductor at the end of time $t = 2t_0$ is

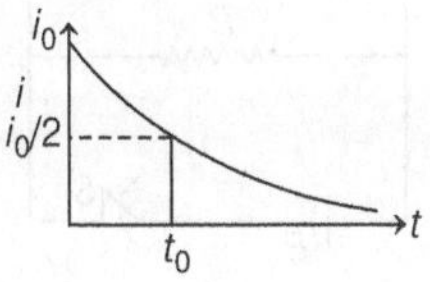

(a) $\frac{1}{4}$ (b) $\frac{3}{4}$ (c) $\frac{1}{16}$ (d) $\frac{15}{16}$

8 The current in a coil of self-inductance 2.0 H is increasing according to $i = 2 \sin t^2$ A. The amount of energy spent during the period when the current changes from 0 to 2A is

(a) 2 J (b) 4 J (c) 8 J (d) 16 J

9 In the circuit shown in the figure the switched S_1 and S_2 are closed at time $t = 0$. After time $t = (0.1) \ln 2$ s, switch S_2 is opened. Find the current in the circuit at time $t = (0.2) \ln 2$ s.

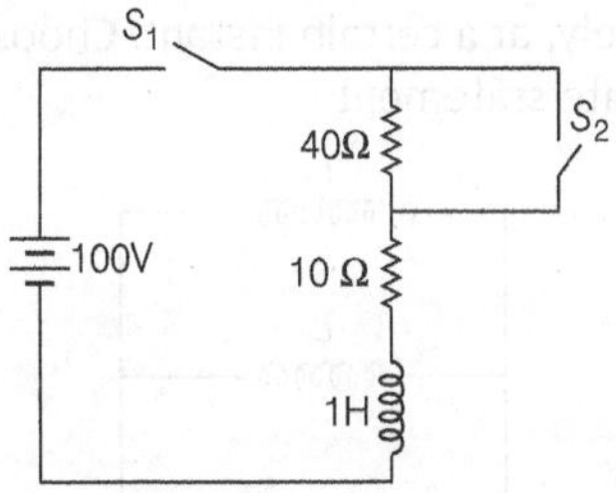

(a) $\frac{63}{32}$ A (b) $\frac{67}{32}$ A (c) $\frac{33}{16}$ A (d) $\frac{31}{16}$ A

10 In the figure shown below, the switch S has been in position 1 for a long time. It is then thrown to position 2. The resulting current through the inductor is sketched in figure on right for four sets of values of R and L, Which curve goes with which set of values?

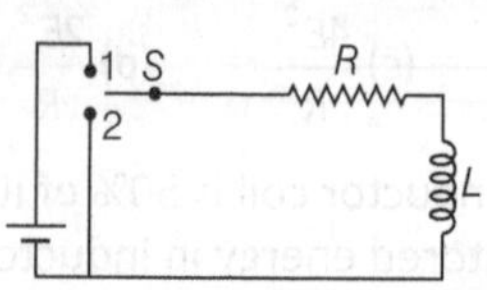

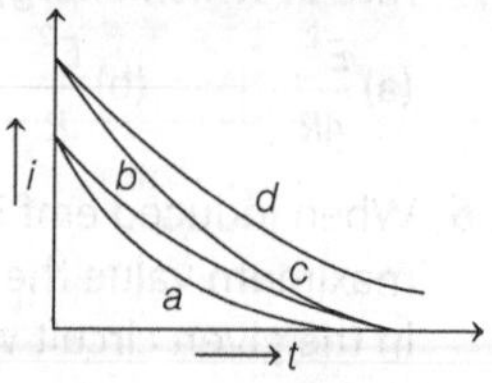

(i) R_0, L_0 (ii) $2R_0, L_0$
(iii) $R_0, 2L_0$ (iv) $2R_0, 2L_0$

(a) a, 2; b, 4; c, 1; d,3 (b) a, 2; b, 1; c, 4; d,3
(c) a, 4; b, 2; c, 1; d,3 (d) a, 4; b, 2; c, 3; d, 1

11 A solenoid of inductance L and resistance r is connected in parallel to a resistance R and a battery of emf E. Initially the switch is closed for long time and at $t = 0$, switch S is opened . Then which of the following statements is wrong?

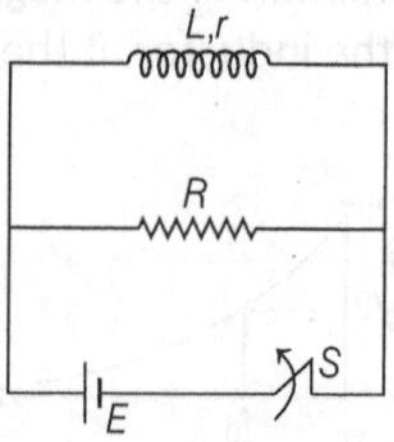

(a) Current through solenoid at any time t, after opening the switch is $\frac{E}{r} e^{-\frac{(R+r)}{L}t}$

(b) Induced emf across solenoid at time $t = 0$ is $\frac{E(R+r)}{r}$

(c) Amount of heat generated in solenoid is $\frac{E^2 L}{2r(r+R)}$

(d) Potential difference across solenoid at $t = 0$ is E

12 The switch S of the circuit shown in the figure is closed at $t = 0$. i_1 and i_2 are the electric current in the branch containing two ideal inductors L_1 and L_2 respectively, at a certain instant. Choose the most appropriate statement

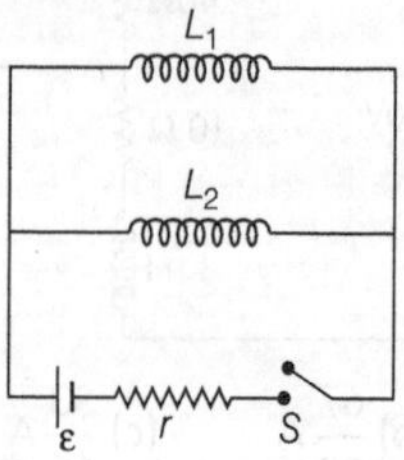

(a) At $t = 0$, (just after the switch is closed) $\frac{di_1}{dt} = \frac{\varepsilon}{L_1}$ and $\frac{di_2}{dt} = \frac{\varepsilon}{L_2}$

(b) At $t = 0$, (just after the switch is closed) $i_1 = 0, i_2 = 0$

(c) After long time $i_1 = \frac{\varepsilon L_2}{(L_1 + L_2)r}$ and $i_2 = \frac{\varepsilon L_1}{(L_1 + L_2)r}$

(d) All the above are true

13 The given figure shows an inductor and resistor fixed on a conducting wire. A movable conducting wire PQ starts moving on the fixed rails from $t = 0$ with constant velocity 1 m/s. The work done by the external force on the wire PQ in 2 seconds is

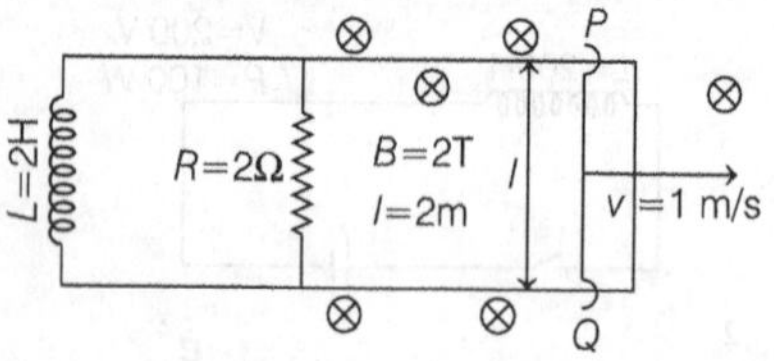

(a) 16 J (b) 32 J (c) 48 J (d) 64 J

14 Switch S shown in figure is closed for $t < 0$ and is opened at $t = 0$. When currents through L_1 and L_2 are equal, their common value is

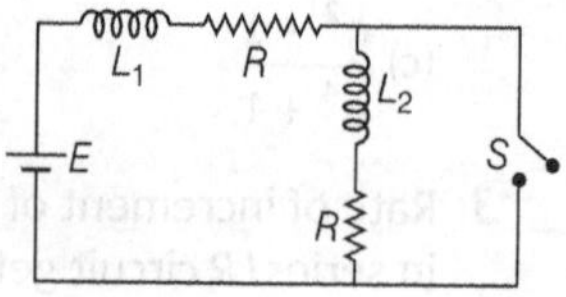

(a) $\frac{E}{R}$ (b) $\frac{E(L_2 + L_1)}{RL_1}$

(c) $\frac{EL_1}{R(L_1 + L_2)}$ (d) $\frac{E(L_1 + L_2)}{RL_2}$

15 The figure below shown a battery with emf 15 V in a circuit with R_1 =30 Ω, R_2 = 10 Ω, R_3 = 20 Ω and L = 3 H. The switch S is initially in the open position and is then closed at time $t = 0$. Then the graph which shows the correct variation of current through battery after switch S is closed

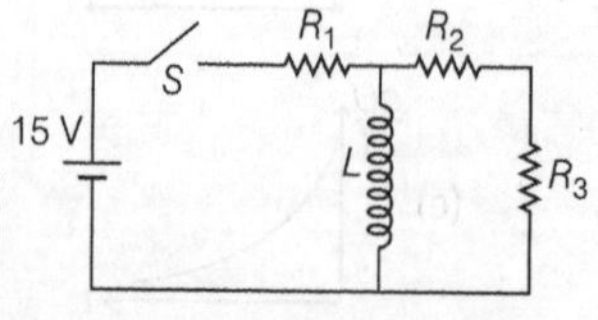

(a)
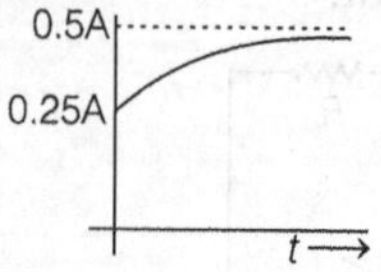

(b)
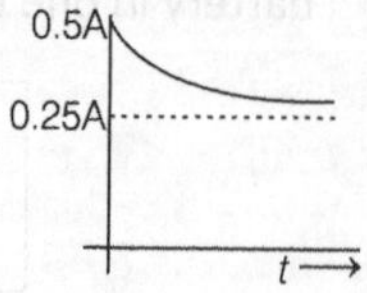

(c)
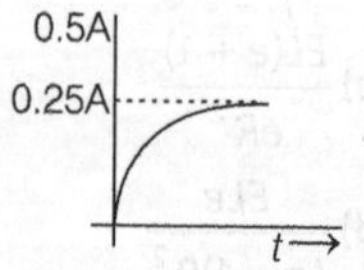

(d)
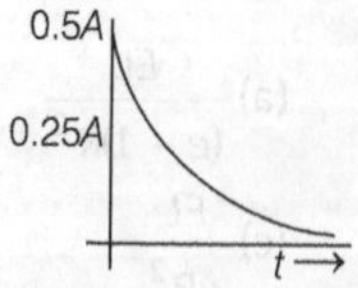

16 In the circuit the key (K) is closed at $t = 0$. The current through the key (K) at the instant $t = 10^{-3}$ ln 2 s is

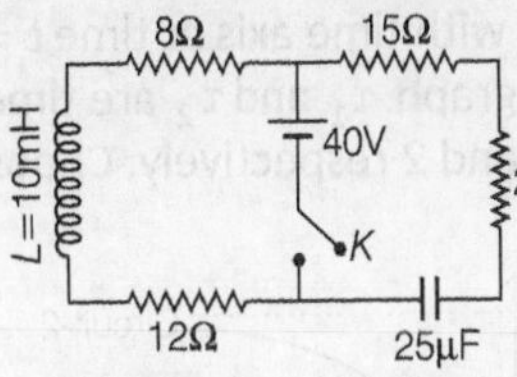

(a) 2 A (b) 2.5 A (c) 3 A (d) 4 A

17 Complete toroidal coil of rectangular cross section is shown in figure. Current i is flowing in each turn and number of turns are N. The value of coefficient of self inductance is

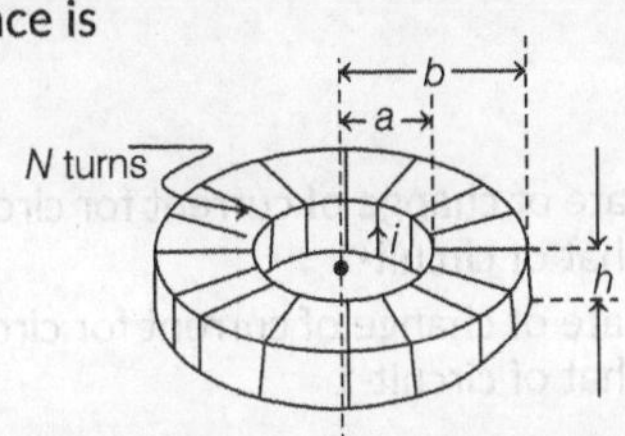

(a) $\frac{\mu_0 N^2 h}{4\pi} \ln\left(\frac{b}{a}\right)$ (b) $\frac{3\mu_0 N^2 h}{2\pi} \ln\left(\frac{b}{a}\right)$

(c) $\frac{3\mu_0 N^2 h}{4\pi} \ln\left(\frac{b}{a}\right)$ (d) $\frac{\mu_0 N^2 h}{2\pi} \ln\left(\frac{b}{a}\right)$

18 A conducting square loop $PQRS$ of zero resistance but containing an inductor of inductance L is placed near a long wire carrying current $i_0 \sin\omega t$, as shown in the figure. The peak value of induced current in the loop is

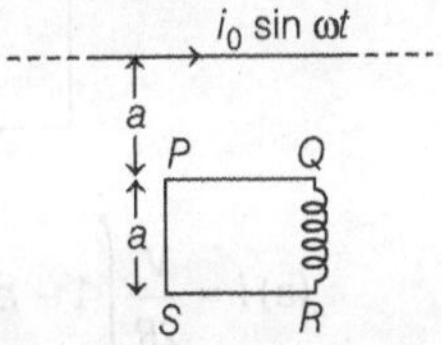

(a) $\frac{\mu_0 a i_0 (\ln 2)}{\omega L}$ (b) $\frac{\mu_0 a i_0 (\ln 2)}{2\pi L}$

(c) $\frac{\mu_0 a i_0 (\ln 2)}{2\pi \omega L}$ (d) $\frac{2\mu_0 a i_0 (\ln 2)}{\pi L}$

19 In the given figure, the mutual inductance of coil and the very long straight wire is M, the coil has resistance R and the self inductance L. The wire lies in the same plane as that of the coil. The current in the wire varies according to the law $i = at$, where a is a constant and t is the time. The time dependence of current in the coil is (consider clockwise current in loop as positive)

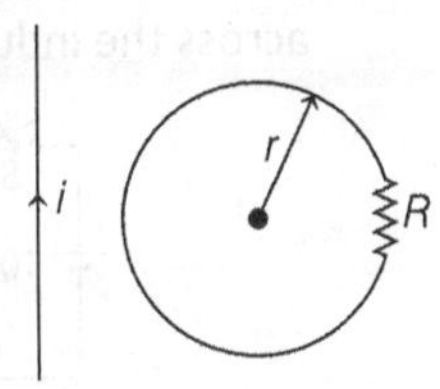

(a) $-\frac{Ma}{R} e^{-tR/L}$ (b) $-\frac{Ma}{R}(1 - e^{-tR/L})$

(c) $\frac{Ma}{R} e^{-tR/L}$ (d) $\frac{Ma}{R}(1 - e^{-tR/L})$

20 Find the difference between the equivalent inductance in the following figures if coupling coefficient is $1/\sqrt{2}$.

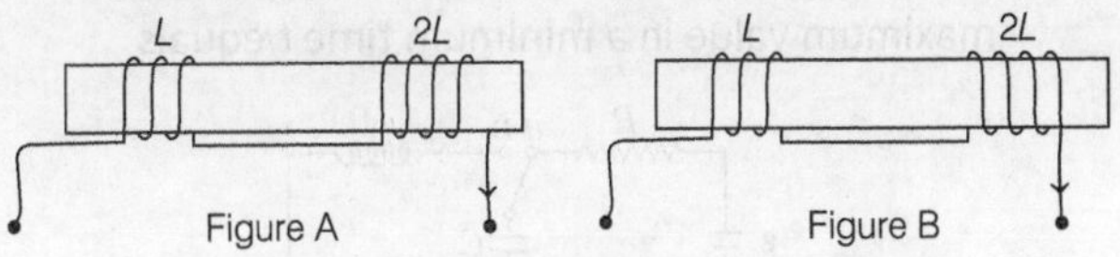

(a) $2L$ (b) $3L$ (c) $4L$ (d) $5L$

21 Two fixed identical metallic spheres A and B of radius $R = 50$ cm each are placed on a non-conducting plane at a very large distance from each other and they are connected by a coil of inductance $L = 9$ mH as shown in figure. One of the spheres (say A) is imparted an initial charge and the other is kept uncharged. The switch S is closed at $t = 0$. After what minimum time t does the charge on the first sphere decrease to half of its initial value?

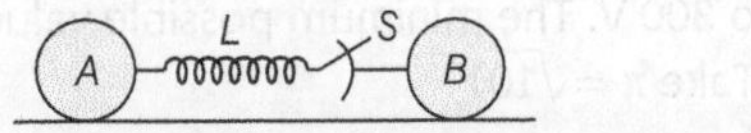

(a) $\pi \times 10^{-6}$ s (b) $\frac{\pi}{4} \times 10^{-6}$ s

(c) $\frac{\pi}{2} \times 10^{-6}$ s (d) $2\pi \times 10^{-6}$ s

22 An ideal DC source of emf E is connected with an uncharged capacitor and inductor. If switch is closed at $t = 0$, what is the maximum charge on the capacitor in subsequent flow of charge?

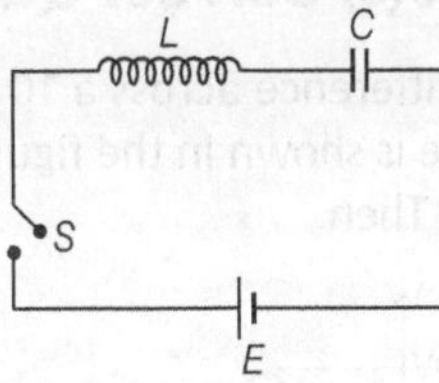

(a) $2\,CE$ (b) CE (c) $1.5\,CE$ (d) $4\,CE$

23 In the circuit shown in figure, the switch has been in position 1 for long time. Now the switch is shifted to position 2 at $t = 0$. The charge on capacitor at $t = \frac{\pi}{6}$ s is

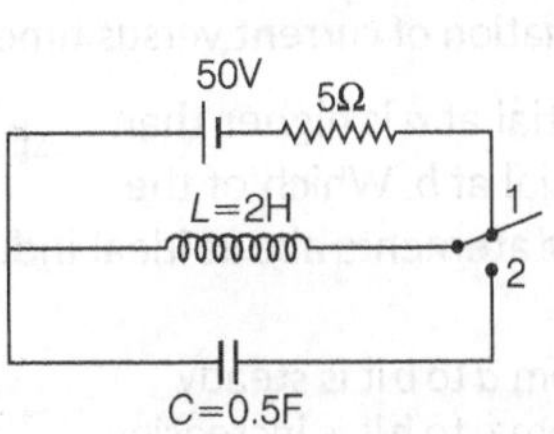

(a) 0 (b) 5 C

(c) $5\sqrt{3}$ C (d) 10 C

24 The switch in the circuit pictured is in position a for a long time. At $t = 0$ the switch is moved from a to b. The energy in inductor will becomes half of its maximum value in a minimum time t equals

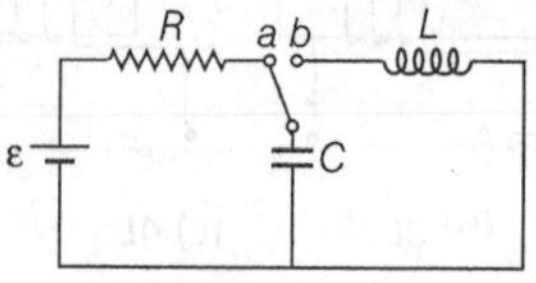

(a) $2\pi\sqrt{LC}$ (b) $\frac{\pi}{4}\sqrt{LC}$ (c) $\frac{\pi}{2}\sqrt{LC}$ (d) $\pi\sqrt{LC}$

25 In the circuit shown, initially both switches are open and the 900 μF capacitor is charged to 100 V and 100 μF capacitor is uncharged. Now switch S_1 is closed for time t_1 after which it is opened and at same instant switch S_2 is closed for time t_2 and then opened. It is found that 100 μF capacitor is charged to 300 V. The minimum possible value of $t_1 + t_2$ is (Take $\pi = \sqrt{10}$)

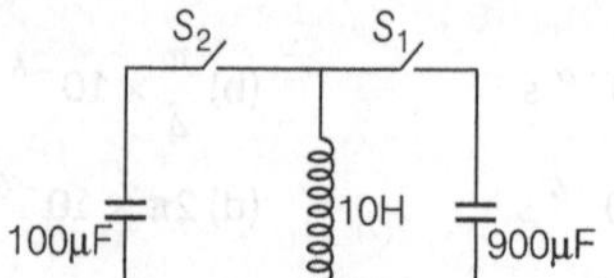

(a) 0.05 s (b) 0.15 s (c) 0.20 s (d) 0.25 s

Multiple Choice(s) Correct Questions

1 The potential difference across a 10 H inductor as a function of time is shown in the figure. At $t = 0$, current is zero. Then

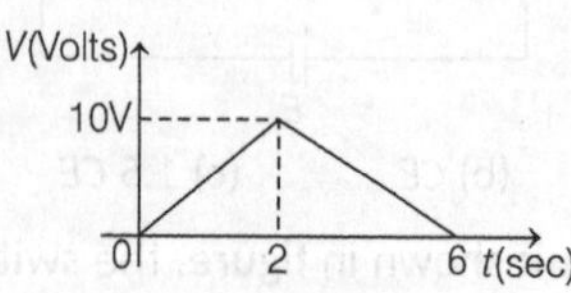

(a) The current in the inductor at $t = 6$ s is 3 A.
(b) The current in the inductor at $t = 1$ s is 1/4 A.
(c) The current in the inductor at $t = 4$ s is 5/2 A.
(d) The variation of current versus time is parabola.

2 The potential at a is higher than the potential at b. Which of the following statements about ideal inductor can be true?

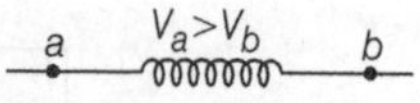

(a) If i is from a to b it is steady
(b) If i is from a to b it is increasing
(c) If i is from b to a it is decreasing
(d) If i is from b to a it is increasing

3 Growth of current in two different L-R circuits are depicted by the i-t graphs shown. Angle subtended by the curves with time axis at time $t = 0$ are also shown in the graph. τ_1 and τ_2 are time constants for the circuits 1 and 2 respectively. Choose the correct alternative

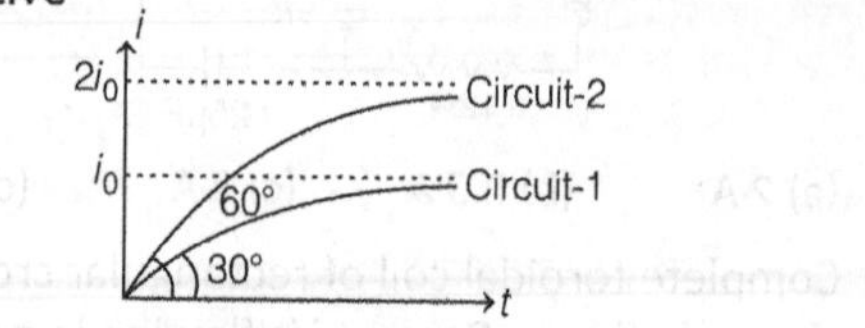

(a) $\frac{\tau_1}{\tau_2} = \frac{2}{3}$

(b) $\frac{\tau_1}{\tau_2} = \frac{3}{2}$

(c) Initial rate of change of current for circuit-2 is 2 times that of circuit-1

(d) Initial rate of change of current for circuit-2 is 3 times that of circuit-1

4 In the circuit shown switch S is closed at $t = 0$. At time (t) which of the following is/are correct

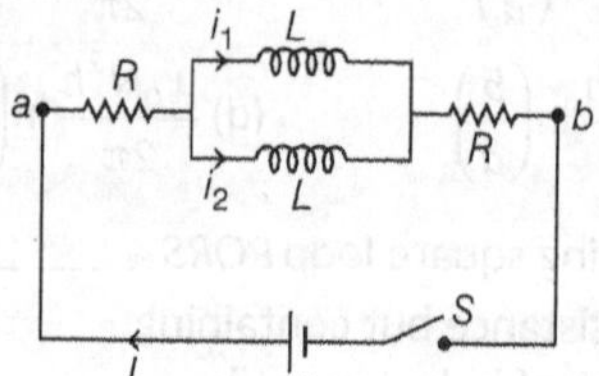

(a) $i = \frac{V}{2R}\left(1 - e^{-\frac{4Rt}{L}}\right)$ (b) $i_1 = i_2 = \frac{V}{2R}\left(1 - e^{-\frac{4Rt}{L}}\right)$

(c) At $t = 0$, $\frac{dV_{ab}}{dt} = 0$ (d) $i = \sqrt{i_1^2 + i_2^2}$

5 In the circuit shown, switch S_1 is initially open and switch S_2 is initially closed. At time $t = 0$, S_1 is closed and at time $t = 0.25$ s, S_2 is opened. The voltage across the inductor, V_L

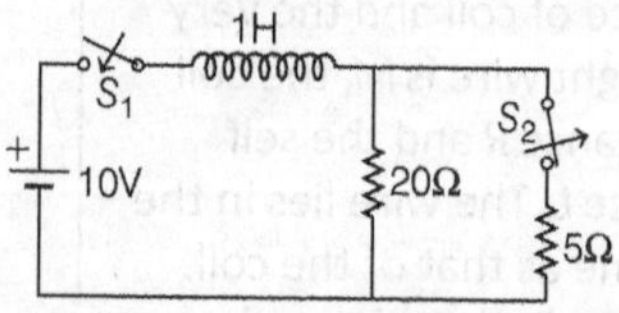

(a) Just after switch S_1 is closed, $V_L = 10$ V

(b) Just before switch S_2 is opened, $V_L = \left(\frac{10}{e}\right)$ V

(c) Just after switch S_2 is opened, $V_L = \left(40 - \frac{50}{e}\right)$ V

(d) Just after switch S_2 is opened, $V_L = \left(60 - \frac{50}{e}\right)$ V

6 The switch is in position 1 for a long time. Then it is suddenly shifted to 2 at $t = 0$. Inductors are ideal and battery has no internal resistance.

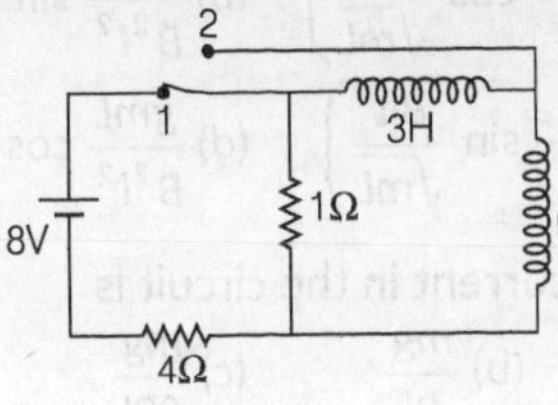

(a) Before switch being shifted to 2, current in 3 H inductor is 2/3 A.

(b) Before switch being shifted to 2, current in 1 Ω resistor is zero.

(c) After switch is shifted to 2, current in 1 Ω resistor is $2e^{-\frac{t}{9}}$ A.

(d) The total heat dissipated in 1 Ω resistor after $t = 0$ is 12 J.

7 In the adjacent circuit diagram, initially switch S is opened and the circuit is in steady state. At time $t = 0$, the switch S is closed and the new steady state is reached. Choose the correct options (s).

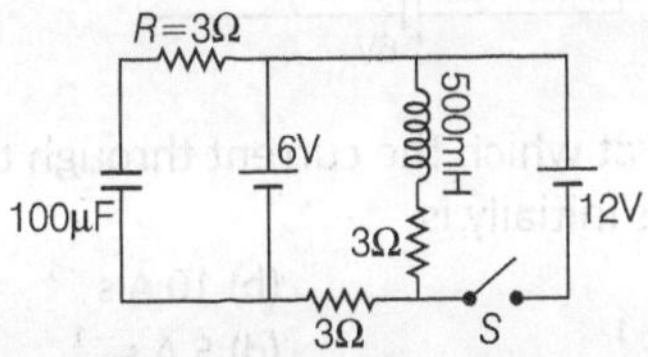

(a) Current in the inductor when the circuit reaches the new steady state is 4A.

(b) The net change in the magnetic flux in the inductor is 1.5 Wb

(c) The potential difference across the inductor is 9 V when the circuit reaches the new steady state

(d) The charge stored in the capacitor in the new steady state is 1.2 mC

8 Two resistors, one inductor and a capacitor are connected in a circuit with a battery and switch as shown in figure. The charge on capacitor and current in inductor is zero at $t = 0$. Now switch is closed at $t = 0$, then choose the correct option(s).

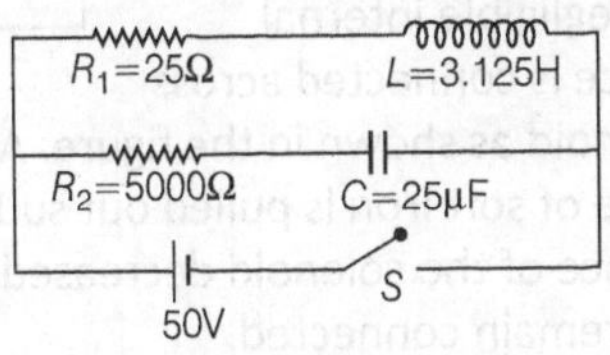

(a) The ratio of maximum current in the branch of inductor to the branch of capacitor is 200.

(b) At $t = \frac{\ln 2}{8}$, the current in the branch of capacitor is 200 times the current in the branch of inductor.

(c) At $t = \frac{1}{8}\ln\left(\frac{5}{4}\right)$, the potential drop across inductor is 4 times the potential drop across capacitor.

(d) The potential drop across inductor is maximum at $t = 0$.

9 In the arrangement as shown in the figure, S_1 and S_3 are already closed for a long time. Now at $t = 0$ the S_2 is closed and S_1, S_3 are opened. [$\varepsilon = 1\,V, L = 1\,H, R = 1\,\Omega, C = 1\,F$]

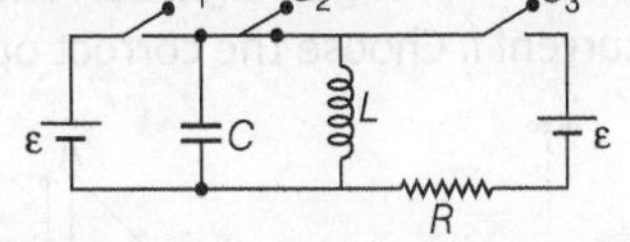

(a) After S_2 is closed the maximum current through the inductor is 2 A.

(b) After S_2 is closed the maximum current through the indicator is $\sqrt{2}$A.

(c) Maximum charge on the capacitor is $(2 + \sqrt{2})$ C

(d) Maximum charge on the capacitor is $\sqrt{2}$ C

10 A circuit containing capacitors C_1 and C_2, shown in the figure is in the steady state with key K_1 closed. At the instant $t = 0$, K_1 is opened and K_2 is closed. The ratio of energy in the inductor and that of capacitor C_1 becomes one third at time 't' for the first time. If charge on capacitor C_1 at that instant is q_1 and that on capacitor C_2 is q_2, then choose the correct statement(s)

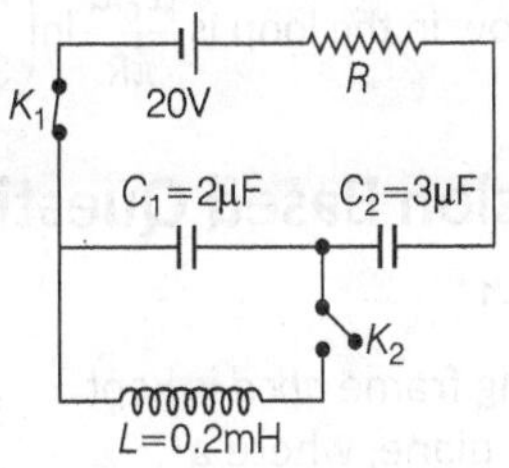

(a) Angular frequency of oscillations of the LC circuit will be 5×10^4 rad/s.

(b) Time t will be 21 μs.

(c) Charge on capacitor C_1 at that instant will be, $q_1 = 12\sqrt{3}$ μC.

(d) Charge on capacitor C_2 at that instant will be, $q_2 = 24\mu C$.

11 Two parallel rectangular superconducting plates of length l, width b and separation a ($l >> b >> a$) are joined at each end to form a one-turn coil of negligible resistance. The steady state current is i.

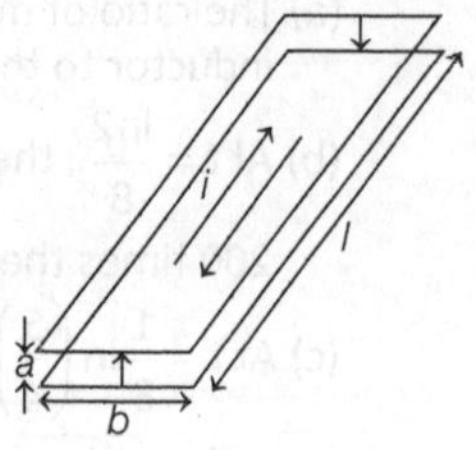

(a) Magnetic field between the plates is $\mu_0 i / b$

(b) Self inductance of coil is $\mu_0 al / 2b$

(c) The energy stored in magnetic field will be $\mu_0 a l i^2 / 2b$

(d) The magnitude of the force per unit area between the two plates is $\mu_0 i^2 / 2b^2$

12 A triangular loop $ABCA$ of resistance R is placed at a distance a from a long straight current carrying wire having current i. Choose the correct options.

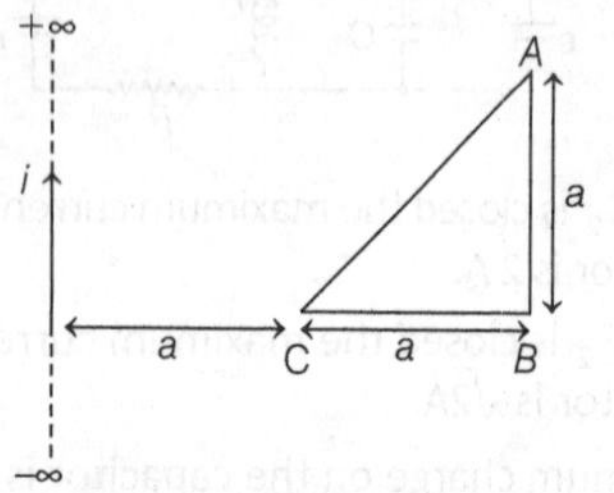

(a) Mutual inductance of the system in the given position is $\frac{\mu_0 a}{2\pi}(1 - \ln 2)$

(b) Mutual inductance of the system in the given position is $\frac{\mu_0 a}{2\pi}(1 + \ln 2)$

(c) If the coil is rotated by 180° about side AB, the charge flow in the loop is $\frac{\mu_0 ia}{2\pi R}\ln\left(\frac{27}{16}\right)$

(d) If the coil is rotated by 180° about side AB, the charge flow in the loop is $\frac{\mu_0 ia}{\pi R}\ln\left(\frac{4}{3}\right)$

Comprehension Based Questions

Comprehension-1

A conducting frame $abcd$ is kept in a vertical plane, where a uniform magnetic field B is present as shown. A conducting rod ef of mass m and length l can slide smoothly on it. It always remains horizontal. The resistance of the loop is negligible and has inductance L. The rod is released from rest and allowed to fall under gravity and inductor has no initial current.

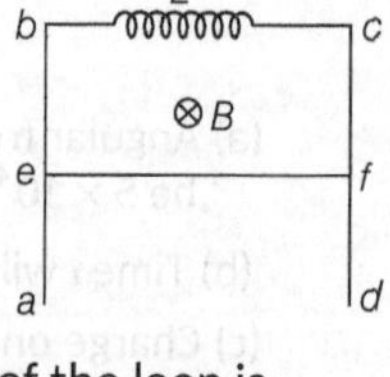

1 Position of rod $x(t)$ assuming initial position to be $x = 0$ and vertically downward as positive X-axis.

(a) $\frac{gmL}{B^2l^2}\left(1 - \cos\frac{Blt}{\sqrt{mL}}\right)$ (b) $\frac{gmL}{B^2l^2}\sin\frac{Blt}{\sqrt{mL}}$

(c) $\frac{gmL}{B^2l^2}\left(1 - \sin\frac{Blt}{\sqrt{mL}}\right)$ (d) $\frac{gmL}{B^2l^2}\cos\frac{Blt}{\sqrt{mL}}$

2 Maximum current in the circuit is

(a) $\frac{2mg}{Bl}$ (b) $\frac{mg}{Bl}$ (c) $\frac{mg}{2Bl}$ (d) $\frac{3mg}{2Bl}$

3 Maximum velocity of the rod is

(a) $\frac{2g\sqrt{mL}}{Bl}$ (b) $\frac{g\sqrt{mL}}{Bl}$ (c) $\frac{3g\sqrt{mL}}{4Bl}$ (d) $\frac{Bl}{g\sqrt{ml}}$

Comprehension-2

There in no current part of this circuit for time $t < 0$. Switch S is closed at $t = 0$

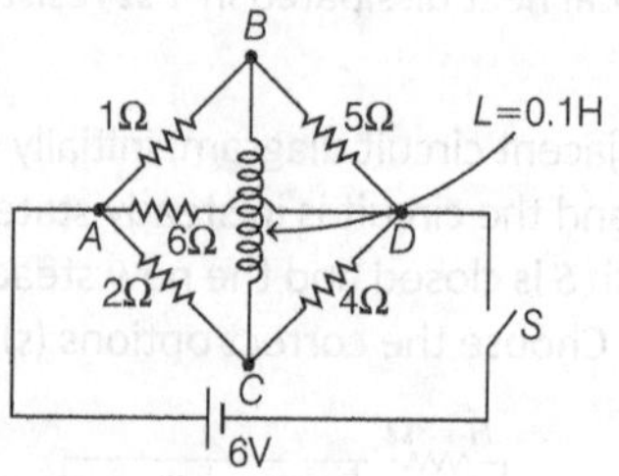

4 The rate at which the current through the inductor increases initially is

(a) zero (b) 10 A s^{-1}

(c) 1 A s^{-1} (d) 5 A s^{-1}

5 Current through the 6Ω resistor

(a) increases linearly with time

(b) increases non-linearly with time

(c) decreases non-linearly with time

(d) remains constant

6 The current through the inductor after a long time will be

(a) zero (b) infinite

(c) 6/13 A (d) None of these

Comprehension-3

A solenoid of resistance R and inductance L has a piece of soft iron inside it. A battery of emf E and of negligible internal resistance is connected across the solenoid as shown in the figure. At an instant, the piece of soft iron is pulled out suddenly so that inductance of the solenoid decreased to ηL with battery remain connected.

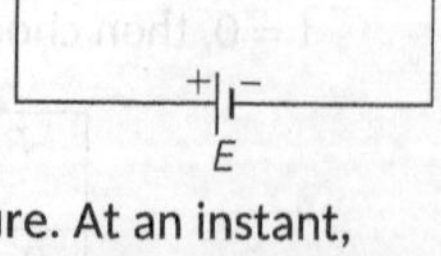

7 The work done to pull out the soft iron piece is

(a) $\frac{\eta LE^2}{2R^2}$ (b) $\frac{(1-\eta)LE^2}{2R^2}$

(c) $\frac{(1-\eta)LE^2}{\eta R^2}$ (d) $\frac{(1-\eta)LE^2}{2\eta R^2}$

8 Assuming $t = 0$ is the instant when iron piece has been pulled out, the current as a function of time is

(a) $\frac{E}{R}\left[1-\left(1-\frac{1}{\eta}\right)e^{-\frac{t}{\lambda}}\right]$ (b) $\frac{E}{R}\left[1+\left(1+\frac{1}{\eta}\right)e^{-\frac{t}{\lambda}}\right]$

(c) $\frac{E}{R}\left[1-\left(1+\frac{1}{\eta}\right)e^{-\frac{t}{\lambda}}\right]$ (d) $\frac{E}{R}\left[1+\left(1-\frac{1}{\eta}\right)e^{-\frac{t}{\lambda}}\right]$

(where $\lambda = \eta L/R$)

9 Power supplied by the battery as a function of time is

(a) $\frac{E^2}{R}\left[1-\left(1-\frac{1}{\eta}\right)e^{-\frac{t}{\lambda}}\right]$ (b) $\frac{E^2}{R}\left[1+\left(1+\frac{1}{\eta}\right)e^{-\frac{t}{\lambda}}\right]$

(c) $\frac{E^2}{R}\left[1-\left(1+\frac{1}{\eta}\right)e^{-\frac{t}{\lambda}}\right]$ (d) $\frac{E^2}{R}\left[1+\left(1-\frac{1}{\eta}\right)e^{-\frac{t}{\lambda}}\right]$

Comprehension-4

A thin ring (mass m, radius r_0) of negligible resistance ($R = 0$) is held over a cylindrical bar magnet that is in vertical position. The axis of the ring coincides with the axis of the magnet. The magnetic field surrounding the ring has a cylindrical symmetry and the co-ordinates of the magnetic induction vector are given by the following equations:

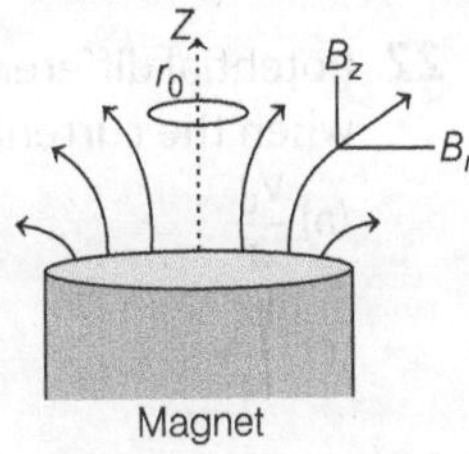

$B_z = B_0(1-\alpha z)$ and $B_r = B_0\beta r$, where B_0, α, β are constants and z and r denote the vertical and radial directions as shown in figure. Initially, the ring carries no current. The ring is released and it starts to move downwards, preserving its vertical axis.

Let the initial coordinates of the centre of the ring be $z = 0$ and $r = 0$. In describing the motion, neglect air resistance. Here L is the self-inductance of ring.

10 Mark the correct statement

(a) There will be no current in the ring while ring is in motion.

(b) Net emf is induced in the ring while it is in motion.

(c) Net magnetic flux through the ring is constant at every instant

(d) Net magnetic flux through the ring is variable while ring is in motion.

11 The net magnetic force in the ring has magnitude

(a) $\frac{2B_0^2\alpha\beta r_0^4\pi^2 z}{L}$ (b) $\frac{B_0^2\beta r_0^3\pi^2 z}{\alpha L}$

(c) $\frac{B_0^2\beta r_0^4\pi^2 z^2}{\beta L}$ (d) $\frac{2B_0^2 r_0^4\pi^2 z^2}{\alpha\beta L}$

12 Mark the correct statement

(a) The ring executes SHM about its initial position as equilibrium position

(b) The ring executes periodic and oscillatory motion about its initial position as equilibrium position

(c) Angular frequency of oscillation is $\omega = \pi r_0^2 B_0\sqrt{\frac{2\alpha\beta}{mL}}$

(d) Angular frequency of oscillation is $\omega = \pi\sqrt{\frac{\alpha\beta r_0^2\beta}{mL}}$

Comprehension-5

In figure there is a frame consisting of two square loops having resistors and inductors as shown.

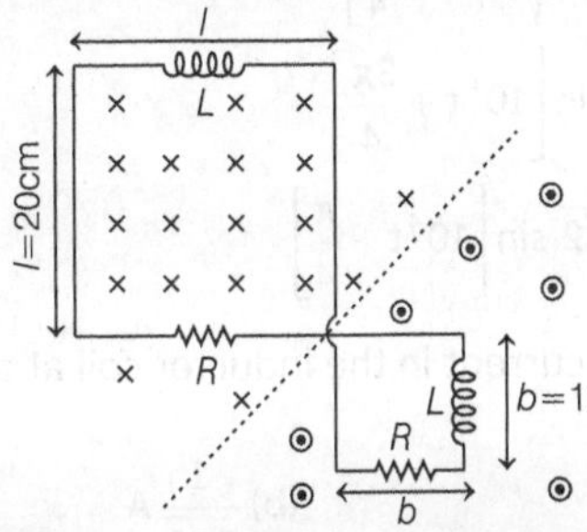

This frame is placed in a uniform but time-varying magnetic field in such a way that one of the loops is placed in crossed magnetic field and the other is placed in dot magnetic field. Both magnetic fields are perpendicular to the planes of the loops.

The magnetic field is given by $B = (20 + 10t)$ Wb m^{-2} in both regions. [$l = 20$ cm, $b = 10$ cm, and $R = 10\ \Omega$, $L = 10$ H),

13 The direction of induced current in the bigger loop will be

(a) clockwise

(b) anti-clockwise

(c) first clockwise for some time, then anti-clockwise, and so on

(d) first anti-clockwise for some time, then clockwise, and so on

14 The induced emf in the frame only due to the variation of magnetic field will be

(a) 0.1 V (b) 0.3 V (c) 0.4 V (d) 0.5 V

15 The current in the frame as a function of time will be

(a) $\frac{1}{20}(1-e^{-t})$ (b) $\frac{1}{40}(1-e^{-t})$

(c) $\frac{1}{20}e^{-t}$ (d) $\frac{1}{10}e^{-t}$

Comprehension-6

Switches S_1, S_2 remain open and switch S_3 remains closed for long time such that capacitor becomes fully charged and current in inductor coil becomes maximum. Now switches S_1, S_2 are simultaneously closed and S_3 is simultaneously opened at $t = 0$. Assume that battery and inductor coil are ideal.

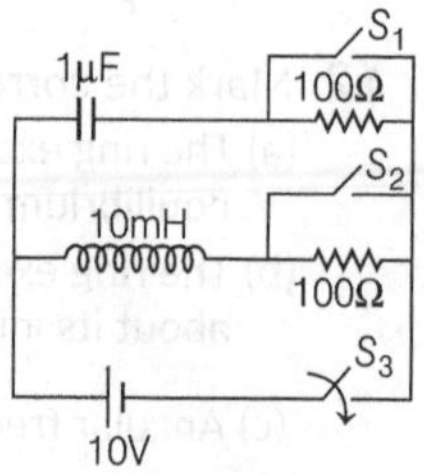

16 Charge (in μC) on capacitor as a function of time is

(a) $q = 10\sqrt{2}\sin\left[10^4 t + \frac{3\pi}{4}\right]$

(b) $q = 10\sin\left[10^4 t + \frac{\pi}{4}\right]$

(c) $q = 10\sin\left[10^4 t + \frac{3\pi}{4}\right]$

(d) $q = 10\sqrt{2}\sin\left[10^4 t + \frac{\pi}{4}\right]$

17 Maximum current in the inductor coil at any time $(t > 0)$ is

(a) $\frac{1}{10}$ A (b) $\frac{1}{5\sqrt{2}}$ A

(c) $\frac{1}{5}$ A (d) 1 A

18 Time $(t > 0)$ when energy stored in inductor would be minimum for the first time is

(a) $\frac{\pi}{4}\times 10^{-4}$ s (b) $\frac{\pi}{2}\times 10^{-4}$ s

(c) $\frac{3\pi}{4}\times 10^{-4}$ s (d) $\pi\times 10^{-4}$ s

Comprehension-7

Initially switch S is kept at position (1) when steady state is achieved. Initially charge on the capacitor is zero and current in L_1 inductor is also zero. Now switch S is shifted to position (2) at $t = 0$. $(L_1 = L_2 = L)$

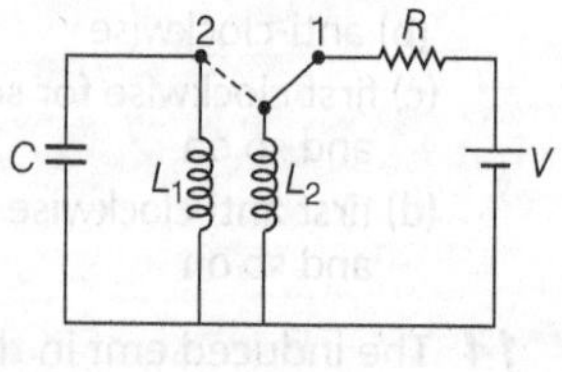

19 Maximum charge on the capacitor is

(a) $\sqrt{\frac{3}{2}CL}\left(\frac{V}{R}\right)$ (b) $\sqrt{\frac{1}{2}CL}\left(\frac{V}{R}\right)$

(c) $\sqrt{CL}\left(\frac{V}{R}\right)$ (d) $\sqrt{2CL}\left(\frac{V}{R}\right)$

20 Amount of energy stored in the inductors when charge on capacitor is maximum, are

(a) $\frac{LV^2}{8R^2}, \frac{LV^2}{8R^2}$ (b) $\frac{LV^2}{7R^2}, \frac{3LV^2}{28R^2}$

(c) $\frac{LV^2}{5R^2}, \frac{LV^2}{20R^2}$ (d) $\frac{LV^2}{10R^2}, \frac{3LV^2}{20R^2}$

Comprehension-8

Two capacitors of capacitance C and $3C$ are charged to potential difference V_0 and $2V_0$, respectively and connected to an inductor of inductance L as shown in Figure Initially, the current in the inductor is zero. Now, switch S is closed.

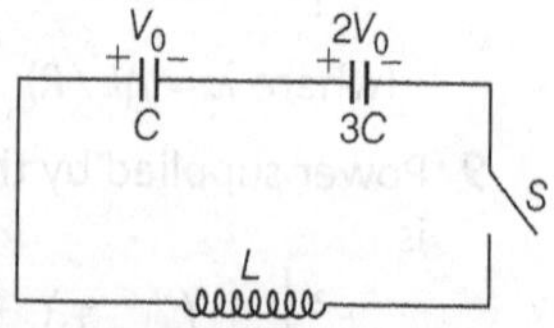

21 The maximum current in the inductor is

(a) $\frac{3V_0}{2}\sqrt{\frac{3C}{L}}$ (b) $V_0\sqrt{\frac{3C}{L}}$ (c) $2V_0\sqrt{\frac{3C}{L}}$ (d) $V_0\sqrt{\frac{C}{L}}$

22 Potential difference across capacitor of capacitance C when the current in the circuit is maximum is

(a) $\frac{V_0}{4}$ (b) $\frac{3V_0}{4}$

(c) $\frac{5V_0}{4}$ (d) None of these

23 Potential difference across capacitor of capacitance $3C$ when the current in the circuit is maximum is

(a) $\frac{V_0}{4}$ (b) $\frac{3V_0}{4}$

(c) $\frac{5V_0}{4}$ (d) None of these

Match The Columns Questions

1

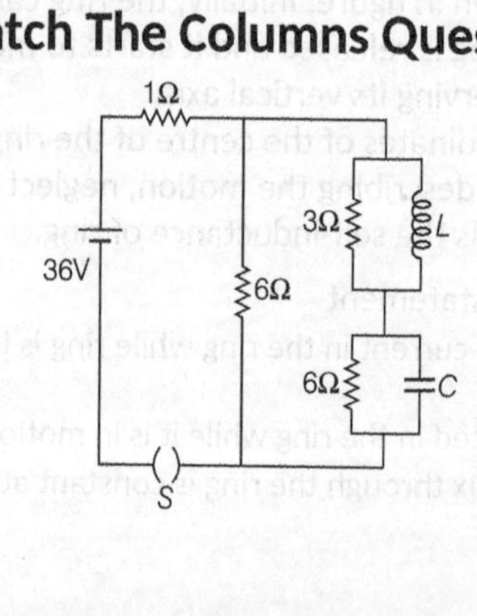

Column-I	Column-II
A. Current through battery just after closing of switch (in A)	P. 12
B. Current through capacitor just after closing of switch (in A)	Q. 8
C. Switch is closed and when steady state of current is achieved the current through battery (in A)	R. 9
D. After steady state switch is re-opened. Just after reopening of switch the ratio of current through inductor and capacitor	S. 1

2 A homogenous field of magnetic induction B is perpendicular and into the plane of a sufficiently long track of gauge length l (separation between tracks) which is inclined at an angle α to the horizontal. A conducting rod of mass m slides on the two frictionless rails of the track as shown in the figure. The rod is released from rest. The circuit formed by the rod and the track is closed by the moving switch of terminals 1, 2 and 3. (Neglect the resistance everywhere except shown resistances)

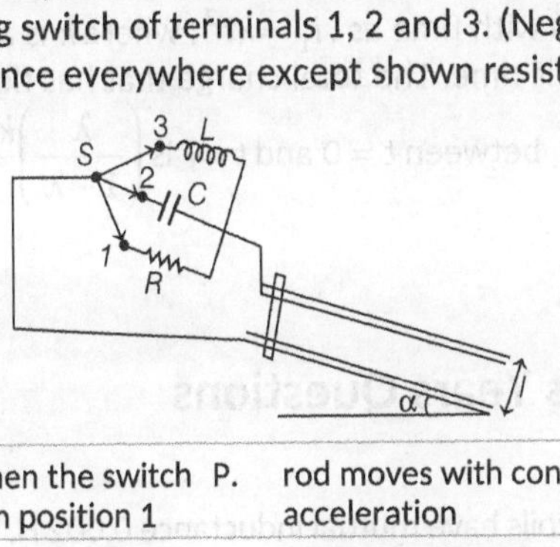

A. When the switch is in position 1	P. rod moves with constant acceleration
B. When the switch is in position 2	Q. rod moves with decreasing acceleration and finally attains a terminal velocity (constant)
C. When the switch is in position 3	R. rod will perform simple harmonic motion
	S. rod moves with constant velocity

3 Match the column-I with column-II. Take mutual inductance = 0 in all cases.

Column-I	Column-II
A. 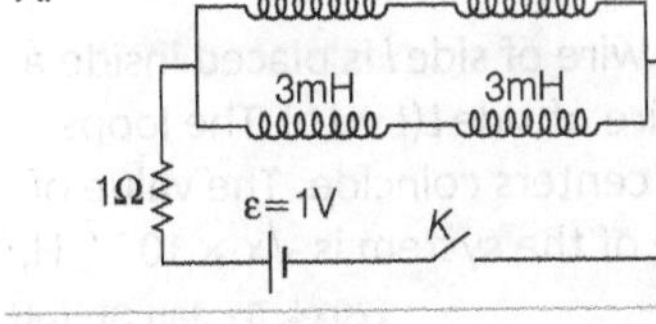	P. at $t = 3$ ms current through the battery is $\left(\frac{e-1}{e}\right)$ A
B. 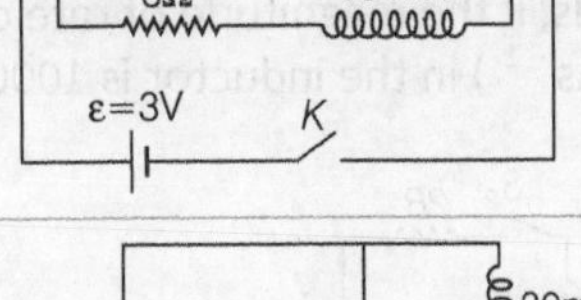	Q. at $t = 3$ ms current through any inductor is $\frac{1}{2}\left(\frac{e-1}{e}\right)$ A
C. 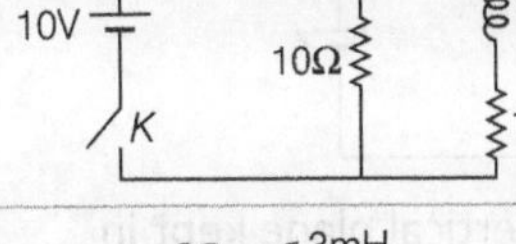	R. at $t = 3$ ms current through any inductor is $\left(\frac{e-1}{e}\right)$ A
D. 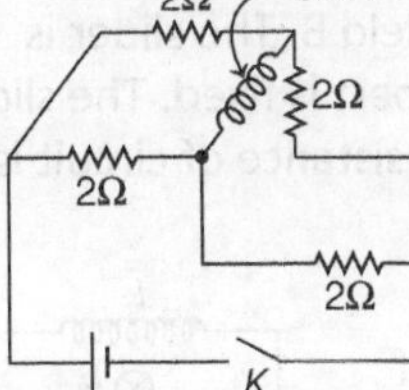	S. Just after closing switch current through any inductor is zero.
	T. Current through battery after very longtime is 1 A.

Numerical Value Questions

1 The figure shows part of a bigger circuit. The capacity of the capacitor is 6 μF and decreasing at the constant rate of 0.5 μF/s. The potential difference across the capacitor is changing as under

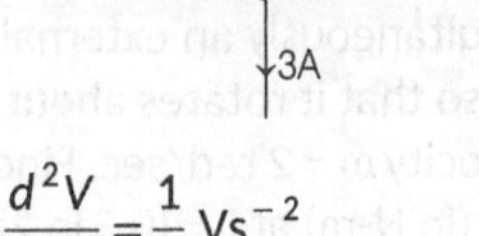

$$\frac{dV}{dt} = 2\,\text{Vs}^{-1},\ \frac{d^2V}{dt^2} = \frac{1}{2}\,\text{Vs}^{-2}$$

The current in the 4Ω resistor is decreasing at the rate of 1 μA/s. What is the potential difference (in μV) across the inductor at this moment?

2 After the current in the circuit has reached its final steady state value, the switch S is closed. Find magnitude of current (in A) through the switch S, (ln 2)/30 sec after S is closed.

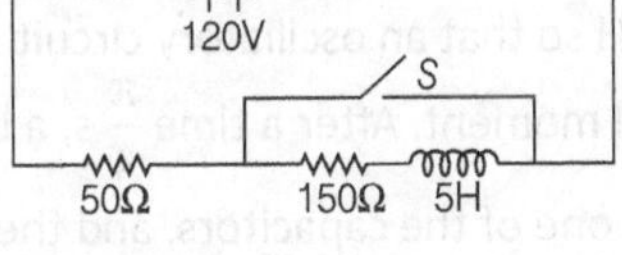

3 In the circuit shown, switch S_2 remains closed for a long time, with S_1 open. It is given that $R = 10\ \Omega$, $L = 1$ mH and $\varepsilon = 3$V. Now switch S_1 is also closed. Immediately afterwards, if the magnitude of rate of change of current (in As^{-1}) in the inductor is 1000 x, find x.

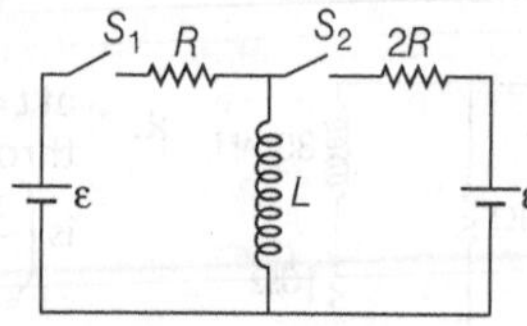

4 Figure shows a circuit in vertical plane kept in uniform horizontal magnetic field B. The slider is movable while the remaining part is fixed. The slider has mass $m = 1$ kg. Electrical resistance of circuit is equal to zero.

Take $B = 10$ T, $l = 1$ m, $L = 1$ H, $g = 10\ ms^{-2}$. In the absence of spring, maximum distance travelled by slide is X_1 and in the presence of spring maximum distance travelled by slider is X_2. For $k = 200$ N/m, find value of X_1/X_2.

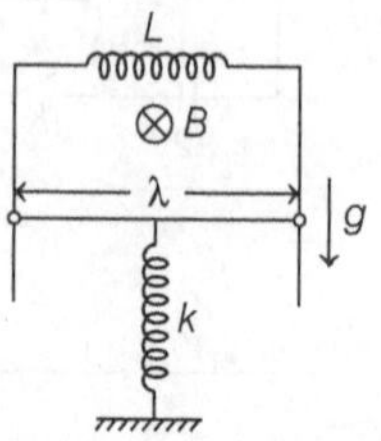

5 The circuit shows a resistance $R = 0.01\ \Omega$ and inductance $L = 3$ mH connected to a conducting rod PQ of length $l = 2$ m which can slide on a perfectly conducting circular arc of radius l with its centre at P. Assume that friction and gravity are absent and a constant uniform magnetic field $B = 0.1$ T exists as shown in the figure. At $t = 0$, the circuit is switched on and simultaneously an external torque is applied on the rod so that it rotates about P with a constant angular velocity $\omega = 2$ rad/sec. Find the magnitude of this torque (in N-m) at $t = (0.3 \ln 2)$ second.

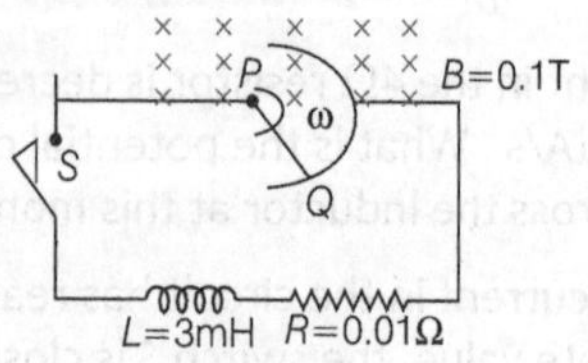

6 A bank of two series connected capacitors of capacitance $C = 500\ \mu F$ each is charged to a voltage 20 V and is connected to a coil of inductance $L = 1000$ H so that an oscillatory circuit is formed at the initial moment. After a time $\frac{\pi}{4}$ s, a breakdown occurs in one of the capacitors, and the resistance between its plates becomes zero. The amplitude of charge oscillations on the undamaged capacitor is $\sqrt{\alpha}$ mC. Fill α in OMR sheet.

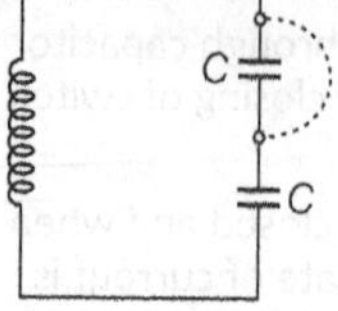

7 The 300 μF capacitor in figure is initially charged to 16 V, the 1200 μF capacitor is uncharged and the switches are both open. What is the maximum voltage (in volts) to which you can charge the 1200 μF capacitor by the proper closing and opening of the two switches.

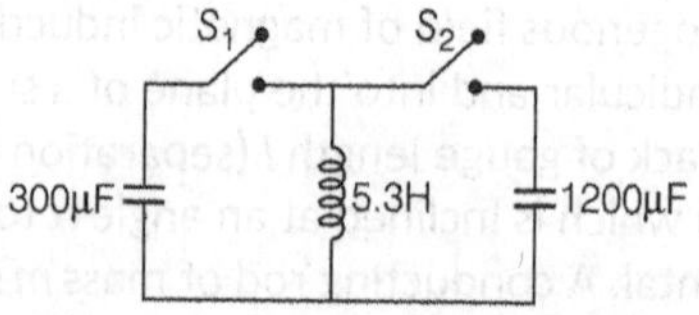

8 Two coils, 1 and 2, have a mutual inductance $= M$ and resistance R each. A current flows in coil 1, which varies with time as : $i_1 = kt^2$, where k is a constant and t is time. The total charge that has flown through coil 2, between $t = 0$ and $t = T$ is $\left(\frac{\lambda}{1-\lambda}\right)\frac{kMT^2}{R}$. Find $\left(\frac{1}{\lambda}\right)$.

Previous Years Questions

JEE Main

1 Two coils have mutual inductance 0.002 H. The current changes in the first coil according to the relation $i = i_0 \sin \omega t$, where $i_0 = 5$A and $\omega = 50\pi$ rad/s. The maximum value of emf in the second coil is $\frac{\pi}{\alpha}$ V. The value of α is .... **[2024, 27 Jan Shift-I]**

2 A capacitor of capacitance 100 μF is charged to a potential of 12 V and connected to a 6.4 mH inductor to produce oscillations. The maximum current in the circuit would be **[2024, 29 Jan Shift-I]**

(a) 2.0 A (b) 1.5 A
(c) 1.2 A (d) 3.2 A

3 A small square loop of wire of side l is placed inside a large square loop of wire of side $L(L = l^2)$. The loops are coplanar and their centers coincide. The value of the mutual inductance of the system is $\sqrt{x} \times 10^{-7}$ H, where $x = \ldots$. **[2024, 31 Jan Shift-I]**

4 A 12 V battery connected to a coil of resistance 6 Ω through a switch, drives a constant current in the circuit. The switch is opened in 1 ms. The emf induced across the coil is 20 V. The inductance of the coil is **[2023, 15 April Shift-I]**

(a) 5 mH (b) 10 mH (c) 12 mH (d) 8 mH

5 Find the mutual inductance in the arrangement, when a small circular loop of wire of radius R is placed inside a large square loop of wire of side L ($L >> R$). The loops are coplanar and their centres coincide **[2023, 29 Jan, Shift-I]**

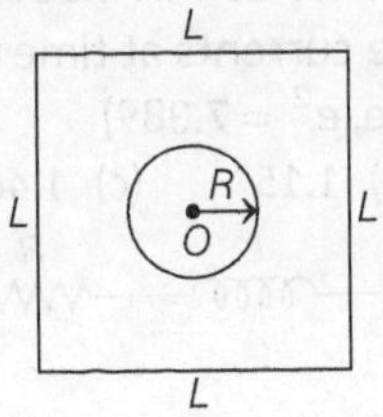

(a) $M = \frac{2\sqrt{2}\mu_0 R^2}{L}$ (b) $M = \frac{2\sqrt{2}\mu_0 R}{L^2}$

(c) $M = \frac{\sqrt{2}\mu_0 R}{L^2}$ (d) $M = \frac{\sqrt{2}\mu_0 R^2}{L}$

6 Two concentric circular coils with radii l cm and 1000 cm, and number of turns 10 and 200 respectively are placed coaxially with centers coinciding. The mutual inductance of this arrangement will be .... $\times 10^{-8}$ H. (Take, $\pi^2 = 10$) **[2023, 6 April Shift-II]**

7 Three identical resistors with resistance $R = 12\ \Omega$ and two identical inductors with self inductance $L = 5$ mH are connected to an ideal battery with emf of 12 V as shown in figure. The current through the battery long after the switch has been closed will be .... A. **[2023, 24 Jan, Shift-II]**

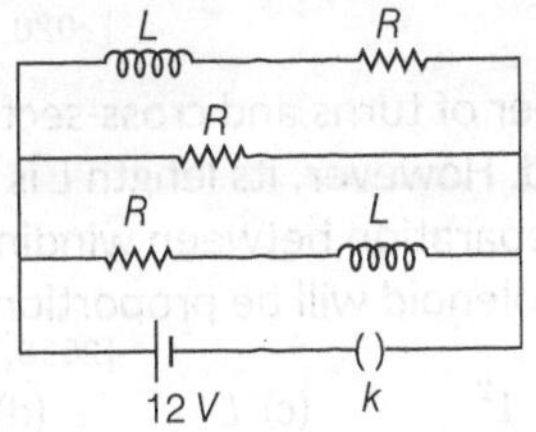

8

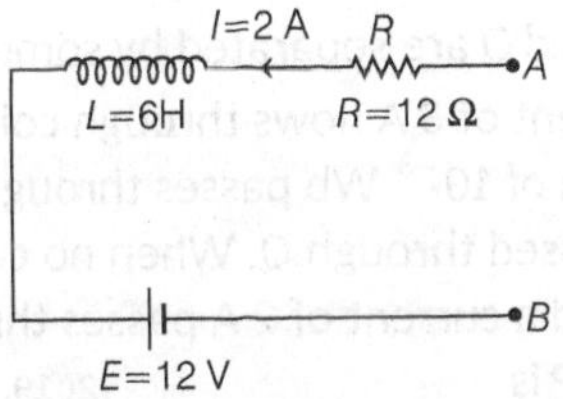

[2023, 30 Jan Shift-II]

As per the given figure, if $dI/dt = -1$ A/s, then the value of V_{AB} at this instant will be .... V.

9 A coil has an inductance of 2H and resistance of 4 Ω. A 10 V is applied across the coil. The energy stored in the magnetic field after the current has built up to its equilibrium value will be .... $\times 10^{-2}$ J. **[2023, 11 April Shift-II]**

10 In the given figure, an inductor and a resistor are connected in series with a battery of emf E volt, $E^a / 2b$ J/s represents the maximum rate at which the energy is stored in the magnetic field (inductor). The numerical value of b/a will be .... **[2023, 13 April Shift-I]**

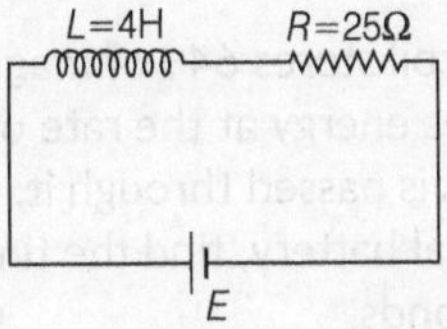

11 An oscillating LC circuit consists of a 75 mH inductor and a 1.2 μF capacitor. If the maximum charge to the capacitor is 2.7 μC. The maximum current in the circuit will be .... mA. **[2023, 8 April Shift-I]**

12 For the given circuit, the current through battery of 6 V just after closing the switch S will be .... A. **[2022, 28 July Shift-II]**

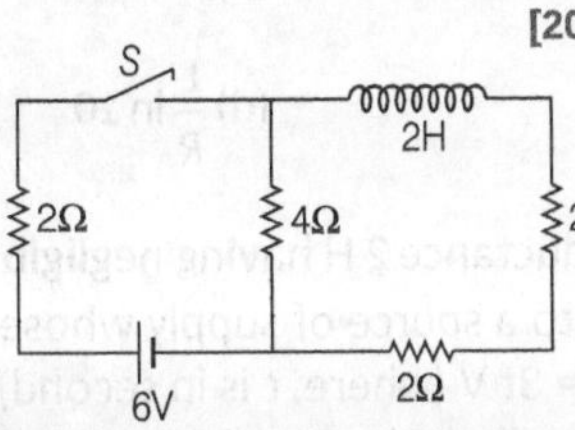

13 A small square loop of wire of side l is placed inside a large square loop of wire L ($L >> l$). Both loops are coplanar and their centres coincide at point O as shown in figure. The mutual inductance of the system is **[2022, 25 July Shift-I]**

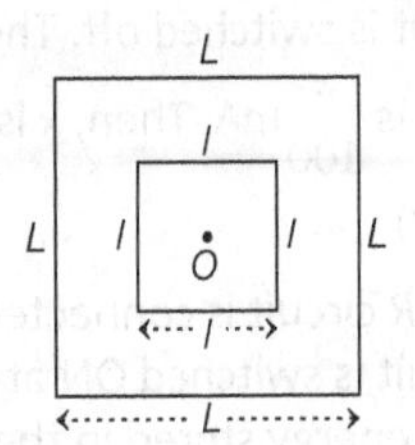

(a) $\frac{2\sqrt{2}\mu L^2}{\pi l}$ (b) $\frac{\mu_0 l^2}{2\sqrt{2}\,\pi L}$ (c) $\frac{2\sqrt{2}\mu_0 l^2}{\pi L}$ (d) $\frac{\mu_0 L^2}{2\sqrt{2}\,\pi l}$

14 The current in a coil of self inductance 2.0 H is increasing according to $I = 2\sin t^2$ A. The amount of energy spent during the period when current changes from 0 to 2 A is ... J. **[2022, 25 June Shift-I]**

15 A small square loop of side a and one turn is placed inside a larger square loop of side b and one turn ($b >> a$). The two loops are coplanar with their centres coinciding. If a current I is passed in the square loop of side b, then the coefficient of mutual inductance between the two loops is **[2021, 31 Aug. Shift-I]**

(a) $\frac{\mu_0}{4\pi} 8\sqrt{2} \frac{a^2}{b}$ (b) $\frac{\mu_0}{4\pi} \frac{8\sqrt{2}}{a}$

(c) $\frac{\mu_0}{4\pi} 8\sqrt{2} \frac{b^2}{a}$ (d) $\frac{\mu_0}{4\pi} \frac{8\sqrt{2}}{b}$

16 An inductor coil stores 64 J of magnetic field energy and dissipates energy at the rate of 640 W when a current of 8A is passed through it. If this coil is joined across an ideal battery, find the time constant of the circuit in seconds. **[2021, 26 Aug. Shift-I]**

(a) 0.4 (b) 0.8
(c) 0.125 (d) 0.2

17 The time taken for the magnetic energy to reach 25% of its maximum value, when a solenoid of resistance R, inductance L is connected to a battery, is **[2021, 18 March Shift-II]**

(a) $\frac{L}{R} \ln 5$ (b) infinite

(c) $\frac{L}{R} \ln 2$ (d) $\frac{L}{R} \ln 10$

18 A coil of inductance 2 H having negligible resistance is connected to a source of supply whose voltage is given by $V = 3t$ V (where, t is in second). If the voltage is applied when $t = 0$, then the energy stored in the coil after 4 s is .... J. **[2021, 25 Feb Shift-I]**

19 An inductor of 10 mH is connected to a 20 V battery through a resistor of 10 kΩ and a switch. After a long time, when maximum current is set up in the circuit, the current is switched off. The current in the circuit after 1 μs is $\frac{x}{100}$ mA. Then, x is equal to .... (Take, $e^{-1} = 0.37$) **[2021, 25 July Shift-I]**

20 A series L-R circuit is connected to a battery of emf V. If the circuit is switched ON at $t = 0$, then the time at which the energy stored in the inductor reaches $\left(\frac{1}{n}\right)$ times of its maximum value, is **[2020, 4 Sep Shift-II]**

(a) $\frac{L}{R} \ln\left(\frac{\sqrt{n}+1}{\sqrt{n}-1}\right)$ (b) $\frac{L}{R} \ln\left(\frac{\sqrt{n}}{\sqrt{n}+1}\right)$

(c) $\frac{L}{R} \ln\left(\frac{\sqrt{n}-1}{\sqrt{n}}\right)$ (d) $\frac{L}{R} \ln\left(\frac{\sqrt{n}}{\sqrt{n}-1}\right)$

21 A part of a complete circuit is shown in the figure. At some instant, the value of current I is 1 A and it is decreasing at the rate of 10^2 As^{-1}. The value of the potential difference $V_P - V_Q$ (in volt) at that instant, is ....

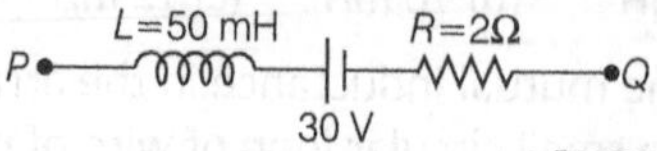

[2020, 6 Sep Shift-I]

22 An emf of 20 V is applied at time $t = 0$ to a circuit containing in series 10 mH inductor and 5Ω resistor. The ratio of the currents at time $t = \infty$ and at $t = 40$ s is close to (Take, $e^2 = 7.389$) **[2020, 7 Jan Shift-II]**

(a) 1.06 (b) 1.15 (c) 1.46 (d) 0.84

23

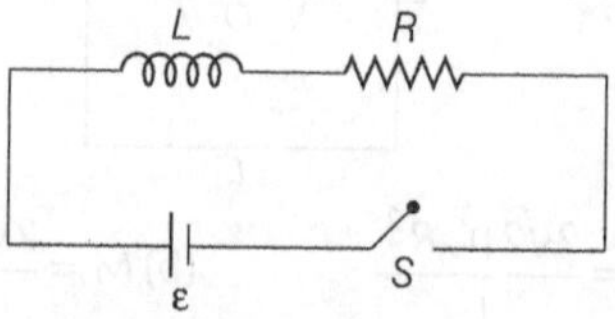

As shown in the figure, a battery of emf ε is connected to an inductor L and resistance R in series. The switch is closed at $t = 0$. The total charge that flows from the battery, between $t = 0$ and $t = t_c$ (t_c is the time constant of the circuit) is **[2020, 8 Jan Shift-II]**

(a) $\frac{\varepsilon L}{R^2}\left(1 - \frac{1}{e}\right)$ (b) $\frac{\varepsilon L}{R^2}$

(c) $\frac{\varepsilon R}{eL^2}$ (d) $\frac{\varepsilon L}{eR^2}$

24 In a fluorescent lamp choke (a small transformer) 100 V of reverse voltage is produced when the choke current changes uniformly from 0.25A to 0 in a duration of 0.025 ms.The self-inductance of the choke (in mH) is estimated to be .... **[2020, 9 Jan Shift-I]**

25 The total number of turns and cross-section area in a solenoid is fixed. However, its length L is varied by adjusting the separation between windings. The inductance of solenoid will be proportional to **[2019, 9 April Shift-I]**

(a) $1/L$ (b) L^2 (c) L (d) $1/L^2$

26 Two coils P and Q are separated by some distance. When a current of 3 A flows through coil P, a magnetic flux of 10^{-3} Wb passes through Q. No current is passed through Q. When no current passes through P and a current of 2 A passes through Q, the flux through P is **[2019, 9 April Shift-II]**

(a) 6.67×10^{-3} Wb (b) 6.67×10^{-4} Wb
(c) 3.67×10^{-3} Wb (d) 3.67×10^{-4} Wb

27 The self-induced emf of a coil is 25 V. When the current in it is changed at uniform rate from 10 A to 25 A in 1s, the change in the energy of the inductance is **[2019, 10 Jan Shift-II]**

(a) 437.5 J (b) 740 J
(c) 637.5 J (d) 540 J

28 There are two long coaxial solenoids of same length l. The inner and outer coils have radii r_1 and r_2 and number of turns per unit length n_1 and n_2, respectively. The ratio of mutual inductance to the self-inductance of the inner coil is **[2019, 11 Jan Shift-I]**

(a) $\frac{n_2}{n_1} \cdot \frac{r_1}{r_2}$ (b) $\frac{n_2}{n_1} \cdot \frac{r_2^2}{r_1^2}$

(c) $\frac{n_2}{n_1}$ (d) $\frac{n_1}{n_2}$

29 A copper wire is wound on a wooden frame, whose shape is that of an equilateral triangle. If the linear dimension of each side of the frame is increased by a factor of 3, keeping the number of turns of the coil per unit length of the frame the same, then the self-inductance of the coil **[2019, 11 Jan Shift-II]**

(a) increases by a factor of 3
(b) decreases by a factor of $9\sqrt{3}$
(c) increases by a factor of 27
(d) decreases by a factor of 9

30 A 20 H inductor coil is connected to a 10 ohm resistance in series as shown in figure. The time at which rate of dissipation of energy (Joule's heat) across resistance is equal to the rate at which magnetic energy is stored in the inductor, is **[2019, 8 April Shift-I]**

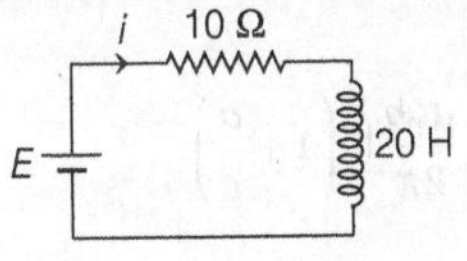

(a) $\frac{2}{\ln 2}$ (b) $\frac{1}{2}\ln 2$
(c) $2\ln 2$ (d) $\ln 2$

31 In the circuit shown,

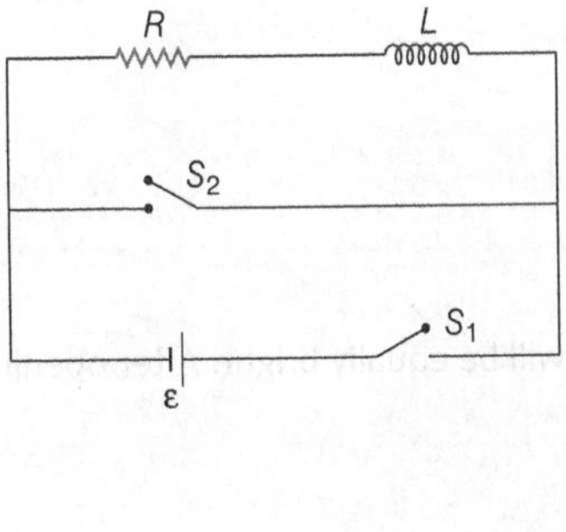

The switch S_1 is closed at time $t = 0$ and the switch S_2 is kept open. At some later time (t_0), the switch S_1 is opened and S_2 is closed. The behaviour of the current I as a function of time 't' is given by **(2019)**

(a)
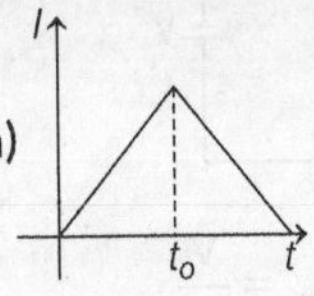

(b)
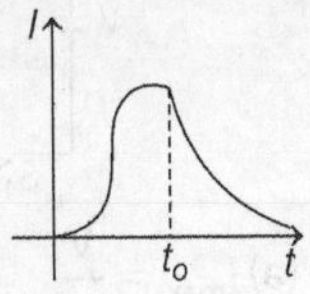

(c)
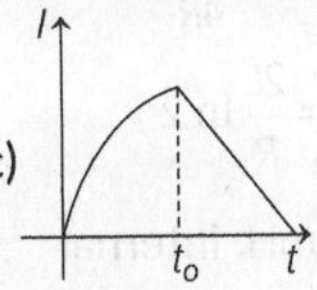

(d)
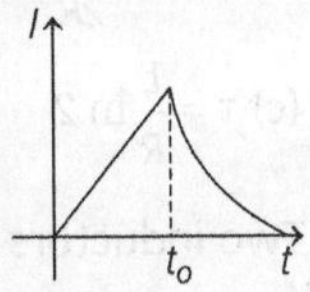

JEE Advanced

1. Consider an L-C circuit, with inductance $L = 0.1$ H and capacitance $C = 10^{-3}$ F, kept on a plane. The area of the circuit is 1 m^2. It is placed in a constant magnetic field of strength B_0 which is perpendicular to the plane of the circuit. At time $t = 0$, the magnetic field strength starts increasing linearly as $B = B_0 + \beta t$ with $\beta = 0.04$ Ts^{-1}. The maximum magnitude of the current in the circuit is .... mA. **(2022)**

2. The inductors of two LR circuits are placed next to each other, as shown in the figure. The values of the self-inductance of the inductors, resistances, mutual-inductance and applied voltages are specified in the given circuit. After both the switches are closed simultaneously, the total work done by the batteries against the induced EMF in the inductors by the time the currents reach their steady state values is________ mJ. **(2020)**

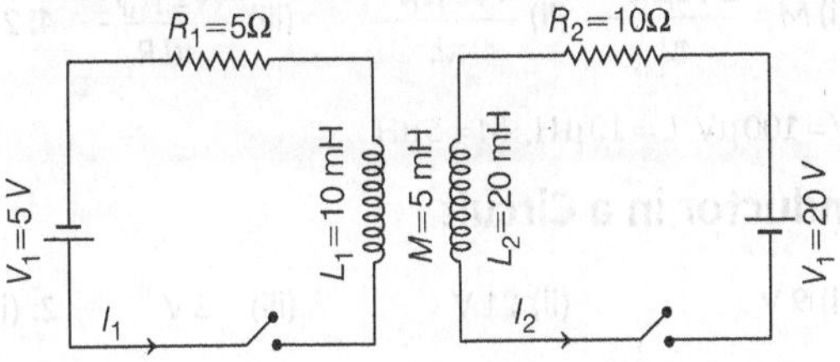

3. In the figure below, the switches S_1 and S_2 are closed simultaneously at $t = 0$ and a current starts to flow in the circuit. Both the batteries have the same magnitude of the electromotive force (emf) and the polarities are as indicated in the figure. Ignore mutual inductance between the inductors. The current I in the middle wire reaches its maximum magnitude I_{max} at time $t = \tau$. Which of the following statements is (are) true ? **(2018)**

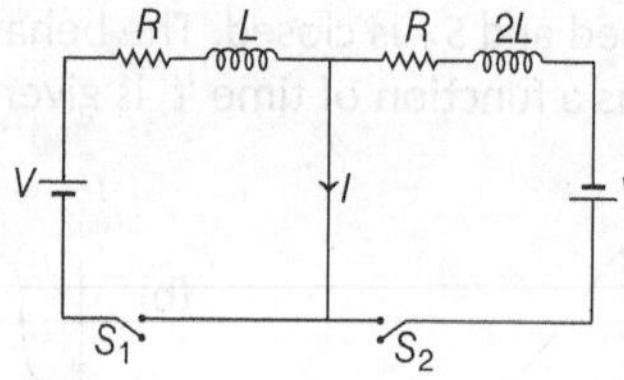

(a) $I_{max} = \dfrac{V}{2R}$ (b) $I_{max} = \dfrac{V}{4R}$

(c) $\tau = \dfrac{L}{R}\ln 2$ (d) $\tau = \dfrac{2L}{R}\ln 2$

4. Two inductors L_1 (inductance 1mH, internal resistance $3\,\Omega$) and L_2 (inductance 2 mH, internal resistance $4\,\Omega$), and a resistor R (resistance $12\,\Omega$) are all connected in parallel across a 5V battery. The circuit is switched on at time $t=0$. The ratio of the maximum to the minimum current (I_{max}/I_{min}) drawn from the battery is **(2016)**

5. A circular wire loop of radius R is placed in the x-y plane centred at the origin O. A square loop of side a ($a << R$) having two turns is placed with its centre at $z = \sqrt{3}\,R$ along the axis of the circular wire loop, as shown in figure.
The plane of the square loop makes an angle of 45° with respect to the Z-axis.
If the mutual inductance between the loops is given by $\dfrac{\mu_0 a^2}{2^{p/2} R}$, then the value of p is **(2012)**

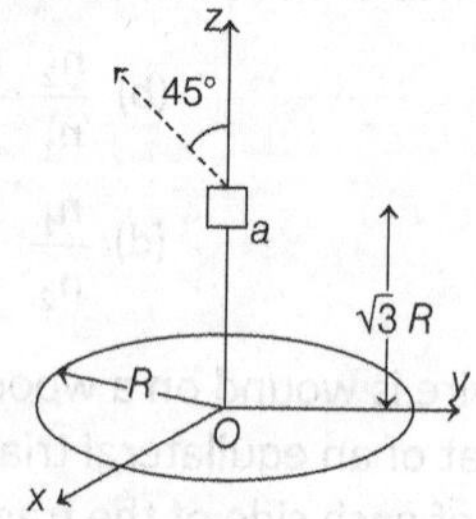

Answer Key

Level 1

6.1 Self-Inductance

1. 0.2 H 2. 0.4 H 3. – 0.14 V 4. (i) 78.96 mH, (ii) 78.96 H 5. $\dfrac{2B\pi R^2}{L}$ 6. $\dfrac{\mu_0 l}{2\pi}\ln\dfrac{b}{a}$

6.2 Mutual Inductance

1. (i) decreases (ii) decreases (iii) increases 2. (i) $\dfrac{\mu_0\pi a_1^2}{2a_2}$ (ii) 0 (iii) $\dfrac{\mu_0\pi a_1^2\cos\theta}{2a_2}$

3. (i) $M = \dfrac{2\sqrt{2}\mu_0 l^2}{\pi L}$ (ii) $\dfrac{4\sqrt{2}\,\mu_0 l^2}{\pi L}$ (iii) $\dfrac{4\sqrt{2}\,\mu_0 l^2}{\pi LR}$ 4. 2.0×10^{-2} H 5. $M = \dfrac{\mu_0 b}{2\pi}\ln\left(1+\dfrac{a}{c}\right)$

6. $V = 100\,\mu V, L = 10\,\mu H, M = 5\,\mu H$

6.3 Inductor in a Circuit

1. (i) 9 V (ii) 21 V (iii) – 3 V 2. (i) $i = \dfrac{\varepsilon t}{L}$ (ii) $\dfrac{\varepsilon^2 t^2}{2L}$ 3. $(42 + 20t)$ V

6.4 *L-R* Circuit at $t = 0$ and $t = \infty$

1. (i) $i_3 = 0, i_1 = i_2 = \dfrac{\varepsilon}{2R}, \dfrac{di}{dt} = \dfrac{\varepsilon}{2L}$ (ii) $i_1 = \dfrac{2\varepsilon}{3R}, i_2 = i_3 = \dfrac{\varepsilon}{3R}, \dfrac{di}{dt} = 0.$

2. $\dfrac{di}{dt} = -\dfrac{6\varepsilon}{L}$ 3. $i_1 = \dfrac{2V}{R}$(up), $i_2 = i_3 = \dfrac{V}{R}$ (down)

4. After closing the key, initially bulb B_1 is brighter but after a long time both bulbs will be equally bright. After opening the key, brightness of both the bulbs will go on decreasing.

6.5 Growth of Current in Series *L-R* Circuit

1. (i) 0.17 A (ii) 0.03 J 2. 4 H 3. 0.66 V 4. $\frac{2}{e}$ A/s, $\frac{2}{e}$ V

5. (i) -2.5×10^3 V/s (ii) $-2.5\times10^3\times e^{-5}$ V/s

6. (i) 12.6 mW, (ii) 8 mW, (iii) 4.6 mW 7. (i) 35 ms (ii) 61 ms (iii) 61 ms

8. $i_0 e^{-\frac{Rt}{L}}+\frac{\varepsilon}{R}\left(1-e^{-\frac{Rt}{L}}\right)$ 9. $\frac{\varepsilon}{3R}\left(1-e^{-\frac{3Rt}{2L}}\right)$

6.6 Decay of Current in *L-R* Circuit (Without Battery)

1. (i) 0.14 s, (ii) 28 Ω 2. (i) $\frac{\varepsilon(R_1+R_2)}{R_1R_2}$ (ii) $\frac{L}{R_1+R_2}$ (iii) $\frac{\varepsilon}{R_1 e}$ 3. $\frac{L\varepsilon^2}{2R_1^2}$ 4. $\frac{LI}{2R}$

6.7 Combination of Inductors

1. 6 H, 4 H 2. $i_1=\frac{EL_2}{R(L_1+L_2)}$, $i_2=\frac{EL_1}{R(L_1+L_2)}$ 3. (i) $L_1+\frac{L_2L_3}{L_2+L_3}+L_4$ (ii) 1 H 4. 3 *L* 5. 0.1 H

6.8 Magnetic Energy Density

1. 2.55×10^{-14} J 2. $\frac{\mu_0 i^2}{16\pi}$

6.9 L-C Oscillations

1. (i) $\left|\frac{di}{dt}\right|=10^4$ A/s (ii) 0 (iii) $i_{max}=2.0$ A (iv) $|Q|=173\,\mu$C

2. (i) 8 mH, (ii) 398 Hz, (iii) $I=\frac{1}{\sqrt{10}}\cos\left(2500t+\frac{\pi}{4}\right)$, $Q=\frac{40}{\sqrt{10}}\sin\left(2500t+\frac{\pi}{4}\right)\mu$C

3. (i) 5×10^4 rad/s (ii) 1.05×10^{-5} s, (iii) 17.32 μC

Level 2

Single Choice Correct Questions

1. (b)	2. (a)	3. (c)	4. (b)	5. (d)	6. (d)	7. (d)	8. (b)	9. (a)	10. (d)
11. (c)	12. (b)	13. (c)	14. (a)	15. (d)	16. (a)	17. (d)	18. (b)	19. (a)	20. (d)
21. (d)	22. (b)	23. (a)	24. (a)	25. (a)	26. (a)	27. (c)	28. (d)	29. (c)	30. (b)
31. (a)	32. (c)	33. (a)	34. (d)	35. (c)	36. (a)	37. (d)	38. (d)	39. (b)	40. (b)
41. (b)	42. (b)	43. (d)	44. (c)	45. (a)	46. (a)	47. (c)	48. (a)		

Numerical Value Questions

1. 1	2. 100	3. 1	4. 3	5. 8	6. 3	7. 2
8. 4	9. 2	10. 5				

Level 3

Single Choice Correct Questions

1. (d)	2. (b)	3. (a)	4. (c)	5. (a)	6. (a)	7. (d)	8. (b)	9. (b)	10. (a)
11. (d)	12. (d)	13. (b)	14. (c)	15. (a)	16. (a)	17. (d)	18. (b)	19. (b)	20. (c)
21. (b)	22. (a)	23. (b)	24. (b)	25. (c)					

Multiple Choice(s) Correct Questions

1. (a, b, c, d) 2. (b, c) 3. (b, d) 4. (a, c) 5. (a, b, c) 6. (b, d) 7. (a, b)
8. (a, c, d) 9. (b, d) 10. (a, c, d) 11. (a, c, d) 12. (a, c)

Comprehension Based Questions

1. (a) 2. (a) 3. (b) 4. (b) 5. (d) 6. (c) 7. (d) 8. (a) 9. (a) 10. (c)
11. (a) 12. (c) 13. (b) 14. (d) 15. (b) 16. (a) 17. (b) 18. (c) 19. (b) 20. (a)
21. (a) 22. (c) 23. (c)

Match the Columns Questions

1. A-P; B-Q; C-R; D-S 2. A - Q ; B - P ; C - R 3. A- (P, Q, S, T) ; B (P, Q, S, T) ; C (R, S) ; D-(S, T)

Numerical Value Questions

1. 4 2. 2.10 3. 2 4. 3 5. 4 6. 50 7. 8 8. 2

Previous Years Questions

JEE Main

1. (2) 2. (b) 3. (128) 4. (b) 5. (a) 6. (4) 7. (3) 8. (30) 9. (625) 10. (25)
11. (9) 12. (1) 13. (c) 14. (4) 15. (a) 16. (d) 17. (c) 18. (144) 19. (74) 20. (d)
21. (33) 22. (a) 23. (d) 24. (10) 25. (a) 26. (b) 27. (a) 28. (c) 29. (c) 30. (c)
31. (b)

JEE Advanced

1. (4) 2. (55) 3. (b,d) 4. (8) 5. (7)

SOLUTIONS

Level 1

6.1 Self-Inductance

1. $N\phi = Li \Rightarrow 100 \times 10^{-5} = L(5 \times 10^{-3}) \Rightarrow L = 0.2\text{ H}$

2. $\varepsilon_{avg} = L\dfrac{\Delta i}{\Delta t} \Rightarrow 16 = L\dfrac{(4-2)}{0.05} \Rightarrow L = 0.4\text{ H}$

3. $\varepsilon = -L\dfrac{di}{dt} = -10 \times 10^{-3} \times (6t + 2)$

   At $t = 2$ s, $\varepsilon = -10^{-2}(6 \times 2 + 2) = -0.14$ V

4. (i) $L = \mu_0 n^2 V = 4\pi \times 10^{-7} \times \left(\dfrac{2000}{0.5}\right)^2 \times \pi(0.05)^2\,(0.5)$

   $= 78.96$ mH

   (ii) $L = \mu_0 \mu_r n^2 V = 1000\,(78.96 \times 10^{-3}) = 78.96$ H

5. $\phi = Li \Rightarrow \Delta\phi = L\Delta i \Rightarrow BA - (-BA) = L(i - 0)$

   $\Rightarrow \quad i = \dfrac{2BA}{L} = \dfrac{2B\pi R^2}{L}$

6. Magnetic field at a distance r from the axis $= \dfrac{\mu_0 i}{2\pi r}$

   Flux through small strip on the rectangle

   $d\phi = \left(\dfrac{\mu_0 i}{2\pi r}\right)(l dr)\cos 0°$

   Flux through rectangle

   $\phi = \int d\phi = \dfrac{\mu_0 il}{2\pi}\displaystyle\int_a^b \dfrac{dr}{r}$

   $\Rightarrow \quad \phi = \dfrac{\mu_0 il}{2\pi}\ln\left(\dfrac{b}{a}\right)$

   Self-inductance,

   $L = \dfrac{\phi}{i} = \dfrac{\mu_0 l}{2\pi}\ln\left(\dfrac{b}{a}\right)$

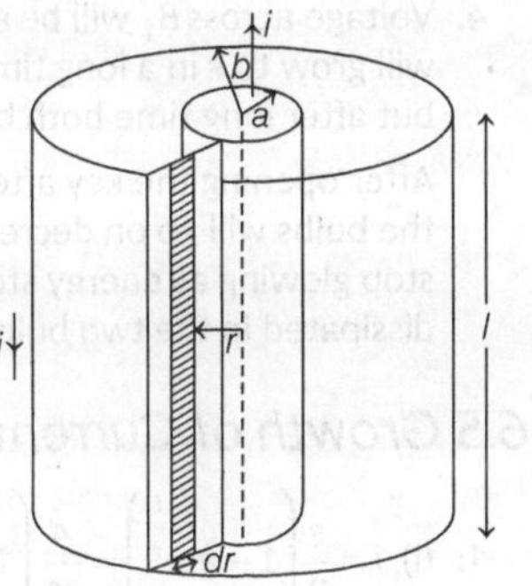

6.2 Mutual Inductance

1. (i) Mutual inductance decreases as flux linked decreases.
   (ii) Mutual inductance decreases as $M \propto N$
   (iii) Mutual inductance increases as $M \propto \mu_r$

2. Let current through the bigger loop be i. Flux through smaller loop $= \phi = \left(\dfrac{\mu_0 i}{2a_2}\right)\pi a_1^2 \cos\theta$,

   $M = \dfrac{\phi}{i} = \dfrac{\mu_0 \pi a_1^2 \cos\theta}{2a_2}$

   (i) $\theta = 0° \Rightarrow M = \dfrac{\mu_0 \pi a_1^2}{2a_2}$

   (ii) $\theta = 90° \Rightarrow M = 0 \qquad \{\because \cos 90° = 0\}$

   (iii) $M = \dfrac{\mu_0 \pi a_1^2 \cos\theta}{2a_2}$

3. (i) Let current in the large loop be i.
   Magnetic field at the centre

   $= 4\left[\dfrac{\mu_0 i}{4\pi\left(\dfrac{L}{2}\right)}(\sin 45° + \sin 45°)\right]$

   $= 2\sqrt{2}\dfrac{\mu_0 i}{\pi L}$

   Flux through the smaller loop

   $= \left(2\sqrt{2}\dfrac{\mu_0 i}{\pi L}\right) l^2 \cos 0° = 2\sqrt{2}\dfrac{\mu_0 i l^2}{\pi L}$

   $M = \dfrac{\phi}{i} = \dfrac{2\sqrt{2}\,\mu_0 l^2}{\pi L}$

   (ii) $\varepsilon_2 = M\dfrac{di_1}{dt} = \dfrac{2\sqrt{2}\mu_0 l^2\,(2)}{\pi L} = \dfrac{4\sqrt{2}\,\mu_0 l^2}{\pi L}$

   (iii) $i_2 = \dfrac{\varepsilon_2}{R} = \dfrac{4\sqrt{2}\,\mu_0 l^2}{\pi L R}$

4.

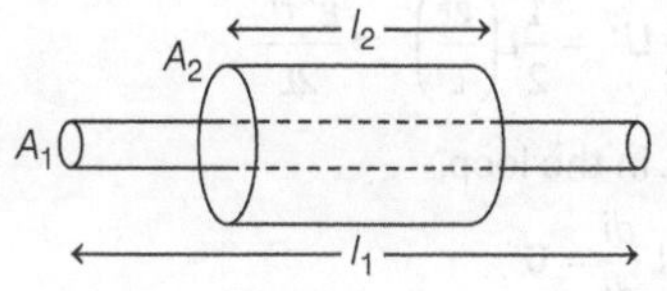

   $n_1 = \dfrac{N_1}{l_1}$

   $= \dfrac{4000}{0.2}$

   $= 20000$

   and $n_2 = \dfrac{N_2}{l_2} = \dfrac{2000}{0.1} = 20000$

   Let current in the bigger solenoid be i.
   Magnetic field inside bigger solenoid $= \mu_0 n_2 i$

   $\phi =$ Flux through smaller solenoid $= (\mu_0 n_2 i)\left(\dfrac{n_1 l_1}{2}\right) A_1 \cos 0°$

   $M = \dfrac{\phi}{i} = \dfrac{\mu_0 n_1 n_2 A_1 l_1}{2}$

   $= \dfrac{4 \times 3.14 \times 10^{-7} \times 20000 \times 20000 \times 4 \times 10^{-4} \times 20 \times 10^{-2}}{2}$

   $= 2 \times 10^{-2}$ H

5. Let current in the long wire be i.

   $\int d\phi = \displaystyle\int_c^{c+a} \left(\dfrac{\mu_0 i}{2\pi x}\right)(b\,dx)\cos 0°$

   $\phi = \dfrac{\mu_0 ib}{2\pi}\ln\left(\dfrac{a+c}{c}\right)$

   $M = \dfrac{\phi}{i} = \dfrac{\mu_0 b}{2\pi}\ln\left(\dfrac{a+c}{c}\right)$

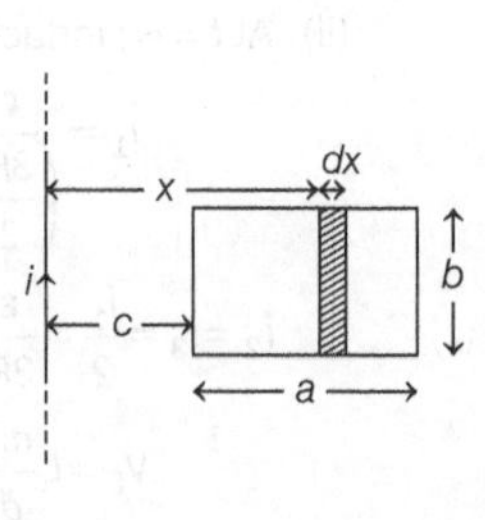

6. $\phi_1 = L_1 i_1 \Rightarrow 10^{-5} = L_1(1) \Rightarrow L_1 = 10^{-5}$ H

$$L_2 = L_1 = 10^{-5}\text{ H} = 10\,\mu\text{H}$$

$$M = K\sqrt{L_1 L_2} = 0.5\sqrt{10^{-5} \times 10^{-5}} = 5\,\mu\text{H}$$

$$\varepsilon_2 = M\frac{di_1}{dt} = 0.5 \times 10^{-5}\left[\frac{1-(-1)}{0.1}\right] = 100\,\mu\text{V}$$

6.3 Inductor in a Circuit

1. $V_A - 3\frac{di}{dt} - 5 - i(2) = V_B$

$$\Rightarrow V_A - V_B = 5 + 2i + 3\frac{di}{dt}$$

(i) $V_A - V_B = 5 + 2(2) + 0 = 9$ V

(ii) $V_A - V_B = 5 + 2(2) + 3(4) = 21$ V

(iii) $V_A - V_B = 5 + 2(2) + 3(-4) = -3$ V

2. (i) Applying KVL in the loop,

$$+\varepsilon - L\frac{di}{dt} = 0$$

$$\Rightarrow \int_0^i di = \frac{\varepsilon}{L}\int_0^t dt \Rightarrow i = \frac{\varepsilon t}{L}$$

(ii) $U = \frac{1}{2}Li^2 = \frac{1}{2}L\left(\frac{\varepsilon t}{L}\right)^2 = \frac{\varepsilon^2 t^2}{2L}$

3. Using KVL in the loop,

$$+\varepsilon - iR - L\frac{di}{dt} = 0$$

$$\Rightarrow \quad \varepsilon = iR + L\frac{di}{dt} = (3+5t)4 + 6(5) = (42+20t)\text{ V}$$

6.4 LR Circuit at $t = 0$ and $t = \infty$

1. (i) At $t = 0$, inductor acts as open circuit.

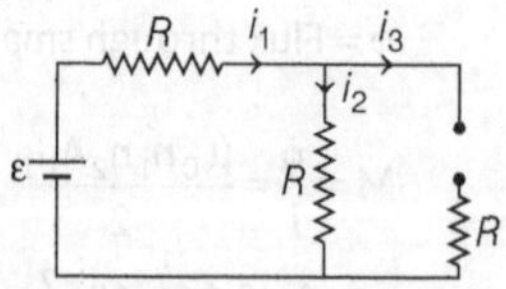

$$i_3 = 0;$$

$$i_1 = i_2 = \frac{\varepsilon}{2R}$$

$$V_C - V_D = L\frac{di_3}{dt} = i_2 R \Rightarrow \frac{di_3}{dt} = \frac{\varepsilon}{2L}$$

(ii) At $t = \infty$; inductor acts as short-circuit.

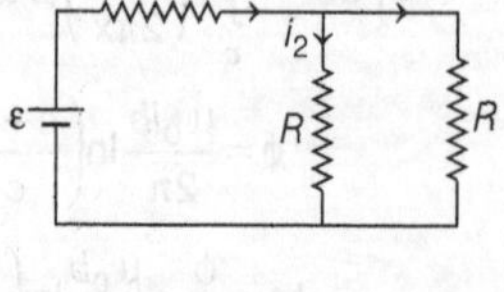

$$i_1 = \frac{\varepsilon}{\left(\frac{3R}{2}\right)} = \frac{2\varepsilon}{3R};$$

$$i_2 = i_3 = \frac{i_1}{2} = \frac{\varepsilon}{3R}$$

$$V_L = L\frac{di_3}{dt} = 0 \Rightarrow \frac{di_3}{dt} = 0$$

2. When S_1 is closed for a long time and S_2 is open, current through inductor $= \frac{\varepsilon}{R}$ (down) Current through inductor doesn't change instantly.

Just after closing S_2 and opening S_1,

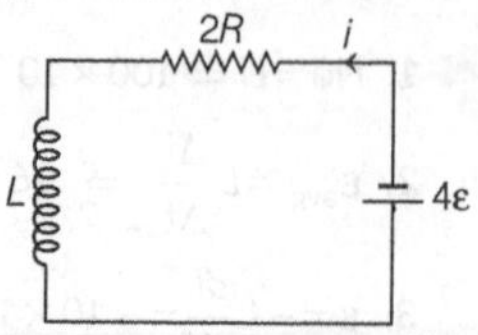

$$-4\varepsilon - L\frac{di}{dt} - i(2R) = 0$$

$$\Rightarrow \frac{di}{dt} = -\left(\frac{4\varepsilon + 2iR}{L}\right) = -\frac{6\varepsilon}{L}$$

3. In steady state, inductor acts as short circuit.

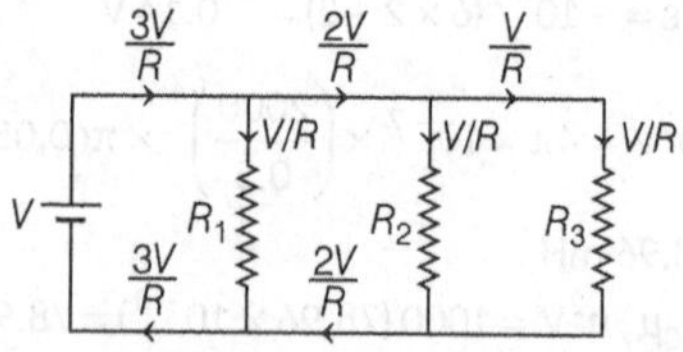

Just after opening the switch, currents through the inductors will be unchanged.

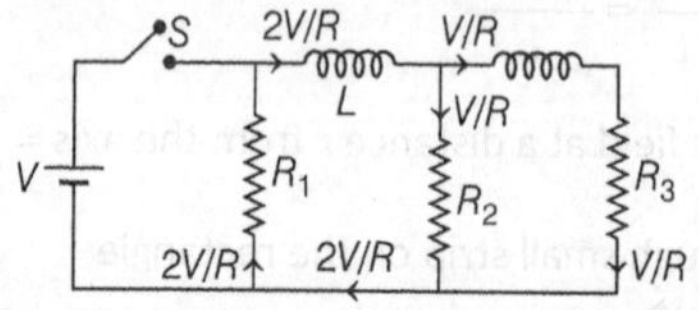

4. Voltage across B_1 will be ε instantly but voltage across B_1 will grow to ε in a long time. So, initially bulb B_1 is brighter but after long time both bulbs will be equally brighter.

After opening the key after a long time, brightness of both the bulbs will go on decreasing and long time later they will stop glowing as energy stored in the inductor will get dissipated in the two bulbs.

6.5 Growth of Current in Series LR Circuit

1. (i) $i = \frac{\varepsilon}{R}\left(1 - e^{-\frac{t}{\tau}}\right) = \frac{4}{20}\left(1 - e^{-\frac{0.2}{0.1}}\right) = 0.17$ A

(ii) $U = \frac{1}{2}Li^2 = \frac{1}{2}(2)(0.17)^2 = 0.03$ J

2. $i = \frac{\varepsilon}{R}\left(1 - e^{-\frac{t}{\tau}}\right) \Rightarrow 63 \times 10^{-3} = \frac{0.4}{4}\left(1 - e^{-\frac{t}{\tau}}\right)$

$$\Rightarrow \tau = 1\text{ s}$$

Now, $\tau = \frac{L}{R} \Rightarrow L = \tau R = (1)(4) = 4$ H

3. $\tau = \frac{L}{R} = \frac{5}{100} = 0.05$ s

$$i = \frac{\varepsilon}{R}\left(1 - e^{-\frac{t}{\tau}}\right) = \frac{2}{100}\left(1 - e^{-\frac{20\times10^{-3}}{5\times10^{-2}}}\right) = 6.6\text{ mA}$$

$$V = iR = (6.6 \times 10^{-3})(100) = 0.66\text{ V}$$

4. $i=\frac{\varepsilon}{R}\left(1-e^{-\frac{Rt}{L}}\right) \Rightarrow \frac{di}{dt}=\frac{\varepsilon}{L}e^{-\frac{Rt}{L}}$

At $t=50$ ms; $\frac{di}{dt}=\frac{2}{1}e^{-\left(\frac{20\times 50\times 10^{-3}}{1}\right)}=\left(\frac{2}{e}\right)$ A/s

$L\frac{di}{dt}=1\left(\frac{2}{e}\right)=\left(\frac{2}{e}\right)$ V

5. $V=L\frac{di}{dt}=\varepsilon e^{-\frac{Rt}{L}};\ \frac{dV}{dt}=-\frac{\varepsilon R}{L}e^{-\frac{Rt}{L}}$

(i) At $t=0$; $\frac{dV}{dt}=-\frac{5\times 10}{20\times 10^{-3}}=-2.5\times 10^{3}$ V/s

(ii) At $t=10$ ms; $\frac{dV}{dt}=-\frac{5\times 10}{20\times 10^{-3}}e^{-\left(\frac{10\times 10\times 10^{-3}}{20\times 10^{-3}}\right)}$

$=-2.5\times 10^{3}\times e^{-5}$ V/s

6. $i=\frac{\varepsilon}{R}\left(1-e^{-\frac{Rt}{L}}\right)=\frac{2}{200}\left(1-e^{-\frac{200\times 10\times 10^{-3}}{2}}\right)=6.3$ mA

(i) $P=\varepsilon i=2\times 6.3\times 10^{-3}=12.6$ mW

(ii) $P=i^2R=(6.3\times 10^{-3})^2\,(200)=8$ mW

(iii) $\frac{dV}{dt}=\varepsilon i-i^2R=4.6$ mW

7. (i) $i=\frac{\varepsilon}{R}\left(1-e^{-\frac{t}{\tau}}\right)=\frac{\varepsilon}{2R}\Rightarrow t=\tau\ln 2=50\times 0.693=35$ ms

(ii) $P=i^2R=\frac{1}{2}i_{max}^2R\Rightarrow i=\frac{i_{max}}{\sqrt{2}}$

$\Rightarrow \frac{\varepsilon}{\sqrt{2}R}=\frac{\varepsilon}{R}\left(1-e^{-\frac{t}{\tau}}\right)\Rightarrow t=-\tau\ln\left(1-\frac{1}{\sqrt{2}}\right)$

$\Rightarrow\quad t=61$ ms

(iii) $U=\frac{1}{2}Li^2=\frac{1}{2}\left(\frac{1}{2}Li_{max}^2\right)\Rightarrow i=\frac{i_{max}}{\sqrt{2}}$

$\Rightarrow t=61$ ms

8. Let current at any instant be i.

Applying KVL in the loop,

$+\varepsilon-iR-L\frac{di}{dt}=0$

$\Rightarrow\quad \int_{i_0}^{i}\frac{di}{\varepsilon-iR}=\frac{1}{L}\int_{0}^{t}dt$

$\Rightarrow \ln\left(\frac{\varepsilon-iR}{\varepsilon-i_0R}\right)=-\frac{R}{L}t$

$\Rightarrow\quad i=i_0e^{-\frac{Rt}{L}}+\frac{\varepsilon}{R}\left(1-e^{-\frac{Rt}{L}}\right)$

9. Using KVL,

$+\varepsilon-(i-x)R-iR=0$ ...(i)

$-L\frac{dx}{dt}-xR+(i-x)R=0$ ...(ii)

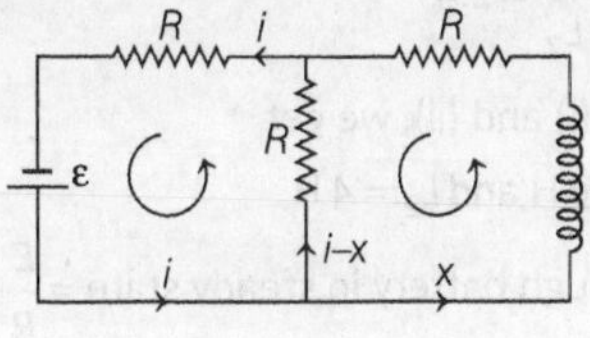

From Eqs. (i) and (ii), we get

$$\int_0^x\frac{dx}{\varepsilon-3xR}=\frac{1}{2L}\int_0^t dt\Rightarrow x=\frac{\varepsilon}{3R}\left(1-e^{-\frac{3Rt}{2L}}\right)$$

6.6 *Decay of Current in LR Circuit (Without Battery)*

1. (i) $i=i_0e^{-\frac{t}{\tau}}\Rightarrow 1=2e^{-\frac{0.1}{\tau}}$

$\Rightarrow \tau=0.14$ sec

(ii) $\tau=\frac{L}{R}\Rightarrow R=\frac{L}{\tau}=\frac{4}{0.14}=28\,\Omega$

2. (i) In steady state, inductor acts as short circuit.

$i=\frac{\varepsilon}{R_{eq}}=\frac{\varepsilon(R_1+R_2)}{R_1R_2}$

(ii) $\tau=\frac{L}{R_{eq}}=\frac{L}{R_1+R_2}$

(iii) At $t=0$; current through inductor $=\frac{\varepsilon}{R_1}$

$i=\frac{\varepsilon}{R_1}e^{-\frac{t}{\tau}}$

At $t=\tau$; $i=\frac{\varepsilon}{eR_1}$

3. Initial current through inductor $=\frac{\varepsilon}{R_1}$

Initial energy stored in the inductor $=\frac{1}{2}L\left(\frac{\varepsilon}{R_1}\right)^2=\frac{\varepsilon^2L}{2R_1^2}$

Total heat produced in R_2 = Initial energy stored in inductor

$=\frac{L\varepsilon^2}{2R_1^2}$

4. $U=\frac{1}{2}Li^2=\frac{1}{4}\left(\frac{1}{2}LI^2\right)\Rightarrow i=\frac{I}{2}$

$i=Ie^{-\frac{t}{\tau}}=\frac{I}{2}\Rightarrow t=\tau\ln 2$

$i=\frac{dq}{dt}=Ie^{-\frac{t}{\tau}}\Rightarrow\int dq=I\int_0^{\tau\ln 2}e^{-\frac{t}{\tau}}dt\ \Rightarrow q=\frac{\tau I}{2}=\frac{LI}{2R}$

6.7 Combination of Inductors

1. Let inductances be L_1 and L_2.

$$L_1 + L_2 = 10 \quad ...(i)$$

$$\frac{L_1 L_2}{L_1 + L_2} = 2.4 \quad ...(ii)$$

Solving Eqs. (i) and (ii), we get

$$L_1 = 6\text{ H and } L_2 = 4\text{ H}$$

2. Current through battery in steady state $= \frac{E}{R}$

For inductors in parallel, $i \propto \frac{1}{L}$

So, $i_1 = \left(\frac{L_2}{L_1 + L_2}\right)\frac{E}{R}$ and $i_2 = \left(\frac{L_1}{L_1 + L_2}\right)\frac{E}{R}$

3. (i) $L_{eq} = L_1 + \frac{L_2 L_3}{L_2 + L_3} + L_4$

(ii) $\frac{1}{L_{eq}} = \frac{1}{3} + \frac{1}{3} + \frac{1}{3} \Rightarrow L_{eq} = 1\text{ H}$

4. $L_{eq} = L_1 + L_2 + 2M$ where, $M = K\sqrt{L_1 L_2}$

$$\Rightarrow L_{eq} = L + L + 2\left(\frac{1}{2}\right)\sqrt{(L)(L)} = 3L$$

5. $M = K\sqrt{L_1 L_2} = 1\sqrt{(0.1)(0.1)}$ {$\because K = 1$ for tight coupling}

$$= 0.1\text{ H}$$

6.8 Magnetic Energy Density

1. Energy density $= \frac{B^2}{2\mu_0} = \frac{\left(\frac{\mu_0 i}{2\pi r}\right)^2}{2\mu_0} = \frac{\mu_0 i^2}{8\pi^2 r^2}$

Energy stored = Energy density × Volume

$$= \frac{4\pi \times 10^{-7} \times 4^2}{8\pi^2 (0.1)^2} \times 1 \times 10^{-9} = 2.55 \times 10^{-14}\text{ J}$$

2. Lets take a cylindrical shell of radius r and thickness dr.

Energy stored in cylindrical shell per unit length

$$= dU = \left(\frac{B^2}{2\mu_0}\right)(2\pi r dr)(1)$$

$$\Rightarrow \int dU = \int_0^R \frac{1}{2\mu_0}\left(\frac{\mu_0 ir}{2\pi R^2}\right)^2 (2\pi r dr)$$

$$\Rightarrow \quad U = \frac{\mu_0 i^2}{4\pi R^4}\int_0^R r^3 dr = \frac{\mu_0 i^2}{16\pi}$$

6.9 L-C Oscillations

1. (i) Potential difference across inductor

= Potential difference across capacitor

$$\Rightarrow L\left|\frac{di}{dt}\right| = \frac{Q}{C}$$

$$\Rightarrow \left|\frac{di}{dt}\right| = \frac{Q}{LC} = \frac{100 \times 10^{-6}}{2 \times 10^{-3} \times 5 \times 10^{-6}} = 10^4\text{ A/s}$$

(ii) $\frac{Q^2}{2C} + \frac{1}{2}Li^2 = \frac{Q^2_{max}}{2C}$

when $Q = Q_{max} \Rightarrow i = 0$

(iii) $\frac{1}{2}Li^2_{max} = \frac{Q^2_{max}}{2C} \Rightarrow i_{max} = \frac{Q_{max}}{\sqrt{LC}} = 2\text{A}$

(iv) $\frac{Q^2}{2C} + \frac{1}{2}Li^2 = \frac{1}{2}Li^2_{max}$

$$\Rightarrow \quad \frac{Q^2}{2C} + \frac{1}{2}L\left(\frac{i_{max}}{2}\right)^2 = \frac{1}{2}Li^2_{max}$$

$$\Rightarrow \quad Q = \left(\sqrt{\frac{3LC}{4}}\right)i_{max} = 173\,\mu\text{C}$$

2. (i) $\frac{Q_0^2}{2C} = 200\,\mu\text{J}$ and $\frac{1}{2}Li_0^2 = 200\,\mu\text{J}$

Total energy $= \frac{1}{2}Li^2_{max} = 400\,\mu\text{J}$

$$\Rightarrow \quad L = \frac{2 \times 400 \times 10^{-6}}{\left(\frac{1}{\sqrt{10}}\right)^2} = 8\text{ mH}$$

(ii) $f = \frac{1}{2\pi}\frac{1}{\sqrt{LC}} = 398\text{ Hz}$

(iii) $\frac{Q^2_{max}}{2C} = 400\,\mu\text{J} \Rightarrow Q_{max} = 40\sqrt{10}\,\mu\text{C}$

$$Q = Q_{max}\sin(\omega t + \phi)$$

At $t = 0$; $40\sqrt{5} = 40\sqrt{10}\sin(\omega t + \phi) \Rightarrow \phi = \frac{\pi}{4}$

$$\Rightarrow Q = (40\sqrt{10}\,\mu\text{C})\sin\left(2500t + \frac{\pi}{4}\right)$$

and $i = \left(\frac{1}{\sqrt{10}}\text{A}\right)\cos\left(2500t + \frac{\pi}{4}\right)$

3. (i) $\omega = \frac{1}{\sqrt{LC_1}} = \frac{1}{\sqrt{0.2 \times 10^{-3} \times 2 \times 10^{-6}}} = 5 \times 10^4\text{ rad/s}$

(ii) $\frac{1}{2}Li^2 + \frac{Q^2}{2C} = \frac{Q^2_{max}}{2C}$

$$\Rightarrow \frac{1}{3}\left(\frac{Q^2}{2C}\right) + \frac{Q^2}{2C} = \frac{Q^2_{max}}{2C} \Rightarrow Q = \frac{\sqrt{3}}{2}Q_{max}$$

$$Q = Q_{max}\cos\omega t$$

$$\Rightarrow \frac{\sqrt{3}Q_{max}}{2} = Q_{max}\cos\omega t \Rightarrow t = \frac{\pi}{6\omega}$$

$$\Rightarrow 1.05 \times 10^{-5}\text{s}$$

(iii) Charge on capacitor C_1 in steady state,

$$Q_{max} = C_{eq}V = \left(\frac{2(2)}{2+2}\right) \times 20 = 20\,\mu\text{C}$$

$$Q = \frac{\sqrt{3}Q_{max}}{2} = 17.32\,\mu\text{C}$$

Level 2

Single Choice Correct Questions

1. $L \propto N^2 \Rightarrow \frac{L_1}{L_2} = \left(\frac{N_1}{N_2}\right)^2 \Rightarrow \frac{108}{L_2} = \left(\frac{600}{500}\right)^2 \Rightarrow L_2 = 75$ mH

2. $L = \mu_0 n^2 v = \mu_0 \left(\frac{N}{l}\right)^2 Al$ ...(i)

$B = \mu_0 ni = \frac{\mu_0 Ni}{l}$ ...(ii)

Dividing Eq. (i) by Eq.(ii)

$$i = \frac{BAN}{L}$$

3. $L = \mu_0 n^2 V = \mu_0 \left(\frac{N}{l}\right)^2 \pi r^2 l$ and $N = \frac{l}{2\pi r}$

$\Rightarrow \quad L = \frac{\mu_0 l}{4\pi} \Rightarrow L \propto l$

Since length is same, self-inductance will be same.

4. $\phi = Mi \Rightarrow 1.8 \times 10^{-3} = M(2) \Rightarrow M = 9 \times 10^{-4}$ H

$\phi = Mi \Rightarrow \phi = (9 \times 10^{-4})(3) = 2.7 \times 10^{-3}$ Wb

5. $\varepsilon_1 = M_{12} \frac{di_2}{dt} \Rightarrow 25 \times 10^{-3} = M(15) \Rightarrow M = \frac{5}{3} \times 10^{-3}$ H

$\phi_2 = Mi_1 \Rightarrow \phi_2 = \frac{5}{3} \times 10^{-3} \times 3.6 = 6.00$ m Wb

6. $\varepsilon = M\frac{di}{dt} = M(10 \times 100\pi \cos(100\pi t))$

$\varepsilon_{max} = (1000\pi)M = 5\pi \Rightarrow M = 5$ mH

7. Let current in one of the solenoids be i.

ϕ = flux through the other solenoid

$$\phi = \left(\mu_0 \left(\frac{N_1}{l}\right) i\right) N_2 A$$

$$M = \frac{\phi}{i} = \frac{\mu_0 N_1 N_2 A}{l}$$

$$= \frac{4\pi \times 10^{-7} \times 300 \times 400 \times 10 \times 10^{-4}}{20 \times 10^{-2}}$$

$$= 2.4\pi \times 10^{-4} \text{ H}$$

8. Let current in the ring be i.

$$B = \frac{\mu_0 i R^2}{2(R^2 + (\sqrt{3}R)^2)^{3/2}} = \frac{\mu_0 i}{16R}$$

ϕ = Flux through the loop $= \left(\frac{\mu_0 i}{16R}\right) \pi r^2 \cos 53°$

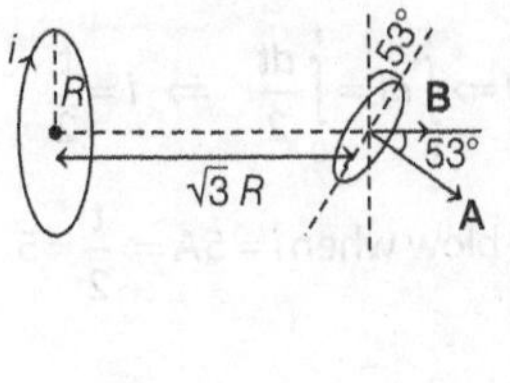

$$= \left(\frac{3\mu_0 \pi r^2}{80R}\right) i$$

$$M = \frac{\phi}{i} = \frac{3\mu_0 \pi r^2}{80R}$$

9. Flux linkage will be maximum in situation (a). So mutual inductance will be maximum in situation (a).

10. $\tan\theta = \frac{y}{x-a} = \frac{(b/2)}{h}$

$\Rightarrow \; 2y = \frac{b(x-a)}{h}$

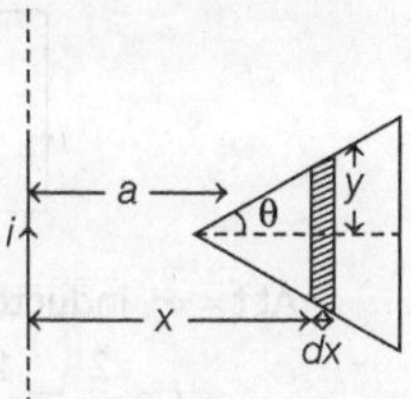

Let current in the long wire be i.

$d\phi$ = Flux through rectangular strip

$= \left(\frac{\mu_0 i}{2\pi x}\right)(2y dx)$

$$\int d\phi = \frac{\mu_0 ib}{2\pi h} \int_a^{a+h} \left(1 - \frac{a}{x}\right) dx$$

$$\phi = \frac{\mu_0 ib}{2\pi h}\left[h - a\ln\left(\frac{a+h}{a}\right)\right]$$

$$M = \frac{\phi}{i} = \frac{\mu_0 b}{2\pi h}\left[h - a\ln\left(\frac{a+h}{a}\right)\right]$$

$$= 1.22 \times 10^{-8} \text{ H}$$

11. $V_A - 5(1) - 15 - 5 \times 10^{-3}(-10^{-3}) = V_B$

$\Rightarrow V_B - V_A = -15$ V

12. $V_A - V_B = iR + L\frac{di}{dt}$

$140 = 5R + 10L \Rightarrow R + 2L = 28$ ...(i)

$60 = 5R - 10L \Rightarrow R - 2L = 12$ ...(ii)

Solving Eqs. (i) and (ii), we get

$$L = 4 \text{ H}$$

13. $U = \frac{1}{2}Li^2 \Rightarrow \frac{dU}{dt} = \frac{1}{2}L\left(2i\frac{di}{dt}\right) = 2 \times 2 \times 4 = 16$ J/s

14. $P = 8i^2 \Rightarrow \left(8\frac{di}{dt}\right)i = 8i^2$

$\Rightarrow \int_{i_0}^{2i_0} \frac{di}{i} = \int_0^t dt \Rightarrow t = \ln 2$

15. $V = 2t \Rightarrow 2\frac{di}{dt} = 2t \Rightarrow \int_0^i di = \int_0^t t dt$

$\Rightarrow \quad i = \frac{t^2}{2}$

At $\quad t = 2$ s; $i = \frac{(2)^2}{2} = 2$A

$U = \frac{1}{2}Li^2 = \frac{1}{2}(2)(2)^2 = 4$ J

$$\frac{dU}{dt}=\frac{1}{2}L\left(2i\frac{di}{dt}\right)=Li\frac{di}{dt}=2\left(\frac{t^2}{2}\right)\left(\frac{2t}{2}\right)$$

At $t=1\text{ s};\ \frac{dU}{dt}=1\text{ J/s}$

16. At $t=0$, inductor acts as open circuit.

$$i=\frac{2}{30}=\frac{1}{15}\text{ A}$$

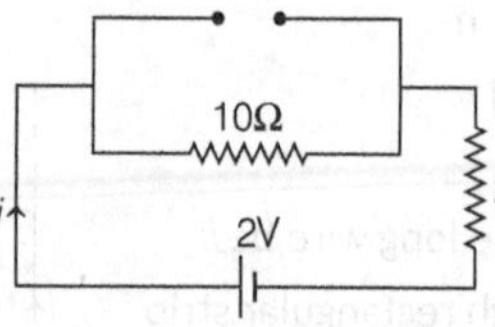

At $t=\infty$, inductor acts as short-circuit.

$$i=\frac{2}{20}=\frac{1}{10}\text{ A}$$

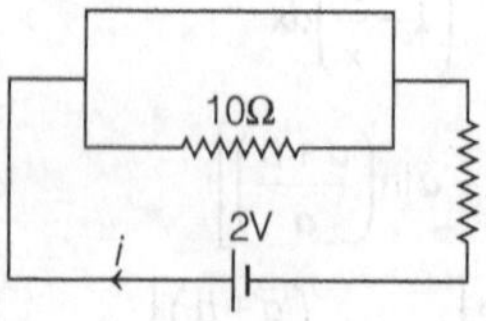

17. Steady state current through inductor $=\dfrac{12}{\left[\dfrac{8(4)}{8+4}\right]}$

$$=4.5\text{ A}$$

Current in a inductor doesn't change suddenly.

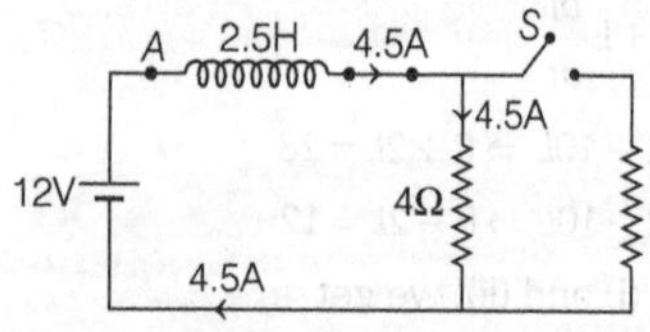

$$V_A-12+(4.5)4=V_B$$
$$V_A-V_B=-6\text{ V}$$

So, $V_L=6\text{V}$ and point B is at higher potential.

18. Let currents through inductors L_1 and L_2 be i_1 and i_2 respectively.

$$\frac{i_1}{i_2}=\frac{L_2}{L_1}$$

$$U_1=\frac{1}{2}L_1i_1^2 \text{ and } U_2=\frac{1}{2}L_2i_2^2$$

$$\Rightarrow\quad \frac{U_1}{U_2}=\frac{L_1}{L_2}\left(\frac{L_2}{L_1}\right)^2=\frac{L_2}{L_1}$$

19. Current in inductor branch will gradually increase to its steady state value.

20. $(2L)\left(\frac{E}{R}\right)+L\left(-\frac{E}{R}\right)=(2L+L)i$

$$i=\frac{E}{3R},\text{ anti-clockwise}$$

21. At $t=0$, current through inductor is zero but there is emf $\left(L\frac{di}{dt}\right)$ induced in the inductor.

22. $i=\frac{\varepsilon}{R}\left(1-e^{-\frac{Rt}{L}}\right)=\frac{15}{10}\left(1-e^{-\frac{10t}{5}}\right)=1.5\,(1-e^{-2t})$

At $t=1;\ i_1=1.5\,(1-e^{-2})$

At $t=\infty;\ i_2=1.5$

$$\frac{i_2}{i_1}=\frac{1}{1-e^{-2}}=\frac{e^2}{e^2-1}$$

23. $V=L\frac{di}{dt}=L\left(\frac{\varepsilon}{L}e^{-\frac{Rt}{L}}\right)=\varepsilon e^{-\frac{Rt}{L}}$

At $t=\ln\sqrt{2};\ V=6e^{-\left(\frac{10\ln\sqrt{2}}{5}\right)}=3\text{ V}$

24. $i=\frac{\varepsilon}{R}\left(1-e^{-\frac{t}{\tau}}\right)=\frac{1}{2}\left(\frac{\varepsilon}{R}\right)$

$$\Rightarrow\quad t=\tau\ln 2=\left(\frac{100\times10^{-3}}{2}\right)\ln 2=(50\ln 2)\text{ ms}$$

25. Applying KVL, $+E-iR-L\frac{di}{dt}=0$

$$\Rightarrow\quad L\frac{di}{dt}=E-iR\ \Rightarrow\ e=E-iR$$

So, e vs i graph will be straight line with negative slope.

26. $U=\frac{1}{2}Li^2\Rightarrow\frac{dU}{dt}=\frac{1}{2}L\left(2i\frac{di}{dt}\right)=Li\frac{di}{dt}$

We have to maximize $\frac{dU}{dt}$. So,

$$\frac{d^2U}{dt^2}=Li\frac{d^2i}{dt^2}+L\left(\frac{di}{dt}\right)^2=0$$

$$\Rightarrow\frac{\varepsilon}{R}(1-e^{-t/\tau})\left(-\frac{\varepsilon R}{L^2}e^{-t/\tau}\right)+\left(\frac{\varepsilon}{L}e^{-t/\tau}\right)^2=0$$

$$\Rightarrow\quad t=\tau\ln 2$$

Now, $i=\frac{\varepsilon}{R}\left(1-e^{-\frac{\tau\ln 2}{\tau}}\right)=\frac{\varepsilon}{2R}=1\text{ A}$

27. $U=\frac{1}{2}Li^2$ and $P=i^2R$

$$\frac{U}{P}=\frac{1}{2}\left(\frac{L}{R}\right)=\frac{\tau}{2}\Rightarrow\tau=\frac{2U}{P}$$

28. $+E-L\frac{di}{dt}=0\Rightarrow\int_0^i di=\int_0^t\frac{dt}{2}\ \Rightarrow\ i=\frac{t}{2}$

The fuse will blow when $i=5\text{A}\Rightarrow\frac{t}{2}=5\ \Rightarrow t=10\text{ sec}$

29. At $t = 2$, Resistance of rod $= 1(5 \times 2) = 10\ \Omega$

Steady state current at this position $= \dfrac{30}{(20+10)} = 1\text{ A}$

At $t = 0$, current $= \dfrac{30}{20} = 1.5\text{ A}$

Because of inductor current will go from 1.5 A to 1 A in very long time. So at $t = 2\text{s}$, current will be more than 1 A.

30. In steady state inductor acts as short circuit and capacitor acts as open circuit.

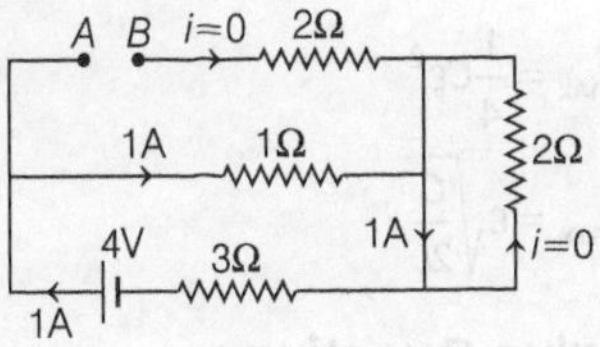

$$V_A - V_B = 1(1) = 1\text{ V}$$

$$U_L = \frac{1}{2}Li^2 = \frac{1}{2}(0.1)(1)^2 = \frac{1}{20}\text{ J}$$

$$U_C = \frac{1}{2}CV^2 = \frac{1}{2}\times 1\times 10^{-6} \times (1)^2 = \frac{10^{-6}}{2}\text{ J}$$

$$\Rightarrow \frac{U_L}{U_C} = 10^5$$

31. Charge on capacitor in steady state $= C\varepsilon$

Current through inductor in steady state $= 0$

$$E = (C\varepsilon)\varepsilon = C\varepsilon^2$$

$$U = U_L + U_C = 0 + \frac{(C\varepsilon)^2}{2C} = \frac{1}{2}C\varepsilon^2$$

$$Q = E - U = \frac{1}{2}C\varepsilon^2$$

32. Using KVL,

$$+E - iR - L\frac{di}{dt} - \frac{q}{C} = 0$$

$$\Rightarrow +4 - 2(1) - 1(4) - \frac{q}{3\times 10^{-6}} = 0$$

$$\Rightarrow \quad q = 6\ \mu\text{C}$$

33. At $t = 0$, capacitor acts as short circuit and inductor acts as open circuit.

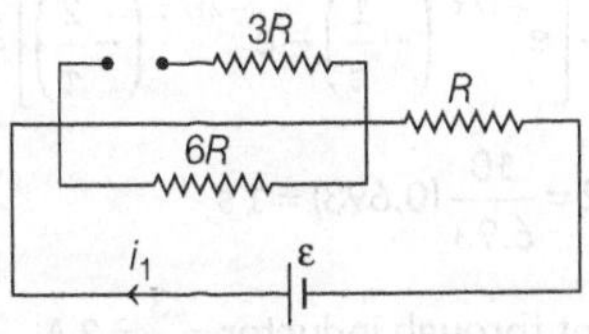

$$i_1 = \frac{\varepsilon}{R}$$

At $t = \infty$, capacitor acts as open circuit and inductor acts as short circuit.

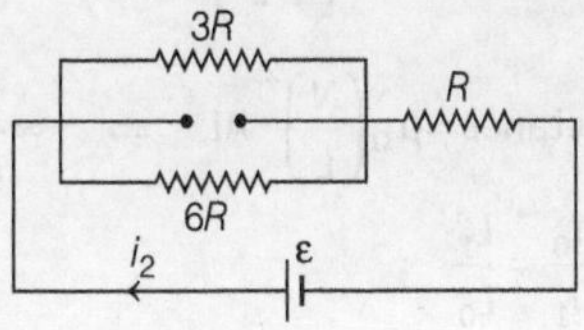

$$i_2 = \frac{\varepsilon}{R + \dfrac{(6R)(3R)}{6R+3R}} = \frac{\varepsilon}{3R}$$

$$\frac{i_1}{i_2} = \frac{3}{1}$$

34. $i_{AB} = \dfrac{10}{2}\left(1 - e^{-\frac{2t}{2}}\right) = 5(1 - e^{-t})$

$$i_{CD} = \frac{10}{1}e^{-\frac{t}{(1)(1)}} = 10e^{-t}$$

$$i_{AB} = i_{CD} \Rightarrow 5(1 - e^{-t}) = 10e^{-t}$$

$$\Rightarrow \quad t = \ln 3\text{ s}$$

35. $i = i_0 e^{-\frac{t}{\tau}}$

$$\Rightarrow \quad 18 = 20\,e^{-\frac{2}{\tau}} \Rightarrow \tau = \frac{2}{\ln\left(\dfrac{10}{9}\right)}$$

36. $i_0 = \dfrac{E}{R} = 0.1\text{ A}$

$$i = i_0 e^{-\left(\frac{Rt}{L}\right)} \Rightarrow i = 0.1e^{-\left(\frac{100\times 1\times 10^{-3}}{100\times 10^{-3}}\right)} = \frac{0.1}{e}\text{ A}$$

37. When switch is in position 1, steady state current is $\dfrac{E}{R}$.

When switch is shifted to position 2, new steady state current is also $\dfrac{E}{R}$. So current in the circuit will not change.

38. $i = \dfrac{E}{R}e^{-\left(\frac{Rt}{L}\right)}$

At $\quad t = 0;\ i_1 = \dfrac{E}{R}$

At $\quad t = \dfrac{2L}{R};\ i_2 = \dfrac{E}{e^2R}$

Heat dissipated in resistor = Loss in energy of inductor

$$= \frac{1}{2}Li_1^2 - \frac{1}{2}Li_2^2$$

$$= \frac{LE^2}{2R^2}\left(\frac{e^4 - 1}{e^4}\right)$$

39. $\frac{1}{2}Li_{max}^2 = \frac{1}{2}mv_0^2 \Rightarrow i_{max} = \left(\sqrt{\frac{m}{L}}\right)v_0$

40. I = Self-inductance $= \mu_0\left(\frac{N}{L}\right)^2 AL \Rightarrow I \propto \frac{1}{L}$

$\Rightarrow \quad \frac{I_0}{I_1} = \frac{L_1}{L_0}$

$\phi = I_0 i_0 = I_1 i_1 \Rightarrow i_1 = \left(\frac{I_0}{I_1}\right)i_0 = \left(\frac{L_1}{L_0}\right)i_0$

41. $\tau_1 = \frac{L}{2R}$ and $\tau_2 = \frac{L}{3R}$

$\Rightarrow \frac{\tau_1}{\tau_2} = \frac{3}{2}$

42. $f = \frac{1}{2\pi\sqrt{L_{eq}C_{eq}}} = \frac{1}{2\pi\sqrt{(3L)(3C)}} = \frac{1}{6\pi\sqrt{LC}}$

43. $U = \frac{1}{2}CV^2 = \frac{1}{2}(6\times10^{-6})(6)^2 = 108\,\mu J$

$\frac{1}{2}Li^2 = \frac{1}{3}(108\times10^{-6})$

$\Rightarrow \frac{1}{2}\times 0.2\times10^{-3}\times i^2 = \frac{1}{3}(108\times10^{-6})$

$\Rightarrow \quad i = 0.6$ A

44. At $t = 0, i_0 = \frac{E}{R} = \frac{10}{2} = 5$A

$\omega = \frac{1}{\sqrt{LC}} = \frac{1}{\sqrt{1\times1\times10^{-6}}} = 1000$ rad/s

$i = i_0\cos\omega t = 5\cos(1000\,t)$

45. $U = \frac{q^2}{2C} + \frac{1}{2}Li^2 = \frac{(4)^2}{2(1)} + \frac{1}{2}(4)(\sqrt{5})^2 = 18$ J

$\frac{q_{max}^2}{2C} = 18 \Rightarrow q_{max} = 6$C

$\frac{1}{2}Li_{max}^2 = 18 \Rightarrow i_{max} = 3$A

46. $q = q_0\cos\omega t \Rightarrow i = \frac{dq}{dt} = -q_0\omega\sin\omega t$

$\frac{di}{dt} = -q_0\omega^2\cos\omega t$

$\left(\frac{di}{dt}\right)_{max} = q_0\omega^2 = \frac{q_0}{LC}$

47. q_0 = Initial charge on capacitor $= C\varepsilon$

$q = q_0\cos\omega t$

$\Rightarrow \quad i = \frac{dq}{dt} = -q_0\omega\sin\omega t$

For i to be maximum, $\sin\omega t = 1$

$\Rightarrow \quad \omega t = \frac{\pi}{2} \Rightarrow t = \frac{\pi}{2\omega} = \frac{\pi}{2}\sqrt{LC}$

48. When current is maximum, potential difference across inductor $\left(L\frac{di}{dt}\right)$ is zero. So, potential difference across the two capacitors will be same.

$C\varepsilon + 0 = (C + C)V \Rightarrow V = \frac{\varepsilon}{2}$

Loss in energy of capacitors

$= \left(\frac{1}{2}C\varepsilon^2 + 0\right) - \left(\frac{1}{2}(C + C)\left(\frac{\varepsilon}{2}\right)^2\right) = \frac{1}{4}C\varepsilon^2$

$\frac{1}{2}Li_{max}^2 = \frac{1}{4}C\varepsilon^2$

$\Rightarrow \quad i_{max} = \varepsilon\sqrt{\frac{C}{2L}}$

Numerical Value Questions

1. Just after closing the switch inductor acts as open circuit.

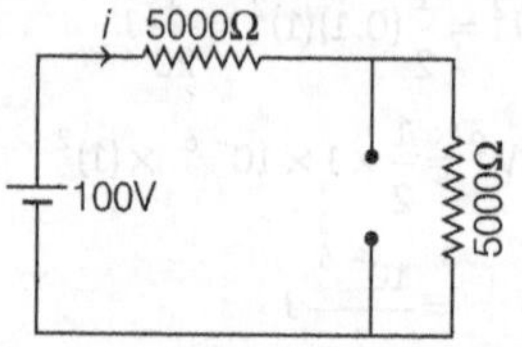

$i = \frac{100}{(5000 + 5000)} = \frac{1}{100}$ A

$P = Vi = 100\left(\frac{1}{100}\right) = 1$ W

2. $L = \mu_0 n^2 V = \mu_0\left(\frac{N}{l}\right)^2\pi r^2 l = \frac{\mu_0(Nr)^2\pi}{l}$

$1\times10^{-3} = \frac{4\pi\times10^{-7}(Nr)^2\pi}{1}$

$\Rightarrow \quad N\pi r = 50$

Length of wire $= N(2\pi r) = 2\times50 = 100$ m

3. $P = i^2R = \left[\frac{V}{R}(1 - e^{-t/\tau})\right]^2 R$

$\frac{dP}{dt} = \frac{V^2}{R}\left[2\left(1 - e^{-t/\tau}\right)\left(-e^{-t/\tau}\right)\left(-\frac{1}{\tau}\right)\right]$

$\frac{d^2P}{dt^2} = \frac{2V^2}{\tau R}\left[e^{-t/\tau}\left(-\frac{1}{\tau}\right) - e^{-2t/\tau}\left(-\frac{2}{\tau}\right)\right] = 0$

$\Rightarrow t = \tau\ln 2 = \frac{10}{6.93}(0.693) = 1$ s

4. Initial current through inductor $= \frac{3}{1} = 3$ A

Energy stored in inductor $= \frac{1}{2}(2\times10^{-3})(3)^2 = 9$ mJ

Since R and R_0 are in series, heat will be dissipated in the ratio of their resistances.

Heat generated in coil $= \left(\frac{1}{1+2}\right)(9 \text{ mJ}) = 3 \text{ mJ}$.

5. $\phi = Li \Rightarrow \Delta\phi = L\Delta i$

$\Rightarrow BA\cos 0° - BA\cos 90° = L(i-0)$

$\Rightarrow \quad i = \frac{BA}{L}$

$$W_{ext} = \Delta U = U_2 - U_1 = \frac{1}{2}L\left(\frac{BA}{L}\right)^2 - 0 = \frac{B^2A^2}{2L} = 8\text{J}$$

6. $V_1 = L_1\frac{di}{dt}$ and $V_2 = L_2\frac{di}{dt}$

$$\frac{V_1}{V_2} = \frac{L_1}{L_2} = \frac{\mu_0 N_1^2 A/l}{\mu_0\mu_r N_2^2 A/l} = \left(\frac{600}{200}\right)^2\left(\frac{1}{3}\right) = \frac{3}{1}$$

7. For finding mutual inductance let current in the circular loop be i.

$$\phi = \left(\frac{\mu_0 i}{2R}\right)a^2 \Rightarrow M = \frac{\phi}{i} = \frac{\mu_0 a^2}{2R}$$

$$\varepsilon = M\frac{di}{dt} = \frac{\mu_0 a^2}{2R}\left(\frac{i_0}{\tau}\right)$$

$$= \frac{4\pi\times10^{-7}\times1\times10^{-4}\times200}{2\times0.1\times2\times10^{-2}\times\pi} = 2\,\mu\text{V}$$

8. Let current in one of the loops be i.

M = Magnetic dipole moment of this loop $= i\pi r^2$

A current carrying loop acts as a bar magnet. Magnetic field at an equitorial point $= \left(\frac{\mu_0}{4\pi}\right)\frac{M}{a^3}$

$$\phi = \left(\left(\frac{\mu_0}{4\pi}\right)\frac{M}{a^3}\right)\pi r^2 = \left(\frac{\mu_0\pi r^4}{4a^3}\right)i$$

Mutual Inductance $= \frac{\phi}{i} = \frac{\mu_0\pi r^4}{4a^3}$

So, $\quad k = 4$

9. When only S_1 is closed, $T_1 = RC = 0.05$ ...(i)

When only S_2 is closed, $T_2 = \frac{L}{R} = 2$ ...(ii)

From Eqs. (i) and (ii), we get

$$LC = 0.1$$

When only S_3 is closed, $T = 2\pi\sqrt{LC}$

$$= 2\sqrt{10}\sqrt{0.1} = 2\text{ s}$$

10. $i_1 = \frac{V}{R}e^{-\frac{t}{RC}}$ and $i_2 = \frac{V}{R}\left(1 - e^{-\frac{Rt}{L}}\right)$

$$i = i_1 + i_2 = \frac{V}{R}\left(1 + e^{-\frac{t}{RC}} - e^{-\frac{Rt}{L}}\right)$$

Since i is constant $\Rightarrow e^{-\frac{t}{RC}} - e^{-\frac{Rt}{L}} = 0$

$$\Rightarrow \quad R = \sqrt{\frac{L}{C}} = 5\Omega$$

Single Choice Correct Questions

1. $q = t^3 - t^2 + 4t \Rightarrow i = \frac{dq}{dt} = 3t^2 - 2t + 4$

$$\frac{di}{dt} = 6t - 2$$

At $t = 1$ s; $q = 4$C, $i = 5$A, $\frac{di}{dt} = 4$

$$V_A - \frac{q}{C} - L\frac{di}{dt} - iR = V_B$$

$$\Rightarrow \quad V_A - V_B = \frac{4}{2} + \frac{1}{2}(4) + 5\left(\frac{3}{5}\right) = 7\text{ V}$$

2. $R = \frac{V^2}{P} = \frac{(200)^2}{100} = 400\ \Omega;\ \tau = \frac{L}{R} = \frac{200}{400} = 0.5$ sec

$$i = \frac{V}{R}(1 - e^{-2t})$$

$$\Rightarrow \quad P = i^2R = \frac{V^2}{R}(1 - e^{-2t})^2$$

$$\frac{P_1}{P_2} = \frac{(1-e^{-2})^2}{(1-e^{-4})^2} = \left(\frac{e^2}{e^2+1}\right)^2$$

3. $\quad U = \frac{1}{2}Li^2$

$$\Rightarrow \frac{dU}{dt} = \left(L\frac{di}{dt}\right)i = L\left(\frac{E}{L}e^{-t/\tau}\right)\frac{E}{R}(1 - e^{-t/\tau})$$

$$= \frac{E^2}{R}(e^{-t/\tau} - e^{-2t/\tau})$$

At $t = 0$, $\frac{dU}{dt} = 0$ and $t = \infty$, $\frac{dU}{dt} = 0$

4. $i = \frac{dq}{dt} = \frac{E}{R}(1 - e^{-t/\tau})$

$$\Rightarrow \quad \int dq = \frac{E}{R}\int_0^\tau (1 - e^{-t/\tau})\,dt$$

$$\Rightarrow \quad q = \frac{E}{R}[t + \tau e^{-t/\tau}]_0^\tau = \frac{E\tau}{eR} = \frac{EL}{eR^2}$$

5. $U = \frac{1}{2}Li^2 \Rightarrow \frac{dU}{dt} = \left(L\frac{di}{dt}\right)i = (E - iR)i$

To maximize $\frac{dU}{dt}$, $\frac{d^2U}{dt^2} = E\frac{di}{dt} - 2i\frac{di}{dt}R = 0 \Rightarrow i = \frac{E}{2R}$

$$\left(\frac{dU}{dt}\right)_{max} = \left(E - \left(\frac{E}{2R}\right)R\right)\frac{E}{2R} = \frac{E^2}{4R}$$

6. $V = \varepsilon - iR = 2 - i$

At $t = 0$; $i = 0$; $V_{max} = 2$

$V = \frac{V_{max}}{2} \Rightarrow 2 - i = 1 \Rightarrow i = 1\text{ A}$

$U = \frac{1}{2}Li^2 = \frac{1}{2} \times 5 \times 10^{-3} \times (1)^2 = 2.5\text{ mJ}$

7. $i = i_0 e^{-\frac{t}{\tau}} \Rightarrow \frac{i_0}{2} = i_0 e^{-\frac{t_0}{\tau}} \Rightarrow t_0 = \tau \ln 2$

At $t = 2t_0; i = i_0 e^{-\left(\frac{2\tau \ln 2}{\tau}\right)} = \frac{i_0}{4}$

Energy lost by inductor $= \frac{1}{2}Li_0^2 - \frac{1}{2}L\left(\frac{i_0}{4}\right)^2 = \left(\frac{1}{2}Li_0^2\right)\left(\frac{15}{16}\right)$

Fraction of energy lost $= \frac{15}{16}$

8. $U = \frac{1}{2}Li^2; \quad U_1 = 0; \quad U_2 = \frac{1}{2}(2)(2)^2 = 4\text{ J}$

Energy spent $= U_2 - U_1 = 4\text{ J}$

9. For $t \le 0.1 \ln 2$; $i = \frac{100}{10}\left(1 - e^{-\frac{10t}{1}}\right) = 10(1 - e^{-10t})$

At $t = 0.1 \ln 2$; $i = 5\text{ A}$

For $t > 0.1 \ln 2$

$$+100 - 50i - 1\frac{di}{dt} = 0$$

$$\int_5^i \frac{di}{100 - 50i} = \int_{0.1 \ln 2}^{0.2 \ln 2} dt \Rightarrow i = \frac{67}{32}\text{ A}$$

10. Initial current $= \frac{E}{R} \Rightarrow i_0 \propto \frac{1}{R}$

c and d have more initial current than a and b. So resistance of c and d will be lesser than resistance of a and b.

$\tau = \frac{L}{R}$; Lesser time constant means faster decay of the current.

11. At $t = 0$; current through inductor $= \frac{E}{r}$

So, $i = \frac{E}{r} e^{-\frac{(R+r)t}{L}}$

Energy stored in inductor at $t = 0$,

$$U = \frac{1}{2}L\left(\frac{E}{r}\right)^2$$

Heat produced in solenoid $= \left(\frac{r}{R+r}\right)\left(\frac{1}{2}L\left(\frac{E}{r}\right)^2\right) = \frac{E^2 L}{2r(R+r)}$

Induced emf across solenoid at $t = 0$,

$$\varepsilon = i(R+r) = \frac{E}{r}(R+r)$$

Potential difference across solenoid at $t = 0$,

$$V = iR = \frac{ER}{r}$$

12. At $t = 0$, all currents are zero.

So, $L_1 \frac{di_1}{dt} = L_2 \frac{di_2}{dt} = E$

$\Rightarrow \frac{di_1}{dt} = \frac{E}{L_1}$ and $\frac{di_2}{dt} = \frac{E}{L_2}$

After long time,

Current through battery $= \frac{\varepsilon}{r}$.

This current will split in the two inductors in the inverse ratio of their inductances.

13. Motional emf $= Blv = 2 \times 2 \times 1 = 4\text{ V}$

Current through $R = \frac{4}{2} = 2\text{ A}$

and $L\frac{di}{dt} = Blv \Rightarrow \int di = 2\int dt$

$\Rightarrow i = 2t$

Energy dissipated in $R = i^2Rt = (2)^2(2)(2) = 16\text{ J}$

Energy stored in $L = \frac{1}{2}Li^2 = \frac{1}{2} \times 2 \times (2 \times 2)^2 = 16\text{ J}$

$$W_{ext} = 16 + 16 = 32\text{ J}$$

14. $\phi_1 = \phi_2 \Rightarrow L_1 i_0 = (L_1 + L_2)i$

$\Rightarrow L_1\left(\frac{E}{R}\right) = (L_1 + L_2)i \Rightarrow i = \frac{EL_1}{R(L_1 + L_2)}$

15. At $t = 0$; inductor acts as open circuit.

So, $i = \frac{15}{(30 + 10 + 20)} = 0.25\text{ A}$

At $t = \infty$, inductor acts as short-circuit.

$\Rightarrow i = \frac{15}{30} = 0.5\text{ A}$

So current will go from 0.25 A to 0.5 A exponentially.

16. $i_L = \frac{40}{20}\left(1 - e^{-\frac{20t}{10 \times 10^{-3}}}\right) = 2(1 - e^{-2000t})$

$$i_c = \frac{40}{40} e^{\left(\frac{-t}{(40 \times 25 \times 10^{-6})}\right)} = e^{-1000t}$$

$$i = i_L + i_c = 2(1 - e^{-2000t}) + e^{-1000t}$$

At $t = 10^{-3} \ln 2; i = 2\left(1 - \frac{1}{4}\right) + \frac{1}{2} = 2\text{ A}$

17. $B(2\pi r) = \mu_0 Ni \Rightarrow B = \frac{\mu_0 Ni}{2\pi r}$

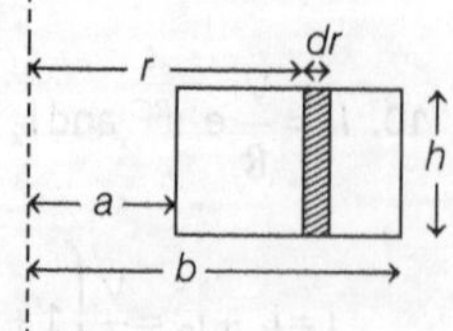

$$\int d\phi = \int_a^b \left(\frac{\mu_0 Ni}{2\pi r}\right)(hdr)$$

$$\phi = \frac{\mu_0 Nhi}{2\pi} \ln\left(\frac{b}{a}\right)$$

Total flux $= N\phi = \dfrac{\mu_0 N^2 hi}{2\pi}\ln\left(\dfrac{b}{a}\right)$

$$L = \frac{N\phi}{i} = \frac{\mu_0 N^2 h}{2\pi}\ln\left(\frac{b}{a}\right)$$

18. $\int d\phi = \int_a^{2a} \dfrac{\mu_0 (i_0 \sin\omega t)}{2\pi x} a dx$

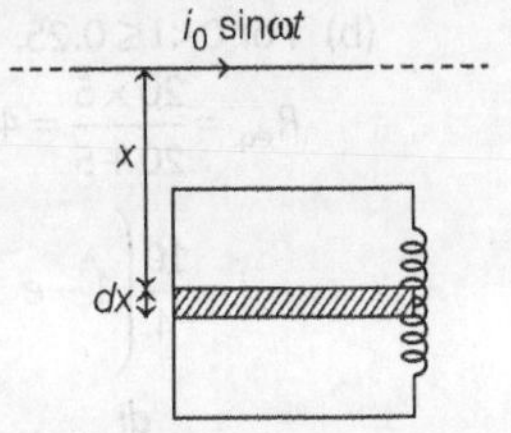

$\Rightarrow \quad \phi = \left(\dfrac{\mu_0 a i_0 \sin\omega t}{2\pi}\right)\ln 2$

$$i = \frac{\phi}{L} = \left(\frac{\mu_0 a i_0 \ln 2}{2\pi L}\right)\sin\omega t$$

$$i_{max} = \frac{\mu_0 a i_0 \ln 2}{2\pi L}$$

19. $\phi = Mi = Mat$

$$\varepsilon = \left|\frac{d\phi}{dt}\right| = Ma$$

$$i = -\frac{\varepsilon}{R}\left(1 - e^{-\frac{Rt}{L}}\right)$$

($\because$ Negative sign as induced current will be anti-clockwise)

$$i = -\frac{Ma}{R}\left(1 - e^{-\frac{Rt}{L}}\right)$$

20. In figure A, $L_A = L_1 + L_2 + 2M$

$$= L + 2L + 2\left(\frac{1}{\sqrt{2}}\right)\sqrt{L(2L)} = 5L$$

In figure B, $L_B = L_1 + L_2 - 2M$

$$= L + 2L - 2\left(\frac{1}{\sqrt{2}}\right)\sqrt{L(2L)} = L$$

$$L_A - L_B = 5L - L = 4L$$

21. Let charge on sphere A be q_0 initially.

At $t = t$, let charge on sphere B be q and hence $(q_0 - q)$ on sphere A.

$$V_A - V_B = L\frac{di}{dt}$$

$\Rightarrow \quad \dfrac{q_0 - q}{C} - \dfrac{q}{C} = L\dfrac{d^2q}{dt^2}$

$\Rightarrow \quad \dfrac{d^2q}{dt^2} = -\dfrac{2}{LC}\left(q - \dfrac{q_0}{2}\right)$

$\Rightarrow q - \dfrac{q_0}{2} = \dfrac{q_0}{2}\cos\omega t$ where $\omega = \sqrt{\dfrac{2}{LC}}$

$\Rightarrow \quad q = \dfrac{q_0}{2}(1 + \cos\omega t)$

$$\omega = \sqrt{\frac{2 \times 9 \times 10^9}{9 \times 10^{-3} \times 0.5}} = 2 \times 10^6 \text{ rad/s}$$

$$\frac{q_0}{2} = \frac{q_0}{2}(1 + \cos\omega t) \Rightarrow \cos\omega t = 0$$

$\Rightarrow \quad \omega t = \dfrac{\pi}{2}$

$\Rightarrow \quad t = \dfrac{\pi}{2 \times 2 \times 10^6}$

$\Rightarrow \quad t = \dfrac{\pi}{4} \times 10^{-6}$ s

22. $+E - L\dfrac{di}{dt} - \dfrac{q}{C} = 0$

$\Rightarrow \quad \dfrac{d^2q}{dt^2} = -\dfrac{1}{LC}(q - CE)$

$\Rightarrow \quad q - CE = CE\cos(\omega t + \phi)$

$\Rightarrow \quad q = CE(1 + \cos(\omega t + \phi))$

$\Rightarrow \quad q_{max} = 2CE$ when $\cos(\omega t + \phi) = 1$

23. $i_0 = \dfrac{50}{5} = 10$ A

$$\frac{q_{max}^2}{2C} = \frac{1}{2}Li_0^2 \Rightarrow q_{max} = 10\text{C}$$

$$q = q_{max}\sin\omega t$$

where $\omega = \dfrac{1}{\sqrt{LC}} = 1$ rad/s

$\Rightarrow \quad q = 10\sin\left(\dfrac{\pi}{6}\right) = 5\text{C}$

24. $\dfrac{1}{2}Li^2 = \dfrac{1}{2}\left(\dfrac{1}{2}Li_{max}^2\right) \Rightarrow i = \dfrac{i_{max}}{\sqrt{2}}$

$i = i_{max}\sin\omega t$, where $\omega = \dfrac{1}{\sqrt{LC}}$

$\Rightarrow \dfrac{i_{max}}{\sqrt{2}} = i_{max}\sin\omega t \Rightarrow \sin\omega t = \dfrac{\pi}{4}$

$\Rightarrow \quad t = \dfrac{\pi}{4}\sqrt{LC}$

25. Initial energy stored in the 900 μF capacitor

$$= \frac{1}{2} \times 900 \times 10^{-6} \times (100)^2 = 4.5 \text{ J}$$

Final energy stored in the 100 μF capacitor

$$= \frac{1}{2} \times 100 \times 10^{-6} \times (300)^2 = 4.5 \text{ J}$$

So the entire energy of the 900 μF capacitor has been transferred to the 100 μF capacitor.

In an LC circuit, the transfer of electrical energy into magnetic energy and *vice versa* takes place in time $\dfrac{T}{4}$

where, $\quad T = 2\pi\sqrt{LC}$.

$$T_1 = 2\pi\sqrt{10 \times 900 \times 10^{-6}} = 0.6 \text{ s}$$

$$T_2 = 2\pi\sqrt{10 \times 100 \times 10^{-6}} = 0.2 \text{ s}$$

$$(t_1 + t_2)_{min} = \frac{T_1}{4} + \frac{T_2}{4} = 0.2 \text{ s}$$

Multiple Choice(s) Correct Questions

1. For $t \le 2$; $V = 5t \Rightarrow 10\frac{di}{dt} = 5t$

$$\Rightarrow \int_0^i di = \frac{1}{2}\int_0^t t\,dt \Rightarrow i = \frac{t^2}{4}$$

For $2 \le t \le 6$; $V = -2.5t + 15$

$$\Rightarrow 10\int_1^i di = \int_2^t (-2.5t + 15)dt$$

$$\Rightarrow \quad i = -0.125t^2 + 1.5t - 1.5$$

At $t = 6; i = 3\text{A}$

At $t = 1; i = \frac{1}{4}\text{A}$

At $t = 4; i = \frac{5}{2}\text{A}$

Current *versus* time graph will be parabola.

$$V = L\frac{di}{dt} \Rightarrow \int_0^i di = \frac{1}{L}\int_0^t V dt$$

$\Rightarrow i = \frac{1}{L}$(Area under V-t graph from $t = 0$ to $t = t$)

2. Inductor opposes the change in current. If i is from a to b, it has to be increasing.

If i is from b to a, it has to be decreasing.

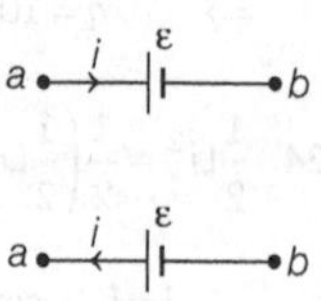

3. $i = i_0\left(1 - e^{-\frac{t}{\tau}}\right) \Rightarrow \frac{di}{dt} = \frac{i_0}{\tau}e^{-\frac{t}{\tau}}$

For circuit 1 at $t = 0$, $\frac{di_1}{dt} = \frac{i_0}{\tau_1} = \tan 30°$ ...(i)

For circuit 2 at $t = 0$, $\frac{di_2}{dt} = \frac{2i_0}{\tau_2} = \tan 60°$ ...(ii)

Dividing Eq. (i) by Eq. (ii), we get

$$\frac{\tau_1}{\tau_2} = \frac{3}{2}$$

At $t = 0$, $\frac{\frac{di_2}{dt}}{\frac{di_1}{dt}} = \frac{\tan 60°}{\tan 30°} = 3 \Rightarrow \frac{di_2}{dt} = 3\left(\frac{di_1}{dt}\right)$

4. $R_{eq} = 2R; L_{eq} = \frac{L}{2}$ So, $\tau = \frac{L_{eq}}{R_{eq}} = \frac{L}{4R}$

Current through battery, $i = \frac{V}{2R}\left(1 - e^{-\left(\frac{4Rt}{L}\right)}\right)$

$$i_1 = i_2 = \frac{i}{2} = \frac{V}{4R}\left[1 - e^{-\left(\frac{4Rt}{L}\right)}\right]$$

At any time, $V_{ab} = V =$ constant

$$\Rightarrow \frac{dV_{ab}}{dt} = 0$$

5. (a) Just after closing S_1, inductor acts as open circuit. Current in the circuit will be zero. So, $V_L = 10\text{ V}$

(b) For $0 < t \le 0.25$,

$$R_{eq} = \frac{20 \times 5}{20 + 5} = 4\,\Omega$$

$$i = \frac{10}{4}\left(1 - e^{-\frac{4t}{1}}\right) = 2.5(1 - e^{-4t})$$

$$V_L = L\frac{di}{dt} = 1(2.5)(e^{-4t})(4) = 10e^{-4t}$$

Just before S_2 is opened, $V_L = 10e^{-4(0.25)} = \left(\frac{10}{e}\right)\text{V}$

(c) Just after S_2 is opened, current through inductor will be unchanged.

$$i = 2.5(1 - e^{-4(0.25)}) = 2.5\left(1 - \frac{1}{e}\right)$$

$$V_L = 10 - 20i = 10 - 20\left[2.5\left(1 - \frac{1}{e}\right)\right]$$

$$= \left(\frac{50}{e} - 40\right)\text{V}$$

6. When the switch is in position 1 for long time, both inductors act as short-circuit.

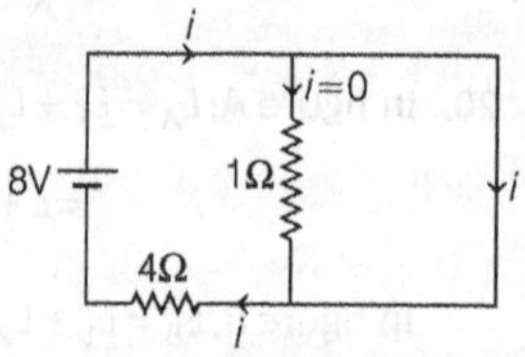

$$i = \frac{8}{4} = 2\text{ A}$$

and current in 1 Ω is zero.

After switch is shifted to position 2, 3H inductor will be shorted.

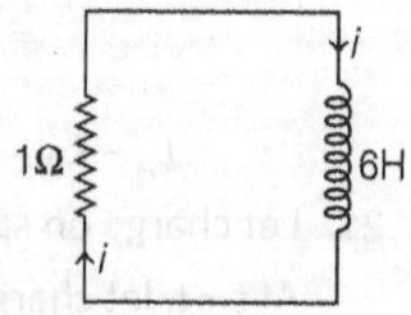

$i = i_0 e^{-\frac{t}{\tau}}$, where

$i_0 = 2\text{A}$ and $\tau = \frac{L}{R} = 6\text{ s}$

$$\Rightarrow \quad i = 2e^{-\frac{t}{6}}$$

Total heat dissipated in 1Ω = Energy stored in 6H inductor initially

$$= \frac{1}{2}(6)(2)^2 = 12\text{ J}$$

7. When the switch S is open for long time,

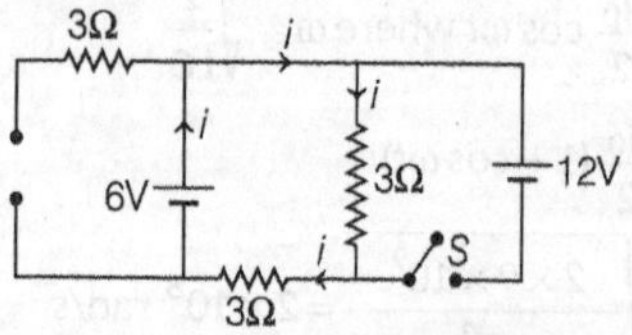

$$i = \frac{6}{(3+3)} = 1\text{ A}$$

Flux through inductor $= \phi_1 = Li = 0.5 \times 1 = 0.5\text{ Wb}$

Long time after closing switch S,

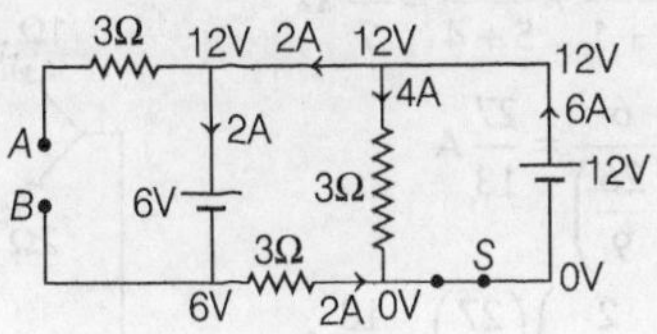

Current through inductor = 4 A

$$\phi_2 = (0.5)\ (4) = 2\ \text{Wb}$$

$$\Delta\phi = \phi_2 - \phi_1 = 2 - 0.5 = 1.5\ \text{Wb}$$

$$V_A - V_B = 12 - 6 = 6\ \text{V}$$

$$q = C(V_A - V_B) = 100 \times 10^{-6} \times 6 = 600\ \mu\text{C}$$

P.d across inductor = 0

8. $i_L = \dfrac{V}{R_1}\left(1 - e^{-\frac{R_1 t}{L}}\right) = \dfrac{50}{25}\left(1 - e^{-\frac{25t}{3.125}}\right) = 2(1 - e^{-8t})$

$$i_c = \frac{V}{R_2} e^{-\frac{t}{R_2 C}} = \frac{50}{5000} e^{\left(-\frac{t}{(5000 \times 25 \times 10^{-6})}\right)} = 0.01\, e^{-8t}$$

(a) $(i_L)_{max} = 2\text{A}$ and $(i_C)_{max} = 0.01$ A

$$\frac{(i_L)_{max}}{(i_C)_{max}} = \frac{2}{0.01} = 200$$

(c) $V_L = L\dfrac{di}{dt} = 3.125 \times 2 \times e^{-8t} \times 8 = 50e^{-8t}$

$$V_C = \frac{q}{C} = 50(1 - e^{-8t})$$

$$\text{At } t = \frac{1}{8}\ln\left(\frac{5}{4}\right);\ V_L = 50\left(\frac{4}{5}\right) = 40\ \text{V}$$

$$V_C = 50\left(1 - \frac{4}{5}\right) = 10\ \text{V, So, } V_L = 4V_C$$

(d) V_L is maximum at $t = 0$.

9. At $t = 0$; charge on capacitor $= C\varepsilon = 1 \times 1 = 1$ C

At $t = 0$; current through inductor $= \dfrac{\varepsilon}{R} = \dfrac{1}{1} = 1$ A

$$\text{At } t = 0;\ U = \frac{q^2}{2C} + \frac{1}{2}Li^2 = \frac{(1)^2}{2(1)} + \frac{1}{2}(1)(1)^2 = 1\ \text{J}$$

After closing S_2, $\dfrac{1}{2}Li_{max}^2 = 1 \Rightarrow i_{max} = \sqrt{2}$ A

$$\frac{q_{max}^2}{2C} = 1 \Rightarrow q_{max} = \sqrt{2}\ \text{C}$$

10. At $t = 0$, $q = C_{eq}V = \left(\dfrac{2(3)}{2+3}\right)20 = 24\ \mu\text{C}$

$$\omega = \frac{1}{\sqrt{LC_1}} = \frac{1}{\sqrt{0.2 \times 10^{-3} \times 2 \times 10^{-6}}} = 5 \times 10^4\ \text{rad/s}$$

$$q_1 = q_0 \cos\omega t = (24\ \mu\text{C})\cos(5 \times 10^4 t)$$

$$U_L + U_C = \frac{q_0^2}{2C_1}$$

$$\Rightarrow \frac{U_C}{3} + U_C = \frac{q_0^2}{2C} \Rightarrow U_C = \frac{3q_0^2}{8C}$$

$$\Rightarrow \frac{q^2}{2C} = \frac{3q_0^2}{8C} \Rightarrow q = \frac{\sqrt{3}q_0}{2}$$

$$\frac{\sqrt{3}q_0}{2} = q_0 \cos\omega t$$

$$\Rightarrow \omega t = \frac{\pi}{6} \Rightarrow t = \frac{\pi}{6\omega} = 10.5\ \mu\text{s}$$

$$q_1 = \frac{\sqrt{3}(24)}{2} = 12\sqrt{3}\ \mu\text{C}$$

11. Let magnetic field be B between the plates and zero outside the plates.

Applying Ampere's law around the dotted loop.

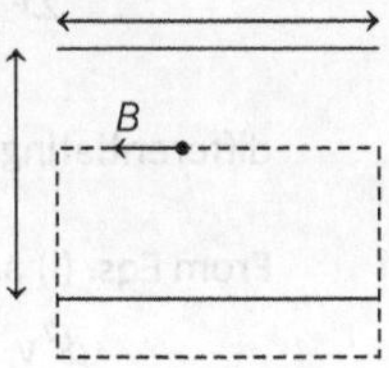

$$B \times b = \mu_0 i \Rightarrow B = \frac{\mu_0 i}{b}$$

Flux linked with coil, $\phi = BA = \left(\dfrac{\mu_0 i}{b}\right)(al)$

$$L = \frac{\phi}{i} = \frac{\mu_0 al}{b}$$

$$U = \frac{1}{2}Li^2 = \frac{1}{2}\left(\frac{\mu_0 al}{b}\right)I^2 = \frac{\mu_0 ali^2}{2b}$$

$$F = -\frac{dU}{da} = -\frac{\mu_0 li^2}{2b}$$

Force per unit area $= \dfrac{F}{bl} = \dfrac{\mu_0 i^2}{2b^2}$

12. $\tan\theta = \dfrac{y}{x-a} = \dfrac{a}{a}$

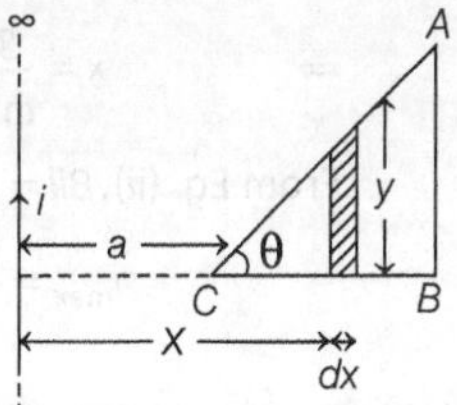

$$\Rightarrow y = x - a$$

$$\int d\phi_1 = \int \frac{\mu_0 i}{2\pi x} y dx$$

$$= \frac{\mu_0 i}{2\pi}\int_a^{2a}\left(1 - \frac{a}{x}\right)dx$$

$$\Rightarrow \phi_1 = \frac{\mu_0 i}{2\pi}[a - a\ln 2]$$

$$M = \frac{\phi}{i}$$

$$\Rightarrow M = \frac{\mu_0 a}{2\pi}(1 - \ln 2)$$

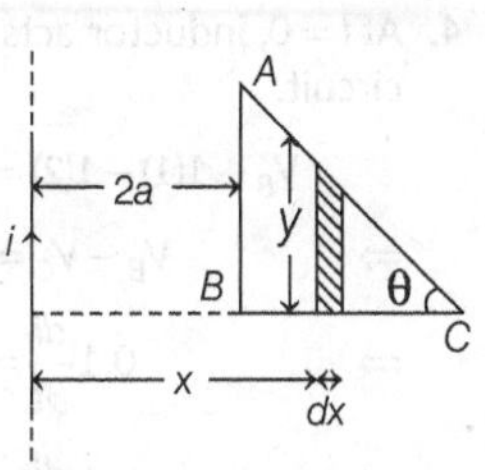

$$\tan\theta = \frac{y}{3a - x} = \frac{a}{a}$$

$$\Rightarrow y = 3a - x$$

$$\int d\phi_2 = \int_{2a}^{3a} \frac{\mu_0 i}{2\pi x}(3a - x)\, dx \cos 180^\circ$$

$$\phi_2 = \frac{\mu_0 ia}{2\pi}\left(1 - 3\ln\left(\frac{3}{2}\right)\right)$$

$$\text{charge flown} = q = \frac{\Delta\phi}{R} = \frac{\mu_0 ia}{2\pi R}\ln\left(\frac{27}{16}\right)$$

Comprehension Based Questions

1., **2.** and **3.**

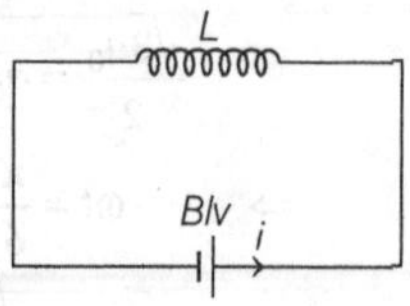

Let velocity of rod at any instant be v.

Motional emf $= Blv$

$$L\frac{di}{dt} = Blv \qquad \text{...(i)}$$

$$\Sigma F = ma \Rightarrow mg - Bil = m\frac{dv}{dt}$$

differentiating $\quad -Bl\frac{di}{dt} = m\frac{d^2v}{dt^2} \qquad \text{...(ii)}$

From Eqs. (i) and (ii),

$$\frac{d^2v}{dt^2} = -\left(\frac{B^2l^2}{mL}\right)v$$

$\Rightarrow \quad v = A\sin\omega t$ where, $\omega = \frac{Bl}{\sqrt{mL}}$

$\Rightarrow \quad \frac{dv}{dt} = A\omega\cos\omega t$, At $t = 0$; $\frac{dv}{dt} = g$

$\Rightarrow \quad g = A\omega \Rightarrow A = \frac{g}{\omega}$

$\Rightarrow \quad v = \frac{g}{\omega}\sin\omega t \Rightarrow \frac{dx}{dt} = \frac{g}{\omega}\sin\omega t$

$\Rightarrow \quad \int dx = \frac{g}{\omega}\int \sin\omega t\, dt$

$\Rightarrow \quad x = \frac{g}{\omega^2}(1 - \cos\omega t)$

From Eq. (ii), $Bil = mg - m(A\omega\cos\omega t)$

$$i_{max} = \frac{mg + mA\omega}{Bl} \text{ when } \cos\omega t = -1$$

$$= \frac{2mg}{Bl}$$

4. At $t = 0$, inductor acts as open circuit.

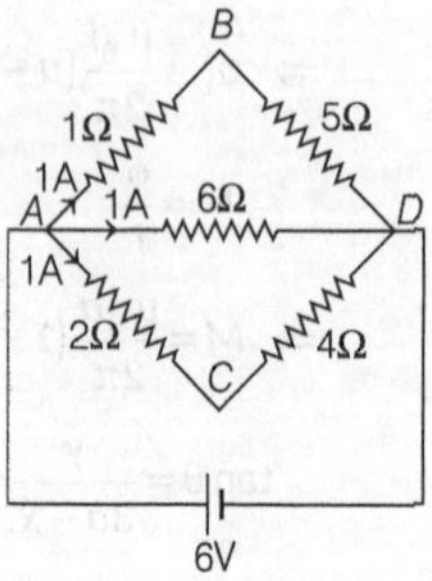

$$V_B + 1(1) - 1(2) = V_C$$

$\Rightarrow \quad V_B - V_C = 1\text{ V}$

$\Rightarrow \quad 0.1\frac{di}{dt} = 1$

$\Rightarrow \quad \frac{di}{dt} = -10\text{ A/s}$

5. Potential difference across 6Ω resistance is 6V (constant). So current will be constant.

6. After a long time, inductor acts as short-circuit.

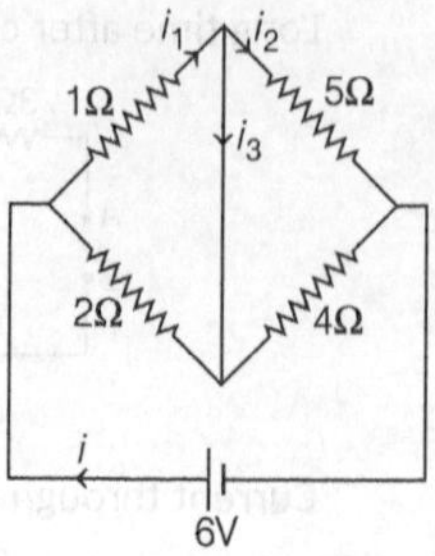

$$R_{eq} = \frac{2\times 1}{2+1} + \frac{5\times 4}{5+4} = \frac{26}{9}\,\Omega$$

$$i = \frac{6}{\left(\frac{26}{9}\right)} = \frac{27}{13}\text{ A}$$

$$i_1 = \left(\frac{2}{2+1}\right)\left(\frac{27}{13}\right) = \frac{18}{13}\text{ A}$$

$$\text{and } i_2 = \left(\frac{4}{4+5}\right)\left(\frac{27}{13}\right) = \frac{12}{13}\text{ A}$$

Current through inductor $= i_1 - i_2 = \frac{6}{13}$ A

7. $L_1 = L, L_2 = nL, \phi = L_1 i_1 = L_2 i_2, i_1 = \frac{E}{R}$

$\Rightarrow \quad i_2 = \frac{L_1}{L_2}i_1 = \frac{i_1}{\eta}$

$$W = \Delta U = \frac{1}{2}L_2 i_2^2 - \frac{1}{2}L_1 i_1^2 = \frac{LE^2}{2\eta R^2}(1-\eta)$$

8. As current increases on pulling out the iron piece, the current will decrease to achieve its steady state value $\frac{E}{R}$ again. At any time

$$+E - IR - \eta L\frac{di}{dt} = 0 \Rightarrow \int_{i_2}^{i}\frac{di}{E - iR} = \int_0^t \frac{dt}{\eta L}$$

Solving, we get

$$i = \frac{E}{R}\left[1 - \left(1 - \frac{1}{\eta}\right)e^{-\frac{t}{\lambda}}\right]$$

9. $P = Ei = \frac{E^2}{R}\left[1 - \left(1 - \frac{1}{\eta}\right)e^{-\frac{t}{\lambda}}\right]$

10. $\phi = B_z(\pi r_0^2) + Li$

$$\frac{d\phi}{dt} = iR = 0 \qquad \{\because R = 0\}$$

$\Rightarrow \quad \phi = \text{constant}$

11. Initial condition, $\phi = B_0(\pi r_0^2)$

$\Rightarrow \quad B_0\pi r_0^2 = B_0(1 - \alpha z)\pi r_0^2 + Li$

$\Rightarrow \quad i = \frac{B_0\alpha\pi r_0^2 z}{L}$

Force on the ring $= B_r i(2\pi r_0) = \frac{2B_0^2\alpha\beta r_0^4\pi^2 z}{L}$

Force due to B_z on the ring is zero.

12. Force on the ring $= Kz$ where, $K = \frac{2B_0^2\alpha\beta r_0^4\pi^2}{L}$

At equilibrium position; $mg = Kz_0$

At general position, $mg - Kz = ma$

$$\Rightarrow \quad a = -\frac{K}{m}(z - z_0)$$

So, the ring will execute SHM with $\omega = \sqrt{\frac{K}{m}}$

13. Since the magnetic field is increasing in inside direction in bigger loop, so the current will be induced in anti-clockwise direction to oppose the increasing flux.

14. $\phi = BA = B(l^2 + b^2)$

$$|\varepsilon| = \left|\frac{d\phi}{dt}\right| = \frac{dB}{dt}(l^2 + b^2) = 0.5\text{ V}$$

15. $i = \frac{\varepsilon}{2R}\left(1 - e^{-\frac{2Rt}{2L}}\right)$

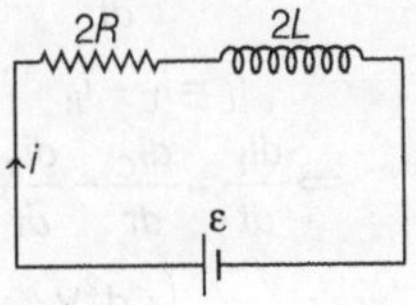

$$= \frac{1}{40}(1 - e^{-t})$$

16., 17. and 18.

At $t = 0$; $q_0 = CV = 10(1) = 10\,\mu\text{C}$

$$i_0 = \frac{\varepsilon}{R} = \frac{10}{100} = 0.1\text{ A}$$

$$U = \frac{q_0^2}{2C} + \frac{1}{2}Li_0^2$$

$$= \frac{(10 \times 10^{-6})^2}{2 \times 1 \times 10^{-6}} + \frac{1}{2} \times 10 \times 10^{-3}(0.1)^2$$

$$= 100\,\mu\text{J}$$

$$\frac{q_{max}^2}{2C} = 100 \times 10^{-6} \quad \Rightarrow \quad q_{max} = 10\sqrt{2}\,\mu\text{C}$$

So, $q = q_{max}\sin(\omega t + \phi)$ where $\omega = \frac{1}{\sqrt{LC}} = 10^4$ rad/s

$$i = \frac{dq}{dt} = q_{max}\omega\cos(\omega t + \phi)$$

So, $i_{max} = q_{max}\omega = (10\sqrt{2} \times 10^{-6})(10^4) = \frac{1}{5\sqrt{2}}$ A

At $t = 0$; $i = -0.1 = \frac{1}{5\sqrt{2}}\cos\phi \Rightarrow \phi = \frac{3\pi}{4}$

So, $q = (10\sqrt{2}\,\mu\text{C})\sin\left(10^4 t + \frac{3\pi}{4}\right)$

Energy stored in inductor would be minimum when $\cos(\omega t + \phi) = 0$

$$\Rightarrow \quad 10^4 t + \frac{3\pi}{4} = \frac{3\pi}{2}$$

$$\Rightarrow \quad t = \frac{3\pi}{4} \times 10^{-4}\text{ sec}$$

19. At $t = 0$, current through $L_2 = i_0 = \frac{V}{R}$

When charge on capacitor is maximum, current through capacitor branch is zero.

So, $L_1(0) + L_2\left(\frac{V}{R}\right) = (L_1 + L_2)i \quad \Rightarrow \quad i = \frac{V}{2R}$

Loss in energy of inductors

$$= \frac{1}{2}L\left(\frac{V}{R}\right)^2 - \frac{1}{2} \times 2L \times \left(\frac{V}{2R}\right)^2 = \frac{LV^2}{4R^2}$$

$$\Rightarrow \frac{q_{max}^2}{2C} = \frac{LV^2}{4R^2} \quad \Rightarrow \quad q_{max} = \left(\sqrt{\frac{1}{2}CL}\right)\left(\frac{V}{R}\right)$$

20. Energy stored in each inductor $= \frac{1}{2}L\left(\frac{V}{2R}\right)^2 = \frac{LV^2}{8R^2}$

21., 22. and 23.

For current to be maximum $\frac{di}{dt} = 0$

So, potential difference across inductor will be zero and potential difference across the capacitors will be same. From conservation of charge on plates 2 and 3

$$3CV + CV = 6CV_0 - CV_0 \quad \Rightarrow \quad V = \frac{5V_0}{4}$$

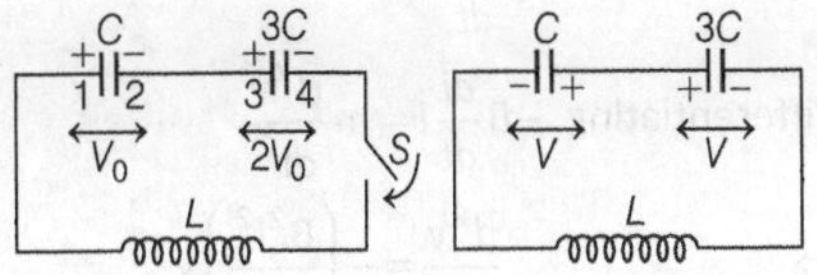

Loss in energy of capacitors = Energy stored in inductor

$$\frac{1}{2}CV_0^2 + \frac{1}{2}(3C)(2V_0)^2 - \frac{1}{2} \times 4C\left(\frac{5V_0}{4}\right)^2 = \frac{1}{2}LI^2$$

$$\Rightarrow \quad I = \frac{3V_0}{2}\sqrt{\frac{3C}{L}}$$

Match The Columns Questions

1. Just after closing the switch, inductor acts as open circuit and capacitor acts as short circuit. So 6Ω is shorted.

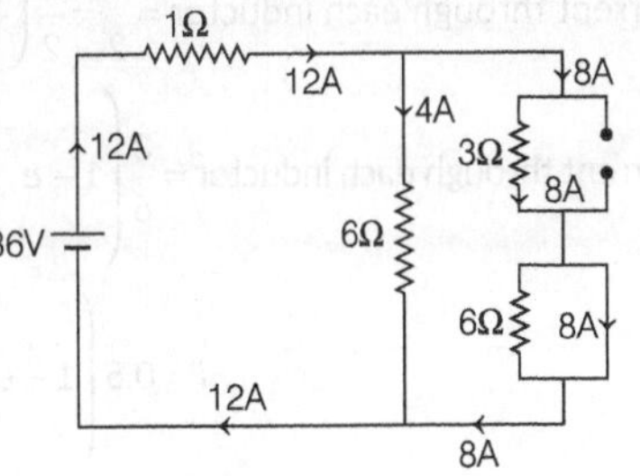

$$R_{eq} = 1 + \frac{6(3)}{6 + 3} = 3\Omega$$

Current through battery = 12 A

Current through capacitor = 8 A

In steady state, inductor acts as short-circuit and capacitor as open circuit.

$$i = \frac{36}{R_{eq}} = \frac{36}{1 + \dfrac{6 \times 6}{6 + 6}} = 9\text{ A}$$

2. (A) $Blv = iR \Rightarrow i = \dfrac{Blv}{R}$

$mg \sin\alpha - Bil = ma$

$$\Rightarrow \quad a = g\sin\alpha - \left(\frac{B^2l^2}{mR}\right)v$$

As v increases, a decreases and after a long time when $a = 0$, rod achieves terminal velocity.

(B) $Blv = \dfrac{q}{C} \Rightarrow q = BlCv \Rightarrow i = \dfrac{dq}{dt} = BlCa$

$mg \sin\alpha - Bil = ma$

$$\Rightarrow \quad a = \frac{mg\sin\alpha}{m + B^2l^2C}$$

So, rod moves with constant acceleration.

(C) $Blv = L\dfrac{di}{dt}$

$$mg\sin\alpha - Bil = m\frac{dv}{dt}$$

$$\text{differentiating, } -B\frac{di}{dt}l = m\frac{d^2v}{dt^2}$$

$$\Rightarrow \quad \frac{d^2v}{dt^2} = -\left(\frac{B^2l^2}{mL}\right)v$$

$$\Rightarrow \quad v = v_{max}\sin\omega t$$

So, rod will perform SHM.

3. (A) $L_{eq} = 3\text{ mH}$

$$i = \frac{\varepsilon}{R}\left(1 - e^{-\frac{Rt}{L}}\right) = \left(1 - e^{-\frac{t}{3\times10^{-3}}}\right)$$

At $t = 3$ ms; $i = 1 - e^{-1} = \dfrac{e-1}{e}$

Current through each inductor $= \dfrac{i}{2} = \dfrac{1}{2}\left(\dfrac{e-1}{e}\right)$

(B) Current through each inductor $= \dfrac{3}{6}\left(1 - e^{-\frac{6t}{18\times10^{-3}}}\right)$

$$i = 0.5\left(1 - e^{-\frac{t}{3\times10^{-3}}}\right)$$

At $t = 3$ ms; $i = \dfrac{1}{2}\left(\dfrac{e-1}{e}\right)$

Current through battery $= 2i = \left(\dfrac{e-1}{e}\right)$

(C) i = current through inductor $= \dfrac{10}{10}\left(1 - e^{-\frac{10t}{30\times10^{-3}}}\right)$

At $t = 3$ ms, $i = \left(\dfrac{e-1}{e}\right)$ A

Current through battery $= \dfrac{10}{10} + \left(\dfrac{e-1}{e}\right) = \dfrac{2e-1}{e}$

(D) It is balanced Wheatstone bridge. So, no current through inductor at any time.

Numerical Value Questions

1. For capacitor, $q = CV$

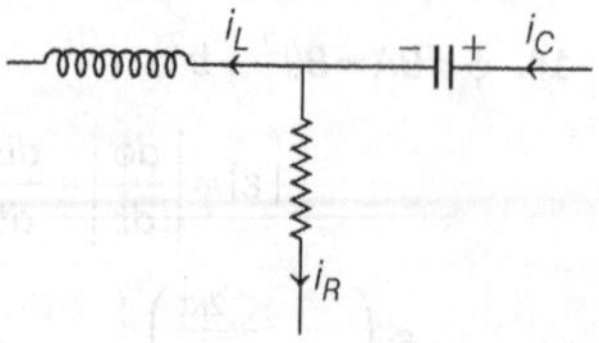

$$i_C = \frac{dq}{dt} = C\frac{dV}{dt} + V\frac{dC}{dt}$$

$$i_L = i_C - i_R$$

$$\Rightarrow \frac{di_L}{dt} = \frac{di_C}{dt} - \frac{di_R}{dt}$$

$$= \left(\frac{Cd^2V}{dt^2} + \frac{dC}{dt}\frac{dV}{dt} + \frac{dV}{dt}\frac{dC}{dt} + V\frac{d^2C}{dt^2}\right) - \frac{di_R}{dt}$$

$$= 6\times10^{-6}\times\frac{1}{2}\times(-0.5\times10^{-6})^2\times2$$
$$+ 2(-0.5\times10^{-6}) + 0 - (-1\times10^{-6})$$

$$= 2\times10^{-6}\text{ As}^{-1}$$

$$V_L = L\frac{di_L}{dt} = 2(2\times10^{-6}) = 4\,\mu\text{V}$$

2. i_0 = Current through inductor just after closing the switch

$$= \frac{120}{200} = \frac{3}{5}\text{ A}$$

$$i = i_0 e^{-\frac{Rt}{L}}$$

$$\Rightarrow \quad i = \frac{3}{5}e^{-\frac{150\ln 2}{30\times5}} = 0.3\text{ A}$$

Current through 50 Ω resistor $= \dfrac{120}{50} = 2.4$ A

Current through switch $S = 2.4 - 0.3 = 2.10$ A

3. Just before and after closing switch S_1, current through inductor will be same. So, $i_3 = \dfrac{\varepsilon}{2R}$

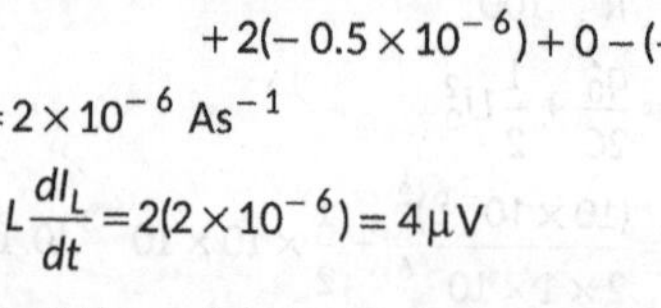

For left loop; $+\varepsilon - i_1R - L\dfrac{di_3}{dt} = 0$ ...(i)

For right loop; $+\varepsilon - i_2(2R) - L\dfrac{di_3}{dt} = 0$ ...(ii)

$$i_3 = i_1 + i_2 = \frac{\varepsilon}{2R} \quad ...(iii)$$

Solving Eqs. (i), (ii) and (iii), we get

$$\frac{di_3}{dt} = \frac{2\varepsilon}{3L} = 2000 \text{ As}^{-1}$$

4. In absence of spring, $L\frac{di}{dt} = Blv$

$$\Sigma F = ma \Rightarrow mg - Bil = m\frac{dv}{dt}$$

Differentiating both sides w.r.t. t,

$$\Rightarrow \quad -B\frac{di}{dt}l = m\frac{d^2v}{dt^2}$$

$$\Rightarrow \quad \frac{d^2v}{dt} = -\left(\frac{B^2l^2}{mL}\right)v$$

$$\Rightarrow v = A\omega \sin\omega t \text{ where, } \omega = \frac{Bl}{\sqrt{mL}}$$

$$a = \frac{dv}{dt} = A\omega^2 \cos\omega t$$

At $\quad t = 0\,; a = g = A\omega^2 \Rightarrow A = \frac{g}{\omega^2}$

So, $\quad X_1 = \frac{g}{\omega^2} = \frac{mgL}{B^2l^2}$

In presence of spring, $L\frac{di}{dt} = Blv$

$$\Sigma F = ma \Rightarrow mg - Bil - kx = ma$$

$$\Rightarrow \quad -B\frac{di}{dt}l - k\frac{dx}{dt} = m\frac{d^2v}{dt^2}$$

$$\Rightarrow \quad \frac{d^2v}{dt^2} = -\left(\frac{B^2l^2}{mL} + \frac{k}{m}\right)v$$

$$\Rightarrow \quad v = A\omega \sin\omega t, \text{ where } \omega = \sqrt{\frac{B^2l^2}{mL} + \frac{k}{m}}$$

$$a = \frac{dv}{dt} = A\omega^2 \cos\omega t$$

At $\quad t = 0; a = g = A\omega^2 \Rightarrow A = \frac{g}{\omega^2}$

So, $X_2 = \frac{g}{\omega^2} = \frac{mgL}{B^2l^2 + kL}$

$$\frac{X_1}{X_2} = \frac{B^2l^2 + kL}{B^2l^2} = 3$$

5. $\varepsilon = \frac{1}{2}B\omega l^2 = \frac{1}{2} \times 0.1 \times 2 \times (2)^2 = 0.4 \text{ V}$

$$i = \frac{\varepsilon}{R}\left(1 - e^{-\frac{Rt}{L}}\right) = \frac{0.4}{0.01}\left(1 - e^{-\frac{0.01 \times 0.3 \ln 2}{3 \times 10^{-3}}}\right) = 20 \text{ A}$$

$$\tau = \int_0^l (Bidx)x = \frac{Bil^2}{2} = 4 \text{ N-m}$$

6. $q_0 = \frac{CV}{2} = \frac{500 \times 10^{-6}}{2} \times 20 = 5 \text{ mC}$

$$-\frac{q}{C} - \frac{q}{C} - L\frac{di}{dt} = 0$$

$$\Rightarrow \quad \frac{d^2q}{dt^2} = -\left(\frac{2}{LC}\right)q$$

$$\Rightarrow \quad q = q_0 \cos\omega t \text{ where, } \omega = \sqrt{\frac{2}{LC}} = 2 \text{ rad/s}$$

At $\quad t = \frac{\pi}{4};\, q = q_0 \cos\left(2\left(\frac{\pi}{4}\right)\right) = 0$

$$i = q_0\omega \sin\omega t = 5 \times 10^{-3} \times 2 \sin\left(\frac{\pi}{2}\right)$$

$$= 10 \text{ mA}$$

So, at breakdown, both capacitors are uncharged and entire energy is stored in the inductor.

$$\frac{1}{2}Li^2 = \frac{q_{max}^2}{2C}$$

$$\Rightarrow \quad \frac{1}{2} \times 1000 \times (10 \times 10^{-3})^2 = \frac{q_{max}^2}{2 \times 500 \times 10^{-6}}$$

$$\Rightarrow \quad q_{max} = \sqrt{50} = 5\sqrt{2} \text{ mC}$$

7. $\frac{1}{2} \times 1200 \times 10^{-6} \times V^2 = \frac{1}{2} \times 300 \times 10^{-6} \times (16)^2$

$$\Rightarrow \quad V = 8 \text{ V}$$

8. $\Delta q = \frac{\Delta\phi}{R} = M\frac{\Delta i}{R} = \frac{M(kT^2 - 0)}{R} = \frac{KMT^2}{R}$

So, $\quad \frac{\lambda}{1 - \lambda} = 1$

$$\Rightarrow \quad \lambda = \frac{1}{2} \Rightarrow \frac{1}{\lambda} = 2$$

Previous Years Questions

JEE Main

1. $L = 0.002 \text{ H}, i = i_0 \sin\omega t, i_0 = 5\text{A}, \quad \omega = 50\pi \text{ rad/s}$

Induced emf is, $E = -L\frac{di}{dt}$

Also, $\frac{di}{dt} = \omega L \cos\omega t$

$$E = -i_0\omega L \cos\omega t$$

When, $\cos\omega t = -1, E$ will be maximum

$$E_{max} = -5 \times 50\pi \times 0.002 \times (-1)$$

$$= 5 \times 50\pi \times 0.002$$

$$= \frac{5 \times 50\pi \times 2}{1000} = \frac{\pi}{2} \text{ V}$$

$\therefore \quad \alpha = 2$

2. By energy conservation,

$$\frac{1}{2}CV^2 = \frac{1}{2}LI_{max}^2$$

$$I_{max}^2 = \frac{CV^2}{L}$$

$$I_{max} = \sqrt{\frac{C}{L}}.V$$

$$C = 100\,\mu F = 100 \times 10^{-6}\text{ F}$$

$$L = 6.4 \times 10^{-3}\text{ H}, V = 12\text{ V}$$

$$I_{max} = \sqrt{\frac{100 \times 10^{-6}}{6.4 \times 10^{-3}}}\,V$$

$$= \sqrt{\frac{100 \times 10^{-6}}{6.4 \times 10^{-3}}} \times 12$$

$$= \sqrt{\frac{100}{6400}} \times 12$$

$$= \frac{10}{80} \times 12 = \frac{120}{80}$$

$$= \frac{12}{8} = \frac{3}{2}$$

$$I_{max} = 1.5\text{ A}$$

3. For two concentric coplanar square loops,

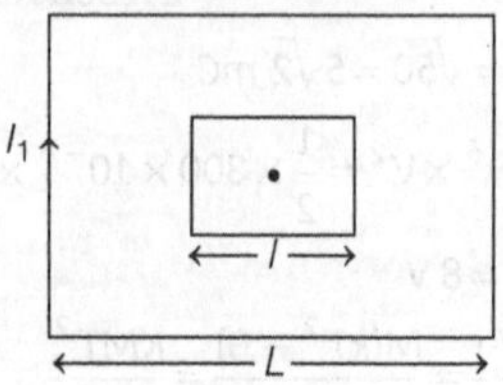

Magnetic field at centre due to outer loop is,

$$B_1 = \frac{\mu_0}{4\pi} \cdot \frac{8\sqrt{2}I_1}{L}$$

So, coefficient of mutual inductance is,

$$M = \frac{B_1 A_2}{I_1} = \frac{\mu_0}{4\pi} \frac{8\sqrt{2}}{L} \times l^2$$

Here, $\frac{\mu_0}{4\pi} = 10^{-7}$ and $l^2 = L$

So, $M = 8\sqrt{2} \times 10^{-7}\text{ H}$

Now given,

$$M = \sqrt{x} \times 10^{-7} = 8\sqrt{2} \times 10^{-7}$$

$\therefore$ $\sqrt{x} = 8\sqrt{2}$

or $x = 64 \times 2 = 128$

4. The steady state current flowing in the circuit until opening the switch is,

$$i = \frac{E}{R} = \frac{12}{6} = 2\text{ A}$$

The final current becomes zero, when the switch is opened.

We know that induced emf,

$$e = -L\frac{dI}{dt}$$

$$20 = -L\left[\frac{0-(2)}{1 \times 10^{-3}}\right]$$

$\Rightarrow$ $20 = L \times 2 \times 10^3$

$\Rightarrow$ $L = 10^{-2}\text{ H} = 10\text{ mH}$

5.

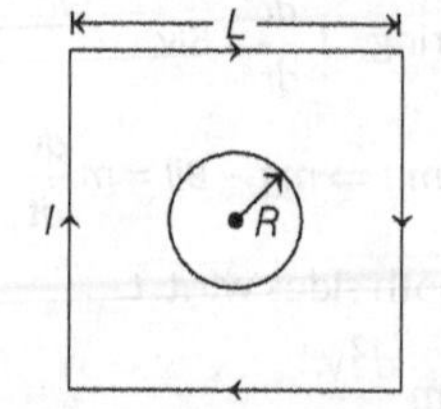

Mutual inductance,

$$M = \frac{\text{Number of Flux Linkages}}{\text{Current}} = \frac{B_1 A_2}{I_1}$$

B_1 = Field of square due to current I in it

$$= \left(\frac{\mu_0}{4\pi} \times \frac{2I\sin 45°}{L/2}\right) \times 4$$

$$= \frac{\mu_0 2\sqrt{2}I}{\pi L}$$

So, $$M = \frac{\frac{\mu_0 2\sqrt{2}I}{\pi L} \times \pi R^2}{I} = \frac{\mu_0 2\sqrt{2}R^2}{L}$$

6. Given,

$$a = 1000\text{ cm}, b = 1\text{ cm}$$

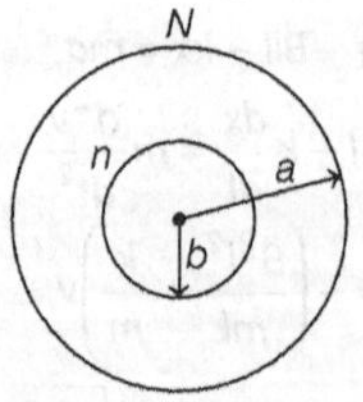

$$b << a$$

We will take larger coil as primary

$$B = \frac{\mu_0 i_p N}{2a}$$

Flux passing through secondary coil,

$$\phi_s = BA = \frac{\mu_0 i_p N}{2a} \times \pi b^2 \times n$$

Mutual Inductancel,

$$M = \frac{\phi_s}{i_p}$$

$$M = \frac{\mu_0 N n \pi b^2}{2a}$$

$$M = \frac{4\pi \times 10^{-7} \times 200 \times 10 \times \pi \times 1 \times 10^{-4}}{2 \times 1000 \times 10^{-2}}$$

$$= 4\pi^2 \times 10^{-9}$$

or $M = 4 \times 10^{-8}\text{ H}$ (using $\pi^2 = 10$)

7. After a long time, induced emf in the coil will be zero.

So, we have equivalent circuit,

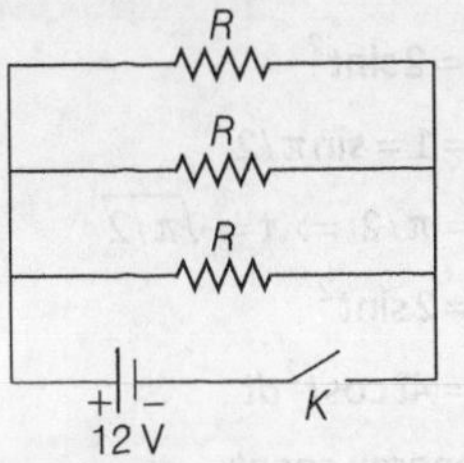

Equivalent resistance R_{eq} of circuit is given by,

$$\frac{1}{R_{eq}} = \frac{1}{R_1} + \frac{1}{R_2} + \frac{1}{R_3}$$

$$= \frac{3}{12} = \frac{1}{4}$$

or $\quad R_{eq} = 4\Omega$

Circuit current,

$$I = \frac{V}{R_{eq}} = \frac{12}{4} = 3\text{ A}$$

8. $\Rightarrow V_A - IR - \frac{LdI}{dt} - 12 = V_B$

$\Rightarrow V_A - V_B = 2 \times 12 + 6(-1) + 12$

$\Rightarrow V_A - V_B = 24 - 6 + 12$

$\Rightarrow V_A - V_B = 30\text{ V}$

$\Rightarrow \quad \Delta V = 30\text{ V}$

9. Given

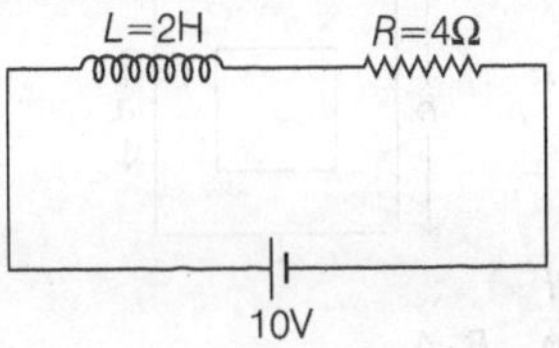

at $t = \infty$

L = Short circuit

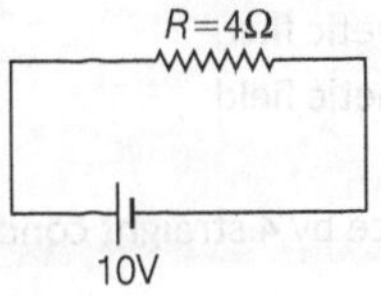

$$I = \frac{V}{R} = \frac{10}{4}$$

$$\text{Energy stored} = \frac{1}{2}LI^2$$

$$= \frac{1}{2} \times 2 \times \frac{100}{16} = 6.25$$

$$= 625 \times 10^{-2}\text{ J}$$

10. Stored energy,

$$U = \frac{1}{2}LI^2$$

We know that,

$$I = I_0(1 - e^{-t/\tau}) \qquad \text{...(i)}$$

Rate of energy,

$$P = \frac{dU}{dt}$$

$$\Rightarrow \quad P = \frac{d}{dt}\left(\frac{1}{2}LI^2\right)$$

$$\Rightarrow \quad P = LI \cdot \frac{dI}{dt}$$

$$\frac{dP}{dt} = L\left[I\frac{d^2I}{dt^2} + \left(\frac{dI}{dt}\right)^2\right]$$

From maximum rate, $\frac{dP}{dt} = 0$

$$\Rightarrow \quad I\frac{d^2I}{dt^2} = -\left(\frac{dI}{dt}\right)^2 \qquad \text{...(ii)}$$

From Eq. (i) $\frac{dI}{dt} = \frac{I_0}{\tau^2}e^{-\frac{t}{\tau}}$

∴ From Eq. (ii), we get

$$I_0(1 - e^{-t/\tau}) \times \frac{I_0}{\tau^2}e^{-\frac{t}{\tau}} = -\frac{I_0^2}{\tau^2}e^{\frac{2t}{\tau}}$$

Let, $\quad e^{-\frac{t}{\tau}} = X,\ X = 2X^2$

$$\Rightarrow \quad X = \frac{1}{2}$$

∴ Maximum power

$$P = LI\frac{dI}{dt} = LI\left(1 - \frac{1}{2}\right)\left(\frac{I}{\tau} \times \frac{1}{2}\right)$$

$$\Rightarrow \quad P = \frac{LI_0^2}{4 \times \frac{L}{R}} = \frac{I_0^2 R}{4}$$

$$\Rightarrow \quad P = \frac{E^2}{4R} = \frac{E^a}{2b} \qquad \text{[given]}$$

∴ $\quad a = 2, b = 2R = 2 \times 25 = 50$

∴ $\quad \frac{b}{a} = \frac{50}{2} = 25$

11. In an oscillatory *L-C* circuit initial energy stored is;

$$U_{E\max} = \frac{1}{2}\frac{Q_{\max}^2}{C}$$

And maximum energy of inductor when capacitor is fully empty and current in circuit is maximum is;

$$U_{B_{\max}} = \frac{1}{2}LI_{\max}^2$$

Assuming N_0 loss of energy,

$$U_{E_{\max}} = U_{B_{\max}}$$

$$\frac{1}{2}\frac{Q_{\max}^2}{C} = \frac{1}{2}LI_{\max}^2$$

$$\Rightarrow \quad I_{max}^2 = \frac{Q_{max}^2}{LC}$$

$$\Rightarrow \quad I_{max} = Q_{max} / \sqrt{LC}$$

$$= \frac{2.7 \times 10^{-6}}{\sqrt{75 \times 10^{-3} \times 1.2 \times 10^{-6}}}$$

$$= \frac{2.7 \times 10^{-6}}{\sqrt{9 \times 10^{-8}}} = \frac{2.7 \times 10^{-6}}{3 \times 10^{-4}}$$

$$= 0.9 \times 10^{-2} = 9 \text{ mA}$$

12. Just after closing the switch S, the current in the inductor branch is zero for this short duration of time at $t = 0$. So, the circuit reduced to as shown below.

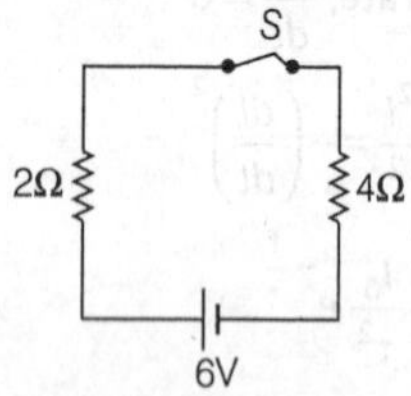

The equivalent resistance of circuit,

$$R_{eq} = 4 + 2 = 6\Omega$$

Current through battery,

$$I = \frac{V}{R_{eq}} = \frac{6}{6} = 1 \text{ A}$$

13.

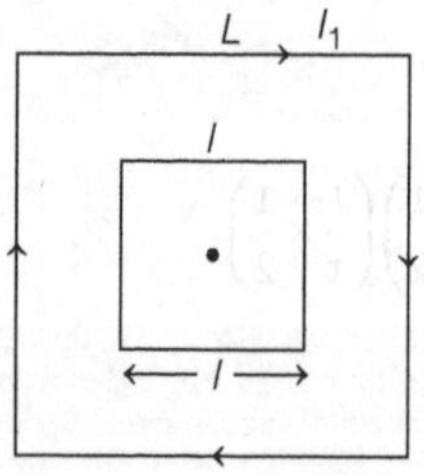

Magnetic field due to one of side at near centre is

$$B_1 = \frac{\mu_0}{4\pi} \cdot \frac{2I_1 \sin 45°}{L/2}$$

Hence, net magnetic field at centre is

$$B = 4B_1 = \frac{\mu_0 I_1 2\sqrt{2}}{4\pi L} \times 4$$

Flux linked with inner coil,

$$\phi_B = B \cdot A = \frac{\mu_0 I_1 \times 2\sqrt{2} \times 4}{4\pi L} \times l^2$$

Mutual inductance of coils is

$$M = \frac{\phi}{I_1} = \frac{\mu_0 \times 2\sqrt{2} \times 4 \times l^2}{4\pi L}$$

$$M = \frac{\mu_0 \times 2\sqrt{2} \times l^2}{\pi L} = \frac{2\sqrt{2}\mu_0 l^2}{\pi L}$$

14. Self inductance of coil, $L = 2.0$ H

Current, $I = 2\sin t^2$

At $t = 0, I = 0$A

When, $I = 2$A

Then, $\quad 2 = 2\sin t^2$

$$\Rightarrow \quad \sin t^2 = 1 = \sin \pi/2$$

$$\Rightarrow \quad t^2 = \pi/2 \Rightarrow t = \sqrt{\pi/2}$$

Since, $\quad I = 2\sin t^2$

$$dI = 4t\cos t^2 dt$$

∴ Amount of energy spent,

$$E = \int LI\, dI$$

$$= \int_0^{\sqrt{\pi/2}} 2 \times 2\sin t^2 \times 4t\cos t^2 dt$$

$$= 8\int_0^{\sqrt{\pi/2}} t\sin(2t^2)\, dt$$

Put, $2t^2 = x$ | when, $t = 0$, $x = 0$

$4t dt = dx$ | when, $t = \sqrt{\pi/2}$

$tdt = \frac{dx}{4}$ | $x = 2 \times \frac{\pi}{2} = \pi$

$$= 8\int_0^{\pi} \sin x \frac{dx}{4} = 4\text{J}$$

15. Given, side of one square loop $= a$

Side of 2nd square loop $= b$

$$b >> a$$

Current $= i$

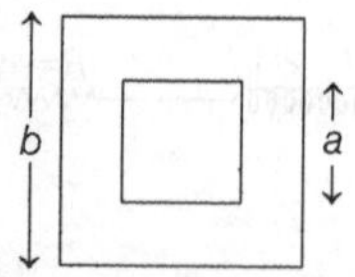

Since, $\phi = Mi$

$$M = \frac{\phi}{i} = \frac{B \cdot A}{i}$$

where, M = mutual inductance,

ϕ = magnetic flux,

B = magnetic field

and $\quad A$ = area.

Mutual inductance by 4 straight conductor,

$$M = \frac{4B \cdot A}{i}$$

$$M = \frac{4\left[\frac{\mu_0}{4\pi}\frac{i}{b/2}(\sin\pi/4 + \sin\pi/4)\right]a^2}{i}$$

$$= \left(\frac{\mu_0}{4\pi}\frac{1}{b}8\sqrt{2}a^2\right) = \left(\frac{\mu_0}{4\pi}8\sqrt{2}\frac{a^2}{b}\right)$$

16. Magnetic energy is stored in an inductor, whereas energy is dissipated through resistor.

Given, $\quad U_m = 64$ J

$$i = 8 \text{ A and } P = 640 \text{ W}$$

As, magnetic energy, $U_m = \frac{1}{2}Li^2$

$$\Rightarrow \quad 64 = \frac{1}{2} \times L \times 64 \Rightarrow L = 2\text{ H}$$

Energy dissipated, $P = i^2 R$

$$\Rightarrow \quad 640 = 64R \Rightarrow R = 10\,\Omega$$

Time constant of *R-L* circuit is given by

$$\tau = \frac{L}{R}$$

$$\Rightarrow \quad \tau = \frac{2}{10} = \frac{1}{5} = 0.2\text{ s}$$

17. The expression of the magnetic energy stored in the solenoid, $U = LI^2/2$

The maximum value of the magnetic energy stored in the solenoid,

$$U_0 = LI_0^2/2$$

Given, $\quad U = 25\% \times U_0$

$$\Rightarrow \quad \frac{LI^2}{2} = \frac{1}{4} \times \frac{LI_0^2}{2} \Rightarrow I = \frac{I_0}{2}$$

Therefore, using the formula for the decay current in *L-R* circuit,

$$I = I_0(1 - e^{-t/\tau}) \Rightarrow \frac{I_0}{2} = I_0(1 - e^{-t/\tau})$$

$$e^{-t/\tau} = 1/2 \Rightarrow t = \tau \ln 2$$

$$\Rightarrow \quad t = \frac{L}{R}\ln 2$$

18. Given, inductance of coil, $L = 2\text{H}$

Supply voltage, $V = 3t$ V

Let *E* be the energy stored in the coil.

Since, emf $V = L \cdot \frac{dI}{dt}$

$$3t = L\frac{dI}{dt} \Rightarrow 3t\,dt = L\,dI$$

On integrating both sides, we get

$$3\frac{t^2}{2} = LI$$

At $t = 4$ s,

$$\frac{3}{2} \times 4^2 = LI \Rightarrow \frac{3}{2} \times \frac{16}{L} = I$$

$$\Rightarrow \quad 24/L = I \quad \text{...(i)}$$

As, $\quad E = 1/2\,LI^2$

$$\therefore \quad E = 1/2\,L\frac{24^2}{L^2} \quad \text{[From Eq. (i)]}$$

$$= \frac{1}{2}\frac{24^2}{L} = \frac{24^2}{2 \times 2} = 144\text{ J}$$

19. In case of circuit having inductor and resistor,

$$I = I_0 e^{-t/\tau} \quad \text{...(i)}$$

$$I = I_0 e^{\frac{-tR}{L}} = \frac{V}{R}e^{-t\frac{R}{L}}$$

$$\Rightarrow \quad I = \frac{20}{10 \times 10^3} e^{-\frac{1 \times 10^{-6} \times 10 \times 10^3}{10 \times 10^{-3}}}$$

$$= 2 \times 10^{-3} e^{-1} = 2e^{-1}\text{ mA}$$

$$= 2 \times 0.37\text{ mA} = 0.74\text{ mA}$$

$$= 74/100\text{ mA}$$

Comparing with given value, i.e.

$$I = \frac{x}{100}\text{ mA, we get}$$

$$x = 74$$

20. Let *t* be the required time at which the energy stored in inductor becomes $\left(\frac{1}{n}\right)$ times of its maximum value.

According to question, for given *L-R* circuit,

$$U = \frac{1}{n}U_{\max}$$

$$\frac{1}{2}LI^2 = \frac{1}{n} \times \frac{1}{2}LI_{\max}^2$$

$$\frac{1}{2}L\left[I_{\max}\left(1 - e^{\frac{-Rt}{L}}\right)\right]^2 = \frac{1}{n} \times \frac{1}{2}LI_{\max}^2$$

$$\Rightarrow \quad e^{-\frac{Rt}{L}} = \frac{\sqrt{n} - 1}{\sqrt{n}}$$

$$\Rightarrow \quad t = \frac{L}{R}\ln\left(\frac{\sqrt{n}}{\sqrt{n} - 1}\right)$$

Hence, option (d) is correct.

21. Given that, at any instant, $I = 1$ A

$$\frac{dI}{dt} = -10^2\text{ A/s (as current is decreasing)}$$

Applying KVL from point *P* to point *Q*,

$$V_P + \frac{LdI}{dt} - 30 + IR = V_Q$$

$$V_P - V_Q = 30 - 1 \times 2 - 50 \times 10^{-3} \times (-10^2) = 33\text{ V}$$

22. In an *L-R* circuit, current growth occurs as

$$I = I_0\left(1 - e^{-\frac{R}{L}t}\right) \quad \text{...(i)}$$

$$\frac{I}{I_0} = \left(1 - e^{-\frac{5}{10 \times 10^{-3}} \times 40}\right) = 1 - e^{-2 \times 10^4}$$

$$\Rightarrow \quad \frac{I_0}{I} = \frac{1}{1 - e^{-2 \times 10^4}} \approx 1$$

$$\therefore \quad \frac{I_0}{I} \approx 1.06\text{ (nearest option)}$$

23. In an *L-R* circuit as shown in the figure, instantaneous current at time *t*.

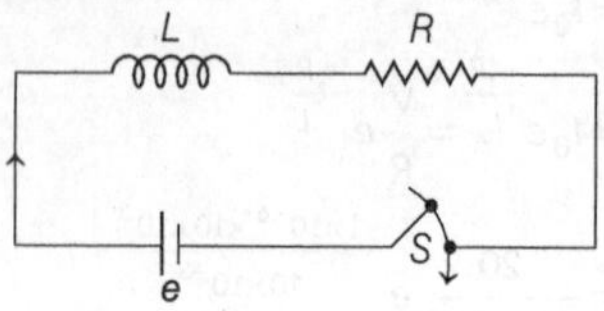

$$i = I(1 - e^{-\frac{R.t}{L}})$$

where, $\frac{L}{R} = t_c$ = time constant of the circuit.

Now, charge that flows from $t = 0$ to $t = t_c$ from battery,

$$q = \int_0^{t_c} i dt = I\int_0^{t_c} (1 - e^{-\frac{R}{L}.t})dt = I\frac{L}{R}e^{-1}$$

Here, I is maximum current which occurs at $t = \infty$ and its value is,

$$I = \frac{\varepsilon}{R}$$

So, $$q = \frac{\varepsilon}{R}.\frac{L}{R}.\frac{1}{e} = \frac{\varepsilon L}{eR^2}$$

24. From an inductor (choke),

$$E_{\text{induced}} = L\frac{dI}{dt} \Rightarrow L = \frac{E \times \Delta t}{\Delta t}$$

Here, $E = 100$ V, $\Delta I = 0.25$ A

and $\Delta t = 0.025$ ms $= 0.025 \times 10^{-3}$ s

So, $$L = \frac{100 \times 0.025 \times 10^{-3}}{0.25} = 100 \times 10^{-4} = 10 \text{ mH}$$

25. Self inductance L_{sol} of a solenoid is given by

$$L_{sol} = \mu_0 n^2 \pi r^2 L$$

(Here, $n = N/L$ and L = length of solenoid)

or $$L_{sol} = \frac{\mu_0 N^2 \pi r^2}{L}$$

Clearly, $L_{sol} \propto \frac{1}{L}$ ($\because$ All other parameters are fixed)

26. As, coefficient of mutual induction is same for both coils

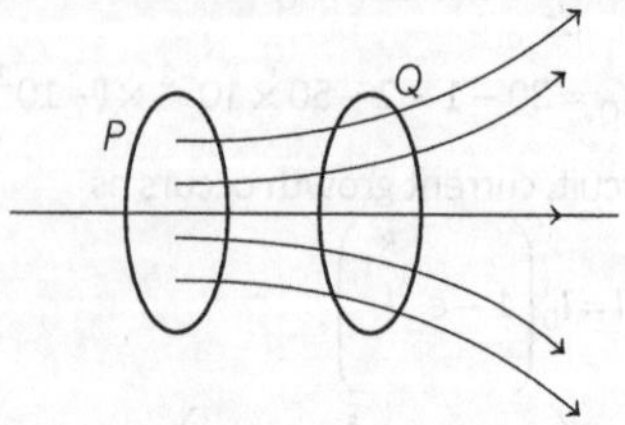

$\therefore$ $$M_{PQ} = M_{QP}$$

$\Rightarrow$ $$\frac{N_P \phi_{PQ}}{I_Q} = \frac{N_Q \phi_{QP}}{I_P} \quad \text{...(i)}$$

Here, $N_P = N_Q = 1$,

$\phi_{PQ} = ?$, $\phi_{QP} = 10^{-3}$ Wb

$I_Q = 2$A, $I_P = 3$A

Substituting values in Eq (i), we get

$$\phi_{PQ} = \frac{I_Q \cdot \phi_{QP}}{I_P} = \frac{2}{3} \times 10^{-3} = 0.667 \times 10^{-3}$$
$$= 6.67 \times 10^{-4} \text{ Wb}$$

27. Energy stored in an inductor of inductance L and current I is given by

$$E = \frac{1}{2}LI^2$$

When, current is being changed from I_1 to I_2, change in energy will be

$$\Delta E = E_2 - E_1 = \frac{1}{2}LI_2^2 - \frac{1}{2}LI_1^2 \quad \text{...(i)}$$

As I_1 and I_2 are given, we need to find value of L.

Now, induced emf in a coil is $\varepsilon = L\frac{dI}{dt}$

Here, $\varepsilon = 25$ V,

$dI = I_2 - I_1 = (25 - 10) = 15$ A

and $dt = 1$ s

$\Rightarrow$ $$25 = L \times \frac{15}{1}$$

or $$L = \frac{25}{15} = 5/3 \text{ H}$$

Putting values of L, I_1 and I_2 in Eq. (i), we get

$$\Delta E = \frac{1}{2} \times \frac{5}{3} \times [25^2 - 10^2] = \frac{1}{2} \times \frac{5}{3} \times 525$$

$$\Delta E = 437.5 \text{ J}$$

28. Mutual inductance for a coaxial solenoid of radius r_1 and r_2 and number of turns n_1 and n_2, respectively is given as,

$M = \mu_0 n_1 n_2 \pi r_1^2 l$ (for internal coil of radius r_1)

Self inductance for the internal coil,

$$L = \mu_0 n_1^2 \pi r_1^2 l$$

$\therefore$ $$\frac{M}{L} = \frac{n_1 n_2}{n_1^2} = \frac{n_2}{n_1}$$

29. Self-inductance of a coil is given by the relation $L = \mu_0 n^2 A \cdot l$

where, n is number of turns per unit length. Shape of the wooden frame is equilateral triangle.

$\therefore$ Area of equilateral triangle, $A = \frac{\sqrt{3}}{4}a^2$ (where, a is side of equilateral triangle)

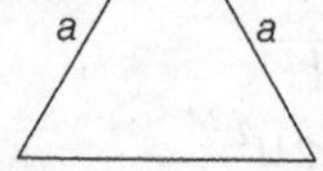

$\therefore$ Self-inductance,

$$L = \mu_0 n^2 \left[\frac{\sqrt{3}}{4}a^2\right].l$$

Here, $l = 3a \times N$ (where, N is total turns)

$$\therefore \quad L = \mu_0 n^2 \left[\frac{\sqrt{3}}{4}a^2\right] \times 3aN \text{ or } L \propto a^3$$

When each side of frame is increased by a factor 3 keeping the number of turns per unit length of the frame constant.

Then, $a' = 3a$

$\therefore \quad L' \propto (a')^3$ or $L' \propto (3a)^3$

or $\quad L' \propto 27a^3$ or $L' = 27L$

So, self-inductance will becomes 27 times.

30. Given circuit is a series *L-R* circuit

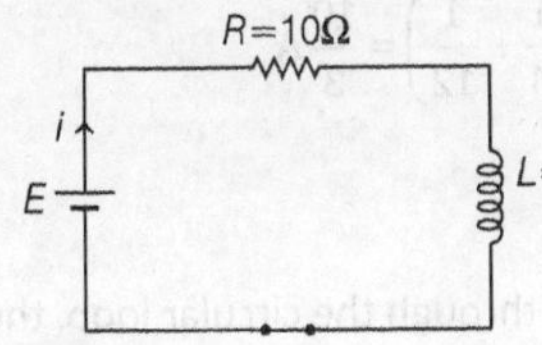

In an *L - R* circuit, current increases is

$$i = \frac{E}{R}\left(1 - e^{-\frac{R}{L}t}\right)$$

Now, energy stored in inductor is

$$U_L = \frac{1}{2}Li^2$$

where, L = self inductance of the coil

and energy dissipated by resistor is

$$U_R = i^2R$$

Given, rate of energy stored in inductor is equal to the rate of energy dissipation in resistor. So, after differentiating, we get

$$iL\frac{di}{dt} = i^2R$$

$$\Rightarrow \quad \frac{di}{dt} = \frac{R}{L}i$$

$$\Rightarrow \quad \frac{E}{R}\cdot\frac{R}{L}e^{-\frac{R}{L}t} = \frac{R}{L}\cdot\frac{E}{R}\left(1 - e^{-\frac{R}{L}t}\right)$$

$$\Rightarrow \quad 2e^{-\frac{R}{L}t} = 1 \Rightarrow e^{-\frac{R}{L}t} = \frac{1}{2}$$

Taking log on both sides, we have

$$\Rightarrow \quad \frac{-R}{L}t = \ln\left(\frac{1}{2}\right)$$

$$\Rightarrow \quad \frac{R}{L}t = \ln 2$$

$$\Rightarrow \quad t = \frac{L}{R}\ln 2 = \frac{20}{10}\ln 2$$

$$\Rightarrow \quad t = 2\ln 2$$

31. Initially in the given *RL* circuit with a source, when S_1 is closed and S_2 is open at $t \le t_0$.

$$I_1 = \frac{V}{R}\left[1 - \exp\left(\frac{-R}{L}t\right)\right]$$

In this case, inductor L is charging.

When switch S_2 is closed and S_1 is open (after $t > t_0$), the inductor will be discharged through resistor.

In this case ($t > t_0$),

$$I_2 = \frac{V}{R}\exp\left[-\frac{R}{L}(t - t_0)\right]$$

Thus, the variation of I with t approximately is shown below

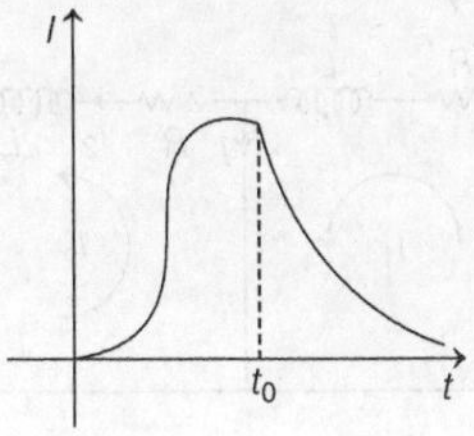

JEE Advanced

1. Emf induced in the circuit is

$$|E| = \left|\frac{d\phi}{dt}\right| = \frac{d}{dt}[(B_0 + \beta t)A] = \beta \times A = 0.04\text{V}$$

So, the circuit can be rearranged as

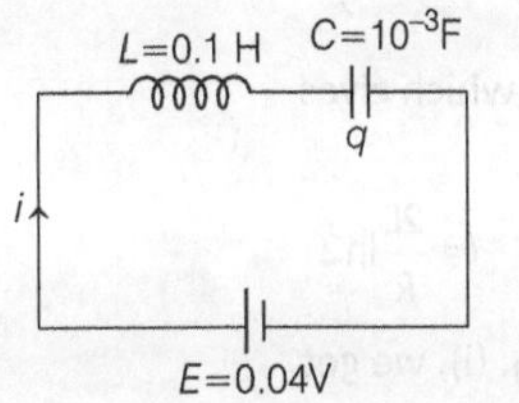

Using Kirchhoff's law we can write

$$E = L\frac{di}{dt} + \frac{q}{C}$$

$$L\frac{di}{dt} = E - \frac{q}{C}$$

$$\text{or} \quad \frac{d^2q}{dt^2} = -\frac{1}{LC}(q - CE)$$

Using SHM concept we can write

$$q = CE + A\sin(\omega t + \phi) \qquad \left(\text{where, } \omega = \frac{1}{\sqrt{LC}}\right)$$

At $t = 0$, $q = 0$ and $i = 0$

So, $\quad A = CE$ and $\phi = -\frac{\pi}{2}$

$$q = CE - CE\cos\omega t$$

So, $\quad i = \frac{dq}{dt} = CE\omega\sin\omega t$

So, $\quad i_{max} = \frac{10^{-3} \times 0.04}{\sqrt{0.1 \times 10^{-3}}} = 4\text{ mA}$

2. Mutual inductance is producing flux in same direction as self-inductance.

$$\therefore \quad U = \frac{1}{2}L_1 I_1^2 + \frac{1}{2}L_2 I_2^2 + M I_1 I_2$$

$$\Rightarrow \quad U = \frac{1}{2}\times(10\times10^{-3})1^2 + \frac{1}{2}\times(20\times10^{-3})\times 2^2 + (5\times10^{-3})\times1\times2$$

$$= 55 \text{ mJ}$$

3. $I_1 = \frac{V}{R}\left(1 - e^{-\frac{tR}{L}}\right)$

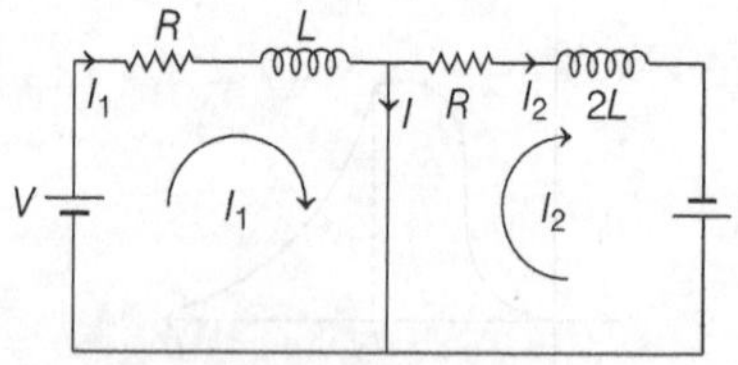

$$I_2 = \frac{V}{R}\left(1 - e^{-\frac{tR}{2L}}\right)$$

From principle of superposition,

$$I = I_1 - I_2 \Rightarrow I = \frac{V}{R}e^{-\frac{tR}{2L}}\left(1 - e^{-\frac{tR}{2L}}\right) \quad \text{...(i)}$$

I is maximum when $\frac{dI}{dt} = 0$, which gives

$$e^{-\frac{tR}{2L}} = \frac{1}{2} \quad \text{or} \quad t = \frac{2L}{R}\ln 2$$

Substituting this time in Eq. (i), we get

$$I_{max} = \frac{V}{4R}$$

4.

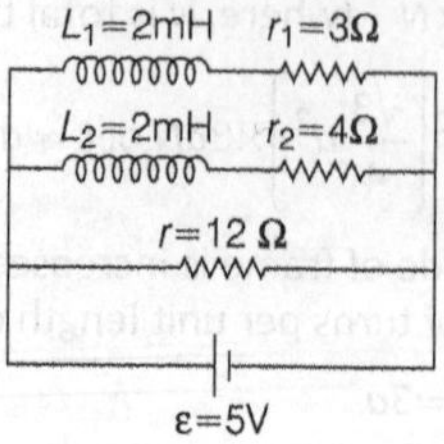

$$I_{min} = \frac{\varepsilon}{R} = \frac{5}{12}\text{A} \quad \text{(Initially at } t \text{)}$$

$$I_{max} = \frac{\varepsilon}{R_{eq}} = \varepsilon\left(\frac{1}{r_1} + \frac{1}{r_2} + \frac{1}{R}\right) \quad \text{(finally in steady state)}$$

$$= 5\left(\frac{1}{3} + \frac{1}{4} + \frac{1}{12}\right) = \frac{10}{3}\text{A}$$

$$\frac{I_{max}}{I_{min}} = 8$$

5. If I current flows through the circular loop, then magnetic field at the location of square loop is:

$$B = \frac{\mu_0 I R^2}{2(R^2 + Z^2)^{3/2}}$$

Substituting the value of $Z = \sqrt{3}R$,

we have, $$B = \frac{\mu_0 I}{16R}$$

Now, total flux through the square loop is

$$\phi_T = NBS\cos\theta = (2)\left(\frac{\mu_0 I}{16R}\right)a^2\cos 45°$$

Mutual inductance,

$$M = \frac{\phi_T}{I} = \frac{\mu_0 a^2}{2^{7/2}R}$$

$$\therefore \quad p = 7$$

CHAPTER~07

ALTERNATING CURRENT

LEVEL 01 Starter Level

7.1 Peak, Average and RMS Value

1 The equation of current in AC circuit is $i = 4\sin\left(100\pi t + \frac{\pi}{3}\right)$ A. Calculate

(i) peak value (ii) rms value
(iii) frequency (iv) initial phase
(v) current at $t = 0$

2 The household supply of electricity is 220 V, 50 Hz. Calculate the peak voltage and the minimum possible time in which the voltage can change from the rms value to zero.

3 Find the average and rms value of current $i = i_m \sin\omega t$ from

(i) $t = 0$ to $t = \frac{\pi}{\omega}$

(ii) $t = \frac{\pi}{2\omega}$ to $t = \frac{3\pi}{2\omega}$

4 Find average and rms value of the saw-tooth voltage of peak value V_0 from $t = 0$ to $t = T$.

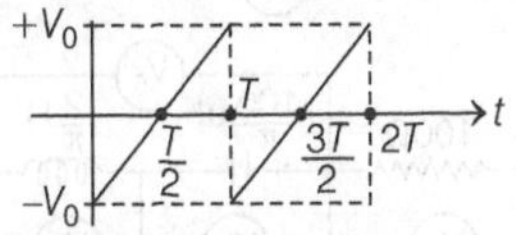

5 Find the effective(rms) value of the following currents.

(i) $i = i_1 \cos\omega t + i_2 \sin\omega t$
(ii) $i = 2\sin 100\pi t + 2\cos(100\pi t + 30°)$
(iii) $i = a + b\sin\omega t$

7.2 Power Consumed in AC Circuit

1 In an AC circuit the instantaneous values of current and applied voltage are respectively $i = (2\text{A})\sin(250\pi\text{s}^{-1})t$ and $\varepsilon = (10\text{V})\sin\left[(250\pi\text{s}^{-1})t + \frac{\pi}{3}\right]$. Find

(i) the instantaneous power drawn from the source at $t = \frac{2}{3}$ ms

(ii) average power

2 If $i = i_0 \sin\omega t$ and $E = E_0 \cos\omega t$, find average power consumed in the circuit.

7.3 Purely Resistive, Capacitive and Inductive Circuits

1 A resistor of resistance 5Ω is connected to an AC source $\varepsilon = (20\text{V})\sin\left[(250\pi\text{s}^{-1})t + \frac{\pi}{3}\right]$. Find

(i) the current and
(ii) the average power consumed by the bulb.

2 A capacitor of capacitance 100 μF is connected with AC source having voltage $\varepsilon = (80\text{V})\sin\left(250t + \frac{\pi}{6}\right)$.

Find

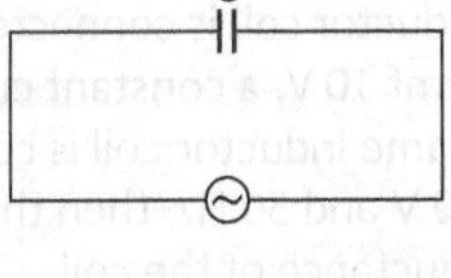

(i) capacitive reactance
(ii) rms current
(iii) instantaneous current
(iv) average power

3 An inductor of inductance $L = 5$ H is connected to an AC source having voltage $\varepsilon = (100\text{V})\sin\left(10t + \frac{\pi}{4}\right)$.

Find

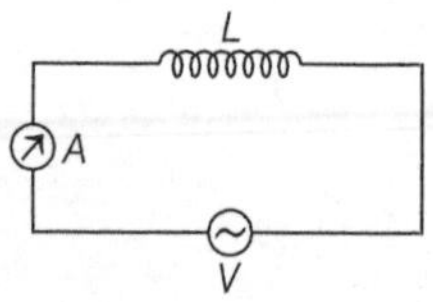

(i) inductive reactance
(ii) ammeter reading
(iii) instantaneous current
(iv) average power

7.4 *RC*, *RL* and *LC* Series Circuits

1 In a *RC* series circuit, the voltage of source is 200V and its frequency is 50 Hz. If $R = 100\ \Omega$ and $C = \frac{100}{\pi}\ \mu$F. Find

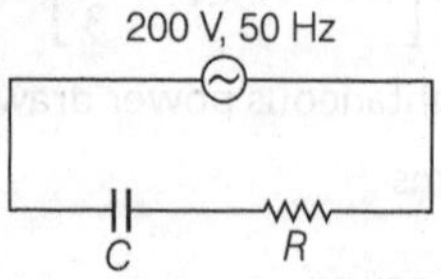

(i) power factor (ii) maximum current
(iii) voltage across *R* (iv) voltage across *C*
(v) power dissipated

2 In the above question if source voltage, $V_s(t) = 200\sqrt{2}\sin(100\pi t)$, find
(i) $i(t)$, (ii) $V_R(t)$ and (iii) $V_C(t)$.

3 A $\frac{9}{100\pi}$ H inductor and a 12Ω resistance are connected in series to a 225 V, 50 Hz AC source. Calculate the current in the circuit and the phase angle between the current and the source voltage.

4 A coil draws a current of 2.0 A and a power of 80 W from an AC source of 50 V and $\frac{5}{\pi}$ Hz. Find the inductance and resistance of the coil.

5 When an inductor coil is connected to an ideal battery of emf 10 V, a constant current 2.5 A flows. When the same inductor coil is connected to an AC source of 10 V and 50 Hz, then the current is 2A. Find out inductance of the coil.

6 A 20 V, 5 W lamp (lamp to be treated as a resistor) is used on AC mains of 200 V and $\frac{50\sqrt{11}}{\pi}$ (cycle per second).
(i) What resistance should be put in series with the lamp, so that the lamp can run on its rated voltage?
(ii) Find capacitance or inductance to be put in series to run the lamp on its rated voltage.
(iii) Which is more economical (the capacitor, the inductor or the resistor)?

7 A circuit consisting of an inductance and a resistance joined to a 250 V AC supply. It draws a current of 10 A. If the power used in the circuit is 1500 W, then calculate the wattless current.

8 A coil has a power factor of 0.866 at 60 Hz. What will be power factor at 180 Hz?

9 A choke coil and a resistance are connected in series in an AC circuit and a potential difference of 130 V is applied to the circuit. If the potential difference across the resistance is 50 V, what would be the potential difference across the choke coil?

10 A circuit containing a 0.5 H inductor and a 400 μF capacitor in series is connected to a 250 V, 100 rad/s supply. The resistance of the circuit is negligible.
(i) Find the current amplitude and rms current.
(ii) Find potential drop across each element.
(iii) What is the total average power absorbed by the circuit?

7.5 *RLC* Series Circuit

1 An inductor 2 H, a capacitor 100 μF and a resistor 75 Ω are connected in series across a source of emf $V = 250\sin 100t$. Here *t* is in second. Find
(i) impedance (ii) current and
(iii) power consumed in the circuit.

2. In the circuit shown in the figure, find

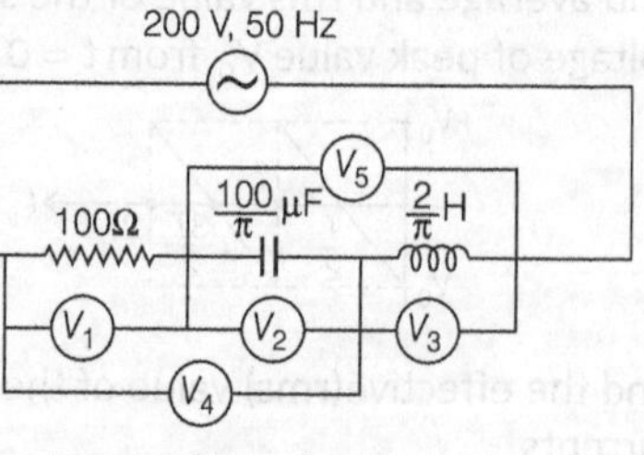

(i) the reactance of the circuit
(ii) impedance of the circuit
(iii) the current
(iv) readings of the ideal AC voltmeters

3 A series circuit consists of a resistance, inductance and capacitance. The applied voltage and the current at any instant are given by $E = 100\cos(5000t - 10°)$ and $i = 5\cos(5000t - 370°)$. The inductance is 0.01 H. Calculate the value of capacitance and resistance.

4 An inductance of 2.0 H, a capacitance of 18 μF and a resistance of 10 kΩ are connected to an AC source of 20 V with adjustable frequency.
(i) What frequency should be chosen to maximise the current in the circuit?
(ii) What is the value of this maximum current ?

5 An inductor coil and a capacitor are connected in series with an AC source of rms voltage 24 V. When the frequency of the source is varied, a maximum rms current of 6.0 A is observed. If this inductor coil is connected to a DC source of 12 V and having internal resistance 4.0 Ω, what will be the current in steady state?

6 An electromagnetic wave of wavelength 300 m can be transmitted by a transmission centre. A condenser of capacity 2.5 μF is available. Find the inductance of the required coil for a resonant circuit. Use $\pi^2 = 10$.

7 A series *L-C-R* circuit with $L = 0.12$ H. $C = 480$ nF, $R = 23\ \Omega$ is connected to a 230 V variable frequency supply.
(i) What is the source frequency for which current amplitude is maximum? Obtain this maximum value.
(ii) What is the source frequency for which average power absorbed by the circuit is maximum? Obtain the value of this maximum power.
(iii) For which frequencies of the source is the power transferred to the circuit half the power at resonant frequency?
(iv) What is the Q-factor of the given circuit?

7.6 Transformer

1 A power transmission line feeds input power at 2300 V to a step-down transformer having 4000 turns in its primary coil. What should be the number of turns in the secondary coil to get output power at 230 V?

2 The output voltage of an ideal transformer, connected to a 240 V AC mains is 24 V. When this transformer is used to light a bulb with rating 24V, 24W, calculate the current in the primary coil of the circuit.

3 A small town with a demand of 800 kW of electric power at 220 V is situated 15 km away from an electric power plant generating power at 440 V. The resistance of the two wire line carrying power is 0.5 Ω per km. The town gets power from the line through a 4000 V - 220 V step-down transformer at a sub-station in the town.
(i) Estimate the line power loss in the form of heat.
(ii) How much power must be plant supply, assuming there is a negligible power loss due to leakage?
(iii) Characterise the step-up transformer at the plant.

LEVEL 02 JEE Main Level

Single Choice Correct Questions

1 In an AC circuit, the current is given by $i = 4\sin(100\pi t + 30°)$ A. The current becomes maximum first time (after $t = 0$) at t equal to

(a) $\left(\frac{1}{200}\right)$ s (b) $\left(\frac{1}{300}\right)$ s
(c) $\left(\frac{1}{50}\right)$ s (d) None of these

2 A resistance of 20Ω is connected to a source of an alternating potential $V = 220\sin(100\pi t)$. The time taken by the current to change from the peak value to rms value, is

(a) 0.2 s (b) 0.25 s
(c) 2.5×10^{-2} s (d) 2.5×10^{-3} s

3 The current in a circuit varies with time as $i = 2\sqrt{t}$ then, the rms value of the current for the interval $t = 2$ s to $t = 4$ s is

(a) $\sqrt{3}$ A (b) $2\sqrt{3}$A
(c) $\frac{\sqrt{3}}{2}$ A (d) $(4 - 2\sqrt{2})$ A

4 In a circuit an AC current and a DC current are supplied together. The expression of the instantaneous current is given as: $i = 3 + 4\sin\left(\omega t + \frac{\pi}{3}\right)$. The rms value of current is

(a) 5 A (b) $\sqrt{17}$ A
(c) $\frac{5}{\sqrt{2}}$ A (d) $\frac{7}{\sqrt{2}}$ A

5 In the given figure if $i_1 = 3 \sin\omega t$ and $i_2 = 4 \cos \omega t$, then i_3 is

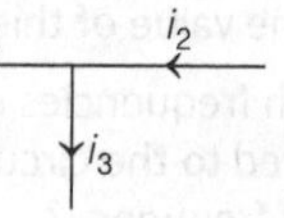

(a) $5 \sin(\omega t + 53°)$ (b) $5 \sin(\omega t + 37°)$
(c) $5 \sin(\omega t + 45°)$ (d) $5 \cos(\omega t + 53°)$

6 An alternating voltage is given by $e = e_1 \sin\omega t + e_2 \cos \omega t$. Then the root mean square value of voltage is given by

(a) $\sqrt{e_1^2 + e_2^2}$ (b) $\sqrt{e_1 e_2}$
(c) $\sqrt{\frac{e_1 e_2}{2}}$ (d) $\sqrt{\frac{e_1^2 + e_2^2}{2}}$

7 A periodic voltage V varies with time t as shown in the figure. T is the time period. The rms value of the voltage is

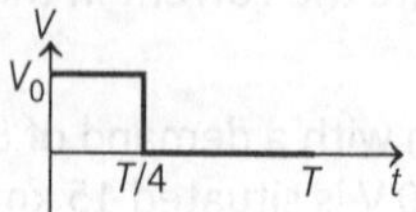

(a) $\frac{V_0}{8}$ (b) $\frac{V_0}{2}$ (c) V_0 (d) $\frac{V_0}{4}$

8 In a certain circuit $E = 200 \cos(314t)$ and $i = \sin\left(314t + \frac{\pi}{4}\right)$. Their vector representation is

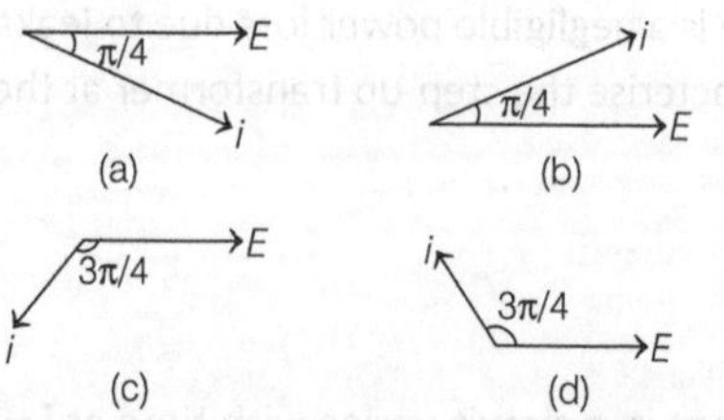

9 The correctly marked ammeter for AC current is shown in

(a) 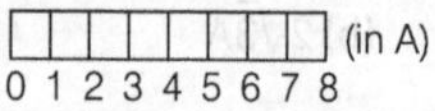

(b) 

(c) 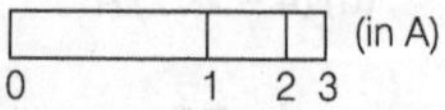

(d) 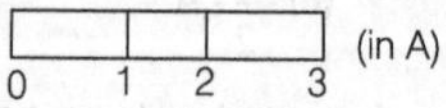

10 The potential difference V and current i flowing through the AC circuit is given by $V = 5 \cos\left(\omega t - \frac{\pi}{6}\right)$ V and $i = 10 \sin \omega t$ A. The average power dissipated in the circuit is

(a) $12.5\sqrt{3}$ W (b) 12.5 W
(c) 25 W (d) 50 W

11 A direct current of 2 A and an alternating current having a maximum value of 2 A flow through two identical resistances. The ratio of heat produced in the two resistances in the same time interval will be

(a) 1 : 1 (b) 1 : 2 (c) 2 : 1 (d) 4 : 1

12 An AC ammeter is used to measure current in a circuit. When a given direct current passes through the circuit, the AC ammeter reads 3 A. When another alternating current passes through the circuit, the AC ammeter reads 4 A, then, the reading of this ammeter if DC and AC flow through the circuit simultaneously, is

(a) 3 A (b) 1 A (c) 7 A (d) 5 A

13 An alternating voltage $V = 300\sqrt{2} \sin(100t)$ is connected to a 1 μF capacitor through an AC ammeter. The reading of the ammeter will be

(a) 10 mA (b) 30 mA (c) $30\sqrt{2}$ mA (d) $20\sqrt{2}$ mA

14 A coil of inductance 0.1 H is connected to an alternating voltage generator of voltage $E = 100 \sin(100t)$ V. The current flowing through the coil will be

(a) $10\sqrt{2} \sin(100t)$ A (b) $10 \cos(100t)$ A
(c) $-10 \sin(100t)$ A (d) $-10 \cos(100t)$ A

15 At a frequency ω_0 the reactance of a certain capacitor equals that of a certain inductor. If the frequency is changed to $2\omega_0$, what is the ratio of the reactance of the inductor to that of the capacitor?

(a) 4 : 1 (b) $\sqrt{2}$: 1 (c) 1 : $2\sqrt{2}$ (d) 1 : 2

16 A capacitor of capacitance 100 μF and a resistance of 100Ω is connected in series with AC supply of 220 V, 50 Hz. The current leads the voltage by

(a) $\tan^{-1}\left(\frac{1}{2\pi}\right)$ (b) $\tan^{-1}\left(\frac{1}{\pi}\right)$
(c) $\tan^{-1}\left(\frac{2}{\pi}\right)$ (d) $\tan^{-1}\left(\frac{4}{\pi}\right)$

17 In a series RC circuit shown in figure, the applied voltage is 10V and the voltage across capacitor is found to be 8V. Then the voltage across R, and the phase difference between current and the applied voltage will respectively be

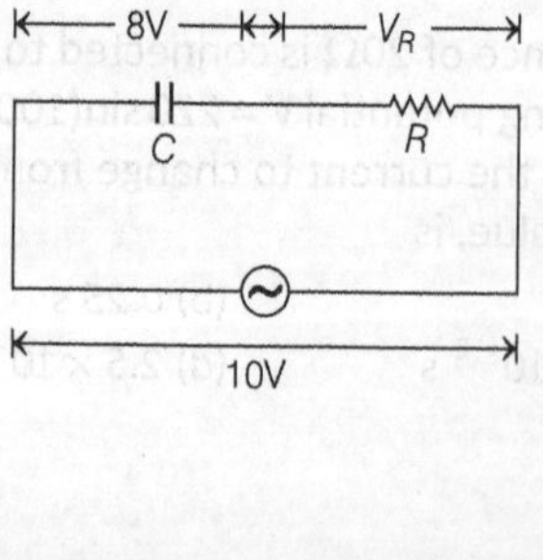

(a) 6V, $\tan^{-1}\left(\frac{4}{3}\right)$ (b) 3V, $\tan^{-1}\left(\frac{3}{4}\right)$

(c) 6V, $\tan^{-1}\left(\frac{5}{3}\right)$ (d) None of these

18 A bulb and a capacitor are connected in series to a source of alternating current. If its frequency is increased, while keeping the voltage of the source constant, then

(a) bulb will give more intense light

(b) bulb will give less intense light

(c) bulb will give light of same intensity as before

(d) bulb will stop radiating light

19 A charged capacitor discharges through a resistance R with time constant τ. The two are now placed in series across in AC source of angular frequency $\omega = \frac{1}{\tau}$. The impedance of the circuit will be

(a) $\frac{R}{\sqrt{2}}$ (b) R

(c) $\sqrt{2}R$ (d) $2R$

20 An AC source of angular frequency ω is fed across a resistor of resistance R and a capacitor of capacitance C in series. The current registered is i. If now the frequency of the source is changed to $\frac{\omega}{3}$ (but maintaining the same voltage), the current in the circuit is found to be $\frac{i}{2}$. The ratio of capacitive reactance to resistance at the original frequency is

(a) $\frac{1}{\sqrt{2}}$ (b) $\frac{\sqrt{3}}{5}$

(c) $\sqrt{\frac{3}{2}}$ (d) $\sqrt{\frac{3}{5}}$

21 In a simple LR circuit with AC source the potential difference at any instant across inductor and resistance are V_L and V_R, respectively and AC source has potential difference V_{AC} at the same instant. Then

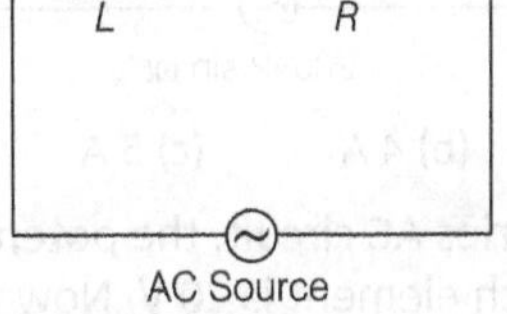

(a) $V_L^2 + V_R^2 = V_{AC}^2$ (b) $V_L + V_R = V_{AC}$

(c) $V_L^2 - V_R^2 = V_{AC}^2$ (d) $V_L^3 + V_R^3 = V_{AC}^3$

22 Switch S is closed at $t = 0$. After sufficiently long time, an iron rod is inserted into the inductor L. Then, the light bulb

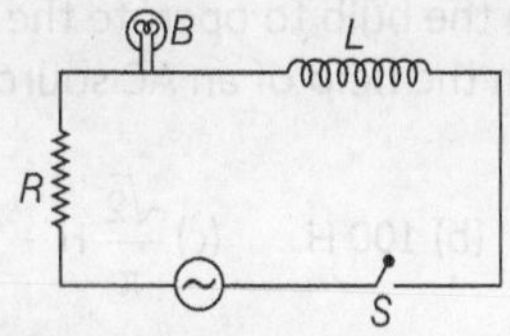

(a) glows more brightly

(b) gets dimmer

(c) glows with the same brightness

(d) gets momentarily dimmer and then glows more brightly

23 Current in this circuit as a function of time will be

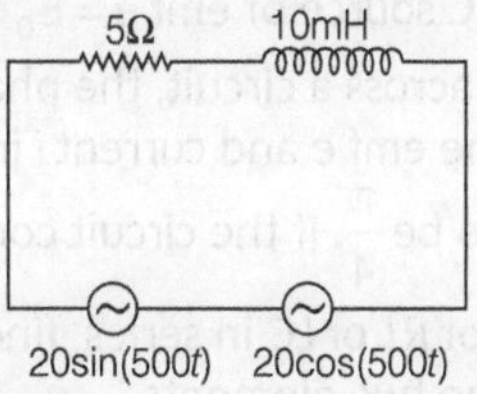

(a) $2\sqrt{2}\sin 500t$ (b) $4\sin 500t$

(c) $4\sin(500t + 45°)$ (d) $2\sqrt{2}\sin(500t + 45°)$

24 A coil has an inductance of 0.7 H and is joined in series with a resistance of 220 Ω. When the alternating emf of 220 V at 50 Hz is applied to it then the phase through which current lags behind the applied emf and the wattless component of current in the circuit will be, respectively

(a) 30°, 1 A (b) 45°, 0.5 A

(c) 60°, 1.5 A (d) None of these

25 Time constant of the given circuit is τ. If the battery is replaced by an AC source having voltage $V = V_0 \cos \omega t$, power factor of the circuit will be

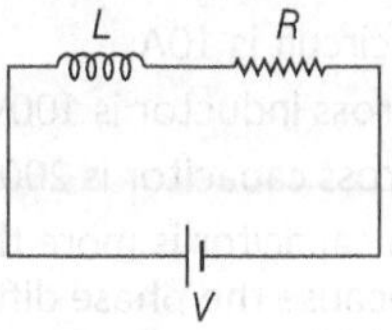

(a) $\omega\tau$ (b) $\frac{1}{\sqrt{1+(\omega\tau)^2}}$ (c) $\sqrt{1-(\omega\tau)^2}$ (d) zero

26 When 100 V DC is applied across a solenoid a current of 1 A flows in it. When 100 V AC is applied across the same coil, the current drops to 0.5 A. If the frequency of the AC source is 50 Hz, the impedance and inductance of the solenoid are

(a) 100Ω, 0.93 H (b) 200Ω, 1.0 H

(c) 10Ω, 0.86 H (d) 200Ω, 0.55 H

27 A bulb is rated of 100 V, 100W, it can be treated as a resistor. Find out the inductance of an inductor (called choke coil) that should be connected in series with the bulb to operate the bulb at its rated power with the help of an AC source of 200V and 50 Hz.

(a) $\frac{\pi}{\sqrt{3}}$ H (b) 100 H (c) $\frac{\sqrt{2}}{\pi}$ H (d) $\frac{\sqrt{3}}{\pi}$ H

28 The self-inductance of a choke coil is 10 mH. When it is connected with a 10V DC source, then the loss of power is 20 W. When it is connected with 10V AC source loss of power is 10 W. The frequency of A.C. source will be

(a) 50 Hz (b) 60 Hz (c) 80 Hz (d) 100 Hz

29 When an AC source of emf $e = E_0 \sin(100t)$ is connected across a circuit, the phase difference between the emf e and current i in the circuit is observed to be $\frac{\pi}{4}$. If the circuit consists possibly only of RC or RL or LC in series, find the relationship between the two elements

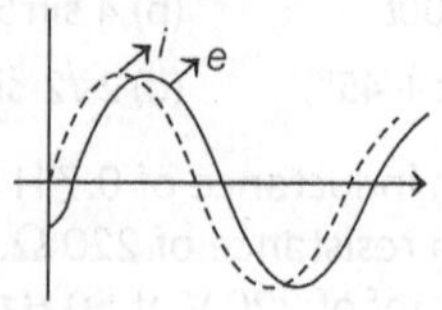

(a) $R = 1$ kW, $C = 10\mu$F (b) $R = 1$ kW, $C = 1\mu$F
(c) $R = 1$ kW, $L = 0.1$ H (d) $R = 1$ kW, $L = 1$ H

30 For shown circuit

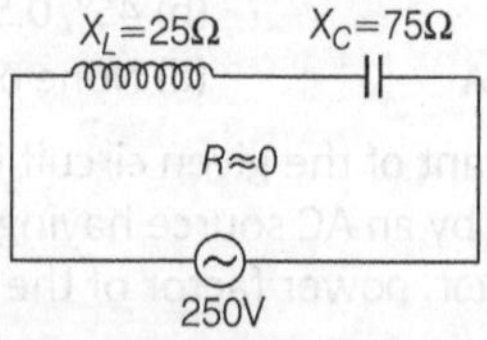

(a) current in circuit is 10A
(b) voltage across inductor is 100V
(c) voltage across capacitor is 200V
(d) voltage on capacitor is more than that of supply voltage because the phase difference between V_L and V_C is 180°

31 For the circuit shown alongside, the average power developed in one cycle is

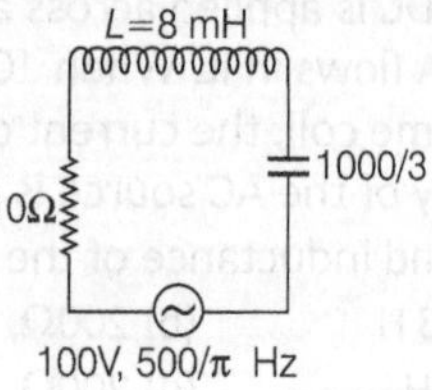

(a) 250 W (b) 800 W (c) 160 W (d) 15 W

32 The power factor of the circuit is $1/\sqrt{2}$. The capacitance of the circuit is equal to

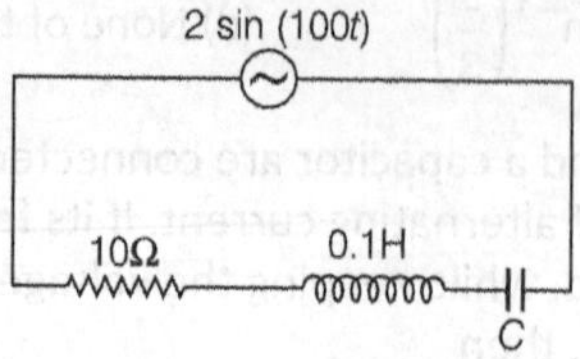

(a) 400 μF (b) 300 μF
(c) 500 μF (d) 200 μF

33 In series R-L-C circuit, the rms voltage across the resistor and inductor are 400 V and 700 V, respectively. If the equation for the applied voltage is $E = 500\sqrt{2} \sin \omega t$, then the peak voltage across the capacitor is

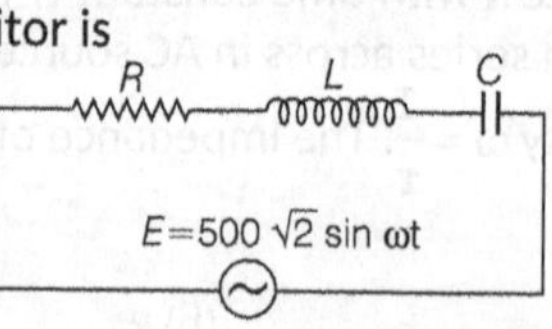

(a) 1200 V (b) $1200\sqrt{2}$ V
(c) 400 V (d) $400\sqrt{2}$V

34 In the circuit shown in the figure, neglecting source resistance, the voltmeter and ammeter readings will respectively be

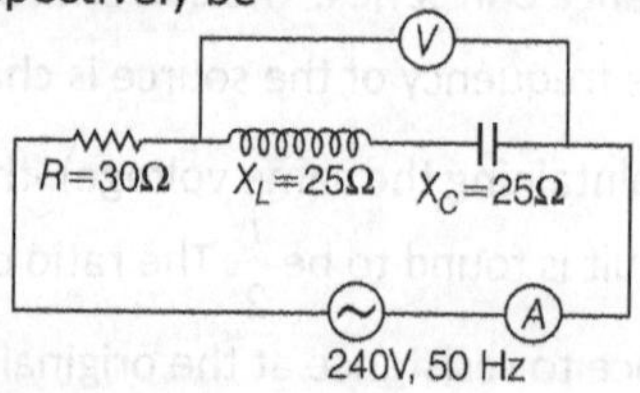

(a) 0 V, 8 A (b) 150 V, 8 A
(c) 150 V, 3 A (d) 0 V, 3 A

35 In the given L-C-R series circuit. Find the reading of the hot wire ammeter.

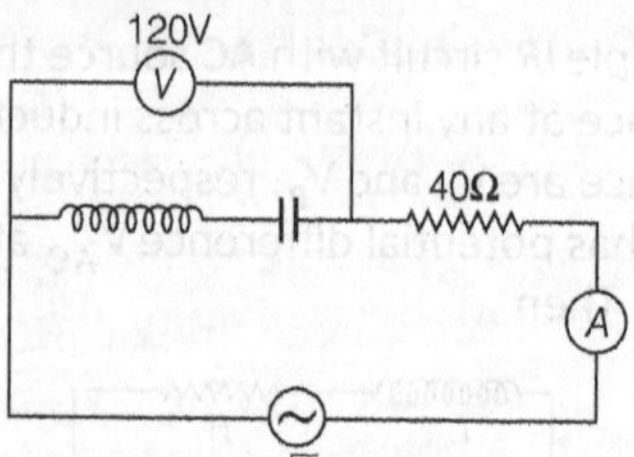

(a) 2 A (b) 4 A (c) 5 A (d) 9 A

36 In R-L-C series AC circuit, the potential differences across each element is 20 V. Now the value of the resistance alone is doubled then potential differences, across R, L and C respectively.

(a) 20 V, 10 V, 10 V (b) 20 V, 20 V, 20 V
(c) 20 V, 40 V, 40 V (d) 10 V, 20 V, 20 V

37 An AC circuit consists of $R=3\Omega$, $L(X_L=7\Omega)$ and $C(X_C=3\Omega)$ in series. Potential difference across R and C is V_1 and that across L, C and R is V_2. Phase difference between V_1 and V_2 is

(a) 45° (b) 82°
(c) 143° (d) 98°

38 Power factor of an *L-R* series circuit is 0.6 and that of a *RC* series circuit is 0.5. If the element (*L*, *C* and *R*) of the two circuits are joined in series the power factor of this circuit is found to be 1. The ratio of the resistance in the *L-R* circuit to the resistance in the *RC* circuit is

(a) $\frac{6}{5}$ (b) $\frac{5}{6}$ (c) $\frac{4}{3\sqrt{3}}$ (d) $\frac{3\sqrt{3}}{4}$

39 An *L-C-R* series circuit with 100Ω resistance is connected to an AC source of 400 V and angular frequency 300 rad/s. When only the capacitance is removed, the current lags behind the voltage by 60°. When only the inductance is removed, the current leads the voltage by 60°. The current and power dissipated in the *L-C-R* circuit is

(a) 400 W, 2 A (b) 800 W, 4 A
(c) 800 W, 2 A (d) 1600 W, 4 A

40 A series *R-L-C* circuit is used in a radio to tune to an FM station broadcasting at 100 MHz. The resistance in the circuit is 10 Ω and the inductance is 2.0 μH. What is the best estimate of the capacitance that should be used?

(a) 0.2 pF (b) 0.5 pF
(c) 1.25 pF (d) 0.6 pF

41 An *L-C-R* series circuit is connected to an AC source of variable angular frequency ω and a fixed voltage amplitude. The current amplitude in the circuit is found to be the same for two angular frequencies, ω_1 and ω_2. The resonance angular frequency of this circuit must be

(a) $[\omega_1\omega_2]^{\frac{1}{2}}$ (b) $\frac{\omega_1+\omega_2}{2}$

(c) $\frac{\omega_1\omega_2}{\omega_1+\omega_2}$ (d) None of these

42 In a series resonant *L-C-R* circuit, the voltage across *R* is 100 V and $R=1\,k\Omega$ with $C=2\,\mu F$. The resonant frequency ω is 200 rad/s. At resonance the voltage across *L* is

(a) 2.5×10^{-2} V (b) 40 V
(c) 250 V (d) 4×10^{-3} V

43 A capacitor and a coil in series are connected to a 6 V AC source. By varying the frequency of the source, maximum current of 600 mA is observed. If the same coil is now connected to a cell of emf 6 V and internal resistance of 2Ω, the current through it in steady state will be

(a) 0.5 A (b) 0.6 A (c) 1.0 A (d) 2.0 A

44 In *L-C-R* circuit current resonant frequency is 600 Hz and half power points are at 650 Hz and 550 Hz. The quality factor is

(a) $\frac{1}{6}$ (b) $\frac{1}{3}$
(c) 6 (d) 3

45 Phase difference between the voltage of source and current from the source in the given AC circuit is given by

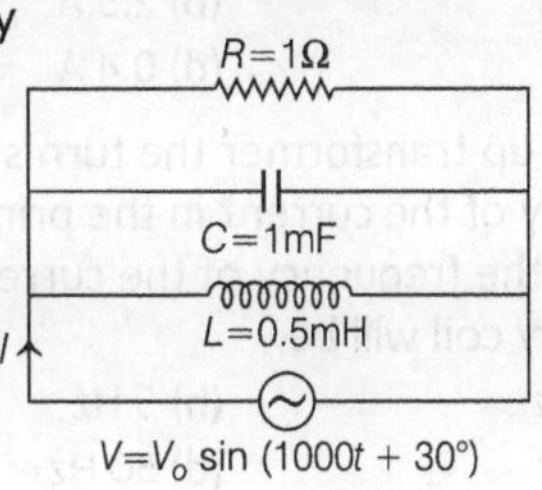

(a) 30° (b) 37°
(c) 45° (d) 53°

46 The current *i* in the circuit at any time *t* is

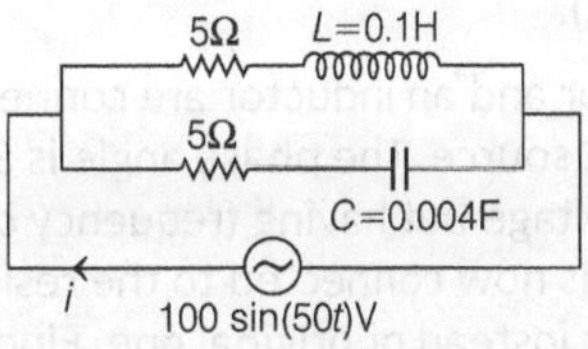

(a) 20 A (b) $20\sin\left(50t+\frac{\pi}{4}\right)$ A

(c) $20\sin\left(50t-\frac{\pi}{4}\right)$ A (d) $20\sin(50t)$ A

47 In the shown AC circuit phase difference between currents i_1 and i_2 is

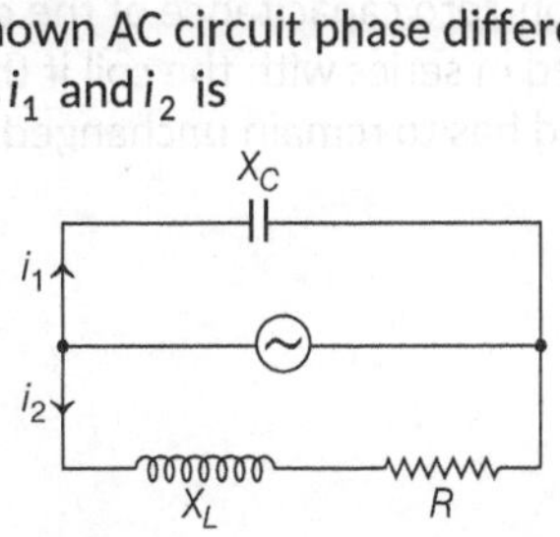

(a) $\frac{\pi}{2}-\tan^{-1}\frac{X_L}{R}$ (b) $\tan^{-1}\frac{X_L-X_C}{R}$

(c) $\frac{\pi}{2}+\tan^{-1}\frac{X_L}{R}$ (d) $\tan^{-1}\frac{X_L-X_C}{R}+\frac{\pi}{2}$

48 In the circuit diagram shown, $X_C = 100\ \Omega$, $X_L = 200\ \Omega$ and $R = 100\ \Omega$. Effective current through the source is

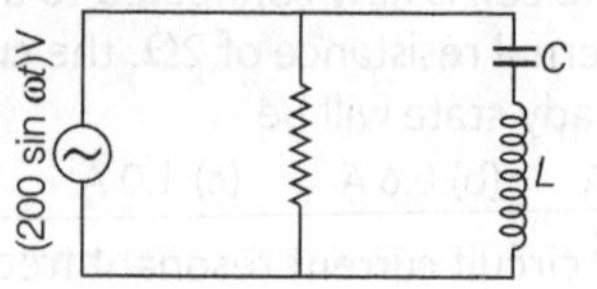

(a) $\sqrt{2}$ A (b) $2\sqrt{2}$ A (c) 2 A (d) $\frac{1}{2}$ A

49 The secondary coil of an ideal step-down transformer is delivering 500 W power at 12.5 A current. If the ratio of turns in the primary coil to the secondary coil is 5 : 1 then the current flowing in the primary coil will be

(a) 62.5 A (b) 2.5 A
(c) 6 A (d) 0.4 A

50 In a step-up transformer the turn's ratio is 10. If the frequency of the current in the primary coil is 50 Hz, then the frequency of the current in the secondary coil will be

(a) 500 Hz (b) 5 Hz
(c) 60 Hz (d) 50 Hz

Numerical Value Questions

1 If $i = 2\sin \omega t + 4\cos \omega t + \sqrt{6}$ A; then find rms value of i (in A).

2 A resistor and an inductor are connected in series to an AC source. The phase angle is 30°. A source of same voltage but having frequency double of the original is now connected to the resistor and inductor instead of original one. Find new power (in W) if original power was 7 W.

3 A coil of inductance $L = 5$ H and resistance $R = 55\ \Omega$ is connected in series to the mains alternating voltage of frequency $f = 50$ Hz in series. What can be the non-zero capacitance of the capacitor (in μF) connected in series with the coil if the power dissipated has to remain unchanged? (take, $\pi^2 = 10$)

4 In an *L-R-C* series circuit at resonance current in the circuit $3\sqrt{2}$ A. If now frequency of the source is changed such that now current lags by 45° than applied voltage in the circuit. Find the new current in the circuit.

5 A circuit shown in the figure contains a box having either a capacitor or an inductor. The power factor of the circuit is 0.8, while current lags behind the voltage. The potential difference across the capacitor is 2000 V. The circuit draws 2 A current. Find the inductance/capacitance of the box in S.I. unit. (take $\pi = 3.2$)

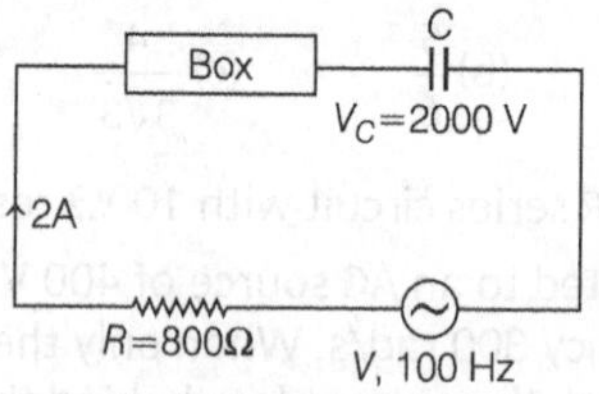

6 When a box A is connected across an AC source of 200 V, 0.4 A of current flows in circuit. When a capacitor of reactance 400 Ω is connected in series with box and connected across AC source, the power factor of circuit becomes 1. If power factor of box A is $n \times 10^{-1}$. Find n.

7 A series *L-C-R* circuit with $R = 120\ \Omega$ has an angular frequency 8×10^5 rad/s at resonance, voltages across resistance and inductor are 60 V and 40 V, respectively. If frequency at which the circuit current leads the voltage by a phase of 45° is $k \times 10^5$ rad/s, then find the value of k.

8 Consider a circuit with an alternating source and contains inductor and capacitor. Given reading of A_1 and A_2 as 3 A and 4 A, respectively. Find the reading of A_2 in ampere.

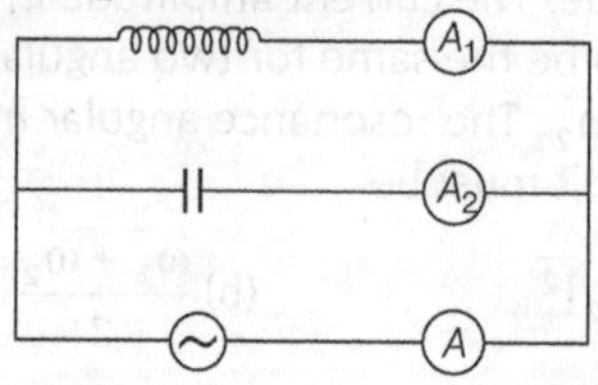

LEVEL 03 JEE Advanced Level

Single Choice Correct Questions

1 The rms current value of a semicircular wave which has a maximum value i_0 is

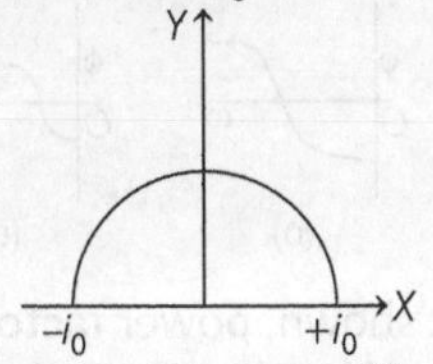

(a) $\frac{i_0}{\sqrt{3}}$ (b) $\sqrt{\frac{2}{3}}i_0$

(c) $\frac{i_0}{\sqrt{2}}$ (d) $2i_0$

2 If i_1, i_2, i_3 and i_4 are the respective rms values of the time varying current as shown in the four cases I, II, III and IV. Then identify the correct relations.

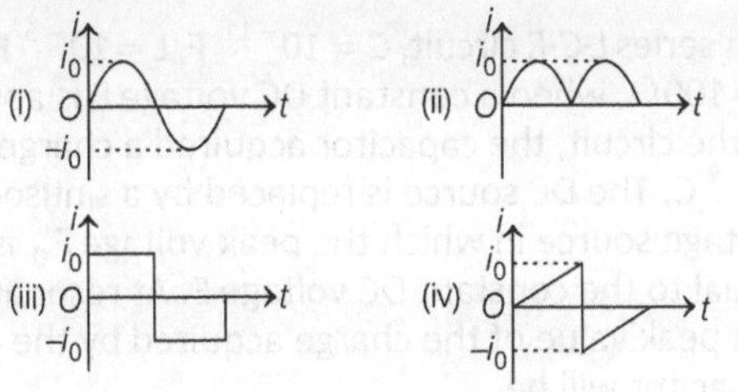

(a) $i_1 = i_2 = i_3 = i_4$ (b) $i_3 > i_1 = i_2 > i_4$

(c) $i_3 > i_4 > i_2 = i_1$ (d) $i_3 > i_2 > i_1 > i_4$

3 A DC voltage with appreciable riple expressed as $V = V_1 + V_2 \cos \omega t$ is applied to a resistor R. The amount of heat generated per second is given by

(a) $\frac{V_1^2 + V_2^2}{2R}$ (b) $\frac{2V_1^2 + V_2^2}{2R}$

(c) $\frac{V_1^2 + 2V_2^2}{2R}$ (d) None of these

4 In an AC circuit, the instantaneous voltage $\varepsilon(t)$ and current $i(t)$ are given by $\varepsilon(t) = 5[\cos \omega t + \sqrt{3} \sin \omega t]$ V and $i(t) = 5 \sin\left(\omega t + \frac{\pi}{4}\right)$ A, then

(a) current leads voltage by $\frac{\pi}{4}$

(b) voltage leads current by $\frac{\pi}{3}$

(c) voltage leads current by $\frac{\pi}{6}$

(d) current leads voltage by $\frac{\pi}{12}$

5 An AC circuit contains a variable inductor L, connected in series with a light bulb of resistance R as shown. Assume that the resistance of the light bulb is independent of its temperature. Now it is desired to reduce the power of the light bulb to one fourth then (frequency of AC source is $\frac{R}{2\pi L_0}$ where L_0 is initial inductance)

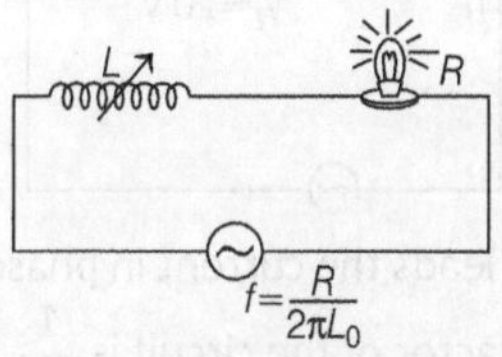

(a) inductance of the circuit should be increased by a factor of 2.

(b) inductance of the circuit should be increased by a factor of $\sqrt{3}$.

(c) impedance of the circuit should be increased by a factor of 4.

(d) power factor of the circuit should be reduced to half.

6 When a resistance R is connected in series with an element A, the electric current is found to be lagging behind the voltage by angle θ_1. When the same resistance is connected in series with element B, current leads voltage by θ_2. When R, A, B are connected in series, the current now leads voltage by θ. Assume same AC source is used in all cases, then

(a) $\theta = \theta_2 - \theta_1$

(b) $\tan\theta = \tan\theta_2 - \tan\theta_1$

(c) $\theta = \frac{(\theta_1 + \theta_2)}{2}$

(d) None of the above

7 In the circuit shown the value of L is 5H and power factor of circuit is 0.8. It is also given that voltage drop across the capacitor is 2/5 times the voltage drop across inductor. Impedance of the circuit is

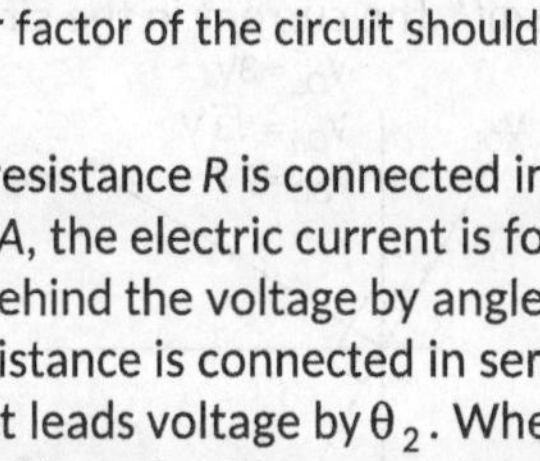

(a) 1570 Ω (b) 1256 Ω

(c) 1875 Ω (d) 1625 Ω

8 A coil with inductance L and resistance R is connected to an alternating source. The capacity of a capacitor connected in series with the coil such that active power of circuit does not change is given by $C = \dfrac{1}{n\omega^2 L}$. Find value of n.

(a) 1 (b) 2
(c) $\sqrt{2}$ (d) 4

9 In the given circuit,

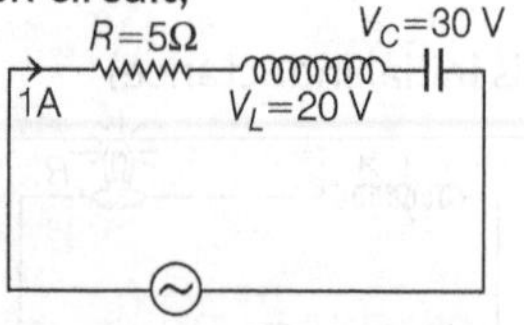

(a) voltage leads the current in phase.

(b) power factor of the circuit is $\dfrac{1}{\sqrt{5}}$.

(c) applied voltage is 15 V.

(d) average power dissipated is greater than 5 W.

10 The given figure represents the phasor diagram of a series L-C-R circuit connected to an AC source. At the instant t', when the source voltage is given by $V = V_0 \cos\omega t'$ the current in the circuit will be

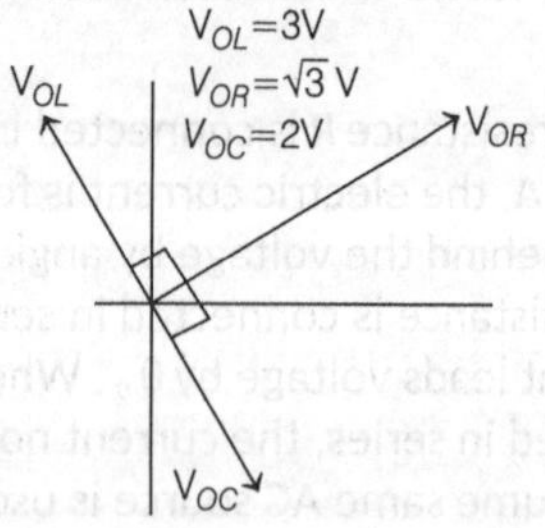

(a) $i = i_0 \cos\left(\omega t' + \dfrac{\pi}{6}\right)$ (b) $i = i_0 \cos\left(\omega t' - \dfrac{\pi}{6}\right)$

(c) $i = i_0 \cos\left(\omega t' + \dfrac{\pi}{3}\right)$ (d) $i = i_0 \cos\left(\omega t' - \dfrac{\pi}{3}\right)$

11 An inductor ($X_L = 2\ \Omega$), a capacitor($X_C = 8\Omega$) and a resistance (8Ω) are connected in series with an AC source. The voltage output of AC source is given by $V = 10 \cos 100\pi t$. The instantaneous potential difference between A and B, when it is half of the voltage output from source at that instant will be

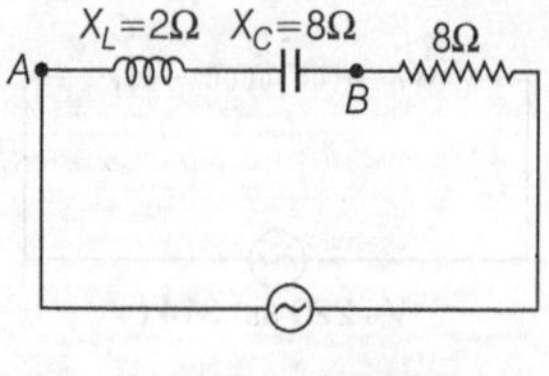

(a) 5V (b) 4.8 V
(c) 7.2 V (d) 8 V

12 An inductor, a capacitor and a resistance are joined in series to an AC source. The frequency of AC is gradually increased. The phase difference ϕ between the emf and the current is plotted against the angular frequency ω. Which of the following best represents the resulting curve?

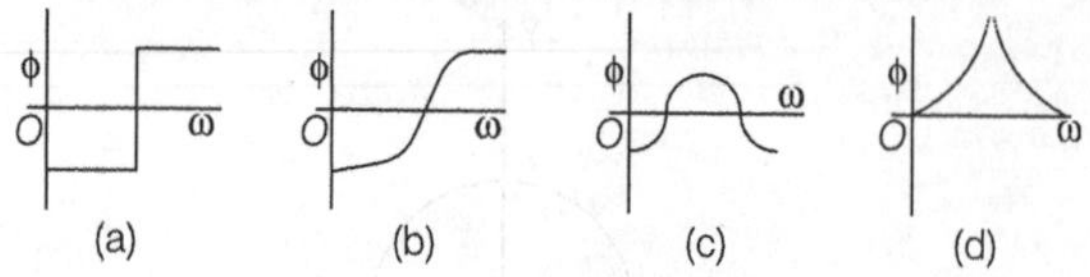

13 In the circuit shown, power factor of circuit is 1 and power factor of box is 3/5. Find reading of ammeter

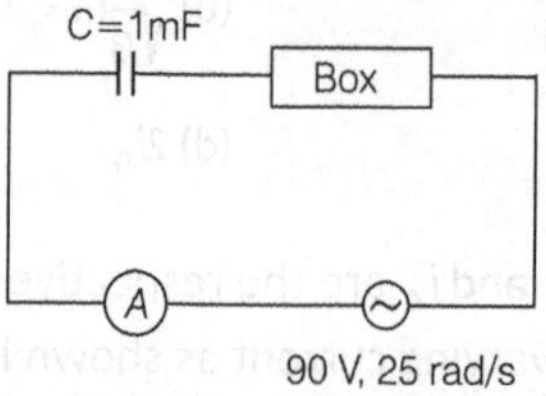

(a) 5A (b) 6A (c) 4A (d) 3A

14 In a series L-C-R circuit, $C = 10^{-11}$ F, $L = 10^{-5}$ H and $R = 100\Omega$, when a constant DC voltage E is applied to the circuit, the capacitor acquired a charge 10^{-9} C. The DC source is replaced by a sinusoidal voltage source in which the peak voltage E_0 is equal to the constant DC voltage E. At resonance the peak value of the charge acquired by the capacitor will be

(a) 10^{-15} C (b) 10^{-6} C (c) 10^{-10} C (d) 10^{-8} C

15 Two impedances Z_1 and Z_2, when connected separately across a 230 V, 50 Hz supply consumed 100 W and 60 W at power factors of 0.5 lagging and 0.6 leading respectively. If these impedances are now connected in series across the same supply, find

(i) total power absorbed

(ii) the value of the impedance to be added in series, so as to raise the overall power factor to unity.

(a) 19W, 295Ω (b) 19W, 95Ω
(c) 99W, 195Ω (d) 75W, 175Ω

16 In series R-L-C circuit shown in the figure bulb shines. When inductor is short circuited then light emission of bulb does not change. How does it change when capacitor is short circuited.

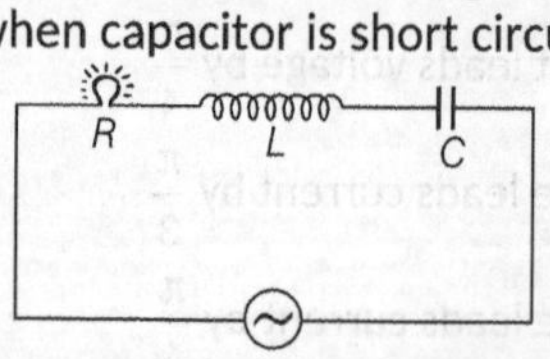

(a) Remains and same (b) Increases
(c) Decreases (d) Cannot be predicted

17 The figure shows variation of R, X_L and X_C with frequency f in a series L, C, R circuit. Then for what frequency point, the circuit is inductive?

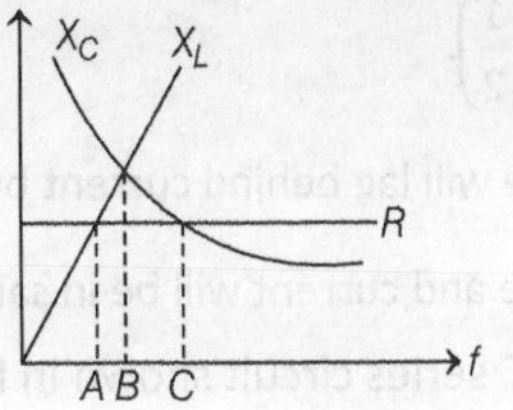

(a) A (b) B
(c) C (d) All points

18 The diagram shows a capacitor C and a resistor R connected in series to an AC source. V_1 and V_2 are voltmeters and A is an ammeter, now consider the following statements.

(I) Readings in A and V_2 are always in phase.
(II) Reading in V_1 is ahead in phase with reading in V_2.
(III) Readings in A and V_1 are always in phase.

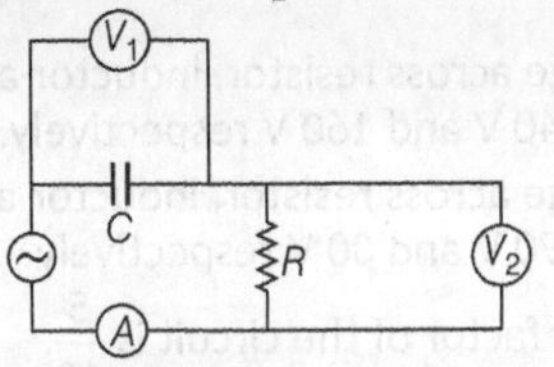

Which of these statements are/is correct?
(a) I only (b) II only
(c) I and II only (d) II and III only

19 A coil (which can be modelled as a series circuit) has been designed for high Q performance at a rated voltage and a specified frequency. If the frequency of operation is doubled and the coil is operated at the same rated voltage, then the Q factor and the active power P consumed by the coil will be affected as below
(a) P is doubled, Q is halved
(b) P is halved, Q is doubled
(c) P remains constant but Q increases 4 times
(d) P decreases 4 times but Q is doubled

20 A series L-C-R circuit is resonating with a source whose emf varies with time as described in diagram-1. If we replace source by another source whose emf varies with time according to diagram-2, then

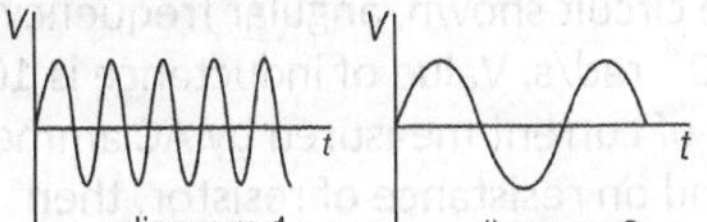

diagram 1 diagram 2

(a) for getting resonance again, decrease R
(b) current will remain in phase with source voltage
(c) for getting resonance again, decrease C
(d) current will lead source voltage after replacing the source

21 In a R-L-C resonant circuit, if the maximum stored energy is increased by 10% and at the same time the energy dissipated per cycle is reduced by 10%, it will result in which of the following ?
(a) An 11% decrease in quality factor
(b) An increase in the resonant frequency by 11%
(c) A 22% increase in quality factor
(d) A decrease in the resonant frequency by 22%

22 An L-C-R circuit has $L = 10$ mH, $R = 3\Omega$ and $C = 1\mu$F connected in series to a source of $(15\cos\omega t)$ V. Compute the average energy dissipated per cycle (in 10^{-4} J) at a frequency that is 10% lower than the resonance frequency. Give the answer in nearest integer.
(a) 2 (b) 3 (c) 5 (d) 8

23 For the AC circuit shown in figure, find the frequency (ω_0) of the AC voltage source so that current through the source will be in same phase as of voltage of source.

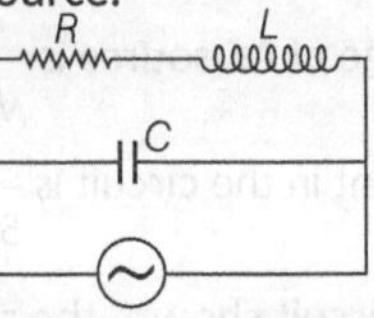

(a) $\sqrt{\dfrac{1}{LC}+\dfrac{R^2}{L^2}}$ (b) $\sqrt{\dfrac{1}{LC}-\dfrac{R^2}{L^2}}$

(c) $\dfrac{1}{\sqrt{LC}}$ (d) $\sqrt{\dfrac{1}{LC}+\dfrac{R^2}{4L}+\dfrac{R}{2L}}$

24 In the circuit shown, when DC of 250 V is applied, 1 A current passes through the circuit and when an alternating voltage source of 250 V and 2250 rad/s is applied, current of 1.25 A flows. If maximum current flows through the circuit at a frequency of 4500 rad/s, then the value of L and C will be respectively

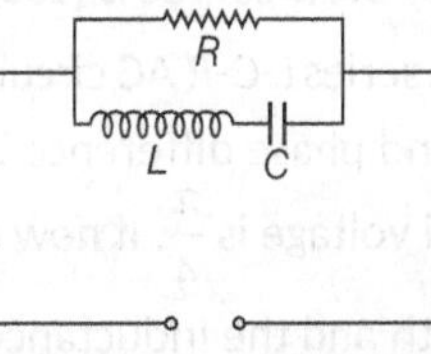

(a) 0.295 H, 10^{-4} F (b) 0.0752 H, 0.01 F
(c) 0.0392 H, 0.005 F (d) 0.0494 H, 10^{-6} F

Multiple Choice(s) Correct Questions

1 In the figure shows $R = 100\ \Omega$, $L = \frac{2}{\pi}$ H and $C = \frac{8}{\pi}\ \mu$F are connected in series with an AC source of 200 V and frequency f. V_1 and V_2 are two hot wire voltmeters. If the reading of V_1 and V_2 are same, then

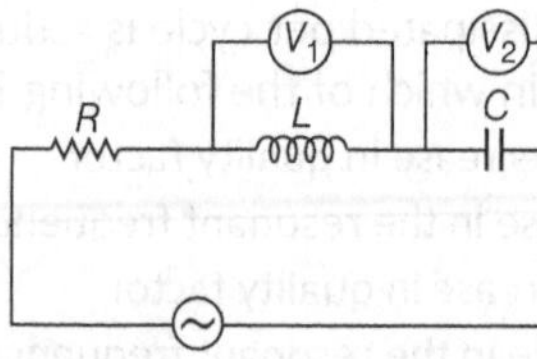

(a) $f = 125$ Hz
(b) $f = 250\pi$ Hz
(c) Current through R is 2 A
(d) $V_1 = V_2 = 1000$ V

2 In an LCR series AC circuit, voltage across resistance is 2 V. The inductive and capacitive reactances are 10Ω and 5Ω respectively. The phase difference between voltage across the circuit and current is 30°, then pick up the correct statement(s)

(a) The resistance of resistor is $5\sqrt{3}\ \Omega$.
(b) The voltage of AC source is $4\sqrt{3}$ V.
(c) The voltage of AC source is $\frac{4}{\sqrt{3}}$ V.
(d) The current in the circuit is $\frac{2}{5\sqrt{3}}$ A.

3 For the AC circuit shown, the reading of ammeter and voltmeter are 5A and $50\sqrt{5}$ V respectively, then

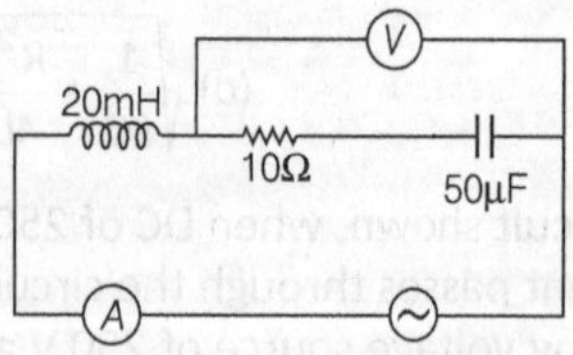

(a) average power delivered by the source is 250W
(b) rms value of AC source is 50 V
(c) rms value of AC source is 100 V
(d) frequency of AC source is $(100/2\pi)$ Hz

4 In a certain series L-C-R AC circuit it is found that $X_L = 2X_C$ and phase difference between the current and voltage is $\frac{\pi}{4}$. If now capacitance is made (1/4)th and the inductance and resistance are doubled then which of the following are not correct?

(a) Voltage will lead current by a phase of $\tan^{-1}\left(\frac{1}{2}\right)$.
(b) Voltage will lag behind current by a phase of $\tan^{-1}\left(\frac{1}{2}\right)$.
(c) Voltage will lag behind current by a phase of $\frac{\pi}{4}$.
(d) Voltage and current will be in same phase.

5 In an R-L-C series circuit shown in figure the readings of voltmeters V_1 and V_2 are 64 V and 120 V respectively. The source voltage is 130 V, for this situation mark out the correct statements (s).

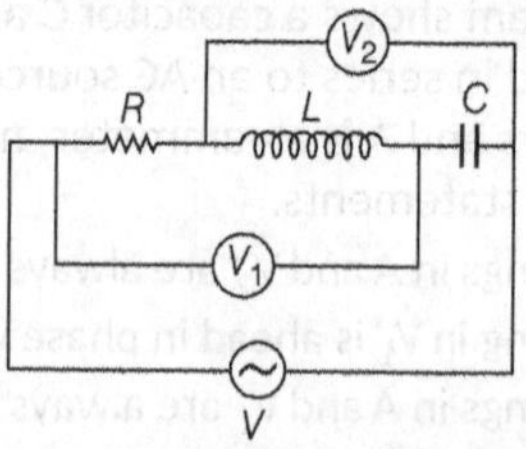

(a) Voltage across resistor, inductor and capacitor are 50 V, 40 V and 160 V respectively.
(b) Voltage across resistor, inductor and capacitor are 10 V, 90 V and 30 V respectively.
(c) Power factor of the circuit is $\frac{5}{13}$.
(d) The circuit is capacitive in nature.

6 The graph shows variation of source voltage (V) and steady state current (i) drawn by a series R-L-C circuit. Identify correct statement(s).

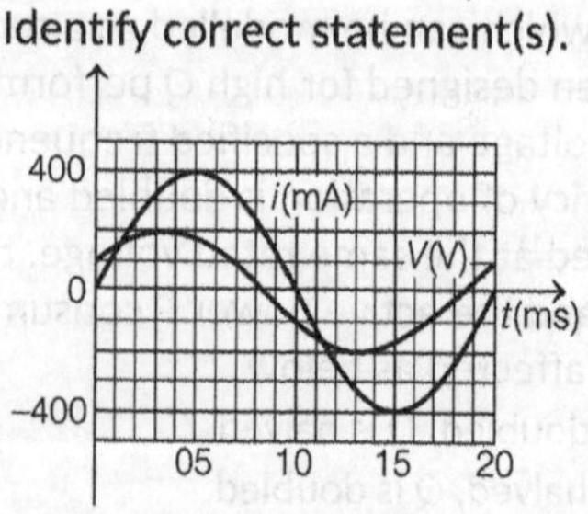

(a) Current lags the voltage
(b) Resistance in circuit is $250\sqrt{3}\ \Omega$
(c) If capacitive reactance is 74Ω, then inductive reactance will be 324Ω.
(d) Average power dissipated in circuit will be $20\sqrt{3}$ W.

7 In the circuit shown, angular frequency of source is $\omega = 10^4$ rad/s. Value of inductance is 10 mH. If value of current measured by AC ammeter does not depend on resistance of resistor, then

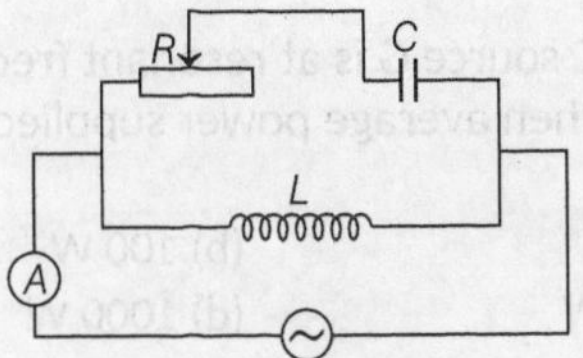

$\omega = 10^4$ rad/s

(a) value of capacitance of capacitor is 1 μF
(b) value of capacitance of capacitor is 2 μF
(c) impedance of circuit is 100Ω
(d) impedance of circuit is 1000Ω

Comprehension Based Questions

Comprehension-1

In a series *LR* circuit, connected with a sinusoidal AC source, the maximum potential difference across *L* and *R* are 3 V and 4 V, respectively.

1 At an instant the potential difference across resistor is 2 V. The potential difference in volt, across the inductor at the same instant will be
(a) 3 cos 30° (b) 3 cos 60°
(c) 3 cos 45° (d) None of these

2 At the same instant, the magnitude of the potential difference (in V), across the AC source may be
(a) 3 cos 67° (b) 5 cos 83°
(c) 6 cos 97° (d) 0

3 If the current at this instant is decreasing the magnitude of potential difference at that instant across the AC source is
(a) increasing (b) decreasing
(c) constant (d) cannot be said

Comprehension-2

A steady current 4 A flows in an inductor coil when connected to a 12 V DC source as shown in figure (i). If the same coil is connected to an AC source of 12 V, 50 rad s^{-1}, a current of 2.4 A flows in the circuit as shown in figure (ii). Now after these observations, a capacitor of capacitance 20 mF is connected in series with the coil and with the same AC source as shown in figure (iii).

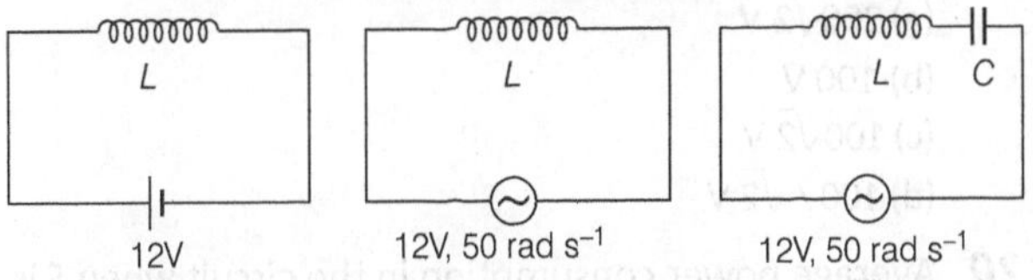

(i) (ii) (iii)

4 The resistance of the coil is
(a) 1Ω (b) 2Ω (c) 3Ω (d) 4Ω

5 The average power supplied to the circuit after connecting capacitance in series is
(a) 24 W
(b) 72 W
(c) 144 W
(d) 120 W

Comprehension-3

Figure shows a two branched parallel circuit with $R_A = 8\ \Omega$, $X_L = 6\ \Omega$, $R_B = 6\ \Omega$ and $X_C = 8\ \Omega$. The total current supplied by alternating source V is $i = 14$ A.

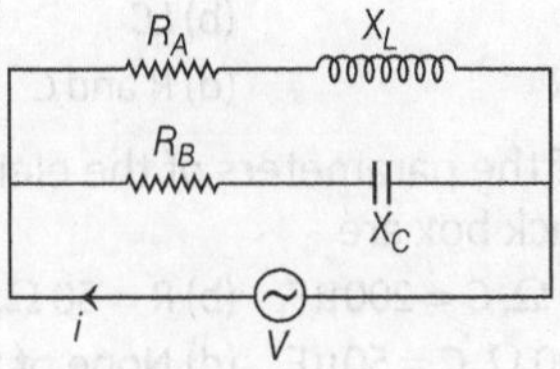

6 Current passing through the inductor (X_L) is
(a) Zero (b) 7 A
(c) $7\sqrt{2}$ A (d) 14 A

7 Power dissipated in the circuit is
(a) Zero (b) 750 W
(c) 1372 W (d) 1500 W

Comprehension-4

An AC generator with an adjustable frequency is connected to an inductor *L*, capacitor, $C = 5.50\ \mu F$ and a variable resistor *R*. When *R* is 100 Ω, the amplitude of the current produced in the circuit by the AC generator is half of its maximum possible value. This situation occurs at two different frequencies of generator *viz* 1.30 kHz and 1.50 kHz.

8 The inductance *L* of the circuit is
(a) 2.35 mH (b) 4.70 mH
(c) 1.175 mH (d) 9.40 mH

9 The phase difference between voltage and current in the above mentioned situation is
(a) $\frac{\pi}{4}$ (b) $\frac{\pi}{6}$
(c) $\frac{\pi}{3}$ (d) $\frac{\pi}{2}$

Comprehension-5

A voltage source $V = V_0 \sin(100t)$ is connected to a black box in which there can be either one element out of *L*, *C*, *R* or any two of them connected in series. At steady state the variation of current in the circuit and the source voltage are plotted together with time, using an oscilloscope, as shown.

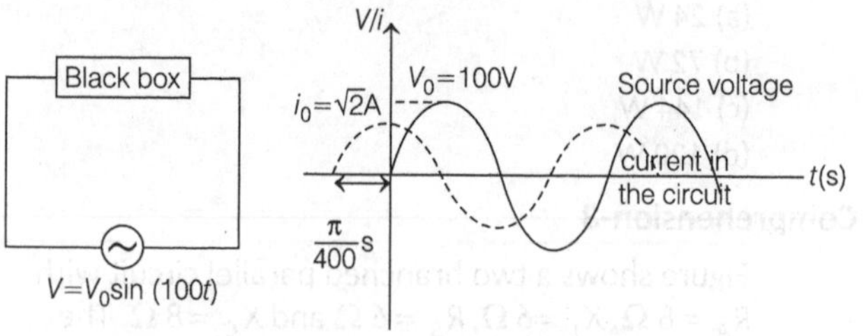

10 The element(s) present in black box is/are

(a) only C (b) LC
(c) L and R (d) R and C

11 Values of the parameters of the elements, present in the black box are

(a) $R = 50\,\Omega, C = 200\,\mu F$ (b) $R = 50\,\Omega, L = 2\,mH$
(c) $R = 400\,\Omega, C = 50\,\mu F$ (d) None of these

12 If AC source is removed, the circuit is shorted and then at $t = 0$, a battery of constant emf is connected across the black box. The current in the circuit will

(a) increase exponentially with time constant = 0.02 s.
(b) decrease exponentially with time constant = 0.01 s.
(c) oscillate with angular frequency $20\ s^{-1}$.
(d) first increase and then decrease.

Comprehension-6

An AC generator G of 100 V rating with an adjustable frequency of oscillation is used in the circuit, as shown.

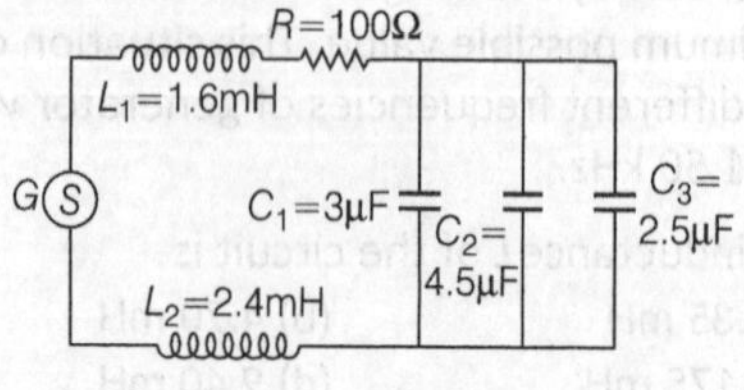

13 Current drawn from the AC source will be maximum if its angular frequency is

(a) 10^5 rad/s (b) 10^4 rad/s
(c) 5000 rad/s (d) 500 rad/s

14 To increase resonant frequency of the circuit, some of the changes in the circuit are carried out. Which change(s) would certainly result in the increase in resonant frequency ?

(a) R is increased.
(b) L_1 is increased and C_1 is decreased.
(c) L_2 is decreased and C_2 is increased.
(d) C_3 is removed from the circuit.

15 If the AC source G is at resonant frequency of the circuit, then average power supplied by the source is

(a) 50 W (b) 100 W
(c) 500 W (d) 1000 W

16 Average energy stored by the inductor L_2 (source is at resonance frequency) is equal to

(a) zero (b) 1.2 mJ
(c) 2.4 mJ (d) 4 mJ

17 Thermal energy produced by the resistance R in time duration 1 μs, using the source at resonant condition, is

(a) 0 J
(b) 1 μJ
(c) 100 μJ
(d) not possible to calculate from the given information.

Comprehension-7

In the L-C-R circuit shown in figure unknown resistance and alternating voltage source are connected. When switch S is closed then there is a phase difference of $\frac{\pi}{4}$ between current and applied voltage and voltage across resistor is $100/\sqrt{2}$ V. When switch is open, current and applied voltage are in same phase. Neglecting resistance of connecting wire answer the following questions

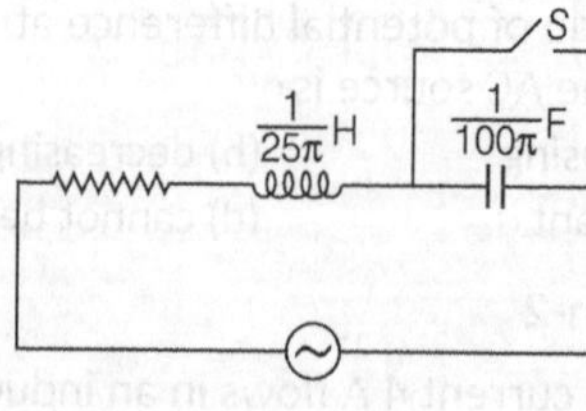

18 Resonance frequency of circuit is

(a) 50 Hz
(b) 25 Hz
(c) 75 Hz
(d) Data insufficient for calculation

19 Peak voltage of applied voltage source is

(a) $200\sqrt{2}$ V
(b) 100 V
(c) $100\sqrt{2}$ V
(d) $100/\sqrt{2}$ V

20 Average power consumption in the circuit when S is open

(a) 2500 W (b) 3000 W
(c) 5000 W (d) 1250 W

Match The Columns Questions

1 In Column I, variation of current i with time t is given in figures. In Column II root mean square current i_{rms}, and average current is given. Match the Column I with corresponding quantities given in Column II.

Column I	Column II
A. 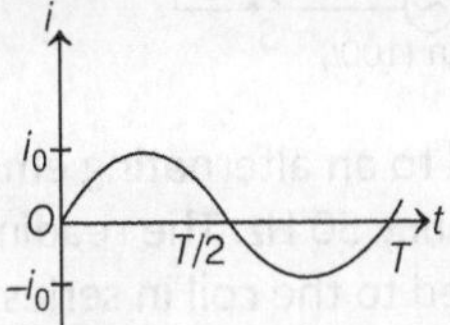	P. $i_{\text{rms}} = \dfrac{i_0}{\sqrt{3}}$
B. 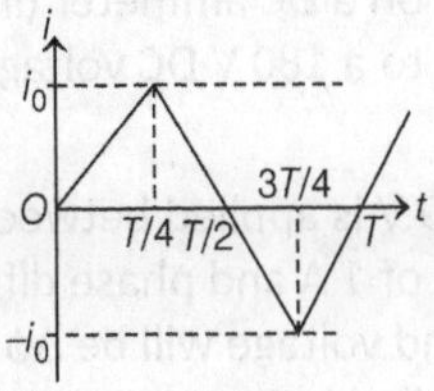	Q. Average current for positive half cycle is i_0
C. 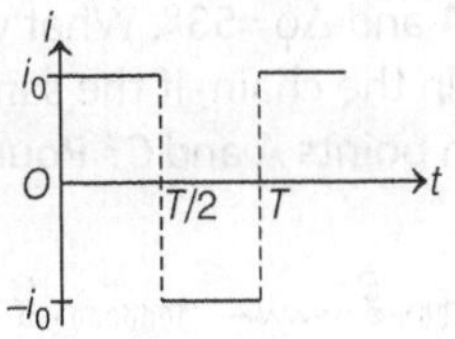	R. Average current for positive half cycle is $\dfrac{i_0}{2}$
D. 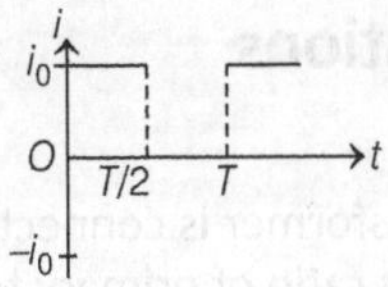	S. Full cycle average current is zero

2 Instantaneous voltage and instantaneous current in a LR circuit in AC is $V = 100\sin(100t)$ and $i = 10\sin\left(100t - \dfrac{\pi}{4}\right)$. Match the following table

Column I	Column II
A. R	P. $\dfrac{1}{10\sqrt{2}}$ SI unit
B. X_L	Q. $5\sqrt{2}$ SI unit
C. L	R. $10\sqrt{2}$ SI unit
D. average power in one cycle	S. None

3 Consider all possibilities [L, R, C are non-zero]

Column I	Column II
A. In LR series AC circuit	P. Current lags inductor voltage by $\dfrac{\pi}{2}$
B. In RC series AC circuit	Q. Current lags voltage by an angle less than $\dfrac{\pi}{2}$
C. In L-C-R series ac circuit	R. Current leads voltage by an angle less than $\dfrac{\pi}{2}$
D. In purely resistive AC circuit	S. Current and voltage are in phase

4 In Column I some AC circuits with meter readings are given and in Column II some circuit quantities are given. Match the entries of Column I with the entries of Column II.

Column I	Column II
A. 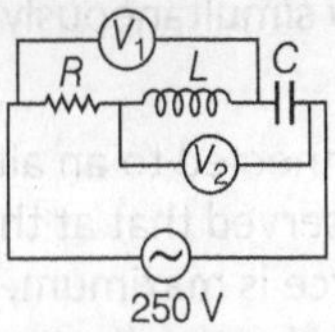 $V_1 = 158.11\text{V}$; $V_2 = 200\text{V}$	P. $V_R = 150$ V
B. 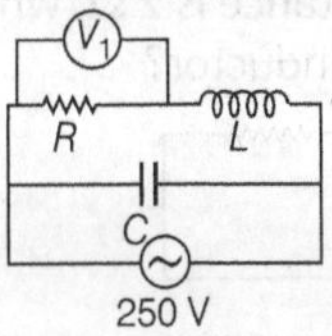 $V_1 = 150$ V	Q. $V_L = 50$ V
C. 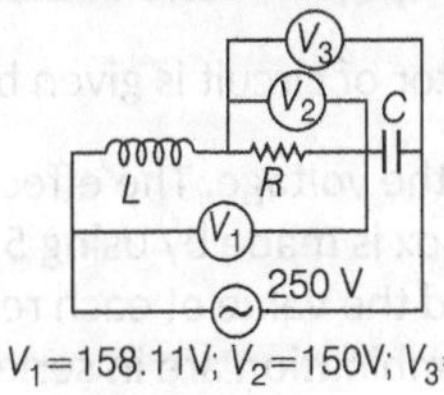 $V_1 = 158.11\text{V}$; $V_2 = 150\text{V}$; $V_3 = 291.6\text{V}$	R. $V_C = 250$ V
D. 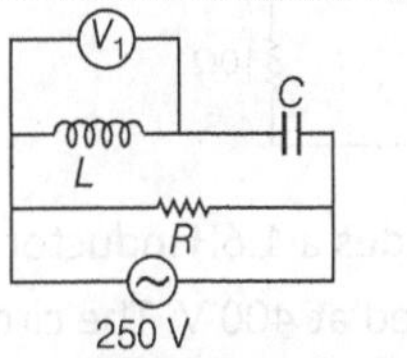 $V_1 = 0$	S. Power factor of the circuit is $\dfrac{3}{5}$

Numerical Value Questions

1 Three alternating voltage sources $V_1 = 3\sin\omega t$, $V_2 = 5\sin(\omega t + \phi_1)$ V and $V_3 = 5\sin(\omega t - \phi_2)$ V connected across a resistance $R = \sqrt{\frac{7}{3}}\ \Omega$ as shown in the figure (where ϕ_1 and ϕ_2 corresponds to 30° and 127° respectively). Find the peak current(in A) through the resistor.

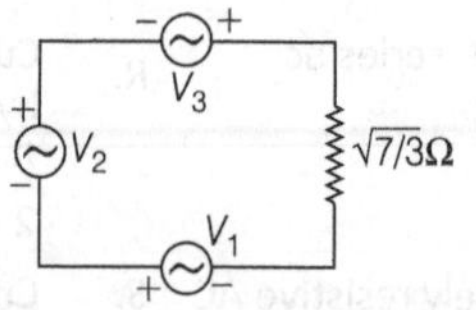

2 A DC ammeter and an AC thermal ammeter are connected to a circuit in series. When a DC is passed through the circuit, the DC ammeter shows $i_1 = 6$ A. When an AC flows through the circuit, the AC ammeter shows $i_2 = 8$A. What will the difference in final readings (in A) of ammeters, if the DC and the AC flow simultaneously through the circuit?

3 In a series *LR* circuit connected to an alternating voltage source, it is observed that at the instant voltage across the source is maximum, voltage across the inductor is 3 V and voltage across the resistance is 4 V. If resistance is 2 Ω, what is reactance (in Ω) of the inductor?

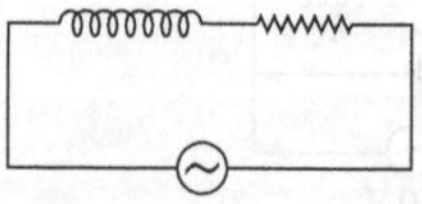

4 In the circuit shown power factor of box is given by 0.5 and power factor of circuit is given by $\frac{\sqrt{3}}{2}$. Current is leading the voltage. The effective resistance of the box is made by using 5 resistances of equal value. Find the value of each resistance (Assume all the combination are in series).

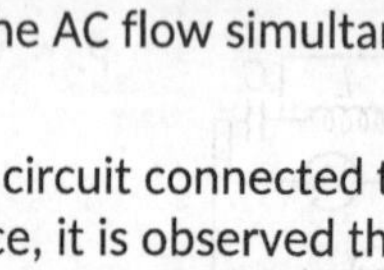

5 An *R-L-C* circuit includes a 1.6H inductor and a 250 μF capacitor rated at 400 V. The circuit is connected across a sine-wave generator whose peak voltage is 32V. What minimum resistance (in Ω) must the circuit have to ensure that the capacitor voltage does not exceed its rated value when the generator is at the resonant frequency?

6 An uncharged capacitor $C = 100\ \mu$F is connected in series with $R = 50\ \Omega$ and with AC source as shown in the figure. If switch *S* is closed at $t = 0$, the maximum value of $(V_A - V_B)$ is *K* V. Calculate *K*.

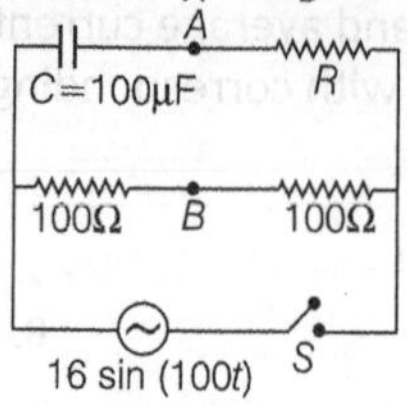

7 A coil is connected to an alternating emf of voltage 24 V and of frequency 50 Hz. The reading on the ammeter connected to the coil in series is 10 mA. If a 1 μF capacitor is connected to the coil in series, the ammeter shows 10 mA again. What would be the approx reading on a DC ammeter (in mA), if the coil was connected to a 180 V DC voltage supply? (Take $\pi^2 = 10$)

8 If an AC voltage 100 V is applied between points *A* and *B*, then current of 1 A and phase difference between current and voltage will be $\Delta\phi = 37°$. If the same voltage is applied between points *B* and *C*, then current of 5 A and $\Delta\phi = 53°$. What will be the impedance (in Ω) in the chain, if the same voltage is applied between points *A* and *C*? Round off to nearest integer.

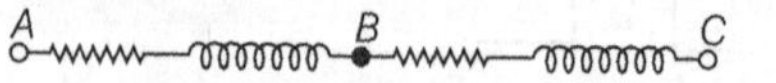

Previous Years Questions

JEE Main

1 Primary side of a transformer is connected to 230 V, 50 Hz supply. Turns ratio of primary to secondary winding is 10 : 1. Lord resistance connected to secondary side is 46 Ω. The power consumed in it is **[2024, 27 Jan Shift-II]**

(a) 11.5 W (b) 10.0 W (c) 12.5 W (d) 12.0 W

2 A series *L-C-R* circuit with $L = \frac{100}{\pi}$ mH, $C = \frac{10^{-3}}{\pi}$ F and $R = 10\ \Omega$, is connected across an AC source of 220 V, 50 Hz supply. The power factor of the circuit would be .... **[2024, 27 Jan Shift-II]**

3 In an AC circuit, voltage and current are given by $V = 100\sin(100t)$ V and $I = 100\sin\left(100t + \frac{\pi}{3}\right)$ mA respectively. The average power dissipated in one cycle is **[2024, 29 Jan Shift-II]**

(a) 25 W (b) 2.5 W (c) 5 W (d) 10 W

4 Given below are two statements

Statement I An AC circuit undergoes electrical resonance if it contains either a capacitor or an inductor.

Statement II An AC circuit containing a pure capacitor or a pure inductor consumes higher power due to its non-zero power factor.

In the light of the above statements, choose the correct answer from the options given below. **[2023, 13 April Shift-II]**

(a) Statement I is true but Statement II is false
(b) Both Statement I and Statement II are true
(c) Statement I is false but Statement II is true
(d) Both Statement I and Statement II are false

5 In an LC oscillator, if values of inductance and capacitance become twice and eight times respectively, then the resonant frequency of oscillator becomes x times its initial resonant frequency ω_0. The value of x is **[2023, 25 Jan Shift-I]**

(a) 1/16 (b) 16
(c) 4 (d) 1/4

6 For the given figures, choose the correct options **[2023, 29 Jan Shift-II]**

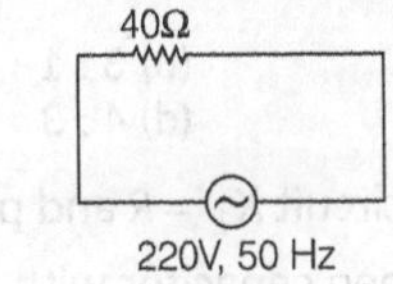

Fig. (a)

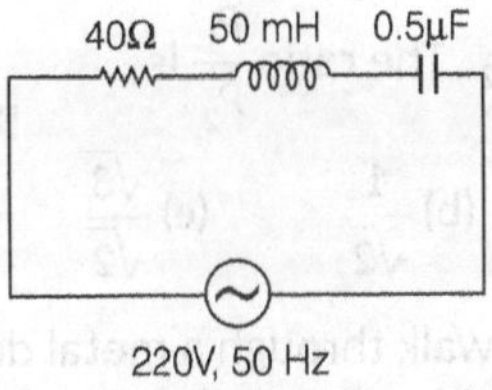

Fig. (b)

(a) The rms current in circuit (b) can be larger than that in (a)
(b) The rms current in Fig. (a) is always equal to that in Fig. (b)
(c) At resonance, current in (b) is less than that in (a)
(d) The rms current in circuit (b) can never be larger than that in (a)

7 In a series L-R circuit with $X_L = R$, power factor is P_1. If a capacitor of capacitance C with $X_C = X_L$ is added to the circuit the power factor becomes P_2. The ratio of P_1 to P_2 will be **[2023, 30 Jan Shift-I]**

(a) 1 : 1 (b) 1 : 2
(c) 1 : 3 (d) $1 : \sqrt{2}$

8 In the given circuit, rms value of current (I_{rms}) through the resistor R is **[2023, 30 Jan Shift-II]**

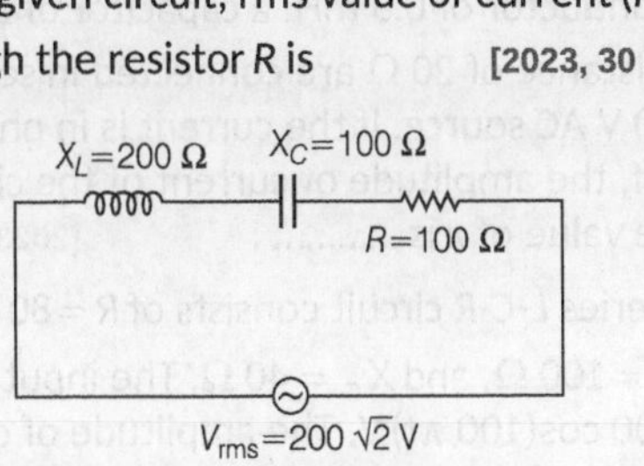

(a) 20 A (b) $2\sqrt{2}$ A (c) 2 A (d) $\frac{1}{2}$ A

9 In the circuit shown in the figure, the ratio of the quality factor and the bandwidth is .... **[2023, 24 Jan Shift-I]**

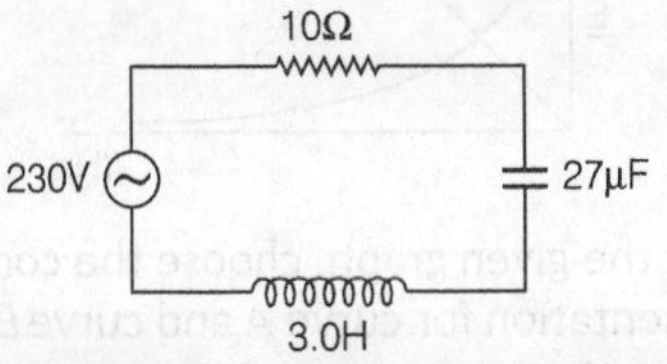

10 An L-C-R series circuit of capacitance 62.5 nF and resistance of 50 Ω, is connected to an A.C. source of frequency 2.0 kHz. For maximum value of amplitude of current in circuit, the value of inductance is .... mH. (Take, $\pi^2 = 10$) **[2023, 25 Jan Shift-I]**

11 A series L-C-R circuit is connected to an AC source of 220 V, 50 Hz. The circuit contains a resistance $R = 80\ \Omega$, an inductor of inductive reactance $X_L = 70\Omega$, and a capacitor of capacitive reactance $X_C = 130\Omega$. The power factor of circuit is $\frac{x}{10}$. The value of x is .... **[2023, 25 Jan Shift-II]**

12 An inductor of inductance 2 μH is connected in series with a resistance, a variable capacitor and an AC source of frequency 7 kHz. The value of capacitance for which maximum current is drawn into the circuit is $\frac{1}{x}$ F, where the value of x is .... $\left(\text{Take, } \pi = \frac{22}{7}\right)$ **[2023, 29 Jan Shift-II]**

13 A series L-C-R circuit is connected to an AC source of 220 V, 50 Hz. The circuit contain a resistance $R = 100\ \Omega$ and an inductor of inductive reactance $X_L = 79.6\ \Omega$. The capacitance of the capacitor needed to maximise the average rate at which energy is supplied will be .... μF. **[2023, 1 Feb Shift-I]**

14 An inductor of 0.5 mH, a capacitor of 20 μF and resistance of 20 Ω are connected in series with a 220 V AC source. If the current is in phase with the emf, the amplitude of current of the circuit is $\sqrt{x}$ A. The value of x is .... **[2023, 31 Jan Shift-I]**

15 A series *L-C-R* circuit consists of $R = 80\ \Omega$, $X_L = 100\ \Omega$, and $X_C = 40\ \Omega$. The input voltage is 2500 cos(100 πt) V. The amplitude of current, in the circuit is .... A. **[2023, 31 Jan Shift-II]**

16

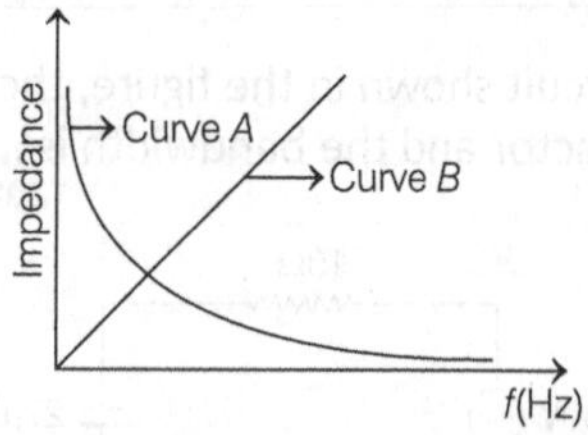

As per the given graph, choose the correct representation for curve *A* and curve *B*.
{Where, X_C = reactance of pure capacitive circuit connected with AC source
X_L = Reactance of pure inductive circuit connected with AC source
R = Impedance of pure resistive circuit connected with AC source.
Z = Impedance of the *L-C-R* series circuit} **[2023, 11 April Shift-I]**

(a) $A = X_L, B = R$ (b) $A = X_L, B = Z$
(c) $A = X_C, B = X_L$ (d) $A = X_C, B = R$

17 A series combination of resistor of resistance 100 Ω, inductor of inductance 1 H and capacitor of capacitance 6.25 μF is connected to an AC source. The quality factor of the circuit will be .... **[2023, 8 April Shift-II]**

18 An ideal transformer with purely resistive load operates at 12 kV on the primary side. It supplies electrical energy to a number of nearby houses at 120 V. The average rate of energy consumption in the houses served by the transformer is 60 kW. The value of resistive load (R_S) required in the secondary circuit will be .... mΩ. **[2023, 6 April Shift-I]**

19 In an AC generator, a rectangular coil of 100 turns each having area $14 \times 10^{-2}\ m^2$ is rotated at 360 rev/min about an axis perpendicular to a uniform magnetic field of magnitude 3.0 T. The maximum value of the emf produced will be .... V. $\left(\text{Take, } \pi = \frac{22}{7}\right)$ **[2023, 30 Jan Shift-I]**

20 A circuit element *X* when connected to an AC supply of peak voltage 100 V gives a peak current of 5 A which is in phase with the voltage. A second element *Y* when connected to the same AC supply also gives the same value of peak current which lags behind the voltage by $\frac{\pi}{2}$. If *X* and *Y* are connected in series to the same supply, what will be the rms value of the current in ampere? **[2022, 29 July Shift-II]**

(a) $\frac{10}{\sqrt{2}}$ (b) $\frac{5}{\sqrt{2}}$ (c) $5\sqrt{2}$ (d) $\frac{5}{2}$

21 An alternating emf $E = 440 \sin 100\pi t$ is applied to a circuit containing an inductance of $\frac{\sqrt{2}}{\pi}$ H. If an AC ammeter is connected in the circuit, its reading will be **[2022, 29 July Shift-I]**

(a) 4.4 A (b) 1.55 A (c) 2.2 A (d) 3.11 A

22 A direct current of 4 A and an alternating current of peak value 4 A flow through resistance of 3 Ω and 2 Ω, respectively. The ratio of heat produced in the two resistances in same interval of time will be **[2022, 27 July Shift-I]**

(a) 3 : 2 (b) 3 : 1
(c) 3 : 4 (d) 4 : 3

23 In a series *L-R* circuit $X_L = R$ and power factor of the circuit is P_1. When capacitor with capacitance *C* such that $X_L = X_C$ is put in series, the power factor becomes P_2. The ratio $\frac{P_1}{P_2}$ is **[2022, 26 July Shift-I]**

(a) $\frac{1}{2}$ (b) $\frac{1}{\sqrt{2}}$ (c) $\frac{\sqrt{3}}{\sqrt{2}}$ (d) 2 : 1

24 When you walk through a metal detector carrying a metal object in your pocket, it raises an alarm. This phenomenon works on **[2022, 25 July Shift-II]**

(a) Electromagnetic induction
(b) Resonance in AC circuits
(c) Mutual induction in AC circuits
(d) Interference of electromagnetic waves

25 To increase the resonant frequency in series *L-C-R* circuit, **[2022, 25 July Shift-I]**

(a) source frequency should be increased
(b) another resistance should be added in series with the first resistance.
(c) another capacitor should be added in series with the first capacitor.
(d) the source frequency should be decreased.

26 An inductor of 0.5 mH, a capacitor of 200 μF and a resistor of 2 Ω are connected in series with a 220 V AC source. If the current is in phase with the emf, the frequency of AC source will be ...... $\times 10^2$ Hz. **[2022, 29 June Shift-II]**

27 A telegraph line of length 100 km has a capacity of 0.01 μF/km and it carries an alternating current at 0.5 kilo cycle per second. If minimum impedance is required, then the value of the inductance that needs to be introduced in series is ...... mH. (If, $\pi = \sqrt{10}$) **[2022, 28 June Shift-I]**

28 If wattless current flows in the AC circuit, then the circuit is **[2022, 25 June Shift-I]**
(a) purely resistive circuit
(b) purely inductive circuit
(c) *L-C-R* series circuit
(d) *R-C* series circuit only

29 Given below are two statements.

Statement I The reactance of an AC circuit is zero. It is possible that the circuit contains a capacitor and an inductor.

Statement II In AC circuit, the average power delivered by the source never becomes zero.

In the light of the above statements, choose the correct option. **[2022, 24 June Shift-II]**
(a) Both Statement I and Statement II are true.
(b) Both Statement I and Statement II are false.
(c) Statement I is true but Statement II is false.
(d) Statement I is false but Statement II is true.

30 As shown in the figure an inductor of inductance 200 mH is connected to an AC source of emf 220 V and frequency 50 Hz.

The instantaneous voltage of the source is 0 V when the peak value of current is $\frac{\sqrt{a}}{\pi}$ A. The value of *a* is .... **[2022, 24 June Shift-I]**

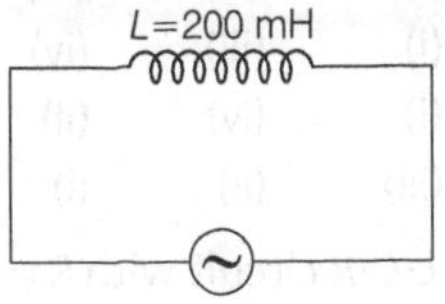

31 A resistance of 40 Ω is connected to a source of alternating current rated 220 V, 50 Hz. Find the time taken by the current to change from its maximum value to the rms value **[2022, 24 June Shift-I]**
(a) 2.5 ms (b) 1.25 ms (c) 2.5 s (d) 0.25 s

32 A transformer operating at primary voltage 8 kV and secondary voltage 160 V serves a load of 80 kW. Assuming the transformer to be ideal with purely resistive load and working on unit power factor, the loads in the primary and secondary circuits would be **[2022, 28 July Shift-II]**
(a) 800 Ω and 1.06 Ω (b) 10 Ω and 500 Ω
(c) 800 Ω and 0.32 Ω (d) 1.06 Ω and 500 Ω

33 At very high frequencies, the effective impedance of the given circuit will be ....Ω. **[2021, 31 Aug Shift-II]**

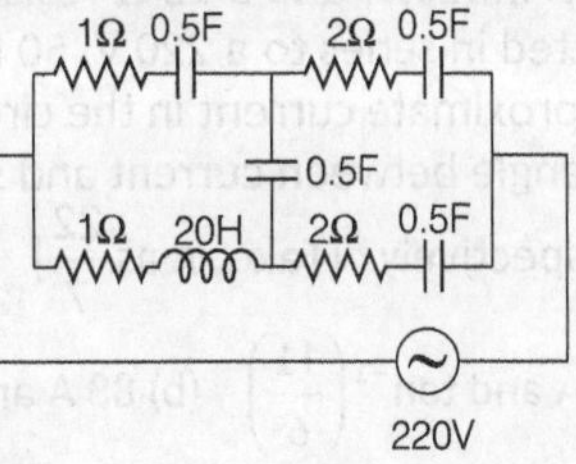

34 An AC circuit has an inductor and a resistor of resistance *R* in series, such that $X_L = 3R$. Now, a capacitor is added in series such that $X_C = 2R$. The ratio of new power factor with the old power factor of the circuit is $\sqrt{5}: x$ The value of *x* is .... **[2021, 27 Aug Shift-II]**

35 The alternating current is given by

$$i = \left\{\sqrt{42}\sin\left(\frac{2\pi}{T}t\right) + 10\right\} \text{A}$$

The rms value of this current is ...... A. **[2021, 27 Aug Shift-I]**

36 In the given circuit the AC source has $\omega = 100 \text{ rad s}^{-1}$. Considering the inductor and capacitor to be ideal, what will be the current *I* flowing through the circuit? **[2021, 26 Aug Shift-II]**

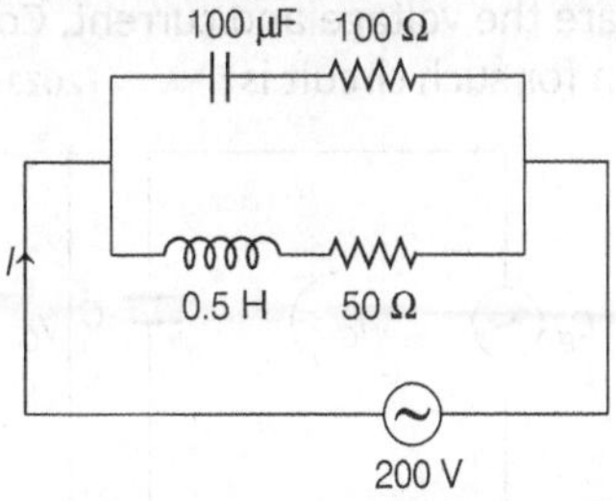

(a) 5.9 A (b) 4.24 A (c) 0.94 A (d) 6 A

37 A series *L-C-R* circuit driven by 300 V at a frequency of 50 Hz contains a resistance $R = 3\text{ k}\Omega$, an inductor of inductive reactance $X_L = 250\,\pi\Omega$ and an unknown capacitor. The value of capacitance to maximise the average power should be (Take, $\pi^2 = 10$) **[2021, 26 Aug Shift-I]**
(a) 4 μF (b) 25 μF (c) 400 μF (d) 40 μF

38 A 100 Ω resistance, a 0.1 μF capacitor and an inductor are connected in series across a 250 V supply at variable frequency. Calculate the value of inductance of inductor at which resonance will occur. Given that the resonant frequency is 60 Hz. **[2021, 27 July Shift-II]**

(a) 0.70 H (b) 70.3 mH
(c) 7.03×10^{-5} H (d) 70.3 H

39 A 0.07 H inductor and a 12 Ω resistor are connected in series to a 220 V, 50 Hz AC source. The approximate current in the circuit and the phase angle between current and source voltage are, respectively. [Take, π as $\frac{22}{7}$] **[2021, 27 July Shift-I]**

(a) 8.8 A and $\tan^{-1}\left(\frac{11}{6}\right)$ (b) 88 A and $\tan^{-1}\left(\frac{11}{6}\right)$
(c) 0.88 A and $\tan^{-1}\left(\frac{11}{6}\right)$ (d) 8.8 A and $\tan^{-1}\left(\frac{6}{11}\right)$

40 Two circuits are shown in the figures (a) and (b). At a frequency of .... rad/s, the average power dissipated in one cycle will be same in both the circuits. **[2021, 25 July Shift-II]**

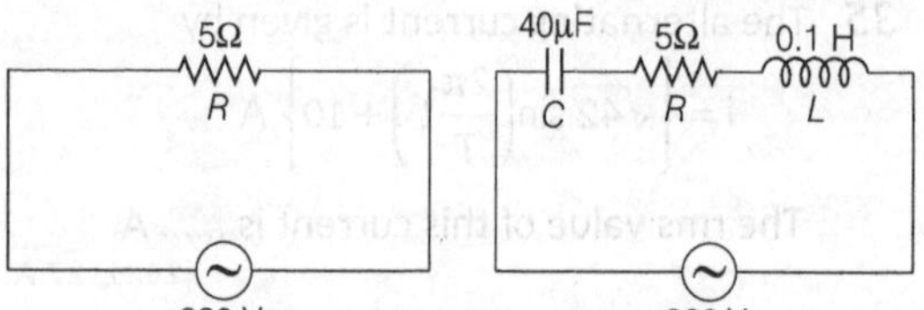

220 V Fig. (a) 220 V Fig. (b)

41 In a circuit consisting of a capacitance and a generator with alternating emf $E_g = E_{g_0} \sin\omega t$, V_C and I_C are the voltage and current. Correct phasor diagram for such circuit is **[2021, 22 July Shift-II]**

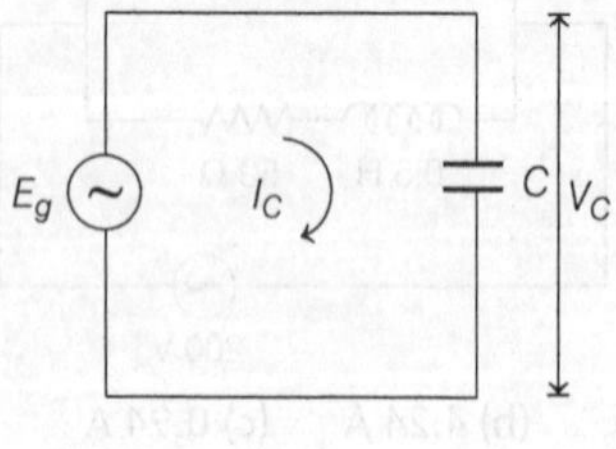

(a)
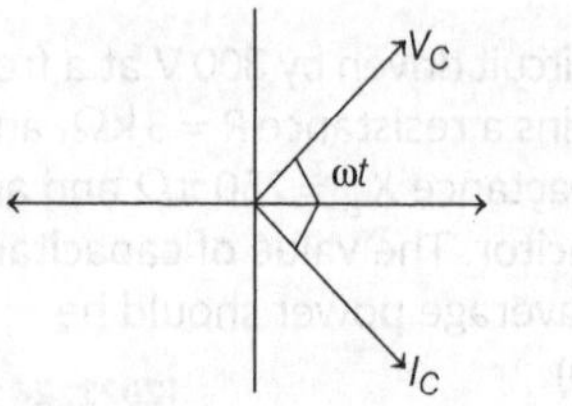

(b)
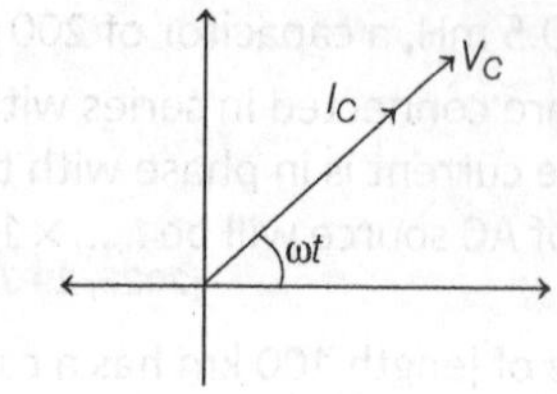

(c)
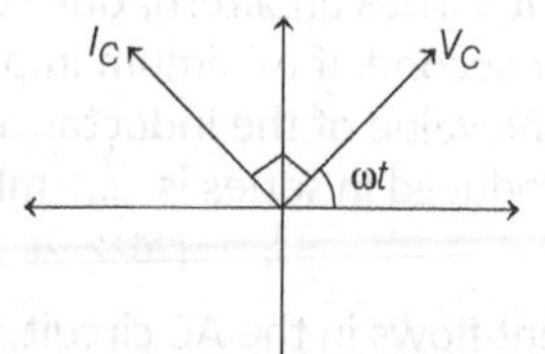

(d)
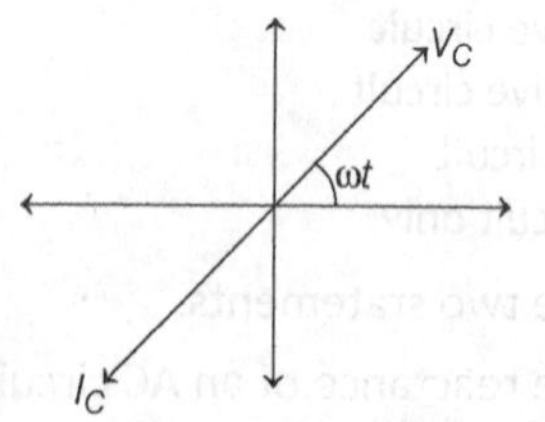

42 Match Column I with Column II. **[2021, 22 July Shift-II]**

	Column I		Column II
A.	$\omega L > \frac{1}{\omega C}$	(i)	Current is in phase with EMF
B.	$\omega L = \frac{1}{\omega C}$	(ii)	Current lags behind the applied EMF
C.	$\omega L < \frac{1}{\omega C}$	(iii)	Maximum current occurs
D.	Resonant frequency	(iv)	Current leads the EMF

Choose the correct answer from the options given below.

Codes

	A	B	C	D
(a)	(ii)	(i)	(iv)	(iii)
(b)	(ii)	(i)	(iii)	(iv)
(c)	(iii)	(i)	(iv)	(ii)
(d)	(iv)	(iii)	(ii)	(i)

43 For a series *L-C-R* circuit with $R = 100\,\Omega$, $L = 0.5$ mH and $C = 0.1$ pF connected across 220 V-50 Hz AC supply, the phase angle between current and supplied voltage and the nature of the circuit is **[2021, 20 July Shift-II]**

(a) 0°, resistive circuit
(b) ≈ 90°, predominantly inductive circuit
(c) 0° resonance circuit
(d) ≈ 90°, predominantly capacitive circuit

44 A series *L-C-R* circuit of $R = 5\Omega$, $L = 20$ mH and $C = 0.5\mu F$ is connected across an AC supply of 250 V, having variable frequency. The power dissipated at resonance condition is ...... $\times 10^2$ W. **[2021, 20 July Shift-II]**

45 AC voltage $V(t) = 20 \sin\omega t$ volt of frequency 50 Hz is applied to a parallel plate capacitor. The separation between the plates is 2 mm and the area is 1 m^2. The amplitude of the oscillating displacement current for the applied AC voltage is .... (Take, $\varepsilon_0 = 8.85 \times 10^{-12}$ F/m) **[2021, 20 July Shift-I]**

(a) 21.14 μA (b) 83.37 μA
(c) 27.79 μA (d) 55.58 μA

46 In an *L-C-R* series circuit, an inductor 30 mH and a resistor 1Ω are connected to an AC source of angular frequency 300 rad/s. The value of capacitance for which, the current leads the voltage by 45° is $\frac{1}{x} \times 10^{-3}$ F. Then, the value of *x* is .... **[2021, 20 July Shift-I]**

47 In a series *L-C-R* circuit, the inductive reactance (X_L) is 10 Ω and the capacitive reactance (X_C) is 4 Ω. The resistance (*R*) in the circuit is 6 Ω. The power factor of the circuit is **[2021, 18 March Shift-II]**

(a) $\frac{1}{2}$ (b) $\frac{1}{2\sqrt{2}}$ (c) $\frac{1}{\sqrt{2}}$ (d) $\frac{\sqrt{3}}{2}$

48 In a series *L-C-R* resonance circuit, if we change the resistance only, from a lower to higher value, **[2021, 18 March Shift-I]**

(a) the bandwidth of resonance circuit will increase
(b) the resonance frequency will increase
(c) the quality factor will increase
(d) the quality factor and the resonance frequency will remain constant

49 An AC source rated 220 V, 50 Hz is connected to a resistor. The time taken by the current to change from its maximum to the rms value is **[2021, 18 March Shift-I]**

(a) 2.5 ms (b) 25 ms (c) 2.5 s (d) 0.25 ms

50 What happens to the inductive reactance and the current in a purely inductive circuit, if the frequency is halved ? **[2021, 17 Mdarch Shift-II]**

(a) Both inductive reactance and current will be halved.
(b) Inductive reactance will be halved and current will be doubled.
(c) Inductive reactance will be doubled and current will be halved.
(d) Both inductive reactance and current will be doubled.

51 Match Column-I with Column-II. **[2021, 17 March Shift-II]**

Column-I	Column-II
A. Phase difference between current and voltage in a purely resistive AC circuit	1. $\frac{\pi}{2}$; current leads voltage
B. Phase difference between current and voltage in a pure inductive AC circuit	2. zero
C. Phase difference between current and voltage in a pure capacitive AC circuit	3. $\frac{\pi}{2}$; current lags voltage
D. Phase difference between current and voltage in an *L-C-R* series circuit	4. $\tan^{-1}\left(\frac{X_C - X_L}{R}\right)$

Choose the most appropriate answer from the options given below.

	A	B	C	D
(a)	1	3	4	2
(b)	2	4	3	1
(c)	2	3	4	1
(d)	2	3	1	4

52 An AC current is given by $I = I_1 \sin\omega t + I_2 \cos\omega t$. A hot wire ammeter will give a reading **[2021, 17 March Shift-I]**

(a) $\sqrt{\frac{I_1^2 - I_2^2}{2}}$ (b) $\sqrt{\frac{I_1^2 + I_2^2}{2}}$
(c) $\frac{I_1 + I_2}{\sqrt{2}}$ (d) $\frac{I_1 + I_2}{2\sqrt{2}}$

53 A sinusoidal voltage of peak value 250 V is applied to a series *L-C-R* circuit, in which $R = 8\ \Omega$, $L = 24$ mH and $C = 60\mu F$. The value of power dissipated at resonant condition is *x* kW. The value of *x* to the nearest integer is .... **[2021, 16 March Shift-I]**

54 Find the peak current and resonant frequency of the following circuit (as shown in figure). **[2021, 26 Feb Shift-II]**

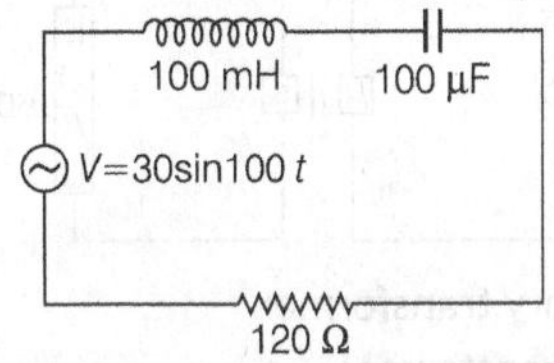

(a) 0.2 A and 50 Hz (b) 0.2 A and 100 Hz
(c) 2 A and 100 Hz (d) 2 A and 50 Hz

55 An alternating current is given by the equation $i = i_1 \sin \omega t + i_2 \cos \omega t$. The rms current will be **[2021, 26 Feb Shift-I]**

(a) $\frac{1}{\sqrt{2}}(i_1^2 + i_2^2)^{1/2}$ (b) $\frac{1}{\sqrt{2}}(i_1 + i_2)^2$

(c) $\frac{1}{2}(i_1^2 + i_2^2)^{1/2}$ (d) $\frac{1}{\sqrt{2}}(i_1 + i_2)$

56 In a series *L-C-R* resonant circuit, the quality factor is measured as 100. If the inductance is increased by two fold and resistance is decreased by two fold, then the quality factor after this change will be .... **[2021, 26 Feb Shift-I]**

57 The angular frequency of alternating current in an *L-C-R* circuit is 100 rad/s. The components connected are shown in the figure. Find the value of inductance of the coil and capacity of condenser. **[2021, 25 Feb Shift-I]**

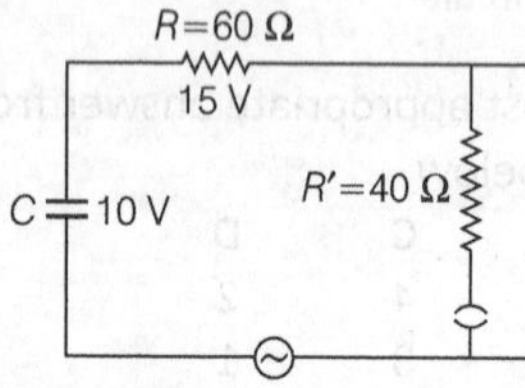

(a) 0.8 H and 150 μF
(b) 0.8 H and 250 μF
(c) 1.33 H and 250 μF
(d) 1.33 H and 150 μF

58 A transmitting station releases waves of wavelength 960 m. A capacitor of 2.56 μF is used in the resonant circuit. The self-inductance of coil necessary for resonance is .... $\times 10^{-8}$ H. **[2021, 25 Feb Shift-I]**

59 A resonance circuit having inductance and resistance 2×10^{-4} H and 6.28 Ω respectively oscillates at 10 MHz frequency. The value of quality factor of this resonator is .... [Take, $\pi = 3.14$] **[2021, 24 Feb Shift-I]**

60 For the given circuit, comment on the type of transformer used. **[2021, 16 March Shift-II]**

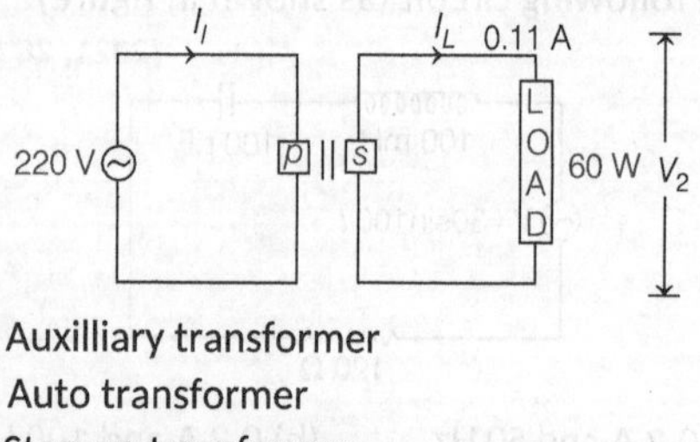

(a) Auxilliary transformer
(b) Auto transformer
(c) Step-up transformer
(d) Step down transformer

61 In an AC-circuit, an inductor, a capacitor and a resistor are connected in series with $X_L = R = X_C$. Impedance of this circuit is **[2020, 2 Sep Shift-II]**

(a) $2R^2$ (b) Zero
(c) R (d) $R\sqrt{2}$

62 An inductance coil has a reactance of 100 Ω. When an AC signal of frequency 1000 Hz is applied to the coil, the applied voltage leads the current by 45°. The self-inductance of the coil is **[2020, 2 Sep Shift-II]**

(a) 1.1×10^{-2} H (b) 1.1×10^{-1} H
(c) 5.5×10^{-5} H (d) 6.7×10^{-7} H

63 A 750 Hz, 20 V (rms) source is connected to a resistance of 100 Ω, an inductance of 0.1803 H and a capacitance of 10 μF all in series combination. The time in which the resistance (heat capacity 2 J/°C) will get heated by 10°C is close to. (Assume no loss of heat to the surroundings) **[2020, 3 Sep Shift-I]**

(a) 418 s (b) 245 s
(c) 365 s (d) 348 s

64 An elliptical loop having resistance *R*, of semi-major axis *a* and semi-minor axis *b* is placed in a magnetic field as shown in the figure. If the loop is rotated about the *X*-axis with angular frequency ω, then the average power loss in the loop due to joule's heating is **[2020, 3 Sep Shift-I]**

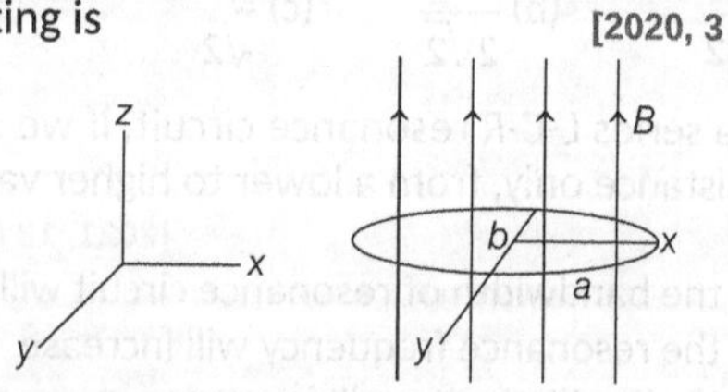

(a) $\frac{\pi^2 a^2 b^2 B^2 \omega^2}{2R}$ (b) zero

(c) $\frac{\pi a b B \omega}{R}$ (d) $\frac{\pi^2 a^2 b^2 B^2 \omega^2}{R}$

65 An AC circuit has $R = 100$ Ω, $C = 2$ μF and $L = 80$ mH connected in series. The quality factor of the circuit is **[2020, 6 Sep Shift-I]**

(a) 2 (b) 0.5
(c) 20 (d) 400

66 In a series *L-R* circuit, power of 400W is dissipated from a source of 250 V, 50 Hz. The power factor of the circuit is 0.8. In order to bring the power factor to unity, a capacitor of value *C* is added in series to the *L* and *R*. Taking the value of *C* as $\left(\frac{n}{3\pi}\right)$ μF, then value of *n* is .... **[2020, 6 Sep Shift-II]**

67 An L-C-R circuit behaves like a damped harmonic oscillator. Comparing it with a physical spring-mass damped oscillator having damping constant b, the correct equivalence would be **[2020, 7 Jan Shift-I]**

(a) $L \leftrightarrow \frac{1}{b}, C \leftrightarrow \frac{1}{m}, R \leftrightarrow \frac{1}{k}$

(b) $L \leftrightarrow m, C \leftrightarrow \frac{1}{k}, R \leftrightarrow b$

(c) $L \leftrightarrow m, C \leftrightarrow k, R \leftrightarrow b$

(d) $L \leftrightarrow k, C \leftrightarrow b, R \leftrightarrow m$

68 In L-C circuit, the inductance $L = 40$ mH and capacitance $C = 100\mu F$. If a voltage $V(t) = 10\sin(314t)$ is applied to the circuit, the current in the circuit is given as **[2020, 9 Jan Shift-II]**

(a) $0.52\cos 314t$ (b) $0.52\sin 314t$

(c) $10\cos 314t$ (d) $5.2\cos 314t$

69 An electrical power line, having a total resistance of 2Ω, delivers 1 kW at 220 V. The efficiency of the transmission line is approximately **[2020, 5 Sep Shift II]**

(a) 91% (b) 85% (c) 96% (d) 72%

70 An alternating voltage $V(t) = 220\sin 100\pi t$ volt is applied to a purely resistive load of 50 Ω. The time taken for the current to rise from half of the peak value to the peak value is **[2019, 8 April Shift-I]**

(a) 5 ms (b) 2.2 ms (c) 7.2 ms (d) 3.3 ms

71 A circuit connected to an AC source of emf $e = e_0 \sin(100t)$ with t in seconds, gives a phase difference of $\frac{\pi}{4}$ between the emf e and current i. Which of the following circuits will exhibit this? **[2019, 8 April Shift-II]**

(a) RC circuit with $R = 1\,k\Omega$ and $C = 1\,\mu F$

(b) RL circuit with $R = 1\,k\Omega$ and $L = 1$ mH

(c) RC circuit with $R = 1\,k\Omega$ and $C = 10\,\mu F$

(d) RL circuit with $R = 1\,k\Omega$ and $L = 10$ mH

72

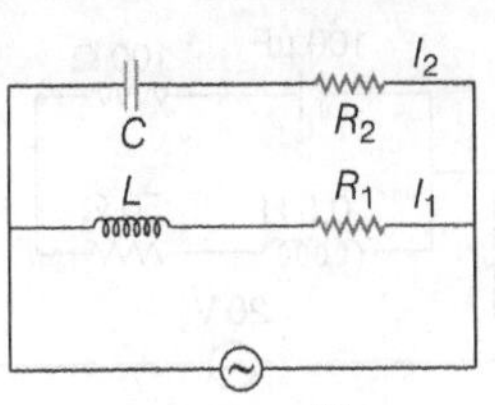

In the above circuit, $C = \frac{\sqrt{3}}{2}\,\mu F$, $R_2 = 20\,\Omega$, $L = \frac{\sqrt{3}}{10}$ H and $R_1 = 10\,\Omega$. Current in L-R_1 path is I_1 and in C-R_2 path is I_2. The voltage of AC source is given by $V = 200\sqrt{2}\sin(100t)$ volts. The phase difference between I_1 and I_2 is **[2019, 12 Jan Shift-II]**

(a) 30° (b) 60° (c) 0° (d) 90°

73 A series AC circuit containing an inductor (20 mH), a capacitor (120 μF) and a resistor (60 Ω) is driven by an AC source of 24 V/50 Hz. The energy dissipated in the circuit in 60 s is **[2019, 9 Jan Shift-II]**

(a) 3.39×10^3 J (b) 5.65×10^2 J

(c) 2.26×10^3 J (d) 5.17×10^2 J

74 A transformer consisting of 300 turns in the primary and 150 turns in the secondary gives output power of 2.2 kW. If the current in the secondary coil is 10 A, then the input voltage and current in the primary coil are **[2019, 10 April Shift-I]**

(a) 440 V and 5 A (b) 220 V and 20 A

(c) 220 V and 10 A (d) 440 V and 20 A

75 A power transmission line feeds input power at 2300 V to a step-down transformer with its primary windings having 4000 turns. The output power is delivered at 230 V by the transformer. If the current in the primary of the transformer is 5A and its efficiency is 90%, the output current would be **[2019, 9 Jan Shift II]**

(a) 45 A (b) 50 A (c) 25 A (d) 35 A

JEE Advanced

1 A series L-C-R circuit is connected to a 45 sin (ωt) Volt source. The resonant angular frequency of the circuit is 10^5 rad s^{-1} and current amplitude at resonance is I_0. When the angular frequency of the source is $\omega = 8 \times 10^4$ rad s^{-1}, the current amplitude in the circuit is $0.05 I_0$. If $L = 50$ mH, match each entry in List-I with an appropriate value from List-II and choose the correct option **(2023)**

List-I	List-II
P. I_0 in mA	1. 44.4
Q. The quality factor of the circuit	2. 18
R. The bandwidth of the circuit in rad s^{-1}	3. 400
S. The peak power dissipated at resonance in Watt	4. 2250
	5. 500

	P	Q	R	S
(a)	2	3	5	1
(b)	3	1	4	2
(c)	4	5	3	1
(d)	4	2	1	5

2. The instantaneous voltages at three terminals marked X, Y and Z are given by $V_X = V_0 \sin\omega t$, $V_Y = V_0 \sin\left(\omega t + \frac{2\pi}{3}\right)$ and $V_Z = V_0 \sin\left(\omega t + \frac{4\pi}{3}\right)$.

An ideal voltmeter is configured to read rms value of the potential difference between its terminals. It is connected between points X and Y and then between Y and Z. The reading(s) of the voltmeter will be **[2017]**

(a) $(V_{YZ})_{\text{rms}} = V_0\sqrt{\frac{1}{2}}$

(b) $(V_{XY})_{\text{rms}} = V_0\sqrt{\frac{3}{2}}$

(c) independent of the choice of the two terminals

(d) $(V_{XY})_{\text{rms}} = V_0$

3. In the circuit shown, $L = 1\,\mu\text{H}$, $C = 1\,\mu\text{F}$ and $R = 1\,\text{k}\Omega$. They are connected in series with an AC source $V = V_0 \sin\omega t$ as shown. Which of the following options is/are correct? **[2017]**

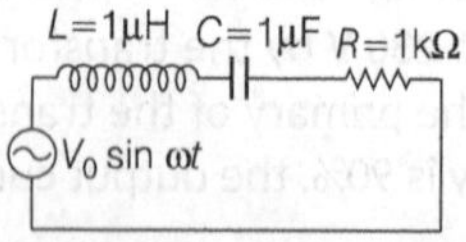

(a) At $\omega \approx 0$, the current flowing through the circuit becomes nearly zero

(b) The frequency at which the current will be in phase with the voltage is independent of R

(c) The current will be in phase with the voltage if $\omega = 10^4\ \text{rads}^{-1}$

(d) At $\omega >> 10^6\ \text{rads}^{-1}$, the circuit behaves like a capacitor

4. At time $t = 0$, terminal A in the circuit shown in the figure is connected to B by a key and an alternating current $I(t) = I_0 \cos(\omega t)$, with $I_0 = 1\ \text{A}$ and $\omega = 500\ \text{rad s}^{-1}$ starts flowing in it with the initial direction shown in the figure. At $t = 7\pi/6\omega$, the key is switched from B to D.

Now onwards only A and D are connected. A total charge Q flows from the battery to charge the capacitor fully. If $C = 20\ \mu\text{F}, R = 10\ \Omega$ and the battery is ideal with emf of 50 V, identify the correct statement(s). **[2014]**

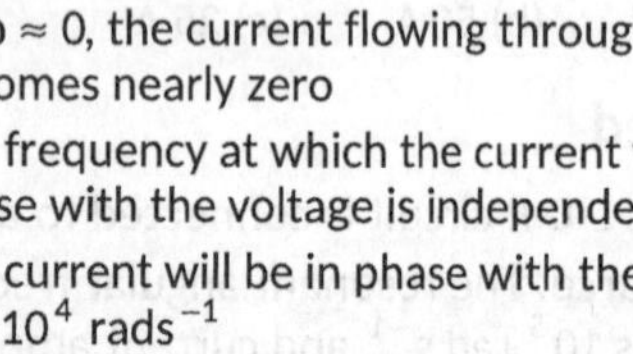

(a) Magnitude of the maximum charge on the capacitor before $t = \dfrac{7\pi}{6\omega}$ is 1×10^{-3} C

(b) The current in the left part of the circuit just before $t = \dfrac{7\pi}{6\omega}$ is clockwise

(c) Immediately after A is connected to D, the current in R is 10 A

(d) $Q = 2 \times 10^{-3}$ C

Direction (Q. Nos. 5 and 6)

A thermal power plant produces electric power of 600 kW at 4000 V, which is to be transported to a place 20 km away from the power plant for consumers' usage. It can be transported either directly with a cable of large current carrying capacity or by using a combination of step-up and step-down transformers at the two ends. The drawback of the direct transmission is the large energy dissipation. In the method of using transformers, the dissipation is much smaller. In this method, a step-up transformer is used at the plant side so that the current is reduced to a smaller value.

At the consumers' end, a step-down transformer is used to supply power to the consumers at the specified lower voltage. It is reasonable to assume that the power cable is purely resistive and the transformers are ideal with a power factor unity. All the current and voltages mentioned are rms values. **[2013]**

5. If the direct transmission method with a cable of resistance $0.4\ \Omega\ \text{km}^{-1}$ is used, the power dissipation (in %) during transmission is

(a) 20 (b) 30 (c) 40 (d) 50

6. In the method using the transformers, assume that the ratio of the number of turns in the primary to that in the secondary in the step-up transformer is 1 : 10. If the power to the consumers has to be supplied at 200V, the ratio of the number of turns in the primary to that in the secondary in the step-down transformer is

(a) 200 : 1 (b) 150 : 1 (c) 100 : 1 (d) 50 : 1

7. In the given circuit, the AC source has $\omega = 100$ rad/s. Considering the inductor and capacitor to be ideal, the correct choice(s) is(are) **[2012]**

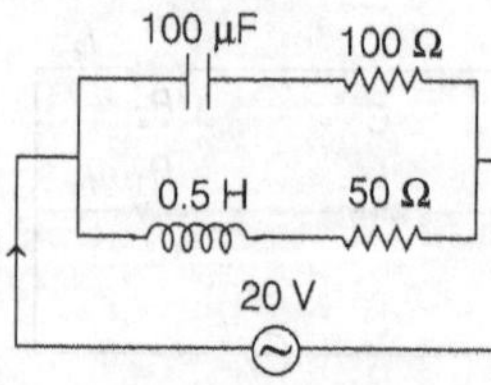

(a) the current through the circuit, I is approximately 0.3 A

(b) the current through the circuit, I is approximately $0.3\sqrt{2}$ A

(c) the voltage across 100 Ω resistor $= 10\sqrt{2}$ V

(d) the voltage across 50 Ω resistor = 10 V

Answer Key

Level 1

7.1 Peak, Average and RMS Value

1. (i) 4A (ii) $2\sqrt{2}$ A (iii) $f = 50$ Hz (iv) $\frac{\pi}{3}$ (v) $2\sqrt{3}$ A
2. $220\sqrt{2}$ V, 2.5 ms
3. (i) $i_{avg} = \frac{2i_m}{\pi}, i_{rms} = \frac{i_m}{\sqrt{2}}$ (ii) $i_{avg} = 0, i_{rms} = \frac{i_m}{\sqrt{2}}$
4. $V_{avg} = 0, V_{rms} = \frac{V_0}{\sqrt{3}}$
5. (i) $\sqrt{\frac{i_1^2 + i_2^2}{2}}$ (ii) $\sqrt{2}$ A (iii) $\left[a^2 + \frac{1}{2}b^2\right]^{\frac{1}{2}}$

7.2 Power Consumed in AC Circuit

1. 10 W, 5 W
2. 0

7.3 Purely Resistive, Capacitive and Inductive Circuits

1. (i) $i = (4A)\sin\left[(250\pi s^{-1})t + \frac{\pi}{3}\right]$ (ii) 40 W
2. (i) 40Ω (ii) $\sqrt{2}$ A (iii) $2\sin\left(250t + \frac{2\pi}{3}\right)$ A (iv) 0
3. (i) 50Ω (ii) $\sqrt{2}$ A (iii) $2\sin\left(10t - \frac{\pi}{4}\right)$ A (iv) 0

7.4 *RC*, *RL* and *LC* Series Circuits

1. (i) $\frac{1}{\sqrt{2}}$ (ii) 2A (iii) $100\sqrt{2}$ V (iv) $100\sqrt{2}$ V (v) 200 W
2. (i) $2\sin(100\pi t + 45°)$ (ii) $200\sin(100\pi t + 45°)$ (iii) $200\sin(100\pi t - 45)$
3. (a) 15 A (b) 37° i.e., the current will lag the applied voltage by 37° in phase.
4. 1.5 H, 20 Ω
5. $3/100\pi$ H
6. (i) 720 Ω (ii) 3.79 μF or 2.4 H (iii) Use of inductance or capacitance is more economical as it consumes no power while resistance consumes power.
7. 8 A
8. 0.5
9. 120 V
10. (i) 10 A, $10\sqrt{2}$ A (ii) $V_L = 500$ V $V_C = 250$ V (iii) 0

7.5 *R-L-C* Series Circuit

1. (i) 125 Ω (ii) $2\sin(100t - 53°)$ (iii) 150 W
2. (i) 100 Ω (ii) $100\sqrt{2}$ (iii) $\sqrt{2}$ A (iv) $V_1 = 100\sqrt{2}$ V, $V_2 = 100\sqrt{2}$ V, $V_3 = 200\sqrt{2}$ V, $V_4 = 200$ V, $V_5 = 100\sqrt{2}$ V
3. 4 μF, 20 Ω
4. (i) $\frac{250}{3\pi}$ Hz (ii) 2 mA
5. 1.5 A
6. 1×10^{-8} H
7. (i) 663.14 Hz, 14.14 A (ii) 663.14 Hz, 2300 W (iii) 4071.9 rad/s, 4263.6 rad/s (iv) 21.74

7.6 Transformer

1. 400
2. 0.1 A
3. (i) 600 kW (ii) 1400 kW (iii) 440 V - 7000 V

Level 2

Single Choice Correct Questions

1. (b)	2. (d)	3. (b)	4. (b)	5. (a)	6. (d)	7. (b)	8. (a)	9. (b)	10. (b)
11. (c)	12. (d)	13. (b)	14. (d)	15. (a)	16. (b)	17. (a)	18. (a)	19. (c)	20. (d)
21. (b)	22. (b)	23. (b)	24. (b)	25. (b)	26. (d)	27. (d)	28. (c)	29. (a)	30. (d)

31. (b)	32. (c)	33. (d)	34. (a)	35. (b)	36. (a)	37. (d)	38. (d)	39. (d)	40. (c)
41. (a)	42. (c)	43. (a)	44. (c)	45. (c)	46. (d)	47. (c)	48. (c)	49. (b)	50. (d)

Numerical Value Questions

1. 4 2. 4 3. 1 4. 3 5. 2.5 6. 6 7. 4
8. 1

Level 3

Single Choice Correct Questions

1. (b)	2. (b)	3. (b)	4. (d)	5. (d)	6. (b)	7. (a)	8. (b)	9. (b)	10. (b)
11. (b)	12. (b)	13. (d)	14. (d)	15. (c)	16. (c)	17. (c)	18. (c)	19. (d)	20. (d)
21. (c)	22. (c)	23. (b)	24. (d)						

Multiple Choice(s) Correct Questions

1. (a, c, d) 2. (a, c, d) 3. (a, b) 4. (a, b, c) 5. (a, c, d) 6. (a, b, c, d) 7. (b, c)

Comprehension Based Questions

1. (a)	2. (b)	3. (a)	4. (c)	5. (a)	6. (c)	7. (c)
8. (a)	9. (c)	10. (d)	11. (a)	12. (b)	13. (c)	14. (d)
15. (b)	16. (b)	17. (d)	18. (b)	19. (c)	20. (c)	

Match the Columns Questions

1. A → S; B → P, R, S; C → Q, S; D → Q
2. A → Q; B → Q; C → P; D → S
3. A → P, Q; B → R; C → P, Q, R, S; D → S
4. A → P, Q ,R, S; B → P, R; C → P, Q, R, S; D → R

Numerical Value Questions

1. 3 2. 4 3. 1.73 4. 1 5. 6.4 6. 8 7. 100
8. 119

Previous Years Questions

JEE Main

1. (a)	2. (1)	3. (b)	4. (d)	5. (d)	6. (d)	7. (d)	8. (c)	9. (10)	10. (100)
11. (8)	12. (3872)	13. (40)	14. (242)	15. (25)	16. (c)	17. (4)	18. (240)	19. (1584)	20. (d)
21. (c)	22. (b)	23. (b)	24. (b)	25. (c)	26. (5)	27. (100)	28. (b)	29. (c)	30. (242)
31. (a)	32. (c)	33. (2)	34. (1)	35. (11)	36. (*)	37. (a)	38. (d)	39. (a)	40. (500)
41. (c)	42. (a)	43. (d)	44. (125)	45. (c)	46. (3)	47. (c)	48. (a)	49. (a)	50. (b)
51. (d)	52. (b)	53. (4)	54. (a)	55. (a)	56. (400)	57. (b)	58. (10)	59. (2000)	60. (c)
61. (c)	62. (a)	63. (d)	64. (a)	65. (a)	66. (400)	67. (b)	68. (a)	69. (c)	70. (d)
71. (c)	72. (a)	73. (d)	74. (a)	75. (a)					

JEE Advanced

1. (b) 2. (b,c) 3. (a,b) 4. (c,d) 5. (b) 6. (a) 7. (a,c)

SOLUTIONS

Level 1

7.1 Peak, Average and RMS Value

1. $i = 4\sin\left(100\pi t + \dfrac{\pi}{3}\right) = I_m \sin(\omega t + \phi)$

(i) peak value = 4A

(ii) rms value = peak value/$\sqrt{2} = 2\sqrt{2}$ A

(iii) frequency $= \dfrac{\omega}{2\pi} = \dfrac{100\pi}{2\pi} = 50$ Hz

(iv) Initial phase $= \phi = \dfrac{\pi}{3}$

(v) at $t = 0, i = 4\sin\left(\dfrac{\pi}{3}\right) = 2\sqrt{3}$ A

2. Peak voltage $= \sqrt{2} \times$ (RMS voltage) $= 220\sqrt{2}$ V

$$\omega = 2\pi f = 100\pi$$

$$V = V_m \sin \omega t = 220\sqrt{2}\sin(100\pi t)$$

$$\Rightarrow \quad 220 = 220\sqrt{2}\sin(100\pi t)$$

$$\Rightarrow \quad 100\pi t = \frac{\pi}{4}$$

$$\Rightarrow \quad t = \frac{1}{400}\text{ s} = 2.5\text{ ms}$$

3. $$i_{avg} = \frac{\int_{t_1}^{t_2} i_m \sin \omega t\, dt}{\int_{t_1}^{t_2} dt} = \frac{i_m}{\omega}\left(\frac{\cos \omega t_1 - \cos \omega t_2}{t_2 - t_1}\right)$$

$$i_{rms} = \sqrt{\frac{\int_{t_1}^{t_2} i_m^2 \sin^2 \omega t\, dt}{\int_{t_1}^{t_2} dt}} = i_m \sqrt{\frac{\int_{t_1}^{t_2}\left(\frac{1 - \cos 2\omega t}{2}\right)dt}{\int_{t_1}^{t_2} dt}}$$

$$= i_m \sqrt{\frac{\left[\frac{t}{2} - \frac{\sin 2\omega t}{4\omega}\right]_{t_1}^{t_2}}{[t]_{t_1}^{t_2}}}$$

(i) For $t_1 = 0$ to $t_2 = \dfrac{\pi}{\omega}$

$$i_{avg} = \frac{2i_m}{\pi} \text{ and } i_{rms} = \frac{i_m}{\sqrt{2}}$$

(ii) For $t_1 = \dfrac{\pi}{2\omega}$ to $t_2 = \dfrac{3\pi}{2\omega}$

$$i_{avg} = 0 \text{ and } i_{rms} = \frac{i_m}{\sqrt{2}}$$

4. $$V_{avg} = \frac{\int_0^T V dt}{\int_0^T dt} = \frac{\text{Area under } V\text{-}t \text{ graph from 0 to } T}{T}$$

$$= \frac{-\frac{1}{2}V_0\left(\frac{T}{2}\right) + \frac{1}{2}V_0\left(\frac{T}{2}\right)}{T} = 0$$

$$y = mx + c$$

$$\Rightarrow V = \left(\frac{V_0}{\frac{T}{2}}\right)t - V_0$$

$$V_{rms} = \sqrt{\frac{\int_0^T \left(\left(\frac{2V_0}{T}\right)t - V_0\right)^2 dt}{\int_0^T dt}} = \frac{V_0}{\sqrt{3}}$$

5. (i) $i = i_1 \sin\left(\omega t + \dfrac{\pi}{2}\right) + i_2 \sin \omega t$

$$\text{Peak current} = \sqrt{i_1^2 + i_2^2 + 2i_1 i_2 \cos\left(\frac{\pi}{2}\right)} = \sqrt{i_1^2 + i_2^2}$$

$$\text{RMS current} = \frac{\text{Peak current}}{\sqrt{2}} = \sqrt{\frac{i_1^2 + i_2^2}{2}}$$

(ii) $i = 2\sin(100\pi t) + 2\cos(100\pi t + 30°)$

$= 2\sin(100\pi t) + 2\sin(100\pi t + 30° + 90°)$

$$\text{Peak current} = \sqrt{2^2 + 2^2 + 2(2)(2)\cos 120°}$$

$= 2$A

$$\text{RMS current} = \frac{\text{Peak current}}{\sqrt{2}} = \frac{2}{\sqrt{2}} = \sqrt{2}\text{ A}$$

(iii) $i^2 = a^2 + b^2 \sin^2 \omega t + 2ab \sin \omega t$

$$i_{rms} = \sqrt{\langle i^2 \rangle} = \sqrt{a^2 + b^2\left(\frac{1}{2}\right) + 2ab(0)} = \sqrt{a^2 + \frac{b^2}{2}}$$

7.2 Power Consumed in AC Circuit

1. (i) $P = Vi = 10\sin\left(250\pi t + \dfrac{\pi}{3}\right) \times 2\sin(250\pi t)$

At $t = \dfrac{2}{3}$ ms,

$$P = 20\sin\left(\frac{\pi}{6} + \frac{\pi}{3}\right)\sin\left(\frac{\pi}{6}\right) = 10\text{ W}$$

(ii) $P_{avg} = V_{rms}\, i_{rms} \cos \phi$

$$= \left(\frac{10}{\sqrt{2}}\right)\left(\frac{2}{\sqrt{2}}\right)\cos\left(\frac{\pi}{3}\right) = 5\text{ W}$$

2. $i = i_0 \sin \omega t, E = E_0 \sin\left(\omega t + \frac{\pi}{2}\right)$

$$P_{avg} = V_{rms} i_{rms} \cos \phi = \left(\frac{E_0}{\sqrt{2}}\right)\left(\frac{i_0}{\sqrt{2}}\right)\cos\left(\frac{\pi}{2}\right) = 0$$

7.3 Purely Resistive, Capacitive and Inductive Circuits

1. (i) $i = \frac{\varepsilon}{R} = \frac{20}{5}\sin\left(250\pi t + \frac{\pi}{3}\right)$

$= (4A)\sin\left(250\pi t + \frac{\pi}{3}\right)$

(ii) $P_{avg} = i_{rms}^2 R = \left(\frac{4}{\sqrt{2}}\right)^2 (5) = 40\text{ W}$

2. (i) $X_C = \frac{1}{\omega C} = \frac{1}{250 \times 100 \times 10^{-6}} = 40\,\Omega$

(ii) $i_{rms} = \frac{V_{rms}}{X_C} = \frac{\frac{80}{\sqrt{2}}}{40} = \sqrt{2}\text{ A}$

(iii) $i = \frac{80}{40}\sin\left(250t + \frac{\pi}{6} + \frac{\pi}{2}\right) = 2\sin\left(250t + \frac{2\pi}{3}\right)\text{A}$

(iv) $P_{avg} = V_{rms}\, i_{rms} \cos\left(\frac{\pi}{2}\right) = 0$

3. (i) $X_L = \omega L = 10 \times 5 = 50\,\Omega$

(ii) Ammeter reads rms value of current.

$$i_{rms} = \frac{\frac{100}{\sqrt{2}}}{50} = \sqrt{2}\text{ A}$$

(iii) $i = \frac{100}{50}\sin\left(10t + \frac{\pi}{4} - \frac{\pi}{2}\right) = 2\sin\left(10t - \frac{\pi}{4}\right)$

(iv) $P_{avg} = V_{rms}\, i_{rms} \cos\left(\frac{\pi}{2}\right) = 0$

7.4 RC, RL and LC Series Circuits

1. (i) $X_C = \frac{1}{\omega C} = \frac{1}{100\pi\left(\frac{100}{\pi}\right) \times 10^{-6}} = 100\Omega$

$Z = \sqrt{R^2 + X_C^2} = 100\sqrt{2}\,\Omega$

Power factor $= \frac{R}{Z} = \frac{100}{100\sqrt{2}} = \frac{1}{\sqrt{2}}$

(ii) maximum current $= \frac{200\sqrt{2}}{100\sqrt{2}} = 2A$

(iii) $(V_R)_{rms} = i_{rms} R = \left(\frac{2}{\sqrt{2}}\right)(100) = 100\sqrt{2}\text{ V}$

(iv) $(V_C)_{rms} = i_{rms}\, X_c = \left(\frac{2}{\sqrt{2}}\right) \times (100) = 100\sqrt{2}\text{ V}$

(v) $P_{avg} = V_{rms} i_{rms} \cos \phi = 200 \times \frac{2}{\sqrt{2}} \times \frac{1}{\sqrt{2}} = 200\text{ W}$

2. $V_s(t) = 200\sqrt{2}\sin(100\pi t)$

(i) $i(t) = \frac{200\sqrt{2}}{100\sqrt{2}}\sin\left(100\pi t + \frac{\pi}{4}\right) = 2\sin\left(100\pi t + \frac{\pi}{4}\right)$

(ii) $V_R(t) = i(t) \times R = 200\sin\left(100\pi t + \frac{\pi}{4}\right)$

(iii) $V_C(t) = i(t) X_C$ (with a phase lag of 90°)

$= 200\sin\left(100\pi t + \frac{\pi}{4} - \frac{\pi}{2}\right)$

$= 200\sin\left(100\pi t - \frac{\pi}{4}\right)$

3. $X_L = \omega L = 2\pi f L = 2\pi(50)\left(\frac{9}{100\pi}\right) = 9\Omega$

$Z = \sqrt{R^2 + X_L^2} = \sqrt{(12)^2 + (9)^2} = 15\,\Omega$

$i = \frac{V}{Z} = \frac{225}{15} = 15A$

$\phi = \tan^{-1}\left(\frac{X_L}{R}\right) = \tan^{-1}\left(\frac{9}{12}\right) = 37°$

Current will lag behind the applied voltage by 37°.

4. $P = i_{rms}^2 R \Rightarrow 80 = (2)^2 R \Rightarrow R = 20\,\Omega$

$Z = \frac{V}{i} \Rightarrow \sqrt{(20)^2 + (X_L)^2} = \frac{50}{2} \Rightarrow X_L = 15\Omega$

$X_L = (2\pi f)L \Rightarrow 15 = 2\pi\left(\frac{5}{\pi}\right)L \Rightarrow L = 1.5\text{ H}$

5. For DC source, an inductor act as a conducting wire.

So, $i = \frac{V}{R} \Rightarrow 2.5 = \frac{10}{R} \Rightarrow R = 4\,\Omega$

For AC source, $i = \frac{V}{\sqrt{R^2 + X_L^2}} \Rightarrow 2 = \frac{10}{\sqrt{(4)^2 + (X_L)^2}}$

$\Rightarrow \quad X_L = 3\,\Omega$

$X_L = (2\pi f)L \Rightarrow L = \frac{3}{100\pi}$

6. For lamp, $R = \frac{V^2}{P} = \frac{(20)^2}{5} = 80\,\Omega$

$i = \frac{P}{V} = \frac{5}{20} = 0.25\text{ A}$

Impedance, $Z = \frac{V}{i} = \frac{200}{0.25} = 800\,\Omega$

(i) $Z = R + R_S$

$\Rightarrow 800 = 80 + R_S$

$\Rightarrow R_S = 720\Omega$

(ii) $Z = \sqrt{R^2 + X_C^2}$

$\Rightarrow 800 = \sqrt{(80)^2 + (X_C)^2} \Rightarrow X_C = 240\sqrt{11}\Omega$

$\Rightarrow X_C = \frac{1}{2\pi f C} \Rightarrow C = \frac{125}{33}\mu\text{F} = 3.79\,\mu\text{F}$

$\Rightarrow X_L = (2\pi f)L \Rightarrow L = 2.4\text{ H}$

(iii) Inductor and capacitor are more economical as they consume no power while resistor consumes power.

7. $P = V_{rms} i_{rms} \cos\phi \Rightarrow 1500 = 250 \times 10 \times \cos\phi$

$$\Rightarrow \cos\phi = \frac{3}{5}$$

$$\text{Wattless current} = i \sin\phi = 10\sqrt{1 - \left(\frac{3}{5}\right)^2} = 8\text{ A}$$

8. $$\text{Power factor} = \cos\phi = \frac{R}{\sqrt{R^2 + (2\pi fL)^2}}$$

For $f = 60$ Hz,

$$\Rightarrow \sqrt{\frac{3}{2}} = \frac{R}{\sqrt{R^2 + (120\pi L)^2}} \Rightarrow R = 120\sqrt{3}\pi L$$

For $f = 180$ Hz,

$$\text{New power factor} = \frac{R}{\sqrt{R^2 + (360\pi L)^2}} = 0.5$$

9. $V^2 = V_R^2 + V_L^2 \Rightarrow (130)^2 = (50)^2 + V_L^2$

$$\Rightarrow \quad V_L = 120\text{ V}$$

10. $X_L = \omega L = 100 \times 0.5 = 50\,\Omega$

$$X_C = \frac{1}{\omega C} = \frac{1}{100 \times 400 \times 10^{-6}} = 25\,\Omega$$

(i) $$i_{rms} = \frac{V_{rms}}{|X_L - X_C|} = \frac{250}{25} = 10\text{ A}$$

$$i_m = i_{rms} \times \sqrt{2} = 10\sqrt{2}\text{ A}$$

(ii) $V_L = iX_L = 10 \times 50 = 500$ V

$V_C = iX_C = 10 \times 25 = 250$ V

(iii) $P_{avg} = V_{rms} i_{rms} \cos\phi = 0$ $\{\because \phi = 90°\}$

7.5 R-L-C Series Circuit

1. $R = 75\,\Omega$, $X_L = \omega L = 200\Omega$, $X_C = \frac{1}{\omega C} = 100\,\Omega$

(i) $Z = \sqrt{R^2 + (X_L - X_C)^2} = 125\Omega$

(ii) $$i = \frac{V}{Z}\left[\text{with a phase lag of } \tan^{-1}\left(\frac{X_L - X_C}{R}\right)\right]$$

$$= \frac{250}{125}\sin(100t - 53°) = 2\sin(100t - 53°)$$

(iii) $$P = i_{rms}^2 R = \left(\frac{2}{\sqrt{2}}\right)^2 (75) = 150\text{ W}$$

2. $$R = 100\Omega,\ X_L = \omega L = 100\pi\left(\frac{2}{\pi}\right) = 200\Omega$$

$$\text{and } X_C = \frac{1}{\omega C} = \frac{1}{100\pi\left(\frac{100}{\pi} \times 10^{-6}\right)} = 100\Omega$$

(i) Reactance $= X_L - X_C = 200 - 100 = 100\Omega$

(ii) $Z = \sqrt{R^2 + (X_L - X_C)^2} = 100\sqrt{2}\,\Omega$

(iii) $$i_{rms} = \frac{V}{Z} = \frac{200}{100\sqrt{2}} = \sqrt{2}\text{ A}$$

(iv) $V_1 = iR = \sqrt{2}(100) = 100\sqrt{2}$ V

$V_2 = iX_C = \sqrt{2}(100) = 100\sqrt{2}$ V

$V_3 = iX_L = \sqrt{2}(200) = 200\sqrt{2}$ V

$V_4 = i\sqrt{R^2 + X_C^2} = \sqrt{2}(100\sqrt{2}) = 200$ V

$V_5 = i|X_L - X_C| = 100\sqrt{2}$ V

3. $\phi = (5000t - 10°) - (5000t - 370°) = 360°$

So, the circuit is at resonance.

$$Z = R = \frac{E}{i} = \frac{100}{5} = 20\Omega$$

$$\omega = \frac{1}{\sqrt{LC}} \Rightarrow C = \frac{1}{\omega^2 L} = 4\mu\text{F}$$

4. (i) $$f = \frac{1}{2\pi\sqrt{LC}} = \frac{1}{2\pi\sqrt{2 \times 18 \times 10^{-6}}} = \frac{250}{3\pi}\text{ Hz}$$

(ii) $$i_{max} = \frac{V}{R} = \frac{20}{10 \times 10^3} = 2\text{ mA}$$

5. At resonance,

$$i_{max} = \frac{V}{R} \Rightarrow 6 = \frac{24}{R} \Rightarrow R = 4\Omega$$

So, resistance of inductor coil is 4Ω.

When inductor coil is connected across DC source,

$$i = \frac{\varepsilon}{R + r} \Rightarrow i = \frac{12}{4 + 4} = 1.5\text{ A}$$

6. $$f = \frac{c}{\lambda} = \frac{3 \times 10^8}{300} = 10^6\text{ Hz}$$

$$\text{Resonance frequency, } f = \frac{1}{2\pi\sqrt{LC}}$$

$$\Rightarrow \quad 10^6 = \frac{1}{2\pi\sqrt{L(2.5 \times 10^{-6})}}$$

$$\Rightarrow \quad L = 1 \times 10^{-8}\text{ H}$$

7. (i) $$f_R = \frac{1}{2\pi\sqrt{LC}} = 663.14\text{ Hz}$$

and $\omega_R = 2\pi f_R = 4166.67$ rad/s

$$i_{max} = \frac{230\sqrt{2}}{23} = 14.14\text{ A}$$

(ii) Average power is also maximum at resonance frequency $f_R = 663.14$ Hz

$$P_{max} = \frac{(230)^2}{23} = 2300\text{ W}$$

(iii) $$P = \frac{P_{max}}{2} \Rightarrow \frac{V^2 R}{Z^2} = \frac{1}{2}\left(\frac{V^2}{R}\right)$$

$$\Rightarrow Z = \sqrt{2}R$$

$$\Rightarrow X_C - X_L = \pm R$$

$$\Rightarrow \frac{1}{\omega C} - \omega L = \pm R$$

Solving we get,

$$\omega_1 = \frac{-RC + \sqrt{R^2C^2 + 4LC}}{2LC} = 4071.9 \text{ rad/s}$$

$$\omega_2 = \frac{RC + \sqrt{R^2C^2 + 4LC}}{2LC} = 4263.6 \text{ rad/s}$$

(iv) $Q = \frac{1}{R}\sqrt{\frac{L}{C}} = 21.74$

7.6 Transformer

1. $\frac{N_1}{N_2} = \frac{V_1}{V_2} \Rightarrow \frac{4000}{N_2} = \frac{2300}{230} \Rightarrow N_2 = 400$

2. $i_2 = \frac{P_2}{V_2} = \frac{24}{24} = 1 \text{ A}$

$\Rightarrow V_1 i_1 = V_2 i_2 \Rightarrow 240 i_1 = 24(1)$

$\Rightarrow \quad i_1 = 0.1 \text{ A}$

3. (i) $i = \frac{P}{V} = \frac{800 \times 10^3}{4000} = 200 \text{ A}$

$P_{Loss} = i^2 R = (200)^2 \times (2 \times 15 \times 0.5) = 600 \text{ kW}$

(ii) Power supplied by plant $= 600 + 800 = 1400$ kW

(iii) Voltage drop $= iR = 200 \times (2 \times 15 \times 0.5) = 3000$ V

Hence secondary voltage $= 3000 + 4000 = 7000$ V

Power generated is at primary voltage of 440 V.

Hence, the transformer rating is 440 V – 7000 V.

Level 2

Single Choice Correct Questions

1. For current to be maximum; $100\pi t + 30° = 90°$

$\Rightarrow \quad 100\pi t = \frac{\pi}{3}$

$\Rightarrow \quad t = \frac{1}{300} \text{ s}$

2. $i_{rms} = \frac{i_m}{\sqrt{2}} = i_m \sin \omega t_2 \Rightarrow \omega t_2 = \frac{\pi}{4}$

and $i_m = i_m \sin \omega t_1 \Rightarrow \omega t_1 = \frac{\pi}{2}$

Hence, $\omega(t_1 - t_2) = \frac{\pi}{2} - \frac{\pi}{4} \Rightarrow t_2 - t_1 = \frac{\pi}{4\omega}$

$= 2.5 \times 10^{-3}$ s

3. $$i_{rms} = \sqrt{\frac{\int_2^4 (2\sqrt{t})^2 dt}{\int_2^4 dt}} = \sqrt{\frac{4\left[\frac{t^2}{2}\right]_2^4}{[t]_2^4}} = 2\sqrt{3} \text{ A}$$

4. $i^2 = 9 + 16\sin^2\left(\omega t + \frac{\pi}{3}\right) + 24\sin\left(\omega t + \frac{\pi}{3}\right)$

$$i_{rms} = \sqrt{<i^2>} = \sqrt{9 + 16\left(\frac{1}{2}\right) + 24(0)} = \sqrt{17} \text{ A}$$

5. $i_3 = i_1 + i_2 = 3\sin\omega t + 4\sin\left(\omega t + \frac{\pi}{2}\right)$

$$i_{max} = \sqrt{3^2 + 4^2 + 2(3)(4)\cos\left(\frac{\pi}{2}\right)} = 5A$$

$$\phi = \tan^{-1}\left(\frac{4\sin\left(\frac{\pi}{2}\right)}{3 + 4\cos\left(\frac{\pi}{2}\right)}\right) = 53°$$

$\Rightarrow \quad i = 5\sin(\omega t + 53°)$

6. $e^2 = e_1^2 \sin^2\omega t + e_2^2 \cos^2\omega t + 2e_1 e_2 \sin\omega t \cos\omega t$

$\Rightarrow \quad e^2 = e_1^2 \sin^2\omega t + e_2^2 \cos^2\omega t + e_1 e_2 \sin 2\omega t$

$\Rightarrow \quad <e^2> = e_1^2\left(\frac{1}{2}\right) + e_2^2\left(\frac{1}{2}\right) + e_1 e_2(0)$

$\Rightarrow \quad e_{rms} = \sqrt{<e^2>} = \sqrt{\frac{e_1^2 + e_2^2}{2}}$

7. $$V_{rms} = \sqrt{\frac{\int_0^{T/4} V^2 dt + \int_{T/4}^{T} V^2 dt}{\int_0^T dt}} = \sqrt{\frac{V_0^2\left(\frac{T}{4}\right) + 0}{T}} = \frac{V_0}{2}$$

8. $E = 200\sin\left(314t + \frac{\pi}{2}\right), i = \sin\left(314t + \frac{\pi}{4}\right)$

So, E is leading i by a phase of $\frac{\pi}{4}$.

9. AC ammeter is based on heating effect of current. So, deflection, $\theta \propto i^2$.

10. $V = 5\sin\left(\omega t - \frac{\pi}{6} + \frac{\pi}{2}\right) = 5\sin\left(\omega t + \frac{\pi}{3}\right)$

$i = 10\sin\omega t$

$$P_{avg} = V_{rms} i_{rms} \cos\phi = \left(\frac{5}{\sqrt{2}}\right)\left(\frac{10}{\sqrt{2}}\right)\cos\left(\frac{\pi}{3}\right)$$

$= 12.5$ W

11. $P_1 = i^2 R = (2)^2 R = 4R$

$P_2 = i_{rms}^2 R = \left(\frac{2}{\sqrt{2}}\right)^2 R = 2R$

$\Rightarrow P_1 : P_2 = 2 : 1$

12. $i = 3 + 4\sqrt{2}\sin\omega t$

$\Rightarrow i^2 = 9 + 32\sin^2\omega t + 24\sqrt{2}\sin\omega t$

$$\Rightarrow \langle i^2 \rangle = 9 + 32\left(\frac{1}{2}\right) + 0$$

$$i_{rms} = \sqrt{9+16} = 5\text{A}$$

13. AC ammeter measures rms current.

$$i_{rms} = \frac{V_{rms}}{X_C} = \frac{\frac{(300\sqrt{2})}{\sqrt{2}}}{\left(\frac{1}{100 \times 10^{-6}}\right)} = 30 \text{ mA}$$

14. $i_m = \frac{E_m}{X_L} = \frac{100}{(100 \times 0.1)} = 10\text{ A}$

Current in a inductor lags voltage by $\frac{\pi}{2}$.

So, $i = 10 \sin\left(100t - \frac{\pi}{2}\right)$

$$= -10\cos(100t)\text{ A}$$

15. $X_L = X_C \Rightarrow \omega_0 L = \frac{1}{\omega_0 C}$

$\Rightarrow \quad \omega_0^2 LC = 1$

$$\frac{X_L'}{X_C'} = \frac{2\omega_0 L}{\left(\frac{1}{2\omega_0 C}\right)} = 4\omega_0^2 LC = 4:1$$

16. $\phi = \tan^{-1}\left(\frac{X_C}{R}\right) = \tan^{-1}\left(\frac{1}{2\pi fCR}\right) = \tan^{-1}\left(\frac{1}{\pi}\right)$

17. $V^2 = V_C^2 + V_R^2 \Rightarrow (10)^2 = 8^2 + V_R^2$

$\Rightarrow \quad V_R = 6\text{ V}$

$$\phi = \tan^{-1}\left(\frac{V_C}{V_R}\right) = \tan^{-1}\left(\frac{8}{6}\right) = \tan^{-1}\left(\frac{4}{3}\right)$$

18. $X_C = \frac{1}{\omega C} \Rightarrow X_C \propto \frac{1}{\omega}$

As frequency is increased, X_C decreases. So, impedance of circuit decreases and current increases. Hence, brightness of bulb will increase.

19. Time constant $= \tau = RC$

$$X_C = \frac{1}{\omega C} = \frac{1}{\left(\frac{1}{\tau}\right)C} = R$$

$$Z = \sqrt{R^2 + X_C^2} = \sqrt{R^2 + R^2} = \sqrt{2}R$$

20. $X_C = \frac{1}{\omega C}$; $X_C' = \frac{1}{\left(\frac{\omega}{3}\right)C} = 3X_C$

$$i = \frac{V}{\sqrt{R^2 + X_C^2}} \quad \text{...(i)}$$

and $$\frac{i}{2} = \frac{V}{\sqrt{R^2 + (3X_C)^2}} \quad \text{...(ii)}$$

Solving Eqs. (i) and (ii), we get

$$\frac{X_C}{R} = \sqrt{\frac{3}{5}}$$

21. At any instant, $V_{AC} = V_L + V_R$

22. When iron rod is inserted, inductance of inductor increases. Hence, impedance of circuit will increase and bulb will get dimmer due to decreased current.

23. $V = 20\sin(500t) + 20\sin\left(500t + \frac{\pi}{2}\right)$

$$= 20\sqrt{2}\sin\left(500t + \frac{\pi}{4}\right)$$

$$X_L = \omega L = 500 \times 10 \times 10^{-3} = 5\,\Omega$$

$$Z = \sqrt{R^2 + X_L^2} = 5\sqrt{2}\,\Omega$$

$$\phi = \tan^{-1}\left(\frac{X_L}{R}\right) = \frac{\pi}{4}$$

So, current will lag behind applied by $\frac{\pi}{4}$.

$$i = \frac{20\sqrt{2}}{5\sqrt{2}}\sin\left(500t + \frac{\pi}{4} - \frac{\pi}{4}\right)$$

$$= 4\sin(500t)$$

24. $X_L = \omega L = 2\pi(50)(0.7) = 220\,\Omega$

$$\phi = \tan^{-1}\left(\frac{X_L}{R}\right) = 45°$$

$$i = \frac{220}{\sqrt{(220)^2 + (220)^2}} = \frac{1}{\sqrt{2}}\text{ A}$$

Wattless component of current $= i\sin\phi = \frac{1}{\sqrt{2}}\left(\frac{1}{\sqrt{2}}\right)$

$$= 0.5\text{ A}$$

25. Time constant $= \frac{L}{R} = \tau \Rightarrow L = \tau R$

Power factor $= \cos\phi = \frac{R}{\sqrt{R^2 + (\omega L)^2}} = \frac{1}{\sqrt{1 + (\omega\tau)^2}}$

26. For DC source, $i = \frac{V}{R} \Rightarrow 1 = \frac{100}{R} \Rightarrow R = 100\,\Omega$

For AC source, $i = \frac{V}{\sqrt{R^2 + X_L^2}} \Rightarrow 0.5 = \frac{100}{\sqrt{(100)^2 + X_L^2}}$

$\Rightarrow \quad X_L = 100\sqrt{3}\,\Omega$

$$Z = \sqrt{(100)^2 + (100\sqrt{3})^2} = 200\,\Omega$$

and $\quad X_L = 100\sqrt{3} = 2\pi(50)L \Rightarrow L = 0.55\text{ H}$

27. Resistance of bulb, $R = \frac{V^2}{P} = \frac{(100)^2}{100} = 100\,\Omega$

$$i = \frac{P}{V} = \frac{100}{100} = 1\text{ A}$$

$$i=\frac{V}{\sqrt{R^2+X_L^2}} \Rightarrow 1=\frac{200}{\sqrt{(100)^2+(100\pi L)^2}}$$

$$\Rightarrow \quad L=\frac{\sqrt{3}}{\pi}\text{ H}$$

28. For DC source, $P=\frac{V^2}{R} \Rightarrow 20=\frac{(10)^2}{R}$

$$\Rightarrow \quad R=5\,\Omega$$

For AC source, $P=\frac{V^2R}{Z^2}=\frac{V^2R}{R^2+X_L^2}$

$$\Rightarrow \quad 10=\frac{(10)^2\,(5)}{(5)^2+X_L^2} \Rightarrow X_L=5\,\Omega$$

Now, $X_L=2\pi fL$

$$\Rightarrow \quad 5=2\pi f(10\times10^{-3}) \Rightarrow f=80\text{ Hz}$$

29. Figure shows that current i leads to emf e by a phase angle of $\frac{\pi}{4}$. So, the circuit has to be RC only.

$$\phi=\tan^{-1}\left(\frac{X_C}{R}\right) \Rightarrow \frac{\pi}{4}=\tan^{-1}\left(\frac{1}{100C(10^3)}\right)$$

$$\Rightarrow \quad C=10^{-5}\text{ F}=10\,\mu\text{F}$$

30. $Z=|X_C-X_L|=75-25=50\Omega$

$$i=\frac{V}{Z}=\frac{250}{50}=5\text{ A}$$

$$V_L=iX_L=5\times25=125\text{ V}$$

$$V_C=iX_C=5\times75=375\text{ V}$$

$$V_C>V$$

31. $X_L=\omega L=2\pi\left(\frac{500}{\pi}\right)(8\times10^{-3})=8\Omega$

$$X_C=\frac{1}{\omega C}=\frac{1}{2\pi\left(\frac{500}{\pi}\right)\left(\frac{1000}{3}\right)\times10^{-6}}=3\Omega$$

$$Z=\sqrt{R^2+(X_L-X_C)^2}=\sqrt{(10)^2+(8-3)^2}$$

$$=5\sqrt{5}\,\Omega$$

$$i_{\text{rms}}=\frac{V_{\text{rms}}}{Z}=\frac{100}{5\sqrt{5}}=\frac{20}{\sqrt{5}}\text{ A}$$

$$P_{\text{avg}}=i_{\text{rms}}^2R=\left(\frac{20}{\sqrt{5}}\right)^2(10)=800\text{ W}$$

32. $X_L=\omega L=100\times0.1=10\,\Omega$

$$\cos\phi=\frac{1}{\sqrt{2}} \Rightarrow \phi=\frac{\pi}{4}$$

$$\tan\phi=\frac{|X_L-X_C|}{R} \Rightarrow 1=\frac{|10-X_C|}{10} \Rightarrow X_C=20\,\Omega$$

$$X_C=\frac{1}{\omega C} \Rightarrow 20=\frac{1}{100C} \Rightarrow C=500\,\mu\text{F}$$

33. $E_{\text{rms}}=\frac{500\sqrt{2}}{\sqrt{2}}=500\text{ V}$

$$E=\sqrt{V_R^2+(V_L-V_C)^2}$$

$$\Rightarrow \quad 500=\sqrt{(400)^2+(700-V_C)^2}$$

$$\Rightarrow \quad V_C=400\text{ V}$$

or $\quad V_C=1000\text{ V}$

Peak voltage across capacitor $=\sqrt{2}\,V_C$

$$=400\sqrt{2}\text{ V or }1000\sqrt{2}\text{ V}$$

34. $V=i|X_L-X_C|=0,\ Z=\sqrt{R^2+(X_L-X_C)^2}=30\,\Omega$

$$i=\frac{V_R}{R}=\frac{240}{30}=8\text{ A}$$

35. $V^2=V_R^2+(V_L-V_C)^2 \Rightarrow (200)^2=V_R^2+(120)^2$

$$\Rightarrow V_R=160\text{V}$$

$$i=\frac{V_R}{R}=\frac{160}{40}=4\text{ A}$$

36. $V_R=V_L=V_C=20\text{ V} \Rightarrow iR=iX_L=iX_C \Rightarrow Z=R$

If resistance is doubled, $Z'=2R \quad \Rightarrow \quad i'=\frac{i}{Z}$

$$V_R'=\left(\frac{i}{2}\right)(2R)=20\text{ V}$$

$$V_L'=\left(\frac{i}{2}\right)X_L=\frac{20}{2}=10\text{V}$$

$$V_C'=\left(\frac{i}{2}\right)X_C=\frac{20}{2}\,10\text{ V}$$

37. $\tan\phi=\frac{X_L-X_C}{R} \Rightarrow \phi=\tan^{-1}\left(\frac{7-3}{3}\right)=53°$

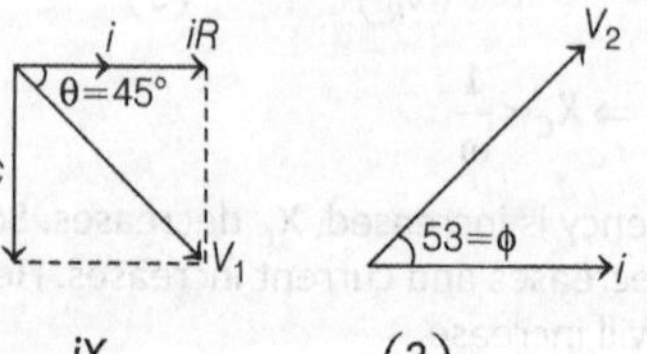

$$\tan\theta=\frac{iX_C}{iR} \Rightarrow \theta=\tan^{-1}\left(\frac{3}{3}\right)=45°$$

Phase difference between V_1 and $V_2=53°+45°=98°$

38. For LR circuit,

$$\cos\phi=0.6 \Rightarrow \tan\phi=\frac{4}{3}=\frac{X_L}{R_1} \Rightarrow X_L=\frac{4R_1}{3}$$

For RC circuit,

$$\cos\phi=0.5 \Rightarrow \tan\phi=\sqrt{3}=\frac{X_C}{R_2} \quad \Rightarrow \quad X_C=\sqrt{3}R_2$$

For series L-C-R circuit,

$$\cos\phi=1 \Rightarrow X_L=X_C \Rightarrow \frac{4R_1}{3}=\sqrt{3}R_2$$

$$\Rightarrow \frac{R_1}{R_2}=\frac{3\sqrt{3}}{4}$$

39. When only capacitance is removed,

$$\tan\phi = \frac{X_L}{R} \Rightarrow \tan 60° = \frac{X_L}{100} \Rightarrow X_L = 100\sqrt{3}\ \Omega$$

When only inductance is removed,

$$\tan\phi = \frac{X_C}{R} \Rightarrow \tan 60° = \frac{X_C}{100} \Rightarrow X_C = 100\sqrt{3}\ \Omega$$

$$Z = \sqrt{R^2 + (X_L - X_C)^2} = 100\ \Omega$$

$$i_{\text{rms}} = \frac{400}{100} = 4\text{A}$$

$$P = i_{\text{rms}}^2 R = (4)^2 (100) = 1600\text{ W}$$

40. $f_R = \frac{1}{2\pi\sqrt{LC}} \Rightarrow 100 \times 10^6 = \frac{1}{2\pi\sqrt{2\times 10^{-6} \times C}}$

$\Rightarrow C = 1.25\text{ pF}$

41. $i_1 = i_2 \Rightarrow \frac{V}{\sqrt{R^2 + \left(\omega_1 L - \frac{1}{\omega_1 C}\right)^2}} = \frac{V}{\sqrt{R^2 + \left(\omega_2 L - \frac{1}{\omega_2 C}\right)^2}}$

$$\Rightarrow \quad \left|\omega_1 L - \frac{1}{\omega_1 C}\right| = \left|\omega_2 L - \frac{1}{\omega_2 C}\right|$$

$$\Rightarrow \quad (\omega_1 - \omega_2)L = \left(\frac{\omega_1 - \omega_2}{\omega_1\omega_2}\right)\frac{1}{C}$$

$$\Rightarrow \quad \frac{1}{\sqrt{LC}} = \sqrt{\omega_1\omega_2}$$

$$\Rightarrow \quad \omega_R = \sqrt{\omega_1\omega_2}$$

42. At resonance, $X_L = X_C \Rightarrow Z = R$

$$i = \frac{V_R}{R} = \frac{100}{1000} = 0.1\text{ A}$$

$$X_L = X_C = \frac{1}{\omega C}$$

$$= \frac{1}{200 \times 2 \times 10^{-6}} = 2500\ \Omega$$

$$V_L = iX_L = 0.1 \times 2500 = 250\text{ V}$$

43. At resonance, $X_L = X_C$ and $Z = R$

$$i = \frac{V}{R} \Rightarrow 600 \times 10^{-3} = \frac{6}{R}$$

$\Rightarrow \quad R = 10\Omega$

For DC source,

$$i = \frac{V}{R+r} = \frac{6}{10+2} = 0.5\text{ A}$$

44. Quality factor $= \frac{f_R}{\Delta f} = \frac{600}{(650-550)} = 6$

45. $X_L = \omega L = 1000 \times 0.5 \times 10^{-3} = 0.5\,\Omega$

$$X_C = \frac{1}{\omega C} = \frac{1}{1000 \times 10^{-3}} = 1\,\Omega$$

$$R = 1\,\Omega$$

$$\tan\phi = \frac{\frac{V_0}{X_L} - \frac{V_0}{X_C}}{\frac{V_0}{R}} = \frac{\frac{1}{X_L} - \frac{1}{X_C}}{\frac{1}{R}}$$

$$= 1$$

$\Rightarrow \quad \phi = 45°$

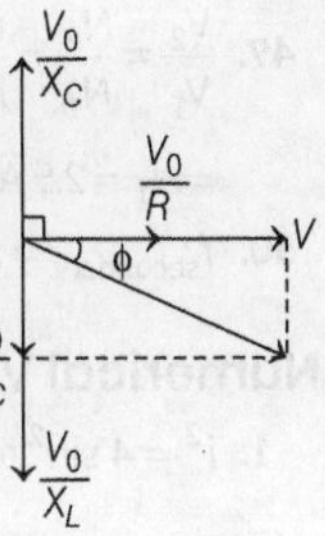

46. $X_L = \omega L = 50 \times 0.1 = 5\Omega$

$$X_C = \frac{1}{\omega C}$$

$$= \frac{1}{50 \times 0.004} = 5\Omega$$

For LR branch, $Z = \sqrt{R^2 + X_L^2} = 5\sqrt{2}\ \Omega$

$$i_L = \frac{100}{5\sqrt{2}} = 10\sqrt{2}\text{ A and } \tan\phi = \frac{X_L}{R} = 1$$

$$i_L = 10\sqrt{2}\sin\left(50t - \frac{\pi}{4}\right)$$

For RC branch, $Z = \sqrt{R^2 + X_C^2} = 5\sqrt{2}\ \Omega$

$$i_C = \frac{100}{5\sqrt{2}} = 10\sqrt{2}\text{ A and } \tan\phi = \frac{X_C}{R} = 1$$

$\Rightarrow \quad \phi = \frac{\pi}{4}$

$$i_C = 10\sqrt{2}\sin\left(50t + \frac{\pi}{4}\right)$$

$$i = i_L + i_C = 10\sqrt{2}\sin\left(50t - \frac{\pi}{4}\right) + 10\sqrt{2}\sin\left(50t + \frac{\pi}{4}\right)$$

$$= 20\sin(50t)\text{ A}$$

47. $\tan\phi = \frac{i_2 X_L}{i_2 R} = \frac{X_L}{R}$

$$\Rightarrow \phi = \tan^{-1}\left(\frac{X_L}{R}\right)$$

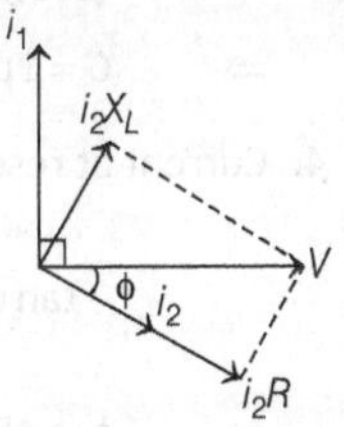

Phase difference between i_1 and i_2

$$= \frac{\pi}{2} + \tan^{-1}\left(\frac{X_L}{R}\right)$$

48. $i_R = \frac{\frac{200}{\sqrt{2}}}{100} = \sqrt{2}\text{ A}$

$$i_C = i_L = \frac{V}{|X_L - X_C|} = \frac{\frac{200}{\sqrt{2}}}{100} = \sqrt{2}\text{ A}$$

$$i_{\text{eff}} = \sqrt{i_R^2 + i_C^2}$$

$$= \sqrt{(\sqrt{2})^2 + (\sqrt{2})^2} = 2\text{ A}$$

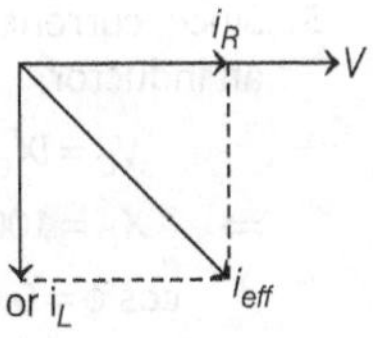

49. $\frac{V_2}{V_1}=\frac{N_2}{N_1}=\frac{i_1}{i_2}\Rightarrow\frac{1}{5}=\frac{i_1}{12.5}$

$\Rightarrow i_1=2.5\text{ A}$

50. $f_{secondary}=f_{primary}=50\text{ Hz}$

Numerical Value Questions

1. $i^2=4\sin^2\omega t+16\cos^2\omega t+6+4\sqrt{6}\sin\omega t+8\sqrt{6}\cos\omega t+8\sin 2\omega t$

$<i^2>=4\left(\frac{1}{2}\right)+16\left(\frac{1}{2}\right)+6+0+0+0$

$i_{rms}=\sqrt{<i^2>}=4\text{ A}$

2. $\tan\phi=\frac{X_L}{R}\Rightarrow\tan 30°=\frac{\omega L}{R}\Rightarrow R=\sqrt{3}\omega L$

$i=\frac{V}{\sqrt{R^2+(\omega L)^2}}=\frac{\sqrt{3}V}{2R}$

With new source, $i'=\frac{V}{\sqrt{R^2+(2\omega L)^2}}=\frac{\sqrt{3}V}{\sqrt{7}R}$

$P=i^2R\Rightarrow\frac{P_1}{P_2}=\left(\frac{i_1}{i_2}\right)^2\Rightarrow\frac{7}{P_2}=\left(\frac{\sqrt{7}}{2}\right)^2$

$\Rightarrow P_2=4\text{ W}$

3. $X_L=\omega L=(100\pi)(5)=500\pi,\ R=55\Omega$

$P=i^2R$, For power to remain unchanged, current should be unchanged. So, impedance should be constant.

$\sqrt{R^2+X_L^2}=\sqrt{R^2+(X_L-X_C)^2}$

$\Rightarrow\quad X_L=|X_L-X_C|$

$\Rightarrow\quad X_C=2X_L$

$\Rightarrow\quad\frac{1}{(100\pi)C}=2(500\pi)$

$\Rightarrow\quad C=1\,\mu\text{F}$

4. Current at resonance, $i=\frac{V}{R}=3\sqrt{2}\text{ A}$

$\tan\phi=\frac{X_L-X_C}{R}$

$\Rightarrow\quad\tan 45°=\frac{X_L-X_C}{R}\Rightarrow X_L-X_C=R$

New impedance, $Z'=\sqrt{R^2+(X_L-X_C)^2}=\sqrt{2}R$

New current, $i'=\frac{V}{Z'}=\frac{V}{\sqrt{2}R}=\frac{3\sqrt{2}}{\sqrt{2}}=3\text{A}$

5. Since, current is lagging behind voltage, the box must have an inductor.

$V_C=iX_C\Rightarrow 2000=2X_C$

$\Rightarrow\quad X_C=1000\ \Omega$

$\cos\phi=0.8$

$\Rightarrow\quad\tan\phi=\frac{3}{4}=\frac{X_L-1000}{800}$

$\Rightarrow\quad X_L=1600\ \Omega$

$X_L=\omega L\Rightarrow 1600=2\pi(100)L\Rightarrow L=2.5\text{ H}$

6. Impedance of box A, $Z=\frac{V}{i}=\frac{200}{0.4}=500\Omega$

For power factor to become 1, $X_L=X_C=400\ \Omega$

$Z=\sqrt{R^2+X_L^2}\Rightarrow 500=\sqrt{R^2+(400)^2}$

$\Rightarrow\quad R=300\ \Omega$

Power factor of box A, $\cos\phi=\frac{R}{Z}=\frac{300}{500}=0.6$

7. $V_R=60\text{ V},\ V_L=V_C=40\text{ V}$

$V_R=iR\Rightarrow 60=i(120)\Rightarrow i=0.5\text{ A}$

$V_L=iX_L\Rightarrow 40=(0.5)X_L\Rightarrow X_L=80\Omega$

$X_C=X_L=80\Omega\Rightarrow\frac{1}{\omega C}=80$ and $\omega L=80$

At new frequency, $\tan\phi=\frac{X_C'-X_L'}{R}$

$\Rightarrow\quad\tan 45°=\frac{\frac{1}{\omega' C}-\omega' L}{R}$

$\Rightarrow\quad\frac{80\omega}{\omega'}-\frac{\omega'(80)}{\omega}=120$

$\Rightarrow\quad\omega'=\frac{\omega}{2}=2\times10^5\text{ rad/s}$

8. Reading of ammeter $A=|i_1-i_2|=|3-4|=1\text{ A}$

Level 3

Single Choice Correct Questions

1. $x^2+y^2=i_0^2\Rightarrow y=\sqrt{i_0^2-x^2}$

$i_{rms}=\sqrt{\frac{1}{2i_0}\int_{-i_0}^{+i_0}y^2dx}=\frac{1}{\sqrt{2i_0}}\sqrt{\int_{-i_0}^{+i_0}(i_0^2-x^2)dx}=\left(\sqrt{\frac{2}{3}}\right)i_0$

2. $i_1=\frac{i_0}{\sqrt{2}}=i_2,\ i_3=i_0,\ i_4=\frac{i_0}{\sqrt{3}}$

So, $i_3>i_1=i_2>i_4$

3. $P=\frac{V^2}{R}=\frac{1}{R}(V_1+V_2\cos\omega t)^2$

$=\frac{1}{R}(V_1^2+V_2^2\cos^2\omega t+2V_1V_2\cos\omega t)$

$<P>=\frac{1}{R}\left(V_1^2+V_2^2\left(\frac{1}{2}\right)+0\right)=\frac{2V_1^2+V_2^2}{2R}$

4. $\varepsilon=5\cos\omega t+5\sqrt{3}\sin\omega t=10\sin\left(\omega t+\frac{\pi}{6}\right)$

$i=5\sin\left(\omega t+\frac{\pi}{4}\right)$

$$\Delta\phi = \left(\omega t + \frac{\pi}{4}\right) - \left(\omega t + \frac{\pi}{6}\right) = \frac{\pi}{12}$$

So, current leads voltage by $\frac{\pi}{12}$

5. $X_L = \omega L = 2\pi\left(\frac{R}{2\pi L_0}\right)L_0 = R$

$$i = \frac{V}{\sqrt{R^2 + X_L^2}} = \frac{V}{\sqrt{2}R}$$

$P = i^2R$ and $\frac{P}{4} = i'^2R \Rightarrow i' = \frac{i}{2}$

$$\Rightarrow \frac{V}{\sqrt{R^2 + X_L'^2}} = \frac{V}{2\sqrt{2}R}$$

$$\Rightarrow X_L = \sqrt{7}R$$

$$\Rightarrow Z' = 2Z$$

Power factor $= \cos\phi = \frac{R}{Z}$

If impedance is doubled, power factor will be reduced to half.

6. $\tan\theta_1 = \frac{X_L}{R}$; $\tan\theta_2 = \frac{X_C}{R}$

$$\tan\theta = \frac{X_C - X_L}{R} = \tan\theta_2 - \tan\theta_1$$

7. $X_L = \omega L = 314 \times 5 = 1570\,\Omega$

$V_C = \frac{2}{5}V_L \Rightarrow iX_C = \frac{2}{5}iX_L \Rightarrow X_C = 628\,\Omega$

$$\cos\phi = 0.8 \Rightarrow \tan\phi = \frac{3}{4} = \frac{X_L - X_C}{R}$$

$$\Rightarrow R = 1256\,\Omega$$

$$\cos\phi = \frac{R}{Z} \Rightarrow 0.8 = \frac{1256}{Z} \Rightarrow Z = 1570\,\Omega$$

8. $P = \frac{V^2R}{Z^2} = \text{constant} \Rightarrow Z = \text{constant}$

$$\Rightarrow \sqrt{R^2 + X_L^2} = \sqrt{R^2 + (X_C - X_L)^2} \Rightarrow X_C = 2X_L$$

$$\Rightarrow \frac{1}{\omega C} = 2\omega L \Rightarrow C = \frac{1}{2\omega^2 L}$$

9. $V_R = iR = 1(5) = 5\text{V}, V_L = 20\text{V}, V_C = 30\text{ V}$

$$V = \sqrt{V_R^2 + (V_C - V_L)^2} = 5\sqrt{5}\text{ V}$$

Since $V_C > V_L$, current leads voltage in phase.

Power factor $= \frac{V_R}{V} = \frac{5}{5\sqrt{5}} = \frac{1}{\sqrt{5}}$

$$P_{\text{avg}} = i^2R = (1)^2(5) = 5\text{W}$$

10. $\tan\phi = \frac{X_L - X_C}{R} = \frac{iX_L - iX_C}{iR} = \frac{V_L - V_C}{V_R} = \frac{3-2}{\sqrt{3}} = \frac{1}{\sqrt{3}}$

$$\Rightarrow \phi = \frac{\pi}{6}$$

Since $V_L > V_C$, current will lag behind applied voltage by $\frac{\pi}{6}$.

So, $i = i_0 \cos\left(\omega t' - \frac{\pi}{6}\right)$

11. $Z = \sqrt{R^2 + (X_L - X_C)^2} = 10\,\Omega,\ i = \frac{V}{Z} = \frac{10}{10} = 1\text{ A}$

$$\tan\phi = \frac{X_L - X_C}{R} \Rightarrow \phi = \tan^{-1}\left(\frac{6}{8}\right) = 37°$$

$$i = \cos(100\pi t + 37°)$$

$$V_{AB} = i(X_C - X_L) = 1(6) = 6\text{V}$$

$$\Rightarrow V_{AB} = 6\cos(100\pi t + 37° - 90°)$$

Now, $V_{AB} = \frac{V}{2} \Rightarrow 6\cos(100\pi t - 53°)$

$$= \frac{1}{2}(10\cos(100\pi t)) \Rightarrow \cos(100\pi t) = \frac{24}{25}$$

$$V_{AB} = 5 \times \frac{24}{25} = \frac{24}{5}\text{V}$$

12. $\tan\phi = \frac{X_L - X_C}{R} = \frac{\omega L - \frac{1}{\omega C}}{R}$

$$\phi = \tan^{-1}\left(\frac{\omega L - \frac{1}{\omega C}}{R}\right)$$

13. $X_C = \frac{1}{\omega C} = \frac{1}{25 \times 1 \times 10^{-3}} = 40\,\Omega$

Power factor of circuit = 1

$\Rightarrow X_L$ of box $= X_C = 40\,\Omega$

Power factor of box $= \cos\phi = 0.6 \Rightarrow \phi = 53°$

$$\tan\phi = \frac{X_L}{R} \Rightarrow \frac{4}{3} = \frac{40}{R} \Rightarrow R = 30\,\Omega$$

$$i = \frac{V}{Z} = \frac{90}{30} = 3\text{ A}$$

14. For DC source, $q = CE \Rightarrow 10^{-9} = 10^{-11}E \Rightarrow E = 100\text{ V}$

For AC source, $V = 100\sin\omega t$

At resonance, $X_L = X_C \Rightarrow \omega(10^{-5}) = \frac{1}{\omega(10^{-11})}$

$$\Rightarrow \omega = 10^8\text{ rad/s}$$

So, $X_C = X_L = 10^8(10^{-5}) = 1000\,\Omega$

$$i_m = \frac{V_m}{R} \Rightarrow i_m = \frac{100}{100} = 1\text{ A}$$

$$(V_C)_m = i_mX_C = 1 \times 1000 = 1000\text{ V}$$

$$q_m = C(V_C)_m = 10^{-11} \times 10^3 = 10^{-8}\text{ C}$$

15. $P = \dfrac{V_{rms}^2}{Z}\cos\phi$

$\Rightarrow \quad 100 = \dfrac{(230)^2}{Z_1}(0.5)$

$\Rightarrow \quad Z_1 = 264.5\ \Omega$

$\cos\phi = \dfrac{R}{Z} \Rightarrow 0.5 = \dfrac{R}{264.5} \Rightarrow R = 132.25\ \Omega$

$\tan\phi = \dfrac{X_L}{R} \Rightarrow X_L = \sqrt{3}R = 229\ \Omega$

Similarly, we get $Z_2 = 529\ \Omega, R_2 = 317.4\ \Omega$

$X_C = 423.2\ \Omega$

When connected in series, $R = R_1 + R_2 = 449.65\ \Omega$

$X_C - X_L = 194.2\ \Omega$

$\therefore \quad Z = \sqrt{R^2 + (X_C - X_L)^2} = 489.79\ \Omega$

$P = i_{rms}^2 R = \left(\dfrac{230}{489.79}\right)^2 (449.65) = 99\ \text{W}$

For power factor to be unity

$X = X_C - X_L = 194.2\ \Omega$

16. When inductor is short-circuited, light emission of bulb doesn't change. So, $Z_1 = Z_2$

$\Rightarrow \sqrt{R^2 + (X_L - X_C)^2} = \sqrt{R^2 + X_C^2}$

$\Rightarrow X_L = 2X_C$

When capacitor is short-circuited, $Z = \sqrt{R^2 + X_L^2}$

So, impedance increases and light emission of bulb will decrease.

17. Circuit is inductive when $X_L > X_C$

18. For resistor current and voltage are in phase. So, reading in A and V_2 are always in phase. Voltage across capacitor is $\dfrac{\pi}{2}$ ahead of current through it.

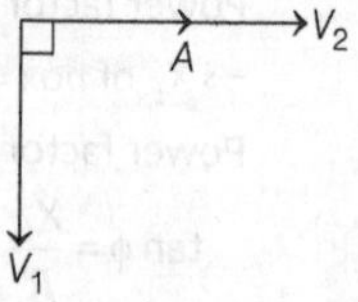

19. $Q = \dfrac{\omega L}{R}$, so if ω is doubled, Q will be doubled.

$i = \dfrac{V}{\sqrt{R^2 + (\omega L)^2}}; i = \dfrac{V}{\omega L}$ $\because$ [$\omega L >> R$ as the coil has high Q-factor]

So, when ω is doubled, i will be halved and $P = i^2 R$ will become one-fourth.

20. $f_2 > f_1 \Rightarrow X_C > X_L \Rightarrow$ current will lead source voltage.

21. $Q = \dfrac{\text{Energy stored per cycle}}{\text{Energy dissipated per cycle}}$

$Q' = \dfrac{1.1 \times \text{Energy stored}}{0.9 \times \text{Energy dissipated}} \times 1.22Q$

% change in $Q = \dfrac{Q' - Q}{Q} \times 100 = 22\%$

22. $\omega = \dfrac{1}{\sqrt{LC}} = \dfrac{1}{\sqrt{10 \times 10^{-3} \times 1 \times 10^{-6}}} = 10^4\ \text{rad/s}$

$\omega' = (90\%)\omega = 9000\ \text{rad/s}$

$X_L' = \omega' L = 90\ \Omega;\ X_C' = \dfrac{1}{\omega' C} = \dfrac{1000}{9}\ \Omega$

$Z = \sqrt{R^2 + (X_C' - X_L')^2} = 21.32\ \Omega$

$i = \dfrac{V}{Z} = \dfrac{\frac{15}{\sqrt{2}}}{21.32} = 0.497\ \text{A}$

$P = i^2 R = (0.497)^2 \times 3 = 0.74\ \text{W}$

Energy dissipated per cycle $= P_{avg} \times \left(\dfrac{2\pi}{\omega}\right)$

$= 5.16 \times 10^{-4}\ \text{J}$

23. $i_C = \dfrac{V}{X_C}$, 90° ahead of source voltage

$i_L = \dfrac{V}{\sqrt{R^2 + X_L^2}}$, $\phi = \tan^{-1}\left(\dfrac{X_L}{R}\right)$ behind the source voltage.

For V and i to be in phase,

$i_C = i_L \sin\phi$

$\Rightarrow \quad \dfrac{V}{X_C} = \dfrac{V}{\sqrt{R^2 + X_L^2}}\left(\dfrac{X_L}{\sqrt{R^2 + X_L^2}}\right)$

$\Rightarrow R^2 + X_L^2 = X_L X_C$

$\Rightarrow R^2 + (\omega L)^2 = (\omega L)\left(\dfrac{1}{\omega C}\right)$

$\Rightarrow \quad \omega = \sqrt{\dfrac{1}{LC} - \dfrac{R^2}{L^2}}$

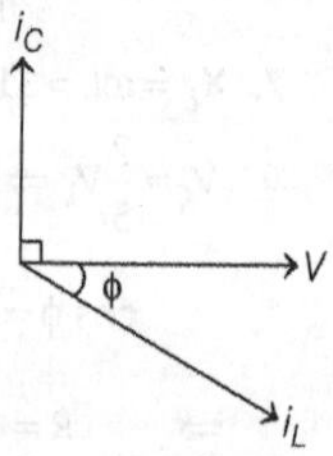

24. For DC source, $i = \dfrac{V}{R} \Rightarrow 1 = \dfrac{250}{R}$

$\Rightarrow \quad R = 250\Omega$

For AC source, $i = \sqrt{\left(\dfrac{V}{R}\right)^2 + \left(\dfrac{V}{X_L - X_C}\right)^2}$

$\Rightarrow 1.25 = 250\sqrt{\left(\dfrac{1}{250}\right)^2 + \left(\dfrac{1}{X_L - X_C}\right)^2}$

$\Rightarrow \quad |X_L - X_C| = \dfrac{1000}{3}\ \Omega$

$\Rightarrow \quad \left|2250L - \dfrac{1}{2250C}\right| = \dfrac{1000}{3}$ ...(i)

and $\omega_0 = \dfrac{1}{\sqrt{LC}} \Rightarrow 4500 = \dfrac{1}{\sqrt{LC}}$ ...(ii)

Solving Eqs. (i) and (ii), we get

$L = \dfrac{4}{81}\ \text{H}$ and $C = 1\ \mu\text{F}$

Multiple Choice(s) Correct Questions

1. $V_1 = V_2 \Rightarrow iX_L = iX_C \Rightarrow X_L = X_C$

$$\Rightarrow (2\pi f)\left(\frac{2}{\pi}\right) = \frac{1}{(2\pi f)\left(\frac{8}{11}\times 10^{-6}\right)}$$

$$\Rightarrow \quad f = 125 \text{ Hz}$$

$$i = \frac{V}{Z} = \frac{V}{R} = \frac{200}{100} = 2\text{A}$$

$$V_1 = V_2 = iX_L = 2\left[2\pi f\left(\frac{2}{\pi}\right)\right] = 1000 \text{ V}$$

2. $\tan\phi = \dfrac{X_L - X_C}{R} \Rightarrow \tan 30° = \dfrac{10-5}{R} \Rightarrow R = 5\sqrt{3}\,\Omega$

$$V_R = iR \Rightarrow 2 = i(5\sqrt{3}) \Rightarrow i = \frac{2}{5\sqrt{3}}\text{A}$$

$$Z = \sqrt{R^2 + (X_L - X_C)^2} = 10\Omega$$

$$V_{AC} = iZ = \left(\frac{2}{5\sqrt{3}}\right)\times 10 = \frac{4}{\sqrt{3}}\text{V}$$

3. $V = i\sqrt{R^2 + X_C^2} \Rightarrow 50\sqrt{5} = 5\sqrt{10^2 + X_C^2} \Rightarrow X_C = 20\,\Omega$

$$X_C = \frac{1}{\omega C} = 20 \Rightarrow \omega = 1000 \text{ rad/s} \Rightarrow f = \frac{1000}{2\pi}\text{Hz}$$

$$X_L = \omega L = 1000 \times 20 \times 10^{-3} = 20\,\Omega$$

$$Z = \sqrt{R^2 + (X_L - X_C)^2} = 10\Omega$$

$$V_{AC} = iZ = 5 \times 10 = 50 \text{ V}$$

$$P_{avg} = i^2R = (5)^2(10) = 250 \text{ W}$$

4. $\tan\phi = \dfrac{X_L - X_C}{R} \Rightarrow \tan\left(\dfrac{\pi}{4}\right) = \dfrac{2X_C - X_C}{R} \Rightarrow X_C = R$

$$X_C' = \frac{1}{\omega\left(\frac{C}{4}\right)} = 4X_C;\; X_L' = \omega(2L) = 4R$$

$$\tan\phi' = \frac{X_L' - X_C'}{R'} = \frac{4R - 4R}{2R} = 0 \Rightarrow \phi' = 0°$$

So, voltage and current will be in same phase.

5. $V_1 = \sqrt{V_R^2 + V_L^2} = 64 \text{ V};\; V_2 = |V_L - V_C| = 120 \text{ V}$

and $V^2 = V_R^2 + (V_L - V_C)^2 \Rightarrow (130)^2 = V_R^2 + (120)^2$

$$\Rightarrow \quad V_R = 50 \text{ V}$$

$$\sqrt{(50)^2 + V_L^2} = 64 \Rightarrow V_L = \sqrt{1596} \simeq 40 \text{ V}$$

$$|V_L - V_C| = 120 \text{ V} \Rightarrow V_C = 160 \text{ V}$$

$$\text{Power factor} = \frac{V_R}{V} = \frac{50}{130} = \frac{5}{13}$$

Since, $V_C > V_L$, circuit is capacitive in nature.

6. $\omega = \dfrac{2\pi}{T} = \dfrac{2\pi}{20\times 10^{-3}} = 100\pi$

$$i = (400\text{ mA})\sin(100\pi t)$$

$$V = 200\sin(100\pi t + \phi)$$

At $t = 0;\; 100 = 200\sin\phi \Rightarrow \phi = \dfrac{\pi}{6}$

So, $V = 200\sin\left(100\pi t + \dfrac{\pi}{6}\right)$

$$\text{Impedance, } Z = \frac{V}{i} = \frac{200}{400\times 10^{-3}} = 500\,\Omega$$

$$\cos\phi = \frac{R}{Z} \Rightarrow \cos\left(\frac{\pi}{6}\right) = \frac{R}{500}$$

$$\Rightarrow \quad R = 250\sqrt{3}\,\Omega$$

$$\tan\phi = \frac{X_L - X_C}{R}$$

$$\Rightarrow \quad X_L - X_C = R\tan\phi = (250\sqrt{3})\left(\frac{1}{\sqrt{3}}\right) = 250\,\Omega$$

$$P_{avg} = i_{rms}^2 R = \left(\frac{400}{\sqrt{2}}\times 10^{-3}\right)^2 (250\sqrt{3}) = 20\sqrt{3} \text{ W}$$

7. $X_L = \omega L = 10^4 \times 10 \times 10^{-3} = 100\Omega,$

$i_L = \dfrac{V}{X_L}$, 90° behind applied voltage

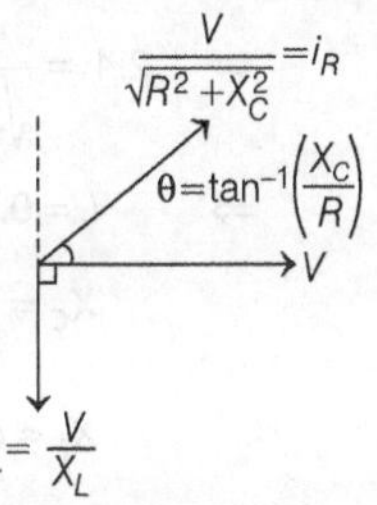

$i_R = \dfrac{V}{\sqrt{R^2 + X_C^2}},\; \tan^{-1}\left(\dfrac{X_C}{R}\right)$

ahead of applied voltage

$$i^2 = i_L^2 + i_R^2 + 2i_L i_R \cos(90° + \phi)$$

$$= \left(\frac{V}{X_L}\right)^2 + \left(\frac{V}{\sqrt{R^2 + X_C^2}}\right)^2 + 2\left(\frac{V}{X_L}\right)\left(\frac{V}{\sqrt{R^2 + X_C^2}}\right)\left(-\frac{X_C}{\sqrt{R^2 + X_C^2}}\right)$$

$$= V^2\left(\frac{1}{X_L^2} + \left(\frac{1}{R^2 + X_C^2}\right)\left(1 - \frac{2X_C}{X_L}\right)\right)$$

Since, i is independent of R, $1 - \dfrac{2X_C}{X_L} = 0$

$$\Rightarrow X_C = \frac{X_L}{2} = 50\,\Omega,$$

$$X_C = \frac{1}{\omega C} \Rightarrow C = 2\,\mu\text{F}$$

$$Z = \frac{V}{i} = X_L = 100\,\Omega$$

Comprehension Based Questions

1. Let $V_R = 4\cos\omega t$, $V_L = 3\cos\left(\omega t + \frac{\pi}{2}\right) = -3\sin\omega t$

   At the given instant,

   $V_R = 2 = 4\cos\omega t \Rightarrow \omega t = 60°$

   $V_L = -3\sin 60° = -3\cos 30°$

   $|V_L| = 3\cos 30°$

2. $V_S = V_R + V_L = 4\cos\omega t - 3\sin\omega t = 5\cos(\omega t + 37°)$

   At the given instant,

   $V_S = 5\cos(60° + 37°) = 5\cos 97°$, $|V_S| = 5\cos 83°$

3. From phasor diagram, it is clear that when instantaneous current will decrease, the magnitude of potential difference will increase.

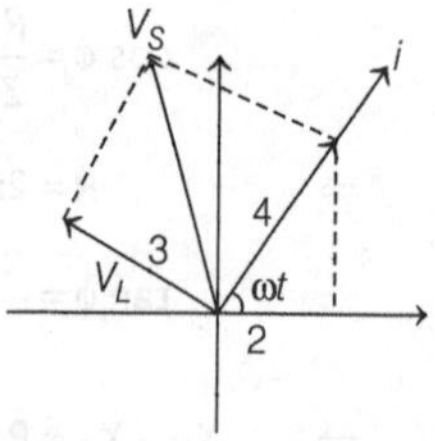

4. For DC source, $i = \frac{V}{R}$

   $\Rightarrow 4 = \frac{12}{R}$

   $\Rightarrow R = 3\,\Omega$

5. For AC source, $i = \frac{V}{\sqrt{R^2 + X_L^2}}$

   $\Rightarrow 2.4 = \frac{12}{\sqrt{3^2 + (50L)^2}}$

   $\Rightarrow L = 0.08\text{ H}$

   $X_C = \frac{1}{\omega C} = \frac{1}{50 \times 20 \times 10^{-3}} = 1\,\Omega$

   $X_L = \omega L = 4\,\Omega$

   $i = \frac{V}{\sqrt{R^2 + (X_L - X_C)^2}} = \frac{12}{3\sqrt{2}} = 2\sqrt{2}\text{ A}$

   $P_{avg} = i^2 R = (2\sqrt{2})^2 (3) = 24\text{ W}$

6. $Z_A = \sqrt{R_A^2 + X_L^2} = 10\,\Omega$; $Z_B = \sqrt{R_B^2 + X_C^2} = 10\Omega$

   $i_A = \frac{V}{10}$, $\tan^{-1}\left(\frac{6}{8}\right) = 37°$ behind the applied voltage

   $i_B = \frac{V}{10}$, $\tan^{-1}\left(\frac{8}{6}\right) = 53°$ ahead of the applied voltage.

   So, $i = \sqrt{i_A^2 + i_B^2} \Rightarrow 14 = \sqrt{\left(\frac{V}{10}\right)^2 + \left(\frac{V}{10}\right)^2}$

   $\Rightarrow V = 70\sqrt{2}\text{ V}$

   $i_A = \frac{V}{10} = 7\sqrt{2}\text{ A}$

7. $P = i_A^2 R_A + i_B^2 R_B = (7\sqrt{2})^2(8) + (7\sqrt{2})^2(6) = 1372\text{ W}$

8. $f_R = \frac{f_1 + f_2}{2} = \frac{1.30 + 1.50}{2} = 1.40\text{ kHz}$

   $f_R = \frac{1}{2\pi\sqrt{L(5.50 \times 10^{-6})}} = 1.40 \times 10^3 \Rightarrow L = 2.35\text{ mH}$

9. $i = \frac{V_m}{\sqrt{R^2 + (X_L - X_C)^2}} = \frac{V_m}{2R} \Rightarrow X_L - X_C = \sqrt{3}R$

   $\phi = \tan^{-1}\left(\frac{X_L - X_C}{R}\right) = \frac{\pi}{3}$

10. Since, current is leading voltage by a phase $\phi < \frac{\pi}{2}$, it has to be *RC* circuit.

11. $\phi = \omega t = 100\left(\frac{\pi}{400}\right) = \frac{\pi}{4}$

    $\phi = \tan^{-1}\left(\frac{X_C}{R}\right) = \frac{\pi}{4} \Rightarrow X_C = R$

    $i_0 = \sqrt{2} = \frac{100}{\sqrt{R^2 + R^2}} \Rightarrow R = 50\,\Omega$

    $X_C = \frac{1}{100C} = 50 \Rightarrow C = 200\,\mu\text{F}$

12. If be *RC* discharging circuit with time constant, $\tau = RC = 50 \times 200 \times 10^{-6} = 0.01$ s.

    So, current will decrease exponentially.

13. $L_{eq} = L_1 + L_2 = 4\text{ mH}$, $C_{eq} = 10\,\mu\text{F}$

    $\omega = \frac{1}{\sqrt{L_{eq}C_{eq}}} = 5000\text{ rad/s}$

14. When C_3 is removed, C_{eq} decreases. So, resonant frequency increases.

15. At resonance, $i = \frac{V}{R} = \frac{100}{100} = 1\text{ A}$

    $P_{avg} = i^2 R = 100\text{ W}$

16. $\langle U \rangle = \frac{1}{2}L\langle i^2 \rangle = \frac{1}{2} \times 2.4 \times 10^{-3} \times 1^2 = 1.2\text{ mJ}$

17. $T = \frac{2\pi}{\omega} = \frac{2\pi}{5000} = 1.26\text{ ms}$

    The given time duration of 1 μs is much smaller than the time period. So, it is not possible to calculate thermal energy produced by the resistance.

18. When switch is open, circuit is at resonance. So,

    $\omega_R = \frac{1}{\sqrt{LC}} = \frac{1}{\sqrt{\left(\frac{1}{25\pi}\right)\left(\frac{1}{100\pi}\right)}} = 50\pi$

    $f_R = \frac{\omega_R}{2\pi} = 25\text{ Hz}$

19. $X_L = \omega_R L = 50\pi\left(\frac{1}{25\pi}\right) = 2\Omega$

    When switch is closed, it is series *LR* circuit.

So, $\tan\phi = \frac{X_L}{R} \Rightarrow \tan\left(\frac{\pi}{4}\right) = \frac{2}{R} \Rightarrow R = 2\Omega$

$V_R = iR \Rightarrow \frac{100}{\sqrt{2}} = i(2) \Rightarrow i = \frac{50}{\sqrt{2}}$ A

$V_S = i\sqrt{R^2 + X_L^2} = \left(\frac{50}{\sqrt{2}}\right)2\sqrt{2} = 100$ V

Peak voltage of source $= \sqrt{2}\,V_S = 100\sqrt{2}$ V

20. $P_{avg} = i^2R = \left(\frac{100}{2}\right)^2 (2) = 5000$ W

Match The Columns Questions

1. (A) For sinusoidal curve, $i_{rms} = \frac{i_0}{\sqrt{2}}$ and average current for positive half cycle is $\frac{2i_0}{\pi}$.

(B) For $t = 0$ to $t = \frac{T}{2}$

$$i_{avg} = \frac{\int_0^{T/2} i\,dt}{\int_0^{T/2} dt} = \frac{\text{Area under } i\text{-}T \text{ curve}}{T/2} = \frac{\frac{1}{2}\times\frac{T}{2}\times i_0}{\frac{T}{2}} = \frac{i_0}{2}$$

So, average current for positive half cycle is $\frac{i_0}{2}$ and average current for all cycle is zero.

For $t = 0$ to $t = \frac{T}{4}$, $i = \left(\frac{i_0}{\frac{T}{4}}\right)t = \frac{4i_0t}{T}$

$$i_{rms} = \sqrt{\frac{\int_0^{T/4} i^2 dt}{\int_0^{T/4} dt}} = \sqrt{\frac{64i_0^2}{T^3}\int_0^{T/4} t^2 dt} = \frac{i_0}{\sqrt{3}}$$

(C) For positive half cycle, $i_{avg} = i_{rms} = i_0$ and for full cycle average current is zero.

(D) For positive half cycle, $i_{avg} = i_{rms} = i_0$

For full cycle,

$$i_{avg} = \frac{\int i\,dt}{\int dt} = \frac{i_0\left(\frac{T}{2}\right)}{T} = \frac{i_0}{2}$$

$$i_{rms} = \sqrt{\frac{\int_0^{T/2} i_0^2 dt}{\int_0^{T} dt}} = \frac{i_0}{\sqrt{2}}$$

2. (A) $Z = \frac{V_m}{i_m} = \frac{100}{10} = 10\Omega$

$\cos\phi = \frac{R}{Z} \Rightarrow \cos\left(\frac{\pi}{4}\right) = \frac{R}{10} \Rightarrow R = 5\sqrt{2}\ \Omega$

(B) $\tan\phi = \frac{X_L}{R} \Rightarrow \tan\left(\frac{\pi}{4}\right) = \frac{X_L}{5\sqrt{2}}$

$\Rightarrow X_L = 5\sqrt{2}\ \Omega$

(C) $X_L = \omega L \Rightarrow 5\sqrt{2} = 100L$

$\Rightarrow L = \frac{1}{10\sqrt{2}}$ H

(D) $P_{avg} = V_{rms}\,i_{rms}\cos\phi = \left(\frac{100}{\sqrt{2}}\right)\left(\frac{10}{\sqrt{2}}\right)\cos\left(\frac{\pi}{4}\right)$

$= \frac{500}{\sqrt{2}}$ W

3. (A) For *LR* series circuit, *i* lags *V* by an angle less than $\frac{\pi}{2}$ and *i* lags V_L by an angle $\frac{\pi}{2}$.

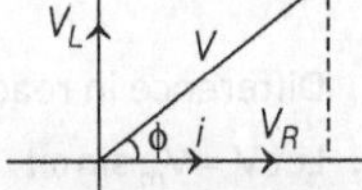

(B) For *RC* series circuit, *i* leads *V* by an angle less than $\frac{\pi}{2}$.

(C) Depending on the values of *L*, *C* and *R*, circuit would be either capacitive, inductive or purely resistive. So, all possibilities can be there.

(D) In purely resistive circuit, current and voltage are in phase.

4. (A) $V_1 = \sqrt{V_R^2 + V_L^2} = 158.11$ V ...(i)

$V_2 = |V_L - V_C| = 200$ V ...(ii)

$V_3 = \sqrt{V_R^2 + (V_L - V_C)^2} = 250$ V ...(iii)

Solving Eqs. (i), (ii) and (iii), we get

$V_R = 150$ V, $V_L = 50$ V, $V_C = 250$ V

Power factor $= \cos\phi = \frac{V_R}{V} = \frac{150}{250} = \frac{3}{5}$

(B) $V_1 = V_R = 150$ V

$V_3 = \sqrt{V_R^2 + V_L^2} = 250\text{ V} \Rightarrow V_L = 200$ V

$V_3 = V_C \Rightarrow V_C = 250$ V

(C) $V_1 = \sqrt{V_L^2 + V_R^2} = 158.11\text{ V} \Rightarrow V_L = 50$ V

$V_2 = V_R = 150$ V

$V_3 = \sqrt{V_R^2 + V_C^2} = 291.6\text{ V} \Rightarrow V_C = 250$ V

Power factor $= \cos\phi = \frac{V_R}{V} = \frac{150}{250} = \frac{3}{5}$

(D) $V_L = V_1 = 0$

$V = |V_L - V_C| = 250\text{ V} \Rightarrow V_C = 250$ V

$V_R = V = 250$ V

Numerical Value Questions

1. $V = V_1 + V_2 + V_3$

$\Rightarrow V = 3\sin\omega t + 5\sin(\omega t + 30°) + 5\sin(\omega t - 127°)$

$$\text{Peak voltage} = \sqrt{\begin{aligned}&(3 + 5\cos 30° - 5\sin 37°)^2\\ &+ (5\sin 30° - 5\cos 37°)^2\end{aligned}}$$

$$= \sqrt{\frac{75}{4} + \frac{9}{4}} = \sqrt{21}\text{ V}$$

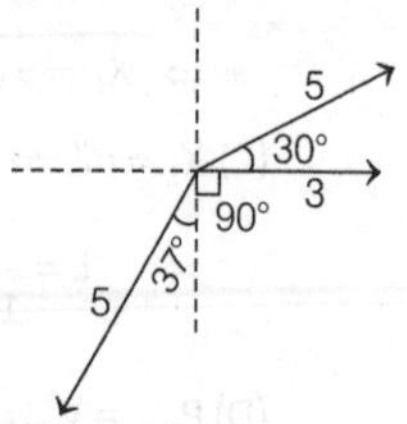

$$\text{Peak current} = \frac{\sqrt{21}}{\sqrt{\frac{7}{3}}} = 3\text{A}$$

2. If DC and AC flow simultaneously, then

$i = 6 + (8\sqrt{2})\sin\omega t$

Reading of DC ammeter $= 6A$

$$\text{Reading of AC ammeter} = \sqrt{6^2 + \frac{(8\sqrt{2})^2}{2}} = 10\text{ A}$$

Difference in reading $= 10 - 6 = 4$ A

3. Let $V = V_m \sin\omega t$

$V_R = i_m R\sin(\omega t - \phi)$

$$V_L = i_m X_L \sin\left(\omega t - \phi + \frac{\pi}{2}\right)$$

When V is maximum, $\sin\omega t = 1 \Rightarrow \omega t = \dfrac{\pi}{2}$

$$\Rightarrow \quad V_R = i_m R\sin\left(\frac{\pi}{2} - \phi\right) = 4 \quad \text{...(i)}$$

$$V_L = i_m X_L \sin\left(\frac{\pi}{2} - \phi + \frac{\pi}{2}\right) = 3 \quad \text{...(ii)}$$

Dividing Eq. (ii) by Eq. (i), we get

$$\left(\frac{X_L}{R}\right)\tan\phi = \frac{3}{4} \Rightarrow \left(\frac{X_L}{R}\right)\left(\frac{X_L}{R}\right) = \frac{3}{4}$$

$$\Rightarrow \quad X_L = \left(\frac{\sqrt{3}}{2}\right)R$$

$$\Rightarrow \quad X_L = \sqrt{3} = 1.73\,\Omega$$

4. Since current is leading voltage, box will be containing capacitor and resistor.

For box, power factor $= \cos\phi = 0.5$

$$\Rightarrow \quad \phi = \frac{\pi}{3}$$

$$\tan\phi = \frac{X_C}{R} \Rightarrow X_C = \sqrt{3}R$$

For circuit, power factor $= \cos\phi' = \dfrac{\sqrt{3}}{2}$

$$\Rightarrow \quad \phi' = \frac{\pi}{6}$$

$$\tan\phi' = \frac{X_C}{R + 10}$$

$$\Rightarrow \quad \frac{1}{\sqrt{3}} = \frac{\sqrt{3}R}{R + 10} \Rightarrow R = 5\,\Omega$$

Now, $\quad R = 5R_1 \Rightarrow 5 = 5R_1 \Rightarrow R_1 = 1\,\Omega$

5. $\omega_R = \dfrac{1}{\sqrt{LC}} = 50$ rad/s

$X_L = X_C = (1.6)(50) = 80\,\Omega$

$V_L = iX_L \Rightarrow 400 = i(80) \Rightarrow i = 5$ A

$$i = \frac{V}{Z} = \frac{V}{R} \quad \Rightarrow \quad 5 = \frac{32}{R}$$

$\Rightarrow R = 6.4\,\Omega$

6. $i_1 = \dfrac{V}{2r} = \dfrac{16\sin(100t)}{2(100)}$

$$\text{Voltage across } r = i_1 r = \frac{16\sin(100t)}{200} \times 100$$

$$= 8\sin(100t)$$

$$X_C = \frac{1}{\omega C},\; Z = \sqrt{R^2 + X_C^2}$$

$$i_2 = \frac{16}{Z}\sin(100t + \phi) \text{ where}$$

$$\phi = \cos^{-1}\left(\frac{R}{Z}\right)$$

$$\text{Voltage across } R = i_2 R = \frac{16R}{Z}\sin(100t + \phi)$$

$$(V_A - V_B)_{max} = \sqrt{8^2 + \left(\frac{16R}{Z}\right)^2 - 2(8)\left(\frac{16R}{Z}\right)\cos\phi}$$

$$= \sqrt{8^2 + \left(\frac{16R}{Z}\right)^2 - 2(8)\left(\frac{16R}{Z}\right)\left(\frac{R}{Z}\right)} = 8\text{V}$$

7. For coil, $i = \dfrac{V}{\sqrt{R^2 + X_L^2}}$ ...(i)

When capacitor is connected in series with the coil,

$$i = \frac{V}{\sqrt{R^2 + (X_L - X_C)^2}} \quad \text{...(ii)}$$

From Eqs. (i) and (ii), we get

$$X_L = X_C - X_L$$

$$\Rightarrow \quad X_L = \frac{X_C}{2}$$

$$= \frac{1}{100\pi \times 10^{-6} \times 2}$$

$$= \frac{5000}{\pi}\,\Omega$$

From Eq. (i),

$$10\times 10^{-3}=\frac{24}{\sqrt{R^2+\left(\frac{5000}{\pi}\right)^2}}\Rightarrow R=1806\ \Omega$$

$$i_{DC}=\frac{180}{1806}\simeq 0.1\ \text{A}=100\ \text{mA}$$

8. For points A and B; $Z=\sqrt{R_1^2+X_{L_1}^2}=\frac{100}{1}$ ...(i)

and $\tan 37^\circ=\frac{X_{L_1}}{R_1}$ ...(ii)

From Eqs. (i) and (ii), we get

$$R_1=80\ \Omega \text{ and } X_{L_1}=60\ \Omega$$

For points B and C; $Z=\sqrt{R_2^2+X_{L_2}^2}=\frac{100}{5}$ ...(iii)

and $\tan 53^\circ=\frac{X_{L_2}}{R_2}$ ...(iv)

From Eqs. (iii) and (iv), we get

$$R_2=12\ \Omega \text{ and } X_{L_2}=16\ \Omega$$

For points A and C,

$$Z=\sqrt{(R_1+R_2)^2+(X_{L_1}+X_{L_2})^2}$$
$$=\sqrt{(92)^2+(76)^2}$$
$$\simeq 119\ \Omega$$

Previous Years Questions

JEE Main

1. $\frac{N_1}{N_2}=\frac{V_1}{V_2}\Rightarrow\frac{10}{1}=\frac{230}{V_2}$

$$\Rightarrow\quad V_2=23\ \text{V}$$

$$P_2=\frac{V_2^2}{R_2}=\frac{23\times 23}{46}=\frac{23}{2}=11.5\ \text{W}$$

2.

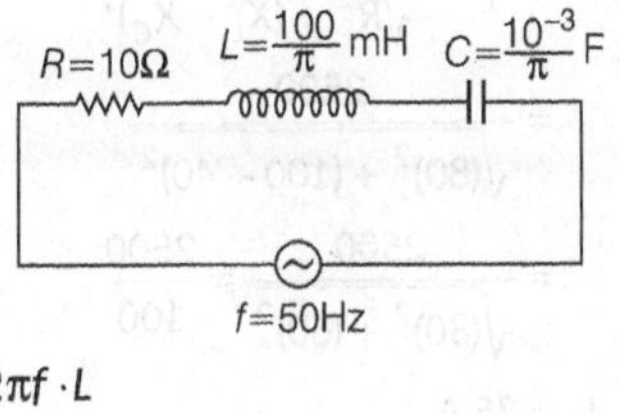

$$X_L=\omega L=2\pi f\cdot L$$
$$X_L=\frac{100}{\pi}\times 2\pi\times 50\times 10^{-3}$$
$$X_L=100\times 100\times 10^{-3}=10\ \Omega$$
$$X_C=\frac{1}{\omega C}=\frac{1}{2\pi f\cdot C}=\frac{1}{2\pi\times 50\times\frac{10^{-3}}{\pi}}=\frac{1}{100\times 10^{-3}}$$
$$X_C=\frac{1}{10^{-1}}=10\ \Omega$$

Power factor

$$\Rightarrow\quad \cos\phi=\frac{R}{Z}=\frac{R}{\sqrt{R^2+(X_L-X_C)^2}}$$
$$=\frac{10}{\sqrt{100+(10-10)^2}}=\frac{10}{10}=1$$

3. In an AC circuit,

$$V=100\sin(100t)\ \text{V}$$
$$I=100\sin(100t+\pi/3)\ \text{mA}$$

$\therefore$ Phase difference between V and I

$$\phi=\pi/3$$

$\therefore$ Average power dissipation

$$P_{av}=V_{rms}\times I_{rms}\times\cos\phi$$
$$=\frac{100}{\sqrt{2}}\times\frac{100}{\sqrt{2}}\times 10^{-3}\times\cos\pi/3$$
$$=2.5\ \text{W}$$

4. Both Statement I and Statement II are false

$\Rightarrow$ In purely inductive circuit $\cos\phi=0$

$\therefore$ Power consumed $=0$

for resonance both L and R be available in circuit.

For resonance $\phi=0$ mean and inductor must be present will be

5. In L-C oscillator, resonance frequency is given as,

$$\omega_0=\frac{1}{\sqrt{LC}}\quad\text{...(i)}$$

When $L'=2L$ and $C'=8C$,

then $\omega_0'=\frac{1}{\sqrt{L'C'}}=\frac{1}{\sqrt{2L\times 8C}}$

$$=\frac{1}{4\sqrt{LC}}=\frac{\omega_0}{4}\quad\text{[From Eq. (i)]}$$
$$=\left(\frac{1}{4}\right)\omega_0=x\omega_0\quad\text{(Given)}$$
$$\Rightarrow\quad x=\frac{1}{4}$$

6. In circuit (b),

Inductive reactance

$$X_L=2\pi fL=2\pi\times 50\times 50\times 10^{-3}\ \Omega=15.7\ \Omega$$

And capacitive reactance,

$$X_C=\frac{1}{2\pi fC}=\frac{1}{2\pi\times 50\times 0.5\times 10^{-6}}=6366\ \Omega$$

As $X_L\neq X_C$, there is no resonance in circuit (b). So, impedance of circuit b is always greater than (a).

$\Rightarrow I_{rms}$ is always smaller in circuit (b).

7. Power factor, $\cos\phi=\frac{R}{Z}$;

So, power factor,

$$P_1=\frac{R}{\sqrt{X_L^2+R^2}}=\frac{R}{\sqrt{R^2+R^2}}\quad(\because X_L=R)$$

So, $P_1 = \frac{1}{\sqrt{2}}$

Now, When a capacitor is added in circuit such that,

$$X_L = X_C$$

Then, power factor will be

$$\Rightarrow \quad P_2 = \frac{R}{\sqrt{R^2 + (X_L - X_C)^2}} = \frac{R}{\sqrt{R^2}} = \frac{R}{R} = 1$$

Hence ratio is, $\frac{P_1}{P_2} = \frac{1}{\sqrt{2}}$

8. Given, $X_L = 200\ \Omega$,

$$X_C = 100\ \Omega, R = 100\ \Omega$$

$$V_{rms} = 200\sqrt{2}\ V$$

Impedance,

$$Z = \sqrt{R^2 + (X_L - X_C)^2}$$

$$= \sqrt{(100)^2 + (200 - 100)^2}$$

$$= \sqrt{100^2 + 100^2} = 100\sqrt{2}\ \Omega$$

$$\therefore \quad I_{rms} = \frac{V_{rms}}{Z} = \frac{200\sqrt{2}}{100\sqrt{2}} = 2\ A$$

9. For an R-L-C circuit,

Bandwidth $= R / L$

Quality factor $= \frac{\sqrt{L}}{R\sqrt{C}}$

$$\text{So, ratio} = \frac{\text{Quality factor}}{\text{Bandwidth}} = \frac{\left(\frac{\sqrt{L}}{R\sqrt{C}}\right)}{\left(\frac{R}{L}\right)} = \frac{\sqrt{L}}{R\sqrt{C}} \times \frac{L}{R}$$

$$= \frac{\sqrt{3} \times 3}{10^2 \times \sqrt{27 \times 10^{-6}}}$$

$$= \frac{3\sqrt{3}}{10^2 \times 3\sqrt{3} \times 10^{-3}} = 10$$

10. In L-C-R series circuit,

$$C = 62.5\ \text{nF} = 6.25 \times 10^{-8} F$$

$$R = 50\ \Omega$$

$$f = 2\ \text{kHz} = 2 \times 10^3\ \text{Hz}$$

At resonance condition, maximum value of current flows. Hence, resonance frequency,

$$f = \frac{1}{2\pi\sqrt{LC}} \Rightarrow L = \frac{1}{4\pi^2 f^2 C}$$

$$= \frac{1}{4 \times 10 \times (2 \times 10^3)^2 \times (6.25) \times 10^{-8}}$$

$$= \frac{1}{10}\ \text{H} = 100\ \text{mH}$$

11. In series L-C-R circuit,

$$V = 220\ V, f = 50\ \text{Hz}, R = 80\ \Omega,$$

$$X_L = 70\ \Omega, X_C = 130\ \Omega$$

$$\therefore \text{Power factor, } \cos\phi = \frac{R}{Z} = \frac{R}{\sqrt{R^2 + (X_C - X_L)^2}}$$

$$= \frac{80}{\sqrt{80^2 + (130 - 70)^2}}$$

$$= \frac{80}{\sqrt{80^2 + 60^2}} = \frac{80}{100} = \frac{8}{10} = \frac{x}{10} \quad \text{(given)}$$

$$\therefore \quad x = 8$$

12. Current drawn in L-C-R series circuit is maximum at resonance.

And at resonance, $\omega = \frac{1}{\sqrt{LC}}$

Substituting given values, $2\pi(7000) = \frac{1}{\sqrt{2 \times 10^{-6} \times C}}$

$$\Rightarrow \quad C = \frac{1}{3872}\ F.$$

13. Given that,

$$V = 220\ V, f = 50\ \text{Hz}, R = 100\ \Omega$$

$$X_L = 79.6\ \Omega$$

or $\quad C = \frac{1}{100\pi \times 79.6} \Rightarrow C = 40 \times 10^{-6}\ F$

14. Given that, current in phase with the emf, then electrical circuit is in resonance.

Current, $I_{rms} = \frac{V_{rms}}{R} = \frac{220}{20} = 11 A$

Amplitude of current,

$$I_0 = \sqrt{2} \times I_{rms} = \sqrt{2} \times 11 = \sqrt{2} \times \sqrt{121}$$

$$I_0 = \sqrt{242}\ A$$

15. Given that,

$$R = 80\ \Omega, X_L = 100\ \Omega,$$

$$X_C = 40\ \Omega$$

$$V_0 = 2500\ V,$$

Amplitude of current,

$$I_0 = \frac{V_0}{Z} = \frac{V_0}{\sqrt{R^2 + (X_L - X_C)^2}}$$

$$= \frac{2500}{\sqrt{(80)^2 + (100 - 40)^2}}$$

$$= \frac{2500}{\sqrt{(80)^2 + (60)^2}} = \frac{2500}{100}$$

$$I_0 = 25\ A$$

16.

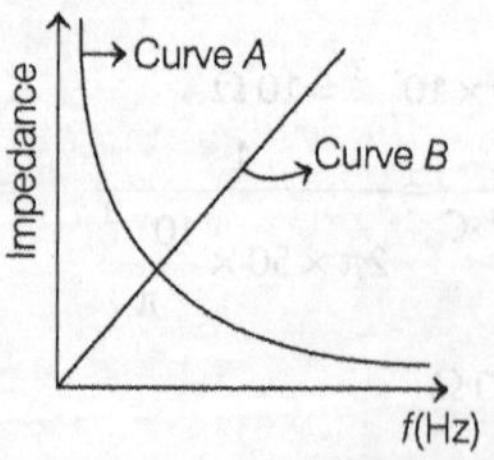

$X_L = \omega L = 2\pi fL$

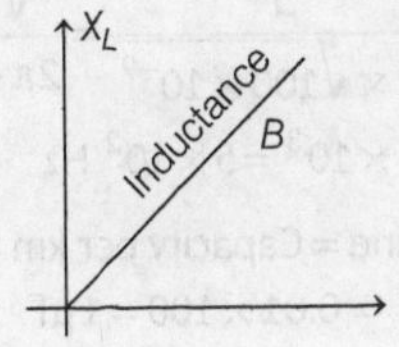

$$X_C = \frac{1}{\omega C} = \frac{1}{2\pi fC}$$

R = constant

$A \to X_C \qquad X_C = A$

$B \to X_L \qquad X_L = B$

Option (c) is correct.

17. Quality factor of an *L-C-R* circuit is

$$Q = \frac{1}{R}\sqrt{\frac{L}{C}}$$

Substituting given values, we get

$$Q = \frac{1}{100}\left(\frac{1}{6.25 \times 10^{-6}}\right)^{1/2} = 4$$

18. Given, $\frac{V_S}{V_P} = \frac{N_S}{N_P}$

$$\frac{120}{12000} = \frac{N_S}{N_P}$$

$$\frac{N_S}{N_P} = \frac{1}{100} \qquad \text{...(i)}$$

For an ideal transformer, input power = Output power

and power is given by

$$P = VI$$

$$I_P V_P = I_S V_S = 60000 \text{ W}$$

$$12000 \times I_P = 60000$$

$$I_P = 5 \text{ A}$$

Now, $R_P = \frac{V_P}{I_P} = \frac{12000}{5} = 2400\ \Omega$

For secondary coil,

$$P_S = V_S \cdot I_S$$

$$I_S = \frac{P_S}{V_S} = \frac{60000}{120} = 500\text{A}$$

$$\frac{V_P}{V_S} = \frac{I_P R_S}{I_S R_S}$$

$$\Rightarrow \quad R_S = \frac{I_P}{I_S} \times \frac{V_S}{V_P} \times RP$$

$$= \frac{I_P}{I_S} \times \frac{N_S}{N_P} \times R_P$$

$$= \frac{5}{500} \times \frac{1}{100} \times 2400$$

$$R_S = 240 \times 10^{-3}\ \Omega = 240\ \text{m}\Omega$$

19. Number of turns in rectangular coil,

$$N = 100$$

Area, $A = 14 \times 10^{-2}\ \text{m}^2$

Rotation frequency,

$$f = 360 \text{ rev/min} = \frac{360}{60} \text{ rev/s}$$

$$= 6 \text{ rev/s}$$

Magnetic field, $B = 3.0$ T

$\therefore$ Maximum value of emf produced,

$$e = NBA\omega = NBA(2\pi f)$$

$$= 100 \times 3 \times 14 \times 10^{-2} \times 2 \times \frac{22}{7} \times 6$$

$$= 1584 \text{ V}$$

20. Given, for the first element *X*,

Peak voltage, $V_0 = 100$ V.

Peak current, $I_0 = 5$A

$$\therefore \quad R = \frac{V_0}{I_0} = \frac{100}{5} = 20\ \Omega$$

(Since, current is in phase with voltage, hence element *X* is resistor).

For second element *Y*,

Current lags behind the voltage, hence *Y* is inductor.

$$\therefore \quad X_L = \frac{V_0}{I_0} = \frac{100}{5} = 20\ \Omega$$

When X (resistor) and Y(inductor) are connected in series with supply voltage $V_0 = 100$ V, then

Impedance of the circuit,

$$Z = \sqrt{R^2 + X_L^2} = \sqrt{20^2 + 20^2} = 20\sqrt{2}\ \Omega$$

$\therefore$ rms value of alternating current,

$$I_{\text{rms}} = \frac{V_{\text{rms}}}{Z} = \frac{\frac{V_0}{\sqrt{2}}}{20\sqrt{2}} = \frac{\frac{100}{\sqrt{2}}}{20\sqrt{2}} = \frac{5}{2} \text{ A}$$

21. Given, $E = 440 \sin 100\pi t$ ($E_0 = 440$ V and $\omega = 100\pi$)

$$L = \frac{\sqrt{2}}{\pi} \text{H}$$

We know, the reading of an AC ammeter is I_{rms}.

So, let's calculate I_{rms}.

$$X_L = \omega L = 100\pi \frac{\sqrt{2}}{\pi} = 100\sqrt{2}\ \Omega$$

$$\therefore \text{ Peak value of current} = I_0 = \frac{E_0}{X_L} = \frac{440}{100\sqrt{2}}$$

$$\Rightarrow \quad I_0 = \frac{4.4}{\sqrt{2}} = \frac{4.4\sqrt{2}}{2} = 2.2\sqrt{2}\text{A}$$

$$I_{\text{rms}} = \frac{I_0}{\sqrt{2}} = \frac{2.2\sqrt{2}}{\sqrt{2}} = 2.2 \text{ A}$$

22. Given, for direct current,

$$I_1 = 4 \text{ A}, R_1 = 3\ \Omega$$

For alternating peak current, $I_0 = 4\,A$

$$I_{rms} = \frac{I_0}{\sqrt{2}} = \frac{4}{\sqrt{2}} = 2\sqrt{2}\,A$$

Resistance, $R_2 = 2\Omega$

$$\frac{\text{Heat produced across } R_1(H_1)}{\text{Heat produced across } R_2(H_2)} = \frac{I_1^2 R_1 t}{I_2^2 R_2 t}$$

$$\Rightarrow \quad \frac{H_1}{H_2} = \frac{I_1^2 R_1}{(I_{rms})^2 R_2} = \frac{4^2 \times 3}{(2\sqrt{2})^2 \times 2} = \frac{4 \times 4 \times 3}{8 \times 2} = \frac{3}{1}$$

$\therefore \quad H_1 : H_2 = 3 : 1$

23. Given in L-R series circuit,

Power factor, $P_1 = \cos\phi = \frac{R}{Z}$

$$\Rightarrow \quad P_1 = \frac{R}{\sqrt{R^2 + X_L^2}} = \frac{R}{\sqrt{R^2 + R^2}} \quad (\because X_L = R)$$

$$P_1 = 1/\sqrt{2}$$

Again, when capacitor of capacitance C, such that $X_L = X_C$ is put in series, then it given AC circuit becomes L-C-R series resonance circuit.

$\therefore$ Power factor, $P_2 = \cos\phi = \frac{R}{Z}$

$$\Rightarrow \quad P_2 = \frac{R}{\sqrt{R^2 + (X_L - X_C)^2}}$$

$$= \frac{R^2}{\sqrt{R^2 + 0}} = 1 \quad (\because X_L = X_C)$$

$$\therefore \quad \frac{P_1}{P_2} = \frac{1/\sqrt{2}}{1} = \frac{1}{\sqrt{2}}$$

24. When a person walks through a metal detector carrying a metal object in his pocket, then impedance of AC circuit changes. It results in appereciable change in current in the AC current due to its resonance condition, which causes production of sound in the form of a beep.

Thus, metal detector works on the principle of resonance in AC circuits.

25. Resonant frequency of an L-C-R circuit is given by

$$\omega_r = \frac{1}{\sqrt{LC}}$$

So, resonance frequency does not depend on resistance of circuit and frequency of supply.

To increase resonance frequency, we have to reduce inductance or capacitance of circuit. As capacitance reduces when capacitors are connected in series (i.e. $\frac{1}{C_{series}} = \frac{1}{C_1} + \frac{1}{C_2}$), we can add another capacitor in series to increase resonant frequency.

26. As current is in phase with emf, so the circuit is in resonance,

and frequency of source = frequency of resonance

$$= \frac{1}{2\pi\sqrt{LC}} = \frac{1}{2 \times \pi \times \sqrt{0.5 \times 10^{-3} \times 200 \times 10^{-6}}}$$

$$= \frac{1}{2\pi \times \sqrt{100 \times 10^{-9}}} = \frac{\sqrt{10^9}}{2\pi\sqrt{100}}$$

$$= 0.5 \times 10^3 = 5 \times 10^2 \text{ Hz}$$

27. Total capacity of line = Capacity per km × Length in km

$$= 0.01 \times 100 = 1\,\mu F$$

Angular frequency of current,

$$\omega = 2\pi f = 2 \times \pi \times 0.5 \times 10^3$$

$$= 2 \times \pi \times 500 = 1000\pi \text{ rad / s}$$

For impedance to be minimum circuit should be operating under resonance condition,

$$\Rightarrow \quad \omega L = \frac{1}{\omega C}$$

Or inductance of circuit, $L = \frac{1}{\omega^2 C}$

$$\Rightarrow \quad L = \frac{1}{10^6 \pi^2 \times 10^{-6}} = \frac{1}{10} \text{ H} = 100 \text{ mH}$$

28. For wattless current, $P_{avg} = 0$

i.e. $\quad V_{rms} \times I_{rms} \times \cos\phi = 0$

$\Rightarrow \quad \cos\phi = 0 \Rightarrow \phi = \pi/2$

We know that, for purely inductive circuit, phase difference between alternating current and alternating voltage is $\frac{\pi}{2}$ because alternating voltage in purely inductive circuit leads $\frac{\pi}{2}$ angle from alternating current.

29. A L-C resonance circuit have zero reactance since, $X_L = X_C$. Therefore, it is possible that the circuit contains a capacitor and an inductor.

In purely inductive or capacitive circuit, voltage lags or leads the current by 90°. So, power in both circuit over one full periodic cycle will be equal to zero.

Thus, Statement I is true but Statement II is false.

30. Given, $L = 200 \text{ mH} = 0.2 \text{ H}$

$$V_{rms} = 220 \text{ V}, \quad f = 50 \text{ Hz}$$

$\therefore$ Inductive reactance,

$$X_L = 2\pi f L = 2\pi \times 50 \times 0.2 = 20\pi\ \Omega$$

Peak current, $I_0 = \frac{V_0}{X_L} = \frac{\sqrt{2}\,V_{rms}}{20\,\pi} = \frac{\sqrt{2} \times 220}{20\pi}$

$$I_0 = \frac{11\sqrt{2}}{\pi}$$

$$\Rightarrow \quad I_0 = \frac{\sqrt{242}}{\pi} \text{ A} \quad \text{... (i)}$$

Since, in inductive circuit, there is a phase difference of $\frac{\pi}{2}$ between alternating current and voltage. Hence, when instantaneous voltage is zero, then current reaches at its peak value, which is given by Eq. (i),

$$I_0 = \frac{\sqrt{242}}{\pi} = \frac{\sqrt{a}}{\pi} \text{ A} \quad \text{(given)}$$

$\therefore \quad a = 242$

31. Given, $R = 40\ \Omega$,

$V_{rms} = 220\text{ V} \Rightarrow f = 50\text{ Hz}$

Instantaneous value of alternating current,

$$I = I_0 \sin\omega t$$

For maximum value of alternating current, $I = I_0$

$\therefore \quad I_0 = I_0 \sin\omega t$

$\Rightarrow \quad \sin\omega t = 1$

$\Rightarrow \quad \omega t = \dfrac{\pi}{2} \Rightarrow t = \dfrac{\pi}{2\omega}$

If t' be the time at rms value, then

$$I_{rms} = I_0 \sin\omega t'$$

$\Rightarrow \quad \dfrac{I_0}{\sqrt{2}} = I_0 \sin\omega t'$

$\Rightarrow \quad \dfrac{\pi}{4} = \omega t' \Rightarrow t' = \dfrac{\pi}{4\omega}$

$\therefore$ Time taken to change the value of current from maximum value to rms value

$$= t - t' = \frac{\pi}{2\omega} - \frac{\pi}{4\omega}$$

$$= \frac{\pi}{4\omega} = \frac{\pi}{4 \times 2\pi f} = 2.5\text{ ms}$$

32. Given, $V_1 = 8\text{ kV} = 8000\text{ V}$

$V_2 = 160\text{ V}$

$P_2 = 80\text{ kW} = 80 \times 1000\text{ W}$

Since, transformer is ideal with purely resistive load and have unity power factor, so

$$P_1 = P_2 = 80000\text{ W}$$

$\Rightarrow \quad V_1 I_1 = V_2 I_2 = 80000\text{ W}$

$\Rightarrow \quad I_1 = \dfrac{80000}{V_1} = \dfrac{80000}{8000} = 10\text{ A}$

and $\quad I_2 = \dfrac{80000}{V_2} = \dfrac{80000}{160} = 500\text{ A}$

Primary load, $R_1 = \dfrac{V_1}{I_1} = \dfrac{8000}{10} = 800\ \Omega$

and secondary load, $R_2 = \dfrac{V_2}{I_2} = \dfrac{160}{500} = 0.32\Omega$

33. We know that, at very high frequency capacitive reactance becomes negligible i.e. short circuit (SC) and inductive reactance becomes very large i.e. open circuit (OC).

i.e. $\quad X_C \to 0$ and $X_L \to \infty$.

Now, the circuit can be rearranged as shown in figure.

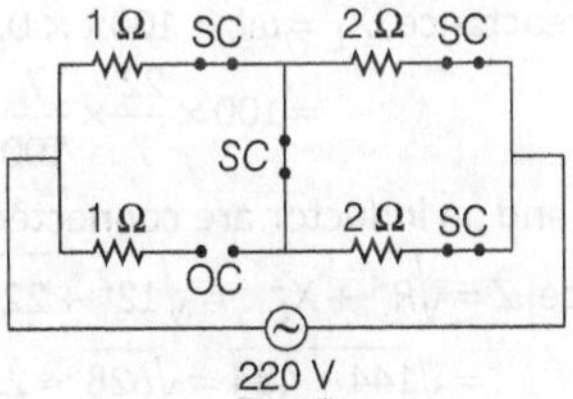

Fig. (i)

Final circuit is

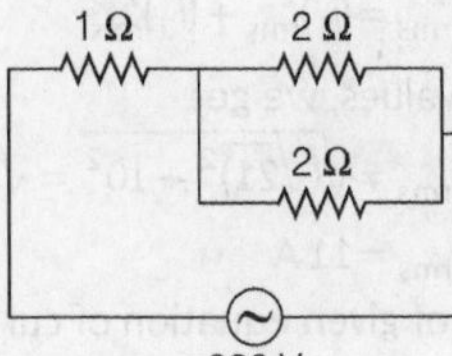

Fig. (ii)

Hence, equivalent resistance,

$$R_{eq} = 1 + \frac{2 \times 2}{2+2} = 2\Omega$$

Thus, correct answer is 2.

34. Given, resistance of resistor $= R$

Inductance, $X_L = 3R$

Capacitance $X_C = 2R$

As we know that,

Power factor, $\cos\phi = \dfrac{R}{Z}$

where, Z is impedance, $Z = \sqrt{R^2 + (X_L - X_C)^2}$

For **case I**, an inductance connected in series with resistance

$$\cos\phi_1 = \frac{R}{Z_1} = \frac{R}{\sqrt{R^2 + (X_L - 0)^2}} = \frac{R}{\sqrt{R^2 + (3R)^2}}$$

$$= \frac{R}{R\sqrt{10}} = \frac{1}{\sqrt{10}} \quad \text{...(i)}$$

For **case II**, A capacitor is also connected in series with resistance

$\therefore \quad \cos\phi_2 = \dfrac{R}{Z_2} = \dfrac{R}{\sqrt{R^2 + (3R - 2R)^2}}$

$$= \frac{R}{\sqrt{R^2 + R^2}} = \frac{R}{R\sqrt{2}} = \frac{1}{\sqrt{2}} \quad \text{...(ii)}$$

Now, ratio of Eqs. (ii) and (i), we get

$$\frac{\cos\phi_2}{\cos\phi_1} = \frac{\frac{1}{\sqrt{2}}}{\frac{1}{\sqrt{10}}} = \sqrt{\frac{10}{2}} = \sqrt{5} : 1$$

$\therefore \quad x = 1$

35. Given, equation of alternating current,

$$i = \left[\sqrt{42} \sin\left(\frac{2\pi}{T} t\right) + 10\right] \text{A}$$

From given equation, we get

$$i = i_1 + i_2$$

where, $i_1 = \sqrt{42} \sin\left(\dfrac{2\pi}{T} t\right)$ A and $i_2 = 10$ A

Now, i_1 is oscillating current, whereas i_2 is direct current and its value does not change with time.

$$(i_1)_{rms} = \frac{\sqrt{42}}{\sqrt{2}} = \sqrt{21}\text{ A}$$

$$(i_2)_{rms} = 10\text{ A}$$

We know that, $i_{rms}^2 = (i_1)_{rms}^2 + (i_2)_{rms}^2$

Substituting the values, we get

$$i_{rms} = \sqrt{(\sqrt{21})^2 + 10^2} = \sqrt{121}$$

$$\Rightarrow \quad i_{rms} = 11\text{ A}$$

Thus, RMS value of given equation of current is 11 A.

36. Given, angular frequency, $\omega = 100$ rad/ s

Capacitance of capacitor, $C = 100\,\mu\text{F} = 100 \times 10^{-6}$ F

Inductance of inductor coil, $L = 0.5$ H

Resistance in upper branch, $R_1 = 100\,\Omega$

Resistance in lower branch, $R_2 = 50\,\Omega$

In the given circuit consider current in upper branch be i_1 and current flowing in lower branch be i_2. The net current flowing in circuit will be I.

Impedance of upper branch can be calculated as

$$Z_1 = \sqrt{X_C^2 + R_1^2} = \sqrt{\left(\frac{1}{\omega C}\right)^2 + R_1^2}$$

$$= \sqrt{\left(\frac{1}{100 \times 100 \times 10^{-6}}\right)^2 + 100^2}$$

$$= \sqrt{100^2 + 100^2} = 100\sqrt{2}\,\Omega$$

Impedance of lower branch can be calculated as

$$= \sqrt{(\omega L)^2 + R_2^2} = \sqrt{(100 \times 0.5)^2 + 50^2}$$

$$= \sqrt{50^2 + 50^2} = 50\sqrt{2}\,\Omega$$

Current flowing in upper branch,

$$i_1 = \frac{V}{Z_1} = \frac{200}{100\sqrt{2}} = \sqrt{2}\text{ A}$$

Phase of current in upper branch,

$$\cos\phi_1 = \frac{R_1}{Z_1} = \frac{100}{100\sqrt{2}} = \frac{1}{\sqrt{2}}$$

$$\Rightarrow \quad \phi_1 = 45°$$

Thus, in upper branch, current leads voltage by 45° as capacitor is present.

Current flowing in lower branch i_2 is

$$i_2 = \frac{V}{Z_2} = \frac{200}{50\sqrt{2}} = 2\sqrt{2}\text{ A}$$

Phase of current in lower branch is

$$\cos\phi_2 = \frac{R_2}{Z_2} = \frac{50}{50\sqrt{2}} \Rightarrow \phi_2 = 45°$$

Thus, in lower branch current lags voltage by 45° as inductor is present.

Thus, the net current, $I = \sqrt{i_1^2 + i_2^2}$

$$I = \sqrt{(\sqrt{2})^2 + (2\sqrt{2})^2}$$

$$I = \sqrt{10} = 3.16\text{ A}$$

Thus, no option in the given question is correct.

If $I = i_1 + i_2$ is taken then

$I = \sqrt{2} + 2\sqrt{2} = 4.24$ A is obtained which is incorrect method of solution.

37. The circuit diagram can be drawn as,

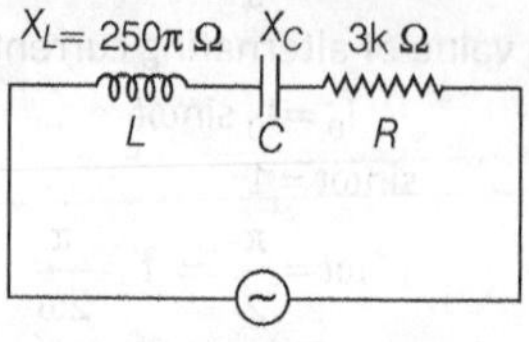

Average power of an L-C-R circuit is given by

$$P_{av} = V_{rms}\, i_{rms} \cos\phi$$

For P_{av} to be maximum, $\cos\phi = 1$ ...(i)

We know that, $\cos\phi = \frac{R}{Z}$,

where, R = resistance

and Z = impedance of L-C-R circuit.

Now, $Z = \sqrt{(X_L - X_C)^2 + R^2}$

As, $\cos\phi = 1 = \frac{R}{Z}$ [using Eq. (i)]

$$\Rightarrow \quad R = Z$$

$$\Rightarrow \quad R = \sqrt{(X_L - X_C)^2 + R^2}$$

Squaring both sides, we get

$$R^2 = (X_L - X_C)^2 + R^2$$

$$\Rightarrow \quad (X_L - X_C)^2 = 0$$

$$\Rightarrow \quad X_L = X_C$$

Since, $X_C = \frac{1}{\omega C} = \frac{1}{2\pi f C}$

and $X_L = 250\pi\,\Omega$ (given)

$$\Rightarrow \quad 250\pi = \frac{1}{2\pi \times 50 \times C}$$

$$\Rightarrow \quad C = \frac{1}{2\pi^2 \times 50 \times 250}$$

$$\Rightarrow \quad C = 4 \times 10^{-6}\text{ F} = 4\,\mu\text{F}$$

38. Resonant frequency, $f_0 = \frac{L}{2\pi\sqrt{LC}}$

$$L = \frac{1}{4\pi^2 f_0^2 C}$$

$$= \frac{1}{4\pi^2 \times (60)^2 \times 0.1 \times 10^{-6}} = 70.3\text{ H}$$

39. Angular frequency, $\omega = 2\pi f = 2\pi \times 50 = 100\pi$ Hz

$\because$ Inductive reactance, $X_L = \omega L = 100\pi \times 0.07$

$$\Rightarrow \quad = 100 \times \frac{22}{7} \times \frac{7}{100} = 22\,\Omega$$

$\because$ A resistor and an inductor are connected in series,

$\therefore$ Impedance, $Z = \sqrt{R^2 + X_L^2} = \sqrt{12^2 + 22^2}$

$$= \sqrt{144 + 484} = \sqrt{628} \approx 25\,\Omega$$

$\therefore$ Current, $I = \frac{V}{Z} = \frac{220}{25} = 8.8$ A

Also, phase angle between current and source voltage can be given as

$$\tan\phi = \left(\frac{X_L}{R}\right) \Rightarrow \tan\phi = \frac{22}{12}$$

$$\Rightarrow \quad \phi = \tan^{-1}\left(\frac{11}{6}\right)$$

40. P_a and P_b be the power in circuit (a) and (b)

$$\therefore \quad P_a = \frac{V^2}{R} = \frac{(220)^2}{5} = 9680 \text{ W}$$

In R - L - C circuit,

$$P_{av} = \frac{V^2}{Z}\cos\phi$$

$$P_{av} = \frac{V^2}{Z}\frac{R}{Z} = \frac{V^2 R}{Z^2} \quad \left[\because \cos\phi = \frac{R}{Z}\right] \ldots\text{(i)}$$

Put in Eq. (i), we get

$$P_{av} = \frac{(220)^2 \times 5}{5^2 + (X_L - X_C)^2}$$

$$\Rightarrow 5^2 + (X_L - X_C)^2 = \frac{(220)^2 \times 5}{484 \times 20} \quad [\because P_{av} = P_a]$$

$$= \frac{484 \times 100 \times 5}{484 \times 20} = 25$$

$$\Rightarrow \quad X_L = X_c$$

$$\Rightarrow \quad \omega L = \frac{1}{\omega C}$$

$$\Rightarrow \quad \omega = \frac{1}{\sqrt{LC}} = \frac{1}{\sqrt{0.1 \times 40 \times 10^{-6}}} = 500 \text{ rad s}^{-1}$$

41. Given, input alternating Emf $(E_g) = E_{g_0}\sin\omega t$

As we know that, capacitive current leads voltage by $\frac{\pi}{2}$ rad

$\therefore$ Phasor diagram will be

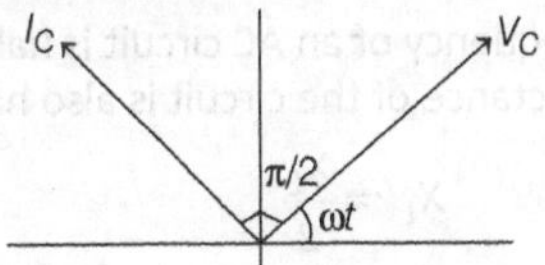

where, V_C and I_C are voltage and current in capacitive circuit.

42. Given,

(A) $\quad \omega L > \frac{1}{\omega C}$

Since, inductive resistance > capacitive resistance, hence Inductive current lag behind applied voltage.

(B) $\quad \omega L = \frac{1}{\omega C}$

Since, inductive resistance = capacitive resistance Hence, this circuit behaves like a L-C-R series resonant circuit. Therefore, $Z = R$ and phase difference = 0.

$\therefore$ Circuit will be purely resistive and resistive current remains in phase with voltage.

(C) $\quad \omega L < \frac{1}{\omega C}$

Since, inductive resistance < capacitive resistance, hence capacitive current lead with applied voltage.

(D) As we know that, at resonance impedance $(Z) = R$ (resistance)

$\therefore$ Circuit current will be maximum.

Hence, option (a) is the correct.

43. According to question, there is a series L-C-R circuit.

$\because$ Inductive reactance, $X_L = \omega L = 2\pi f L$

$$= 2\pi \times 50 \times 0.5 \times 10^{-3}$$

$$\Rightarrow \quad X_L = 50\pi \times 10^{-3}\,\Omega$$

$\because$ Capacitive reactance, $X_C = \frac{1}{\omega C} = \frac{1}{2\pi f C}$

$$\Rightarrow \quad X_C = \frac{1}{2\pi \times 50 \times 10^{-12} \times 0.1} = \frac{10^{11}}{\pi}\,\Omega$$

On comparing X_L with X_C, we can write

$$X_C >> X_L$$

and $\quad |X_C - X_L| >> R$

which means that the circuit is predominantly capacitive circuit.

44. Given, resistance, $R = 5\,\Omega$

Inductance, $L = 20$ mH

Capacitance, $C = 0.5\,\mu$F

Voltage, $V = 250$ V

$$I_{rms} = \frac{V}{Z} = \frac{V}{R} \quad [\text{At resonance, } Z = R]$$

Power dissipated, $P = I_{rms}^2 R$

or $\quad P = \frac{V^2}{R} = \frac{250 \times 250}{5} = 125 \times 10^2$ W

45. Given,

AC voltage, $V(t) = 20\sin\omega t$ volt.

Frequency, $f = 50$Hz

Separation between the plates, $d = 2$ mm $= 2 \times 10^{-3}$ m

Area, $A = 1\text{ m}^2$

As, $\quad C = \frac{\varepsilon_0 A}{d}$

where, ε_0 = absolute electrical permittivity of free space

$$= 8.854 \times 10^{-12}\text{ N}^{-1}\text{ kg}^2\text{m}^{-2}$$

$$\Rightarrow \quad C = \frac{\varepsilon_0 \times 1}{2 \times 10^{-3}} \quad \ldots\text{(i)}$$

Capacitive reactance $(X_C) = 1/\omega C \quad$ ...(ii)

From Eqs. (i) and (ii), we get

$$X_C = \frac{2 \times 10^{-3}}{2 \times 50\pi \times \varepsilon_0} \quad (\because \omega = 2\pi f)$$

$$= \frac{2 \times 10^{-3}}{25 \times 4\pi\varepsilon_0}$$

$$\Rightarrow \quad X_C = \frac{2 \times 10^{-3}}{25} \times 9 \times 10^9 \Rightarrow X_C = \frac{18}{25} \times 10^6 \ \Omega$$

By using Ohm's law,

As, $I_0 = \frac{V_0}{X_C} = \frac{20 \times 25}{18} \times 10^{-6} = 27.78 \times 10^{-6}$

$$\Rightarrow \quad I_0 = 27.78 \ \mu A$$

∴ The amplitude of the oscillating displacement current for applied AC voltage will be approximately 27.79 μA.

46. Given,

Inductance, $L = 30$ mH

Resistance, $R = 1 \ \Omega$

Angular frequency, $\omega = 300$ rad/s

We know that in *L-C-R* circuit, $\tan\phi = \frac{X_C - X_L}{R}$

where, $\phi =$ phase angle $= 45°$

$X_C =$ capacitive reactance $= \frac{1}{\omega C}$

$X_L =$ inductive reactance $= \omega L$

$$\Rightarrow \quad \tan 45° = \frac{X_C - X_L}{R}$$

$$\Rightarrow \quad X_C - X_L = R \quad [\because \tan 45° = 1]$$

$$\Rightarrow \quad \frac{1}{\omega C} - \omega L = R$$

$$\Rightarrow \quad \frac{1}{\omega C} - 300 \times 30 \times 10^{-3} = 1$$

$$\Rightarrow \quad \frac{1}{\omega C} = 10 \Rightarrow \omega C = \frac{1}{10}$$

$$\Rightarrow \quad C = \frac{1}{10\omega} \Rightarrow C = \frac{1}{10 \times 300}$$

$$\Rightarrow \quad C = \frac{1}{3} \times 10^{-3} \text{ F} \quad \text{...(i)}$$

According to question, the value of capacitance is $\frac{1}{x} \times 10^{-3}$ F. So, on comparing it with Eq. (i), we can say $x = 3$.

47. Given, inductive reactance, $X_L = 10 \ \Omega$

Capacitive reactance, $X_C = 4 \Omega$

Resistance, $R = 6 \Omega$

Therefore, power factor $= \cos\theta$

$$= \frac{R}{Z} = \frac{R}{\sqrt{R^2 + (X_L - X_C)^2}}$$

$$= \frac{6}{\sqrt{6^2 + (10 - 4)^2}} = \frac{1}{\sqrt{2}}$$

48. Bandwidth of *L-C-R* series resonance circuit, $\beta = R / L$

As we increase the value of the resistance from lower to the higher of the circuit, the bandwidth of resonance circuit will also increase.

So, the option (a) is correct.

Resonance frequency, $\omega = \frac{1}{\sqrt{LC}}$

Since, the resonance frequency is independent of the resistance.

So, the option (b) is incorrect.

We know that,

Quality factor, $Q = \frac{\omega L}{R}$

The quality factor is inversely proportional to the resistance of the circuit. So, increasing the value of resistance, the quality factor is decreased. So, the option (c) and (d) are incorrect.

49. Given, the frequency of the AC source, $f = 50$ Hz

Angular frequency of the circuit,

$$\omega = 2\pi f$$

$$\Rightarrow \quad \omega = 2\pi(50) \Rightarrow \omega = 100\pi$$

As we know the general expression of the current in AC circuit,

$$I = I_0 \sin\omega t$$

$$\Rightarrow \quad \frac{I_0}{\sqrt{2}} = I_0 \sin(100 \ \pi t)$$

$$\Rightarrow \quad \sin(100 \ \pi t) = \frac{1}{\sqrt{2}}$$

$$\Rightarrow \quad 100 \ \pi t = \sin^{-1}\left(\frac{1}{\sqrt{2}}\right)$$

$$\Rightarrow \quad 100 \ \pi t = \frac{\pi}{4} \Rightarrow t = \frac{1}{400} \text{ sec}$$

$$\Rightarrow \quad t = 2.5 \times 10^{-3} \text{ s} = 2.5 \text{ ms}$$

50. As we know, the inductive reactance is directly proportional to the frequency of the AC circuit

i.e., $X_L = \omega L$

$$\Rightarrow \quad X_L = 2\pi f L \quad (\because \omega = 2\pi f)$$

Here, *f* is the frequency of the AC circuit,

L is the inductive resistance

and X_L is the inductive reactance.

When the frequency of an AC circuit is halved, then the inductive reactance of the circuit is also halved.

i.e. $X_L' = \frac{X_L}{2}$

Using Ohm's law, $I = \frac{V}{X_L}$

When the frequency is halved, then the current

$$I' = \frac{V}{X_L'} \Rightarrow I' = \frac{V}{X_L/2}$$

$$I' = 2I$$

The current becomes doubled.

51. A. In a purely resistive AC circuit, the phase difference between the current and voltage is zero.

B. In a purely inductive AC circuit, the current lags the voltage, so the phase difference between the current and voltage is $\pi/2$.

C. In a purely capacitive AC circuit the current leads the voltage, so the phase difference between the current and voltage is $\pi/2$.

D. The phase difference between current & voltage in an L- C- R series circuit is

$$\phi = \tan^{-1}\frac{(X_C - X_L)}{R}$$

$\therefore$ The correct match is

A-(2), B-(3), C-(1), D-(4).

52. Given, $I = I_1 \sin\omega t + I_2 \cos\omega t$ ...(i)

We know that rms value of current is given by

$$I_{rms} = \sqrt{\frac{\int I^2 dt}{T}}$$

$$\Rightarrow \quad I_{rms} = \sqrt{\frac{\int_0^T (I_1 \sin\omega t + I_2 \cos\omega t)^2 dt}{T}} \quad \text{[using Eq. (i)]}$$

Squaring on both sides of the above equation, we get

$$\Rightarrow \quad (I_{rms})^2 = \frac{\int_0^T (I_1 \sin\omega t + I_2 \cos\omega t)^2 dt}{T}$$

$$\Rightarrow \quad (I_{rms})^2 = \frac{\int_0^T I_1^2 (\sin^2\omega t + I_2 \cos^2\omega t + 2I_1 I_2 \sin\omega t \cos\omega t) dt}{T}$$

$$\Rightarrow \quad I_{rms} = \sqrt{\frac{I_1^2}{2} + \frac{I_2^2}{2} + 0} \Rightarrow I_{rms} = \sqrt{\frac{I_1^2 + I_2^2}{2}}$$

53. Given, $V_0 = 250$ V, $R = 8\,\Omega, L = 24$ mH

and $C = 60\,\mu$F

We know that, at resonance power ,

$$P = \frac{V_{rms}^2}{R}$$

$$\Rightarrow \quad P = \frac{(250/\sqrt{2})^2}{8} \quad \left[\because V_{rms} = \frac{V_0}{\sqrt{2}} = \frac{250}{\sqrt{2}}\,\text{V}\right]$$

$$= (250)^2/16$$

$$= \frac{62500}{16} = 3906.25 \text{ W} \approx 4 \text{ kW}$$

$x = 4$

Comparing with the given value in the question i.e., x kW, the value of $x = 4$.

54. Given, inductance, $L = 100$ mH $= 100 \times 10^{-3}$ H

Capacitance, $C = 100\,\mu\text{F} = 100 \times 10^{-6}$ F

Resistance, $R = 120\,\Omega$

Maximum voltage, $V_0 = 30$ V

Angular frequency, $\omega = 100\,\text{rads}^{-1}$

Impedance, $Z = \sqrt{(X_L - X_C)^2 + R^2}$

Here, $X_L = \omega L = 100 \times 100 \times 10^{-3} = 10\,\Omega$

$$\therefore \quad X_C = \frac{1}{\omega C} = \frac{1}{100 \times 100 \times 10^{-6}} = 100\,\Omega$$

$$\Rightarrow \quad Z = \sqrt{(X_C - X_L)^2 + R^2}$$

$$= \sqrt{(100 - 10)^2 + (120)^2}$$

$$= \sqrt{(90^2 + 120^2} = 153.3\,\Omega$$

As we know that, peak current,

$$I_0 = \frac{V_0}{Z} = \frac{30}{153.3} = 0.195 \text{ A} \simeq 0.2 \text{ A}$$

Resonance frequency,

$$\therefore \quad f = \frac{1}{2\pi\sqrt{LC}} = \frac{1}{2\pi\sqrt{100 \times 10^{-3} \times 100 \times 10^{-6}}}$$

$$\Rightarrow \quad f = \frac{1}{2\pi\sqrt{10^{-5}}} = \frac{1}{2\pi \times 10^{-2}\sqrt{10^{-1}}}$$

$$= \frac{100\,\pi}{2\,\pi} = 50 \text{ Hz}$$

55. Given, $i = i_1 \sin\omega t + i_2 \cos\omega t$

Let I_{rms} be the rms current.

$$\therefore \quad I_{rms} = \left(\frac{i_1^2 + i_2^2}{2}\right)^{1/2}$$

$$\Rightarrow \quad I_{rms} = \frac{1}{\sqrt{2}}(i_1^2 + i_2^2)^{1/2}$$

56. Given, initial quality factor $(Q_i) = 100$

Let initial inductance $(x_{Li}) = x$

Final inductance $(x_{Lf}) = 2x$

and initial resistance $(R_i) = R$

Final resistance $(R_f) = \frac{R}{2}$

Final quality factor $= Q_f$

Since, $Q_i = \frac{X_L}{R}$ and $Q_f = \frac{2X_L}{R/2}$

$$\Rightarrow \quad Q_f = \frac{4X_L}{R} = 4Q_i = 4 \times 100 = 400$$

Hence, final quality factor will be 400.

57. Given, angular frequency,

$\omega = 100\,\text{rads}^{-1}$

$R = 60\,\Omega, V_R = 15$ V,

$R' = 40\,\Omega, V_{R'} = V_L = 20$ V

and $V_C = 10$ V

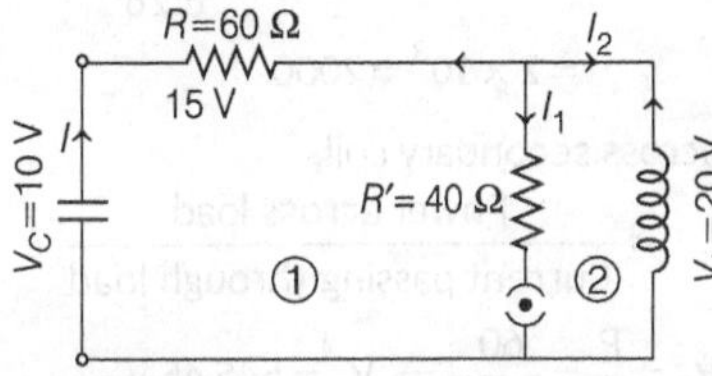

By using Ohm's law,

$V = IR \Rightarrow I = V/R$

$\Rightarrow \quad I = 15/60 = 1/4$ A ... (i)

and $I_1 = \frac{V_{R'}}{R'} = 20/40 = (1/2)\text{ A}$ ... (ii)

As, $X_C = \frac{V_C}{I} = \frac{10}{1/4} = 40\,\Omega$

and $X_C = \frac{1}{\omega C}$

$\Rightarrow C = \frac{1}{X_C\omega} = \frac{1}{40\times 100}$

$= 0.25\times 10^{-3}\text{ F} = 0.25\text{ mF} = 250\,\mu\text{F}$

By using KCL in loop 2,

$I_2 = I - I_1$

$= 1/4 - 1/2 = -1/4\text{ A}$

$\therefore X_L = \frac{V_L}{|I_2|} = \frac{20}{1/4} = 80\,\Omega \Rightarrow \omega L = 80$

$\Rightarrow L = \frac{80}{\omega} = \frac{80}{100} = 0.8\text{ H}$

58. Given, wavelength of transmission signal,

$\lambda = 960\text{ m}$

Capacitance, $C = 2.56\,\mu\text{F} = 2.56\times 10^{-6}\text{ F}$

As we know resonance frequency,

$$f = \frac{1}{2\pi\sqrt{LC}}$$

Also, frequency $(f) = \frac{\text{speed }(v)}{\text{wavelength }(\lambda)}$

$\therefore \frac{v}{\lambda} = \frac{1}{2\pi\sqrt{LC}} \Rightarrow \sqrt{LC} = \frac{\lambda}{v\times 2\pi}$

On squaring both sides, we get

$\Rightarrow LC = \frac{\lambda^2}{v^2\times 4\pi^2} \Rightarrow L = \frac{\lambda^2}{v^2\times 4\pi^2\times C}$

$\Rightarrow L = \frac{(960)^2}{(3\times 10^8)^2\times 4\pi^2\times 2.56\times 10^{-6}}$

$\therefore L = 10\times 10^{-8}\text{ H}$

59. Given, $L = 2\times 10^{-4}\text{ H}, R = 6.28\,\Omega,$

$f_0 = 10\text{ MHz} = 10\times 10^6\text{ Hz}$

$\therefore$ Quality factor $= \omega_0\frac{L}{R} = 2\pi f_0\frac{L}{R}$

$= 2\pi\times 10\times 10^6\times\frac{2\times 10^{-4}}{6.28}$

$= 2\times 10^3 = 2000$

60. Voltage across secondary coil,

$= \frac{\text{Power across load}}{\text{Current passing through load}}$

$\Rightarrow V_2 = \frac{P}{I_L} = \frac{60}{0.11} \Rightarrow V_2 = 545.45\text{ V}$

Voltage across primary coil, $V_1 = 220\text{V}$

$\Rightarrow V_2 > V_1$

It means that step-up transformer is used.

61. Given, inductor, capacitor and resistors are connected in series and have same reactance i.e., $X_L = X_C = R$

Since, impedance $(Z) = \sqrt{R^2 + (X_L - X_C)^2}$

$\therefore Z = \sqrt{R^2 + (R-R)^2} = R$

62. Given, reactance, $X_L = 100\,\Omega$

Frequency of AC, $f = 1000\text{ Hz}$

As voltage leads current by 45°, so there must be some resistance in the coil otherwise

$\Delta\phi = 90°.$

Using, $\tan\phi = \frac{X_L}{R}$

We have, $\tan 45° = \frac{X_L}{R}$ or $X_L = R$

$\therefore$ Reactance of circuit containing resistance and inductance is

$\sqrt{X_L^2 + R^2} = 100\,\Omega$

$\Rightarrow \sqrt{X_L^2 + X_L^2} = 100\,\Omega$ or $X_L = 50\sqrt{2}\,\Omega$

But $X_L = L\omega$

$\Rightarrow L = \frac{X_L}{\omega} = \frac{X_L}{2\pi f} = \frac{50\sqrt{2}}{2\pi\times 1000}$

$\Rightarrow L = 1.125\times 10^{-2}\text{ H}$

Hence, correct option is (a).

63. Given, frequency, $f = 750\text{ Hz}$

$V_{\text{rms}} = 20\text{V}, R = 100\,\Omega, L = 0.1803\text{ H}$ and $C = 10\,\mu\text{F}$

So, impedance of L-C-R circuit is

$$Z = \sqrt{R^2 + \left(2\pi fL - \frac{1}{2\pi fC}\right)^2}$$

$$= \sqrt{(100)^2 + \left(2\pi\times 750\times 0.1803 - \frac{1}{2\pi\times 750\times 10\times 10^{-6}}\right)^2}$$

$\approx 834\,\Omega$

Now, power lost by L-C-R circuit, which occurs in resistance is given by

$P = V_{\text{rms}} I_{\text{rms}}\cos\phi$

As, $\cos\phi = \frac{R}{Z}$ and $I_{\text{rms}} = \frac{V_{\text{rms}}}{Z}$

$\therefore P = \frac{V_{\text{rms}}^2\cdot R}{Z^2} = \frac{(20)^2\times 100}{(834)^2} = 0.0575\text{ Js}^{-1}$

Heat developed in resistor,

$H = Pt = S(\Delta\theta)$

where, t = time, S = heat capacity = 2 J/°C

$\Delta\theta$ = temperature change = 10 °C

$\Rightarrow t = \frac{S\Delta\theta}{P} = \frac{2\times 10}{0.0575} = 348\text{ s}$

Hence, option (d) is correct.

64. Average power developed which eventually gets lost as heat due to resistance of loop is given by

$$P_{avg} = \frac{V_{rms}^2}{R} = \frac{(V_{max}/\sqrt{2})^2}{R} = \frac{V_{max}^2}{2R}$$

Also, $V_{max} = NBA\omega$

In given loop, $N = 1, A = \pi ab$

So, $$P_{avg} = \frac{(BA\omega)^2}{2R} = \frac{B^2\pi^2a^2b^2\omega^2}{2R}$$

Hence, option (a) is correct.

65. Given that, $R = 100\,\Omega, C = 2\,\mu F, L = 80$ mH

For a series L - C - R AC circuit,

Quality factor, $$\phi = \frac{1}{R}\sqrt{\frac{L}{C}} = \frac{1}{100}\sqrt{\frac{80\times10^{-3}}{2\times10^{-6}}}$$

$$\phi = 2$$

66. Given, for L - R circuit

$$V_{rms} = 250\text{ V}, f = 50\text{ Hz}, P = 400\text{ W}$$

and $\cos\phi = 0.8$

As, we know, power is given by

$$P = V_{rms} i_{rms} \cos\phi$$

$$\Rightarrow \quad P = V_{rms}\frac{V_{rms}}{Z}\cos\phi$$

$$\Rightarrow \quad Z = \frac{V_{rms}^2}{P}\cos\phi$$

$$\Rightarrow \quad Z = \frac{(250)^2}{400}\times 0.8 = 125\,\Omega$$

Also, $\cos\phi = \frac{R}{Z} \Rightarrow 0.8 = \frac{R}{125} \Rightarrow R = 100\,\Omega$

Impedance, $$Z = \sqrt{R^2 + X_L^2}$$

$$\Rightarrow \quad 125 = \sqrt{(100)^2 + X_L^2}$$

$$X_L = 75\,\Omega$$

Now, to obtain power factor unity, X_C must be equal to X_L.

i.e. $$X_C = X_L = 75\,\Omega$$

$$\Rightarrow \quad \frac{1}{\omega C} = 75$$

$$\Rightarrow \quad C = \frac{1}{\omega\times75} = \frac{1}{2\pi\times50\times75}$$

$$\Rightarrow \quad C = \frac{1}{7500\pi}\text{F or } C = \frac{400}{3\pi}\mu\text{F}$$

Given, $$C = \frac{n}{3\pi}\mu\text{F}$$

On comparing the both, we get

$$n = 400$$

67. For an L-C-R circuit,

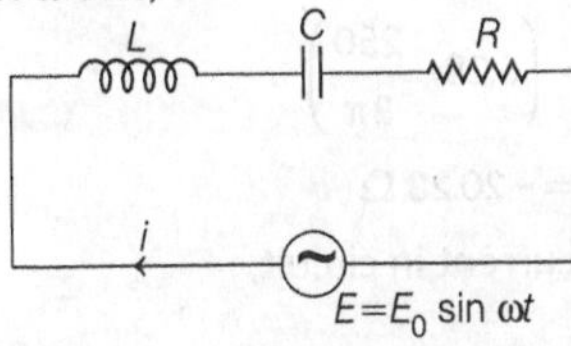

By KVL, we have

$$-L\frac{di}{dt} - \frac{q}{C} - iR + E = 0$$

Above can be rearranged as

$$L\frac{d^2q}{dt^2} + R\cdot\frac{dq}{dt} + \frac{1}{C}q = E_0\sin\omega t \qquad \text{...(i)}$$

Now, for a damped harmonic oscillator, we have

$$ma = -kx - bv + F_0\cos\omega t$$

Rearranging above equation, we have

$$m\frac{d^2x}{dt^2} + b\cdot\frac{dx}{dt} + kx = F_0\cos\omega t \qquad \text{...(ii)}$$

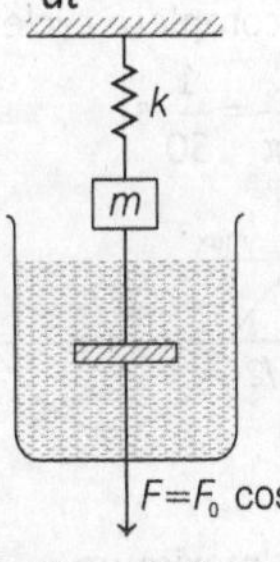

On comparing Eqs. (i) and (ii), we get the following analogy,

$$L \equiv m, R \equiv b \text{ and } \frac{1}{C} \equiv k$$

$$\text{or } L \leftrightarrow m, C \leftrightarrow \frac{1}{k} \text{ and } R \leftrightarrow b$$

68.

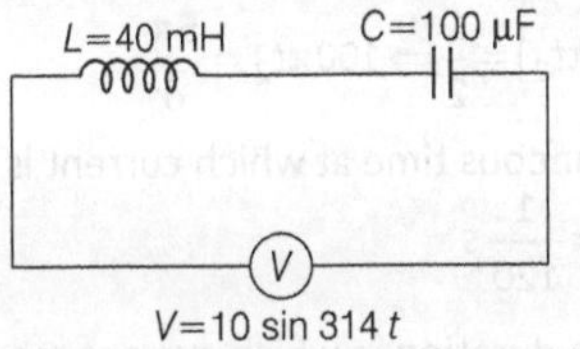

Impedance of given ciruit,

$$Z = \sqrt{(X_C - X_L)^2} = X_C - X_L = \frac{1}{\omega C} - \omega L$$

$$= \frac{1}{314\times100\times10^{-6}} - 314\times40\times10^{-3}$$

$$= 19.28\,\Omega$$

As $X_C > X_L$, circuit is captive, hence current in circuit leads emf by $\pi/2$ radians.

Current in circuit is given by

$$I = I_{max}\sin\left(\omega t + \frac{\pi}{2}\right) = \frac{V_{max}}{Z}\cos\omega t$$

$$\Rightarrow \quad I = 0.52\cos 314t$$

69. Given, $P = 1\text{ kW} = 1000\text{ W}$

$$V = 220\text{ V}, R = 2\,\Omega$$

Current, $$I = \frac{P}{V} = \frac{1000}{220}\text{ A}$$

Power loss, $P_{loss} = I^2R = \left(\frac{1000}{220}\right)^2 \times 2 = 41.32$ W

Now, the efficiency of transmission line,

$$\eta = \left(\frac{P}{P+P_{loss}}\right) \times 100 = \left(\frac{1000}{1000+41.32}\right) \times 100$$

$$\eta = 96.03\% \approx 96\%$$

Hence, correct option is (c).

70. In an AC resistive circuit, current and voltage are in phase.

So, $$I = \frac{V}{R} \Rightarrow I = \frac{220}{50}\sin(100\pi t) \quad \text{...(i)}$$

$\therefore$ Time period of one complete cycle of current is

$$T = \frac{2\pi}{\omega} = \frac{2\pi}{100\pi} = \frac{1}{50}\text{ s}$$

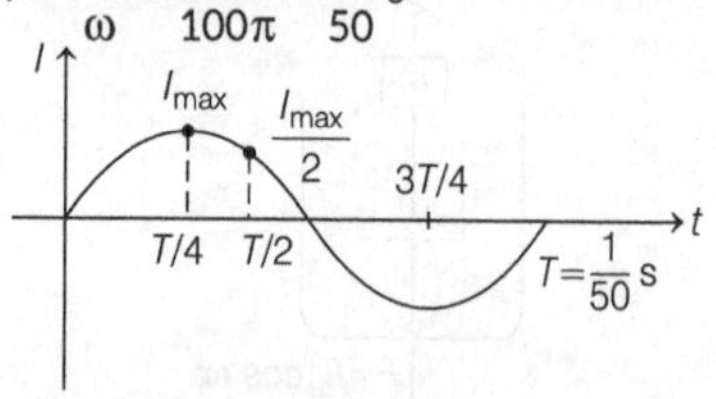

So, current reaches its maximum value at

$$t_1 = \frac{T}{4} = \frac{1}{200}\text{ s}$$

When current is half of its maximum value, then from Eq. (i), we have

$$I = \frac{I_{max}}{2} = I_{max}\sin(100\pi t_2)$$

$$\Rightarrow \sin(100\pi t_2) = \frac{1}{2} \Rightarrow 100\pi t_2 = \frac{5\pi}{6}$$

So, instantaneous time at which current is half of maximum value is $t_2 = \frac{1}{120}$ s

Hence, time duration in which current reaches half of its maximum value after reaching maximum value is

$$\Delta t = t_2 - t_1 = \frac{1}{120} - \frac{1}{200} = \frac{1}{300}\text{ s} = 3.3\text{ ms}$$

71. Since, $\tan\frac{\pi}{4} = 1 = \frac{X_C \text{ or } X_L}{R}$

$\therefore$ For *R-C* circuit, we have

$$1 = \frac{1}{C\omega R} \quad \text{or} \quad \omega = \frac{1}{CR} \quad \text{...(i)}$$

Similarly, for *R-L* circuit, we have

$$1 = \frac{\omega L}{R} \Rightarrow \omega = \frac{R}{L} \quad \text{...(ii)}$$

It is given in the question that,

$$\omega = 100 \text{ rad/s}$$

Thus, again by substituting the given values of *R*, *C* or *L* option wise in the respective Eqs. (i) and (ii), we get that only for option (c),

$$\omega = \frac{1}{CR} = \frac{1}{10 \times 10^{-6} \times 10^3}$$

or $$\omega = 100 \text{ rad/s}$$

72. Phase difference between I_2 and V, i.e. $C-R_2$ circuit is given by

$$\tan\phi = \frac{X_C}{R_2} \Rightarrow \tan\phi = \frac{1}{C\omega R_2}$$

Substituting the given values, we get

$$\tan\phi = \frac{1}{\frac{\sqrt{3}}{2} \times 10^{-6} \times 100 \times 20} = \frac{10^3}{\sqrt{3}}$$

$\therefore \phi_1$, is nearly 90°.

Phase difference between I_1 and V, i.e. in $L-R_1$ circuit is given by

$$\tan\phi_2 = -\frac{X_L}{R_1} = -\frac{L\omega}{R}$$

Substituting the given values, we get

$$\tan\phi_2 = -\frac{\frac{\sqrt{3}}{10} \times 100}{10} = -\sqrt{3}$$

As, $$\tan\phi_2 = -\sqrt{3}$$

$\therefore$ $$\phi_2 = 120°$$

Now, phase difference between I_1 and I_2 is

$\Delta\phi = \phi_2 - \phi_1 = 120° - 90° = 30°$

73. The given series *R-L-C* circuit is shown in the figure below.

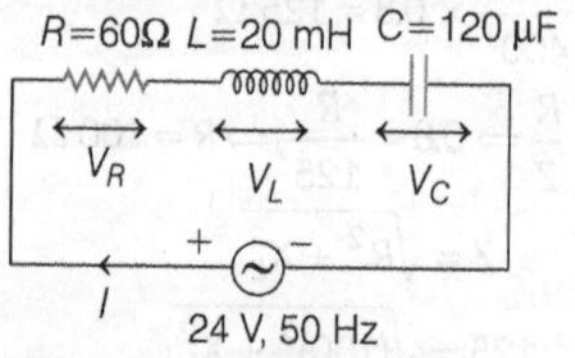

Here,

V_R = potential across resistance (R)

V_L = potential across inductor (L) and

V_C = potential across capacitor (C).

Impedance of this series circuit is,

$$Z = \sqrt{R^2 + (X_L - X_C)^2} \quad \text{...(i)}$$

$\because$ $$X_L = \omega L = (2\pi f)(L)$$

$$= 2\pi \times 50 \times 20 \times 10^{-3}\ \Omega$$

$$X_L = 6.28\ \Omega \quad \text{...(ii)}$$

and $$X_C = \frac{1}{\omega C} = \frac{1}{2\pi f C}$$

$$= \frac{1}{2\pi \times 50 \times 120 \times 10^{-6}} = \frac{250}{3\pi}\ \Omega \quad \text{...(iii)}$$

and $$X_L - X_C = \left(6.28 - \frac{250}{3\pi}\right)$$

$$= -20.23\ \Omega \quad \text{...(iv)}$$

RMS value of current in circuit,

$$I_{rms} = \frac{V_{rms}}{Z} = \frac{24}{\sqrt{R^2 + (X_L - X_C)^2}}$$

$$I_{rms} = \frac{24}{\sqrt{60^2 + (-20.23)^2}} = \frac{24}{63.18}$$

$$I_{rms} = 0.379 \text{ A}$$

Therefore, energy dissipated

$$= I_{rms}^2 \times R \times t$$

$$E = (0.379)^2 \times 60 \times 60$$

or $= 517.10 = 5.17 \times 10^2$ J

74. Given,

Number of turns in primary, $N_1 = 300$

Number of turns in secondary, $N_2 = 150$

Output power, $P_2 = 2.2$ kW $= 2.2 \times 10^3$ W

Current in secondary coil, $I_2 = 10$ A

Output power, $P_2 = I_2 V_2$

$$\Rightarrow \quad V_2 = \frac{P_2}{I_2} = \frac{2.2 \times 10^3}{10} = 220 \text{ V} \quad \text{... (i)}$$

We know that,

$$\frac{N_1}{N_2} = \frac{\text{Input voltage}}{\text{Output voltage}} = \frac{V_1}{V_2} \Rightarrow V_1 = \left(\frac{N_1}{N_2}\right) V_2$$

$$\Rightarrow \quad V_1 = \left(\frac{300}{150}\right) \times (220 \text{ V}) \quad \text{[using Eq. (i)]}$$

$$V_1 = 440 \text{ V} \quad \text{... (ii)}$$

Again, $\frac{V_1}{V_2} = \frac{I_2}{I_1}$

$$\Rightarrow \quad I_1 = \left(\frac{V_2}{V_1}\right) I_2 = \frac{220}{440} \times 10 \quad \text{[using Eqs. (i) and (ii)]}$$

$$\Rightarrow \quad I_1 = 5 \text{ A}$$

75. For a transformer, there are two circuits which have N_p and N_s (number of coil turns), I_p and I_s (currents) respectively as shown below.

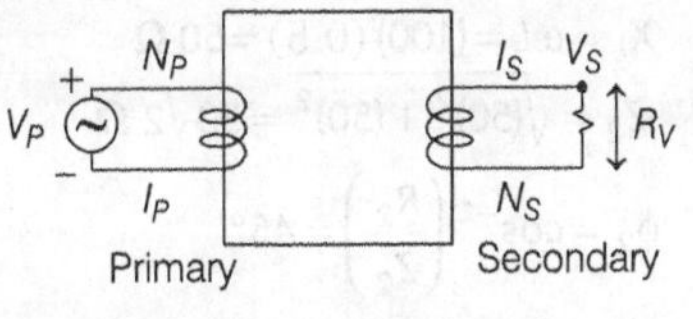

Here, input voltage, $V_p = 2300$ V

Number of turns in primary coil, $N_P = 4000$

Output voltage, $V_S = 230$ volt

Output power, $P_S = V_S \cdot I_S$

Input power, $P_P = V_P I_P$

∴ The efficiency of the transformer is

$$\eta = \frac{\text{Output (secondary) power}}{\text{Input (primary) power}}$$

$$\Rightarrow \quad \eta = \frac{V_S \cdot I_S}{V_P \cdot I_P} \times 100$$

$$\Rightarrow \quad \eta = \frac{(230)(I_S)}{(2300)(5)} \times 100$$

$$90 = \frac{230 I_S}{(2300) \times 5} \times 100 \Rightarrow I_S = 45 \text{ A}$$

JEE Advanced

1. $E = 45 \sin(\omega t)$

$$\omega_r^2 = \frac{1}{LC}$$

$$(10^5)^2 = \frac{1}{50 \times 10^{-3} \times C} \quad 10^{10} = \frac{1}{5 \times 10^{-2} C}$$

$$\Rightarrow \quad C = 2 \times 10^{-9} \text{ F}$$

at $\omega = 8 \times 10^4$ rad/s

$$X_L = \omega L = 8 \times 10^4 \times 50 \times 10^{-3} = 4000\ \Omega$$

$$X_C = \frac{1}{\omega C} = \frac{1}{8 \times 10^4 \times 2 \times 10^{-9}} = 6250\ \Omega$$

$$X = X_C - X_L = 2250\ \Omega$$

Also $0.05 I_0 = \frac{45}{Z}$

$$0.05 \times \frac{45}{R} = \frac{45}{Z} \Rightarrow Z = \frac{R}{0.05}$$

$$\sqrt{R^2 + X^2} = 20R$$

$$R^2 + X^2 = 400R^2$$

$$\Rightarrow \quad R = 112.6\ \Omega \quad (\text{as } X = 2250\ \Omega)$$

(P) $I_0 = \frac{45}{112.6}$ A $= \frac{45 \times 1000}{112.6}$ mA ≈ 400 mA

(Q) $Q_{factor} = \frac{\omega_r \times L}{R} = \frac{10^5 \times 50 \times 10^{-3}}{112.6} = 44.4$

(R) B and width $= R/L = 2250$ rad/s

(S) Peak power at resonance $= \frac{(45)^2}{R} = \frac{(45)^2}{112.6} \approx 18\ \omega$

2. $V_{XY} = V_X - V_Y = V_0 \sin\left(\omega t + \frac{2\pi}{3}\right) - V_0 \sin \omega t$

$$= V_0 \sin\left(\omega t + \frac{2\pi}{3}\right) + V_0 \sin(\omega t + \pi)$$

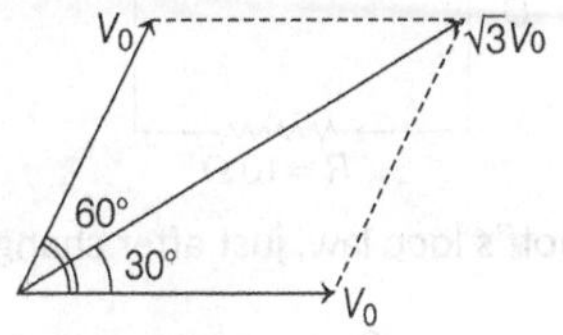

$$\Rightarrow \quad \phi = \pi - \frac{2\pi}{3} = \frac{\pi}{3}$$

$$\Rightarrow \quad V_{XY} = \sqrt{3} V_0 \sin(\omega t + 30°)$$

Therefore, $(V_{XY})_{rms} = \frac{\sqrt{3} V_0}{\sqrt{2}}$.

Similarly we can find $(V_{YZ})_{rms}$

3. At $\omega \approx 0$, $X_C = \dfrac{1}{\omega C} = \infty$. Therefore, current is nearly zero.

Further at resonance frequency, current and voltage are in phase. This resonance frequency is given by

$$\omega_r = \frac{1}{\sqrt{LC}} = \frac{1}{\sqrt{10^{-6} \times 10^{-6}}} = 10^6 \text{ rad/s}$$

We can see that this frequency is independent of R.

Further, $X_L = \omega L, X_C = \dfrac{1}{\omega C}$

At, $\omega = \omega_r = 10^6$ rad s, $X_L = X_C$.

For $\omega > \omega_r, X_L > X_C$. So, circuit is inductive.

4. $\dfrac{dQ}{dt} = I \Rightarrow Q = \int I\,dt = \int (I_0 \cos \omega t)\,dt$

$$\therefore \quad Q_{max} = \frac{I_0}{\omega} = \frac{1}{500} = 2 \times 10^{-3} \text{ C}$$

At $\quad t = \dfrac{7\pi}{6\omega}$ or $\omega t = \dfrac{7\pi}{6}$

Current comes out to be negative from the given expression. So, current is anti-clockwise. Charge supplied by source from $t = 0$ to $t = \dfrac{7\pi}{6\omega}$

$$Q = \int_0^{\frac{7\pi}{6\omega}} \cos(500t)\,dt$$

$$= \left[\frac{\sin 500t}{500}\right]_0^{\frac{7\pi}{6\omega}} = \frac{\sin\frac{7\pi}{6}}{500} = -1 \text{ mC}$$

Just after switching

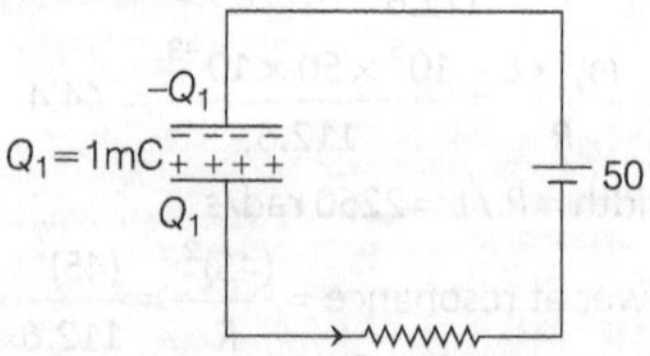

In steady state

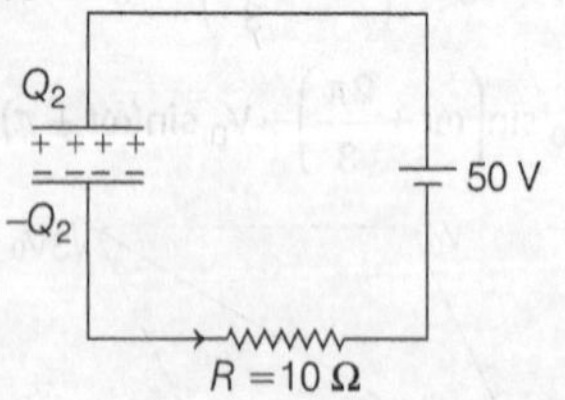

Apply Kirchhoff's loop law, just after changing the switch to position D

$$50 + \frac{Q_1}{C} - IR = 0$$

Substituting the values of Q_1, C and R, we get

$$I = 10 \text{ A}$$

In steady state $\quad Q_2 = CV = 1$ m C

$\therefore$ Net charge flown from battery = 2 m C

5.
$$P = Vi$$

$$\therefore \quad i = \frac{P}{V} = \frac{600 \times 10^3}{4000} = 150 \text{ A}$$

Total resistance of cables, $R = 0.4 \times 20 = 8\,\Omega$

$\therefore$ Power loss in cables $= i^2 R = (150)^2 (8)$

$$= 180000 \text{ W} = 180 \text{ kW}$$

This loss is 30% of 600 kW.

6. During step-up, $\dfrac{N_p}{N_s} = \dfrac{V_p}{V_s}$

or $\quad \dfrac{1}{10} = \dfrac{4000}{V_s}$ or $V_s = 40000$ V

In step down transformer,

$$\frac{N_p}{N_s} = \frac{V_p}{V_s} = \frac{40000}{200} = \frac{200}{1}$$

7.

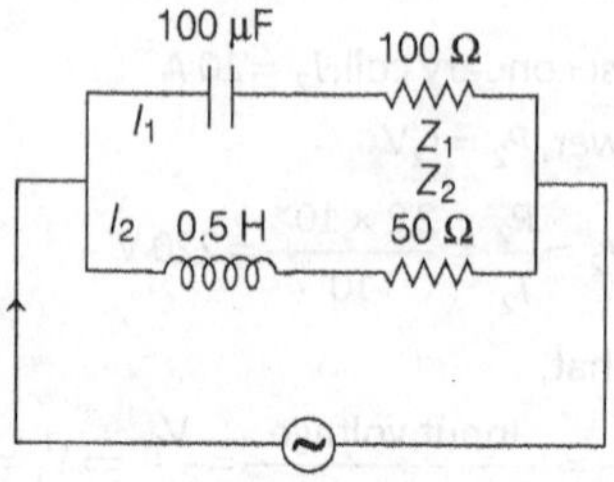

Circuit 1

$$X_C = \frac{1}{\omega C} = 100\,\Omega$$

$$\therefore \quad Z_1 = \sqrt{(100)^2 + (100)^2} = 100\sqrt{2}\,\Omega$$

$$\phi_1 = \cos^{-1}\left(\frac{R_1}{Z_1}\right) = 45°$$

In this circuit, current leads the voltage.

$$I_1 = \frac{V}{Z_1} = \frac{20}{100\sqrt{2}} = \frac{1}{5\sqrt{2}} \text{ A}$$

$$V_{100\,\Omega} = (100) I_1 = (100)\frac{1}{5\sqrt{2}} \text{ V} = 10\sqrt{2} \text{ V}$$

Circuit 2

$$X_L = \omega L = (100)(0.5) = 50\,\Omega$$

$$Z_2 = \sqrt{(50)^2 + (50)^2} = 50\sqrt{2}\,\Omega$$

$$\phi_2 = \cos^{-1}\left(\frac{R_2}{Z_2}\right) = 45°$$

In this circuit, voltage leads the current.

$$I_2 = \frac{V}{Z_2} = \frac{20}{50\sqrt{2}} = \frac{\sqrt{2}}{5} \text{ A}$$

$$V_{50\,\Omega} = (50) I_2 = 50\left(\frac{\sqrt{2}}{5}\right) = 10\sqrt{2} \text{ V}$$

Further, I_1 and I_2 have a mutual phase difference of 90°.

$$\therefore \quad I = \sqrt{I_1^2 + I_2^2} = 0.34 \text{ A}$$

CHAPTER~08

ELECTROMAGNETIC WAVES

LEVEL 01 Starter Level

8.1 Displacement Current

1 A parallel plate capacitor has circular plates, each of radius 5.0 cm. It is being charged so that electric field in the gap between its plates rises steadily at the rate of 10^{12} V-m^{-1}s^{-1}. What is the displacement current?

2 The voltage between the plates of a parallel-plate capacitor of capacitance 1.0 μF is changing at the rate of 5 V-s^{-1}. What is the displacement current in the capacitor?

3 A parallel plate capacitor of area 50 cm^2 and plate separation 3.0 mm is charged initially to 80 μC. Due to radioactive source nearby, the medium between the plates gets slightly conducting and the plate loses charge initially at the rate of 1.5×10^{-8} C s^{-1}. What is the magnitude and direction of displacement current? What is the magnetic field between the plates?

4 A parallel plate capacitor with circular plates of radius 1 m has a capacitance of 1 nF. At $t = 0$, it is connected for charging in series with a resistor $R = 1\ \text{M}\Omega$ across a 2 V battery as shown in figure. Calculate the magnetic field at a point P halfway between the centre and the periphery of the plates, after $t = 10^{-3}$ s.

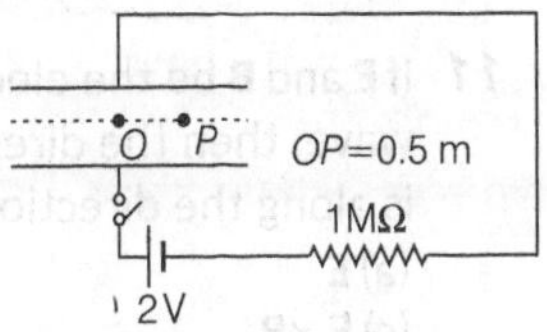

5 A parallel capacitor made of circular plates of radius 10.0 cm has a capacitance of 200 pF. The capacitor is connected to a 200 V AC supply with an angular frequency of 200 rad s^{-1}.

(i) What is the rms value of conduction current?

(ii) Is the conduction current equal to displacement current ?

(iii) Find peak value of displacement current.

(iv) Determine the amplitude of magnetic field at a point 2.0 cm from the axis between the plates.

8.2 Properties of EM Waves

1 Electromagnetic waves travel in a medium with a speed of 2×10^8 m/s. The relative permeability of the medium is 1. What is the relative permittivity of the medium?

2 A plane electromagnetic wave of frequency 25 MHz travels in free space along the x-direction. At a particular point in space and time, $\mathbf{E} = 6.3\hat{\mathbf{j}}$ V/m. What is $\mathbf{B}$ at this point?

3 The magnetic field in a plane electromagnetic wave is given by

$$B_y = 2 \times 10^{-7} \sin(0.5 \times 10^3 x + 1.5 \times 10^{11} t)\ \text{T}$$

(i) What is the wavelength and frequency of the wave?

(ii) Write an expression for the electric field.

4 Light with an energy flux of 18 W/cm^2 falls on a non-reflecting surface at normal incidence. If the surface has an area of 20 cm^2, find the average force exerted on the surface during a 30 min time span.

5. A plane electromagnetic wave in the visible region is moving along the z-direction. The frequency of the wave is 10^{15} Hz and the electric field at any point is varying sinusoidally with time with an amplitude of 2 Vm^{-1}. Calculate the average values of the densities of the electric and the magnetic fields.

6. The electric field in an electromagnetic wave is given by $E = 50 \sin \frac{2\pi}{\lambda}(ct - x)\ NC^{-1}$. Find the energy contained in a cylinder of cross-section 10 cm^2 and length 50 cm along the X-axis.

7 Calculate the electric and magnetic fields produced by the radiation coming from a 100 W bulb at a distance of 3 m. Assume that the efficiency of the bulb is 2.5% and it is a point source.

LEVEL 02 JEE Main Level

Single Choice Correct Questions

1 Displacement current is
(a) continuous when electric field is changing in the circuit
(b) continuous when magnetic field is changing in the circuit
(c) continuous in both types of fields
(d) continuous through wires and resistance only.

2 The charging current for a capacitor is 1 A then what is the displacement current ?
(a) 1 A (b) 0.5 A (c) 0 (d) 2 A

3 A parallel plate capacitor with plate area A and seperation between the plates *d*, is charged by a constant current *i*. Consider a plane surface of area A/4 parallel to the plates and drawn symetrically between the plates what is the displacement current through this area?
(a) i (b) $2i$ (c) $\frac{i}{4}$ (d) $\frac{i}{2}$

4 A parallel plate capacitor consists of two circular plates each of radius 2 cm, separated by a distance of 0.1 mm. If voltage across the plates is varying at the rate of 5×10^{13} V/s, then the value of displacement current is
(a) 5.50 A (b) 5.56×10^2 A
(c) 5.56×10^3 A (d) 2.28×10^4 A

5 A capacitor is having a capacity of 2 pF. Electric field across the capacitor is changing with a value of 10^{12} V/s. The displacement current is
(a) 2A (b) 3A (c) 6A (d) 9A

6 A variable frequency AC source is connected to a capacitor. Then on increasing the frequency
(a) both conduction current and displacement current will increase
(b) both conduction current and displacement current will decrease
(c) conduction current will increase and displacement current will decrease
(d) conduction current will decrease and displacement current will increase.

7 The relation between electric field *E* and magnetic field induction *B* in an electromagnetic wave is
(a) $E = \sqrt{\frac{\mu_0}{\varepsilon_0}}B$ (b) $E = cB$ (c) $E = \frac{B}{c}$ (d) $E = \frac{B}{c^2}$

8 An electromagnetic wave is propagating along *Y*-axis. Then,
(a) oscillating electric field is along *X*-axis and oscillating magnetic field is along *Y*-axis
(b) oscillating electric field is along *Z*-axis and oscillating magnetic field is along *X*-axis
(c) both oscillating electric and magnetic fields are along *Y*-axis, but phase difference between them is 90°
(d) both oscillating electric and magnetic fields are mutually perpendicular in arbitrary directions

9 In electromagnetic wave the phase difference between electric and magnetic field vectors **E** and **B** is
(a) zero (b) $\frac{\pi}{2}$ (c) π (d) $\frac{\pi}{4}$

10 In a plane EM wave, the electric field oscillates sinusoidally at a frequency of 2.5×10^{10} Hz and amplitude 480 V/m. The amplitude of oscillating magnetic field will be
(a) $1.52 \times 10^{-8}\ Wb/m^2$ (b) $1.52 \times 10^{-7}\ Wb/m^2$
(c) $1.6 \times 10^{-6}\ Wb/m^2$ (d) $1.6 \times 10^{-7}\ Wb/m^2$

11 If **E** and **B** be the electric and magnetic field of EM wave, then the direction of propagation of EM wave is along the direction of
(a) **E** (b) **B**
(c) **E** × **B** (d) **B** × **E**

12 If ε_0 and μ_0 represent the permittivity and permeability of vacuum and ε and μ represent the permittivity and permeability of medium, then refractive index of the medium is given by
(a) $\sqrt{\frac{\varepsilon_0\mu_0}{\varepsilon\mu}}$ (b) $\sqrt{\frac{\varepsilon\mu}{\varepsilon_0\mu_0}}$
(c) $\sqrt{\frac{\varepsilon}{\mu_0\varepsilon_0}}$ (d) $\sqrt{\frac{\mu_0\varepsilon_0}{\varepsilon}}$

13 An electromagnetic wave going through vacuum is described by

$$E = E_0 \sin(kx - \omega t); B = B_0 \sin(kx - \omega t)$$

(a) $E_0 B_0 = \omega k$ (b) $E_0 \omega = B_0 k$
(c) $E_0 k = B_0 \omega$ (d) None of these

14 A plane EM wave of frequency 25 MHz travels in free space in x-direction. At a particular point in space and time $E = 6.3\ \hat{j}$ V/m then $\mathbf{B}$ at that point is

(a) 2.1×10^{-8} T $(-\hat{k})$ (b) 2.1×10^{-8} T$(\hat{k})$
(c) 2.1 T$(\hat{k})$ (d) 2.1×10^{-8} T$(\hat{i})$

15 Which of the following pairs of space and time varying E and B fields would generate a plane electro magnetic wave travelling in $-z$-direction

(a) E_x, B_y (b) E_y, B_x (c) E_x, B_z (d) E_z, B_x

16 Choose the wrong statement for EM wave. They

(a) are transverse
(b) travel in free space with the speed of light
(c) are produced by accelerated charges
(d) travel with same speed in all medium

17 Which of the following statements about electromagnetic waves is/are correct?

(i) X-rays in vacuum travel faster than light waves in vacuum.
(ii) The energy of X-ray photon is greater than that of a light photon
(iii) Light can be polarised but X-ray cannot.

(a) 1 and 2 (b) 2 and 3
(c) 1, 2 and 3 (d) 2 only

18 In an electromagnetic wave, the direction of the magnetic field induction **B** is

(a) parallel to electric field **E**
(b) perpendicular to electric field **E**
(c) anti-parallel to poynting vector **S**
(d) random

19 The magnetic field in a plane EM wave is given by $B = (100\mu\text{T}) \sin\left[(2\times 10^{15}\ \text{s}^{-1})\left(t - \frac{x}{c}\right)\right]\hat{\mathbf{j}}$. The equation for electric field is

(a) $\mathbf{E} = 100\mu\text{N/C} \sin\left[(2\times 10^{15}\ \text{s}^{-1})\left(t - \frac{x}{c}\right)\right](-\hat{\mathbf{k}})$

(b) $\mathbf{E} = 3\times 10^{10}\ \mu\text{N/C} \sin\left[(2\times 10^{15}\ \text{s}^{-1})\left(t - \frac{x}{c}\right)\right](-\hat{\mathbf{k}})$

(c) $\mathbf{E} = 3\times 10^{10}\ \mu\text{N/C} \sin\left[(2\times 10^{15}\ \text{s}^{-1})\left(t - \frac{x}{c}\right)\right]\hat{\mathbf{k}}$

(d) $\mathbf{E} = 100\mu\text{N/C} \sin\left[(2\times 10^{15}\ \text{s}^{-1})\left(t - \frac{x}{c}\right)\right]\hat{\mathbf{k}}$

20 The shortest wavelength is for

(a) γ-rays (b) X-rays
(c) ultraviolet rays (d) microwaves

21 The electromagnetic radiations are in descending order of wavelength in the following sequence

(a) infrared waves, radiowaves, X-rays, visible light rays
(b) radiowaves, infrared waves, visible light rays, X-rays
(c) radiowaves, visible light rays, infrared waves, X-rays
(d) X-rays, visible light rays, infrared wave, radiowaves.

22 The waves related to tele-communication are

(a) infrared (b) visible light
(c) microwaves (d) ultraviolet rays

23 The frequencies of X-rays, γ-rays and ultraviolet rays are respectively a, b and c. Then

(a) $a < b, b < c$ (b) $a > b, b > c$
(c) $a > b, b > a$ (d) $a < b, b > c$

24 Which of the following are not electromagnetic waves ?

(a) cosmic rays (b) gamma rays
(c) β-rays (d) X-rays

25 Poynting vector **P** for an EM wave is

(a) $\mathbf{P} = \mathbf{E}\times\mathbf{B}$ (b) $\mathbf{P} = \mathbf{E}\times\mathbf{H}$
(c) $\mathbf{P} = \frac{\mathbf{E}}{\mathbf{B}}$ (d) $\mathbf{P} = \frac{\mathbf{E}}{\mathbf{H}}$

26 A flood light is covered with a filter that transmits red light. The electric field of the emerging beam is represented by a sinusoidal plane wave, $E_x = 36 \sin(1.20\times 10^7 z - 3.6\times 10^{15} t)$ V/m. The average intensity of the beam will be

(a) 0.86 W/m^2 (b) 1.72 W/m^2
(c) 3.44 W/m^2 (d) 6.88 W/m^2

27 The average value of electric energy density in an electromagnetic wave is (E_0 is peak value)

(a) $\frac{1}{2}\varepsilon_0 E_0^2$ (b) $\frac{E_0^2}{2\varepsilon_0}$
(c) $\varepsilon_0 E_0^2$ (d) $\frac{1}{4}\varepsilon_0 E_0^2$

28 A lamp radiates power P_0 uniformly in all directions, the amplitude of electric field strength E_0 at a distance r from it is

(a) $\frac{P_0}{2\pi\varepsilon_0 c r^2}$ (b) $\sqrt{\frac{P_0}{2\pi\varepsilon_0 c r^2}}$
(c) $\sqrt{\frac{P_0}{4\pi\varepsilon_0 c r^2}}$ (d) $\sqrt{\frac{P_0}{8\pi\varepsilon_0 c r}}$

29 In an electromagnetic wave, the amplitude of electric field is 1 V/m. The frequency of wave is 5×10^{14}. The wave is propagating along Z-axis. The average energy density of electric field in (J/m^3), will be
(a) 2.2×10^{-12} (b) 4.4×10^{-12}
(c) 6.6×10^{-12} (d) 8.8×10^{-12}

30 The sun delivers 10^3 W/m^2 of electromagnetic flux to the earth's surface. The total power that is incident on a roof of dimensions 8m × 20m will be
(a) 2.56×10^4 W (b) 6.4×10^5 W
(c) 4.0×10^5 W (d) 1.6×10^5 W

31 The intensity of light from a source is $\frac{500}{\pi}$ W/m^2. Find the amplitude of electric field in this wave
(a) $\sqrt{3} \times 10^2$ N/ (b) $2\sqrt{3} \times 10^2$ N/C
(c) $\frac{\sqrt{3}}{2} \times 10^2$ N/C (d) $2\sqrt{3} \times 10$ N/C

32 For any EM wave if E=100 V/m and B=3.33×10^{-7} T. Then the rate of energy flow per unit area is
(a) 3.33×10^5 J/m^2 (b) 26.5 VA/m^2
(c) 3×10^8 J/m^2 (d) None of these

33 A lamp emits monochromatic green light uniformly in all directions. The lamp is 3% efficient in converting electrical power to electromagnetic waves and consumes 100 W of power. The amplitude of electric field associated with the electromagnetic radiation at a distance of 5 m from the lamp will be
(a) 1.34 V/m (b) 2.68 V/m (c) 4.02 V/m (d) 5.36 V/m

34 The energy stored in a 90 cm length of laser beam operating at 10 mW, is
(a) 3×10^8 J (b) 3×10^9 J
(c) 3×10^{11} J (d) 3×10^{-11} J

35 A plane electromagnetic wave of intensity 10 W/m^2 strikes a small mirror of area 20 cm^2, held perpendicular to the approaching wave. The radiation force on the mirror will be
(a) 6.6×10^{-11} N (b) 1.33×10^{-11} N
(c) 6.6×10^{-10} N (d) 1.33×10^{-10} N

Previous Years Questions

JEE Main

1 A plane electromagnetic wave propagating in x-direction is described by E_y =(200 Vm^{-1}) $\sin[1.5 \times 10^7 t - 0.05x]$. The intensity of the wave is (Use $\varepsilon_0 = 8.85 \times 10^{-12}$ C^{2}N^{-1} m^{-2})
[2024, 27 Jan Shift-I]
(a) 53.1 Wm^{-2} (b) 106.2 Wm^{-2}
(c) 26.6 Wm^{-2} (d) 35.4 Wm^{-2}

2 An object is placed in a medium of refractive index 3. An electromagnetic wave of intensity 6×18^8 W/m^2 falls normally on the object and it is absorbed completely. The radiation pressure on the object would be (speed of light in free space = 3×10^8 m/s)
[2024, 27 Jan Shift-II]
(a) 2 Nm^{-2} (b) 18 Nm^{-2} (c) 36 Nm^{-2} (d) 6 Nm^{-2}

3 Match List-I with List-II

	List-I		List-II
A.	$\oint \mathbf{B} \cdot d\mathbf{l} = \mu_0 i_0 + \mu_0 \varepsilon_0 \frac{d\phi_E}{dt}$	I.	Gauss' law for electricity
B.	$\oint \mathbf{E} \cdot d\mathbf{l} = \frac{d\phi_B}{dt}$	II.	Gauss' law for magnetism
C.	$\oint \mathbf{E} \cdot d\mathbf{A} = \frac{Q}{\varepsilon_0}$	III.	Faraday law
D.	$\oint \mathbf{B} \cdot d\mathbf{A} = 0$	IV.	Ampere-Maxwell law

Choose the correct answer from the options given below
[2024, 29 Jan Shift-I]
(a) A-I, B-II, C-III, D-IV (b) A-IV, B-III, C-I, D-II
(c) A-II, B-III, C-I, D-IV (d) A-IV, B-I, C-III, D-II

4 A plane electromagnetic wave of frequency 35 MHz travels in free space along the x-direction. At a particular point (in space and time) $\mathbf{E} = 9.6 \hat{\mathbf{j}}$ V/m. The value of magnetic field at this point is
[2024, 29 Jan Shift-II]
(a) $3.2 \times 10^{-8} \hat{\mathbf{k}}$ T (b) $9.6 \times 10^{-8} \hat{\mathbf{k}}$ T
(c) $3.2 \times 10^{-8} \hat{\mathbf{i}}$ T (d) $9.6 \hat{\mathbf{j}}$ T

5 Which of the following Maxwell's equation is valid for time varying conditions but not valid for static conditions
[2023, 13 April Shift-I]
(a) $\oint \mathbf{E} \cdot d\mathbf{l} = 0$ (b) $\oint \mathbf{D} \cdot d\mathbf{A} = Q$
(c) $\oint \mathbf{B} \cdot d\mathbf{l} = \mu_0 I$ (d) $\oint \mathbf{E} \cdot d\mathbf{l} = -\frac{\partial \phi_B}{\partial t}$

6 In an electromagnetic wave, at an instant and at a particular position, the electric field is along the negative Z-axis and magnetic field is along the positive X-axis. Then, the direction of propagation of electromagnetic wave is
[2023, 13 April Shift-II]
(a) at 45° angle from positive Y-axis
(b) positive Z-axis
(c) negative Y-axis
(d) positive Y-axis

7 The electric field in an electromagnetic wave is given as $\mathbf{E} = 20 \sin\omega\left(t - \frac{x}{c}\right)\hat{\mathbf{j}}$ NC^{-1}, where ω and c are angular frequency and velocity of electromagnetic wave respectively. The energy contained in a volume of 5×10^{-4} m^3 will be (Given, $\varepsilon_0 = 8.85 \times 10^{-12}$ C^2 / Nm^2) **[2023, 11 April Shift-I]**

(a) 28.5×10^{-13} J (b) 17.7×10^{-13} J
(c) 8.85×10^{-13} J (d) 88.5×10^{-13} J

8 The ratio of average electric energy density and total average energy density of electromagnetic wave is **[2023, 1 Feb Shift-II]**

(a) 1/2 (b) 2 (c) 1 (d) 3

9 Match List-I with List-II.

List-I	List-II
A. Gauss's law in Electrostatics	I. $\oint \mathbf{E} \cdot d\mathbf{l} = -\frac{d\phi_B}{dt}$
B. Faraday's law	II. $\oint \mathbf{B} \cdot d\mathbf{A} = 0$
C. Gauss's law in magnetism	III. $\oint \mathbf{B} \cdot d\mathbf{l} = \mu_0 i_0 + \mu_0 \varepsilon_0 \frac{d\phi_E}{dt}$
D. Ampere-Maxwell law	IV. $\oint \mathbf{E} \cdot d\mathbf{s} = \frac{q}{\varepsilon_0}$

Choose the correct answer from the options given below. **[2023, 25 Jan Shift -II]**

(a) A-III, B-IV, C-I, D-II (b) A-IV, B-I, C-II, D-III
(c) A-I, B-II, C-III, D-IV (d) A-II, B-III, C-IV, D-I

10 A point source of 100 W emits light with 5% efficiency. At a distance of 5 m from the source, the intensity produced by the electric field component is **[2023, 30 Jan Shift-II]**

(a) $\frac{1}{10\pi} \frac{W}{m^2}$ (b) $\frac{1}{20\pi} \frac{W}{m^2}$
(c) $\frac{1}{2\pi} \frac{W}{m^2}$ (d) $\frac{1}{40\pi} \frac{W}{m^2}$

11 The electric field and magnetic field components of an electromagnetic wave going through vacuum is described by

$$E_x = E_0 \sin(kz - \omega t);\ B_y = B_0 \sin(kz - \omega t)$$

Then the correct relation between E_0 and B_0 is given by **[2023, 24 Jan Shift-II]**

(a) $kE_0 = \omega B_0$ (b) $E_0 B_0 = \omega k$
(c) $\omega E_0 = kB_0$ (d) $E_0 = kB_0$

12 If **E** and **k** represent electric field and propagation vectors of the EM waves in vacuum, then magnetic field vector is given by (ω = angular frequency) **[2023, 24 Jan Shift-I]**

(a) $\omega(\mathbf{k} \times \mathbf{E})$ (b) $\mathbf{k} \times \mathbf{E}$
(c) $\frac{1}{\omega}(\mathbf{k} \times \mathbf{E})$ (d) $\omega(\mathbf{E} \times \mathbf{k})$

13 An electromagnetic wave is transporting energy in the negative z-direction. At a certain point and certain time, the direction of electric field of the wave is along positive y-direction. What will be the direction of the magnetic field of the wave at that point and instant? **[2023, 25 Jan Shift-I]**

(a) Positive direction of x (b) Negative direction of y
(c) Negative direction of x (d) Positive direction of z

14 Given below are two statements.

Statement I Electromagnetic waves are not deflected by electric and magnetic field.

Statement II The amplitude of electric field and the magnetic field in electromagnetic waves are related to each other as $E_0 = \sqrt{\frac{\mu_0}{\varepsilon_0}} B_0$.

In the light of the above statements, choose the correct answer from the options given below **[2023, 29 Jan Shift-II]**

(a) Statement I is false but Statement II is true
(b) Statement I is true but Statement II is false
(c) Both Statement I and Statement II are true
(d) Both Statement I and Statement II are false

15 Which of the following are true?

A. Speed of light in vacuum is dependent on the direction of propagation.
B. Speed of light in a medium is independent of the wavelength of light.
C. The speed of light is independent of the motion of the source.
D. The speed of light in a medium is independent of intensity.

Choose the correct answer from the options given below **[2023, 29 Jan Shift-I]**

(a) B and C only (b) B and D only
(c) C and D only (d) A and C only

16 A point source of light is placed at the centre of curvature of a hemispherical surface. The source emits a power of 24 W. The radius of curvature of hemisphere is 10 cm and the inner surface is completely reflecting. The force on the hemisphere due to the light falling on it is .... $\times 10^{-8}$ N. **[2023, 30 Jan Shift-I]**

17 In a medium, the speed of light wave decreases to 0.2 times to its speed in free space. The ratio of relative permittivity to the refractive index of the medium is $x : 1$. The value of x is ....
(Given, speed of light in free space $= 3 \times 10^8$ m s^{-1} and for the given medium $\mu_r = 1$) **[2023, 31 Jan Shift-I]**

18 Match List-I with List-II.

List-I	List-II
A. Microwave	I. 400 nm to 1 nm
B. Ultraviolet	II. 1 nm to 10^{-3} nm
C. X-Ray	III. 1 mm to 700 nm
D. Infrared	IV. 0.1 m to 1 mm

Choose the correct answer from the options given below. **[2023, 15 April Shift-I]**

(a) A-IV, B-I, C-II, D-III (b) A-I, B-IV, C-II, D-III
(c) A-IV, B-II, C-I, D-III (d) A-IV, B-I, C-III, D-II

19 Given below are two statements, one is labelled as Assertion (A) and the other is labelled as Reason (R).

Assertion (A) EM waves used for optical communication have longer wavelengths than that of microwave, employed in Radar technology.

Reason (R) Infrared EM waves are more energetic than microwaves, (used in Radar)

In the light of the above statements, choose the most appropriate answer from the options given below. **[2023, 12 April Shift-I]**

(a) Both A and R are true and R is the correct explanation of A
(b) Both A and R are true but R is not the correct explanation of A
(c) A is true but R is false
(d) A is false but R is true

20 Match List I with List II.

List I	List II
A. Microwave	I. Radioactive decay of the nucleus
B. Gamma rays	II. Rapid acceleration and deceleration of electron in aerials
C. Radio waves	III. Inner shell electrons
D. X-rays	IV. Klystron valve

Choose the correct answer from the options given below : **[2023, 1 Feb Shift-I]**

(a) A-IV, B-I, C-II, D-III (b) A-I, B-II, C-III, D-IV
(c) A-IV, B-III, C-II, D-I (d) A-I, B-III, C-IV, D-II

21 Nearly 10% of the power of a 110 W light bulb is converted to visible radiation. The change in average intensities of visible radiation, at a distance of 1 m from the bulb to a distance of 5 m is $a \times 10^{-2}$ W/m^2. The value of a will be .... **[2022, 29 July Shift-II]**

22 Sun light falls normally on a surface of area 36 cm^2 and exerts an average force of 7.2×10^{-9} N within a time period of 20 min. Considering a case of complete absorption, the energy flux of incident light is **[2022, 28 July Shift-II]**

(a) 25.92×10^2 W/cm^2 (b) 8.64×10^{-6} W/cm^2
(c) 6.0 W/cm^2 (d) 0.06 W/cm^2

23 A beam of light travelling along X-axis is described by the electric field $E_y = 900 \sin\omega(t - x/c)$. The ratio of electric force to magnetic force on a charge q moving along Y-axis with a speed of 3×10^7 ms^{-1} will be (Given, speed of light $= 3 \times 10^8$ ms^{-1}) **[2022, 27 July Shift-I]**

(a) 1 : 1 (b) 1 : 10
(c) 10 : 1 (d) 1 : 2

24 The oscillating magnetic field in a plane electromagnetic wave is given by $B_y = 5 \times 10^{-6} \sin 1000\pi (5x - 4 \times 10^8 t)$ T. The amplitude of electric field will be **[2022, 26 July Shift-II]**

(a) 15×10^2 Vm^{-1} (b) 5×10^{-6} Vm^{-1}
(c) 16×10^{12} Vm^{-1} (d) 4×10^2 Vm^{-1}

25 The magnetic field of a plane electromagnetic wave is given by

$$\mathbf{B} = 2 \times 10^{-8} \sin(0.5 \times 10^3 x + 1.5 \times 10^{11} t)\hat{j}\,\mathrm{T}$$

The amplitude of the electric field would be **[2022, 26 July Shift-I]**

(a) 6 Vm^{-1} along X-axis (b) 3 Vm^{-1} along Z-axis
(c) 6 Vm^{-1} along Z-axis (d) 2×10^{-8} Vm^{-1} along Z-axis

26 Light wave travelling in air a long x-direction is given by $E_y = 540 \sin \pi \times 10^4 (x - ct)$ Vm^{-1}. Then, the peak value of magnetic field of wave will be (Given, $c = 3 \times 10^8$ ms^{-1}) **[2022, 25 July Shift-II]**

(a) 18×10^{-7} T (b) 54×10^{-7} T
(c) 54×10^{-8} T (d) 18×10^{-8} T

27 The displacement current of 4.425 μA is developed in the space between the plates of parallel plate capacitor when voltage is changing at a rate of 10^6 Vs^{-1}. The area of each plate of the capacitor is 40 cm^2. The distance between each plate of the capacitor is $x \times 10^{-3}$ m. The value of x is .... (Permittivity of free space, $E_0 = 8.85 \times 10^{-12}$ C^2 N^{-1}m^{-2}) **[2022, 29 June Shift-II]**

28 The intensity of the light from a bulb incident on a surface is 0.22 W/m^2. The amplitude of the magnetic field in this light wave is ...... $\times 10^{-9}$ T. (Given, permittivity of vacuum, $\varepsilon_0 = 8.85 \times 10^{-12}$ C^2 N^{-1}-m^{-2}, speed of light in vacuum, $c = 3 \times 10^8$ ms^{-1}) **[2022, 29 June Shift-I]**

29 A RADAR sends an electromagnetic signal of electric field $E_0 = 2.25$ V/m and magnetic field $B_0 = 1.5 \times 10^{-8}$ T which strikes a target on line of sight at a distance of 3 km in a medium. After that, a pail of signal (echo) reflects back towards the RADAR with same velocity and by same path. If the signal was transmitted at time $t = 0$ from RADAR, then after how much time echo will reach to the RADAR? **[2022, 28 June Shift-I]**

(a) 2.0×10^{-5} s (b) 4.0×10^{-5} s
(c) 1.0×10^{-5} s (d) 8.0×10^{-5} s

30 Given below are two statements

Statement I A time varying electric field is a source of changing magnetic field and *vice-versa*. Thus, a disturbance in electric or magnetic field creates electromagnetic waves.

Statement II In a material medium. The EM wave travels with speed $v = \frac{1}{\sqrt{\mu_0 \varepsilon_0}}$.

In the light of the above statements, choose the correct answer from the options given below **[2022, 27 June Shift-II]**

(a) Both Statement I and Statement II are true.
(b) Both Statement I and Statement II are false.
(c) Statement I is true but Statement II is false.
(d) Statement I is false but Statement II is true.

31 In free space, an electromagnetic wave of 3 GHz frequency strikes over the edge of an object of size $\frac{\lambda}{100}$, where λ is the wavelength of the wave in free space. The phenomenon, which happens there will be **[2022, 26 June Shift-I]**

(a) reflection (b) refraction
(c) diffraction (d) scattering

32 The electromagnetic waves travel in a medium at a speed of 2.0×10^8 m/s. The relative permeability of the medium is 1.0. The relative permittivity of the medium will be **[2022, 25 June Shift-II]**

(a) 2.25 (b) 4.25
(c) 6.25 (d) 8.25

33 An electric bulb is rated as 200 W. What will be the peak magnetic field at 4 m distance produced by the radiations coming from this bulb? Consider this bulb as a point source with 3.5% efficiency. **[2022, 24 June Shift-II]**

(a) 1.19×10^{-8} T (b) 1.71×10^{-8} T
(c) 0.84×10^{-8} T (d) 3.36×10^{-8} T

34 A plane electromagnetic wave travels in a medium of relative permeability 1.61 and relative permittivity 6.44. If magnitude of magnetic intensity is 4.5×10^{-2} Am^{-1} at a point, what will be the approximate magnitude of electric field intensity at that point?

(Given, permeability of free space $\mu_0 = 4\pi \times 10^{-7}$ NA^{-2}, speed of light in vacuum, $c = 3 \times 10^8$ ms^{-1}) **[2022, 24 June Shift-I]**

(a) 16.96 Vm^{-1} (b) 2.25×10^{-2} Vm^{-1}
(c) 8.48 Vm^{-1} (d) 6.75×10^6 Vm^{-1}

35 Electric field of plane electromagnetic wave propagating through a non-magnetic medium is given by $E = 20\cos(2 \times 10^{10} t - 200x)$ V/m. The dielectric constant of the medium is equal to

(Take, $\mu_r = 1$) **[2021, 1 Sep. Shift-II]**

(a) 9 (b) 2
(c) $\frac{1}{3}$ (d) 3

36 A light beam is described by $E = 800 \sin\left(\omega t - \frac{x}{c}\right)$. An electron is allowed to move normal to the propagation of light beam with a speed 3×10^7 ms^{-1}. What is the maximum magnetic force exerted on the electron? **[2021, 26 Aug Shift-II]**

(a) 1.28×10^{-17} N (b) 1.28×10^{-18} N
(c) 12.8×10^{-17} N (d) 12.8×10^{-18} N

37 The magnetic field vector of an electromagnetic wave is given by $\mathbf{B} = B_0 \frac{\hat{\mathbf{i}} + \hat{\mathbf{j}}}{\sqrt{2}} \cos(kz - \omega t)$T where $\hat{\mathbf{i}}$, $\hat{\mathbf{j}}$ represents unit vector along X and Y-axis respectively. At $t = 0$, two electric charges q_1 of 4π C and q_2 of 2π C located at $\left(0, 0, \frac{\pi}{k}\right)$ and $\left(0, 0, \frac{3\pi}{k}\right)$ respectively, have the same velocity of $0.5\, c\, \hat{\mathbf{i}}$. (where, c is the velocity of light). The ratio of the force acting on charge q_1 to q_2 is **[2021, 31 Aug Shift-I]**

(a) $2\sqrt{2} : 1$ (b) $1 : \sqrt{2}$
(c) $2 : 1$ (d) $\sqrt{2} : 1$

38 The electric field in an electromagnetic wave is given by $E = (50\ NC^{-1}) \sin \omega \left(t - \frac{x}{c}\right)$

The energy contained in a cylinder of volume V is 5.5×10^{-12} J. The value of V is .... cm^3. (Given $\varepsilon_0 = 8.85 \times 10^{-12}$ $C^2N^{-1}m^{-2}$). **[2021, 31 Aug. Shift-I]**

39 A plane electromagnetic wave with frequency of 30 MHz travels in free space. At particular point in space and time, electric field is 6 V/m. The magnetic field at this point will be $x \times 10^{-8}$ T. The value of x is .... **[2021, 27 Aug. Shift-II]**

40 Electric field in a plane electromagnetic wave is given by $E = 50\sin(500x - 10 \times 10^{10} t)$ V/m.

The velocity of electromagnetic wave in this medium is

(Given, c = speed of light in vacuum) **[2021, 27 Aug. Shift-I]**

(a) $\frac{3}{2}c$ (b) c (c) $\frac{2}{3}c$ (d) $\frac{c}{2}$

41 The electric field in a plane electromagnetic wave is given by

$$\mathbf{E} = 200\cos\left[\left(\frac{0.5 \times 10^3}{m}\right)x - \left(1.5 \times 10^{11}\frac{\text{rad}}{s} \times t\right)\right]\frac{V}{m}\hat{\mathbf{j}}$$

If this wave falls normally on a perfectly reflecting surface having an area of 100 cm^2. If the radiation pressure exerted by the EM wave on the surface during a 10 min exposure is $\frac{x}{10^9}$. Find the value of x. **[2021, 26 Aug. Shift-I]**

42 The relative permittivity of distilled water is 81. The velocity of light in it will be

(Take, $\mu_r = 1$) **[2021, 27 July Shift-I]**

(a) 4.33×10^7 m/s (b) 2.33×10^7 m/s

(c) 3.33×10^7 m/s (d) 5.33×10^7 m/s

43 A linearly polarised electromagnetic wave in vacuum is $E = 3.1\cos[(1.8)z - (5.4 \times 10^6)t]\hat{\mathbf{i}}$ N/C is incident normally on a perfectly reflecting wall at $z = a$. Choose the correct option. **[2021, 25 July Shift-I]**

(a) The wavelength is 5.4 m

(b) The frequency of electromagnetic wave is 54×10^4 Hz.

(c) The transmitted wave will be $3.1\cos[(1.8)z - (5.4 \times 10^6)t]\hat{\mathbf{i}}$ N/C

(d) The reflected wave will be $3.1\cos[(1.8)z + (5.4 \times 10^6)t]\hat{\mathbf{i}}$ N/C

44 Intensity of sunlight is observed as 0.092 Wm^{-2} at a point in free space. What will be the peak value of magnetic field at that point?

($\varepsilon_0 = 8.85 \times 10^{-12}$ C^{-2}N^{-1}m^{-2}) **[2021, 22 July Shift-II]**

(a) 2.77×10^{-8} T (b) 1.96×10^{-8} T

(c) 8.31 T (d) 5.88 T

45 In an electromagnetic wave, the electric field vector and magnetic field vector are given as $\mathbf{E} = E_0\hat{\mathbf{i}}$ and $\mathbf{B} = B_0\hat{\mathbf{k}}$, respectively. The direction of propagation of electromagnetic wave is along **[2021, 20 July Shift-II]**

(a) $\hat{k}$ (b) $\hat{j}$

(c) $-\hat{k}$ (d) $-\hat{j}$

46 A plane electromagnetic wave propagating along y-direction can have the following pair of electric field (**E**) and magnetic field (**B**) components. **[2021, 18 March Shift-II]**

(a) E_y, B_y or E_z, B_z (b) E_y, B_x or E_x, B_y

(c) E_x, B_z or E_z, B_x (d) E_x, B_y or E_y, B_x

47 A plane electromagnetic wave of frequency 100 MHz is travelling in vacuum along the x-direction. At a particular point in space and time, $\mathbf{B} = 2.0 \times 10^{-8}\,\hat{\mathbf{k}}$T (where, $\hat{\mathbf{k}}$ is unit vector along z-direction). What is **E** at this point? **[2021, 18 March Shift-I]**

(a) $0.6\,\hat{j}$ V/m (b) $6.0\,\hat{k}$ V/m

(c) $6.0\,\hat{j}$ V/m (d) $0.6\,\hat{k}$ V/m

48 The electric field intensity produced by the radiation coming from a 100 W bulb at a distance of 3 m is E. The electric field intensity produced by the radiation coming from 60 W at the same distance is $\sqrt{\frac{x}{5}}E$, where the value of x is .... **[2021, 17 March Shift-I]**

49 Seawater at a frequency $f = 9 \times 10^2$ Hz, has permittivity $\varepsilon = 80\varepsilon_0$ and resistivity $r = 0.25\,\Omega$-m. Imagine a parallel plate capacitor is immersed in seawater and is driven by an alternating voltage source $V(t) = V_0\sin(2\pi ft)$. Then, the conduction current density becomes 10^x times the displacement current density after time $t = \frac{1}{800}$ s. The value of x is .... $\left(\text{Take, } \frac{1}{4\pi\varepsilon_0} = 9 \times 10^9\,\text{N-m}^2\text{C}^{-2}\right)$ **[2021, 17 March Shift-II]**

50 A plane electromagnetic wave of frequency 500 MHz is travelling in vacuum along y-direction. At a particular point in space and time, $\mathbf{B} = 8.0 \times 10^{-8}\,\hat{\mathbf{z}}$T. The value of electric field at this point is

(speed of light $= 3 \times 10^8$ ms^{-1};

$\hat{\mathbf{x}}, \hat{\mathbf{y}}, \hat{\mathbf{z}}$ are unit vectors along x, y and z-direction). **[2021, 16 March Shift-I]**

(a) $-24\hat{x}$ V/m (b) $2.6\hat{x}$ V/m

(c) $24\hat{x}$ V/m (d) $-2.6\hat{x}$ V/m

51 For an electromagnetic wave travelling in free space, the relation between average energy densities due to electric (U_e) and magnetic (U_m) fields is **[2021, 16 March Shift-I]**

(a) $U_e = U_m$ (b) $U_e > U_m$
(c) $U_e < U_m$ (d) $U_e \neq U_m$

52 A radiation is emitted by 1000 W bulb and it generates an electric field and magnetic field at P, placed at a distance of 2 m. The efficiency of the bulb is 1.25%. The value of peak electric field at P is $x \times 10^{-1}$ V/m. Value of x is .... (Rounded-off to the nearest integer)
[Take, $\varepsilon_0 = 8.85 \times 10^{-12}\ C^2N^{-1}m^{-2}, c = 3 \times 10^8\ ms^{-1}$] **[2021, 26 Feb Shift-I]**

53 The peak electric field produced by the radiation coming from the 8 W bulb at a distance of 10 m is $\frac{x}{10}\sqrt{\frac{\mu_0 c}{\pi}}\frac{V}{m}$. The efficiency of the bulb is 10% and it is a point source. The value of x is .... **[2021, 25 Feb Shift-II]**

54 An electromagnetic wave of frequency 3 GHz enters a dielectric medium of relative electric permittivity 2.25 from vacuum. The wavelength of this wave in that medium will be .... $\times 10^{-2}$ cm. **[2021, 24 Feb Shift-II]**

55 An electromagnetic wave of frequency 5 GHz, is travelling in a medium whose relative electric permittivity and relative magnetic permeability both are 2. Its velocity in this medium is ...... $\times 10^7$ m/s. **[2021, 24 Feb 2021 Shift-I]**

56 Match List-I with List-II.

	List-I		List-II
A.	Source of microwave frequency	1.	Radioactive decay of nucleus
B.	Source of infrared frequency	2.	Magnetron
C.	Source of gamma rays	3.	Inner shell electrons
D.	Source of X-rays	4.	Vibration of atoms and molecules
		5.	LASER
		6.	R-C circuit

Choose the correct answer from the options given below. **[2021, 24 Feb Shift-II]**

	A	B	C	D		A	B	C	D
(a)	6	4	1	5	(b)	6	5	1	4
(c)	2	4	6	3	(d)	2	4	1	3

57 A plane electromagnetic wave, has frequency of 2.0×10^{10} Hz and its energy density is $1.02 \times 10^{-8}\ J/m^3$ in vacuum. The amplitude of the magnetic field of the wave is close to
(Take, $\frac{1}{4\pi\varepsilon_0} = 9 \times 10^9 \frac{Nm^2}{C^2}$ and speed of light $= 3 \times 10^8\ ms^{-1}$) **[2020, 2 Sep Shift-I]**

(a) 190 nT (b) 160 nT (c) 180 nT (d) 150 nT

58 In a plane electromagnetic wave, the directions of electric field and magnetic field are represented by $\hat{\mathbf{K}}$ and $2\hat{\mathbf{i}} - 2\hat{\mathbf{j}}$, respectively. What is the unit vector along direction of propagation of the wave? **[2020, 2 Sep Shift-II]**

(a) $\frac{1}{\sqrt{2}}(\hat{i} + \hat{j})$ (b) $\frac{1}{\sqrt{2}}(\hat{j} + \hat{k})$
(c) $\frac{1}{\sqrt{5}}(\hat{i} + 2\hat{j})$ (d) $\frac{1}{\sqrt{5}}(2\hat{i} + \hat{j})$

59 The magnetic field of a plane electromagnetic wave is $\mathbf{B} = 3 \times 10^{-8} \sin[200\pi(y + ct)]\hat{\mathbf{i}}$ T, where $c = 3 \times 10^8\ ms^{-1}$ is the speed of light. The corresponding electric field is **[2020, 3 Sep Shift-I]**

(a) $E = 9\sin[200\pi(y + ct)]\hat{k}$ V/m
(b) $E = -10^{-6}\sin[200\pi(y + ct)]\hat{k}$ V/m
(c) $E = 3 \times 10^{-8}\sin[200\pi(y + ct)]\hat{k}$ V/m
(d) $E = -9\sin[200\pi(y + ct)]\hat{k}$ V/m

60 The electric field of a plane electromagnetic wave propagating along the x-direction in vacuum is $\mathbf{E} = E_0\hat{\mathbf{j}}\cos(\omega t - kx)$. The magnetic field $\mathbf{B}$, at the moment $t = 0$ is **[2020, 3 Sep Shift-II]**

(a) $B = E_0\sqrt{\mu_0\varepsilon_0}\cos(kx)\hat{j}$ (b) $B = \frac{E_0}{\sqrt{\mu_0\varepsilon_0}}\cos(kx)\hat{j}$
(c) $B = \frac{E_0}{\sqrt{\mu_0\varepsilon_0}}\cos(kx)\hat{k}$ (d) $B = E_0\sqrt{\mu_0\varepsilon_0}\cos(kx)\hat{k}$

61 The electric field of a plane electromagnetic wave is given by $\mathbf{E} = E_0(\hat{\mathbf{x}} + \hat{\mathbf{y}})\sin(kz - \omega t)$
Its magnetic field will be given by **[2020, 4 Sep Shift-II]**

(a) $\frac{E_0}{c}(\hat{x} + \hat{y})\sin(kz - \omega t)$ (b) $\frac{E_0}{c}(-\hat{x} + \hat{y})\sin(kz - \omega t)$
(c) $\frac{E_0}{c}(\hat{x} - \hat{y})\sin(kz - \omega t)$ (d) $\frac{E_0}{c}(\hat{x} - \hat{y})\cos(kz - \omega t)$

62 An electron is constrained to move along the Y-axis with a speed of 0.1 c (c is the speed of light) in the presence of electromagnetic wave, w4hose electric field is $\mathbf{E} = 30\hat{\mathbf{j}}\sin(1.5 \times 10^7 t - 5 \times 10^{-2}x)$ V/m.

The maximum magnetic force experienced by the electron will be

(Given, $c = 3 \times 10^8\ ms^{-1}$ and electron charge $= 1.6 \times 10^{-19}$ C) **[2020, 5 Sep Shift-I]**

(a) 2.4×10^{-18} N (b) 4.8×10^{-19} N

(c) 1.6×10^{-19} N (d) 3.2×10^{-18} N

63 Suppose that intensity of a laser is $\left(\frac{315}{\pi}\right)$ W/m^2. The rms electric field (in V/m) associated with this source is close to the nearest integer is ..... . (Take, $\varepsilon_0 = 8.86 \times 10^{-12}\ C^2Nm^{-2}$ and $c = 3 \times 10^8\ ms^{-1}$) **[2020, 6 Sep Shift-I]**

64 For a plane electromagnetic wave, the magnetic field at a point x and time t is

$\mathbf{B}(x, t) = [1.2 \times 10^{-7} \sin(0.5 \times 10^3 x + 1.5 \times 10^{11} t)\hat{\mathbf{k}}]$ T

The instantaneous electric field **E** corresponding to **B** is (Given, speed of light, $c = 3 \times 10^8$ m / s) **[2020, 6 Sep Shift-II]**

(a) $E(x, t) = [-36 \sin(0.5 \times 10^3 x + 1.5 \times 10^{11} t)\hat{j}]\frac{V}{m}$

(b) $E(x, t) = [36 \sin(1 \times 10^3 x + 0.5 \times 10^{11} t)\hat{j}]\frac{V}{m}$

(c) $E(x, t) = [36 \sin(0.5 \times 10^3 x + 1.5 \times 10^{11} t)\hat{k}]\frac{V}{m}$

(d) $E(x, t) = [36 \sin(1 \times 10^3 x + 1.5 \times 10^{11} t)\hat{j}]\frac{V}{m}$

65 If the magnetic field in a plane electromagnetic wave is given by

$\mathbf{B} = 3 \times 10^{-8} \sin(1.6 \times 10^3 x + 48 \times 10^{10} t)\hat{\mathbf{j}}$T, then what will be expression for electric field? **[2020, 7 Jan Shift-I]**

(a) $E = 60 \sin(1.6 \times 10^3 x + 48 \times 10^{10} t)\hat{k}$ V/m

(b) $E = 3 \times 10^{-8} \sin(1.6 \times 10^3 x + 48 \times 10^{10} t)\hat{i}$ V/m

(c) $E = 3 \times 10^{-8} \sin(1.6 \times 10^3 x + 48 \times 10^{10} t)\hat{j}$ V/m

(d) $E = 9 \sin(1.6 \times 10^3 x + 48 \times 10^{10} t)\hat{k}$V/m

66 The electric field of a plane electromagnetic wave is given by

$$\mathbf{E} = E_0 \frac{\hat{i} + \hat{j}}{\sqrt{2}} \cos(kz + \omega t)$$

At $t = 0$, a positively charged particle is at the point $(x, y, z) = (0, 0, \pi/k)$.

If its instantaneous velocity at $(t = 0)$ is $v_0\hat{\mathbf{k}}$, the force acting on it due to the wave is **[2020, 7 Jan Shift-II]**

(a) zero (b) antiparallel to $\frac{\hat{i} + \hat{j}}{\sqrt{2}}$

(c) parallel to $\frac{\hat{i} + \hat{j}}{\sqrt{2}}$ (d) parallel to $\hat{k}$

67 A plane electromagnetic wave of frequency 25 GHz is propagating in vacuum along the z-direction. At a particular point in space and time, the magnetic field is given by $\mathbf{B} = 5 \times 10^{-8}\ \hat{\mathbf{j}}$ T. The corresponding electric field **E** is (speed of light, $c = 3 \times 10^8\ ms^{-1}$) **[2020, 8 Jan Shift-II]**

(a) $-1.66 \times 10^{-16}\ \hat{i}$ V/m

(b) $1.66 \times 10^{-16}\ \hat{i}$ V/m

(c) $-15\hat{i}$ V/m

(d) $15\ \hat{i}$ V/m

68 A plane electromagnetic wave is propagating along the direction $\frac{\hat{i} + \hat{j}}{\sqrt{2}}$ with its polarisation along the direction $\hat{\mathbf{k}}$. The correct form of the magnetic field of the wave would be (here B_0 is an appropriate constant) **[2020, 9 Jan Shift-II]**

(a) $B_0\hat{k}\cos\left(\omega t - k\frac{\hat{i} + \hat{j}}{\sqrt{2}}\right)$

(b) $B_0\frac{\hat{j} - \hat{i}}{\sqrt{2}}\cos\left(\omega t + k\frac{\hat{i} + \hat{j}}{\sqrt{2}}\right)$

(c) $B_0\frac{\hat{i} - \hat{j}}{\sqrt{2}}\cos\left(\omega t - k\frac{\hat{i} + \hat{j}}{\sqrt{2}}\right)$

(d) $B_0\frac{\hat{i} + \hat{j}}{\sqrt{2}}\cos\left(\omega t - k\frac{\hat{i} + \hat{j}}{\sqrt{2}}\right)$

69 Choose the correct option relating wavelengths of different parts of electromagnetic wave spectrum **[2020, 4 Sep Shift-I]**

(a) $\lambda_{\text{X-rays}} < \lambda_{\text{microwaves}} < \lambda_{\text{radio waves}} < \lambda_{\text{visible}}$

(b) $\lambda_{\text{visible}} > \lambda_{\text{X-rays}} > \lambda_{\text{radio waves}} > \lambda_{\text{microwaves}}$

(c) $\lambda_{\text{radio waves}} > \lambda_{\text{microwaves}} > \lambda_{\text{visible}} > \lambda_{\text{X-rays}}$

(d) $\lambda_{\text{visible}} < \lambda_{\text{microwaves}} < \lambda_{\text{radio waves}} < \lambda_{\text{X-rays}}$

70 The correct match between the entries in table are **[2020, 5 Sep Shift-II]**

	Column I (Radiation)		Column II (Wavelength)
(A)	Microwaves	(I)	100 m
(B)	γ-rays	(II)	10^{-15} m
(C)	AM radiowaves	(III)	10^{-10} m
(D)	X-rays	(IV)	10^{-3} m

	A	B	C	D
(a)	II	I	IV	III
(b)	I	III	IV	II
(c)	III	II	I	IV
(d)	IV	II	I	III

71 A plane electromagnetic wave travels in free space along the *x*-direction. The electric field component of the wave at a particular point of space and time is $E = 6\text{Vm}^{-1}$ along *y*-direction. Its corresponding magnetic field component, *B* would be **[2019, 8 April Shift-I]**

(a) 2×10^{-8} T along *z* - direction
(b) 6×10^{-8} T along *x* - direction
(c) 6×10^{-8} T along *z* - direction
(d) 2×10^{-8} T along *y* - direction

72 The magnetic field of an electromagnetic wave is given by

$\mathbf{B} = 1.6 \times 10^{-6} \cos(2 \times 10^7 z + 6 \times 10^{15} t)(2\hat{\mathbf{i}} + \hat{\mathbf{j}})\, \text{Wbm}^{-2}$

The associated electric field will be **[2019, 8 April Shift-II]**

(a) $E = 4.8 \times 10^2 \cos(2 \times 10^7 z - 6 \times 10^{15} t)(-2\hat{j} + \hat{i})\, \text{Vm}^{-1}$
(b) $E = 4.8 \times 10^2 \cos(2 \times 10^7 z - 6 \times 10^{15} t)(2\hat{j} + \hat{i})\, \text{Vm}^{-1}$
(c) $E = 4.8 \times 10^2 \cos(2 \times 10^7 z + 6 \times 10^{15} t)(\hat{i} - 2\hat{j})\, \text{Vm}^{-1}$
(d) $E = 4.8 \times 10^2 \cos(2 \times 10^7 z + 6 \times 10^{15} t)(-\hat{i} + 2\hat{j})\text{Vm}^{-1}$

73 50 W/m^2 energy density of sunlight is normally incident on the surface of a solar panel. Some part of incident energy (25%) is reflected from the surface and the rest is absorbed. The force exerted on 1 m^2 surface area will be close to ($c = 3 \times 10^8$ m/s) **[2019, 9 April Shift-II]**

(a) 20×10^{-8} N (b) 35×10^{-8} N
(c) 15×10^{-8} N (d) 10×10^{-8} N

74 Light is incident normally on a completely absorbing surface with an energy flux of 25 W cm^{-2}. If the surface has an area of 25 cm^2, the momentum transferred to the surface in 40 min time duration will be **[2019, 10 April Shift-II]**

(a) 3.5×10^{-6} N-s
(b) 6.3×10^{-4} N-s
(c) 1.4×10^{-6} N-s
(d) 5.0×10^{-3} N-s

75 The magnetic field of a plane electromagnetic wave is given by

$\mathbf{B} = B_0[\cos(kz - \omega t)]\hat{\mathbf{i}} + B_1 \cos(kz + \omega t)\hat{\mathbf{j}}$

where, $B_0 = 3 \times 10^{-5}$ T and $B_1 = 2 \times 10^{-6}$ T. The rms value of the force experienced by a stationary charge $Q = 10^{-4}$ C at $z = 0$ is closest to **[2019, 9 April Shift-I]**

(a) 0.1 N (b) 3×10^{-2} N
(c) 0.6 N (d) 0.9 N

76 The electric field of a plane electromagnetic wave is given by

$$\mathbf{E} = E_0 \hat{\mathbf{i}} \cos(kz) \cos(\omega t)$$

The corresponding magnetic field **B** is then given by **[2019, 10 April Shift-I]**

(a) $B = \frac{E_0}{C} \hat{j} \sin(kz) \sin(\omega t)$
(b) $B = \frac{E_0}{C} \hat{j} \sin(kz) \cos(\omega t)$
(c) $B = \frac{E_0}{C} \hat{k} \sin(kz) \cos(\omega t)$
(d) $B = \frac{E_0}{C} \hat{j} \cos(kz) \sin(\omega t)$

77 An electromagnetic wave is represented by the electric field $\mathbf{E} = E_0 \hat{\mathbf{n}} \sin[\omega t + (6y - 8z)]$. Taking unit vectors in *x*, *y* and *z*- directions to be $\hat{\mathbf{i}}, \hat{\mathbf{j}}, \hat{\mathbf{k}}$, the direction of propagation $\hat{\mathbf{s}}$, is **[2019, 12 April Shift-I]**

(a) $\hat{s} = \frac{3\hat{i} - 4\hat{j}}{5}$ (b) $\hat{s} = \frac{-4\hat{k} + 3\hat{j}}{5}$
(c) $\hat{s} = \left(\frac{-3\hat{j} + 4\hat{k}}{5}\right)$ (d) $\hat{s} = \frac{4\hat{j} - 3\hat{k}}{5}$

78 A plane electromagnetic wave having a frequency $\nu = 23.9$ GHz propagates along the positive *z* -direction in free space. The peak value of the electric field is 60 V/m. Which among the following is the acceptable magnetic field component in the electromagnetic wave? **[2019, 12 April Shift-II]**

(a) $B = 2 \times 10^7 \sin(0.5 \times 10^3 z + 1.5 \times 10^{11} t)\, \hat{i}$
(b) $B = 2 \times 10^{-7} \sin(0.5 \times 10^3 z - 1.5 \times 10^{11} t)\, \hat{i}$
(c) $B = 60 \sin(0.5 \times 10^3 x + 1.5 \times 10^{11} t)\hat{k}$
(d) $B = 2 \times 10^{-7} \sin(1.5 \times 10^2 x + 0.5 \times 10^{11} t)\, \hat{j}$

79 A plane electromagnetic wave of frequency 50 MHz travels in free space along the positive *x* - direction. At a particular point in space and time, $\mathbf{E} = 6.3\, \hat{\mathbf{j}}$ V/m. The corresponding magnetic field **B**, at that point will be **[2019, 9 Jan Shift-I]**

(a) $18.9 \times 10^8 \hat{k}$ T
(b) $6.3 \times 10^{-8} \hat{k}$ T
(c) $18.9 \times 10^{-8} \hat{k}$ T
(d) $2.1 \times 10^{-8} \hat{k}$ T

80 In free space, the energy of electromagnetic wave in electric field is U_E and in magnetic field is U_B. Then **[2019, 9 Jan Shift-II]**

(a) $U_E = U_B$ (b) $U_E > U_B$
(c) $U_E < U_B$ (d) $U_E = U_B / 2$

81 If the magnetic field of a plane electromagnetic wave is given by

$B = 100 \times 10^{-6} \sin\left[2\pi \times 2 \times 10^{15}\left(t - \frac{x}{c}\right)\right]$ then the maximum electric field associated with it is (Take, the speed of light $= 3 \times 10^8$ m/s) **[2019, 10 Jan Shift-I]**

(a) 6×10^4 N/C (b) 4×10^4 N/C

(c) 3×10^4 N/C (d) 4.5×10^4 N/C

82 The electric field of a plane polarised electromagnetic wave in free space at time $t = 0$ is given by an expression.

$$\mathbf{E}(x, y) = 10\hat{\mathbf{j}} \cos[(6x + 8z)]$$

The magnetic field $\mathbf{B}(x, z, t)$ is given by (where, c is the velocity of light) **[2019, 10 Jan Shift-II]**

(a) $\frac{1}{c}(6\hat{k} - 8\hat{i}) \cos[(6x + 8z + 10ct)]$

(b) $\frac{1}{c}(6\hat{k} - 8\hat{i}) \cos[(6x + 8z - 10ct)]$

(c) $\frac{1}{c}(6\hat{k} + 8\hat{i}) \cos[(6x - 8z + 10ct)]$

(d) $\frac{1}{c}(6\hat{k} + 8\hat{i}) \cos[(6x + 8z - 10ct)]$

83 An electromagnetic wave of intensity 50 Wm^{-2} enters in a medium of refractive index 'n' without any loss. The ratio of the magnitudes of electric fields and the ratio of the magnitudes of magnetic fields of the wave before and after entering into the medium are respectively, given by **[2019, 11 Jan Shift-I]**

(a) $\left(\frac{1}{\sqrt{n}}, \sqrt{n}\right)$ (b) $(\sqrt{n}, \sqrt{n})$

(c) $\left(\frac{1}{\sqrt{n}}, \frac{1}{\sqrt{n}}\right)$ (d) $\left(\sqrt{n}, \frac{1}{\sqrt{n}}\right)$

84 A 27 mW laser beam has a cross-sectional area of 10 mm^2. The magnitude of the maximum electric field in this electromagnetic wave is given by [Take, permittivity of space, $\varepsilon_0 = 9 \times 10^{-12}$ SI units and speed of light, $c = 3 \times 10^8$ m/s] **[2019, 11 Jan Shift-II]**

(a) 1 kV/m (b) 0.7 kV/m

(c) 2 kV/m (d) 1.4 kV/m

85 A light wave is incident normally on a glass slab of refractive index 1.5. If 4% of light gets reflected and the amplitude of the electric field of the incident light is 30 V/m, then the amplitude of the electric field for the wave propogating in the glass medium will be **[2019, 12 Jan Shift-I]**

(a) 30 V/m (b) 6 V/m

(c) 10 V/m (d) 24 V/m

JEE Advanced

1 The electric field associated with an electromagnetic wave propagating in a dielectric medium is given by

$$\mathbf{E} = 30(2\hat{\mathbf{x}} + \hat{\mathbf{y}}) \sin\left[2\pi\left(5 \times 10^{14} t - \frac{10^7}{3} z\right)\right] \text{Vm}^{-1}.$$

Which of he following option(s) is (are) correct? [Given : The speed of light in vacuum, $c = 3 \times 10^8\ \text{ms}^{-1}$] **(2023)**

(a) $B_x = -2 \times 10^{-7} \sin\left[2\pi\left(5 \times 10^{14} t - \frac{10^7}{3} z\right)\right]$ Wb m^{-2}

(b) $B_y = 2 \times 10^{-7} \sin\left[2\pi\left(5 \times 10^{14} t = \frac{10^7}{3} z\right)\right]$ Wb m^{-2}

(c) The wave is polarised in the XY-plane with polarisation angle 30° with respect to the X-axis

(d) The refractive index of the medium is 2.

Answer Key

Level 1

8.1 Displacement Current

1. 0.07 A
2. 5 μA
3. 1.5×10^{-8} A opposite to the direction of conduction current, 0
4. 0.74×10^{-13} T
5. (i) 8 μA (ii) Yes (iii) 11.31 μA (iv) 4.525×10^{-12} T

8.2 Properties of EM Waves

1. 2.25
2. $B = (2.1 \times 10^{-8}\ \text{T})\hat{k}$
3. (i) 1.26 cm, 23.9 GHz
   (ii) $E_z = 60 \sin(0.5 \times 10^3 x + 1.5 \times 10^{11} t)$ V/m
4. 1.2×10^{-6} N
5. 8.85×10^{-12} Jm^{-3}, 8.85×10^{-12} Jm^{-3}
6. 5.5×10^{-12} J
7. $E_0 = 4.07$ V/m, $B_0 = 1.36 \times 10^{-8}$ T

Level 2

Single Choice Correct Questions

1. (a)	2. (a)	3. (c)	4. (c)	5. (a)	6. (a)	7. (b)	8. (b)	9. (a)	10. (c)
11. (c)	12. (b)	13. (c)	14. (b)	15. (b)	16. (d)	17. (d)	18. (b)	19. (b)	20. (a)
21. (b)	22. (c)	23. (d)	24. (c)	25. (b)	26. (b)	27. (d)	28. (b)	29. (a)	30. (d)
31. (b)	32. (b)	33. (b)	34. (d)	35. (d)					

Previous years Questions

JEE Main

1. (a)	2. (d)	3. (b)	4. (a)	5. (d)	6. (c)	7. (c)	8. (a)	9. (b)	10. (d)
11. (a)	12. (c)	13. (a)	14. (b)	15. (c)	16. (4)	17. (5)	18. (a)	19. (d)	20. (a)
21. (84)	22. (d)	23. (c)	24. (d)	25. (c)	26. (a)	27. (8)	28. (43)	29. (b)	30. (c)
31. (d)	32. (a)	33. (b)	34. (*)	35. (a)	36. (a)	37. (c)	38. (500)	39. (2)	40. (c)
41. (354)	42. (c)	43. (d)	44. (a)	45. (d)	46. (c)	47. (c)	48. (3)	49. (6)	50. (a)
51. (a)	52. (137)	53. (2)	54. (667)	55. (15)	56. (d)	57. (b)	58. (a)	59. (d)	60. (d)
61. (b)	62. (b)	63. (194)	64. (a)	65. (d)	66. (b)	67. (d)	68. (c)	69. (c)	70. (d)
71. (a)	72. (c)	73. (a)	74. (d)	75. (c)	76. (a)	77. (c)	78. (b)	79. (d)	80. (a)
81. (c)	82. (b)	83. (d)	84. (d)	85. (d)					

JEE Advanced

1. (a, d)

SOLUTIONS

Level 1

8.1 Displacement Current

1. $i_d = \varepsilon_0 \dfrac{d\phi}{dt} = \varepsilon_0 \dfrac{d(EA)}{dt} = A\varepsilon_0 \dfrac{dE}{dt}$

$= 3.14 \times (0.05)^2 \times 8.85 \times 10^{-12} \times 10^{12}$

$= 0.07$ A

2. $\phi = EA \Rightarrow \phi = \dfrac{VA}{d} \Rightarrow \phi = \dfrac{CV}{\varepsilon_0}$

$i_d = \varepsilon_0 \dfrac{d\phi}{dt} = \varepsilon_0 \left(\dfrac{C}{\varepsilon_0}\right)\dfrac{dV}{dt} = 1 \times 10^{-6} \times 5 = 5\,\mu A$

3. $i_d = \varepsilon_0 \dfrac{d\phi}{dt} = \dfrac{\varepsilon_0 d(EA)}{dt}$

$= \varepsilon_0 A \dfrac{d}{dt}\left(\dfrac{q}{A\varepsilon_0}\right) = \dfrac{dq}{dt} = 1.5 \times 10^{-8}$ A

As electric field is decreasing due to loss of charge, direction of displacement current is opposite of the direction of conduction current. So, total current will be zero. Hence, magnetic field will be zero between the plates.

4. $i_d = i_c = \dfrac{V}{R} e^{-\frac{t}{RC}} = \dfrac{2}{10^6} e^{-\frac{10^{-3}}{10^6 \times 10^{-9}}}$

$= 0.74 \times 10^{-6}$ A

Using Ampere-Maxwell law,

$\oint \mathbf{B} \cdot \mathbf{dl} = \mu_0 (i_c + i_d)$

$\Rightarrow B(2\pi r) = \mu_0 \left(0 + \dfrac{i_d}{\pi R^2} \pi r^2\right)$

$\Rightarrow B = \dfrac{\mu_0 i_d r}{2\pi R^2} = \dfrac{4\pi \times 10^{-7} \times 0.74 \times 10^{-6} \times 0.5}{2\pi (1)^2}$

$= 0.74 \times 10^{-13}$ T

5. (i) $i_c = \dfrac{V}{X_L} = (\omega C)\,V = 200 \times 200 \times 10^{-12} \times 200 = 8\,\mu A$

(ii) Yes, $i_c = i_d$

(iii) $i_d = \sqrt{2} i_c = 11.31\,\mu A$

(iv) Using Ampere-Maxwell law

$\oint \mathbf{B} \cdot \mathbf{dl} = \mu_0 (i_c + i_d)$

$\Rightarrow B(2\pi (0.02)) = \mu_0 \left[0 + \left(\dfrac{11.31 \times 10^{-6}}{\pi (0.1)^2}\right) \times \pi (0.02)^2\right]$

$\Rightarrow \quad B = 4.525 \times 10^{-12}$ T

8.2 Properties of EM Waves

1. $v = \dfrac{c}{\sqrt{\mu_r \varepsilon_r}} \Rightarrow 2 \times 10^8 = \dfrac{3 \times 10^8}{\sqrt{1 \times \varepsilon_r}} \Rightarrow \varepsilon_r = 2.25$

2. $\dfrac{E}{B} = c \Rightarrow B = \dfrac{E}{c} = \dfrac{6.3}{3 \times 10^8} = 2.1 \times 10^{-8}$ T

Direction of propagation $= \hat{\mathbf{E}} \times \hat{\mathbf{B}} \Rightarrow \hat{\mathbf{i}} = \hat{\mathbf{j}} \times \mathbf{B} \Rightarrow \hat{\mathbf{B}} = \hat{\mathbf{k}}$

$\mathbf{B} = (2.1 \times 10^{-8}\ \text{T})\,\hat{\mathbf{k}}$

3. (i) $\lambda = \dfrac{2\pi}{k} = \dfrac{2\pi}{0.5 \times 10^3} = 1.26$ cm

$f = \dfrac{\omega}{2\pi} = \dfrac{1.5 \times 10^{11}}{2\pi} = 23.9$ GHz

(ii) $\dfrac{E}{B} = c \Rightarrow E = Bc = 2 \times 10^{-7} \times 3 \times 10^8 = 60$ V/m

Direction of propagation $= \hat{\mathbf{E}} \times \hat{\mathbf{B}}$

$\Rightarrow -\hat{\mathbf{i}} = \hat{\mathbf{E}} \times \hat{\mathbf{j}} \Rightarrow \hat{\mathbf{E}} = \hat{\mathbf{k}}$

So, $E_z = 60 \sin(0.5 \times 10^3 x + 1.5 \times 10^{11} t)$

4. $F = \dfrac{IA}{c} = \dfrac{18 \times 10^4 \times 20 \times 10^{-4}}{3 \times 10^8} = 1.2 \times 10^{-6}$ N

5. $u_E = \dfrac{1}{2}\varepsilon_0 E^2; \langle u_E \rangle = \dfrac{1}{2}\varepsilon_0 \langle E^2 \rangle$

$= \dfrac{1}{2} \times 8.85 \times 10^{-12} \times (\sqrt{2})^2$

$= 8.85 \times 10^{-12}$ Jm^{-3}

$u_B = u_E = 8.85 \times 10^{-12}$ Jm^{-3}

6. $u_{avg} = \dfrac{1}{2}\varepsilon_0 E_0^2 = \dfrac{1}{2} \times 8.85 \times 10^{-12} \times (50)^2 = 1.1 \times 10^{-8}$ Jm^{-3}

Energy $= u_{avg} \times V = (1.1 \times 10^{-8}) \times (10 \times 10^{-4} \times 50 \times 10^{-2})$

$= 5.5 \times 10^{-12}$ J

7. $I = \dfrac{P}{4\pi r^2} = \dfrac{100 \times \left(\dfrac{2.5}{100}\right)}{4 \times 3.14 \times 3^2} = 0.022$ W/m^2

Half of this intensity is produced by the electric field and half by the magnetic field.

$\dfrac{I}{2} = \dfrac{1}{2}\varepsilon_0 E_{rms}^2 C \Rightarrow E_{rms} = 2.9$ V/m

$E_0 = \sqrt{2}\, E_{rms} = 4.07$ V/m

$B_0 = \dfrac{E_0}{c} = 1.36 \times 10^{-8}$ T

Level 2

Single Choice Correct Questions

1. $i_d = \varepsilon_0 \frac{d\phi_E}{dt}$ **2.** (a) $i_d = i_c = 1\text{ A}$

3. $i_d = i$

Displacement current through area $\frac{A}{4} = \frac{i}{A} \times \left(\frac{A}{4}\right) = \frac{i}{4}$

4. $q = CV \Rightarrow \frac{dq}{dt} = C\frac{dV}{dt} = \frac{A\varepsilon_0}{d}\frac{dV}{dt}$

$$= \frac{3.14 \times (2\times 10^{-2})^2 \times 8.85 \times 10^{-12}}{0.1 \times 10^{-3}} \times 5 \times 10$$

$= 5.56 \times 10^3$ A

5. $i_d = \varepsilon_0 \frac{d\phi_E}{dt} = \varepsilon_0 \frac{d(EA)}{dt} = \frac{A\varepsilon_0}{d}\frac{dV}{dt} = 2\times 10^{-12} \times 10^{12} = 2\text{ A}$

6. $i_d = i_c = \frac{V}{X_C} = (\omega C)V$

If ω increases, then both i_d and i_c will increase.

7. $\frac{E}{B} = c \Rightarrow E = cB$

8. Direction of propagation $= \mathbf{E} \times \hat{\mathbf{B}}$

$\hat{\mathbf{j}} = \hat{\mathbf{k}} \times \hat{\mathbf{i}}$

9. **E** and **B** oscillate in phase.

10. $\frac{E}{B} = c \Rightarrow B = \frac{E}{c} = \frac{480}{3\times 10^8} = 1.6 \times 10^{-6}\text{ Wb/m}^2$

11. Direction of propagation is along $\mathbf{E} \times \mathbf{B}$.

12. $v = \frac{c}{\sqrt{\mu_r \varepsilon_r}} \Rightarrow$ Refractive index $= \sqrt{\mu_r \varepsilon_r} = \sqrt{\frac{\mu\varepsilon}{\mu_0 \varepsilon_0}}$

13. $\frac{E_0}{B_0} = v = \frac{\omega}{k} \Rightarrow E_0 k = B_0 \omega$

14. $B = \frac{E}{c} \Rightarrow B = \frac{6.3}{3\times 10^8} = 2.1 \times 10^{-8}$ T

$\mathbf{v} = \mathbf{E} \times \mathbf{B} \Rightarrow \hat{\mathbf{i}} = \hat{\mathbf{j}} \times \hat{\mathbf{B}} \Rightarrow \hat{\mathbf{B}} = \hat{\mathbf{k}}$

$\mathbf{B} = 2.1 \times 10^{-8}$ T $(\hat{\mathbf{k}})$

15. $\hat{\mathbf{v}} = \hat{\mathbf{E}} \times \hat{\mathbf{B}} = \hat{\mathbf{j}} \times \hat{\mathbf{i}} = -\hat{\mathbf{k}}$

16. $v = \frac{c}{\sqrt{\mu_r \varepsilon_r}}$

18. $\mathbf{B} \perp \mathbf{E}$

19. $\frac{E}{B} = c \Rightarrow E = cB = 3\times 10^8 \times 100 \times 10^{-6} = 3 \times 10^4$ N/C

$\hat{\mathbf{v}} = \hat{\mathbf{E}} \times \hat{\mathbf{B}} \Rightarrow \hat{\mathbf{i}} = \hat{\mathbf{E}} \times \hat{\mathbf{j}} \Rightarrow \hat{\mathbf{E}} = -\hat{\mathbf{k}}$

So, $\mathbf{E} = 3\times 10^{10}\ \mu\text{N/C} \sin\left[2\times 10^5\left(t - \frac{x}{c}\right)\right](-\hat{\mathbf{k}})$

20. γ-rays have least wavelength.

23. $b > a > c$

26. $i_{avg} = \frac{1}{2}\varepsilon_0 E_0^2 c = \frac{1}{2} \times 8.85 \times 10^{-12} \times (36)^2 \times 3 \times 10^8$

$= 1.72\text{ W/m}^2$

27. $u_E = \frac{1}{2}\varepsilon_0 E^2 = \frac{1}{2}\varepsilon_0 E_0^2 \sin^2(\omega t - kx)$

$< u_E > = \frac{1}{2}\varepsilon_0 E_0^2 \left(\frac{1}{2}\right) = \frac{1}{4}\varepsilon_0 E_0^2$

28. $i_{avg} = \frac{1}{2}\varepsilon_0 E_0^2 c = \frac{P_0}{4\pi r^2}$

$\Rightarrow \quad E_0 = \sqrt{\frac{P_0}{2\pi\varepsilon_0 c r^2}}$

29. $< u_E > = \frac{1}{4}\varepsilon_0 E_0^2 = \frac{1}{4} \times 8.85 \times 10^{-12} \times (1)^2$

$= 2.2 \times 10^{-12}\text{ J/m}^3$

30. $P = iA = 10^3 \times 160 = 1.6 \times 10^5$ W

31. $i = \frac{1}{2}\varepsilon_0 E_0^2 c = \frac{1}{2} \times 8.85 \times 10^{-12} \times E_0^2 \times 3 \times 10^8$

$\Rightarrow \quad \frac{500}{\pi} = \frac{1}{2}\varepsilon_0 E_0^2 (3\times 10^8)$

$\Rightarrow \quad \frac{1000}{\pi\varepsilon_0} = E_0^2(3\times 10^8)$

$\Rightarrow \quad 4000 \times 9 \times 10^9 = E_0^2(3\times 10^8)$

$\Rightarrow \quad E_0 = 2\sqrt{3} \times 10^2$ N/C

32. $H = \frac{B}{\mu_0} = \frac{3.33\times 10^{-7}}{4\pi \times 10^{-7}} = 0.265\text{ A-m}^{-1}$

Rate of energy flow per unit area $= \mathbf{E} \times \mathbf{H}$

$= 100(0.265) = 26.5\text{ V Am}^{-2}$

33. $I = \frac{P}{4\pi r^2} = \frac{100 \times \left(\frac{3}{100}\right)}{4\pi(5)^2} = 9.55 \times 10^{-3}\text{ W/m}^2$

$\frac{I}{2} = \frac{1}{2}\varepsilon_0 E_{rms}^2 c \Rightarrow \frac{9.55 \times 10^{-3}}{2}$

$= \frac{1}{2} \times 8.85 \times 10^{-12} E_{rms}^2 (3 \times 10^8)$

$\Rightarrow \quad E_{rms} = 1.89$ V/m

$E_0 = \sqrt{2}E_{rms} = 2.68$ V/m

34. Energy = Power × Time

$= 10 \times 10^{-3} \times \frac{90 \times 10^{-2}}{3 \times 10^8} = 3 \times 10^{-11}$ J

35. $F = \frac{2IA}{c} = \frac{2 \times 10 \times 20 \times 10^{-4}}{3 \times 10^8} = 1.33 \times 10^{-10}$ N

Previous Years Questions

JEE Main

1. EM wave

$$E = 200 \sin [1.5 \times 10^7 t - 0.05x] \frac{N}{C}$$

$$I = \frac{1}{2} \varepsilon_0 E_0^2 \cdot c = \frac{1}{2} \varepsilon_0 E_0^2 \cdot \left(\frac{\omega}{k}\right)$$

$$= \frac{1}{2} \times 8.85 \times 10^{-12} \times [200]^2 \times \frac{1.5 \times 10^7}{0.05}$$

$$I = 53.1 \text{ W/m}^2$$

2. Given, $I = 6 \times 10^8 \text{ W/m}^2$

$$\mu = 3$$

$$\text{Radiation pressure} = \frac{I}{v} = \frac{I\mu}{c} = \frac{6 \times 10^8 \times 3}{3 \times 10^8} = 6 \text{ N/m}^2$$

3. (1) Ampere-Maxwell's law,

$$\oint \mathbf{B} \cdot d\mathbf{l} = \mu_0 i_c + \mu_0 \varepsilon_0 d \frac{\phi_E}{dt}$$

(2) Faraday's law, $\oint \mathbf{E} \cdot d\mathbf{l} = d \frac{\phi_B}{dt}$

(3) Gauss' law for electricity,

$$\Rightarrow \quad \oint \mathbf{E} \cdot d\mathbf{A} = \frac{Q}{\varepsilon_0}$$

(4) Gauss' law for magnetism,

$$\oint \mathbf{B} \cdot d\mathbf{A} = 0$$

A-IV, B-III, C-I, D-II

4. Given,

$$f = 35 \text{ MHz} = 3.5 \times 10^7 \text{ Hz}$$

$$\mathbf{E} = 9.6 \hat{j} \text{ V/m}$$

$$\therefore \quad E = 9.6 \text{ V/m}$$

$$B = \frac{E}{c} = \frac{9.6}{3 \times 10^8} = 3.2 \times 10^{-8} \text{ T}$$

Since, EM wave is travelling along X-axis i.e., along $\hat{i}$.
Thus, magnetic field must be directed along $\hat{k}$ because E and B are perpendicular to each other and also perpendicular to the direction of propagation of EM wave.

$$\therefore \quad \mathbf{B} = 3.2 \times 10^{-8} \hat{k} \text{ T}$$

5. $\oint \mathbf{E} \cdot d\mathbf{l} = -\frac{\partial \phi_B}{\partial t}$

6. $\mathbf{E} \times \mathbf{B} = \hat{c}$, option (c) is correct

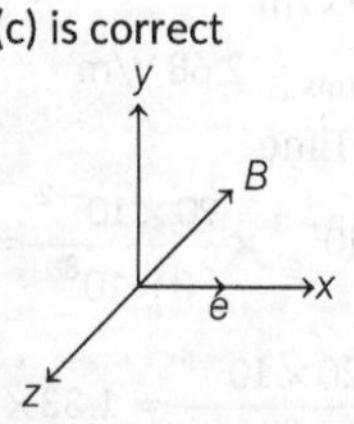

The direction of propagation of electromagnetic wave is negative Y-axis $(-\hat{j})$

7. Given,

$$E = 20 \sin\omega\left(t - \frac{x}{c}\right) \quad \text{...(i) [Given]}$$

$$E = E_0 \sin\omega\left(t - \frac{x}{c}\right) \quad \text{...(ii)}$$

On comparing Eqs. (i) and (ii), we get

$$E_0 = 20$$

$$\text{Energy density} = \frac{1}{2} \varepsilon_0 E_0^2 = \frac{1}{2} \times 8.85 \times 10^{-12} \times 400 \text{ J/m}^3$$

Energy contained in the given volumes

$$= 200 \times 8.85 \times 10^{-12} \times 5 \times 10^{-4}$$

$$= 8.85 \times 10^{-12} \times 10^{-4} \times 1000$$

$$= 8.85 \times 10^{-13} \text{ J}$$

8. For electromagnetic wave,
Average energy density,

$$U_E = \frac{1}{2} \varepsilon_0 E_{\text{rms}}^2 = \frac{1}{2} \varepsilon_0 \left(\frac{E_0}{\sqrt{2}}\right)^2$$

$$U_E = \frac{1}{4} \varepsilon_0 E_0^2$$

Where, E_0 is peak value of Electric field.
Total average energy density,

$$U_T = \frac{1}{2} \varepsilon_0 E_0^2$$

$$\text{Ratio, } \frac{U_E}{U_T} = \frac{1}{2}$$

9. A → IV, B → I, C → II, D → III
According to Gauss's law in electrostatics,

$$\phi = \oint \mathbf{E} \cdot dS = \frac{q}{\varepsilon_0}$$

According to Faraday's law,

$$\oint \mathbf{E} \cdot d\mathbf{l} = -\frac{d\phi_B}{dt}$$

According to Gauss's law in magnetism,

$$\oint \mathbf{B} \cdot d\mathbf{A} = 0$$

According to Ampere-Maxwell law,

$$\oint \mathbf{B} \cdot d\mathbf{l} = \mu_0 (I_c + I_d) = \mu_0 I_c + \mu_0 \varepsilon_0 \frac{d\phi_E}{dt}$$

10. A point source of 100 W emits light with 5% efficiency.
∴ Efficient power produced by point source,

$$P' = 5\% \text{ of } 100 \text{ W} = \frac{5}{100} \times 100 = 5 \text{ W}$$

At a distance, $r = 5$ m, intensity produced by point source.

$$I = \frac{P'}{4\pi r^2} = \frac{5}{4\pi \times 5^2} = \frac{1}{20\pi}$$

Since, $U_E = U_B$
Hence, intensity produced by the electric field component.

$$I_E = \frac{I}{2} = \frac{1}{2} \times \frac{1}{20\pi} = \frac{1}{40\pi} \text{ (W/m}^2\text{)}$$

11. As, $\frac{E_0}{B_0} = c = \frac{\omega}{k} \Rightarrow kE_0 = \omega B_0$

12. Magnetic field vector is perpendicular to both direction of propagation of electromagnetic wave and direction of electric field vector.

Also, $\frac{E}{B} = c$ and $\frac{\omega}{k} = c$

So, magnetic field vector can be given by

$$B = \frac{1}{\omega}(\mathbf{k} \times \mathbf{E}) \qquad \left(\because B = \frac{E}{c} = \frac{E}{\omega / k} = \frac{kE}{\omega} \right)$$

13. Electromagnetic wave is transporting energy in the negative z-direction. This means that EM wave is propagating along negative z-direction $(-\hat{k})$. Direction of electric field is given along $+y$-direction $(\hat{j})$.

Since, electric field vector and magnetic field vector are perpendicular to each other and also perpendicular to the direction of propagation of EM wave.

If $\hat{x}$ be the unit vector along the direction of magnetic field, then

$$\hat{j} \times \hat{x} = -\hat{k}$$

Clearly, $\hat{x} = \hat{i}$

14. Electromagnetic waves are photon stream and they are not deflected by electric or magnetic fields.

Also, $\frac{E_0}{B_0} = c = \frac{1}{\sqrt{\varepsilon_0 \mu_0}}$

15. Speed of light does not depend on the direction of propagation in vacuum.

Speed of light depends on wavelength of light in a medium.

Speed of light is independent of motion of source or intensity of source.

16. Radiation pressure over a perfectly reflecting surface is given by $p = \frac{2I}{c}$

Now, Intensity $I = \frac{\text{Energy}}{\text{Area} \times \text{time}} = \frac{\text{Power}}{\text{Area}}$

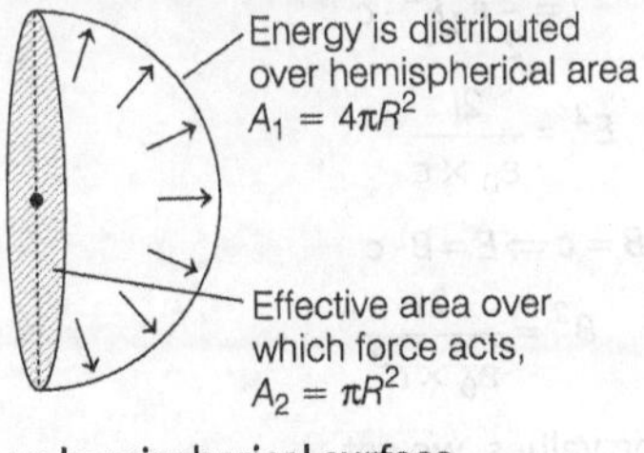

So, force on hemispherical surface,

$$F = p \times A_2 = \frac{2I}{c} \times A_2 = \frac{2(p / A_1) \times A_2}{c}$$

$$= \frac{2 \times 24 \times \pi R^2}{4\pi R^2 \times 3 \times 10^8} = 4 \times 10^{-8}\ \text{N}$$

17. Given that speed in medium, $v = 0.2\,c$

Refractive index, $n = \frac{c}{v}$

$$n = \frac{c}{0.2\,c} = 5$$

$\therefore \quad n = \sqrt{\mu_r \varepsilon_r}$

or $\quad n^2 = \mu_r \varepsilon_r$ or $\frac{\varepsilon_r}{n} = \frac{n}{\mu_r} = \frac{5}{1}$

On comparing with $\frac{\varepsilon_r}{n} = \frac{x}{1}$, we get

$$x = 5$$

18.

EM Wave	Wavelength range
Microwave	0.1 m to 1 mm
Ultraviolet	400 nm to 1 nm
X-rays	1 nm to 10^{-3} nm
Infrared	1 mm to 700 nm

Hence,

A$\rightarrow$ IV, B$\rightarrow$ I, C$\rightarrow$ II, D$\rightarrow$ III

19. Optical communication is performed in the frequency range of 1 THz to 1000 THz.

From microwave to UV range.

So, EM wave used for optical communication have shorter wavelength than that of microwaves used in RADAR.

Also, $\nu_{\text{infrared}} > \nu_{\text{microwave}}$

$\therefore$ Infrared EM waves are more energetic than microwave.

Hence, A is false and R is true.

20.

S.No.	Radiation		Production
A.	Microwave	IV.	Special electronic devices such as klystron tube.
B.	Gamma rays	I.	Due to decay of radioactive nuclei
C.	Radiowaves	II.	Oscillating circuits
D.	X-rays	III.	Due to transition of inner shell electrons

Thus, correct sequence from List I to List II is A-IV, B-I, C-II, D-III.

21. Effective power of light bulb converted into visible radiation,

$$P' = 10\% \text{ of } 110\ \text{W} = \frac{10}{100} \times 110\ \text{W} = 11\ \text{W}$$

Change in average intensities of visible radiation,

$$I_1 - I_2 = \frac{P'}{4\pi r_1^2} - \frac{P'}{4\pi r_2^2}$$

Here, $r_1 = 1$ m and $r_2 = 5$ m

$$= \frac{P'}{4\pi}\left(\frac{1}{r_1^2} - \frac{1}{r_2^2}\right) = \frac{11}{4\pi}\left(\frac{1}{1^2} - \frac{1}{5^2}\right) = \frac{11}{4 \times \frac{22}{7}}\left(\frac{24}{25}\right)$$

$$= \frac{7}{8} \times \frac{24}{25} = \frac{21}{25} = 0.84$$

$$= 84 \times 10^{-2}\ \text{W/m}^2 = a \times 10^{-2}\ \text{W/m}^2 \qquad \text{(given)}$$

$\therefore \quad a = 84$

22. Given, surface area, $A = 36\text{cm}^2 = 36 \times 10^{-4}\text{m}^2$

Force exerted, $F = 7.2 \times 10^{-9}$ N

Time period, $t = 20$ min

In case of complete absorption, the pressure exerted by incident light is

$$p = \frac{I}{c},$$

where, I = Energy flux of incident light.

$$\Rightarrow \quad \frac{F}{A} = \frac{I}{c}$$

$$\Rightarrow \quad I = \frac{Fc}{A} = \frac{7.2 \times 10^{-9} \times 3 \times 10^8}{36 \times 10^{-4}}$$

$$= 6 \times 10^2 \text{ or } 600 \text{ W/m}^2$$

So, energy flux of incident light is 600 W / m^2 or 0.06 W/cm^2

23. Electric field component of beam of light travelling along X-axis is given as

$$E_y = 900 \sin\omega\left(t - \frac{x}{c}\right)$$

Speed of charge moving along Y-axis,

$$v = 3 \times 10^7 \text{ m/s}$$

Speed of light, $c = 3 \times 10^8$ m/s

$$\therefore \quad \frac{\text{Electric force } (F_e)}{\text{Magnetic force } (F_m)} = \frac{qE}{Bqv}$$

$$\Rightarrow \quad \frac{F_e}{F_m} = \frac{E}{Bv} = \frac{E/B}{v} = \frac{c}{v} \quad \left(\because \frac{E}{B} = c\right)$$

$$= \frac{3 \times 10^8}{3 \times 10^7} = \frac{10}{1}$$

$$\Rightarrow \quad F_e : F_m = 10 : 1$$

24. The oscillating magnetic field in an EM wave is given as $B_y = 5 \times 10^{-6} \sin 1000\pi(5x - 4 \times 10^8 t)$ T

Amplitude of magnetic field, $B_0 = 5 \times 10^{-6}$ T

Here, speed of EM wave, $c = \omega / k$

$$= \frac{1000\pi \times 4 \times 10^8}{1000\pi \times 5} = 0.8 \times 10^8 \text{ m/s} = 8 \times 10^7 \text{ m/s}$$

We know that, $E_0 = B_0 c$

$$= 5 \times 10^{-6} \times 8 \times 10^7 = 400 \text{ V/m}$$

$$= 4 \times 10^2 \text{ V/m}$$

25. Magnetic field of a plane electromagnetic wave is given as, $\mathbf{B} = 2 \times 10^{-8} \sin(0.5 \times 10^3 x + 1.5 \times 10^{11} t)\hat{\mathbf{j}}$ T

The amplitude of magnetic field vector, $B_0 = 2 \times 10^{-8}$ T

We know that, amplitude of electric field vector E_0 and magnetic field vector B_0 are related as

$E_0 = B_0 c$ (Where, c is speed of light)

$$= 2 \times 10^{-8} \times 3 \times 10^8 = 6 \text{ V/m}$$

From the given expression of magnetic field vector $\mathbf{B}$ of EM wave, it is clear that EM wave is travelling along X-axis and magnetic field vector vibrates along y direction, hence electric field vector will vibrate along z-direction because in EM wave, **E** and **B** are perpendicular to each other and also perpendicular to direction of motion of EM wave.

26. Given, $E_y = 540 \sin \pi \times 10^4 (x - ct) \text{Vm}^{-1}$

Peak value of electric field of light wave,

$$E_0 = 540 \text{ Vm}^{-1}$$

If B_0 be the peak value of magnetic field, then

$$B_0 = \frac{E_0}{c} = \frac{540}{3 \times 10^8}$$

$$= 180 \times 10^{-8} \text{ T} = 18 \times 10^{-7} \text{ T}$$

27. Displacement current is given by

$$I_d = \varepsilon_0 \frac{d\phi_E}{dt} = \varepsilon_0 \frac{d}{dt}(EA)$$

$$= \varepsilon_0 A \cdot \frac{d}{dt}\left(\frac{V}{d}\right)$$

or $$I_d = \frac{\varepsilon_0 A}{d}\left(\frac{d}{dt}V\right) \quad \text{...(i)}$$

Here, given $\frac{dV}{dt} = 10^6 \text{ Vs}^{-1}$

$$I_d = 4.425 \times 10^{-6} \text{ A}$$

$$A = 40 \times 10^{-4} \text{m}^2$$

$$\varepsilon_0 = 8.85 \times 10^{-12} \text{ C}^2\text{N}^{-1}\text{m}^{-2}$$

Substituting values in Eq. (i), we get

$$d = \frac{8.85 \times 10^{-12} \times 40 \times 10^{-4} \times 10^6}{4.425 \times 10^{-6}}$$

$$= 8 \times 10^{-3} \text{ m}$$

so, $$x = 8$$

28. Intensity, I and magnitude of electric field, E are related as

$$I = \frac{1}{2}\varepsilon_0 E^2 \cdot c$$

$$\Rightarrow \quad E^2 = \frac{2I}{\varepsilon_0 \times c}$$

Also, $E / B = c \Rightarrow E = B \cdot c$

So, $$B^2 = \frac{2I}{\varepsilon_0 \times c^3}$$

Substituting values, we get

$$\Rightarrow \quad B^2 = \frac{2 \times 0.22}{8.85 \times 10^{-12} \times 27 \times 10^{24}}$$

$$\Rightarrow \quad B = \sqrt{\left(\frac{2 \times 0.22}{8.85 \times 27 \times 10^{12}}\right)}$$

$$= 0.429 \times 10^{-7}$$

$$= 42.9 \times 10^{-9} \text{ T}$$

or $$B \approx 43 \times 10^{-9} \text{ T}$$

29. For the signal send by RADAR,

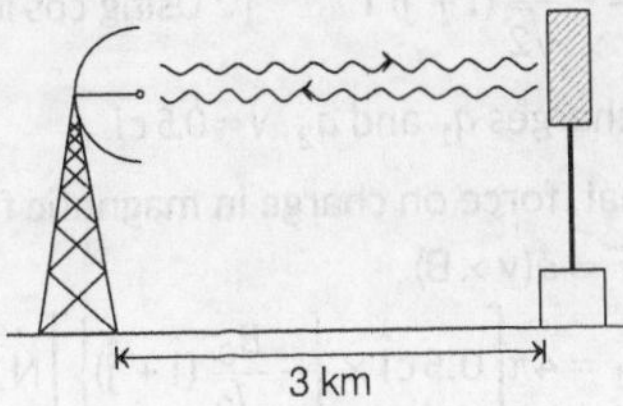

Electric and magnetic field magnitudes are

$$E_0 = 2.25\ \text{V/m}, B_0 = 1.5\times10^{-8}\ \text{T}$$

Speed of Electromagnetic signal in medium,

$$c = \frac{E_0}{B_0} = \frac{2.25}{1.5\times10^{-8}} = 1.5\times10^8\ \text{m/s}$$

Time taken by signal for to and fro from RADAR,

$$t = \frac{2d}{v} = \frac{2\times3\times10^3\ \text{m}}{1.5\times10^8\ \text{m/s}} = 4\times10^{-5}\ \text{s}$$

30. A time varying electric field is source of production of varying magnetic field and *vice-versa*. When electric fields come in contact with magnetic field, then this combination forms EM wave. In air, the speed of light is given by

$$c = \frac{1}{\sqrt{\mu_0\varepsilon_0}} \text{ and}$$

In material medium, the speed of light is given by

$$v = \frac{1}{\sqrt{\mu_0\varepsilon_0\mu_r\varepsilon_r}}$$

where, μ_r and ε_r are the relative permeability and relative permittivity of medium respectively.

So, statement (II) is false.

31. Given, frequency, $f = 3\text{GHz} = 3\times10^9$ Hz

$$\text{Wavelength, } \lambda = \frac{c}{f} = \frac{3\times10^8}{3\times10^9} = \frac{1}{10}\text{m}$$

$$\text{The size of the object is given by, } \frac{\lambda}{100} \approx \left(\frac{1}{10}\right)^3$$

This satisfies the condition of Rayleigh's scattering.

32. Speed of EM wave in medium, $v = 2\times10^8$ m/s

Speed of EM wave in air or vacuum, $c = 3\times10^8$ m/s

Relative permeability, $\mu_r = 1$

We know that refractive index of medium, $\mu = \sqrt{\mu_r\varepsilon_r}$

$$\Rightarrow \frac{c}{v} = \sqrt{\mu_r\varepsilon_r} \qquad \left[\because \mu = \frac{c}{v}\right]$$

$$\Rightarrow \frac{3\times10^8}{2\times10^8} = \sqrt{1\times\varepsilon_r}$$

$$\Rightarrow 1.5 = \sqrt{\varepsilon_r} \Rightarrow 2.25 = \varepsilon_r$$

$$\Rightarrow \varepsilon_r = 2.25$$

33. Power of electric bulb, $P = 200$ W

Efficiency, $\eta = 3.5\% = 0.035$

$r = 4$ m

$\therefore$ Intensity of radiation at $r = 4$ m

$$I = \frac{\text{Power}}{\text{Area}}\times\eta = \frac{200}{4\pi r^2}\times0.035$$

$$= \frac{200}{4\times3.14\times4^2}\times0.035$$

$$= 3.48\times10^{-2}\ \text{W/m}^2$$

But, $I = \dfrac{cB_0^2}{2\mu_0}$

$$\Rightarrow B_0^2 = \frac{2\mu_0 I}{c}$$

$$\Rightarrow B_0 = \sqrt{\frac{2\mu_0 I}{c}}$$

$$= \sqrt{\frac{2\times4\pi\times10^{-7}\times3.48\times10^{-2}}{3\times10^8}}$$

$$= 1.71\times10^{-8}\ \text{T}$$

34. Given, relative permeability, $\mu_r = 1.61$

relative permittivity, $\varepsilon_r = 6.44$

Magnetic intensity, $B = 4.5\times10^{-2}$ T

We know that,

$$c = \frac{1}{\sqrt{\mu_0\varepsilon_0}} \text{ and } v = \frac{1}{\sqrt{\mu\varepsilon}}$$

$$\therefore \frac{c}{v} = \sqrt{\frac{\mu\varepsilon}{\mu_0\varepsilon_0}} = \sqrt{\left(\frac{\mu}{\mu_0}\right)\left(\frac{\varepsilon}{\varepsilon_0}\right)} = \sqrt{\mu_r\varepsilon_r}$$

$$\Rightarrow \frac{c}{v} = \sqrt{1.61\times6.44}$$

$$\Rightarrow v = \frac{c}{\sqrt{1.61\times6.44}} \Rightarrow v = \frac{3\times10^8}{\sqrt{1.61\times6.44}}$$

But speed of electromagnetic wave,

$$v = \frac{E}{B}$$

$$\Rightarrow E = Bv = 4.5\times10^{-2}\times\frac{3\times10^8}{\sqrt{1.61\times6.44}}$$

$$= 4.2\times10^6\ \text{N/C}$$

35. Given, electric field,

$$E = 20\cos(2\times10^{10}t - 200x)\ \text{V/m}$$

Comparing with the standard equation,

$$E = E_0\cos(\omega t - kx)\ \text{V/m, we get}$$

Wave constant, $k = 200$

Angular frequency, $\omega = 2\times10^{10}$ rad / s

$$\text{Speed of the wave, } v = \frac{\omega}{k} = \frac{2\times10^{10}}{200}$$

$$= 10^8\ \text{m/s}$$

$$\text{Refractive index, } \mu = \frac{c}{v} = \frac{3\times10^8}{10^8} = 3$$

As we know the relation between the refractive index and dielectric constant,

$$\mu = \sqrt{\varepsilon_r \mu_r}$$

Substituting the value in the above equations, we get

$$3 = \sqrt{\varepsilon_r (1)}$$

$$\varepsilon_r = 9$$

Thus, the dielectric constant of the medium is 9.

36. Equation for light beam is given as

$$E = 800 \sin\left(\omega t - \frac{x}{c}\right)$$

Here, c is speed of light.
Comparing with standard equation, we get

$$E_0 = 800 \text{ Vm}^{-1}$$

As we know, the magnitude of magnetic field is given as

$$E_0 = B_0 c$$

$$\Rightarrow \quad 800 = B_0 \times 3 \times 10^8$$

$$\Rightarrow \quad B_0 = \frac{800}{3 \times 10^8} \text{ T}$$

Maximum magnetic force exerted on electron will be

$$F_{max} = evB_0$$

$$= (1.6 \times 10^{-19}) \times (3 \times 10^7) \times \frac{800}{3 \times 10^8}$$

(Given, $v = 3 \times 10^7 \text{ ms}^{-1}$)

$$F_{max} = 12.8 \times 10^{-18} \text{N}$$

$$= 1.28 \times 10^{-17} \text{N}$$

37. The equation of magnetic field vector of an electromagnetic field is

$$B = \frac{B_0}{\sqrt{2}}(\hat{i} + \hat{j}) \cos(kz - \omega t) \text{T}$$

Electric charges

$$q_1 \text{ at } P\left(0, 0, \frac{\pi}{k}\right) = 4\pi C$$

$$q_2 \text{ at } Q\left(0, 0, \frac{3\pi}{k}\right) = 2\pi C$$

At $t = 0$ and $P\left(0, 0, \frac{\pi}{k}\right)$, where $z = \frac{\pi}{k}$,

Magnetic field vector,

$$B = \frac{B_0}{\sqrt{2}}(\hat{i} + \hat{j}) \cos\left(k\frac{\pi}{k} - 0\right) \text{T}$$

$$= \frac{B_0}{\sqrt{2}}(\hat{i} + \hat{j}) \cos \pi \text{T} = -\frac{B_0}{\sqrt{2}}(\hat{i} + \hat{j}) \text{T}$$

and at $t = 0$ and $Q\left(0, 0, \frac{3\pi}{k}\right)$, where $z = \frac{3\pi}{k}$.

Magnetic field vector,

$$B = \frac{B_0}{\sqrt{2}}(\hat{i} + \hat{j}) \cos\left(k\frac{3\pi}{k} - 0\right)$$

$$= -\frac{B_0}{\sqrt{2}}(\hat{i} + \hat{j}) \text{ T} \qquad [\because \text{Using } \cos \pi = \cos 3\pi = -1]$$

Velocity of charges q_1 and q_2, $v = 0.5c\hat{i}$

We know that, force on charge in magnetic field is given by

$$F = q(v \times B)$$

$$\therefore \quad \text{For } q_1, F_1 = 4\pi\left[0.5c\hat{i} \times \left\{-\frac{B_0}{\sqrt{2}}(\hat{i} + \hat{j})\right\}\right] \text{N}$$

$$F_1 = -\frac{2\pi c B_0}{\sqrt{2}} \hat{k} \text{ N}$$

Similarly, for q_2

$$\Rightarrow \quad F_2 = 2\pi\left[0.5c\hat{i} \times \left\{-\frac{B_0}{\sqrt{2}}(\hat{i} + \hat{j})\right\}\right] \text{N}$$

$$\Rightarrow \quad F_2 = -\frac{\pi c B_0}{\sqrt{2}} \hat{k} \text{ N}$$

Hence, ratio of magnitudes of F_1 to F_2,

$$\frac{F_1}{F_2} = \frac{\frac{2\pi c B_0}{\sqrt{2}}}{\frac{\pi c B_0}{\sqrt{2}}} = \frac{2}{1} \Rightarrow F_1 : F_2 = 2:1$$

38. Given, electric field in electromagnetic wave,

$$E = 50 \sin\omega(t - x/c)$$

Energy contained in cylinder,

$$U = 5.5 \times 10^{-12} \text{ J}$$

Let, volume = V
and permittivity in free space,

$$\varepsilon_0 = 8.85 \times 10^{-12} \text{ N}^{-1}\text{C}^2 \text{ m}^{-2}$$

As we know that,

$$\frac{\text{Energy } (U)}{\text{Volume } (V)} = \frac{1}{2}\varepsilon_0 E_0^2$$

$$\therefore \quad V = \frac{2U}{\varepsilon_0 E_0^2} = \frac{2 \times 5.5 \times 10^{-12}}{8.854 \times 10^{-12} \times (50)^2}$$

$$= \frac{11}{8.854 \times 50^2} = 4.97 \times 10^{-4}$$

$$= 497 \times 10^{-6} = 500 \text{ cm}^3$$

39. Given, frequency of electromagnetic wave (*f*)

$$= 30 \text{ MHz}$$

$$= 30 \times 10^6 \text{ Hz}$$

Electric field, E = 6 V/m
Magnetic field, $B = x \times 10^{-8}$ T
Speed of light in air, $c = 3 \times 10^8 \text{ ms}^{-1}$

We know that, $B = \frac{E}{c}$

$$\Rightarrow \quad B = \frac{6}{3 \times 10^8}$$

$$\Rightarrow \quad B = 2 \times 10^{-8} \text{ T}$$

$$\therefore \quad x = 2$$

40. Given, equation of electromagnetic wave,
$E = 50\sin(500x - 10\times10^{10}t)$ V/m

The standard equation of electromagnetic wave,
$$E = E_0\sin(kx - \omega t)\ \text{V/m}$$
Comparing with standard equation, we get
$E_0 = 50$ V/m, $\omega = 10^{10}$ rad s^{-1},
$k = 500$ rad m^{-1}

Speed of wave in medium will be
$$v = \frac{\omega}{k}$$
$$= \frac{10\times10^{10}}{500} = 2\times10^8\ \text{ms}^{-1}$$
$$= \frac{2}{3}\times3\times10^8\ \text{m/s} = \frac{2}{3}c$$

41. The electric field in a plane electromagnetic wave is given by
$$E = 200\cos\left[\frac{(0.5\times10^3)x}{m} - (1.5\times10^{11}\frac{\text{rad}}{s}\times t)\right]\frac{V}{m}\hat{j}$$
$\therefore E_0 = 200$ V / m

Intensity provided by electric field is given by
$$I = \frac{1}{2}\varepsilon_0 E_0^2 c$$
The radiation pressure exerted by electromagnetic wave on surface is given by
$$P = \frac{2I}{c} = \frac{2\times\frac{1}{2}\varepsilon_0 E_0^2 c}{c} = \varepsilon_0 E_0^2$$
$$\Rightarrow \quad P = \varepsilon_0 E_0^2 = 8.85\times10^{-12}\times(200)^2$$
$$= \frac{354}{10^9}$$
According to question,
$$\frac{x}{10^9} = \frac{354}{10^9}$$
$$\therefore \quad x = 354$$

42. Given, relative permittivity of distilled water = 81

$\because$ We know that, $v = \frac{c}{\sqrt{\varepsilon_r \mu_r}}$

where, v = speed of light in medium,
c = speed of light in air,
ε_r = relative permittivity
and μ_r = relative permeability.
$$\Rightarrow \quad v = \frac{3\times10^8}{\sqrt{1\times81}} \quad [\because \mu_r = 1]$$
$$= \frac{3\times10^8}{9} = \frac{10^8}{3}$$
$$= 3.33\times10^7\ \text{ms}^{-1}$$

43. Given,
Linearly polarised electromagnetic wave,
$$E = 3.1\cos[(1.8)z - (5.4\times10^6)t]\hat{i}\ \text{N/C}$$
The given wave is travelling along +ve X-axis.
Angular frequency, $\omega = 5.4\times10^6$ rads^{-1}
Wave constant, $k = 1.8$ m^{-1}
As, we know that,
If incident wave is $x = A\sin(\omega t - kx)$
Then, for normal incidence, reflected wave
$$x_r = A\sin(\omega t + kx)$$
Hence, reflected wave will be
$$E_r = 3.1\cos[(1.8)z + (5.4\times10^6)t]\hat{i}\ \text{N/C}.$$

44. Given, intensity of sunlight,
$$I = 0.092\ \text{W/m}^2$$
As we know that,
$$I = \frac{\varepsilon_0 c}{2}E_0^2$$
$$E = \sqrt{2\frac{I}{\varepsilon_0 c}}$$
The peak value of electric field (E_0) and magnetic field (B_0) are related as

Since, $$B_0 = \frac{E_0}{c} = \frac{1}{c}\sqrt{\frac{2I}{\varepsilon_0 c}}$$
$$= \frac{1}{3\times10^8}\sqrt{\frac{2\times0.092}{8.85\times10^{-12}\times3\times10^8}}$$
$$= \frac{1}{3\times10^8}\sqrt{0.0069\times10^4}$$
$$= \frac{1}{3\times10^8}\times\sqrt{69}$$
$$= 2.77\times10^{-8}\ \text{T}$$

45. In an electromagnetic wave, the electric field vector and magnetic field vector are given as
$$E = E_0\hat{i} \quad \text{...(i)}$$
and $$B = B_0\hat{k} \quad \text{...(ii)}$$
$\because$ Direction of electromagnetic wave is given by direction of $E\times B$ because it is perpendicular to both E and B vectors.
So, unit vector in direction of $E\times B$ will be
$$= \frac{E\times B}{|E\times B|} \quad \text{...(iii)}$$
From Eqs. (i), (ii) and (iii), we get
$$\frac{E_0\hat{i}\times B_0\hat{k}}{E_0 B_0\sin 90^\circ} = \hat{i}\times\hat{k} = -\hat{j}$$

46. Electric field, magnetic field and the direction of wave propagation are mutually perpendicular to each other.
For electromagnetic waves,
$$E\times B = C$$

The direction of wave propagation is in along $+y$-direction. Therefore, the possible direction of electric field and magnetic field are (E_x, B_z) and (E_z, B_x).

47. Given, $f = 100$ MHz

$$B = (2.0 \times 10^{-8})\hat{k} T$$

The speed of the light in free space,

$$c = (3 \times 10^8)\hat{i} \text{ m/s}$$

(the direction of wave propagates in x-direction)

Magnitude of electric field,

$$E = Bc = 2 \times 10^{-8} \times 3 \times 10^8$$

$$\Rightarrow \quad E = 6 \text{ V/m}$$

If $\hat{n}$ be the direction of E, then $\hat{i} = \hat{n} \times \hat{k}$

$$\Rightarrow \quad \hat{n} = \hat{j}$$

Hence, the electric field at this point is $6\hat{j}$ V/m.

48. Intensity of the electromagnetic radiation is given as

$$I = \frac{\text{Energy}}{\text{Area} \times \text{Time}} = \frac{\text{Power}}{\text{Area}}$$

$$= U_{avg} c = \frac{1}{2} c\varepsilon_0 E_0^2$$

Here, U_{avg} = average energy density,

c = speed of radiation in air (or vacuum),

ε_0 = permittivity of the free space

and E_0 = peak value of the electric field.

$$\Rightarrow \quad P \propto E_0^2$$

$$\Rightarrow \quad \frac{P_1}{P_2} = \frac{E_1^2}{E_2^2} \Rightarrow \frac{E_1}{E_2} = \sqrt{\frac{P_1}{P_2}}$$

Substituting the values in the above equation, we get

$$\Rightarrow \quad \frac{E_1}{E_2} = \sqrt{\frac{60}{100}}$$

$$\Rightarrow \quad E_1 = \sqrt{\frac{3}{5}} E_2$$

$$= \sqrt{\frac{3}{5}} = E \quad (\because E_2 = E)$$

Comparing with $\sqrt{\frac{x}{5}} E$, we get

$$x = 3$$

49. As we know, conduction current,

$$I_c = \frac{[v_0 \sin(2\pi ft)]}{\rho \frac{d}{A}}$$

$$\Rightarrow \quad I_c = \frac{A[v_0 \sin(2\pi ft)]}{\rho d} \quad \text{... (i)}$$

As we know the displacement current equation,

$$I_d = \frac{\varepsilon_0 \varepsilon_r A}{d} \frac{d}{dt}[v_0 \sin(2\pi ft)]$$

$$I_d = \frac{\varepsilon_0 \varepsilon_r A}{d} v_0(2\pi f)[\cos(2\pi ft)] \quad \text{... (ii)}$$

Divide Eq. (ii) by Eq. (i), we get

$$\frac{I_d}{I_c} = \varepsilon_0 \varepsilon_r \times \rho 2\pi f \cot(2\pi ft)$$

Substituting the values in the above equation, we get

$$\frac{I_d}{I_c} = \frac{1}{4\pi \times 9 \times 10^9} \times (80) \times 2\pi \times 900(0.25) \cot\left(2\pi(900)\frac{1}{800}\right)$$

$$\frac{I_d}{I_c} = \frac{1}{10^6}$$

Comparing with 10^x, we get $x = 6$.

50. Given, frequency,

$$f = 500 \text{ MHz} = 5 \times 10^8 \text{ Hz}$$

$$B = 8.0 \times 10^{-8} \hat{z} \text{ T}$$

$\therefore$ Magnitude of peak value of magnetic field is given by

$$B_0 = 8 \times 10^{-8} \text{ T}$$

We know that,

$$\frac{E_0}{B_0} = c$$

where, E_0 is the magnitude of peak value of electric field and c is the speed of electromagnetic wave in air (or vacuum).

$$\Rightarrow E_0 = cB_0 = 3 \times 10^8 \times 8 \times 10^{-8} = 24 \text{V/m}$$

Since, the direction of propagation of electromagnetic wave is perpendicular to the direction of E and B both.

$\therefore$ Direction of propagation is given by $\hat{E} \times \hat{B}$.

As, the wave is travelling in y-direction, and the magnetic field is in z-direction.

$$\Rightarrow \quad \hat{E} \times \hat{z} = \hat{y}$$

$$\hat{E} = -\hat{x}$$

$\therefore$ The value of electric field will be $-24\hat{x}$ V/m.

51. We know that,

$$U_e = \frac{1}{2} \varepsilon_0 E^2 \quad \text{...(i)}$$

where, U_e = average energy density due to electric field,

ε_0 = electrical permittivity of free space

and E = electric field.

$$\text{and} \quad U_m = \frac{B^2}{2\mu_0} \quad \text{...(ii)}$$

where, U_m = average energy density due to magnetic field,

μ_0 = magnetic permeability of free space and

B = magnetic field.

$$\text{Also,} \quad E = cB \quad \left(\because c = \frac{1}{\sqrt{\mu_0 \varepsilon_0}}\right)$$

$$\Rightarrow \quad E = \frac{B}{\sqrt{\mu_0 \varepsilon_0}}$$

Put this value in Eq. (i), we get

$$U_e = \frac{1}{2}\varepsilon_0 \times \frac{1}{\mu_0\varepsilon_0}B^2$$

$$\Rightarrow \quad U_e = \frac{B^2}{2\mu_0}$$

$$\Rightarrow \quad U_e = U_m \quad \text{[using Eq. (ii)]}$$

52. Given, power of bulb,

$P = 1000$ W

Distance $d = 2$ m

Efficiency of bulb = 1.25%,

$\varepsilon_0 = 8.854 \times 10^{-12}\, C^2N^{-1}m^{-1}$,

$c = 3 \times 10^8\, ms^{-1}$

$$\therefore \text{Intensity, } (I) = \frac{\text{Power}(P)}{\text{Area}(A)} = \frac{1}{2}\varepsilon_0 E^2 c$$

$$\Rightarrow \quad \frac{1.25}{100} \times \frac{1000}{4\pi(2)^2} = \frac{1}{2} \times 8.854 \times 10^{-12} \times E^2 \times 3 \times 10^8$$

$$\Rightarrow \quad E = \sqrt{\frac{12.5}{16\pi} \times \frac{2}{8.854 \times 10^{-4} \times 3}}$$

$$= 13.7\, NC^{-1} = 137 \times 10^{-1}\, NC^{-1} \text{ or } Vm^{-1}$$

$$\therefore \quad x = 137$$

53. Intensity, $I = \frac{1}{2}c\varepsilon_0(E_0)^2$

$$\therefore \text{Intensity} = \frac{\text{Power}}{\text{Area}} = \frac{8}{(4\pi \times 10^2)}$$

$$\because \quad \frac{8}{4\pi \times 10^2} \times \frac{1}{2} = \frac{1}{4} \times C \times \frac{1}{\mu_0 C^2} \times E_0^2$$

$$\left[\text{Multiplying by } \frac{1}{2} \text{ and } \varepsilon_0 = \frac{1}{\mu_0 c^2}\right]$$

$$\Rightarrow \quad E_0 = \frac{2}{10}\sqrt{\frac{\mu_0 c}{\pi}} \Rightarrow x = 2$$

54. Given, frequency of wave,

$f = 3$ GHz $= 3 \times 10^9$ Hz

Relative permittivity, $\varepsilon_r = 2.25$

Since, $f = c/\lambda$

$$\Rightarrow \quad \lambda = \frac{c}{f} = \frac{3 \times 10^8}{3 \times 10^9} = 0.1 \text{ m}$$

$\because \lambda_m$ (wavelength of wave in a medium) $= \lambda/\mu$

and as we know that, $\mu = \sqrt{\mu_r \varepsilon_r}$

As, dielectric is non-magnetic, $\mu_r = 1$

$$\Rightarrow \quad \mu = \sqrt{2.25} = 1.5$$

$$\Rightarrow \quad \lambda_m = \frac{0.1}{1.5} = \frac{1}{15} = 0.0667 \text{ m}$$

$$= 6.67 \text{ cm} = 667 \times 10^{-2} \text{ cm}$$

55. Given, $\mu_r = \varepsilon_r = 2$

where, μ_r is relative permeability,

ε_r is relative permittivity.

Speed of electromagnetic wave v is given by

$$v = \frac{c}{n}$$

where, n = refractive index

$$= \sqrt{\mu_r \varepsilon_r} = \sqrt{4} = 2$$

$$\Rightarrow \quad v = \frac{3 \times 10^8}{2} = 15 \times 10^7 \text{ m/s}$$

$$\because \quad x \times 10^7 = 15 \times 10^7$$

$$\Rightarrow \quad x = 15$$

56. As we know that;

A. Source of microwave frequency is magnetron.
B. Source of infrared frequency is vibration of atoms and molecules.
C. Source of gamma ray is radioactive decay of nucleus.
D. Source of X-ray is transition of electron in inner shells.

$\therefore$ The correct match is A → (2), B → (4), C → (1), D → (3).

57. Energy density of magnetic field of an electromagnetic wave is given by

$$u_B = \frac{1}{2}\left(\frac{B_0^2}{\mu_0}\right)$$

Here, $\mu_0 = 4\pi \times 10^{-7}$ units,

and $u_B = 1.02 \times 10^{-8}\, Jm^{-3}$

So, amplitude of magnetic field,

$$B_0 = \sqrt{2\mu_0 u_B}$$

$$= \sqrt{2 \times 4\pi \times 10^{-7} \times 1.02 \times 10^{-8}}$$

$$= 16 \times 10^{-8}\, T = 160\, nT$$

Hence, correct option is (b).

58. Direction of propagation of an electromagnetic wave is given by $\hat{E} \times \hat{B}$.

$\therefore$ A unit vector in the direction of propagation

$$= \frac{E \times B}{|E \times B|} = \frac{\hat{k} \times (2\hat{i} - 2\hat{j})}{|E \times B|}$$

$$\left[\begin{aligned} \because E \times B &= \hat{k} \times (2\hat{i} - 2\hat{j}) \\ &= 2(\hat{k} \times \hat{i}) - 2(\hat{k} \times \hat{j}) \\ &= 2(\hat{j}) - 2(-\hat{i}) \\ &= 2\hat{j} + 2\hat{i} \\ \therefore |E \times B| &= \sqrt{2^2 + 2^2} = 2\sqrt{2} \end{aligned}\right]$$

$$= \frac{2\hat{j} + 2\hat{i}}{2\sqrt{2}} = \frac{\hat{i} + \hat{j}}{\sqrt{2}}$$

Hence, correct option is (a).

59. We have the following facts :

An electromagnetic wave propagates in direction of vector $E \times B$.

Phase gives velocity of wave.

Electric field vector of EM wave is given by

$$E = cB$$

Here, $B = B_0 \sin[200\pi(y + ct)]\hat{i}$

$$= 3 \times 10^{-8} \sin[200\pi(y + ct)]\hat{i}$$

$\Rightarrow \quad E_0 = cB_0 = 3 \times 10^8 \times 3 \times 10^{-8} = 9 \text{ V/m}$

Phase $= y + ct =$ constant

$$\Rightarrow \quad \frac{dy}{dt} = -c$$

i.e., wave propagates in negative y-direction.

$\Rightarrow \quad E \times B$ is parallel to $-\hat{j}$

$\Rightarrow \quad \hat{E} \times \hat{i} = \lambda(-\hat{j})$

So, $\hat{E} = -\hat{k}$

Hence, electric field vector is given by

$$E = E_0 \sin(ky + \omega t)(-\hat{k})$$

$$= -9 \sin[200\pi(y + ct)]\hat{k} \text{ V/m}$$

Hence, option (d) is correct.

60. Given, $\mathbf{E} = E_0 \hat{j} \cos(\omega t - kx)$

This equation represents electric field vector of a wave which travels in positive x-direction, i.e. along $\hat{i}$.

As, $E \times B =$ direction of wave propagation,

we have $\quad \hat{j} \times B = \hat{i}$

$\therefore$ B is along $\hat{k}$

Also, $\quad \dfrac{E_0}{B_0} = c = \dfrac{1}{\sqrt{\mu_0 \varepsilon_0}}$

so $\quad B_0 = E_0(\sqrt{\mu_0 \varepsilon_0})$

So, $\quad B = B_0 \hat{k} \cos(\omega t - kx)$

or $\quad B = E_0(\sqrt{\mu_0 \varepsilon_0})\hat{k} \cdot \cos kx$

Hence, correct option is (d).

61. Electric field vector of the given EM wave is

$$E = E_0 (\hat{x} + \hat{y}) \sin(kz - \omega t)$$

$\therefore$ Amplitude of electric field $= E_0$

and unit vector of electric field,

$$\hat{E} = \frac{\hat{x} + \hat{y}}{\sqrt{1^2 + 1^2}} = \frac{\hat{x} + \hat{y}}{\sqrt{2}}$$

The coefficient of k in the given equation is z. So, wave travels along positive z-direction. So, unit vector into the direction of propagation of EM wave $\hat{c} = \hat{z}$.

Now, for magnetic field vector of the given EM wave, we can conclude

Amplitude of magnetic field, $_0 = E_0 / c$

and unit vector of magnetic field $= \hat{B}$

So, the expected equation of magnetic field vector will be

$$B = B_0(\hat{B}) \sin(kz - \omega t)$$

$$= \frac{E_0}{c}(\hat{B}) \sin(kz - \omega t) \quad \text{...(i)}$$

Also, $\quad \hat{E} \times \hat{B} = \hat{c} = \hat{z} \quad \text{...(ii)}$

Now, let's check the given alternatives

(a) $B = \dfrac{E_0}{c}(\hat{x} + \hat{y}) \sin(kz - \omega t)$

Here, $\hat{B} = \dfrac{\hat{x} + \hat{y}}{\sqrt{1^2 + 1^2}} = \dfrac{\hat{x} + \hat{y}}{\sqrt{2}}$

So, $\hat{E} \times \hat{B} = \left(\dfrac{\hat{x} + \hat{y}}{\sqrt{2}}\right) \times \left(\dfrac{\hat{x} + \hat{y}}{\sqrt{2}}\right)$

$$= \frac{1}{2}[(\hat{x} \times \hat{x}) + (\hat{x} \times \hat{y}) + (\hat{y} \times \hat{x}) + (\hat{y} \times \hat{y})]$$

$$= \frac{1}{2}[(0) + (\hat{z}) + (-\hat{z}) + (0)]$$

$$= \frac{1}{2}[\hat{z} - \hat{z}] = 0$$

which is impossible for an EM wave.

So, this option is wrong.

(b) $B = \dfrac{E_0}{c}(-\hat{x} + \hat{y}) \sin(kz - \omega t)$

Here, $\hat{B} = \dfrac{-\hat{x} + \hat{y}}{\sqrt{1^2 + 1^2}} = \dfrac{-\hat{x} + \hat{y}}{\sqrt{2}}$

So, $\hat{E} \times \hat{B} = \left(\dfrac{\hat{x} + \hat{y}}{\sqrt{2}}\right) \times \left(-\dfrac{\hat{x} + \hat{y}}{\sqrt{2}}\right)$

$$\frac{1}{2}[-(\hat{x} \times \hat{x}) + (\hat{x} \times \hat{y}) - (\hat{y} \times \hat{x}) + (\hat{y} \times \hat{y})]$$

$$= \frac{1}{2}[-(0) + (\hat{z}) - (-\hat{z}) + (0)]$$

$$= \frac{1}{2}[\hat{z} + \hat{z}] = \frac{1}{2}(2\hat{z}) = \hat{z}$$

which satisfies for Eq. (ii).

So, this option is correct.

(c) $B = \dfrac{E_0}{c}(\hat{x} - \hat{y}) \sin(kz - \omega t)$

Here, $\hat{B} = \dfrac{\hat{x} - \hat{y}}{\sqrt{1^2 + 1^2}} = \dfrac{\hat{x} - \hat{y}}{\sqrt{2}}$

So, $\hat{E} \times \hat{B} = \left(\dfrac{\hat{x} + \hat{y}}{\sqrt{2}}\right) \times \left(\dfrac{\hat{x} - \hat{y}}{\sqrt{2}}\right)$

$$= \frac{1}{2}[(\hat{x} \times \hat{x}) - (\hat{x} \times \hat{y}) + (\hat{y} \times \hat{x}) - (\hat{y} \times \hat{y})]$$

$$= \frac{1}{2}[(0) - (\hat{z}) + (-\hat{z}) - (0)]$$

$$= \frac{1}{2}[-\hat{z} - \hat{z}]$$

$$= \frac{1}{2}(-2\hat{z}) = -\hat{z}$$

which doesn't satisfy for eq. (ii).

So, this option is wrong.

(d) $B = \frac{E_0}{c}(\hat{x} - \hat{y})\cos(kz - \omega t)$

This option is wrong, as the function in eq. (i) is a "sine" function, not a "cosine" function.

Hence, option (b) is correct.

62. The moving electron is shown in the following figure.

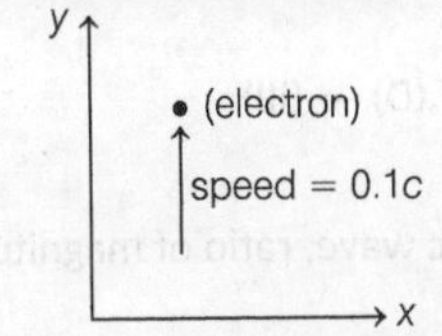

In electromagnetic wave,

$$B_{max} = \frac{E_{max}}{c}$$

We know that, magnetic force on a moving charge (electron) is given by

$$F = q\mathbf{v} \times \mathbf{B}$$

Here, angle between v and B is 90°.

So, $F_{max} = qvB_{max}\sin\theta$

$$= qvB_{max}\sin 90° = \frac{qvE_{max}}{c}$$

Given, $c = 3 \times 10^8$ m/s,

$v = 0.1c$

Charge on electron, $q = 1.6 \times 10^{-19}$ C

Substituting these values in above equation, we get

$$F_{max} = \frac{1.6 \times 10^{-19} \times 0.1 \times 3 \times 10^8 \times 30}{3 \times 10^8}$$

$$= 4.8 \times 10^{-19} \text{ N}$$

Hence, correct option is (b).

63. Given, intensity, $I = \left(\frac{315}{\pi}\right)$ W/m^2

Absolute permittivity,

$$\varepsilon_0 = 8.86 \times 10^{-12} \text{ C}^2\text{Nm}^{-2}$$

Speed of light, $c = 3 \times 10^8$ m/s

As, intensity, $I = \frac{1}{2}\varepsilon_0 E_0^2 c$

or $E_0 = \sqrt{\frac{2I}{\varepsilon_0 c}} = \sqrt{\frac{2 \times \left(\frac{315}{\pi}\right)}{8.86 \times 10^{-12} \times 3 \times 10^8}}$

$E_0 \approx 275$ V/m

$\therefore E_{rms} = \frac{E_0}{\sqrt{2}} = \frac{275}{\sqrt{2}} \approx 194$ V/m

64. Given that,

$B(x,t)$

$$= [1.2 \times 10^{-7} \sin(0.5 \times 10^3 x + 1.5 \times 10^{11} t)\hat{k}]\text{T}$$

Speed of light, $c = 3 \times 10^8$ m/s

Maximum value of electric field,

E_0 = (maximum value of B_0) × (speed of light)

$$= B_0 \times c = 1.2 \times 10^{-7} \times 3 \times 10^8 = 36 \text{ V/m}$$

Since, wave is propagating in negative *x*-direction and magnetic field is in *z*-direction. So, electric field vector must be in negative *y*-direction as direction of wave propagation is in the direction of $\mathbf{E} \times \mathbf{B}$.

So, electric field at a point *x* and time *t* is given by

$$E(x,t) = -36\sin(0.5 \times 10^3 x + 1.5 \times 10^{11} t)\hat{j} \text{V/m}$$

Here, phase of E will be same that of B.

Hence, correct option is (a).

65. An electromagnetic wave is a travelling wave in which electric vector E is perpendicular to magnetic vector B and both of these vectors are also perpendicular to the direction of propagation of electromagnetic wave.

So, it is given that

$$B = 3 \times 10^{-8} \sin(1.6 \times 10^3 x + 48 \times 10^{10} t)\hat{j} \text{ T}$$

$$= B_0 \sin(kx + \omega t)\hat{j}\text{T}$$

Here, $k = 1.6 \times 10^3$ units

and $\omega = 48 \times 10^{10}$ units

Then, it can be implied that electromagnetic wave is travelling along $-X$-axis (this is obtained from phase $kx + \omega t$) and its magnetic vector B is directed along $+Y$-axis (this is indicated by unit vector $\hat{j}$).

Hence, electric field vector is along $+Z$-axis and its magnitude is given by

$$E_0 = c \cdot B_0 = 3 \times 10^8 \times 3 \times 10^{-8} = 9 \text{ V/m}$$

$\therefore$ Expression for $E = 9\sin(kx + \omega t)\hat{k}$

$$= 9\sin(1.6 \times 10^3 x + 48 \times 10^{10} t)\hat{k} \text{ V/m}$$

66. We are given with following situation

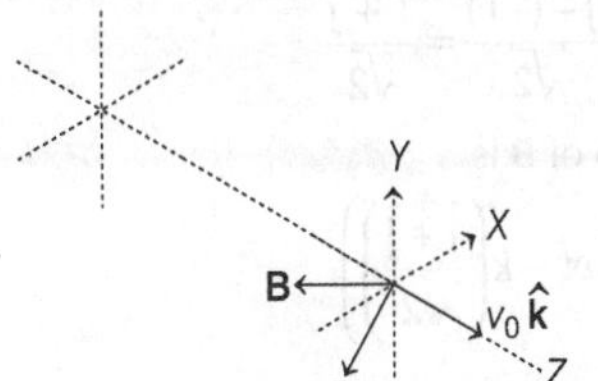

Given, $E = E_0\left(\frac{\hat{i} + \hat{j}}{\sqrt{2}}\right) \cdot \cos(kz + \omega t)$

So, electromagnetic wave is propagating along *Z*-axis and its electric vector E is perpendicular to *Z*-axis; and is along angle bisector of IIIrd quadrant of *xy*-plane as shown in the figure. So, magnetic vector B is along angle bisector of IInd quadrant of *xy*-plane and is perpendicular to both E and v vectors.

Now, force due to electric field is along E vector and force due to magnetic field is obtained by Fleming's left hand rule.

Thus, direction of magnetic force is also along E. So, force on charged particle will be along E or along $-\left(\frac{\hat{i}+\hat{j}}{\sqrt{2}}\right)$ vector.

Hence, force on charged particle is antiparallel to $\left(\frac{\hat{i}+\hat{j}}{\sqrt{2}}\right)$ vector.

67. Given,

$$\mathbf{B} = 5 \times 10^{-8}\,\hat{j} \text{ and } \mathbf{v} = 3 \times 10^{8}\,\hat{k}$$

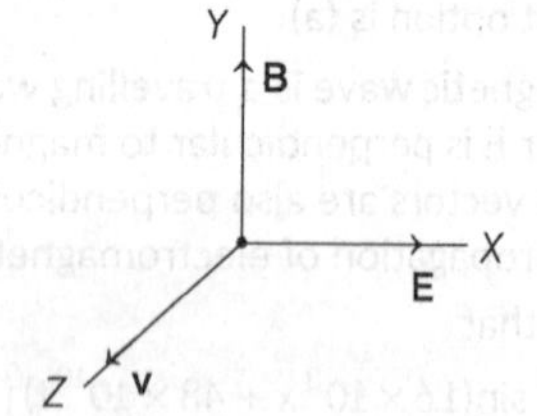

Using $\mathbf{E} = \mathbf{B} \times \mathbf{v}$, we have

$$\mathbf{E} = (5 \times 10^{-8}\,\hat{j}) \times (3 \times 10^{8}\,\hat{k}) = 15\hat{i}\ \text{Vm}^{-1}$$

68. Given, direction of propagation of electromagnetic wave is along $\frac{\hat{i}+\hat{j}}{\sqrt{2}}$ also direction of its electric field vector E (or direction of its polarisation) is $\hat{k}$.

As, direction of propagation of wave is along $\mathbf{E} \times \mathbf{B}$, so direction of B is such that

$$\hat{k} \times \mathbf{B} = \frac{\hat{i}+\hat{j}}{\sqrt{2}}$$

From options,

$$\hat{k} \times \left(\frac{\hat{i}-\hat{j}}{\sqrt{2}}\right) = \frac{\hat{k}\times\hat{i} - \hat{k}\times\hat{j}}{\sqrt{2}}$$

$$= \frac{\hat{j}-(-\hat{i})}{\sqrt{2}} = \frac{\hat{i}+\hat{j}}{\sqrt{2}}$$

So, correct expression of **B** is

$$\mathbf{B} = B_0\left(\frac{\hat{i}-\hat{j}}{\sqrt{2}}\right) \cdot \cos\left(\omega t - k\left(\frac{\hat{i}+\hat{j}}{\sqrt{2}}\right)\right)$$

69. $\lambda_{\text{X-rays}} = 0.01\ \text{Å to } 100\ \text{Å}$

$\lambda_{\text{visible}} = 3800\ \text{Å to } 7000\ \text{Å}$

$\lambda_{\text{microwaves}} = 10^{7}\ \text{Å to } 3 \times 10^{9}\ \text{Å}$

$\lambda_{\text{radio waves}} = 10^{7}\ \text{Å to } 10^{15}\ \text{Å}$

So, it is clear from the values that

$\lambda_{\text{radio waves}} > \lambda_{\text{microwaves}} > \lambda_{\text{visible}} > \lambda_{\text{X-rays}}$

So, correct option is (c).

70. Energy is inversely proportional to wavelength,

i.e., $E = \frac{hc}{\lambda} \Rightarrow E \propto \frac{1}{\lambda}$

Energies of given radiations have the following order:

$$E_{\gamma\text{-rays}} > E_{\text{X-rays}} > E_{\text{microwaves}} > E_{\text{AM radiowaves}}$$

$$\therefore\ \lambda_{\gamma\text{-rays}} < \lambda_{\text{X-rays}} < \lambda_{\text{microwaves}} < \lambda_{\text{AM radiowaves}}$$

Thus, microwaves $\rightarrow 10^{-3}$ m

γ-rays $\rightarrow 10^{-15}$ m

AM radiowaves $\rightarrow 100$ m

X-rays $\rightarrow 10^{-10}$ m

∴ (A) → (IV), (B) → (II), (C) → (I), (D) → (III).

Hence, correct option is (d).

71. Key Idea For an electromagnetic wave, ratio of magnitudes of electric and magnetic field is

$$E/B = c$$

where, *c* is the speed of electromagnetic wave in vacuum.

Given, $E = 6\ \text{V/m}$, $c = 3 \times 10^{8}\ \text{ms}^{-1}$

So, $B = \frac{E}{c} = \frac{6}{3 \times 10^{8}} = 2 \times 10^{-8}\ \text{T}$

Also, direction of propagation of electromagnetic wave is given by

$$\hat{n} = \mathbf{E} \times \mathbf{B}$$

Here, $\hat{n} = \hat{i}$ and E = Unit vector of electric field ($\hat{j}$)

B = unit vector of magnetic field.

$$\Rightarrow\quad \hat{i} = \hat{j} \times \mathbf{B}$$

$$\therefore\quad \mathbf{B} = \hat{k}$$

Hence, magnetic field components

$\mathbf{B} = 2 \times 10^{-8}\hat{k}\ \text{T} = 2 \times 10^{-8}\ \text{T}$ (along *z*-direction)

72 Given,

$$\mathbf{B} = 1.6 \times 10^{-6} \cos(2 \times 10^{7} z + 6 \times 10^{15} t)(2\hat{i} + \hat{j})\ \text{Wbm}^{-2}$$

From the given equation, it can be said that the electromagnetic wave is propagating negative *z*-direction, i.e. $-\hat{k}$.

Equation of associated electric field will be

$$\mathbf{E} = (|\mathbf{B}|\,c)\cos(kz + \omega t) \cdot \hat{n}$$

where, $\hat{n}$ = a vector perpendicular to **B**.

So, $|\mathbf{E}| = |\mathbf{B}| \cdot c$

$$= 1.6 \times 10^{-6} \times 3 \times 10^{8} = 4.8 \times 10^{2}\ \text{V/m}$$

Since, we know that for an electromagnetic wave, **E** and **B** are mutually perpendicular to each other.

So, $\mathbf{E} \cdot \mathbf{B} = 0$

From the given options, when $\hat{n} = \hat{i} - 2\hat{j}$

$$\mathbf{E} \cdot \mathbf{B} = (2\hat{i} + \hat{j}) \cdot (\hat{i} - 2\hat{j}) = 0$$

Also, when $\hat{\mathbf{n}} = -\hat{i} + 2\hat{j}$

$$\mathbf{E} \cdot \mathbf{B} = (2\hat{i} + \hat{j}) \cdot (-\hat{i} + 2\hat{j}) = 0$$

But, we also know that the direction of propagation of electromagnetic wave is perpendicular to both **E** and **B**, i.e. it is in the direction of **E** × **B**.

Again, when $\hat{n} = \hat{i} - 2\hat{j}$

$$\mathbf{E} \times \mathbf{B} = (2\hat{i} + \hat{j}) \times (\hat{i} - 2\hat{j}) = -\hat{k}$$

and when $\hat{n} = -\hat{i} + 2\hat{j}$

$$\mathbf{E} \times \mathbf{B} = (2\hat{i} + \hat{j}) \times (-\hat{i} + 2\hat{j}) = \hat{k}$$

But, it is been given in the question that the direction of propagation of wave is in $-\hat{k}$.

Thus, associated electric field will be

$$\mathbf{E} = 4.8 \times 10^2 \cos(2 \times 10^7 z + 6 \times 10^{15} t)\ (\hat{i} - 2\hat{j})\ \text{Vm}^{-1}$$

73. Radiation pressure or momentum imparted per second per unit area when light falls is

$$p = \begin{cases} \dfrac{2I}{c}\ ; & \text{for reflection of radiation} \\ \dfrac{I}{c}\ ; & \text{for absorption of radiation} \end{cases}$$

where, I is the intensity of the light.

In given case, there is 25% reflection and 75% absorption, so radiation pressure

= force per unit area

$$= \frac{25}{100} \times \frac{2I}{c} + \frac{75}{100} \times \frac{I}{c} = \frac{1}{2} \times \frac{I}{c} + \frac{3}{4} \times \frac{I}{c}$$

$$= \frac{5}{4} \times \frac{I}{c} = \frac{5}{4} \times \frac{50}{3 \times 10^8}$$

$$= 20.83 \times 10^{-8}\ \text{N}$$

$$\approx 20 \times 10^{-8}\ \text{N}$$

74. Radiation pressure over an absorbing surface is,

$$p = \frac{I}{c}$$

where, I = intensity or energy flux

and c = speed of light.

If A = area of surface, then force due to radiation on the surface is

$$F = p \times A = \frac{IA}{c}$$

If force F acts for a duration of Δt seconds, then momentum transferred to the surface is

$$\Delta p = F \times \Delta t = \frac{IA}{c} \times \Delta t$$

Here, $I = 25\ \text{W cm}^{-2}$, $A = 25\ \text{cm}^2$,

$c = 3 \times 10^8\ \text{ms}^{-1}$,

$\Delta t = 40\ \text{min} = 2400\ \text{s}$

So, momentum transferred to the surface,

$$\Delta p = \frac{25 \times 25 \times 2400}{3 \times 10^8} = 5 \times 10^{-3}\ \text{N-s}$$

75. Given, magnetic field of an electromagnetic wave is

$$\mathbf{B} = B_0[\cos(kz - \omega t)]\,\hat{i} + B_1[\cos(kz + \omega t)]\,\hat{j}$$

Here, $B_0 = 3 \times 10^{-5}$ T and $B_1 = 2 \times 10^{-6}$ T

Also, stationary charge, $Q = 10^{-4}$ C at $z = 0$

As charge is released from the rest at $z = 0$, in this condition.

Maximum electric field, $E_0 = cB_0$ and $E_1 = cB_1$

So, $E_0 = c \times 3 \times 10^{-5}$

and $E_1 = c \times 2 \times 10^{-6}$

Now, the direction of electric field of an electromagnetic wave is perpendicular to **B** and to the direction of propagation of wave (**E** × **B**) which is $\hat{k}$.

So, for E_0,

$$\mathbf{E}_0 \times \mathbf{B}_0 = \hat{k}$$

$$\Rightarrow \quad \mathbf{E}_0 \times \hat{i} = \hat{k}$$

$$\Rightarrow \quad \mathbf{E}_0 = -\hat{j}$$

Similarly, for E_1 $\mathbf{E}_1 \times \mathbf{B}_1 = \mathbf{k}$

$$\Rightarrow \quad \mathbf{E}_1 \times \mathbf{j} = \mathbf{k}$$

$$\Rightarrow \quad \mathbf{E}_1 = \hat{i}$$

$$\therefore \quad \mathbf{E}_0 = c \times 3 \times 10^{-5}(-\hat{j})\text{NC}^{-1}$$

$$\mathbf{E} = c \times 2 \times 10^{-6}(+\hat{i})\text{NC}^{-1}$$

∴ Maximum force experienced by stationary charge is

$$F_{max} = Q\mathbf{E} = Q(\mathbf{E}_0 + \mathbf{E}_1)$$

$$= Q \times c\,[-3 \times 10^{-5}\hat{j} + 2 \times 10^{-6}\hat{i}]$$

$$\Rightarrow \quad |F_{max}| = 10^{-4} \times 3 \times 10^8 \times \sqrt{(3 \times 10^{-5})^2 + (2 \times 10^{-6})^2}$$

$$= 3 \times 10^4 \times 10^{-6}\sqrt{900 + 4}$$

$$= 3 \times 10^{-2} \times \sqrt{904} \approx 0.9\ \text{N}$$

∴ rms value of experienced force is

$$F_{rms} = \frac{F_{max}}{\sqrt{2}} = \frac{0.9}{\sqrt{2}} = 0.707 \times 0.9$$

$$= 0.6363\ \text{N} \approx 0.6\ \text{N}$$

76. Key Idea For an electromagnetic wave, its electric field vector (**E**) and magnetic field vector (**B**) is mutually perpendicular to each other and also to its direction of propagation.

We know that, **E** × **B** represents direction of propagation of an electromagnetic wave

$$\Rightarrow \quad (\mathbf{E} \times \mathbf{B}) \parallel v$$

∴ From the given electric field, we can state that direction of propagation is along Z-axis and direction of **E** is along X-axis.

Thus, from the above discussion, direction of **B** must be Y-axis.

From Maxwell's equation,

$$\nabla \times \mathbf{E} = -\frac{\partial \mathbf{B}}{\partial t}$$

Here, $$\frac{\partial \mathbf{E}}{\partial Z} = -\frac{\partial B}{\partial t} \quad \text{... (i)}$$

and $$B_0 = \frac{E_0}{C} \quad \text{... (ii)}$$

Given, $\mathbf{E} = E_0 \,\hat{\mathbf{i}} \cos kz \cos \omega t$

$$\Rightarrow \quad \frac{-\partial \mathbf{E}}{\partial Z} = kE_0 \sin kz \cos \omega t$$

$\therefore$ Using Eq. (i), we get

$$\frac{\partial \mathbf{B}}{\partial t} = kE_0 \sin kz \cos \omega t$$

Integrating both sides of the above equation w.r.t. t, we get

$$\Rightarrow \quad \mathbf{B} = \frac{k}{\omega} E_0 \sin kz \sin \omega t$$

$$= \frac{E_0}{C} \sin kz \sin \omega t$$

$$\Rightarrow \quad \mathbf{B} = \frac{E_0}{C} \sin(kz) \sin(\omega t)\,\hat{\mathbf{j}}$$

77. Key Idea Standard expression of electromagnetic wave is given by

$$\mathbf{E} = E_0 \hat{\mathbf{n}} \,[\sin(\omega t - \mathbf{k} \cdot \hat{\mathbf{r}})] \quad \text{...(i)}$$

Here, $\mathbf{k}$ is the propagation vector.

Direction of propagation in this case is $\hat{\mathbf{k}}$.

Given expression of electromagnetic wave,

$$\mathbf{E} = E_0 \hat{\mathbf{n}} \sin[\omega t + (6y - 8z)]$$

$$\Rightarrow \quad \mathbf{E} = E_0 \hat{\mathbf{n}} \sin[\omega t - (8z - 6y)] \quad \text{...(ii)}$$

Comparing Eq. (ii) with Eq. (i), we get

$$\mathbf{k} \cdot \hat{\mathbf{r}} = 8z - 6y \quad \text{...(iii)}$$

Here, $$\hat{\mathbf{r}} = x\hat{\mathbf{i}} + y\hat{\mathbf{j}} + z\hat{\mathbf{k}}$$

and $$\mathbf{k} = k_x \hat{\mathbf{i}} + k_y \hat{\mathbf{j}} + k_z \hat{\mathbf{k}}$$

$$\therefore \quad \mathbf{k} \cdot \hat{\mathbf{r}} = xk_x + yk_y + zk_z \quad \text{...(iv)}$$

From Eqs. (iii) and (iv), we get

$$xk_x = \text{zero} \Rightarrow k_x = 0$$

$$yk_y = -6y \Rightarrow k_y = -6$$

$$zk_z = 8z \Rightarrow k_z = 8$$

Hence, $\mathbf{k} = -6\hat{\mathbf{j}} + 8\hat{\mathbf{k}}$

So, direction of propagation,

$$\hat{\mathbf{s}} = \hat{\mathbf{k}} = \frac{\mathbf{k}}{|\mathbf{k}|} = \frac{-6\hat{\mathbf{j}} + 8\hat{\mathbf{k}}}{\sqrt{6^2 + 8^2}}$$

$$= \frac{-6\hat{\mathbf{j}} + 8\hat{\mathbf{k}}}{10}$$

$$= \frac{-3\hat{\mathbf{j}} + 4\hat{\mathbf{k}}}{5}$$

78. In an electromagnetic wave, magnetic field and electric field are perpendicular to each other and both are also perpendicular to the direction of propagation of wave.

Now, given direction of propagation is along z-direction. So, magnetic field is in either x or y direction. Also, angular wave number for wave is

$$k = \frac{2\pi}{\lambda} = \frac{2\pi\nu}{c} = \frac{2\pi \times 23.9 \times 10^9}{3 \times 10^8}$$

$$\approx 0.5 \times 10^3 \text{ m}^{-1}$$

and angular frequency ω for wave is

$$\omega = 2\pi\nu = 2\pi \times 23.9 \times 10^9 \text{ Hz}$$

$$= 1.5 \times 10^{11} \text{ Hz}$$

Magnitude of magnetic field is

$$B_0 = \frac{E_0}{c} = \frac{60}{3 \times 10^8} = 2 \times 10^{-7} \text{ T}$$

As the general equation of magnetic field of an electromagnetic wave propagating in $+z$- direction is given as,

$$\mathbf{B} = B_0 \sin(kz - \omega t)\hat{\mathbf{i}} \text{ or } \hat{\mathbf{j}}$$

Thus, substituting the values of B_0, k and ω, we get

$$\Rightarrow \mathbf{B} = 2 \times 10^{-7} \sin(0.5 \times 10^3 z - 1.5 \times 10^{11} t)\,\hat{\mathbf{i}} \text{ or } \hat{\mathbf{j}}$$

79. Since, the magnitude of electric field vector and magnetic field vector of electromagnetic wave is related as,

$$\frac{|\mathbf{E}|}{|\mathbf{B}|} = c$$

where, c is the speed of light in vacuum.

Here, $|\mathbf{E}| = 6.3$ and $c = 3 \times 10^8$ m/s.

$$\Rightarrow \quad |\mathbf{B}| = \frac{|\mathbf{E}|}{c} = \frac{6.3}{3 \times 10^8} = 2.1 \times 10^{-8}$$

Now, as we know for a EM wave, $\mathbf{E}$ and $\mathbf{B}$ are perpendicular to each other as well as to direction of propagation of wave $(\mathbf{E} \times \mathbf{B})$.

As here, direction of $\mathbf{E}$ is $+y$-direction i.e. $\hat{\mathbf{j}}$ and direction of propagation of wave is in $+x$-direction i.e., $\hat{\mathbf{i}}$

$\therefore$ If $\mathbf{B}$ has to be perpendicular to $\mathbf{E}$ and direction of propagation, then it must in $+z$-direction i.e., $\hat{\mathbf{k}}$.

Thus, magnetic field, $\mathbf{B} = 2.1 \times 10^{-8}\,\hat{\mathbf{k}}$ T.

80. Energy density of an electomagnetic wave in electric field,

$$U_E = \frac{1}{2}\varepsilon_0 \cdot E^2 \quad \text{...(i)}$$

Energy density of an electromagnetic wave in magnetic field,

$$U_B = \frac{B^2}{2\mu_0} \quad \text{...(ii)}$$

where, E = electric field,

B = magnetic field,

ε_0 = permittivity of medium and

μ_0 = magnetic permeability of medium.

From the theory of electro-magnetic waves, the relation between μ_0 and ε_0 is

$$c = \frac{1}{\sqrt{\mu_0 \varepsilon_0}} \quad \text{...(iii)}$$

where, c = velocity of light

$$= 3 \times 10^8 \text{ m/s}$$

and $$\frac{E}{B} = c \quad \text{...(iv)}$$

Dividing Eq. (i) by Eq. (ii), we get

$$\frac{U_E}{U_B} = \frac{\frac{1}{2}\varepsilon_0 E^2}{\frac{1}{2}B^2 \times \frac{1}{\mu_0}} = \frac{\mu_0 \varepsilon_0 E^2}{B^2} \quad \text{...(v)}$$

Using Eqs. (iii), (iv) and (v), we get

$$\frac{U_E}{U_B} = \frac{c^2}{c^2} = 1$$

Therefore, $U_E = U_B$

81. Given, instantaneous value of magnetic field

$$B = 100 \times 10^{-6} \sin\left[2\pi \times 2 \times 10^{15}\left(t - \frac{x}{c}\right)\right]$$

and speed of light, $c = 3 \times 10^8 \text{ ms}^{-1}$

For an electromagnetic wave,

$$E_{max} = B_{max} \times c$$

where, E_{max} = maximum value of the electric field.

We get, $E_{max} = 100 \times 10^{-6} \times 3 \times 10^8$

$$= 3 \times 10^4 \frac{\text{N}}{\text{C}}$$

82. We are given electric field as

$$\mathbf{E} = 10\,\hat{j}\cos(6x + 8z) \quad \text{... (i)}$$

where, phase angle is independent of time,

i.e., phase angle at $t = 0$ is $\phi = 6x + 8z$.

Phase angle for B will also be $6x + 8z$ because for an electromagnetic wave **E** and B oscillate in same phase.

Thus, direction of wave propagation

$$= \frac{6\hat{i} + 8\hat{k}}{\sqrt{6^2 + 8^2}} = \frac{6\hat{i} + 8\hat{k}}{10} \quad \text{...(ii)}$$

Let magnetic field vector,

$\mathbf{B} = a\hat{i} + b\hat{j} + d\hat{k}$, then direction of wave propagation is given by

$$\frac{\mathbf{E} \times \mathbf{B}}{|E'||B|} = \frac{10\hat{j} \times (a\hat{i} + b\hat{j} + d\hat{k})}{10 \times (a^2 + b^2 + d^2)^{1/2}}$$

$$= \frac{-10a\hat{k} + 10d\hat{i}}{10(a^2 + b^2 + d^2)^{1/2}} \quad \text{...(iii)}$$

As, $$|B| = \frac{|E|}{c} = \frac{10}{c}$$

We get, $|B| = \sqrt{a^2 + b^2 + d^2} = 10/c$

By putting this value in Eqs. (iii) and (ii), we get direction of propagation

$$\Rightarrow \quad \frac{c10(d\,\hat{i} - a\hat{k})}{10 \times 10} = \frac{6\,\hat{i} \times 8\hat{k}}{10}$$

$$\Rightarrow \quad d = 6/c$$

and $$a = -8/c$$

Hence, $$\mathbf{B} = \frac{6}{c}\hat{k} - \frac{8}{c}\hat{i} = \frac{1}{c}(6\hat{k} - 8\,\hat{i})$$

As the general equation of magnetic field of an EM wave propagating in positive y-direction is given as,

$$B = B_0 \cos(Ry - \omega t))$$

$$\therefore \quad \mathbf{B} = \frac{1}{c}(6\hat{k} - 8\,\hat{i})\cos(6x + 8z - 10ct)$$

Alternate Solution Given, electric field is $E(x, y)$, i.e. electric field is in xy-plane which is given as

$$\because \quad \mathbf{E} = 10\,\hat{j}\cos(6x + 8z)$$

Since, the magnetic field given is $\mathbf{B}(x, z, t)$, this means **B** is in xz-plane.

$\therefore$ Propagation of wave is in y-direction.

[$\because$ for an electromagnetic wave, $\mathbf{E} \perp \mathbf{B} \perp$ propagation direction]

As Poynting vector suggests that $\mathbf{E} \times \mathbf{B}$ is parallel to $(6\,\hat{i} + 8\hat{k})$.

Let $\mathbf{B} = (x\hat{i} + z\hat{k})$,

then $\mathbf{E} \times \mathbf{B} = \hat{j} \times (x\,\hat{i} + z\hat{k}) = 6\,\hat{i} + 8\hat{k}$

or $-x\hat{k} + z\,\hat{i} = 6\,\hat{i} + 8\hat{k}$

or $x = -8$ and $z = 6$

$$\therefore \quad \mathbf{B} = \frac{1}{c}(6\hat{k} - 8\hat{i})\cos(6x + 8z - 10ct) \quad \left[\because \frac{|E|}{|B|} = c\right]$$

83. In the free space, the speed of electromagnetic wave is given as,

$$c = \frac{1}{\sqrt{\mu_0 \varepsilon_0}} = \frac{E_0}{B_0} \quad \text{...(i)}$$

where, E_0 and B_0 are the amplitudes of varying electric and magnetic fields, respectively.

Now, when it enters in a medium of refractive index 'n', its speed is given as,

$$v = \frac{1}{\sqrt{\mu\varepsilon}} = \frac{1}{\sqrt{K\varepsilon_0 \mu}} = \frac{E}{B} \quad \text{...(ii)}$$

where, K is dielectric strength of the medium.

Using Eqs. (i) and (ii), we get

$$\frac{v}{c} = \frac{1}{\sqrt{K}} \quad \text{...(iii)}$$

($\because$ For a transparent medium, $\mu_0 \approx \mu$)

Also, refractive index of medium is 'n' and is given as

$$\frac{c}{v} = n$$

or $$\frac{v}{c} = \frac{1}{n} \quad \text{...(iv)}$$

$\therefore$ From Eqs. (iii) and (iv), we get

$$n=\sqrt{K} \text{ or } K=n^2 \quad \text{...(v)}$$

The intensity of a EM wave is given as,

$$I=\frac{1}{2}\varepsilon_0 E_0^2 c$$

and in the medium, it is given as

$$I'=\frac{1}{2}K\varepsilon_0 E^2 v$$

It is given that, $I=I'$

$$\Rightarrow \quad \frac{1}{2}\varepsilon_0 E_0^2 c=\frac{1}{2}K\varepsilon_0 E^2 v$$

or

$$\left(\frac{E_0}{E}\right)^2=\frac{Kv}{c} \quad \text{...(vi)}$$

From Eqs. (iv), (v) and (vi), we get

$$\left(\frac{E_0}{E}\right)^2=\frac{n^2}{n}=n \quad \text{or} \quad E_0/E=\sqrt{n}$$

Similarly, $\frac{1}{2}\frac{B_0^2}{\mu_0}c=\frac{1}{2}\cdot\frac{B^2}{\mu_0}v$

$$\Rightarrow \quad \frac{B_0}{B}=\frac{1}{\sqrt{n}}$$

Alternate Solution

We know that,

$$\left(\frac{E_0}{B_0}\right)_{\text{air/vacuum}}=c \quad \text{and} \quad \left(\frac{E}{B}\right)_{\text{medium}}=v$$

Also, $n=\frac{c}{v}$

$$\frac{E_0/B_0}{E/B}=\frac{c}{v}=n$$

$$\Rightarrow \quad \frac{E_0/E}{B_0/B}=n$$

This is possible only if $\frac{E_0}{E}=\sqrt{n}$ and $\frac{B_0}{B}=\frac{1}{\sqrt{n}}$.

84. Given,

Power of laser beam

$$(P)=27\text{mW}=27\times10^{-3}\text{ W}$$

Area of cross-section (A)

$$=10\text{ m m}^2=10\times10^{-6}\text{m}^2$$

Permittivity of free space $(\varepsilon_0)=9\times10^{-12}$ SI unit

Speed of light $(c)=3\times10^8$ m/s

Intensity of electromagnetic wave is given by the relation

$$I=\frac{1}{2}nc\varepsilon_0 E^2$$

where, n is refractive index, for air $n=1$.

$$\therefore \quad I=\frac{1}{2}c\cdot\varepsilon_0 E^2 \quad \text{...(i)}$$

Also, $I=\frac{P}{A}$ ...(ii)

From Eqs. (i) and (ii), we get

$$\frac{1}{2}c\varepsilon_0 E^2=\frac{P}{A}$$

or $E^2=\frac{2P}{Ac\varepsilon_0}$

or $E=\sqrt{\frac{2\times27\times10^{-3}}{10\times10^{-6}\times3\times10^8\times9\times10^{-12}}}$

$$\approx 1.4\times10^3\text{ V/m}=1.4\text{ k V/m}$$

85. Energy of a light wave $\propto$ Intensity of the light wave

Since, intensity $=\varepsilon v A^2$

where, ε is the permittivity of the medium in which light is travelling with velocity v and A is its amplitude.

Since, only 4% of the energy of the light gets reflected.

$\therefore$ 96% of the energy of the light is transmitted.

$$E_{\text{transmitted}}(E_t)=96\%\text{ of }E_{\text{incident}}(E_i)$$

$$\varepsilon_0\varepsilon_r vA_t^2=\frac{96}{100}\times\varepsilon_0\times c\times A_1^0$$

$$A_t^2=\frac{96}{100}\cdot\frac{\varepsilon_0}{\varepsilon_r}\cdot\frac{c}{v}A_i^2$$

$$A_t^2=\frac{96}{100}\cdot\frac{v^2}{c^2}\cdot\frac{c}{v}A_i^2 \quad \left[\because \sqrt{\frac{\varepsilon_0}{\varepsilon_r}}=\frac{v}{c}\right]$$

$$A_t^2=\frac{96}{100}\cdot\frac{v}{c}\cdot A_i^2$$

$$=\frac{96}{100}\times\frac{1}{3/2}\times30^2 \quad \left[\because \mu=\frac{c}{v}=1.5\right]$$

$$A_t=\sqrt{\frac{64}{100}\times30^2}$$

$$A_t=24\text{ V/m}$$

JEE Advanced

1. (A) $(B_{x_0})=\frac{(E_x)_0}{c}=\frac{60}{3\times10^8}=2\times10^{-7}$

(B) $(B_{y_0})=\frac{(E_y)_0}{c}=\frac{30}{3\times10^8}=1\times10^{-7}$

(C) Wave is polarised in xy-plane, polarisation angle is $\tan^{-1}\left(\frac{1}{2}\right)$

(D) Refractive index of medium $=\frac{C}{V}$

When

$$V=\frac{\omega}{R}=\frac{5\times10^{14}}{10^7/3}$$

$$=15\times10^7=1.5\times10^8$$

$$\therefore \quad \mu=\frac{C}{V}=2$$